Fodor's

PACIFIC NORTHWEST

30

Welcome to the Pacific Northwest

Little did we realize that the emergence of a novel coronavirus in early 2020 would abruptly bring almost all travel to a halt. Although our Fodor's writers around the world have continued working to bring you the best of the destinations they cover, we still anticipate that more than the usual number of businesses will close permanently in the coming months, perhaps with little advance notice. We don't expect things to return to "normal" for some time. As you plan your upcoming travels to the Pacific Northwest, please confirm that places are still open and let us know when we need to make updates by writing to us at editors@fodors.com.

TOP REASONS TO GO

★ **Hip Cities:** Quirky Portland, eclectic Seattle, and gorgeous Vancouver entice.

★ **Coastal Fun:** Beaches, whale sightings, tidal pools, headland walks.

★ **Mountains:** Mt. Rainier, Mt. Hood, Mt. Olympus, and Mt. St. Helens inspire awe.

★ **Craft Beverages:** Wineries, microbreweries, artisan coffee, and boutique distilleries.

★ **Seafood:** Fresh local crab, razor clams, sea scallops, oysters, and salmon.

★ **Scenic Drives:** On the Oregon Coast, in the Cascade Range, through evergreen forests.

Contents

Fodor's Features

MAPS

Chapter 1

EXPERIENCE THE PACIFIC NORTHWEST

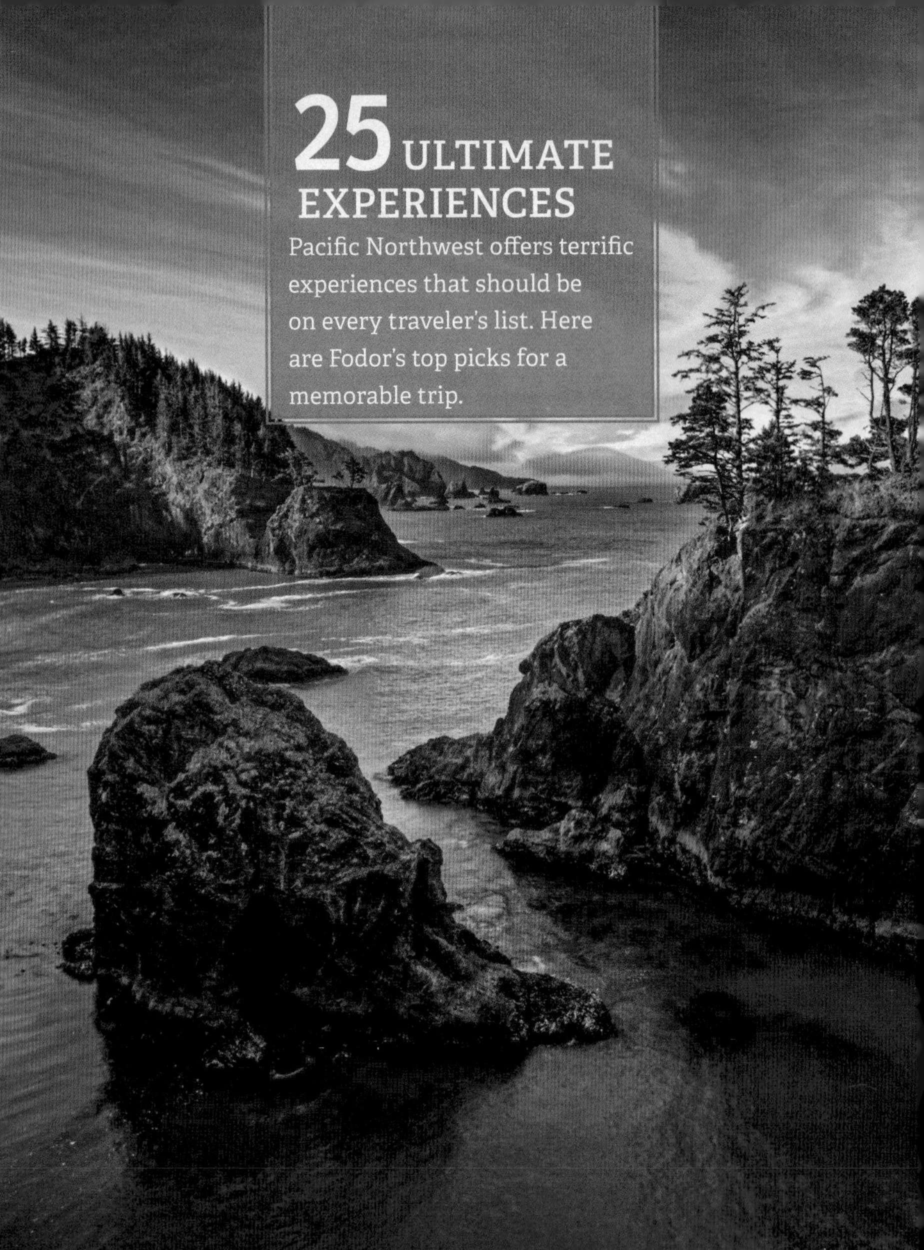

25 ULTIMATE EXPERIENCES

Pacific Northwest offers terrific experiences that should be on every traveler's list. Here are Fodor's top picks for a memorable trip.

1 Explore Oregon's Rugged Coast

Oregon's shoreline is unlike any other on the continent. The northern half draws visitors to Astoria, Cannon Beach, and the Tillamook Creamery. The southern stretches woo solitude seekers. (Ch. 4)

2 Whistler, British Columbia

The 11-minute gondola ride between Whistler and Blackcomb Mountains is the highest of its kind, with an elevation of 436 meters. (Ch. 20)

3 Crater Lake, Oregon

Crater Lake reaches depths of nearly 2,000 feet and sunlight filters down 400 feet, making it one of the most striking sights in the West. (Ch. 8)

4 Seaplane Flight, Vancouver and Victoria

Whether heading to Victoria, Tofino, or the Gulf Islands, this is an impressive way to enjoy the magnificent scenery of the Pacific Northwest. (Ch. 20)

5 Storm-Watching in Tofino, Vancouver

Winter on the West Coast brings with it the lashings of violent coastal storms and fury of unpredictable weather. Storm season is from November to March. (Ch. 20)

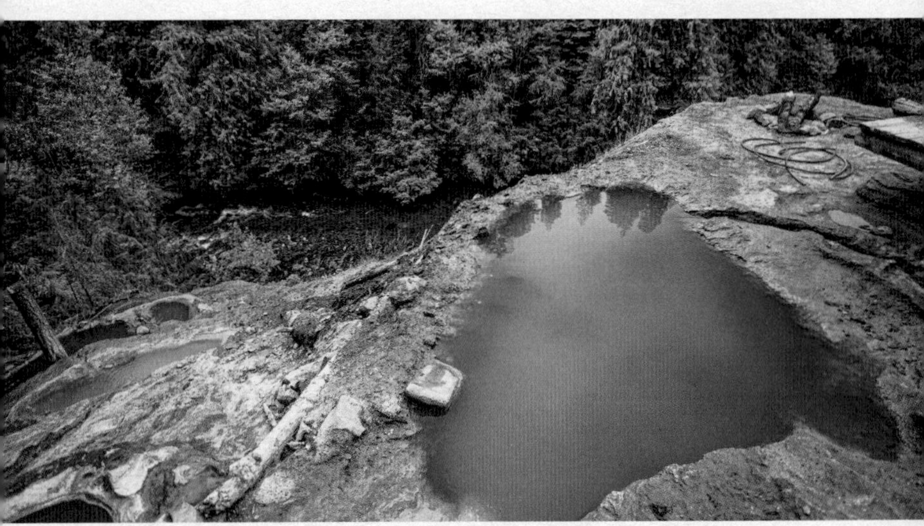

6 Dip in Natural Hot Springs, Oregon

The volcanic forces that shape Oregon's landscapes come with steamy perks: dozens of soothing hot springs, from rustic cabin resorts to lush national forests. (Ch. 5)

7 Visit the "Alps of Oregon"

Riding the Wallowa Lake Tramway—the steepest tram in North America—to the 8,150-foot summit of Mt. Howard feels like taking a gondola lift all the way to the Alps. (Ch. 10)

8 Race a Dune Buggy, Oregon

The Oregon Dunes National Recreation Area stretches for more than 40 miles between Florence and Coos Bay. A dune buggy is the quickest way to explore this expanse. (Ch. 4)

9 Capilano Suspension Bridge, Vancouver

Set against the rain forest of Vancouver's North Shore mountains, the swaying cedar plank bridge is suspended 70 meters above the Capilano River. (Ch. 20)

10 Burke Museum of Natural History, Seattle

Founded by a team of naturalists, the Burke Museum has living exhibits touching on paleontology, archaeology, biology, and contemporary culture. (Ch. 10)

11 Sea to Sky Highway, British Columbia

Drive the Sea to Sky Highway along Howe Sound. In Squamish, the Stawamus Chief is one of the largest granite monoliths in the world. (Ch. 20)

12 Time Travel at the Painted Hills, Oregon

Part of the John Day Fossil Beds National Monument, the distinctive stripes seen in the Painted Hills represent more than 30 million years of geological history. (Ch. 4)

13 Chihuly Gardens and Glass, Seattle

Considered to be among the modern masters in glasswork, artist Dale Chihuly is behind Seattle's unique and vibrant technicolor sculptural garden. (Ch. 10)

14 Wine Tasting in Willamette Valley

This swath of countryside in Oregon is home to more than 500 wineries and has earned a reputation as one of the finest producers of Pinot Noir in the world. (Ch. 5)

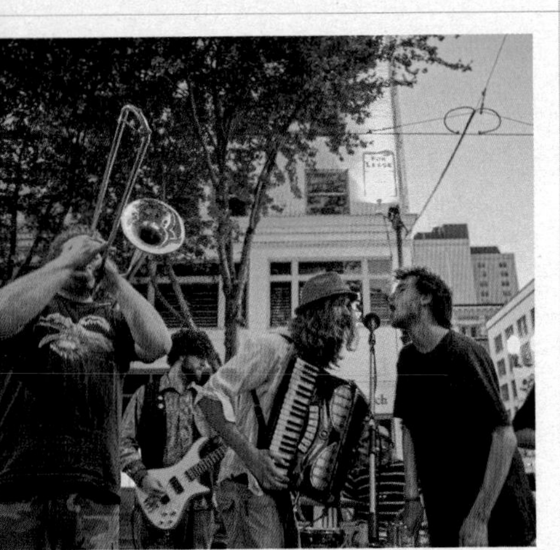

15 Portland, Oregon

A doughnut shop (Voodoo Doughnut), a sprawling temperate rainforest (Forest Park), and a bookstore (Powell's City of Books) are top attractions here. (Ch. 3)

16 Space Needle, Seattle

Erected for the 1962 World's Fair, this 602-foot-tall internationally renowned Space Age-era relic remains a quintessential Seattle experience. (Ch. 10)

17 Volunteer Park, Seattle

Seattle's largest park is 534 acres of winding woodland trails, picturesque sea cliff views, sprawling open meadows, and other natural landscapes. (Ch. 10)

18 Bard on the Beach, Vancouver

In summer, take a picnic to the billowing tents at Vanier Park to experience Western Canada's largest Shakespeare festival. Time it for a night when there are fireworks. (Ch. 20)

19 Tour the Columbia River Gorge, Oregon

The Columbia River Gorge's basalt cliffs rise from moss-covered forests along both sides of the West's grandest waterway, providing some spectacular vistas. (Ch. 6)

20 Richmond Oval, Richmond, BC

Visit the Richmond Oval, site of the speed skating competition during the 2010 Winter Olympics. The glass-and-steel building houses the Olympic ice rinks and fitness center. (Ch. 20)

21 Shakespeare in Ashland, Oregon

One of the country's best regional performing arts organizations, Ashland's Tony Award–winning Oregon Shakespeare Festival puts on more than 700 shows every year. (Ch. 8)

22 Polar Bear Swim, Vancouver

Every year, revelers take to the frigid waters of English Bay for the annual Polar Bear Swim. This New Year's Day event is one of the largest in the world. (Ch. 20)

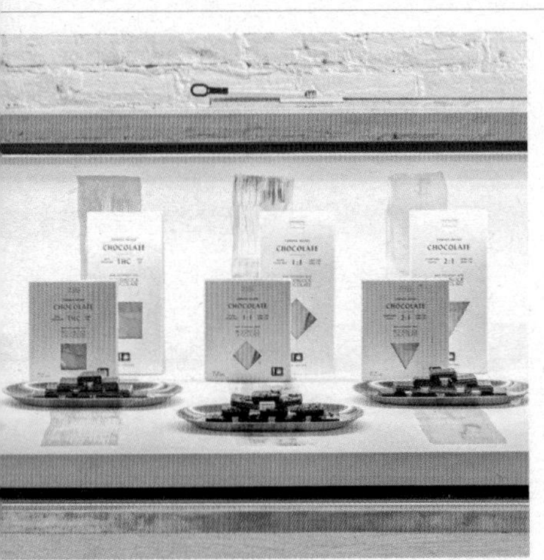

23 Get High Legally

In 2012 and 2014, respectively, Washington and Oregon were among the first to legalize cannabis for recreational use, and today claim the highest densities of licensed vendors in the country. (Ch. 3, 10)

24 Museum of Anthropology

This museum, located at the University of British Columbia campus on Point Grey in Vancouver, has one of the country's finest collections of Northwest Coast First Nations art. (Ch. 20)

25 Grouse Mountain Skyride, Vancouver

To reach the top of Grouse Mountain, you can climb the Grouse Grind, or take the Skyride gondola, part of the largest aerial tramway system in North America. (Ch. 20)

WHAT'S WHERE

1 Portland. Portland has become a magnet for fans of artisanal food, coffee, and music, and its parks and miles of bike lanes make it a prime spot for outdoors enthusiasts.

2 The Oregon Coast. Oregon's roughly 300 miles of rugged shoreline are every bit as scenic as the more crowded and famous California coast.

3 The Willamette Valley and Wine Country. Just beyond the Portland city limits and extending south for 120 miles to Eugene, the Willamette Valley is synonymous with exceptional winemaking and an increasingly noteworthy food scene.

4 The Columbia River Gorge and Mt. Hood. Less than an hour east of Portland, the Columbia Gorge extends for about 160 miles along the Oregon-Washington border.

5 Central Oregon. The swatch of Oregon immediately east of the Cascade Range takes in a varied landscape, with the outdoorsy city of Bend as the regional hub. Make time for the funky mountain town of Sisters.

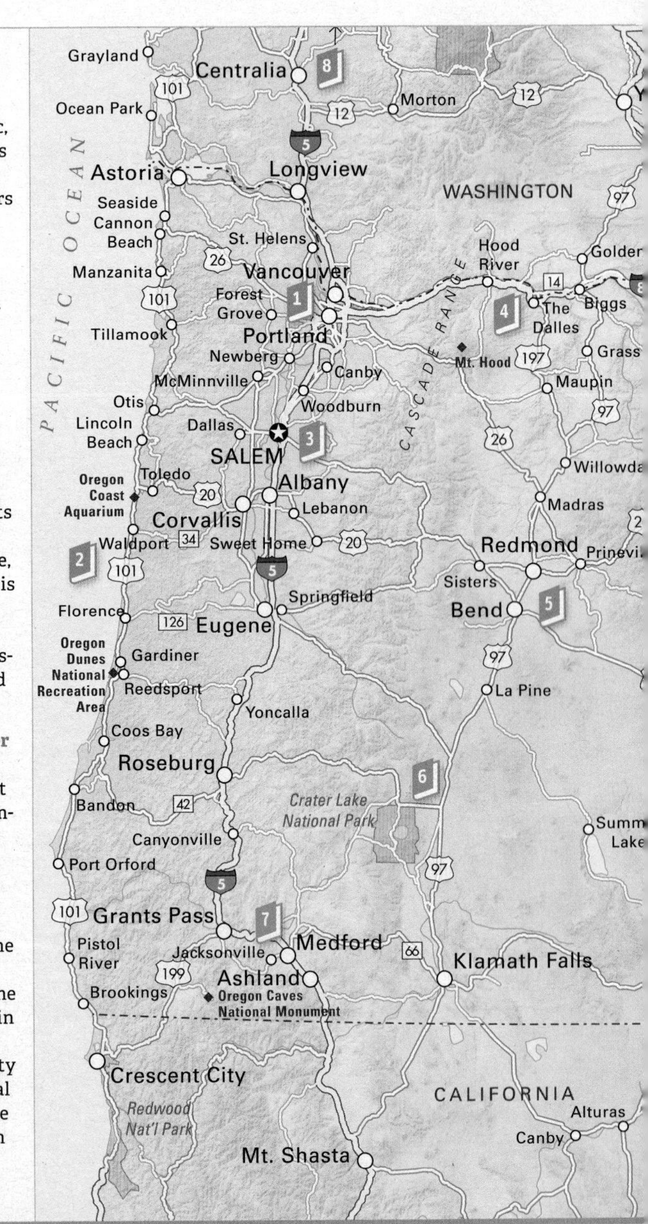

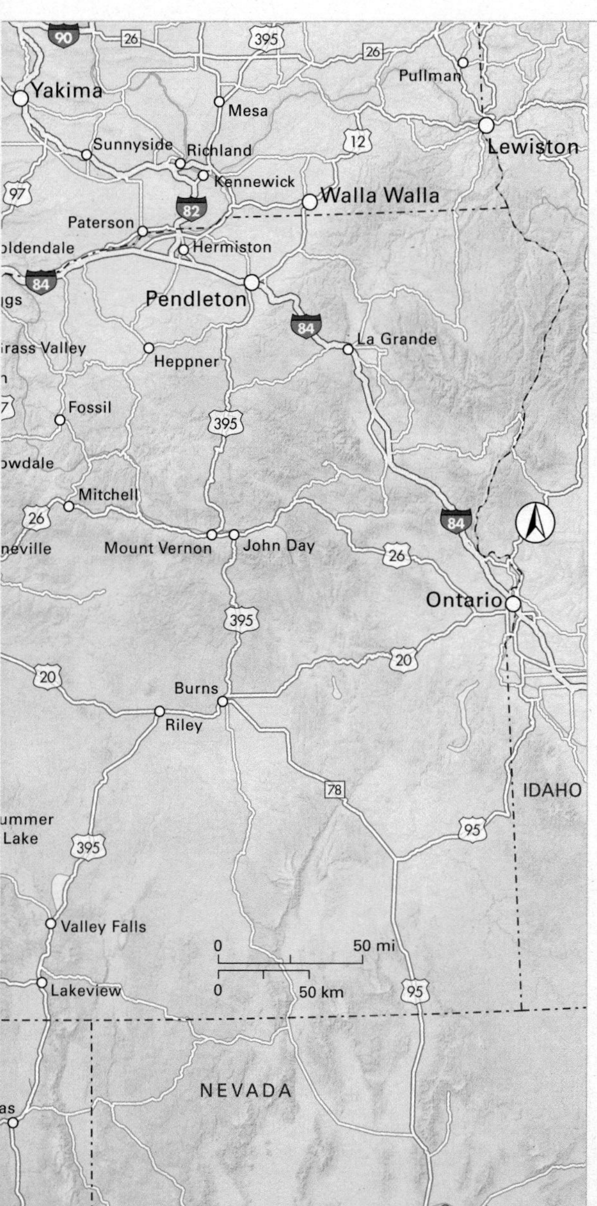

6 Crater Lake National Park. The 21-square-mile sapphire-blue expanse is the nation's deepest lake and a scenic wonder. You can drive the loop road around the lake, hike, or take a boat tour.

7 Southern Oregon. Artsy Ashland and Old West–looking Jacksonville have sophisticated restaurants, shops, and wineries. Nearby, Oregon Caves National Monument is a fascinating natural attraction, while the Klamath Falls region has some of the best wildlife-viewing in the state.

8 Seattle. Pacific Northwest's hub of arts and culture, this city has a vibrant mix of swanky restaurants and cocktail bars, coffee shops, and hotels.

9 Washington Cascade Mountains and Valleys. Outside Seattle, you can tour the waterfront and museums of Tacoma and bike past tulip fields in the Skagit Valley. Olympia is a good base for exploring Mt. Rainier and Mt. St. Helens, and up north, Bellingham is a picturesque waterfront town with a bounty of outdoors activities and great restaurants.

WHAT'S WHERE

10 The San Juan Islands. This relaxing and stunningly beautiful archipelago is prime whale-watching and kayaking territory, and you'll find art galleries, quirky cafés, and upscale inns amid the islands' largest towns.

11 Olympic National Park. Centered on Mt. Olympus and framed on three sides by water, this 922,651-acre park covers much of Washington's forest-clad Olympic Peninsula.

12 Olympic Peninsula and Washington Coast. Wilderness envelops most of the Olympic Peninsula, with the Olympic Mountains at its core. Rugged terrain and few roads limit interior accessibility, but U.S. Highway 101 offers breathtaking forest, ocean, and mountain vistas.

13 North Cascades National Park. This 505,000-acre expanse of mountain wilderness is part of an area with more than half of the glaciers in America.

14 North Central Washington. Along the beautiful North Cascades Highway, you'll encounter spectacular scenery

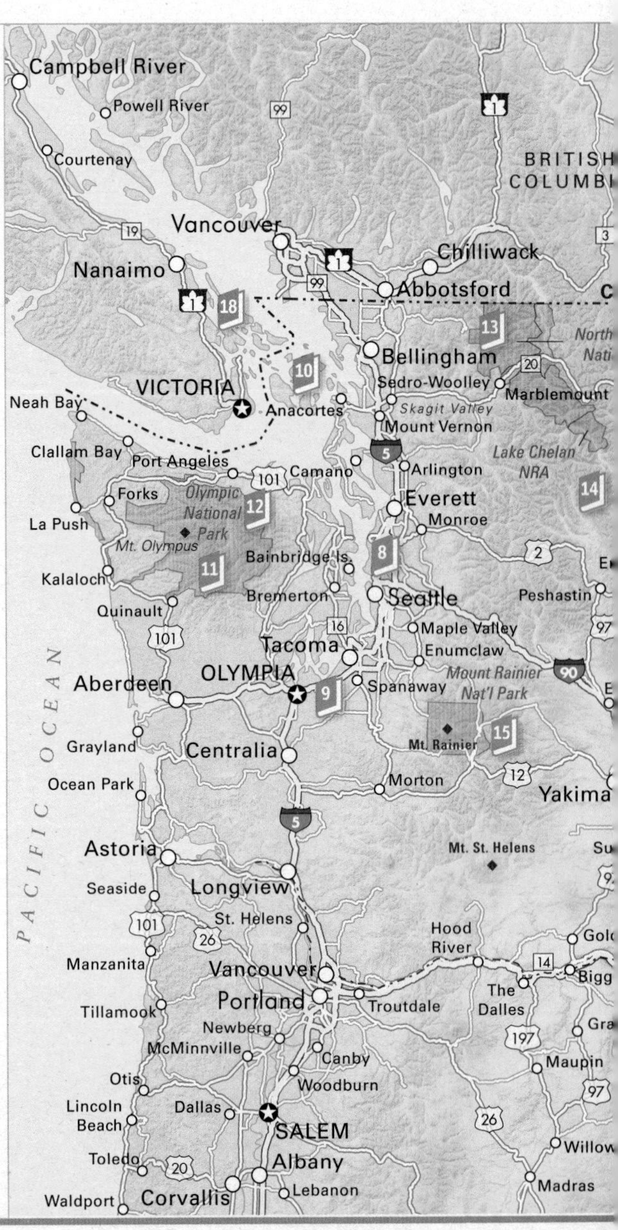

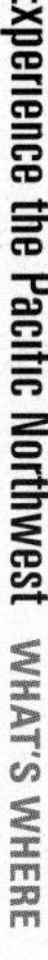

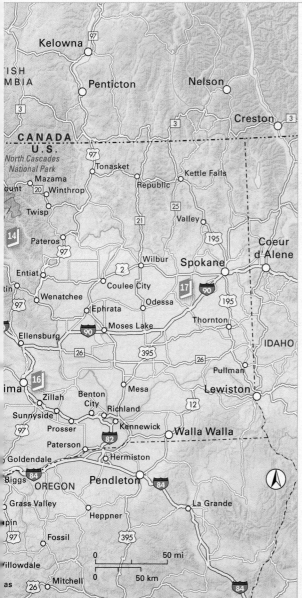

and logging towns such as Sedro-Woolley and Marblemount, as well as Winthrop.

15 Mount Rainier National Park. The fifth-highest mountain in the Lower 48, Mt. Rainier is massive and unforgettable.

16 Washington Wine Country. This fertile valley east of the Cascades has long been known for apple and cherry orchards, and more recently as a prized winemaking area—including the vineyards around Yakima, Zillah, Prosser, and Benton City.

17 Spokane and Eastern Washington. Characterized by rolling, dry, treeless hills and anchored by the state's second-largest city, Spokane, this area takes in the vast Columbia River valley and an eclectic mix of cities and towns, including wine-centric Walla Walla.

18 Vancouver and Victoria. Vancouver is a glorious city with tall fir trees, rock spires, the ocean at your doorstep, and a vibrant atmosphere. Victoria—with its stately Victorian houses, walkable Downtown and waterfront, and hip boutiques and restaurants—is a stunner.

What to Eat and Drink

WASHINGTON STATE WINE
Woodinville is the destination for oenophiles in the Pacific Northwest, with many wineries to tour and vintners to learn from. If you can't make it out for a tasting in Woodinville, check menus for sips of Washington's acclaimed wines, including Walla, which is often compared to Napa Valley in quality.

OYSTERS, BRITISH COLUMBIA AND WASHINGTON
From Kusshi to Fanny Bay to Kumamotos, West Coast oysters are mild, sweet, and smaller than other oysters and are said to be great for beginners. So if you've never tried one, now is the time and this is definitely the place to do it. Oyster bars around Vancouver include Fanny Bay Oyster Bar and Shellfish Market on Cambie Street in Downtown. The cold, clean waters of the Pacific Northwest are also nutrient-rich, and produce crisp, briny oysters that are the pride of the region. The Olympia oyster, specifically, garners the most praise. Not only is the state home to America's largest shellfish farm, you can also find these flavorful delights throughout Seattle.

SPOT PRAWNS, BRITISH COLUMBIA
Once mainly exported to Asia for use as a filler for fish stock and chowder, this humble crustacean is now a prized local delicacy and the focus of an entire annual festival that takes place each spring. The harvest season, which starts in May in BC's coastal waters, typically lasts just six to eight weeks, so if you're visiting at that time you'll find the sweet shellfish on special menus around Vancouver.

DIM SUM, RICHMOND, BC
The Cantonese-style menu of bite-sized dumplings, steamed buns, rice noodle rolls, and pots of oolong tea is served midday at Asian restaurants around the city, in particular the nearby suburb of Richmond, which is also home of the "Dumpling Trail," a collection of restaurants serving the specialty.

WHITE SPOT LEGENDARY BURGER, BRITISH COLUMBIA
This local burger joint has been around since 1928 when founder Nat Bailey transformed his Model T into Canada's first food truck, serving hot dogs and peanuts at Lookout Point in Stanley Park. He opened his first location at the corner of Granville and 67th which then expanded to become Canada's longest running restaurant chain. The burgers are a legend among locals and feature secret Triple "O" sauce.

JAPADOG, VANCOUVER
A favorite of the late Anthony Bourdain, this street-food vendor offers hot dogs with a Japanese twist at stands and food trucks around Vancouver's Downtown core, including one small restaurant (there are now also two stands in LA). It's popular with the film

Nanaimo bars, Vancouver

industry and acclaimed by celebrities and locals alike, who line up for the Oroshi, a bratwurst topped with a special soya sauce glaze and freshly grated daikon radish. You can also try the best-selling Terimayo topped with nori seaweed, teriyaki sauce, and wasabi mayo–this is a fun fusion of Japanese flavors and tastes.

NANAIMO BARS

Nanaimo bars, featuring a chocolate graham cracker coconut base, creamy custard in the middle, and chocolate ganache on top, are named for the Vancouver Island city. These yummy treats can be found at coffee shops and bakeries in Vancouver and on Vancouver Island.

GEODUCK

Less famous than the salmon and oysters, but the most symbolic for locals as it is specific to the Northwest, eating this giant saltwater clam (pronounced gooey-duck) is the purest taste of local merroir (flavor of the sea). Its flavor is surprisingly sweet and crunchy. You can eat it cooked or raw, though you might be put off by its unique appearance.

SEATTLE DOG

The city's signature late-night food can be found at hot dog carts outside bars in Capitol Hill, Belltown, and Pioneer Square. The classic topping is not ketchup or mustard, but cream cheese.

PHO, SEATTLE

If you've ever wondered how Seattle survives the damp and dark of winter here, this subtle, fragrant Vietnamese noodle soup, found every few blocks, is the answer. Vietnamese food in general is very popular in the city, but hot soup complements rainy days, especially as many of the pho eateries are warm and cozy inside. Enjoy the slow-cooked, thick or thin noodles with beef or vegetables.

CHEHALEM WINES, OREGON

The team at Chehalem Winery puts their values into actions, earning LIVE, Salmon-Safe, and B Corp certifications—a fancy way of demonstrating their commitment to the land and community. Their signature single-lot Pinot Noir and white varieties are worth a swirl, too. Make an appointment to tour the winery or visit the rustic tasting room in downtown Newberg.

Best Islands in the Pacific Northwest

SAN JUAN ISLANDS: ORCAS ISLAND, WA
The San Juan Islands are a bit farther afield, located north of Seattle, in the Salish Sea, which separates Washington State from Vancouver Island, British Columbia. Orcas Island is the largest of the San Juans, heavily forested and full of hiking trails and a variety of water sports.

SALT SPRING ISLAND, BRITISH COLUMBIA
One of the Gulf Islands in the Strait of Georgia, which separates Vancouver Island from the mainland, Salt Spring Island is full of cute places to stay, camping, restaurants, arts and crafts, gardens, hiking, and kayaking.

GALIANO ISLAND, BRITISH COLUMBIA
Another one of the Southern Gulf Islands between Vancouver Island and the mainland, Galiano Island has old-growth forests and beaches. Foodies take note: it is also where the farm-to-table restaurant pilgrimme won third-best new restaurant in Canada.

SAUVIE ISLAND, OR
Sauvie Island is the largest island in the Columbia River. Just 10 miles northwest of downtown Portland, Sauvie Island (pronounced SOH-vee) is superaccessible by car, bus, or even bike. Most of the island is state-designated wildlife areas, but it is also a working farm island where summer means picking berries and hitting the sandy beach for a dip in the river. Parking passes for public beach parking are a must, and day passes or a summer pass can be purchased from stores on the island (there are signs along the road to the beach). Also note that there are clothing-optional beaches located at the end of the strip.

BAINBRIDGE ISLAND, WA
Essentially a suburb of Seattle, Bainbridge is easily accessible by a 35-minute ferry ride from Downtown Seattle. With a variety of outdoor activities plus dining and shopping, Bainbridge makes a fun and easy day trip if you are visiting Seattle and want to experience the Puget Sound, but don't have time to roam farther.

LOPEZ ISLAND, WA
The third-largest of the San Juans, Lopez Island is quiet, remote, and known as the friendly island, where everyone waves. Visit for the flat, easy cycling, great kayaking, beautiful beaches, the Lopez Island Vineyards, and the spectacular mountainous scenery.

Vachon Island

VASHON ISLAND, WA
Only a 20-minute ferry ride from Seattle, Vashon Island feels far more distant. It's a quiet escape that is close to the city, but still remote enough to maintain a real farming community and experience the quiet Pacific Northwest life—think charming farm stands where people leave bone broth or goat cheese and you pay by the honor system. There are wineries and restaurants, which all lean a bit toward the luxe these days but Vashon still maintains a sense of authentic hippie spirit.

HAIDA GWAII, BRITISH COLUMBIA
Remote and protected, Haida Gwaii is an archipelago off the coast of British Columbia full of old-growth forests, breathtaking landscape—and such a diverse variety of plant life and wildlife that it is sometimes referred to as Canada's Galapagos.

CORTES ISLAND AND QUADRA ISLAND, BRITISH COLUMBIA
Cortes Island and Quadra Island are part of the Discovery Passage, the channel that links Vancouver Island and the Discovery Islands. The smaller, Cortes Island, is full of nature—there is hiking, boating, swimming from ocean beaches and freshwater lakes, some with white-sand beaches, and a vibrant artistic community. Nearby Quadra Island also offers beaches, lakes, and lots of nature.

VANCOUVER ISLAND
One of the biggest destinations in British Columbia, Vancouver Island has a lot going for it aside from the fact that it's Meghan and Harry's new home. There's a big First Nations presence; heaps of charm and culture in Victoria (BC's capital city); great hiking and nature; a robust wine region and vibrant food scene.

Best Places for Book Lovers in the Pacific Northwest

POWELL'S
Powell's "City of Books" in Portland claims to be the largest independent bookseller in the world. Powell's is a beloved bookstore and a visit to their largest and most famous downtown location is a memorable experience. Don't miss the Pearl Room upstairs, which is filled with rare books.

THE ELLIOTT BAY BOOK COMPANY
A beloved and thriving independent bookstore located in Seattle's Capitol Hill neighborhood, Elliott Bay Book Company has an extensive selection of books, inspiring tables of staff favorites, and an excellent café, Little Oddfellows, which is operated by their next-door neighbor Oddfellows Cafe.

MONOGRAPH BOOKWERKS
Set in a vine-covered, redbrick storefront, Monograph Bookwerks is an artist-owned art book and ephemera gem in northeast Portland just off popular Alberta Street that is a dream shop for artists and booklovers alike. Only open on the weekends, be sure to time your visit right—après weekend brunch.

SYLVIA BEACH HOTEL
An eclectic, literary-themed hotel located on the Oregon Coast overlooking Nye Beach. Named after Sylvia Beach, the American expat who opened the iconic Parisian bookstore Shakespeare and Company in 1919, Sylvia Beach Hotel is truly a place for book lovers: all the rooms named after authors and there is not a TV—or any Wi-Fi—in sight.

SEATTLE PUBLIC LIBRARY-CENTRAL LIBRARY
Designed by Dutch architect Rem Koolhaas, the Seattle Public Central Library is a must-visit landmark for book lovers and architecture enthusiasts alike.

MUNRO'S BOOKS
Started by Nobel Prize–winning Canadian author Alice Munro and her ex-husband Tom, Munro's Books is the largest independent bookstore on Vancouver Island.

VANCOUVER PUBLIC LIBRARY
A Moshe Safdie–designed building that is reminiscent of a Roman coliseum, the Vancouver Public Library has been the set for various TV shows and movies. Don't miss the rooftop garden and viewing deck during the summertime.

Phinney Books

PHINNEY BOOKS
Phinney Books is a neighborhood bookstore in Seattle's Phinney Ridge neighborhood that is absolutely worth a visit. Opened in 2014 by Tom Nissley, a former Amazon employee who won big on Jeopardy!, Phinney Books is a fun spot with a thoughtful selection of books and a "True" and "Made-Up" section. What's not to love?

MACLEOD'S BOOKS
Located in Vancouver's popular Gastown neighborhood, the family-owned MacLeod's Books is like stepping into a time capsule. With an almost-overwhelming number of used and rare books, there is definitely something for everyone.

MOTHER FOUCAULT'S
Mother Foucault's in Portland, OR, is a serious book spot selling a mix of used, rare, and vintage books. If you are looking for Kafka in German and Sartre in French this is your spot. Mother Foucault's also hosts a variety of poetry readings and literary events.

Best Hikes in the Pacific Northwest

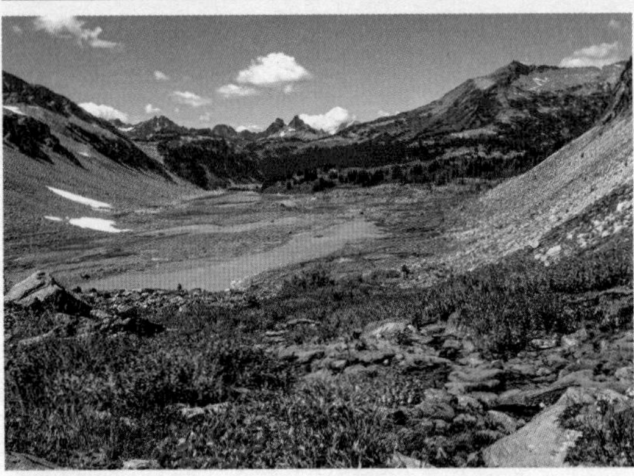

SPIDER GAP, WA
Serious hikers should explore the many trails in the Spider Gap area. Stay in nearby Leavenworth, a Bavarian-style village with a European alpine feel.

SKYLINE TRAIL, WA
A world-famous 5½-mile loop at the base of Mt. Rainier, Skyline Trail offers glacier views, waterfalls, and summertime wildflowers.

PACIFIC RIM NATIONAL PARK, BC
Located on the west coast of Vancouver Island, the Pacific Rim National Park offers the classic Pacific Northwest trifecta of a dramatic coastline, beautiful old-growth forests, and amazing hiking trails. The park consists of three sections: Long Beach Area, The West Coast Trail, and The Broken Group Islands. Just up the coastline, one of the best trails to hit is the Wild Pacific Trail, it is located in Ucluelet, which is also having a bit of a moment as its more famous neighbor, Tofino, has become more pricey.

MOUNT SI/ LITTLE SI, WA
Only a 40-minute drive from Seattle, Mount Si is located in the North Bend area, a region made famous by the cult '90s television series *Twin Peaks*. The popular 8-mile hike up Mount Si offers a real challenge, while Little Si is perfect for more moderate/family hikes.

MULTNOMAH FALLS AREA, OR
No trip to the Portland area is complete without a visit to the Columbia River Gorge and Multnomah Falls. Just outside of Portland, Multnomah Falls is not only incredibly scenic, it also offers some moderate hiking opportunities.

GARIBALDI LAKE, BC
Twelve miles south of Whistler, old-growth forests lead to the stunning glacier-fed Garibaldi Lake, which features fantastic intermediate–expert level hiking and mountain biking. If there's time, head to Joffre Lakes Provincial Park east of Pemberton, just outside of Whistler.

OLYMPIC PENINSULA, WA

The Olympic Peninsula offers many excellent hiking options and some hot springs, too. Loop through the Hoh Rainforest, a temperate rain forest with possibly the most complex ecosystem in the country, hike around Lake Crescent, or head out to the surreal Shi Shi Beach for some scenic coastal hiking and camping.

FOREST PARK, OR

Portland is home to one of the largest urban forests, Forest Park, which is full of excellent hikes and outdoor experiences right in the city. Popular trails can be found around the Pittock Mansion (which is also worth a visit) and the Audubon Society.

THE OREGON COAST/ PORT ORFORD

Oregon's coast is famous for its rugged beauty and long stretches of beach. It's full of hikes and outdoor experiences. If you have limited time, a day trip from Portland for a walk along Cannon Beach to see Haystack Rock emerging from the ocean or a hike along the trails in Ecola State Park for sweeping ocean views can be incredibly memorable. If you have more time, head to Port Orford along Oregon's scenic southern coast.

Portland with Kids

Many of Oregon's best kids-oriented attractions and activities are in greater Portland. Just getting around the Rose City—via streetcars and light-rail trains on city streets and kayaks, excursion cruises, and jet boats on the Willamette River—is fun. For listings of family-oriented concerts, performances by the Oregon Children's Theatre, and the like, check the free *Willamette Weekly* newspaper.

MUSEUMS AND ATTRACTIONS

On the east bank of the Willamette River near the new pedestrians-welcome Tilikum Crossing bridge, the **Oregon Museum of Science and Industry** (OMSI) is a leading interactive museum, with touch-friendly exhibits, an Omnimax theater, the state's biggest planetarium, and a 240-foot submarine moored just outside in the river. Along Portland's leafy Park Blocks, both the **Oregon History Museum** and the **Portland Art Museum** have exhibits and programming geared toward kids.

In Old Town, kids enjoy walking amid the ornate pagodas and dramatic foliage of the **Lan Su Chinese Garden.** This is a good spot for a weekend morning, followed by a visit to the **Portland Saturday Market,** where food stalls and musicians keep younger kids entertained, and the cool jewelry, toys, and gifts handcrafted by local artisans appeal to teens. Steps from the market is the **Oregon Maritime Museum,** set within a vintage stern-wheeler docked on the river. And just up Burnside Street from the market, **Powell's City of Books** contains enormous sections of kids' and young adults' literature.

PARKS

Portland is dotted with densely wooded parks—many of the larger ones have ball fields, playgrounds, and picnic areas. The most famous urban oasis in the city, **Forest Park** (along with adjoining **Washington Park**) offers a wealth of engaging activities. You can ride the MAX light-rail right to the park's main hub of culture, a complex comprising the **Oregon Zoo, Portland Children's Museum,** and **World Forestry Discovery Center Museum.** Ride the narrow-gauge railroad from the zoo for 2 miles to reach the **International Rose Test Garden** and **Japanese Garden.** From here it's an easy downhill stroll to **Northwest 23rd and 21st avenues'** pizza parlors, ice-cream shops, and bakeries.

OUTDOOR ADVENTURES

Tour boats ply the **Willamette River,** and a couple of marinas near OMSI rent **kayaks** and conduct **drag-boat races** out on the water. There are also several shops in town that rent **bikes** for use on the city's many miles of dedicated bike lanes and trails. There's outstanding **white-water rafting** just southeast of Portland, along the Clackamas River. On your way toward the Clackamas, check out **North Clackamas Aquatic Park** and **Oaks Amusement Park,** which have rides and wave pools galore.

Nearby **Mt. Hood** has camping, hiking, and biking all summer, and three of the most family-friendly ski resorts in the Northwest—**Timberline** is especially popular for younger and less experienced boarders and skiers. From summer through fall, the pick-your-own berry farms and pumpkin patches on **Sauvie Island** make for an engaging afternoon getaway—for an all-day outing, continue up U.S. 30 all the way to **Astoria,** at the mouth of the Columbia River, to visit the **Columbia River Maritime Museum** and **Fort Stevens State Park,** where kids love to scamper about the remains of an early-20th-century shipwreck.

Seattle with Kids

Seattle is great for kids. After all, a place where floatplanes take off a few feet from houseboats, and where harbor seals might be spotted on a routine ferry ride, doesn't have to try too hard to feel like a wonderland. And if the rain falls, there are plenty of great museums to keep the kids occupied. A lot of child-centric sights are easily reached via public transportation, and the piers and the aquarium can be explored on foot from most Downtown hotels. A few spots (Woodland Park Zoo, the Ballard Locks, and Discovery Park) are easier to visit by car.

MUSEUMS

Several museums cater specifically to kids, and many are conveniently clustered at the Seattle Center. The Center's winning trio is the **Pacific Science Center,** which has interactive exhibits and IMAX theaters; the **Children's Museum,** which has exhibits on Washington State and foreign cultures plus plenty of interactive art spaces; and, of course, the **Space Needle.** For older, hipper siblings there's a skate park; the Vera Project, a teen music and art space; and the **Museum of Pop Culture (MoPOP),** which features exhibits on pop culture and music history.

Downtown there are miles of waterfront to explore along the piers. The **Seattle Aquarium** is here and has touch pools and otters—what more could a kid want?

PARKS AND OUTDOOR ATTRACTIONS

Discovery Park has an interpretive center, a Native American cultural center, easy forest trails, and accessible beaches. **Alki Beach** in West Seattle is lively and fun; a wide paved path is the perfect surface for wheels of all kinds—you can rent bikes and scooters, or take to the water on rented paddleboats and kayaks. **Volunteer Park** has wide lawns and shallow pools made for splashing toddlers.

The **Woodland Park Zoo** has nearly 300 different species of animals, from jaguars to mountain goats, cheap parking, and an adjacent playground; stroller rentals are available. Watching an astonishing variety of boats navigate the ship canal at the **Ballard Locks** will entertain visitors of any age.

HOTELS

Downtown, the **Hotel Monaco** offers a happy medium between sophisticated and family-friendly. The colorful, eccentric decor will appeal to kids but remind adults that they're in a boutique property. Fun amenities abound, like optional goldfish in the rooms, and toys in the lobby. Surprisingly, one of the city's most high-end historic properties, the **Fairmont Olympic,** is also quite kid-friendly. The hotel's decor is a little fussy, but the grand staircases in the lobby will awe most little ones, and there's a great indoor pool area. In addition, the hotel offers babysitting, a kids' room-service menu, and toys and board games.

Outdoor Adventures

Hiking

In the Pacific Northwest, hiking is potentially a year-round sport, though only experts should attempt hiking in the snowy higher elevations in winter. One of the greatest aspects of this region is the diverse terrain, from high alpine scrambles that require stamina to flowered meadows that invite a relaxed pace to stunning coastal areas that offer a mix of level and precipitous terrain.

Of course, many of the best trails in the region are in national parks (Crater Lake, Olympic, Mount Rainier, and North Cascades among them). We've focused on trails elsewhere in the region, including some spectacular hidden gems.

BEST HIKES

Forest Park, Portland, OR. You can easily walk to the network of more than 80 miles of densely forested trails, many leading to spectacular vistas, from Downtown hotels, making this 5,000-acre urban wilderness one of the most accessible in the country. A good place to start is Washington Park, with its Japanese Garden and International Rose Test Garden.

Oswald West State Park, Manzanita, OR. The trails at this state park, just south of popular Cannon Beach, lead to sweeping headlands, to a sheltered beach popular for surfing, and to the top of Neahkahnie Mountain, from which you have a view of more than 20 miles of coastline.

Smith Rock State Park, Redmond, OR. Although world-famous for rock climbing, this maze of soaring rock formations has a number of trails well suited to casual hikers; the 3-mile Smith Rocks Loop hike is a favorite.

Table Rock, Central Point, OR. Comprising a pair of monolithic rocky peaks outside Medford, Table Rock makes a great quick and relaxing scramble—from the top, you're treated to wonderful views of the Cascades.

Wallowa Mountains, Enterprise, OR. This range of granite peaks in eastern Oregon, near Hells Canyon, is rife with crystalline alpine lakes and meadows, rushing rivers, and thickly forested valleys that fall between mountain ridges. Trails lead from both Enterprise and La Grande.

Beacon Rock State Park, North Bonneville, WA. Although Multnomah Falls, on the Oregon side of the Columbia Gorge, provides access to plenty of cool trails, the hiking at this park across the river provides bigger wows and fewer crowds. Scaling the 848-foot rock for which the park is named is fun and easy, but you can also access longer and more challenging day hikes to Hamilton Mountain and Table Mountain.

Cape Disappointment State Park, Ilwaco, WA. One of the top spots on the Washington coast for a beach hike, Cape Disappointment is at the mouth of the Columbia River and also contains exhibits documenting Lewis and Clark's journey, which ended here.

Moran State Park, Orcas Island, WA. Explore the 14 hiking trails at Moran State Park, which contains the largest mountain in the San Juan Islands, for exhilarating views of the islands, the Cascades, the Olympics, and Vancouver Island.

Snow Lake, Snoqualmie, WA. Relative proximity to Seattle makes this 8-mile trail into the dramatic Alpine Lakes Wilderness a bit crowded on weekends, but don't let that deter you—this hike is one of the state's true stunners.

Beaches

Unless you're a truly hardy soul, or you've brought your wet suit, taking a trip to the beach in the Pacific Northwest probably won't involve much swimming—water temperatures in these parts rarely exceed 55°F, even in late summer. However, residents of this part of the world love going to the coast. The mountainous coastline in Oregon—which frequently inspires comparisons with everywhere from Big Sur to New Zealand—is home to rugged, curvy, smooth-as-glass beaches ideal for tide pooling, strolling, and surfing. And you'll find similarly spectacular scenery as you continue into Washington, along the Long Beach Peninsula, up around the coast of Olympic National Park, and in the many islands of Puget Sound. Across the border, both Victoria and Vancouver have lovely, graceful beaches set against gorgeous mountain backdrops. Throughout the region, from spring through fall, there's a good chance of spotting whales swimming and diving just offshore (and plenty of tour boats offer cruises that afford better views).

BEST BEACHES

Cannon Beach, OR. The nearest coastal town to Portland also contains some of the state's most breathtaking beaches, including a stretch that fringes downtown. The 235-foot-tall Haystack Rock rises monumentally above the beach, and on the north side of town, Ecola State Park is a long stretch of rocky headlands punctuated by secluded beaches.

Cape Kiwanda State Natural Area, Pacific City, OR. Yet another formation called Haystack Rock, this one soaring to 327 feet, defines the coast at this dramatic stretch of beach that's part of Oregon's famed Three Capes Loop scenic drive. Massive waves pound the wide beach here, which has dozens of tidal pools at low tide.

Cape Perpetua Scenic Area, Yachats, OR. This 2,700-acre oceanfront wilderness on the central coast of Oregon is home to an 800-foot-high coastal lookout point, steep and easy hiking trails (including one through a fern-filled rain forest), an educational nature center, and a rocky but beautiful beach.

Oregon Dunes National Recreation Area, Reedsport, OR. Smooth, wind-sculpted dunes—some rising as high as 500 feet—are the highlight of this recreation area near Florence, the largest expanse of coastal sand dunes on the continent.

Port Orford, OR. The westernmost town in the continental United States, this artsy small hamlet along the southern coast is home to several great little beaches, including Battle Rock Park, which is just steps from downtown, and Paradise Point State Beach, a long stretch of sand extending north from Port Orford headland.

Alki Point and Beach, Seattle, WA. The quintessential sunning, beachcombing, and kite-flying stretch of sand, this West Seattle park encompasses 2½ miles of beachfront and is steps from several restaurants.

Second and Third Beaches, Olympic National Park, WA. These national park beaches are ideal for tide pooling, kayaking, surfing, and watching gray whales frolic offshore in spring and fall.

Kitsilano Beach, Vancouver, BC. A lovely urban beach in the quiet and charming Kitsilano neighborhood, the shore here has plenty of diversions (tennis, a huge pool) and gorgeous views of the city skyline and North Shore Mountains in the distance.

Biking

The Pacific Northwest is ideal for—and hugely popular with—biking enthusiasts. You'll find rental shops, bike-share programs, and a handful of tour operators in Portland and Seattle, and in all of these cities as well as Vancouver, Victoria, Eugene, Tacoma, and other municipalities, dedicated bike lanes and separate multiuse trails (for bikes, runners, and pedestrians) proliferate. And although bikes aren't permitted on many hiking trails, including many of those in national parks, roads in parks and many other scenic regions have wide shoulders and are well suited to cycling adventures.

BEST BIKING ROUTES

Columbia Historic Highway, OR. Just 17 miles east of Portland, this narrow, rolling highway climbs through the spectacular Columbia Gorge, past Multnomah Falls, and by the Vista House at Crown Point, a dramatic scenic overlook.

Portland and Sauvie Island, OR. Portland has miles of bike lanes, a bike-share program, and plenty of rental shops. In town, biking is a great way to explore leafy East Side neighborhoods like Hawthorne, Mississippi, and Alberta, which all abound with hip shops and cafés. Nearby are the rural and relatively flat roads of Sauvie Island, with its bounty of pick-your-own berry farms.

U.S. 97, near Bend, OR. The 40 miles or so north from Lava Butte through Bend and on up to Smith Rock State Park have awesome high-desert scenery and receive plenty of sunshine year-round.

Burke-Gilman Trail, Seattle, WA. Extending along an abandoned rail line through Seattle, including part of the lively Ballard community, this 27-mile multiuse trail draws plenty of bikers year-round. The city itself has many miles of bike lanes and paths and a popular bike-share program.

Highway 20, North Cascades National Park, WA. You'll want to be in good shape before tackling the hilly North Cascades Highway, but few roads in the state offer more mesmerizing scenery.

Lopez Island, San Juan Islands, WA. All the islands in Puget Sound, including Whidbey and Bainbridge to the south, are massively popular with cyclists, but rural Lopez Island—with its gently rolling terrain and very little auto traffic—is especially well suited to two-wheel traffic.

Mount Vernon and La Conner, WA. Biking around these two picturesque Skagit County communities is popular year-round, but this activity is especially fun in spring, when Tulip Country Bike Tours arranges trips through the region's glorious tulip fields.

Lochside Regional Trail, Victoria, BC. A fun way to get from the ferry terminal at Swartz Bay to Downtown Victoria, and to access a number of wineries, this 29-km (18-mile) level route is along a former rail track.

Lower Seymour Valley Conservation Reserve, Vancouver, BC. Easily reached from Downtown Vancouver, the reserve in the soaring North Shore Mountains comprises some 25 km (15½ miles) of trails through leafy rain forests, plus an easier, paved, 10-km (6-mile) track.

Seaside Route, Vancouver, BC. The 32-km (20-mile) Seaside Route, which curves around the seawall through False Creek and Stanley Park and then south into Kitsilano, is particularly dramatic.

WHALE-WATCHING IN THE PACIFIC NORTHWEST

The thrill of seeing whales in the wild is, for many, one of the most enduring memories of a trip to the Pacific Northwest. In this part of the world, you'll generally spot two species—gray whales and killer "orca" whales.

About 20,000 grays migrate up the West Coast in spring and back down again in early winter (a smaller group of gray whales live off the Oregon coast all summer). From late spring through early autumn about 80 orcas inhabit Washington's Puget Sound and BC's Georgia Strait. Although far fewer in number, the orcas live in pods and travel in predictable patterns; therefore chances are high that you will see a pod on any given trip. Some operators claim sighting rates of 90 percent; others offer guaranteed sightings, meaning that you can repeat

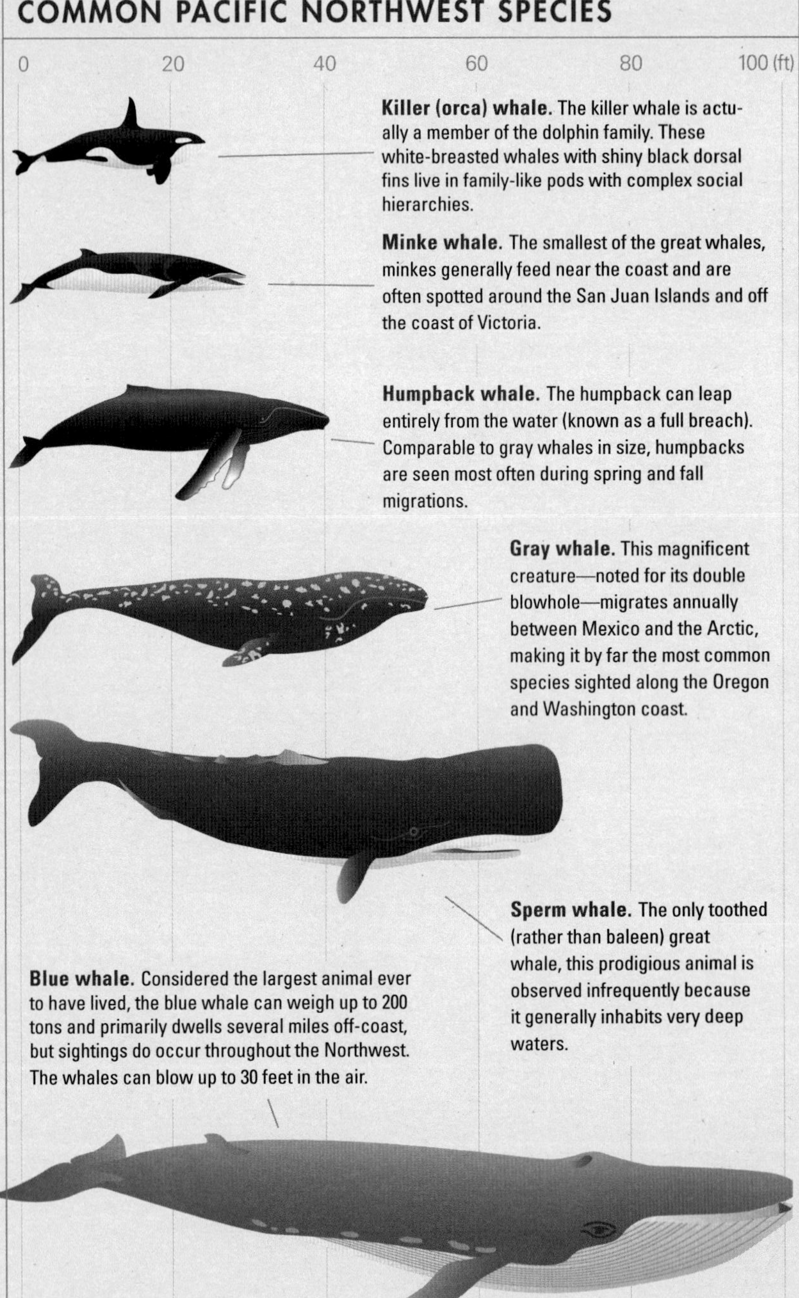
COMMON PACIFIC NORTHWEST SPECIES
0
20
40
60
80
100 (ft)
Killer (orca) whale. The killer whale is actually a member of the dolphin family. These white-breasted whales with shiny black dorsal fins live in family-like pods with complex social hierarchies.
Minke whale. The smallest of the great whales, minkes generally feed near the coast and are often spotted around the San Juan Islands and off the coast of Victoria.
Humpback whale. The humpback can leap entirely from the water (known as a full breach). Comparable to gray whales in size, humpbacks are seen most often during spring and fall migrations.
Gray whale. This magnificent creature—noted for its double blowhole—migrates annually between Mexico and the Arctic, making it by far the most common species sighted along the Oregon and Washington coast.
Sperm whale. The only toothed (rather than baleen) great whale, this prodigious animal is observed infrequently because it generally inhabits very deep waters.
Blue whale. Considered the largest animal ever to have lived, the blue whale can weigh up to 200 tons and primarily dwells several miles off-coast, but sightings do occur throughout the Northwest. The whales can blow up to 30 feet in the air.

TAKING A TOUR

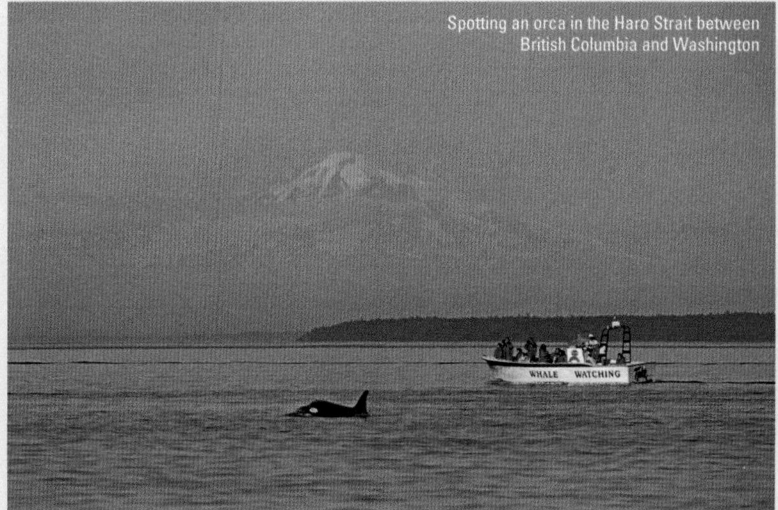

Spotting an orca in the Haro Strait between British Columbia and Washington

CHOOSING YOUR BOAT

The type of boat you choose does not affect how close you can get to the whales. For the safety of whales and humans, government regulations require boats to stay at least 100 meters (328 feet) from the pods, though closer encounters are possible if whales approach a boat when its engine is off.

Motor Launches. These cruisers carry from 30 to more than 80 passengers. They are comfortable, with washrooms, protection from the elements, and even snack-and-drink concessions. They can be either glass-enclosed or open-air.

Zodiacs. Open inflatable boats, Zodiacs carry about 12 passengers. They are smaller and more agile than cruisers and offer both an exciting ride bouncing over the waves and an eye-level view of the whales. Passengers are supplied with warm, waterproof survival suits. **Note: Zodiac tours are not recommended for people with back or neck problems, pregnant women, or small children.**

Most companies have naturalists on board as guides, as well as hydrophones that, if you get close enough, allow you to listen to the whales singing and vocalizing. Although the focus is on whales, you also have a good chance of spotting marine birds, Dall's porpoises, dolphins, seals, and sea lions, as well as other marine life. And, naturally, there's the scenery of forested islands, distant mountains, and craggy coastline.

MOTION SICKNESS

Seasickness isn't usually a problem in the sheltered waters of Puget Sound and the Georgia Strait, but seas can get choppy off the Washington and Oregon coasts. If you're not a good sailor, it's wise to wear a seasickness band or take anti-nausea medication. Ginger candy often works, too.

THE OREGON AND WASHINGTON COAST

A full breach in open waters is a thrilling sight

WHEN TO GO

Mid-December through mid-January is the best time for viewing the southbound migration, with April through mid-June the peak period for the northbound return (when whales swim closer to shore). Throughout summer, several hundred gray whales remain in Oregon waters, often feeding within close view of land. Mornings are often the best time for viewing, as it's more commonly overcast at this time, which means less glare and calmer seas. Try to watch for vapor or water expelled from whales' spouts on the horizon.

WHAT IT COSTS

Trips are generally 2 hours and prices for adults range from about $25 to $40.

RECOMMENDED OUTFITTERS

Depoe Bay, with its sheltered, deepwater harbor, is Oregon's whale-watching capital, and here you'll find several outfitters.

Dockside Charters (☎ *800/733–8915* 🌐 *www.docksidedepoebay.com*) has an excellent reputation. Green-oriented **Eco Tours of Oregon** (☎ *888/868–7733,* 🌐 *www.ecotours-of-oregon.com*) offers full day tours that depart from Portland hotels and include a stop along the coast at Siletz Bay, a 75-minute charter boat tour, lunch, and stops at state parks near Newport and Lincoln City.

Along the Washington coast, several of the fishing-charter companies in Westport offer seasonal whale-watching cruises, including **Ocean Sportfishing Charters** (☎ *800/562–0105,* 🌐 *www.oceansportfishing.com*).

BEST VIEWING FROM SHORE

Washington: On Long Beach Peninsula, the North Head Lighthouse at the mouth of the Columbia River, makes an excellent perch for whale sightings. Westport, farther up the coast at the mouth of Grays Harbor, is another great spot.

Oregon Coast: You can spot gray whales all summer long and especially during the spring migration—excellent locales include Neahkanie Mountain Overlook near Manzanita, Cape Lookout State Park, the Whale Watching Center in Depoe Bay, Cape Perpetua Interpretive Center in Yachats, and Cape Blanco Lighthouse near Port Orford.

PUGET SOUND AND GEORGIA STRAIT

Killer whales in the Puget Sound

WHEN TO GO

Prime time for viewing the three pods of orcas that inhabit this region's waterways is March through September. Less commonly, you may see minke, gray, and humpback whales around the same time.

WHAT IT COSTS

Trips in the San Juan waters are from 3 to 6 hours and prices range from $60 to $120 per adult. Trips in Canada are generally 4 to 6 hours and prices range from $125 to $175 per adult.

RECOMMENDED OUTFITTERS

Many tours depart from Friday Harbor on San Juan Island, among them **Eclipse Charters** (☎ *360/376–6566* 🌐 *www.orcasislandwhales.com*), **San Juan Excursions** (☎ *800/809–4253* 🌐 *www.watchwhales.com*), and **Western Prince Cruises** (☎ *800/757–6722* 🌐 *www.orcawhalewatch.com*). **San Juan Cruises** (☎ *800/443-4552* 🌐 *www.whales.com*) offers both day- and overnight whale-watching cruises between Bellingham and Victoria.

One rather fortuitous approach to whale-watching is simply to ride one of the **Washington State Ferries** (☎ *888/808–7977* 🌐 *www.wsdot.wa.gov/ferries*) out of Anacortes through the San Juans. During the summer killer-whale season, naturalists work on the ferries and talk about the whales and other wildlife.

In Canada, **Wild Whales Vancouver** (☎ *604/699-2011* 🌐 *www.whalesvancouver.com*) departs from Granville Island on both glass-domed and open-air vessels. **Vancouver Whale Watch** (☎ *604/274–9565* 🌐 *www.vancouverwhalewatch.com*) is another first-rate company.

Victoria has an even greater number of whale-watching outfitters. **Great Pacific Adventures** (☎ *877/733–6722* 🌐 *www.greatpacificadventures.com*), **Springtide Whale Tours** (☎ *800/470–3474* 🌐 *www.victoriawhalewatching.com)* and **Prince of Whales** (☎ *888/383–4884* 🌐 *www.princeofwhales.com*) use boats equipped with hydrophones. The latter also offers trips on a 74-passenger cruiser.

BEST VIEWING FROM SHORE

A prime spot for viewing orcas is Lime Kiln State Park, on the west side of San Juan Island. On the Canadian side, you can sometimes see whales right off Oak Bay in Victoria.

What to Watch and Read

THE GOONIES
The beloved Richard Donner–directed teen adventure comedy was filmed entirely on the northern Oregon Coast, including Cannon Beach and Astoria, which is home to the historic jail in the movie and now serves as the Oregon Film Museum.

THE LATHE OF HEAVEN
The late sci-fi novelist and Portlander Ursula K. Le Guin set this award-winning 1971 novel in a futuristic and dystopian version of Portland (in 2002). There have been two TV movies made from the book.

MY OWN PRIVATE IDAHO
Locally based LGBTQ indie director Gus Van Sant's 1991 drama, starring Keanu Reeves and River Phoenix, was filmed primarily in Portland, with many scenes at what is now the posh Sentinel hotel. It's perhaps the most celebrated of several movies that Van Sant set and shot in Portland, including *Drugstore Cowboy* and *Paranoid Park*.

PORTLANDIA
This hit satirical sketch TV series, starring Carrie Brownstein and Fred Armisen, ran on the IFC channel from 2011 through 2018. The show was filmed at a number of recognizable spots around town, including the Vera Katz Eastbank Esplanade (in the opening credits), Prasad restaurant, Olympia Provisions, Paxton Gate, Caravan–The Tiny House Hotel, and Land Gallery.

THE GREY FOX
The godfather of Vancouver cinema, director Phillip Borsos made his feature debut in 1982 with *The Grey Fox*, a revisionist Western film portraying the infamous bandit Bill Miner as he plots Canada's first great train robbery in the early 1900s. True to life, the movie was filmed on location along the BC Railway. Regarded as one of the country's cinematic masterworks, Borsos manages to transcend period-piece clichés with his elegant depiction of this pivotal moment in British Columbian history.

JUNO
For the coming-of-age dramedy *Juno*, Canadian director Jason Reitman casts Vancouver's suburbs as Minnesota, where fellow Canadian-turned-Hollywood star Ellen Page plays a confident teen navigating her junior year of high school—four seasons defined by an unplanned pregnancy and her tangled relationship with a yuppie couple looking to adopt. This 2007 Academy Award winner is one of the best-regarded films in which Vancouver once again passes for its southern neighbor.

MUSIC OF THE '90S
It may not be a book or movie, but the music of the Pacific Northwest is just as impactful. Seattle will always be proud of its association with Kurt Cobain, the late great golden boy of grunge. Nirvana was signed to iconic Seattle label Sub Pop who gave rise to the grunge movement, and was also the home of bands like Mudhoney. Alice in Chains and Pearl Jam also formed in the mid-90s. Hole, fronted by the legendary Courtney Love came out with *Live Through This* in 1994, their best-known and most accessible album. Tracks like "Miss World" were written in Seattle. Kathleen Hanna of Bikini Kill, the Julie Ruin, and Le Tigre, is credited as being one of the most influential female punk artists; not just in the Pacific Northwest, but anywhere. The birthers of the Riot Grrrl movement, Bikini Kill put out the perfectly '90s punk album *Revolution Girl Style Now!* in 1991, inspiring acts like Sleater-Kinney (originally out of Olympia, Washington), and influencing contemporaries like Nirvana. Hip-hop was also prevalent during this time, with one of most notable PNW-based acts being Sir Mix-A-Lot.

Chapter 2

TRAVEL SMART

2

Updated by
Shelley Arenas

★ CAPITAL:
Washington: Olympia; Oregon: Salem; British Columbia: Victoria

POPULATION:
Washington: 7.57 million; Oregon: 4.24 million; British Columbia: 5.07 million

LANGUAGE:
English in the U.S.; English and French in Canada

$ CURRENCY:
U.S. dollar (USD) in Washington and Oregon; Canadian dollar (CAD) in BC.

COUNTRY CODE:
1

⚠ EMERGENCIES:
911

DRIVING:
On the right.

ELECTRICITY:
120v

TIME:
Pacific Time Zone

WEB RESOURCES:
www.experiencewa.com,
www.traveloregon.com,
www.hellobc.com

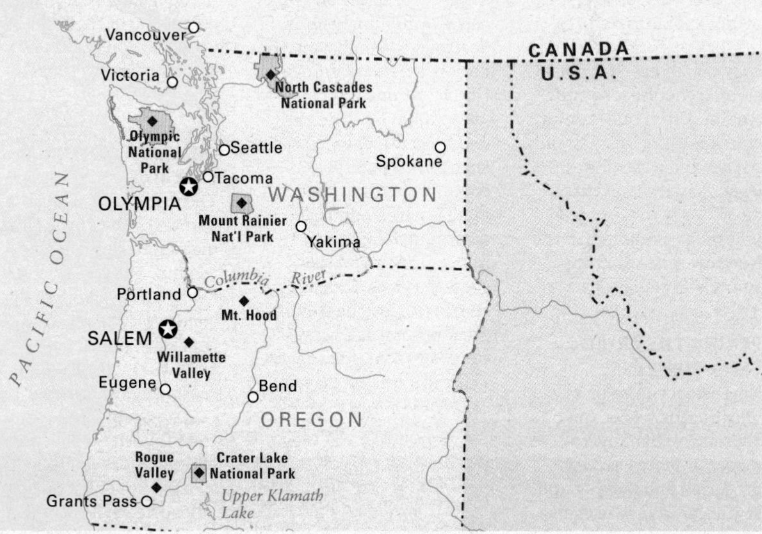

Know Before You Go

With the Pacific Ocean as its western boundary, the Pacific Northwest is an international region encompassing the states of Washington and Oregon in the United States and British Columbia in Canada. It's an intriguing, if somewhat mysterious, destination.

HERE COMES THE RAIN AGAIN

The Pacific Northwest has two distinct climates—wet and mild on the west side of the Cascade Mountain Range, dry with hot summers and cold winters on the east. There are also microclimates, including the unique Puget Sound Convergence Zone, which accounts for occasionally big snowfalls on the west side. That snow rarely sticks around for more than a day or two, but even a couple of flakes in the forecast sends people rushing to stores to stock up for the coming snowpocalypse. If it does arrive, schools close and workers often take a snow day. While the rainy, dreary days of the west side are legendary, it's true that mostly only tourists use umbrellas. Summers in the Northwest are dazzling: sunny and warm.

PAYING THE PRICE

Visiting the Pacific Northwest can be pricey. Washington's sales tax adds more than 10% to most purchases except groceries, and lodging and rental car taxes are even higher. Oregon has no state sales tax, but you'll pay surcharges on lodging and rental cars there as well. In British Columbia, expect both taxes and higher prices. Gas is significantly more in Canada, and thrifty drivers fill up on the U.S. side before crossing the border. (Note that the U.S. dollar nearly always goes further in Canada, usually between 20% and 35% more, depending on exchange rate.) Costs for dining out can be especially high in the metro areas, due to higher real estate and labor costs. Minimum wage in Seattle is the highest in the nation, a necessity since the city's housing costs are so high. But there are ways to save when visiting, such as discount passes for tourist attractions, monthly free-admission days at museums, and public transit and ride-share services. During the short but glorious summer season, hotel and rental car prices soar, so consider visiting in the off-season.

CANNABIS CONSIDERATIONS

Marijuana use is legal in Washington and Oregon and all of Canada. You can't take your stash across the international border, so plan on finishing your BC bud before returning to the United States. Age restrictions match those for alcohol: 21 in Washington and Oregon, 19 in BC. Pot shops are licensed by the government just like liquor stores, and identification is checked at the door. Friendly budtenders answer your questions about the various products. It's rare that hotels allow pot smoking inside (many don't allow smoking at all), though a few advertise they are "420 friendly." Only BC allows pot smoking in public, and only in places where no children are present. Rules or not, it's pretty common (and some would say annoying) to smell pot when out in public, especially in parks and other outdoor venues. If you're partaking, be respectful of those around you. And don't toke and drive: obviously that's against the law.

THE SPORTS FAN GAME IS STRONG

The Pacific Northwest is home to some of the most passionate sports fans around. The NFL's Seattle Seahawks are backed by community team spirit that is both visible and audible. During football season, every Friday is Blue Friday, when fans wear their favorite team's attire. Making it to two back-to-back Super Bowls has helped keep the "12th Man" strong. More than half a million people turned out for the Super Bowl victory parade in 2014, and league noise records have been set by the roaring crowd at home games. If you can't make it to a game in person, join in the camaraderie by watching the Seahawks or the Mariners live at a sports bar. The city is also justifiably proud of the Seattle Sounders FC soccer team, which won Major League Soccer's prestigious MLS Cup in 2016 and 2019. The club has its own fan traditions, including the famous March to the Match that anyone can join and starts at Occidental Park an hour before each home match. While Seattleites are sometimes known for being introverted and distant (the so-called Seattle Freeze), that melts away on game day. The city also loves its women's basketball team, the Seattle Storm. Portlanders show up for the NBA Trailblazers, and BC fans strongly support the NHL's Vancouver-based Canucks, though Seattle's new NHL team will undoubtedly spark some cross-border rivalry when games begin in 2021.

GETTING OUT ON THE WATER

A visit to the Pacific Northwest isn't complete if you don't experience it from one of the many waterways. You can head out on your own with a kayak, canoe, or electric boat to explore the calm lakes and bays around Seattle and Vancouver, get your adrenaline pumping with whitewater rafting down mountain rivers, enjoy a narrated cruise around big cities, bypass city traffic with a water taxi, or take ferries across the Puget Sound and Salish Sea. The ferries make it possible to reach islands that are otherwise only accessible by seaplane or private boat, including Washington's San Juan Islands, the Gulf Islands in BC, and Vancouver Island, home of the province's capital city of Victoria. Ferries get crowded in summer; plan ahead and make reservations when available.

WHAT TO WEAR

Both Seattle and Portland are informal cities, and there's almost nowhere you could go that you'd be out of place in a T-shirt and jeans. You'll rarely see anyone in formal attire, and it's required only at a few high-end restaurants. It's been years since grunge's heyday, but locals still wear flannel and fleece, as they are the perfect materials for the damp, cool weather.

EAT, DRINK, AND SHOP LOCAL

With the region's bounty of locally grown produce, freshly caught seafood, and abundant wineries and breweries, it's easy to find "farm-to-table" restaurants featuring the best of the Northwest. Definitely check out such eateries to experience their chefs' inspiration. Take some time to explore the scene at local markets, too.

EXPECT TO SEE HOMELESS PEOPLE

All along the West Coast, including in the Pacific Northwest, there are high numbers of homeless people living in larger cities. They often sleep in tents under freeway overpasses at night and panhandle during the day. This can be shocking for first-time visitors. Homelessness is a complex issue and there haven't been easy or quick solutions in these cities so far.

TRANSPORTATION TIPS

If you're traveling by car, don't expect to get anywhere quickly during rush hour in the bigger cities. Both Seattle and Portland usually rank highly on the national "worst traffic" lists.

BRING ALONG YOUR BEST (CANINE) FRIEND

Some Northwest cities have more dogs than children, and businesses know that Fido is everybody's friend. Hotels, bars, and even some restaurants have made their dog-friendliness not just policy, but a point of pride. Off-leash dog parks are plentiful in cities and welcome your visiting pup. State and provincial parks usually allow dogs on leashes (with some areas off-limits) but national parks generally don't, even on a leash. Nearby national forests often do. If you're crossing the international border with your dog, be sure and bring a valid rabies vaccination certificate.

Getting Here and Around

 Air

It takes about 5 hours to fly nonstop to Seattle or Portland from New York, 4 hours from Chicago, and 2½ hours from Los Angeles. Flights from New York to Vancouver take about 6 hours nonstop; from Chicago, 4½ hours nonstop; and from Los Angeles, 3 hours nonstop. Flying from Seattle to Portland takes just under an hour; flying from Portland to Vancouver takes an hour and 15 minutes; and from Seattle to Vancouver about 45 minutes.

AIRPORTS

The main gateways to the Pacific Northwest are Portland International Airport (PDX), Sea-Tac International Airport (SEA), and Vancouver International Airport (YVR). The small Paine Field Airport (PAE) opened in 2019 to rave reviews for its luxurious style and passenger comfort. Located 36 miles north of Sea-Tac and served by two airlines, Alaska and Delta, it's a convenient alternative for traveling to and from Spokane, Portland, Las Vegas, Phoenix, Denver, and six cities in California.

FLIGHTS

Many international carriers serve the Pacific Northwest with direct flights. These include Air France, All Nippon Airways, British Airways, Cathay Pacific, Emirates, Icelandair, Japan Airlines, and Lufthansa. Vancouver has the most connections with international cities, but Seattle's a close second. U.S. carriers serving the area include Alaska Airlines, American, Delta, and United. JetBlue has daily direct flights from New York's JFK Airport, Logan International in Boston, and Los Angeles's Long Beach Airport to both Seattle and Portland. Frontier Airlines, Skywest (via Delta), and United Express provide frequent service between cities in Washington, Oregon, Idaho, Montana, and California. Southwest Airlines has frequent nonstop service to Seattle and Portland from cities in California, Nevada, Arizona, and Texas, as well as Baltimore, Chicago, and some other parts of the country. The major regional carrier in western Canada is Air Canada (and its subsidiary, Air Canada Express), which has flights from Seattle and Portland to Vancouver and Victoria, along with many direct flights between Vancouver and major U.S. cities outside the Northwest.

Boat and Ferry

Ferries play an important part in the transportation network of the Pacific Northwest. Some are the sole connection to islands in Puget Sound and to small towns and islands along the west coast of British Columbia. Each day ferries transport thousands of commuters to and from work in the coastal cities. Always comfortable, convenient, and providing spectacular views, ferries are also one of the best ways for you to get a feel for the region and its ties to the sea.

Generally, the best times for travel are 9–3 and after 7 pm on weekdays. In July and August you may have to wait hours to take a car aboard one of the popular ferries, such as those to the San Juan Islands. Walk-on space is almost always available; if possible, leave your car behind. Reservations aren't taken for most domestic routes in Washington.

WASHINGTON AND OREGON

Washington State Ferries carries millions of passengers and vehicles each year on 10 routes between 20 points on Puget Sound, the San Juan Islands, and Sidney, British Columbia. Onboard services vary depending on the size of the ferry, but many have a cafeteria, vending machines, newspaper and tourist-information kiosks, arcade games, and restrooms with family facilities. There are discounted fares in off-peak months.

Black Ball Transport's MV *Coho* makes daily crossings year-round from Port Angeles, WA, to Victoria. The *Coho* can carry 800 passengers and 100 cars across the Strait of Juan de Fuca in 1½ hours. Clipper Vacations operates the passenger-only *Victoria Clipper* jet catamaran service between Seattle and Victoria year-round and between Seattle and the San Juan Islands May through September. **■ TIP→ Victoria Clipper fares are less expensive if booked at least one day in advance, and great package deals are often available online.**

Argosy cruising vessels make sightseeing, dinner, weekend brunch, and special-event cruises around Elliott Bay, Lake Union, Lake Washington, the Ballard Locks, and other Seattle waterways.

From Portland, the *Portland Spirit*, *Willamette Star*, and *Crystal Dolphin* offer sightseeing and dinner cruises on the Willamette and Columbia Rivers. The high-speed *Explorer* takes day trips from Portland to the Columbia River, and offers a one-way option for cyclists to return via a 45-mile historic highway route. Departing from Cascade Locks, Oregon (45 minutes east of Portland), the stern-wheeler *Columbia Gorge* cruises the Columbia River.

BRITISH COLUMBIA

British Columbia Ferries operates passenger and vehicle service between the mainland and Victoria and elsewhere. Most ferries take reservations.

Bus

BoltBus service runs between Vancouver, Bellingham, Seattle, Portland, and southern Oregon and features sleek new buses with extra legroom, reserved seating, power outlets, and Wi-Fi. Experience Oregon in Eugene operates charter bus services and scheduled sightseeing tours that last from a few hours to several days. Greyhound serves many towns in Washington, Oregon, and British Columbia, and provides frequent service on popular runs. Quick Shuttle runs buses from Sea-Tac Airport, Downtown Seattle, and Bellingham to various Vancouver spots and hotels.

SIGHTSEEING

Gray Line operates a variety of popular hop-on hop-off bus tours in Seattle, Portland, Victoria, and Vancouver, along with day trips to Multnomah Falls and the Columbia River Gorge, Willamette Valley, Whistler Village, and Vancouver and Victoria attractions.

Car

Driver's licenses from other countries are valid in the United States and Canada. International driving permits (IDPs)—available from the American and Canadian automobile associations and Canada's National Auto Club, and, in the United Kingdom, from the Automobile Association, Royal Automobile Club, and some post office branches—are a good idea. Valid only in conjunction with your regular driver's license, these permits are universally recognized; having one may spare you from difficulties with local authorities.

Getting Here and Around

Travel Times from Seattle by Car	
Portland	3–3½ hours
Vancouver	2½–3 hours
Victoria	2½–3 hour drive to Vancouver; 1½-hour ferry ride from Vancouver
Mount Rainier National Park (Paradise or Longmire entrances)	2½ hours
North Cascades National Park	3–3½ hours
Olympic National Park	2½ hours to Port Angeles; 1 hour from Port Angeles to Hurricane Ridge; 2 hours from Port Angeles to Hoh Rain Forest
Mt. St. Helens	3–3½ hours
Spokane	4½–5 hours
Yakima Valley	2–2½ hours

Bookstores, gas stations, convenience stores, and rest stops sell maps (about $5) and multiregion road atlases (about $15). Along larger highways, roadside stops with restrooms, fast-food restaurants, and sundries stores are well spaced. Police and tow trucks patrol major highways and lend assistance.

BORDER CROSSING

You will need a valid passport to cross the border; passport cards and enhanced driver's licenses are also accepted for land and sea crossings only. In addition, drivers must carry owner registration and proof of insurance coverage, which is compulsory in Canada. The Canadian Non-Resident Inter-Provincial Motor Vehicle Liability Insurance Card, available from any U.S. insurance company, is accepted as evidence of financial responsibility in Canada. If you are driving a car that is not registered in your name, carry a letter from the owner that authorizes your use of the vehicle.

Travel Times from Portland by Car	
Bend	3½–4 hours
Crater Lake National Park	4½–5 hours
Columbia River Gorge/Mt. Hood	1½ hours
Willamette Valley	1½–2 hours

The main entry point into British Columbia from the United States by car is on Interstate 5 at Blaine, Washington, 30 miles south of Vancouver. Three highways enter British Columbia from the east: Highway 1, or the Trans-Canada Highway; Highway 3, or the Crowsnest Highway, which crosses southern British Columbia; and Highway 16, the Yellowhead Highway, which runs through northern British Columbia from the Rocky Mountains to Prince Rupert. From Alaska and the Yukon, take the Alaska Highway (from Fairbanks) or the Klondike Highway (from Skagway or Dawson City).

Border-crossing procedures are usually quick and simple. Every British Columbia border crossing is open 24 hours (except the one at Aldergrove, which is open from 8 am to midnight). The Interstate 5 border crossing at Blaine, Washington (also known as the Douglas, or Peace Arch, border crossing), is one of the busiest border crossings between the United States and Canada. An alternate route, the Pacific Highway border crossing (aka the "truck crossing"), is just east of the Peace Arch crossing and serves all vehicles, not just trucks. For updated information on border wait times, check local radio traffic reports and watch for electronic signs on the main highways.

GASOLINE

Gas stations are plentiful in major metropolitan areas and along major highways like Interstate 5. Most stay open late except in rural areas, where Sunday hours are limited and where you may drive long stretches without a refueling opportunity. This is particularly true in Oregon, where you are not allowed to pump your own gas, and therefore won't be able to find an automated pump in an emergency.

Keep an eye on the gauge when traveling to wilderness areas and off-the-beaten-path trails, particularly if you'll be heading down Forest Service roads. A good rule of thumb is to fill up before you get off (or too far away from) a major highway like Interstate 5 or Interstate 90. Making a wide loop around Olympic National Park can burn a lot of fuel, and there are very few towns between Port Angeles to the north and Aberdeen to the south. The eastern stretches of Washington and Oregon can be virtually empty, so always fill up before you exit major highways.

RENTAL CARS

Unless you only visit Seattle, Portland, and Vancouver, you will need to rent a car for at least part of your trip. It's possible to get around the big cities by public transportation and taxis, but once you go outside city limits, your options are limited. National lines like Greyhound do provide service between major towns, and Amtrak has limited service between points in Washington, Oregon, and British Columbia (allowing you to get from, say, Seattle to Portland, by train), but it is nearly impossible to get to and around the major recreation areas and national parks of each state without your own wheels. For example, there is no public transportation from Seattle to Mount Rainier National Park.

Rates in Seattle begin at $22 a day ($108 per week) for an economy car. This does not include the 17.8% tax. The tax on rentals at Sea-Tac Airport, which includes an airport concession fee, is more than 30%, so try to rent from a Downtown branch, where base rental rates are often lower, too. Rates in Portland are similar, not including the 17% tax and $6 daily fee for rentals at the airport. Rates in Vancouver begin at about C$20 a day or C$115 a week, usually including unlimited mileage. Note that summer rates in all cities can be absurd (up to $75 per day for a compact); book as far in advance as possible, and if you find a good deal, grab it. Car rentals in British Columbia also incur a 12% sales tax. An additional 17% Concession Recovery Fee, charged by the airport authority for retail space in the terminal, is levied at airport locations.

All the major agencies are represented in the region. If you're planning to cross the U.S.–Canadian border with your rental car, discuss it with the agency to see what's involved.

ROAD CONDITIONS

Winter driving can present challenges. In coastal areas, the mild, damp climate contributes to frequently wet roadways. Snowfalls generally occur in low-lying Portland, Seattle, and Vancouver only once or twice a year, but when snow does fall, traffic grinds to a halt and roadways become treacherous and stay that way until the snow melts.

Tire chains, studs, or snow tires are essential equipment for winter travel in mountain areas. If you're planning to drive into high elevations, be sure to check the weather forecast beforehand. Even the main-highway mountain passes can close because of snow conditions. In winter, state and provincial highway departments operate snow-advisory telephone lines that give pass conditions.

Getting Here and Around

RULES OF THE ROAD

In the Pacific Northwest you must be 21 to rent a car. Car seats are compulsory for infants and toddlers; older children are required to sit in booster seats until they are at least 4 feet, 9 inches tall *or*13 years old in Washington or 8 years old in Oregon. In British Columbia, children up to 40 pounds or 18 kilos in weight must use a child seat; booster seats are required for children up to nine years old or 145 cm tall. In the United States nonresidents need a reservation voucher, passport, driver's license, and insurance for each driver.

Cruise

Seattle's cruise industry welcomes some of the world's largest ships to its docks on Elliott Bay.

Vancouver is the major embarkation point for Alaska cruises, and virtually all Alaska-bound cruise ships call there; some also call at Victoria and Prince Rupert.

Train

Amtrak, the U.S. passenger rail system, has daily service to the Pacific Northwest from the Midwest and California. The Empire Builder takes a northern route through Minnesota and Montana from Chicago to Spokane, from which separate legs continue to Seattle and Portland. The Coast Starlight begins in Los Angeles; makes stops throughout California, western Oregon, and Washington; and terminates in Seattle.

The Amtrak Cascades trains travel between Seattle and Vancouver and between Seattle, Portland, and Eugene. The trip from Seattle to Portland takes roughly 3½ hours and costs \$27–\$65 for a coach seat each way; this is a pleasant alternative to a mind-numbing drive down Interstate 5. The trip from Seattle to Vancouver takes roughly 4½ hours and costs \$34–\$80 one-way. The Empire Builder's northern leg between Seattle and Spokane takes eight hours and costs \$46–\$127 each way. The southern leg travels between Portland and Spokane (7½ hours, \$46–\$127 one-way), with part of the route running through the Columbia River Gorge. From Portland to Eugene, the trip is just under three hours; the cost is \$22–\$52.

Essentials

Lodging

The lodgings we list are the cream of the crop in each price category. Prices are for a standard double room in high season and excluding tax and service charges. Seattle room tax is 15.6%. Elsewhere in Washington it ranges from 10% to 16%. Portland room tax is 11.5% (13.5% at hotels with 50 or more rooms) while elsewhere in Oregon it ranges from 7% to 12%. Vancouver room tax is 16% with elsewhere in British Columbia ranging from 13% to 15%.

BED-AND-BREAKFASTS

The Pacific Northwest is known for its vast range of bed-and-breakfasts, which are found everywhere from busy urban areas to casual country farms and coastal retreats. Many B&Bs here provide full gourmet breakfasts, and some have kitchens that guests can use. Other popular amenities to ask about are fireplaces, jetted bathtubs, outdoor hot tubs, and area activities.

CAMPING

Oregon, Washington, and British Columbia have excellent government-run campgrounds. Some accept advance camping reservations. National park campsites—even backcountry sites—fill up quickly and should be reserved in advance. Note that federal forests allow free camping almost anywhere along trails—a good fail-safe if you're unable to secure last-minute arrangements at designated sites, and don't mind hauling your gear.

Privately operated campgrounds sometimes have extra amenities such as laundry rooms and swimming pools. For more information, contact the state or local tourism department.

HOTELS

Most of the larger hotels throughout the region will be part of a major American or Canadian chain, but there are still a handful of lodges dotted around the area that are family-owned and have plenty of local flavor.

Dining

Pacific Northwest cuisine highlights regional seafood and locally grown, organic produce, often prepared in styles that reflect an Asian influence (Seattle, Victoria, and Vancouver have large Asian populations) or incorporate European (often French or Italian) influences.

MEALS AND MEALTIMES

Unless otherwise noted, the restaurants listed here are open daily for lunch and dinner.

WINES, BEER, AND SPIRITS

Oregon, Washington, and British Columbia all have thriving wineries, and many restaurants in major cities and many small towns, and even in wilderness areas, take their wine lists very seriously. Most of Washington's vineyards are east of the Cascades in the south-central part of the state; you'll also find more than 100 wineries in Woodinville, near Seattle. Oregon's wineries mostly lie in the valleys between the southern Cascades and the coast. British Columbia wine-making has become increasingly prominent, with many wineries in the Okanagan Valley. The Washington State Wine Commission (🌐 *www.washingtonwine.org*) and the Oregon Wine Board (🌐 *www.oregonwine.org*) both maintain websites with facts, history, and information on local wineries. The British Columbia Wine Institute's website (🌐 *www.winebc.com*) has facts and information on individual wineries.

Essentials

Oregon has more than 200 microbreweries, and Washington has no shortage of excellent local microbrews. Both states have festivals and events celebrating their brews—Seattle's Fremont neighborhood has its own Oktoberfest. The website for the Washington Brewers Guild (🌐 *www.washingtonbeer.com*) has info on breweries in the state and events throughout the Pacific Northwest. The Oregon Brewers Guild (🌐 *www.oregoncraftbeer.org*) also has links to breweries and information on events.

You must be 21 to buy alcohol in Washington and Oregon. The legal drinking age in British Columbia is 19.

Customs and Duties

You're always allowed to bring goods of a certain value back home without having to pay any duty or import tax. But there's a limit on the amount of tobacco and liquor you can bring back duty-free, and some countries have separate limits for perfumes; for exact figures, check with your customs department. The values of so-called duty-free goods are included in these amounts. When you shop abroad, save all your receipts, as customs inspectors may ask to see them as well as the items you purchased. If the total value of your goods is more than the duty-free limit, you'll have to pay a tax (most often a flat percentage) on the value of everything beyond that limit.

Health

A novel coronavirus brought all travel to a virtual standstill in the first half of 2020. Although the illness is mild in most people, some experience severe and even life-threatening complications. Once travel started up again, albeit slowly and cautiously, travelers were asked to be particularly careful about hygiene and to avoid any unnecessary travel, especially if they are sick.

Older adults, especially those over 65, have a greater chance of having severe complications from COVID-19. The same is true for people with weaker immune systems or those living with some types of medical conditions, including diabetes, asthma, heart disease, cancer, HIV/AIDS, kidney disease, and liver disease. Starting two weeks before a trip, anyone planning to travel should be on the lookout for some of the following symptoms: cough, fever, chills, trouble breathing, muscle pain, sore throat, new loss of smell or taste. If you experience any of these symptoms, you should not travel at all.

And to protect yourself during travel, do your best to avoid contact with people showing symptoms. Wash your hands often with soap and water. Limit your time in public places, and, when you are out and about, wear a cloth face mask that covers your nose and mouth. Indeed, a mask may be required in some places, such as on an airplane or in a confined space like a theater, where you share the space with a lot of people.

You may wish to bring extra supplies, such as disenfecting wipes, hand sanitizer (12-ounce bottles were allowed in carry-on luggage at this writing), and a first-aid kit with a thermometer.

Given how abruptly travel was curtailed in March 2020, it is wise to consider protecting yourself by purchasing a travel insurance policy that will reimburse you for any costs related to COVID-19 related cancellations. Not all travel insurance policies protect against pandemic-related cancellations, so always read the fine print.

Packing

It's all about layers here, as there's no other way to keep up with the weather, which can morph from cold and overcast to warm and sunny and back again in the course of a few hours, especially in spring and early fall. Summer days are warm and more consistent, but evenings can cool off substantially. Bring an umbrella or raincoat for unpredictable fall and winter weather. Hikers will want to bring rain gear and a hat with them, even if they're visiting in summer; insect repellent is also a good idea if you'll be hiking along mountain trails or beaches.

Passports

All people traveling by air between the United States and Canada are required to present a passport to enter or reenter the United States. To enter Canada (or more precisely, to reenter the United States from Canada) by land or sea you need to present either a valid passport or a U.S. Passport Card—sort of a "passport lite" that is only valid for land or sea crossings from Canada, Mexico, the Caribbean, or Bermuda. Enhanced drivers licenses, issued by Washington and other border states, can also be used for land or sea crossings.

U.S. passports are valid for 10 years. You must apply in person if you're getting a passport for the first time; if your previous passport was lost, stolen, or damaged; or if your previous passport has expired and was issued more than 15 years ago or when you were under 16. All children under 18 must appear in person to apply for or renew a passport. Both parents must accompany any child under 14 (or send a notarized statement with their permission) and provide proof of their relationship to the child.

The cost to apply for a new passport is $145 for adults, $115 for children under 16; renewals are $110. Allow up to eight weeks for processing, both for first-time passports and renewals. For an expediting fee of $60, you can reduce this time to about three weeks. If your trip is less than two weeks away, you can get a passport even more rapidly by going to a passport office with the necessary documentation. Private expediters can get things done in as little as 48 hours, but charge hefty fees for their services.

Safety

The most dangerous element of the Northwest is the great outdoors. Don't hike alone, and make sure you bring enough water plus basic first-aid items. If you're not an experienced hiker, stick to tourist-friendly spots like the more accessible parts of the national parks; if you have to drive 30 miles down a Forest Service road to reach a trail, it's possible you might be the only one hiking on it.

Taxes

Oregon has no sales tax, although many cities and counties levy a tax on lodging and services. Room taxes, for example, vary from 7% to 13.5%. The state retail sales tax in Washington is 6.5%, but there are also local taxes that can raise the total tax to almost 10%, depending on the goods or service and the municipality; Seattle's retail sales tax is 9.5%. A Goods and Services Tax (GST) of 5% applies on virtually every transaction in Canada except for the purchase of basic groceries.

In British Columbia an additional Provincial Sales Tax (PST) of 7% applies to most goods and services.

Great Itineraries

The Northwest Coast and Cities in 10 Days

The hip and urbane cities of Seattle and Portland bookend this itinerary, with the verdant Olympic Peninsula, rugged Oregon Coast, and undulating Willamette Valley Wine Country at the heart, giving you the best of the city and the country in one trip.

DAYS 1 AND 2: SEATTLE

Start in **Seattle,** where you can spend a couple of nights exploring this picturesque and dynamic city's highlights. Most of the must-see attractions—**Pike Place Market, Seattle Art Museum,** the **Seattle Aquarium**—are steps from Downtown hotels, and it's only a short walk or monorail ride to reach the **Seattle Center,** with its iconic **Space Needle** and such family-friendly draws as the **Pacific Science Center, Children's Museum,** and **Museum of Pop Culture (MoPOP).** You could cram several of these attractions into one busy day, but it's better to spread them out over two days. Or spend your second day exploring some of the city's lively neighborhoods, including Capitol Hill, with its scenic **Volunteer Park,** and Ballard, where you can check out the **Lake Washington Ship Canal** and the **Hiram M. Chittenden Locks.**

DAY 3: BAINBRIDGE ISLAND AND PORT TOWNSEND

(2 hours by car ferry and car from Seattle)

Take the 35-minute car ferry from Seattle across Puget Sound to laid-back and beautiful **Bainbridge Island,** stopping for lunch and browsing the shops in the village of Winslow and touring **Bloedel Reserve.** Continue on Highways 305, 3, and 104, stopping in the cute Scandinavian town of **Poulsbo,** and continuing to the northeastern corner of the Olympic Peninsula, where the charming towns of **Port Townsend** and **Port Angeles** make good overnight bases and have several fine dinner options.

DAYS 4 AND 5: OLYMPIC NATIONAL PARK

(1 hour by car from Port Townsend, 15 minutes by car from Port Angeles)

The next morning, launch into a full day at **Olympic National Park.** Explore **Hurricane Ridge** (the nearest section to Port Angeles), continue west to the waterfalls and hiking trails of **Sol Duc Valley,** then head to glacially formed **Lake Crescent** for an overnight stay at the venerable **Lake Crescent Lodge** or nostalgic **Log Cabin Resort.** Start Day 5 with a drive west on U.S. 101 to **Forks** and on to **La Push** via Highway 110, a total of about 50 miles. A stroll to **Second Beach** or **Third Beach** will offer a taste of the wild Pacific coastline. Back on U.S. 101, head south for 15 miles to the **Hoh Rain Forest** turn-off, then drive another 18 miles through the verdant forest to reach the visitors center and trails. Returning back to U.S. 101, continue south to **Lake Quinault.** Check into the **Lake Quinault Lodge,** then drive up the river 6 miles to one of the rain-forest trails through the lush Quinault Valley.

DAYS 6 AND 7: THE OREGON COAST

(2½ hours from Lake Quinault to Astoria)

Leave Lake Quinault early on Day 6 for the scenic drive south on U.S. 101. Here the road winds through coastal spruce forests, periodically rising on headlands to offer Pacific Ocean panoramas. Spend your first night in the up-and-coming town of **Astoria,** just across the Columbia River from Washington. The next day, after visiting Astoria's excellent **Columbia Maritime Museum,** continue south on U.S. 101, where small coastal resort towns like **Cannon Beach** and **Manzanita** beckon with cafés, shops, and spectacular beach parks. Be sure to walk out to the gorgeous beach at **Oswald West State Park,** just north of Manzanita. Take a detour onto the **Three Capes Loop,** a stunning 35-mile byway off U.S. 101. Stop in **Newport,** 130 miles south of Astoria, for your second night on the coast—this bustling town has several good restaurants and is home to the **Oregon Coast Aquarium.**

DAY 8: EUGENE AND THE WILLAMETTE VALLEY

(2½ hours by car from Newport to Eugene or 4 hours by car stopping at Oregon Dunes)

From Newport, continue south along the coast on U.S. 101 for 50 miles, stopping in the charming village of **Florence** for lunch. Then head south another 20 miles to briefly get a look at the soaring mountains of sand that make up **Oregon Dunes National Recreation Area** before backtracking back to Florence and cutting inland on Highway 126 about 60 miles to the artsy, friendly college town of **Eugene,** which is at the southern end of the Willamette Valley wine region. Eugene has plenty of overnight options, or you could continue north 90 miles on Interstate 5 to spend the night in the heart of the wine country at **Newberg** or **McMinnville,** where you'll find dozens of wineries, several fine restaurants, and a few upscale inns and hotels.

DAYS 9 AND 10: PORTLAND

(1 hour 45 minutes by car from Eugene, 30 minutes by car from Newberg)

On Day 9, visit some of the Willamette Valley's wineries, and then, from either Eugene or Newberg, continue into the hip, outdoorsy, and food-driven city of **Portland.** Be sure to visit the several attractions found at green and beautiful **Washington Park,** the chic shops and restaurants of the **West End** and **Pearl District,**

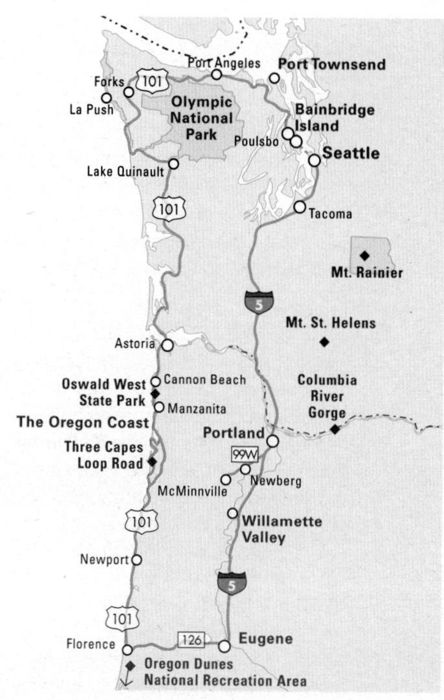

and the **Portland Art Museum,** situated along Downtown's dapper Park Blocks. Like Seattle, the Rose City is renowned for its quirky, inviting neighborhoods, filled with locavore-minded restaurants, artisanal-coffee roasters, swanky cocktail lounges, and smart boutiques—the **Central East Side, Hawthorne, Division Street, Mississippi,** and **Alberta** are among the best areas for exploring. From Portland, it's a straight three-hour drive back up to Seattle; if you have an extra day, consider a detour east into the magnificent **Columbia River Gorge.** En route to Seattle, you could also easily detour to **Mt. St. Helens, Mt. Rainier,** and the surprisingly vibrant and engaging city of **Tacoma.**

Great Itineraries

Oregon in 10 Days

With 10 days, you can get a taste of Oregon's largest city, eco-conscious Portland, while also getting a nice sense of the state's geographical diversity—the mountainous and sweeping coast, gorgeous Crater Lake, the rugged Cascade Mountains, and the eastern high-desert regions.

DAYS 1 AND 2: PORTLAND

Start by spending a couple of days in Portland, where you can tour the museums and attractions that make up **Washington Park,** as well as the **Lan Su Chinese Garden** in Old Town, and the excellent museums and cultural institutions along Downtown's leafy **Park Blocks.** This city of vibrant, distinctive neighborhoods offers plenty of great urban exploring, with Nob Hill, Hawthorne, Alberta, and the Mississippi Avenue Arts District among the best areas for shopping, café-hopping, and people-watching. If you have a little extra time, consider spending a couple of hours just south of the city in the **Willamette Valley Wine Country,** an easy jaunt from Portland.

DAYS 3 AND 4: OREGON COAST

(1½ hours by car from Portland to Cannon Beach)

Leave Portland early on Day 3 for the drive west about 100 miles on U.S. 30 to the small city of **Astoria,** which has several excellent spots for lunch and the **Columbia River Maritime Museum.** Pick the main scenic highway down the Oregon Coast, U.S. 101, and continue south, stopping at **Fort Stevens State Park** and **Fort Clatsop** in **Lewis and Clark National Historic Park.** End the day in charming **Cannon Beach** (26 miles south of Astoria), which has a wealth of oceanfront hotels and inns, many with views of one of the region's seminal features, 235-foot-tall **Haystack Rock.** Be sure to check out the stunning beach scenery at nearby **Ecola State Park** and **Oswald West State Park.**

The following morning, continue south down U.S. 101. In **Tillamook** (famous for its cheese), take a detour onto the **Three Capes Loop,** a stunning 35-mile byway. Stop in small and scenic **Pacific City** (at the south end of the loop) for lunch. Once you're back on U.S. 101, continue south to **Newport,** spending some time at the excellent **Oregon Coast Aquarium** as well as Oregon State University's fascinating **Hatfield Marine Science Center.** Your final stop is the charming village of **Florence,** 160 miles (about four hours by car) from Cannon Beach.

DAY 5: EUGENE

(2½ hours by car from Florence to Eugene with detour at Oregon Dunes)

Spend the morning driving 20 miles south of Florence along U.S. 101 to scamper about the sandy bluffs at **Oregon Dunes National Recreation Area** near Reedsport. Then backtrack to Florence for lunch in Old Town before taking Highway 126 east for 60 miles to the attractive college city of **Eugene,** staying at one of the charming inns or bed-and-breakfasts near the leafy campus of the University of Oregon. Take a walk to the summit of **Skinner Butte,** which affords fine views of the city, and plan to have dinner at one of the top-notch restaurants at the **5th Street Public Market.** Budget some additional time in Eugene the following morning to visit two excellent University of Oregon museums, the **Jordan Schnitzer Museum of Art** and the **Oregon Museum of Natural History.**

DAYS 6 AND 7: CRATER LAKE AND ASHLAND

(3 hours by car from Eugene to Crater Lake National Park or Prospect)

From Eugene, take Interstate 5 south for 75 miles to Roseburg, then head east along Highway 138 (the Umpqua River Scenic Byway), which twists and turns over the Cascade Range for 85 miles to the northern entrance of **Crater Lake National Park.** Once inside the park, you can continue along Rim Drive for another half hour for excellent views of the lake. Overnight in the park or in nearby **Prospect.**

The following morning, take the lake boat tour to **Wizard Island** and hike through the surrounding forest. In the afternoon, head southwest on Highway 62 to Interstate 5, then continue on to **Ashland,** 95 miles (about two hours) from Crater Lake. Plan to stay the night in one of Ashland's many superb bed-and-breakfasts. Have dinner and attend one of the **Oregon Shakespeare Festival** productions (March through October).

DAYS 8 AND 9: BEND

(3½ hours by car from Ashland)

Get an early start out of Ashland, driving east along scenic Highway 140, which skirts picturesque **Upper Klamath Lake,** and then north on U.S. 97, stopping if you have time at **Collier Memorial State Park,** to reach the outdoorsy resort town of **Bend.** Here you can spend two nights checking out the parks, mountain hikes, microbreweries, and restaurants of the state's largest city east of the Cascades. Be sure to visit the outstanding **High Desert Museum,** the **Old Mill District,** and **Mt. Bachelor Ski Area.**

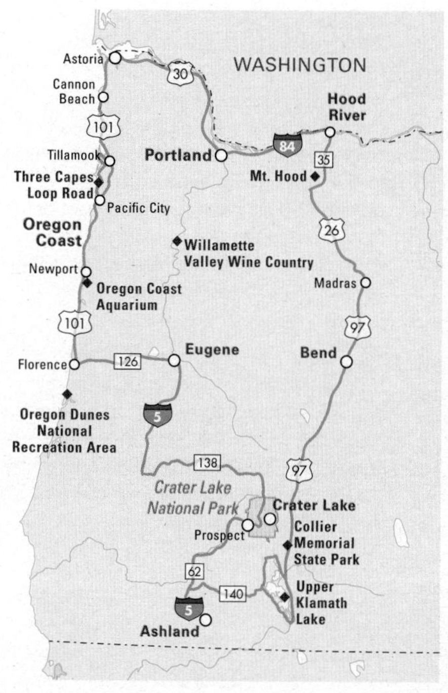

DAY 10: HOOD RIVER

(3 hours by car from Bend)

From Bend, continue north up U.S. 97, and then northwest up U.S. 26 to **Mt. Hood,** 105 miles total. Have lunch at the historic **Timberline Lodge,** admiring the stunning views to the south of the Cascade Range. Pick up Highway 35 and drive around the east side of Mt. Hood and then north 40 miles to the dapper town of **Hood River,** in the heart of the picturesque Columbia Gorge. Spend the night at one of the attractive inns, and try one of this town's stellar restaurants for dinner. From here it's just a 60-mile drive west along a scenic stretch of Interstate 84 to reach Portland.

Great Itineraries

Washington in 10 Days

It's hard to say which is more alluring for Washington visitors: the sculpted bays of Puget Sound, the volcanic peaks of the Cascade Range, or the lively neighborhoods and first-rate attractions, locavore-minded restaurants, and trendy music clubs of Seattle. Here's a tour that reveals all of the state's charms.

DAYS 1 AND 2: SEATTLE

Begin with two days of touring this world-class hub of acclaimed arts, culture, and dining, visiting Downtown's must-see sights, including **Pike Place Market,** the **Seattle Art Museum,** and—a bit north—the **Seattle Center** and its iconic **Space Needle.** Set aside at least a half day to investigate some of the city's liveliest neighborhoods, including **Capitol Hill,** with its indie shops, hipster bars, and diverse cafés, and similarly inviting **Ballard** and **Fremont.** If you have extra time, consider a quick day trip south to up-and-coming **Tacoma,** with its several excellent museums (including the **LeMay Car Museum** and **International Museum of Glass**), or journey northeast to the nearby wine-tasting hub of **Woodinville,** with more than 130 wineries and tasting rooms.

DAYS 3 AND 4: OLYMPIC NATIONAL PARK

(3 hours by car ferry and car from Seattle, via Bainbridge Island)

Get an early start from Seattle on Day 3, taking the ferry from Downtown across Puget Sound to scenic **Bainbridge Island** for lunch and shopping in the village of **Winslow,** and perhaps a quick tour of **Bloedel Reserve,** before continuing the drive to historic **Port Angeles,** which you can use as an overnight base for exploring **Olympic National Park.** **Hurricane Ridge** is the park's nearest section, but on Day 4, depending on how ambitious you are, you could drive west to the **Hoh Rain Forest** section of the park, as well as the coastal areas out at **La Push,** and possibly all the way down to **Lake Quinault** (125 miles from Port Angeles). Try to visit at least one of the rain forests, where you can hike amid huge stands of Douglas firs and Sitka spruces.

DAY 5: WHIDBEY ISLAND

(1½ hours by car and car ferry from Port Angeles)

Drive from Port Angeles to the Victorian-era town of **Port Townsend,** a good stop for lunch and a look at the **Northwest Maritime Center,** and then catch the ferry to **Whidbey Island,** where there are plenty of sophisticated shops, galleries, restaurants, and inns in the laid-back, friendly hamlets of **Langley, Greenbank,** and **Coupeville** (where you disembark the ferry). Bird lovers shouldn't miss **Ebey's Landing National Historic Reserve.** To be closer to where you're headed on Day 6, you might consider staying just north of Whidbey on **Fidalgo Island,** which is home to **Anacortes,** where ferries leave for the San Juan Islands.

DAYS 6 AND 7: THE NORTHERN CASCADES

(2½ hours by car from Whidbey Island to North Cascades National Park)

Leave the Puget Sound region, perhaps stopping in the picturesque Skagit Valley towns of **La Conner** or **Mount Vernon** for lunch, and head for Washington's stunning, skyscraping Cascades Range, passing through the old logging town of **Sedro-Woolley** and making your way up the dramatic **North Cascades Highway** (Highway 20) into **North Cascades National Park.** After descending from the high mountain passes, you could stop in

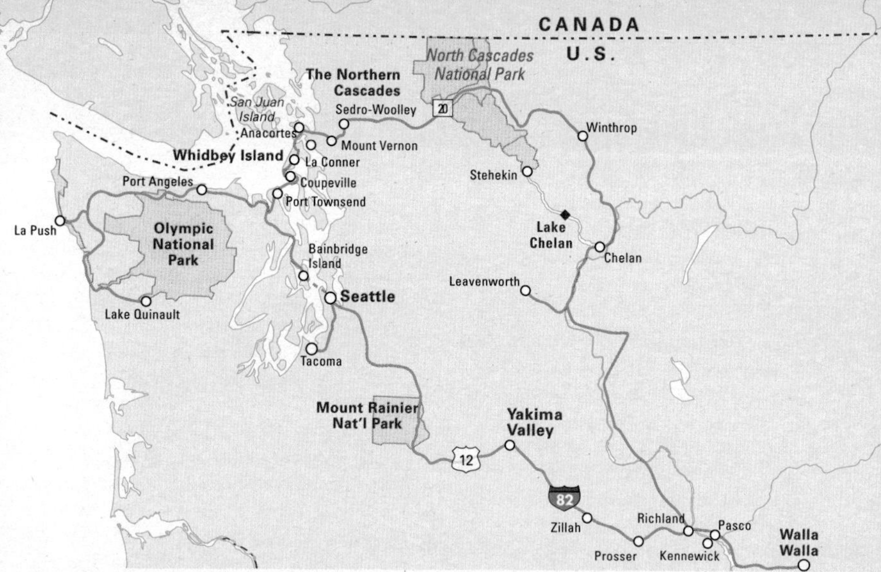

Mazama to stay at **Freestone Inn & Cabins** or stay a bit farther east in the wild-west theme town of **Winthrop.**

On Day 7, turn south and follow the upper Columbia River down into **Chelan** (2½ hours from North Cascades), the base area for exploring fjordlike, 55-mile-long **Lake Chelan,** the state's deepest lake, which you can explore by boat or even floatplane. Stay in Chelan, up at the north end of the lake at **Stehekin**, south of the lake in the town of **Wenatchee,** or an hour southwest of Chelan in the endearingly cute, if kitschy, Bavarian-style town of **Leavenworth,** with its gingerbread architecture and cozy German restaurants.

DAY 8: WALLA WALLA

(4 hours by car from Chelan)

From the Lake Chelan area, it's a long but pleasant 200-mile drive southeast, much of it along the mighty Columbia River, to reach what's developed into the most impressive of the Pacific Northwest's wine-producing areas, **Walla Walla.** This once-sleepy college and farming town has blossomed with stylish restaurants and shops, and you'll find dozens of tasting rooms, both in town and in the surrounding countryside.

DAY 9: YAKIMA VALLEY

(2½ hours from Walla Walla)

Your wine tour continues as you return west from Walla Walla through the **Tri-Cities** communities of Pasco, Kennewick, and Richland, following Interstate 82 to **Yakima.** Good stops for visiting wineries include **Richland, Benton City, Prosser,** and **Zillah.** Yakima itself is a good overnight stop.

DAY 10: MOUNT RAINIER NATIONAL PARK

(2½ hours from Yakima)

On the morning of Day 10, take U.S. 12 west from Yakima 102 miles to Ohanapecosh, the southern entrance to **Mount Rainier National Park.** When you arrive, take the 31-mile, two-hour drive on Sunrise Road, which reveals the "back" (northeast) side of Rainier. From there, continue south and west around the park 160 miles on Highways 410, 12, and 706 to reach the Longmire entrance. A rustic room at historic **Paradise Inn** or **National Park Inn** is your base for the night. On the following day, energetic hikers could tackle one of the four- to six-hour trails that lead up among the park's many peaks. Or, if it's your last day of traveling, try one of the shorter ranger-led walks through wildflower meadows. It's about a two-hour drive back to Seattle.

Great Itineraries

Vancouver and Victoria in 7 Days

Easily reached from Washington via a combination of ferry and roads, Vancouver and Victoria are a pair of gems. The former is a fast-growing, contemporary city—Canada's third largest—with a mix of enchanting outdoor activities and world-class cultural and culinary diversions. Much smaller, Victoria is surprisingly relaxed and compact for a provincial capital. It's renowned for its colorful gardens, well-groomed bike paths, and picturesque Inner Harbour.

DAYS 1 THROUGH 4: VANCOUVER

Start with two or three days in Vancouver itself. You'll want to dedicate a full day to touring 1,000-acre **Stanley Park,** with its 9-km (5½-mile) seawall for walking, cycling, and skating, and the **Vancouver Aquarium,** a family favorite. From the park, you're at the edge of Vancouver's bustling **West End,** which is rife with interesting shopping and breezy cafés. Continue up the city's main retail drag, **Robson Street,** to reach some of Vancouver's top museums, including the **Vancouver Art Gallery** and the **Bill Reid Gallery of Northwest Coast Art.**

On additional days in Vancouver, explore the Victorian-era **Gaslamp Quarter** and adjacent **Chinatown,** home to the very interesting **Dr. Sun Yat-Sen Classical Chinese Garden.** Stroll over to hip and exciting **Yaletown,** a trendy warren of dining and shopping, and catch the Aquabus across False Creek to **Granville Island,** a former industrial wasteland that's become arguably—along with Stanley Park—Vancouver's premier attraction. Here you can eat and shop your way through 50,000-square-foot **Granville Island Public Market,** taking a seat outside and admiring the yachts and sailboats plying False Creek. It's also well worth detouring from the Downtown area to stroll through the charming **Kitsilano** neighborhood, near Granville Island, a gentrified patch of dining and shopping with a lovely beach park affording fine views of the city skyline. On this side of town, you're within easy driving or busing distance to a pair of top attractions, the **Museum of Anthropology** on the campus of University of British Columbia, and **Queen Elizabeth Park,** the highest point in the city.

On your final day in Vancouver, explore the mountains and parks of the **North Shore,** hiking across **Capilano Suspension Bridge** and through the adjoining rain forest, and taking the aerial tram to the top of **Grouse Mountain.** You could visit these attractions before catching the ferry from Horseshoe Bay across the Georgia Strait to Nanaimo and making the two-hour drive south to Victoria. Or if you're headed to Victoria directly from Downtown Vancouver, you could instead drive south from Vancouver to Tsawwassen and catch a ferry to Swartz Bay, from which it's a 30-minute drive south to Victoria.

DAYS 5 THROUGH 7: VICTORIA

(4 hours from Vancouver via Horseshoe Bay–Nanaimo ferry, 3 hours via Tsawwassen–Swartz Bay ferry)

British Columbia's verdant and welcoming capital city, Victoria, is compact enough to explore mostly on foot, although with a car you can more easily reach some of the city's interesting outlying attractions, as well as the wineries of the Saanich Peninsula. Give yourself a couple of days to see the top sights, including the artful architecture of

Chinatown; the **Emily Carr House,** dedicated to one of the nation's most celebrated artists; and the fascinating **Royal British Columbia Museum,** where you could easily spend a few hours. Plan to have high tea at the regal **Fairmont Empress** hotel, which overlooks the city's picturesque **Inner Harbour.**

This is a great area for biking, with older residential areas like **Oak Bay, Rockland,** and **Fairfield** popular for touring on foot or on two wheels. Highlights include **Abkhazi Garden** and **Craigdarroch Castle.**

Set aside a full day for a side trip outside of Victoria proper to the **Saanich Peninsula,** with its wineries, bike paths, and perhaps the most impressive attraction in the entire region, 55-acre **Butchart Gardens.**

ALTERNATIVES

En route from Vancouver to Victoria, many travelers tack on a couple of days in the nearby **Gulf Islands,** which are just off Vancouver Island and bear a strong resemblance in scenery and personality to the **San Juan Islands.**

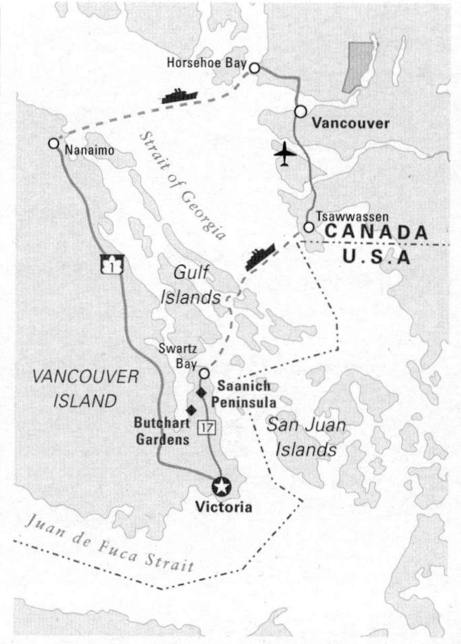

Contacts

Air

AIRPORT INFORMATION

Paine Field Airport (PAE). ✉ *3300 100th St. SW, Everett* ☎ *425/ 622–9040* 🌐 *www.flypainefield.com*. **Portland International Airport (PDX).** ☎ *503/460–4234, 877/739–4636* 🌐 *www.flypdx.com*. **Sea-Tac International Airport (SEA).** ☎ *206/787–5388, 800/544–1965* 🌐 *www.portseattle.org/seatac*. **Vancouver International Airport (YVR).** ☎ *604/207–7077* 🌐 *www.yvr.ca*.

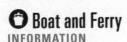

Boat and Ferry

INFORMATION

Black Ball Transport
☎ *250/386–2202 in Victoria, 360/457–4491 in Port Angeles* 🌐 *www.cohoferry.com.*

British Columbia Ferries
☎ *888/223–3779* 🌐 *www.bcferries.com.*

King County Water Taxi
☎ *206/477–3979* 🌐 *www.kingcounty.gov/depts/transportation/water-taxi.aspx.*

Washington State Ferries
☎ *206/464–6400, 888/808–7977* 🌐 *www.wsdot.wa.gov/ferries.*

Bus

INFORMATION

BoltBus
☎ *877/265–8287* 🌐 *www.boltbus.com.*

Experience Oregon
☎ *541/600–8641* 🌐 *www.experienceoregon.com.*

Gray Line
☎ *503/241–7373 in Portland, 604/451–1600 in Vancouver, 250/385–6553 in Victoria, 800/564-4160 in Seattle* 🌐 *www.grayline.com.*

Greyhound Lines
☎ *800/231–2222 in U.S., 800/661–8747 in Canada* 🌐 *www.greyhound.com.*

Quick Shuttle
☎ *800/665–2122* 🌐 *www.quickcoach.com.*

Car

EMERGENCY INFORMATION

Oregon State Police
☎ *503/378–3720* 🌐 *www.oregon.gov/OSP.*

Washington State Patrol
☎ *911 for emergencies* 🌐 *www.wsp.wa.gov.*

Cruise

INFORMATION

Argosy Cruises
☎ *206/623–1445, 888/623–1445* 🌐 *www.argosycruises.com.*

Clipper Vacations
☎ *800/888–2535* 🌐 *www.clippervacations.com.*

Portland Spirit River Cruises
☎ *503/224–3900* 🌐 *www.portlandspirit.com.*

Train

INFORMATION

Amtrak
☎ *800/872–7245* 🌐 *www.amtrak.com.*

Visitor Information

Tourism Vancouver Island
🌐 *www.vancouverisland.travel.*

Tourism Victoria
✉ *Visitors Centre, 812 Wharf St., Victoria* ☎ *250/953–2033, 800/663–3883* 🌐 *www.tourismvictoria.com.*

Travel Oregon
✉ *Portland International Airport Welcome Center, 7000 NE Airport Way, Portland* ☎ *800/547–7842,* 🌐 *www.traveloregon.com.*

Washington Tourism Alliance
☎ *800/544–1800* 🌐 *www.experiencewa.com.*

Chapter 3

PORTLAND

Updated by
Andrew Collins

Sights
★★★☆☆

Restaurants
★★★★★

Hotels
★★★★☆

Shopping
★★★★☆

Nightlife
★★★★★

WELCOME TO PORTLAND

TOP REASONS TO GO

★ **Play in the parks:** Head to Washington Park's Japanese Garden and International Rose Test Garden; stroll along the Willamette in Tom McCall Waterfront Park, or ramble amid the evergreens atop Mt. Tabor.

★ **View works of art:** Take part in the First Thursday Pearl District and Last Thursday Alberta Street art walks. Galleries stay open late, often with receptions and openings. And don't miss the superb Portland Art Museum.

★ **Embrace Portland's indie retail spirit:** Check out the many hip pockets of cool, maker-driven boutiques, especially in Nob Hill, the Pearl District, Hawthorne, and North Mississippi Avenue.

★ **Sample the liquid assets:** Visit a few of the dozens of superb local producers of craft spirits and beer, artisanal coffee and tea, and fine wine.

★ **Eat locally:** Plenty of visitors to Portland build their entire daily itineraries around eating; food trucks, cafés, and restaurants showcase the city's farm-to-table, locavore ethic.

1 **Downtown.** At the center of it all, Portland's Downtown boasts the Portland Art Museum, the Portland'5 Centers for the Arts, and the Portland Farmers' Market along with a slew of notable restaurants and the bulk of the city's hotels. Nearest to the Pearl District, Downtown's West End has become an increasingly stylish dining and retail area in recent years. Due west of Downtown lies enormous Washington Park.

2 **Old Town/Chinatown.** Home to some great examples of Asian-inspired public art, the Lan Su Chinese Garden, and a fun if sometimes rowdy nightlife scene, this historic port district is also home to the famed Portland Saturday Market and the trendy Pine Street Market food hall.

3 **Pearl District.** Bordering Old Town to the west and Downtown to the north, this former warehouse district is now a posh warren of both historic and contemporary condos and commercial buildings housing upscale restaurants, bars, and retailers, including world-renowned Powell's City of Books.

4 **Nob Hill.** From offbeat to upscale, Nob Hill and adjacent Slabtown's shopping, restaurants, and bars draw a discerning crowd.

5 **Forest Park.** Immediately west of Nob Hill, Forest Park is the nation's largest urban forest. Trailheads are easily accessible from Nob Hill as well as Washington Park, to the south.

6 **West Hills and Southwest.** This expansive, green section of the city is home to Washington Park, which contains many must-sees, including the Hoyt Arboretum, International Rose Test Garden, Japanese Garden, and Portland Children's Museum.

7 **North.** The city's "fifth quadrant" sits on the peninsula formed by the confluence of the Willamette River and the Columbia River. Part working class, part creative class, it's home to the hip North Mississippi Avenue and North Williams Avenue dining and retail strips.

8 **Northeast.** Containing the Moda basketball arena, the Oregon Convention Center, the Alberta Arts District, and some of the city's least and most affluent neighborhoods,

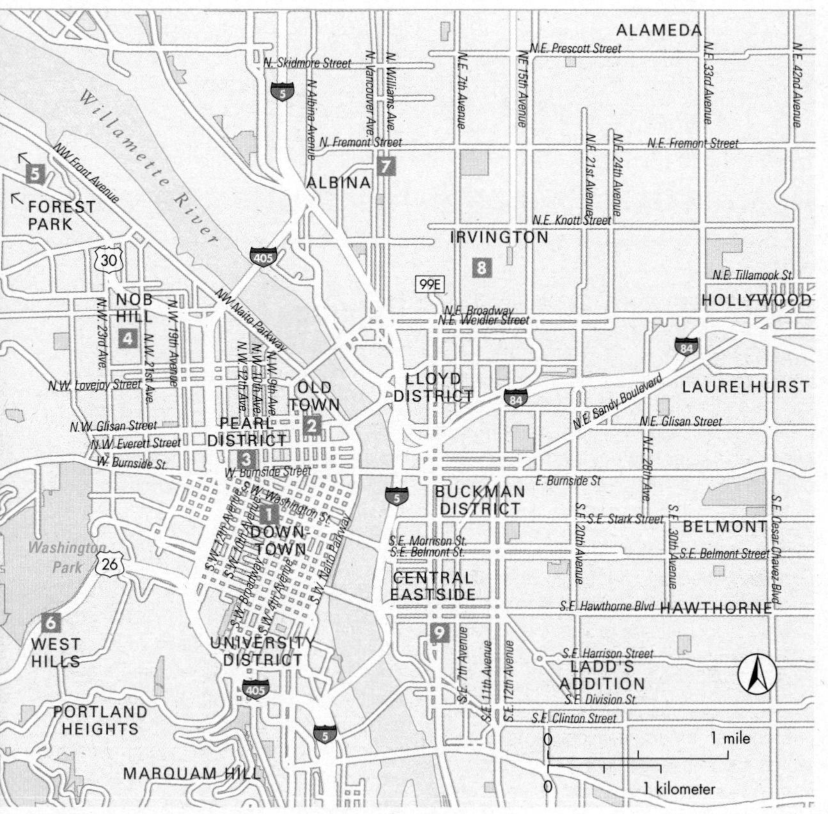

Portland's Northeast quadrant is also one of the city's most diverse neighborhoods.

9 Southeast. The several vibrant pockets of foodie-approved restaurants and independently owned shops—especially on Belmont, Hawthorne, and Division, and in the formerly industrial Central East Side—are highlights of this large quadrant that includes a number of attractive and historic residential areas. This neighborhood also has kid-popular draws like the Oregon Museum of Science and Industry (OMSI), Tilikum Crossing bridge, and Mount Tabor Park.

What distinguishes Portland, Oregon, from the rest of America's cityscapes? For some, it's the wealth of cultural offerings and never-ending culinary choices; for others, it's Portland's proximity to the ocean and mountains, or simply the beauty of having all this in one place.

Strolling through Downtown or one of Portland's many diverse and dynamic outlying neighborhoods, there's an unmistakable vibrancy to this city—one that's encouraged by clean air, infinite trees, and an appealing blend of historic and modern architecture. Portland's various nicknames—Rose City, Bridgetown, Beervana—tell its story.

Rich cultural offerings, endless recreational activities, and a friendly vibe make Portland universally alluring, but the white-hot food scene is arguably its top visitor attraction, especially its fervent embrace of the locavore movement. On a related note, the city maintains a strong appreciation for artisanal craftsmanship, which encompasses everything from coffee, beer, chocolate, and other edibles (recreational marijuana was legalized in Oregon in 2015) to furniture, jewelry, apparel, and household goods. These touchstones of modern urbanism have made Portland the kind of place that younger creative spirits, tech workers, and artists want to visit and live in.

Planning

When to Go

Portland's mild climate is best from June through September, when rain is a rarity and sunny days seem to go on forever. Hotels can fill up quickly during this period, and although a recent hotel building boom has greatly helped to increase supply and soften rates, it's still a good idea to book reservations in advance. Spring and fall are also excellent times to visit. The weather is still usually quite pleasant, prices for accommodations often drop considerably, and crowds are far fewer at popular attractions and restaurants. In winter, snow is uncommon in the city but abundant in the nearby mountains, which are hugely popular with skiers and snowboarders.

Average daytime summer highs are in the 70s, but heat waves usually two or three times per summer can lead to several consecutive days of temperatures topping out near or above 100 degrees; winter temperatures generally reach the 40s and low 50s during the day. Rainfall varies greatly from one locale to another. In the coastal mountains, for example, 160 inches of rain fall annually, creating temperate rain forests. Portland has an average of only 36 inches of rainfall a year—less than New York, Chicago, or Miami. In winter, however, even if it doesn't often rain hard, rainy or misty weather is common and can sometimes go on for days (especially in November and December). More than 75% of Portland's annual precipitation occurs from October through March.

Getting Here and Around

AIR

It takes about 5 hours to fly nonstop to Portland from New York, 4 hours from Chicago and Atlanta, and 2½ hours from Los Angeles. Flying to Seattle takes just under an hour, and flying to Vancouver takes just over an hour.

Portland International Airport (PDX) is an efficient, modern airport with service to most major national and a handful of international destinations. It's a relatively uncrowded facility, and both check-in and security lines tend to proceed quickly. It's also easily accessible from Downtown Portland, both by car and TriMet/MAX light rail.

AIRPORT

Portland International Airport (*PDX*) This is the city's—and the region's—major airport. You'll find a pretty good selection of local restaurants and shops inside the terminal. ✉ *7000 N.E. Airport Way, Portland* ☎ *877/739–4636, 503/460–4234* 🌐 *www.pdx.com.*

GROUND TRANSPORTATION

Taking the MAX, Portland's light rail train, to and from Portland International Airport is straightforward. The Red Line MAX stops right at the terminal, and the approximately 35- to 45-minute ride to Downtown costs $2.50. Trains run daily from early morning until around midnight—MAX won't be available to some very late-arriving passengers, but it generally runs early enough to catch even the first flights of the day out of Portland, which typically depart around 6 am. You purchase your ticket before boarding at one of the vending machines in the terminal and at every MAX stop, or by downloading the TriMet Hop Fastpass app and paying with your phone; tickets are also good on TriMet buses and the Portland Streetcar, and transfers within 2½ hours of the time of purchase are free. Uber and Lyft have dedicated pick-up areas at the airport; the cost for either between the airport and Downtown averages around $25 to $35 (a taxi generally runs about $10 more).

CONTACTS TriMet/MAX. ☎ *503/238–7433* 🌐 *www.trimet.org.*

CAR

Although traffic has increased dramatically in recent years (Portland ranks as one of the worst cities in the country for traffic congestion), the city is a fairly easy city to navigate by car, and if you're planning to explore neighboring regions—such as the coast, Willamette wine country, and Columbia Gorge—it's best to do so by car, as public transportation options to these areas, especially the coast, is very limited. That said, parking Downtown can get expensive and a car isn't necessary for getting around the city itself. One practical strategy is going without a car during the days you plan to spend in the city center, and then renting a car just for those days when you're venturing outside the city or exploring some of the East Side neighborhoods, which have ample free parking. Most major rental agencies have Downtown offices, and renting Downtown can save you plenty of money, as you avoid paying the hefty taxes and surcharges that you must pay at the airport agencies.

Portland is easily reached via the West Coast's major interstate highway, Interstate 5, which connects Portland to Seattle (which is a three-hour drive north) and Eugene (a little over a two-hour drive south). Interstate 84 begins in Downtown Portland and runs east into the Columbia Gorge and eventually to Idaho. U.S. 26 is the main route to the Oregon Coast west from Downtown, and to Mt. Hood going east. The city's bypass freeways are Interstate 205, which links Interstate 5 and Interstate 84 before crossing the Columbia River north into Washington, and Interstate 405, which arcs around western Downtown. Most city-center streets are one way, and some Downtown streets—including 5th and 6th Avenues—are limited primarily to bus and MAX traffic (with just one lane for cars, and limited turns).

PARKING

Compared with many other major U.S. cities, Portland has a relatively abundant parking, even Downtown, both metered and in garages. The most affordable and accessible option is to park in one of several city-owned "Smart Park" lots. Rates start at $1.80 per hour (short-term parking, four hours or less), with a $16 daily maximum; weekends and evenings, the daily maximum is just $5. The best part about Smart Park is that about 400 participating merchants validate tickets, covering the first two hours of parking when you spend at least $25 in their establishments.

There are numerous privately owned lots around the city as well; fees for these vary and can be quite pricey, and Downtown hotels also charge significantly (as much as $40 to $55 nightly).

Downtown street parking is metered only, and enforcement is vigilant. You can use cash or a credit card to pay ($2 per hour) at machines located on each block (display your receipt on the inside of your curbside window) or by downloading the Parking-Kitty app and paying with your phone. Metered spaces are mostly available for one to three hours, with a few longer-term spaces available on certain streets.

Outside the Downtown core, you'll find a mix of free and metered parking, with rates ranging from $1 to $2 depending on the neighborhood. In some free parking areas, time limits (usually an hour to three hours) are enforced. On the east side of the river, with the exception of the Central East Side (which has a number of metered blocks), free unmetered parking is the norm.

TRIMET/MAX

TriMet operates an extensive system of buses, streetcars, and light-rail trains. The North–South streetcar line runs from Nob Hill through the Pearl District, Downtown, and Portland State University campus to South Waterfront. The A and B Loop streetcar lines cross the Willamette River to the East Side via Broadway Bridge and the Tilikum Crossing Bridge.

MAX light rail links the city's eastern, southern, and western suburbs as well as North Portland with Downtown, Washington Park and the Oregon Zoo, the Lloyd Center district, and the Hollywood District and the airport. From Downtown, trains operate daily about 5 am–1 am, with a fare of $2.50 for up to 2½ hours of travel (transfers to other MAX trains, buses, and streetcars are free within this time period), and $5 for an unlimited all-day ticket, which is also good systemwide. A one-month pass costs $100. The ticket for riding without a fare is stiff.

You can pay your fare by purchasing a reloadable Hop Fastpass card at a number of grocery and convenience stores around town, downloading Hop Fastpass app and paying with your phone, or paying in cash on buses (exact change required) or at ticket vending machines at streetcar and MAX light rail stops. If you buy a physical ticket, hold onto it whether you're transferring or not; it also serves as proof that you have paid your fare. The most central bus routes operate every 10 to 15 minutes throughout the day. Bikes are allowed in designated areas of MAX trains, and there are bike racks on the front of all buses that everyone is free to use.

CONTACTS TriMet/MAX. ✉ *Ticket office at Pioneer Courthouse Sq., 701 S.W. 6th Ave., Downtown* ☎ *503/238–7433* 🌐 *www.trimet.org.*

Tours

BIKE TOURS

Portland is famously bike friendly, with miles of dedicated bike lanes and numerous rental shops. Also, a couple of great companies offer guided rides around the city, covering everything from eating and brewpub-hopping to checking out local parks and historic neighborhoods.

Cycle Portland Bike Tours and Rentals

BICYCLE TOURS | Trust your guide at this well-established outfitter to know Portland's popular and lesser-known spots. Tour themes include Essential Portland, Foodie Field Trip, and Brews Cruise, but you can also customize a tour. The well-stocked on-site bike shop serves beer on tap. ✉ *117 N.W. 2nd Ave., Old Town/Chinatown* ☎ *503/902–5035, 844/739–2453* 🌐 *www.portlandbicycletours.com* 🎫 *From $39.*

WALKING TOURS

Walk the Portland beat with guides who share their personal Portland knowledge, including history, food, brews, arts, and sights.

Portland Walking Tours

WALKING TOURS | A slew of tours are offered by this company, but it's the Beyond Bizarre tour that generates the most buzz. Ghost-hunter wannabes and paranormal junkies make this a popular tour that often sells out. There's also the Underground Portland tour, which highlights the city's sinister history, and a Chocolate Decadence excursion. ✉ *131 N.W. 2nd Ave., Old Town/Chinatown* ☎ *503/774–4522* 🌐 *www.portlandwalkingtours.com* 🎫 *From $19.*

Sights

One of the greatest things about Portland is that there's so much to explore, from both conventional attractions—museums, parks, and other amusements—to lively, pedestrian-friendly neighborhoods abundant with interesting, and usually independently owned, shops, restaurants, and bars. What makes discovering Portland's treasures even more enticing is that most of its attractions, transportation options, and events are relatively accessible and affordable.

The variety of Portland's parks is immense and includes one of the largest urban natural areas in the country (Forest Park). Other favorite Portland green spaces include Laurelhurst, Mt. Tabor, Powell Butte, and Washington parks.

Restaurants

Rising-star chefs and the foodies who adore them have been flocking to Portland for the better part of the past two decades. In this playground of sustainability and creativity, many of the city's hottest restaurants change menus weekly—sometimes even daily—depending upon the ingredients they have delivered to their door that morning from local farms. The combination of fertile soils, temperate weather, and nearby waters contributes to a year-round bountiful harvest (be it lettuces or hazelnuts, mushrooms or salmon) that is within any chef's reach.

And these chefs are not shy about putting new twists on old favorites. Restaurants like Le Pigeon, Beast, Ox, Ned Ludd, Tasty n Alder, and Bullard have all taken culinary risks by presenting imaginatively executed, often globally inspired fare while utilizing sustainable ingredients. There's a strong willingness in and around Portland for chefs to explore their creative boundaries. The city also excels when it comes to international dining, especially when it comes to Asian eateries, such as Pok Pok, Nodoguru, Aviary, Han Oak, and Langbaan. Other strengths include artisanal bakeries and pizzerias, coffeehouses, craft ice cream and doughnut shops, and vegan (or at least vegetarian) restaurants, and Portland also soars when it comes to gastropubs.

Many of Portland's longtime favorites and higher-end spots are concentrated in Downtown, the Pearl District, and Nob Hill. But many of the city's most exciting food scenes are on the East Side, along Alberta Street, Mississippi Avenue, Williams Avenue, Fremont Street, Burnside Street, 28th Avenue, Belmont Street, Hawthorne Boulevard, and Division Street, and sprinkled throughout the Central East Side or tucked away in many neighborhoods in between. Serious food enthusiasts will definitely want to make some trips to these vibrant, if out-of-the-way, neighborhoods. *Restaurant reviews have been shortened. For full information, visit Fodors.com.*

What It Costs in U.S. Dollars

$	$$	$$$	$$$$
AT DINNER			
under $16	$16–$22	$23–$30	over $30

Hotels

Portland has an unusually rich variety of distinctive, design-driven boutique hotels and historic properties, and though you'll find the usual mix of budget-oriented, midrange, and upscale chains here, if you'd rather avoid cookie-cutter brand-name properties, you're in the right place. The city has undergone a major hotel building boom since 2015, with most of these new and often chic and trendy boutique properties having opened Downtown, but the Central East Side, Lloyd District, Old Town, and Pearl District have also seen several notable new lodging additions. The influx of rooms has helped greatly to reduce hotel rates, which had become quite steep at one point—it's much easier to find good deals, even during the busy summer months. Portland has a few bed-and-breakfasts and an enormous supply of Airbnbs; the latter provide a great way to stay in some of the trendy East Side neighborhoods that lack hotels, such as Alberta, North Mississippi, Hawthorne, and Laurelhurst.

Downtown Portland is about a 20- to 25-minute drive from the airport. There are a number of chain properties near the airport, all offering much lower rates than comparable Downtown hotels. *Hotel reviews have been shortened. For full information visit Fodors.com.*

What It Costs in U.S. Dollars

$	$$	$$$	$$$$
HOTELS			
under $150	$150–$225	$226–$300	over $300

Nightlife

Given the city's unabashed passion for craft cocktails, beer, and local wines, it makes sense that Portland abounds with cool lounges and bars. Hard-core clubbing and dancing has a bit less of a following here than more casual barhopping, and Portlanders do like to combine noshing and sipping—you'll find an abundance of nightspots serving exceptional food (and often offering great happy-hour deals on victuals and drinks), and quite a few full-service restaurants with popular side bars and lounges. Nightlife and dining really overlap in the Rose City.

Portland has become something of a base for up-and-coming alternative-rock bands, which perform in clubs scattered throughout the city. Portland's top neighborhoods for barhopping are, not surprisingly, its favored dining districts, too—the West End, Pearl District, and Nob Hill on the west side of the Willamette River, within walking distance (or a streetcar ride) of Downtown hotels. On the East Side, head to the Alberta Arts District, North Mississippi Avenue, East Burnside Street in the 20s, the Central East Side, Belmont Street, Hawthorne Boulevard, Division Street, and Foster-Powell.

Performing Arts

Portland is quite the creative town. Every night top-ranked dance, theater, and musical performers take the stage somewhere in the city. Expect to find never-ending choices for things to do, from watching independent films, performance art, and plays to checking out some of the Northwest's (and the country's) hottest bands at one of the city's many nightclubs or concert venues. For a city of this size, there is truly an impressive—and accessible—scope of talent from visual artists, performance artists, and musicians. The arts are alive, with outdoor sculptural works strewn around the city, ongoing festivals, and premieres of traveling Broadway shows. One of the city's artistic strengths is its bounty of independent neighborhood theaters—many of these are historic, serve craft beer and light food, and show a mix of mainstream and independent films and film festivals.

Shopping

The shopping landscape in Portland has changed significantly in recent years, perhaps not quite as dramatically as the much-buzzed-about culinary scene, but in similar (pardon the pun) fashion. Specifically, those same hip and indie-spirited neighborhoods around the city that have become hot spots for food and drink—areas like the Pearl District, Downtown West End, Alberta, North Mississippi, North Williams, Central East Side, Hawthorne, and Division—are also enjoying a steady influx of distinctive, well-curated boutiques specializing in edgy fashion and jewelry, handcrafted home accessories and household goods, and artisanal foods.

Activities

Portlanders avidly gravitate to the outdoors and they're well acclimated to the elements year-round. Once the sun starts to shine in spring and into summer, the city fills with hikers, joggers, and mountain bikers, who flock to Portland's hundreds of miles of parks, paths, and trails. The Willamette and Columbia rivers are popular for boating and water sports.

As for competitive sports, Portland is home to the Timbers, a major league soccer team with a devout local fan base, and NBA basketball's beloved Trail Blazers.

Visitor Information

"A&E, The Arts and Entertainment Guide," published each Friday in the *Oregonian* (🌐 *www.oregonlive.com*), contains listings of performers, productions, events, and club entertainment. *Willamette Week* (🌐 *wweek.com*), published free each Wednesday and widely available throughout the metropolitan area, contains similar, but hipper, listings. The *Portland Mercury* (🌐 *www.portlandmercury.com*), also free, is an even edgier entertainment publication distributed every other Wednesday. The glossy newsstand magazine *Portland Monthly* (🌐 *www.pdxmonthly.com*) covers Portland culture and lifestyle and provides great nightlife, entertainment, and dining coverage for the city.

CONTACTS Travel Portland Information Center. ✉ *Director Park, 877 S.W. Taylor St., Downtown* ☎ *503/427–1372, 888/503–3291* 🌐 *www.travelportland.com.*

Downtown

Portland has one of the most attractive, inviting Downtown centers in the United States. It's clean, compact, and filled with fountains, plazas, and parks, including a particularly pretty expanse of greenery along the Willamette River. Architecture fans find plenty to admire in its mix of old and new. Whereas many urban U.S. business districts clear out at night and on weekends, Portland's Downtown is decidedly mixed-use, with plenty of residential and commercial buildings, and an appealing mix of hotels, shops, museums, restaurants, and bars, especially in the hip West End district. You can easily walk from one end of Downtown to the other, and the city's superb public transportation system—which includes MAX light rail, buses, and the streetcar—makes it easy to get here from other parts of the city. A day pass is recommended.

Sights

★ Portland Art Museum

MUSEUM | The treasures at the Pacific Northwest's oldest arts facility span 35 centuries of Asian, European, and American art—it's an impressive collection for a midsize city. A high point is the Center for Native American Art, with regional and contemporary art from more than 200 indigenous groups. The **Jubitz Center for Modern and Contemporary Art** contains six floors devoted entirely to modern art, including a small but superb photography gallery, with the changing selection chosen from more than 5,000 pieces in the museum's permanent collection. The film center presents the annual Portland International Film Festival in March. Also, take a moment to linger in the peaceful outdoor sculpture garden. Kids under 17 are admitted free. ✉ *1219 S.W. Park Ave., Downtown* ☎ *503/226–2811, 503/221–1156 film schedule* 🌐 *www.portlandartmuseum.org* 🎟 *$20; free on the first Thurs. of every month from 5–8 pm* ⏲ *Closed Mon.*

★ Portland Farmers Market

MARKET | **FAMILY** | On Saturdays year-round, local farmers, bakers, chefs, and entertainers converge at the South Park Blocks near the PSU campus for Oregon's largest open-air farmers' market—it's one of the most impressive in the country. It's a great place to sample the regional bounty and to witness the local-food obsession that's revolutionized Portland's culinary scene. There's plenty of food you can eat on the spot, plus nonperishable local items (wine, hazelnuts, chocolates, vinegars) you can take home with you. There's a smaller Wednesday market, May through November, on a different section of the Park Blocks (between S.W. Salmon and S.W. Main). On Mondays, June through September, the market is held at Pioneer Courthouse Square, and at other times the Portland Farmers Market is held in different locations around town, including Nob Hill/Northwest, Kenton/North Portland, King/Alberta, and Lents/Southeast, and some 40 other farmers' markets take place throughout metro Portland—see the website for a list. ✉ *South Park Blocks at S.W. Park Ave. and Montgomery St., Downtown* ☎ *503/241–0032* 🌐 *www.portlandfarmersmarket.org* ⏲ *Closed Sun.–Fri.*

★ West End

NEIGHBORHOOD | Sandwiched between the Pioneer Square area and the swanky Pearl District, this triangular patch of vintage buildings—interspersed with a handful of contemporary ones—has evolved since the early 2000s into one of the city's most eclectic hubs of fashion, nightlife, and dining. Boutique hotels like the Ace and Sentinel rank among the city's trendiest addresses. Along Harvey Milk Street, formerly the heart of Portland's LGBTQ scene, there's still a popular gay bar, but now you'll also find noteworthy restaurants and lounges like Clyde Common, Bamboo Sushi, and Multnomah Whiskey Library. Among the many independent shops, check out Cacao chocolate shop, Frances May clothier, and Union Way—an enclosed pedestrian mall with a handful of tiny storefronts. ✉ *S.W. 13th to S.W. 9th Aves., between W. Burnside St. and S.W. Yamhill St., West End.*

Restaurants

★ Bullard

$$$$ | **STEAKHOUSE** | In a city with the density of restaurants that Portland has, it takes a lot to stoke the level of buzz surrounding the opening of Bullard, a festive next-generation steak house in the lobby of the Woodlark Hotel. Drawing on his roots in Texas, *Top Chef* alum Doug Adams brings a Southwest-meets-Oregon flair ("Tex-Oregana," according to *The Oregonian*'s food critic) to signature dishes such as beef carpaccio and San Antonio chicken that lives up to the hype. **Known for:** mains large enough for two; house-smoked meats; pickleback shots. $ *Average main: $35* ✉ *Woodlark Hotel, 813 S.W. Alder St., Downtown* ☎ *503/222–1670* 🌐 *www.bullardpdx.com.*

★ Departure Restaurant + Lounge

$$$ | **ASIAN** | This extravagant rooftop restaurant and lounge on the top floor of The Nines hotel seems fresh out of LA—a look and feel that is, indeed, a departure from Portland's usual no-fuss vibe. The retro-chic interior has an extravagant, space-age, airport-lounge feel, and the outdoor patio—furnished with low, white couches and bright-orange tables and chairs—offers panoramic views of the Downtown skyline. **Known for:** chef's tasting service with wine pairings; dedicated vegan menu; fantastic skyline views. $ *Average main: $25* ✉ *The Nines hotel, 525 S.W. Morrison St., Downtown* ☎ *503/802–5370* 🌐 *www.departureportland.com* ⏲ *No lunch.*

★ Imperial

$$$ | **PACIFIC NORTHWEST** | Tall concrete pillars, exposed brick and ductwork, soft overhead lighting, and rustic wood tables and floors create a warehouse vibe at one of Portland's most defining restaurants, located inside the Hotel Lucia. Open for breakfast, lunch, and dinner, and serving up exemplary contemporary Pacific Northwest fare, menu highlights include Dungeness crab omelet, duck meatballs, grilled king salmon with corn puree and chanterelles, and meaty fare from the wood-fired rotisserie grill. **Known for:** Flat Top happy-hour burger; stellar cocktail program; wood-fired rotisserie-grill fare. $ *Average main: $25* ✉ *Hotel Lucia, 410 S.W. Broadway, Downtown* ☎ *503/228–7221* 🌐 *www.imperialpdx.com.*

★ King Tide Fish & Shell

$$$ | **SEAFOOD** | One of only a handful of serious seafood restaurants in Portland, this casually upscale restaurant in the Kimpton RiverPlace Hotel overlooks the Willamette River and Tom McCall Waterfront Park, offering seating in a proper dining room as well as on a sweeping veranda (for the best views). Offering plenty of enticing starters (pickled deviled eggs with Dungeness crab, mussels with smoked-pork dashi, hamachi tostadas) as well as raw bar platters and a typically weighty whole fish catch of the day, the menu is well suited to sharing several dishes among friends. **Known for:** extensive late-night and happy hour menus; local king salmon with your choice of several sauces; a peaceful riverfront setting away from the bustle of Downtown. $ *Average main: $28* ✉ *Kimpton RiverPlace Hotel, 1510 S.W. Harbor Way, Downtown* ☎ *503/295–6166* 🌐 *www.kingtidefishandshell.com.*

★ Maurice

$$ | **CAFÉ** | Described by baker-owner Kristen Murray as a "modern pastry luncheonette," this dainty West End café has just a handful of wooden booth and counter seats and a minimalist-inspired white-on-white aesthetic. The menu features exquisite French–Scandinavian pastries, cakes, and sandwiches, as well as a full gamut of drinks, including wine,

Downtown and West Hills
A
B
C
D
E
F
1
2
3
4
5
6
7
8
9
N.W. Davis St.
N.W. Couch St.
N.W. 10th Ave.
N.W. 9th Ave.
CHINATOWN DISTRICT
W. Burnside St.
S.W. Harvey Milk St.
S.W. 15th Ave.
S.W. 13th Ave.
S.W. Washington St.
S.W. Alder St.
TO PROVIDENCE PARK
S.W. 14th Ave.
S.W. 10th Ave.
MAX LIGHT RAIL
6th Ave. Transit Mall
5th Ave. Transit Mall
S.W. 4th Ave.
S.W. 12th Ave.
S.W. 11th Ave.
S.W. 9th Ave.
S.W. Park Ave.
S.W. Morrison St.
CENTRAL CITY STREETCAR
405
S.W. Yamhill St.
S.W. Taylor St.
S.W. Park Ave.
S.W. Main St.
BUS
S.W. Salmon St.
First Congregationalist Church
WEST HILLS
3rd Ave.
S.W.
S.W. Main St.
South Park Blocks
S.W. Broadway
S.W. 6th Ave.
S.W. 5th Ave.
S.W. Madison St.
S.W. Jefferson St.
26
S.W. 4th Ave.
0
1/4 mile
0
1/4 kilometer
S.W. Columbia St.
S.W. 2nd Ave.
S.W. Clay St.
S.W. Market St.
S.W. Mill St.
Harrison St.

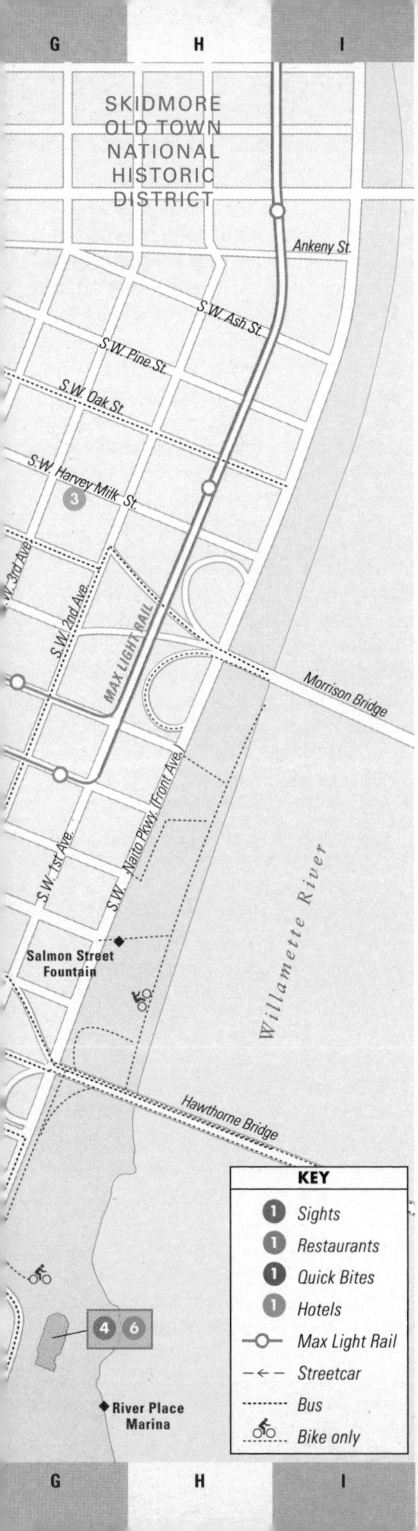

SKIDMORE OLD TOWN NATIONAL HISTORIC DISTRICT

Ankeny St.
S.W. Ash St.
S.W. Pine St.
S.W. Oak St.
S.W. Harvey Milk St.
S.W. 3rd Ave.
S.W. 2nd Ave.
MAX LIGHT RAIL
Morrison Bridge
S.W. 1st Ave.
S.W. Naito Pkwy. (Front Ave.)
Willamette River
Salmon Street Fountain
Hawthorne Bridge
River Place Marina

KEY
Sights
Restaurants
Quick Bites
Hotels
Max Light Rail
Streetcar
Bus
Bike only

Sights

1 International Rose Test Garden A5
2 Oregon Holocaust Memorial A5
3 Portland Art Museum ... C6
4 Portland Children's Museum A6
5 Portland Farmers Market B8
6 Portland Japanese Garden A5
7 West End D2

Restaurants

1 Bullard D3
2 Departure Restaurant + Lounge E4
3 Imperial E3
4 King Tide Fish & Shell G9
5 Maurice D1

Quick Bites

1 Good Coffee D3

Hotels

1 Ace Hotel D2
2 Heathman Hotel D5
3 Hi-Lo Hotel, Autograph Collection G3
4 Kimpton Hotel Monaco Portland F3
5 Kimpton Hotel Vintage Portland E3
6 Kimpton RiverPlace Hotel G9
7 The Nines F4
8 Sentinel Hotel C3
9 The Woodlark D3

beer, cocktails, teas, and coffee. **Known for:** ever-changing, handwritten menu; assorted Swedish fika (snack) pastries; revelatory black-pepper cheesecake. *$ Average main: $20 ✉ 921 S.W. Oak St., West End ☎ 503/224–9921 ⊕ www.mauricepdx.com ⊙ Closed Mon. No dinner.*

Coffee and Quick Bites

★ Good Coffee

$ | **CAFÉ** | The Woodlark Hotel yielded its plant-filled lobby to the latest outpost from Portland roaster Good Coffee. The marble bar complements the sprawling seating area—a living room for an army of young freelancers, who set up shop at the communal table, on the blue banquet seats lining the street-facing windows, and the plush couches and armchairs. **Known for:** one of Portland's best cappuccinos; intriguing seasonal drink menu; tea lattes and matcha. *$ Average main: $5 ✉ Woodlark Hotel, 813 S.W. Alder St., Downtown ☎ 503/548–2559 ⊕ www.goodwith.us ⊙ No dinner.*

Hotels

Ace Hotel

$$ | **HOTEL** | The quintessential Portland hipster lodging, this flagship location of the buzzy Ace Hotels brand contains a Stumptown Coffee café as well as the very good Clyde Common restaurant and Pépé Le Moko bar, is a block from Powell's Books and the Pearl District, and is right in the heart of Downtown's ever-trendy West End neighborhood. **Pros:** prime West End location; unique design and artwork in each room; free city bicycles available for guests. **Cons:** offbeat decor and hipster vibe isn't for everybody; the cheapest rooms don't have private baths; on a sometimes noisy street. *$ Rooms from: $195 ✉ 1022 S.W. Harvey Milk St., West End ☎ 503/228–2277 ⊕ www.acehotel.com 🛏 78 rooms 🍴 No meals.*

★ Heathman Hotel

$$$$ | **HOTEL** | The choice of countless celebs and dignitaries since it opened in 1927, this wonderfully atmospheric, art-filled hotel has undergone a stylish and contemporary redesign. **Pros:** stellar restaurant; central location adjoining Portland'5 Centers for the Arts, and a block from Portland Art Museum; outstanding art collection. **Cons:** some rooms are small; expensive parking; bar and restaurant can be crowded when there are performances next door. *$ Rooms from: $309 ✉ 1001 S.W. Broadway, Downtown ☎ 503/241–4100 ⊕ www.heathmanhotel.com 🛏 150 rooms 🍴 No meals.*

★ Hi-Lo Hotel, Autograph Collection

$$$ | **HOTEL** | This dapper, old-meets-new boutique hotel—part of Marriott's indie-spirited Autograph Collection—occupies a masterfully converted 1910 Oregon Pioneer Building, a six-story structure with high ceilings, big windows, and the city's oldest restaurant, Huber's café, on the ground floor. **Pros:** close to Pearl District, West End, and Old Town; cool old building with midcentury modern vibe; very nice fitness center for a small hotel. **Cons:** street noise can be a problem; expensive valet parking; mid-rise building with not much of a view from lower floors. *$ Rooms from: $259 ✉ 320 S.W. Harvey Milk St., Downtown ☎ 971/222–2100 ⊕ www.hi-lo-hotel.com 🛏 120 rooms 🍴 No meals.*

★ Kimpton Hotel Monaco Portland

$$$ | **HOTEL** | This artsy Downtown Portland outpost of the Kimpton-operated Monaco boutique-hotel brand offers eclectic textiles and patterns, bright spaces and bold colors, interesting amenities like in-room yoga mats, extensive pet-welcoming items, and an evening social hour with local wines, spirits, and beers, and the overall sense that staying here is a lot of fun. **Pros:** vibrant, arty decor; convenient, central location; well-equipped fitness center and a full-service Aveda spa. **Cons:** design style may not

suit all; pricey overnight parking; on a busy Downtown street. *Rooms from: $230 ✉ 506 S.W. Washington St., Downtown ☎ 503/222–0001, 888/207–2201 🌐 www.monaco-portland.com 221 rooms No meals.*

Kimpton Hotel Vintage Portland

$$$ | **HOTEL** | This historic landmark hotel with a stylish two-story lobby takes its theme from Oregon vineyards, with rooms named after local wineries, complimentary wine served every evening, and an extensive collection of Oregon vintages served in the superb Bacchus wine bar and Il Solito restaurant. **Pros:** terrific on-site Italian restaurant and wine bar; several over-the-top spectacular suites; smart, contemporary room decor. **Cons:** pricey parking; some street noise on the lower levels on the Washington Street side; small gym. *Rooms from: $239 ✉ 422 S.W. Broadway, Downtown ☎ 503/228–1212, 800/263–2305 🌐 www.hotelvintage-portland.com 115 rooms No meals.*

★ Kimpton RiverPlace Hotel

$$$ | **HOTEL** | With textured wall coverings, pillows made of Pendleton wool, and a color palette of slate blue, mustard yellow, and a variety of browns, this Kimpton-operated boutique hotel on the banks of the Willamette River captures the look and feel of the Pacific Northwest. **Pros:** stellar views and park-side riverfront location; outstanding seafood restaurant; several apartment-style suites with kitchens are great for families or extended stays. **Cons:** not many restaurants or shops within easy walking distance; some river views from rooms are blocked by trees; expensive parking. *Rooms from: $249 ✉ 1510 S.W. Harbor Way, Downtown ☎ 503/228–3233, 888/869–3108 🌐 www.riverplacehotel.com 84 rooms No meals.*

★ The Nines

$$$$ | **HOTEL** | On the top nine floors of a former landmark department store, this swanky Marriott Luxury Collection has the city's poshest accommodations, with luxe decor and two notable restaurants. **Pros:** stunning views; swanky vibe and cool design; outstanding Departure Restaurant on the rooftop. **Cons:** rooms facing the atrium can be noisy; expensive valet-only parking; on a very busy downtown block. *Rooms from: $359 ✉ 525 S.W. Morrison St., Downtown ☎ 503/222–9996, 877/229–9995 🌐 www.thenines.com 331 rooms No meals.*

★ Sentinel Hotel

$$$ | **HOTEL** | The discerning common areas in this landmark, early-20th-century buildings capture Portland's maker aesthetic, with locally sourced textiles, furnishings, and goods. **Pros:** indie style meets luxury; well-equipped gym; spacious, well-designed rooms. **Cons:** pricey valet parking; uneven service in lobby bar; construction (through 2023) next door can get a little noisy. *Rooms from: $239 ✉ 614 S.W. 10th Ave., Downtown ☎ 503/224–3400, 888/246–5631 🌐 www.sentinelhotel.com 100 rooms No meals.*

★ The Woodlark

$$$ | **HOTEL** | The latest offering from the überhip Provenance Hotels brand connects a pair of stately early-1900s Downtown buildings that have been outfitted with well-curated local art, midcentury modern furnishings, and a slew of wellness amenities, from a first-rate fitness center to in-room streaming workout videos. **Pros:** exceptional dining and bars; artful, chic aesthetic; prime central location. **Cons:** some rooms are small; construction next door (through 2023) can get a little noisy; pricey valet parking. *Rooms from: $255 ✉ 813 S.W. Alder St., Downtown ☎ 503/548–2559, 833/624–2188 🌐 www.woodlarkhotel.com 150 rooms No meals.*

Nightlife

BARS AND LOUNGES

★ Abigail Hall

BARS/PUBS | Inspired by the legacy of Oregon suffragist Abigail Scott Duniway, the first woman registered to vote in Multnomah County, this elegant hotel lounge looks like a time capsule for a reason. A historian helped the design team re-create the early-1900s floral aesthetic of the historic Ladies Reception Hall, which originally inhabited this room. Behind the bar, the bartenders seem less tied to the history of the space, mixing up more than a dozen creative cocktails with quippy names. ✉ *Woodlark Hotel, 813 S.W. Alder St., Downtown* ☎ *503/548–2559* 🌐 *www.abigailhallpdx.com.*

★ Headwaters at the Heathman

BARS/PUBS | At the elegant Heathman Hotel, you can enjoy Russian tea service in the eucalyptus-paneled Tea Court or beer, wine, and cocktails in the marble Headwaters lounge, a venerable old-world space that received a revamp in 2016 when local celeb chef Vitaly Paley took over. This is one of the city's most popular see-and-be-seen venues, especially before or after shows at nearby theaters and concert halls. ✉ *Heathman Hotel, 1001 S.W. Broadway, Downtown* ☎ *503/790–7752* 🌐 *www.headwaterspdx.com.*

★ Multnomah Whiskey Library

BARS/PUBS | Smartly dressed bartenders roll drink carts around the seductively clubby room—with beam ceilings, wood paneling, leather chairs, a wood-burning fireplace, and crystal chandeliers—pouring cocktails table-side. The emphasis, of course, is whiskey and bourbon—Multnomah has such an extensive collection in its "library" that staff need rolling ladders to access the bottles perched on the tall shelves lining the exposed-brick walls. ✉ *1124 S.W. Alder St., West End* ☎ *503/954–1381* 🌐 *www.mwlpdx.com.*

LIVE MUSIC

McMenamins Crystal Ballroom

MUSIC CLUBS | With a 7,500-square-foot spring-loaded dance floor built on ball bearings to ramp up the energy, this historic former dance hall draws local, regional, and national acts every night but Monday. Past performers include Sleater-Kinney, Jefferson Airplane, Emmylou Harris, Tame Impala, and Angel Olsen. ✉ *1332 W. Burnside St., West End* ☎ *503/225–0047* 🌐 *www.crystalballroompdx.com.*

Performing Arts

PERFORMANCE VENUES

★ Arlene Schnitzer Concert Hall

ARTS CENTERS | The 2,776-seat Arlene Schnitzer Concert Hall, built in 1928 in an Italian rococo revival style, hosts rock concerts, choral groups, lectures, and concerts by the Oregon Symphony and others. "The Schnitz," as locals call it, is one of the venues that make up the Portland'5 Centers for the Arts umbrella organization. ✉ *1037 S.W. Broadway, Downtown* ☎ *503/248-4335* 🌐 *www.portland5.com.*

★ Portland'5 Centers for the Arts

ARTS CENTERS | The city's top performing arts complex hosts opera, ballet, rock shows, symphony performances, lectures, and Broadway musicals in its five venues: the Arlene Schnitzer Concert Hall, the Keller Auditorium, and the three-in-one Antoinette Hatfield Hall, which comprises the Brunish, Newmark, and Winningstad theaters. The majority of the region's top performing companies call these venues home, including the Portland Opera, the Oregon Symphony, the Oregon Ballet Theatre, and the Portland Youth Philharmonic. ✉ *Box office, 1111 S.W. Broadway, Downtown* ☎ *503/248–4335* 🌐 *www.portland5.com.*

CLASSICAL MUSIC

ORCHESTRAS

★ Oregon Symphony

MUSIC | FAMILY | Established in 1896, the symphony is Portland's largest classical group—and one of the largest orchestras in the country. Its season officially starts in September and ends in May, with concerts held at Arlene Schnitzer Concert Hall, but throughout the summer the orchestra and its smaller ensembles can be seen at Waterfront Park and Washington Park for special outdoor summer performances. It also presents about 40 classical, pop, children's, and family concerts each year. ✉ *Ticket Office, 909 S.W. Washington St., Downtown* ☎ *503/228–1353* 🌐 *www.orsymphony.org.*

Shopping

CLOTHING

★ Frances May

CLOTHING | Commanding a prime corner shop in the fashion-forward West End, this grandmother-and-granddaughter-owned clothing retailer is one of the Pacific Northwest's most defining trendsetters—a favorite of stylish locals who come for that cool, understated look (casual to dressy) that Portlanders are known for. You'll find made-here labels like gender-neutral, organic line Olderbrother, as well as European faves like Acne and APC. Frances May also stocks jewelry, art books, and the city's own OLO Fragrances. ✉ *1003 S.W. Washington St., West End* ☎ *503/227–3402* 🌐 *www.francesmay.com.*

★ Wildfang

CLOTHING | Founded by two former Nike employees, this queer-owned, women-centric retailer makes its values immediately clear, with its "Wild Feminist" T-shirt among its best-sellers. Wildfang's house collection of punkish, tomboy-inspired apparel shares this gallery-like shop with other minimally stylish brands that challenge gender conventions in the fashion world. ✉ *404 S.W. 10th Ave., West End* ☎ *503/964–6746* 🌐 *www.wildfang.com.*

HOUSEHOLD GOODS AND FURNITURE

★ Canoe

GIFTS/SOUVENIRS | Form meets function at this design boutique with a niche selection of clean-lined, modern goods and gifts for every room in the home. You'll find curvy thick-glass bowls, modern lamps with sheer paper shades, polished-stone trays, Bigelow natural-bristle toothbrushes, and Chemex coffee kettles, with some goods produced locally and exclusively for Canoe, and others imported from Asia and northern Europe. ✉ *1233 S.W. 10th Ave., Downtown* ☎ *503/889–8545* 🌐 *www.canoe.design.*

Tender Loving Empire

GIFTS/SOUVENIRS | The retail shop of the eponymous Portland record label founded by Jared and Brianne Mees carries not only music but also cool hand-printed cards, posters, and T-shirts, along with an artistic selection of handcrafted lifestyle goods, from pastel miniature vases and squiggle-shaped earrings to ceramic fox trinkets and illustrated prints. You'll find additional locations on Hawthorne, in Nob Hill, at Bridgeport Village, and in the airport. ✉ *412 S.W. 10th Ave., West End* ☎ *503/548–2925* 🌐 *www.tenderlovingempire.com.*

Activities

BIKING

BIKETOWN Portland

BICYCLING | Portland's bike-share program, in partnership with Nike, is affordable and easy to use. There are more than 125 stations throughout the city, and some 1,000 bikes, each with a small basket (helmets are not provided, however, so consider bringing your own). Just choose a plan (single rides start at 8 cents per minute), sign up (there's a one-time $5 fee), and you'll receive an account and PIN number that allows you to take out a bike. ✉ *Portland* ☎ *866/512–2453* 🌐 *www.biketownpdx.com.*

Old Town/Chinatown

Old Town/Chinatown, officially known as the Skidmore Old Town National Historic District, is where Portland was born. The 20-square-block section—bounded by Oak Street to the south, Broadway to the west, and Hoyt Street to the north—includes buildings of varying ages and architectural designs. Before it was renovated, this was skid row. Vestiges of it remain in parts of Chinatown; older buildings are gradually being remodeled, and lately the immediate area has experienced a small surge in development, but the neighborhood can also feel a bit seedy in places. Portland doesn't have an LGBTQ district per se—the scene permeates just about every neighborhood of this extremely LGBTQ-welcoming city. But you'll find the highest concentration of Portland's gay nightspots in Old Town (and a few others close by in Downtown). MAX serves the area with stops at the Old Town/Chinatown and Skidmore Fountain stations.

Sights

Chinatown Gateway
PUBLIC ART | Located on West Burnside Street and Northwest 4th Avenue, this ornate arch is guarded by two bronze lions and decorated mythical creatures. It marks the entrance to Portland's once-thriving Chinatown. ✉ *22 NW 4th Ave., Old Town/Chinatown.*

★ Lan Su Chinese Garden
GARDEN | In a twist on the Joni Mitchell song, the city of Portland and private donors took down a parking lot and unpaved paradise when they created this wonderland near the Pearl District and Old Town/Chinatown. It's the largest Suzhou-style garden outside China, with a large lake, bridged and covered walkways, koi- and water lily–filled ponds, rocks, bamboo, statues, waterfalls, and courtyards. A team of 60 artisans and designers from China literally left no stone unturned—500 tons of stone were brought here from Suzhou—in their efforts to give the windows, roof tiles, gateways (including a "moongate"), and other architectural aspects of the garden some specific meaning or purpose. Also on the premises are a gift shop and an enchanting two-story teahouse, operated by local Tao of Tea company, overlooking the lake and garden. ✉ *239 N.W. Everett St., Old Town/Chinatown* ☎ *503/228–8131* 🌐 *www.lansugarden.org* 🎫 *$12.95.*

Oregon Nikkei Legacy Center Museum
MUSEUM | This Japanese American historical museum, just a short walk from the related historical plaza in Waterfront Park, pays homage to the dynamic Nikkei (Japanese emigrant) community that has thrived in Portland for generations. The museum occupies the stately 19th-century Merchant Hotel building, and the excellent rotating exhibits use art, photography, personal histories, and artifacts to touch on all aspects of the Japanese American experience in Portland and the Northwest, including the dark period during World War II of forced relocation to concentration camps situated throughout the U.S. West. **■ TIP→ You can also view an excellent interactive permanent history exhibit on the Nikkei Center's website.** ✉ *121 N.W. 2nd Ave., Old Town/Chinatown* ☎ *503/224–1458* 🌐 *www.oregonnikkei.org* 🎫 *$5* 🕙 *Closed Mon.*

★ Pine Street Market
MARKET | In a city where restaurants rank among the top sightseeing attractions, this bustling food hall in a handsome late-Victorian Old Town building offers visitors a one-stop opportunity to try food from some of Portland's most celebrated chefs. In one massive room, you'll find nine small restaurants with

counter service and plenty of common seating. Highlights include one of the first U.S. branches of Tokyo's famed **Marukin Ramen,** juicy Southern-style burgers and throwback cocktails at **Bless Your Heart** (from John Gorham of Tasty n Sons fame), Spanish-inspired tapas and rotisserie chicken at **Pollo Bravo**, and a soft-serve ice-cream stand called **Wiz Bang Bar** operated by Salt & Straw. Bring your appetite, and brace yourself for long lines on weekends. ✉ *126 S.W. 2nd Ave., Old Town/Chinatown* 🌐 *www.pinestreetpdx.com* 🎫 *Free.*

Portland Chinatown Museum

MUSEUM | Begun as a temporary exhibit on the city's Chinatown—more than 10% of Portland's population identified as Chinese American in the 1900s, making it the second-largest such community in the country—at the Oregon Historical Society Museum, this museum opened a 2,500-square-foot permanent space in late 2018 in the heart of Chinatown. Exhibits here document the community's continuously important contribution to the city, including the vibrant Chinese American–owned businesses that have prospered here since Portland's founding, as well as art, music, food, and important aspects of the community. The museum also presents rotating art and history exhibits as well as occasional concerts, lectures, and oral-history presentations. ✉ *127 N.W. 3rd Ave., Old Town/Chinatown* ☎ *503/224–0008* 🌐 *www.portlandchinatownmuseum.org* 🎫 *$8* 🕓 *Closed Mon.–Wed.*

★ Portland Saturday Market

MARKET | **FAMILY** | On weekends from March to Christmas Eve, the west side of the Burnside Bridge and the Skidmore Fountain area hosts North America's largest ongoing open-air handicraft market, with some 400 vendors. If you're looking for jewelry, yard art, housewares, and decorative goods made from every material under the sun, check out the amazing collection of works by talented artisans on display here. The market also opens for holiday shopping during the week preceding Christmas Day, a period known as the Festival of the Last Minute. Entertainers and food booths add to the festive feel. ■ **TIP→ Be careful not to mistake this market for the food-centric PSU Portland Farmers Market, which also takes place on Saturday, on the other side of Downtown.** ✉ *2 S.W. Naito Pkwy. at foot of S.W. Ankeny, in Waterfront Park, Old Town/Chinatown* ☎ *503/222–6072* 🌐 *www.portlandsaturdaymarket.com* 🎫 *Free* 🕓 *Closed Jan., Feb., and weekdays.*

Restaurants

★ Lechon

$$$ | **SOUTH AMERICAN** | The menu of wood-fired, *carne*-intensive dishes at this bustling spot reads like a greatest hits of South American recipes, from Peruvian fried-chicken bites with fermented hot honey to brisket empanadas with ancho aioli to Argentinean-style 28-day dry-aged rib-eye steaks with cilantro butter. An added appeal is the location inside a handsome historic building just across the street from Tom McCall Waterfront Park, making it one of the closest dining options to the city's riverfront. **Known for:** plenty of seafood and vegetarian options; an emphasis on locally sourced and organic ingredients; great late-night tapas menu. 💲 *Average main: $25* ✉ *113 S.W. Naito Pkwy., Old Town/Chinatown* ☎ *503/219–9000* 🌐 *www.lechonpdx.com* 🕓 *No lunch weekends.*

Coffee and Quick Bites

Voodoo Doughnut

$ | **BAKERY** | The long lines outside this Old Town 24/7 doughnut shop, marked by its distinctive pink-neon sign, attest to the fact that this irreverent bakery is almost as famous a Portland landmark as Powell's Books. The aforementioned sign depicts one of the shop's biggest sellers,

Sights

1 Chinatown Gateway **B4**
2 Lan Su Chinese Garden **C3**
3 Oregon Nikkei Legacy Center Museum **C3**
4 Pine Street Market **C5**
5 Portland Chinatown Museum **B3**
6 Portland Saturday Market **D4**

Restaurants

1 Lechon **D5**

Quick Bites

1 Voodoo Doughnut ... **C4**

Hotels

1 The Hoxton Portland..... **B4**
2 Society Hotel........ **B3**

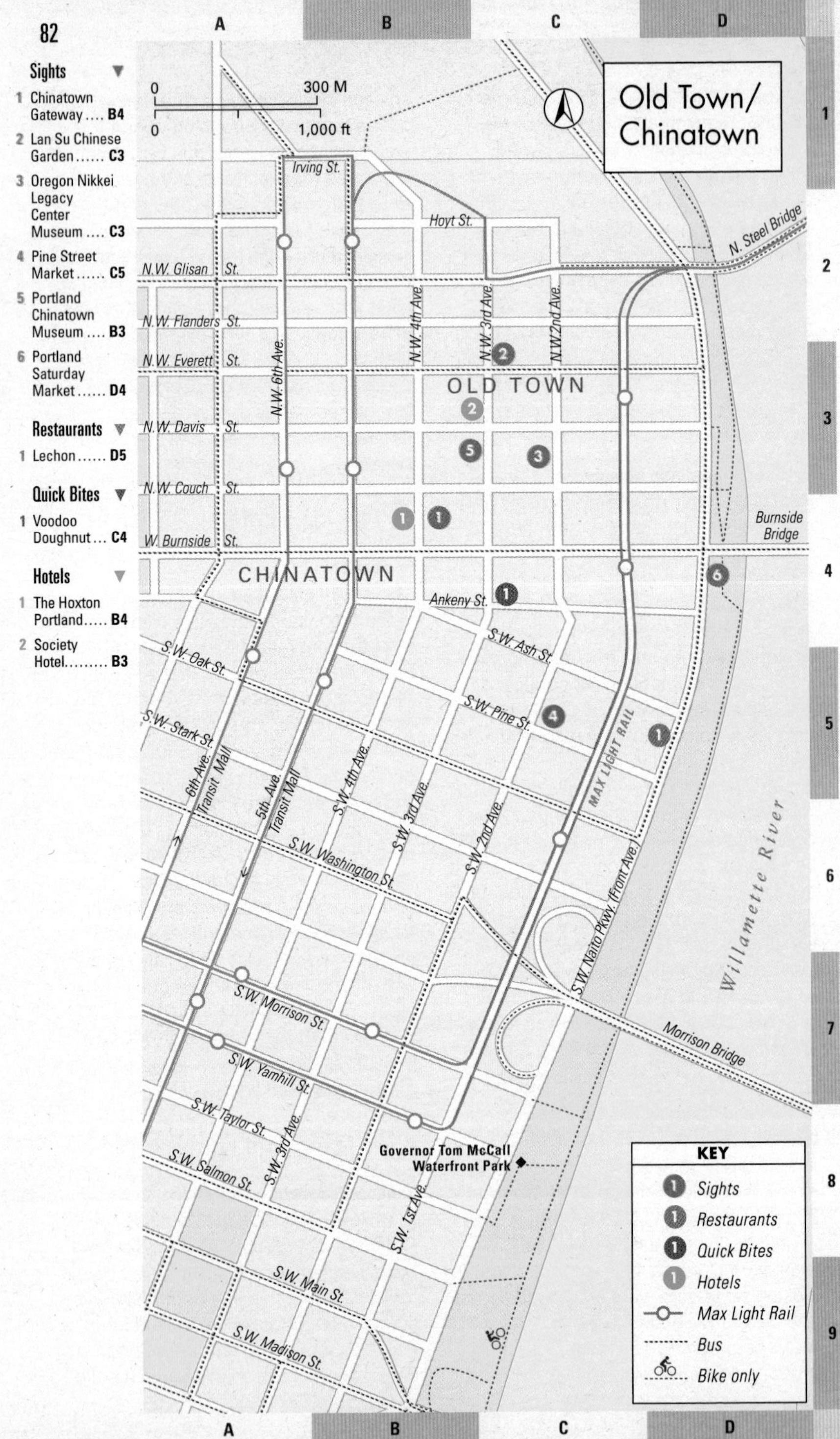

a raspberry jelly–topped chocolate voodoo-doll doughnut, but all the creations here, some of them witty, some ribald, bring smiles to the faces of customers—even those who have waited 30 minutes in the rain. **Known for:** offbeat doughnut flavors; the bacon maple bar doughnut; long lines. *Average main: $4* ✉ *22 S.W. 3rd Ave., Old Town/Chinatown* ☎ *503/241–4704* *www.voodoodoughnut.com.*

Hotels

The Hoxton Portland

$$ | **HOTEL** | London's hipper-than-thou Hoxton brand opened this see-and-be-seen hotel in 2018 on the border between Old Town and Downtown. **Pros:** close to Pearl District and West End; stunningly designed bars and restaurant; rates include "healthy breakfast bag" (with fruit, juice, and house-made granola). **Cons:** many rooms are quite small; surrounding Old Town can be boisterous and loud; expensive valet parking. *Rooms from: $189* ✉ *15 N.W. 4th Ave., Old Town/Chinatown* ☎ *503/770–0500* *www.thehoxton.com* *119 rooms* *Free breakfast.*

★ Society Hotel

$ | **HOTEL** | This quirky, bargain-priced boutique hotel with simple, stylish, and affordable rooms and a gorgeous roof deck is just steps from Old Town nightlife and Lan Su Chinese Garden, and occupies an 1880s former boardinghouse for sailors. **Pros:** budget-friendly rates; gorgeous rooftop deck; airy lobby café with artisanal coffee and pastries. **Cons:** rooms are very small; nearby bars can get noisy at night; no on-site parking. *Rooms from: $129* ✉ *203 N.W. 3rd Ave., Old Town/Chinatown* ☎ *503/445–0444* *www.thesocietyhotel.com* *39 rooms* *No meals.*

Nightlife

BARS AND LOUNGES

★ Ground Kontrol Classic Arcade

BARS/PUBS | **FAMILY** | Revisit your teen years at this massive, old-school Old Town arcade filled with more than 100 classic arcade games and about 50 pinball machines, including vintage Atari, Super Nintendo, and Killer Queen. There are two full bars and a kitchen serving reliably good nachos, sandwiches, and ice cream sundaes—and now that you are no longer a teen, you can have as much as you like. Over 21 after 5 pm. ✉ *115 N.W. 5th Ave., Old Town/Chinatown* ☎ *503/796–9364* *www.groundkontrol.com.*

★ Stag

BARS/PUBS | Drawing a diverse crowd of hipsters, tourists, and old-school clubbers, this Old Town hot spot cheekily bills itself a "gay gentlemen's lounge." Mounted antlers, leather chairs, and exposed-brick walls lend a rustic air, and male strippers dance on a small stage toward the back of the main room; a side bar contains a pool table. ✉ *317 N.W. Broadway, Old Town/Chinatown* ☎ *971/407–3132* *www.stagpdx.com.*

LIVE MUSIC

Roseland Theater

MUSIC | This spacious theater holds 1,410 people (standing-room only except for the 21+ balcony seating area), primarily stages rock, alternative, and blues shows, plus occasional comedians. Legends like Miles Davis and Prince have performed here, and more recent acts have included Hot Chip, Ingrid Michaelson, and Cat Power. ✉ *10 N.W. 6th Ave., Old Town/Chinatown* ☎ *855/227–8499* *www.roselandpdx.com.*

Lan Su Chinese Garden, Old Town/Chinatown

Shopping

CLOTHING

Compound Gallery

SHOES/LUGGAGE/LEATHER GOODS | One of a few spots in Old Town that specialize in urban streetwear fashion, this expansive boutique carries Herschel backpacks, Japanese Kidrobot vinyl art toys, and clothing, footwear, and hats from trendy brands like Stüssy, UNDFTD, and Bape. The shop also collaborates on new products with local designers and artists. ✉ *107 N.W. 5th Ave., Old Town/Chinatown* ☎ *503/796–2733* 🌐 *www.compoundgallery.com.*

HOUSEHOLD GOODS AND FURNITURE

Pendleton Home Store

CLOTHING | At this flagship lifestyle store—the headquarters are in the same building—of the world-famous textile and furniture purveyor, you can browse the company's new products before they're available online or in Pendleton's other shops around the country. The company's classic camp blankets—many of them with patterns inspired by Native American weavings and U.S. national parks—are a huge draw, but you'll also find pillows, pet beds, hats, backpacks, totes, sweaters, and other apparel. ✉ *210 N.W. Broadway, Old Town/Chinatown* ☎ *503/535–5444* 🌐 *www.pendleton-usa.com.*

SPECIALTY SHOPS

Serra Dispensary

SPECIALTY STORES | A beautifully designed cannabis shop in which carefully curated marijuana is displayed in blue ceramic dishes inside blond-wood cases, Serra stands out for its knowledgeable staff and decidedly artisanal aesthetic. They'll lend you a bronze magnifying glass if you want a closer inspection of the products, which also include cannabis-infused local chocolates, gummies, and other edibles. There's a similar branch in Southeast on Belmont Street. ✉ *220 S.W. 1st Ave., Old Town/Chinatown* ☎ *971/279–5613* 🌐 *www.shopserra.com.*

Pearl District

Bordering Old Town to the west and Downtown and the West End to the north, the trendy Pearl District comprises a formerly rough-and-tumble warren of warehouses and railroad yards. Much of the Pearl is new construction, but dozens of the district's historic industrial buildings have been converted into handsome, loft-style housing and commercial concerns, too. You'll find some of the city's most buzzed-about restaurants, galleries, and shops in this neighborhood—the monthly First Thursday evening art walk is an especially fun time to visit. The Portland Streetcar line passes through here, with stops at ecologically themed Jamison Square and Tanner Springs parks.

Sights

★ Oregon Jewish Museum and Center for Holocaust Education

MUSEUM | FAMILY | This institution, which interprets the stories and lives of the state's vibrant Jewish community, also functions as an educational and inspirational resource that focuses on promoting tolerance and combating discrimination and persecution. The museum was established in 1999 and is the force behind Washington Park's poignant Oregon Holocaust Memorial, but it wasn't until 2017 that it moved into this beautiful new permanent home inside the 1916 DeSoto Building, on the leafy Park Blocks. The gallery on the upper floor contains permanent collections, including artifacts and artwork, and oral histories of the state's earliest Jewish residents as well as the profoundly moving historical exhibit on both the Holocaust and the valiant struggles of Jewish, Asian American, African American, Hispanic, LGBTQ, and other minority communities in the face of often strenuous intolerance in Oregon. **■ TIP→ The ground floor features Lefty's, an excellent little lunch spot that has delicious sandwiches, salads, soups, rugelach, and other treats.** ✉ *724 N.W. Davis St., Old Town/Chinatown* ☎ *503/226–3600* 🌐 *www.ojmche.org* 🎫 *$8* ⏲ *Closed Mon.*

★ Powell's City of Books

STORE/MALL | A local legend, and rightfully so, Powell's is the largest independent bookstore in the world, with more than 1.5 million new and used books along with a good selection of locally made gifts and goodies. It's a top draw for any visitor, but serious book lovers can easily spend a few hours inside. The three-level store covers an entire city block on the edge of the Pearl District—maps are available at the info kiosks and rooms are color-coded according to book type. On the top floor, the Rare Book Room is a must-see, even if you're not planning to splurge for an 1829 volume of the Waverly Novels or an autobiography signed by Anwar Sadat; there are rare prints and mint-condition first editions in just about every genre. Be sure to look for the pillar bearing signatures of prominent sci-fi authors who have passed through the store that's protected by a jagged length of Plexiglas. Also check online for upcoming author readings, which take place three to five times a week and draw some of the world's top literary names. You'll find a branch of the popular Portland coffeehouse, World Cup, on the ground floor. There are also branches in Portland International Airport as well as a large outpost in the heart of the Hawthorne District, with its own coffeehouse, the Fresh Pot. ✉ *1005 W. Burnside St., Pearl District* ☎ *503/228–4651* 🌐 *www.powells.com.*

Restaurants

★ Deschutes Brewery Portland Public House

$$ | AMERICAN | The Portland branch of the Bend-based Deschutes Brewery typically has more than 25 beers on tap, including nationally acclaimed mainstays Mirror Pond Pale Ale, Inversion IPA, and

One-of-a-kind items at Portland Saturday Market

Black Butte Porter, plus seasonal and experimental brews. On the food side, the kitchen has really upped its game in recent years, making this a worthy destination for elevated pub fare, such as Manila clams steamed in cider, porter-braised and smoked pork shoulder with grits, and plenty of sandwiches and salads. **Known for:** limited-release and seasonal beers; the IPA pretzel with cheese sauce and porter mustard; marionberry cobbler. *Average main: $18 ✉ 210 N.W. 11th Ave., Pearl District ☎ 503/296–4906 🌐 www.deschutes-brewery.com.*

★ Mediterranean Exploration Company

$$ | MEDITERRANEAN | Developed by cookbook author and celeb-chef John Gorham, this vegetarian-friendly tribute to Mediterranean cuisine occupies a handsome former warehouse on historic 13th Avenue in the Pearl. MEC (for short) is an energy-filled, open space with a mix of communal and individual tables (the food is served family-style)—it's surprisingly affordable considering the extraordinary quality and generous portions, particularly if you opt for the $50 tasting menu. **Known for:** chicken and lamb kebabs; Middle East–inspired cocktails; cardamom ice cream served with a pour-over of robust Turkish coffee. *Average main: $22 ✉ 333 N.W. 13th Ave., Pearl District ☎ 503/222–0906 🌐 www.mediterraneanexplorationcompany.com ⏲ No lunch.*

Oven and Shaker

$$ | PIZZA | A joint venture between James Beard Award–nominated chef Cathy Whims and renowned cocktail mixologist Ryan Magarian, this aptly named late-night spot specializes in creatively topped wood-fired pizzas and deftly crafted cocktails that rely heavily on local spirits and fresh juices. The salads and appetizers are also terrific, especially the radicchio version of a classic Caesar salad. **Known for:** great early-evening and late-night pizza deals; Tuscan brownie sundae with vanilla gelato, chocolate sauce; the Maple Pig pizza with apple butter, pork belly, smoked ham, maple mascarpone, and ricotta. *Average main: $19 1134 N.W. Everett St., Pearl District 503/241–1600 www.ovenandshaker.com.*

Coffee and Quick Bites

★ Nuvrei

$ | **BAKERY** | You'll find some of the tastiest sweets—including heavenly pistachio-rose croissants and blueberry-blackberry scones—in town at this cozy patisserie and café a few blocks south of Jamison Square. Be sure to check out the ever-changing selection of fluffy macarons. **Known for:** house-made macarons; savory quiches and croissants; double-chocolate flourless cookies. *Average main: $9 404 N.W. 10th Ave., Pearl District 503/972–1701 www.nuvrei.com No dinner.*

★ Canopy by Hilton Portland

$$$ | **HOTEL** | This contemporary member of Hilton's hip Canopy boutique brand eagerly encourages guests to chill out and relax in the hotel's extensive—and gorgeous—industrial-chic lounges, one of which features complimentary evening beer and wine. **Pros:** quiet but central location near Pearl District; beautifully designed living room–inspired common spaces; rooftop gym with stunning views. **Cons:** a 10- to 15-minute walk from heart of Downtown; breakfast isn't complimentary; expensive valet parking. *Rooms from: $259 425 N.W. 9th Ave., Pearl District 971/351–0230 www.canopy3.hilton.com 153 rooms No meals.*

BARS AND LOUNGES

★ Botanist Bar PDX

BARS/PUBS | This classy, food-forward basement lounge opened in 2019 to rave reviews for its use of high-quality artisanal spirits and fresh juice, shrubs, and spirits. The bar snacks here are substantive and delicious—whitefish ceviche, tuna poke nachos, Korean barbecue chicken. A popular boozy brunch is offered on Sunday. *1300 N.W. Lovejoy St., Pearl District 971/533–8064 www.botanistbarpdx.com.*

Pink Rabbit

BARS/PUBS | This elegant space with ambient pink lighting and suspended bubble lamps, named for a song by indie band The National, serves playfully named but seriously crafted cocktails like the sherry-and-gin-centric Sucker's Luck and the mezcal-driven Quiet Company. The Asian-influenced bar snacks are distinctively delicious—try taro tots with Thai ranch and chili sauce or the oxtail burger. The darkly seductive space makes an inviting milieu before or after a show at nearby Portland Center Stage. *232 N.W. 12th Ave., Pearl District www.pinkrabbitpdx.com.*

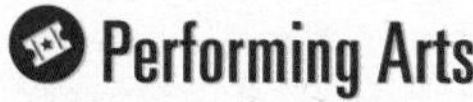

THEATER

★ Portland Center Stage

THEATER | Housed in a handsomely restored 1891 armory, Portland Center Stage puts on around 10 contemporary and classic works on two stages in the LEED-certified green building between September and June. These are first-rate productions with exceptional onstage and behind-the-scenes talents. *Gerding Theater at the Armory, 128 N.W. 11th Ave., Pearl District 503/445–3700 www.pcs.org.*

CLOTHING

★ Keen Garage

SHOES/LUGGAGE/LEATHER GOODS | Known for its wildly popular and often playfully colorful hiking sandals, boots, and water shoes, this spacious showroom occupies a splendidly restored 1907 steamship factory that also houses this eco-concious company's headquarters. In addition to just about any kind of footwear you could need to tackle Pacific Northwest's great outdoors, you'll also find backpacks and messenger bags along with socks, pants, shirts, and other rugged outerwear. There's also a phone booth in the store from which you can call politicians in Washington to express support for a variety of environmental issues, from land and water conservation to clean air. ✉ *505 N.W. 13th Ave., Pearl District* ☎ *971/200–4040* 🌐 *www.keenfootwear.com.*

GALLERIES

★ First Thursday

ART GALLERIES | This gallery walk the first Thursday of every month gives art appreciators a chance to check out new exhibits while enjoying music, wine, and light appetizers. Typically the galleries, which are largely located in the Pearl District, are open in the evening from 6 to 9, but hours vary. Beyond the galleries, you'll find a lively scene of street musicians, local art vendors, and food and craft beer stalls along N.W. 13th Avenue between roughly Hoyt and Kearney Streets, which is pedestrians-only during First Thursday. ✉ *Pearl District* ☎ *503/227–8519* 🌐 *www.explorethepearl.com.*

PDX Contemporary Art

ART GALLERIES | One of the Pearl District's longest-running and most respected art spaces, this large gallery features rotating exhibitions in a range of materials from an impressive roster of both local and national artists. The striking space, inside one of the neighborhood's oldest buildings, was designed by famous Portland architect Brad Cloepfil (famous for the Seattle Art Museum, Museum of Arts and Design in New York City, and many others). ✉ *925 N.W. Flanders St., Pearl District* ☎ *503/222–0063* 🌐 *www.pdxcontemporaryart.com.*

HOUSEHOLD GOODS AND FURNITURE

★ Made Here PDX

GIFTS/SOUVENIRS | This spacious showroom across from Powell's carries an impressive and eclectic assortment of locally made culinary goods, housewares, fashion, jewelry, arts and crafts—even handcrafted skis and snowboards. The quality of everything here is consistently high—it's a perfect way to get a sense of Portland's vibrant "maker" culture, all under one roof. There's a second location on North Mississippi Avenue. ✉ *40 N.W. 10th Ave., Pearl District* ☎ *503/224–0122* 🌐 *www.madehereonline.com.*

Nob Hill and Vicinity

Fashionable since the 1880s and still filled with Victorian houses, Nob Hill is a mixed-use cornucopia of old Portland charm and new Portland retail and dining. With its cafés, restaurants, galleries, and boutiques, it's a great place to stroll, shop, and people-watch. At the southern end of 23rd, on the blocks nearest Burnside, you'll mostly encounter upscale chain shops, whereas more independent and generally less pricey retail proliferates farther north, which includes the more recently developed and up-and-coming Slabtown district.

Sights

Bull Run Distilling

WINERY/DISTILLERY | A pioneer of Portland's burgeoning craft spirits scene, head distiller Lee Medoff opened this Slabtown distillery in a 7,000-square-foot warehouse in 2010, with a dream of creating an iconic single-malt Oregon whiskey. Today Bull Run operates two of the largest commercial stills in the state, turning out acclaimed whiskeys, vodkas, and aquavit. ✉ *2259 N.W. Quimby St., Slabtown* ☎ *503/224–3483* 🌐 *www.bullrundistillery.com* ⏲ *Closed Mon. and Tues.*

Slabtown

NEIGHBORHOOD | A formerly industrial slice of Northwest, this mini neighborhood epitomizes New Portland, with a walking-scale grid of stylish apartment buildings and repurposed warehouses filled with some of the city's most hyped restaurants. Come hungry, as the food scene is the star of Slabtown. Tasty highlights include cocktail lounges like Solo Club and Bar West, inventive tapas at Spanish eatery Ataula, craft beer at the bi-level Breakside Brewery, and handmade pasta at Grassa. While Slabtown loosely refers to the blocks stretching north from Lovejoy Street to the Willamette River, most of the action is sandwiched between Northrup and Thurman Streets. ✉ *Blocks stretching north of Lovejoy St., Slabtown.*

Restaurants

★ Ataula

$$$ | **TAPAS** | The son of a cook from Spain's Aragon region, renowned chef-owner José Chesa brings his passion for Spanish cuisine to this small restaurant on a side street just off N.W. 23rd Avenue. The food is served tapas-style, with everything meant to be shared, including the heaping paella platters. **Known for:** picturesque sidewalk seating; the dessert of toasted bread with olive oil, chocolate, and salt; outstanding wine list. *Ⓢ Average main: $29* ✉ *1818 N.W. 23rd Pl., Slabtown* ☎ *503/894–8904* 🌐 *www.ataulapdx.com* ⏲ *Closed Mon. No lunch.*

★ Paley's Place

$$$$ | **FRENCH** | Open since 1995 in an old Victorian house, this nationally acclaimed bistro helped put Portland's farm-forward restaurant scene on the map. Helmed by James Beard Award–winning chef-owner Vitaly Paley, who also operates Downtown's Imperial restaurant, Paley's serves Pacific Northwest meets French cuisine prepared with organic ingredients. **Known for:** iconic restaurant in a converted Victorian; glass case filled with an extensive cheese selection; porch and patio seating. *Ⓢ Average main: $34* ✉ *1204 N.W. 21st Ave., Slabtown* ☎ *503/243–2403* 🌐 *www.paleysplace.net* ⏲ *No lunch.*

Hotels

★ Inn @ Northrup Station

$$$ | **HOTEL** | **FAMILY** | Near the Pearl District, bright colors, bold patterns, and retro designs characterize this Nob Hill hotel, which contains luxurious apartment-style suites with full kitchens or kitchenettes as well as patios (or balconies) adjoining most units, and a garden terrace for all guests to use. **Pros:** roomy suites have kitchens and feel like home; steps from Nob Hill shopping, dining, and the streetcar; free parking and streetcar tickets. **Cons:** the bold color scheme isn't for everyone; a 30-minute walk, or 15-minute streetcar ride, from Downtown; in demand, so it can be hard to get a reservation. *Ⓢ Rooms from: $239* ✉ *2025 N.W. Northrup St., Nob Hill* ☎ *503/224–0543, 800/224–1180* 🌐 *www.northrupstation.com* *70 suites* *Free breakfast.*

Silver Cloud Inn–Portland

$$ | **HOTEL** | The sole Portland branch of a small, Seattle-area, midpriced hotel chain is just a block from the lively upper end of N.W. 23rd Avenue and a great alternative to the bustle of Downtown. **Pros:** free parking; close to Nob Hill and Slabtown boutiques and dining as well as Forest Park hiking trails; easy access to bus and streetcar. **Cons:** gym but no pool; a bit of a distance from Downtown; front rooms face a busy street. *Ⓢ Rooms from: $189* ✉ *2426 N.W. Vaughn St., Nob Hill* ☎ *503/242–2400, 800/205–6939* 🌐 *www.silvercloud.com* *81 rooms* *Free breakfast.*

Pearl District, Nob Hill, and Forest Park

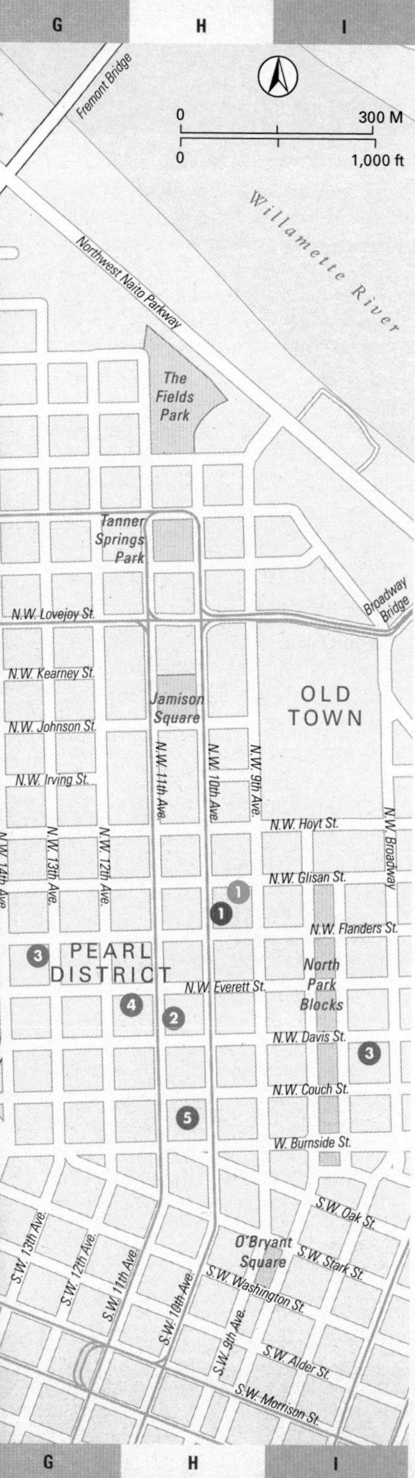

Sights ▼

1 Bull Run Distilling **B3**

2 Forest Park **A1**

3 Oregon Jewish Museum and Center for Holocaust Education **I7**

4 Pittock Mansion **A7**

5 Powell's City of Books.. **H7**

6 Slabtown................. **B1**

Restaurants ▼

1 Ataula **B1**

2 Deschutes Brewery Portland Public House **H7**

3 Mediterranean Exploration Company... **G6**

4 Oven and Shaker **H7**

5 Paley's Place **C4**

Quick Bites ▼

1 Nuvrei **H6**

2 Smith Teamaker.......... **F2**

Hotels ▼

1 Canopy by Hilton Portland.................. **H6**

2 Inn @ Northrup Station **D4**

Nightlife

BARS AND LOUNGES

★ Pope House Bourbon Lounge

BARS/PUBS | Of the half-dozen hopping bars clustered around the intersection of 21st Avenue and Glisan Street, this whiskey lover's haven is the clear standout. Set in a Victorian home, with a covered porch and pocket-size patio, Pope House prides itself on its collection of more than 40 different Kentucky bourbon brands that pair well with the selection of Southern-accented small plates. ✉ *2075 N.W. Glisan St., Nob Hill* ☎ *503/222–1056* 🌐 *www.popehouselounge.com.*

★ Solo Club

BARS/PUBS | A Mediterranean air flows through this jewelry box of a bar, which specializes in highball cocktails and *amari*, Italian after-dinner digestifs. The bi-level Solo Club, with salt-block-adorned pillars and turquoise tiles, has a piazza-like patio that appeals to the parents of toy poodles, corgis, and other adorable dogs. ✉ *2110 N.W. Raleigh St., Slabtown* ☎ *971/254–9806* 🌐 *www.thesoloclub.com.*

Shopping

HOUSEHOLD GOODS AND FURNITURE

★ Vía Raíz

HOUSEHOLD ITEMS/FURNITURE | "Made in Mexico" is the manifesto at Vía Raíz. The Spanish name of this tiny, 220-square-foot boutique translates to "via roots," which sums up the shopkeeper's approach to elevating contemporary Mexican designers and artisans. Expect a rotating display of modern crafts, art, accessories, home goods, and coffee table books. ✉ *2774 N.W. Thurman St., Slabtown* ☎ *503/303–3450* 🌐 *www.viaraiz.com.*

JEWELRY

★ Betsy & Iya

JEWELRY/ACCESSORIES | Bright Santa Fe-esque colors and sleek geometric forms define the handmade earrings, bracelets, rings, cuffs, necklaces, and other stylish accessories at this beloved jewelry studio. On weekdays during production hours (between 10 am and 5 pm), complimentary artisan-led tours show you the magic happening in the production space, where you might glimpse anything from stone setting to metal soldering. ✉ *1777 N.W. 24th Ave., Slabtown* ☎ *503/227–5482* 🌐 *www.betsyandiya.com.*

Activities

BIKE RENTALS

Fat Tire Farm

BICYCLING | For treks in Forest Park, rent mountain bikes at Fat Tire Farm, which is close to the park's Leif Erikson trailhead. The staff here really knows their stuff, from repair and maintenance help to advice on the best trails and routes. ✉ *2714 N.W. Thurman St., Nob Hill* ☎ *503/222–3276* 🌐 *www.fattirefarm.com.*

Forest Park

One of the largest woodland city parks in the country, Forest Park stretches 8 miles along the hills overlooking the Willamette River west of Downtown. More than 80 miles of trails through forests of Douglas fir, hemlock, and cedar (including a few patches of old growth) offer numerous options for those looking to log some miles or spend some time outside.

Sights

★ Forest Park

NATIONAL/STATE PARK | One of the nation's largest urban wildernesses (5,157 acres), this city-owned, car-free park has more than 50 species of birds and mammals and more than 80 miles of trails through forests of Douglas fir, hemlock, and cedar. Running the length of the park is the 30-mile Wildwood Trail, which extends into adjoining Washington Park (and is a handy point for accessing Forest Park), starting at the Vietnam Veterans Memorial in Hoyt Arboretum. You can access a number of spur trails from the Wildwood Trail, including the 11-mile Leif Erikson Drive, which picks up from the end of N.W. Thurman Street and is a popular route for jogging and mountain biking. ■ **TIP→ You can find information and maps at the Forest Park Conservancy office, at 833 S.W. 11th Avenue, Suite 800, and on the website.** ✉ *End of N.W. Thurman St., Forest Park* ✣ *Entrance at Leif Erikson Dr.* ☎ *503/223–5449* 🌐 *www.forestparkconservancy.org.*

★ Pittock Mansion

HOUSE | Henry Pittock, the founder and publisher of the *Oregonian* newspaper, built this 22-room, castlelike mansion, which combines French Renaissance and Victorian styles. The opulent manor, built in 1914, is filled with art and antiques. The 46-acre grounds, northwest of Washington Park and 1,000 feet above the city, offer superb views of the skyline, rivers, and the Cascade Range, including Mt. Hood and Mt. St. Helens. The mansion is a half-mile uphill trek from the nearest bus stop. The mansion is also a highly popular destination among hikers using Forest Park's well-utilized Wildwood Trail. ✉ *3229 N.W. Pittock Dr., Forest Park* ☎ *503/823–3623* 🌐 *www.pittockmansion.org* 🎫 *$12* ⏲ *Closed Jan.*

West Hills and Southwest

Forming a natural western border of Downtown and Nob Hill, the West Hills extend as a high (up to around 1,000 feet in elevation) ridgeline from Southwest to Northwest Portland. Part of this lofty neighborhood is residential, containing some of the largest and finest homes in the city, many of them with knockout views of the Downtown skyline and Mt. St. Helens and Mt. Hood in the distance. Technically, Downtown Portland is in the city's Southwest quadrant as are most of the attractions included in the West Hills section of town. But when locals mention Southwest, they're generally referring to the area south and southwest of Downtown, a mostly middle- to upper-middle-class residential district with a few commercial pockets.

Sights

★ International Rose Test Garden

GARDEN | **FAMILY** | This glorious park within Washington Park comprises three terraced gardens, set on 4½ acres, where more than 10,000 bushes and some 550 varieties of roses grow. The flowers, many of them new varieties, are at their peak in June, July, September, and October. From the gardens you can take in views of the Downtown skyline and, on clear days, the slopes of Mt. Hood, 50 miles to the east. Summer concerts take place in the garden's amphitheater. It's a pretty but hilly 30- to 40-minute walk from Downtown, or you can get here via MAX light rail (either to Washington Park or Kings Hill/S.W. Salmon Street stations); then transfer to Bus No. 63 or Washington Park shuttle (May–October only). ✉ *400 S.W. Kingston Ave., Washington Park* ☎ *503/227–7033* 🌐 *www.portlandoregon.gov/parks.*

Oregon Holocaust Memorial

MEMORIAL | This memorial to those who perished during the Holocaust bears the names of surviving families who live in Oregon and southwest Washington. A bronzed baby shoe, a doll, broken spectacles, and other strewn possessions await notice on the cobbled courtyard. Soil and ash from six Nazi concentration camps is interred beneath the black granite wall. The memorial is operated by the Oregon Jewish Museum and Center for Holocaust Education in Old Town, which hosts rotating history and art exhibits, films, concerts, and lectures. ✉ *S.W. Washington Way and S.W. Wright Ave., Washington Park* ☎ *503/226–3600* 🌐 *www.ojmche.org*.

Portland Children's Museum

MUSEUM | FAMILY | Colorful sights and sounds entertain kids of all ages where hands-on play is the order of the day. Visit nationally touring exhibits; catch a story time, a sing-along, or a puppet show in the theater; create sculptures in the clay studio; splash hands in the waterworks display; or make a creation from junk in the Maker Studio. The museum shares the same parking lot as the Oregon Zoo and can also be reached via the MAX light rail Washington Park stop. ✉ *4015 S.W. Canyon Rd., Washington Park* ☎ *503/223–6500* 🌐 *www.portlandcm.org* 🎫 *$11*.

★ **Portland Japanese Garden**

GARDEN | One of the most authentic Japanese gardens outside Japan, this serene landscape unfolds over 12½ acres of Washington Park, just a short stroll up the hill from the International Rose Test Garden. Designed by a Japanese landscape master, there are five separate garden styles: Strolling Pond Garden, Tea Garden, Natural Garden, Sand and Stone Garden, and Flat Garden. The Tea House was built in Japan and reconstructed here. An ambitious expansion designed by renowned Japanese architect Kengo Kuma added a tea garden café, library, art gallery, and a new gift shop in 2017. The east side of the Pavilion has a majestic view of Portland and Mt. Hood. Take MAX light rail to Washington Park station, and transfer to Bus No. 63 or the Washington Park Shuttle (May–October only). **■ TIP→ Knowledgeable volunteers guide daily public tours, which are free with admission; call ahead for times.** ✉ *611 S.W. Kingston Ave., Washington Park* ☎ *503/223–1321* 🌐 *www.japanesegarden.com* 🎫 *$19.95*.

North

Somewhat dismissed historically as the city's "fifth quadrant," North Portland has come into its own in recent years, as the comparatively low cost of real estate has made it popular with young entrepreneurs, students, and other urban pioneers. North Mississippi and North Williams Avenues, which are about 10 short blocks apart, have become home to some of the hottest food, drink, and music venues in the city, and farther-out areas like Kenton and St. Johns are becoming increasingly popular.

Sights

★ **Cathedral Park**

NATIONAL/STATE PARK | Whether it's the view of the imposing and stunning Gothic St. John's Bridge, which rises some 400 feet above the Willamette River, or the historic significance of Lewis and Clark having camped here in 1806, this 23-acre park is divine. Though there's no church, the park gets its name from the picturesque arches supporting the bridge. It's rumored that the ghost of a young girl haunts the bridge, and that may be true, but if you're told that it was designed by the same man who envisioned the Golden Gate Bridge, that's just a popular misconception. Dog lovers, or those who aren't, should take note of the off-leash area. ✉ *N. Edison St. and N. Pittsburg Ave., St. Johns* 🌐 *www.portlandoregon.gov/parks*.

★ **North Mississippi Avenue**

NEIGHBORHOOD | One of North Portland's strips of indie retailers, the liveliest section of North Mississippi Avenue stretches for several blocks and includes a mix of old storefronts and sleek new buildings that house cafés, brewpubs, collectives, shops, music venues, and an excellent food-cart pod, Mississippi Marketplace. Bioswale planter boxes, found-object fences, and café tables built from old doors are some of the innovations you'll see along this eclectic thoroughfare. At the southern end of the strip, stop by the ReBuilding Center, an outlet for recycled building supplies that has cob (clay-and-straw) trees and benches built into the facade. ✉ *N. Mississippi Ave., North Mississippi Ave.* ✣ *Between N. Fremont and N. Skidmore Sts.* 🌐 *www.mississippiave.com.*

★ Sauvie Island

ISLAND | **FAMILY** | If it's a day to take advantage of gorgeous weather, then drive about a half hour northwest of Downtown, or 15 minutes north of St. Johns, to Sauvie Island. The largely agrarian 33-square-mile piece of paradise in the Columbia River has a wildlife refuge, three beaches (including Collins Beach, which is clothing-optional), superb biking and hiking trails, and several farms offering seasonal "u-pick" bounty (and one, Bella Organic, offering an autumn pumpkin patch and corn maze). One excellent hike, and one of the few with free parking, is the Wapato Greenway, which is just 3 miles north of the bridge onto the island. The trail leads through a white oak savannah and around a pond, and you may see green horned owls, nuthatches, and deer. Part of the trail leads to a peaceful dock on the Multnomah Channel, where you can tie a boat or kayak. To get to the beaches, after crossing the Sauvie Island bridge, turn right; follow N.W. Sauvie Island Road to Reeder Road and follow signs. There's plenty of parking at the beaches, but a permit is required ($10 for a one-day permit, $30 annual, available at the general store at the base of the bridge). Keep in mind that visitors are banned from bringing alcohol onto the island from May to September. ✉ *N.W. Sauvie Island Rd., Sauvie Island* ✣ *Take U.S. 30 north from Portland to the Sauvie Island Bridge* 🌐 *www.sauvieisland.org.*

Restaurants

★ Eem

$$ | **THAI** | This impossibly delicious mash-up of Thai street food and Texas barbecue, a collaboration between the talents behind locally renowned restaurants Langbaan and Matt's BBQ, excels in both its playful approach and smoking-good execution. Potted plants and hanging basket lamps impart a subtle, relaxed beach bar vibe, perfect for enjoying tiki-esque cocktails with inspired names like Arranged Marriage and Act of God. **Known for:** colorful tropical drinks; chopped barbecue-fried rice with shishito peppers; rich curries with smoked brisket, lamb shoulder, and other barbecue staples. [$] *Average main: $16* ✉ *3808 N. Williams Ave., North Williams Ave.* ☎ *971/295–1645* 🌐 *www.eempdx.com.*

★ Interurban

$ | **MODERN AMERICAN** | A laid-back North Mississippi gastropub with an L-shaped indoor bar and a bi-level back patio with lush landscaping and a shaded pergola, Interurban is both a convivial drinkery and a fine spot for affordable, well-crafted American fare served from midafternoon until 2 am (hours start earlier on weekends, with brunch kicking off at 10 am). The kitchen creates consistently good and creative food, such as steak tartare and smoked-trout BLT sandwiches, and there's an extensive selection of cocktails and microbrews. **Known for:** terrific afternoon and late-night happy hour menu; salted-caramel French toast at brunch; pretty back patio. [$] *Average main: $15* ✉ *4057 N. Mississippi Ave., North Mississippi Ave.* ☎ *503/284–6669* 🌐 *www.interurbanpdx.com* ⏲ *No lunch weekdays.*

★ Lovely's Fifty-Fifty

$ | **PIZZA** | This unpretentious and airy neighborhood spot with wooden booths and whimsical fire-engine-red chairs is really two delicious dining options in one: the dining room serves inventively

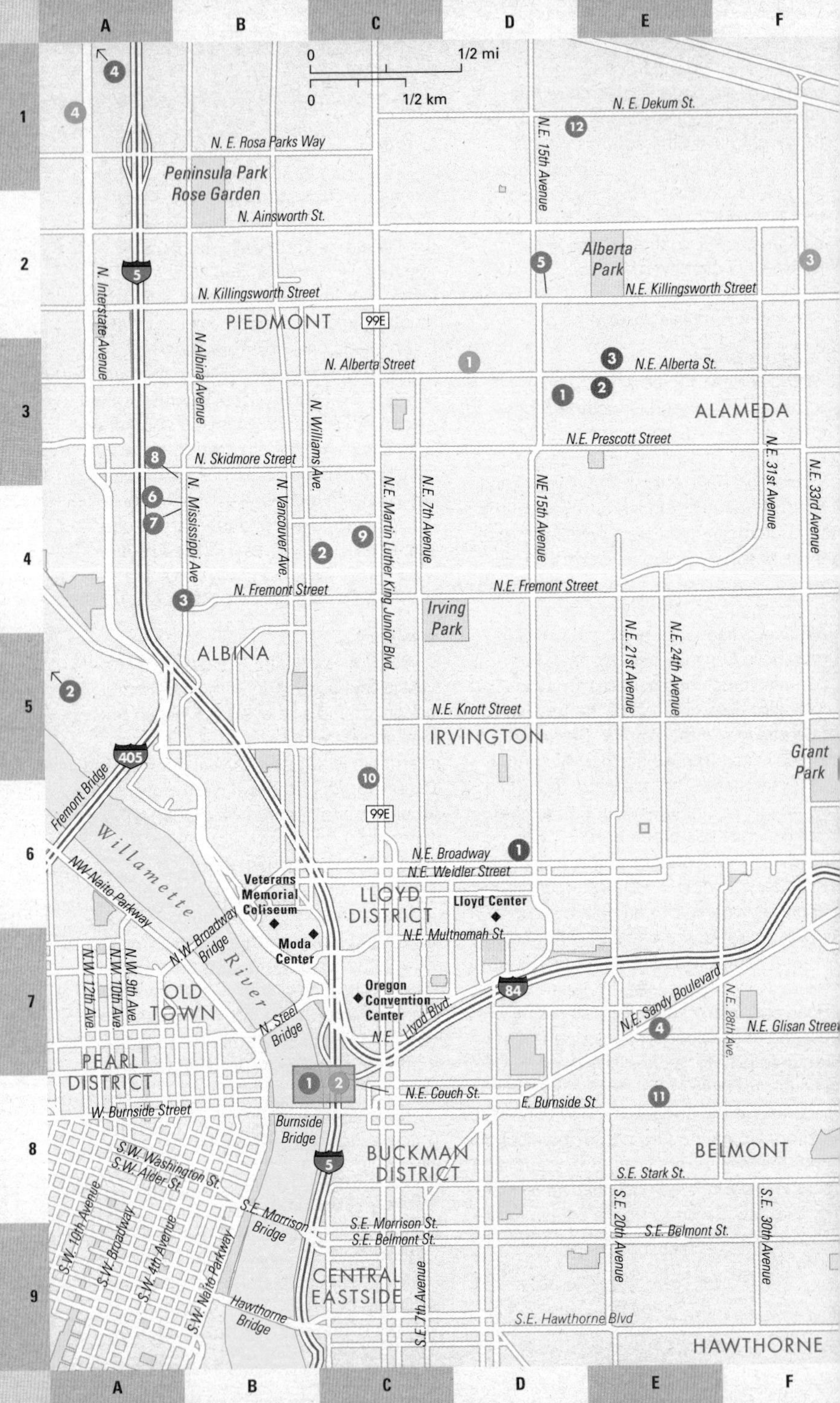

A
B
C
D
E
F
1
2
3
4
5
6
7
8
9
0
1/2 mi
1/2 km
N. E. Dekum St.
N.E. 15th Avenue
N. E. Rosa Parks Way
Peninsula Park
Rose Garden
N. Ainsworth St.
Alberta
Park
N.E. Killingsworth Street
N. Interstate Avenue
N. Killingsworth Street
PIEDMONT
99E
N Albina Avenue
N. Alberta Street
N.E. Alberta St.
ALAMEDA
N. Williams Ave.
N.E. Prescott Street
N. Skidmore Street
N. Mississippi Ave
N. Vancouver Ave.
N.E. Martin Luther King Junior Blvd.
N.E. 7th Avenue
NE 15th Avenue
N.E. 31st Avenue
N.E. 33rd Avenue
N. Fremont Street
N.E. Fremont Street
Irving
Park
ALBINA
N.E. 21st Avenue
N.E. 24th Avenue
N.E. Knott Street
IRVINGTON
Grant
Park
Fremont Bridge
Willamette
River
NW Naito Parkway
N.E. Broadway
N.E. Weidler Street
Veterans
Memorial
Coliseum
LLOYD
DISTRICT
Lloyd Center
Moda
Center
N.E. Multnomah St.
N.W. Broadway
Bridge
N.W. 12th Ave.
N.W. 10th Ave.
N.W. 9th Ave.
OLD
TOWN
Oregon
Convention
Center
N.E. Lloyd Blvd.
N.E. Sandy Boulevard
N.E. 28th Ave.
N.E. Glisan Stree
N. Steel
Bridge
PEARL
DISTRICT
N.E. Couch St.
E. Burnside St
W. Burnside Street
Burnside
Bridge
S.W. Washington St.
S.W. Alder St.
BUCKMAN
DISTRICT
BELMONT
S.E. Stark St.
S.E. 20th Avenue
S.E. 30th Avenue
S.E. Morrison
Bridge
S.E. Morrison St.
S.E. Belmont St.
S.E. Belmont St.
S.W. 10th Avenue
S.W. Broadway
S.W. 4th Avenue
S.W. Naito Parkway
CENTRAL
EASTSIDE
S.E. 7th Avenue
Hawthorne
Bridge
S.E. Hawthorne Blvd
HAWTHORNE

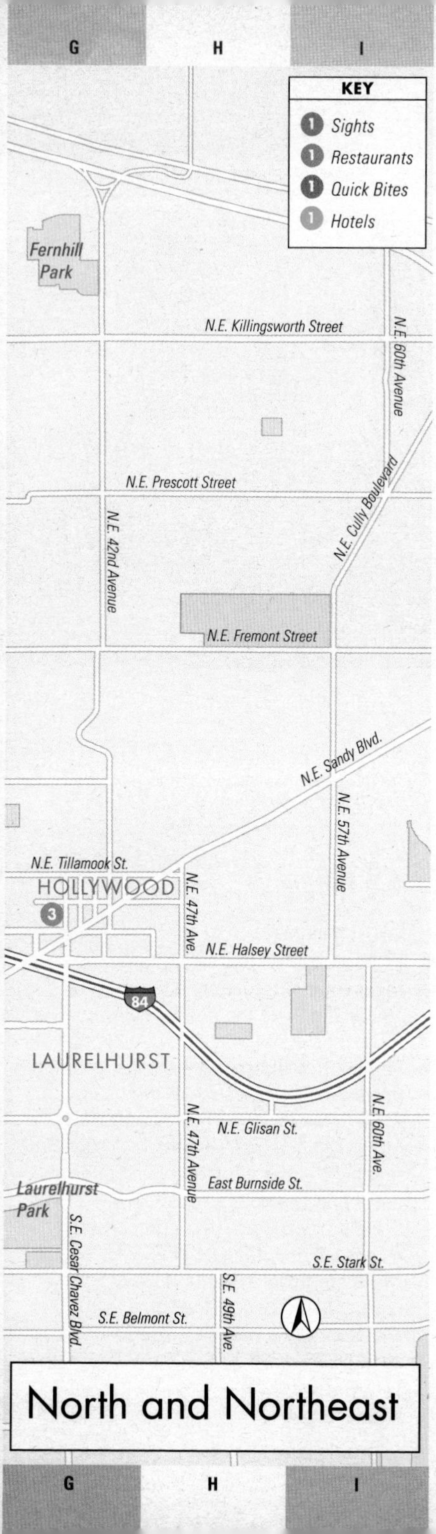

KEY

1 Sights
1 Restaurants
1 Quick Bites
1 Hotels

Fernhill Park
N.E. Killingsworth Street
N.E. 60th Avenue
N.E. Prescott Street
N.E. Cully Boulevard
N.E. 42nd Avenue
N.E. Fremont Street
N.E. Sandy Blvd.
N.E. 57th Avenue
N.E. Tillamook St.
HOLLYWOOD
3
N.E. 47th Ave.
N.E. Halsey Street
84
LAURELHURST
N.E. Glisan St.
N.E. 47th Avenue
N.E. 60th Ave.
East Burnside St.
Laurelhurst Park
S.E. Cesar Chavez Blvd.
S.E. Stark St.
S.E. 49th Ave.
S.E. Belmont St.

North and Northeast

Sights

1 Alberta Arts District **D3**
2 Cathedral Park **A5**
3 North Mississippi Avenue **B4**
4 Sauvie Island **A1**

Restaurants

1 Dóttir **C8**
2 Eem........................ **C4**
3 Gado Gado.............. **G6**
4 Han Oak.................. **E7**
5 Hat Yai................... **D2**
6 Interurban **A4**
7 Lovely's Fifty Fifty **A4**
8 Matt's BBQ **A3**
9 Ned Ludd **C4**
10 Ox Restaurant........... **C6**
11 Screen Door............. **E8**
12 Tamale Boy.............. **E1**

Quick Bites

1 Eb & Bean **D6**
2 Proud Mary.............. **E3**
3 Salt & Straw Ice Cream................ **E3**

Hotels

1 Caravan–The Tiny House Hotel **D3**
2 KEX Portland **C8**
3 McMenamins Kennedy School **F2**
4 Viking Motel............. **A1**

Portland's famous food carts

topped, crisp, wood-fired pizzas, and a small takeout counter dispenses homemade hard and soft-serve organic ice cream with flavors like hazelnut toffee and candied kumquat. Among the pizzas, you can't go wrong with the pie layered in shaved-and-roasted potatoes, sage, taleggio, and pancetta, and topped with an egg. **Known for:** innovative flavors of house-made ice cream; perfectly crispy wood-fired pizzas; beautiful seasonal salads with local greens. *$ Average main: $15 ✉ 4039 N. Mississippi Ave., North Mississippi Ave. ☎ 503/281–4060 🌐 www.lovelysfiftyfifty.com ⏲ Closed Mon. No lunch.*

★ Matt's BBQ

$ | **BARBECUE** | Located in the Prost! Marketplace on North Mississippi, you'll often have to stand in line (it's worth it!) to experience the top food-cart *and* (Texas-style) barbecue joint in Portland. **Known for:** the hotmess sandwich (with brisket, sausage, jalapeños, and slaw); combo platters featuring brisket, ribs, sausage, pulled pork, and sides; outstanding craft-beer offerings elsewhere in this cart pod. *$ Average main: $10 ✉ Prost! Marketplace, 4233 N. Mississippi Ave., North Mississippi Ave. ☎ 503/504–0870 🌐 www.mattsbbqpdx.com.*

Hotels

Viking Motel

$ | **HOTEL** | When this clean, family-run, mid-century motel opened in the late 1970s, it served the nearby shipyard; today, this eco-friendly property is one of Portland's best bargain lodgings, catering to savvy visitors who take the nearby MAX to Downtown Portland. **Pros:** low rates that include free parking and Wi-Fi; friendly owners who take great pride in the property's upkeep; just off Interstate 5 and a block from MAX light rail station. **Cons:** a 15-minute drive or 20-minute MAX ride from Downtown; very basic rooms; dated decor. *$ Rooms from: $95 ✉ 6701 N. Interstate Ave., North ☎ 503/285–4896, 800/308–5097 🌐 www.vikingmotelportland.com 26 rooms 🍽 No meals.*

Portland's Food Carts

Throughout Portland at any given mealtime, more than 500 food carts are dishing up steaming plates of everything from Korean bibimbap to brick-oven pizza to Texas-style barbecue to Oaxacan *tlayudas* (flatbread with toppings). The food-cart scene that's become a fixture in countless North American cities in recent years owes much of its popularity to Portland, which fervently embraced the movement in the 1990s.

Brightly colored and mostly stationary, the carts tend to cluster in former parking lots in pods ranging from 3 to nearly 60 establishments, oftentimes ringing a cluster of picnic tables or a covered awning. The city's rampant boom has led to the closure or relocation of some key cart pods, but others have opened, often farther from the city center, and you'll always find a handful of notable carts at any of the many farmers' markets around town. Arguably the most famous pod in the city, downtown's S.W. 9th and Alder cart community shut down in 2019 to make way for an impending Ritz-Carlton hotel development, but as of this writing, it's slated to reopen at some point along the North Park Blocks on the edge of the Pearl District and Old Town.

With plate prices averaging $7 to $10, carts provide a quick, inexpensive, and delicious alternative to traditional sit-down restaurants, and it's an easy way to sample Portland's extensive ethnic food offerings.

For up-to-date information on hours and locations, and the latest on openings, moves, and closures, check out the extensive local blog **Food Carts Portland** (🌐 *www.foodcartsportland.com*) and its corresponding apps.

Some Top Pods

Prost! Marketplace (4233 N. Mississippi Ave.): A snug encampment of about 15 pods that's adjacent to the excellent German-beer hall **Prost!** (where you'll also find restrooms), this fixture along North Mississippi contains some of the city's most vaunted carts, including the smoky Texas-style chopped brisket of **Matt's BBQ**, exceptional Mexico City–style street tacos from **Little Conejo**, and two-fisted smoked-meat sandwiches from **Pastrami Zombie**. There's also an expansive (and covered) wood-deck beer garden with taps from some of the best craft brewers in the Pacific Northwest.

Southeast, Portland Mercado (S.E. 73rd Ave. and Foster Rd.): A convivial collection of some 40 businesses, including food carts and crafts and gift vendors, the Mercado is devoted to Latin culture and heritage. Feast on *ropa vieja* (braised beef) and other Cuban delicacies at **Que Bolá?**; Venezuelan egg and sweet-pepper arepas at **La Arepa**; and Oaxacan mole blue-corn enchiladas at **Tierra del Sol**.

The Bite on Belmont (4255 S.E. Belmont): There are just 9 or 10 carts at this cozy but festive cart colony in Southeast, but the variety and quality is right up there with the best in the city, starting with **Viking Soul Food** and its delectable Norwegian meatballs and house-smoked-salmon wraps. There are also gooey-good casseroles with plenty of mix-in ingredients available (bacon, jalapeños) at **Herb's Mac & Cheese**, *bulgogi* cheesesteak sandwiches and Hawaiian plate lunches at **Namu**, and pints of local beer at **Hindsight Tap Cart**.

Nightlife

BARS

The Box Social

BARS/PUBS | Aptly located in a boxy glass-and-steel contemporary building in the trendy North Williams Corridor, this low-key, self-proclaimed "drinking parlor" stands out in particular for its nicely balanced whiskey cocktails. Note the extensive use of house-made, sometimes barrel-aged, bitters, and the long list of premium whiskeys and small-batch bourbons. ✉ *3971 N. Williams Ave., North Williams Ave.* ☎ *503/288–1111* 🌐 *www.bxsocial.com.*

BREWPUBS AND MICROBREWERIES

★ Ecliptic Brewing

BREWPUBS/BEER GARDENS | Fans of boldly flavored brews flock to this spacious, airy brewery and pub at the south end of the Mississippi strip, which also has a spacious patio that's abuzz with revelers on summer afternoons. Founder John Harris is as obsessed with astronomy as he is with beer, hence the cosmic names of beers, which include Quasar Pale Ale and Phobos Single Hop Red Ale. **■ TIP→ Brewery tours are offered at noon three times a week.** ✉ *825 N. Cook St., North Mississippi Ave.* ☎ *503/265–8002* 🌐 *www.eclipticbrewing.com.*

LIVE MUSIC

★ Mississippi Studios

MUSIC CLUBS | An intimate and inclusive neighborhood music venue, with a seated balcony and old Oriental rugs covering the standing-room-only floor, community-oriented Mississippi Studios offers high-quality live music performances every night of the week in a wide range of genres. Between sets, you can jump back and forth from the adjacent BarBar, a hip, comfortable bar serving delicious burgers and vegan fare and a covered back patio. ✉ *3939 N. Mississippi Ave., North Mississippi Ave.* ☎ *503/288–3895* 🌐 *www.mississippistudios.com.*

Shopping

CLOTHING AND ACCESSORIES

Queen Bee Creations

SPECIALTY STORES | Since 1996, this stalwart along the rapidly developing North Williams strip has been creating fairly priced products to help you carry and organize your stuff in style. Many of these items—which include honeybee faux-leather messenger bags, canvas weekenders, and convertible tote-backpacks—are waterproof or water resistant, and everything is handcrafted in Portland. Wallets, eyeglass cases, notebooks, and other useful accessories are also available. ✉ *3961 N. Williams Ave., North Williams Ave.* ☎ *503/232–1755* 🌐 *www.queenbee-creations.com.*

FOOD

★ The Meadow

FOOD/CANDY | Food writer Mark Bitterman (not to be confused with food writer Mark Bittman) knows a thing or two about salt—he's written popular books on the subject, and he's the owner of this tiny purveyor of gourmet finishing salts, some of them smoked or infused with unusual flavors, like cherry and plums, or saffron. At this flagship location (there's a second Meadow in Nob Hill, and others in Manhattan and Tokyo) you can also purchase the additional magical touches you might need to create the perfect dinner party, from Oregon and European wines and vermouths, to fresh-cut flowers, aromatic cocktail bitters, and high-quality, single-origin chocolates. ✉ *3731 N. Mississippi Ave., North Mississippi Ave.* ☎ *503/974–8349* 🌐 *www.themeadow.com.*

HOUSEHOLD GOODS AND FURNITURE

★ Beam & Anchor

HOUSEHOLD ITEMS/FURNITURE | Set on a busy street corner several blocks from the North Side's trendy North Mississippi strip, this once-dilapidated warehouse houses an upstairs workshop for makers of artisanal goods and an inspiring downstairs retail space where you'll find a carefully curated selection of lifestyle goods for every room in the home, many of them produced locally—some as local as upstairs. Among the hipster treasures, look for warm and soft camp blankets and Navajo rugs with vibrant prints, women's jewelry in a variety of simple-but-beautiful styles, Portland Apothecary bath salts and soaps, and quite a few larger pieces of distinctive furniture. ✉ *2710 N. Interstate Ave., North Mississippi Ave.* ☎ *503/367–3230* 🌐 *www.beamandanchor.com.*

Northeast

Still the epicenter of the city's relatively small—compared with other U.S. cities the size of Portland—African American community, Northeast has slowly gentrified over the last half century. In the Irvington, Laurelhurst, and Alameda neighborhoods, you'll find some of the largest, most historic homes in town. Northeast's outer reaches include one of the city's top neighborhoods for indie retail and dining, the Alberta Arts District, as well as inviting neighborhoods like Hollywood and Beaumont. This huge quadrant extends north to the Columbia River and way out east to the city border, and is home to some intriguing attractions like the Grotto and Rocky Butte.

Sights

★ Alberta Arts District

NEIGHBORHOOD | FAMILY | Arguably the first of Portland's several hipster-favored East Side neighborhoods to earn national attention, the Alberta Arts District (aka Alberta) has morphed from a downcast commercial strip into an offbeat row of hippie-driven counterculture and then more recently into a considerably more eclectic stretch of both indie arts spaces and downright sophisticated bistros and galleries. Favorite stops include Pine State Biscuits, Salt & Straw ice cream, the Bye and Bye bar, Tin Shed Garden Cafe, Aviary restaurant, Bollywood Theater restaurant, Urdaneta restaurant, Proud Mary coffeehouse, Ampersand art gallery and books, PedX shoes, and Grayling jewelry. Extending a little more than a mile, Northeast Alberta offers plenty of one-of-a-kind dining and shopping; you'll find virtually no national chains along here. The area is also home to some of the best people-watching in Portland, especially during the Last Thursday (of the month) art walks, held from 6 pm until 9 pm. The Alberta Street Fair in August showcases the neighborhood's offerings with arts-and-crafts displays and street performances. **■ TIP→ Northeast Alberta is about a mile from the smaller but similarly intriguing North Mississippi and North Williams corridors; fans of indie dining and shopping could easily spend a full day strolling or biking among both areas.** ✉ *N.E. Alberta St., Alberta Arts District* ✣ *Between N.E. Martin Luther King Jr. Blvd. and N.E. 30th Ave.* 🌐 *www.albertamainst.org.*

Restaurants

★ Dóttir

$$ | SCANDINAVIAN | Iceland bumps happily into the Pacific Northwest in this Nordic restaurant inside the hip KEX hotel, where roasted cabbage has never tasted so heavenly (it's flavored with whey caramel and apple vinegar)—follow this, perhaps, with the hearty (designed for two or more to share) plate of loin, belly, braised shoulder, and sausage of lamb with spiced lentils. The warmly lighted, atmospheric seating in the dining room–cum–lobby is at tables or the long, elliptical bar, a space that encourages lingering and socializing over one of "Grandma Helga's" chocolate-butterscotch doughnuts with black cardamom sugar and a glass of Campari. **Known for:** fantastic, often veggie- and seafood-centric starters; cool, living room-esque vibe; several house-brewed craft ales. $ *Average main: $22* ✉ *KEX Portland, 100 N.E. Martin Luther King Blvd., Central East Side* ☎ *971/346–2992* 🌐 *www.kexhotels.com.*

★ Gado Gado

$$ | INDONESIAN | Bold colors play a central role in the look and culinary approach of this trendy restaurant, from the tropical-print wallpaper to the ornately ornamented tableware, and above all else in the consistently delicious Indonesian fare. Roti with coconut-cream corn, braised-beef *rendang* with kumquats, and Coca-Cola clams steamed with chilies and lemongrass reflect the kitchen's creative and sometimes surprising interpretation of a cuisine that's gotten very little play in Portland until recently. **Known for:** family-style ($55 per person) "rice table" featuring a wide selection of chef favorites; whole wok-fried Dungeness crabs; weekend brunch with mimosas. $ *Average main: $17* ✉ *1801 N.E. Cesar E. Chavez Blvd., Hollywood/Rose City Park* ☎ *503/206–8778* 🌐 *www.gadogadopdx.com* ⏲ *Closed Tues. No lunch weekdays.*

★ Han Oak

$$$ | KOREAN | Begun as a pop-up and still with somewhat limited hours, this clean and contemporary space lined with shelves of beautiful plates, glassware, and cookbooks produces some of the most exciting Korean fare on the West Coast. The carefully plated food is arranged as artful vignettes, and everything bursts with flavor, from hand-cut noodle soups to Korean fried chicken wings. **Known for:** fresh-fruit "slushy" cocktails; communal seating (that's expanded to outside in summer); pork-and-chive dumplings. $ *Average main: $26* ✉ *511 N.E. 24th Ave., Kerns* ☎ *971/255-0032* 🌐 *www.hanoakpdx.com* ⏲ *Closed Tues.–Thurs. No lunch.*

★ Hat Yai

$ | THAI | Operated by the acclaimed chef behind Langbaan and Eem, this cozy and casual counter-service eatery takes its name from a small Thai city near the Malaysian border and its concept from that region's spicy and delicious fried chicken with sticky rice and rich Malayu-style curries with panfried roti bread. Other treats here uncommon to Thai restaurant culture in the States include fiery turmeric curry with mussels and heady lemongrass oxtail soup. **Known for:** the roti dessert with condensed milk; perfectly crunchy free-range fried chicken; good selection of Asian beers. $ *Average main: $14* ✉ *1605 N.E. Killingsworth St., Woodlawn/Concordia* ☎ *503/764–9701* 🌐 *www.hatyaipdx.com.*

★ Ned Ludd

$$$ | PACIFIC NORTHWEST | Named for the founder of the Luddites, the group that resisted the technological advances of the Industrial Revolution, this Northwest-inspired kitchen prepares its food the most low-tech way possible: in a wood-burning brick oven, over an open flame. Sourcing most of its ingredients locally (or carefully, if they come from afar), Ned Ludd's menu varies completely depending on the season and weather, and the from-the-earth theme continues through to the decor, which incorporates salvaged wood, dried flowers, and small succulent plants under glass domes. **Known for:** whole roasted trout with charred leeks; nice selection of craft ciders; a $60 per person family-style dinner option that features some of the kitchen's most interesting food. $ *Average main: $27* ✉ *3925 N.E. Martin Luther King Blvd., North Williams Ave.* ☎ *503/288–6900* 🌐 *www.nedluddpdx.com* ⏲ *No lunch.*

★ Ox Restaurant

$$$$ | ARGENTINE | Specializing in "Argentine-inspired Portland food," Ox is all about prime cuts of meat—along with flavorful garden-fresh side dishes—prepared to perfection. In a dimly lit dining room with hardwood floors, exposed brick walls, and a bar against the front window, the flannel-shirt-and-white-apron-clad waitstaff serves beef, lamb, pork, and fish dishes cooked over flames in a large, hand-cranked grill. **Known for:** the asado Argentino platter (lots of amazing meaty grills); creative side dishes, a few of which could make a full meal; vanilla tres leches cake dessert. *$ Average main: $36 ✉ 2225 N.E. Martin Luther King Blvd., Lloyd District/Convention Center ☎ 503/284–3366 🌐 www.oxpdx.com ⊗ No lunch.*

★ Screen Door

$$ | SOUTHERN | The line that forms outside this Southern-cooking restaurant during weekend brunch and dinner is as epic as the food itself, but you can more easily score a table if you come for weekday breakfast or lunch; a spacious second location opened in the Pearl District in early 2020. A large, packed dining room with canned pickles and peppers along the walls, this Portland hot spot does justice to authentic Southern cooking, especially when it comes to the crispy buttermilk-battered fried chicken with creamy mashed potatoes and collard greens cooked in bacon fat. **Known for:** fried chicken (with waffles at breakfast or brunch); seasonal side dishes, from praline bacon to spiced zucchini fritters; banoffee pie with shortbread-pecan crust. *$ Average main: $20 ✉ 2337 E. Burnside St., East Burnside/28th Ave. ☎ 503/542–0880 🌐 www.screendoorrestaurant.com.*

★ Tamale Boy

$ | MEXICAN | Though the cooks at this lively counter-service restaurant are adept at preparing tamales—both the Oaxacan style wrapped in banana leaves and the more conventional style wrapped in corn husks (try the version filled with roasted pasilla peppers, onions, corn kernels, and queso fresco)—the kitchen also turns out fabulous ceviche and *alambre de camarones* (adobo shrimp with bacon and Oaxacan cheese over flat corn tortillas). Be sure to check out the colorful murals that decorate the space and don't miss the chance to dine on the spacious side patio. **Known for:** El Diablo margarita with roasted-habanero-infused tequila and mango puree; table-side guacamole; hearty and filling tamales. *$ Average main: $11 ✉ 1764 N.E. Dekum St., Woodlawn/Concordia ☎ 503/206–8022 🌐 www.tamaleboy.com.*

Coffee and Quick Bites

★ Eb & Bean

$ | CAFÉ | Choosing your flavor of silky, premium frozen yogurt at this hip dessert café is relatively easy, as there are only a few flavors offered at any given time, unique though they often are (honey-grapefruit and mango lassi, for example). It's the formidable list of toppings that may leave you overwhelmed, albeit happily so, highlights of which include coconut-pecan cookie, organic sour fruity bears, marionberry compote, cold-brew bourbon sauce, and nondairy peanut butter magic shell. **Known for:** inventive dairy-based and vegan flavors; seasonal fruit toppings (figs, blueberries, etc.); made-from-scratch waffle cones. *$ Average main: $5 ✉ 1425 N.E. Broadway St., Lloyd District/Convention Center ☎ 503/281–6081 🌐 www.ebandbean.com.*

★ Proud Mary

$ | AUSTRALIAN | Launched in 2009 in Melbourne, Australia, this third-wave coffeehouse that sources its beans sustainably from around the world opened a U.S. location on Alberta Street in 2017. In this light-filled postindustrial space, you can savor perfectly prepared espresso drinks alongside tasty breakfast and lunch fare, such as Singapore chili crab omelets and grilled croissant brioches with cured ham, blackened corn, and poached egg. **Known for:** avocado and other breakfast toasts; healthy, inventive salads; flat whites. *$ Average main: $12 ✉ 2012*

N.E. Alberta St., Alberta Arts District ☎ 503/208–3475 🌐 www.proudmarycoffee.com ⏲ No dinner.

★ Salt & Straw Ice Cream

$ | CAFÉ | FAMILY | This artisanal ice-cream shop began here with this still always-packed café in the Alberta Arts District and continues to wow the public with its wildly inventive classics as well as seasonal flavors (freckled-chocolate zucchini bread and green fennel and maple are a couple of recent examples). Locally produced Woodblock chocolate bars and house-made salted-caramel sauce are among the toppings, and the related Wiz Bang Bar in Old Town's Pine Street Market offers delicious soft serve. **Known for:** strawberry-honey-balsamic ice cream with black pepper; monthly rotating specialty flavors; flavor collaborations with local chefs and restaurants. *$ Average main: $5 ✉ 2035 N.E. Alberta St., Alberta Arts District ☎ 971/208–3867 🌐 www.saltandstraw.com.*

Hotels

Caravan–The Tiny House Hotel

$$ | B&B/INN | This cluster of itty-bitty custom-built houses-on-wheels offers visitors the chance to experience Portland's unabashed offbeat side. **Pros:** a quirky, only-in-Portland experience; in the heart of Alberta's hip retail-dining district; all units have kitchenettes. **Cons:** these houses really are tiny; 15-minute drive or 35-minute bus ride from Downtown; often books up weeks in advance (especially weekends). *$ Rooms from: $155 ✉ 5009 N.E. 11th Ave., Alberta Arts District ☎ 503/288–5225 🌐 www.tinyhousehotel.com 5 cottages No meals.*

★ KEX Portland

$ | HOTEL | Opened in fall 2019, the first U.S. outpost of the hip, design-driven Reykjavík hotel–hostel has been developed expressly with the aim of encouraging travelers and locals to mix and mingle together, whether in the inviting lobby-restaurant or with friends in the cedar sauna. **Pros:** cool Icelandic design; hip bar and restaurant; reasonably priced. **Cons:** many rooms are bunk-style and share bathrooms; the very social vibe isn't for everyone; no on-site parking. *$ Rooms from: $140 ✉ 100 N.E. Martin Luther King Blvd., Central East Side ☎ 971/346–2992 🌐 www.kexportland.com 29 rooms No meals.*

★ McMenamins Kennedy School

$ | HOTEL | FAMILY | In a renovated elementary school near Northeast Portland's trendy Alberta District, Oregon's famously creative McMenamin brothers hoteliers created a quirky and fantastical multiuse facility with guest rooms that feature original schoolhouse touches like chalkboards and cloakrooms and literature-inspired themes, a movie theater, a restaurant, a warm outdoor soaking pool, a brewery, and several small bars. **Pros:** funky and authentic Portland experience; room rates include movies and use of year-round soaking pool; free parking. **Cons:** rooms have showers but no tubs; no TVs in rooms; 20-minute drive or 40-minute bus ride from Downtown. *$ Rooms from: $145 ✉ 5736 N.E. 33rd Ave., Northeast ☎ 503/249–3983, 888/249–3983 🌐 www.mcmenamins.com/kennedy-school 57 rooms No meals.*

Nightlife

BARS AND LOUNGES

★ Expatriate

BARS/PUBS | Operated by Kyle Webster and his wife, celeb-chef partner Naomi Pomeroy of Beast (across the street), this intimate, candlelit spot has a devoted following for its balanced, boozy cocktails and addictively delicious Asian bar snacks, like Burmese curried noodles. Each of the eight nightly cocktails are meticulously crafted. *✉ 5424 N.E. 30th Ave., Woodlawn/Concordia ☎ 503/805–3750 🌐 www.expatriatepdx.com.*

Performing Arts

PERFORMANCE VENUES

Moda Center

MUSIC | This 20,000-seat facility is home to the Portland Trail Blazers basketball team and the site of other sporting events and rock concerts. It's right on the MAX light rail line, just across from Downtown. ✉ *1 N. Center Ct., Lloyd District/Convention Center* ☎ *503/235–8771* 🌐 *www.rosequarter.com.*

FILM

★ Hollywood Theatre

FILM | A landmark movie theater that showed silent films when it opened in 1926, the not-for-profit Hollywood Theatre screens everything from obscure foreign art films to old American classics and second-run Hollywood hits, and hosts an annual Academy Awards viewing party. It also hosts a slew of film series and festivals, including the QDoc LGBTQ documentary film festival, the Grindhouse Film Festival, the Northwest Animation Festival, the Portland Latin American Film Festival, and POW, which showcases top women directors. ✉ *4122 N.E. Sandy Blvd., Hollywood/Rose City Park* ☎ *503/281–4215* 🌐 *www.hollywoodtheatre.org.*

Shopping

GALLERIES

★ Last Thursdays on Alberta

ART GALLERIES | **FAMILY** | The Alberta Arts District hosts an arts walk on the last Thursday of each month. This quirky procession along 15 blocks of one of the city's favorite thoroughfares for browsing art galleries, distinctive boutiques, and hipster bars and restaurants features street performers and buskers, crafts makers, and food vendors. During the three summer events, from June through August, the street is closed to traffic from 6 to 9 pm, and many more arts and crafts vendors show their work. ✉ *N.E. Alberta St. and N.E. 22nd Ave., Alberta Arts District.*

HOUSEHOLD GOODS AND FURNITURE

★ Crafty Wonderland

CRAFTS | Although the Alberta branch of this whimsically named arts and crafts gallery is smaller than the original Downtown location, it still showcases the handmade cards, books, apparel, jewelry, household goods, and toys of more than 60 carefully selected makers. Crafty Wonderland also hosts two huge annual markets, featuring works by about 250 artists, in May and December at the Oregon Convention Center. ✉ *2022 N.E. Alberta St., Alberta Arts District* ☎ *503/281–4616* 🌐 *www.craftywonderland.com.*

JEWELRY

★ Grayling Jewelry

JEWELRY/ACCESSORIES | All of the locally made pieces at this friendly boutique have been carefully and exquisitely designed with sensitive skin in mind—every piece is nickel-free. The simply elegant lariat necklaces, chain-cuff earrings, and wrap rings are done mostly in silver and gold and displayed in a clean, unobtrusive storefront on Alberta Street. ✉ *1609 N.E. Alberta St., Alberta Arts District* ☎ *503/548–4979* 🌐 *www.graylingjewelry.com.*

Activities

BASKETBALL

Portland Trail Blazers

BASKETBALL | The NBA's Portland Trail Blazers play their 82-game season—with half the games at home—in the Moda Center, which can hold up to 20,000 spectators. The MAX train pulls up just a couple of blocks from the arena's front door. ✉ *Moda Center, 1 N. Center Ct., Rose Quarter, Lloyd District/Convention Center* ☎ *503/797–9600* 🌐 *www.nba.com/blazers.*

Southeast

Vibrant pockets of foodie-minded eateries, craft cocktail bars, and funky indie boutiques make the closer-in sections of Southeast, especially the formerly industrial Central East Side, a must-visit. You'll also find the funky commercial sections of Hawthorne, Division, and Belmont west of the 30th Avenue in this part of town, as well as the family-popular OMSI science museum and Tilikum Crossing Bridge. As you move farther east and south, you'll discover beautiful Mt. Tabor Park and up-and-coming Montavilla and Foster-Powell, which is also where you'll find sizable Asian and Latino communities. To the south, the historic and mostly residential neighborhoods of Sellwood and Moreland contain a smattering of notable shops as well as some pretty parks.

Sights

★ Central East Side

NEIGHBORHOOD | This expansive 681-acre tract of mostly industrial and commercial buildings was largely ignored by all but local workers until shops, galleries, and restaurants began opening in some of the neighborhood's handsome, high-ceilinged buildings beginning in the 1990s. These days, it's a legitimately hot neighborhood for shopping and coffeehouse-hopping by day, and dining and bar-going at night, and a slew of high-end apartment buildings have added a residential component to the Central East Side. ✉ *Willamette River to S.E. 12th Ave. from Burnside to Division Sts., Central East Side* ✣ *Reachable via the East Side Streetcar, walking from Downtown, or taking any of several buses across the Hawthorne or Burnside bridges* 🌐 *www.ceic.cc.*

★ Division Street

NEIGHBORHOOD | Back in the early 1970s, Division Street (aka "Southeast Division") was earmarked for condemnation as part of a proposed—and thankfully never built—freeway that would have connected Downtown to Mt. Hood. For many years, this street sat forlornly, just a long stretch of modest buildings and empty lots. These days, Southeast Division—no longer threatened with condemnation—is one of the hottest restaurant rows on the West Coast, and sleek three- and four-story contemporary condos and apartments are popping up like dandelions. If culinary tourism is your thing, head to the 10 blocks of Southeast Division from about 30th to 39th Avenues, where you'll find such darlings of the culinary scene as Pok Pok, Ava Gene's, Bollywood Theater, Olympia Provisions Public House, an outpost of Salt & Straw ice cream, Little T bakery, Lauretta Jean's, and several others. The main draw here is mostly food-and-drink related; there are several great bars, and the excellent Oui! Wine Bar at SE Wine Collective urban winery. You'll also find a growing number of other noteworthy restaurants and bars extending all the way to 12th Avenue to the west, and 50th Avenue to the east. As well as "Division" and "Southeast Division," you may hear some locals refer to the western end of the neighborhood as "Division/Clinton" referring to Clinton Street, a block south of Division, where you will find lovely early- to mid-20th-century bungalows and houses and a few noteworthy eateries (Broder, La Moule, Magna Kusina, Jaqueline), mostly from 27th to 20th Avenue. ✉ *S.E. Division St., and parts of S.E. Clinton St., from 12th to 50th Aves., Division/Clinton* ✣ *Bus 2 crosses the Hawthorne Bridge from Downtown and continues along Division Street; there's also free street parking, although increased development has made it a bit harder to find* 🌐 *www.divisionstreetportland.com.*

★ Hawthorne District

NEIGHBORHOOD | Stretching from the foot of Mt. Tabor to S.E. 12th Avenue (where you'll find a terrific little food-cart pod), with some blocks far livelier than others, this eclectic commercial thoroughfare was at the forefront of Portland's hippie and LGBTQ scenes in the 1960s and 1970s. As the rest of Portland's East Side has become more urbane and popular among hipsters, young families, students, and the so-called creative class over the years, Hawthorne has retained an arty, homegrown flavor. An influx of trendy eateries and retailers opening alongside the still-colorful and decidedly low-frills thrift shops and old-school taverns and cafés makes for a hodgepodge of styles and personalities—you could easily spend an afternoon popping in and out of boutiques, and then stay for happy hour at a local nightspot or even later for dinner. Highlights include a small (but still impressive) branch of Powell's Books, House of Vintage emporium, Bagdad Theater, Farmhouse Kitchen Thai, Apizza Scholls, OK Omens wine bar, and the Sapphire Hotel lounge. ✉ *S.E. Hawthorne Blvd., between S.E. 12th and S.E. 50th Aves., Hawthorne* ✥ *Bus 14 runs from Downtown along the length of Hawthorne, and there's plenty of free street parking* 🌐 *www.thinkhawthorne.com.*

★ Mt. Tabor Park

NATIONAL/STATE PARK | **FAMILY** | A playground on top of a volcano cinder cone? Yup, that's here. The cinders, or glassy rock fragments, unearthed in this 190-acre park's construction were used to surface the respite's roads; the ones leading to the very top are closed to cars, but popular with cyclists. They're also popular with cruisers—each August there's an old-fashioned soapbox derby. Picnic tables and tennis, basketball, and volleyball courts make Mt. Tabor Park a popular spot for outdoor recreation, but plenty of quiet, shaded trails and wide-open grassy lawns with panoramic views of the Downtown skyline appeal to sunbathers, hikers, and nature lovers. The whole park is closed to cars on Wednesday. ■ **TIP→ Just down the hill on the west side of Mt. Tabor, you'll find the lively cafés and restaurants of the hip Hawthorne District.** ✉ *S.E. 60th Ave. and S.E. Salmon St., Mt. Tabor* 🌐 *www.portlandoregon.gov/parks.*

★ Oregon Museum of Science and Industry (*OMSI*)

MUSEUM | **FAMILY** | Hundreds of engaging exhibits draw families to this outstanding interactive science museum, which also contains the Empirical Theater (featuring Portland's biggest screen), and the Northwest's largest planetarium. The many permanent and touring exhibits are loaded with enough hands-on play for kids to fill a whole day exploring robotics, ecology, rockets, animation, and outer space. Moored in the Willamette River as part of the museum is a 240-foot submarine, the USS *Blueback,* which can be toured for an extra charge. OMSI also offers some very cool event programming for adults, including the hugely popular monthly OMSI After Dark nights, where "science nerds" can enjoy food, drink, and science fun, and the twice-monthly OMSI Science Pub nights, where local and national experts lecture on a wide range of topics in the museum's Empirical Theater. ■ **TIP→ OMSI's excellent restaurant, Theory, open for lunch, offers great views of the Willamette River and Downtown skyline, and Empirical Café is a great stop for a light bite or drink.** ✉ *1945 S.E. Water Ave., Central East Side* ☎ *503/797–4000, 800/955–6674* 🌐 *www.omsi.edu* 🎟 *Museum $15, planetarium $7.50, Empirical Theater Show $8.50, submarine $7.50, parking $5* ⏲ *Closed Mon. early Sept.–early Mar.*

★ Portland Mercado

MARKET | This colorful and community-driven complex of indoor and outdoor food stalls and markets, flanked by a row of picnic tables, is Portland's own little Latin America with business owners from Mexico, Brazil, Cuba, Venezuela, and elsewhere throughout Central and South America. A great destination for eating and socializing, the colorfully painted Mercado is also a business incubator that helps Latin American entrepreneurs

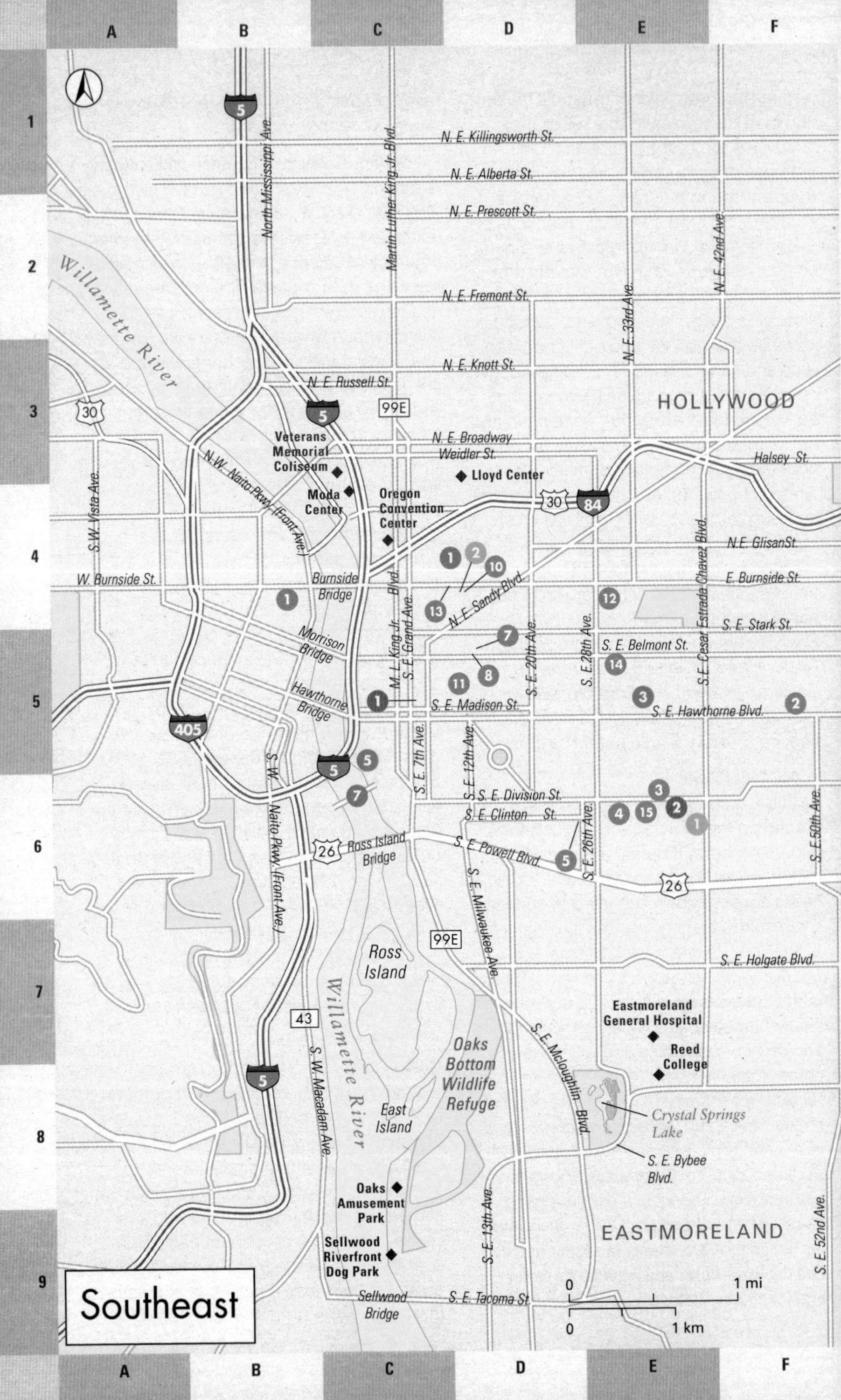

Southeast
N. E. Killingsworth St.
N. E. Alberta St.
N. E. Prescott St.
N. E. Fremont St.
N. E. Knott St.
N. E. Russell St.
N. E. Broadway
Weidler St.
Halsey St.
N.E. GlisanSt.
E. Burnside St.
S. E. Stark St.
S. E. Belmont St.
S. E. Madison St.
S. E. Hawthorne Blvd.
S. E. Division St.
S. E. Clinton St.
S. E. Powell Blvd.
S. E. Holgate Blvd.
S. E. Tacoma St.
W. Burnside St.
North Mississippi Ave.
Martin Luther King Jr. Blvd.
N. E. 33rd Ave.
N. E. 42nd Ave.
S.W. Vista Ave.
N.W. Naito Pkwy. (Front Ave.)
S. W. Naito Pkwy. (Front Ave.)
S. W. Macadam Ave.
M. L. King Jr. Blvd.
S. E. Grand Ave.
S. E. 7th Ave.
S. E. 12th Ave.
S. E. 20th Ave.
S. E. 28th Ave.
S. E. 26th Ave.
S.E. Cesar Estrada Chavez Blvd.
S. E. 50th Ave.
S. E. 52nd Ave.
S. E. 13th Ave.
S. E. Milwaukee Ave.
S. E. Mcloughlin Blvd.
N. E. Sandy Blvd.
S. E. Bybee Blvd.
HOLLYWOOD
EASTMORELAND
Willamette River
Veterans Memorial Coliseum
Moda Center
Oregon Convention Center
Lloyd Center
Burnside Bridge
Morrison Bridge
Hawthorne Bridge
Ross Island Bridge
Sellwood Bridge
Ross Island
East Island
Oaks Bottom Wildlife Refuge
Oaks Amusement Park
Sellwood Riverfront Dog Park
Eastmoreland General Hospital
Reed College
Crystal Springs Lake
5
405
84
30
99E
26
43
0
1 mi
1 km
A B C D E F
1 2 3 4 5 6 7 8 9

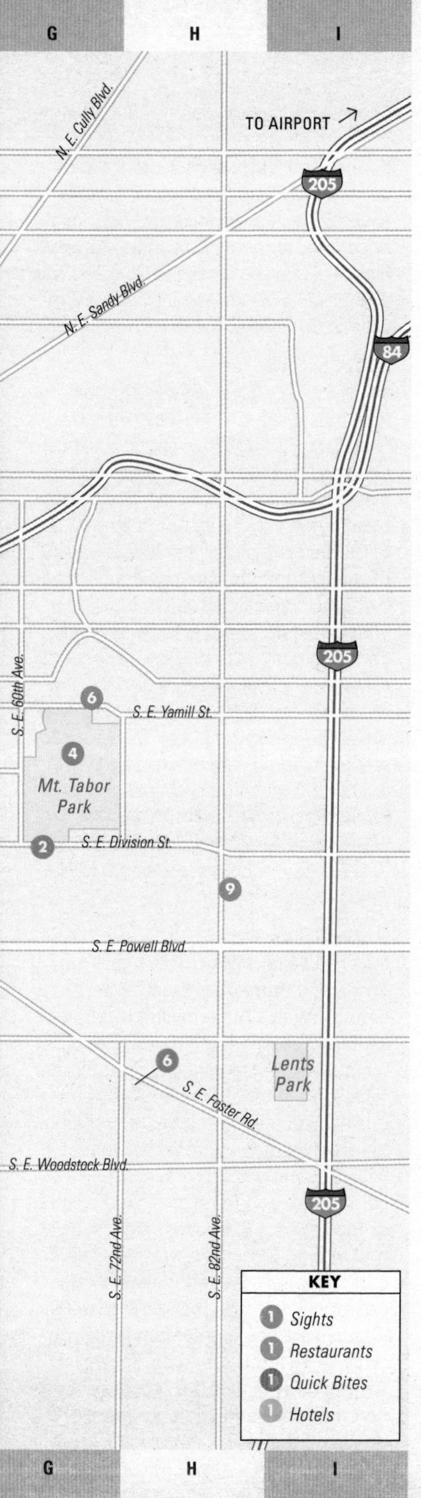

Sights

1 Central East Side **D4**
2 Division Street **G6**
3 Hawthorne District **E5**
4 Mt. Tabor Park **G5**
5 Oregon Museum of Science and Industry **C5**
6 Portland Mercado **H7**
7 Tilikum Crossing Bridge **C6**

Restaurants

1 Afuri Ramen **B4**
2 Apizza Scholls............ **F5**
3 Ava Gene's................ **E6**
4 Bollywood Theater **E6**
5 Broder.................... **D6**
6 Coquine **G5**
7 Delores................... **D5**
8 Farm Spirit............... **D5**
9 Ha & VL **H6**
10 Hey Love **D4**
11 Kachka **D5**
12 Langbaan **E4**
13 Le Pigeon **D4**
14 Nodoguro **E5**
15 Pok Pok **E6**

Quick Bites

1 Coava Coffee Roasters **C5**
2 Lauretta Jean's........... **E6**

Hotels

1 Evermore Guesthouse............... **E6**
2 Jupiter NEXT **D4**

thrive both here and throughout Portland, and it's a thriving anchor of the diverse Foster Powell neighborhood. Be sure to step inside the central interior space to view displays with facts and historic photos about the city's and region's Latin American community. Vendor highlights include Sandino Coffee Roasters, Kaah Neighborhood Market, Tierra del Sol (Oaxacan), Que Bola (Cuban), and Barrio neighborhood bar. ✉ *7238 S.E. Foster Rd., Foster/Powell* ☎ *971/200–0581* 🌐 *www.portlandmercado.org.*

★ Tilikum Crossing Bridge

BRIDGE/TUNNEL | Downtown Portland's collection of striking bridges gained a new member in 2015 with the opening of this sleek, cable-stayed bridge a few steps from Oregon Museum of Science and Industry (OMSI). Nicknamed "the Bridge of the People," the Tilikum is unusual in that it's the largest car-free bridge in the country—it's open only to public transit (MAX trains, buses, and streetcars), bikes, and pedestrians. The 1,720-foot-long bridge connects Southeast Portland with the South Waterfront district and rewards those who stroll or cycle across it with impressive skyline views. ✉ *Tilikum Crossing, Southeast* ✥ *Eastbank Esplanade just south of OMSI on the East Side, and S.W. Moody Ave. in South Waterfront.*

Restaurants

★ Afuri Ramen

$$ | RAMEN | When the acclaimed Japanese ramen chain Afuri decided to open an outpost in the United States in 2016, it chose this modern, high-ceilinged dining room in food-obsessed Portland in part because the exacting culinary team appreciated the city's pristine, glacially fed water supply, which plays a significant part in the steaming, savory portions of *yuzu shio* (with chicken broth, yuzu citrus, shimeji mushrooms, seasoned egg, chashu, endive, and nori), one of a half dozen deeply satisfying ramen bowls. The kitchen also turns out flavorful skewers of shishito peppers and chicken thighs, pork dumplings, sushi, and other izakaya-style fare, all of it consistently exceptional. **Known for:** authentic Japanese ramen; meat and veggie skewers; flights of premium sake. Ⓢ *Average main: $18* ✉ *923 S.E. 7th Ave., Central East Side* ☎ *503/468–5001* 🌐 *www.afuri.us.*

Apizza Scholls

$$ | PIZZA | The pies at Apizza Scholls, which have been lauded by Anthony Bourdain, Rachael Ray, and thousands of everyday pizza lovers, deserve the first-class reputation they enjoy. The greatness of the pies rests not in innovation or complexity, but in the simple quality of the ingredients, such as dough made by hand in small batches and baked to crispy-outside, tender-inside perfection and toppings—including basil, pecorino romano, and house-cured bacon—that are fresh and delicious. **Known for:** interesting beer list; the bacon bianca pizza (white, with no sauce); occasionally long waits for a table (reservations are a good idea). Ⓢ *Average main: $18* ✉ *4741 S.E. Hawthorne Blvd., Hawthorne* ☎ *503/233–1286* 🌐 *www.apizzascholls.com* ⏲ *No lunch weekdays.*

★ Ava Gene's

$$$$ | MODERN ITALIAN | This highly acclaimed Roman-inspired Italian eatery—with a buzzy dining room with a vaulted ceiling and two long rows of banquette seats—ranks among the top tables in town both in popularity and quality. The menu emphasizes regional, home-style recipes from throughout Italy, but focuses on local produce—you could make an impressive feast of three or four *giardini* (gardens) sides, such as melon with tomatillos, ground cherries, and prosciutto, while the satisfyingly hearty mains might include tagliatelle with chicken ragù or lamb grilled with artichokes and celery root. **Known for:** flatbreads with creative toppings; a top-notch cocktail and wine program; $85

Tilikum Crossing Bridge is the country's largest car-free bridge, meaning it's only open to public transit, bikes, and pedestrians.

per person family-style "chef's selection" option. 💲 *Average main: $32* ✉ *3377 S.E. Division St., Division/Clinton* ☎ *971/229–0571* 🌐 *www.avagenes.com* 🕓 *No lunch weekdays.*

Bollywood Theater

$ | INDIAN | Set beneath a soaring beamed ceiling, and with a welcoming mix of worn wooden seating, kitschy decor, bright fabrics, and intoxicating smells, this lively restaurant along Division Street's hoppin' restaurant row specializes in Indian street food. Order at the counter, and your food—perhaps *vada pav* (spicy potato dumplings with chutney), *gobi* Manchurian (Indo-Chinese fried cauliflower with lemon, curry leaves, and sweet-and-sour sauce), or Goan-style shrimp served with a full complement of chutneys, paratha bread, and dal—will be brought out to you. **Known for:** delicious breads and vegetable side dishes; small Indian gourmet market with spices and curries; mango lassi. 💲 *Average main: $14* ✉ *3010 S.E. Division St., Division/Clinton* ☎ *503/477–6699* 🌐 *www.bollywoodtheaterpdx.com.*

★ Broder

$ | SCANDINAVIAN | This adorable neighborhood café—one of the most outstanding brunch spots in town—serves fresh and delicious Scandinavian food with fun-to-pronounce names like *friterade applen* (apple fritter) and *aebleskivers* (Danish pancakes). All the food—the hashes, *lefse* potato crepes, the baked egg scrambles, the Swedish breakfast boards—is delicious, with the Swedish meatballs in sherry cream sauce and salmon fish cakes with caraway vinaigrette being especially tasty among the midday choices. **Known for:** light-filled dining room with rustic-modern furniture; often long waits for a table, especially for breakfast; the largest selection of aquavit in the western United States. 💲 *Average main: $13* ✉ *2508 S.E. Clinton St., Division/Clinton* ☎ *503/736–3333* 🌐 *www.broderpdx.com* 🕓 *No dinner.*

★ **Coquine**

$$$ | **FRENCH** | A sunny neighborhood café serving brunch daily, Coquine blossoms into a romantic, sophisticated French–Pacific Northwest bistro in the evening. Early in the day, sup on sourdough pancakes with huckleberry compote, or black cod–based fisherman's stew with garlic toast, while in the evening, you might encounter pappardelle noodles with pork ragu or roasted whole chicken padron peppers, sungold tomatoes, pole beans, and pickled red onion. **Known for:** four- and seven-course tasting menus (with optional wine pairings); a dim sum–style candy tray offered during the dessert course; cheerful setting near Mt. Tabor. *Average main: $27* *6839 S.E. Belmont St., Mt. Tabor* *503/384–2483* *www.coquinepdx.com* *No dinner Mon. and Tues.*

★ **Delores**

$$ | **POLISH** | Former *Top Chef* contestant BJ Smith, who established himself as one of Portland's premier barbecue chefs, runs this modern take on Polish food—a tribute to his late mom, for whom the restaurant is named. Many of the artfully plated dishes here showcase Smith's talent for grilling, including smoked kielbasa hash (a brunch favorite) and chicken-fried rabbit with mustard cream, but you'll also discover ethereal plates of stuffed cabbage rolls and *kopytka* (Polish gnocchi with corn puree and pickled shallots). **Known for:** duck-confit pierogis; Monday family-style ($25 per person) Marczewski Night with polka and traditional Polish food (named in honor of the owner's grandmother); weekend brunch. *Average main: $20* *1401 S.E. Morrison St., Belmont* *503/231–3609* *www.delorespdx.com* *Closed Mon. No lunch weekdays.*

★ **Farm Spirit**

$$$$ | **VEGETARIAN** | Dinners at this chef-driven vegan restaurant are truly an event—in fact, admission to these several-course repasts, which you can experience at your own table in the dining room or at a lively communal counter (this choice is a bit pricier but includes more courses) overlooking the kitchen, is by advance ticket purchase only. The highly inventive menu changes daily but utilizes about 95% Northwest ingredients and might feature delicata squash with smoked pumpkinseed or fire-roasted plums with oat cream and rosemary. **Known for:** interesting wine, beer, and juice flights; no-tipping policy; nut- and gluten-free menus by advance notice. *Average main: $89* *1403 S.E. Belmont St., Belmont* *971/255–0329* *www.farmspiritpdx.com* *Closed Sun.–Tues. No lunch.*

★ **Ha & VL**

$ | **VIETNAMESE** | This humble, no-frills banh mi shop amid the many cheap and authentic Asian restaurants on S.E. 82nd stands out not just for its filling sandwiches (these crispy-bread creations come with fillings like spicy Chinese sausage, pork meat loaf, or sardines) but also for the daily featured soup, such as peppery pork-ball noodle soup on Wednesday and Vietnamese turmeric soup, with shrimp cake and sliced pork, on Sunday. There's also a diverse selection of thick milk shakes—top flavors include avocado, mango, and durian. **Known for:** milk shakes in unusual flavors; pork-ball noodle soup (on Wednesday only); barbecue pork loin banh mi sandwiches. *Average main: $9* *2738 S.E. 82nd Ave., No. 102, Montavilla/82nd Ave.* *503/772–0103* *Closed Tues. No dinner.*

★ **Hey Love**

$$ | **ASIAN FUSION** | The food-and-drink component of the stylish Jupiter Next hotel has quickly become one of the East Side's hottest destinations for hobnobbing over drinks and creative bar fare, much of it—salmon poke, Wagyu steak fajitas—framed around Asian and Latin American elements. The space is adorned with hanging and potted greenery and Oriental rugs, which provide a

decidedly funky aesthetic. **Known for:** fried chicken chow mein; late-night dining and people-watching; a cast-iron macadamia nut–white chocolate cookie with coconut caramel and sea-salt ice cream. *Average main: $19 ✉ 920 E. Burnside St., Central East Side ☎ 503/206–6223 🌐 www.heylovepdx.com.*

★ Kachka

$$ | RUSSIAN | This Central East Side establishment decorated to resemble a *dacha* (a Russian country/vacation house) turns out wonderfully creative and often quite light Russian fare, including plenty of shareable small plates, like crispy beef tongue with sweet onion sauce, orange, and pomegranate; panfried sour-cherry *vareniki* (Ukrainian dumplings), and—of course—caviar with blini and all the usual accompaniments. Another crowd-pleaser on the menu is the classic chicken Kiev, prepared the old-fashioned way, oozing with butter. **Known for:** extensive craft vodka list; the cold "zakuski" assorted appetizer experience ($30 per person); hearty Ukrainian dumplings. *Average main: $22 ✉ 960 S.E. 11th Ave., Central East Side ☎ 503/235–0059 🌐 www.kachkapdx.com.*

★ Langbaan

$$$$ | THAI | Guests reach this tiny, wood-paneled, 24-seat gem with an open kitchen by walking through the adjoining PaaDee restaurant and pushing open a faux bookshelf that's actually a door. Of course, you won't even get this far unless you've called ahead to reserve a table; the restaurant serves the most interesting and consistently delicious Southeast Asian food in Portland via a weekly changing 10-course, $95 tasting menu that features unusual dishes like duck breast and tongue skewer with duck yolk jam and fermented fish sauce, or turmeric broth with Arctic char and clams. **Known for:** some of the most inventive Thai food in the country; a carefully curated wine list; wonderfully creative and flavorful desserts. *Average main: $95 ✉ 6 S.E. 28th Ave., East Burnside/28th Ave. ☎ 971/344–2564 🌐 www.langbaanpdx.com ⏲ Closed Mon.–Wed. No lunch.*

★ Le Pigeon

$$$$ | FRENCH | Specializing in adventurous Northwest-influenced French dishes of extraordinary quality, this cozy and unassuming restaurant consistently ranks among the city's most acclaimed dining venues. The menu changes regularly but often features items like beef-cheek Bourguignon, chicken and oxtail with semolina gnocchi, and seared foie gras with chestnuts, raisins, bacon, and cinnamon toast (especially exceptional). James Beard award–winning chef Gabriel Rucker also operates Canard, next door, which serves lighter and less pricey breakfast, lunch, and dinner fare. **Known for:** open kitchen in which diners at the counter can interact with chefs; one of the best burgers in town; grilled dry-aged pigeon with a seasonally changing preparation. *Average main: $34 ✉ 738 E. Burnside St., Central East Side ☎ 503/546–8796 🌐 www.lepigeon.com ⏲ No lunch.*

★ Nodoguro

$$$$ | JAPANESE | A nightly changing selection of exquisitely plated, imaginative Japanese cuisine is served in this small, sophisticated dining room on an otherwise unpretentious stretch of Belmont Street. The 15- to 25-course omakase menus are available exclusively by advance-ticket purchase, and pairings featuring fine sakes and natural wines are available. **Known for:** elaborate 2½-hour feasts; an emphasis on sublime fish and shellfish; knowledgeable and gracious service. *Average main: $125 ✉ 2832 S.E. Belmont St., Belmont 🌐 www.nodoguropdx.com ⏲ Closed Mon. and Tues. No lunch.*

★ Pok Pok

$$ | THAI | Andy Ricker, the owner of one of Portland's most talked-about restaurants, regularly travels to Southeast Asia to research street food and home-style recipes to include on the menu of this always-hopping spot. Diners have the option of sitting outside under tents, or in the funky, cavelike interior, while they enjoy enticing dishes like green papaya salad, charcoal-roasted game hen, and Ike's Vietnamese chicken wings, which are deep-fried in caramelized fish sauce and garlic. **Known for:** Ike's Vietnamese chicken wings; charcoal-roasted game hen and other meaty fare; fiery-hot food (although there are plenty of milder dishes—you just have to ask). *Average main: $19 3226 S.E. Division St., Division/Clinton 503/232–1387 www.pokpokdivision.com.*

Coffee and Quick Bites

★ Coava Coffee Roasters

$ | **CAFÉ** | The light and open, bamboo wood–filled flagship location of Coava Coffee Roasters offers some of the highest-quality single-origin, pour-over coffees in the city. There's a second branch in Hawthorne, and a separate coffee bar a few blocks away on S.E. **Known for:** honey lattes; coffee roasted to the most exacting standards; sustainable sourcing and production processes. *Average main: $5 1300 S.E. Grand Ave., Central East Side 503/894–8134 www.coavacoffee.com No dinner.*

★ Lauretta Jean's

$ | **CAFÉ** | This pie-focused operation began as a stall at Portland's Saturday Farmers Market at PSU and now comprises a couple of charming, homey, brick-and-mortar cafés, one Downtown, but the most atmospheric along Division Street in Southeast. Though it's the delicious pies—with feathery-light crusts and delicious fillings like tart cherry, salted pecan, and chocolate-banana cream—that have made Lauretta Jean's a foodie icon in Portland, these cheerful eateries also serve exceptional brunch fare, including the LJ Classic, a fluffy biscuit topped with an over-easy egg, Jack cheese, bacon, and strawberry jam. **Known for:** salted-caramel apple pie; short but well-curated cocktail list; breakfast sandwich that features the bakery's fluffy biscuits. *Average main: $8 3402 S.E. Division St., Division/Clinton 503/235–3119 www.laurettajeans.com No dinner.*

Hotels

Evermore Guesthouse

$ | **B&B/INN** | Just a block from the trendy dining along Southeast Portland's hip Division Street, this beautifully restored, 1909 Arts and Crafts–style mansion contains spacious, light-filled rooms, some with private balconies, claw-foot soaking tubs, and good-size sitting areas; one detached suite has a full kitchen, and a cozy and romantic third-floor room has skylights and pitched ceilings. **Pros:** located in hip, charming neighborhood with many bars and restaurants; reasonably priced with free off-street parking; free laundry and basic breakfast. **Cons:** some rooms face busy Cesar Chavez Boulevard; a 15-minute drive or 30-minute bus ride from Downtown; least expensive rooms are shared bath. *Rooms from: $145 3860 S.E. Clinton St., Richmond 503/206–6509, 877/600–6509 www.evermoreguesthouse.com 6 rooms Free breakfast.*

Jupiter NEXT

$$ | **HOTEL** | Across the street from its sister, the original mod-hip Jupiter Hotel (which is a good bet if you need cheap but basic and rather noisy digs), this futuristic-looking mid-rise offers a more upscale—but still moderately priced—lodging experience, complete with several airy outdoor spaces and a sceney lobby bar and restaurant, Hey Love. **Pros:** guest rooms have cool photo collages of Portland landmarks; fun and lively common spaces; excellent restaurant and bar. **Cons:** youthful vibe and quirky design doesn't appeal to everyone; lobby and bar can be loud and busy on weekends; a short drive or bus ride from Downtown. *Rooms from: $155 900 E. Burnside*

St., Central East Side ☎ 503/230–9200 🌐 www.jupiterhotel.com 68 rooms No meals.

BARS AND LOUNGES

★ Bible Club

BARS/PUBS | There's a speakeasy-like quality to this hip, vintage-style bar with signs referencing Prohibition and the 18th Amendment. The Bible Club serves up some of the most creative cocktails in the Sellwood and Westmoreland area, as well as a good mix of Oregon beers. Out back there's an expansive seating area with picnic tables and an additional outdoor bar. ✉ *6716 S.E. 16th Ave., Sellwood/Moreland* ☎ *971/279–2198* 🌐 *www.bibleclubpdx.com* ☞ *Closed Mon.–Tues.*

★ Crush

BARS/PUBS | A favorite LGBTQ hangout in the Central East Side, Crush serves up tasty pub grub, strong cocktails, and DJ-fueled dance parties. The front section is mellow and good for conversation, while the back area contains a small but lively dance floor. ✉ *1400 S.E. Morrison St., Belmont* ☎ *503/235–8150* 🌐 *www.crushbar.com.*

★ ENSO Winery

WINE BARS—NIGHTLIFE | Based in a large garagelike space in Southeast Portland's trendy Buckman neighborhood, ENSO is the creation of young and talented winemaker Ryan Sharp, who sources grapes from Washington, California, and Oregon to produce superb wines that are quickly earning notice in the national wine press. Notable varietals include Petite Sirah, Malbec, Dry Riesling, and the especially popular L'American blend of Zinfandel, Petite Sirah, and Mourvèdre. The high-ceilinged, industrial-chic tasting lounge—with exposed air ducts, a timber-beam ceiling, and a wall of windows (open on warm days)—has become one of the neighborhood's favorite wine bars, serving local Olympia Provisions charcuterie, Woodblock chocolates, Steve's Cheese Bar cheeses, and Little T Baker breads, plus local microbrews and a few wines, mostly from other Portland producers. ✉ *1416 S.E. Stark St., Central East Side* ☎ *503/683–3676* 🌐 *www.ensowinery.com.*

★ Oui! Wine Bar at SE Wine Collective

WINE BARS—NIGHTLIFE | This hive of boutique wine-making has an inviting tasting room–cum–wine bar in which you can sample the vinos of several up-and-coming producers. You could carve out a full meal from the extensive menu's tapas, salads, baguette sandwiches, and cheese and meat plates. Although Oregon is chiefly known for Pinot Noir, Pinot Gris, and Chardonnay, the wineries at the collective produce a richly varied assortment of varietals, from racy Sauvignon Blancs to peppery Cabernet Francs. ✉ *2425 S.E. 35th Pl., Division/Clinton* ☎ *503/208–2061* 🌐 *www.sewinecollective.com.*

BREWPUBS AND MICROBREWERIES

★ Cascade Brewing

BREWPUBS/BEER GARDENS | This laid-back brewpub and pioneer of the Northwest sour-beer movement is a good place for friends and sour-beer lovers to share tart flights of several varieties, including Blackcap Raspberry, Kriek, and potent (10.1% ABV) Sang Noir. You'll find 24 rotating taps, small plates, and sandwiches to complement the sour beers, and ample outdoor seating. ✉ *939 S.E. Belmont St., Central East Side* ☎ *503/265–8603* 🌐 *www.cascadebrewingbarrelhouse.com.*

LIVE MUSIC

Doug Fir Lounge

MUSIC CLUBS | Part retro diner and part log cabin, the Doug Fir serves food and booze and hosts DJs and live rock shows from both up-and-coming and established bands most nights of the week. It adjoins the trendy Hotel Jupiter. ✉ *830 E. Burnside*

St., Central East Side ☎ 503/231–9663 🌐 www.dougfirlounge.com.

★ **Revolution Hall**

MUSIC CLUBS | Southeast Portland's stately early-1900s former Washington High School building has been converted into a state-of-the-art concert hall, featuring noted pop and world-beat music acts and comedians, from Steve Earle to Tig Notaro, plus film festivals and other intriguing events. There are two bars on-site, including a roof deck with great views of the Downtown skyline. ✉ *1300 S.E. Stark St., Central East Side* ☎ *503/288–3895* 🌐 *www.revolutionhall.com.*

FILM

★ **Bagdad Theater**

FILM | Built in 1927, the stunningly restored, eminently quirky Bagdad Theater shows first-run Hollywood films on a huge screen and serves pizza, burgers, sandwiches, and McMenamins ales. The Bagdad is a local favorite. ✉ *3702 S.E. Hawthorne Blvd., Hawthorne* ☎ *503/249–7474* 🌐 *www.mcmenamins.com/bagdad-theater-pub.*

THEATER

★ **Milagro Theatre Group**

THEATER | This well-established nonprofit company in the Central East Side showcases the region's vibrant, and growing, Latino voice through theatrical performances, featuring everything from classic dramas and musicals to experimental works and world premieres. ✉ *525 S.E. Stark St., Central East Side* ☎ *503/236–7253* 🌐 *www.milagro.org.*

CLOTHING

★ **Una**

CLOTHING | The fashion-minded devotees of this chic, upscale women's boutique swear by its staff's discerning eye for international jewelry and clothes. Creations by dozens of vaunted designers are displayed here—hammered sterling silver link collars from Annie Costello Brown, Japanese wool and flax dresses from Vlas Blomme, and Italian leather bags from Massimo Palomba, plus enticing home accessories. ✉ *922 S.E. Ankeny St., Central East Side* ☎ *503/235–2326* 🌐 *www.unanegozio.com.*

FOOD

★ **Jacobsen Salt Co.**

FOOD/CANDY | Established in 2011 on the Oregon Coast, this artisanal saltworks has become wildly successful and prolific, and you can sample its carefully balanced finishing salts as well as Portland-made Bee Local Honey in this handsome gourmet shop. There's also a wide selection of salty treats—salted caramels, black licorice, and other goodies. ✉ *602 S.E. Salmon St., Central East Side* ☎ *503/719–4973* 🌐 *www.jacobsensalt.com.*

HOUSEHOLD GOODS AND FURNITURE

★ **Urbanite**

ANTIQUES/COLLECTIBLES | In this huge warehouse packed with both vintage and contemporary furniture and accessories, you'll find wares from about 40 different designers and sellers. You could easily lose yourself in here for a couple of hours, admiring the antique signs and containers, midcentury lamps, cushy armchairs, industrial tables and drawers, and curious knickknacks. ✉ *1005 S.E. Grand Ave., Central East Side* ☎ *971/801–2361* 🌐 *www.urbanitepdx.com.*

Chapter 4

OREGON COAST

Updated by
Andrew Collins

Sights	Restaurants	Hotels	Shopping	Nightlife
★★★★★	★★★★☆	★★★★☆	★★★☆☆	★★★☆☆

WELCOME TO OREGON COAST

TOP REASONS TO GO

★ **Beaches:** Think broad expanses ideal for strolling, creature-teeming tide pools, stunning stretches framed by cliffs and boulders, and the dramatic sands of Oregon Dunes National Recreation Area.

★ **Sip craft beverages:** The coast has developed an impressive bounty of craft breweries, along with a number of first-rate artisanal distilleries, coffeehouses, and cideries.

★ **Rugged hikes:** Breathtaking trails line the coast, many of them leading to lofty mountain summits or rocky ledges that offer great wildlife viewing.

★ **Small-town charms:** You'll find some of the state's most quirky and charming communities along the coast, from hipster-approved Astoria to arty and secluded Port Orford to rustic yet sophisticated Yachats.

★ **Local seafood:** The region has vastly upped its dining game, with talented chefs featuring local crab, razor clams, rockfish, albacore, salmon, and other riches of the Oregon Coast.

1 **Astoria.** A historic working-class fishing town that abounds with hip cafés, indie boutiques, and restored hotels.

2 **Seaside.** Family-friendly town with a touristy but bustling boardwalk and old-time amusements.

3 **Cannon Beach.** Art-fueled and refined with some of Oregon's swankiest coastal accommodations.

4 **Manzanita.** A cozy seaside hamlet with a laid-back vibe and gorgeous natural scenery.

5 **Tillamook.** This lush, agrarian valley is home to a famous cheese maker and the stunning Three Capes Scenic Loop.

6 **Pacific City.** A colorful fleet of dories dots the wide beach of this tiny village that's popular for outdoor recreation.

7 **Lincoln City.** Visitors can indulge in gaming, shopping, golfing, and beachcombing in this sprawling, family-oriented resort town.

8 **Depoe Bay.** A coastal town with a teeny-tiny harbor, it's the best place in Oregon for whale-watching.

9 **Newport.** Home to a stellar aquarium and one of Oregon's largest fishing fleets, expect sophisticated dining and beachfront hotels.

10 **Yachats.** This less-developed town is a true seaside gem with astounding coastal views and a noteworthy restaurant scene.

11 **Florence.** With a bustling downtown that hugs the Siuslaw River, this cute village is also the northern gateway to the Oregon dunes.

12 **Coos Bay and North Bend.** These historic industrial towns offer southern access to Oregon dunes and are close to several beautiful state parks on the ocean.

13 **Bandon.** A world-class golfing destination that's also known for spectacular boulder-strewn beaches, offshore islands, and lighthouse gazing.

14 **Port Orford.** Gorgeous beach landscapes and a growing arts scene are the hallmarks of this ruggedly situated and low-key spot.

15 **Gold Beach.** Entry point for the fabled Rogue River with a nice range of casual seafood eateries and midprice resorts.

16 **Brookings.** Sterling state parks, lots of redwoods, and plenty of sunshine are accented by a burgeoning restaurant scene.

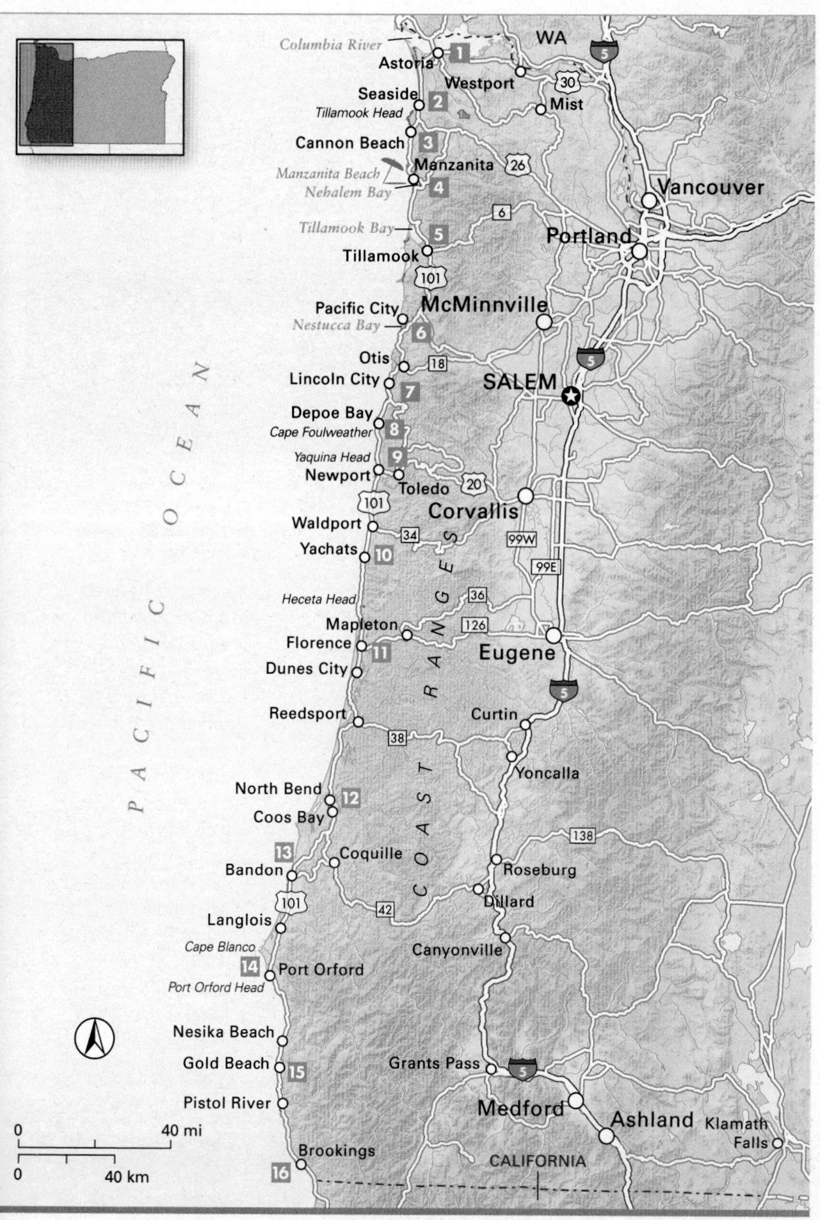

Columbia River
WA
Astoria
Westport
Seaside
Tillamook Head
Mist
Cannon Beach
Manzanita
Manzanita Beach
Nehalem Bay
Vancouver
Tillamook Bay
Portland
Tillamook
Pacific City
McMinnville
Nestucca Bay
Otis
Lincoln City
SALEM
Depoe Bay
Cape Foulweather
Yaquina Head
Newport
Toledo
Corvallis
Waldport
Yachats
Heceta Head
Mapleton
Florence
Eugene
Dunes City
Reedsport
Curtin
Yoncalla
North Bend
Coos Bay
Coquille
Bandon
Roseburg
Dillard
Langlois
Cape Blanco
Canyonville
Port Orford
Port Orford Head
Nesika Beach
Gold Beach
Grants Pass
Pistol River
Medford
Ashland
Klamath Falls
Brookings
CALIFORNIA
PACIFIC OCEAN
COAST RANGES
0
40 mi
0
40 km

EXPLORING OREGON'S BEST BEACHES

Oregon's 300 miles of public coastline is the backdrop for thrills, serenity, rejuvenation, and romance. From wide expanses of sand dotted with beach chairs to surf-shaped cliffs, the shoreline is often compared to New Zealand.

Most awe-inspiring are the massive rock formations just offshore in the coast's northern and southern sections. Beaches along the north coast, from Astoria to Pacific City, are perfect for romantic strolls. The central-coast beaches, from Lincoln City to Florence, are long and wide, providing perfect conditions for sunbathers, children, clam diggers, horseback riders, and surfers. The southern coast from Oregon Dunes National Recreation Area to Brookings is less populated, ideal for an escape.

In late July and August the climate is generally kind to sun worshippers. During the shoulder months, keep layers of clothing handy for temperature swings. Winter can be downright blustery.

GLASS FLOATS: FINDERS KEEPERS

Since 1997, between mid-October and Memorial Day, more than 2,000 handcrafted glass floats made by local artists have been hidden along Lincoln City's 7½-mile public beach. If you happen to come upon one, call the local tourism office (*800/452–2151*) to register it, and find out which artist made it. Although antique glass floats are extremely rare, these new versions make great souvenirs.

THE OREGON COAST'S BEST BEACHES

Cannon Beach. In the shadow of glorious **Haystack Rock,** this family-friendly beach is wide, flat, and perfect for bird-watching, exploring tide pools, building sand castles, and romantic walks in the sea mist. Each June the city holds a **sand-castle contest,** drawing artists and thousands of visitors. The rest of the year the beach is far less populated. The dapper beachfront town has several of the region's swankiest hotels and finest restaurants, as well as spots for surfing, hiking, and beachcombing.

Pacific City. Like Cannon Beach, this town also has a huge (less famous) Haystack Rock that provides the perfect scenic backdrop for horseback riders, beach strollers, and people with shovels chasing sand-covered clams. With safe beach breaks that are ideal for beginners and larger peaks a bit to the south, this is also a great spot for surfers. Winter-storm-watchers love Pacific City, where winds exceeding 75 mph twist Sitka spruce, and tides deposit driftwood and logs on the beach.

Oregon Dunes National Recreation Area. One reason the Pacific Northwest isn't known for its amusement parks is because nature hurls more thrills than any rattling contraption could ever provide. This certainly is true at this 40-mile stretch of coastal sand dunes, the largest expanse in North America. From Florence to Coos Bay, the dunes draw more than 1.5 million visitors each year. For those who just want to swim, relax, hike, and marvel at the amazing expanse of dunes against the ocean, there are spaces off-limits to motorized vehicles. One of the best places to view the dunes and beach is the gorgeous **Umpqua River Lighthouse.**

Samuel H. Boardman State Scenic Corridor. It doesn't get any wilder than this—or more spectacular. The 12-mile strip of forested, rugged coastline between Gold Beach and Brookings is dotted with smaller sand beaches, some more accessible than others. Here visitors will find the amazing **Arch Rock** and **Natural Bridges** and can hike 27 miles of the **Oregon Coast Trail.** Beach highlights include **Whaleshead Beach, Secret Beach,** and **Thunder Rock Cove,** where you might spy migrating gray whales. From the 345-foot-high **Thomas Creek Bridge,** you can take a moderately difficult hike down to admire the gorgeous, jagged rocks off **China Beach.**

If you aren't from the Pacific Northwest, Oregon's spectacular coastline might still be a secret: it's less visited and less talked about than California's coast, but certainly no less beautiful. In recent decades, however, the state's reputation for scenic drives and splendid hikes, reasonably priced oceanfront hotels and vacation rentals, low-key towns with friendly, creative vibes, and consistently fresh and well-prepared seafood has garnered increased attention. The true draw here is the beaches, where nature lovers delight at their first sight of a migrating whale or a baby harbor seal sitting on a rock.

Oregon's coastline is open to all; not a grain of its more than 300 miles of white-sand beaches is privately owned. The coast's midsize towns and small villages (you won't find any large cities) are linked by U.S. 101, which runs the length of the state. It winds past sea-tortured rocks, brooding headlands, hidden beaches, historic lighthouses, and tiny ports. This is one of the most picturesque driving routes in the country, and it should not be missed. Embracing it is the vast, indigo-blue Pacific Ocean, which presents a range of moods with the seasons. On summer evenings it might be smooth enough to reflect a romantic sunset. In winter the ocean might throw a thrilling tantrum for storm watchers sitting snug and safe in a beachfront cabin.

Active visitors indulge in thrills from racing up a sand dune in a buggy to making par at Bandon Dunes, one of the world's finest links-style golf courses. Bicyclists pedal along misty coastline vistas, cruising past historic lighthouses. Hikers enjoy breezy, open trails along the sea as well as lush, evergreen-studded treks into the adjoining Coast Range. Opportunities abound as well for excursions on jet boats along southern-coast rivers and whale-watching tours along the wildlife-rich central coast. If the weather turns, don't overlook indoor venues like the Oregon Coast Aquarium and Columbia River Maritime Museum.

The region's culinary scene has improved markedly in recent years, with destination-worthy restaurants as well as craft breweries and hip cafés popping up everywhere. Shoppers appreciate the art galleries of Newport and Cannon Beach; for more family-oriented fun, giggle in the souvenir shops of Lincoln City and Seaside while eating fistfuls of caramel corn or chewing saltwater taffy.

MAJOR REGIONS

The **North Coast** is the primary beach playground for residents of Portland, and you'll find a growing number of sophisticated eateries, craft breweries and cocktail bars, colorful art galleries and indie retailers, and smartly restored boutique hotels along this ruggedly beautiful stretch of coastline. What distinguishes the region historically from other areas of the coast are its forts, its graveyard of shipwrecks, historic sites related to Lewis and Clark's early visit, and a town—**Astoria**—that blends the misty temperament and cannery heritage of Monterey, California, with Portland's progressive, hipster personality. To the south, bustling **Seaside** is Oregon's long-time go-to for family-friendly fun, while nearby **Cannon Beach** feels a just a bit fancier than any other town in the area. Farther south are the sleepy and scenic little villages of **Manzanita** and **Pacific City**, as well as **Tillamook,** home to thriving dairy farms and an iconic cheese factory that's a favorite visitor attraction.

The **Central Coast** is Oregon's top destination for families, shoppers, casino goers, kite flyers, deep-sea fishing enthusiasts, and dune-shredding daredevils. Although it's a bit touristy and bisected by a rather tatty commercial stretch of U.S. 101, **Lincoln City** offers a wealth of shops devoted to souvenirs and knickknacks, and visitors can even blow their own glass float at a few local studios. **Depoe Bay** is popular for whale-watching excursions, and **Newport** is designated the Dungeness crab capital of the world as well as home to bustling bay-front and picturesque ocean beaches, plus plenty of excellent dining and lodging options. As you venture farther south, you'll roll through gorgeous and less-developed **Yachats** and charming **Florence** to reach the iconic mountains of sand that fall within Oregon Dunes National Recreation Area. Even if you're not intent on making tracks in the sand, the dunes provide vast, unforgettable scenery.

Coos Bay-Charleston-North Bend, or Bay Area, is considered to be the gateway to this gorgeous stretch known as the **Southern Coast**. The upper portion is continuation of the Oregon Dunes National Recreation Area, and is the location of its visitor center. In **Bandon** golfers flock to one of the most celebrated clusters of courses in the world at Bandon Dunes. Lovers of lighthouses, sailing, fishing, crabbing, elk viewing, camping, and water sports may wonder why they didn't venture south sooner to explore **Port Orford, Gold Beach,** and **Brookings.**

Planning

When to Go

November through May are generally rainy months (albeit with sporadic stretches of dry and sometimes even sunny days), but once the fair weather comes, coastal Oregon is one of the most gorgeous places on earth. July through September offer wonderful, dry days for beachgoers. Autumn is also a great time to visit, as the warm-enough weather is perfect for crisp beachcombing walks followed by hearty harvest meals paired with ales from the area's growing crop of craft breweries.

Even with the rain, coastal winter and spring do have quite a following. Many hotels are perfectly situated for storm watching, and provide all the trappings for a romantic experience. Think of a toasty (albeit likely gas) fireplace, a smooth Oregon Pinot, and your loved one, settled in to watch the waves dance upon a jagged rocky stage.

Festivals

Astoria Music Festival

FESTIVALS | Fans of opera and classical works flock to this increasingly popular festival, which mounts more than 20 performances, over 16 days in late June and early July. 🌐 *www.astoriamusicfestival.org.*

Cannon Beach Sandcastle Contest

FESTIVALS | It can be tough to find a room—or parking spot—during this single-day mid-June festival that's been going strong for more than 55 years and showcases the amazingly detailed sand constructions of both professional and amateur teams. 🌐 *www.cannonbeach.org.*

Cranberry Festival

FESTIVALS | In Bandon each September, this three-day festival in celebration of the town's most famous product (well, after seafood) comprises a fair and parade. 🌐 *www.bandon.com/cranberry-festival.*

Newport Seafood and Wine Festival

FESTIVALS | This renowned foodie gathering takes place the last full weekend in late February and bills itself the premier seafood and wine event of the Oregon Coast. Dozens of wineries are represented at this expansive celebration, which also features myriad crafts and eateries. 🌐 *www.seafoodandwine.com.*

Getting Here and Around

By far the most practical way to reach and to explore the coast is by car. There's only one small regional airport with limited commercial service, the regional bus lines provide fairly slow and infrequent service from other parts of the state, and there's zero train service. Several two-lane state highways connect the central and northern sections of the coast with the state's two largest cities, Portland and Eugene; the southern portion of the coast is more remote and requires longer drives.

AIR

From Portland, which has Oregon's largest airport, the drive is about 2 hours to Astoria and Cannon Beach, and 2½ hours to Lincoln City and Newport. If you're headed farther south, you have a few other options, including flying into the regional airport in Eugene, which is served by most major airlines and is a 90-minute drive from Florence; flying into the tiny Southwest Oregon Regional Airport in the coast town of North Bend, which is an hour south of Florence and 2½ hours north of Brookings; flying into Rogue Valley International Airport in Medford, which is a 2½-hour drive from Brookings and a 3-hour drive from Bandon; and flying into Del Norte County Airport in Crescent City, California, which is just a 30-minute drive south of Brookings (and has scheduled service only to Oakland).

Southwest Oregon Regional Airport has flights to San Francisco and—from June to early October—Denver on United Express. The airport has Hertz and Enterprise car-rental agencies as well as cab companies serving the area, including Coos Bay and Bandon.

A few shuttle services connect the airports in Portland and Eugene to the coast, but these tend to be far less convenient than renting a car, and not necessarily more economical. Caravan Shuttle runs a daily shuttle service from Portland International Airport to Lincoln City and on down to Waldport (nearly to Yachats). Hub Airport Shuttle provides door-to-door van service from the Eugene airport to the Central Coast, from Florence down to around Bandon.

CONTACTS Caravan Shuttle. ☎ *541/994–9645* 🌐 *www.caravanshuttle.com.* **Hub Airport Shuttle.** ☎ *541/461–7959* 🌐 *www.hubairportshuttle.com.* **Southwest Oregon Regional Airport.** ✉ *1100 Airport La., North Bend* ☎ *541/756–8531* 🌐 *www.cooscountyairportdistrict.com.*

BUS

There is bus travel to the coast from Portland and Eugene, but this is a fairly slow and cumbersome way to explore the area. NW Connector is a nonprofit organization that coordinates travel among five rural transit services in the northwestern corner of the state. From its website, you can plan and book trips from Portland to Astoria, with connecting service between the two along the coast, stopping in Seaside, Cannon Beach, Manzanita, and other communities. You can also purchase three- and seven-day travel passes from drivers on any of the NW Connector buses. Additionally, Point has daily bus service from Portland to Cannon Beach, and then up the coast to Astoria; and daily buses from Klamath Falls to Brookings, via Ashland, Medford, and Crescent City, California; Amtrak handles the company's reservations and ticketing. Pacific Crest Bus Lines connects Florence, Coos Bay, and Reedsport with Eugene and Bend every day.

CONTACTS NW Connector. 🌐 *www.nworegontransit.org.* **Pacific Crest Bus Lines.** ☎ *800/872–7245 ticketing through Amtrak, 800/231–2222 ticketing through Greyhound* 🌐 *www.pacificcrestbuslines.com.* **Point.** ☎ *800/872–7245 ticketing through Amtrak, 541/484–4100 information* 🌐 *www.oregon-point.com.*

CAR

Beautiful U.S. 101 hugs the entire Oregon coastline from Brookings near the California border in the south to Astoria on the Columbia River in the north. The road can be slow in places, especially where it passes through towns and curves over headlands and around coves. In theory, you could drive the entire 345-mile Oregon stretch of U.S 101 in a little under eight hours, but that's without stopping—and, of course, the whole point of driving the coast is stopping regularly to enjoy it. If you want to do a full road trip of the Oregon Coast, give yourself at least three days and two nights; that's enough time to see a few key attractions along the way, enjoy the many scenic viewpoints, and stop to eat and overnight in some small towns along the route.

Several two-lane roads connect key towns on the coast—Astoria, Cannon Beach, Tillamook, Lincoln City, Newport, Waldport (near Yachats), Florence (and nearby Reedsport), and Bandon—with the major towns in the Willamette and Rogue valleys (Portland, Corvallis, Eugene, Roseburg). All these roads climb over the Coast Range, meaning the drives tend to be winding and hilly but quite picturesque. Keep in mind that winter storms in the mountains occasionally create slick conditions and even road closures. Always use numbered, paved state roads when crossing the mountains from the valley to the coast, especially in winter; what might appear to be a scenic alternative or shortcut on a map or GPS device is likely an unmaintained logging or forest road that leads through a secluded part of the mountains, without cell service.

Restaurants

Deciding which restaurant has the best clam chowder or Dungeness crab cakes is just one of the culinary fact-finding expeditions you can embark upon along the Oregon Coast. Chefs here take full advantage of the wealth of sturgeon, salmon, steelhead, and trout that abound in coastal rivers as well as the fresh rockfish, halibut, albacore, and lingcod caught in the Pacific. You'll also find fresh mussels, bay shrimp, oysters, and razor clams.

What's changed of late is a notable influx of chef-driven restaurants serving creatively prepared, often globally influenced dishes along with beverage programs that showcase craft spirits, beers, and wines from the Pacific Northwest. The increase in buzz-worthy dining aside, restaurants still tend to be casual and low-key, with a wide range of price points. *Restaurant reviews have been shortened. For full information visit Fodors.com.*

What It Costs in U.S. Dollars

$	$$	$$$	$$$$
RESTAURANTS			
under $16	$16–$22	$23–$30	over $30
HOTELS			
under $150	$150–$200	$201–$250	over $250

Hotels

Compared with other coastal destinations in the United States, the Oregon Coast offers a pretty good value. You can typically find clean but basic motels and rustic inns, often with beachfront locations, that have nightly rates well below $150, even in high season, although you'll also find a smattering of high-end resorts and boutique inns with summer rates well over $300 nightly. Spring and fall rates often drop by 20% to 30% and the value is even greater in winter. The lodging landscape is dominated by family- or independently owned motels and hotels, a diminishing number of distinctive B&Bs (many have become rentals or private homes in recent years), and a great variety vacation rentals. Airbnb has the greatest selection of rentals along the coast, but you'll also find well-regarded agencies in many communities, and the reputable Oregon-based online agency Vacasa also has dozens of listings.

Properties in much of the North and Central Coast fill up fast in the summer, so book in advance. Many lodgings require a minimum two-night stay on a summer weekend. *Hotel reviews have been shortened. For full information, visit Fodors.com.*

Visitor Information

CONTACTS Oregon Coast Visitors Association. ☎ *541/574–2679, 888/628–2101* 🌐 *www.visittheoregoncoast.com.*

Astoria

96 miles northwest of Portland.

The mighty Columbia River meets the Pacific at Astoria, the oldest city west of the Rockies and a bustling riverfront getaway with a creative spirit and a surprisingly urbane personality for a city of less than 10,000. Astoria cultivates a bit of Portland's hipster vibe, especially when it comes to shopping and nightlife, and its once workaday downtown and cannery wharfs now house trendy restaurants and distinctive lodgings.

It's named for John Jacob Astor, owner of the Pacific Fur Company, whose members arrived in 1811 and established Fort Astoria. In its early days, it was a placid amalgamation of small town and hardworking port city. Its rivers rich with salmon, the city relied on its fishing and canning industries. Settlers built sprawling Victorian houses on the flanks of Coxcomb Hill; many of the homes have since been restored and used as backdrops in movies (*The Goonies,* notably) or been converted into Airbnbs or vacation rentals. Astoria still retains the soul of a fisherman's town, celebrated each February during its FisherPoets Gathering. It's easy to find spectacular views from a number of points in town, both of the river and the richly forested countryside to the south and east, yet it remains a working waterfront, albeit with a superb museum dedicated to the Columbia River. There is little public beach access in the town proper; to reach the Pacific, drive a few miles west to Fort Stevens in the adjacent village of Warrenton.

GETTING HERE AND AROUND

The northernmost town on the Oregon Coast, Astoria is just across the Columbia River from southwestern Washington via U.S. 101 (over the stunning Astoria-Megler Bridge) and a two-hour drive from Portland on U.S. 30. It only takes about 20 extra minutes to get here from Portland via the more scenic route of U.S. 101 south and U.S. 26 east.

ESSENTIALS

VISITOR INFORMATION Travel Astoria. ✉ *111 W. Marine Dr.* ☎ *503/325–6311, 800/875–6807* 🌐 *www.travelastoria.com.*

Sights

★ Astoria Column

MEMORIAL | For the best view of the city, the Coast Range, volcanic Mt. St. Helens, and the Pacific Ocean, scamper up the 164 spiral stairs to the top of the Astoria Column. When you get to the top, you can throw a small wooden plane and watch it glide to earth; each year some 35,000 gliders are tossed. The 125-foot-high structure sits atop Coxcomb Hill, and was patterned after Trajan's Column in Rome. There are little platforms to rest on if you get winded, or, if you don't want to climb, the column's 500 feet of artwork, depicting important Pacific Northwest historical milestones, are well worth a study. ✉ *1 Coxcomb Dr.* ☎ *503/325–2963* 🌐 *www.astoriacolumn.org* 🎫 *$5 parking (good for 1 yr).*

Astoria Riverfront Trolley

TOUR—SIGHT | **FAMILY** | Also known as "Old 300," this is a beautifully restored 1913 streetcar that travels for 4 miles along Astoria's historic riverfront, stopping at several points between the Astoria River Inn and the foot of 39th Street (although you can easily flag it down at any point along the route by offering a friendly wave). The hour-long ride gives you a close-up look at the waterfront from the Port of Astoria to the East Morring Basin; the Columbia River; and points of interest in between. ☎ *503/325–6311, 800/875–6807* 🌐 *www.old300.org* 🎫 *$1, $2 all-day pass* ⏲ *Limited service Oct.–Apr. (call first).*

Clatsop County Historical Society Museums

MUSEUM | In a 1904 Colonial Revival building originally used as the city hall, the Clatsop County Historical Society Museum has two floors of exhibits detailing the history of the early pioneers, Native Americans, and logging and marine industries of Clatsop County, the oldest American settlement west of the Mississippi. Artifacts include finely crafted 19th-century Chinook and Clatsop baskets, otter pelts, a re-created Prohibition-era saloon, and historic logging and fishing tools. The Historical Society also operates two other excellent downtown history museums, the Flavel House (441 8th St.), a graciously restored Queen Anne–style mansion where visitors can imagine what life was like for the wealthy in late-19th-century Astoria; and the Uppertown Firefighters Museum (2968 Marine Dr.), which is filled with old equipment, including hand-pulled and horse-drawn fire engines, and a collection of photos of some of the town's most notable fires make up the exhibits. ✉ *1618 Exchange St.* ☎ *503/325–2203* 🌐 *www.cumtux.org* 🎫 *$4 ($6 Flavel House, free Uppertown Firefighters Museum).*

★ Columbia River Maritime Museum

MUSEUM | **FAMILY** | One of C
coastal attractions illuminat
history of the Pacific North
provides visitors with a sen
of guiding ships into the m
Columbia River. Vivid exhib
it was like to pilot a tugboa
in a Coast Guard rescue or
River Bar. You can tour the

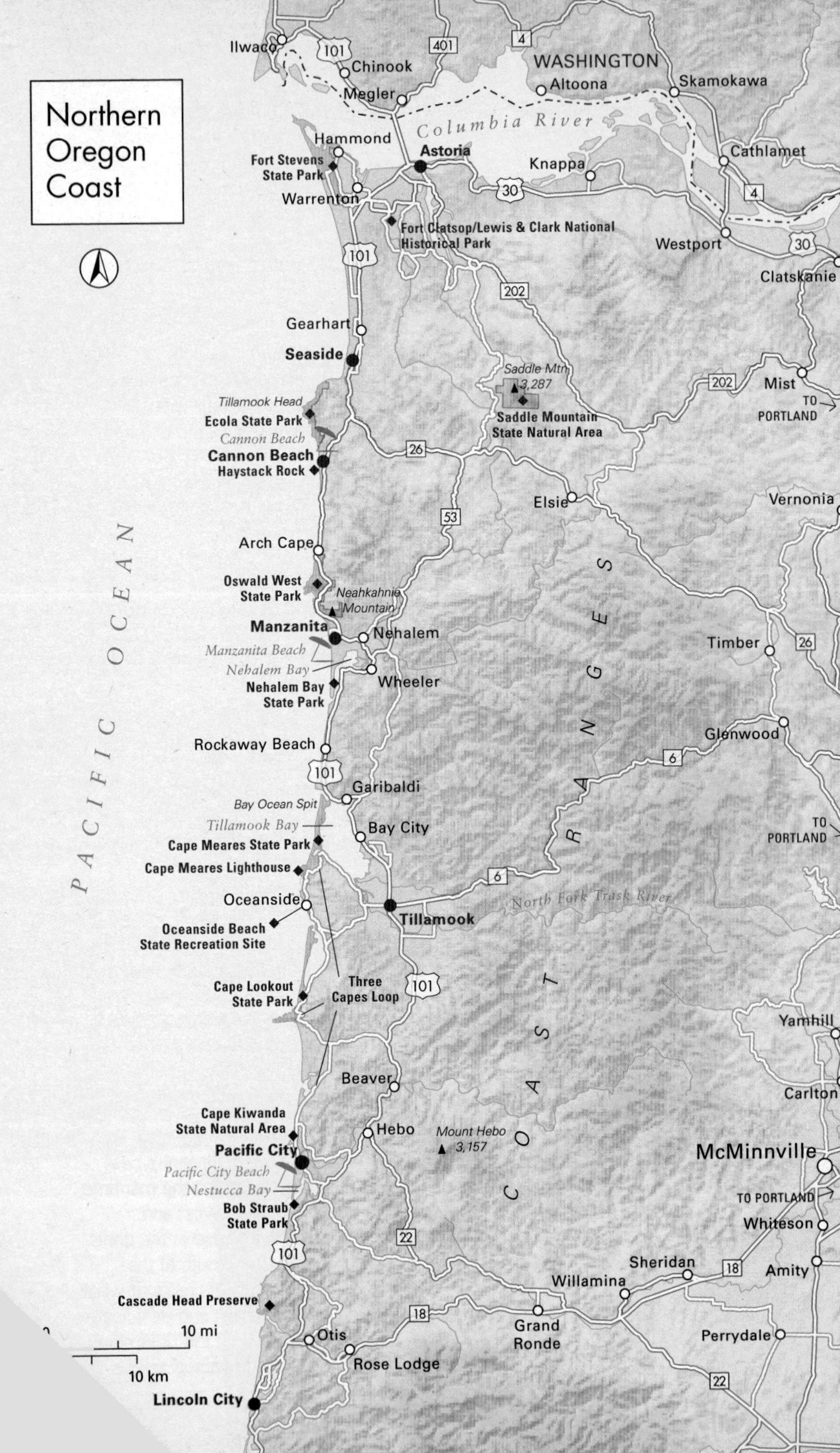

Northern Oregon Coast
Ilwaco
Chinook
Megler
WASHINGTON
Altoona
Skamokawa
Columbia River
Hammond
Astoria
Fort Stevens State Park
Warrenton
Knappa
Cathlamet
Fort Clatsop/Lewis & Clark National Historical Park
Westport
Clatskanie
Gearhart
Seaside
Saddle Mtn 3,287
Saddle Mountain State Natural Area
Mist
TO PORTLAND
Tillamook Head
Ecola State Park
Cannon Beach
Cannon Beach
Haystack Rock
Elsie
Vernonia
PACIFIC OCEAN
Arch Cape
Oswald West State Park
Neahkahnie Mountain
Manzanita
Nehalem
Manzanita Beach
Nehalem Bay
Wheeler
Nehalem Bay State Park
Timber
COAST RANGES
Glenwood
Rockaway Beach
Garibaldi
Bay Ocean Spit
Tillamook Bay
Bay City
TO PORTLAND
Cape Meares State Park
Cape Meares Lighthouse
Oceanside
Tillamook
North Fork Trask River
Oceanside Beach State Recreation Site
Three Capes Loop
Cape Lookout State Park
Yamhill
Beaver
Carlton
Cape Kiwanda State Natural Area
Hebo
Mount Hebo 3,157
Pacific City
McMinnville
Pacific City Beach
Nestucca Bay
TO PORTLAND
Bob Straub State Park
Whiteson
Sheridan
Amity
Willamina
Cascade Head Preserve
Grand Ronde
10 mi
Otis
Perrydale
10 km
Rose Lodge
Lincoln City
101
401
4
30
202
26
53
6
22
18

of a World War II–era U.S. Navy destroyer and the 1951 U.S. Coast Guard lightship *Columbia.* Also on display is a 44-foot Coast Guard motor lifeboat, artifacts from the region's illustrious riverboat heyday, and details about Astoria's seafood-canning history. One especially captivating exhibit displays the personal belongings of some of the ill-fated passengers of the 2,000 ships that have foundered here since the early 19th century. In addition, the theater shows an excellent documentary about the river's heritage as well as rotating 3-D films about sea life. At the east end of the property, the city's former railroad depot now houses the museum's Barbey Maritime Center, which offers classes and workshops on maritime culture and wooden boatbuilding. ✉ *1792 Marine Dr.* ☎ *503/325–2323* 🌐 *www.crmm.org* 🎫 *$14.*

★ Fort Clatsop at Lewis and Clark National Historical Park

MEMORIAL | **FAMILY** | See where the 30-member Lewis and Clark Expedition endured a rain-soaked winter in 1805–06, hunting, gathering food, making salt, and trading with the local Clatsops, Chinooks, and Tillamooks. This memorial is part of the 3,200-acre Lewis and Clark National Historical Park and is a faithful replica of the log fort depicted in Clark's journal. The fort lies within a forested wonderland, with an exhibit hall, gift shop, film, and trails. Park rangers dress in period garb during the summer and perform such early-19th-century tasks as making fire with flint and steel. Hikers enjoy the easy 1½-mile Netul Landing Trail and the more rigorous but still fairly flat 6½-mile Fort to Sea Trail. ✉ *92343 Fort Clatsop Rd.* ☎ *503/861–2471* 🌐 *www.nps.gov/lewi* 🎫 *$7.*

Fort Stevens State Park

MILITARY SITE | **FAMILY** | This earthen fort at Oregon's northwestern tip was built during the Civil War to guard the Columbia River against attack. None came until World War II, when a Japanese submarine fired upon it. The fort still has cannons and an underground gun battery, of which tours are available in summer (call for details). This 4,300-acre park has year-round camping, with full hookup sites, 11 cabins, and 15 yurts. There are also bike paths, boating, swimming, hiking trails, and a short walk to a gorgeous, wide beach where the corroded skeleton—or the tiny bit that remains of it—of the *Peter Iredale* pokes up through the sand. This century-old English four-master shipwreck is a reminder of the nearly 2,000 vessels claimed by these treacherous waters. ✉ *100 Peter Iredale Rd., Hammond* ☎ *503/861–3170* 🌐 *www.oregonstateparks.org* 🎫 *Day use $5 per vehicle.*

Hanthorn Cannery Museum

MUSEUM | Drive or walk over the rickety-seeming (but actually completely sturdy) bridge onto historic Pier 39, which juts out into the Columbia River on the east side of downtown, to visit this small but interesting museum that occupies the oldest extant cannery building in Astoria. It was once operated by Bumble Bee Seafood, and some 30,000 cans of salmon were processed here annually during the plant's late-19th-century heyday. Exhibits and artifacts, including three vintage gill-net boats, some wonderful old photos, and equipment and cans tell the story of the town's—and facility's—canning history. Also on the pier is Coffee Girl café and Rogue Ales Public House. ✉ *100 39th St.* ☎ *503/325–2502* 🌐 *www.canneryworker.org* 🎫 *Free.*

Oregon Film Museum

MUSEUM | **FAMILY** | Housed in the old Clatsop County Jail, this small but engaging museum celebrates Oregon's long history of filmmaking and contains artifacts from and displays about prior productions. The location is apt because it was featured prominently in the famous cult film *The Goonies*, which the town celebrates each June with a one-day Goonies festival. The state's film productions date back to 1908 for *The Fisherman's Bride*. Since then, Oregon has helped give birth to such classics as

The General, The Great Race, One Flew Over the Cuckoo's Nest, Paint Your Wagon, Animal House, and *Twilight,* leading some to call the state Hollywood North. *Kindergarten Cop, The Ring II, Free Willy I* and *II,* and *Short Circuit* are among those filmed in Astoria. ✉ *732 Duane St.* ☎ *503/325–2203* 🌐 *www.oregonfilmmuseum.org* 🎫 *$6.*

Restaurants

Astoria Coffeehouse & Bistro

$$ | **ECLECTIC** | A source of fine coffee drinks and baked goods, this colorful storefront café has both sidewalk seating and a living-room-like interior decorated with old photos. The always-bustling restaurant serves consistently well-prepared food, a mix of American classics and international treats, including a decadent Monte Cristo sandwich at breakfast, and tuna poke with mango and avocado, slow-roasted-beet salad with chèvre and apples, and pad Thai with fresh salmon late in the day. **Known for:** Sunday brunch; excellent drinks, from coffees to cocktails; decadent pastries and baked goods. $ *Average main: $19* ✉ *243 11th St.* ☎ *503/325–1787* 🌐 *www.astoriacoffeehouse.com.*

Blue Scorcher Bakery Café

$ | **CAFÉ** | **FAMILY** | "Joyful work, delicious food, and strong community" is the rallying cry of this family-friendly café known for everything from *huevos scorcheros* (poached eggs with rice, beans, cheese, and salsa) and organic, handcrafted breads to a variety of foods using local, fair trade, and organic ingredients. The offerings change with the seasons, but there are always vegan and gluten-free options, and the inviting dining room's big windows and children's play area overlook downtown and the Columbia River in the distance. **Known for:** delicious desserts; children's play area; funky, light-filled dining room. $ *Average main: $8* ✉ *1493 Duane St.* ☎ *503/338–7473* 🌐 *www.bluescorcher.com* ⏲ *No dinner.*

Bridgewater Bistro

$$$ | **SEAFOOD** | In the same complex as the Cannery Pier Hotel, this stylish restaurant has great views of the river and bridge to Washington. Inside, high ceilings are supported by ancient fir timbers, and an extensive menu is strong on creative seafood and meat grills, including roasted spice-encrusted duck breast with orange marmalade glaze, and seared wild local salmon with an arugula-strawberry salad and a star anise–balsamic vinaigrette. **Known for:** Sunday brunch; Columbia River views; fresh, creatively prepared seafood. $ *Average main: $28* ✉ *20 Basin St., Suite A* ☎ *503/325–6777* 🌐 *www.bridgewaterbistro.com.*

★ **Buoy Beer Co**

$$ | **AMERICAN** | One of the most acclaimed craft brewers on the coast, Buoy Beer also serves exceptionally tasty contemporary pub fare in its warm and inviting taproom, set in a converted 1920s grain warehouse on Astoria's riverfront walk—huge windows afford dramatic views of the Columbia. Seafood figures prominently in many dishes here, including rockfish-and-chips and bacon-clam chowder, but you'll also find delicious burgers and meat and cheese boards. **Known for:** hoppy handcrafted IPAs and strong German-style beers; river and sea lion views; panfried oysters with jalapeño jam and goat cheese. $ *Average main: $17* ✉ *1 8th St.* ☎ *503/325–4540* 🌐 *www.buoybeer.com.*

Carruthers

$$$ | **MODERN AMERICAN** | The warm lighting, massive fireplace, marble-top bar, and glass-brick transom windows impart a cosmopolitan vibe to this high-ceilinged downtown bistro that turns out sophisticated, contemporary lunch, dinner, and Sunday brunch fare. Highlights include seared sea scallops with apple-fennel orzo and braised short ribs with andouille and white cheddar grits, but there's also a terrific bar menu of lighter bites—blackened-rockfish tacos, seafood mac and

cheese, and the like. **Known for:** great happy hour; well-crafted cocktails; Sunday brunch. *Average main: $27* *1198 Commercial St.* *503/741–3443* *No dinner Sun.*

Coffee Girl

$ | **CAFÉ** | This cozy café inside a 19th-century cannery building on historic Pier 39 has big windows overlooking the river—you can always take your well-crafted espresso or latte with you for a stroll around the pier. Open until late afternoon each day, Coffee Girl also serves tasty quiches, pastries, soups, bagels with lox, and grilled panini sandwiches. **Known for:** unusual river wharf setting; house-baked granola; top-quality coffee drinks. *Average main: $6* *100 39th St.* *503/325–6900* *www.thecoffeegirl.com.*

Columbian Cafe & Voodoo Room

$ | **ECLECTIC** | Locals love this funky diner-and-nightclub complex that defies categorization by offering inventive, fresh seafood, spicy vegetarian dishes, and meats cured and smoked on the premises. Located next to the historic Columbian Theater, the café serves simple food, such as crepes with broccoli, cheese, and homemade salsa for lunch. **Known for:** cocktails and very good pizza in the Voodoo Room bar; good people-watching; vintage movies in the adjacent Columbian Theater. *Average main: $12* *1114 Marine Dr.* *503/325–2233* *www.columbianvoodoo.com/cafe* *No credit cards.*

Hotels

★ Cannery Pier Hotel

$$$$ | **HOTEL** | From every room in this captivating property there's a gorgeous view of the mighty Columbia River flowing toward the Pacific Ocean, and it's almost hypnotic to watch the tugboats shepherding barges to and fro. **Pros:** spectacular river views; complimentary afternoon wine and lox; hotel hot tub and day spa. **Cons:** pricey; a bit of a walk from downtown; some traffic noise from nearby highway bridge. *Rooms from: $259* *10 Basin St.* *503/325–4996, 888/325–4996* *www.cannerypierhotel.com* *54 rooms* *Free breakfast.*

Clementine's B&B

$ | **B&B/INN** | This lovingly restored 1888 Italianate Victorian home is just a couple of blocks up the hill from Flavel House Museum and a short walk from several fine restaurants and shops. **Pros:** superb, multicourse breakfast included; handy downtown location; exudes historic charm. **Cons:** the traditional lacy room decor isn't for everyone; rooms are compact; steep steps up to the front door. *Rooms from: $139* *847 Exchange St.* *503/325–2005* *www.clementines-bb.com* *5 rooms* *Free breakfast.*

Commodore Hotel

$ | **HOTEL** | An economical but stylish downtown boutique hotel, the Commodore is a favorite with young and artsy souls from Portland and Seattle thanks to its vintage-chic aesthetic, large wall murals and photos, and hip Street 14 Café off the lobby. **Pros:** hip setting; wallet-friendly rates; excellent Street 14 Café on-site. **Cons:** least expensive rooms share a bath; simple decor; on busy downtown street. *Rooms from: $89* *258 14th St.* *503/325–4747* *www.commodoreastoria.com* *18 rooms* *No meals.*

Hotel Elliott

$$ | **HOTEL** | This atmospheric, five-story hotel stands in the heart of Astoria's historic district and retains the elegance of yesteryear, updated with modern comforts like cozy underfloor heating in the bathrooms and fireplaces and Jacuzzi tubs in the deluxe rooms. **Pros:** captures the city's historic atmosphere beautifully; every effort made to infuse the rooms with upscale amenities; roof deck with stunning views. **Cons:** no on-site dining; some rooms are on the small side; on a busy street downtown. *Rooms from:*

$179 *357 12th St.* *503/325–2222* *www.hotelelliott.com* *32 rooms* *Free breakfast.*

★ Norblad Hotel

$ | HOTEL | Formerly a boardinghouse, this attractively renovated, offbeat hotel occupies a stately two-story 1920s building a few steps from Fort George Brewery and offers a mix of small, European-style rooms with shared baths down the hall and a few spacious suites with a private bath. **Pros:** nice common areas and kitchen; short walk from downtown shopping and dining; bargain-priced rooms. **Cons:** fairly basic decor; offbeat, arty vibe isn't for everyone; many rooms share a bath. *Rooms from: $79* *443 14th St.* *503/325–6989* *www.norbladhotel.com* *17 rooms* *No meals.*

Nightlife

★ Fort George Brewery

BREWPUBS/BEER GARDENS | The spacious taproom and brewery set in a former 1920s auto showroom has plenty of indoor and outdoor seating where you can sample some of the best craft beers on the coast, including a number of limited-release collaborations with other top regional brewers. There's also tasty pub fare. *1483 Duane St.* *503/325–7468* *www.fortgeorgebrewery.com.*

Inferno Lounge

BARS/PUBS | Just about every seat in this hip bar situated on a pier that juts into the Columbia River offers stupendous water views. Catch the sunset with a well-crafted cocktail and perhaps a few nibbles—Thai shrimp tacos, pork potstickers—from the tapas menu. This place known for house-infused spirits buzzes until midnight or later. *77 11th St.* *503/741–3401.*

★ Reveille Ciderworks

BARS/PUBS | Stop by this friendly downtown taproom with big patio with food trucks to sample superb handcrafted ciders made from a variety of heirloom Northwest apples. These Belgian saison- and English ale-style hard ciders come with a range of complex flavor profiles, from dry and crisp to chai spiced to full-on fruit bombs infused with marionberry or cranberry. *1343 Duane St., Suite B* *971/704–2161* *www.astoriacider.com.*

Performing Arts

Liberty Theatre

CONCERTS | A massive amber chandelier glows above the 630 seats of this magnificent Italian Renaissance theater that's been a fixture in downtown Astoria since 1925. Painstakingly restored in 2006 and known for its dozen interior murals of Venice, the former vaudeville movie house shows local and nationally prominent dance, classical music, and theater as well as occasional film screenings throughout the year. *1203 Commercial St.* *503/325–5922* *www.libertyastoria.org.*

Shopping

Astoria Sunday Market

OUTDOOR/FLEA/GREEN MARKETS | Every Sunday between mid-May and mid-October, the town closes three blocks of 12th Street to traffic from 10 to 3 so that as many as 200 vendors can sell goods they've grown or made. There are booths and tables full of fresh fruits, vegetables, farm products, arts, crafts, and treats of all kinds, plus excellent live music. *12th and Commercial Sts.* *503/325–1010* *www.astoriasundaymarket.com.*

Doe & Arrow

CLOTHING | This beautifully curated purveyor of urbane women's and men's fashion as well as arty jewelry, hip home accessories, and eco-friendly grooming products occupies a large corner space in downtown's Historic Astor Hotel building. *380 14th St.* *503/741–3132* *www.doeandarrow.com.*

Josephson's

FOOD/CANDY | Open since 1920, this venerable smokehouse uses alder for all processing and specializes in Pacific Northwest Chinook salmon. The mouthwatering fish that's smoked on the premises includes hot smoked pepper or wine-maple salmon, as well as smoked halibut, sturgeon, tuna, oysters, mussels, rainbow trout, and salmon jerky. ✉ *106 Marine Dr.* ☎ *503/325–2190* 🌐 *www.josephsons.com.*

Seaside

12 miles south of Astoria on U.S. 101.

Established in 1899 as the Oregon Coast's first resort town, Seaside has significantly spruced up its honky-tonk reputation for gaudy arcades and kitschy souvenir shops and now supports a notable selection of mostly midrange hotels, condominiums, and restaurants within walking distance of its traditional paved promenade, aka "the Prom," which stretches 1½ miles along the beachfront. It still has fun games, candy shops, and plenty of carny noise to appeal to kids and teens, but it's also more well-rounded than in the past and offers access to some beautiful natural scenery. Only 90 miles from Portland, Seaside can get crowded, so it's not the place to come for solitude. Peak times include mid-March to early April during spring break; and late June, when the annual Miss Oregon Pageant is in full swing. Just south of town, waves draw surfers to the Cove, a spot jealously guarded by locals, and the dramatic hike along the Oregon Coast Trail to Tillamook Head connects with Cannon Beach's famous Ecola State Park.

GETTING HERE AND AROUND

Seaside is about a 90-minute drive from Portland via U.S 26 and a 20-minute drive south of Astoria on coastal U.S. 101.

VISITOR INFORMATION

CONTACTS Seaside Visitors Bureau. ✉ *7 N. Roosevelt Ave.* ☎ *503/738–3097, 888/306–2326* 🌐 *www.seasideor.com.*

Sights

Seaside Aquarium

ZOO | **FAMILY** | The first thing you hear at this small but fun 1930s-era aquarium is the clapping and barking of the harbor seals just inside the door (which you can feed). Located on the 1½-mile beachfront Promenade, the aquarium has jellyfish, giant king crab, octopus, moray eels, wolf eels, and other sea life swimming in more than 30 tanks. The discovery center draws curious kids and grown-ups alike for its hands-on touch tanks of starfish, anemones, and urchins, as well as for a close-up exploration of the most miniature marine life. No restrooms on-site. ✉ *200 N. Promenade* ☎ *503/738–6211* 🌐 *www.seasideaquarium.com* 🎫 *$8.50.*

Restaurants

Firehouse Grill

$ | **PACIFIC NORTHWEST** | This bustling diner-style café in a former firehouse in downtown Seaside hits the mark with its hearty breakfast fare, including fluffy biscuits with gravy, salmon Benedicts, cinnamon French toast, meat-loaf scrambles, and a couple of lighter options, such as house-made granola with fresh fruit. Open only until early afternoon, the restaurant also turns out excellent burgers, panfried oysters, and cod tacos and fish-and-chips at lunch. **Known for:** hearty, creative breakfast fare; cod tacos and fish-and-chips; Sleepy Monk coffee and first-rate Bloody Marys. 💲 *Average main: $13* ✉ *841 Broadway* ☎ *503/717–5502* 🌐 *www.firehousegrill.org* 🕓 *Closed Tues. and Wed. No dinner.*

★ Osprey Café

$ | **ECLECTIC** | The delicious made-from-scratch breakfast and lunch items at this cheerful café with several outdoor seats reflects the owner's extensive travels around the world, from the Central American arepas with shredded chicken, black beans, and avocado to Indonesian *nasi goreng* to flavorful chilaquiles. There are plenty of classic American dishes, too (the Hangtown fry and Cobb salad are both excellent), and creative cocktails offer a way to liven up your weekend brunch. **Known for:** quiet location near south end of "the Prom"; interesting globally inspired daily specials; weekend brunch. *$ Average main: $12 ✉ 2281 Beach Dr. ☎ 503/739–7054 ⏲ Closed Wed. No dinner.*

Hotels

McMenamins Gearhart Hotel

$$ | **HOTEL** | The quirky McMenamins hotel group operates this 34-room boutique inn on the upper floor of the Cape Cod–style Kelly House and in the modern Annex building, in the low-key beach community of Gearhart (a 10-minute drive north of Seaside)—it's next to the esteemed Gearhart Golf Links. **Pros:** short walk from beach; rooms have distinctive and arty flair; excellent 18-hole golf course. **Cons:** ocean view is blocked by condos across the street; 10-minute drive north of Seaside; restaurant on-site is uneven. *$ Rooms from: $155 ✉ 1157 N. Marion Ave., 4 miles north of Seaside, Gearhart ☎ 503/717–8159, 855/846–7583 🌐 www.mcmenamins.com/gearhart-hotel 34 rooms No meals.*

★ Rivertide Suites

$$ | **HOTEL** | **FAMILY** | Although it's not right on the beach, the Rivertide's splendid and spacious accommodations are within walking distance of Seaside's many restaurants, candy shops, and old-time amusements, making it a great choice for families. **Pros:** rates include breakfast and evening manager's reception; lots of different activity-based packages available; near plenty of shopping and boardwalk activities. **Cons:** it's on a river rather than the beach; rooms on lower floors have less of a view; family-friendly vibe isn't ideal for everyone. *$ Rooms from: $169 ✉ 102 N. Holladay Dr. ☎ 503/717–1100, 877/871–8433 🌐 www.rivertidesuites.com 70 suites Free breakfast.*

Sandy Cove Inn

$ | **HOTEL** | This small, nicely maintained motel is fun and colorfully decorated, and it's just a couple of blocks away from the quieter and more scenic southern end of Seaside's promenade as well as Seaside Golf Course. **Pros:** relatively quiet, low-key location; distinctive room themes; excellent value. **Cons:** not directly on the beach; about 1 mile south of downtown shops and dining; two-night minimum stay at busy times. *$ Rooms from: $149 ✉ 241 Ave. U ☎ 503/738–7473 🌐 www.sandycoveinn.net 15 rooms No meals.*

Nightlife

Seaside Brewing

BREWPUBS/BEER GARDENS | This chatter-filled taproom inside the old city jail is as worthy a stop for well-crafted, European-influenced beers, including a potent Belgian Tripel and sweet but lightly hoppy vanilla cream ale, as for the extensive menu of pub fare. Texas-style brisket and sausages are among the top noshables. *✉ 851 Broadway St. ☎ 503/717–5451 🌐 www.seasidebrewery.com.*

Shopping

Phillips Candy Kitchen

FOOD/CANDY | **FAMILY** | There are at least a half-dozen candy shops in Seaside's tiny downtown, and shopping for sweets is a favorite pastime here among kids and adults. Phillips has been a favorite since 1897 and presently stocks homemade saltwater taffy, candied fruit slices, caramel popcorn, fudge, stroopwafel, and hand-dipped chocolates in an astonishing array of flavors. *✉ 217 Broadway ☎ 503/738–5402 🌐 www.phillipscandies.com Free.*

Activities

HIKING

★ Saddle Mountain State Natural Area

HIKING/WALKING | One of the most accessible mountain peaks in the Coast Range, 3,290-foot Saddle Mountain is reached via a challenging but beautiful 2½-mile climb, with a 1,640-foot elevation gain—the reward, on clear days, is a view of the ocean to the west and the Cascade peaks—including Mt. Hood—far to the east. Wear sturdy shoes, and be prepared for sections with steep upgrades. There's a zippy change in the altitude as you climb higher, but the wildflowers make it all worthwhile. The trailhead is well signed off U.S. 26, the main highway back to Portland. ✉ *Saddle Mountain Rd.* ✣ *Off U.S. 26, 20 miles east of Seaside* ☎ *503/368–5943* ⊕ *www.oregonstateparks.org.*

Tillamook Head

HIKING/WALKING | A moderately challenging 7½-mile loop from U.S. 101, south of Seaside, brings you through lushly forested Elmer Feldenheimer Forest Reserve and into the northern end of Cannon Beach's Ecola State Park to a nearly 1,000-foot-high viewing point, a great place to see the **Tillamook Rock Light Station,** which stands a mile or so off the coast. The lonely beacon, built in 1881 on a straight-sided rock, towers 41 feet above the ocean and was abandoned in 1957. You can also reach this viewing area by hiking north from Indian Beach in Ecola State Park in Cannon Beach. ✉ *End of Sunset Blvd.* ⊕ *www.oregonstateparks.org.*

Cannon Beach

9 miles south of Seaside.

Cannon Beach is a mellow but relatively affluent town where locals and part-time residents—many of the latter reside in Portland—come to enjoy shopping, gallery touring, and dining, the sea air, and the chance to explore the spectacular state parks at either end of the area: Ecola to the north and Oswald West to the south. Shops and galleries selling surfing gear, upscale clothing, local art, wine, coffee, and candies line Hemlock Street, Cannon Beach's main thoroughfare. In late June the town hosts the Cannon Beach Sandcastle Contest, for which thousands throng the beach to view imaginative and often startling works in this most transient of art forms. On the downside, this so-called Carmel of the Oregon Coast is more expensive and often more crowded than other towns along U.S. 101.

GETTING HERE AND AROUND

It's a 90-minute drive east from Portland on U.S. 26 to reach Cannon Beach, which is a 10-minute drive south of Seaside. To make a scenic loop, consider returning to Portland by way of Astoria and U.S. 30 (about 2¼ hours) or Tillamook and Highway 6 (about 2½ hours).

ESSENTIALS

VISITOR INFORMATION Cannon Beach Chamber of Commerce. ✉ *207 N. Spruce St.* ☎ *503/436–2623* ⊕ *www.cannonbeach.org.*

Sights

EVOO Cannon Beach

COLLEGE | Offering fun and interactive culinary experiences as well as a well-stocked gourmet shop, EVOO offers cooking classes as well as demonstration dinners and lunches set around seasonal or specific food themes throughout the year, from artisanal bread making to the art of pasta. The food is always based on what's local and in season, and these meals are always delicious and a great opportunity to learn and meet friends. These experiences are by ticket only and start at $149 per person and include a full meal, with wine pairings. ✉ *188 S. Hemlock St.* ☎ *503/436–8555, 877/436–3866* ⊕ *www.evoo.biz.*

Beaches

★ Cannon Beach and Ecola State Park

BEACHES | FAMILY | Beachcombers love Cannon Beach for its often low foamy waves and the wide stretch of sand that wraps the quaint community, making it ideal for fair-weather play or for hunting down a cup of coffee and strolling in winter. This stretch can get feisty in storms, however, which also makes Cannon Beach a good place to curl up indoors and watch the show. Haystack Rock rises 235 feet over the beach on the south side of downtown, one of nearly 2,000 protected rocks that are part of the Oregon Ocean Island Wildlife Refuge, providing a nesting habitat for birds. Continue south past Tolovana Park—a playground located in the flood plain—to find the quiet side of Cannon Beach with a bevy of tide pools and few other souls. To the north of town, the beach gives way to Ecola State Park, a breathtakingly beautiful series of coves and rocky headlands where William Clark spotted a beached whale in 1806 and visitors still come to view them offshore during the twice-yearly migrations. From here, Sitka spruce and barbecues feature along the sands. There are a few excellent trails that hug the sometimes steep cliffs that rise above sand, including a 6½-mile trail first traced by Lewis and Clark, which runs from this spot past the Tillamook Head lookout and then eventually all the way to Seaside. **Amenities:** parking; toilets. **Best for:** partiers; sunset; walking. ✉ *Ocean Ave.* ☎ *503/436–2844* 🌐 *www.oregonstateparks.org* 🎫 *Ecola State Park day use $5 per vehicle.*

Restaurants

Castaways

$$$ | CARIBBEAN | At the north end of town, making it a perfect drop-in after a hike at Ecola State Park, this colorfully decorated spot with its own little tiki bar serves big portions of creatively prepared Caribbean and Creole fare, along with a fittingly extensive selection of tropical cocktails (the yellowbird, with fresh-squeezed tangerine and lime juice and Tia Maria, is a favorite). Kick things off with Dungeness crab fritters with mango salsa and Bahamian brown stew, before tucking into a heartier main dish, perhaps Jamaican jerk chicken or New Orleans jambalaya. **Known for:** a pineapple-guava red curry dish with a daily changing protein; easygoing island vibe; Caribbean-inspired cocktails. 💲 *Average main: $24* ✉ *316 Fir St.* ☎ *503/436–4444* 🕓 *Closed Tues. No lunch.*

★ Irish Table

$$$ | IRISH | Adjacent to the Sleepy Monk café, this cozy restaurant with a timber-beam ceiling and warm lighting serves seasonal food with an Irish twist, such as potato-kale soup, a much-heralded Irish lamb stew, and an always outstanding fresh fish of the day. Start with the curried mussels, and soak up the sauce with slices of piping-hot soda bread, and keep in mind that there's a rich assortment of drinks, including Irish whiskey and a wine list featuring plenty of noted Oregon options. **Known for:** Irish whiskey selection; friendly service; addictive warm soda bread. 💲 *Average main: $25* ✉ *1235 S. Hemlock St.* ☎ *503/436–0708* 🕓 *Closed Wed. and Jan. No lunch.*

★ Sleepy Monk

$ | CAFÉ | In a region renowned for artisanal coffee, this small roaster brews some of the best espresso and coffee drinks in the state, and thus attracts java aficionados on caffeine pilgrimages from near and far eager to sample its certified-organic, fair-trade beans. Local, fresh pastries are stacked high and there's also a good selection of herbal and green teas. **Known for:** outstanding coffee; cozy dining room with some outdoor seats; savory and sweet baked goods. 💲 *Average main: $5* ✉ *1235 S. Hemlock St.* ☎ *503/436–2796* 🌐 *www.sleepymonkcoffee.com* 🕓 *Closed Wed. No dinner.*

Wayfarer Restaurant

$$$$ | **PACIFIC NORTHWEST** | The dazzling beach and ocean views, especially at sunset, are just part of the story at this casually elegant restaurant at the Surfsand Resort; it's also a reliable if very traditional destination for a leisurely feast of local seafood and steaks, such as panko-breaded Pacific razor clams with rémoulade, seared Chinook salmon with risotto, and the prodigious 22-ounce "tomahawk" rib-eye steak with a Pinot Noir butter. There's a nice list of Oregon wines, and breakfast—featuring delicious crab cake Benedicts and cinnamon roll French toast—is offered daily. **Known for:** great ocean views; classic Northwest seafood and steaks; hearty breakfasts. *Average main: $34* *1190 Pacific Dr.* *503/436–1108* *www.wayfarer-restaurant.com.*

Hotels

Arch Cape Inn & Retreat

$$$ | **B&B/INN** | Between the lively beach communities of Manzanita and Cannon Beach, this utterly romantic getaway—situated well away from the summer hordes—lies along some of the most gorgeous stretch of coast in the region. **Pros:** elegant, distinctive rooms; peaceful location away from the crowds; most rooms have terrific ocean views. **Cons:** 200 yards from the beach; no kids under 18 permitted; not within walking distance of town. *Rooms from: $209* *31970 E. Ocean La.* *503/436–2800* *www.archcapeinn.com* *10 rooms* *Free breakfast.*

Ecola Creek Lodge

$$ | **HOTEL** | With a quiet, shady courtyard just off the main road leading into the north side of town, this small, reasonably priced 1940s hotel offers suites and rooms with a mix of configurations, from two-bedroom units with kitchens to cozy standard rooms. **Pros:** simple and tasteful decor; rooms come in wide range of layouts; good value. **Cons:** not on the beach; slight walk from downtown shopping; some rooms are a little small. *Rooms from: $160* *208 E. 5th St.* *503/436–2776, 800/873–2749* *www.ecolacreeklodge.com* *22 rooms* *No meals.*

Ocean Lodge

$$$$ | **HOTEL** | Designed to capture the feel of a 1940s beach resort, this rustic but upscale lodge is perfect for special occasions and romantic getaways; its rooms—most with oceanfront views—feature wood beams, gas fireplaces, and balconies or decks. **Pros:** beachfront waterfront location; spacious rooms; free passes to local gym and yoga studio. **Cons:** expensive in summer; balconies are shared with neighboring rooms; about a mile from downtown. *Rooms from: $289* *2864 S. Pacific St.* *503/436–2241, 888/777–4047* *www.theoceanlodge.com* *45 rooms* *Free breakfast.*

★ Stephanie Inn

$$$$ | **RESORT** | One of the coastline's most beautiful views is paired with one of its most splendid hotels, where the focus is firmly on romance, superior service, and luxurious rooms. **Pros:** incredibly plush accommodations; on a gorgeous stretch of beach; fabulous on-site restaurant and spa. **Cons:** among the highest rates of any hotel in the state; not for families with younger children; about a mile from downtown. *Rooms from: $469* *2740 S. Pacific St.* *503/436–2221, 855/977–2444* *www.stephanieinn.com* *41 rooms* *Free breakfast.*

Tolovana Inn

$ | **HOTEL** | **FAMILY** | Set on the beach at the quieter southern end of town, the large, rambling Tolovana Inn is one of the better-priced options in this tony seaside community, especially considering that most rooms enjoy partial or full views of the Pacific. **Pros:** panoramic beach views; gym, day spa, pool, and other resort amenities; some units have kitchens.

Cons: a 10-minute drive from downtown; some rooms are relatively small; economy rooms have no water view. *Rooms from: $139* ✉ *3400 S. Hemlock St.* ☎ *503/436–2211, 800/333–8890* 🌐 *www.tolovanainn.com* *175 rooms* *No meals.*

Nightlife

★ Cannon Beach Hardware and Public House

BARS/PUBS | At this oddly endearing gastropub a block from the beach, the view from your table may be of bins filled with assorted lamb knobs or pliers—this is an actual hardware store (with a good supply of gifts, to boot). To drink you'll find a nice list of regional craft brews on tap, plus eclectic cocktails and Northwest wines, and good burgers, sandwiches, seafood apps, and other tavern fare are available. ✉ *1235 S. Hemlock St.* ☎ *503/436–4086* 🌐 *www.cannonbeachhardware.com.*

Shopping

Cannon Beach Art Galleries

ART GALLERIES | The numerous art galleries that line Cannon Beach's Hemlock Street are an essential part of the town's spirit and beauty. A group of about a dozen galleries featuring beautifully innovative works in ceramic, bronze, photography, painting, and other mediums have collaborated to form the Cannon Beach Gallery Group. You'll find information about exhibits and special events on the website. ✉ *Hemlock St.* 🌐 *www.cbgallerygroup.com.*

Manzanita

15 miles south of Cannon Beach.

Manzanita is a secluded and gorgeously situated seaside community with only around 650 full-time residents—but a fast-growing popularity among weekenders from the Willamette Valley translates to one of the largest selections of vacation rentals along the northern Oregon Coast. The village is on a sandy peninsula, peppered with tufts of grass, on the northwestern side of Nehalem Bay, a noted windsurfing destination. It's a fairly laid-back town, but its growing crop of notable restaurants and boutiques has given it an increasingly fashionable reputation, and nature lovers appreciate its proximity to beautiful Oswald West State Park.

GETTING HERE AND AROUND

Tiny Manzanita is an easy and picturesque 20-minute drive south of Cannon Beach on coastal U.S. 101; from Portland, it takes just less than two hours to get here.

Beaches

Manzanita Beach and Nehalem Bay State Park

BEACHES | **FAMILY** | The long stretch of white sand that separates the Pacific Ocean from the town of Manzanita is as loved a stretch of coastline as the next, its north side reaching into the shadows of Neahkanie Mountain, right where the mountain puts its foot in the ocean (the mountain itself, which makes for a great hike, lies within Oswald West State Park). The beach is frequented by vacationers, day-trippers, kite flyers, and dogs on its north end, but it extends a breezy 7 miles to the tip of Nehalem Bay State Park, which is accessible on foot over sand or by car along the road (the auto entrance is off Gary Street at Sandpiper Lane). At the south end of the park's parking lot, a dirt horse trail leads all the way to a peninsula's tip, a flat walk behind grassy dunes—you can book horseback excursions from Oregon Beach Rides, which has a stable inside the park. Cross to the right for a secluded patch of windy sand on the ocean, or to the left for a quiet, sunny place in the sun on Nehalem Bay, out of the wind. **Amenities:** toilets. **Best**

for: sunset; walking. ✉ *Foot of Laneda Ave.* ☎ *503/368–5154* 🌐 *www.oregonstateparks.org* 🎫 *Nehalem Bay State Park day use $5 per vehicle.*

Restaurants

Bread and Ocean Bakery

$$ | **AMERICAN** | This small bakery with a simple, cheerful dining room and several more tables on the sunny patio is hugely popular for breakfast and lunch—and dinners some evenings—with the many folks who rent cottages in the friendly beach town. Start the morning with a slice of quiche or breakfast frittata; tuck into a hefty deli sandwich at lunch, and consider the Dungeness crab cakes or slow-cooked pot roast in the evening. **Known for:** picnic lunches (great for the beach or a hike); gourmet groceries, wines, and beers to go or eat in; huge and chewy cinnamon rolls. [$] *Average main: $18* ✉ *154 Laneda Ave.* ☎ *503/368–5823* 🌐 *www.breadandocean.com* ⏲ *Closed Mon. and Tues. No dinner Sun.–Wed.*

★ **Salmonberry Saloon**

$$ | **MODERN AMERICAN** | With a sweeping wooden deck to watch the magnificent sunsets over Nehalem Bay and Manzanita's sand dunes, this lively saloon in tiny, historic Wheeler could probably get away with serving merely ordinary food. But the owners offer a remarkably ambitious beverage program (especially when it comes to the wine selection) and exceptional seafood-focused tavern fare, such as *brodetto* (Italian fish stew) of local crabs, shrimp, and clams with shaved fennel and toast, and rockfish–melted cheddar sandwiches. **Known for:** dazzling sunset views; nicely curated list of often hard-to-find wines; creative local seafood fare. [$] *Average main: $20* ✉ *380 Marine Dr., Wheeler* ☎ *503/714–1423* 🌐 *www.salmonberrysaloon.com* ⏲ *Closed Tues.*

Yolk

$ | **MODERN AMERICAN** | The locally sourced, all-day breakfasts at this hip café on Manzanita's main drag include hefty platters of buttery biscuits with fennel sausage–mushroom gravy and lemon-ricotta pancakes with marionberries. For lunch, try the lamb burger with feta and a dill-mint aioli. **Known for:** all-day breakfast; extensive menu; huge portions. [$] *Average main: $14* ✉ *503 Laneda Ave.* ☎ *503/368–9655* ⏲ *Closed Tues. and Wed. No dinner.*

Hotels

Coast Cabins

$$$ | **RENTAL** | The options at this tranquil little compound within walking distance of the beach and Manzanita's lively shopping-dining strip include six luxury cabins and three loft-style contemporary condos, all of them appointed with carefully chosen, stylish contemporary furnishings. **Pros:** chicly appointed, spacious accommodations; plenty of cushy amenities; there's a nice little gym. **Cons:** not on the beach; not all units have hot tubs; pricey. [$] *Rooms from: $235* ✉ *635 Laneda Ave.* ☎ *503/368–7113* 🌐 *www.coastcabins.com* 🛏 *10 units* 🍽 *No meals.*

★ **Inn at Manzanita**

$$ | **B&B/INN** | **FAMILY** | Shore pines around this 1987 Scandinavian structure give upper-floor patios a tree-house feel, and it's just half a block from the beach. **Pros:** tranquil setting with a Japanese garden atmosphere; very close to the beach and downtown shops; several rooms good for families. **Cons:** two-night minimum stay on weekends; can book up fast in summer; no water view from some rooms. [$] *Rooms from: $179* ✉ *67 Laneda Ave.* ☎ *503/368–6754* 🌐 *www.innatmanzanita.com* 🛏 *13 rooms* 🍽 *No meals.*

Old Wheeler Hotel

$ | **B&B/INN** | One of the better values along this section of the Oregon Coast, this small and simple 1920s hotel offers eight clean, economical rooms in the center of Wheeler, a tiny historic village on the Nehalem River just a 10-minute drive south of Manzanita. **Pros:** antiques-filled rooms lend a charming atmosphere; some rooms overlook Nehalem Bay; wallet-friendly rates. **Cons:** not many businesses within walking distance; not on the beach; no restaurant on-site. *Rooms from: $129 ✉ 495 U.S. 101, Wheeler ☎ 503/368–6000 🌐 www.oldwheelerhotel.com 8 rooms Free breakfast.*

Activities

RECREATIONAL AREAS

★ Oswald West State Park

PARK—SPORTS-OUTDOORS | Adventurous travelers will enjoy a sojourn at one of the best-kept secrets on the Pacific coast, at the base of Neahkahnie Mountain. Park in one of the two free lots on U.S. 101 and hike a half-mile trail to dramatic Short Sand Beach, aka "Shorty's," one of the top spots along the Oregon Coast for surfing. It's a spectacular beach with caves and tidal pools. There are several trails from the beach, all offering dazzling scenery; the relatively easy 2½-mile trail to Cape Falcon overlook joins with the Oregon Coast Trail and offers impressive views back toward Shorty's Beach. The arduous 5½-mile trail to the 1,680-foot summit of Neahkahnie Mountain (access the trailhead about 2 miles south of the parking lots marked only by a "Hikers" sign, or get there via Short Sand Beach) provides dazzling views south for many miles toward the surf, sand, and mountains fringing Manzanita and, in the distance, Tillamook. Come in December or March and you might spot pods of gray whales. ✉ *U.S. 101, Arch Cape ✣ 5 miles north of downtown Manzanita ☎ 503/368–3575 🌐 www.oregonstateparks.org Free.*

HORSEBACK RIDING

Oregon Beach Rides

HORSEBACK RIDING | **FAMILY** | Saddle up for horseback rides at Nehalem Bay State Park, available Memorial Day through Labor Day weekends. Guides take you on a journey along the beach in Manzanita, and reserved rides can last from one to several hours. There's even a romantic sunset trot. It's appropriate for ages six and up. ✉ *Nehalem Bay State Park, 34600 Gary St., Nehalem ☎ 971/237–6653 🌐 www.oregonbeachrides.com Reservations essential.*

Tillamook

27 miles south of Manzanita.

More than 100 inches of annual rainfall and the confluence of three rivers contribute to the lush green pastures around Tillamook, probably best known for its thriving dairy industry and cheese factory, and an increasingly noteworthy locavore-driven culinary scene that extends into the nearby villages of Oceanside, Netarts, and Pacific City—for tips on where to explore in the region, visit the Tillamook Coast Visitors Association's North Coast Food Trail website (🌐 *www.northcoastfoodtrail.com*). The town itself lies several miles inland from the ocean and doesn't offer much in the way of beachy diversions, but it is the best jumping-off point for driving the dramatic Three Capes Loop, which passes over Cape Meares, Cape Lookout, and Cape Kiwanda and offers spectacular views of the ocean and coastline. The small village of Oceanside, just north of Cape Lookout, has several cute restaurants and shops and a lovely beachfront.

GETTING HERE AND AROUND

Tillamook is a 90-minute drive from Portland on U.S. 26 to Highway 6. It's a winding, pretty, 45-minute drive south of Cannon Beach on U.S. 101, and a one-hour drive north of Lincoln City along the same coastal highway.

VISITOR INFORMATION

VISITOR INFORMATION Tillamook Coast Visitors Association. ✉ *4506 3rd St.* ☎ *503/842–2672* 🌐 *www.tillamookcoast.com.*

Sights

★ Cape Lookout State Park

BEACH—SIGHT | Located about 8 miles south of the beach town Netarts, this pristine and diverse park includes a moderately easy (though often muddy) 2-mile trail—marked on the highway as "wildlife viewing area"—that leads through giant spruces, western red cedars, and hemlocks, and ends with views of Cascade Head to the south and Cape Meares to the north. Wildflowers, more than 150 species of birds, and occasional whales throughout the summer months make this trail a favorite with nature lovers. The section of the park just north of the trail comprises a long, curving stretch of beach with picnic areas and campsites. ✉ *Cape Lookout Rd. at Netarts Bay Rd.* ☎ *503/842–4981* 🌐 *www.oregonstateparks.org* 🎫 *Day-use parking $5.*

Cape Meares State Scenic Viewpoint

LIGHTHOUSE | On the northern tip of the Three Capes Loop, this small but spectacular park and vista is the site of the restored **Cape Meares Lighthouse,** built in 1890 and open to the public May through September. It provides a sweeping view from a 200-foot-tall cliff to the caves and sea lion rookery on the rocks below, and this is a great perch for seeing whales during their migrations. A many-trunked Sitka spruce known as the Octopus Tree grows near the lighthouse parking lot. ✉ *3500 Cape Meares Loop, Oceanside* ☎ *503/842–3182* 🌐 *www.oregonstateparks.org* 🎫 *Free.*

★ Tillamook Cheese Creamery

FACTORY | **FAMILY** | Cheese and ice cream lovers of all ages have long made a stop by the largest cheese-making plant on the West Coast, as much to enjoy free samples and snack on delicious ice cream (try the marionberry, if you're stumped about what to order). In 2018 Tillamook completely revamped and expanded its visitor facilities. You can still learn about cheese making through informative signs and by watching the process from a glassed-in mezzanine, but the gift shop has been expanded into an impressive gourmet market that stocks Tillamook's many varieties of cheddar, produced in part with milk from thousands of local Holstein and brown Swiss cows, as well as chocolates, charcuterie, and all sorts of other mostly Oregon-made snacks and beverages, including wine and craft beer. Additionally, the ice cream café has been reimagined as a huge food hall with soaring windows, plenty of seating, and a full kitchen serving Tillamook cheeseburgers, pizzas, mac and cheese, and the like. ✉ *4175 U.S. 101 N* ☎ *503/815–1300, 800/542–7290* 🌐 *www.tillamook.com.*

Tillamook Naval Air Station Museum

MUSEUM | **FAMILY** | In the world's largest wooden structure, a former blimp hangar south of town displays a fine collection of vintage aircraft from World War II, including a vast trove of artifacts and memorabilia, including war uniforms, photos, and remains from the Hindenburg. The 20-story-high building is big enough to hold half a dozen football fields. ✉ *6030 Hangar Rd.* ☎ *503/842–1130* 🌐 *www.tillamookair.com* 🎫 *$10.50* ⏲ *Closed Mon. and Tues.*

Beaches

Oceanside Beach State Recreation Site

BEACHES | **FAMILY** | This relatively small, sandy cove is a great stop at the midpoint of the cape's loop. It's especially popular with beachcombers in summer for both its shallow, gentle surf and the low-tide bowls and tide pools that make it a great play beach for kids. When the water recedes, it also uncovers a tunnel through the north rock face ensconcing the beach, allowing passage to a second, rocky cove. There are a few fun, casual spots for ice cream and light bites steps from the beach. Parking in summer, however, is tough. The small lot fills quickly, and a walk through the hilly side streets is sometimes required. **Amenities:** none. **Best for:** walking; partiers. ✉ *Pacific Ave. at Rosenberg Loop, Oceanside* ☎ *503/842–3182* 🌐 *www.oregonstateparks.org.*

Restaurants

Hidden Acres Greenhouse & Café

$ | **AMERICAN** | Set along a stretch of U.S. 101 that courses south of downtown Tillamook, a bit inland and through a lush, agrarian valley, this aptly named oasis of plants, garden gifts, fountains, and art is a delightful spot for a daytime meal that's usually refreshingly far from beach crowds. Count on made-to-order tuna, club, turkey-cranberry, and other sandwiches and wraps (everything can be served on a bed of local greens in place of bread), as well as granola parfait, avocado toast, and Tillamook cheese egg sandwiches at breakfast. **Known for:** charming greenhouse-nursery setting; scones, pies, and other sweets; coffee drinks and smoothies. $ *Average main: $10* ✉ *6760 S Prairie Rd.* ☎ *503/842–1197* ⊗ *Closed Sun. No dinner.*

Roseanna's Cafe

$$ | **SEAFOOD** | In a rustic 1915 building on the beach, this café brightened with candlelight and fresh flowers sits opposite Three Arch Rock, a favorite resting spot for sea lions and puffins. The menu includes snapper, halibut, and salmon prepared with several sauce options, baked oysters, and Gorgonzola seafood pasta, and the meal's not complete without marionberry cobbler. **Known for:** marionberry cobbler; baked Washington oysters; lovely water views. $ *Average main: $22* ✉ *1490 Pacific Ave., Oceanside* ☎ *503/842–7351* 🌐 *www.roseannascafe.com* ⊗ *Closed Tues. and Wed. and most of Dec.*

Shopping

Jacobsen Salt Co

FOOD/CANDY | This little wood-frame contemporary shop on Netarts Bay adjoins the saltworks of this company that's rapidly becoming internationally renowned for pure and artisanally infused sea salts (with flavors like black garlic, vanilla bean, and ghost chili). You can also purchase the company's honey, salted caramels, peppercorns, and other goodies. ✉ *9820 Whiskey Creek Rd.* ☎ *503/946–9573* 🌐 *www.jacobsensalt.com.*

Activities

The **Three Capes Loop,** an enchanting 35-mile byway off U.S. 101, winds along the coast between Tillamook and Pacific City, passing three distinctive headlands—Cape Meares, Cape Lookout, and Cape Kiwanda. Bayocean Road heading west from Tillamook passes what was the thriving resort town of Bayocean, which washed into the sea more than 50 years ago. A road still crosses the levee to Bayocean, and along the beach on the other side you can find the remnants of an old hotel to the north. The panoramic views from the north end of the peninsula are worth the walk. A warm and windless road returns hikers on the bay side.

Pacific City

24 miles south of Tillamook.

There's a lot to like about Pacific City, not the least of which is that it's 3 miles off Oregon's busy coastal highway, U.S. 101. That means there's usually no backup at the town's only traffic light—a blinking-red, four-way stop in the center of town. There's just the quiet, happy atmosphere of a town whose 1,000-or-so residents live in the midst of extraordinary beauty. It's home to one of the region's most celebrated contemporary resorts, Headlands Coastal Lodge & Spa, along with some wonderful opportunities for recreation. The beach at Pacific City is one of the few places in the state where fishing dories (flat-bottom boats with high, flaring sides) are launched directly into the surf instead of from harbors or docks.

GETTING HERE AND AROUND

Between Tillamook and Lincoln City, the unincorporated village of Pacific City is just off U.S. 101 on the south end of the beautiful Three Capes Loop. It is a two-hour drive from Portland on U.S. 26 to Highway 6, or a 75-minute drive from Salem via Highway 22.

ESSENTIALS

VISITOR INFORMATION Pacific City-Nestucca Valley Chamber of Commerce. ☎ *503/392–4340, 888/549–2632* 🌐 *www.pcnvchamber.org.*

Sights

★ Bob Straub State Park

PARK—SPORTS-OUTDOORS | This 484-acre expanse of coastal wilderness includes a wind-swept walk along the flat white-sand beach that leads to the mouth of the Nestucca River, one of the best fishing rivers on the North Coast. The beach along the Pacific is frequently windy, but it's separated from the stiller, warmer side of the peninsula by high dunes. Multiple trails cross the dunes into a forest that leads to small beaches on the Nestucca. Relax here with a book, and easily find stillness and sunshine. It's possible to skip the Pacific stroll all together, and find trails to the Nestucca straight from the parking lot, but it's hard to resist the views from the top of the dunes. If you choose the ocean side, pitch your beach camp in the dunes, not the flat sand, and you'll find respite from the wind. ✉ *End of Sunset Dr.* ☎ *503/842–3182* 🌐 *www.oregonstateparks.org.*

Cape Kiwanda State Natural Area

BEACH—SIGHT | Huge waves pound the jagged sandstone cliffs and caves here, and the much-photographed, 327-foot-high **Haystack Rock** (not to be confused with the 235-foot-tall rock of the same name up in Cannon Beach) juts out of the Pacific Ocean to the south. Surfers ride some of the longest waves on the coast, hang gliders soar above the shore, and beachcombers explore tidal pools and massive sand dunes, and take in unparalleled ocean views. ✉ *Cape Kiwanda Dr.* ☎ *503/842–3182, 800/551–6949* 🌐 *www.oregonstateparks.org.*

Beaches

★ Cape Kiwanda State Natural Area and Pacific City Beach

BEACHES | The town's public beach adjoins Cape Kiwanda State Natural Area, the southernmost section of famously picturesque Three Capes Loop, and extends south to Bob Straub State Park. Adjacent to Cape Kiwanda's massive 240-foot-tall dune, it's a fun place for kids to scamper to its summit just for the thrill of sliding back down again. Hikers also get a thrill from the top, where the view opens on a tiny cove and tide pools below, and the walk down is infinitely easier than the climb. The beach is also popular with tailgaters—it's one of the few places on the Oregon Coast where it's legal to park your vehicle on the sand. Other parking is available off Cape Kiwanda Drive, near the Pelican Pub. For quieter outings, try the Bob Straub. **Amenities:** none. **Best for:** partiers; walking. ✉ *Cape Kiwanda Dr.* ☎ *503/842–3182* 🌐 *www.oregonstateparks.org.*

Restaurants

Grateful Bread Bakery

$ | **AMERICAN** | **FAMILY** | This airy and bright café uses the cod caught by the local dories for its fish sandwiches, and everything served during its popular breakfasts and lunches is made fresh and from scratch, including delicious breads, biscuits, and pastries. Favorite dishes include gingerbread pancakes and *gallo pinto* (a Costa Rican plate of black beans, scrambled eggs, homemade salsa, and corn tortillas) at breakfast, and locally caught albacore tuna melts and bacon-cheddar burgers at lunch. **Known for:** made-from-scratch pastries; filling breakfasts of smoked-salmon scrambles and gingerbread pancakes; local tuna and cod sandwiches. *Average main: $13* *34805 Brooten Rd.* *503/965–7337* *www.gratefulbreadbakery.com* *Closed Tues. and Wed. No dinner.*

★ **Meridian Restaurant & Bar**

$$$$ | **MODERN AMERICAN** | With its soaring windows, cathedral ceiling, earthy tones, and vibrant timber beams and flooring, this stylish and airy farm-to-table restaurant has become one of the coast's top destinations for a romantic meal—or even just a memorable breakfast or happy hour overlooking the Pacific. The kitchen sources as much as possible from local farms and seafood purveyors with its seasonal menu, which might feature char-grilled, wine-braised octopus with basil-watercress salsa verde, or petrale sole topped with a light citrus beurre blanc, capers, and local pink shrimp. **Known for:** shareable charcuterie, veggie, and cheese plates; huge windows with water and beach views; excellent wine list and craft cocktails. *Average main: $31* *Headlands Coastal Lodge, 33000 Cape Kiwanda Dr.* *503/483–3000* *www.headlandslodge.com.*

Pelican Pub & Brewery

$$ | **AMERICAN** | **FAMILY** | This craft beer lover's favorite, which overlooks the ocean by Haystack Rock, has garnered considerable kudos for its beers, including the Kiwanda Cream Ale and deep, rich Tsunami Stout, while the pub turns out reliably good comfort fare, such as flatbread pizzas, burgers, and cioppino. Many dishes are infused with homemade beverages, such as pale-malt-crusted salmon and the root beer float. **Known for:** occasional brewers' dinner with international food and house beer pairings; good children's menu; root beer floats. *Average main: $19* *33180 Cape Kiwanda Dr.* *503/965–7007* *www.pelicanbrewing.com.*

Hotels

★ **Headlands Coastal Lodge & Spa**

$$$$ | **RESORT** | Newly built in 2018 at the foot of Cape Kiwanda dunes and overlooking the bustling beachfront of Pacific City, this stylish, casually posh boutique resort offers an impressive selection of wellness pursuits, including yoga classes, surfing lessons, Peloton indoor exercise bikes, and a full slate of soothing spa treatments. **Pros:** first-rate spa and restaurant on-site; fabulous beachfront location; hip, contemporary vibe and aesthetic. **Cons:** quite pricey in summer; busy, sometimes noisy, location; glass-walled bathrooms are cool but don't allow a lot of privacy. *Rooms from: $425* *33000 Cape Kiwanda Dr.* *503/483–3000* *www.headlandslodge.com* *51 rooms* *No meals.*

Inn at Cape Kiwanda

$$$ | **HOTEL** | Most of the 35 upscale, fireplace-warmed rooms at this handsome boutique hotel have a view across the street of Pacific City's beach and Haystack Rock in the distance. **Pros:** great views; light and contemporary rooms; terrific restaurants nearby. **Cons:** water views blocked in some rooms by the new hotel across the street; can be a somewhat noisy location in summer; there's a big parking lot between hotel and beach. *Rooms from: $244*

⊠ *33105 Cape Kiwanda Dr.* ☎ *888/965–7001, 503/965–7001* ⊕ *www.innatcapekiwanda.com* *35 rooms* *No meals.*

Lincoln City

16 miles south of Pacific City, 90 miles southwest of Portland.

Lincoln City is an unpretentious, highly social destination whose diversions appeal to families and couples who enjoy hobnobbing and playing on the beach, poking their fingers in tide pools, and trying to harness wind-bucking kites. Once a series of small villages, Lincoln City incorporated into one sprawling municipality without a center in 1965. For its legions of fans, the endless tourist amenities make up for a lack of a small-coastal-town charm. Clustered like barnacles on offshore reefs are fast-food restaurants, gift shops, supermarkets, candy stores, antiques markets, dozens of motels and hotels, a factory-outlet mall, and a busy casino. Lincoln City is the most popular destination city on the Oregon Coast, but its only real geographic claim to fame is the 445-foot-long D River, stretching from its source in Devil's Lake to the Pacific; *Guinness World Records* lists the D as the world's shortest river.

Just south of Lincoln City, quieter and less-developed Gleneden Beach is a small vacation town known primarily for the famed Salishan Resort, which is perched high above placid Siletz Bay.

GETTING HERE AND AROUND

Lincoln City is a 2-hour drive from Portland on Highway 99W and Highway 18, and a 2½-hour drive south of Astoria along coastal U.S. 101.

ESSENTIALS

VISITOR INFORMATION Lincoln City Visitors & Convention Bureau. ⊠ *801 S.W. U.S. 101, Suite 401* ☎ *541/996–1274* ⊕ *www.oregoncoast.org.*

Sights

★ Cascade Head Preserve

HIKING/WALKING | At this pristine, slightly off-the-beaten-path property managed by the Nature Conservancy, a dense, green trail winds through a rain forest where 100-inch annual rainfalls nourish 250-year-old Sitka spruces, mosses, and ferns. Emerging from the forest, hikers come upon grassy and treeless Cascade Head, an undulating maritime prairie. There are magnificent views down to the Salmon River and east to the Coast Range. Continuing along the headland, black-tailed deer often graze and turkey vultures soar in the sometimes strong winds. It's a somewhat steep and strenuous but tremendously rewarding hike—allow at least three hours to make the full nearly 7-mile round-trip hike, although you can make it out to the beginning of the headland and back in an hour. ⊠ *Savage Rd. at N 3 Rocks Rd., Otis* ✣ *Off U.S. 101 between Lincoln City and Pacific City* ⊕ *www.nature.org* *Free* ⏲ *Upper trail closed Jan.–mid-July.*

Restaurants

★ Blackfish Café

$$$ | PACIFIC NORTHWEST | This dapper but unpretentious bistro is known for simple-but-succulent dishes that blend fresh ingredients from local fishermen and gardeners, such as skillet-roasted Chinook salmon basted with fennel-lime butter, Oregon blue-cheese potatoes, and center-cut New York steak au jus with red wine and porcini butter. The Blackfish Ding Dong dessert, with mixed-berry sauce and whipped cream, is the best way to finish a meal. **Known for:** Chinook salmon; Ding Dong dessert; fresh ingredients. [$] *Average main: $28* ⊠ *2733 N.W. U.S. 101* ☎ *541/996–1007* ⊕ *www.blackfishcafe.com* ⏲ *Closed Mon. and Tues.*

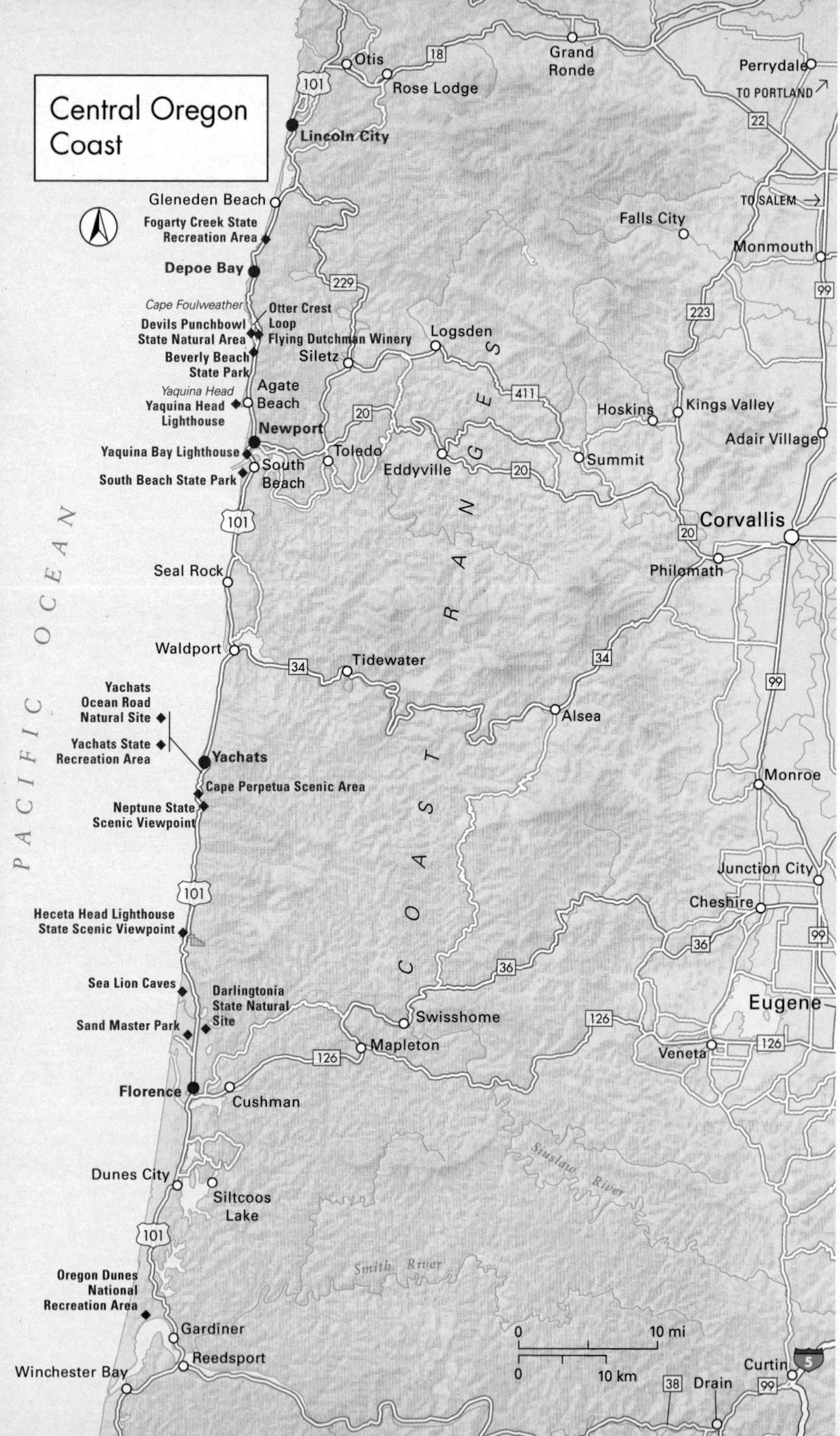

Central Oregon Coast
PACIFIC OCEAN
COAST RANGES
Otis
Rose Lodge
Grand Ronde
Perrydale
TO PORTLAND
Lincoln City
Gleneden Beach
Fogarty Creek State Recreation Area
Depoe Bay
Cape Foulweather
Otter Crest Loop
Devils Punchbowl State Natural Area
Flying Dutchman Winery
Beverly Beach State Park
Logsden
Siletz
Yaquina Head
Yaquina Head Lighthouse
Agate Beach
Newport
Yaquina Bay Lighthouse
South Beach
South Beach State Park
Toledo
Eddyville
Summit
Hoskins
Kings Valley
Adair Village
Falls City
Monmouth
TO SALEM
Corvallis
Philomath
Seal Rock
Waldport
Tidewater
Alsea
Yachats Ocean Road Natural Site
Yachats State Recreation Area
Yachats
Cape Perpetua Scenic Area
Neptune State Scenic Viewpoint
Monroe
Junction City
Cheshire
Heceta Head Lighthouse State Scenic Viewpoint
Sea Lion Caves
Darlingtonia State Natural Site
Sand Master Park
Swisshome
Mapleton
Eugene
Veneta
Florence
Cushman
Siuslaw River
Dunes City
Siltcoos Lake
Smith River
Oregon Dunes National Recreation Area
Gardiner
Reedsport
Winchester Bay
Drain
Curtin
0
10 mi
0
10 km
101
18
22
99
229
223
411
20
34
36
126
38
5

Klementine's Kitchen
$$ | **MODERN AMERICAN** | Set in an unassuming building along busy U.S. 101 a little north of the Siletz River, this cheerful restaurant with a gas fireplace is a tribute to the owners' Cajun roots, which influence but don't completely define the menu. You'll find authentic versions of Louisiana classics like red beans and rice and crab-and-shrimp gumbo, but other specialties more reflect the bounty of fresh Northwest ingredients—note the blueberry-and-beet salad with chèvre. **Known for:** several dishes featuring Dungeness crab, shrimp, and catfish; warmly welcoming service; butterscotch pudding with a dusting of pink rock salt. *Average main: $17 4660 S.E. U.S. 101 541/418–5371 www.klementineskitchen.com Closed Mon. and Tues. No lunch.*

Side Door Café
$$$ | **PACIFIC NORTHWEST** | This dining room, set in an old brick and tile factory with a high ceiling, exposed beams, a fireplace, and many windows, shares its space with Eden Hall performance venue. The menu changes often, but favorites that tend to appear regularly include fire-roasted rack of lamb with vegetable risotto and Northwest bouillabaisse with a lemongrass-saffron-tomato broth. **Known for:** funky and historic industrial setting; seafood-intensive seasonal cuisine; creative quesadillas (bay shrimp; chicken, pear, Gorgonzola) at lunch. *Average main: $24 6675 Gleneden Beach Loop Rd., Gleneden Beach 541/764–3825 www.sidedoorcafe.com Closed Sun. and Mon.*

Hotels

★ Coho Oceanfront Lodge
$$ | **HOTEL** | **FAMILY** | Set on a romantic cliff, the clean and contemporary Coho is a perfect hybrid of family-friendly lodging and a quiet, intimate hideaway for couples—14 of the 65 suites and rooms are relegated to adults, while family-oriented suites have Wii or PS3 game systems, and all have complimentary snack baskets and French press coffeemakers. **Pros:** seating and fire pits overlooking the ocean; family-friendly; DVD and games available in lobby to take to your room. **Cons:** no restaurant; bathrooms can be on the small side; not ideal if seeking a quiet, secluded getaway. *Rooms from: $165 1635 N.W. Harbor Ave. 541/994–3684, 800/848–7006 www.thecoholodge.com 65 rooms Free breakfast.*

Historic Anchor Inn
$ | **B&B/INN** | This quirky bungalow might not be for everyone, but for those who appreciate a warm, spirited inn with a decidedly inventive and whimsical touch, this is a remarkable find. **Pros:** a memorable, truly unique property; central location; on-site pub. **Cons:** not on the beach; very quirky and rustic; on a busy road. *Rooms from: $119 4417 S.W. U.S. 101 541/996–3810 www.historicanchorinn.com 19 rooms Free breakfast.*

Inn at Spanish Head
$$$ | **RESORT** | Driving up to this midcentury condo hotel, you'd think it might be a fairly intimate place, but on further investigation you'll see that the property takes up the entire side of a bluff like a huge staircase. **Pros:** sweeping views of the ocean through floor-to-ceiling windows; good restaurant; easy beach access via elevator. **Cons:** decor varies greatly from room to room; not within walking distance of many restaurants or shops; can get pricey on summer weekends. *Rooms from: $239 4009 S.E. U.S. 101 541/996–2161, 800/452–8127 www.spanishhead.com 120 units No meals.*

★ Salishan Lodge and Golf Resort
$$$ | **RESORT** | Secluded and refined, this upscale resort designed in the 1960s by renowned architect John Gray is set in a hillside forest preserve near Siletz Bay and offers spacious, art-filled

rooms with wood-burning fireplaces, balconies, and large whirlpool tubs. **Pros:** elegantly designed rooms and public spaces; secluded, beautiful natural setting; outstanding spa, golf course, and restaurants. **Cons:** ocean views are few; not within walking distance of town; some rooms receive noise from U.S. 101. *Rooms from: $239* *7760 N. U.S. 101, Gleneden Beach* *541/764–3600, 800/452–2300* *www.salishan.com* *205 rooms* *No meals.*

Nightlife

Black Squid Beer House

BREWPUBS/BEER GARDENS | Bring your dog and grab a seat on the plant-filled brick patio, or grab a seat (and feel free to bring your own food) in the homey taproom. This highly popular bottle shop and drinkery offers a well-chosen selection of ales on tap from both established and cult-favorite microbreweries, plus Northwest wines and cider. There's often live music, too. *3001 U.S. 101* *541/614–0733* *www.blacksquidbeerhouse.com.*

Chinook Winds Casino Resort

CASINOS | Oregon's only beachfront casino resort has a great variety of slot machines, blackjack, poker, keno, and off-track betting, plus big-name entertainers performing in the showroom. *1777 N.W. 44th St.* *541/996–5825* *www.chinookwindscasino.com.*

Shopping

★ Alder House Glassblowing

CRAFTS | The imaginative crafts folk at this studio turn molten glass into vases and bowls, which are available for sale. It is the oldest glass-blowing studio in the state. It's closed November–April. *611 Immonen Rd.* *541/996–2483* *www.alderhouse.com.*

Culinary Center

FOOD/CANDY | The talented chefs here offer everything from small, hands-on classes to full-blown cooking demonstrations for dozens. Frequent themes include baking pizza, making sushi, and even dim sum. *801 S.W. U.S. 101, Suite 401* *541/557–1125* *www.oregoncoast.org/culinary.*

Lincoln City Glass Center

CERAMICS/GLASSWARE | Blow a glass float or make a glorious glass starfish, heart, or fluted bowl of your own design (prices start at $65 for a glass float). The studio's expert artisans will guide you every step of the way. It's a fun, memorable keepsake of the coast. *4821 S.W. U.S. 101* *541/996–2569* *www.lincolncityglasscenter.com.*

Activities

GOLF

Salishan Golf Resort

GOLF | With a layout designed by Peter Jacobsen, this par-71 course is a year-round treat for hackers and aficionados alike. The front nine holes are surrounded by a forest of old-growth timber, while the back nine holes provide old-school, links-style play. There's an expansive pro shop and a great bar and grill, too. High-season greens fees are $99–$119. *7760 N. U.S. 101, Gleneden Beach* *541/452–2300* *www.salishan.com.*

Depoe Bay

12 miles south of Lincoln City.

This small but lively town founded in the 1920s bills itself the whale-watching capital of the world. With a narrow channel and deep water, its tiny harbor is also one of the most protected on the coast (and is said to be the nation's smallest navigable harbor).

GETTING HERE AND AROUND

Depoe Bay lies right between Newport and Lincoln City along U.S. 101—it's a 20-minute drive to either town.

ESSENTIALS

VISITOR INFORMATION Depoe Bay Chamber of Commerce. ✉ *223 S.W. U.S. 101, Suite B* ☎ *541/765–2889, 877/485–8348* 🌐 *www.depoebaychamber.org.*

Sights

Fogarty Creek State Recreation Area
NATIONAL/STATE PARK | Bird-watching and viewing the tidal pools are the key draws here, but hiking and picnicking are also popular at this park along U.S. 101. Wooden footbridges wind through the dense forest and tall cliffs rise above the beach. ✉ *U.S. 101* ✣ *3 miles north of Depoe Bay* ☎ *541/265–4560* 🌐 *www.oregonstateparks.org* 🎫 *Free.*

Whale, Sealife and Shark Museum
MUSEUM | FAMILY | This small but excellent museum on Depoe Bay's tiny harbor is the creation of experienced marine biologist Carrie Newell, who also operates the excellent Whale Research EcoExcursions tour company from the premises. Inside you'll find fascinating exhibits on whales, of course, but also sea lions, sea otters, seals, migratory birds, and the abundance of creatures that inhabit the Oregon Coast's tidal pools. Cut-out murals on the building's exterior depict several "resident" gray whales who spend time in Depoe Bay's waters each summer. The museum also runs a cute little café next door, Whale Bite, that's a fun stop for breakfast or lunch. ✉ *234 S.E. U.S. 101* ☎ *541/912–6734* 🌐 *www.oregonwhales.com* 🎫 *$5.*

The Whale Watching Center
INFO CENTER | FAMILY | Here in the most famous whale-watching town in Oregon, this helpful little information center perched on a oceanfront bluff in the heart of town is a valuable resource, whether you're looking for tips on the latest sightings during the peak winter and spring migratory seasons or you simply want to learn about these amazing creatures. The center is staffed with state park naturalists who regularly give talks and can answer your questions, and there's an observation deck that offers fantastic views—you might see gray, humpback, and orcas along with a wide variety of seabirds and other sea mammals. ✉ *119 U.S. 101* ☎ *541/765–3304* 🌐 *www.oregonstateparks.org.*

Restaurants

★ Restaurant Beck
$$$ | PACIFIC NORTHWEST | Immensely gifted chef-owner Justin Wills presents a short but memorable menu of creatively prepared, modern, Pacific Northwest cuisine each night in this romantic, contemporary dining room at the Whale Cove Inn. The menu changes regularly, with chef Wills sourcing largely from local farms, ranches, and fisheries, but you might start with vanilla-cured foie gras or pork belly with caramelized-miso ice cream, followed by Wagyu beef coulotte with parsnip puree, mizuna, chive oil, parsley root, and citrus. **Known for:** panoramic views of Whale Cove; exceptional desserts; one of the best wine lists on the coast. 💲 *Average main: $29* ✉ *Whale Cove Inn, 2345 U.S. 101* ☎ *541/765–3220* 🌐 *www.restaurantbeck.com* ⏲ *No lunch.*

Tidal Raves Seafood Grill
$$$ | SEAFOOD | Serving consistently well-prepared modern seafood fare, Tidal Raves uses local and sustainable fish and shellfish in preparations inspired by places far and near. A few steaks and vegetarian dishes round out the lengthy menu, which also includes such local classics as Dungeness crab cakes, panko-crusted razor clams, and rockfish and shrimp green curry with steamed peanut rice, and the dapper bi-level dining room has tall windows overlooking the ocean. **Known for:** local Dungeness crab cakes; ocean views; notable cocktail and wine selection. 💲 *Average main: $25* ✉ *279 U.S. 101* ☎ *541/765–2995* 🌐 *www.tidalraves.com.*

En Route

Five miles south of Depoe Bay off U.S. 101 (watch for signs), the **Otter Crest Loop**, another scenic byway, winds along the cliff tops. Only parts of the loop are open to motor vehicles, but you can drive to points midway from either end and turn around. The full loop is open to bikes and hiking. British explorer Captain James Cook named the 500-foot-high **Cape Foulweather**, at the south end of the loop, on a blustery March day in 1778—a small visitor center and gift shop at this site affords mesmerizing views and opportunities to spot whales and other marine life. Backward-leaning shore pines lend mute witness to the 100-mph winds that still strafe this exposed spot. At the viewing point at the **Devil's Punchbowl**, 1 mile south of Cape Foulweather, you can peer down into a collapsed sandstone sea cave carved out by the powerful waters of the Pacific. About 100 feet to the north in the rocky tidal pools of the beach known as **Marine Gardens**, purple sea urchins and orange starfish can be seen at low tide. The Otter Crest Loop rejoins U.S. 101 about 4 miles south of Cape Foulweather near **Yaquina Head**, which has been designated an Outstanding Natural Area. Harbor seals, sea lions, cormorants, murres, puffins, and guillemots frolic in the water and on the rocks below the gleaming, white tower of the **Yaquina Bay Lighthouse.**

Hotels

Channel House

$$$ | **B&B/INN** | You can enjoy some of the best whale-watching on the Oregon Coast from your own private balcony and hot tub from many of the spacious rooms in this upscale, contemporary, oceanfront inn that's in the heart of town. **Pros:** you can often see whales right from your room; close to local shops and restaurants; many rooms have decks with hot tubs. **Cons:** no kids under 16; slightly busy location on U.S. 101; steep rates, especially in summer. *Rooms from: $250 ✉ 35 Ellingson St. ☎ 541/765–2140 🌐 www.channelhouse.com 15 rooms Free breakfast.*

Clarion Surfrider Resort

$ | **HOTEL** | The economical Clarion Surfrider Resort comprises a few two-story clapboard buildings perched on a bluff overlooking the ocean and Fogarty Creek State Park, and amenities include a seafood restaurant and lounge, indoor pool, and exercise room. **Pros:** impressive ocean views; reasonable rates; decent seafood restaurant and bar on-site. **Cons:** rooms have attractive but cookie-cutter chain furniture; not within walking distance of town; smallish bathrooms. *Rooms from: $139 ✉ 3115 N.W. U.S. 101 ☎ 541/764–2311 🌐 www.choicehotels.com 55 rooms Free breakfast.*

★ Whale Cove Inn

$$$$ | **B&B/INN** | This small and exquisitely decorated high-end inn overlooks the picturesque cove for which it's named and contains just eight spacious suites, each with a balcony that has a large hot tub with a dazzling view of the water. **Pros:** astoundingly good restaurant; stunning building with cushy and spacious suites; terrific ocean views. **Cons:** not a good fit for kids (only those 16 and over are permitted); pricey; not within walking distance of town. *Rooms from: $520 ✉ 2345 U.S. 101 ☎ 541/765–4300, 800/628–3409 🌐 www.whalecoveinn.com 8 suites Free breakfast.*

Activities

OUTFITTERS

★ Whale Research EcoExcursions
TOUR—SPORTS | FAMILY | Knowledgeable marine biologists and naturalists captain the informative and exciting whale-watching excursions offered by this highly respected outfitter that also operates the Whale, Sea Life and Shark Museum from which these 90-minute tours depart. *234 U.S. 101* *541/912–6734* *www.oregonwhales.com* *From $45.*

Newport

12 miles south of Depoe Bay.

Known as the Dungeness crab capital of the world, Newport offers accessible beaches, a popular aquarium, the coast's premier performing-arts center, and a significant supply of both elegant and affordable accommodations and restaurants.

GETTING HERE AND AROUND

Newport is a 2½-hour drive from Portland by way of Interstate 5 south to Albany and U.S. 20 west; the town is a 40-minute drive south along U.S. 101 from Lincoln City, and a 75-minute drive north of Florence.

ESSENTIALS

VISITOR INFORMATION Discover Newport. *541/265–8801* *www.discovernewport.com.*

TOURS

Marine Discovery Tours
Sea-life cruises, priced from $42 and departing throughout the day, are conducted on a 65-foot excursion boat *Discovery,* with inside seating for 49 people and two viewing levels. The cruise season is March through October. *345 S.W. Bay Blvd.* *541/265–6200* *www.marinediscoverytours.com* *From $36.*

Sights

Beverly Beach State Park
NATIONAL/STATE PARK | Seven miles north of Newport, this beachfront park extends from Yaquina Head, where you can see the lighthouse, to the headlands of Otter Rock. It's a great place to fly a kite, surf the waves, or hunt for fossils. The campground is well equipped, with a wind-protected picnic area and a yurt meeting hall. *N.E. Beverly Dr.* *Off U.S. 101, 6 miles north of Newport* *541/265–9278* *www.oregonstateparks.org* *Free.*

★ Devil's Punchbowl State Natural Area
NATIONAL/STATE PARK | A rocky shoreline separates the day-use area from the surf at this park named for a dramatic rock formation—likely formed by a collapsed sea cave—through which you can observe the violently churning surf. It's a popular setting for whale-watching, and there are excellent tidal pools. *1st St., Otter Rock* *Off U.S. 101, 8 miles north of Newport* *541/265–4560* *www.oregonstateparks.org* *Free.*

Hatfield Marine Science Center
COLLEGE | FAMILY | Interactive and interpretive exhibits at Oregon State University appeal to the kid in everyone. More than just showcasing sea life, the center contains exhibits and tide-pool touch tanks, and it holds classes that teach the importance of scientific research in managing and sustaining coastal and marine resources. The staff regularly leads guided tours of the adjoining estuary. *2030 S. Marine Science Dr.* *541/867–0100* *seagrant.oregonstate.edu* *Closed Tues. and Wed. in winter.*

Oregon Coast Aquarium
ZOO | FAMILY | This 4½-acre complex brings visitors face-to-face with the creatures living in offshore and near-shore Pacific marine habitats: frolicking sea otters, colorful puffins, pulsating jellyfish, and even a several-hundred-pound octopus. There's a hands-on interactive area for children, including tide pools perfect

for "petting" sea anemones and urchins. The aquarium houses one of North America's largest seabird aviaries, including glowering turkey vultures. Permanent exhibits include Passages of the Deep, where visitors walk through a 200-foot underwater tunnel with 360-degree views of sharks, wolf eels, halibut, and a truly captivating array of sea life; and SeaPunk, a nautical take on steampunk with interactive artwork. Large coho salmon and sturgeon can be viewed in a naturalistic setting through a window wall 9 feet high and 20 feet wide. The sherbet-colored nettles are hypnotizing. ✉ *2820 S.E. Ferry Slip Rd.* ☎ *541/867–3474* 🌐 *www.aquarium.org* 🎫 *$24.95.*

South Beach State Park

NATIONAL/STATE PARK | Fishing, crabbing, boating, windsurfing, hiking, and beachcombing are popular activities at this park that begins just across the Yaquina Bay Bridge from Newport and contains a long, lovely stretch of beach. Kayaking tours along Beaver Creek are available for a fee. There's a popular campground, too. ✉ *U.S. 101 S* ☎ *541/867–4715* 🌐 *www.oregonstateparks.org.*

Yaquina Bay Lighthouse

LIGHTHOUSE | **FAMILY** | The state's oldest wooden lighthouse was only in commission for three years (1871–74), because it was determined that it was built in the wrong location. Today the well-restored lighthouse with a candy-apple-red top shines a steady white light from dusk to dawn. Open to the public, it's believed to be Newport's oldest structure, and the only Oregon lighthouse with living quarters attached. ✉ *S.W. Government St. at S.W. 9th St.* ☎ *541/265–5679* 🌐 *www.yaquinalights.org* 🎫 *Free, donations suggested* ⏲ *Closed Mon. and Tues. in winter.*

★ Yaquina Head Lighthouse

LIGHTHOUSE | **FAMILY** | The tallest lighthouse on the Oregon Coast has been blinking its beacon since its head keeper first walked up its 114 steps to light the wicks on the evening of August 20, 1873. Next to the 93-foot tower is an interpretive center. Bring your camera and call ahead to confirm tour times. ✉ *750 N.W. Lighthouse Dr.* ☎ *541/574–3100* 🌐 *www.yaquinalights.org* 🎫 *Free, donations suggested.*

 Restaurants

Canyon Way Restaurant and Bookstore

$$ | **SEAFOOD** | Cod, Dungeness crab cakes, bouillabaisse, and Yaquina Bay oysters—along with homemade pastas—are among the specialties of this weekday-only Newport institution just up the hill from the historic Bayfront and connected to a well-stocked bookstore. The adjacent Club 1216 has live music on Friday nights. **Known for:** dog-friendly patio; deli counter for takeout; excellent bookstore. 💲 *Average main: $18* ✉ *1216 S.W. Canyon Way* ☎ *541/265–8319* 🌐 *www.canyonway.com* ⏲ *No dinner Mon.–Thurs. Closed weekends.*

★ Clearwater Restaurant

$$$ | **SEAFOOD** | Part of the fun of dining in this handsome, bi-level restaurant with huge windows overlooking the bay is watching—and listening to—the big posse of sea lions gamboling about on the docks out back, but Clearwater also serves terrifically good seafood. You can't go wrong with any of the shareable starters, including tuna poke bowls and quinoa-crusted avocado fries, but save room for one or two of the signature mains—maybe jumbo sea scallops with roasted-chestnut puree or local Dungeness crab with garlic soba noodles. **Known for:** view of sea lions and Yaquina Bay; coconut curry stew loaded with local seafood; tableside s'mores. 💲 *Average main: $25* ✉ *325 S.W. Bay Blvd., Portland* ☎ *541/272–5550* 🌐 *www.clearwaterrestaurant.com.*

Georgie's Beachside Grill

$$ | **SEAFOOD** | **FAMILY** | This stand-alone restaurant serves up some wonderfully innovative dishes and is one of few in town with ocean views—windows line a half-moon of table seating, and tiered booths allow decent views even in the back of the room. From the sea scallops blackened in house-mixed herbs to flame-broiled halibut with pineapple salsa, the food here lives up to the setting. **Known for:** sweeping ocean views; excellent breakfasts; reasonably priced seafood. *Average main: $21* *Hallmark Resort, 744 S.W. Elizabeth St.* *503/265–9800* *www.georgiesbeachsidegrill.com.*

★ Local Ocean Seafoods

$$ | **SEAFOOD** | At this sustainable fish market and sleek, airy grill with retractable windows that look out across picturesque Yaquina Bay, the operators purchase fish directly from the boats in the fishing fleet right outside. The menu includes such fish lovers' fare as tuna mignon (bacon-wrapped albacore with pan-seared vegetables), panko-buttermilk-crusted oysters, and Fishwives Stew (a tomato broth stew loaded with both shell- and finfish), and nothing is deep-fried—even the fish-and-chips are panfried. **Known for:** market with fresh-caught seafood to go; superb wine list; house-smoked fish and shellfish. *Average main: $22* *213 S.E. Bay Blvd.* *514/574–7959* *www.localocean.net.*

★ Ove Northwest

$$$ | **PACIFIC NORTHWEST** | The former executive chef of Local Ocean Seafoods opened this stellar Nye Beach restaurant that dazzles with both its ocean views and exquisite modern Pacific Northwest cuisine. The menu changes seasonally but might feature bruschetta with Matiz sardines, pickled fennel, and fromage blanc, and lingcod with Manila clams, Spanish chorizo, and a delicate tomato-saffron cream sauce. **Known for:** sophisticated farm-to-table fare; creative vegetable starters; sunset views over Nye Beach. *Average main: $24* *749 N.W. 3rd St.* *541/264–2990* *www.ovenorthwest.com* *Closed Sun. and Mon.*

Panini Bakery

$ | **CAFÉ** | The owner of this bustling bakery and espresso bar prides himself on hearty and home-roasted meats, hand-cut breads, sourdough pizza, and friendly service. The coffee's organic, the eggs free-range, the orange juice fresh squeezed, and just about everything is made from scratch. **Known for:** made-from-scratch food; outdoor seating; pizzas with interesting toppings. *Average main: $9* *232 N.W. Coast Hwy.* *541/272–5322* *www.paninibakery.com* *No credit cards.*

Tables of Content

$$$$ | **PACIFIC NORTHWEST** | The thoughtful prix-fixe menu at this offbeat restaurant in the outstanding Sylvia Beach Hotel changes nightly, but there's a good chance one of the handful of entrée options will be fresh local seafood, perhaps a moist grilled salmon fillet in a Dijonnaise sauce, served with sautéed vegetables, fresh-baked breads, and rice pilaf; a decadent dessert is also included. Note that dinners, which are at 6 or 7 pm depending on the day, can be long, so young children may get restless. **Known for:** convivial family-style dining; rich desserts; locally sourced seafood. *Average main: $32* *267 N.W. Cliff St.* *541/265–5428* *sylviabeachhotel.com/restaurant/.*

Hotels

★ Inn at Nye Beach

$$$ | **HOTEL** | With a prime beachfront location on a bluff in historic Nye Beach, this chic, eco-friendly, boutique hotel has large rooms with a clean, contemporary look and plenty of perks, including DVD players, premium tea and French press coffee, "green" bath amenities, microwaves and refrigerators, and wonderfully comfy beds. **Pros:** ocean views from infinity hot tub; direct beach access; stylish and spacious rooms. **Cons:** the complimentary breakfast is fairly basic; some rooms don't overlook ocean; no

Passages of the Deep, at Newport's Oregon Coast Aquarium, is a 200-foot underwater tunnel with 360-degree views of an amazing array of sea life.

restaurant on-site. *Rooms from: $235* *729 N.W. Coast St.* *541/265–2477, 800/480–2477* *www.innatnyebeach.com* *22 rooms* *Free breakfast.*

Newport Belle B&B

$$ | **B&B/INN** | This floating B&B is in a fully operational stern-wheeler that's permanently moored at the Newport Marina, where guests have front-row seats to all the boating activity around Yaquina Bay, and it's a short walk from Oregon Coast Aquarium. **Pros:** one-of-a-kind lodging experience; great harbor views; walking distance from Rogue Brewer's pub. **Cons:** not suitable for kids; need a car to get into town; small rooms. *Rooms from: $165* *Dock H, 2126 S.E. Marine Science Dr.* *541/867–6290* *www.newportbelle.com* *Closed Nov.–Mar.* *5 rooms* *Free breakfast.*

Sylvia Beach Hotel

$$ | **HOTEL** | This quirky 1913-vintage beachfront hotel offers a colorful range of antiques-filled rooms named for famous writers—a pendulum swings over the bed in the Poe room, while the Christie, Twain, Tolkien, Woolf, and Colette rooms feature fireplaces, decks, and great water views. **Pros:** loads of personality; great place to disconnect; very good restaurant. **Cons:** no TV, telephone, or Internet access; idiosyncratic decor isn't to everyone's taste; least-expensive rooms don't have ocean views. *Rooms from: $160* *267 N.W. Cliff St.* *541/265–5428, 888/795–8422* *sylviabeachhotel.com* *20 rooms* *Free breakfast.*

Performing Arts

★ **Newport Symphony Orchestra**

MUSIC | The only year-round, professional symphony orchestra on the Oregon Coast performs a popular series of concerts in the 328-seat Newport Performing Arts Center fall through spring, and special events in the summer, including a popular free community concert every July 4. *777 W. Olive St.* *541/574–0614* *www.newportsymphony.org.*

Yachats

24 miles south of Newport.

The small but utterly enchanting town of Yachats (pronounced "yah- *hots*") lies at the mouth of the Yachats River, and from its rocky shoreline, which includes the highest point directly located on the Oregon Coast (Cape Perpetua), trails lead to beaches and dozens of tidal pools. A relaxed alternative to the more touristy communities to the north, Yachats abounds with coastal pleasures, but without nearly as much traffic: Airbnbs and oceanfront hotels, an impressive bounty of terrific restaurants, quiet beaches, tidal pools, surf-pounded crags, fishing, and crabbing.

GETTING HERE AND AROUND

Yachats lies between Newport and Florence on coastal U.S. 101—it's a 40-minute drive from either town, and a three-hour drive via Interstate 5 and Highway 34 from Portland.

ESSENTIALS

VISITOR INFORMATION Yachats Visitors Center. ✉ *241 U.S. 101* ☎ *800/929–0477, 541/547–3530* 🌐 *www.yachats.org.*

Sights

★ Cape Perpetua Scenic Area
TRAIL | FAMILY | The highest vehicle-accessible lookout on the Oregon Coast, Cape Perpetua towers 800 feet above the rocky shoreline. Named by Captain Cook on St. Perpetua's Day in 1778, the cape is part of a 2,700-acre scenic area popular with hikers, campers, beachcombers, and naturalists. General information, educational movies and exhibits, and trail maps are available at the **Cape Perpetua Visitors Center,** ½ mile south of Devil's Churn. The easy 1-mile **Giant Spruce Trail** passes through a fern-filled rain forest to an enormous 600-year-old Sitka spruce. Easier still is the marked Auto Tour; it begins just north of the visitor center and winds through Siuslaw National Forest to the ¼-mile **Whispering Spruce Trail.** Views from the rustic rock shelter here extend 50 miles north to south, and some 40 miles out to sea. For a more rigorous trek, hike the **St. Perpetua Trail** to the shelter. Other trails lead from the visitor center down along the shore, including a scenic pathway to **Devil's Churn,** next to which a small snack bar sells sandwiches, sweets, and coffee. ✉ *2400 U.S. 101* ✣ *3 miles south of Yachats* ☎ *541/547–3289* 🌐 *www.fs.usda.gov/siuslaw* 🎫 *Parking fee $5.*

Neptune State Scenic Viewpoint
VIEWPOINT | Visitors have fun searching for whales and other sea life, watching the surf, or hunting for agates at this stretch of shoreline reached via four pulloffs a bit south of Cape Perpetua. The benches set above the beach on the cliff provide a great view of Cumming Creek. At low tide, beachcombers have access to a natural cave and tidal pools. And there's a grassy area that's ideal for picnicking at the northernmost pulloff, by Gwynn Creek. ✉ *U.S. 101* ✣ *4 miles south of Yachats* ☎ *541/547–3416* 🌐 *www.oregonstateparks.org* 🎫 *Free.*

★ Yachats Ocean Road State Natural Site
VIEWPOINT | Drive this 1-mile loop just across the Yachats River from downtown Yachats, and discover one of the most scenic viewpoints on the Oregon Coast. Park along Yachats Ocean Road and scamper out along the broad swath of sand where the Yachats River meets the Pacific Ocean. There's fun to be had playing on the beach, poking around tide pools, and watching blowholes, summer sunsets, and whales spouting. ✉ *Yachats Ocean Rd.* ☎ *541/867–7451* 🌐 *www.oregonstateparks.org.*

Beaches

Yachats State Recreation Area
BEACHES | The public beach in downtown Yachats is more like the surface of the moon than your typical beach. A wooden

platform overlooks the coastline, where the waves roll in sideways and splash over the rocks at high tide. As is the case throughout most of the town, the beach itself is paralleled by an upland walking trail and dotted with picnic tables, benches, and interpretive signs. Visit to spot the sea lions that frequent this stretch of coast. Or join the intrepid beachcombers who climb the rocks for a closer look at tide pools populated by sea urchins, hermit crabs, barnacles, snails, and sea stars. **Amenities:** parking; toilets. **Best for:** walking; sunset. ✉ *Ocean View Dr.* ✣ *Off 2nd St. and U.S. 101* ☎ *541/867–7451* 🌐 *www.oregonstateparks.org.*

Restaurants

★ Beach Street Kitchen

$ | **MODERN AMERICAN** | Duck into this sunny corner café across the street from where the Yachats River empties into the sea for some of the tastiest made-from-scratch breakfast and lunch fare on the central Oregon Coast, along with a full selection of craft beer, wine, and cocktails. From the wild-mushroom frittata and baked French toast with Oregon blueberries in the morning to a killer beef barbacoa sandwich at lunch, the food here is consistently stellar, and the rustic-contemporary dining room, with tables fashioned out of Sitka spruce, is utterly inviting. **Known for:** water views; best espresso drinks in town; carefully sourced ingredients. $ *Average main: $13* ✉ *84 Beach St.* ☎ *541/547–4409* 🌐 *www.beachstreetkitchen.com* 🕓 *Closed Tues. and Wed. No dinner.*

Bread and Roses Baking

$ | **BAKERY** | Artisanal breads are handmade in small batches here, along with pastries, muffins, scones, cookies, cinnamon rolls, and desserts. In the bright, yellow-cottage bakery you can also try the daily soup and sandwiches at lunchtime, or just while away the morning with pastries and good coffee. **Known for:** proximity to Yachats State Recreation Area; delicious pastries and baked goods; organic, fair-trade coffee. $ *Average main: $9* ✉ *238 4th St.* ☎ *541/547–4454* 🌐 *www.bnrbakery.com* 🕓 *Closed Tues. and Wed. No dinner.*

The Drift Inn

$$ | **AMERICAN** | **FAMILY** | This funky, convivial restaurant with affordable, basic overnight accommodations on the upper floor is a reliable bet for all three meals of the day; it's also great for watching live music below a ceiling full of umbrellas, with views of the Yachats River and ocean. Family-friendly and lively, the Drift Inn features fresh razor clams, halibut fish-and-chips, juicy steaks, wood-fired pizzas, and other well-prepared American fare. **Known for:** nice range of Oregon wines and beer; live music nightly; substantial breakfasts. $ *Average main: $20* ✉ *124 U.S. 101 N* ☎ *541/547–4477* 🌐 *www.the-drift-inn.com.*

Luna Sea Fish House

$$ | **SEAFOOD** | **FAMILY** | Sustainable, line-caught wild seafood—including albacore, cod, halibut, and, when in season, Dungeness crab—straight from the owner's boat is the draw at this festive weathered restaurant with colorful indoor and outdoor seating areas. Fish-and-chips of all stripes, including clam and salmon, are served, but the fish tacos and a sinful dish called slumgullion—clam chowder baked with cheese and bay shrimp—are the most popular choices. **Known for:** pet-friendly outdoor patio; slumgullion (a rich clam-and-shrimp chowder baked with cheese); live music many evenings. $ *Average main: $17* ✉ *153 N.W. U.S. 101* ☎ *541/547–4794, 888/547–4794* 🌐 *www.lunaseafishhouse.com.*

Ona Restaurant

$$$ | **MODERN AMERICAN** | Relatively snazzy for such a laid-back town, this bustling downtown bistro overlooking the confluence of the Yachats River and the Pacific is nonetheless unpretentious and relaxed. The specialty is locally and seasonally sourced Oregon seafood,

such as Manila clams steamed with grape tomatoes, dry vermouth, garlic, and butter, or rare seared albacore with togarashi, smoked maitake mushrooms, and tamari green beans—try a glass of wine from the excellent regional wine list. **Known for:** artfully plated contemporary seafood fare; luscious desserts; nice happy hour deals. *Average main: $25 131 U.S. 101 N 541/547–6627 www.onarestaurant.com Closed Mon.–Wed. in winter.*

★ Yachats Brewing

$$ | **ECLECTIC** | Inside this lively establishment with pitched-timber ceilings, skylights, and a solarium-style beer garden, you'll find one of the state's most impressive craft breweries and a taproom specializing in house-fermented, -pickled, and-smoked ingredients. It may sound like a slightly odd concept, but the food is creative and absolutely delicious, with dishes like elk-huckleberry sausage sandwiches; a salad of maple-smoked salmon, quail eggs, pickled beets, and seasonal farm veggies; and *khao man gai* (aromatic poached chicken with kimchi and spicy fermented soy sauce) leading the way. **Known for:** unusual craft beers and probiotic drinks; house-fermented foods; burgers and pizzas with interesting seasonal toppings. *Average main: $17 348 U.S. 101 N 541/547–3884 www.yachatsbrewing.com.*

Hotels

Deane's Oceanfront Lodge

$ | **HOTEL** | This simple single-story, family-run motel is set on a sweeping stretch of beachfront midway between downtown Yachats and Waldport. **Pros:** charming rooms; direct ocean views and beach access; reasonable rates. **Cons:** small rooms; not within walking distance of dining and shopping; books up fast in summer. *Rooms from: $89 7365 U.S. 101 N 541/547–3321 www.deaneslodge.com 18 rooms No meals.*

★ Overleaf Lodge

$$$ | **HOTEL** | On a rocky shoreline at the north end of Yachats, this rambling romantic three-story hotel enjoys spectacular sunsets and contains splendidly comfortable and spacious accommodations that have a variety of options, including fireplaces, corner nooks, and whirlpool tubs with ocean views. **Pros:** fantastic oceanfront setting; one of the best full-service spas on the coast; complimentary wine tastings on Friday and Saturday evenings. **Cons:** no restaurant; a bit of a walk from town; rooms with best views can be quite spendy. *Rooms from: $239 280 Overleaf Lodge La. 541/547–4885, 800/338–0507 www.overleaflodge.com 58 rooms Free breakfast.*

Florence

25 miles south of Yachats; 64 miles west of Eugene.

The closest beach town to Oregon's second-largest city, Eugene, charming and low-key Florence delights visitors with its restored riverfront Old Town and proximity to one of the most remarkable stretches of Oregon coastline. Some 75 creeks and rivers empty into the Pacific Ocean in and around town, and the Siuslaw River flows right through the historic village center. When the numerous nearby lakes are added to the mix, it makes for one of the richest fishing areas in Oregon. Salmon, rainbow trout, bass, perch, crabs, and clams are among the water's treasures. Fishing boats and pleasure crafts moor in Florence's harbor, forming a pleasant backdrop for the town's restored buildings. Old Town has notable restaurants, antiques stores, fish markets, and other diversions. South of town, the miles of white sand dunes that make up Oregon Dunes National Recreation Area lend themselves to everything from solitary hikes to rides aboard all-terrain vehicles.

GETTING HERE AND AROUND

It's a 75-minute drive west to Florence on Highway 126 from Eugene and a stunningly scenic 40-minute drive south on U.S. 101 from Yachats. It takes about an hour to drive U.S. 101 south to Coos Bay, a stretch that takes in all of Oregon Dunes National Recreation Area.

ESSENTIALS

VISITOR INFORMATION Florence Area Chamber of Commerce. ✉ *290 U.S. 101* ☎ *541/997–3128* 🌐 *www.florencechamber.com.*

Sights

Darlingtonia State Natural Site
GARDEN | FAMILY | A few miles north of Florence, you'll find this interesting example of the rich plant life found in the marshy terrain near the coast. It's also a surefire child pleaser. A short paved nature trail leads through clumps of insect-catching cobra lilies, so named because they look like spotted cobras ready to strike. This area is most interesting in May, when the lilies are in bloom. ✉ *U.S. 101, at Mercer Lake Rd.* ☎ *541/997–3851* 🌐 *www.oregonstateparks.org.*

★ Heceta Head Lighthouse State Scenic Viewpoint
VIEWPOINT | A ½-mile trail from the beachside parking lot leads to the oft-photographed Heceta Head Lighthouse built in 1894, whose beacon, visible for more than 21 miles, is the most powerful on the Oregon Coast. More than 7 miles of trails traverse the rocky landscape north and south of the lighthouse, which rises some 200 feet above the ocean. For a mesmerizing view of the lighthouse and Heceta Head, pull over at the scenic viewpoint just north of Sea Lion Caves. ✉ *U.S. 101, Yachats* ✣ *11 miles north of Florence* ☎ *541/547–3416* 🌐 *www.oregonstateparks.org* 🎫 *Day use $5, lighthouse tours free.*

★ Oregon Dunes National Recreation Area
NATIONAL/STATE PARK | FAMILY | The Oregon Dunes National Recreation Area is the largest expanse of coastal sand dunes in North America, extending for 40 miles, from Florence to Coos Bay. The area contains some of the best ATV riding in the United States and encompasses some 31,500 acres. More than 1.5 million people visit the dunes each year, many of whom are ATV users. **Honeyman Memorial State Park,** 515 acres within the recreation area, is a base camp for dune-buggy enthusiasts, mountain bikers, hikers, boaters, horseback riders, and dogsledders (the sandy hills are an excellent training ground). There's a campground, too. The dunes are a vast playground for children, particularly the slopes surrounding cool **Cleawox Lake.** If you have time for just a quick scamper in the sand, stop by the Oregon Dunes Overlook off U.S. 101, 11 miles south of Florence and 11 miles north of Reedsport—it's on the west side of the road, just north of Perkins Lake. ✉ *Visitor Center, 855 U.S. 101, Reedsport* ☎ *541/271–6000* 🌐 *www.fs.usda.gov/siuslaw* 🎫 *Day use $5.*

Sea Lion Caves
CAVE | FAMILY | In 1880 a sea captain named Cox rowed a small skiff into a fissure in a 300-foot-high sea cliff. Inside, he was startled to discover a vaulted chamber in the rock, 125 feet high and 2 acres in size. Hundreds of massive sea lions—the largest bulls weighing 2,000 pounds or more—covered every available surface. Cox's discovery would become one of the Oregon Coast's premier attractions, if something of a tourist trap. An elevator near the cliff-top ticket office and kitschy gift shop descends to the floor of the cavern, near sea level, where vast numbers of Steller's and California sea lions relax on rocks and swim about (their cute, fuzzy pups can be viewed from behind a wire fence). This is the only known hauling-out area and rookery for wild sea lions on the mainland in the Lower 48, and it's an awesome sight and

sound when they're in the cave, typically only in fall and winter (in spring and summer the mammals usually stay on the rocky ledges outside the cave). You'll also see several species of seabirds here, including migratory pigeon guillemots, cormorants, and three varieties of gulls. Gray whales are sometimes visible during their October–December and March–May migrations. ✉ *91560 U.S. 101* ✣ *10 miles north of Florence* ☎ *541/547–3111* 🌐 *www.sealioncaves.com* 🎫 *$14.*

Umpqua Lighthouse State Park

LIGHTHOUSE | Some of the highest sand dunes in the country are found in this 50-acre park between Florence and Coos Bay, near the small town of Reedsport. The first **Umpqua River Lighthouse,** built on the dunes at the mouth of the Umpqua River in 1857, lasted only four years before it toppled over in a storm. It took local residents 33 years to build another one. The "new" lighthouse, built on a bluff overlooking the south side of Winchester Bay and operated by the U.S. Coast Guard, stands at 65 feet and is still going strong, flashing a warning beacon out to sea every five seconds. The **Douglas County Coastal Visitors Center** adjacent to the lighthouse has a museum and can arrange lighthouse tours. ✉ *Lighthouse Rd., Reedsport* ✣ *Umpqua Hwy., west side of U.S. 101* ☎ *541/271–4118, 541/271–4631 lighthouse tours* 🌐 *www.oregonstateparks.org* 🎫 *Tours and museum $8.*

Restaurants

Bridgewater Fishhouse

$$ | **SEAFOOD** | Freshly caught seafood—20 to 25 choices nightly—is the mainstay of this creaky-floored, Victorian-era restaurant in Florence's Old Town. Whether you opt for patio dining during summer or lounge seating in winter, the eclectic fare of pastas, burgers, salads, and seafood-packed stews is consistently well prepared, and a live jazz band provides some foot-tapping fun many evenings. **Known for:** live music; happy hour deals; lighter fare in Zebra Lounge. $ *Average main: $19* ✉ *1297 Bay St.* ☎ *541/997–1133* 🌐 *www.bridgewaterfishhouse.com* 🕑 *Closed Tues.*

Harbor Light Restaurant

$$ | **AMERICAN** | **FAMILY** | Located about 20 miles south of Florence in Reedsport, this homey, family-friendly restaurant—think log-cabin-style building decorated with mounted Oregon fish—is a great place to fuel up before playing on the nearby dunes. The food here is straightforward and traditional, from marionberry-stuffed French toast and seafood omelets at breakfast to prosciutto-wrapped prawns and blue-cheese-topped flat-iron steak in the evening, and the use of fresh, often local ingredients results in some of the healthiest and tastiest fare along this stretch of the coast. **Known for:** delicious blackberry, chocolate, and caramel milk shakes; filling breakfasts; proximity to Oregon Dunes National Recreation Area. $ *Average main: $20* ✉ *930 U.S. 101, Reedsport* ☎ *541/271–3848* 🌐 *www.harborlightrestaurant.com.*

Homegrown Public House

$$ | **MODERN AMERICAN** | This convivial, intimate gastropub in Old Town Florence—a couple of blocks north of the riverfront—specializes in locally sourced, creatively prepared American fare and offers a well-chosen list of Oregon beers on tap, plus local spirits, iced teas, and kombucha. Stop by for lunch to enjoy the lightly battered albacore fish and hand-cut fries with tartar sauce, or a cheeseburger topped with Rogue blue and served with marinated vegetables and local greens. **Known for:** great selection of Oregon craft beers on tap; seafood curry; popular happy hour. $ *Average main: $17* ✉ *294 Laurel St.* ☎ *541/997–4886* 🌐 *homegrownpublichouse.com/* 🕑 *Closed Mon.*

The Hukilau

$$ | **ASIAN FUSION** | Well-prepared Pacific Rim–fusion fare and fun tiki-inspired cocktails complete with paper umbrellas, are the draw at this hip, supercasual spot festooned with surfboards, Hawaiian shirts, and tropical artwork. Boldly flavored dishes like Hawaiian-style loco moco, pineapple teriyaki chicken, and Spam musubi may have you feeling like you've been airlifted to Maui, and there's tasty sushi, too. **Known for:** Hawaiian-inspired appetizers; creative sushi; tropical cocktails. *Average main: $19 ✉ 185 U.S. 101 ☎ 541/991–1071 🌐 www.hukilauflorence.com ⏱ Closed Sun. and Mon.*

River Roasters

$ | **CAFÉ** | This small, homey café serves cups of drip-on-demand coffee—you select the roast and they grind and brew it on the spot. Beans are roasted on-site, muffins and breads are freshly baked, and a view of the Siuslaw River can be savored from the deck out back. **Known for:** deck with river views; lots of flavored latte options; premium house-roasted coffee. *Average main: $4 ✉ 1240 Bay St. ☎ 541/997–3443 🌐 www.coffeeoregon.com.*

★ **Waterfront Depot Restaurant and Bar**

$$ | **SEAFOOD** | The detailed chalkboard menu of always intriguing nightly specials says it all: from the fresh, crab-encrusted halibut to classic duck-and-lamb cassoulet to Bill's Flaming Spanish Coffee, this is a place serious about fresh food and fine flavors. Originally located in the old Mapleton train station, moved in pieces and reassembled in Old Town Florence, the atmospheric tavern has a great view of the Siuslaw River and the Siuslaw River Bridge. **Known for:** patio seating on the river; creative daily specials; excellent wine list. *Average main: $21 ✉ 1252 Bay St. ☎ 541/902–9100 🌐 www.thewaterfrontdepot.com ⏱ No lunch.*

Hotels

★ **Heceta Head Lighthouse B&B**

$$$$ | **B&B/INN** | On a windswept promontory, this unusual late-Victorian property is one of Oregon's most remarkable bed-and-breakfasts; it's located at Heceta Head Lighthouse State Scenic Viewpoint and owned by a gifted chef who prepares an elaborate seven-course breakfast each morning, with seasonal offerings. **Pros:** unique property with a magical setting; exceptionally good food; the promise of potential ghost sightings. **Cons:** remote location; expensive, especially considering some rooms share a bath; tends to book up well in advance. *Rooms from: $280 ✉ 92072 U.S. 101 ✣ 12 miles north of Florence ☎ 541/547–3696, 866/547–3696 🌐 www.hecetalighthouse.com 6 rooms 🍽 Free breakfast.*

River House Inn

$ | **B&B/INN** | On the beautiful Siuslaw River, this property has terrific accommodations and is near quaint shops and restaurants in Florence's Old Town. **Pros:** spacious rooms; great views from most rooms; close proximity to dining and shopping. **Cons:** not on the beach; in-town location can be a little busy at times; some rooms receive traffic noise from U.S. 101 bridge. *Rooms from: $140 ✉ 1202 Bay St. ☎ 541/997–3933, 888/824–2454 🌐 www.riverhouseflorence.com 40 rooms 🍽 Free breakfast.*

Bay Area: Coos Bay and North Bend

45 miles south of Florence on U.S. 101.

The Coos Bay–Charleston–North Bend metropolitan area, collectively known as the Bay Area (population 32,000), is the gateway to rewarding recreational experiences. The small adjoining cities of North Bend and Coos Bay lie on the largest natural harbor between San Francisco Bay and Seattle's Puget Sound.

To see the most picturesque part of the Bay Area, head west from Coos Bay on Newmark Avenue for about 7 miles to **Charleston,** which is home to some beautiful state parks and a bustling marina with casual restaurants and fishing charters. Though it's a Bay Area community, this quiet fishing village at the mouth of Coos Bay is a world unto itself. As it loops into town, the road becomes the Cape Arago Highway and leads to the area's stunning parks.

GETTING HERE AND AROUND

The area lies along a slightly inland stretch of U.S. 101 that's a one-hour drive south of Florence and a 30-minute drive north of Bandon; from the Umpqua Valley and Interstate 5 corridor, Coos Bay is just under two hours' drive west from Roseburg on Highway 42.

Southwest Oregon Regional Airport in North Bend has commercial flights from Denver (summer only) and San Francisco.

ESSENTIALS

VISITOR INFORMATION Oregon's Adventure Coast. ✉ *50 Central Ave., Coos Bay* ☎ *541/269–0215* 🌐 *www.oregonsadventurecoast.com.*

Sights

Cape Arago Lighthouse

LIGHTHOUSE | FAMILY | On a rock island just offshore from Charleston near Sunset Bay State Park, this lighthouse has had several iterations; the first lighthouse was built here in 1866, but it was destroyed by storms and erosion. A second, built in 1908, suffered the same fate. The current white tower, built in 1934, is 44 feet tall and towers 100 feet above the ocean. If you're here on a foggy day, listen for its unique foghorn. The lighthouse is connected to the mainland by a bridge. Neither is open to the public, but there's an excellent spot to view this lonely guardian and much of the coastline. From U.S. 101 take Cape Arago Highway to Gregory Point, where it ends at a turnaround, and follow the short trail. ✉ *Cape Arago Hwy., Charleston* ✣ *Just north of Sunset Bay State Park.*

Cape Arago State Park

NATIONAL/STATE PARK | The distant barking of sea lions echoes in the air at a trio of coves connected by short but steep trails. The park overlooks the **Oregon Islands National Wildlife Refuge,** where offshore rocks, beaches, islands, and reefs provide breeding grounds for seabirds and marine mammals, including seal pups (the trail is closed in spring to protect them). ✉ *End of Cape Arago Hwy., Coos Bay* ☎ *541/888–3778* 🌐 *www.oregonstateparks.org* 🎫 *Free.*

★ Coos History Museum & Maritime Collection

MUSEUM | FAMILY | This contemporary 11,000-square-foot museum with expansive views of the Coos Bay waterfront contains an impressive collection of memorabilia related to the region's history, from early photos to vintage boats, all displayed in an airy, open exhibit hall with extensive interpretive signage. You'll also find well-designed exhibits on Native American history, agriculture, and industry such as logging, shipwrecks, boatbuilding, natural history, and mining. ✉ *1210 N. Front St., Coos Bay* ☎ *541/756–6320* 🌐 *www.cooshistory.org* 🎫 *$7* 🕙 *Closed Mon.*

★ Shore Acres State Park

NATIONAL/STATE PARK | An observation building on a grassy bluff overlooking the Pacific marks the site that held the mansion of lumber baron Louis J. Simpson. The view over the rugged wave-smashed cliffs is splendid, but the real glory of Shore Acres lies a few hundred yards to the south, where an entrance gate leads into what was Simpson's private garden. Beautifully landscaped and meticulously maintained, the gardens incorporate formal English and Japanese designs. From March to mid-October the grounds are ablaze with blossoming daffodils, rhododendrons, azaleas, roses, and dahlias. In December the garden is decked out with a dazzling display of holiday lights. ✉ *89526 Cape*

Arago Hwy., Coos Bay 541/888–2472 gardens, 541/888–3732 www.oregonstateparks.org $5 parking.

South Slough National Estuarine Research Reserve

NATURE PRESERVE | FAMILY | The 5,900-acre reserve's fragile ecosystem supports everything from algae to bald eagles and black bears. More than 300 species of birds have been sighted at the reserve, which has an interpretive center with interesting nature exhibits, guided walks (summer only), and nature trails that give you a chance to see things up close. *61907 Seven Devils Rd., Coos Bay 4 miles south of Charleston 541/888–5558 www.oregon.gov/dsl/ss Free Visitor center closed Sun. and Mon.*

Restaurants

Blue Heron Bistro

$$ | GERMAN | The specialty at this bustling downtown bistro is hearty German fare, but you'll also find a number of local seafood items, as well as sandwiches and lighter dishes, from panfried oysters to meatball sandwiches. The skylit, tile-floor dining room has natural wood and mounted animal heads on the walls, and there's a pet-friendly patio outside. **Known for:** great selection of German and local craft beers; pleasant outdoor seating; Sunday brunch. *Average main: $20 100 W. Commercial St., Coos Bay 541/267–3933 www.blueheronbistro.net.*

Miller's at the Cove

$$ | SEAFOOD | Often packed with local fishermen and dock workers as well as tourists en route to and from Sunset Bay and nearby state parks, this lively and fun—if at times raucous—sports bar and tavern makes a great dinner or lunch stop for fresh seafood, and watching a game on TV. Favorites here include the fish-and-chips (available with local snapper or cod), oyster burgers, Dungeness crab melts, meatball subs, clam chowder, and Baja-style fish or crab tacos. **Known for:** laid-back atmosphere; tasty fish tacos; craft beer by the pitcher. *Average main: $16 63346 Boat Basin Rd., Charleston 541/808–2404 www.millersatthecove.rocks.*

Hotels

★ Bay Point Landing

$$ | RESORT | With striking contemporary architecture and a pristine setting on a section of Coos Bay near Charleston and the ocean, this 100-acre compound is the first luxury glamping venue on the Oregon Coast, though you don't need a tent or sleeping bag to enjoy a stay in its airy cabins and tricked-out Airstream trailers. **Pros:** gorgeous contemporary design; lots of cushy amenities; picturesque bay-side setting. **Cons:** need a car to get to shops and restaurants; some cabins have limited water views; a bit spendy. *Rooms from: $179 92443 Cape Arago Hwy., Coos Bay 541/351–9160 www.baypointlanding.com 25 units No meals.*

Coos Bay Manor

$ | B&B/INN | FAMILY | Built in 1912 on a quiet residential street, this 15-room Colonial Revival manor contains original hardwood floors, detailed woodwork, high ceilings, and antiques and period reproductions. **Pros:** elegantly decorated; family-friendly; central location near restaurants and shops. **Cons:** on a quiet street but still in a busy downtown area; a 15-minute drive from the ocean; traditional, historic vibe isn't everyone's taste. *Rooms from: $145 955 S. 5th St., Coos Bay 541/269–1224, 800/269–1224 www.coosbaymanor.com 6 rooms Free breakfast.*

Mill Casino Hotel

$ | RESORT | Even if you're not a big fan of gambling, this attractive hotel on the bay and boardwalk in North Bend (a short distance north of downtown Coos Bay) makes a handy and fairly economical

You can experience the Umpqua Sand Dunes via ATV in the 31,500-acre Oregon Dunes National Recreation Area.

base for exploring this stretch of the coast. **Pros:** attractive, contemporary rooms; location close to downtown dining and shopping; nice bay views from many rooms. **Cons:** casino can be noisy and smoky; 25-minute drive from the ocean; rooms in older buildings feel a bit dated. *$ Rooms from: $125 ✉ 3201 Tremont Ave., North Bend ☎ 541/756–8800, 800/953–4800 🌐 www.themillcasino.com 🛏 203 rooms 🍽 No meals.*

Bandon

25 miles south of Coos Bay.

Referred to by some who cherish its romantic lure as Bandon-by-the-Sea, Bandon is both a harbor town and a popular beach-vacation town, famous for its cranberry products and its artists' colony, complete with galleries and shops. Two national wildlife refuges, Oregon Islands and Bandon Marsh, are within the town limits, and a drive along Beach Loop Road, just southwest of downtown, affords mesmerizing views of awesome coastal rock formations, especially around Coquille Point and Face Rock State Scenic Viewpoint. The Bandon Dunes links-style golf courses are a worldwide attraction, often ranked among the top courses in the nation.

Tiny Bandon bills itself as Oregon's cranberry capital—10 miles north of town you'll find acres of bogs and irrigated fields where tons of the tart berries are harvested every year. Each September there's the Cranberry Festival, featuring a parade and a fair.

GETTING HERE AND AROUND

Bandon, on U.S. 101, is a half-hour drive south of Coos Bay and North Bend, and a 2-hour drive north up the coast from the California border; allow just under 2 hours to get here from Roseburg in the Umpqua Valley via Highway 42, and 4½ hours from Portland.

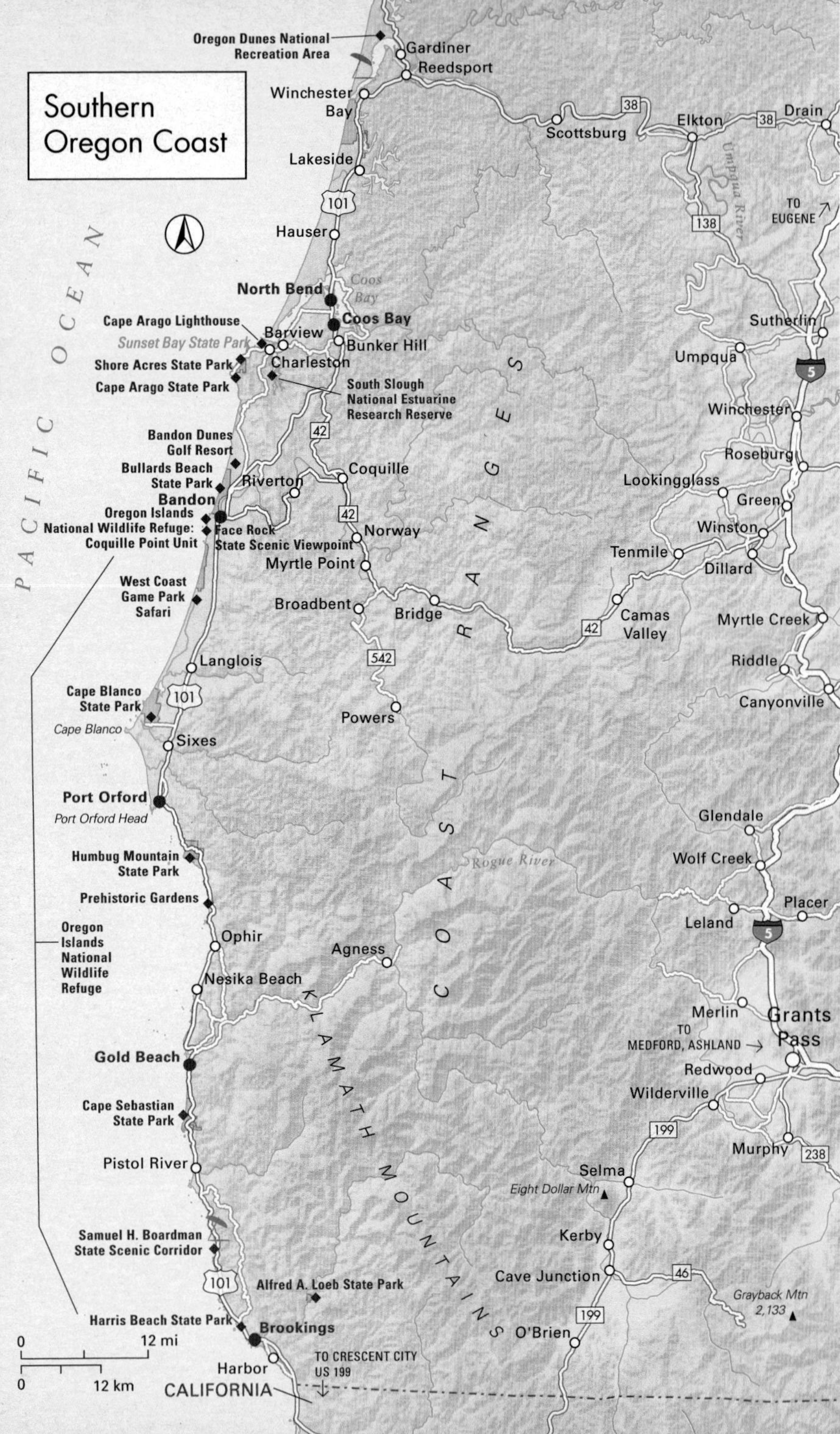

Southern Oregon Coast
PACIFIC OCEAN
Oregon Dunes National Recreation Area
Gardiner
Reedsport
Winchester Bay
38
Scottsburg
Elkton
38
Drain
Lakeside
101
Umpqua River
138
TO EUGENE
Hauser
Coos Bay
North Bend
Coos Bay
Cape Arago Lighthouse
Barview
Sunset Bay State Park
Bunker Hill
Charleston
Shore Acres State Park
Cape Arago State Park
South Slough National Estuarine Research Reserve
Sutherlin
Umpqua
5
Winchester
42
Bandon Dunes Golf Resort
Bullards Beach State Park
Coquille
Riverton
Roseburg
Lookingglass
Green
Bandon
Oregon Islands National Wildlife Refuge: Coquille Point Unit
Face Rock State Scenic Viewpoint
42
Norway
Winston
Myrtle Point
Tenmile
Dillard
West Coast Game Park Safari
Broadbent
Bridge
Camas Valley
42
Myrtle Creek
COAST RANGES
542
Langlois
Riddle
Canyonville
Cape Blanco State Park
101
Powers
Cape Blanco
Sixes
Port Orford
Port Orford Head
Glendale
Humbug Mountain State Park
Rogue River
Wolf Creek
Prehistoric Gardens
Placer
Leland
5
Oregon Islands National Wildlife Refuge
Ophir
Agness
Nesika Beach
KLAMATH MOUNTAINS
Merlin
Grants Pass
TO MEDFORD, ASHLAND
Gold Beach
Redwood
Wilderville
Cape Sebastian State Park
199
Murphy
238
Pistol River
Selma
Eight Dollar Mtn
Samuel H. Boardman State Scenic Corridor
Kerby
Cave Junction
46
101
Alfred A. Loeb State Park
Grayback Mtn 2,133
199
Harris Beach State Park
Brookings
O'Brien
0
12 mi
0
12 km
Harbor
TO CRESCENT CITY US 199
CALIFORNIA

ESSENTIALS

VISITOR INFORMATION Bandon Chamber of Commerce. ✉ *300 2nd St.* ☎ *541/347–9616* 🌐 *www.bandon.com.*

Sights

Bandon Historical Society Museum

MUSEUM | In the old city hall building, this museum depicts the area's early history, including Native American artifacts, logging, fishing, cranberry farming, and the disastrous 1936 fire that destroyed the city. The well-stocked gift shop has books, knickknacks, jewelry, myrtlewood, and other little treasures. ✉ *270 Fillmore St.* ☎ *541/347–2164* 🌐 *www.bandonhistoricalmuseum.org* 🎟 *$3* ⏲ *Closed Sun. in winter.*

Bullards Beach State Park

NATIONAL/STATE PARK | At this rugged park along the north bank of the Coquille River (just across from downtown Bandon but reached via a 3½-mile drive up U.S. 101), you can tour the signal room inside the octagonal **Coquille Lighthouse,** built in 1896 and no longer in use; due to safety concerns, visitors can no longer tour the tower, but the signal room is open. From turnoff from U.S. 101, the meandering 2-mile drive to reach it passes through the Bandon Marsh, a prime bird-watching and picnicking area. The 4½-mile stretch of beach beside the lighthouse is a good place to search for jasper, agate, and driftwood—the firm sand is also popular for mountain biking. There's a campground with a wide variety of tent and RV sites as well as pet-friendly yurts. ✉ *52470 U.S. 101* ☎ *541/347–2209* 🌐 *www.oregonstateparks.org* 🎟 *Free.*

Face Rock State Scenic Viewpoint

BEACH—SIGHT | The stone sculptures of Face Rock Wayside, formed only by wind and rain, have names such as Elephant Rock, Table Rock, and Face Rock. To reach them, follow signs from Bandon south along Beach Loop Road; then walk down a stairway to the sand and enjoy the stone sights along this dramatic stretch of beach. ✉ *Beach Loop Rd. at Face Rock Dr.* 🎟 *Free.*

★ Oregon Islands National Wildlife Refuge: Coquille Point Unit

NATURE PRESERVE | **FAMILY** | Each of the colossal rocks jutting from the ocean between Bandon and Brookings is protected as part of the 19-acre Coquille Point section of this huge refuge that, in total, comprises 1,853 rocks, reefs, islands, and two headland areas spanning 320 miles up and down the Oregon Coast. Thirteen species of seabirds—totalling 1.2 million birds—nest here, and harbor seals, California sea lions, Steller sea lions, and Northern elephant seals also breed within the refuge. Coquille Point, which sits at the edge of Kronenberg County Park close to downtown Bandon, is one of the best places to observe seabirds and harbor seals. The dramatic point atop a steep sea cliff overlooks a series of offshore rocks, and a paved trail that winds over the headland ends in stairways to the beach on both sides, allowing for a loop across the sand when tides permit. Visitors are encouraged to steer clear of harbor seals and avoid touching seal pups. **■TIP→ A complete list of Oregon Islands Refuge viewpoints and trails is available online, and the refuge headquarters is located up the coast in Newport.** ✉ *11th St. W at Portland Ave. SW* ☎ *541/867–4550* 🌐 *www.fws.gov/refuge/oregon_islands.*

West Coast Game Park Safari

NATURE PRESERVE | **FAMILY** | The "walk-through safari" on 21 acres has free-roaming wildlife (it's the visitors who are behind fences); more than 450 animals and about 75 species, including lions, tigers, snow leopards, lemurs, bears, chimps, cougars, and camels, make it one of the largest wild-animal petting parks in the United States. The big attractions here are the young animals: bear cubs, tiger cubs, whatever is suitable for actual handling. ✉ *46914 U.S.*

101 ☎ 541/347–3106 🌐 www.westcoastgameparksafari.com 🎫 $20.50 ⏲ Closed weekdays Jan.–Feb.

Restaurants

Alloro Wine Bar

$$$$ | **MODERN ITALIAN** | Although it bills itself as a wine bar, this casually upscale dining room with local art on the walls is also one of the southern Oregon Coast's most sophisticated little restaurants, with a dinner menu that emphasizes freshly made pastas, often served with local seafood (the wild sea scallops with orange zest–infused spaetzle is a standout). Wines by the glass and bottle are discounted 25% during early evening happy hour. **Known for:** homemade (gluten-free on request) pasta with seafood; extensive Italian and southern Oregon wine list; knowledgeable staff. *$ Average main: $32 ✉ 375 2nd St. SE ☎ 541/347–1850 🌐 www.allorowinebar.com ⏲ Closed Wed. and Sun. No lunch.*

Edgewaters Restaurant

$$ | **SEAFOOD** | This second-story bar above Edgewaters Restaurant has some of the best west-facing views of the Coquille River and the ocean beyond—you can sometimes see migrating whales. It makes a great happy-hour stop with its tall ceilings, warm fireplace, and many windows, while the main dining downstairs also has great views and serves a great array of fresh seafood, pastas, and creative salads. **Known for:** fish- or prawns-and-chips; impressive river and sunset views; seafood chowder. *$ Average main: $22 ✉ 480 1st St. ☎ 541/347–8500 🌐 www.edgewaters.net ⏲ No lunch Tues.–Thurs. Closed Mon. in winter.*

Lord Bennett's

$$$ | **AMERICAN** | His lordship has a lot going for him: a cliff-top setting, a comfortable and spacious dining area in a dramatic contemporary building, sunsets visible through picture windows overlooking Face Rock Beach, and occasional live music on weekends. The modern American menu features plenty of local seafood; try the nut-crusted halibut, blackened red snapper with potato-horseradish crust, or wild prawns with garlic butter and sherry. **Known for:** Sunday brunch; some of the best steaks in the area; dazzling ocean views. *$ Average main: $29 ✉ 1695 Beach Loop Rd. ☎ 541/347–3663 🌐 www.lordbennetts.com ⏲ No lunch Mon.–Sat.*

★ Tony's Crab Shack & Seafood Grill

$$ | **SEAFOOD** | Started in 1989 as a bait and tackle shop (which still exists next door), this casual short-order seafooder has become a staple of Bandon's small but picturesque riverfront boardwalk, renowned for its crab cakes, fish tacos, crab and bay shrimp sandwich, and house-smoked salmon. Open only until 6 pm, it's a reliable bet for lunch or a very early dinner. **Known for:** scenic riverfront location; combo crab, steamer clam, and shrimp platters; grilled oysters on the half shell with garlic butter. *$ Average main: $19 ✉ 155 1st St. ☎ 541/347–2875 🌐 www.tonyscrabshack.com.*

Hotels

★ Bandon Dunes Golf Resort

$$$ | **RESORT** | This golfing lodge provides a comfortable place to relax after a day on the world-famous links, with accommodations ranging from single rooms or cottages to four-bedroom condos, many with beautiful views of the famous golf course. **Pros:** if you're a golfer, this adds to an incredible overall experience; if not, you'll have a wonderful stay anyway; lots of on-site dining options. **Cons:** the weather can be wet and wild in the shoulder-season months; not within walking distance of town; no a/c in rooms. *$ Rooms from: $240 ✉ 57744 Round Lake Dr. ☎ 541/347–4380, 888/345–6008 🌐 www.bandondunesgolf.com 🛏 186 rooms 🍽 Free Breakfast.*

Bandon Inn

$$ | **HOTEL** | This comfy, casual motel offers views of Old Town Bandon and the mouth of Coquille River from every room, each with a small balcony from which to take in the scenery and the town's famous Fourth of July fireworks. **Pros:** steps from downtown dining and shopping; good value; nice views of town and river. **Cons:** walls are a little thin; not directly on the water; busy downtown location. *Rooms from: $154* *355 U.S. 101* *541/347–4417, 800/526–0209* *www.bandoninn.com* *57 rooms* *Free breakfast.*

Shopping

★ **Face Rock Creamery**

FOOD/CANDY | Launched in 2013, this local creamery has rapidly developed a following for its classic and flavored handmade cheddar as well as its cheese curds and spreadable fromage blanc. At the downtown creamery, you'll also find a wide range of gourmet food items, soups and sandwiches, and ice cream—it's a perfect stop for picnic supplies. The milk comes from a 600-acre dairy farm just 15 miles from Bandon. *680 2nd St. SE* *541/347–3223* *www.facerockcreamery.com.*

Activities

GOLF

★ **Bandon Dunes Golf Resort**

GOLF | This windswept, links-style playland for the nation's golfing elite is no stranger to well-heeled athletes flying in to North Bend on private jets to play on the resort's four distinct courses, including the beloved Pacific Dunes layout, many of whose rolling, bunker-laced fairways meander atop high bluffs with breathtaking ocean views. The steep greens fees vary a good bit according to season; they drop sharply during the November–April off-season. The expectation (although not requirement) at Bandon Dunes is that you walk the course with a caddy—adding a refined, traditional touch. Caddy fees are $100 per bag, per round, plus gratuity. *57744 Round Lake Dr.* *541/347–4380, 888/345–6008* *www.bandondunesgolf.com* *$255–$345* *Bandon Dunes Course: 18 holes, 5716 yards, par 72; Bandon Trails Course: 18 holes, 5751 yards, par 71; Old Macdonald Course: 18 holes, 5658 yards, par 71; Pacific Dunes Course: 18 holes, 5775 yards, par 71.*

Port Orford

30 miles south of Bandon.

The westernmost incorporated community in the contiguous United States, Port Orford is surrounded by pristine forests, rivers, lakes, and beaches. Its secluded setting and dramatic natural scenery make it an ideal place to live or visit among artists, hikers, and others who appreciate solitude. The jetty at Port Orford offers little protection from storms, so every night the fishing boats are lifted out and stored on the docks. The town of about 1,150 is a prolific center of commercial fishing (mostly for crab, tuna, snapper, and salmon), diving boats gather sea urchins for Japanese markets—fishing enthusiasts also like to cast a line off the Port Orford dock or the jetty for smelt, sardine, herring, lingcod, and halibut. Dock Beach is a favorite spot for sport divers because of the near-shore, protected reef, and for whale-watchers in fall and early spring.

GETTING HERE AND AROUND

Port Orford is a 30-minute drive south of Bandon and a one-hour drive north of Brookings along U.S. 101.

ESSENTIALS

VISITOR INFORMATION Port Orford Visitors Center. *520 Jefferson St.* *541/332–4106* *www.enjoyportorford.com.*

Sights

Battle Rock Park and Port Orford Heads State Park

NATIONAL/STATE PARK | FAMILY | Stroll the mocha-colored sand and admire pristine Battle Rock right in the heart of downtown Port Orford. Named for a battle between white settlers and the Dene Tsut Dah that took place here in 1850, this spot sits just below Port Orford Heads State Park. Atop the bluff that is Port Orford Heads, a trail loops the rocky outcropping between the Pacific and the Port Orford Lifeboat Station, taking in the hillside below, from which crews once mounted daring rescues on the fierce sea. The lifeboat station and adjoining museum is open for free tours Wednesday–Monday, 10–3:30. Their motto? "You have to go out... you don't have to come back." ⊠ *Port Orford Hwy.* ✣ *Follow signs from U.S. 101* ☎ *541/332–6774* ⊕ *www.oregonstateparks.org.*

Cape Blanco State Park

NATIONAL/STATE PARK | FAMILY | Said to be the westernmost point in Oregon and perhaps the windiest—gusts clocked at speeds as high as 184 mph have twisted and battered the Sitka spruces along the 6-mile road from U.S. 101 to the **Cape Blanco Lighthouse.** The lighthouse, atop a 245-foot headland, has been in continuous use since 1870, longer than any other in Oregon. **Hughes House** is all that remains of the Irish settler Patrick Hughes's dairy farm complex built in 1860. The lighthouse and Hughes House are open in summer only. No one knows why the Spaniards sailing past these reddish bluffs in 1603 called them *blanco* (white). One theory is that the name refers to the fossilized shells that glint in the cliff face. Campsites at the 1,880-acre park are available on a first-come, first-served basis. Four cabins are available for reservation. ⊠ *91814 Cape Blanco Rd., Sixes* ☎ *541/332–2973* ⊕ *www.oregonstateparks.org* 🎫 *Day use and Hughes House tour free; lighthouse tour $2.*

★ Humbug Mountain State Park

NATIONAL/STATE PARK | This secluded, 1,850-acre park, especially popular with campers, usually has warm weather, thanks to the nearby mountains that shelter it from ocean breezes. A 6-mile loop leads to the top of 1,756-foot Humbug Mountain, one of the highest points along the state's coastline. It's a pretty, moderately challenging hike, but the summit is fairly overgrown and doesn't provide especially panoramic views. The campground has tent and RV sites. ⊠ *U.S. 101* ✣ *6 miles south of Port Orford* ☎ *541/332–6774* ⊕ *www.oregonstateparks.org.*

Prehistoric Gardens

LOCAL INTEREST | FAMILY | As you round a bend between Port Orford and Gold Beach, you'll see one of those sights that make grown-ups groan and kids squeal with delight: a huge, open-jawed Tyrannosaurus rex, with a green Brontosaurus peering out from the forest beside it. You can view 23 other life-size dinosaur replicas on the trail that runs through the property. ⊠ *36848 U.S. 101* ☎ *541/332–4463* ⊕ *www.prehistoricgardens.com* 🎫 *$12.*

Restaurants

Crazy Norwegians Fish and Chips

$ | SEAFOOD | FAMILY | This quirky and casual hole-in-the-wall in Port Orford excels at what it does: good old-fashioned fish-and-chips. With everything from shrimp to cod to halibut paired with fries, the Crazy Norwegians serve it up with a side of pasta salad or coleslaw. **Known for:** to-go meals to take to the beach or park; the crazy combo platter (jumbo prawns, cod, and clams); stellar fish-and-chips. 💲 *Average main: $13* ⊠ *259 6th St.* ☎ *541/332–8601* ⊕ *the-crazy-norwegians-fish-and-chips.business.site/* 🕒 *Closed Mon.*

★ **Redfish**
$$$ | **MODERN AMERICAN** | Two walls of windows allow diners at this stylish downtown bistro spectacular ocean panoramas, but the views inside are pretty inviting, too, from the modern artwork provided by sister establishment Hawthorne Gallery to the artfully presented and globally influenced food. Start with the local clams sautéed in butter or the five-spice baked duck eggrolls, before graduating to double-cut pork chops with cranberry-apple chutney or house-made gnocchi with pesto and hazelnuts. **Known for:** crab cakes Benedict at weekend brunch; stunning water views; a noteworthy cocktail, wine, and craft beer program. *$ Average main: $25 ✉ 517 Jefferson St. ☎ 541/366–2200 🌐 www.redfishportorford.com ⏲ Closed Tues.*

Castaway by the Sea
$ | **HOTEL** | **FAMILY** | This old-school motel with a friendly owner offers fantastic views from nearly every room, most of which have enclosed sun porches—the simplest and least expensive accommodations open to an enclosed breezeway that takes in these same views. **Pros:** within walking distance of local restaurants; panoramic ocean views; reasonable rates. **Cons:** decor is a bit dated; not actually on the beach; quirky decor may not please everyone. *$ Rooms from: $125 ✉ 545 5th St. ☎ 541/332–4502 🌐 www.castawaybythesea.com 13 rooms No meals.*

★ **WildSpring Guest Habitat**
$$$$ | **B&B/INN** | This rustic outpost in the woods above Port Orford blends all the comforts and privacy of a vacation rental with the services of a small resort. **Pros:** relaxing, secluded, and private; gorgeous rooms; eco-conscious practices. **Cons:** need to drive to the beach and stores; not a good fit if you like bigger hotels; two-night minimum on summer weekends. *$ Rooms from: $259 ✉ 92978 Cemetery Loop Rd. ☎ 541/332–0977, 866/333–9453 🌐 www.wildspring.com 5 cabins Free breakfast.*

Gold Beach

28 miles south of Port Orford.

The fabled Rogue River is one of about 150 in the nation to merit federally designated Wild and Scenic status. From spring to late fall, thousands of visitors descend on the town to take one of the daily jet-boat excursions that roar upstream from Wedderburn, an unincorporated hamlet across the bay from Gold Beach, into the Rogue River Wilderness Area. Black bears, otters, beavers, ospreys, egrets, and bald eagles are seen regularly on these trips.

GETTING HERE AND AROUND

It's a 90-minute drive south along U.S. 101 from Coos Bay and North Bend to reach Gold Beach, which is a one-hour drive north of the California border.

ESSENTIALS

VISITOR INFORMATION Gold Beach Visitors Center. *✉ 94080 Shirley La. ☎ 541/247–7526, 800/525–2334 🌐 www.visitgoldbeach.com.*

Cape Sebastian State Scenic Corridor
VIEWPOINT | The parking lots at this scenic area are more than 200 feet above sea level. At the south parking vista, you can see up to 43 miles north to Humbug Mountain. Looking south, you can see nearly 50 miles toward Crescent City, California, and the Point Saint George Lighthouse. A deep forest of Sitka spruce covers most of the park. There's a 1½-mile walking trail. *✉ U.S. 101 ✣ 6 miles south of Gold Beach ☎ 541/469–2021 🌐 www.oregonstateparks.org.*

Restaurants

★ Anna's by the Sea

$$$ | **MODERN CANADIAN** | Dining at Anna's by the Sea is like stepping into one man's artisanal universe: bowed and wood-trimmed ceilings, handmade cheeses, and blackberry honey lemonade, even a hydroponic herb garden, crafted by the owner–head cook. The enchanting, intimate eatery seats only 18, six of those seats stools with a view into the kitchen, and serves what it calls "retro nouvelle Canadian Prairie cuisine," which might include a charcuterie plate of goose prosciutto, smoked local albacore, and beef-tongue pastrami, or Alaskan scallops on a bed of buttered pasta with truffle oil. **Known for:** outstanding selection of Oregon wines and craft spirits; live music; friendly, knowledgeable service. *Average main: $26 ✉ 29672 Stewart St. ☎ 514/247–2100 🌐 www.annasbythesea.com ⏲ Closed Sun.–Tues. No lunch.*

Barnacle Bistro

$ | **AMERICAN** | At this quirky tavern on the main road in downtown Gold Beach, try the lingcod fish-and-chips with ginger-sesame coleslaw and sweet-potato fries, the curry-cider mussels, the shellfish tacos with a Brazilian coconut-peanut sauce, or any of the enormous burgers. It's reliably good pub fare using produce, meat, and seafood sourced locally. **Known for:** beer from nearby Arch Rock Brewery; very reasonable prices; hefty burgers. *Average main: $14 ✉ 29805 Ellensburg Ave. ☎ 541/247–7799 🌐 www.barnaclebistro.com ⏲ Closed Sun. and Mon.*

Wild Oaks Grill

$$ | **BARBECUE** | This bare-bones, counter-service barbecue joint serves up diabolically delicious, house-brined and smoked meaty fare along with sides of fries with decadent toppings (poutine, chili-cheese, and so on). The burgers and sandwiches are delicious, but if you have the appetite for it, consider the sampler of pulled pork, smoked chicken breast, baby back ribs, brisket, and tri-tip with a couple of sides. **Known for:** tri-tip sandwiches; habanero-garlic-Parmesan fries; smoked bacon. *Average main: $16 ✉ 29545 Ellensburg Ave. ☎ 541/425–5460 🌐 www.wildoaksgrill.com.*

Hotels

Pacific Reef and Resort

$ | **HOTEL** | **FAMILY** | This resort offers a little something for everyone: from comfy, clean, economical rooms in the original renovated 1950s hotel to modern two-story condos with expansive ocean views, king-size beds, full kitchens, and outdoor patios. **Pros:** nicely equipped condos with full kitchens; in center of town; glorious water views from the best units. **Cons:** adjoins a rocky beach; on a busy road; could use a little updating. *Rooms from: $89 ✉ 29362 Ellensburg Hwy. ☎ 541/247–6658 🌐 www.pacificreefhotel.com 39 units Free breakfast.*

★ Tu Tu' Tun Lodge

$$$$ | **RESORT** | Pronounced "too- *too*-tin," this renowned and rather lavish boutique resort is a slice of heaven on the Rogue River; its rustic-elegant rooms have private decks overlooking the water; some have hot tubs, others have fireplaces, and a few have both. **Pros:** luxurious, beautifully outfitted rooms; exceptional dining; peaceful location overlooking river. **Cons:** no TVs; not well suited for young kids; 15-minute drive from downtown and the ocean. *Rooms from: $295 ✉ 96550 N. Bank Rogue River Rd. ✣ 7 miles east of Gold Beach ☎ 541/247–6664, 800/864–6357 🌐 www.tututun.com 20 rooms Free breakfast.*

Activities

BOATING

★ Jerry's Rogue Jets

BOATING | **FAMILY** | These jet boats operate from May through September in the most rugged section of the Wild and

Scenic Rogue River, offering 64-, 80-, and 104-mile tours, starting at $50 per person. Whether visitors choose a shorter, six-hour lower Rogue scenic trip or an eight-hour white-water trip, folks have a rollicking good time. Its largest vessels are 40 feet long and can hold 75 passengers. The smaller, white-water boats are 32 feet long and can hold 42 passengers. ✉ *29985 Harbor Way* ☎ *541/247–4571, 800/451–3645* 🌐 *www.roguejets.com.*

Brookings

27 miles south of Gold Beach on U.S. 101.

The coastal gateway to Oregon if you're approaching from California, Brookings is home to a pair of sterling state parks, one overlooking the ocean and another nestled amid the redwoods a bit inland. The only overnight option along the 55-mile stretch between Gold Beach and Crescent City, it's also a handy base, with some reasonably priced hotels and motels, and a growing crop of noteworthy restaurants. A startling 90% of the pot lilies grown in the United States come from a 500-acre area just inland from Brookings. Mild temperatures along this coastal plain provide ideal conditions for flowering plants of all kinds—even a few palm trees, a rare sight in Oregon.

The town is equally famous as a commercial and sportfishing port at the mouth of the turquoise-blue Chetco River. Salmon and steelhead weighing 20 pounds or more swim here.

GETTING HERE AND AROUND

Brookings is the southernmost town on Oregon's coastal 101, just 10 miles north of the California border and a half-hour drive from Crescent City; it's a 2½-hour drive south on U.S. 101 from the Coos Bay and North Bend area. Allow about six hours to get here from Portland via Interstate 5 to Grants Pass and U.S. 199 to Crescent City.

VISITOR INFORMATION

CONTACTS Brookings Harbor Chamber of Commerce. ✉ *703 Chetco Ave.* ☎ *541/469–3181* 🌐 *www.brookingsharborchamber.com.*

Sights

Alfred A. Loeb State Park

NATIONAL/STATE PARK | Some fine hiking trails, one leading to a hidden redwood grove, along with a nice selection of campsites, make up this park a bit inland from Brookings. There's also a grove of myrtlewood trees, which you'll find only in southwest Oregon and northern California. ✉ *N. Bank Chetco River Rd. (Hwy. 784)* ✣ *10 miles east of Brookings* ☎ *541/469–2021* 🌐 *www.oregonstateparks.org* ✍ *Reservations not accepted.*

★ Harris Beach State Park

NATIONAL/STATE PARK | The views from the parking areas, oceanfront trails, and beaches at this popular tract of craggy rock formations and evergreen forest are some of the prettiest along the southern Oregon Coast. The proximity to downtown Brookings makes this an easy place to head for morning beachcombing or a sunset stroll. You might see gray whales migrate in spring and winter. Just offshore, Bird Island, also called Goat Island, is a National Wildlife Sanctuary and a breeding site for rare birds. The campground here, with tent and RV sites, is very popular. ✉ *1655 Old U.S. 101* ☎ *541/469–2021* 🌐 *www.oregonstateparks.org.*

Restaurants

★ Oxenfre Public House

$$ | MODERN AMERICAN | The kitchen at this upbeat, contemporary gastropub with a welcoming outdoor balcony, from which you can see the ocean in the distance, stands out for its commitment to locally sourced produce and seafood and an ambitious craft-cocktail selection. The eclectic, elevated comfort fare here has an international flair—consider the Baja-style Pacific cod tacos with avocado-mango cruda and Thai chili lime crema, or Korean chicken salad with sesame-soy dressing and charred pineapple. **Known for:** first-rate craft cocktails; excellent happy hour deals; ingredients sourced from local purveyors. *Average main: $19 631 Chetco Ave. 541/813–1985 www.oxenpub.com No lunch.*

Pacific Sushi & Grill

$$$ | **SUSHI** | You'll find some of the tastiest sushi on the Oregon Coast at this welcoming Japanese restaurant with weathered-timber walls and booths and a friendly adjoining cocktail lounge. Beyond the flavorful and creative jumbo spider and hamachi jalapeño rolls, you'll find a great selection of Japanese dishes, including tonkotsu ramen with chashu pork and crispy fried karaage-style calamari. **Known for:** creative sushi rolls; cucumber-wasabi martinis; late-night menu in the lounge. *Average main: $23 613 Chetco Ave. 541/251–7707 www.pacificsushi.com Closed Thurs.*

Vista Pub

$ | **AMERICAN** | An affordable, friendly, and attractive family-run tavern in downtown Brookings, Vista Pub is known both for its extensive selection of rotating craft beers and tasty but simple comfort food. Try the hefty bacon-cheddar burgers, beer-cheese soup in a bread bowl, thick-cut fries sprinkled with sea salt, fried locally grown zucchini, and smoked-salmon chowder with bacon. **Known for:** tasty pub fare; excellent craft-beer selection; great burgers. *Average main: $11 1009 Chetco Ave. 541/813–1638 Closed Mon.*

Hotels

Beachfront Inn

$$$ | **HOTEL** | This spotlessly clean three-story Best Western across the street from the Brookings boat basin has direct beach access and ocean views, making it one of the best-maintained and most appealingly located lodging options along the southern coast. **Pros:** fantastic ocean views; quiet location away from busy U.S. 101; very well kept. **Cons:** rooms don't have much personality; not many restaurants within walking distance; a bit pricey in summer. *Rooms from: $219 16008 Boat Basin Rd. 541/469–7779 www.beachfrontinn.com 102 rooms Free breakfast.*

Chapter 5

WILLAMETTE VALLEY AND WINE COUNTRY

Updated by
Margot Bigg

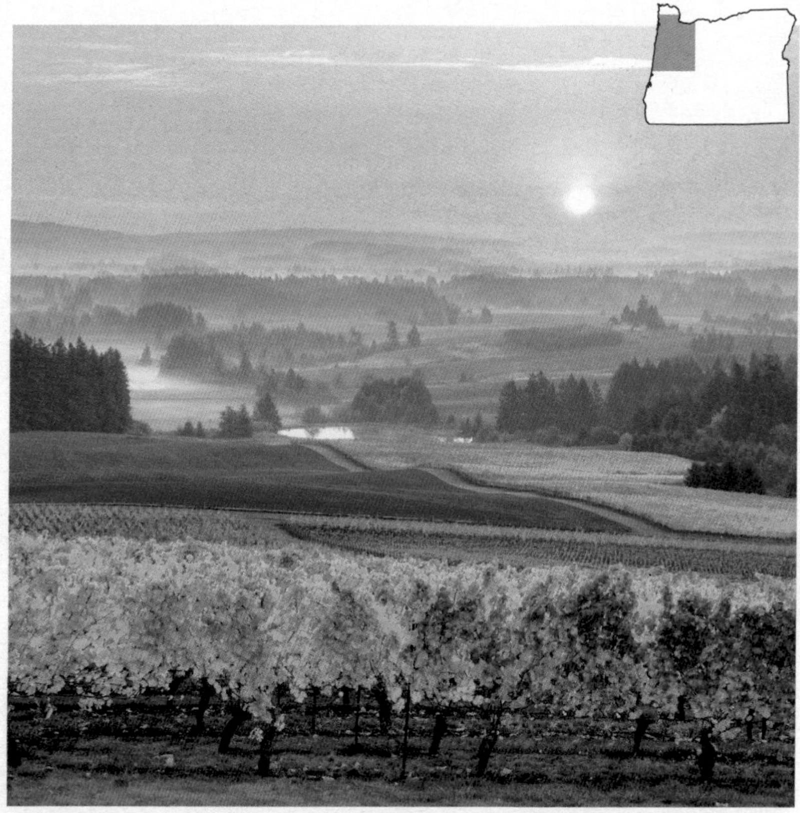

Sights	Restaurants	Hotels	Shopping	Nightlife
★★★★☆	★★★★★	★★★★☆	★★★☆☆	★☆☆☆☆

WELCOME TO WILLAMETTE VALLEY AND WINE COUNTRY

TOP REASONS TO GO

★ **Swirl and sip:** Each region in the Willamette Valley offers some of the finest vintages and dining experiences found anywhere.

★ **Soar through the air:** Newberg's hot-air balloons will give you a bird's-eye view of Yamhill County's wine country.

★ **Run rapids:** Feel the bouncing exhilaration and the cold spray of white-water rafting on the wild, winding McKenzie River outside Eugene.

★ **Walk on the wild side:** Hillsboro's Jackson Bottom Nature Preserve gives walkers a chance to view otters, beavers, herons, and eagles.

★ **Back the Beavers or Ducks:** Nothing gets the blood pumping like an Oregon State Beavers or University of Oregon Ducks football game.

The Willamette Valley is a fertile mix of urban, rural, and wild stretching from Portland at the north to Cottage Grove at the south. It is bordered by the Cascade Range to the east and the Coast Range to the west. The Calapooya Mountains border it to the south and the mighty Columbia River runs along the north. Running north and south, Interstate 5 connects communities throughout the valley. In the mid-1800s the Willamette Valley was the destination of emigrants on the Oregon Trail, and today is home to about two-thirds of the state's population. The Willamette Valley is 150 miles long and up to 60 miles wide, which makes it Oregon's largest wine-growing region.

1 **Forest Grove.** Douglas firs and sequoias surround the area's numerous wineries and tasting rooms.

2 **Newberg.** The gateway to Oregon Wine Country.

3 **Dundee.** A charming town full of wineries and restaurants.

4 **Yamhill and Carlton.** This area is home to some of the world's finest Pinot Noir vineyards.

5 **McMinnville.** The largest city in Yamhill County and the commercial hub of Oregon's wine industry, with shops, hotels, and dining galore.

6 **Independence.** Historic Victorian city in the heart of Oregon's hop country.

7 **Salem.** Oregon's historic state capital and a gateway to great hiking.

8 **Albany.** Listed on the National Register of Historic Places and home to some of Oregon's most historic buildings.

9 **Eugene.** Home to the University of Oregon and a center for athletics, this friendly, bohemian town is a great spot to eat, drink, and spend time outdoors.

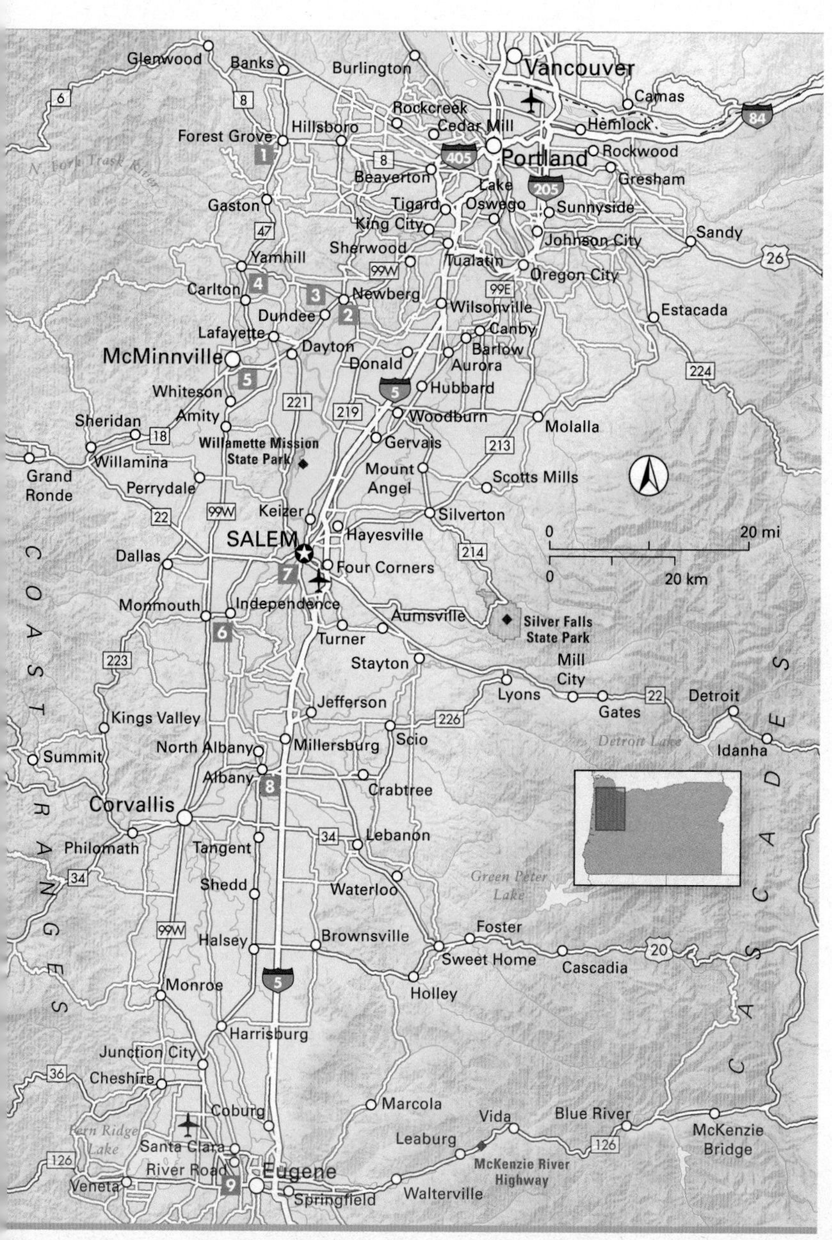
Glenwood
Banks
Burlington
Vancouver
Camas
Hemlock
Rockcreek
Cedar Mill
Hillsboro
Forest Grove
Portland
Rockwood
Gresham
Beaverton
Lake Oswego
Sunnyside
Gaston
Tigard
King City
Johnson City
Sandy
Sherwood
Tualatin
Oregon City
Yamhill
Carlton
Newberg
Wilsonville
Estacada
Dundee
Lafayette
Canby
Dayton
Barlow
McMinnville
Donald
Aurora
Hubbard
Whiteson
Amity
Woodburn
Molalla
Sheridan
Willamette Mission State Park
Gervais
Willamina
Grand Ronde
Mount Angel
Scotts Mills
Perrydale
Keizer
Silverton
SALEM
Hayesville
Dallas
Four Corners
0
20 mi
20 km
Monmouth
Independence
Aumsville
Silver Falls State Park
Turner
Stayton
Mill City
Lyons
Gates
Detroit
Jefferson
Kings Valley
Scio
North Albany
Millersburg
Detroit Lake
Idanha
Summit
Albany
Crabtree
Corvallis
Philomath
Tangent
Lebanon
Shedd
Waterloo
Green Peter Lake
Halsey
Brownsville
Foster
Sweet Home
Cascadia
Monroe
Holley
Harrisburg
Junction City
Cheshire
Marcola
Coburg
Vida
Blue River
McKenzie Bridge
Fern Ridge Lake
Leaburg
Santa Clara
River Road
Eugene
McKenzie River Highway
Veneta
Springfield
Walterville
COAST RANGES
CASCADES
N. Fork Trask River
1
2
3
4
5
6
7
8
9
6
8
8
47
99W
99E
405
205
84
26
224
221
219
5
18
213
22
214
223
22
226
34
34
99W
20
5
36
126
126

The Willamette (pronounced "wil-*lam*-it") Valley has become a wine lover's Shangri-La, particularly in the northern Yamhill and Washington counties between Interstate 5 and the Oregon Coast, a region that is not only carpeted with vineyards but encompasses small hotels and inns, cozy restaurants, and casual wine bars.

The valley divides two mountain ranges (the Cascade and Coast), and contains more than 500 wineries. The huge wine region is made up of seven subappellations: Chehalem Mountains, Ribbon Ridge, Dundee Hills, Yamhill-Carlton, Eola-Amity Hills, The Van Duzer Corridor, and McMinnville. With its incredibly rich soil perfect for growing Pinot Noir, Pinot Gris, Chardonnay, and Riesling, the valley has received worldwide acclaim for its vintages. The region's farms are famous for producing quality fruits, vegetables, and cheeses that are savored in area restaurants. During spring and summer there are many roadside stands dotting the country lanes, and farmers' markets appear in most of the valley's towns. Also delicious are the locally raised lamb, pork, chicken, and beef. The valley also is a huge exporter of plants and flowers for nurseries, with a large number of farms growing ornamental trees, bulbs, and plants.

The valley definitely has an artsy, expressive, and fun side, with its wine and beer festivals, theater, music, crafts, and culinary events. Many residents and visitors are serious runners and bicyclists, particularly in Eugene, so pay close attention while driving.

There's a long-standing collegiate football rivalry between the Oregon State Beavers in Corvallis and University of Oregon Ducks in Eugene; getting a ticket to the annual "Civil War" game between the two teams is a feat in itself. Across the state, but particularly in the Willamette Valley, Oregonians are passionate fans of one team or the other. If you happen to be visiting the area during the event (usually held in October or November), be prepared for some serious traffic and some closed businesses.

MAJOR REGIONS

Just outside Portland, in the **North Willamette Valley,** the suburban areas of Tigard, Hillsboro, and **Forest Grove** have gorgeous wetlands, rivers, and nature preserves. The area has a wealth of golfing, biking, and trails for running and hiking and it's not unusual to spot red-tail hawks, beavers, and ducks on your route. Shopping, fine dining, and proximity to Portland make this a great area in which to begin your exploration of the Willamette Valley and its wine country.

Yamhill County, at the northern end of the Willamette Valley, has a fortunate confluence of perfect soils, a benign climate, and talented winemakers who craft world-class vintages. In recent years several new wineries have been built in Yamhill County's hills, as well as on its flatlands. While vineyards flourished in the northern Willamette Valley in the 19th century, viticulture didn't arrive in Yamhill County until the 1960s and 1970s, with such pioneers as Dick Erath (Erath Vineyards Winery), David and Ginny Adelsheim (Adelsheim Vineyard), and David and Diana Lett (The Eyrie Vineyards). The focus of much of the county's enthusiasm lies in the Red Hills of Dundee, where the farming towns of **Newberg, Dundee, Yamhill-Carlton,** and **McMinnville** have made room for upscale hotels and bed-and-breakfasts, wine bars, and tourists seeking that perfect swirl and sip.

The Yamhill County wineries are only a short drive from Portland, and the roads, especially Route 99W and Route 18, can be crowded on weekends as they link suburban Portland communities to Newport and Lincoln City on the Oregon Coast.

While most of the wineries are concentrated in Washington and Yamhill counties, there are several finds in the **mid–Willamette Valley** that warrant extending a wine enthusiast's journey, with plenty of breweries, flower farms, and state parks along the way. Popular spots to stop include **Salem, Independence,** and **Albany.** The large cluster of factory outlet shops in Woodburn on Interstate 5 will have you thinking about some new Nikes, and Oregon State University will have you wearing orange and black long after Halloween is over. Be aware that many communities in this region are little more than wide spots in the road.

Lane County rests at the southern end of the **South Willamette Valley,** encompassing **Eugene,** Springfield, Drain, **McKenzie Bridge,** and Cottage Grove. Visitors can enjoy a wide range of outdoor activities such as running, fishing, swimming, white-water rafting, and deep-woods hiking along the McKenzie River, while Eugene offers great food, shopping, and the arts. There are plenty of wineries to enjoy, too, as well as cheering on the Oregon Ducks. To the west lies the Oregon Dunes Recreation Area, and to the east are the beautiful central Oregon communities of Sisters, Bend, and Redmond.

Planning

When to Go

July to October are the best times to wander the country roads in the Willamette Valley, exploring the grounds of its many wineries. Fall is spectacular, with leaves at their colorful peak in late October. Winters are usually mild, but they can be relentlessly overcast and downright rainy. Visitors not disturbed by dampness or chill will find excellent deals on lodging. In the spring rains continue, but the wildflowers begin to bloom, which pays off at the many gardens and nature parks throughout the valley.

FESTIVALS

International Pinot Noir Celebration

FESTIVALS | During the International Pinot Noir Celebration, held the last full weekend in July, wine lovers flock to McMinnville to sample fine regional vintages along with Pinot Noir from around the world. ✉ *Box 1310800, McMinnville* ☎ *800/775–4762* 🌐 *www.ipnc.org.*

Oregon Bach Festival

FESTIVALS | Eugene hosts the world-class Oregon Bach Festival, with two-plus weeks of classical music performances. ✉ *1257 University of Oregon, Eugene* ☎ *541/346–5666, 800/457–1486* 🌐 *oregonbachfestival.com.*

Oregon Country Fair

FESTIVALS | Every July, the weekend after Independence Day, a small patch of fields and forest right outside of Eugene transforms into an enchanting community celebration known as the Oregon Country Fair. This annual event has been going on since the 1960s and maintains much of its flower-child vibe, with all sorts of parades, live music, puppet shows, face painting, and excellent craft shopping. ✉ *24207 Oregon 126, Veneta* ☎ *541/343–4298* 🌐 *www.oregoncountryfair.org.*

Wooden Shoe Tulip Fest

FESTIVALS | Every April, visitors to Woodburn's Wooden Shoe Tulip Farm can tiptoe (or walk, or take a hayride) through spectacular fields of brightly hued tulips. Other festival features include wine tastings, cutout boards for photos, food booths, and a play area for kids. ✉ *33814 S. Meridian Rd., Woodburn* ☎ *503/634–2243* 🌐 *www.woodenshoe.com/events/tulip-fest/.*

Getting Here and Around

AIR TRAVEL

Portland's airport is an hour's drive east of the northern Willamette Valley. The **Aloha Express Airport Shuttle** provides shuttle service. **Eugene Airport** is more convenient if you're exploring the region's southern end. It's served by Delta, Alaska/Horizon, American, and United/United Express. The flight from Portland to Eugene is 40 minutes. Smaller airports for private aircraft are scattered throughout the valley.

Rental cars are available at the Eugene airport from Budget, Enterprise, and Hertz. Taxis and airport shuttles will transport you to downtown Eugene for about $30. **Omni Shuttle** will provide shuttle service to and from the Eugene airport from anywhere in Oregon.

AIR CONTACTS Aloha Express Airport Shuttle. ☎ *503/356–8848* 🌐 *www.alohaexpressshuttle.com.* **Hub Airport Shuttle.** ☎ *541/461–7959* 🌐 *hubairportshuttle.com.*

BUS TRAVEL

Buses operated by Portland's **TriMet** network connect Forest Grove, Hillsboro, and other metro-area suburb communities with Portland and each other; light-rail trains operated by MAX run between Portland and Hillsboro. Many of the **Lane Transit District** buses will make a few stops to the outskirts of Lane County, such as McKenzie Bridge. All buses have bike racks. **Yamhill County Transit Area** provides bus service for Yamhill County, with links to Hillsboro/MAX, Sherwood/TriMet, and Salem/SAMT.

BUS CONTACTS Lane Transit District. *(LTD)* ☎ *541/687–5555* 🌐 *www.ltd.org.* **Yamhill County Transit Area.** ☎ *503/474–4900* 🌐 *www.ycbus.org.*

CAR TRAVEL

Interstate 5 runs north–south the length of the Willamette Valley. Many Willamette Valley attractions sit not too far east or west of Interstate 5. Highway 22 travels west from the Willamette National Forest through Salem to the coast. Highway 99 travels parallel to Interstate 5 through much of the Willamette Valley. Highway 34 leaves Interstate 5 just south of Albany and heads west, past Corvallis and into the Coast Range, where it follows the Alsea River. Highway 126 heads east from Eugene toward the Willamette National Forest; it travels west from town to the coast. U.S. 20 travels west from Corvallis. Most major rental car companies have outposts in Portland and throughout the region.

Restaurants

The buzzwords associated with fine dining in this region are "sustainable," "farm-to-table," and "local." Fresh salmon, Dungeness crab, mussels, shrimp, and oysters are harvested just a couple of hours away on the Oregon Coast. Lamb, pork, and beef are local and plentiful, and seasonal game appears on many menus. Desserts made with local blueberries, huckleberries, raspberries, and marionberries should not be missed. But what really sets the offerings apart are the splendid local wines that receive worldwide acclaim.

Restaurants in the Willamette Valley are low-key and unpretentious. Expensive doesn't necessarily mean better, and locals have a pretty good nose for good value. Reasonably priced Mexican, Indian, Japanese, and Italian do very well. Food carts in the cities are a growing phenomenon. But there's still nothing like a great, sit-down meal at a cozy bistro for some fresh fish or lamb, washed down with a stellar Pinot Noir. *Restaurant reviews have been shortened. For full information visit Fodors.com.*

What It Costs in U.S. Dollars

$	$$	$$$	$$$$
RESTAURANTS			
under $16	$17–$22	$23–$30	over $30
HOTELS			
under $150	$150–$200	$201–$250	over $250

Hotels

One of the great pleasures of touring the Willamette Valley is the incredible selection of small, ornate bed-and-breakfast hotels sprinkled throughout Oregon's wine country. In the summer and fall they can fill up quickly, as visitors come from around the world to enjoy wine tastings at the hundreds of large and small wineries. Many of these have exquisite restaurants right on the premises, with home-baked goods available day and night. There are plenty of larger properties located closer to urban areas and shopping centers, including upscale resorts with expansive spas, as well as national chains that are perfect for travelers who just need a place to lay their heads. *Hotel reviews have been shortened. For full information, visit Fodors.com.*

Tours

Oregon Wine Tours and **EcoTours of Oregon** provide informative guided outings across the Willamette Valley wine country.

CONTACTS EcoTours of Oregon. ☎ *503/245–1428* 🌐 *www.ecotours-of-oregon.com.* **Great Oregon Tours.** ☎ *971/713–1023* 🌐 *greatoregontours.com.*

Visitor Information

CONTACTS Travel Lane County. ✉ *754 Olive St., Eugene* ☎ *541/484–5307, 800/547–5445* 🌐 *www.eugenecascadescoast.org.* **Washington County Visitors Association.** ✉ *12725 S.W. Millikan Way, Suite 210, Beaverton* ☎ *503/644–5555, 800/537–3149* 🌐 *www.oregonswashingtoncounty.com.* **Willamette Valley Visitors Association.** ☎ *866/548–5018* 🌐 *www.oregonwinecountry.org.*

Forest Grove

24 miles west of Portland on Hwy. 8.

This small town is surrounded by stands of Douglas firs and giant sequoia, including the largest giant sequoia in the state. There are nearby wetlands, birding, the Hagg Lake Recreation Area, a new outdoor adventure park, and numerous wineries and tasting rooms. To get to many of the wineries, head south from Forest Grove on Highway 47 and watch for the blue road signs between Forest Grove, Gaston, and Yamhill. To the west of town, you'll find some of the oldest Pinot Noir vines in the valley at David Hill Winery.

GETTING HERE AND AROUND

Forest Grove is about an hour's drive west from Portland International Airport. The **Aloha Express Airport Shuttle** and the **Beaverton Airporter** provide shuttle service.

From Downtown Portland it's a short 35-minute car ride with only a few traffic lights during the entire trip. TriMet Bus Service provides bus service to and from Forest Grove every 15 minutes, connecting to the MAX light rail 6 miles east in Hillsboro, which continues into Portland. Buses travel to Cornelius, Hillsboro, Aloha, and Beaverton.

ESSENTIALS

CONTACTS Forest Grove Chamber of Commerce. ✉ *2417 Pacific Ave.* ☎ *503/357–3006* 🌐 *www.visitforestgrove.com.*

David Hill Vineyards and Winery

WINERY/DISTILLERY | In 1965 Charles Coury came to Oregon from California and planted some of the Willamette Valley's first Pinot Noir vines on the site of what is now the David Hill Winery. The original farmhouse serves as the tasting room and offers splendid views of the Tualatin Valley. They produce Pinot Noir, some of which comes from the original vines planted by Coury, along with Chardonnay, Gewürztraminer, Merlot, Tempranillo, Pinot Gris, and Riesling. The wines are well made and pleasant, especially the eclectic blend called Farmhouse Red and the estate Riesling. ✉ *46350 N.W. David Hill Rd.* ☎ *503/992–8545* 🌐 *www.davidhillwinery.com* 🎫 *Tastings from $10.*

Elk Cove Vineyard

WINERY/DISTILLERY | Founded in 1974 by Pat and Joe Campbell, this established winery covers 600 acres on four separate vineyard sites. The tasting room is set in the beautiful rolling hills at the foot of the coast range overlooking the vines. The focus is on Willamette Valley Pinot Noir, Pinot Gris, and Pinot Blanc. Be sure to also try the limited bottling of their Pinot Noir Rosé if they're pouring it. ✉ *27751 N.W. Olson Rd., Gaston* ☎ *503/985–7760, 877/355–2683* 🌐 *www.elkcove.com* 🎫 *Tastings from $15.*

Montinore Estate

WINERY/DISTILLERY | Locals chuckle at visitors who try to show off their French savvy when they pronounce it "Mont-in-or-ay." The estate, originally a ranch, was established by a tycoon who'd made his money in the Montana mines before he retired to Oregon; he decided to call his estate "Montana in Oregon." Montinore (no "ay" at the end) has 232 acres of vineyards, and its wines reflect the high-quality soil and fruit. Highlights include a crisp Gewürztraminer, a light Müller-Thurgau, an off-dry Riesling, several lush Pinot Noirs, and a delightful white blend called Borealis that's a perfect partner for Northwest seafood. ✉ *3663 S.W. Dilley Rd.* ☎ *503/359–5012* 🌐 *www.montinore.com* 🎫 *Tastings $15.*

SakéOne

WINERY/DISTILLERY | After the founders realized that the country's best water supply for sake was in the Pacific Northwest, they built their brewery in Forest Grove in 1997. It's one of only six sake brewing facilities in America and produces award-winning sake under three labels, in addition to importing from partners in Japan. The tasting room offers three different flights, including one with a food pairing. Be sure to catch one of the tours, offered Friday through Sunday, where your guide will walk you through every phase of the sake-making process, from milling the rice to final filtration and bottling. ✉ *820 Elm St.* ☎ *503/357–7056, 800/550–7253* 🌐 *www.sakeone.com* 🎫 *Tastings from $10.*

★ Scoggin Valley Park and Henry Hagg Lake

NATIONAL/STATE PARK | FAMILY | This beautiful area in the Coast Range foothills has a 15-mile-long hiking trail that surrounds the lake. Bird-watching is best in spring. Recreational activities include fishing, boating, waterskiing, picnicking, and hiking, and a 10½-mile, well-marked bicycle lane parallels the park's perimeter road. *50250 S.W. Scoggins Valley Rd., Gaston 503/846–8715 www.co.washington.or.us/Support_Services/Facilities/Parks/Hagglake Free, parking $7.*

Tree to Tree Adventure Park

AMUSEMENT PARK/WATER PARK | FAMILY | At the first public aerial adventure park in the Pacific Northwest—and only the second of its kind in the United States—the aerial adventure course features 19 ziplines and more than 60 treetop elements and obstacles. You can experience the thrills of moving from platform to platform (tree to tree) via wobbly bridges, tightropes, Tarzan swings, and more. The courses range from beginner to extreme, with certified and trained instructors providing guidance to adventurers. "Woody's Ziptastic Voyage" zipline tour features six extreme ziplines (including one that is 1,280 feet long), a bridge, and a 40-foot rappel. Harnesses and helmets are provided, and no open-toed shoes are allowed. Reservations are required. *2975 S.W. Nelson Rd., Gaston 503/357–0109 tree2treeadventurepark.com Aerial park $55, zip tour $85 Closed mid-Nov.–Feb.*

Hotels

McMenamins Grand Lodge

$ | HOTEL | On 13 acres of pastoral countryside, this converted Masonic rest home has accommodations that run from bunk-bed rooms to a three-room fireplace suite, with some nice period antiques in all. **Pros:** relaxed, friendly brewpub atmosphere; spa and soaking pool; on-site disc golf course. **Cons:** some rooms have shared bathrooms; not much to do in the area; rooms can be noisy. *Rooms from: $60 3505 Pacific Ave. 503/992–9533, 877/992–9533 www.mcmenamins.com/grandlodge 90 rooms No meals.*

Newberg

24 miles south of Portland on Hwy. 99W.

Newberg sits in the Chehalem Valley, known as one of Oregon's most fertile wine-growing locations, and is called the Gateway to Oregon Wine Country. Many of Newberg's early settlers were Quakers from the Midwest, who founded the school that has become George Fox University. Newberg's most famous resident, likewise a Quaker, was Herbert Hoover, the 31st president of the United States. For about five years during his adolescence, he lived with an aunt and uncle at the Hoover-Minthorn House, now a museum listed on the National Register of Historic Places. Now the town is on the map for the nearby wineries, fine-dining establishments, and a spacious, spectacular resort, the Allison. St. Paul, a historic town with a population of about 325, is about 8 miles south of Newberg, and every July holds a professional rodeo.

GETTING HERE AND AROUND

Newberg is just under an hour's drive from Portland International Airport; **Caravan Airport Transportation** (*541/994–9645 www.caravanairporttransportation.com*) provides shuttle service. The best way to visit Newberg and the Yamhill County vineyards is by car. Situated on Highway 99W, Newberg is 90 minutes from Lincoln City, on the Oregon Coast. Greyhound provides bus service to McMinnville.

David Hill Vineyards and Winery in Forest Grove produces Pinot Noir, as well as Chardonnay, Gewürztraminer, Merlot, Tempranillo, Pinot Gris, and Riesling.

Sights

★ Adelsheim Vineyard

WINERY/DISTILLERY | David Adelsheim is the knight in shining armor of the Oregon wine industry—tirelessly promoting Oregon wines abroad, and always willing to share the knowledge he has gained from his long viticultural experience. He and Ginny Adelsheim founded their pioneer winery in 1971. They make their wines from grapes picked on their 230 acres of estate vineyards, as well as from grapes they've purchased. Their Pinot Noir, Pinot Gris, Pinot Blanc, and Chardonnay all conform to the Adelsheim house style of rich, balanced fruit and long, clean finishes. They also make a spicy cool-climate Syrah from grapes grown just outside the beautiful tasting room. **■ TIP→ Tours are available by appointment.** ✉ *16800 N.E. Calkins La.* ☎ *503/538–3652* 🌐 *www.adelsheim.com* 🎫 *Tastings from $15.*

Aramenta Cellars

WINERY/DISTILLERY | Owners Ed and Darlene Looney have been farming this land for more than 40 years. In 2000, they planted grapevines after keeping cattle on the property. The winery and tasting room are built on the foundation of the old barn, and Ed makes the wine while Darlene runs the tasting room. Of the 27 acres planted in vines, 20 acres are leased to Archrey Summit for its Looney Vineyard Pinot Noir, and the Looneys farm 7 acres for their own wines which have very limited distribution. If you're looking for a break from all the Pinot Noir, try the Tillie Claret—a smooth Bordeaux blend made with grapes from eastern Washington and southern Oregon. Aramenta offers a great opportunity to interact with farmers who have worked the land for several generations and to taste some great small-production wine. ✉ *17979 N.E. Lewis Rogers La.* ☎ *503/538–7230* 🌐 *www.aramentacellars.com* 🎫 *Tastings $10.*

Bergstrom Winery

WINERY/DISTILLERY | Focusing on classic Oregon Pinot Noir and Chardonnay, this family-owned winery produces elegant and refined wines that represent some of the best the Willamette Valley has to offer. The tasting room is surrounded by the Silice Vineyard, and offers beautiful views of several neighboring vineyards as well. French-trained winemaker Josh Bergstrom sources fruit from his estate vineyards and from several other local sites to produce a wide range of single-vineyard Pinots. Enjoy your tasting on the deck on a warm summer day. ✉ *18215 N.E. Calkins La.* ☎ *503/554–0468* 🌐 *www.bergstromwines.com* 🎫 *Tastings $30* ⏲ *By appointment.*

Bravuro Cellars

WINERY/DISTILLERY | One of the newest additions to the Newberg tasting-room scene, this boutique winery eschews the Pinot Noir prevalent throughout the region in favor of hot-climate varietals—including Zinfandel, Cab, and even a ruby port—all produced in small batches of around 40 to 60 cases. Bravuro's wines are only available at the tasting room or online, and every bottle is individually numbered. ✉ *108. S. College St.* ☎ *503/822–5116* 🌐 *www.bravurocellars.com.*

Champoeg State Heritage Area

NATIONAL/STATE PARK | Pronounced "sham-*poo*-ee," this 615-acre state park on the south bank of the Willamette River is on the site of a Hudson's Bay Company trading post, granary, and warehouse that was built in 1813. This was the seat of the first provisional government in the Northwest. The settlement was abandoned after a catastrophic flood in 1861, then rebuilt and abandoned again after the flood of 1890. The park's wide-open spaces, groves of oak and fir, modern visitor center, museum, and historic buildings provide vivid insight into pioneer life. Tepees and wagons are displayed here, and there are 10 miles of hiking and cycle trails. ✉ *8239 Champoeg Rd. NE, St. Paul* ☎ *503/678–1251* 🌐 *www.oregonstateparks.org* 🎫 *$5 per vehicle.*

Hoover-Minthorn House Museum

HOUSE | In 1885 Dr. Henry Minthorn invited his orphan nephew Herbert "Bertie" Hoover to come west and join the Minthorn family in Newberg. Built in 1881, the restored frame house, the oldest and most significant of Newberg's original structures, still has many of its original furnishings, including the president's boyhood bed and dresser. Hoover maintained his connection to Newberg, and visited several times after his presidency. ✉ *115 S. River St.* ☎ *503/538–6629* 🌐 *hooverminthorn.org* 🎫 *$5* ⏲ *Closed Jan.; Mar.–Nov., Mon. and Tues.; Dec. and Feb., weekdays.*

99W Drive-in

ARTS VENUE | **FAMILY** | Ted Francis built this drive-in in 1953, and operated it until his death at 98; the business is now run by his grandson. The first film begins at dusk. ✉ *3110 Portland Rd. (Hwy. 99W)* ☎ *503/538–2738* 🌐 *www.99w.com* 🎫 *$9; vehicles with single occupant $14* ⏲ *Closed Mon.–Wed.*

Penner-Ash Wine Cellars

WINERY/DISTILLERY | Lynn Penner-Ash brings years of experience working in Napa and as Rex Hill's winemaker to the winery that she and her husband Ron started in 1998. Although focused primarily on silky Pinot Noir, Penner-Ash also produces very good Syrah, Viognier, and Riesling. From its hilltop perch in the middle of the Dussin vineyard, this state-of-the-art gravity-flow winery and tasting room offers commanding views of the valley below. ✉ *15771 N.E. Ribbon Ridge Rd.* ☎ *503/554–5545* 🌐 *www.pennerash.com* 🎫 *Tastings $25.*

★ Ponzi Vineyards

WINERY/DISTILLERY | One of the founding families of Willamette Valley wine, Dick and Nancy Ponzi planted their original estate vineyard in 1970. While you can still visit the historic estate that looks out over these old vines, your best bet is to drop in at their new visitors facility at the winery just 12 miles south of Hillsboro. Here you'll find red and white flights of the current releases, as well as the occasional older vintage from the library. Enjoy table-side wine service indoors around the fireplace, or out on the covered terrace. Antipasti plates are a nice accompaniment to the wine. Pictures on the walls and displays provide a wonderful visual history of this winery that is still family owned and operated. The Ponzi family also launched the BridgePort Brewing Company in 1984, and runs a wine bar and restaurant in Dundee. ✉ *19500 S.W. Mountain Home Rd., Sherwood* ✣ *7 miles north of Newberg* ☎ *503/628–1227* 🌐 *www.ponziwines.com* 🎫 *Tastings $20.*

Rex Hill Vineyards

WINERY/DISTILLERY | A few hundred feet off the busy highway, surrounded by conifers and overlooked by vineyards, Rex Hill seems to exist in a world of its own. The winery opened in 1982, after owners Paul Hart and Jan Jacobsen converted a former nut-drying facility. It produces first-class Pinot Noir, Pinot Gris, Chardonnay, Sauvignon Blanc, and Riesling from both estate-grown and purchased grapes. The tasting room has a massive fireplace, elegant antiques, and an absorbing collection of modern art. Another highlight is the beautifully landscaped garden, perfect for picnicking. ✉ *30835 N. Hwy. 99W* ☎ *503/538–0666, 800/739–4455* 🌐 *www.rexhill.com* 🎫 *Tastings $15.*

Utopia Vineyard

WINERY/DISTILLERY | Take a trip back in time to when the Oregon wine industry was much smaller and more intimate. Utopia owner and winemaker Daniel Warnhius moved north from California looking for a vineyard site that would produce world-class Pinot Noir, and he found this location with the right combination of location, climate, and soil structure. In the tasting room, you're likely to be served by Daniel himself. In addition to several great Pinot Noirs, they also produce a bright, crisp Chardonnay, and a Pinot Noir Rosé. ✉ *17445 N.E. Ribbon Ridge Rd.* ☎ *503/687–1671* 🌐 *utopiawine.com* 🎫 *Tastings $15* ⏲ *Closed weekdays Dec.–Apr.*

Vidon Vineyard

WINERY/DISTILLERY | This small Newberg-area winery produces seven varieties of Pinot Noir along with small batches of Chardonnay, Pinot Gris, Viognier, Tempranillo, and Syrah. While the wines are enough to merit a visit to Vidon's hilltop tasting room, those with an interest in the science of wine-making will likely get a kick out of chatting with physicist-turned-winemaker Donald Hagge, who has applied his background to come up with some innovative ways to make and store wine. ✉ *17425 N.E. Hillside Dr.* ☎ *503/538–4092* 🌐 *www.vidonvineyard.com* 🎫 *Tastings $20.*

Restaurants

Jory

$$$$ | **MODERN AMERICAN** | This exquisite hotel dining room is named after one of the soils in the Oregon wine country. Chef Sunny Jin sources the majority of his ingredients locally, many from the on-site garden. **Known for:** Oregon-centric wine list; locally sourced ingredients; open kitchen experience. 💲 *Average main: $35* ✉ *The Allison Inn, 2525 Allison La.* ☎ *503/554–2525, 877/294–2525* 🌐 *www.theallison.com.*

Subterra

$$$$ | **AMERICAN** | This casual restaurant offers pizzas, sandwiches, and comfort food at lunch, upping the ante significantly at dinnertime, when it offers three-course prix-fixe menus paired with Pacific Northwest wine. A variety of tapas-style small plates are served throughout the day, too. **Known for:** an extensive list of Oregon wines; three-course dinners paired with local wines; small plates for sharing. *Average main: $32* *1505 Portland Rd.* *503/538–6060* *subterrarestaurant.com.*

Hotels

The Allison Inn & Spa
$$$$ | **RESORT** | At this luxurious, relaxing base for exploring the region's 200 wineries, each bright, comfortable room includes a gas fireplace, original works of art, a soaking tub, impressive furnishings, bay-window seats, and views of the vineyards from the terrace or balcony. **Pros:** outstanding on-site restaurant; excellent gym and spa facilities; located in the middle of wine country. **Cons:** not many nearby off-property activities other than wine tasting; expensive, particularly by local standards; restaurant can book up early. *Rooms from: $445* *2525 Allison La.* *503/554–2525, 877/294–2525* *www.theallison.com* *85 rooms* *No meals.*

Le Puy A Wine Valley Inn
$$$ | **B&B/INN** | This beautiful wine country retreat caters to wine enthusiasts with amenities that include wine bars in each individually decorated room, along with hot tubs and gas fireplaces in some. **Pros:** beautiful surroundings; lots of nice architectural and decorative touches; included breakfast and coffee. **Cons:** a distance from sights other than wineries; strict rules for guests, with no outside food allowed; minimum two-night stays. *Rooms from: $285* *20300 N.E. Hwy. 240* *503/554–9528* *lepuy-inn.com* *8 rooms* *Free breakfast.*

Activities

BALLOONING

Hot-air balloon rides are nothing less than a spectacular, breathtaking thrill—particularly over Oregon's beautiful Yamhill County.

★ Vista Balloon Adventures
BALLOONING | Enjoy floating gently above beautiful Oregon wine country as the sun rises behind the vines. Your FAA-licensed pilot will take the balloon up about 1,500 feet and can often steer the craft down to skim the water, then up to view hawks' nests. A Champagne brunch is served upon returning to the ground. *1050 Commerce Pkwy.* *503/625–7385, 800/622–2309* *www.vistaballoon.com* *$230 per person.*

Dundee

3 miles southwest of Newberg on Hwy. 99W.

Dundee used to be known for growing the lion's share (more than 90%) of the U.S. hazelnut crop. Today, some of Oregon's top-rated wineries are just outside Dundee, and the area is now best known for wine tourism and wine bars, bed-and-breakfast inns, and restaurants.

GETTING HERE AND AROUND

Dundee is just under an hour's drive from Portland International Airport; **Caravan Airport Transportation** provides shuttle service.

What used to be a pleasant drive through quaint Dundee on Highway 99W now can be a traffic hassle, as it serves as the main artery from Lincoln City on the Oregon Coast to suburban Portland. Others will enjoy wandering along the 25 miles of Highway 18 between Dundee and Grande Ronde, in the Coast Range, which goes through the heart of the Yamhill Valley wine country.

CONTACTS Caravan Airport Transportation. *541/994–9645* *www.caravanshuttle.com.*

Continued on page 196

The Willamette Valley is Oregon's premier wine region. With a milder climate than any growing area in California, cool-climate grapes like Pinot Noir and Pinot Gris thrive here, and are being transformed into world-class wines.

There may be fewer and smaller wineries than in Napa, but the experience is often more intimate. The winemaker himself may even pour you wine.

Touring is easy, as most wineries are well marked, and have tasting rooms with regular hours. Whether you're taking a day trip from Portland, or staying for a couple of days, here's how to get the most out of your sipping experience.

By Dave Sandage and John Doerper

Above and right, Willamette Valley

Wine Tasting in the Willamette Valley

OREGON'S WINES: THEN AND NOW

Rex Hill Vineyards

THE EARLY YEARS

The French made wine first—French Canadians, that is. In the 1830s, retired fur trappers from the Hudson's Bay Company started to colonize the Willamette Valley and planted grapes on the south-facing buttes. They were followed by American settlers who made wine.

Although wine-making in the regionlanguished after these early efforts, it never quite vanished. A few wineries hung on, producing wines mainly for Oregonians of European descent.

It wasn't until the 1970s that the state's wine industry finally took off. Only after a group of young California winemakers started making vinifera wines in the Umpqua and Willamette Valleys and gained international acclaim for them, did Oregon's wines really take hold.

WINEMAKING TODAY

Today, Oregon's wine industry is racing ahead. Here the most prolific white and red grapes are Pinot Gris and Pinot Noir, respectively. Other prominent varietals include Riesling, Gewürztraminer, Viognier, Chardonnay, Carbernet Franc, and Syrah.

The wine industry in Oregon is still largely dominated by family and boutique wineries that pay close attention to quality and are often keen to experiment. That makes traveling and tasting at the source an always-interesting experience.

OREGON CERTIFIED SUSTAINABLE WINE

The latest trend in Oregon winemaking is a dedication to responsible grape growing and winemaking. When you see the Oregon Certified Sustainable Wine (OCSW) logo on the back of a wine bottle, it means the winery ensures accountable agricultural and winemaking practices (in conjunction with agencies such as USDA Organic, Demeter Biodynamic, the Food Alliance, Salmon-Safe, and Low Input Viticulture and Enology) through independent third-party certification. For more information on Oregon Certified Sustainable wines and participating wineries, check 🌐 *www.ocsw.org.*

WINE TASTING PRIMER

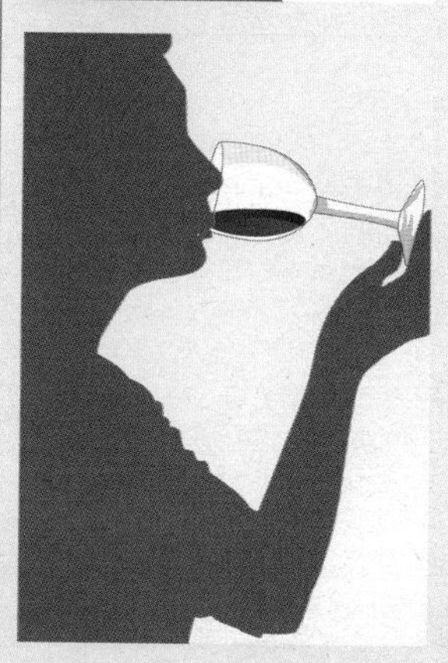

Ordering and tasting wine—whether at a winery, bar, or restaurant—is easy once you master a few simple steps.

LOOK AND NOTE

Hold your glass by the stem and look at the wine in the glass. Note its color, depth, and clarity.

For whites, is it greenish, yellow, or gold? For reds, is it purplish, ruby, or garnet? Is the wine's color pale or deep? Is the liquid clear or cloudy?

SWIRL AND SNIFF

Swirl the wine gently in the glass to intensify the scents, then sniff over the rim of the glass. What do you smell? Try to identify aromas like:

- **Fruits**—citrus, peaches, berries, figs, melon
- **Flowers**—orange blossoms, honey, perfume
- **Spices**—baking spices, pungent, herbal notes
- **Vegetables**—fresh or cooked, herbal notes
- **Minerals**—earth, steely notes, wet stones
- **Dairy**—butter, cream, cheese, yogurt
- **Oak**—toast, vanilla, coconut, tobacco
- **Animal**—leathery, meaty notes

Are there any unpleasant notes, like mildew or wet dog, that might indicate that the wine is "off?"

SIP AND SAVOR

Prime your palate with a sip, swishing the wine in your mouth. Then spit in a bucket or swallow.

Take another sip and think about the wine's attributes. Sweetness is detected on the tip of the tongue, acidity on the sides of the tongue, and tannins (a mouth-drying sensation) on the gums. Consider the body—does the wine feel light in the mouth, or is there a rich sensation? Are the flavors consistent with the aromas? If you like the wine, try to pinpoint what you like about it, and vice versa if you don't like it.

Take time to savor the wine as you're sipping it—the tasting experience may seem a bit scientific, but the end goal is your enjoyment.

WINE TOURING AND TASTING

Wine tasting at Argyle and Rex Hill

WHEN TO GO

In high season (June through October) and on weekends and holidays during much of the year, wine-country roads can be busy and tasting rooms are often crowded. If you prefer a more intimate tasting experience, plan your visit for a weekday.

To avoid the frustration of a fruitless drive, confirm in advance that wineries of interest will be open when you plan to visit.

Choose a designated driver for the day: Willamette wine-country roads are often narrow and curvy, and you may be sharing the road with bicyclists and wildlife as well as other wine tourists.

IN THE TASTING ROOM

Tasting rooms are designed to introduce newcomers to the pleasures of wine and to the wines made at the winery. At popular wineries you'll sometimes have to pay for your tasting, anything from a nominal $3 fee to $30 and up for a tasting that might include a glass you can take home. This fee is often deducted if you buy wine before leaving.

WHAT'S AN AVA?

AVAs (American Viticultural Areas) are geographic winegrowing regions that vaguely reflect the French concept of terroir, or "sense of place." The vineyards within a given AVA have similar characteristics such as climate, soil types, and/or elevation, which impart shared characteristics to the wines made from grapes grown in that area. AVAs are strictly geographic boundaries distinct from city or county designations. AVAs can also be subdivided into sub-AVAs; each of the AVAs mentioned here is actually part of the larger Willamette Valley AVA.

Each taste consists of an ounce or two. Feel free to pour whatever you don't finish into one of the dump buckets on the bar. If you like, rinse your glass between pours with a little water. Remember, those sips add up, so pace yourself. If you plan to visit several wineries, try just a few wines at each so you won't suffer from palate fatigue, when your mouth can no longer distinguish subtleties. It's also a good idea to bring a picnic lunch, which you can enjoy on the deck of a winery, taking in the surrounding wine country vistas.

FALL FOLIAGE

In autumn, Willamette Valley vineyards are particularly stunning as the leaves change color.

DAY TRIP FROM PORTLAND

Ponzi Vineyards

With nearly 150 vineyards, the Chehalem Mountain and Ribbon Ridge AVAs offer widely varied soil types and diverse Pinot Noirs. The region is less than an hour away from Portland.

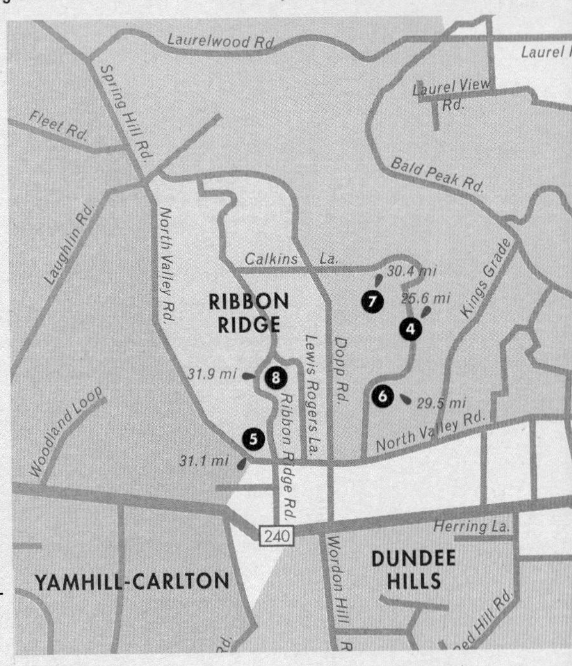

CHEHALEM MOUNTAIN AND RIBBON RIDGE AVAS

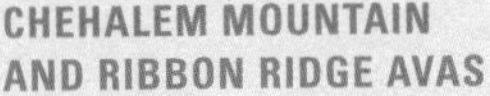

❶ PONZI VINEYARDS

First planted in 1970, Ponzi has some of Oregon's oldest Pinot Noir vines. In addition to current releases, the tasting room sometimes offers older library wines. **Try:** *Arneis, a crisp Italian white varietal.*

✉ 19500 SW Mountain Home Rd., Sherwood
☎ 503/628–1227
🌐 www.ponziwines.com

❷ REX HILL VINEYARDS

Before grapevines, the Willamette Valley was widely planted with fruits and nuts. Enjoy classic Oregon Pinot Noir in this tasting room built around an old fruit and nut drying facility. **Try:** *dark and spicy Dundee Hills Pinot Noir.*

✉ 30835 N. Hwy. 99W, Newberg
☎ 800/739–4455
🌐 www.rexhill.com

❸ BRAVURO CELLARS

Newberg's new-kid-on-the-block winery features small-batch wines made from hot-climate grapes, including Zinfandels, Cabernets Sauvignons, and even port. **Try:** *crisp and refreshing Pinot Blanc.*

✉ 108 S. College St., Newberg
☎ 503/822-5116
🌐 www.bravuracellars.com

❹ VIDON VINEYARD

Run by a particle physicist-turned-winemaker, this hilltop vineyard features a low-key tasting room plus a covered outdoor seating area for taking in bucolic vineyard views. **Try:** *rich but fruity Pinot Noir Maresh*

✉ 17425 NE Hillside Dr., Newberg
☎ 503/538-4092
🌐 www.vidonvineyard.com

❺ UTOPIA VINEYARD

The tasting room at this small Oregon winery is quite intimate—you'll likely be served by the winemaker himself. **Try:** *light and slightly sweet Rosé.*

✉ 17445 N.E. Ribbon Ridge Rd., Newberg
☎ 503/298–7841
🌐 www.utopiawine.com

Adelsheim Vineyard

Rex Hill

Pinot Gris grapes

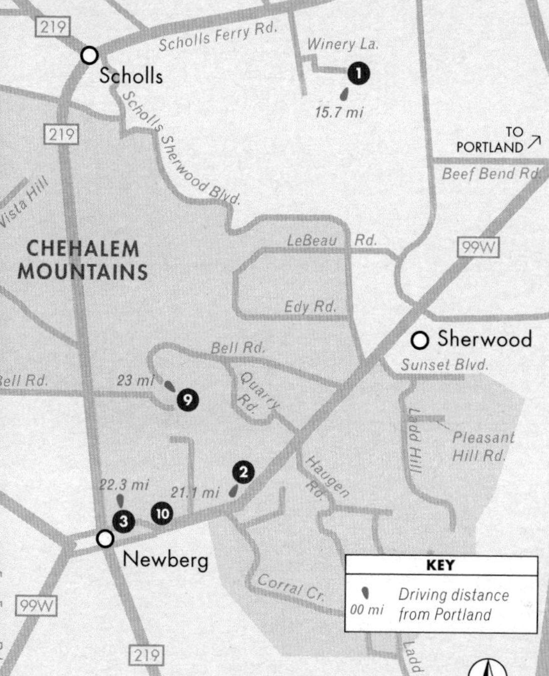

6 ADELSHEIM VINEYARD
One of Oregon's older Pinot Noir producers, Adelsheim has just opened a new tasting room inside its modern winery, with friendly, knowledgeable employees. **Try:** *dark and smoky Elizabeth's Reserve Pinot Noir.*
✉ 16800 N.E. Calkins La., Newberg
☎ 503/538–3652
🌐 www.adelsheim.com

7 BERGSTROM WINERY
A beautiful tasting room, but the real high point here is the classic Oregon Pinot Noir sourced from several of its estate vineyards as well as other local sites. **Try:** *earthy Bergstrom Pinot Noir.*
✉ 18215 N.E. Calkins La., Newberg
☎ 503/554-0468
🌐 www.bergstromwines.com

8 ARAMENTA CELLARS
A small, family-run operation that offers tastings in its winery, built on the foundation of an old barn. The on-site vineyard grows primarily Pinot Noir and Chardonnay. **Try:** *smooth and structured Tillie Claret.*
✉ 17979 N.E. Lewis Rogers La., Newberg
☎ 503/538–7230
🌐 www.aramentacellars.com

STOP FOR A BITE

9 JORY RESTAURANT
Located within the luxurious Allison Inn and Spa, Jory serves creative dishes that highlight the bounty of the Willamette Valley.
✉ 2525 Allison La., Newberg
☎ 503/554-2526
🌐 www.theallison.com

10 SUBTERRA
Underground cellar restaurant with an impressive regional wine list. Lunch is casual comfort food, while prix-fixe three-course meals dominate at dinner time. Small plates to share are available all day.
✉ 1505 Portland Rd., Newberg
☎ 503/538-6060
🌐 www.subterrarestaurant.com

TWO DAYS IN WINE COUNTRY

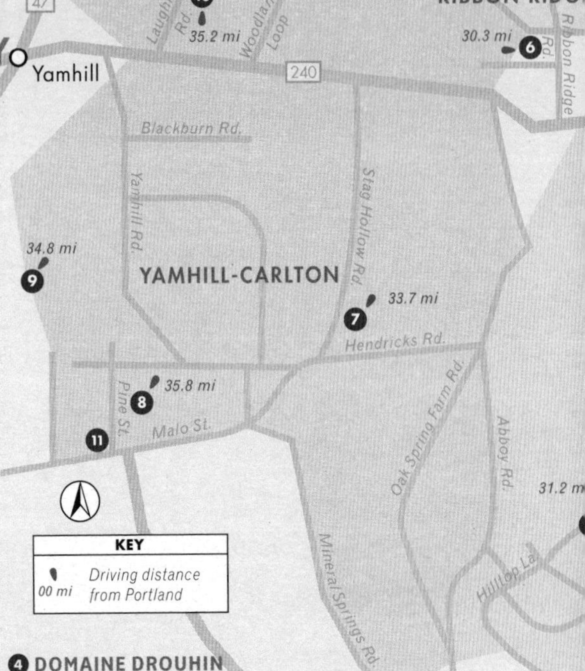

DAY 1

DUNDEE HILLS AVA

The Dundee Hills AVA is home to some of Oregon's best known Pinot Noir producers. Start your tour in the town of Dundee, about 30 miles southwest of Portland, then drive up into the red hills and enjoy the valley views from many wineries.

❶ ARGYLE WINERY

If you don't want to drive off the beaten path, this winery is right on Highway 99W in Dundee. They specialize in sparkling wines, but also make very nice still wines. **Try:** *crisp Brut Rosé.*

✉ 691 Hwy. 99 W, Dundee
☎ 503/538–8520
🌐 www.argylewinery.com

❷ THE BISTRO BAR

This cozy wine bar offers a nice selection of local labels, making it a good choice for those who want to sample a large selection side-by-side. **Try:** *bright and fruity Ponzi Pinot Gris.*

✉ 100 S.W. 7th St., Dundee
☎ 503/554–1500
🌐 www.dundeebistro.com

❸ ARCHERY SUMMIT

An Oregon Pinot Noir pioneer, Archery Summit features memorable wines and equally pleasing views. Call in advance to schedule a tour of the winery and aging caves. Try: *dark and rich Premier Cuvée Pinot Noir.*

✉ 18599 NE Archery Summit Rd., Dayton
☎ 503/864–4300
🌐 www.archerysummit.com

❹ DOMAINE DROUHIN OREGON

Started in the late 1980s by the Drouhin family of Burgundy fame, this winery makes notable Oregon Pinot Noir, as well as Chardonnay. **Try:** *smooth and earthy Willamette Valley Pinot Noir.*

✉ 6750 Breyman Orchards Rd., Dayton
☎ 503/864–2700
🌐 www.domainedrouhin.com

❺ SOKOL BLOSSER

Producing excellent wines since 1971, Sokol Blosser is worth visiting for the wines alone, but its beautiful tasting areas amongst rolling vineyards certainly don't hurt. **Try:** *Dundee Hills Estate Pinot Noir.*

✉ 5000 Sokol Blosser La., Dayton
☎ 800/582–6668
🌐 www.sokolblosser.com

DAY 2

YAMHILL-CARLTON AVA

To the west of the Dundee Hills AVA is the horseshoe-shaped Yamhill-Carlton AVA. Vineyards here are found on the slopes that surround the towns of Yamhill and Carlton. Carlton has become a center of wine tourism, and you could easily spend a day visiting tasting rooms in town.

❻ PENNER-ASH WINE CELLARS

This state-of-the-art winery and tasting room is atop a hill with an excellent view of the valley below. **Try:** *smooth and dark Shea Vineyard Pinot Noir.*

✉ 15771 N.E. Ribbon Ridge Rd., Newberg
☎ 503/554–5545
🌐 www.pennerash.com

Penner-Ash Wine Cellars

Ponzi Wine Bar

Pinot Gris grapes

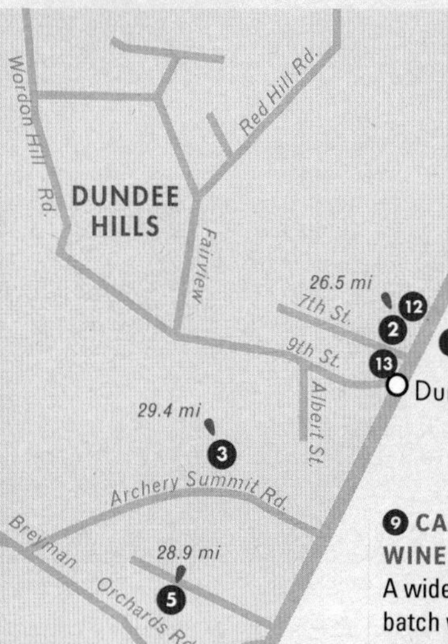

❼ LEMELSON VINEYARDS

Although it specializes in single-vineyard Pinot Noir, Lemelson also makes several crisp white wines. The deck overlooking the vineyards is perfect for picnics. **Try:** *crisp and fruity Riesling.*

✉ 12020 N.E. Stag Hollow Rd., Carlton
☎ 503/852–6619
🌐 www.lemelsonvineyards.com

❽ KEN WRIGHT CELLARS TASTING ROOM

Well-known winemaker Ken Wright is known for producing big reds. The tasting room is in the historic Carlton train station. **Try:** *bold and spicy Del Rio Claret.*

✉ 120 N. Pine St., Carlton
☎ 503/852–7070
🌐 kenwrightcellars.com

❾ CARLTON WINEMAKERS STUDIO

A wide range of small-batch wine producers are showcased at this winery cooperative, with a rotating selection of offerings, including plenty of Pinot. **Try:** *Studio Benchmark Pinot Noirs*

✉ 801 N. Scott St., Carlton
☎ 503/852–6100
🌐 www.winemakersstudio.com

❿ LENNÉ ESTATE

Lenné specializes in highly regarded Pinot Noir, although it's often pouring a couple of non-Pinot wines from other wineries as well. The tasting room in a small stone building overlooks the vineyards. **Try:** *complex and earthy Estate Pinot Noir.*

✉ 18760 Laughlin Rd., Yamhill
☎ 503/956–2256
🌐 www.lenneestate.com

STOP FOR A BITE

⓫ THE HORSE RADISH

Located in downtown Carlton, The Horseradish offers a wide selection of local wines as well as cheese from around the world. The sandwiches and small plates make for a great quick lunch.

✉ 211 W. Main St., Carlton
☎ 503/852–6656
🌐 www.thehorseradish.com

⓬ DUNDEE BISTRO

A favorite of winemakers, Dundee Bistro serves seasonal local ingredients paired with Willamette Valley wines. Enjoy outdoor seating, or watch chefs work in the open kitchen inside.

✉ 100-A S.W. 7th St., Dundee
☎ 503/554–1650
🌐 www.dundeebistro.com

⓭ TINA'S

The warm and intimate Tina's features dishes made with seasonal ingredients, organic vegetables, and free-range meats. Stop by for lunch Tuesday–Friday, or nightly dinner.

✉ 760 Hwy. 99 W, Dundee
☎ 503/538–8880
🌐 www.tinasdundee.com

Sights

★ Archery Summit Winery

WINERY/DISTILLERY | The winery that Gary and Nancy Andrus, owners of Pine Ridge winery in Napa Valley, founded in the 1990s has become synonymous with premium Oregon Pinot Noir. Because they believed that great wines are made in the vineyard, they adopted such innovative techniques as narrow spacing and vertical trellis systems, which give the fruit a great concentration of flavors. In addition to the standard flight of Pinot Noirs in the tasting room, you can call ahead and reserve a private seated tasting or a tasting paired with small bites or a tour of the winery and, weather permitting, a walk out to the vineyard. You're welcome to bring a picnic, and as at many Oregon wineries, you can bring your dog, too. ✉ *18599 N.E. Archery Summit Rd., Dayton* ☎ *503/714–2030* 🌐 *www.archerysummit.com* 🎫 *Tastings from $30.*

Argyle Winery

WINERY/DISTILLERY | A beautiful establishment, Argyle has its tasting room in a Victorian farmhouse set amid gorgeous gardens. The winery is tucked into a former hazelnut processing plant—which explains the Nuthouse label on its reserve wines. Since Argyle opened in 1987, it has consistently produced sparkling wines that are crisp on the palate, with an aromatic, lingering finish and bubbles that seem to last forever. And these sparklers cost about a third of their counterparts from California. The winery also produces Chardonnay, dry Riesling, Pinot Gris, and Pinot Noir. ✉ *691 Hwy. 99W* ☎ *503/538–8520, 888/427–4953* 🌐 *www.argylewinery.com* 🎫 *Tastings from $20.*

The Bistro Bar

WINERY/DISTILLERY | Located right on the main highway between Portland and wine country, The Bistro Bar offers the opportunity to sample wines from both the Ponzi Winery and small local producers without straying far from the beaten path. The tasting menu features current releases of Ponzi wines, as well as a rotating selection of other local wines. If you've had enough wine for a while, you can also get snacks, Italian coffee, or a craft beer to enjoy in the comfortable tasting room. ✉ *100 S.W. 7th St.* ☎ *503/554–1500* 🌐 *www.dundeebistro.com.*

Dobbes Family Estate

WINERY/DISTILLERY | Joe Dobbes makes a lot of wine, but he's definitely not a bulk winemaker. He provides custom wine-making services to many Oregon wineries that are too small to have their own winery or winemaker. But he also makes several lines of his own wine, ranging from his everyday "Wine By Joe" label to the premium Dobbes Family Estate label featuring great Pinot Noir, Syrah, Sauvignon Blanc, Viognier, and Grenache Blanc. In addition to a few single vineyard Pinot Noir bottlings, Dobbes focuses on blends from multiple vineyards to provide consistent, balanced, and interesting wines. Two different tasting fights are available in the tasting room, and seated tastings and tours can be arranged by appointment. ✉ *240 S.E. 5th St.* ☎ *503/538–1141* 🌐 *www.dobbesfamilyestate.com* 🎫 *Tastings $20.*

★ Domaine Drouhin Oregon

WINERY/DISTILLERY | When the French winery magnate Robert Drouhin ("the Sebastiani of France") planted a vineyard and built a winery in the Red Hills of Dundee back in 1987, he set local oenophiles abuzz. His daughter Veronique is now the winemaker and produces silky and elegant Pinot Noir and Chardonnay. Ninety acres of the 225-acre estate has been planted on a hillside to take advantage of the natural coolness of the earth and to establish a gravity-flow winery. No appointment is needed to taste the Oregon wines, but if you can plan ahead for the tour (reservations required), you can taste Oregon and Burgundy side by side. ✉ *6750 N.E. Breyman Orchards Rd., Dayton* ☎ *503/864–2700* 🌐 *www.domainedrouhin.com* 🎫 *Tastings $25* ⏲ *Closed mid-Oct.–May, Mon. and Tues.*

Erath Vineyards Winery

WINERY/DISTILLERY | When Dick Erath opened one of Oregon's pioneer wineries more than a quarter century ago, he focused on producing distinctive Pinot Noir from grapes he'd been growing in the Red Hills since 1972—as well as full-flavored Pinot Gris, Pinot Blanc, Chardonnay, Riesling, and late-harvest Gewürztraminer. The wines are excellent and reasonably priced. In 2006 the winery was sold to Washington State's giant conglomerate Ste. Michelle Wine Estate. The tasting room is in the middle of the vineyards, high in the hills, with views in nearly every direction; the hazelnut trees that covered the slopes not so long ago have been replaced with vines. The tasting-room terrace, which overlooks the winery and the hills, is a choice spot for picnicking. Crabtree Park, next to the winery, is a good place to stretch your legs after a tasting. ✉ *9409 N.E. Worden Hill Rd.* ☎ *503/538–3318, 800/539–9463* 🌐 *www.erath.com* 🎫 *Tastings $30.*

Red Ridge

FARM/RANCH | A good place to clean your palate after all that wine tasting is Red Ridge, home to the first commercial olive mill in the Pacific Northwest. Stop by the gift shop to taste some of the farm's signature oils or head out back to see an old-fashioned (and not-in-use) olive press imported from Spain. ✉ *5510 N.E. Breyman Orchards Rd., Dayton* ☎ *503/864–8502* 🌐 *redridgefarms.com.*

★ Sokol Blosser

WINERY/DISTILLERY | One of Yamhill County's oldest wineries (it was established in 1971) makes consistently excellent wines and sells them at reasonable prices. Set on a gently sloping south-facing hillside and surrounded by vineyards, lush lawns, and shade trees, it's a splendid place to learn about wine with tableside tastings held across a number of indoor and outdoor spaces. Winery tours and summer Sunday vineyard hikes can be booked in advance. ✉ *5000 Sokol Blosser La., Dayton* ✥ *3 miles west of Dundee off Hwy. 99W* ☎ *503/864–2282, 800/582–6668* 🌐 *www.sokolblosser.com* 🎫 *Tastings $15, tours $40.*

Torii Mor Winery

WINERY/DISTILLERY | Established in 1993, Torii Mor makes small quantities of handcrafted Pinot Noir, Pinot Gris, and Chardonnay and is set amid Japanese gardens with breathtaking views of the Willamette Valley. The gardens were designed by Takuma Tono, the same architect who designed the renowned Portland Japanese Garden. The owners, who love all things Japanese, named their winery after the distinctive Japanese gate of Shinto religious significance; they added a Scandinavian mor, signifying "earth," to create an east-west combo: "earth gate." Jacques Tardy, a native of Nuits Saint Georges, in Burgundy, France, is the current head winemaker. Under his guidance Torii Mor wines have become more Burgundian in style. ✉ *18323 N.E. Fairview Dr.* ☎ *503/538–2279* 🌐 *www.toriimorwinery.com* 🎫 *Tastings $35.*

Winderlea

WINERY/DISTILLERY | The tasting room looks over the acclaimed former Goldschmidt vineyard, first planted in 1974, and the view can be enjoyed on the outside deck on a warm summer day. Winemaker Robert Brittan crafts lush Pinot Noir and Chardonnay from several nearby vineyards in both single-vineyard offerings and blends from multiple vineyards. Proceeds from the tasting fee are donated to ¡Salud!, a nonprofit providing health-care services to Oregon's vineyard workers and their families. ✉ *8905 N.E. Worden Hill Rd.* ☎ *503/554–5900* 🌐 *www.winderlea.com* 🎫 *Tastings $25.*

Restaurants

Dundee Bistro

$$$ | **CONTEMPORARY** | Owned by the Ponzi wine family, this bistro showcases Italian-style fare dominated by locally grown and raised produce, while the on-site Fratelli Ponzi Fine Food & Wine Bar serves Ponzi wines from Oregon and Italy. Vaulted ceilings provide an open feeling inside, warmed by abundant fresh flowers and the works of local Oregon artists. **Known for:** part of the Ponzi wine family; wines from Oregon and Italy; Italian fare with options for special diets. *Average main: $25* *100-A S.W. 7th St.* *503/554–1650* *www.dundeebistro.com.*

Red Hills Market

$ | **PACIFIC NORTHWEST** | **FAMILY** | Serving great sandwiches, salads, and pizza, this is the perfect stop for a quick lunch in the middle of a day of wine tasting, or a casual no-frills dinner at the end of the day. In addition to wine, there are cocktails and a great selection of local and imported craft beers. **Known for:** great stop during wine tasting; takeout options; kids' menu. *Average main: $12* *155 S.W. 7th St.* *971/832–8414* *www.redhillsmarket.com.*

★ **Tina's**

$$$$ | **FRENCH** | Opened back in 1991, this Dundee institution has long been known for luring Portlanders away from their own restaurant scene, offering country-French fare cooked lovingly with locally grown produce. Service is as intimate and laid-back as the interiors; a double fireplace divides the dining room, with heavy glass brick shrouded by bushes on the highway side, so you're not bothered by the traffic on Highway 99. **Known for:** attracting Portland foodies; delicious homemade soups; hearty French-country cuisine. *Average main: $35* *760 Hwy. 99W* *503/538–8880* *www.tinasdundee.com.*

Hotels

The Dundee

$$ | **HOTEL** | Right on the main road in Dundee, this boutique property offers spacious, light-filled rooms with living areas and tall ceilings; there's even a "Squad Room" with six bunk beds for traveling groups. **Pros:** contemporary, stylish surroundings; close to many wineries; spacious rooms remodeled in 2019. **Cons:** located on the main highway through town rather than the country; check-in time is later than usual; breakfast is not included. *Rooms from: $199* *1410 N. Hwy. 99W* *503/538–7666* *www.thedundee.com* *22 rooms* *No meals.*

The Vintages Trailer Resort

$ | **RESORT** | **FAMILY** | Just off the road that runs from Dundee to McMinnville, this quirky retro resort boasts 34 lovingly refurbished vintage trailers, most dating from the 1940s–60s. **Pros:** authentic vintage trailers with quirky, retro-chic decor; each comes with its own gas grill; some trailers are dog-friendly. **Cons:** $29 cleaning fee added at check-in; near the highway and can get traffic noise; bathrooms are compact. *Rooms from: $145* *16205 SE Kreder Rd., Dayton* *971/267–2130* *www.the-vintages.com* *34 trailers* *No meals.*

Yamhill-Carlton

14 miles west of Dundee.

Just outside the small towns of Carlton and Yamhill are neatly combed benchlands and hillsides, an American Viticultural Area (AVA) established in 2004, and home to some of the finest Pinot Noir vineyards in the world. Carlton has exploded with many small tasting rooms in the past few years, and you could easily spend an entire day tasting wine within three or four blocks. The area is a gorgeous quilt of nurseries, grain fields,

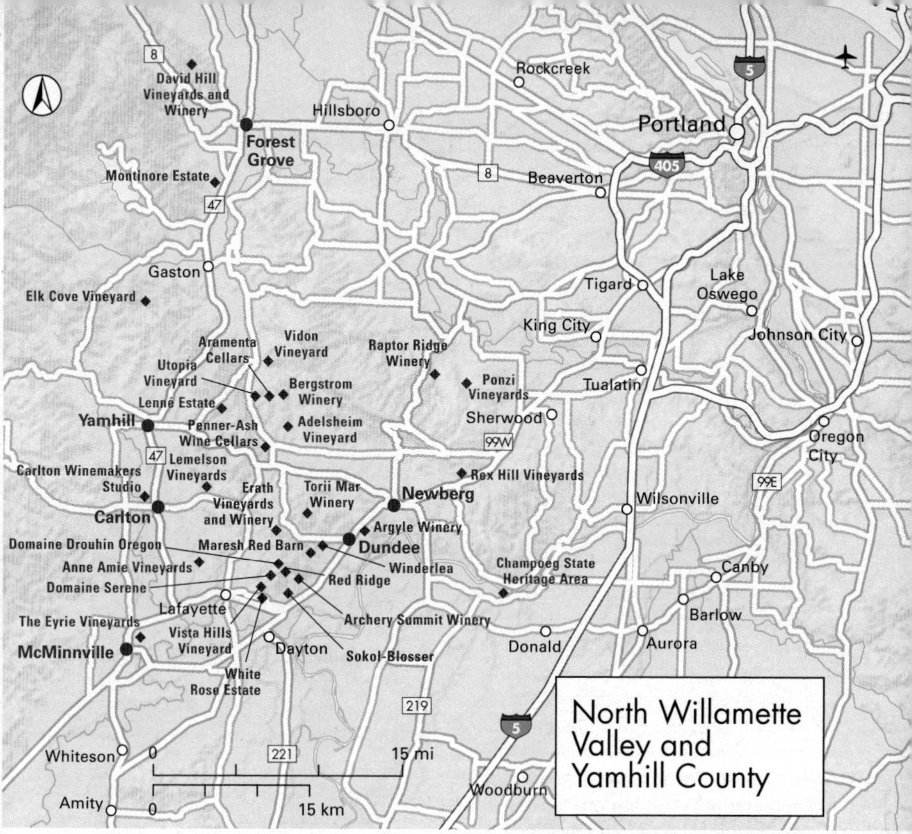

North Willamette Valley and Yamhill County

and orchards. Come here for the wine tasting, but don't expect to find too much else to do.

GETTING HERE AND AROUND

Having your own car is the best way to explore this rural region of Yamhill County, located a little more than an hour's drive from Portland International Airport. The towns of Yamhill and Carlton are about an hour's drive from Downtown Portland, traveling through Tigard, to Newberg and west on Highway 240.

CONTACTS Yamhill County Transit Area. ☎ *503/474–4900* 🌐 *www.ycbus.org.*

Sights

Carlton Winemakers Studio

WINERY/DISTILLERY | Oregon's first cooperative winery was specifically designed to house multiple small premium wine producers. This gravity-flow winery has up-to-date wine-making equipment as well as multiple cellars for storing the different makers' wines. You can taste and purchase bottles from the different member wineries. The emphasis is on Pinot Noir, but more than a dozen other types of wines are poured, from Cabernet Franc to Gewürztraminer to Mourvèdre on a rotating basis. The selection of wines available to taste changes every few days. ✉ *801 N. Scott St., Carlton* ☎ *503/852–6100* 🌐 *www.winemakersstudio.com* *Tastings from $25.*

Ken Wright Cellars Tasting Room

WINERY/DISTILLERY | Carlton's former train depot is now the tasting room for Ken Wright Cellars and his warm-climate label, Tyrus Evan. The winery specializes in single-vineyard Pinot Noirs, each subtly different from the next depending on the soil types and grape clones. The wines are poured side by side, giving you an opportunity to go back and forth to compare them. The Tyrus Evan wines are quite different from the Ken Wright Pinots: they are warm-climate varieties like Cabernet Franc, Malbec, Syrah, and red Bordeaux blends, from grapes Wright buys from vineyards in eastern Washington and southern Oregon. You can also pick up cheeses and other picnic supplies, as well as wine country gifts and souvenirs. ✉ *120 N. Pine St., Carlton* ☎ *503/852–7070* 🌐 *www.kenwrightcellars.com* 🎫 *Tastings from $20.*

Lemelson Vineyards

WINERY/DISTILLERY | This winery was designed from the ground up to be a no-compromises Pinot Noir production facility with an eye to Willamette Valley aesthetics, and the highlight is a diverse range of single-vineyard Pinot Noirs. But don't neglect the bright Pinot Gris and Riesling, perfect with seafood or spicy fare. The spacious high-ceiling tasting room is a great place to relax and take in the view through the floor-to-ceiling windows, or bring a picnic and enjoy the deck on a warm summer day. ✉ *12020 N.E. Stag Hollow Rd., Carlton* ☎ *503/852–6619* 🌐 *www.lemelsonvineyards.com* 🎫 *Tastings from $25.*

Lenné Estate

WINERY/DISTILLERY | The small stone building that houses the tasting room is surrounded by the estate vineyard and looks like something right out of Burgundy. Steve Lutz was looking for the perfect site to grow Pinot Noir and bought the property in 2000. In addition to offering his own rich and elegant estate Pinot Noirs for tasting, he often pours other varietals from other wineries. ✉ *18760 N.E. Laughlin Rd., Yamhill* ☎ *503/956–2256* 🌐 *www.lenneestate.com* 🎫 *$15.*

Restaurants

The Horse Radish

$ | **DELI** | The perfect stop in the middle of a day of wine tasting offers a wide selection of artisanal cheese and meats, as well as a great lunch menu. Pick up some sandwiches and a soup or salad to go, and you'll be all set for a picnic at your favorite winery. **Known for:** live music on Friday and Saturday nights; tasting room featuring Marshall Davis wines; kids' menu. 💲 *Average main: $8* ✉ *211 W. Main St., Carlton* ☎ *503/852–6656* 🌐 *www.thehorseradish.com.*

Hotels

Abbey Road Farm Silo Suites B&B

$$$ | **B&B/INN** | Situated on a small farm and winery overlooking a lush expanse of farmland, this unusual bed-and-breakfast is housed in a trio of old silos that have been converted into a small inn. **Pros:** gorgeous views; delicious gourmet breakfast; casual but chic on-site tasting room. **Cons:** lumpy beds; not much within the immediate area; resident roosters may awaken light sleepers. 💲 *Rooms from: $250* ✉ *10501 NE Abbey Rd., Carlton* ☎ *503/687–3100* 🌐 *abbeyroadfarm.com* *5 rooms* *Free breakfast.*

McMinnville

11 miles south of Yamhill on Hwy. 99W.

The Yamhill County seat, McMinnville lies in the center of Oregon's thriving wine industry. There is a larger concentration of wineries in Yamhill County than in any other area of the state. Among the varieties are Chardonnay, Pinot Noir, and Pinot Gris. Most of the wineries in the area offer tours and tastings. McMinnville's downtown area has a few shops worth a look; many of the historic district buildings, erected 1890–1915, are still standing, and are remarkably well maintained.

GETTING HERE AND AROUND

McMinnville is a little more than an hour's drive from Downtown Portland; **Caravan Airport Transportation** provides shuttle service to Portland International Airport. McMinnville is just 70 minutes from Lincoln City on the Oregon Coast, and 27 miles west of Salem.

ESSENTIALS

VISITOR INFORMATION Visit McMinnville. ✉ *328 N.E. Davis St., Suite 1* ☎ *503/857–0182* 🌐 *visitmcminnville.com.*

Sights

Evergreen Aviation & Space Museum and Wings & Waves Waterpark

MUSEUM | FAMILY | Howard Hughes's *Spruce Goose,* the largest plane ever built and constructed entirely of wood, is on permanent display, but if you can take your eyes off the giant you will also see more than 45 historic planes and replicas from the early years of flight and World War II, as well as the postwar and modern eras. Across the parking lot from the aviation museum is the space museum with artifacts that include a German V-2 rocket and a Titan missile, complete with silo and launch control room. The adjacent Wings and Waves Waterpark (separate admission) has 10 waterslides, including one that starts at a Boeing 747-100 that sits on *top* of the building. The IMAX theater is open daily and features several different films each day. There are a museum store and two cafés, as well as ongoing educational programs and special events. ✉ *500 N.E. Michael King Smith Way* ☎ *503/434–4185* 🌐 *www.evergreenmuseum.org* 🎫 *$27, includes IMAX movie; $29 water park.*

The Eyrie Vineyards

WINERY/DISTILLERY | When David Lett planted the first Pinot Noir vines in the Willamette Valley in 1965, he was setting in motion a series of events that caused Willamette Valley Pinot Noir to be recognized as among the best in the world. Affectionately known as Papa Pinot, Lett, along with several other pioneering winemakers, nurtured the Oregon wine industry to what it is today. Today, David's son Jason Lett is now the winemaker and vineyard manager, and continues to make Pinot Noir, Pinot Gris, and Chardonnay that reflect the gentle touch that has always characterized Eyrie wines. In recent years, many small wineries have sprung up in the neighborhood around this historic winery. ✉ *935 N.E. 10th Ave.* ☎ *503/472–6315, 888/440–4970* 🌐 *www.eyrievineyards.com* 🎫 *Tastings $40* ⏲ *Closed Tues. and Wed.*

★ Maysara Winery

WINERY/DISTILLERY | Set on 497 acres, this sprawling winery specializes in biodynamic farming and wine production, a sustainable alternative to commercial agriculture based on the works of Rudolf Steiner (best known as the force behind Waldorf education). Instead of commercial fertilizers and chemical pesticides, the focus here is on a holistic approach to farming—turkeys roam the fields, fending off insects, and manure and compost are used to enrich the soil. The result is some fantastic Pinots and wines without any worry of chemical residues. Owner Moe Momtazi's belief in sustainability carries into the tasting room, a cavernous space built of stone from the farm and upcycled wood; even the bar stools are made from old wine barrels. ✉ *15765 S.W. Muddy Valley Rd.* ☎ *503/843–1234* 🌐 *maysara.com.*

Restaurants

Joel Palmer House

$$$$ | CONTEMPORARY | Wild mushrooms and truffles are the stars at this 1857 home, named after an Oregon pioneer, that is now on the National Register of Historic Places; there are three small dining rooms, each seating about 15 people. The standard dinner is a seasonal three-course prix-fixe menu, but if you really, really like mushrooms, have your entire table order chef Christopher's Mushroom Madness Menu, a six-course extravaganza. **Known for:** mushrooms, mushrooms, mushrooms; three-course prix-fixe menu; chef Christopher's Mushroom Madness Menu. *Average main: $50 600 Ferry St., Dayton 503/864–2995 www.joelpalmerhouse.com Closed Sun. and Mon. No lunch.*

★ Nick's Italian Cafe
$$$ | **ITALIAN** | Famed for serving Oregon's wine country enthusiasts, this fine-dining venue is a destination for a special evening or lunch. Modestly furnished but with a voluminous wine cellar, Nick's serves spirited and simple food, reflecting the owner's northern Italian heritage. **Known for:** five-course prix fixe with wine pairings; expansive wine cellar; extensive dessert menu. *Average main: $26 521 N.E. 3rd St. 503/434–4471 nicksitaliancafe.com.*

Coffee and Quick Bites

Serendipity Ice Cream
$ | **CAFÉ** | **FAMILY** | Historic Cook's Hotel, built in 1886, is the setting for a true, old-fashioned ice-cream-parlor experience. Try a sundae, and take home cookies made from scratch. **Known for:** locally made ice cream (dairy- and sugar-free varieties); open all year; the shop provides workplace experience and job training for adults with developmental disabilities. *Average main: $4 502 N.E. 3rd St. 503/474–9189 serendipityicecream.com Closed Mon.*

Hotels

★ Atticus Hotel
$$$$ | **HOTEL** | Smack in the middle of downtown McMinnville, this chic boutique hotel offers elegant, high-ceilinged rooms that feature an eclectic mix of local art and amenities and vaguely Edwardian soft furnishings. **Pros:** elegant digs in downtown McMinnville; on-site dining and room service from Red Hills Kitchen; unlimited free espresso at the front desk. **Cons:** no self-parking (except on the street); fee for room service; rooms get some ambient noise. *Rooms from: $315 375 N.E. Ford St. 503/472–1975 atticushotel.com 36 rooms No meals.*

Youngberg Hill
$$$$ | **B&B/INN** | Situated on a hilltop overlooking the ridiculously bucolic outskirts of McMinnville, this family-run winery and B&B features nine elegant rooms, all with gas or electric fireplaces and some with whirlpool hot tubs; a couple of the top-floor units even have private balconies. **Pros:** incredible wine country views; included two-course breakfasts; some rooms have Jacuzzis. **Cons:** no on-site restaurant (except for breakfast); some rooms lack views; removed from town. *Rooms from: $309 10660 S.W. Youngberg Hill Rd. 503/472–2727 youngberghill.com 9 rooms Free breakfast.*

Salem

24 miles from McMinnville, south on Hwy. 99W and east on Hwy. 22, 45 miles south of Portland on I–5.

The state capital has a rich pioneer history, but before that it was the home of the Calapooia Indians, who called it Chemeketa, which means "place of rest." Salem is said to have been renamed by missionaries. Although trappers and farmers preceded them in the Willamette Valley, the Methodist missionaries had come in 1834 to minister to Native Americans, and they are credited with the founding of Salem. In 1842 they established the first academic institution west of the Rockies, which is now known as Willamette University. Salem became the capital when Oregon achieved statehood in 1859 (Oregon City was the capital of the Oregon Territory). Salem serves as the seat to Marion County as well as the home of the state fairgrounds. Government ranks as a major industry here, while the city's setting in the heart of the fertile Willamette Valley stimulates rich agricultural and food-processing industries. More than a dozen wineries are in or near Salem. The main attractions in Salem are west of Interstate 5 in and around the Capitol Mall.

GETTING HERE AND AROUND

Salem is located on Interstate 5 with easy access to Portland, Albany, and Eugene. **Hut Portland Airport Shuttle** provides transportation to Portland International Airport, which is one hour and 15 minutes away. Salem's McNary Field no longer has commercial airline service, but serves general aviation aircraft.

Bus transportation throughout Salem is provided by **Cherriots.** Amtrak operates regularly, and its train station is located at 500 13th Street SE.

ESSENTIALS

CONTACTS Cherriots. *www.cherriots.org.* **Hut Portland Airport Shuttle.** *503/364–4444* *hutshuttle.cim.*

VISITOR INFORMATION Salem Convention & Visitors Center. *181 High St. NE* *503/581–4325, 800/874–7012* *www.travelsalem.com.*

Sights

Bethel Heights Vineyard

WINERY/DISTILLERY | Founded in 1977, Bethel Heights was one of the first vineyards planted in the Eola Hills region of the Willamette Valley. It produces Pinot Noir, Chardonnay, Pinot Blanc, and Pinot Gris. The tasting room has one of the most glorious panoramic views of any winery in the state; its terrace and picnic area overlook the surrounding vineyards, the valley below, and Mt. Jefferson in the distance. *6060 Bethel Heights Rd. NW* *503/581–2262* *www.bethelheights.com* *Tastings $20.*

Bush's Pasture Park and Bush House

HOUSE | These 105 acres of rolling lawn and formal English gardens include the remarkably well-preserved Bush House, an 1878 Italianate mansion at the park's far-western boundary. It has 10 marble fireplaces and virtually all of its original furnishings, and can be visited only on informative tours. Bush Barn Art Center, behind the house, exhibits the work of Northwest artists and has a sales gallery. *600 Mission St. SE* *503/363–4714* *bushhousemuseum.org* *House $6.*

Elsinore Theatre

ARTS VENUE | This flamboyant Tudor Gothic vaudeville house opened on May 28, 1926, with Edgar Bergen in attendance. Clark Gable (who lived in nearby Silverton) and Gregory Peck performed on stage. The theater was designed to look like a castle, with a false-stone front, chandeliers, ironwork, and stained-glass windows. It's now a lively performing arts center with a busy schedule of bookings, and there are concerts on its Wurlitzer pipe organ. *170 High St. SE* *503/375–3574* *www.elsinoretheatre.com.*

Enchanted Forest

AMUSEMENT PARK/WATER PARK | **FAMILY** | South of Salem, the Enchanted Forest is the closest thing Oregon has to a major theme park. The park has several attractions in forestlike surroundings, including a Big Timber Log Ride. On it, you ride logs through flumes that pass through a lumber mill and the woods. The ride—the biggest log ride in the Northwest—has a 25-foot roller-coaster dip and a 40-foot drop at the end. Other attractions include the Ice Mountain Bobsled roller coaster, the Haunted House, English Village, Storybook Lane, the Fantasy Fountains Water Light Show, Fort Fearless, and the Western town of Tofteville. *8462 Enchanted Way SE, Turner* *7 miles south of Salem at Exit 248 off I–5* *503/363–3060, 503/371–4242* *www.enchantedforest.com* *$13.50, $12*

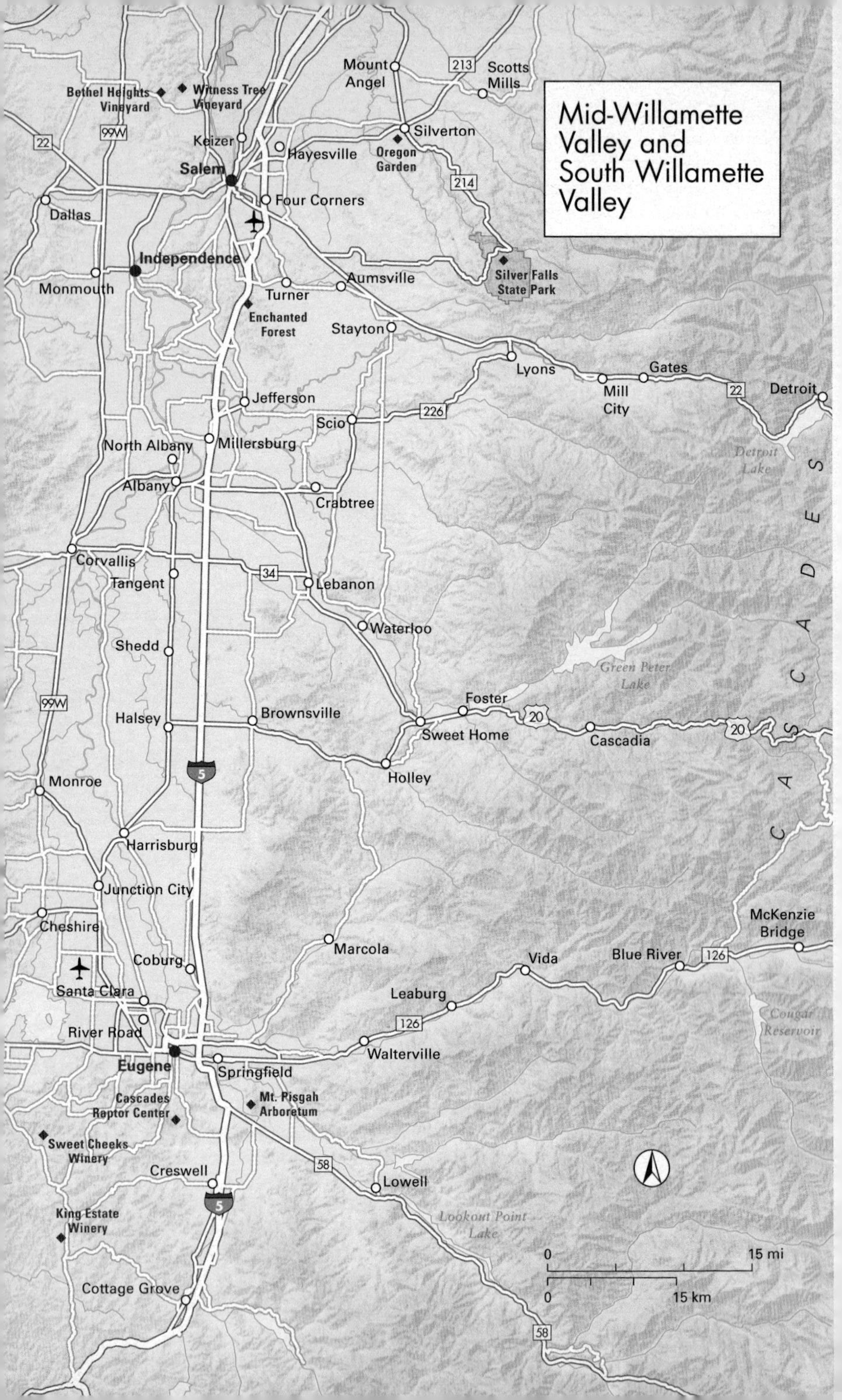

Mid-Willamette Valley and South Willamette Valley
Mount Angel
213
Scotts Mills
Bethel Heights Vineyard
Witness Tree Vineyard
99W
22
Keizer
Silverton
Hayesville
Oregon Garden
Salem
214
Four Corners
Dallas
Independence
Monmouth
Turner
Aumsville
Silver Falls State Park
Enchanted Forest
Stayton
Lyons
Gates
Mill City
22
Detroit
Jefferson
226
Scio
Detroit Lake
North Albany
Millersburg
Albany
Crabtree
Corvallis
34
Tangent
Lebanon
Waterloo
Shedd
Green Peter Lake
99W
Foster
Halsey
Brownsville
Sweet Home
20
Cascadia
20
5
Holley
Monroe
C A S C A D E S
Harrisburg
Junction City
Cheshire
McKenzie Bridge
Marcola
Coburg
Vida
Blue River
126
Santa Clara
Leaburg
126
Cougar Reservoir
River Road
Walterville
Eugene
Springfield
Cascades Raptor Center
Mt. Pisgah Arboretum
Sweet Cheeks Winery
58
Creswell
Lowell
5
King Estate Winery
Lookout Point Lake
0
15 mi
0
15 km
Cottage Grove
58

children, rides cost extra ⏲ Closed Apr. and Labor Day–end of Sept., weekdays, and Nov.–Mar.

Gilbert House Children's Museum

MUSEUM | FAMILY | This is a different kind of kids' museum; an amazing place to let the imagination run wild. Celebrating the life and the inventions of A.C. Gilbert, a Salem native who became a toy manufacturer and inventor, the historic houses included many themed interactive rooms along with a huge outdoor play structure. In addition to the children's activities, many beloved toys created by A.C. Gilbert are on display, including Erector sets and American Flyer trains. The wide range of indoor and outdoor interactive exhibits will appeal to children (and adults) of all ages. ✉ *116 Marion St. NE* ☎ *503/371–3631* 🌐 *www.acgilbert.org* 🎫 *$8* ⏲ *Closed Mon. except during school holidays.*

★ Mount Angel Abbey

RELIGIOUS SITE | This Benedictine monastery on a 300-foot-high butte was founded in 1882 and is the site of one of two Modernist buildings in the United States designed by Finnish architect Alvar Aalto. A masterpiece of serene and thoughtful design, Aalto's library opened its doors in 1970, and has become a place of pilgrimage for students and aficionados of modern architecture. You also can sample beers produced by the abbey's in-house brewery (the aptly named Benedictine Brewery) at its taproom just up the road (closed Monday and Tuesday). ✉ *1 Abbey Dr., St. Benedict* ✣ *18 miles from Salem; east on Hwy. 213 and north on Hwy. 214* ☎ *503/845–3030* 🌐 *www.mountangelabbey.org* 🎫 *Free.*

Oregon Capitol

GOVERNMENT BUILDING | A brightly gilded bronze statue of the *Oregon Pioneer* stands atop the 140-foot-high Capitol dome, looking north across the Capitol Mall. Built in 1939 with blocks of gray Vermont marble, Oregon's Capitol has an elegant yet austere neoclassical feel. East and west wings were added in 1978. Relief sculptures and deft historical murals soften the interior. Guided tours of the rotunda, the House and Senate chambers, and the governor's office leave from the information center under the dome at 10:30 am, 11:30 am, 1:30 pm, and 2:30 pm. ✉ *900 Court St. NE* ☎ *503/986–1388* 🌐 *www.oregonlegislature.gov* 🎫 *Free* ⏲ *Closed weekends and public holidays.*

Oregon Garden

GARDEN | Just outside the town of Silverton, a 25-minute drive from Salem, the Oregon Garden showcases the botanical diversity of the Willamette Valley and Pacific Northwest. Open 365 days a year, the 80-acre garden features themed plots ranging from a conifer forest to medicinal plants. There's also a whimsical children's garden complete with a model train, and another garden featuring the agricultural bounty of the area. A free narrated hop-on hop-off tram tour operates from April through October and stops at six points across the garden. ✉ *879 W. Main St., Silverton* ☎ *503/874–8100, 877/674–2733* 🌐 *www.oregongarden.org* 🎫 *$8–$14 depending on season* ⏲ *Closed Nov.–Mar., Mon.–Thurs.*

Oregon State Hospital Museum of Mental Health

MUSEUM | This former insane asylum served as the primary set for the legendary 1975 blockbuster *One Flew Over the Cuckoo's Nest*, starring Jack Nicholson. In the late- 19th-century facility, volunteers operate this nonprofit museum, which explores the somber history of psychiatry through artifacts such as straitjackets sewn by patients and now-regrettable treatment devices. A popular permanent exhibit is dedicated to the Academy Award–winning film. ✉ *2600 Center St. NE* ☎ *971/599–1674* 🌐 *oshmuseum.org* 🎫 *$7* ⏲ *Closed Mon.*

The Sprague Fountain, also known as the Capitol Fountain, can be found in Salem's Capitol Mall in front of the capitol building.

Silver Falls State Park

NATIONAL/STATE PARK | Hidden amid old-growth Douglas firs in the foothills of the Cascades, this is the largest state park in Oregon (8,700 acres). South Falls, roaring over the lip of a mossy basalt bowl into a deep pool 177 feet below, is the main attraction here, but 13 other waterfalls—half of them more than 100 feet high—are accessible to hikers. The best time to visit is in the fall, when vine maples blaze with brilliant color, or early spring, when the forest floor is carpeted with trilliums and yellow violets. There are picnic facilities and a day lodge; in winter you can cross-country ski. Camping facilities include tent and trailer sites, cabins, and a horse camp. ✉ *20024 Silver Falls Hwy. SE, Sublimity* ☎ *503/873–8681, 800/551–6949* 🌐 *www.oregonstateparks.org* 🎫 *$5 per vehicle.*

Willamette Heritage Center

MUSEUM VILLAGE | FAMILY | Take a trip back in time to experience the story of Oregon's early pioneers and the industrial revolution. The **Thomas Kay Woolen Mill Museum** complex (circa 1889), complete with working waterwheels and mill-stream, looks as if the workers have just stepped away for a lunch break. Teasel gigging, napper flock bins, and the patented Furber double-acting napper are but a few of the machines and processes on display. The **Jason Lee House,** the **John D. Boon Home,** and the **Methodist Parsonage** are also part of the village. There is nothing grandiose about these early pioneer homes, the oldest frame structures in the Northwest, but they reveal a great deal about domestic life in the wilds of Oregon in the 1840s. ✉ *1313 Mill St. SE* ☎ *503/585–7012* 🌐 *www.willametteheritage.org* 🎫 *$8* 🕒 *Closed Sun.*

Willamette Mission State Park

NATIONAL/STATE PARK | Along pastoral lowlands by the Willamette River, this serene park holds the largest black cottonwood tree in the United States. A thick-barked behemoth by a small pond, the 275-year-old tree has upraised arms that bring to mind J.R.R. Tolkien's fictional Ents. Site of Reverend Jason Lee's 1834 pioneer mission, the park also offers quiet strolling and picnicking in an old orchard and along the river. The Wheatland Ferry, at the north end of the park, began carrying covered wagons across the Willamette in 1844 and is still in operation today. ✉ *Wheatland Rd.* ✣ *8 miles north of Salem, I–5 Exit 263* ☎ *503/393–1172, 800/551–6949* 🌐 *www.oregonstateparks.org* 🎫 *$5 per vehicle.*

Willamette University

COLLEGE | Behind the Capitol, across State Street but half a world away, are the brick buildings and grounds of Willamette University, the oldest college in the West. Founded in 1842, Willamette has long been a breeding ground for aspiring politicians. **Hatfield Library,** built in 1986 on the banks of Mill Stream, is a handsome brick-and-glass building with a striking campanile; tall, prim **Waller Hall,** built in 1867, is one of the oldest buildings in the Pacific Northwest. ✉ *900 State St.* ☎ *503/370–6300* 🌐 *www.willamette.edu* ⏲ *Closed weekends.*

Witness Tree Vineyard

WINERY/DISTILLERY | Named for the ancient oak that towers over the vineyard (it was used as a surveyor's landmark in the 1850s), this winery produces premium Pinot Noir made entirely from grapes grown on its 100-acre estate nestled in the Eola Hills northwest of Salem. The vineyard also produces limited quantities of estate Chardonnay, Viognier, Pinot Blanc, Dolcetto, and a sweet dessert wine called Sweet Signé. Tours are available by appointment. ✉ *7111 Spring Valley Rd. NW* ☎ *503/585–7874* 🌐 *www.witnesstreevineyard.com* 🎫 *Tastings from $10* ⏲ *Closed Mon.–Wed. Mar.–mid-Dec. and mid-Dec.–Feb.*

Restaurants

★ DaVinci

$$$ | **ITALIAN** | Salem politicos flock to this two-story downtown gathering spot for Italian-inspired dishes cooked in a wood-burning oven. No shortcuts are taken in the preparation, so don't come if you're in a rush. **Known for:** pasta made in-house; good wines by the glass; live music. 💲 *Average main: $24* ✉ *180 High St. SE* ☎ *503/399–1413* 🌐 *www.davincisofsalem.com* ⏲ *Closed Sun. No lunch.*

Hotels

Grand Hotel in Salem

$$ | **HOTEL** | Salem is short on choices, but this hotel offers large rooms, with comfortable and luxurious furnishings; it's a good base for guests attending shows and meetings at Salem Conference Center or touring the region. **Pros:** spacious rooms; centrally located; free hot breakfast. **Cons:** some street noise; lacks character; check-in times are late. 💲 *Rooms from: $189* ✉ *201 Liberty St. SE* ☎ *503/540–7800, 877/540–7800* 🌐 *www.grandhotelsalem.com* *193 rooms* *Free breakfast.*

Oregon Garden Resort

$$ | **RESORT** | Bright, spacious, classically decorated rooms, each with a fireplace and a private landscaped patio or balcony, neighbor the Oregon Garden (admission is included in the rates). **Pros:** gorgeous grounds; rooms have fireplaces and patios or balconies; spa and plenty of other amenities. **Cons:** a distance from other activities; room decor is simple and old-fashioned; pool is outdoors and seasonal. 💲 *Rooms from: $159* ✉ *895 W. Main St., Silverton* ☎ *503/874–2500* 🌐 *www.oregongardenresort.com* *103 rooms* *Free breakfast.*

Shopping

Reed Opera House

SHOPPING CENTERS/MALLS | These days the 1869 opera house in downtown Salem contains an eclectic collection of locally owned stores, shops, restaurants, bars, and bakeries, everything from art galleries to tattoo parlors. Its Trinity Ballroom hosts special events and celebrations.

✉ *189 Liberty St. NE* ☎ *503/391–4481* 🌐 *www.reedoperahouse.com.*

Woodburn Premium Outlets
SHOPPING CENTERS/MALLS | Located 18 miles north of Salem just off Interstate 5 are more than 100 brand-name outlet stores, including Nike, Adidas, Calvin Klein, Bose, Coach, Ann Taylor, Levi's, Pendleton, and Columbia Sportswear. There's also a small playground and a couple of places to eat. ✉ *1001 Arney Rd., Woodburn* ☎ *503/981–1900, 888/664–7467* 🌐 *www.premiumoutlets.com/outlet/woodburn.*

Independence

13 miles southwest of Salem on Hwy. 22 W and Hwy. 51 S.

Founded by Oregon Trail pioneers (who named the city after their hometown in Missouri), Independence thrived largely as a trading port owing to its location right on the Willamette River and its proximity to Oregon's hop country. Much of the city was built in the 1880s and its National Register of Historic Places–listed Independence Historic District features around 250 buildings spread over about 30 blocks.

GETTING HERE AND AROUND

Independence is located right on the Willamette River, between 99W and Interstate 5 and directly east of the college town of Monmouth. It's about 15 minutes from Salem, while the Portland International Airport is about 90 minutes away without traffic.

ESSENTIALS

VISITOR INFORMATION Independence Downtown Association. ✉ *278 S Main St., Independence* 🌐 *www.downtownindependence.com.*

Sights

Independence Heritage Museum
MUSEUM | Housed in the old First Baptist Church building, built in 1888, this history museum does a striking job at telling the story of Independence and its surrounding regions through the eyes of various communities that have contributed to its history, not just white settlers. Kids love the skeleton of "Betsy the Cow," used in local classrooms to teach anatomy since her bones were first discovered by a group of schoolboys in the 1960s. Pick up a historic district map for a self-guided tour. ✉ *112 S. 3rd St., Independence* ☎ *503/838–1811* 🌐 *www.ci.independence.or.us/museum.*

Redgate Vineyard
WINERY/DISTILLERY | Though the Independence area is more known for hops than vineyards, Red Gate produces a wide variety of wines, from Pinots to Syrah, Tempranillo, and even port-style dessert wines. The small, publike tasting room has some of the most reasonably priced flights in the area. ✉ *8175 Buena Vista Rd., Independence* ☎ *503/428–7115* 🌐 *redgatevineyard.com* 🎟 *Tastings $10* 🕒 *Closed Mon.–Thurs.*

Rogue Farms Tasting Room
WINERY/DISTILLERY | If you want to try out some of Rogue Ales' most popular brews, you can't get much fresher than right on the grounds of the celebrated Oregon brewery's massive hop farm. A selection of 12 beers are on tap at any given time (along with pretzels and sandwiches); there's also a gift shop with merch and beer for sale, plus a series of educational panels that tell the story of hop production in the area. ✉ *3590 Wigrich Rd., Independence* ☎ *503/838–9813* 🌐 *www.rogue.com/locations/rogue-farms-chatoe-tasting-room.*

Restaurants

Jubilee Champagne and Dessert Bar

$ | **WINE BAR** | Though Champagne, Prosecco, and mimosas are the star attraction at this bright, feminine dessert bar, it also offers espresso drinks, tea, and beer. Beautifully presented desserts, from glittery red velvet cake to pastel-hued cupcakes, and macarons, round out the menu, and there are a few savory snacks, including a popular dill-pickle soup, for those wanting something more substantial. **Known for:** sparkling wine, Champagne, and espresso drinks; a huge selection of fresh cakes and pastries; dill pickle soup. *Average main: $8 296 S. Main St., Independence 837–0888 Closed Mon.*

Mangiare Italian Restaurant

$$ | **ITALIAN** | Italian-food lovers frequently make the drive from neighboring towns to dine on Mangiare's celebrated pasta dishes and traditional desserts (it also does pizzas, salads, and even meatball sandwiches). The wine list isn't too shabby, either, with an even balance of Willamette Valley and Italian options. **Known for:** generous portions of pasta; traditional Italian desserts; charming outdoor patio area. *Average main: $19 114 S. Main St., Independence 503/838–0566 www.mangiareitalianrestaurantor.com No lunch Sun.*

Hotels

The Independence

$$ | **HOTEL** | Overlooking the Willamette River, this business-boutique hotel draws decor inspiration from its local geography, with oceanic blues and wavelike patterns paired with locally sourced furnishings (even the mattresses were made in the region). **Pros:** beautiful riverfront location right in town; cyclist-friendly facilities, with workshops and in-room bike storage; lovely restaurant with indoor and outdoor seating. **Cons:** bathrooms have automatic light switches and abrasively bright lights; rooms lack safes; no room service. *Rooms from: $189 201 Osprey La., Independence 503/837–0200 theindependenthotel.com 75 rooms No meals.*

Eugene

63 miles south of Corvallis on I–5.

Eugene was founded in 1846, when Eugene Skinner staked the first federal land-grant claim for pioneers. Eugene is consistently given high marks for its "livability." As the home of the University of Oregon, a large student and former-student population lends Eugene a youthful vitality and countercultural edge. Full of parks and oriented to the outdoors, Eugene is a place where bike paths are used, pedestrians *always* have the right-of-way, and joggers are so plentiful that the city is known as the Running Capital of the World. Shopping and commercial streets surround the Eugene Hilton and the Hult Center for the Performing Arts, the two most prominent downtown buildings. During football season you can count on the U of O Ducks being the primary topic of most conversations.

GETTING HERE AND AROUND

Eugene's airport has rental cars, cabs, and shuttles that make the 15-minute trip to Eugene's city center. By train, Amtrak stops in the heart of downtown. Getting around Lane County's communities is easy with **Lane Transit District** public transportation. Eugene is very bicycle-friendly.

ESSENTIALS

VISITOR INFORMATION Travel Lane County. *754 Olive St. 541/484–5307, 800/547–5445 www.eugenecascadescoast.org.*

Alton Baker Park

CITY PARK | This parcel of open land on the banks of the Willamette River is named after the late publisher of Eugene's newspaper, the *Register-Guard,* and is the site of many community events. Live music is performed in summer at the Cuthbert Amphitheater. There's fine hiking and biking on a footpath that runs along the river for the length of the park, and an 18-hole disc golf course. Also worth seeing is the Whilamut Natural Area, an open space with 13 "talking stones," each with an inscription. ✉ *200 Day Island Rd.* ☎ *541/682–4906* 🌐 *www.altonbakerpark.com.*

Cascades Raptor Center

NATURE PRESERVE | **FAMILY** | This birds-of-prey nature center and hospital hosts more than 30 species of birds. A visit is a great outing for kids, who can learn what owls eat, why and where birds migrate, and all sorts of other raptor facts. Some of the full-time residents include turkey vultures, bald eagles, owls, hawks, falcons, and kites. ✉ *32275 Fox Hollow Rd.* ☎ *541/485–1320* 🌐 *www.eraptors.org* 🎟 *$9* ⏲ *Closed Mon.*

Civic Winery

WINERY/DISTILLERY | This intimate wine shop focuses on small-batch producers, with a solid list of some of Oregon's finest biodynamic growers. Civic also makes a few wines of its own, all fermented naturally, without added yeast, in terra-cotta amphorae using locally sourced biodynamic and organic grapes. ✉ *50 E 11th Ave.* ☎ *541/636–2990* 🌐 *www.civicwinery.com* ⏲ *Closed Mon. and Tues.*

Eugene Saturday Market

MARKET | Held every Saturday from April through the middle of November, the Saturday Market is a great place to browse for handicrafts, try out local food carts, or simply kick back and people-watch while listening to live music at the Market Stage. ✉ *126 E. 8th Ave.* ☎ *541/686–8885* 🌐 *www.eugenesaturdaymarket.org.*

Eugene Science Center

MUSEUM | **FAMILY** | Formerly the Willamette Science and Technology Center (WISTEC), and still known to locals by its former name, Eugene's imaginative, hands-on museum assembles rotating exhibits designed for curious young minds. The adjacent **planetarium,** one of the largest in the Pacific Northwest, presents star shows and entertainment events. ✉ *2300 Leo Harris Pkwy.* ☎ *541/682–7888* 🌐 *www.sciencefactory.org* 🎟 *$5 for exhibit hall or planetarium show, $8 for both* ⏲ *Closed Mon. and during Oregon Ducks home football games; planetarium timings vary.*

Hayward Field

SPORTS VENUE | University of Oregon's historic Hayward Field was demolished and rebuilt from scratch to host the 2021 IAAF World Athletics Championships, and the results have been fantastic. Featuring gargantuan indoor and outdoor practice areas along with extensive world-class facilities for runners and spectators alike, from an antigravity treadmill room to a theater created specifically for optimal viewing of track-and-field events. ✉ *1580 E 15th Ave.*

★ Jordan Schnitzer Museum of Art

MUSEUM | Works from the 20th and 21st centuries are a specialty in these handsome galleries on the University of Oregon campus. They feature works by many leading Pacific Northwest artists, and European, Korean, Chinese, and Japanese works are also on view, as are 300 works commissioned by the Works Progress Administration in the 1930s and '40s. You can also view an ever-changing collection of important works from private collections by internationally recognized artists through the museum's Masterworks On Loan program. ✉ *1430 Johnson La.* ☎ *541/346–3027* 🌐 *jsma.uoregon.edu* 🎟 *$5* ⏲ *Closed Mon. and Tues.*

King Estate Winery

WINERY/DISTILLERY | One of Oregon's largest producers is known for its crisp Pinot Gris and silky Pinot Noir and boasts the world's largest organic vineyard. The visitor center offers wine tasting and production tours, and the restaurant highlights local meats and organic produce grown in the estate gardens. ✉ *80854 Territorial Rd.* ☎ *541/942–9874* 🌐 *www.kingestate.com* 🎫 *Tastings $15.*

Lane County Farmers' Market

MARKET | Across the street from the Eugene Saturday Market, the Lane County market offers produce grown or made in Oregon. Hours and days vary throughout the year. ✉ *Corner of 8th Ave. and Oak St.* ☎ *541/431–4923* 🌐 *www.lanecountyfarmersmarket.org/markets* ⏲ *Closed Jan.*

Mount Pisgah Arboretum

GARDEN | **FAMILY** | This beautiful nature preserve near southeast Eugene includes extensive all-weather trails, educational programs for all ages, and facilities for special events. Its visitor center holds workshops and features native amphibian and reptile terraria; microscopes for exploring tiny seeds, bugs, feathers, and snakeskins; "touch me" exhibits; reference books; and a working viewable beehive. ✉ *34901 Frank Parrish Rd.* ☎ *541/747–3817* 🌐 *www.mountpisgaharboretum.org* 🎫 *Parking $4.*

Ninkasi Brewing Company

WINERY/DISTILLERY | Named after the Sumerian goddess of fermentation, Ninkasi has grown from a little start-up in 2006 to a major supplier of craft beer. Its flagship beer, Total Domination IPA, is signature Northwest, with bold flavor and lots of hops. Visit the tasting room and enjoy a tasting flight or a pint, either indoors or on the patio. The beer menu changes often and includes a few hard-to-find limited-production beers. If you'd like a little food to go with your beer, you'll usually find one of Eugene's many food carts right there on the patio. Free brewery tours are offered daily. ✉ *272 Van Buren St.* ☎ *541/344–2739* 🌐 *www.ninkasibrewing.com.*

Skinner Butte Park

NATIONAL/STATE PARK | **FAMILY** | Rising from the south bank of the Willamette River, this forested enclave provides the best views of any of the city's parks; it also has the greatest historic cachet, since it was here that Eugene Skinner staked the claim that put Eugene on the map. Children can scale a replica of Skinner Butte, uncover fossils, and cool off under a rain circle. Skinner Butte Loop leads to the top of Skinner Butte, traversing sometimes difficult terrain through a mixed-conifer forest. ✉ *248 Cheshire Ave.* ☎ *541/682–4800* 🎫 *Free.*

Sweet Cheeks Winery

WINERY/DISTILLERY | This estate vineyard lies on a prime sloping hillside in the heart of the Willamette Valley appellation. It also supplies grapes to several award-winning wineries. Bring a picnic and enjoy the amazing view from the lawn outside the tasting room, or take advantage of the food available for purchase. Friday-night tastings are embellished with cheese pairings and live music. They also have a second tasting room in the Fifth Street Public Market. ✉ *27007 Briggs Hill Rd.* ☎ *541/349–9463, 877/309–9463* 🌐 *www.sweetcheekswinery.com.*

University of Oregon

COLLEGE | The true heart of Eugene lies southeast of the city center at its university. Several fine old buildings can be seen on the 250-acre campus; **Deady Hall,** built in 1876, is the oldest. More than 400 varieties of trees grace the bucolic grounds, along with outdoor sculptures that include *The Pioneer* and *The Pioneer Mother.* The two bronze figures by Alexander Phimster Proctor were dedicated to the men and women who settled the Oregon Territory and less than a generation later founded the university. ✉ *1585 E. 13th Ave.* ☎ *541/346–1000* 🌐 *www.uoregon.edu.*

University of Oregon Museum of Natural and Cultural History

MUSEUM | Relics on display are devoted to Pacific Northwest anthropology and the natural sciences. Highlights include the fossil collection of Thomas Condon, Oregon's first geologist, and a pair of 9,000-year-old sandals made of sagebrush. ✉ *1680 E. 15th Ave.* ☎ *541/346–3024* 🌐 *mnch.uoregon.edu* 🎫 *$6* 🕒 *Closed Mon.*

★ WildCraft Cider Works

WINERY/DISTILLERY | With a long list of house-crafted ciders, many seasonal, this casual spot is a great place to try out WildCraft's locally celebrated wild-ferment ciders, many of which highlight the diversity of the Willamette Valley's apple bounty. Local favorites include the botanical Wild Rose cider (made with locally harvested rose petals) and "perries," unpasteurized pear ciders stored in wax-sealed bottles. WildCraft also has its own event space with regular live music. Peckish guests can order meals and snacks from Krob Krua, an independently operated Thai restaurant that rents out a section of the cidery. ✉ *232 Lincoln St.* ✥ *The main parking area is off Lawrence St., 1 block west of Lincoln* ☎ *541/735–3506* 🌐 *wildcraftciderworks.com* 🕒 *Closed Sun. and Mon.*

Restaurants

Café 440

$$ | MODERN AMERICAN | Putting a modern twist on classic comfort food, this airy, industrial-chic space features pub food and comfort fare made from locally grown ingredients and a great local beer list. Along with updated classics like mac and cheese, burgers, and fish-and-chips, you'll find innovative versions of ahi poke and salmon cakes. **Known for:** upscale takes on comfort food; homemade desserts; supporting local charities. 💲 *Average main: $22* ✉ *440 Coburg Rd.* ☎ *541/505–8493* 🌐 *www.cafe440.com.*

Grit Kitchen and Wine

$$$ | PACIFIC NORTHWEST | Local, seasonal ingredients are the star attraction at this Whiteaker neighborhood mainstay, with a changing menu featuring complex and unexpected flavors and a wide range of textures. Eat inside and take advantage of the open kitchen to watch the chefs at work, or enjoy a pleasant outdoor dining experience on either of the two decks. **Known for:** the monthly changing four-course feast; locally sourced ingredients; handmade noodles. 💲 *Average main: $27* ✉ *1080 W. 3rd St.* ☎ *541/343–0501* 🌐 *gritkitchen.com* 🕒 *No lunch.*

Marché

$$$ | FRENCH | Located in the bustling Fifth Street Market, this renowned Eugene restaurant works with more than a dozen local farmers to bring fresh, local, organic food to the table. Specialties include salmon, halibut, sturgeon, and beef tenderloin, braised pork shoulder, and outstanding local oysters paired with an extensive wine list featuring lots of Oregon wines. **Known for:** fresh beignets on Sunday; locally sourced ingredients; solid wine list with plenty of local options. 💲 *Average main: $30* ✉ *296 E. 5th Ave.* ☎ *541/342–3612* 🌐 *www.marcherestaurant.com.*

★ Morning Glory Cafe

$ | VEGETARIAN | Eugene's oldest vegetarian restaurant serves up huge, hearty breakfasts and delicious espresso drinks all day along with a great lunchtime menu of soups, salads, and sandwiches. The interiors are decked with local art pieces and there's a small seating area outside for sunny-day dining. **Known for:** breakfast served all day; house-made baked goods; hearty lunch menu with generous portions. 💲 *Average main: $9* ✉ *450 Willamette St.* ☎ *541/687–0709* 🌐 *morninggloryeugene.squarespace.com.*

★ Ristorante Italiano

$$$$ | **ITALIAN** | The chef uses fresh local produce from the restaurant's own farm, but this bistro-style café across from the University of Oregon is best known for its authentic Italian cuisine, with a heavy emphasis on fresh local seafood. The menu changes according to the season, but staples include delicious salads and soups, ravioli, grilled chicken, pizza, and sandwiches plus a variety of specials. **Known for:** Italian fare, with lots of seafood; farm-sourced produce; lovely outdoor seating area. *Average main: $33 Excelsior Inn, 754 E. 13th Ave. 541/342–6963, 800/321–6963 No lunch Sat.*

Hotels

Campbell House

$ | **B&B/INN** | Built in 1892 and later restored with fastidious care, this luxurious bed-and-breakfast features elegant rooms spread across a main house and a carriage house that are surrounded by an acre of landscaped grounds. **Pros:** classic architecture and decor; evening wine receptions; well-kept grounds. **Cons:** rooms lack some of the amenities of nearby hotels; rooms get train noise; uncomfortable mattresses. *Rooms from: $109 252 Pearl St. 541/343–1119, 800/264–2519 www.campbellhouse.com 21 rooms Free breakfast.*

C'est la Vie Inn

$$ | **B&B/INN** | Listed on the National Register of Historic Places, this 1891 Queen Anne Victorian bed-and-breakfast provides old-world comfort and modern-day amenities in its luxurious and romantic guest rooms. **Pros:** intimate ambience; beautiful grounds; helpful staff. **Cons:** few rooms; breakfast is average; not as central as some alternatives. *Rooms from: $175 1006 Taylor St. 541/302–3014 cestlavieinn.com 4 rooms Free breakfast.*

EVEN Hotel Eugene

$ | **HOTEL** | With an excellent gym, an indoor pool, and extensive in-room exercise equipment, this sleek business hotel is ideal for visiting athletes (and anyone who values a good workout); its location near the jogging trails at Alton Baker Park is an added bonus. **Pros:** in-room fitness equipment and modern gym; free and ample on-site parking; 24-hour gift shop selling healthy snacks and fresh-squeezed OJ. **Cons:** lacks local charm of smaller properties; room thermostat; thin walls. *Rooms from: $104 2133 Centennial Plaza 541/342–3836 www.ihg.com/evenhotels 100 rooms No meals.*

Excelsior Inn

$ | **B&B/INN** | Quiet sophistication, attention to architectural detail, and rooms furnished in a refreshingly understated manner, each with a marble-and-tile bath and some with fireplaces, suggest a European inn. **Pros:** romantic accommodations; excellent service and restaurant; close to the University of Oregon campus. **Cons:** some rooms are tiny; limited parking; front desk has limited hours. *Rooms from: $135 754 E. 13th Ave. 541/342–6963, 800/321–6963 www.excelsiorinn.com 14 rooms Free breakfast.*

★ Graduate Eugene

$$$$ | **HOTEL** | The University of Oregon is celebrated with stylish fervor at Graduate Eugene, from the gargantuan wooden duck mascot that greets guests in the lobby to room decor featuring reproductions of local frat and field ephemera; they even have lamps designed to resemble waffle irons (the inspiration for homegrown-brand Nike's first soles). **Pros:** right next to Autzen Stadium in downtown Eugene; tasteful University of Oregon–inspired decor throughout; extensive conference facilities, including rooftop. **Cons:** rooms near ice machines get noise; a trek from the university; no room service. *Rooms from: $277 66 E 6th Ave. 541/342–2000 graduatehotels.com/eugene 295 rooms No meals.*

Inn at the 5th
$$$$ | **HOTEL** | This upscale boutique hotel, set among the shops and restaurants of the trendy Fifth Street Public Market, features subtly elegant rooms and suites. **Pros:** most rooms have fireplaces; great location surrounded by boutiques and restaurants; great amenities, including fitness center. **Cons:** no self-parking; expensive by local standards; some rooms get train noise. *Rooms from: $259* ✉ *205 E. 6th Ave.* ☎ *541/743–4099* 🌐 *www.innat5th.com* *69 rooms* *No meals.*

Performing Arts

Hult Center for the Performing Arts
ARTS VENUE | This is the locus of Eugene's cultural life. Renowned for the quality of its acoustics, the center has two theaters that are home to Eugene's symphony and opera. ✉ *1 Eugene Center* ☎ *541/682–5087 administration, 541/682–5000 tickets* 🌐 *www.hultcenter.org.*

★ **Oregon Bach Festival**
FESTIVALS | Conductor Helmuth Rilling leads the internationally known Oregon Bach Festival every summer. Concerts, chamber music, and social events—held mainly in Eugene at the Hult Center and the University of Oregon School of Music but also in Corvallis and Florence—are part of this three-week event. ✉ *1 Eugene Center* ☎ *541/346–5666* 🌐 *oregonbachfestival.com.*

Shopping

Fifth Street Public Market
SHOPPING CENTERS/MALLS | Tourists coming to the Willamette Valley, especially to Eugene, can't escape without experiencing the Fifth Street Public Market in downtown Eugene. There are plenty of boutiques and crafts shops, a large gourmet food hall with a bakery, and restaurants serving sushi, pizza, and seafood. ✉ *296 E. 5th Ave.* ☎ *541/484–0383* 🌐 *www.5stmarket.com.*

Marley's Monsters EcoShop
HOUSEHOLD ITEMS/FURNITURE | What started as a homegrown Etsy business focusing on eco-friendly, machine-washable, reusable items has quickly mushroomed into a major operation. Here you'll find everything from rolls of cloth "unpaper towels" to reusable sponges in simple whites or fun, colorful patterns; they even do custom orders. ✉ *234 W. 6th Ave.* ☎ *541/505–9417* 🌐 *www.marleysmonsters.com.*

Activities

BIKING AND JOGGING

The **River Bank Bike Path,** originating in Alton Baker Park on the Willamette's north bank, is a level and leisurely introduction to Eugene's topography. It's one of 120 miles of trails in the area. **Prefontaine Trail,** used by area runners, travels through level fields and forests for 1½ miles.

RECREATIONAL AREAS

Dexter State Recreation Site
BOATING | **FAMILY** | A 20-minute drive southeast of Eugene on the western shores of Dexter Reservoir, this recreation site offers disc golf, picnic areas, boat launches, and plenty of hiking. ✥ *Hwy. 58, between mileposts 11 and 12.*

Chapter 6

COLUMBIA RIVER GORGE AND MT. HOOD

Updated by
Andrew Collins

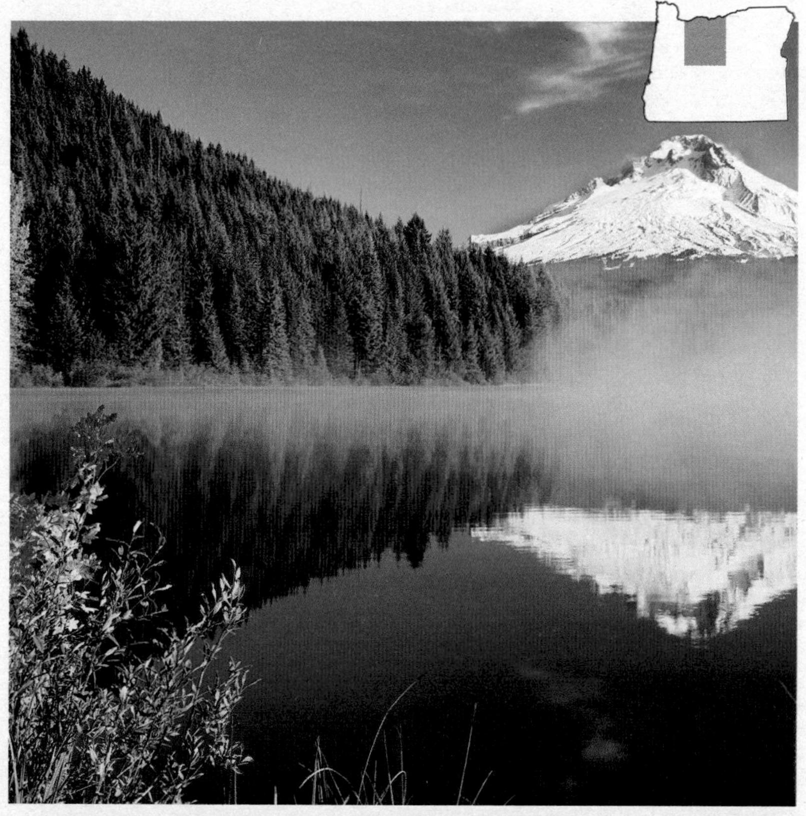

Sights ★★★★★

Restaurants ★★★★☆

Hotels ★★★☆☆

Shopping ★★★☆☆

Nightlife ★★★☆☆

WELCOME TO COLUMBIA RIVER GORGE AND MT. HOOD

TOP REASONS TO GO

★ **Orchards and vineyards:** Dozens of farm stands selling apples, pears, peaches, cherries, and berries, as well as a growing crop of seriously acclaimed wineries, thrive here.

★ **Outdoor rec mecca:** From kiteboarding in the Columbia River to mountain biking the slopes of Mt. Hood to hiking among the roaring waterfalls of the Gorge, this is a region tailor-made for adventure junkies.

★ **Historical-luxe:** Grand dames like Timberline Lodge and the Columbia Gorge Hotel exude history and architectural distinction.

★ **Road-tripping:** From Portland you can make a full 250-mile scenic loop through the Gorge out to Maryhill, Washington, returning to Hood River and then circling Mt. Hood to the south.

★ **Hop havens:** The Gorge-Hood region has a fast-growing proliferation of craft-beer taprooms, from Stevenson's quirky Walking Man Brewing to pFriem, Ferment, and several others in Hood River.

1 **Historic Columbia River Highway.** The country's oldest scenic highway is a great way to see the Gorge.

2 **Cascade Locks.** Early-20th-century dams turned the raging Columbia River into a comparatively docile waterway.

3 **Stevenson, Washington.** This is a quiet base for outdoor adventures and Oregon cliff views.

4 **Hood River.** The hub of the Gorge area has restaurants, lodgings, taprooms, wineries, and amazing mountain views.

5 **White Salmon, Washington.** This scenic spot is handy for wine touring, hiking, and other adventures on the eastern Gorge.

6 **The Dalles.** Old West meets workaday city in north-central Oregon's economic hub.

7 **Goldendale, Washington.** The Gorge's eastern edge has the Maryhill Museum, Maryhill Winery, and Goldendale Observatory State Park.

8 **Mt. Hood.** Mt. Hood is a mecca for mountaineers, sightseers, and year-round skiers. You'll find the alpine resort village of Government Camp, as well as Welches and Zigzag villages.

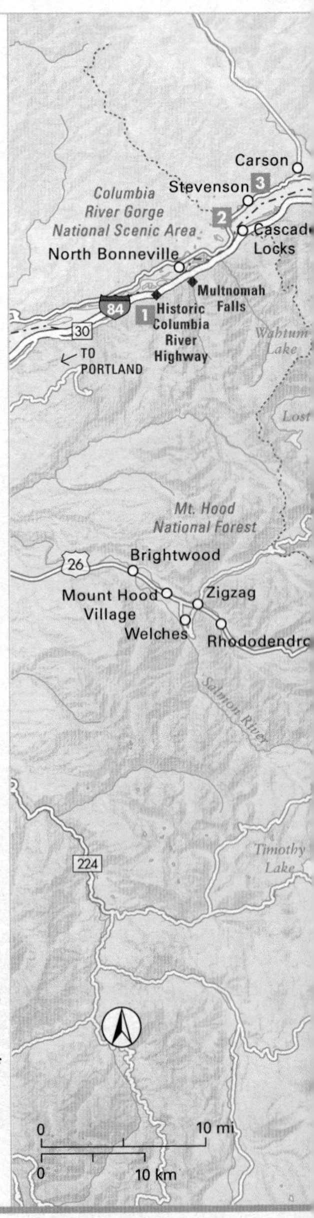

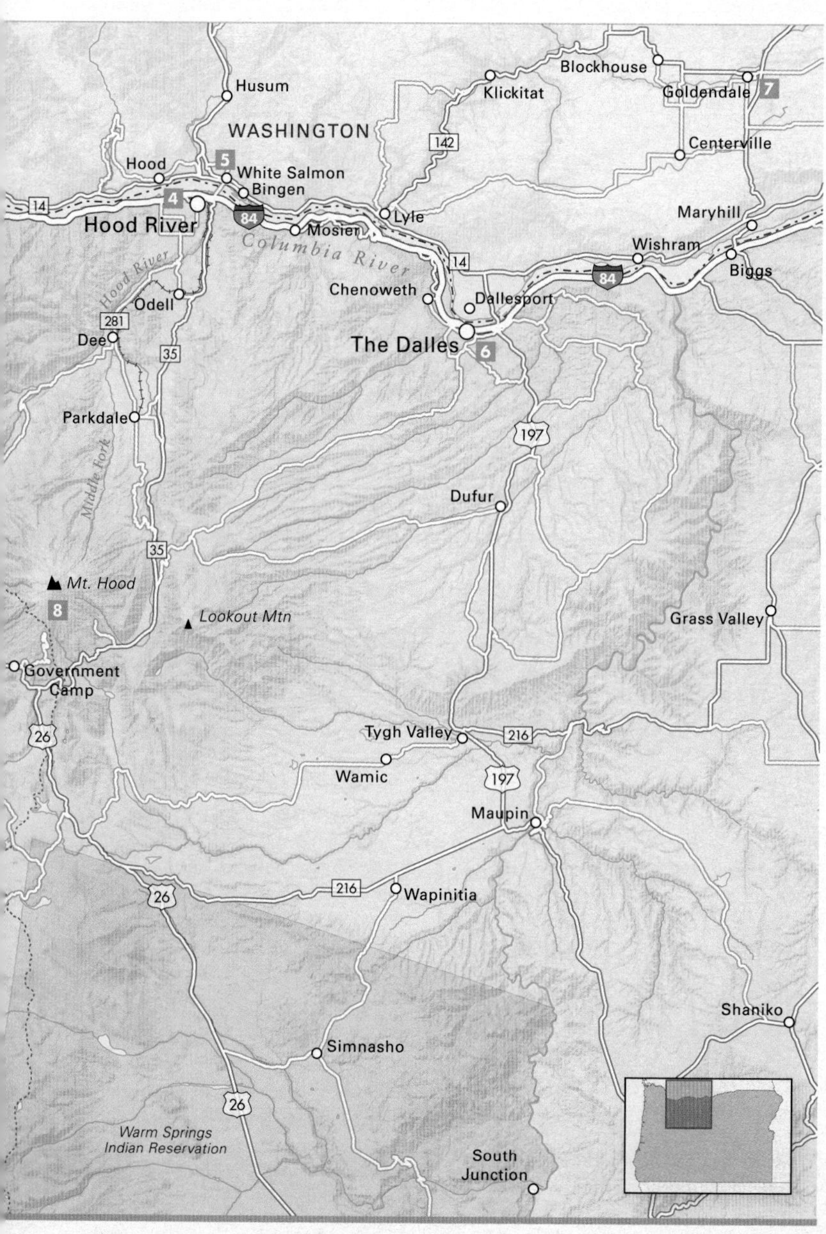
Husum
Klickitat
Blockhouse
Goldendale
7
WASHINGTON
142
Centerville
Hood
5
White Salmon
Bingen
14
4
Hood River
84
Mosier
Lyle
Maryhill
Columbia River
Wishram
14
84
Biggs
Hood River
Odell
Chenoweth
Dallesport
281
Dee
35
The Dalles
6
Parkdale
197
Middle Fork
Dufur
35
Mt. Hood
8
Lookout Mtn
Grass Valley
Government Camp
26
Tygh Valley
216
Wamic
197
Maupin
216
Wapinitia
26
Shaniko
Simnasho
26
Warm Springs Indian Reservation
South Junction

Volcanoes, lava flows, ice-age floodwaters, and glaciers were nature's tools of choice for carving this breathtaking, nearly 100-mile landscape known as the Columbia River Gorge. Proof of human civilization here reaches back 31,000 years, and excavations near The Dalles have uncovered evidence that salmon fishing is a 10,000-year-old tradition in these parts. In 1805 Lewis and Clark discovered the Columbia River, the only major waterway that leads to the Pacific. Their first expedition was a treacherous route through wild, plunging rapids, but their successful navigation set a new exodus in motion.

Today the river has been tamed by a comprehensive system of hydroelectric dams and locks, and the towns in these parts are laid-back though increasingly sophisticated recreation hubs whose residents harbor a fierce pride in their shared natural resources. Sightseers, hikers, bikers, windsurfers, kiteboarders, and skiers have long found contentment in this robust region, officially labeled a National Scenic Area in 1986 and on par with some of the country's top national parks when it comes to eye-popping natural scenery. Rapidly, the region is drawing those in search of farm-to-table cuisine, craft breweries, artisanal bakeries and coffeehouses, and seriously stellar—if still a bit underrated—wineries. Highlights of the areainclude Multnomah Falls, Bonneville Dam, the rich orchard and vineyard lands of Hood River and White Salmon (and the agrarian hamlets nearby), and Maryhill Museum of Art.

To the south of Hood River are all the alpine attractions of the 11,249-foot-high Mt. Hood. With more than 2.5 million people living just up the road in greater Portland, you'd think this mountain playground would be overrun, but it's still easy to find solitude in the 1,067,000-acre national forest surrounding the peak. Some of the world's best skiers take advantage of the powder on Hood, and they stick around in summer for North America's longest ski season at Palmer Snowfield, above Timberline Lodge.

MAJOR REGIONS

When glacial floods carved out most of the **Columbia River Gorge** at the end of the last ice age, they left behind massive, looming cliffs where the river bisects the Cascade mountain range. The size of the canyon and the wildly varying elevations make this small stretch of Oregon as ecologically diverse as anyplace in the state. In a few days along the Gorge you can mountain bike through dry canyons near **The Dalles,** hike through temperate rain forests in the Columbia Gorge along the **Historic Columbia River Highway,** or drive across the Bridge of Gods, which connects **Cascade Locks** with it's twin city, **Stevenson, Washington.** At night you'll be rewarded with historic lodging and good food in one of a half-dozen mellow river towns and one very bustling one, **Hood River. White Salmon, Washington,** is a great base for exploring the Washington side of the Gorge, and farther east, you'll find some notable attractions in Maryhill and **Goldendale.**

Towering at 11,249 feet above sea level, **Mt. Hood** offers the longest ski season in North America, with three major ski resorts that also offer great mountain biking, hiking, and climbing opportunities in the summer. The small resort village of **Government Camp** is located on Mt. Hood, while **Welches and Zigzag** are part of a group of small hamlets known as the Villages of Mt. Hood.

Planning

When to Go

Winter weather in the Mt. Hood area is much more severe than in Portland and the Willamette Valley, and occasionally rough conditions permeate the Gorge, too. Interstate 84 rarely closes because of snow and ice. If you're planning a winter visit, be sure to carry plenty of warm clothes. High winds and single-digit temps are par for the course around 6,000 feet—the elevation of Timberline Lodge on Mt. Hood—in January. Note that chains are sometimes required for traveling over mountain passes.

Temperatures in the Gorge are mild year-round, rarely dipping below 30°F in winter and hovering in the high 70s in midsummer. As throughout Oregon, however, elevation is often a more significant factor than season, and an hour-long drive to Mt. Hood's Timberline Lodge can reduce those midsummer temps by 20–30 degrees. Don't forget that the higher reaches of Mt. Hood retain snow year-round.

In early fall, look for maple, tamarack, and aspen trees around the Gorge, bursting with brilliant red and gold color. No matter the season, the basalt cliffs, the acres of lush forest, and that glorious expanse of water make the Gorge one of the West's great scenic wonders.

Getting Here and Around

The Columbia Gorge, which is easily accessed from Portland, is most easily explored by car. The same is generally true for the Mt. Hood area, but in season, the area ski resorts do have shuttle services from Portland and the airport. Even light exploring of the region, however, requires an automobile—take heart that the driving in these parts is scenic and relatively free of traffic (exceptions being the Historic Columbia River Highway, which can get backed up on weekends). Just keep in mind that winter storms can result in road closures around Mt. Hood and, occasionally, even in the Gorge. It's just a 20-minute drive east of Portland to reach the beginning of the Columbia Gorge, in Troutdale. From Portland it's a one-hour drive to Hood River, a 90-minute drive to Mt. Hood, and a two-hour drive to Goldendale, Washington *(the farthest-away point covered in this chapter)*. If you're trying to visit the region without a car, there are some limited bus options, and you could even take Amtrak to White Salmon–Bingen and then cab it to Hood River, but it'll be tricky to explore the countryside. For tips and details on leaving the car behind, visit 🌐 *www.columbiagorgecarfree.com*.

CAR TRAVEL

Interstate 84 is the main east–west route into the Columbia River Gorge, although you can also reach the area on the Washington side via slower but quite scenic Highway 14, which skirts the north side of the river. U.S. 26, which leads east from Portland, is the main route to Mt. Hood.

The scenic Historic Columbia River Highway (U.S. 30) from Troutdale to just east of Oneonta Gorge (which is, itself, closed indefinitely due to wildfire damage) passes Crown Point State Park and Multnomah Falls. Interstate 84/U.S. 30 continues on to The Dalles. Highway 35 heads south from Hood River to the Mt. Hood area, intersecting with U.S. 26 near Government Camp. From Portland the Columbia Gorge–Mt. Hood Scenic Loop is the easiest way to fully explore the Gorge and the mountain. Take Interstate 84 east to Troutdale and then follow U.S. 26 east to Mt. Hood, Highway 35 north to Hood River, and Interstate 84 back to Portland. Or make the loop in reverse.

Restaurants

A prominent locavore mentality pervades western Oregon generally, and low elevations around the Gorge mean long growing seasons for dozens of local producers. Fresh foods grown, caught, and harvested in the Northwest dominate menus in the increasingly sophisticated restaurants in the Gorge, especially in the charming town of Hood River, but even in smaller White Salmon and up around Mt. Hood. Columbia River salmon is big; fruit orchards proliferate around Hood River; delicious huckleberries flourish in Mount Hood National Forest; and the Gorge nurtures a bounty of excellent vineyards. Additionally, even the smallest towns around the region have their own lively and consistently excellent brewpubs with tasty comfort fare and tap after tap of craft ales. In keeping with the region's green and laid-back vibe, outdoor dining is highly popular. *Restaurant reviews have been shortened. For full information visit Fodors.com.*

What It Costs in U.S. Dollars

	$	$$	$$$	$$$$
RESTAURANTS	under $16	$16–$22	$23–$30	over $30
HOTELS	under $150	$150–$200	$201–$250	over $250

Hotels

The region is close enough that you could spend a day or two exploring the Gorge and Mt. Hood, using Portland hotels as your base. The best way to fully appreciate the Gorge, however, is to spend a night or two—look to Hood River and The Dalles for the largest selections of lodging options, although you'll also find some noteworthy resorts, motels, and B&Bs in some of the towns between Portland and The Dalles (on both sides of the river). There are a couple of run-of-the-mill motels in Goldendale, but otherwise, you won't find any accommodations in the region east of The Dalles.

The slopes of Mt. Hood are dotted with smart ski resorts, and towns like Government Camp and Welches have a mix of rustic and contemporary vacation rentals. The closer you are to Mt. Hood in any season, the earlier you'll want to reserve. With ski country working ever harder to attract summer patrons, Mt. Hood resorts like Timberline Lodge and Mt. Hood Skibowl offer some worthwhile seasonal specials. *Hotel reviews have been shortened. For full information visit Fodors.com.*

Tours

EverGreen Escapes

GUIDED TOURS | The energetic crew at this highly respected tour operator provides both regularly scheduled and customizable tours of the Gorge (with themes that range from wine to hiking) and Mt. Hood, where options include hiking and snowshoeing. ☎ *503/252–1931* 🌐 *www.evergreenescapes.com* 🎫 *From $149.*

Martin's Gorge Tours

GUIDED TOURS | Wine tours, waterfall hikes, and spring wildflower tours are among the popular trips offered by this Portland-based guide. ☎ *503/349–1323* 🌐 *www.martinsgorgetours.com* 🎫 *From $70.*

Visitor Information

CONTACTS Columbia Gorge Tourism Alliance. ☎ *509/427–8911* 🌐 *www.visitcolumbiarivergorge.com.* **Hood-Gorge.com.** 🌐 *www.hood-gorge.com.* **Mt. Hood Territory.** ☎ *800/424–3002, 503/655–8490* 🌐 *www.mthoodterritory.com.*

Historic Columbia River Highway

U.S. 30, paralleling I–84 for 22 miles between Troutdale and Interstate Exit 35.

The oldest scenic highway in the United States is a construction marvel that integrates asphalt path with cliff, river, and forest landscapes. Paralleling the interstate, U.S. 30 climbs to forested riverside bluffs, passes half a dozen waterfalls, and provides access to hiking trails leading to still more falls and scenic overlooks. Completed in 1922, the serpentine highway was the first paved road in the Gorge built expressly for automotive sightseers. Technically, the Historic Columbia River Highway extends some 74 miles to The Dalles, but much of that is along modern Interstate 84—the 22-mile western segment is the real draw. Along this stretch as well as some additional spans closer to Hood River, you'll find pull-outs with parking for dozens of popular day hikes, including Angel's Rest, Bridal Veil Falls, Dry Creek Falls, Latourell Falls, Wahkeena Falls, Horsetail Falls, Mitchell Point, and Starvation Creek. Sadly, the Eagle Creek Fire of 2017—begun accidentally by a careless teenager illegally using fireworks on a trail—burned about 50,000 acres of the Gorge, and a number of once popular trails (including those around Eagle Creek and Oneonta Gorge) are closed indefinitely as the forest restores itself. For an up-to-date list of trail closures and other useful information on hiking and helping to protect this beloved wilderness, visit the excellent website of **Friends of the Columbia Gorge** (🌐 *www.gorgefriends.org*).

GETTING HERE AND AROUND

U.S. 30 heads east out of downtown Troutdale, a suburb about 15 miles east of Portland, but you can also access the route from Interstate 84 along the way, via Exit 22 near Corbett, Exit 28 near Bridal Veil Falls, Exit 31 at Multnomah Falls, and Exit 35, where it rejoins the interstate.

ESSENTIALS

VISITOR INFORMATION Multnomah Falls Visitor Center. ✉ *53000 E. Historic Columbia River Hwy., Bridal Veil* ✣ *Exit 31 off I–84* ☎ *503/695–2376* 🌐 *www.multnomahfallslodge.com.* **West Columbia**

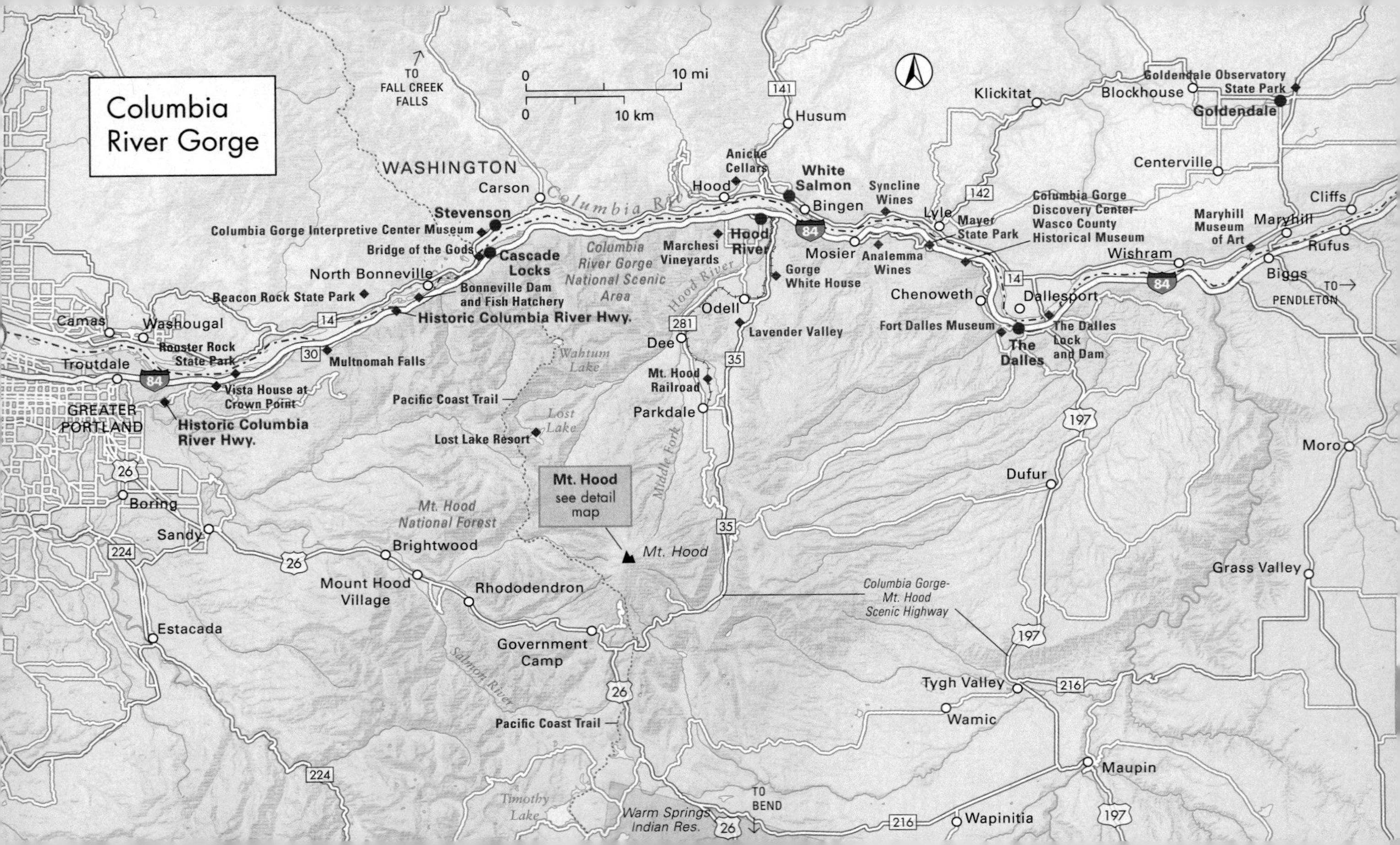
Columbia River Gorge
WASHINGTON
TO FALL CREEK FALLS
0
10 mi
0
10 km
Carson
Stevenson
Columbia Gorge Interpretive Center Museum
Bridge of the Gods
Cascade Locks
North Bonneville
Bonneville Dam and Fish Hatchery
Beacon Rock State Park
Historic Columbia River Hwy.
Camas
Washougal
Rooster Rock State Park
Troutdale
Multnomah Falls
Vista House at Crown Point
GREATER PORTLAND
Historic Columbia River Hwy.
Boring
Sandy
Estacada
Columbia River
Columbia River Gorge National Scenic Area
Wahtum Lake
Pacific Coast Trail
Lost Lake
Lost Lake Resort
Mt. Hood National Forest
Mt. Hood see detail map
Mt. Hood
Brightwood
Mount Hood Village
Rhododendron
Government Camp
Salmon River
Pacific Coast Trail
Timothy Lake
Warm Springs Indian Res.
TO BEND
Husum
Hood
Anicha Cellars
White Salmon
Bingen
Hood River
Marchesi Vineyards
Hood River
Odell
Dee
Mt. Hood Railroad
Parkdale
Middle Fork
Gorge White House
Lavender Valley
Mosier
Syncline Wines
Analemma Wines
Lyle
Mayer State Park
Columbia Gorge Discovery Center-Wasco County Historical Museum
Chenoweth
Dallesport
Fort Dalles Museum
The Dalles
The Dalles Lock and Dam
Klickitat
Blockhouse
Goldendale Observatory State Park
Goldendale
Centerville
Wishram
Maryhill Museum of Art
Maryhill
Cliffs
Rufus
Biggs
TO PENDLETON
Moro
Dufur
Grass Valley
Columbia Gorge-Mt. Hood Scenic Highway
Tygh Valley
Wamic
Maupin
Wapinitia
14
30
84
26
224
141
281
35
142
197
216

Gorge Chamber of Commerce. ✉ *107 E. Historic Columbia River Hwy., Troutdale* ☎ *503/669–7473* 🌐 *www.westcolumbiagorgechamber.com.*

Sights

★ Multnomah Falls

TRAIL | FAMILY | A 620-foot-high double-decker torrent, the second-highest year-round waterfall in the nation, Multnomah is by far the most spectacular of the Gorge cataracts east of Troutdale. You can access the falls and Multnomah Lodge via a parking lot at Exit 31 off Interstate 84, or via the Historic Columbia River Highway; from the parking area, a paved path winds to a bridge over the lower falls. A much steeper, though paved, 1.1-mile trail climbs to a viewing point overlooking the upper falls, and from here, unpaved but well-groomed trails join with others, allowing for as much as a full day of hiking in the mountains above the Gorge, if you're up for some serious but scenic trekking. Even the paved ramble to the top will get your blood pumping, but worth it to avoid the crowds that swarm the lower falls area in every season. ✉ *53000 E. Historic Columbia River Hwy., Bridal Veil* ✥ *15 miles east of Troutdale* ☎ *503/695–2376* 🌐 *traveloregon.com.*

★ Rooster Rock State Park

NATIONAL/STATE PARK | FAMILY | The most famous beach lining the Columbia River is right below Crown Point. Three miles of sandy beaches, panoramic cascades, and a large swimming area make this a popular spot for lazing on the sand, picnicking, and hanging out with friends. Naturists appreciate that one of Oregon's two designated nude beaches is at the east end of Rooster Rock, and that it's completely secluded and clearly marked—the area has a bit of a party vibe and is hugely popular with the LGBTQ community, but all are welcome. The other section of the park, where nudity is not permitted, is also beautiful and draws a good number of families. Rooster Rock is 9 miles east of Troutdale, accessible only via the interstate. ✉ *I–84, Exit 25, Corbett* ☎ *503/695–2261* 🌐 *www.oregonstateparks.org* 🎫 *$5 parking.*

★ Vista House at Crown Point

BUILDING | A two-tier octagonal structure perched on the edge of this 730-foot-high cliff offers unparalleled 30-mile views up and down the Columbia River Gorge. The building dates to 1917, its rotunda and lower level filled with displays about the Gorge and the highway. Vista House's architect Edgar Lazarus was the brother of Emma Lazarus, author of the poem displayed at the base of the Statue of Liberty. ✉ *40700 E. Historic Columbia River Hwy., Corbett* ✥ *10 miles east of Troutdale* ☎ *503/344–1368* 🌐 *www.vistahouse.com.*

Restaurants

Multnomah Falls Lodge

$$ | AMERICAN | Vaulted ceilings, stone fireplaces, and exquisite views of Multnomah Falls are complemented by friendly service and reliably good American fare at this landmark restaurant, which is listed on the National Register of Historic Places. Consider the smoked salmon starter with apple-huckleberry compote, cod fish-and-chips, or the elk burger with aged Tillamook cheddar and garlic-sesame mayo. **Known for:** amazing waterfall views; Sunday Champagne brunch; scenic patio. 💲 *Average main: $22* ✉ *53000 Historic Columbia River Hwy., Bridal Veil* ✥ *Exit 31 off I–84, 15 miles east of Troutdale* ☎ *503/695–2376* 🌐 *www.multnomahfallslodge.com.*

★ Sugarpine Drive-In

$ | MODERN AMERICAN | This modern take on a classic drive-in is a fantastic first stop when setting out from Portland for a drive along the Historic Columbia River Highway—it adjoins a leafy park in Troutdale overlooking the Sandy River.

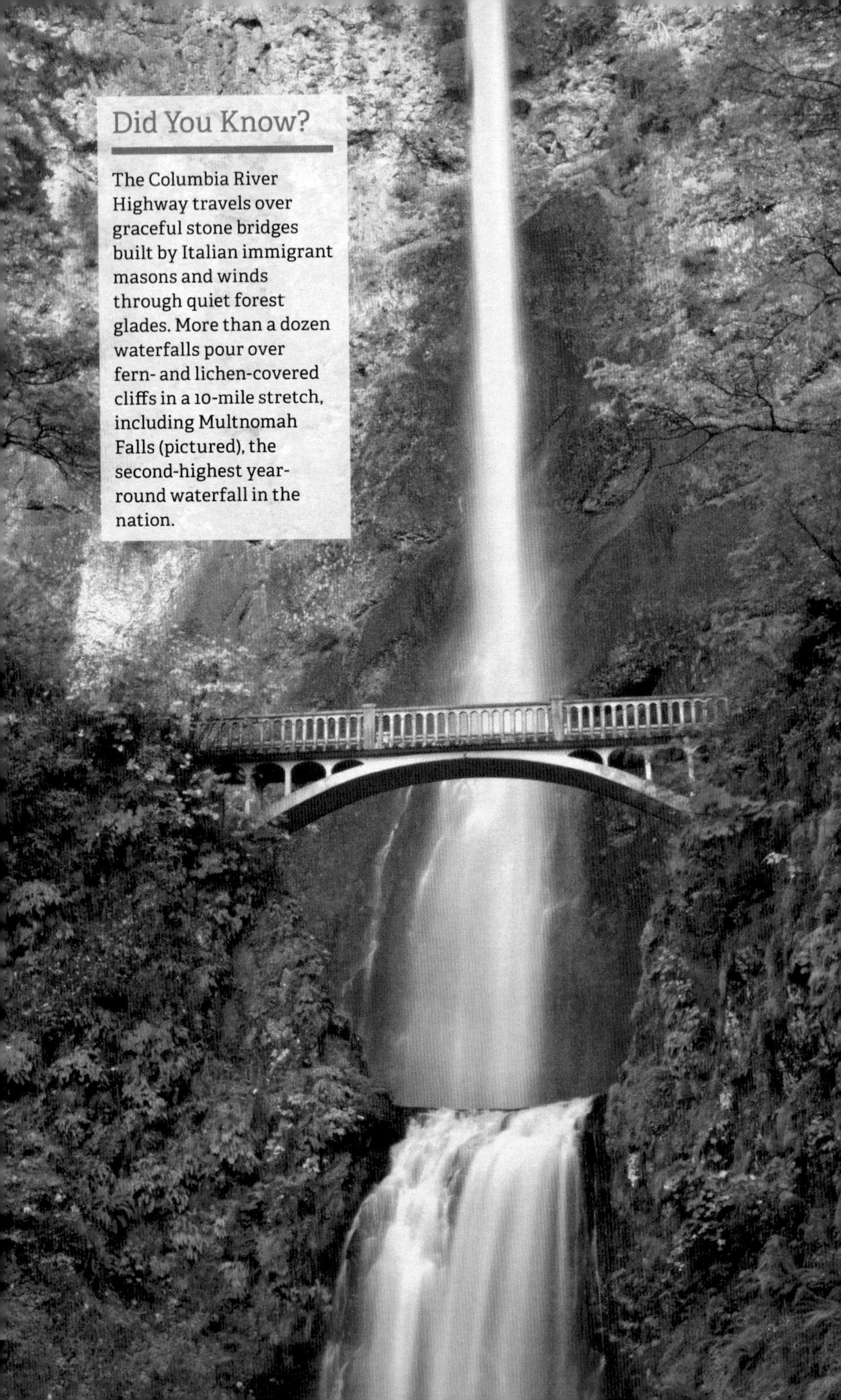

Did You Know?

The Columbia River Highway travels over graceful stone bridges built by Italian immigrant masons and winds through quiet forest glades. More than a dozen waterfalls pour over fern- and lichen-covered cliffs in a 10-mile stretch, including Multnomah Falls (pictured), the second-highest year-round waterfall in the nation.

Favorites from the creative menu of locally sourced fare include pulled-pork barbecue sandwiches, seasonal harvest veggie salads, and the Larch Mountain sundae with vanilla and chocolate soft serve, blondie brownie, blueberry-lavender sauce, and pine-nut honeycomb crunch. **Known for:** creative soft-serve sundaes; craft beer and artisanal ciders; creative locavore-driven food. *Average main: $13 ✉ 1208 E. Historic Columbia River Hwy., Troutdale ☎ 503/665–6558 🌐 www.sugarpinedrivein.com ⏱ Closed Tues. and Wed.*

Hotels

★ McMenamins Edgefield

$ | RESORT | Set in 74 acres of gardens, murals, orchards, and vineyards, this Georgian Revival manor—once home to the county poor farm—is now an offbeat resort that offers intriguing amenities and large but basic rooms filled with vintage furnishings; some rooms are hostel-style or have shared baths. **Pros:** plenty of eating and drinking choices; on-site movie theater and live-music concerts; great spa. **Cons:** this busy place can get pretty crowded; no TVs, phones, or air-conditioning in the rooms; most rooms share baths. *Rooms from: $145 ✉ 2126 S.W. Halsey St., Troutdale ☎ 503/669–8610, 800/669–8610 🌐 www.mcmenamins.com/edgefield 114 rooms No meals.*

Cascade Locks

13 miles east of Multnomah Falls on Historic Columbia River Hwy. and I–84; 30 miles east of Troutdale on I–84.

In pioneer days, boats needing to pass the bedeviling rapids near the town of Whiskey Flats had to portage around them. The locks that gave the town its new name were completed in 1896, allowing waterborne passage for the first time. In 1938 they were submerged beneath the new Lake Bonneville when the Bonneville Lock and Dam became one of the most massive Corps of Engineers projects to come out of the New Deal. The town of Cascade Locks hung onto its name, though. A historic stern-wheeler still leads excursions up and down the river from the town's port district, and the region's Native American tribes still practice traditional dip-net fishing near the current locks.

GETTING HERE AND AROUND

Cascade Locks is 45 miles east of Portland and 20 miles west of Hood River on Interstate 84. The town is also home to Bridge of the Gods ($2 toll), which featured prominently in the 2014 movie *Wild* and is the only auto bridge that spans the Columbia River (it connects with Stevenson, Washington) between Portland and Hood River.

Sights

Bonneville Dam

DAM | FAMILY | President Franklin D. Roosevelt dedicated the first federal dam to span the Columbia in 1937. Its generators (visible from a balcony on a self-guided tour or up close during free guided tours offered daily in summer and on weekends the rest of the year) have a capacity of more than a million kilowatts, enough to supply power to more than 200,000 single-family homes. There's an extensive visitor center on Bradford Island, complete with underwater windows where gaggles of kids watch migrating salmon and steelhead as they struggle up fish ladders. The best viewing times are between April and October. In recent years the dwindling runs of wild Columbia salmon have made the dam a subject of much environmental controversy. *✉ I–84, Exit 40 Follow signs 1 mile to visitor center ☎ 541/374–8820 🌐 www.nwp.usace.army.mil.*

Bonneville Fish Hatchery

FISH HATCHERY | FAMILY | Built in 1909 and operated by the Oregon Department of Fish & Wildlife, the largest state-operated fish hatchery is next door to Bonneville Dam. Visitors can view the fishponds in which Chinook, coho, and steelhead spawn—October and November are the most prolific times. Other ponds hold rainbow trout (which visitors can feed) and mammoth Columbia River sturgeon, some exceeding 10 feet in length. ✉ *70543 N.E. Herman Loop* ✣ *Off exit 40 of I–84* ☎ *541/374–8393* ⊕ *www.myodfw.com.*

Cascade Locks Marine Park and Portland Spirit Cruises

LIGHTHOUSE | This riverfront park is the home port of the 500-passenger stern-wheeler *Columbia Gorge*, which churns upriver, then back again, on one- and two-hour excursions through some of the Columbia River Gorge's most impressive scenery, mid-May to early October; brunch and dinner cruises are also available. The ship's captain discusses the Gorge's fascinating 40-million-year geology and pioneering spirits and legends, such as Lewis and Clark, who once triumphed over this very same river. The park itself, which includes a pedestrian bridge to leafy and tranquil Thunder Island, is a lovely spot for picnicking. ✉ *Marine Park, S.W. Portage Rd.* ☎ *503/224–3900* ⊕ *www.portlandspirit.com* 🎫 *Cruises from $28* ✍ *Reservations essential.*

Restaurants

Brigham Fish Market

$$ | SEAFOOD | This casual seafood market is a great stop for fish and shellfish to go—maybe to enjoy on a hike or a picnic at Rooster Rock—but there's casual seating to dine in. Fish-and-chips are available with several different proteins (halibut, cod, clam, and—most cherished of all—Columbia River salmon), and there are three kinds of chowder, as well as ceviche and a great selection of po'boy sandwiches. **Known for:** fish-and-chips with Columbia River salmon; three kinds of seafood chowder; great takeout spot when exploring the Historic Columbia River Hwy. $ *Average main: $17* ✉ *681 Wa Na Pa St.* ☎ *541/374–9340* ⊕ *www.brighamfish.com* ⊙ *Closed Wed. No dinner.*

★ **Thunder Island Brewing**

$ | AMERICAN | Hikers, boaters, and others exploring the Gorge gather at this laid-back, funky brewpub that in 2019 moved into striking new contemporary building overlooking the Columbia River, the Bridge of the Gods, and the little island for which the brewery is named. Order a glass of hoppy Pacific Crest Trail Pale Ale or malty Scotch Porter, and enjoy it with one of the light dishes from the pub menu. **Known for:** great beer from on-site brewery; cheese platters and hummus plates; stellar river views from outdoor dining area. $ *Average main: $10* ✉ *601 Wa Na Pa St.* ☎ *971/231–4599* ⊕ *www.thunderislandbrewing.com.*

Hotels

Best Western Plus Columbia River Inn

$ | HOTEL | The draw here is an enviable setting with great views of the Columbia River and Bridge of the Gods—many rooms, which are done in soft tans and grays and hung with framed black-and-white photos of the Gorge, overlook the river, as does a deck in back and the breakfast room. **Pros:** excellent river views; handy location midway between Portland and Hood River; spotless, modern rooms. **Cons:** cookie-cutter furnishings; some rooms face away from the river; no restaurant. $ *Rooms from: $140* ✉ *735 Wa Na Pa St.* ☎ *541/374–8777, 800/780–7234* ⊕ *www.bwcolumbiariverinn.com* *62 rooms* *Free breakfast.*

Activities

HIKING

Pacific Crest Trail

HIKING/WALKING | Cascade Locks bustles with grubby thru-hikers refueling along the 2,650-mile Canada-to-Mexico Pacific Crest Trail, which was immortalized in the 2014 movie *Wild* starring Reese Witherspoon. Check out a scenic and strenuous portion of it, heading south from the trailhead at Herman Creek Horse Camp, just east of town. The route heads up into the Cascades, showing off monster views of the Gorge. Backpackers out for a longer trek will find idyllic campsites at Wahtum Lake, 14 miles south. You can also access the trail from the free parking area at Toll House Park, by the Bridge of the Gods. ✉ *Off N.W. Forest La.* ✣ *1 mile east of downtown* ☎ *541/308–1700* 🌐 *www.pcta.org.*

Stevenson, Washington

Across the river from Cascade Locks via the Bridge of the Gods and 1 mile east on Hwy. 14.

With the Bridge of the Gods toll bridge spanning the Columbia River above the Bonneville Dam, Stevenson acts as a sort of "twin city" to Cascade Locks on the Oregon side. Tribal legends and the geologic record tell of the original Bridge of the Gods, a substantial landslide that occurred here sometime between AD 1000 and 1760, briefly linking the two sides of the Gorge before the river swept away the debris. The landslide's steel namesake now leads to tiny Stevenson, where a quiet Main Street is lined with a few casual eateries and shops. Washington's Highway 14 runs through the middle of town, and since the cliffs on the Oregon side are more dramatic, driving this two-lane highway actually offers better views. About 5 miles east and slightly north, the village of Carson also has a handful of notable businesses and is a good access point to hiking north of the Gorge in Gifford Pinchot National Forest.

GETTING HERE AND AROUND

From the Oregon side of the Gorge, cross the Columbia River at the Bridge of the Gods ($2 toll).

ESSENTIALS

VISITOR INFORMATION Skamania County Chamber of Commerce. ✉ *167 N.W. 2nd St., Stevenson* ☎ *509/427–8911, 800/989–9178* 🌐 *www.skamania.org.*

Sights

★ Beacon Rock State Park

NATIONAL/STATE PARK | For several hundred years this 848-foot rock was a landmark for river travelers, including Native Americans, who recognized this point as the last rapids of the Columbia River. Lewis and Clark are thought to have been the first white men to see the volcanic remnant. Even most casual hikers can make the steep but safe trek up to the top of the rock—allow about 45–60 minutes round-trip. More serious hikers should head to the trailhead for Hamilton Mountain, which is reached via a beautiful, though arduous, 8-mile ramble over a roaring waterfall, through dense temperate rain forest, and finally up to the 2,400-foot summit with breathtaking views up and down the Gorge. ✉ *34841 Hwy. 14, Skamania* ✣ *7 miles west of Bridge of the Gods* ☎ *509/427–8265* 🌐 *www.parks.wa.gov* 🎟 *$10 parking.*

Bridge of the Gods

BRIDGE/TUNNEL | For a magnificent vista 135 feet above the Columbia, as well as a short and quick (despite its 15 mph speed limit) route between Oregon and Washington, $2 will pay your way over the grandly named bridge that Reese Witherspoon memorably strolled across in the 2014 movie *Wild*. Hikers cross the bridge from Oregon to reach the Washington segment of the **Pacific Crest Trail**, which picks up just west of the bridge. ✉ *Off Hwy. 14, Stevenson* 🌐 *portofcascadelocks.org/bridge-of-the-gods/.*

Columbia Gorge Interpretive Center Museum

MUSEUM | FAMILY | A petroglyph whose eyes seem to look straight at you, "She Who Watches" or "Tsagaglalal" is the logo for this museum. Sitting among the dramatic basaltic cliffs on the north bank of the Columbia River Gorge, the museum explores the life of the Gorge: its history, culture, architecture, legends, and much more. Younger guests enjoy the reenactment of the Gorge's formation in the DeGroote Theater, and the 37-foot-high fish wheel, a device like a mill wheel equipped with baskets for catching fish, from the 19th century. Historians appreciate studying the water route of the Lewis and Clark Expedition. There's also an eye-opening exhibit that examines current environmental impacts on the area. ✉ *990 S.W. Rock Creek Dr., Stevenson* ☎ *509/427–8211, 800/991–2338* 🌐 *www.columbiagorge.org* 🎟 *$10.*

Big River Grill

$$ | AMERICAN | A tradition with hikers, bikers, fishermen, and scenic drivers out exploring the Gorge, especially for weekend breakfast but also at lunch and dinnertime, this colorful roadhouse in the center of town is festooned with license plates, vintage signs, and kitschy artwork. Grab a seat at the counter or in one of the high-back wooden booths, and tuck into grilled wild salmon sandwich, home-style fried chicken with eggs, home-style meat loaf with buttermilk-garlic mashed potatoes, and other hearty, reasonably priced fare. **Known for:** grilled wild salmon sandwiches; weekend breakfast; hiker and biker crowd. 💲 *Average main: $20* ✉ *192 S.W. 2nd St., Stevenson* ☎ *509/427–4888* 🌐 *www.thebigrivergrill.com.*

Cascade Room at Skamania Lodge

$$$$ | PACIFIC NORTHWEST | At Skamania Lodge's signature restaurant, with its stunning views of sky, river, and cliff scapes, the chef draws on local seafood and regionally sourced meats. Try dishes like a Dungeness crab tower with avocado, beet coulis, and basil oil; and bacon-cured Carlton Farms pork chops. **Known for:** stunning Gorge views; lavish Sunday brunch; hefty steaks and grills. 💲 *Average main: $33* ✉ *Skamania Lodge, 1131 S.W. Skamania Lodge Way, Stevenson* ☎ *509/427–7700* 🌐 *www.skamania.com.*

Red Bluff Tap House

$ | AMERICAN | With exposed-brick walls, varnished wood tables, and a sleek long bar, this downtown gastropub excels both with its extensive craft-beer and drinks selection and its modern take on comfort food. Snack on shareable starters like deep-fried brussels sprouts with pork belly and apple-cider reduction and smoked salmon flatbread, while popular mains include ale-battered seasonal fish-and-chips and bacon-jam Gouda burgers. **Known for:** ample selection of craft beers and Columbia Gorge wines; fish-and-chips; tasty, shareable appetizers. 💲 *Average main: $15* ✉ *256 2nd St., Stevenson* ☎ *509/427–4979* 🌐 *www.redblufftaphouse.com.*

Carson Ridge Luxury Cabins

$$$$ | B&B/INN | For a romantic, cushy getaway in the piney woods near Gifford Pinchot National Forest, book one of these luxurious rustic-chic cabins outfitted with hot tubs and separate walk-in showers, iPod docks, DVD players, fireplaces, sitting areas, and private porches. **Pros:** serene woodland setting; fireplaces and two-person hot tubs in each cabin; across the street from Backwoods Brewing. **Cons:** in a small, slightly remote village; steep rates; not designed for kids. 💲 *Rooms from: $299* ✉ *1261 Wind River Hwy.* ✥ *10-min drive* *northeast of Stevenson ☎ 509/427–7777 ⊕ www.carsonridgecabins.com ⇨ 10 cabins ⦿ Free breakfast.*

★ Skamania Lodge

$$$ | RESORT | FAMILY | This warm, woodsy lodge on an expansive, verdant swath of forest and meadows impresses with a multitude of windows overlooking the surrounding mountains and Gorge, an outstanding array of recreational facilities, and handsome, Pacific Northwest–chic accommodations, many with fireplaces and all with views. **Pros:** secluded and totally relaxing; loads of fun outdoorsy activities; first-rate spa and dining facilities. **Cons:** expensive in high season; can get crowded; set back from the river. *$ Rooms from: $209 ✉ 1131 S.W. Skamania Lodge Way, Stevenson ☎ 509/427–7700, 800/221–7117 ⊕ www.skamania.com ⇨ 254 rooms ⦿ No meals.*

Nightlife

Backwoods Brewing

BREWPUBS/BEER GARDENS | A favorite destination for well-crafted ales and reliably good pub fare before or after hiking at nearby Falls Creek Falls or venturing deeper into Gifford Pinchot National Forest, Backwoods is in the heart of the small town of Carson, a short drive northeast of Stevenson. Top brews include the crispy and piney Logyard IPA, and a seasonal Imperial Maple Porter that warms the soul on rainy winter days. *✉ 1162 Wind River Hwy., Carson ☎ 509/427–3412 ⊕ www.backwoodsbrewingcompany.com.*

Walking Man Brewing

BARS/PUBS | The sunshiny patio and cozy interior are great spots for creative pizzas and sampling the dozen-or-so craft ales. After a couple of pints of the strong Homo Erectus IPA and Walking Stick Stout, you may go a little ape. Live music on summer weekends skews twangy and upbeat. *✉ 240 S.W. 1st St., Stevenson ☎ 509/427–5520 ⊕ www.walkingmanbeer.com.*

Activities

HIKING

Falls Creek Falls

HIKING/WALKING | You'll find one of the most spectacular waterfall hikes in the Northwest in the Wind River section of 1½-million-acre Gifford Pinchot National Forest. The large, free parking area (with restrooms) is at the end of graded, unpaved forest road off paved Wind River Road, about 20 miles north of Stevenson. The trail meanders through dense forest and crosses a couple of sturdy suspension bridges en route to the more spectacular Lower Falls (a relatively easy 3½-mile round-trip). If you're up for more of an adventure, continue to the Upper Falls overlook, which adds about 3 more miles and makes it a loop hike—parts of this section are quite steep. *✉ End of NF 057, Carson ⊕ 16 miles north of Carson via Wind River Rd. and NF 3062 ☎ 509/395–3400 ⊕ www.fs.usda.gov/main/giffordpinchot.*

Hood River

20 miles east of Cascade Locks and 60 miles east of Portland on I–84.

This picturesque riverside community of about 7,700 residents affords visitors spectacular views of the Columbia River and the snowcapped peaks of Mt. Hood and—on the Washington side—Mt. Adams. The bustling downtown of more than 40 buildings dating from the 1890s to the 1930s and more recently developed Columbia River waterfront make this charming town the Gorge's hub for dining, lodging, and shopping and a hugely popular weekend destination among Portlanders. You'll find plenty of urbane farm-to-table restaurants, up-and-coming craft breweries and wine-tasting rooms, and nicely curated boutiques and art galleries. The surrounding countryside abounds with orchards and vineyards, enticing fans of U-pick farmsteads and tasting rooms. Wineries in Hood River and also across the river from roughly White Salmon to Maryhill grow a much broader range of grapes than Oregon's famous Willamette Valley, and wine touring has become one of the area's top draws.

And then there are Hood River's recreational pursuits. For years, the incessant easterly winds blowing through town were nothing more than a slight nuisance. Then somebody bolted a sail to a surfboard, waded into the fat part of the Gorge, and a new recreational craze was born. A fortuitous combination of factors—mainly the reliable gale-force winds blowing against the current—has made Hood River the self-proclaimed windsurfing capital of the world. Especially in summer, the town swarms with colorful "boardheads" from as far away as Europe and Australia.

GETTING HERE AND AROUND

Reach Hood River from Portland via Interstate 84, or from Mt. Hood by heading 40 miles north on Highway 35.

ESSENTIALS

VISITOR INFORMATION Hood River County Chamber of Commerce. ✉ *720 E. Port Marina Dr.* ☎ *541/386–2000, 800/366–3530* 🌐 *www.visithoodriver.com.*

TOURS

MountNbarreL

BICYCLE TOURS | This outfitter's knowledgeable guides offer 6.5- and 8-mile wine country bike tours in two different areas of Hood River, each one stopping for tastings at wineries as well as a U-pick fruit farm. E-bike tours are also available. ✉ *Hood River* ☎ *541/490–8687* 🌐 *www.mountnbarrel.com* 🎫 *From $169.*

Sol Rides Electric Bike Tours

BICYCLE TOURS | Explore the area on state-of-the-art e-bikes on the four guided excursions offered by Sol Rides. There are two options for touring the Columbia Gorge, one trip through Hood River Valley, and a winery tour of Lyle, Washington, just across the Columbia River. ✉ *101 Oak St.* ☎ *503/939–4961* 🌐 *www.solrides.com* 🎫 *From $99.*

Sights

Columbia Center for the Arts

ARTS VENUE | FAMILY | Hood River's premier venue for both visual and performing arts is a great place to start your explorations of the town's growing creative scene. The center's excellent gallery presents rotating exhibits throughout the year and also offers a range of classes. And it's worth checking the CCA's calendar to see what's upcoming in the venue's theater, which offers plays, musicals, and children's theater. ✉ *215 Cascade Ave.* ☎ *541/387–8877* 🌐 *www.columbiaarts.org.*

★ Fruit Loop

SCENIC DRIVE | Either by car or bicycle, tour the quiet country highways of Hood River Valley, which abounds with about 30 fruit stands, a handful of U-pick berry farms, about 10 wineries, and 3 cideries. You'll see apples, pears, cherries, and peaches fertilized by volcanic soil, pure glacier water, and a conducive harvesting climate. Along the 35 miles of farms are a host of outlets for delicious baked goods, wines, flowers, and nuts. While on the loop, consider stopping in the small town of **Parkdale** to lunch, taste beer at Solera Brewery, and snap a photo of Mt. Hood's north face. ✉ *Hood River* ✢ *Begins just east of downtown on Hwy. 35* 🌐 *www.hoodriverfruitloop.com.*

★ Gorge White House

FARM/RANCH | You'll find pretty much everything the Hood River Valley is famous for growing and producing at this picturesque, century-old farm anchored by a Dutch Colonial farmhouse and surrounded by acres of U-pick flowers, apple and peach trees, and blackberry and blueberry bushes. After strolling through the farm fields, stop inside the main house to sample wines—the tasting room carries one of the largest selections of Columbia River wines in the region. Out back, there's a farm store, another tasting room serving local craft beer and cider, and a garden patio with seating and a food-truck-style café serving delicious strawberry salads, burgers, pear-cheddar pizzas, and other light fare. ✉ *2265 Hwy. 35* ☎ *541/386–2828* 🌐 *www.thegorge-whitehouse.com.*

★ Historic Columbia River Highway State Trail–Mark O. Hatfield Trailheads

TRAIL | This peaceful and picturesque 4½-mile section of the old Historic Columbia River Highway begins just east of downtown Hood River at the Mark O. Hatfield West Trailhead and Visitor Center. Known as the Twin Tunnels segment, this paved trail that's closed to vehicular traffic is great for biking, jogging, or strolling. It first twists and turns upwardly through a dense ponderosa-pine forest before passing through the tunnels and descending past jagged volcanic-rock formations and semi-arid terrain into the small town of Mosier. This portion of the trail is one of a few segments of the old highway that's been converted to paved trail—there are currently about 13 miles in all, with additional sections west of Hood River with access at Starvation Creek and Veinto state parks, and well west of here in Cascade Locks, with access from the parking lot at the Bridge of the Gods. ✉ *End of Old Columbia River Rd.* ✣ *2 miles east of downtown Hood River* ☎ *541/387–4010* 🌐 *www.oregonstateparks.org* ☞ *$5 parking.*

Hood River Waterfront Park

CITY PARK | **FAMILY** | The recreational anchor of Hood River's contemporary waterfront district has been opened in phases, starting in 2010, and includes a sheltered sandy cove with a children's play area, picnic tables, a swimming beach, a launch ramp for windsurfing and stand-up paddleboarding, and access to a walking trail that connects with Waucoma Basin Marina to the west (a great spot to watch the sunset over the Gorge) and Nichols Boat Basin to the east. Events take place here and elsewhere along the park all throughout the year, and a number of hip new eateries and bars are steps away. ✉ *650 Portway Ave.* ☎ *541/387–5201* 🌐 *www.hoodriverwaterfront.org.*

Lavender Valley

FARM/RANCH | **FAMILY** | During the warmer months, and especially during the late June–August full-bloom season, saunter the beautiful lavender fields of this farm near Parkdale. The small shop sells honeys, soaps, teas, and dozens of other products infused with lavender grown on-site. ✉ *5965 Boneboro Rd., Parkdale* ☎ *541/386–1906* 🌐 *www.lavendervalley.com* ⏲ *Closed Oct.–Apr.*

★ Lost Lake Resort

BODY OF WATER | One of the most-photographed spots in the region, this lake's waters reflect towering Mt. Hood and the thick forests that line its shore. Open May through mid-October, the blissfully quiet 240-acre wilderness resort in Mt. Hood National Forest offers cabins and campsites for overnight stays, but it's also a popular destination for day-use recreation, offering miles of hiking trails, as well as fishing for rainbow trout, kayaking, rowboating, stand-up paddling, swimming, canoeing, and other nonmotorized boating. There's also a camp store and a grill offering burgers, ice cream, and other light fare. ✉ *9000 Lost Lake Rd.* ✣ *25 miles southwest of Hood River via Hwy. 35 and Hwy. 281* ☎ *541/386–6366* 🌐 *www.lostlakeresort.org* 🎫 *Day use parking $9.*

★ Marchesi Vineyards

WINERY/DISTILLERY | Somewhat unusual for the Pacific Northwest, this boutique winery with a small, airy tasting room and a verdant garden patio specializes in Italian varietals—Moscato, Ramato, Dolcetto, Sangiovese, Barbera, Nebbiolo, and a few others. Owner Franco Marchesi hails from Italy's Piemonte region, and he's earned serious kudos for his finesse as a winemaker. ✉ *3955 Belmont Dr.* ☎ *541/386–1800* 🌐 *www.marchesivineyards.com.*

Mt. Hood Railroad

SCENIC DRIVE | FAMILY | Scenic passenger excursions along a small rail line established in 1906 offer a picturesque and relaxing way to survey Mt. Hood and the Hood River Valley. Chug alongside the Hood River through vast fruit orchards before climbing up steep forested canyons, glimpsing Mt. Hood along the way. There are several trip options, from $35: a four-hour excursion (serves light concessions), dinner, brunch, and several themed trips, like murder mysteries and Old West robberies, and a family-favorite holiday-inspired Train to Christmas Town runs throughout much of November and December. The friendly service enhances the great scenery. ✉ *110 Railroad Ave.* ☎ *541/386–3556, 800/872–4661* 🌐 *www.mthoodrr.com* ⏲ *Closed Jan.–Apr.*

Mt. Hood Winery

WINERY/DISTILLERY | In addition to producing increasingly acclaimed wine—with particularly impressive Pinot Gris, dry Riesling, Zinfandel (which is seldom bottled in these parts), Pinot Noir, Barbera, and Tempranillo—this winery adjacent to the long-running Fruit Company (fruit and gift baskets) has a beautiful, contemporary tasting room with gorgeous Mt. Hood views from inside and the expansive patio. ✉ *2882 Van Horn Dr.* ☎ *541/386–8333* 🌐 *www.mthoodwinery.com* ⏲ *Closed Dec.–Feb.*

Stave & Stone Winery

WINERY/DISTILLERY | With one of the most dramatic settings of any Hood River winery, this lodge-style tasting room is a wonderful locale for sampling Stave & Stone's expressive vinos. The dry, strawberry-inflected Dorothy Pinot Noir Rosé and zesty Pinot Gris have each garnered plenty of awards, but the reds are terrific, too. If you can't make it to the vineyard, there's a cute tasting room in downtown Hood River, too. ✉ *3827 Fletcher Dr.* ☎ *541/946–3750* 🌐 *www.staveandstone.com.*

Viento Wines

WINERY/DISTILLERY | Focused more on whites than most of the winemakers in the Gorge region, Viento has a stunning tasting room with vaulted ceilings, soaring windows, and a large patio overlooking the on-site vineyard of Riesling grapes. This is a lovely space for tasting and chatting with fellow oenophiles. Notable wines here include a crisp Grüner Veltliner, a food-friendly Brut Rosé, and one of the better Oregon Pinot Noirs you'll find in the Hood River region. ✉ *301 Country Club Rd.* ☎ *541/386–3026* 🌐 *www.vientowines.com.*

Western Antique Aeroplane and Automobile Museum

MUSEUM | FAMILY | Housed at Hood River's tiny airport (general aviation only), the museum's impressive, meticulously restored, propeller-driven planes are all still in flying condition. The antique steam cars, Model Ts, and sleek Depression-era sedans are road-worthy, too. Periodic car shows and an annual fly-in draw thousands of history buffs and spectators. ✉ *1600 Air Museum Rd.* ☎ *541/308–1600* 🌐 *www.waaamuseum.org* 🎟 *$16.*

Restaurants

Broder Øst

$ | SCANDINAVIAN | Portland's wildly popular modern Scandinavian restaurant Broder has a branch just off the lobby of downtown's historic Hood River Hotel. Breakfast and lunch are the main event, although dinner is served during the busy summer months, and you may have to wait, especially on weekend mornings, for the chance to sample such delicacies as *abeleskivers* (Danish pancakes) with lingonberry jam and lemon curd or the open-faced gravlax (salmon) sandwich with mustard sauce. **Known for:** Danish favorites like pancakes with lingonberry sauce; covered sidewalk tables overlooking bustling Oak Street; fresh house-baked pastries (weekends only). *Average main: $14 ✉ Hood River Hotel, 102 Oak St. ☎ 541/436–3444 🌐 www.brodereast.com ⏲ No dinner Mon. and Tues. or Sept.–May.*

Celilo Restaurant

$$$ | PACIFIC NORTHWEST | Refined and relaxing, this high-ceilinged restaurant in a contemporary downtown building is popular both for dinner and enjoying a glass of local wine in the bar. Notable examples of the kitchen's deftly crafted Pacific Northwest fare, which emphasizes seasonal ingredients, include pan-seared scallops over goat cheese spaetzle and tender pork schnitzel with house-made choucroute garnie (a traditional Alsatian dish of sauerkraut and sausages). **Known for:** one of the best local wine lists in the Gorge; attractive sidewalk seating; lively and inviting bar. *Average main: $28 ✉ 16 Oak St. ☎ 541/386–5710 🌐 www.celilorestaurant.com ⏲ No lunch Mon.–Thurs. or Nov.–Apr.*

Doppio Coffee + Lounge

$ | CAFÉ | Sunshine fills the small dining room and outdoor seating area of this high-ceilinged, contemporary downtown coffee bar that serves fine espresso drinks as well as local wines and craft beers. It's great for light snacking—there's a nice selection of baked goods and fine chocolates—but there are also substantial grilled panini sandwiches, salads, and soups. **Known for:** rich Ghiradelli hot chocolate; great selection of Columbia Gorge wines by the glass; delicious breakfast sandwiches. *Average main: $8 ✉ 310 Oak St. ☎ 541/386–3000 🌐 www.doppiohoodriver.com ⏲ No dinner.*

★ Kin

$$ | MODERN EUROPEAN | This intimate and charming downtown bistro offers a short but enticing menu of beautifully prepared modern European dishes, such as grilled bread topped with raclette cheese and smoked paprika, and duck confit with sauerkraut, potato, and bacon. Save room for the pot de crème. **Known for:** friendly service; small but well-chosen wine selection; intimate, romantic space. *Average main: $20 ✉ 110 5th St. ☎ 541/387–0111 🌐 www.kineatery.com ⏲ Closed Mon. and Tues. No lunch.*

★ pFriem Family Brewers

$ | PACIFIC NORTHWEST | Inside a striking contemporary building on the Columbia River, pFriem (pronounced "freem") is all about the marriage of Belgium's brewing traditions and Oregon's distinctive, often hoppy, styles. But the on-site restaurant serves stellar pub fare, too, including mussels and fries, lentil burgers with grilled-leek aioli, and house-made bratwurst—it's a legit dining option even if you're not a big fan of craft beer. **Known for:** well-crafted Belgian-influenced beers; plenty of veggie options; dog-friendly patio with fire pit. *Average main: $15 ✉ 707 Portway Ave. ☎ 541/321–0490 🌐 www.pfriembeer.com.*

★ Solstice Wood Fire Pizza Café

$$ | PIZZA | This snazzy, high-ceilinged space along the Hood River waterfront is wildly popular for its wood-fire-grilled pizzas with unusual toppings—such as the Cherry Girl, layered with local cherries, spicy chorizo, goat cheese, mozzarella, and marinara sauce. There are several tasty salads, apps, and non-pizza entrées, too, as well as tantalizing wood-fired s'mores for dessert. **Known for:** creative pizzas; wood-fired mac 'n' cheese; wood-fired s'mores. *Average main: $18 ✉ 501 Portway Ave. ☎ 541/436–0800 🌐 www.solsticewoodfirecafe.com ⏲ Closed Tues.*

Hotels

Best Western Plus Hood River Inn

$$ | HOTEL | This low-slung, rambling hotel beside the Hood River Bridge offers some of the best river views of any hotel in the Gorge, and many units have private balconies or patios on the water; the deluxe accommodations have full kitchens, fireplaces, and Jacuzzi tubs. **Pros:** riverfront location with great views; good restaurant and lounge; spacious rooms. **Cons:** a little pricey in summer; downtown shopping and dining not within walking distance; room decor is a bit cookie-cutter. *Rooms from: $170* *1108 E. Marina Way* *541/386–2200, 800/828–7873* *www.hoodriverinn.com* *194 rooms* *Free breakfast.*

★ Columbia Cliff Villas Hotel

$$ | **HOTEL** | **FAMILY** | This elegant condo-style compound on a sheer cliff overlooking the Columbia River contains some of the plushest accommodations in the region—units have one to three bedrooms, fireplaces, terraces or patios, stone-and-tile bathrooms, and fine linens. **Pros:** private apartment-style accommodations; great river views; sophisticated decor and top-flight amenities. **Cons:** no restaurant or fitness center on-site; need a car to get into town; some rooms experience highway noise. *Rooms from: $199* *3880 Westcliff Dr.* *541/490–8081, 866/912–8366* *www.columbiacliffvillas.com* *37 suites* *No meals.*

Columbia Gorge Hotel & Spa

$$$ | **HOTEL** | Charming though somewhat dated-looking period-style rooms at this grande dame of Gorge hotels are fitted out with plenty of wood, brass, and antiques and overlook the Gorge, impeccably landscaped formal gardens, or a 208-foot-high waterfall. **Pros:** historic structure built by Columbia Gorge Highway visionary Simon Benson; unbeatable Gorge views; full-service spa. **Cons:** smallish rooms with rather dated decor; rooms facing away from river pick up noise from nearby Interstate 84; often books up with weddings on summer and fall weekends. *Rooms from: $219* *4000 Westcliff Dr.* *541/386–5566, 800/345–1921* *www.columbiagorgehotel.com* *40 rooms* *No meals.*

Hood River Hotel

$ | **HOTEL** | In the heart of the lively and hip business district, steps from great restaurants and shops, this handsomely restored 1911 boutique hotel has a grand, Old West facade, behind which are simple rooms with tasteful period-style antiques and a few larger suites that have kitchenettes and large sitting rooms. **Pros:** excellent downtown location; good-value rafting and ski packages; antiques-heavy interiors have feel of a European inn. **Cons:** smallish rooms; no king-size beds; rooms in back have great river views but tend to receive some freeway noise. *Rooms from: $99* *102 Oak St.* *541/386–1900* *www.hoodriverhotel.com* *41 rooms* *Free breakfast.*

★ Sakura Ridge

$$$ | **B&B/INN** | Located on a 72-acre farm on the south side of town, the five warm but sleekly furnished rooms at this contemporary lodge-style B&B offer magical panoramas of Mt. Hood, and the inn's gorgeous gardens, amid a welcome absence of clutter. **Pros:** spectacular mountain views; rustic yet urbane decor; lush gardens and orchards on the grounds. **Cons:** secluded location is a 15-minute drive from downtown; closed in winter. *Rooms from: $225* *5601 York Hill Rd.* *541/386–2636, 877/472–5872* *www.sakuraridge.com* *Closed Nov.–Mar.* *5 rooms* *Free breakfast.*

Nightlife

★ Camp 1805

BARS/PUBS | Yet another delicious reason to spend time around Hood River's sleek new waterfront district, this artisanal producer of rum, vodka, and bracing white whiskey offers an interesting menu of creative cocktails, from new-school mai tais to soothing drinks made with CBD-infused mint oil or elderflower-lavender bitters. There's a noteworthy food menu, too, with pulled-pork nachos and smoked tri-tip sandwiches leading the charge. ✉ *501 Portway Ave., Suite 102* ☎ *541/386–1805* 🌐 *www.camp1805.com.*

Double Mountain Brewery & Taproom
BREWPUBS/BEER GARDENS | Notable for its European-style beers, including the rich Black Irish Stout and the refreshing Kölsch, Double Mountain also produces seasonal cherry-infused Kriek ales and a hoppy India Red Ale. The bustling, homey downtown taproom is also a great source for pizzas, salads, and sandwiches. There's a second location in Portland. ✉ *8 4th St.* ☎ *541/387–0042* 🌐 *www.double-mountainbrewery.com.*

★ **Ferment Brewing Company**
BREWPUBS/BEER GARDENS | One of the latest venues to further Hood River's reputation as something of a mini Brewvana, Ferment uses traditional farmhouse techniques to craft complex beers as well as kombucha, from Bavarian-inspired smoked dunkelweisse to Japanese-style sensa kombucha. The gorgeous, airy tasting room has huge windows overlooking the waterfront, and the kitchen turns out tasty gastropub fare. ✉ *403 Portway Ave.* ☎ *541/436–3499* 🌐 *www.fermentbrewing.com.*

Full Sail Tasting Room and Pub
BARS/PUBS | A glass-walled microbrewery with a windswept deck overlooking the Columbia, Full Sail was a pioneer brewpub in Oregon, helping to put Hood River on the map as a major beer hub. Free, on-site brewery tours are given during the afternoons. ✉ *506 Columbia St.* ☎ *541/386–2247* 🌐 *www.fullsailbrewing.com.*

Activities

KAYAKING

Gorge Paddling Center
KAYAKING | Whether you want to practice your Eskimo roll in the safety of a pool, run the Klickitat River in an inflatable kayak, or try out a stand-up paddleboard on the Columbia, the Gorge's premier kayak guides can arrange the trip or rent you the equipment you need. ✉ *101 N. 1st St.* ☎ *541/806–4190* 🌐 *www.gorgekayaker.com.*

WINDSURFING

Big Winds
WINDSURFING | The retail hub for Hood River's windsurfing and kiteboarding culture also rents gear and provides windsurfing lessons for beginners. Lessons and clinics begin at $89 for windsurfing, and $49 for stand-up paddling. ✉ *207 Front St.* ☎ *541/386–6086, 888/509–4210* 🌐 *www.bigwinds.com.*

White Salmon, Washington

5 miles north of Hood River on Hwy. 14.

Tiny White Salmon, which sits on a bluff with commanding views of the Columbia River as well as the town of Hood River, is handy for exploring the Washington side of the eastern end of the Gorge. A few noteworthy restaurants and shops in the village center cater to hikers, kayakers, and wine- and beer-tasting aficionados checking out this quieter but similarly scenic counterpart to Hood River. Just down the hill in the tiny adjacent village of Bingen, you'll find increasingly more tourism-related businesses. Several first-rate wineries offer tastings in the nearby rural communities of Underwood (just west) and Lyle (just east) along Highway 14. There's also excellent hiking and white-water rafting in the vicinity, and if you drive north of town about 20 miles on Highway 141, you'll reach secluded Trout Lake, the access point for hiking and recreation in and around 12,281-foot Mt. Adams, a soaring "twin" of Mt. Hood that's similarly visible from many points in the Gorge.

GETTING HERE AND AROUND

You reach White Salmon by driving across the Hood River Bridge (toll $2), turning east onto Highway 14, and then north in the small village of Bingen onto Highway 141—it's a 10-minute drive from Hood River. Amtrak's *Empire Builder* also stops once a day in each direction in Bingen–White Salmon, en route from Portland to Spokane.

ESSENTIALS

CONTACTS Mt. Adams Chamber of Commerce. ✉ *1 Heritage Plaza, White Salmon* ✣ *Off Hwy. 14, just west of Hood River Bridge* ☎ *509/493–3630* 🌐 *www.mtadamschamber.com.*

Sights

AniChe Cellars

WINERY/DISTILLERY | Just a short drive west of White Salmon, this friendly boutique winery has one of the prettiest tasting-room settings in the area—it's high on Underwood Mountain, with outdoor seating that affords spectacular views looking east toward Hood River and deep into the Gorge. The cleverly named wines here—Puck, an Albarino, and Three Witches, a Rhône-style blend of Cinsault, Carignan, and Counoise—are paired with little amuse-bouche-style nibbles, typically chocolate, prosciutto, or fruit. ✉ *71 Little Buck Creek Rd., Underwood* ☎ *360/624–6531* 🌐 *www.anichecellars.com* ⏲ *Closed Mon. and Tues.*

Catherine Creek Recreation Area

NATIONAL/STATE PARK | Administered by the U.S. Forest Service, this ruggedly beautiful patch of wilderness in generally sunny and dry Lyle, less than 2 miles east of Coyote Wall, comprises a well-signed network of trails through what had been a sprawling ranch. This is one of the top spots in the region for wildflower viewing in the spring, but there's plenty to see and do here year-round. A paved multiuse trail curves down along a bluff overlooking the river, while longer trails meander up into the foothills. ✉ *Old Hwy. 8, Lyle* ✣ *1½ miles east of junction with Hwy. 14* ☎ *541/308–1700* 🌐 *www.fs.usda.gov/recarea/crgnsa/recarea.*

COR Cellars

WINERY/DISTILLERY | Appreciated for its sleek, glass-walled tasting room and landscaped courtyard as well as for producing complex, eclectic wines, COR is one of several excellent Lyle wineries. The Cabernet Franc is one of the best in the state, but don't overlook the distinctive Merlot-Malbec and co-fermented Pinot Gris and Gewürztraminer blends. ✉ *151 Old Hwy. 8, Lyle* ☎ *509/365–2744* 🌐 *www.corcellars.com* ⏲ *Closed Tues. and Wed.*

★ Coyote Wall–Labyrinth Loop

TRAIL | The Coyote Wall trail, accessed about 5 miles east of town off Highway 14, affords hikers unobstructed views of the Columbia River and the surrounding mountains, including Mt. Hood. The trail leads from a disused section of roadway up a gradual slope, through tall grass and wildflower meadows, from sea level up the side of a sheer cliff that rises to about 1,900 feet elevation. You can descend the way you came up or by looping back down through an intriguing valley of basalt rock formations (known as the Labyrinth)—the full round-trip is about 8 miles, but you could hike part of the way up the trail and back, taking in the impressive vistas, in less than an hour. ✉ *Old Hwy. 8 at Courtney Rd., White Salmon.*

★ Savage Grace Wines

WINERY/DISTILLERY | Celebrated Woodinville winemaker Michael Savage opened this intimate tasting room at the vineyard on which he grows the grapes in several of his most acclaimed bottles, including a vibrant Riesling, a lean and elegant Pinot Noir, and an earthy Grüner Veltliner. Enjoy the sweeping Gorge and Mt. Hood views while you sip. ✉ *442 Kramer Rd., Underwood* ☎ *206/920–4206* 🌐 *www.savagegracewines.com* ⏲ *Closed Mon.–Thurs.*

★ Syncline Wines
WINERY/DISTILLERY | The focus at this intimate winery with lovely seating set among beautiful gardens is predominantly on elegant, full-bodied Rhône-style wines. The friendly, knowledgeable tasting room has garnered plenty of awards for its aromatic Cuvée Elena Grenache-Syrah-Mourvèdre blend, as well as a first-rate stand-alone Syrah, and several racy, dry whites—Picpoul, Grenache Blanc, Grüner Veltliner—that seem tailor-made for the Gorge's warm summer nights. Note that several other outstanding small wineries—Domaine Pouillon and Tetrahedron among them—are in the same rural town, 10 miles east of White Salmon. ✉ *111 Balch Rd., Lyle* ☎ *509/365–4361* 🌐 *www.synclinewine.com* 🕑 *Closed Mon.–Wed.*

Restaurants

Feast Market & Delicatessen
$ | **PACIFIC NORTHWEST** | Although this handsome space with Edison lights and a tile-back bar fits the bill when you're seeking wines and food (coffee, cheeses, sandwiches, prepared foods, cookies) to go, it's also an inviting dine-in restaurant with a spacious back patio offering glorious views of Mt. Hood. The kitchen sources regionally to create many of the enticing dishes, including roasted bone marrow with chimichurri and sea-salt grilled bread, and pan-seared Columbia salmon with red quinoa, leeks, and a pomegranate vinaigrette. **Known for:** gourmet groceries and sandwiches to go; superb beer and wine list; patio views of Mt. Hood. 💲 *Average main: $15* ✉ *151 E. Jewett Blvd., White Salmon* ☎ *509/637–6886* 🌐 *www.feastmarket.org* 🕑 *Closed Sun. No dinner Mon. and Tues.*

Henni's Kitchen & Bar
$$ | **PACIFIC NORTHWEST** | This warm and inviting neighborhood bistro serves well-priced, creatively prepared international fare with a decided Northwest focus—think broccolini with sumac and mint raita, salmon cakes with kimchi and remoulade, and Goat-style organic-chicken yellow curry. The bar serves terrific, innovative cocktails, and food prices during the weekday evening (5–6 pm) happy hour represent one of the best deals around. **Known for:** excellent cocktails; inventive food; fun, lively ambience. 💲 *Average main: $21* ✉ *120 E. Jewett Blvd., White Salmon* ☎ *509/493–1555* 🌐 *www.henniskitchenandbar.com* 🕑 *No lunch.*

★ White Salmon Baking Co
$ | **BAKERY** | The formidable redbrick, wood-fired oven toward the back of this artisanal bakery's airy dining room hints at the delicious treats on offer here, from local-mushroom scrambles over rustic toast in the morning to line-caught-albacore melts and house-made falafel-and-beet-kraut sandwiches at lunch. There's also a vast selection of savory breads, chewy cookies, and a nice selection of espresso drinks, beers, and wines. **Known for:** made-to-order tartines, frittatas, and toasts; wood-fired savory breads and sweets; Monday pizza nights. 💲 *Average main: $9* ✉ *80 N.E. Estes Ave., White Salmon* ☎ *509/281–3140* 🌐 *www.whitesalmonbaking.com* 🕑 *Closed Tues. No dinner.*

Hotels

Lyle Hotel
$ | **HOTEL** | Built in the early 20th century a block from still very active train tracks (rooms are equipped with ear plugs), this friendly and slightly quirky 10-room boutique hotel is a well-situated and affordable base for exploring the many exceptional wineries between Lyle and Maryhill. **Pros:** short drive from several excellent wineries; terrific bar and restaurant on-site; reasonably priced. **Cons:** noise from passing trains; need a car to get around; rooms have shared bathrooms. 💲 *Rooms from: $110* ✉ *100 7th St., Lyle* ☎ *509/365–5953* 🌐 *www.thelylehotel.com* *10 rooms* *No meals.*

★ **Society Hotel Bingen**

$$ | **HOTEL** | This stylish but unpretentious Scandinavian-inspired compound—a converted 1937 schoolhouse and a ring of sleek cabins set around a spa and bathhouse—is a perfect base for hiking, wine touring, and chilling out on the Washington side of the Columbia Gorge. **Pros:** stunning contemporary design; soothing bathhouse with hot tubs and sauna; kitchenettes in cabins. **Cons:** some rooms share bath; not within walking distance of many restaurants; bathhouse can get crowded on weekends. *Rooms from: $155 ✉ 210 N. Cedar St., Bingen ☎ 509/774–4437 🌐 www.thesocietyhotel.com 30 rooms No meals.*

Everybody's Brewing

BREWPUBS/BEER GARDENS | Head to this stylish downtown brewpub with a back patio overlooking Mt. Hood for seriously impressive beers, with the potent Cryo IPA and roasty and rich Cash Oatmeal Stout leading the way. There's live music many evenings, and tasty pub fare, too. *✉ 177 E. Jewett Blvd., White Salmon ☎ 509/637–2774 🌐 www.everybodysbrewing.com.*

WHITE-WATER RAFTING

Wet Planet Whitewater

KAYAKING | This outfitter just outside White Salmon offers half- and full-day white-water rafting trips on the White Salmon, Wind, Klickitat, Farmlands, Hood, and Tieton rivers, which rank among some of the top waterways for this activity in the region. The Wind and Hood rivers contain stretches of hairy Class IV–Class V rapids (previous experience is required), but the other trips are suitable for beginners. The company also offers kayaking instruction and trips. *✉ 860 Hwy. 141, Husum ☎ 509/493–8989, 877/390–9445 🌐 www.wetplanet-whitewater.com.*

The Dalles

20 miles east of Hood River on I–84.

The seat of Wasco County and the economic hub of the region, The Dalles lies on a crescent bend of the Columbia River where it narrows and once spilled over a series of rapids, creating a flagstone effect. French voyagers christened it *dalle*, or "flagstone." The town gained fame early in the region's history as the town where the Oregon Trail branched, with some pioneers departing to travel over Mt. Hood on Barlow Road and the others continuing down the Columbia River. This may account for the small-town, Old West feeling that still permeates the area. In this workaday town, you'll find some excellent museums as well as a mix of independent and chain restaurants and hotels. As you're strolling around, watch for the eight historic downtown murals that depict important events in Oregon's past.

GETTING HERE AND AROUND

From Hood River, it's a 22-mile drive east on Interstate 84 to reach The Dalles. Alternatively, you can take the slightly slower and more scenic Highway 14, on the Washington side of the Columbia, from White Salmon to U.S. 197, which leads you into town via The Dalles Bridge.

ESSENTIALS

VISITOR INFORMATION Dalles Area Chamber of Commerce. *✉ 404 W. 2nd St. ☎ 541/296–2231, 800/255–3385 🌐 www.thedalleschamber.com.*

★ **Analemma Winery**

WINERY/DISTILLERY | It's worth the trip to the rugged Mosier Hills, midway between The Dalles and Hood River, to enjoy some sips at this serene winery and tasting room that's developed a cult following for its exceptional wines. Using grapes grown at upwards of 1,800 feet

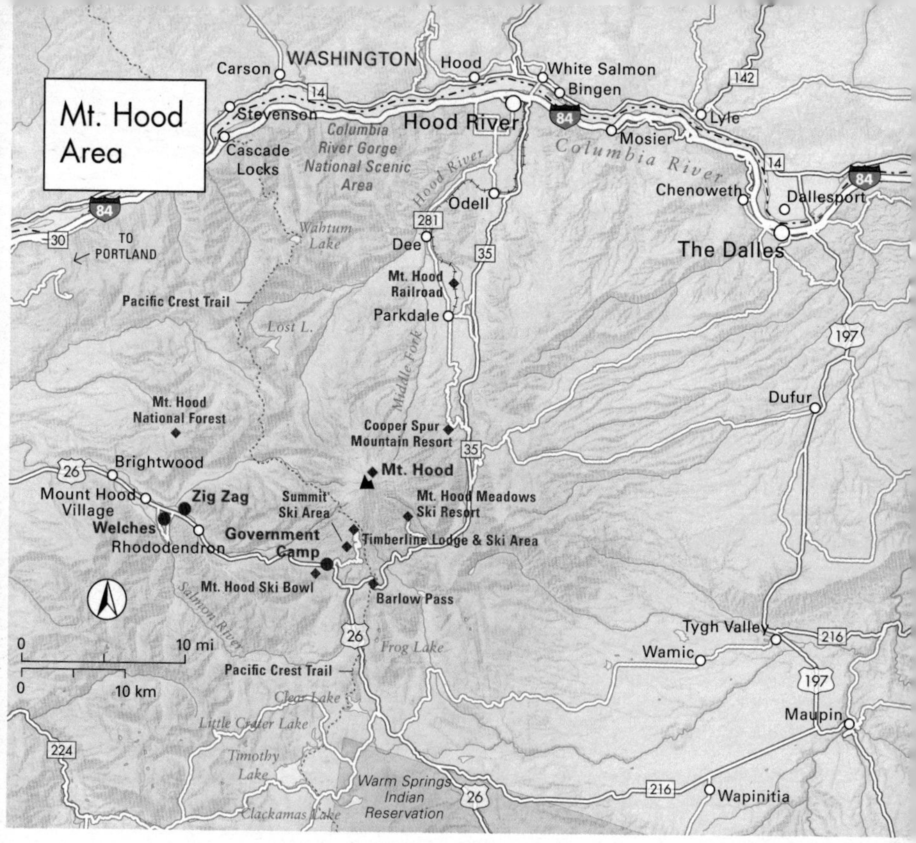

peak no longer spews ash or fire, active vents regularly release steam high on the mountain, which was named in 1792 for the naval officer who helmed the first European sailing expedition up the Columbia River. Mt. Hood offers the longest ski season in North America, with three major ski areas, as well as extensive areas for cross-country skiing and snowboarding. Many of the ski runs turn into mountain-bike trails in summer. The mountain is also popular with climbers and hikers. In fact, some hikes follow parts of the Oregon Trail, and signs of the pioneers' passing are still evident.

GETTING HERE AND AROUND

From Portland U.S. 26 heads east into the heart of Mount Hood National Forest, while Highway 35 runs south from Hood River, skirting the mountain's east face. The roads meet 60 miles east of Portland, near Government Camp, forming an oblong loop with Interstate 84 and the Historic Columbia River Highway. It's about a 75-minute drive from Downtown Portland to Government Camp via U.S. 26. **Sea to Summit**—call for timetables and pickup and drop-off sites—offers shuttle service from Portland International Airport and Downtown Portland hotels to Mt. Hood resorts; the fare is $59 each way, with discounted lift-ticket and ski-rental packages available. Additionally, the **Mt. Hood Express** bus line operates daily and links the villages along the corridor—including Welches, Government Camp, and Timberline Lodge—to the Portland suburb of Sandy, which you can reach via TriMet commuter bus. This option is slower (it takes 2½ to 3 hours each way from the airport or Downtown to Timberline Lodge, for example) than a direct shuttle but costs just $2 ($5 for

A snowboarder catches some air on Mt. Hood.

all-day ticket), plus $2.50 for TriMet bus fare to Sandy.

CONTACTS Mt. Hood Express. ☎ *503/668–3466* 🌐 *www.mthoodexpress.com.* **Sea to Summit.** ☎ *503/286–9333* 🌐 *www.seatosummit.net.*

ESSENTIALS

VISITOR INFORMATION Mount Hood National Forest Headquarters. ✉ *16400 Champion Way, Sandy* ☎ *503/668–1700* 🌐 *www.fs.usda.gov/mthood.* **Mt. Hood Area Chamber of Commerce.** ☎ *503/622–3017* 🌐 *www.mthoodchamber.com.*

TOURS

Mt. Hood Outfitters

ADVENTURE TOURS | The only business on Mt. Hood that rents snowmobiles and offers snowmobile tours is also a well-respected tour company for snowshoe tours and sleigh rides in winter, and mountain hikes, biking trips, and boat excursions on area rivers—the shop is also a good place to buy gear and ask for advice on outdoorsy activities in the area. ✉ *88220 Government Camp Loop Rd., Government Camp* ☎ *503/715–2175* 🌐 *www.mthoodoutfitters.com* 🎫 *From $119; snowmobile tours from $225.*

Sights

★ Mount Hood National Forest

HIKING/WALKING | The highest spot in Oregon and the fourth-highest peak in the Cascades, "the Mountain" is a focal point of the 1.1-million-acre forest and all-season playground. Beginning 20 miles southeast of Portland, it extends south from the Columbia River Gorge for more than 60 miles and includes more than 315,000 acres of designated wilderness. These woods are perfect for hikers, horseback riders, mountain climbers, and cyclists. Within the forest are dozens of campgrounds as well as lakes stocked with brown, rainbow, cutthroat, brook, and steelhead trout. The Sandy, Salmon, Clackamas, and other rivers are known for their fishing, rafting, canoeing, and swimming. Both forest and mountain are crossed by an extensive trail system for hikers, cyclists, and horseback riders. The

Pacific Crest Trail, which begins in British Columbia and ends in Mexico, crosses at the 4,155-foot-high Barlow Pass. As with most other mountain destinations within Oregon, weather can be temperamental, and snow and ice may affect driving conditions as early as mid-September and as late as June. Bring tire chains and warm clothes as a precaution.

Since this forest is close to the Portland metro area, campgrounds and trails are potentially crowded over the summer months, especially on weekends. If you're planning to camp, get info and permits from the Mount Hood National Forest Headquarters. Campgrounds are managed by the U.S. Forest Service and a few private concessionaires, and standouts include a string of neighboring campgrounds on the south side of Mt. Hood: Trillium Lake, Still Creek, Timothy Lake, Little Crater Lake, Clackamas Lake, Summit Lake, Clear Lake, and Frog Lake. Each varies in what it offers and in price. The mountain overflows with day-use areas. From mid-November through April, all designated Winter Recreation Areas require a Sno-Park permit, available from the U.S. Forest Service and many local resorts and sporting goods stores. ✉ *Headquarters, 16400 Champion Way, Sandy* ☎ *503/668–1700* 🌐 *www.fs.usda.gov/mthood* 🎫 *$5 parking.*

Restaurants

Cascade Dining Room

$$$$ | PACIFIC NORTHWEST | Vaulted wooden beams and a wood-plank floor, handcrafted furniture, handwoven drapes, and a lion-sized stone fireplace set the scene in Timberline Lodge's esteemed restaurant, from which views of neighboring mountains are enjoyed, except when snow drifts cover the windows. The atmosphere is traditional and historic, and the menu emphasizes local and organic ingredients in dishes like alpine spaetzle with applewood-smoked bacon, green cabbage, apples, aged Gouda, and your choice of several protein options (salmon, flat-iron steak, etc.). **Known for:** less expensive menu in atmospheric Ram's Head Bar; grand views from many tables; historic setting. Ⓢ *Average main: $42* ✉ *27500 E. Timberline Rd., Timberline Lodge* ☎ *503/272–3104* 🌐 *www.timberlinelodge.com.*

Hotels

★ Timberline Lodge

$$ | RESORT | FAMILY | Guest rooms are simple, rustic, and charming (a handful of them lack private baths), but don't expect a cushy experience—the reason for staying here is the location and setting. **Pros:** a thrill to stay on the mountain itself; great proximity to all snow activity; amazing architecture. **Cons:** rooms are small and the least expensive ones have shared bathrooms; views from rooms are often completely blocked by snow in winter; lots of tourists milling. Ⓢ *Rooms from: $175* ✉ *27500 E. Timberline Rd., Timberline Lodge* ☎ *503/272–3311, 800/547–1406* 🌐 *www.timberlinelodge.com* *70 rooms* *No meals.*

Activities

DOWNHILL SKIING

Cooper Spur Mountain Resort

SKIING/SNOWBOARDING | FAMILY | On the northern slope of Mt. Hood, Cooper Spur caters to families and has one double chair and a tow rope. The longest run is ⅔ mile, with a 350-foot vertical drop, but you'll also find a tubing run as well as groomed cross-country and snowshoeing trails. Facilities and services include rentals, instruction, repairs, and a ski shop, day lodge, snack bar, restaurant, and a handful of log cabin–style overnight accommodations. ✉ *10755 Cooper Spur Rd., Mount Hood* ✣ *Follow signs from Hwy. 35 for 2½ miles to ski area* ☎ *541/352–6692* 🌐 *www.cooperspur.com.*

Timberline Lodge & Ski Area
SKIING/SNOWBOARDING | The longest ski season in North America unfolds at this full-service ski area, where the U.S. ski team conducts summer training. Thanks to the omnipresent Palmer Snowfield, it's the closest thing to a year-round ski area in the Lower 48 (it's typically closed for just a few weeks in September). Timberline is famous for its Palmer chairlift, which takes skiers and snowboarders to the high glacier for summer skiing. There are five high-speed quad chairs, one triple chair, and one double. The top elevation is 8,500 feet, with a 3,700-foot vertical drop, and the longest run is 3 miles. Facilities include a day lodge with fast food and a ski shop; lessons and equipment rental and repair are available. Parking requires a Sno-Park permit. The Palmer and Magic Mile lifts are popular with both skiers and sightseers. ✉ *27500 E. Timberline Rd., Timberline Lodge* ☎ *503/272–3311* 🌐 *www.timberlinelodge.com.*

HIKING

Tamanawas Falls
HIKING/WALKING | This relatively easy (it's 3½ miles round-trip), family-friendly hike on the lower eastern slopes of Mt. Hood is popular from late spring through midautumn, although it's on the hottest days of summer that folks flock here to cool off and splash around in Cold Spring Creek and the roaring Tamanawas Falls. These dramatic cascades tumble from a 150-foot-tall lava cliff and make quite an impression on Instagram feeds. ✉ *Hwy. 35, Mount Hood* ✣ *Just north of Sherwood Campground* ☞ *$5 parking.*

Government Camp

54 miles east of Portland on I–84 and U.S. 26, and 42 miles south of Hood River via Hwy. 35 and U.S. 26.

This alpine resort village with a laid-back vibe has several hotels and restaurants popular with visitors exploring Mt. Hood's ski areas.

GETTING HERE AND AROUND

Government Camp is on U.S. 26, about 55 miles east of Portland, and just down the hill from Timberline Lodge.

Restaurants

Charlie's Mountain View
$ | AMERICAN | Old and new ski swag plasters the walls, lift chairs function as furniture, and photos of famous (and locally famous) skiers and other memorabilia abound in this raucous local institution for après-ski fun and listening to live music on weekend nights. Open-flame-grilled steaks, beer-bratwurst sandwiches, and hamburgers are worthy here, as are generous portions of biscuits and gravy for breakfast (weekends only). **Known for:** live music on weekends; large burgers with lots of toppings; rowdy and fun vibe. [$] *Average main: $14* ✉ *88462 E. Government Camp Loop* ☎ *503/272–3333* 🌐 *www.charliesmountainview.com.*

Glacier Public House
$$ | MODERN AMERICAN | Formerly run by different owners and known as Glacier Haus Bistro, this lively spot in the center of Government Camp reopened in late 2019 as a cool gastropub offering tasty, elevated comfort fare. It's a great go-to before or after a day of skiing or summer outdoor fun, and there's a great list of local wines and craft beers. **Known for:** well-crafted comfort food; family-friendly atmosphere; good selection of craft beer. [$] *Average main: $19* ✉ *88817 E. Government Camp Loop Rd.* ☎ *503/272–3471* 🌐 *www.glacierpublichouse.com* ⊙ *Closed Mon. and Tues.*

Mt. Hood Brewing
$$ | AMERICAN | Producing finely crafted beers—Multorporter Smoked Porter, Ice Axe IPA, Highland Meadow Blond Ale—since the early '90s, this casual brewpub with stone walls, a fireplace, and both booth and table seating buzzes in the early evening for après-ski dining and drinking. It's popular for its creative

comfort food, including poutine with fontina cheese and peppercorn demi-glace, cast-iron-skillet-baked fondue, Alsatian pizza topped with smoked ham and crème fraîche, barbecue pulled-pork-and-porter sandwiches. **Known for:** root-beer—and beer—ice-cream floats; giant salted pretzel with beer-cheese dip; hearty chilis and chowders. $ *Average main: $20* ✉ *87304 E. Government Camp Loop* ☎ *503/272–3172* 🌐 *www.mthood-brewing.com.*

Hotels

Best Western Mt. Hood Inn

$$ | HOTEL | Clean, well maintained, and inexpensive, all rooms have microwaves and refrigerators, and some have kitchenettes and whirlpool tubs. **Pros:** handy location for skiing and hiking; clean and modern rooms; great value. **Cons:** cookie-cutter decor and design; not ski-in, ski-out (but very close); parking can be limited when hotel is full. $ *Rooms from: $160* ✉ *87450 E. Government Camp Loop* ☎ *503/272–3205* 🌐 *www.bestwesternoregon.com* *57 rooms* *Free breakfast.*

★ Collins Lake Resort

$$$ | RESORT | FAMILY | This contemporary 28-acre compound of poshly furnished chalets and "Grand Lodge" town homes with fireplaces and dozens of other amenities is scattered around an alpine lake and offers the cushiest accommodations in the Mt. Hood area. **Pros:** within walking distance of Government Camp restaurants and bars; spacious layouts are ideal for groups and families; fireplaces and private decks in all units. **Cons:** two- or three-night minimum during busy times; can be expensive for just one or two occupants; decor varies from unit to unit. $ *Rooms from: $239* ✉ *88149 E. Creek Ridge Rd.* ☎ *503/928–3498, 800/234–6288* 🌐 *www.collinslakeresort.com* *66 condos* *No meals.*

Shopping

Govy General Store

CONVENIENCE/GENERAL STORES | Good thing this is a really nice grocery store, because it's the only one for miles around. Govy General stocks all the staples, plus a nice selection of gourmet treats like cheeses and chocolates. **■ TIP→ Buy your Sno-Park permit here in winter.** ✉ *30521 E. Meldrum St.* ☎ *541/272–3107* 🌐 *www.govygeneral-store.com.*

Activities

DOWNHILL SKIING

★ Mt. Hood Meadows Ski Resort

SKIING/SNOWBOARDING | The mountain's largest resort has more than 2,150 skiable acres, 85 runs, five double chairs, six high-speed quads, a top elevation of 9,000 feet, a vertical drop of 2,777 feet, and a longest run of 3 miles. If you're seeking varied, scenic terrain with plenty of trails for all skiing abilities, this is your best choice among the region's ski areas. Facilities include a day lodge, nine restaurants, two lounges, a ski-and-snowboard school, a children's learning center with daycare, and two ski shops with equipment rentals. ✉ *Hwy. 35* ↔ *10 miles east of Government Camp* ☎ *503/337–2222* 🌐 *www.skihood.com.*

Mt. Hood Skibowl

SKIING/SNOWBOARDING | FAMILY | The ski area closest to Portland is also known as "America's largest night ski area," with 36 runs lighted each evening. It has 960 skiable acres serviced by four double chairs and five surface tows, a top elevation of 5,100 feet, a vertical drop of 1,500 feet, and a longest run of 3 miles. You can take advantage of two day lodges, a midmountain warming hut, four restaurants, and two lounges. Sleigh rides are conducted, weather permitting, and a hugely popular tubing and adventure park has several tubing hills, plus "cosmic tubing," which features music, 600,000 LED lights, and a laser show. In summer the resort morphs into the Adventure Park at Skibowl, with mountain biking, ziplines, bungee jumping, a five-story free-fall Tarzan Swing, disc golf, and kid-friendly tubing and alpine slides. ✉ *87000 E. U.S. 26* ☎ *503/272–3206* 🌐 *www.skibowl.com.*

Welches and Zigzag

12 miles west of Government Camp and 40 miles east of Portland.

One of a string of small communities known as the Villages of Mt. Hood, Welches' claim to fame is that it was the site of Oregon's first golf course, built near the base of Mt. Hood in 1928 and still going strong (as part of the Mt. Hood Oregon Resort). Vacationers hover around both towns for proximity to Mt. Hood along with easy access to basic services like gas, groceries, and dining. Others come to pull a few trout out of the scenic Zigzag River or to access trails and streams in the adjacent Salmon–Huckleberry Wilderness.

GETTING HERE AND AROUND

Most of Welches is just off U.S. 26, sometimes called the Mt. Hood Corridor, about 45 miles east of Portland.

Sights

North American Bigfoot Center
MUSEUM | FAMILY | In the town of Boring along the main route from Portland to Mt. Hood (about 20 miles before you reach Welches), this museum devoted to all things Bigfoot opened in 2019 by one of the world's foremost researchers on the topic and has quickly become a favorite stop, especially with kids. Inside you'll find a 7½-foot-tall replica of a rather stern-looking Sasquatch (his name is Murphy), along with framed and cast footprints, indigenous masks, photos, books, and other artifacts that help visitors to decide for themselves about the likelihood that this creature actually exists. ✉ *31297 S.E. U.S. 26, Boring* ☎ *503/912–3054* 🌐 *www.northamericanbigfootcenter.com* 🎫 *$8* 🕒 *Closed Tues. and Wed.*

Restaurants

Altitude
$$$ | MODERN AMERICAN | Mt. Hood Oregon Resort's flagship restaurant aims for a sleek, modernist look in its glitzy—for this rustic region at least—dining room with recessed lighting and contemporary art. **Known for:** popular lounge with lighter menu; nice views of resort's greenery; extensive wine list. 💲 *Average main: $26* ✉ *Mt. Hood Oregon Resort, 68010 E. Fairway Ave., Welches* ☎ *503/622–2214* 🌐 *www.mthood-resort.com* 🕒 *No lunch.*

Koya Kitchen
$ | JAPANESE | One of the few options for Asian cuisine near Mt. Hood, this affordable Japanese spot is nestled beneath a grove of towering pines and offers simple yet artfully designed dining areas inside and out. Make a feast of a few of the good-sized sushi rolls (which include veggie options) or tuck into a steaming bowl of Oregon mushroom ramen with tofu, chicken, or pork, or ponzu-avocado fried rice with a sunny fried egg on top. **Known for:** nice selection of sushi; pine-shaded beer garden; ramen and noodle bowls. 💲 *Average main: $13* ✉ *67886 E. U.S. 26, Welches* ☎ *503/564–9345* 🕒 *Closed Mon. and Tues.*

★ **Rendezvous Grill**
$$ | MODERN AMERICAN | "Serious food in a not-so-serious place" is the slogan of this casual roadhouse with surprisingly sophisticated food—it's been a locals' favorite since it opened back in the mid-'90s. For a joint many miles from the coast, the 'Vous sure does a nice job with seafood, turning out appetizing plates of sautéed shrimp, Willapa Bay oysters, Dungeness crab,

and chargrilled wild salmon. **Known for:** creatively prepared comfort fare; cocktails with house-infused spirits; attractive patio seating. *Average main: $21* *67149 E. U.S. 26, Welches* *503/622–6837* *www.thevousgrill.com* *Closed Mon. in winter.*

Hotels

The Cabins Creekside at Welches

$ | **RENTAL** | Affordability, accessibility to recreational activities, and wonderful hosts make these cabins with knotty-pine vaulted ceilings, log furnishings, and full-size kitchens a great lodging choice in the Mt. Hood area. **Pros:** friendly owners who can dispense fly-fishing advice; quiet, off-highway location; close to hiking and skiing. **Cons:** no dining within walking distance; no cabin-side parking; simple but clean, functional furnishings. *Rooms from: $129* *25086 E. Welches Rd., Welches* *503/622–4275* *www.mthoodcabins.com* *10 cabins* *No meals.*

Mt. Hood Oregon Resort

$$ | **RESORT** | In the evergreen-forest foothills of Mt. Hood, this expansive golf and spa resort is popular year-round both with outdoorsy sorts and couples seeking romantic alpine hideaways. **Pros:** every sport available; plenty of choices in room size; closer to Portland than most Mt. Hood area lodgings. **Cons:** can get crowded; less appealing if you're not a golfer; a 20-minute drive from ski areas. *Rooms from: $199* *68010 E. Fairway Ave., Welches* *503/622–3101* *www.mthood-resort.com* *157 rooms* *No meals.*

Mt. Hood Vacation Rentals

$$ | **RENTAL** | Doggedly determined to ensure a great time for the two- and four-pawed vacationer alike, this company welcomes the family pet into the majority of its homes, cabins, and condos, yet the properties are still on the upscale side: you'll find fireplaces or wood-burning stoves, hot tubs, river views, and full kitchens. **Pros:** knowledgeable, hospitable staff; family- and pet-friendly; many secluded sites. **Cons:** bring your own shampoo; two- to five-night minimum stays; there's an additional guest services fee. *Rooms from: $180* *67898 E. Hwy. 26, Welches* *888/424–9168* *www.mthoodrentals.com* *32 units* *No meals.*

Activities

FISHING

The Fly Fishing Shop

FISHING | This heritage shop full of self-proclaimed "fish-aholics" has been peddling flies and guiding trips for three decades. Drop in to ask about the huge variety of customizable float trips, clinics, and by-the-hour walking trips for seasonal steelhead and salmon ($60 an hour). Great nearby rivers include the glacial-fed Sandy and its tributary the Zigzag, which hides some native cutthroat. *67296 E. U.S. 26, Welches* *503/622–4607, 800/266–3971* *www.flyfishusa.com.*

GOLF

Mt. Hood Oregon Resort

GOLF | The three 9-hole tracks at this esteemed resort include the Pine Cone Nine, Oregon's oldest golf course, built on a rented hayfield in 1928—you can mix any combination of the three courses to complete a full 18-hole round. There's also a lighted 18-hole putting course that's popular with families and adults working on their short game. Resort guests receive a 10% discount. *68010 E. Fairway Ave., Welches* *503/622–3151* *www.mthood-resort.com* *$67–$83 for 18 holes* *Pine Cone: 9 holes, 3299 yards, par 36. Foxglove: 9 holes, 3106 yards, par 36. Thistle: 9 holes, 2956 yards, par 34.*

RECREATIONAL AREAS

Salmon–Huckleberry Wilderness

PARK—SPORTS-OUTDOORS | Named for the two main food groups of both black bears and frequent Mt. Hood restaurant diners, this sizeable wilderness area just south of Welches occupies the eroded foothills of the "Old Cascades," ancient mountains made mellow by time, water, and wind. Not surprisingly, trailside huckleberry picking is big here in late August and September. Inquire at the Zigzag Ranger Station for regulations and recommended trails, and to buy National Forest parking passes ($5). ✉ *Mt. Hood National Forest Zigzag Ranger Station, 70220 E. U.S. 26, Zigzag* ☎ *503/622–3191* 🌐 *www.fs.usda.gov/recarea/mthood.*

Chapter 7

CENTRAL OREGON

Updated by
Jon Shadel

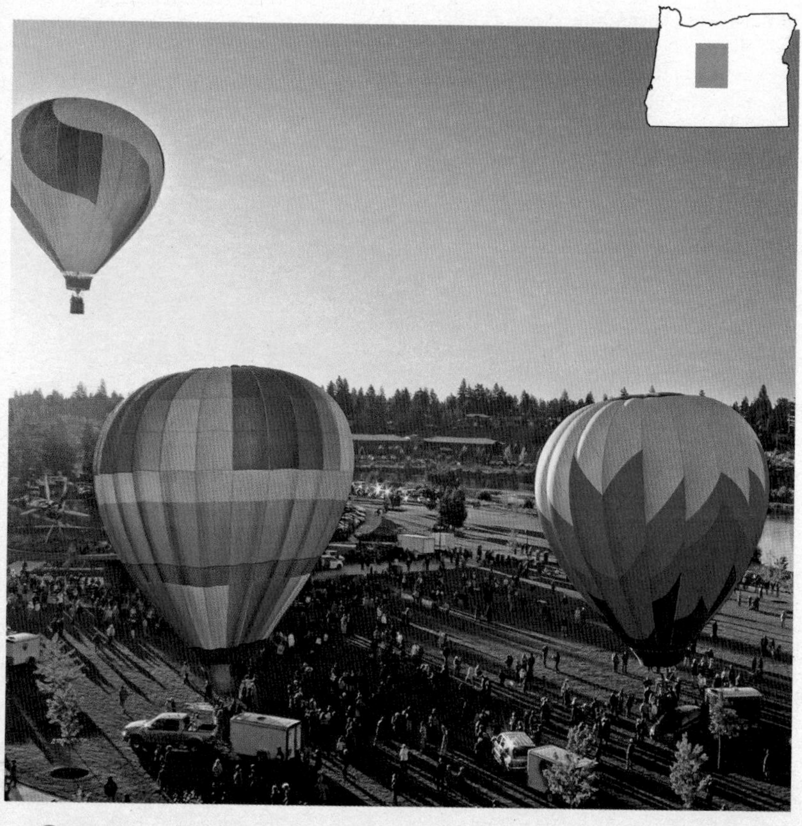

Sights ★★★★★ | Restaurants ★★★☆☆ | Hotels ★★★★☆ | Shopping ★★★☆☆ | Nightlife ★★☆☆☆

WELCOME TO CENTRAL OREGON

TOP REASONS TO GO

★ **Escape into the wild:** Pack your hiking boots, carabiners, snowboard, and camera to explore snowy mountains, rock formations, rivers, lakes, forests, ancient lava flows, and desert badlands.

★ **Get a taste of Bend:** See the refined side of the high desert in Bend's walkable city center, which is packed with upscale restaurants and bars, taprooms, boutiques, and food carts.

★ **Kick back at Sunriver:** This riverfront resort has bike paths, hiking trails, horse stables, hot tubs, four golf courses, and several restaurants.

★ **Tour the brewery scene:** With nearly three dozen breweries—and more on the horizon—you can discover nearly any type of beer that fits your tastes.

★ **Discover the Old West:** Historic ranching towns such as Sisters keep frontier heritage alive with annual festivals.

Central Oregon provides a natural meeting place between the urban west side and the rural east side. It's set below the Columbia River basin and drained by the Deschutes River, which flows from south to north. Skiers and snowboarders flock to winter sports areas on the western edge; anglers head to the Deschutes, the Metolius, and the Cascade Lakes; and climbers, campers, rockhounds, and wanderers explore the arid landscapes on the east side. Bend, the largest town for more than 120 miles in any direction, sits roughly in the center of this region.

1 **Bend.** This quickly gentrifying resort city has a new wave of culinary ambition to fuel outdoor adventurers.

2 **Sisters.** Famous for its namesake rodeo and quilt festival, this kitschy little town looks like an Old West theme park.

3 **Redmond.** The hub for air travel in central Oregon is also the gateway to Smith Rock State Park.

4 **Prineville.** Ranchlands and the Ochoco National Forest border the region's oldest community.

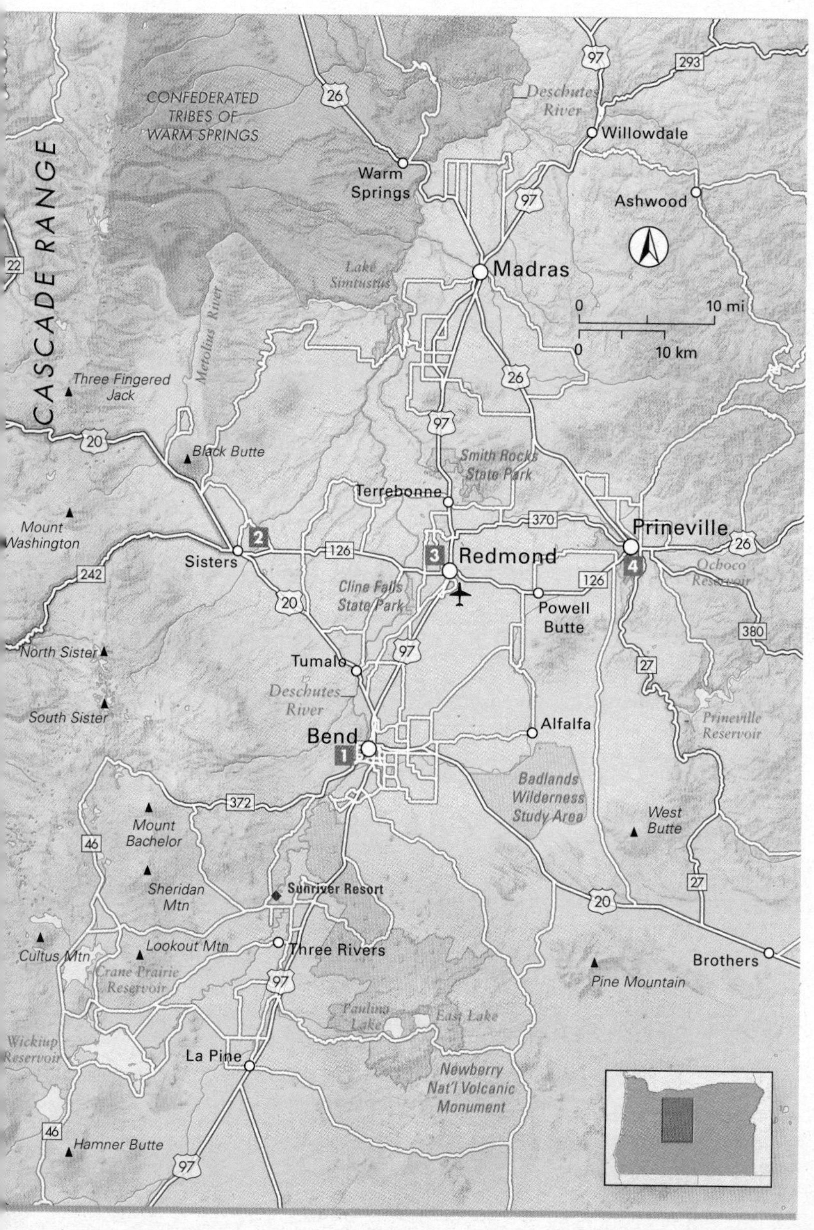
CONFEDERATED TRIBES OF WARM SPRINGS
CASCADE RANGE
Deschutes River
Willowdale
Warm Springs
Ashwood
Madras
Lake Simtustus
Metolius River
0
10 mi
0
10 km
Three Fingered Jack
Black Butte
Smith Rocks State Park
Terrebonne
Mount Washington
Prineville
Sisters
Redmond
Ocheco Reservoir
Cline Falls State Park
Powell Butte
North Sister
Tumalo
Deschutes River
South Sister
Alfalfa
Prineville Reservoir
Bend
Badlands Wilderness Study Area
West Butte
Mount Bachelor
Sheridan Mtn
Sunriver Resort
Lookout Mtn
Three Rivers
Cultus Mtn
Crane Prairie Reservoir
Brothers
Pine Mountain
Paulina Lake
East Lake
Wickiup Reservoir
La Pine
Newberry Nat'l Volcanic Monument
Hamner Butte

As you zip along highways through the straw-colored high deserts and past evergreen forests of ponderosa pines, you may feel like a star in a commercial for some four-wheel-drive vehicle. Yes, central Oregon's sunny landscapes capture the romance of the open road: snowfields so white they sharpen the edges of the mountains; canyons so deep and sudden as to induce vertigo; water that ripples in mountain lakes so clear that boaters can see to the bottom, or rushes through turbulent rapids favored by rafters.

A region born of volcanic tumult is now a powerful lure for the adventurous, the solitude seeking, and even the urbane—Bend has grown into a sophisticated city nearing 100,000 residents, a haven for hikers, athletes, and barflies.

From Bend it's easy to launch to the outdoor attractions that surround it. To the northwest, Camp Sherman is a fisher's destination for rainbow trout or kokanee. The Smith Rocks formation to the north draws climbers and boulderers, and, to the south, Lava Lands and the Lava River Caves fascinate budding geologists more than 6,000 years after they were chiseled out of the earth. Hikers and equestrians trot across the untamed Oregon Badlands Wilderness to the east. Lake Billy Chinook to the north is a startling oasis, where summer visitors drift in houseboats beneath the high walls of the Deschutes River canyon. The Deschutes River itself carries rafters of all descriptions, from young families to solo drifters.

And after a pulse-raising day exploring the rugged setting, you can settle into one of the many rustic but luxurious resorts that compete with each other for upscale amenities. They dot the landscape from the dry terrain around Warm Springs to the high road to Mt. Bachelor.

MAJOR REGIONS

Sunshine, crisp pines, pure air, rushing waters, world-class skiing and snowboarding at Mt. Bachelor, destination golf resorts, a touch of the frontier West at **Sisters,** an air of sophistication in **Bend**—the forested side of **west central Oregon** serves up many recreational flavors. The area draws young couples, seniors, families, athletes, and adventurers, all of whom have no problem filling a week (or more) with memorable activities, from rafting and biking to beer tasting and fine dining.

East of the Cascades, **east central Oregon** changes to desert. The land is austere, covered mostly in sage and juniper, with a few hardy rivers and great extrusions of lava, which flowed or was blasted across the prehistoric landscape. In recent years resorts have emerged to draw Portlanders, especially in winter when the Willamette Valley gets rainy. They venture here to bask in the sun and to soak up the feeling of the frontier, reinforced by ranches and resilient towns like **Redmond** and **Prineville.**

Planning

When to Go

Central Oregon is a popular destination year-round. Skiers and snowboarders come from mid-December through March, when the powder is deepest and driest. During this time, guests flock to the hotels and resorts along Century Drive, which leads from Bend to Mt. Bachelor. In summer, when temperatures reach the upper 80s, travelers are more likely to spread throughout the region. But temperatures fall as the elevation rises, so take a jacket if you're heading out for an evening at the high lakes or Newberry Crater.

You'll pay a premium at the mountain resorts during ski season, and Sunriver and other family and golf resorts are busiest in summer. It's best to make reservations as far in advance as possible; six months in advance is not too early.

Getting Here and Around

AIR

Visitors fly into Redmond Municipal Airport–Roberts Field (RDM), about 17 miles north of downtown Bend. Rental cars are available for pickup at the airport from several national agencies. The Redmond Airport Shuttle provides transportation throughout the region (reservations requested); a ride from the airport to addresses within Bend costs about $40. Taxis are available at curbside, or can be summoned from the call board inside the airport; rideshare services Uber and Lyft both service RDM. Portland's airport is 160 miles northwest of Bend, and daily flights connect the two cities.

AIR CONTACTS Redmond Airport Shuttle. ☎ *541/382–1687, 888/427–4888* 🌐 *www.redmondairportshuttle.net.* **Redmond Municipal Airport–Roberts Field.** (*RDM*) ✉ *2522 S.E. Jesse Butler Circle, Redmond* ☎ *541/548–0646* 🌐 *www.flyrdm.com.*

BUS

The Central Oregon Breeze, a regional carrier, runs one bus a day each way between Portland and Bend, with stops in Redmond and Madras. Cascades East Transit is Bend's intercity bus service, and connects Redmond, La Pine, Madras, Prineville, Bend, and Sisters. Trips from the airport require reservations. Greyhound also serves the area with direct routes from Bend to Eugene and Salem, with connections onward to Portland.

BUS CONTACTS Cascades East Transit. ✉ *334 Hawthorn Ave., Bend* ☎ *541/385–8680, 866/385–8680* 🌐 *www.cascadeseasttransit.com.* **Central Oregon Breeze.** ✉ *2045 N.E. Hwy. 20, Bend* ☎ *541/389–7469, 800/847–0157* 🌐 *www.cobreeze.com.* **Greyhound Bend.** ✉ *334 N.E. Hawthorne Ave., Bend* ☎ *541/923–1732* 🌐 *www.greyhound.com.*

CAR

U.S. 20 heads west from Idaho and east from the coastal town of Newport into central Oregon. U.S. 26 goes southeast from Portland to Prineville, where it heads northeast into the Ochoco National Forest. U.S. 97 heads north from California and south from Washington to Bend. Highway 126 travels east from Eugene to Prineville; it connects with U.S. 20 heading south (to Bend) at Sisters. Major roads throughout central Oregon are well maintained and open throughout the winter season, although it's always advisable to have tire chains in the car. Some roads are closed by snow during winter, including Highway 242. Check the Oregon Department of Transportation's TripCheck (🌐 *www.tripcheck.com*) or call ODOT (☎ *800/977–6368*).

Festivals

★ Bend Film Festival

FESTIVALS | This local film festival, among the most popular in the state, takes place in October. ✉ *Bend* ☎ *541/388–3378* 🌐 *www.bendfilm.org.*

Bend Summer and Fall Festival

FESTIVALS | Downtown Bend is blocked off with food, crafts, art booths, and music in July and October. ✉ *Bend* ☎ *541/508–4280* 🌐 *www.bendsummerfestival.com; www.bendfallfestival.com.*

Oregon Winterfest

FESTIVALS | February brings music, food, brews, wine, ice carving, and other winter sports to Bend's Old Mill District. ✉ *Bend* ☎ *541/323–0964* 🌐 *www.oregonwinterfest.com.*

Pole, Pedal, Paddle

FESTIVALS | Bend's popular ski, bike, run, and kayak or canoe race is held in May. ✉ *Bend* ☎ *541/388–0002* 🌐 *www.pppbend.com.*

Sisters Folk Festival

FESTIVALS | A celebration of American music is held in September. ✉ *Sisters* ☎ *541/549–4979* 🌐 *www.sistersfolkfestival.org.*

Sisters Outdoor Quilt Show

FESTIVALS | The second Saturday in July, Sisters transforms into a western town covered with colorful quilts hanging from building exteriors. ✉ *Sisters* ☎ *541/549–0989* 🌐 *www.sistersoutdoorquiltshow.org.*

Sisters Rodeo

FESTIVALS | Multiple rodeo and community events, held annually for more than 75 years, take place over a weekend in June. ✉ *67637 U.S. 20, south of Sisters, Sisters* ☎ *541/549–0121, 800/827–7522* 🌐 *www.sistersrodeo.com.*

Restaurants

The center of culinary ambition is in downtown Bend, where the restaurant scene has exploded since about 2010. Decent restaurants also serve diners in Sisters, Redmond, Prineville, and the major resorts. Styles vary, but many hew to the Northwest preference for fresh foods grown, caught, and harvested in the region.

Central Oregon also has many down-home places and brewpubs, and family-run Mexican restaurants have emerged to win faithful followings in Prineville, Redmond, Madras, and Bend. *Restaurant reviews have been shortened. For full information visit Fodors.com.*

What It Costs in U.S. Dollars

$	$$	$$$	$$$$
RESTAURANTS			
under $16	$16–$22	$23–$30	over $30
HOTELS			
under $150	$150–$200	$201–$250	over $250

Hotels

Central Oregon has lodging for every taste, from upscale resort lodges to an in-town brewpub village, eclectic bed-and-breakfasts, rustic western inns, and a range of independent and chain hotels and motels. If you're drawn to the rivers, stay in a pastoral fishing cabin along the Metolius near Camp Sherman. If you came for the powder, you'll want a ski-snowboard condo closer to the mountain. For soaking up the atmosphere, you might favor one of downtown Bend's luxurious hotels, or Old St. Francis, the Catholic school–turned-brewpub village. *Hotel reviews have been shortened. For full information, visit Fodors.com.*

Tours

Cog Wild Bicycle Tours
BICYCLE TOURS | Half-, one-, and multi-day mountain bike tours are offered for people of all skill levels and interests. ✉ *LOGE Bend, 19221 S.W. Century Dr., Suite 135, Bend* ☎ *541/385–7002* 🌐 *www.cogwild.com* 🎫 *From $60.*

Sun Country Tours
ADVENTURE TOURS | A longtime provider of raft and tube trips on central Oregon rivers offers rafting excursions that range from two hours to full days May through September. ✉ *531 S.W. 13th St., Bend* ☎ *541/382–1709* 🌐 *www.suncountry-tours.com* 🎫 *From $59.*

★ Wanderlust Tours
ADVENTURE TOURS | Popular and family-friendly half-day or evening excursions are offered around Bend, Sisters, and Sunriver. Options include kayaking, canoeing, snowshoeing, and caving. ✉ *61535 S. Hwy. 97, Suite 13, Bend* ☎ *541/389–8359* 🌐 *www.wanderlust-tours.com* 🎫 *From $80.*

Visitor Information

CONTACTS Central Oregon Visitors Association. ✉ *57100 Beaver Dr., Bldg. 6, Suite 130, Sunriver* ☎ *541/389–8799, 800/800–8334* 🌐 *www.visitcentraloregon.com.*

Bend

160 miles southeast of Portland.

No longer a sleepy timber town, Bend is booming as one of the top recreational playgrounds on the West Coast thanks to its proximity to skiing, rivers, and seemingly endless trails. Invigorated start-up and culinary scenes add fresh energy to the urban core, while active families fleeing California's high cost of living are, in turn, pushing up the cost of real estate here. Even as Oregon's biggest city east of the Cascades grows more cosmopolitan, it remains a monoculture—demographically, it's overwhelmingly white and at times, it seems everybody is an athlete, a tech bro, or a brewer. But thankfully, everyone strives to make a good first impression. Bend's heart is a handsome area of about four square blocks, centered on Wall and Bond Streets. Here you'll find boutique stores, galleries, independent coffee shops, brewpubs, creative restaurants, and historic landmarks such as the Tower Theatre, built in 1940. A few traditional barbershops and taverns are also spread around, keeping it real.

Neighboring Mt. Bachelor, though hardly a giant among the Cascades at 9,065 feet, is blessed by an advantage over its taller siblings—by virtue of its location, it's the first to get snowfall, and the last to see it go. Inland air collides with the Pacific's damp influence, creating skiing conditions immortalized in songs by local rock bands and raves from the ski press.

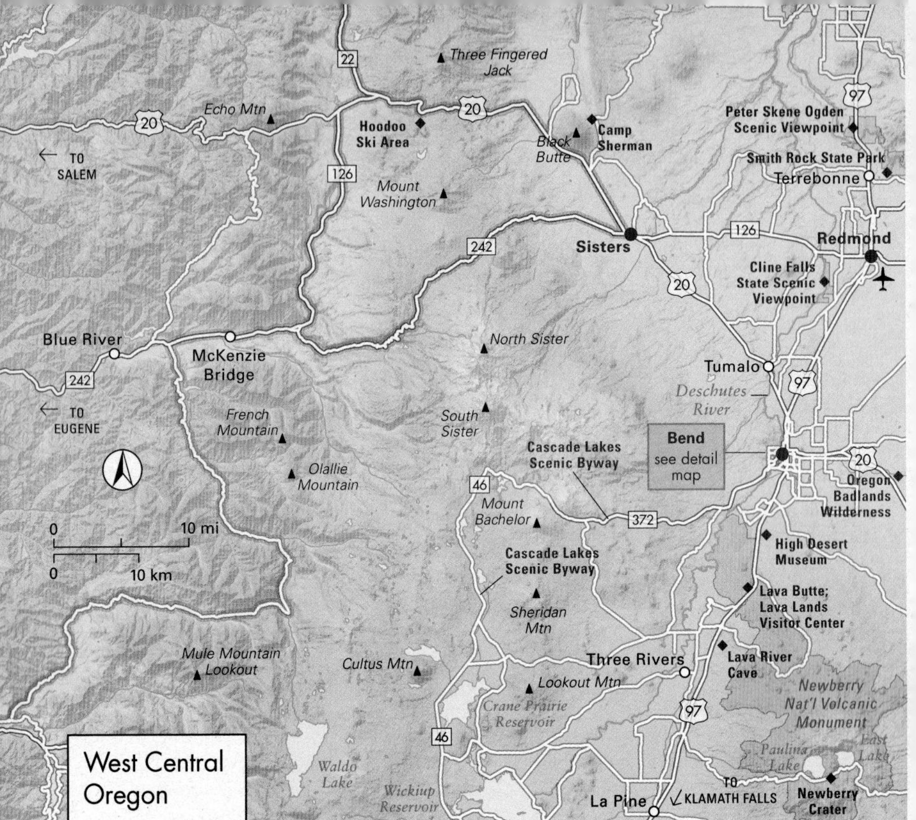

GETTING HERE AND AROUND

Portlanders arrive via car on U.S. 20 or U.S. 26, and folks from the mid–Willamette Valley cross the mountains on Highway 126. Redmond Municipal Airport, 17 miles to the north, is an efficient hub for air travelers, who can rent a car or take a shuttle or cab into town. Greyhound also serves the area with direct routes to Eugene and Salem. The Central Oregon Breeze, a privately operated regional carrier, runs daily between Portland and Bend, with stops in Redmond and Madras. Bend is served by a citywide bus system called Cascades East Transit, which also connects to Redmond, La Pine, Sisters, Prineville, and Madras. To take a Cascades East bus between cities in central Oregon, reservations are not required but recommended. *For more on bus travel to and from Bend, see Getting Here and Around in the Central Oregon Planner.*

If you're trying to head out of or into Bend on a major highway during the morning or 5 pm rush, especially on U.S. 97, you may hit congestion. Parking in downtown Bend is free for the first two hours (three hours at the centrally located parking garage), or park for free in the residential neighborhoods just west of downtown. In addition to the car-rental counters at the airport, Avis, Budget, Enterprise, and Hertz also have rental locations in Bend.

ESSENTIALS

VISITOR INFORMATION Bend Chamber of Commerce. ✉ *777 N.W. Wall St., Suite 200* ☎ *541/382–3221* 🌐 *www.bendchamber.org.* **Visit Bend/Bend Visitor Center.** ✉ *750 N.W. Lava Rd., Suite 160* ☎ *541/382–8048, 877/245–8484* 🌐 *www.visitbend.com.*

Sights

★ Cascade Lakes Scenic Byway

SCENIC DRIVE | For 66 miles, this nationally designated Scenic Byway meanders past a series of high mountain lakes and is good for fishing, hiking, and camping in the summer months. (Much of the road beyond Mt. Bachelor is closed by snow during the colder months.) ✉ *Bend* ✣ *Take Century Dr./Hwy. 372 out of Bend and follow it around Mt. Bachelor. To complete as a loop, take U.S. 97 to return* 🌐 *www.tripcheck.com.*

Deschutes Brewery

WINERY/DISTILLERY | Central Oregon's first and most famous brewery produces and bottles its beer in this facility separate from the popular brewpub. Join one of the four daily tours ($5) and learn from the beer-obsessed staff; be sure to make reservations online or by phone, since groups fill quickly. The tour ends in the tasting room and gift shop, where participants get to try samples of the fresh beer. ✉ *901 S.W. Simpson Ave.* ☎ *541/385–8606* 🌐 *www.deschutesbrewery.com.*

Deschutes Historical Museum

MUSEUM | FAMILY | The Deschutes County Historical Society operates this museum, which was originally built as a schoolhouse in 1914. Exhibits depict historical life in the area, including a pioneer schoolroom, Native American artifacts, and relics from the logging, ranching, homesteading, and railroading eras. ✉ *129 N.W. Idaho Ave.* ☎ *541/389–1813* 🌐 *www.deschuteshistory.org* 🎟 *$5.*

Deschutes National Forest

FOREST | This 1½-million-acre forest has 20 peaks higher than 7,000 feet, including three of Oregon's five highest mountains, more than 150 lakes, and 500 miles of streams. If you want to park your car at a trailhead, some of the sites require a Northwest Forest Pass; day-use passes are also needed May through September at many locations for boating and picnicking. Campgrounds are operated by a camp host. ✉ *63095 Deschutes Market Rd.* ☎ *541/383–5300* 🌐 *www.fs.usda.gov/centraloregon* 🎟 *Park pass $5.*

Drake Park and Mirror Pond

CITY PARK | At its western edge, downtown Bend slopes down to these 13 acres of manicured greensward and trees lining the edge of the Deschutes, attracting flocks of Canada geese as well as strollers from downtown. Various events, such as music festivals, occur in the park during the summer months. Note the 11-foot-high wheel log skidder, harkening back to Bend's logging industry in the early 20th century, when four draft horses pulled the wheel to move heavy logs. ✉ *Bend* ✣ *Bounded on the west by N.W. Brooks St. and Drake Park; N.W. Lava Rd. on the east; N.W. Franklin Ave. to the south; and N.W. Greenwood Ave. to the north* 🌐 *www.downtownbend.org.*

★ High Desert Museum

MUSEUM | FAMILY | The West is actually quite wild, and this combo museum-zoo proves it. Kids will love the up-close-and-personal encounters with Gila monsters, snakes, porcupines, birds of prey, Vivi the bobcat, and Snowshoe the lynx. Characters in costume take part in the Living History series, where you can chat with stagecoach drivers, boomtown widows, pioneers, homesteaders, and sawmill operators. Peruse the 110,000 square feet of indoor and outdoor exhibits, such as Spirit of the West and a historic family ranch, to experience how the past can truly come alive. ✉ *59800 S. Hwy. 97* ✣ *7 miles south of downtown Bend* ☎ *541/382–4754* 🌐 *www.highdesertmuseum.org* 🎟 *$17 Apr.–Oct., $14 Nov.–Mar.*

Newberry National Volcanic Monument and Lava Lands

VOLCANO | FAMILY | The last time hot lava flowed from Newberry Volcano was about 13 centuries ago. The north end of the monument has several large basalt flows, as well as the 500-foot **Lava Butte**

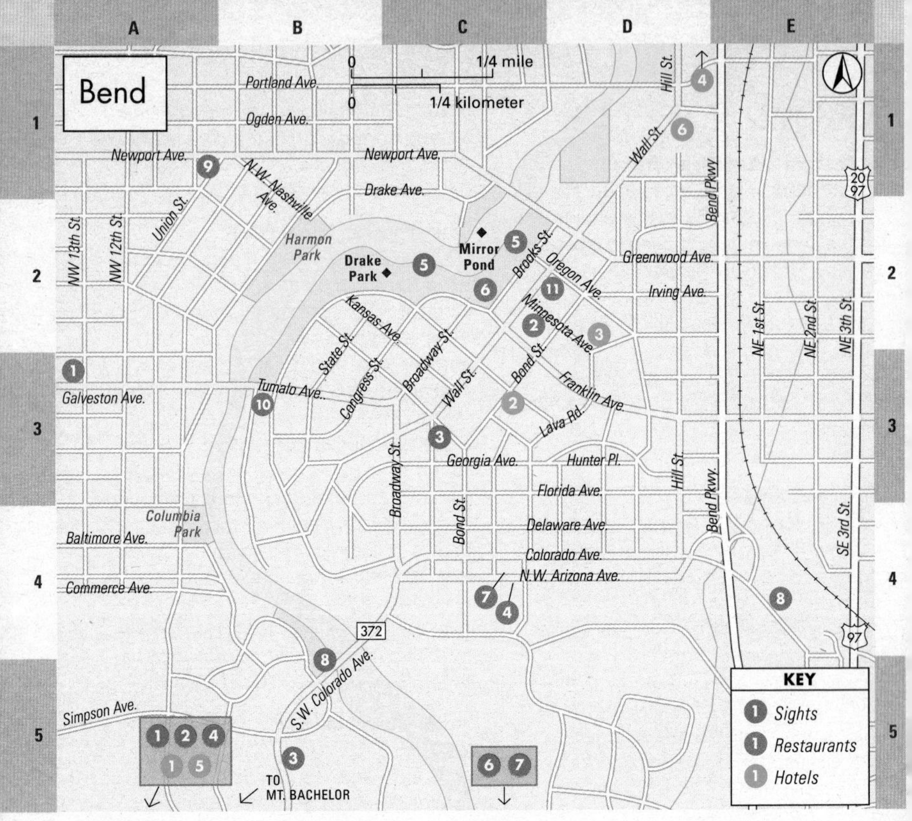

Sights

1 Cascade Lakes Scenic Byway........... **A5**
2 Deschutes Brewery.... **A5**
3 Deschutes Historical Museum.................. **C3**
4 Deschutes National Forest.................... **A5**
5 Drake Park and Mirror Pond......... **C2**
6 High Desert Museum.... **C5**
7 Newberry National Volcanic Monument and Lava Lands.......... **C5**
8 Vector Volcano Classic Arcade.......... **B5**

Restaurants

1 Ariana Restaurant...... **A3**
2 Bos Taurus............... **C2**
3 Deschutes Brewery & Public House......... **B5**
4 Foxtail Bakeshop & Kitchen................. **C4**
5 Pine Tavern............... **C2**
6 Pizza Mondo.............. **C2**
7 The Podski................ **C4**
8 Sparrow Bakery......... **E4**
9 Spork..................... **A1**
10 10 Barrel Brewing West Side................ **B3**
11 Zydeco Kitchen & Cocktails.............. **D2**

Hotels

1 LOGE Bend.............. **A5**
2 Old St. Francis School... **C3**
3 The Oxford Hotel........ **D2**
4 Riverhouse on the Deschutes....... **D1**
5 Sunriver Resort......... **A5**
6 Wall Street Suites...... **D1**

cinder cone—a coal-black and scorched-red, symmetrical mound thrust from the depths 7,000 years ago. The cone is now home to the **Lava Lands Visitor Center,** which features interpretive exhibits that explain the volcanic and early human history of the area. **Lava River Cave,** a 1-mile-long lava tube, takes about 90 minutes to explore on your own with a lantern (available for rent, $5). On the south end of the monument, an unpaved road leads to beautiful views from **Paulina Peak.** Along the shores of **Paulina Lake** and **East Lake,** you can hike, fish, camp, or stay at the rustic resorts. You can also hike a trail to **Paulina Falls,** an 80-foot double waterfall. The monument offers 100 miles of summer trails, and may be accessible during winter months, depending on snowmelt, for snowmobiling, snowshoeing, and skiing. ✉ *58201 S. Hwy. 97* ☎ *541/593–2421* 🌐 *www.fs.usda.gov/centraloregon* 🎟 *$5 per vehicle* 🕑 *Lava River Cave closes Oct. 1 to protect bat population.*

Vector Volcano Classic Arcade

LOCAL INTEREST | **FAMILY** | One of the few spots in central Oregon where you should head indoors to stare at screens, this arcade doubles as a gallery for playing retro arcade games and pinball machines, all while sipping craft beer or kombucha. Thankfully, you won't need to slide any spare change into the 40-plus games from the 1980s and '90s; instead, you pay for an hour or full-day of nostalgia-tripping. ✉ *111 N.W. Oregon Ave.* 🌐 *www.vectorvolcanoarcade.com* 🎟 *Unlimited play for $5–$15* 🕑 *Closed Mon.*

Restaurants

Ariana Restaurant

$$$$ | **AMERICAN** | For the good part of a decade, the 12 tables inside this Craftsman bungalow were the top real estate in the city for celebrating special occasions. Bend's dining scene has evolved considerably since 2004, but Ariana continues to draw national acclaim—landing twice on OpenTable's list of Top 100 Restaurants in America—for its French-, Italian-, and Spanish-inspired dishes. **Known for:** an Oregon take on European classics; intimate dinner-party atmosphere; extensive list of Pacific Northwest wines. 💲 *Average main: $35* ✉ *1304 N.W. Galveston Ave.* ☎ *541/330–5539* 🌐 *www.arianarestaurantbend.com* 🕑 *Closed Mon. No lunch.*

★ Bos Taurus

$$$$ | **STEAKHOUSE** | After 10 Barrel Brewing Co. sold to Anheuser-Busch, the brewery's founding team veered into more upscale territory with the 2018 opening of Bos Taurus. The always-packed modern steak house seems like a central Oregonian's hungry vision of a big-city restaurant—aspiring to be a sort of gallery for some of the finest cuts of meat in town. **Known for:** sourcing top-rated steak from around the world; California- and Washington-centric wine list; attentive service. 💲 *Average main: $50* ✉ *163 N.W. Minnesota Ave.* ☎ *541/241–2735* 🌐 *www.bostaurussteak.com* 🕑 *No lunch.*

Deschutes Brewery & Public House

$ | **AMERICAN** | Established in 1988, Bend's original brewpub remains a happening spot to get a taste of the city's beer scene. The menu includes a diverse lineup of craft brews, including rotating seasonals, and pub food, such as hearty burgers on homemade brioche rolls. **Known for:** central Oregon–inspired brews; sometimes long waits for a table; elk burgers. 💲 *Average main: $15* ✉ *1044 N.W. Bond St.* ☎ *541/382–9242* 🌐 *www.deschutesbrewery.com.*

★ Foxtail Bakeshop & Kitchen

$ | **CAFÉ** | More artful than hearty, brunch is the sleeper hit at this twee bakeshop, where the kitchen struggles to keep up with the weekend demand. A mural of buzzing bees, fluttering bats and butterflies, and a big fox lends a storybook setting to the café's compact dining room, while a spacious patio is prime

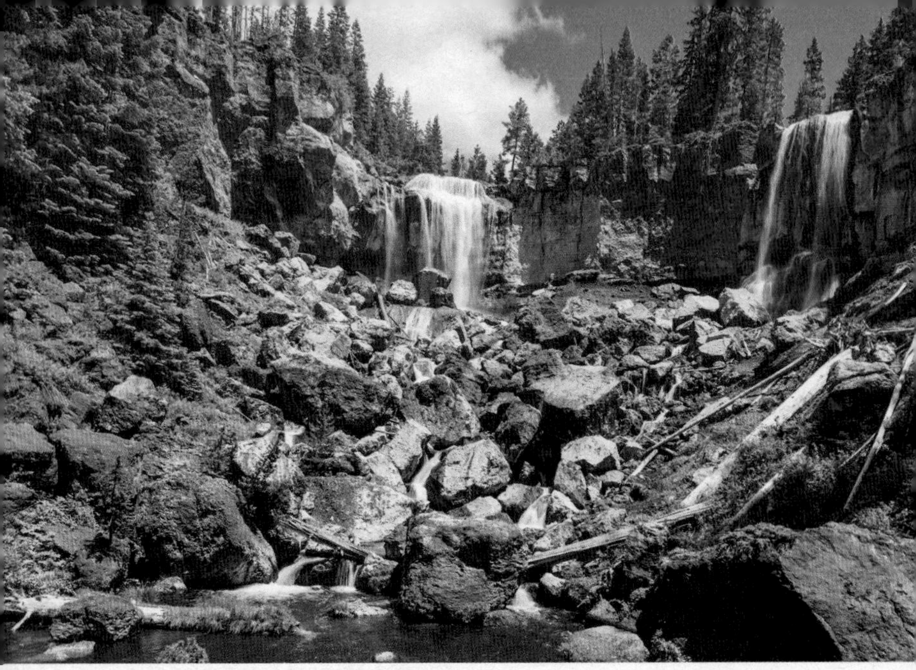

Newberry National Volcanic Monument's Paulina Falls has an 80-foot double waterfall.

real estate on warm mornings. **Known for:** slim menu of savory brunch entrées; sourcing ingredients from nearby farms; long waits during the midmorning rush. *Average main: $14 555 N.W. Arizona St., Suite 60 541/213–2275 www.foxtailbakeshop.com Closed Mon. No dinner.*

Pine Tavern

$$ | AMERICAN | A pair of ponderosa pine trees actually grow through the back dining room in this downtown landmark, which two venturesome women opened in the height of the Great Depression. As the longest-operating restaurant in the city, it keeps old-timers coming back for what hasn't changed: the focus on traditional American cooking and the warm scones with honey butter. **Known for:** an idyllic patio overlooking Mirror Pond; comfort food classics like meat loaf and three-cheese mac; happy hour specials. *Average main: $20 967 N.W. Brooks St. 541/382–5581 www.pinetavern.com.*

Pizza Mondo

$$ | PIZZA | FAMILY | The Maui Wowie and Run Little Piggy are just a few topping combinations at this New York–style pizza restaurant downtown, a fan favorite among families and hungry hikers. Visit the cozy digs for the lunch special—pizza slice, salad, and soda—or order an "after mountain special" (two slices and a beer) in the late afternoon. **Known for:** hand-tossed thin-crust pizza; stellar vegan and "gluten sensitive" pies; limited seating. *Average main: $20 811 N.W. Wall St. 541/330–9093 www.pizzamondo-bend.com.*

★ The Podski

$ | ECLECTIC | This tightly packed cluster of street-food vendors feels less like a typical food-cart pod and more like a year-round party—even the trash cans are decorated with a disco ball. Choose from a half-dozen carts serving dishes like pierogies, charcuterie, vegan toast, and stuffed Korean-style pancakes. **Known for:** Bend's most creative food carts; on-site taproom pouring craft beer; indoor

Central Oregon Brewery Boom

With nearly three dozen breweries and counting, central Oregon rivals the Portland metro area for brewpubs per capita, but it only hit the map as a beer travel destination in recent years.

Since the first microbrewery opened its doors in 1988 (Deschutes Brewery in downtown Bend), the industry has continued to grow and expand. Each brewery and brewpub approaches the craft beer experience in an original manner, often supported by locals and a combination of live music, good food, unique marketing, experimental brews, and standbys that keep pint glasses and growlers filled.

Residents may buoy the industry, but breweries in turn support the community. Local artists design labels, many beer proceeds go to neighborhood causes, and brews are continually concocted with local events and culture in mind.

Bend Ale Trail

Pick up a Bend Ale Trail brochure, or download the app, to guide you through nearly 20 of Bend's breweries. Stop at each brewery, have a taste or a pint, and receive a stamp in your passport. Once you've visited 10 locations, drop by the Bend Visitor Center to receive the prize: a durable silicone pint glass.

seating. *Average main: $12 536 N.W. Arizona Ave. www.thepodski.com No breakfast.*

Sparrow Bakery

$ | **BAKERY** | Groggy locals start lining up every morning for this bakery's signature treat: the Ocean Roll, a croissant-like pastry that's wrapped like a cinnamon roll and filed with cardamom and vanilla. Pastry chefs also hand-make the caramel used in the house espresso drinks. **Known for:** hand-folded croissants and Ocean Rolls; stacked breakfast and lunch sandwiches; French-style bread. *Average main: $10 50 S.E. Scott St. 541/330–6321 www.thesparrowbakery.net No dinner.*

Spork

$ | **INTERNATIONAL** | Interpretations of street food staples from around the world come out of the kitchen at this beloved counter-serve spot, which draws a health-conscious crowd. Originally opened as a mobile kitchen housed in a 1962 Airstream, the restaurant keeps the good vibes alive with its colorful, hippie-industrial decor. **Known for:** eclectic, wide-ranging menu; globally inspired house cocktails; popular for takeout. *Average main: $12 937 N.W. Newport Ave. 541/390–0946 www.sporkbend.com.*

★ 10 Barrel Brewing West Side

$ | **AMERICAN** | One of Bend's favorite brewpubs, 10 Barrel's founders faced threats of boycotts from many fans when they sold the operation to conglomerate Anheuser-Busch in 2014. Thankfully, the tap list at their original outpost remains one of the most creative and varied in this very suds-obsessed city and the beer still pairs best with the signature pizzas. **Known for:** innovative brews; patio with fire pits; noisy dining room. *Average main: $12 1135 N.W. Galveston Ave. 541/678–5228 www.10barrel.com.*

Zydeco Kitchen & Cocktails

$$$ | **AMERICAN** | The blended menu of Northwest specialties and Cajun influences has made this elegant but welcoming restaurant (named after a style of Creole music) a popular lunch and dinner spot

for more than a decade. On the menu, fillet medallions, chicken, and pasta sit alongside jambalaya and redfish dishes. **Known for:** gluten-free menu; expert bartenders; seasonal specials. *$ Average main: $23 ✉ 919 N.W. Bond St. ☎ 541/312–2899 🌐 www.zydecokitchen.com ⏲ No lunch weekends.*

Hotels

LOGE Bend

$$$ | **HOTEL** | No hotel in Bend caters more to outdoor adventurers than LOGE, an old-school motel stylishly renovated in 2018 with recreation-focused amenities that take advantage of the property's proximity to the Deschutes National Forest. **Pros:** close to the Mt. Bachelor ski area; on-site gear rental center; year-round hot tub. **Cons:** motel-style layout; bare-bones café menu; a bit far from the city center. *$ Rooms from: $210 ✉ 19221 S.W. Century Dr. ☎ 541/382–4080 🌐 www.logecamps.com 79 rooms No meals.*

Old St. Francis School

$$$ | **RESORT** | Part of the eclectic McMenamins chain of pubs, movie theaters, and hotels, this fun outpost in a restored 1936 Catholic schoolhouse has classrooms turned into lodging quarters, restaurant and bars, a brewery, a stage, a mosaic-tile soaking pool, and a movie theater with couches and food service. **Pros:** a bohemian-styled destination village; smack in downtown Bend; a semi-secret bar known as the Broom Closet. **Cons:** many rooms feel quite small; few modern appliances; rooms near on-site pubs can get noisy. *$ Rooms from: $215 ✉ 700 N.W. Bond St. ☎ 541/382–5174, 877/661–4228 🌐 www.mcmenamins.com 60 rooms No meals.*

★ The Oxford Hotel

$$$$ | **HOTEL** | Unrivaled for its downtown views and close proximity to the city's top restaurants, this jazz-inspired boutique sets the rhythm for urban lodging in Bend, with in-room vinyl record players and loaner acoustic guitars. **Pros:** generous and environmentally sustainable amenities; luxurious spa and fitness room; loaner bikes in summer months. **Cons:** parking limited to valet or adjacent pay-per-day garage; location is less convenient for outdoor adventures; basement restaurant underwhelms. *$ Rooms from: $425 ✉ 10 N.W. Minnesota Ave. ☎ 541/382–8436 🌐 www.oxfordhotelbend.com 59 rooms No meals.*

Riverhouse on the Deschutes

$$ | **HOTEL** | **FAMILY** | Extensively renovated in 2016, this lodge-inspired hotel and convention center overlooks the Deschutes River and appeals to family travelers with its indoor and outdoor pools, hot tubs, and on-site dining. **Pros:** spacious standard rooms and suites; convenient facilities for family and business travelers; dining and shopping nearby. **Cons:** rooms lack character; not ideal for those looking to walk downtown; room-service menu disappoints. *$ Rooms from: $199 ✉ 3075 N. Business Hwy. 97 ☎ 541/389–3111 221 rooms No meals.*

Sunriver Resort

$$$$ | **RESORT** | **FAMILY** | Central Oregon's premier family playground and luxurious destination resort encapsulates so many things that are distinctive about central Oregon, from the mountain views and winding river to the biking, rafting, golfing, skiing, and family or romantic getaways. **Pros:** many activities for kids and adults; much pampering in elegant lodge facilities; close to The Village at Sunriver. **Cons:** decor looks a tad dated; vibe is very family-centric; gets quite crowded on summer weekends. *$ Rooms from: $259 ✉ 17600 Center Dr., Sunriver ✣ 15 miles south of Bend on Hwy. 97 ☎ 800/801–8765 🌐 www.sunriver-resort.com 245 rooms, 284 houses No meals.*

Wall Street Suites
$$$ | HOTEL | Built in the 1950s as a motel and reopened in 2013 after getting a complete makeover, these spacious suites and rooms are both woodsy and stylishly contemporary, with stunning pine, hardwood, and granite surfaces. **Pros:** room to spread out; pet-friendly; walkable to downtown. **Cons:** basic rooms with few amenities; no lobby common area; still looks like a motel. *Rooms from: $230* *1430 Wall St.* *541/706–9006* *www.wallstreet-suitesbend.com* *17 rooms* *No meals.*

Nightlife

The Ale Apothecary
BREWPUBS/BEER GARDENS | The ancient process of wild fermentation gives an unusual sense of terroir to the oak-barrel-aged sours at The Ale Apothecary, setting this small-batch operation apart from most other IPA-driven beer ventures in the region. The tasting room feels more like a winery's than a brewery's—and it keeps similar hours, too, so check ahead to ensure they're open. *30 S.W. Century Dr., Suite 140* *541/797–6265* *www.thealeapothecary.com.*

Boss Rambler Beer Club
BREWPUBS/BEER GARDENS | Bright pastels and whitewashed shiplap walls make this west-side Bend tasting room look more like an ice cream shop. Indeed, a beachy vibe permeates Boss Rambler's ever-changing tap list—highlighting the house brewer's preference for brewery collaborations and beers intended for sipping on the typically sunny street-side patio. *1009 N.W. Galveston Ave.* *www.bossrambler.com.*

Crux Fermentation Project
BREWPUBS/BEER GARDENS | Housed in a converted auto repair shop, this experimental brewery has no flagship beer. Instead, the brewmaster, a Deschutes Brewery alum, produces an ever-changing variety of pale ales and other craft brews, all of which are on tap in the lively tasting room. On-site food carts and a sprawling patio make this a popular hangout in summer months. *50 S.W. Division St.* *541/385–3333* *www.cruxfermentation.com.*

900 Wall Restaurant and Bar
WINE BARS—NIGHTLIFE | In a historic corner brick building on a downtown Bend crossroads, this sophisticated restaurant and bar serves hundreds of bottles and about 50 different wines by the glass, earning it the Wine Spectator Award of Excellence. *900 N.W. Wall St.* *541/323–6295* *www.900wall.com.*

★ Velvet Lounge
BARS/PUBS | In a city where nightlife seems to end when the Tower Theatre locks up, the nearby Velvet Lounge has earned loyal fans. Join the flannel-clad crowd for a happy-hour brew or an after-show cocktail in the narrow, bi-level bar, which is filled with hanging houseplants and, frequently, the sounds of acoustic-guitar-picking locals. *805 N.W. Wall St.* *541/728–0303* *www.velvetbend.com.*

Shopping

In addition to Bend's compact downtown, the Old Mill District draws shoppers from throughout the region. Chain stores and franchise restaurants have filled in along the approaches to town, especially along U.S. 20 and U.S. 97.

★ Box Factory
SHOPPING CENTERS/MALLS | A converted mill building from the early 1900s houses more than two dozen of Bend's most eclectic shops, restaurants, and studios. Browse leather goods at Danner and the latest opening at the Bend Art Center, or embark on a round-the-block tasting tour of Immersion Brewery, AVID Cider, River Pig Saloon, and Riff, a café dedicated to cold-brewed coffee. *550 S.W. Industrial Way.*

Dudley's Bookshop Cafe

BOOKS/STATIONERY | Bookshelves stacked with new and used titles surround café tables and couches in this two-floor, dual-purpose space that hosts all kinds of activities, from tango classes to philosophical debates. Order an espresso drink at the bar and then browse the city's widest selection of central Oregon trail guides. ✉ *135 N.W. Minnesota Ave.* ☎ *541/749–2010* 🌐 *www.dudleysbookshopcafe.com.*

Goody's

FOOD/CANDY | If the aroma of fresh waffle cones causes a pause on your downtown stroll, you've probably hit one of central Oregon's favorite soda fountain and candy shops. Try the Oreo cookie ice cream, a local favorite, or the homemade chocolate. If you purchase a stuffed toy animal that calls the store home, expect for it to smell sweet for weeks to come. ✉ *957 N.W. Wall St.* ☎ *541/389–5185* 🌐 *www.goodyschocolates.com.*

Hot Box Betty

CLOTHING | This fun, casual shop helps set women's style trends in central Oregon, with its ethically sourced selection of utilitarian apparel and handbags from Pacific Northwest and international brands. ✉ *903 N.W. Wall St.* ☎ *541/383–0050* 🌐 *www.hotboxbetty.com.*

Old Mill District

SHOPPING CENTERS/MALLS | Bend was once the site of one of the world's largest sawmill operations, with a sprawling industrial complex along the banks of the Deschutes. In recent years the abandoned shells of the old factory buildings have been transformed into an attractive shopping center, a project honored with national environmental awards. National chain retailers mingle with restaurants, boutiques, a 16-screen multiplex and IMAX movie theater, and the Les Schwab Amphitheater that attracts nationally renowned artists, local bands, and summer festivals. ✉ *450 S.W. Powerhouse Dr.* ☎ *541/312–0131* 🌐 *www.oldmilldistrict.com.*

Oregon Body & Bath

SPA/BEAUTY | If adventures in the high desert's arid climate have left your skin feeling dry and dehydrated, head to this body and bath boutique in downtown Bend for locally made soaps, lotions, bath bombs, and body butters. The store also stocks home goods, such as fragrant candles and scents. ✉ *1019 N.W. Wall St.* ☎ *541/383–5890* 🌐 *www.oregonbodyandbath.com.*

Pine Mountain Sports

CLOTHING | Part of Bend's fleet of outdoors stores, this shop sells high-quality clothing, energy bars, and the locally famous Hydro Flask water bottles. Recreation equipment such as mountain bikes, backcountry skis, and snowshoes are also available for rent or purchase. ✉ *255 S.W. Century Dr.* ☎ *541/385–8080* 🌐 *www.pinemountainsports.com.*

BIKING

U.S. 97 north to the Crooked River Gorge and Smith Rock and the route along the Cascade Lakes Highway out of Bend provide bikers with memorable scenery and a good workout. Sunriver has more than 30 miles of paved bike paths.

Hutch's Bicycles

BICYCLING | Rent road, mountain, and kids' bikes at this shop as well as a location at 725 N.W. Columbia Street. ✉ *820 N.E. 3rd St.* ☎ *541/382–6248 3rd St. shop, 541/382–9253 Columbia St. shop* 🌐 *www.hutchsbicycles.com.*

BOATING AND RAFTING

A popular summer activity is floating the Deschutes River at your own pace.

Bend Whitewater Park

BOATING | The first white-water park in Oregon, at McKay Park in the Old Mill District, is the result of an extensive renovation to a 1915 dam, which previously made this section of the Deschutes River impassable. Three separate channels

Accommodations at Sunriver Resort Accommodations range from vacation-house rentals to guest rooms and condos.

below the dam cater to rafters, kayakers, tubers, and even surfers. ✉ *166 S.W. Shevlin Hixon Rd.* ☎ *541/389–7275* 🌐 *www.bendparksandrec.org.*

Riverbend Park

BOATING | In Bend, rent an inner tube at Riverbend Park from a kiosk operated from Memorial Day to Labor Day by **Tumalo Creek Kayak & Canoe** and float an hour and a half downriver to Drake Park, where you can catch a shuttle back for a minimal cash fee. ✉ *799 S.W. Columbia St.* ☎ *541/389–7275* 🌐 *www.bendparksandrec.org.*

Tumalo Creek Kayak & Canoe

BOATING | Rent a kayak or stand-up paddleboard and enter the river from the store's backyard, but be prepared to paddle upriver before a leisurely float downstream. Tumalo also operates out of a seasonal shop in Sunriver and a rental kiosk in Riverbend Park. ✉ *805 S.W. Industrial Way, Suite 6* ☎ *541/317–9407* 🌐 *tumalocreek.com.*

SKIING

Many Nordic trails—more than 165 miles of them—wind through the Deschutes National Forest.

Mt. Bachelor

SKIING/SNOWBOARDING | **FAMILY** | This alpine resort area has 60% of downhill runs that are rated advanced or expert, with the rest geared for beginner and intermediate skiers and snowboarders. One of 10 lifts takes skiers all the way to the mountain's 9,065-foot summit. One run has a vertical drop of 3,265 feet for thrill seekers, and the longest of the 88 runs is 4 miles. Facilities and services include equipment rental and repair, a ski school, retail shop, and day care; you can enjoy seven restaurants, three bars, and six lodges. Other activities include cross-country skiing, a tubing park, sled-dog rides, snowshoeing, and in summer, hiking, biking, disc golfing, and chairlift rides. The 35 miles of trails at the **Mt. Bachelor Nordic Center** are suitable for all abilities.

During the off-season, the lift to the **Pine Marten Lodge** provides sightseeing, stunning views, and fine sunset dining. Visitors can play disc golf on a downhill course that starts near the lodge. At the base of the mountain, take dry-land dogsled rides with four-time Iditarod musher Rachael Scdoris. ✉ *13000 S.W. Century Dr.* ☎ *541/382–1709, 541/382–7888* 🌐 *www.mtbachelor.com* 🎫 *Lift tickets $56–$99 per day; kids five and under free.*

Sisters

21 miles northwest of Bend.

If Sisters looks as if you've stumbled onto the set of a western film, that's entirely by design. The town strictly enforces an 1800s-style architecture, which can make its walkable center feel like an Old West theme park. Rustic cabins border ranches on the edge of town, and you won't find a stoplight on any street. Frontier storefronts give way to touristy gift shops, the century-old hotel now houses a restaurant and bar, and a bakery occupies the former general store. Although its population is just a little more than 2,000, Sisters increasingly attracts visitors as well as urban runaways who appreciate its tranquillity and kitsch. If you're driving over from the Willamette Valley, note how the weather seems to change to sunshine when you cross the Cascades at the Santiam Pass and begin descending toward the town.

Black Butte, a perfectly conical cinder cone, rises to the northwest. The Metolius River/Camp Sherman area to the west is a special find for fly-fishermen and abounds with springtime wildflowers.

GETTING HERE AND AROUND

Travelers from Portland and the west come to Sisters over the Santiam Pass on Highway 126. This is also the route for visitors who fly into Redmond Municipal Airport, rent a car, and drive 20 miles west. Those coming from Bend drive 21 miles northwest on U.S. 20. Cascades East, a regional bus carrier, runs routes between Sisters and the Redmond airport by reservation.

ESSENTIALS

VISITOR INFORMATION Sisters Chamber of Commerce. ✉ *291 E. Main Ave.* ☎ *541/549–0251* 🌐 *www.sisterscountry.com.*

Sights

Camp Sherman

RESORT—SIGHT | Surrounded by groves of whispering yellow-bellied ponderosa pines, larch, fir, and cedars and miles of streamside forest trails, this small, peaceful resort community of about 250 full-time residents (plus a few stray cats and dogs) is part of a designated conservation area. The area's beauty and natural resources are the big draw: the spring-fed Metolius River prominently glides through the community. In the early 1900s Sherman County wheat farmers escaped the dry summer heat by migrating here to fish and rest in the cool river environment, making Camp Sherman one of the first destination resorts in central Oregon. As legend has it, to help guide fellow farmers to the spot, devotees nailed a shoebox top with the name "Camp Sherman" to a tree at a fork in the road. Several original buildings still stand from the early days, including some cabins, a schoolhouse, and a tiny railroad chapel. Find the source of local information at the **Camp Sherman Store & Fly Shop**, built in 1918, adjacent to the post office. ✉ *25451 S.W. Forest Service Rd. 1419* ⊕ *10 miles northwest of Sisters on U.S. 20, 5 miles north on Hwy. 14* ☎ *541/595–6711* 🌐 *www.campshermanstore.com.*

Restaurants

The Cottonwood Café

$ | **AMERICAN** | **FAMILY** | Occupying a cute cottage hemmed by a white-picket fence, Sisters' signature brunch spot serves breakfast all day. The menu features such recognizable dishes as scrambles, hash, and eggs Benedict—all elevated by the chef's attention to sourcing ingredients from regional growers and bakers. **Known for:** homey brunch atmosphere; pup-friendly backyard patio with fire pit; standard lunch menu of salads and sandwiches. *Average main: $12 ✉ 403 E. Hood Ave. ☎ 541/549–2699 🌐 www.cottonwoodinsisters.com ⊙ Closed Wed. fall and winter.*

The Open Door

$$ | **WINE BAR** | This wine bar and Mediterranean-inflected restaurant exudes an artsy, small-town eccentricity, with the dining room's mix of mismatched tables and chairs opening into a gallery displaying work from regional craftspeople. The rather tacky art and trinkets all look swell after a few glasses of vino from the well-curated bottle collection. **Known for:** boards with charcuterie from Sisters Meat and Smokehouse; live music on most Monday nights; a leafy patio. *Average main: $16 ✉ 303 W. Hood Ave. ☎ 541/549–6076 🌐 www.theclearwatergallery.com ⊙ Closed Sun.*

Sisters Meat and Smokehouse

$ | **DELI** | A retired fire chief works his smoky magic at this modern butchery and smokehouse, where you can sample the house meats—from pastrami to bologna to cheddar bratwurst—on thick deli-style sandwiches, served with baked beans. For a snack, try the beef jerky, pepperoni sticks, and squeaky cheese curds. **Known for:** smoked and cured meats; counter-serve lunch hot spot; craft beer on tap. *Average main: $12 ✉ 110 S. Spruce St. ☎ 541/719–1186 🌐 www.sistersmeat.com ⊙ No dinner.*

Sno Cap Drive In

$ | **AMERICAN** | Since the golden age of the automobile, this iconic drive-in has served sizzling hamburgers, crispy fries, and handmade milk shakes and ice cream. Stop in for a good helping of roadside Americana, though expect lines in the summer, when travelers driving across the mountain stop here for lunch. **Known for:** historic drive-in; made-to-order burgers; tiny dining area with checkered floors. *Average main: $8 ✉ 380 W. Cascade Ave. ☎ 541/549–6151.*

Coffee and Quick Bites

Sisters Bakery

$ | **BAKERY** | In a rustic western-looking former general store built in 1925, Sisters Bakery smells precisely how you want it to—the scent of fresh-baked pastries, doughnuts, and specialty breads wafts out the door from 6 am to 5 pm. **Known for:** traditional baked treats; simple doughnuts; cash and check only. *Average main: $4 ✉ 251 E. Cascade St. ☎ 541/549–0361 🌐 www.sistersbakery.com 💳 No credit cards.*

Sisters Coffee Co.

$ | **CAFÉ** | When it comes to a correctly prepared latte, there's only one gunner in town—Sisters Coffee Co. operates out of a lofty log cabin, where the only specialty baristas in miles pull shots of the single-origin espresso and prepare perfect pour-overs. It's also the top spot for an early morning bite or to camp out with a laptop on the mezzanine. **Known for:** house-sourced and-roasted beans; classic breakfast muffins; a bakery case filled with pastries and scones. *Average main: $8 ✉ 273 W. Hood Ave. ☎ 541/549–0527 🌐 www.sisterscoffee.com.*

★ FivePine Lodge

$$$ | **RESORT** | **FAMILY** | This upscale western-style resort resembles an alpine village with a cluster of cabins surrounding the main lodge, where every room is rustically decorated with custom-built furnishings. **Pros:** peaceful atmosphere on the fringes of Sisters; on-site brewery and cinema; popular athletic club and spa. **Cons:** limited breakfast options; some cabins are too close to neighbors; main lodge is near U.S. 20, where traffic gets heavy. *Rooms from: $219* *1021 Desperado Trail* *541/549–5900* *www.fivepinelodge.com* *8 suites, 36 cabins* *Free breakfast.*

Metolius River Resort

$$$$ | **RENTAL** | Each of the cabins set amid the pines and aspen at this peaceful resort has splendid views of the sparkling Metolius River, decks furnished with Adirondack chairs, a full kitchen, and a fireplace. **Pros:** peaceful forest setting; feels truly off-grid; wake up to the sound of the river. **Cons:** no additional people (even visitors) allowed; no cell-phone service; bring supplies on winter weekdays when Camp Sherman closes down. *Rooms from: $300* *25551 S.W. Forest Service Rd. 1419, Camp Sherman* *Off U.S. 20, northeast 10 miles from Sisters, turn north on Camp Sherman Rd., stay to left at fork (1419), and then turn right at only stop sign* *800/818–7688* *www.metoliusriverresort.com* *11 cabins* *No meals.*

★ Suttle Lodge

$$$$ | **RESORT** | If the famed director Wes Anderson built a wilderness lodge, it'd probably look something like this whimsically updated lakeside retreat in the Deschutes National Forest, where the vintage summer-camp vibes come with the finest craft cocktails you'll find between here and Portland. **Pros:** the only Sisters-area resort with its own lake; lobby bar and on-site restaurant; year-round accessibility to outdoor sports. **Cons:** no air-conditioning; unreliable Wi-Fi and cell reception; Boathouse restaurant only operates in summer. *Rooms from: $265* *13300 U.S. 20* *13 miles northwest of Sisters* *541/638–7001* *www.thesuttlelodge.com* *11 rooms, 14 cabins* *No meals.*

Sisters Saloon & Ranch Grill

BARS/PUBS | Pass through the swinging saloon doors into this Old West watering hole, originally built more than a century ago as the Hotel Sisters. Head to the bar, which is decorated with a mural of cancan dancers, weathered saddles hanging on the wall, and a mounted stuffed buffalo head. The menu remains rooted in ranch favorites but gets updated with vegetarian-friendly offerings. *190 E. Cascade Ave.* *541/549–7427* *www.sisterssaloon.net.*

Three Creeks Brewing Co.

BREWPUBS/BEER GARDENS | Currently Sisters' only brewery, Three Creeks offers a selection of beers at its brewing facility and brewpub that play on Northwest culture and the outdoor lifestyle. The brewery system is visible from the pub, which serves a range of burgers, pizzas, salads, and other bar mainstays. Order a frothing pint of the popular Knotty Blonde, or try one of their seasonal brews. *721 Desperado Ct.* *541/549–1963* *www.threecreeksbrewing.com.*

Shopping

Hop in the Spa

SPA/BEAUTY | More of a fun novelty than luxe experience, America's first beer spa takes advantage of the medicinal, non-intoxicating qualities of hops and other beer ingredients. Call ahead to schedule a microbrew soak and massage, or one of the other beer-centric spa packages. *371 W. Cascade Ave.* *541/588–6818* *www.hopinthespa.com.*

Paulina Springs Books

BOOKS/STATIONERY | Select a book from the discounted staff recommendation table, or from categories such as history, outdoor recreation, field guides, regional, science, and fiction. Sisters' leading independent bookstore also sells toys and games, and has a substantial young readers section. ✉ *252 W. Hood Ave.* ☎ *541/549–0866* 🌐 *www.paulinasprings-books.com.*

Stitchin' Post

CRAFTS | Owned by a mother-and-daughter team, the famous knitting, sewing, and quilting store opened its doors in 1975. The spacious store not only inspires the senses with colorful fabric, patterns, and yarns, but also conducts classes throughout the year. The **Sisters Outdoor Quilt Show**, annually held the second Saturday of July, is the largest in the world and intertwines its origins with the store's early years. ✉ *311 W. Cascade St.* ☎ *541/549–6061* 🌐 *www.stitchinpost.com.*

Activities

FISHING

Fly-fishing the Metolius River attracts anglers who seek a challenge.

Camp Sherman Store & Fly Shop

FISHING | This local institution—the center of life in the tiny riverside community—sells gear and provides information about where and how best to fish. ✉ *25451 Forest Service Rd. 1419, Camp Sherman* ☎ *541/595–6711* 🌐 *www.campsherman-store.com.*

Fly & Field Outfitters

FISHING | This large Bend-based supplier of gear also sets anglers up with expert guides. ✉ *35 S.W. Century Dr., Bend* ☎ *866/800–2812* 🌐 *www.flyandfield.com.*

RECREATIONAL AREAS

Metolius Recreation Area

PARK—SPORTS-OUTDOORS | On the eastern slope of the Cascades and within the 1.6-million-acre Deschutes National Forest, this bounty of recreational wilderness is drier and sunnier than the western side of the mountains, giving way to bountiful natural history, outdoor activities, and wildlife. There are spectacular views of jagged, 10,000-foot snowcapped Cascade peaks, looming high above the basin of an expansive evergreen valley clothed in pine.

Five miles south of **Camp Sherman** (2 miles to headwaters), the dark and perfectly shaped cinder cone of **Black Butte** rises 6,400 feet. At its base the **Metolius River** springs forth. Witness the birth of this "instant" river by walking a short paved path embedded in ponderosa forest, eventually reaching a viewpoint with the dramatic snow-covered peak of **Mt. Jefferson** on the horizon. At this point, water gurgles to the ground's surface and pours into a wide trickling creek cascading over moss-covered rocks. Within feet it funnels outward, expanding its northerly flow; becomes a full-size river; and meanders east alongside grassy banks and a dense pine forest to join the Deschutes River downstream. Within the 4,600-acre area of the Metolius and along the river, there are ample resources for camping, hiking, biking, and floating. Enjoy fly-fishing for rainbow, brown, and bull trout in perhaps the best spot within the Cascades. ✉ *Camp Sherman* ✢ *Off U.S. 20, 9 miles northwest of Sisters* 🌐 *www.metoliusriver.com.*

SKIING

Hoodoo Ski Area

SKIING/SNOWBOARDING | On a 5,703-foot summit, this winter sports area has more than 800 acres of skiable terrain. With 34 runs and five lifts, skiers of all levels will find suitable thrills. Upper and lower Nordic trails are surrounded by silence, and an inner tube run and night skiing round out the range of activities. At a 60,000-square-foot lodge at the mountain's base, you can take in the view, grab a bite, shop, or rest your weary feet. The ski area has kids' activities

and child-care services available. Lift tickets range from $12 to $61, depending on the type and day. ✉ *U.S. 20* ✣ *20 miles northwest of Sisters* ☎ *541/822–3799* 🌐 *www.hoodoo.com.*

Redmond

20 miles east of Sisters, 17 miles northeast of Bend.

If you find yourself in Redmond, chances are you're on your way somewhere else. The town nearest Eagle Crest Resort and Smith Rock, Redmond is where windswept ranches meet runways, as it serves as the regional hub for air travel. It's experienced notable growth in the past decade, largely owing to its proximity to cross-country skiing, fishing, hiking, mountain biking, and rockhounding. Still, this is no gentrified resort town à la Bend, as a stroll through the compact and historic downtown will attest. A few blocks of vintage buildings remain and Centennial Park serves as an attractive civic center, but north–south traffic mostly hustles through the city core, with the majority of the 30,000 residents in suburban neighborhoods sprawling out to the west. A bevy of taquerias and a couple of breweries make Redmond a convenient pit stop or rather quiet base camp for outdoor adventurers.

GETTING HERE AND AROUND

A couple of highways—U.S. 97 and Highway 126—cross in Redmond. U.S. 97 carries travelers north and south to Washington and California, and Highway 126 runs between Sisters in the west to Prineville in the east. Taxis and the Redmond Airport Shuttle ferry travelers to the Redmond Municipal Airport. Two bus lines, the Central Oregon Breeze and Cascades East Transit, serve Redmond. The Central Oregon Breeze links Bend, Redmond, Madras, and Portland, and Cascades East runs buses to and from Redmond and Madras, Prineville, and Bend. Passengers should call to ensure a ride.

ESSENTIALS

VISITOR INFORMATION Redmond Chamber of Commerce and Convention Visitor's Bureau. ✉ *446 S.W. 7th St.* ☎ *541/923–5191* 🌐 *www.visitredmondoregon.com.*

Sights

Cline Falls State Scenic Viewpoint
VIEWPOINT | Picnicking and fishing are popular at this 9-acre rest area commanding scenic views on the Deschutes River. ✉ *Hwy. 126* ✣ *4 miles west of Redmond* ☎ *800/551–6949* 🌐 *www.oregonstateparks.org.*

★ The Cove Palisades State Park
NATIONAL/STATE PARK | Many people who drive through this part of north-central Oregon are more intent on their distant destinations than on the arid landscape they're passing through. But venture down the two-lane roads to this mini Grand Canyon of red-rock cliffs and gorges 14 miles west of small-town Madras. On a clear day a column of snowcapped Cascades peaks lines the horizon during the drive from town. Lake Billy Chinook, a glittering oasis amid the rocks, snakes through the park. It's formed by the Deschutes, Metolius, and Crooked rivers.

The park is accessible year-round, but high season is summertime, when families camp on the lakeshore and houseboats drift unhurriedly from cliff to cleft. The lake is renowned for its wildlife, from the lake's bull trout to turkey vultures that fill the sky with their cries. Nature lovers also flock to the park in February for the annual eagle watch. The Crooked River Day Use Area is the most immediately accessible part of the park, a great place to cast a line into the water, launch a boat, or raid your picnic basket. Nearby is the Cove Palisades Marina, where you can rent fishing and houseboats, clean fish, and buy sandwiches and boat supplies, including kids' water toys.

In addition to nearly 10 miles of hiking trails, The Cove Palisades has a driving loop around its craggy rim. Near the Ship Rock formation, you may see petroglyphs carved into a boulder by indigenous people centuries ago.

A full-service campgrounds has full hookups, electrical sites with water, and tent sites, boat slips, and cabins. ✉ *7300 Jordan Rd., Culver* ✣ *Off U.S. 97, 27 miles north of Redmond* ☎ *541/546–3412, 800/551–6949, 541/546–3412* 🌐 *www.oregonstateparks.org* 🎫 *Day use $5 per vehicle.*

The Museum at Warm Springs
MUSEUM | If you're driving on U.S. 26 from Portland, stop by the Confederated Tribes of Warm Springs Reservation to check out this museum. It's worth a stop to see the collection of Native American artifacts and exhibits on the culture and history of the Confederated Tribes. ✉ *2189 U.S. 26, Warm Springs* ☎ *541/553–3331* 🌐 *www.museumatwarmsprings.org* 🕓 *Closed Sun. and Mon.*

Peter Skene Ogden State Scenic Viewpoint
VIEWPOINT | Even the most seasoned traveler may develop vertigo peering from the cliff top into a deep river canyon. It is a view that gives insight into why Oregon's high desert looks the way it does, with sheer drops and austere landscapes. You'll want to take pictures, but hang on to your camera. ✉ *U.S. 97 N* ✣ *9 miles north of Redmond* ☎ *800/551–6949* 🌐 *www.oregonstateparks.org.*

★ Smith Rock State Park
NATIONAL/STATE PARK | Eight miles north of Redmond, this park is world famous for rock climbing, with hundreds of routes of all levels of difficulty. A network of

Cove Palisades State Park in north-central Oregon is like a mini Grand Canyon of red-rock cliffs and gorges.

hiking trails serves both climbers and families dropping in for the scenery. In addition to the stunning rock formations, the Crooked River, which helped shape these features, loops through the park. You might spot golden eagles, prairie falcons, mule deer, river otters, and beavers. Due to the environmental sensitivity of the region, the animal leash law is strongly enforced. It can get quite hot in midsummer, so most prefer to climb in the spring and fall. ✉ *9241 N.E. Crooked River Dr., Terrebonne* ✣ *Off U.S. 97* ☎ *541/548–7501, 800/551–6949* 🌐 *www.oregonstateparks.org* 🎟 *Day use $5 per vehicle.*

Restaurants

General Duffy's Waterhole
$ | **ECLECTIC** | **FAMILY** | A glimmer of Portland's street-food scene in Redmond, this no-frills food-cart pod is a neighborhood hangout with a half-dozen vendors clustered around a bar with 20 taps dedicated to West Coast beer and cider. **Known for:** low-key lunch and dinner; plenty of indoor and outdoor seating; filling growlers with to-go beer. 💲 *Average main: $12* ✉ *404 S.W. Forest Ave.* ☎ *541/527–4345* 🌐 *www.generalduffys.com* 🕙 *No breakfast.*

Seventh Street Brew House
$ | **AMERICAN** | **FAMILY** | A hometown hero since the 1990s, Cascade Lakes Brewing operates this no-frills tap house, which ranks among the most popular spots for dinner in Redmond, where Seventh Street doesn't have much competition. Dig into typical pub fare—sandwiches, burgers, tacos, and so on—and try a flight of the hoppy ales. **Known for:** reliable dinner in a town with limited options; sunny, dog-friendly patio; rotating seasonal beers. 💲 *Average main: $12* ✉ *855 S.W. 7th St.* ☎ *541/923–1795* 🌐 *www.cascadelakes.com* 🕙 *No breakfast.*

Terrebonne Depot
$$ | **AMERICAN** | Former food-cart proprietors operate this traditional American restaurant and full bar in an old train depot, where you can chow down on burgers and nachos after braving the

Misery Ridge Trail at nearby Smith Rock State Park. **Known for:** restaurant nearest the iconic Smith Rock; hearty meals for hikers and climbers; sizeable happy-hour dishes for a late lunch. *Average main: $18 400 N.W. Smith Rock Way, Terrebonne 541/527–4339 www.terrebonnedepotrestaurant.com Closed Tues.*

Hotels

Eagle Crest Resort

$$$ | **RESORT** | **FAMILY** | Three golf courses are the big draw at this 1,700-acre destination resort, set on high-desert grounds covered with juniper and sagebrush; accommodations include rental houses as well as rooms and suites in the main lodge. **Pros:** a full-service resort with a spa and restaurants; near Smith Rock State Park; kid- and pet-friendly. **Cons:** clean but not luxurious; noisy, unreliable air-conditioning in some units; gets crowded with families. *Rooms from: $226 1522 Cline Falls Hwy. 5 miles west of Redmond 541/923–2453, 888/306–9643 www.eagle-crest.com 100 rooms, 70 town houses No meals.*

Nightlife

Wild Ride Brew

BREWPUBS/BEER GARDENS | Occupying a block on the edge of downtown, Wild Ride's tasting room and outdoor patio bustle late into the evening thanks to a quartet of food carts serving meals until the bartenders stop pouring. As its name suggests, the brewery takes a cue from the locals' adventurous lifestyles and names its flagship beers for various "wild rides"—from motorcycles to skiing to rock climbing. *332 S.W. 5th St. 541/516–8544 www.wildridebrew.com.*

Activities

ROCK CLIMBING

Smith Rock Climbing Guides

CLIMBING/MOUNTAINEERING | Professionals with emergency medical training take visitors to the Smith Rock formation for climbs of all levels of difficulty; they also supply equipment. Guided climbs—you meet at Smith Rock—can run a half day or full day, and are priced according to the number of people. *Smith Rock State Park, Terrebonne 541/788–6225 www.smithrockclimbingguides.com.*

Prineville

18 miles east of Redmond.

Prineville is the oldest town in central Oregon, and the only incorporated city in Crook County. Tire entrepreneur Les Schwab founded his regional empire here, and this community of around 10,000 remains a key hub for the company. In more recent years, Facebook and Apple have chosen Prineville as the location for data centers. Surrounded by verdant ranch lands and the purplish hills of the Ochoco National Forest, Prineville will likely interest you chiefly as a jumping-off point for some of the region's more secluded outdoor adventures. The area attracts thousands of anglers, boaters, sightseers, and rockhounds to its nearby streams, reservoirs, and mountains. Rimrocks nearly encircle Prineville, and geology fans dig for free agates, limb casts, jasper, and thunder eggs. Downtown Prineville consists of a handful of small buildings along a quiet strip of U.S. 26, dominated by the Crook County Courthouse, built in 1909. Shopping and dining opportunities are mostly on the basic side.

GETTING HERE AND AROUND

Travelers approaching Prineville from the west on Highway 126 descend like a marble circling a funnel, dropping into a tidy grid of a town from a high

Oregon's Ghost Towns

Oregon's many ghost towns captivate the imaginations of road-trippers and photographers with the mysteries of who might've called these frontier communities home. Shaniko, about 75 minutes north of Redmond on U.S. 97, is a picture-perfect example of one of these towns, with a decaying hotel, jail, and schoolhouse among the still-standing structures. Considered the "Wool Capital of the World" at the turn of the century, the town peaked at nearly 500 residents; today Shaniko looks like the abandoned set of a Wild West film.

Other ghost towns in Eastern Oregon include Galena, an 1860s gold mining town near Prairie City; Hardman, an 1870s agricultural hub south of Heppner; and Sumpter, a defunct 1860s gold mining town in the Elkhorn Mountain Range that has become a bit of a destination.

desert plain. It's an unfailingly dramatic way to enter the seat of Crook County, dominated by the courthouse on N.E. Third Street, aka U.S. 26, the main drag. Prineville is 19 miles east of Redmond Municipal Airport. If you're coming to Prineville from the airport, it's easiest to rent a car and drive. Nevertheless, two bus lines, **Central Oregon Breeze** and **Cascades East Transit,** run routes.

ESSENTIALS

VISITOR INFORMATION Ochoco National Forest Office. ✉ *3160 N.E. 3rd St.* ☎ *541/416–6500* 🌐 *www.fs.usda.gov/centraloregon.* **Prineville-Crook County Chamber of Commerce & Visitor Center.** ✉ *185 N.E. 10th St.* ☎ *541/447–6304* 🌐 *www.prinevillechamber.com.*

Sights

A. R. Bowman Memorial Museum

MUSEUM | A tough little stone building (it was once a bank, and banks out here needed to be solid) is the site of the museum of the Crook County Historical Society. The 1910 edifice is on the National Register of Historic Places, with the inside vault and teller cages seemingly untouched. Prominent in the museum are old guns, relics from the lumber mills, and Native American artifacts that define early Prineville. An expansion houses a research library and life-size representations of an Old West street. ✉ *246 N. Main St.* ☎ *541/447–3715* 🌐 *www.bowmanmuseum.org* 🎫 *Free* 🕑 *Closed Jan.*

Ochoco National Forest

FOREST | Twenty-five miles east of the flat, juniper-dotted countryside around Prineville, the landscape changes to forested ridges covered with tall ponderosa pines and Douglas firs. Sheltered by the diminutive Ochoco Mountains and with only about a foot of rain each year, the national forest, established in 1906 by President Theodore Roosevelt, manages to lay a blanket of green across the dry, high desert of central Oregon. This arid landscape—marked by deep canyons, towering volcanic plugs, and sharp ridges—goes largely unnoticed except for the annual influx of hunters during the fall. The Ochoco, part of the old Blue Mountain Forest Reserve, is a great place for camping, hiking, biking, and fishing in relative solitude. In its three wilderness areas—Mill Creek, Bridge Creek, and Black Canyon—it's possible to see elk, wild horses, eagles, and even cougars. ✉ *Office, 3160 N.E. 3rd St. (U.S. 26)* ☎ *541/416–6500* 🌐 *www.fs.usda.gov/ochoco.*

Ochoco Viewpoint

VIEWPOINT | This scenic overlook commands a sweeping view of the city, including the prominent Crook County Courthouse built in 1909, and the hills, ridges, and buttes beyond. ✉ *U.S. 126* ✣ *½ mile west of Prineville.*

Oregon Badlands Wilderness

NATIONAL/STATE PARK | This 29,000-acre swath of Oregon's high desert was designated a national wilderness in 2009, following the longtime advocacy of Oregonians enamored by its harshly beautiful landscape riven by ancient lava flows and home to sage grouse, pronghorn antelope, and elk. Motorized vehicles are prohibited, but visitors can ride horses on designated trails and low-impact hikers are welcome. Bring a camera to capture the jagged rock formations, birds, and wildflowers. ✉ *BLM Office, 3050 N.E. 3rd St. (U.S. 26)* ☎ *541/416–6700* 🌐 *www.blm.gov.*

Prineville Reservoir State Park

NATIONAL/STATE PARK | Mountain streams flow out of the Ochoco Mountains and join together to create the Crooked River, which is dammed near Prineville. Bowman Dam on the river forms this park, where recreational activities include boating, swimming, fishing, hiking, and camping. Some anglers return here year after year, although temperatures can get uncomfortably hot and water levels relatively low by late summer. The reservoir is known for its bass, trout, and crappie, with fly-fishing available on the Crooked River below Bowman Dam. ✉ *19020 S.E. Parkland Dr.* ☎ *541/447–4363, 800/452–5687* 🌐 *www.oregonstateparks.org* *Campsites $21–$31.*

Summit Prairie Drive

SCENIC DRIVE | The scenic drive winds past Lookout Mountain, Round Mountain, Walton Lake, and Big Summit Prairie. The prairie abounds with trout-filled creeks and has one of the finest stands of ponderosa pines in the state; wild horses, coyote, deer, and sometimes even elk roam the area. The prairie can be glorious between late May and June, when wildflowers with evocative names like mule ears, paintbrush, checkermallow, and Peck's mariposa lily burst into bloom. ✉ *Prineville* ✣ *From Prineville, head 16 miles east on U.S. 26, go right on County Rd. 123, turn east and travel 8½ miles to Forest Rd. 42, turn southeast and travel 9½ miles to Forest Rd. 4210* ☎ *541/416–6500.*

Restaurants

Ochoco Brewing Company

$ | **AMERICAN** | **FAMILY** | Burgers are as big a draw as the craft beer at Prineville's prime hangout, which borrows its name from the first brewery known to operate in Oregon in the 1870s. The ⅓-pound grass-fed beef patties come from a ranch just outside town. **Known for:** carb-heavy brewpub favorites; various IPA styles; a few vegetarian options. *Average main: $12* ✉ *380 N. Main St.* ☎ *541/233–0883* 🌐 *www.ochocobrewing.com.*

Tastee Treet

$ | **DINER** | **FAMILY** | The stuff of childhood memories, this old-school establishment is locally renowned for its traditional burgers, hand-cut French fries, and milk shakes. Saunter up to the horseshoe-shaped counter to sit on swiveling stools and chat with locals and out-of-towners, some of whom never miss a chance to drop by while passing through. **Known for:** 1950s-era burger joint; greasy deep-fried appetizers; iconic neon ice-cream cone sign. *Average main: $9* ✉ *493 N.E. 3rd St.* ☎ *541/447–4165* 🌐 *www.tasteetreetprineville.com.*

Hotels

★ Brasada Ranch

$$$$ | **RESORT** | This top-rated but lesser-known luxury resort places an emphasis on feeling good, with a series of 2019 renovations expanding the fitness center and adding an adults-only pool and a new studio space dedicated to wellness classes. **Pros:** on-site restaurants and spa; range of on-site facilities and activities; serene views of mountain horizons. **Cons:** beautiful but somewhat isolated setting; Ranch House suites do not permit kids; not all units have hot tubs. *Rooms from: $289* *16986 S.W. Brasada Ranch Rd., Powell Butte* *855/561–7953* *www.brasada.com* *8 suites, 119 cabins* *No meals.*

Activities

FISHING

It's helpful to check the Oregon Department of Fish and Wildlife's (*ww.dfw.state.or.us*) recreation report before you head out.

Ochoco Reservoir

FISHING | This lake is annually stocked with fingerling trout, and you might also find a rainbow, bass, or brown bullhead tugging on your line. *U.S. 26* *6 miles east of Prineville* *541/447–1209* *www.ccprd.org* *Campsites $20.*

HIKING

Pick up maps at the Ochoco National Forest office for trails through the nearly 5,400-acre Bridge Creek Wilderness and the demanding Black Canyon Trail (11½ miles one way with a hazardous river crossing in spring) in the Black Canyon Wilderness. The 1½-mile Ponderosa Loop Trail follows an old logging road through ponderosa pines growing on hills. In early summer wildflowers take over the open meadows. The trailhead begins at Bandit Springs Rest Area, 29 miles east of Prineville on U.S. 26. A 2-mile, one-way trail winds through old-growth forest and mountain meadows to Steins Pillar, a giant lava column with panoramic views; be prepared for a workout on the trail's poorly maintained second half, and allow at least three hours for the hike. To get to the trailhead, drive east 9 miles from Prineville on U.S. 26, head north (to the left) for 6½ miles on Mill Creek Road (also signed as Forest Service Road 33), and head east (to the right) on Forest Service Road 500.

SKIING

Bandit Springs Sno-Park

SKIING/SNOWBOARDING | A network of cross-country trails starts here at a rest area. Designed for all levels of skiers, the trails traverse areas near the Ochoco Divide and have snow globe–like views of the wilderness area dotted with ponderosa pines. *U.S. 26* *29 miles east of Prineville.*

Prineville Department of Motor Vehicles

SKIING/SNOWBOARDING | The office can provide the required Sno-Park permits. *Ochoco Plaza, 1595 E. 3rd St., Suite A-3* *541/447–7855* *www.oregondmv.com.*

Chapter 8

CRATER LAKE NATIONAL PARK

Updated by
Andrew Collins

Sights
★★★★★

Restaurants
★★★☆☆

Hotels
★★★★☆

Shopping
★★☆☆☆

Nightlife
★★☆☆☆

WELCOME TO CRATER LAKE NATIONAL PARK

TOP REASONS TO GO

★ **The lake:** Cruise inside the caldera basin and gaze into the extraordinary sapphire-blue water of the country's deepest lake, stopping for a ramble around Wizard Island.

★ **Native land:** Enjoy the rare luxury of interacting with totally unspoiled terrain.

★ **The night sky:** Billions of stars glisten in the pitch-black darkness of an unpolluted sky.

★ **Splendid hikes:** Accessible trails spool off the main roads and wind past colorful bursts of wildflowers and cascading waterfalls.

★ **Lake-rim lodging:** Spend the night perched on the lake rim at the rustic yet stately Crater Lake Lodge.

Crater Lake National Park covers 183,224 acres, and only a relatively small portion of it encompasses the lake for which it's named. In southern Oregon less than 75 miles from the California border, the park is surrounded by several Cascade Range forests, including the Winema and Rogue River national forests. The town of Klamath Falls, 50 miles south of the park, has the most convenient Amtrak stop; Ashland and Medford, to the southwest, are 73 miles and 85 miles, respectively, from the park's southern (Annie Spring) entrance. Roseburg is 85 miles northwest of the park's northern entrance, which is open only during the warmer months.

1 Crater Lake. The park's focal point, this scenic destination is known for its deep-blue hue.

2 Wizard Island. Visitors can take boat rides to this protruding landmass rising from the western section of Crater Lake; it's a great place for hiking and picnicking.

3 Mazama Village. About 5 miles south of Rim Drive, the village is your best bet for stocking up on snacks, beverages, and fuel.

4 Cleetwood Cove Trail. The only designated trail to hike down the caldera and reach the lake's edge is on the rim's north side off Rim Drive; boat tours leave from the dock at trail's end.

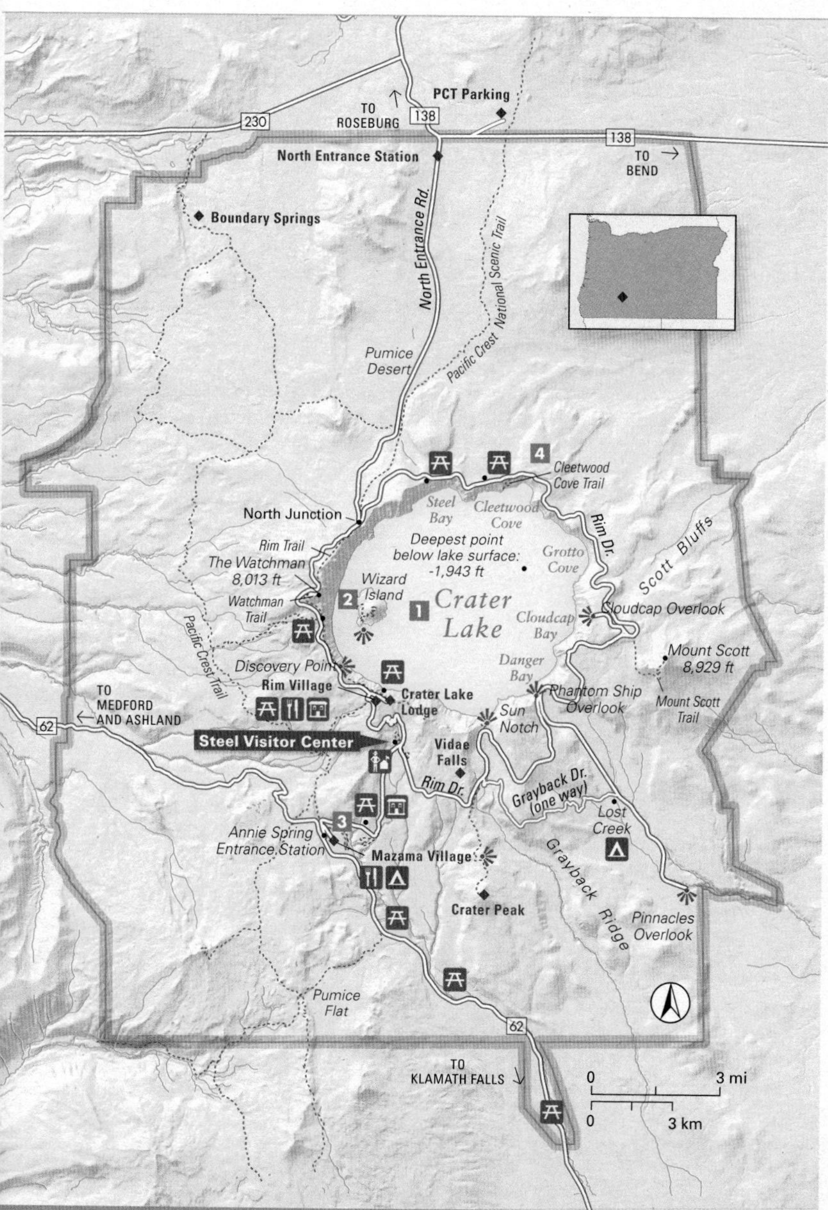

TO ROSEBURG
PCT Parking
230
138
North Entrance Station
TO BEND
Boundary Springs
North Entrance Rd.
Pacific Crest National Scenic Trail
Pumice Desert
4
Cleetwood Cove Trail
North Junction
Steel Bay
Cleetwood Cove
Rim Dr.
Deepest point below lake surface: -1,943 ft
Grotto Cove
Scott Bluffs
Rim Trail
The Watchman 8,013 ft
Wizard Island
2
1
Crater Lake
Watchman Trail
Cloudcap Overlook
Cloudcap Bay
Mount Scott 8,929 ft
Pacific Crest Trail
Discovery Point
Danger Bay
Rim Village
TO MEDFORD AND ASHLAND
62
Crater Lake Lodge
Phantom Ship Overlook
Mount Scott Trail
Sun Notch
Steel Visitor Center
Vidae Falls
Rim Dr.
Grayback Dr. (one way)
Lost Creek
3
Annie Spring Entrance Station
Mazama Village
Grayback Ridge
Crater Peak
Pinnacles Overlook
Pumice Flat
62
TO KLAMATH FALLS
0
3 mi
0
3 km

The pure, crystalline blue of Crater Lake astounds visitors at first sight. More than 5 miles wide and ringed by cliffs almost 2,000 feet high, the lake was created approximately 7,700 years ago, following Mt. Mazama's fiery explosion. Days after the eruption, the mountain collapsed on an underground chamber emptied of lava.

Rain and snowmelt filled the caldera, creating a sapphire-blue lake so clear that sunlight penetrates to a depth of 400 feet (the lake's depth is 1,943 feet). Crater Lake is both the clearest and deepest lake in the United States—and the ninth deepest in the world. For most visitors, the star attractions of Crater Lake are the lake itself and the breathtakingly situated Crater Lake Lodge. Although it takes some effort to reach it, Wizard Island is another outstanding draw. Other park highlights include the natural, unspoiled beauty of the forest and the geological marvels you can access along the Rim Drive.

Planning

When to Go

The park's high season is July and August. September and early October tend to draw smaller crowds. By mid-October until well into June, nearly the entire park closes due to heavy snowfall. The road is kept open just from the South Entrance to the rim in winter, except during severe weather. Early summer snowmelt often creates watery breeding areas for large groups of mosquitoes. Bring lots of insect repellent in June and July, and expect mosquito swarms in the early morning and at sunset. They can also be a problem later in the summer in campgrounds and on the Cleetwood Cove Trail, so pack repellent if you plan on camping or hiking. You might even consider a hat with mosquito netting.

Planning Your Time

CRATER LAKE IN ONE DAY

Begin at the **Steel Visitor Center,** a short drive from Annie Spring, the only park entrance open year-round. The center's interpretive displays and a short video describe the forces that created the lake and what makes it unique. From here begin circling the crater's rim by heading northeast on **Rim Drive,** allowing an hour to stop at overlooks—be sure to check out the Phantom Ship rock formation in the lake—before you reach the trailhead of **Cleetwood Cove Trail,** the only safe and legal way to access the lake. If you're game for a good workout, hike down the trail to reach the dock at trail's end and hop aboard a **tour boat** for a two-hour ranger-guided excursion. If you'd prefer to hike on your own, instead take

AVERAGE HIGH/LOW TEMPERATURES					
JAN.	**FEB.**	**MAR.**	**APR.**	**MAY**	**JUNE**
34/18	35/18	37/19	42/23	50/28	58/34
JULY	**AUG.**	**SEPT.**	**OCT.**	**NOV.**	**DEC.**
68/41	69/41	63/37	52/31	40/23	34/19

the late-morning shuttle boat to **Wizard Island** for a picnic lunch and a trek to the island's summit.

Back on Rim Drive, continue around the lake, stopping at the **Watchman Trail** for a short but steep hike to this peak above the rim, which affords a splendid view of the lake and a broad vista of the surrounding southern Cascades. Wind up your visit at **Crater Lake Lodge.** Allow time to wander the lobby of this 1915 structure that perches right on the rim. Dinner at the lodge's restaurant, overlooking the lake, caps the day—reservations are strongly advised, although you can enjoy drinks, appetizers, and desserts in the Great Hall or out on the back terrace without having booked ahead.

Getting Here and Around

Rogue Valley International–Medford Airport (MFR) is the nearest commercial airport. About 75 miles southwest of the park, it's served by Alaska, Allegiant, American, Delta, and United Airlines and has rental cars. Amtrak trains stop in downtown Klamath Falls, 50 miles south of the park, and car rentals are available in town.

Crater Lake National Park's South Entrance, open year-round, is off Highway 62 in southern Oregon. If driving here from California, follow Interstate 5 north to Medford and head east on Highway 62, or take U.S. 97 north past Klamath Falls, exiting northwest on Highway 62. From Portland, Oregon, allow from 5½ to 6 hours to reach the park's South Entrance, by taking Interstate 5 to Medford. In summer, when the North Entrance is open, the drive from Portland takes just 4½ hours via Interstate 5, Highway 58 (through Oakridge), U.S. 97, and Highway 138. If coming from Portland in summer, staying at an Oakridge, Chemult, or Diamond Lake lodging the night before your arrival will get you fairly close to the park the following morning.

Most of the park is accessible only from late June or early July through mid-October. The rest of the year, snow blocks park roadways and entrances except Highway 62 and the access road to Rim Village from Mazama Village. Rim Drive is typically closed because of snow from mid-October to mid-July, and you could encounter icy conditions at any time of year, particularly in the early morning.

Park Essentials

ACCESSIBILITY

All the overlooks along Rim Drive are accessible to those with impaired mobility, as are Crater Lake Lodge, the facilities at Rim Village, and Steel Visitor Center. A half dozen accessible campsites are available at Mazama Campground.

PARK FEES AND PERMITS

Admission to the park is $30 per vehicle in summer, $20 in winter, good for seven days. For all overnight trips, backcountry campers and hikers must obtain a free wilderness permit at Canfield Ranger Station, which is at the park headquarters adjacent to Steel Visitor Center and open daily 9–5 from mid-April through early November, and 10–4 the rest of the year.

PARK HOURS

Crater Lake National Park is open 24 hours a day year-round; however, snow closes most park roadways from October to June. Lodging and most dining facilities are open usually from late May to mid-October (Rim Village Café the one year-round dining option). The park is in the Pacific time zone.

CELL PHONE RECEPTION

Cell phone reception in the park is unreliable, although generally it works around Crater Lake Lodge, which—along with Mazama Village—also has public phones.

Educational Offerings

RANGER PROGRAMS

★ Boat Tours

ISLAND | FAMILY | The most popular way to tour Crater Lake itself is on a two-hour ranger-led excursion aboard a 37-passenger launch. The first narrated tour leaves the dock at 9:30 am; the last departs at 3:45 pm. Several of the 10 daily boats stop at Wizard Island, where you can get off and reboard three or six hours later. Some of these trips act as shuttles, with no ranger narration. They're perfect if you just want to get to Wizard Island to hike. The shuttles leave at 8:30 and 11:30 and return to Cleetwood Cove at 12:15, 3:05, and 4:35. To get to the dock you must hike down Cleetwood Cove Trail, a strenuous 1.1-mile walk that descends 700 feet in elevation along the way; only those in excellent physical shape should attempt the hike. Bring adequate water with you. Purchase boat-tour tickets at Crater Lake Lodge, Annie Creek Restaurant and gift shop, the top of the trail, and through reservations. Restrooms are available at the top and bottom of the trail. ✉ *Crater Lake National Park* ✣ *Access Cleetwood Cove Trail off Rim Dr., 11 miles north of Rim Village* ☎ *866/292–6720* 🌐 *www.travelcraterlake.com* 🎫 *$28–$55.*

Junior Ranger Program

TOUR—SIGHT | FAMILY | Kids ages 6–12 learn about Crater Lake while earning a Junior Ranger patch in daily sessions during summer months at the Rim Visitor Center, and year-round they can earn a badge by completing the Junior Ranger Activity Book, which can be picked up at either visitor center. ☎ *541/594–3100* 🌐 *www.nps.gov/crla/learn/kidsyouth.*

TOURS

Main Street Adventure Tours

GUIDED TOURS | This Ashland-based outfitter's guided tours in southern Oregon include seven-hour ones to Crater Lake. During these tours, available year-round, participants are driven around part of the lake and, seasonally, given the chance to take a boat tour. Along the way to the park there are stops at the Cole M. Rivers Fish Hatchery, two waterfalls, and Lake of the Woods. ✉ *Ashland* ☎ *541/625–9845* 🌐 *www.ashland-tours.com* 🎫 *From $139.*

Restaurants

There are just a few casual eateries and convenience stores within the park, all near the main (southern) entrance. For fantastic upscale dining on the caldera's rim, head to the Crater Lake Lodge. Outside the park, Klamath Falls has a smattering of good restaurants, and both Medford and Ashland abound with first-rate eateries serving farm-to-table cuisine and local Rogue Valley wines. *Restaurant reviews have been shortened. For full information visit Fodors.com.*

What It Costs in U.S. Dollars			
$	$$	$$$	$$$$
RESTAURANTS			
under $16	$16–$22	$23–$30	over $30
HOTELS			
under $150	$150–$200	$201–$250	over $250

Hotels

Crater Lake's summer season is relatively brief, and Crater Lake Lodge, the park's main accommodation, is generally booked up a year in advance. If you are unable to get a reservation, check availability as your trip approaches—cancellations do happen on occasion. The other in-park option, the Cabins at Mazama Village, also books up early in summer. Outside the park there are a couple of options in nearby Prospect as well as Fort Klamath and Union Creek, and you'll find numerous lodgings a bit farther afield in Klamath Falls, Medford, Ashland, and Roseburg. Additionally, if visiting the park via the North Entrance in summer, you might consider staying in one of the handful of lodgings in Diamond Lake, Oakridge, and Chemult. Even Bend is an option, as it's just a two-hour drive from North Entrance, which is only slightly longer than the drive from Ashland to the main entrance. *Hotel reviews have been shortened. For full information, visit Fodors.com.*

Visitor Information

PARK CONTACT INFORMATION Crater Lake National Park. ☎ *541/594–3000* 🌐 *www.nps.gov/crla.*

PARK LITERATURE AND INFORMATION Crater Lake Natural History Association. ☎ *541/594–3111* 🌐 *www.craterlakeoregon.org.*

VISITOR CENTERS

Rim Visitor Center

INFO CENTER | In summer you can obtain park information at the center, introduce your kids to a number of Junior Ranger activities, or stop into the nearby Sinnott Memorial Overlook, which has a small museum and a 900-foot view down to the lake's surface as well as ranger talks several times per day. In winter, snowshoe walks are offered on weekends and holidays. A short walk away, the Rim Village Gift Store and cafeteria are the only services open in winter. ✉ *Rim Dr.* ✥ *7 miles north of Annie Spring entrance station* ☎ *541/594–3000* 🌐 *www.nps.gov/crla.*

Steel Visitor Center

INFO CENTER | Open year-round, the center, part of the park's headquarters, has restrooms, a small post office, and a shop that sells books, maps, and postcards. There are fewer exhibits than at comparable national park visitor centers, but you can view an engaging 22-minute film, *Crater Lake: Into the Deep,* which describes the lake's formation and geology and examines the area's cultural history. ✉ *Rim Dr.* ✥ *4 miles north of Annie Spring entrance station* ☎ *541/594–3000* 🌐 *www.nps.gov/crla.*

Sights

SCENIC DRIVES

★ Rim Drive

SCENIC DRIVE | Take this 33-mile scenic loop for views of the lake and its cliffs from every conceivable angle. The drive takes two hours not counting frequent stops at overlooks and short hikes that can easily stretch this to a half day. Rim Drive is typically closed due to heavy snowfall from mid-October to mid-June, and icy conditions can be encountered any month of the year, particularly in early morning. ✉ *Crater Lake National Park* ✥ *Drive begins at Rim Village, 7 miles from (Annie Spring) South Entrance; from North Entrance, follow North Entrance Rd. south for 10 miles* 🌐 *www.nps.gov/crla.*

Wildlife in Crater Lake

Wildlife in the Crater Lake area flourishes in the water and throughout the surrounding forest.

Salmon and Trout

Two primary types of fish swim beneath the surface of Crater Lake: kokanee salmon and rainbow trout. Kokanees average about 8 inches in length, but they can grow to nearly 18 inches. Rainbow trout are larger than the kokanee but are less abundant in Crater Lake. Trout—including bull, Eastern brook, rainbow, and German brown—swim in the park's many streams and rivers.

Elk, Deer, and More

Remote canyons shelter the park's elk and deer populations, which can sometimes be seen at dusk and dawn feeding at forest's edge. Black bears and pine martens—cousins of the short-tailed weasel—also call Crater Lake home. Birds such as hairy woodpeckers, California gulls, red-tailed hawks, and great horned owls are more commonly seen in summer in forests below the lake.

HISTORIC SITES

★ Crater Lake Lodge

HOTEL—SIGHT | Built in 1915, this regal log-and-stone structure was designed in the classic style of western national park lodges, and the original lodgepole-pine pillars, beams, and stone fireplaces are still intact. The lobby, fondly referred to as the Great Hall, serves as a warm, welcoming gathering place where you can play games, socialize with a cocktail, or gaze out of the many windows to view spectacular sunrises and sunsets by a crackling fire. Exhibits off the lobby contain historic photographs and memorabilia from throughout the park's history. ✉ *Rim Village* 🌐 *www.travelcraterlake.com.*

SCENIC STOPS

Cloudcap Overlook

VIEWPOINT | The highest road-access overlook on the Crater Lake rim, Cloudcap has a westward view across the lake to Wizard Island and an eastward view of Mt. Scott, the volcanic cone that is the park's highest point. ✉ *Crater Lake National Park* ✣ *2 miles off Rim Dr., 13 miles northeast of Steel Visitor Center.*

Discovery Point

VIEWPOINT | This overlook marks the spot at which prospectors first spied the lake in 1853. Wizard Island is just northeast, close to shore. ✉ *West Rim Dr.* ✣ *1½ miles north of Rim Village.*

Mazama Village

INFO CENTER | In summer, a campground, cabin-style motel, restaurant, gift shop, amphitheater, and gas station are open here. No gasoline is available in the park from mid-October to mid-May. Snowfall determines when the village and its facilities open and close for the season. Hours vary; call ahead. ✉ *Mazama Village Rd.* ✣ *Off Hwy. 62, near Annie Spring entrance station* ☎ *541/594–2255, 866/292–6720* 🌐 *www.travelcraterlake.com.*

Phantom Ship Overlook

VIEWPOINT | From this point you can get a close look at Phantom Ship, a rock formation that resembles a schooner with furled masts and looks ghostly in fog. ✉ *East Rim Dr.* ✣ *7 miles northeast of Steel Visitor Center.*

Wizard Island in Craker Lake is accessible only by boat.

★ Pinnacles Overlook

VIEWPOINT | Ascending from the banks of Sand and Wheeler creeks, unearthly spires of eroded ash resemble the peaks of fairy-tale castles. Once upon a time, the road continued east to a former entrance. A path now replaces the old road and follows the rim of Sand Creek (affording more views of pinnacles) to where the entrance sign still stands. ✉ *Pinnacles Rd.* ✥ *12 miles east of Steel Visitor Center.*

Sun Notch

VIEWPOINT | It's a relatively easy ½-mile loop hike through wildflowers and dry meadow to this overlook, which has views of Crater Lake and Phantom Ship. Mind the cliff edges. ✉ *East Rim Dr.* ✥ *About 4½ miles east of Steel Visitor Center.*

★ Wizard Island

ISLAND | The volcanic eruption that led to the creation of Crater Lake resulted in the formation of this magical island a quarter mile from the lake's western shore. The views at its summit—reached on a somewhat strenuous 2-mile hike—are stupendous.

Getting to the island requires a strenuous 1-mile hike down (and later back up) the steep Cleetwood Cove Trail to the cove's dock. There, board either the shuttle boat to Wizard Island or a Crater Lake narrated tour boat that includes a stop on the island. If you opt for the latter, you can explore Wizard Island a bit and reboard a later boat to resume the lake tour.

The hike to Wizard Summit, 763 feet above the lake's surface, begins at the island's boat dock and steeply ascends over rock-strewn terrain; a path at the top circles the 90-foot-deep crater's rim. More moderate is the 1¾-mile hike on a rocky trail along the shore of Wizard Island, so called because William Steel, an early Crater Lake booster, thought its shape resembled a wizard's hat. ✉ *Crater Lake National Park* ✥ *Access Cleetwood Cove Trail off Rim Dr., 11 miles north of Rim Village* ☎ *541/594–2255, 866/292–6720* 🌐 *www.travelcraterlake.com* 🎟 *Shuttle boat $28, tour boat $55.*

HIKING

Annie Creek Canyon Trail

HIKING/WALKING | This somewhat challenging 1½-mile hike loops through a deep stream-cut canyon, providing views of the narrow cleft scarred by volcanic activity. This is a good area to look for flowers and deer. *Moderate.* ✉ *Mazama Campground, Mazama Village Rd.* ✣ *Trailhead: behind amphitheater between D and E campground loops.*

Boundary Springs Trail

HIKING/WALKING | If you feel like sleuthing, take this moderate 5-mile round-trip hike to the headwaters of the Rogue River. The trail isn't well marked, so a detailed trail guide is necessary. You'll see streams, forests, and wildflowers along the way before discovering Boundary Springs pouring out of the side of a low ridge. *Moderate.* ✉ *Crater Lake National Park* ✣ *Trailhead: pullout on Hwy. 230, near milepost 19, about 5 miles west of Hwy. 138.*

★ Castle Crest Wildflower Trail

HIKING/WALKING | This picturesque 1-mile round-trip trek passes through a spring-fed meadow and is one of the park's flatter hikes. Wildflowers burst into full bloom here in July. You can also access Castle Crest via a similarly easy half-mile loop trail from East Rim Drive. *Easy.* ✉ *Crater Lake National Park* ✣ *Trailhead: either East Rim Dr. or across road from Steel Visitor Center parking lot.*

Cleetwood Cove Trail

HIKING/WALKING | This strenuous 2¼-mile round-trip hike descends 700 feet down nearly vertical cliffs along the lake to the boat dock. Be in very good shape before you tackle this well-maintained trail—it's the hike back up that catches some visitors unprepared. Bring along plenty of water. *Difficult.* ✉ *Crater Lake National Park* ✣ *Trailhead: on Rim Dr., 11 miles north of Rim Village.*

Godfrey Glen Trail

HIKING/WALKING | This 1-mile loop trail is an easy stroll through an old-growth forest with canyon views. Its dirt path is accessible to wheelchairs with assistance. *Easy.* ✉ *Crater Lake National Park* ✣ *Trailhead: Mission Valley Rd., 2½ miles south of Steel Visitor Center.*

★ Mt. Scott Trail

HIKING/WALKING | This strenuous 4½-mile round-trip trail takes you to the park's highest point—the top of Mt. Scott, the oldest volcanic cone of Mt. Mazama, at 8,929 feet. The average hiker needs 90 minutes to make the steep uphill trek—and about 60 minutes to get down. The trail starts at an elevation of about 7,679 feet, so the climb is not extreme, but the trail is steep in spots. The views of the lake and the broad Klamath Basin are spectacular. *Difficult.* ✉ *Crater Lake National Park* ✣ *Trailhead: 14 miles east of Steel Visitor Center on Rim Dr., across from road to Cloudcap Overlook.*

Pacific Crest Trail

HIKING/WALKING | You can hike a portion of the Pacific Crest Trail, which extends from Mexico to Canada and winds through the park for 33 miles. For this prime backcountry experience, catch the trail off Highway 138 about a mile east of the North Entrance, where it heads south and then toward the west rim of the lake and circles it for about 6 miles, then descends down Dutton Creek to the Mazama Village area. You'll need a detailed map for this hike; check online or with the PCT association. *Difficult.* ✉ *Crater Lake National Park* ✣ *Trailhead: at Pacific Crest Trail parking lot, off Hwy. 138, 1 mile east of North Entrance* 🌐 *www.pcta.org.*

★ Watchman Peak Trail

HIKING/WALKING | This is one of the park's best and most easily accessed hikes. Though it's just more than 1½ miles round-trip, the trail climbs more than 400 feet—not counting the steps up to the actual lookout, which has great

Best Campgrounds in Crater Lake

Tent campers and RV enthusiasts alike enjoy the heavily wooded and well-equipped setting of Mazama Campground. Lost Creek is much smaller, with minimal amenities and a more "rustic" Crater Lake experience. Pack bug repellent and patience if camping in the snowmelt season.

Lost Creek Campground. The 16 small, remote tent sites here are usually available on a daily basis; in summer arrive early to secure a spot (it's open early July–mid-October). The cost is $5 nightly. ✉ *3 miles south of Rim Rd. on Pinnacles Spur Rd. at Grayback Dr.* ☎ *541/594–3100.*

Mazama Campground. This campground is set well below the lake caldera in the pine and fir forest of the Cascades not far from the main access road (Highway 62). Drinking water, showers, and laundry facilities help ensure that you don't have to rough it too much. About half the 214 spaces are pull-throughs, some with electricity and a few with hookups. The best tent spots are on some of the outer loops above Annie Creek Canyon. Tent sites cost $21, RV ones $31–$36. ✉ *Mazama Village, near Annie Spring entrance station* ☎ *541/594–2255, 866/292–6720* 🌐 *www.craterlakelodges.com.*

views of Wizard Island and the lake. *Moderate.* ✉ *Crater Lake National Park* ✣ *Trailhead: at Watchman Overlook, Rim Dr., about 4 miles northwest of Rim Village.*

Restaurants

IN THE PARK

Annie Creek Restaurant

$ | **AMERICAN** | **FAMILY** | This family-friendly dining spot in Mazama Village serves hearty if unmemorable comfort fare, and service can be hit or miss. Blue cheese–bacon burgers, Cobb salads, sandwiches, meat loaf, and a tofu stir-fry are all on the menu, and American standards are served at breakfast. **Known for:** pine-shaded outdoor seating area; convenient to lake and the park's southern hiking trails; several varieties of burgers. Ⓢ *Average main: $13* ✉ *Mazama Village Rd. and Ave. C* ✣ *Near Annie Spring entrance station* ☎ *541/594–2255* 🌐 *www.travelcraterlake.com* ⏲ *Closed late Sept.–late May.*

★ Crater Lake Lodge Dining Room

$$$ | **PACIFIC NORTHWEST** | The only upscale restaurant option inside the park (dinner reservations are essential), the dining room is magnificent, with a large stone fireplace and views of Crater Lake's clear-blue waters. Breakfast and lunch are enjoyable here, but the dinner is the main attraction, with tempting dishes that emphasize local produce and Pacific Northwest seafood—think wild mushroom–and–caramelized onion flatbread and pan-seared wild salmon with seasonal veggies. **Known for:** nice selection of Oregon wines; Oregon berry cobbler; views of the lake. Ⓢ *Average main: $28* ✉ *Crater Lake Lodge, 1 Lodge Loop Rd.* ☎ *541/594–2255* 🌐 *www.craterlakelodges.com* ⏲ *Closed mid-Oct.–mid-May.*

PICNIC AREAS

Godfrey Glen Trail

RESTAURANT—SIGHT | In a small canyon abuzz with songbirds, squirrels, and chipmunks, this picnic area has a south-facing, protected location. The half dozen picnic tables here are in a small meadow;

there are also a few fire grills and a pit toilet. ✉ *Crater Lake National Park* ✥ *2½ miles south of Steel Visitor Center.*

Rim Drive

RESTAURANT—SIGHT | About a half dozen picnic-area turnouts encircle the lake; all have good views, but they can get very windy. Most have pit toilets, and a few have fire grills, but none have running water. ✉ *Rim Dr.*

★ Rim Village

RESTAURANT—SIGHT | This is the only park picnic area with running water. The tables are set behind the visitor center, and most have a view of the lake below. There are flush toilets inside the visitor center. ✉ *Rim Dr., Rim Village* ✥ *By Crater Lake Lodge.*

★ Wizard Island

RESTAURANT—SIGHT | The park's best picnic venue is on Wizard Island; pack a lunch and book yourself on one of the early-morning boat tour departures, reserving space on an afternoon return. There are no formal picnic areas and just pit toilets, but you'll discover plenty of sunny and shaded spots where you can enjoy a quiet meal and appreciate the astounding scene that surrounds you. The island is accessible by boat only. ✉ *Crater Lake* ✥ *Boat dock at end of Cleetwood Cove Trail, off Rim Dr., 11 miles north of Rim Village* 🌐 *www.travelcraterlake.com.*

IN THE PARK

The Cabins at Mazama Village

$$ | **HOTEL** | In a wooded area 7 miles south of the lake, this complex is made up of several A-frame buildings and has modest rooms with two queen beds and a private bath. **Pros:** clean and well-kept facility; very close to the lake and plenty of hiking trails; most affordable of the park lodgings. **Cons:** lots of traffic into adjacent campground; no a/c, TVs, or phones in rooms; not actually on Crater Lake (but a short drive away). [$] *Rooms from: $165* ✉ *Mazama Village* ✥ *Near Annie Spring entrance station* ☎ *541/594–2255, 866/292–6720* 🌐 *www.travelcraterlake.com* ⏲ *Closed mid-Oct.–late May* 🛏 *40 rooms* 🍴 *No meals.*

★ Crater Lake Lodge

$$$ | **HOTEL** | The period feel of this 1915 lodge on the caldera's rim is reflected in its lodgepole-pine columns, gleaming wood floors, and stone fireplaces in the common areas, and the simple guest rooms. **Pros:** ideal location for watching sunrise and sunset reflected on the lake; exudes rustic charm; excellent restaurant. **Cons:** books up far in advance; rooms are small and have tubs only, no shower; no air-conditioning, phone, or TV in rooms. [$] *Rooms from: $201* ✉ *1 Lodge Loop Rd.* ✥ *Rim Village, east of Rim Visitor Center* ☎ *541/594–2255, 866/292–6720* 🌐 *www.travelcraterlake.com* ⏲ *Closed mid-Oct.–mid-May* 🛏 *71 rooms* 🍴 *No meals.*

Chapter 9

SOUTHERN OREGON

Updated by
Andrew Collins

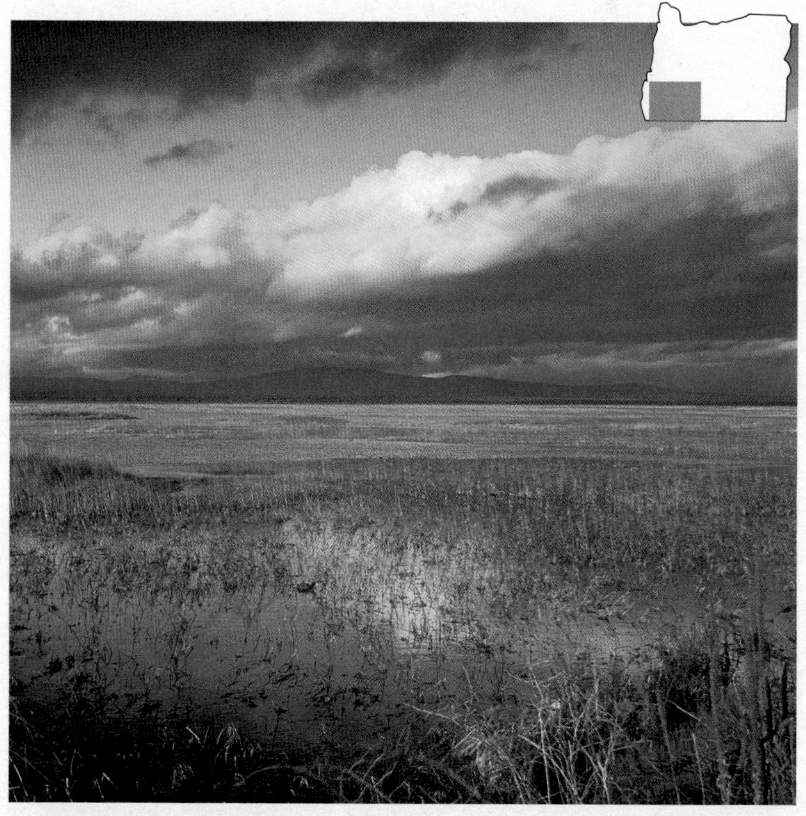

Sights	Restaurants	Hotels	Shopping	Nightlife
★★★★★	★★★★☆	★★★★☆	★★☆☆☆	★★★☆☆

WELCOME TO SOUTHERN OREGON

TOP REASONS TO GO

★ **Discover Oregon's other wine regions:** The once underrated Umpqua and Rogue River wine regions offer a fast-growing bounty of critically acclaimed tasting rooms.

★ **Go underground:** Explore deep into mysterious underground chambers and marble caves at Oregon Caves National Monument.

★ **Shakespeare Festival:** The acclaimed Oregon Shakespeare Festival draws drama lovers to Ashland nine months a year for both classic and contemporary theater.

★ **Enjoy quaint towns:** Southern Oregon's own throwback to the Old West, Jacksonville abounds with well-preserved buildings, while Ashland has one of the state's prettiest downtowns.

★ **Get wet and wild:** Each fall millions of waterfowl descend upon Klamath Basin National Wildlife Refuge Complex. The Rogue River is Oregon's white-water-rafting capital, and the entire region is laced with stunning hiking trails.

1 **Roseburg.** Located on the pristine Umpqua River, there's fishing, waterfall hikes, several excellent wineries, and a wildlife safari nearby.

2 **Grants Pass.** The lively downtown has a growing number of restaurants and boutiques, and it's the launching point for great white-water rafting.

3 **Medford.** The region's largest city and transportation hub boasts reasonably priced lodgings and a burgeoning craft-beer, wine, and distilling scene.

4 **Jacksonville.** Founded during the 1851 gold rush, this historic downtown has lively boutiques and eateries, and several excellent wineries nearby.

5 **Ashland.** The Oregon Shakespeare Festival and an abundance of historic buildings have made this into a hub of arts, dining, and luxury inns.

6 **Cave Junction.** Along the scenic highway from Grants Pass to Crescent City, California, this modest village is home to the Oregon Caves National Monument.

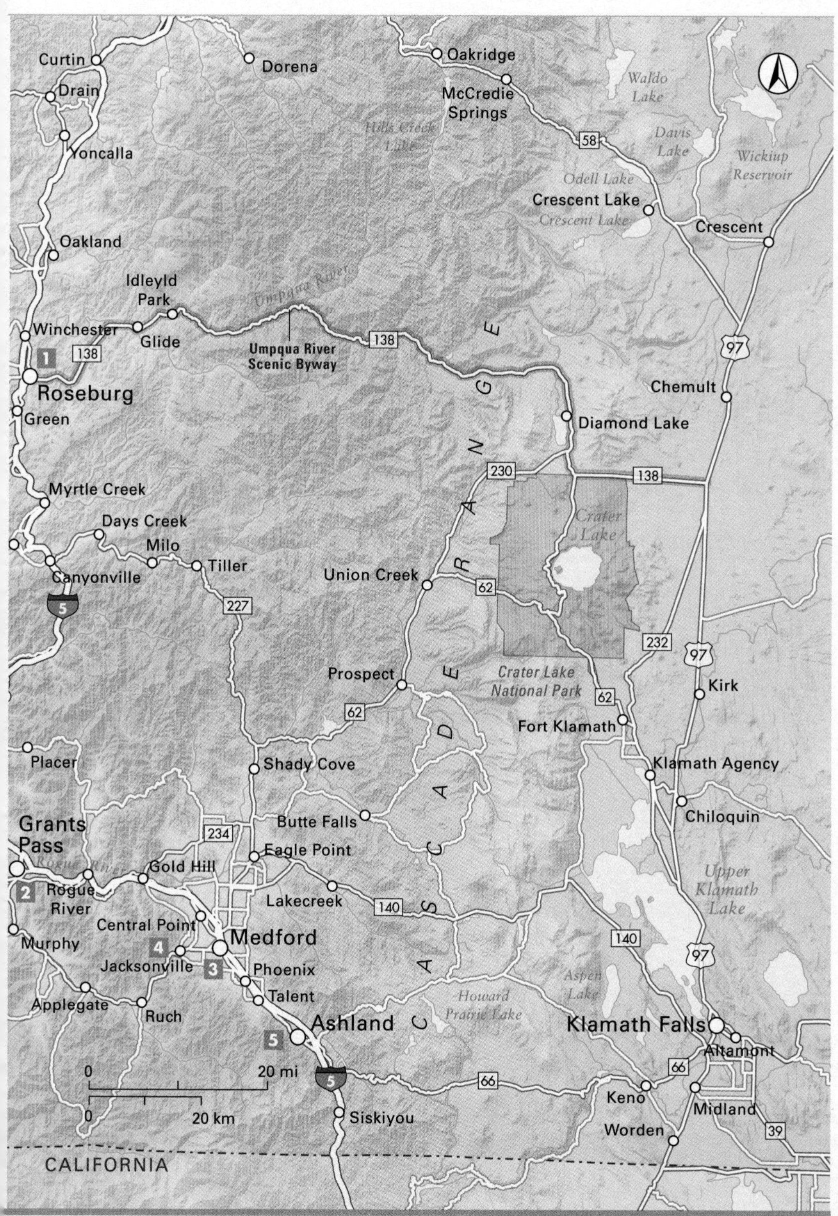
Curtin
Dorena
Oakridge
Drain
McCredie Springs
Hills Creek Lake
Waldo Lake
Davis Lake
Wickiup Reservoir
Yoncalla
58
Odell Lake
Crescent Lake
Crescent Lake
Crescent
Oakland
Idleyld Park
Umpqua River
Winchester
Glide
138
Umpqua River Scenic Byway
138
1
97
Roseburg
Chemult
Green
Diamond Lake
230
138
Myrtle Creek
Crater Lake
Days Creek
Milo
Tiller
Canyonville
Union Creek
62
5
227
232
97
Prospect
Crater Lake National Park
Kirk
62
62
Fort Klamath
Placer
Shady Cove
Klamath Agency
CASCADE RANGE
Chiloquin
Grants Pass
Butte Falls
234
Eagle Point
Rogue River
Gold Hill
Upper Klamath Lake
2
Rogue River
Lakecreek
140
Central Point
Medford
140
Murphy
4
Jacksonville
3
Phoenix
97
Aspen Lake
Applegate
Talent
Howard Prairie Lake
Ruch
Ashland
Klamath Falls
5
Altamont
0
20 mi
5
66
66
Keno
Midland
0
20 km
Siskiyou
Worden
39
CALIFORNIA

Southern Oregon begins where the verdant lowlands of the Willamette Valley give way to a complex collision of mountains, rivers, and ravines. The intricate geography of the "Land of Umpqua," as the area around Roseburg is somewhat romantically known, signals that this is territory distinct from neighboring regions to the north, east, and west.

Wild rivers—the Rogue and the Umpqua are legendary for fishing and boating—and twisting mountain roads traverse this landscape that saw Oregon's most violent Indian wars and became the territory of a self-reliant breed. "Don't-Tread-on-Me" southern Oregonians see themselves as markedly different from fellow citizens of the Pacific Wonderland. In fact, several early-20th-century attempts to secede from Oregon (in cahoots with northern California) and proclaim a "state of Jefferson" survive in local folklore and culture. That being said, Ashland and parts of the surrounding area have steadily become more progressive and urbane in recent decades, as wineries, breweries, art galleries, and farm-to-table restaurants continue to proliferate. The mix of folks from all different political, social, and stylistic bents is a big part of what makes southern Oregon so interesting—and appealing.

Some locals describe this sun-kissed, sometimes surprisingly hot landscape as Mediterranean; others refer to it as Oregon's banana belt. It's a climate built for slow-paced pursuits and a leisurely outlook on life, not to mention agriculture—the region's orchards, farms, and increasingly acclaimed vineyards have lately helped give southern Oregon cachet among food and wine aficionados. The restaurant scene has grown partly thanks to a pair of big cultural draws, Ashland's Oregon Shakespeare Festival and Jacksonville's open-air, picnic-friendly Britt Festivals concert series.

Roseburg, Medford, and Klamath Falls are all popular bases for visiting Crater Lake National Park *(see Chapter 8)*, which lies at the region's eastern edge, about two hours away by car. Formed nearly 8,000 years ago by the cataclysmic eruption of Mt. Mazama, this stunningly clear-blue lake is North America's deepest.

MAJOR REGIONS

The northernmost part of southern Oregon, beginning about 40 miles south of Eugene and the Willamette Valley, the rural and sparsely populated **Umpqua Valley** is the gateway to this part of the state's sunny and relatively dry climate. As you drive down Interstate 5 you'll descend through twisting valleys and climb up over scenic highlands. In summer you can follow the dramatic Rogue-Umpqua River Scenic Byway (Highway 138) east over the Cascades to access Crater Lake from the north—it's the prettiest route to the lake.

Known increasingly for its up-and-coming wineries, including superb Abacela, the Umpqua Valley is home to bustling **Roseburg** and its family-friendly Wildlife Safari park, and the Rogue-Umpqua River Scenic Byway, a particularly scenic route that leads to the northern (summer only) entrance of Crater Lake before doubling back to the southwest toward Medford.

Encompassing the broad, curving, southeasterly swath of towns from Grants Pass through Medford down to Ashland, the mild and sun-kissed **Rogue Valley** is southern Oregon's main population center, and also where you'll find the bulk of the region's lodging, dining, shopping, and recreation.

Interstate 5 cuts through the valley en route to northern California, but venture away from the main thoroughfare and you'll discover the many superb wineries that have lately begun earning the same kind of attention that the state's more famous Willamette Wine Country has been receiving for decades. Foodies are also drawn to the region's abundance of local producers, from nationally acclaimed cheese makers and chocolatiers to farms growing pears, blackberries, and cherries. With warmer temperatures, this area is conducive to growing a wide range of grape varieties—from reds like Syrah, Tempranillo, and Cabernet Sauvignon to increasingly well-known old-world whites like Viognier, Sauvignon Blanc, and Pinot Gris. At the north end of the valley, the bustling river-rafting hub of **Grants Pass** has several excellent restaurants and marks the northern gateway to the Rogue and adjacent Applegate Valley wine regions. Farther south are charmingly historic **Jacksonville,** home to the annual three-week Britt Music Festival, and the small city (population 82,000) of **Medford**, whose downtown has been enjoying a resurgence of late. The artsy college town of **Ashland** is one of Oregon's top restaurant destinations and home to the world-renowned Oregon Shakespeare Festival.

Flanked by about a 2-million-acre Rogue–Siskiyou National Forest, the Rogue Valley is a hub of outdoor recreation, from Oregon Caves National Monument in the sleepy town of **Cave Junction** to fishing and white-water rafting along its clear rivers and mountain biking, hiking, and even skiing in the higher elevations. **Klamath Falls** lies technically a bit east of the Rogue Valley but shares the region's abundance of unspoiled wilderness and opportunities for getting in touch with nature.

Planning

When to Go

Southern Oregon's population centers, which all lie chiefly in the valleys, tend to be warmer and quite a bit sunnier than Eugene and Portland to the north, receiving almost no snow in winter and only 2 to 3 inches of rain per month. In summer, temperatures regularly climb into the 90s, but the low humidity makes for a generally comfortable climate. This makes most of the region quite pleasant to visit year-round, with spring and fall generally offering the best balance of sunny and mild weather.

The exceptions, during the colder months, are southern Oregon's mountainous areas to the east and west, which are covered with snow from fall through spring. Some of the roads leading from the Umpqua and Rogue valleys up to Crater Lake are closed because of snow from mid-October through June, making summer the prime time to visit.

Festivals

Britt Music & Art Festival

FESTIVALS | The Northwest's oldest performing arts showcase features three midsummer weekends of concerts by some 90 international artists, offering everything from classical to bluegrass to pop. ✉ *Britt Festival Pavilion, 350 1st St., Jacksonville* ☎ *541/773–6077, 800/882–7488* 🌐 *www.brittfest.org.*

★ Oregon Shakespeare Festival

FESTIVALS | Ashland's biggest attraction is this festival of Shakespeare and other plays, which runs mid-February through early November. Book tickets and lodging well in advance. ✉ *15 S. Pioneer St., Ashland* ☎ *800/219–8161* 🌐 *www.osfashland.org.*

Winter Wings Festival

FESTIVALS | Each February, nature enthusiasts flock to the Klamath Basin for the Winter Wings Festival, the nation's oldest birding festival. ✉ *Klamath Falls* ☎ *877/541–2473* 🌐 *www.winterwings-fest.org.*

Getting Here and Around

AIR

Medford's Rogue Valley International Airport (MFR) is the state's third-largest facility, with direct flights to Denver, Las Vegas, Los Angeles, Phoenix, Portland, Salt Lake City, San Francisco, and Seattle, and service by Allegiant, Alaska, American, Delta, and United. Most national car-rental branches are at the airport. A few taxi and shuttle companies provide transportation from the airport to other towns in the area, as do Lyft and Uber; these are used mostly by locals, as a car is the only practical way to explore this relatively rural part of Oregon. The one exception is Ashland, where many attractions, restaurants, and accommodations are within walking distance. Cascade Airport Shuttle offers door-to-door service from the airport to Ashland for about $30 to $35. Among taxi companies, Valley Cab serves the Rogue Valley region, with fares costing $2.75 base per trip, plus $3 per mile thereafter.

Roseburg is a 75-mile drive from Oregon's second-largest airport, in Eugene (EUG). Ashland is about 300 miles south of the state's largest airport, in Portland, and 350 miles north of San Francisco. Although it's often cheaper to fly into these larger airports than it is to Medford, what you lose in gas costs, time, and inconvenience will likely outweigh any savings.

CONTACTS Cascade Airport Shuttle. ☎ *541/488–1998, 888/760–7433* 🌐 *www.cascadeshuttle.com.* **Rogue Valley International Airport.** ☎ *541/772–8068* 🌐 *www.jacksoncountyor.org/airport.* **Valley Cab.** ☎ *541/772–1818* 🌐 *www.myvalleycab.com.*

CAR

Unquestionably, your best way to explore the region is by car, although key attractions, hotels, and restaurants in a few downtowns—such as Ashland, Grants Pass, and Jacksonville—are within walking distance of one another. Interstate 5 runs north–south the length of the Umpqua and Rogue river valleys, linking Roseburg, Grants Pass, Medford, and Ashland. Many regional attractions lie not too far east or west of Interstate 5. Jacksonville is a short drive due west from Medford. Highway 138 (aka the Rogue-Umpqua Scenic Byway) winds scenically along the Umpqua River east of Roseburg to the less-visited northern end of Crater Lake National Park. Highway 140 leads from Medford east to Klamath Falls, which you can also reach from Ashland via Highway 66 and Bend via U.S. 97.

Restaurants

Southern Oregon's dining scene varies greatly from region to region, with the more tourism-driven communities of Ashland, Jacksonville, and Grants Pass leading the way in terms of sophisticated farm-to-table restaurants, hip coffeehouses, and noteworthy bakeries and wine bars. Other larger towns in the valleys, including Roseburg and Medford, have grown in culinary as well as craft-brewing stature of late, while Klamath Falls and Cave Junction have few dining options of note. In the top culinary communities you'll find chefs emphasizing Oregon-produced foods; regional wines, including many from the Rogue and Umqua valleys, also find their way onto many menus. *Restaurant reviews have been shortened. For full information visit Fodors.com.*

What It Costs in U.S. Dollars

$	$$	$$$	$$$$
RESTAURANTS			
under $16	$16–$22	$23–$30	over $30
HOTELS			
under $150	$150–$200	$201–$250	over $250

Hotels

Ashland has the region's greatest variety of distinctive lodgings, from the usual midpriced chain properties to plush B&Bs set in restored Arts and Crafts and Victorian mansions. Nearby Jacksonville also has a few fine, upscale inns. Beyond that, in nearly every town in southern Oregon you'll find an interesting country inn or small hotel, and in any of the key communities along Interstate 5—including Roseburg, Grants Pass, and Medford—a wide variety of chain motels and hotels. Rooms in this part of the state book up earliest in summer, especially on weekends. If you're coming to Ashland or Jacksonville, try to book at least a week or two ahead. Elsewhere, you can usually find a room in a suitable chain property on less than a day's notice. *Hotel reviews have been shortened. For full information visit Fodors.com.*

Tours

Hellgate Jetboat Excursions
BOAT TOURS | FAMILY | You'll see some of Oregon's most magnificent scenery on these excursions, which depart from the Riverside Inn in Grants Pass. The 36-mile round-trip runs through Hellgate Canyon and takes two hours. There is also a 5½-hour, 75-mile round-trip from Grants Pass to Grave Creek, with a stop for a meal on an open-air deck (cost of meal not included). Trips are available May through September, conditions permitting. ☎ *541/479–7204* 🌐 *www.hellgate.com* 🎫 *From $33.*

Premier Wine Tours
SPECIAL-INTEREST | Getting to know some of the region's more than 130 wineries can be a challenge to visitors, especially when you factor in having to drive from tasting room to tasting room. This outfitter with knowledgeable guides leads five-hour tours leaving daily from Ashland, Medford, and Jacksonville—the day includes a tour of a winery, picnic lunch, and tasting at a few of the area's top producers. ☎ *541/261–6389* 🌐 *www.southernoregonwinetour.com* 🎫 *From $79.*

Visitor Information

CONTACTS Travel Southern Oregon.
☎ *541/708–1994* 🌐 *www.southernoregon.org.*

Roseburg

73 miles south of Eugene on I–5.

Fishermen the world over hold the name Roseburg sacred. The timber town on the Umpqua River attracts anglers in search of a dozen popular fish species, including bass, brown and brook trout, and Chinook, coho, and sockeye salmon. The native steelhead, which makes its run to the sea in the summer, is king of them all.

The north and south branches of the Umpqua River meet up just north of Roseburg. You can drive alongside the North Umpqua via the Rogue-Umpqua Scenic Byway, which provides access to trails, hot springs, waterfalls, and the Winchester fish ladder. White-water rafting is also popular here, although not to the degree that it is farther south in the Rogue Valley.

About 80 miles west of the northern gateway to Crater Lake National Park and in the Hundred Valleys of the Umpqua, Roseburg and the surrounding countryside are home to about 25 wineries, many of them well regarded and most within easy reach of Interstate 5.

GETTING HERE AND AROUND

Roseburg is the first large town you'll reach driving south from Eugene on Interstate 5. It's also a main access point into southern Oregon via Highway 138 if you're approaching from the east, either by way of Crater Lake or U.S. 97, which leads down from Bend. And from the North Bend–Coos Bay region of the Oregon Coast, windy but picturesque Highway 42 leads to just south of Roseburg. It's a 75-mile drive north to Eugene's airport, and a 95-mile drive south to Rogue Valley Airport in Medford.

ESSENTIALS

VISITOR INFORMATION Roseburg Area Visitor Center. ✉ *410 S.E. Spruce St.* ☎ *541/672–2648* 🌐 *www.roseburgchamber.com.*

Sights

★ Abacela Vineyards and Winery
WINERY/DISTILLERY | The name derives from an archaic Spanish word meaning "to plant grapevines," and that's exactly what this winery's husband-wife team started doing in the late '90s. Abacela has steadily established itself as one of the best Oregon wineries outside the Willamette Valley. Hot-blooded Spanish Tempranillo is Abacela's pride and joy, though inky Malbec and a subtly floral Albariño also highlight a repertoire heavy on Mediterranean varietals, which you can sample in a handsome, eco-friendly tasting room where you can also order light appetizers to snack on. ✉ *12500 Lookingglass Rd.* ☎ *541/679–6642* 🌐 *www.abacela.com.*

Douglas County Museum
MUSEUM | One of the best county museums in the state surveys 10,000 years of human activity in the region. The fossil collection is worth a stop, as is the state's second-largest photo collection, numbering more than 24,000 images, some dating to the 1840s. ✉ *123 Museum Dr.* ☎ *541/957–7007* 🌐 *www.umpquavalleymuseums.org* 🎫 *$8* ⏲ *Closed Sun. and Mon.*

Henry Estate Winery
WINERY/DISTILLERY | One of the earliest wineries to develop into a serious success in southern Oregon, this picturesque estate sits alongside the Umpqua River about 15 miles northwest of Roseburg and turns out exceptional Pinot Noir and Alsace-style Pinot Gris, along with some European wines less often seen in the United States, such as Müller-Thurgau and Veraison. The winery hosts a number of events, including a

Cajun blues festival each June. ✉ *687 Hubbard Creek Rd., Umpqua* ☎ *541/459–5120* 🌐 *www.henryestate.com.*

Rogue-Umpqua River Scenic Byway

SCENIC DRIVE | Roseburg is the starting point for this dramatic route that climbs east through dense stands of old-growth Douglas fir and hemlock trees and into the Cascade Range for about 80 miles en route to the northern entrance to Crater Lake National Park (this section, which runs alongside the North Umpqua Wild and Scenic River, is also known as Highway 138). Just after Diamond Lake, the route turns southwest via Highways 230, 62, and 234 along a stunning stretch of the Rogue River, before ending northeast of Medford in the small town of Eagle Point. If you're planning to drive this entire 172-mile route, give yourself at least six hours (and as many as nine) to stop here and there to enjoy the scenery, and perhaps even hike some portions of the North Umpqua Trail. Signposted trailheads along the drive lead to some magnificent waterfalls—Deadline Falls and Fern Creek Falls are a couple of favorites. Note that this route differs from the Umpqua River Scenic Byway, which you can also access near Roseburg. This stretch of Highway 138 starts about 15 miles north of Roseburg in Oakland and twists and turns for 66 miles over the Coast Range—through famous fishing holes and rugged timber towns—before ending at U.S. 101 (aka the Oregon Coast Highway) in Reedsport, on the central coast. ✉ *Hwy. 138* ✥ *It runs east starting at the junction with Hwy. 99* 🌐 *www.blm.gov/or/districts/roseburg/recreation/ScenicByway.*

★ **Wildlife Safari**

ZOO | **FAMILY** | Come face-to-face with some 500 free-roaming animals at the 600-acre drive-through wildlife park. Inhabitants include alligators, bobcats, cougars, gibbons, lions, giraffes, grizzly bears, Tibetan yaks, Siberian tigers, and more than 100 additional species. There's also a petting zoo, a miniature train, up-close animal feedings and encounters, and engaging wildlife talks. The admission price includes two same-day drive-throughs. This nonprofit zoological park is a respected research facility with full accreditation from the American Zoo and Aquarium Association, with a mission to conserve and protect endangered species through education and breeding programs. Through its cheetah breeding program, for example, more than 215 of these animals have been born here. ✉ *1790 Safari Rd., Winston* ☎ *541/679–6761* 🌐 *www.wildlifesafari.net* 🎫 *$22.*

Restaurants

Brix

$$ | **AMERICAN** | This handsome downtown American bistro with exposed-brick walls, curving leather banquettes, and high ceilings serves reasonably priced breakfast and lunch fare daily, and somewhat more upscale dinners. Highlights include mango-mahi nachos, and Sicilian-style, rare-seared ahi tuna steak with olive tapenade; several more affordable sandwiches, burgers, and salads are available, too. **Known for:** mix of affordable and upscale dishes; impressive wine and cocktail list; pumpkin-cranberry ricotta pancakes at breakfast. $ *Average main: $18* ✉ *527 S.E. Jackson St.* ☎ *541/440–4901* 🌐 *www.facebook.com/brixgrill/* ⏲ *No dinner Sun. and Mon.*

The Parrot House

$$$ | **AMERICAN** | This ornate Victorian house filled with antiques, chandeliers, and framed mirrors and artwork provides a grand setting for everything from a romantic dinner by the fireplace to a relaxed brunch or lunch with friends on the heated patio—you'll find both formal and casual spaces. The farm-to-table menu is similarly varied, with burgers, pizzas, pastas to more elaborately sauced steaks and seafood grills, and there's live music many evenings. **Known for:** setting inside a gracious Victorian house; lavish

Sunday brunch (with buffet and à la carte option); barrel-aged bourbons in the classy Reform Bar. $ *Average main: $28* ✉ *1851 S.E. Stephens St.* ☎ *541/580–0600* 🌐 *www.parrotthouseroseburg.com.*

★ True Kitchen + Bar

$$$ | **MODERN AMERICAN** | A dapper, upmarket downtown bistro with a friendly, easy-going vibe, True excels both in its gastropub menu that often draws on seasonal ingredients and arguably the region's best beverage program, which features a terrific selection of Umpqua Valley wines and Oregon craft beers. The cuisine borrows a bit from different parts of the world, with short-rib bao buns, shrimp and grits, and adobo-lime chicken among the favorites, and several juicy burgers to choose from as well. **Known for:** generous food deals during the daily (bar-seating only) happy hour; impressive craft cocktail list; creatively topped burgers. $ *Average main: $25* ✉ *629 S.E. Main St.* ☎ *541/900–1000* 🌐 *www.truekitchenandbar.com* ⏲ *Closed Sun. No lunch.*

Hotels

Hampton Inn & Suites Roseburg

$$ | **HOTEL** | Although its straight out of the Hampton Inn cookie-cutter mold, this clean and modern property offers the comfiest rooms of any property in town, and it's a quick drive from downtown. **Pros:** nice indoor pool and gym; conveniently located just off the interstate; rooms have microwaves and refrigerators. **Cons:** looks and feels like any other Hampton Inn; no pets allowed; not an especially inspired setting. $ *Rooms from: $162* ✉ *1620 N.W. Mulholland Dr.* ☎ *541/492–1212* 🌐 *www.hampton-inn3.hilton.com* *84 rooms* 🍽 *Free breakfast.*

★ The Steamboat Inn

$$$ | **B&B/INN** | The world's top fly-fishermen converge at this secluded forest inn, high in the Cascades above the North Umpqua River; others come simply to relax in the reading nooks or on the decks of the riverside guest cabins nestled below soaring fir trees. **Pros:** good option if en route to Crater Lake; access to some of the best fishing in the West; an excellent restaurant (open to the general public; call for hours). **Cons:** far from any towns or cities; often books up well in advance in summer; no TV or Wi-Fi. $ *Rooms from: $215* ✉ *42705 N. Umpqua Hwy., Idleyld Park* ✣ *38 miles east of Roseburg on Hwy. 138, near Steamboat Creek* ☎ *541/498–2230* 🌐 *www.thesteamboatinn.com* *20 units* 🍽 *No meals.*

Nightlife

Backside Brewing

BREWPUBS/BEER GARDENS | Situated just north of downtown, this lively, rambling brewpub turns out well-crafted pilsners, red ales, and hazy IPAs. There are pool tables and sports on TV in the spacious taproom and a grassy lawn with picnic tables outside. They serve pretty tasty pizza, too. ✉ *1640 N.E. Odell Ave.* ☎ *541/671–2552.*

Activities

FISHING

You'll find some of the best river fishing in Oregon along the Umpqua, with smallmouth bass, shad, steelhead, salmon (coho, Chinook, and sockeye), and sturgeon—the biggest reaching 10 feet in length—among the most prized catches. In addition to the Steamboat Inn, several outfitters in the region provide full guide services, which typically include all gear, boats, and expert leaders. There's good fishing in this region year-round, with sturgeon and steelhead at their best during the colder months, Chinook and coho salmon thriving in the fall, and most other species prolific in spring and summer.

Kayaking Rainey Falls on the Rogue River

Big K Guest Ranch

FISHING | Set along a 10-mile span of the upper Umpqua River near Elkton (about 35 miles north of Roseburg), Big K is a 2,500-acre guest ranch. Accommodations are geared primarily to groups and corporate retreats, but the ranch offers individual half- and full-day fishing trips starting at $350 for one or two anglers, and two-day/three-night fishing and lodging packages (meals included) for around $940 per person. Adventures include fly-fishing for smallmouth bass and summer steelhead, as well as spin-casting and drift-boat fishing. ✉ *20029 Hwy. 138 W, Elkton* ☎ *541/584–2295* 🌐 *www.big-k.com.*

Oregon Angler

FISHING | One of the state's most respected and knowledgeable guides, Todd Hannah, specializes in jet-boat and drift-boat fishing excursions along the famed "Umpqua Loop," an 18-mile span of river that's long been lauded for exceptional fishing. Full-day trips start around $200 per person. ✉ *Elkton* ☎ *541/459–7922* 🌐 *www.theoregonangler.com.*

RAFTING

There's thrilling Class III and higher white-water rafting along the North Umpqua River, with several outfitters providing trips ranging from a few hours to a few days throughout the year.

North Umpqua Outfitters

WHITE-WATER RAFTING | Since 1987, this trusted provider has offered half-, full-, and two-day rafting and kayaking trips, starting at $105 per person, along the frothy North Umpqua. ✉ *Idleyld Park* ☎ *888/454–9696* 🌐 *www.umpquarivers.com.*

Grants Pass

70 miles south of Roseburg on I–5.

"It's the Climate!" So says a confident 1950s vintage neon sign presiding over Josephine County's downtown. Grants Pass bills itself as Oregon's white-water

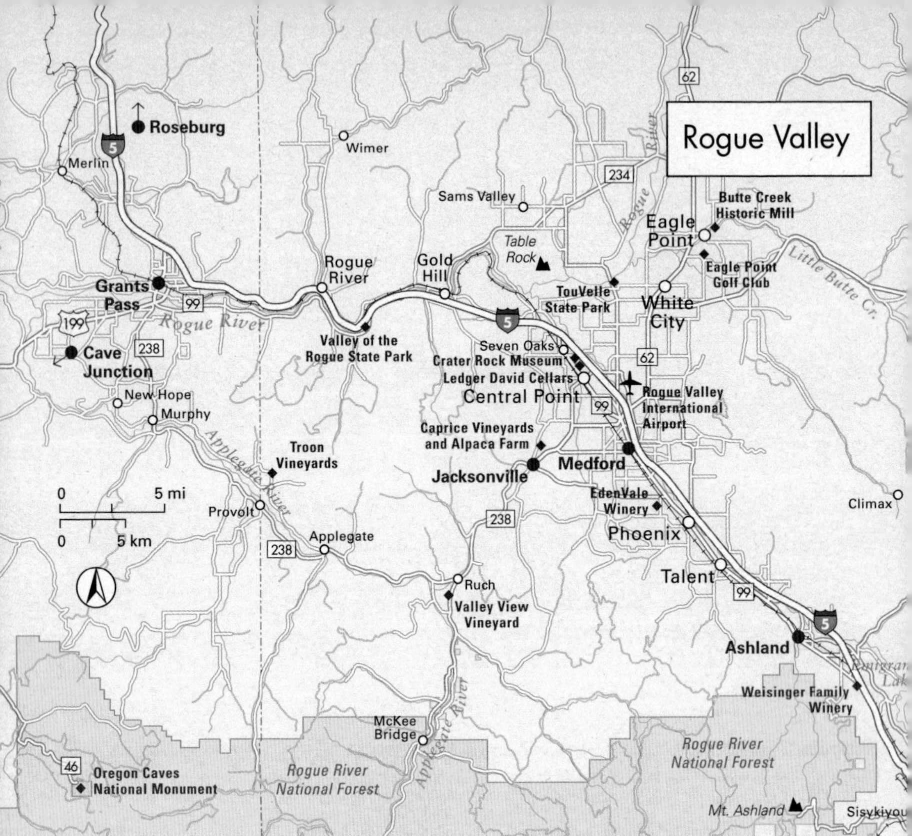

capital: the Rogue River, preserved by Congress in 1968 as a National Wild and Scenic River, runs right through town. Downtown Grants Pass is a National Historic District, an attractive little enclave of 19th-century brick storefronts housing a mix of folksy businesses harking back to the 1950s and newer, trendier cafés and boutiques. It's all that white water, however, that compels most visitors—and not a few moviemakers (*The River Wild* and *Rooster Cogburn* were both filmed here). If the river alone doesn't serve up enough natural drama, the sheer rock walls of nearby Hellgate Canyon rise 250 feet.

GETTING HERE AND AROUND

Grants Pass is easily reached via Interstate 5, and it's also where Highway 238 curves in a southeasterly direction through the Applegate Valley wine region en route to Jacksonville and Medford (a very pretty alternative route to driving south on Interstate 5), and where U.S. 199 cuts southwest toward Oregon Caves National Monument and, eventually, the northernmost section of California's coast (and Redwood National Park). Many visitors to the southern Oregon coastline backtrack inland up U.S. 199 to create a scenic loop drive, ultimately intersecting with Interstate 5 at Grants Pass. Medford's airport is a 30-mile drive south.

ESSENTIALS

VISITOR INFORMATION Experience Grants Pass. ✉ *198 S.W. 6th St.* ☎ *541/476–7574* 🌐 *www.travelgrantspass.com.*

Sights

Del Rio Vineyards & Winery
WINERY/DISTILLERY | In the small town of Gold Hill, about 15 miles east of Grants Pass, one of the Rogue Valley's most established vineyards stands out as much for its elegant wines as for its setting—the tasting room is set inside one of the region's oldest structures, the former Rock Point Hotel, which dates to 1865. In this grand building or out on the breezy patio, you can sample Del Rio's finest bottles, including an age-worthy Claret Bordeaux-style blend, a heady Rhône-style Syrah, and the most appealing rosés in the valley. Del Rio manages about 300 acres of grapes and sends its fruit to more than 20 wineries on the West Coast. ✉ *52 N. River Rd., Gold Hill* ☎ *541/855–2062* 🌐 *www.delriovineyards.com.*

The Oregon Vortex and House of Mystery
MUSEUM | In southern Oregon, between Grants Pass and Medford, there's a place that seems to defy all the laws of physics—where a ball rolls uphill and a person's height appears to change as they move. Optical illusion or some strange paranormal activity? That question has made the Oregon Vortex and House of Mystery a popular diversion since the 1930s. ✉ *4303 Sardine Creek Left Fork Rd., Gold Hill* ✣ *27 miles northeast of Grants Pass on I–5 S* ☎ *541/855–1543* 🌐 *www.oregonvortex.com* 🎟 *$13.75* ⏲ *Closed Nov.–Feb.*

★ **Troon Vineyards**
WINERY/DISTILLERY | Few winemakers in southern Oregon have generated more buzz than Troon, whose swank tasting room and winery is patterned after a French country villa. Troon produces relatively small yields of exceptional wines more typical of Sonoma than Oregon (Malbec and Zinfandel are the heavy hitters), but they also offer less typical U.S. bottles, such as Vermentino orange wines and Tannat. The winery is 14 miles southeast of downtown Grants Pass, in the northern edge of the Applegate Valley; there's a second Troon tasting room in Carlton, in the Willamette Valley. ✉ *1475 Kubli Rd.* ☎ *541/846–9900* 🌐 *www.troonvineyard.com.*

Wildlife Images Rehabilitation Center
ZOO | **FAMILY** | Begun in 1981 as a nonprofit care center for orphaned, injured, and otherwise in-need wildlife, this 24-acre facility on the Rogue River also educates the public by offering tours of the property and opportunities to view the animals, which include bobcats, bears, eagles, owls, otters, and dozens of other species native to the region. ✉ *11845 Lower River Rd.* ☎ *541/476–0222* 🌐 *www.wildlifeimages.org* 🎟 *$14* ⏲ *Closed Mon.–Thurs.*

★ **Wooldridge Creek Winery**
WINERY/DISTILLERY | A trip to this peaceful hillside winery in the Applegate Valley offers the chance to view a herd of adorable dairy goats who provide the milk that Wooldridge uses to produce its organic fresh and aged cheeses. Enjoy a platter of cheeses along with housemade charcuterie while you relax on the patio, sipping the winery's exceptional estate wines, including Malbec, Pinot Noir, Tempranillo, and Chardonnay. If you're in downtown Grants Pass, you can enjoy these same treats at Wooldridge's terrific little tasting room, VinFarm, which also serves a full menu of lunch, dinner, and Sunday brunch items. ✉ *818 Slagle Creek Rd.* ☎ *541/846–6364* 🌐 *www.wcwinery.com.*

Restaurants

Gtano's
$$ | **LATIN AMERICAN** | Although set in a nondescript downtown shopping center, this cozy and welcoming restaurant is cheerful inside, and the kitchen turns out superb Nuevo Latino cuisine. Specialties include the starter of Puerto Rico "nachos," with Jack cheese, black beans, chicken, grilled pineapples,

and mango salsa; and hearty main dishes, such as Peruvian-style grilled pork ribs with aji amarillo sauce, and Bolivian-style steak strips with a smoky roasted-tomato sauce. **Known for:** fresh-fruit margaritas; guacamole prepared table-side; a variety of Mexican burritos, tacos, and enchiladas. *Average main: $18* *218 S.W. G St.* *541/507–1255* *Closed Sun. and Mon.*

★ Ma Mosa's

$ | **AMERICAN** | Sustainability is the name of the game at this lively breakfast and lunch café in downtown Grants Pass, with a cozy dining room of colorfully painted tables and mismatched chairs, and a large adjacent patio with picnic tables and lush landscaping. The kitchen sources from local farms and purveyors to create beer-battered fried chicken and waffles, kale Caesar salads, and line-caught-fish tacos with seasonal slaw and house-made salsa. **Known for:** refreshing mimosa and other cocktails at brunch; pet-friendly patio; coconut rice porridge topped with seasonal fruit and granola. *Average main: $11* *118 N.W. E St.* *541/479–0236* *www.mamosas.com* *Closed Mon. and Tues. No dinner.*

★ Twisted Cork Wine Bar

$$ | **WINE BAR** | With a mission to showcase southern Oregon's fast-growing reputation for acclaimed vino, this dapper, art-filled space lends a bit of urbane sophistication to downtown Grants Pass. In addition to pouring varietals from throughout the Umpqua and Rogue valleys, Twisted Cork carries wines from more than 115 wineries throughout the Northwest, along with a few from California, and it offers a menu of small plates ideal for sharing—fruit-and-cheese plates, cured meats—as well as creative and quite affordable larger plates, including pomegranate-cinnamon flank steak, ginger-glazed salmon, and wild-mushroom flatbread with butternut-mint hummus. **Known for:** local ports and dessert wines; shareable platters of cheese and charcuterie; a good mix of affordable and fancier menu options. *Average main: $19* *210 S.W. 6th St.* *541/295–3094* *www.thetwistedcorkgrantspass.com* *Closed Sun. and Mon.*

Hotels

Lodge at Riverside

$$$ | **HOTEL** | At this contemporary lodge at the southern end of downtown, the pool and many rooms overlook the Rogue River, and all but a few rooms, furnished with stylish country house–inspired armoires, plush beds, and oil paintings, have private balconies or patios; suites have river-rock fireplaces and Jacuzzi tubs. **Pros:** central location overlooking the river; spacious rooms, many with balconies; very good breakfasts. **Cons:** no restaurant on-site; some rooms contend with a bit of traffic noise; rates can get steep in summer. *Rooms from: $205* *955 S.E. 7th St.* *541/955–0600, 877/955–0600* *www.thelodgeatriverside.com* *33 rooms* *Free breakfast.*

★ Weasku Inn

$$$ | **B&B/INN** | Pacific Northwest–inspired art, handmade furnishings, and fine fabrics fill this rambling timber-frame home overlooking the Rogue River, 11 handsomely outfitted cabins, and an A-frame bungalow that comprise the most luxurious accommodations between Ashland and Eugene. **Pros:** set directly on the Rogue River; impeccably decorated; evening wine reception and full hot breakfast included. **Cons:** 10-minute drive east of downtown; you may hear some road noise if you're in the main lodge; no restaurant on-site. *Rooms from: $210* *5560 Rogue River Hwy., Wolf Creek* *541/471–8000, 800/493–2758* *www.weaskuinn.com* *17 rooms* *Free breakfast.*

Wolf Creek Inn & Tavern

$ | **B&B/INN** | Following a multiyear closure and renovation, one of the Pacific

Northwest's most historic inns is once again open for overnight stays in the homey, old-fashioned rooms and meals in the convivial tavern. **Pros:** exudes historic charm; paranormal ghost-hunting tours are available; enchanting restaurant, known especially for its Sunday brunch. **Cons:** in a small town 20 miles north of Grants Pass; you can sometimes hear Interstate 5 traffic in the distance; restaurant is closed some nights for dinner. *Rooms from: $90* ✉ *100 Front St.* ☎ *541/866–2474* 🌐 *www.wolfcreekinn.com* *9 rooms* *No meals.*

Bohemian Bar & Bistro
BARS/PUBS | A chatter-filled, brick-walled modern tavern in the historic district of downtown Grants Pass, Bohemian is a great option for well-prepared cocktails, and it's also a great choice for a late dinner, dessert, or even happy hour snacking in the afternoon. ✉ *233 S.W. G St.* ☎ *541/471–7158* 🌐 *www.bohemianbarandbistro.com.*

The Glass Forge
ART GALLERIES | **FAMILY** | Check out the extensive array of colorful, contemporary glass art, from lamps to vases to paperweights, at this spacious gallery that also offers tours and demonstrations. ✉ *501 S.W. G St.* ☎ *541/955–0815* 🌐 *www.glassforge.com.*

RAFTING

More than a dozen outfitters guide white-water rafting trips along the Rogue River in and around Grants Pass. In fact, this stretch of Class III rapids ranks among the best in the West. The rafting season lasts from about July through August and often into September, and the stretch of river running south from Grants Pass, with some 80 frothy rapids, is exciting but not treacherous, making it ideal for novices, families, and others looking simply to give this enthralling activity a try.

Morrisons Rogue Wilderness Adventures
WHITE-WATER RAFTING | If you're up for an adventure that combines rafting with overnight accommodations, consider booking one of these exciting excursions that run along a 34-mile stretch of the Rogue River. They last for four days and three nights, with options for both lodge and camping stays along the way. Half- and full-day trips are also available. ✉ *325 Galice Rd., Merlin* ☎ *800/336–1647, 541/476–3825* 🌐 *www.rogueriverraft.com* *From $69.*

Orange Torpedo Trips
WHITE-WATER RAFTING | One of the most reliable operators on the Rogue River offers half-day to several-day trips, as well as relaxed dinner-and-wine and morning float trips along a calmer stretch of river. Klamath and North Umpqua river trips are also available. ✉ *210 Merlin Rd., Merlin* ☎ *541/479–5061, 800/635–2925* 🌐 *www.orangetorpedo.com* *From $69.*

RECREATIONAL AREAS

Rogue River–Siskiyou National Forest, Grants Pass
PARK—SPORTS-OUTDOORS | In the Klamath Mountains and the Coast Range of southwestern Oregon, the 2-million-acre forest contains the 35-mile-long Wild and Scenic section of the Rogue River, which races through the Wild Rogue Wilderness Area, and the Illinois and Chetco Wild and Scenic rivers, which run through the 180,000-acre Kalmiopsis Wilderness Area. Activities include white-water rafting, camping, and hiking, but many hiking areas require trail-park passes. You can get advice on exploring the rivers and forest, and buy passes both online and at the Grants Pass Wild Rivers Ranger District office. ✉ *2164 N.E. Spalding Ave.* ☎ *541/471–6500* 🌐 *www.fs.usda.gov/rogue-siskiyou.*

Valley of the Rogue State Park

PARK—SPORTS-OUTDOORS | A 1¼-mile hiking trail follows the bank of the Rogue, the river made famous by novelist and fisherman Zane Grey; it joins with a picturesque 4-mile stretch of the multiuse Rogue River Greenway Trail, which will eventually span 30 miles and connect Grants Pass with Gold Hill and Central Point. There's a campground along 3 miles of shoreline with full RV hookups as well as yurts (some of them pet-friendly). Day visitors appreciate the picnic tables, walking trails, playgrounds, and restrooms. ✉ *3792 N. River Rd., Gold Hill* ✈ *12 miles east of Grants Pass* ☎ *541/582–1118, 800/551–6949* 🌐 *www.oregonstateparks.org.*

Medford

30 miles southeast of Grants Pass on I–5.

Medford is the professional, retail, trade, and service hub for eight counties in southern Oregon and northern California. As such, it offers more professional and cultural venues than might be expected for a city of its size (with a population of about 82,000). The historic downtown has shown signs of gentrification and rejuvenation in recent years, with a rapidly growing craft-brewing and distilling scene having taken hold, and in the outskirts you'll find several major shopping centers and the famed fruit and gourmet-food mail-order company Harry & David.

Lodging tends to be cheaper in Medford than in nearby Ashland or Jacksonville, although cookie-cutter chain properties dominate the hotel landscape. The city is also 75 miles southwest of Crater Lake and 80 miles northeast of the Oregon Caves, making it an affordable and convenient base for visiting either.

GETTING HERE AND AROUND

Medford is in the heart of the Rogue Valley on Interstate 5, and is home to the state's third-largest airport, Rogue Valley International. A car is your best way to get around the city and surrounding area.

ESSENTIALS

VISITOR INFORMATION Travel Medford. ✉ *101 E. 8th St.* ☎ *541/776–4021, 800/469–6307* 🌐 *www.travelmedford.org.*

Sights

Crater Rock Museum

MUSEUM | Jackson County's natural history and collections of the Roxy Ann Gem and Mineral Society are on display at this impressive 12,000-square-foot museum in Central Point (6 miles northwest of Medford). Fossils, petrified wood, scrimshaw, fluorescent rocks, thunder eggs, and precious minerals from throughout Oregon and elsewhere in the West are included, plus works of glass by renowned artist Dale Chihuly. ✉ *2002 Scenic Ave., Central Point* ☎ *541/664–6081* 🌐 *www.craterrock.com* 🎫 *$7* ⏲ *Closed Sun. and Mon.*

Dancin Vineyard

WINERY/DISTILLERY | This gorgeous wine estate with a handsome tasting room and patio is technically in Medford, but it's actually closer to historic downtown Jacksonville and a great stop if you're exploring either area. Dancin turns out an interesting mix of wines, from a jammy Zinfandel to a bright, bramble-accented Barbera that's a perfect match with any of the artisanal pizzas served from the tasting room kitchen. ✉ *4477 S. Stage Rd.* ☎ *541/245–1133* 🌐 *www.dancin.com* ⏲ *Closed Mon. and Tues. (also Wed. in winter).*

EdenVale Winery and Orchards

WINERY/DISTILLERY | Four miles southwest of downtown Medford amid a bucolic patch of fruit orchards, this winery and tasting room adjoins a stately 19th-century white-clapboard farmhouse surrounded by flower beds and vegetable gardens. Inside the tasting room you can sample and buy EdenVale's noted reds, a late-harvest dessert Viognier, a white port, and a first-rate cider produced with estate-grown pears. ✉ *2310 Voorhies Rd.* ☎ *541/512–2955* 🌐 *www.edenvalleyorchards.com.*

Kriselle Cellars

WINERY/DISTILLERY | About 12 miles north of Medford on the way to Crater Lake and near the area's two famous Table Rock hikes, Kriselle offers tastings in an airy, contemporary wood-frame bar with spectacular vineyard and Cascades Range views and spacious patio. The winery produces one of the best Sauvignon Blancs in Oregon, along with a superb Cabernet Franc. ✉ *12956 Modoc Rd., Eagle Point* ☎ *541/830–8466* 🌐 *www.krisellecellars.com.*

★ Ledger David Cellars

WINERY/DISTILLERY | Sandwiched handily between Rogue Creamery and Lillie Belle Chocolates in the small downtown of Central Point, this boutique winery produces an interesting portfolio of wines that earn top praise at competitions and from major critics. Standouts include a bright, balanced Chenin Blanc and a berry-forward, medium-body Sangiovese. Enjoy your tasting on the patio if it's a nice day. ✉ *245 N. Front St., Central Point* ☎ *541/664–2218* 🌐 *www.ledgerdavid.com.*

Rogue River–Siskiyou National Forest, Medford

NATIONAL/STATE PARK | Covering 1.7 million acres, this immense tract of wilderness woodland has fishing, swimming, hiking, and skiing. Motorized vehicles and equipment—even bicycles—are prohibited in the 113,849-acre Sky Lakes Wilderness, south of Crater Lake National Park. Its highest point is the 9,495-foot Mt. McLoughlin. Access to most of the forest is free, but there are fees at some trailheads. ✉ *Forest Office, 3040 Biddle Rd.* ☎ *541/618–2200* 🌐 *www.fs.usda.gov/rogue-siskiyou.*

Rogue River Views

Nature lovers who want to see the Rogue River at its loveliest can take a side trip to the Avenue of the Boulders, Mill Creek Falls, and Barr Creek Falls, off Highway 62, near Prospect, which is about 45 miles northeast of Medford—it's a scenic one-hour drive, and it's on the way to Crater Lake. Here the wild waters of the upper Rogue foam past volcanic boulders and the dense greenery of the Rogue River National Forest.

Rogue Valley Family Fun Center

LOCAL INTEREST | FAMILY | You'll find an impressive array of kids' games and recreation at this complex just off Exit 33 of Interstate 5. Miniature golf, batting cages, a golf driving range, bumper boats, and go-karts are among the offerings, and there's also a video arcade and game room. ✉ *1A Peninger Rd., Central Point* ☎ *541/664–4263* 🌐 *www.rvfamilyfuncenter.com.*

★ Table Rock

LOCAL INTEREST | This pair of monolithic rock formations rise some 700 to 800 feet above the valley floor. Operated by a partnership between the Bureau of Land Management and the Nature Conservancy, the Table Rock formations and surrounding 4,864 acres of wilderness afford panoramic valley views from their summits, and glorious wildflower viewing and migratory bird-watching in spring. This is one of the best venues in the Rogue Valley for hiking; you can reach Lower Table Rock on a moderately challenging trail, and Upper Table Rock via a shorter, less-steep route. ✉ *Off Table Rock Rd., Central Point* ⊕ *About 10 miles north of Medford and just a couple of miles north of TouVelle State Park* ☎ *541/618–2200* 🌐 *www.blm.gov.*

Restaurants

Elements Tapas Bar

$$$ | **TAPAS** | A stylish setting and a taste of impressively authentic Spanish fare—these are the draws of this handsome tapas restaurant in downtown Medford's turn-of-the-20th-century "Goldy" building. Pass around plates of mussels in romesco sauce, apricot-braised-pork empanadas, chorizo-studded Andalucian paella, and lamb-sausage flatbread, while sampling selections from the lengthy beer and cocktail menus. **Known for:** late-night dining; several types of paella (that serves three to four); extensive, international beer, wine, and cocktail selection. *Average main: $25* *101 E. Main St.* *541/779–0135* *www.elementsmedford.com* *No lunch.*

Jaspers Café

$ | **BURGER** | This cute roadhouse-style building a few miles northwest of downtown Medford has made a name for itself serving absurdly large, decadently topped, and deliciously crafted burgers. Polish off the chuck wagon wild-boar burger with maple-glazed bacon, country gravy, cheddar, a hash-brown patty, and a fried egg, and you probably won't be experiencing any hunger pangs for the rest of the day; veggie and game (from lamb to antelope to kangaroo) burgers are offered, too. **Known for:** old-fashioned shakes and malts in about 20 flavors; tasty sides—sweet potatoes, pork pot stickers; excellent craft beer and wine selection. *Average main: $9* *2739 N. Pacific Hwy.* *541/776–5307* *www.jasperscafe.com.*

Hotels

Inn on the Commons

$ | **HOTEL** | This smartly revamped and reasonably priced hotel with a pool and excellent restaurant is within walking distance of downtown Medford's restaurants and shops as well as leafy Hawthorne Park and the Rogue River (which some rooms have views of). **Pros:** prettier and more distinctive decor than most of Medford's chain properties; a branch of Ashland's notable Larks restaurant is on-site; free passes to the health club across the street. **Cons:** some rooms have street and freeway traffic noise; busy downtown location; although nicely updated, it's much older than several new chain properties in town. *Rooms from: $107* *200 N. Riverside Ave.* *541/779–5811, 866/779–5811* *www.innatthecommons.com/* *118 rooms* *Free breakfast.*

Resort at Eagle Point

$$ | **HOTEL** | The setting adjacent to one of the state's top golf courses is a major draw for this small boutique hotel with a dozen contemporary chalet-style suites featuring fireplaces and either balconies or patios. **Pros:** adjacent to and overlooking a beautiful golf course; peaceful setting; location handy for visiting Rogue Valley and Crater Lake. **Cons:** remote setting about a 20-minute drive from Medford; setting is less exciting for non-golfers; no elevator for upper-level rooms. *Rooms from: $150* *Eagle Point Golf Club, 100 Eagle Point Dr., Eagle Point* *541/879–3700* *www.resortateaglepoint.com* *12 rooms* *Free breakfast.*

Rodeway Inn–Medford

$ | **HOTEL** | If you're on a budget and seeking a simple and immaculately clean base camp, check into this friendly, family-run '50s vintage motor court on the city's south side. **Pros:** vintage charm; convenient to sights in Medford as well Jacksonville and Ashland; super low rates. **Cons:** few amenities and luxuries; rather dated (though that's part of the charm); bland setting on busy commercial strip. *Rooms from: $74* *901 S. Riverside Ave.* *541/776–9194* *www.choicehotels.com* *40 rooms* *Free breakfast.*

Nightlife

Common Block Brewing

BREWPUBS/BEER GARDENS | This convivial downtown spot with a huge patio is a great microbrewery pick whether you're a serious beer aficionado or you're just seeking a laid-back spot to quaff a pint or two of Tangerine Squeeze IPA or Wild Turkey Bourbon barrel–aged Stout and enjoy good pizza and elevated pub food. ✉ *315 E. 5th St.* ☎ *541/326–2277* 🌐 *www.commonblockbrewing.com.*

Immortal Spirits & Distillery Company

BARS/PUBS | Part of the boom of craft beverage makers that's redefining downtown Medford, this inviting tasting room with tables fashioned out of barrels and rotating art exhibits offers a full bar and restaurant with creative (and big) burgers and sandwiches and creative cocktails. But you can also just stop in to sample Immortal's first-rate single-barrel whiskey, Genever-style gin, blackberry brandy, and other heady elixirs. ✉ *141 S. Central Ave.* ☎ *541/816–4344* 🌐 *www.immortalspirits.com.*

★ Jefferson Spirits

BARS/PUBS | This hip nightspot has helped to spur downtown Medford's ongoing renaissance by creating a swanky environment for hobnobbing and enjoying creative craft cocktails, like the blue linen, with gin, cucumber, lemon, and local blueberries. Barrel-aged cocktails are a specialty, and you'll also find local and international wines, mostly Oregon beers, and tasty pub fare. There's a similarly inviting branch in downtown Ashland. ✉ *404 E. Main St.* ☎ *541/622–8190* 🌐 *www.jeffersonspirits.com.*

★ The Urban Cork

WINE BARS—NIGHTLIFE | You can sit at a table or on a black leather sofa lining the brick wall as you enjoy one of the extensive selection of southern Oregon wines—more than 120 choices. Try one of the many flight options or order 2-ounce pours of whatever you'd care to try. There's tasting food to pair with your sips as well, including cheese and charcuterie plates, salads, and a flourless chocolate cake. ✉ *330 N. Fir St.* ☎ *541/500–8778* 🌐 *www.theurbancork.com.*

Craterian Theater at the Collier Center for the Performing Arts

ARTS CENTERS | This beautifully restored 750-seat 1920s performing arts center with state-of-the-art acoustics is steps from downtown restaurants and microbreweries and hosts a wide range of concerts and shows, including some big-name talents and national touring companies. ✉ *23 S. Central Ave.* ☎ *541/779–3000* 🌐 *www.craterian.org.*

Harry & David

FOOD/CANDY | Famous for holiday gift baskets, Harry & David is based in Medford and offers hour-long tours of its huge facility on weekdays at 9:15, 10:30, 12:30, and 1:45. The tours cost $5 per person, but the fee is refunded if you spend $40 in the mammoth Harry & David store, great for snagging picnic supplies to carry with you on any winery tour. Reservations are recommended, as space is limited. ✉ *1314 Center Dr.* ☎ *541/864–2278, 877/322–8000* 🌐 *www.harryanddavid.com.*

★ Lillie Belle Farms

FOOD/CANDY | Next door to Rogue Creamery, this artisanal chocolatier handcrafts outstanding chocolates using local, often organic ingredients. A favorite treat is the Smokey Blue Cheese ganache made with Rogue River blue, but don't overlook the dark-chocolate–marionberry bonbons (made with organic marionberries grown on-site) or the delectable hazelnut chews. ✉ *211 N. Front St., Central Point* ☎ *541/664–2815* 🌐 *www.lilliebellefarms.com.*

★ Rogue Creamery

FOOD/CANDY | Just a few miles up the road from Medford in the little town of Central Point, you'll find one of the planet's most respected cheese makers (in 2019, Rogue became the first U.S. cheese maker ever to take the top prize at the prestigious World Cheese Awards). Begun in 1935 by Italian immigrants and now run by David Gremmels, this factory store sells all of the company's stellar cheeses, from Smokey Blue to a lavender-infused cheddar, and you can often watch the production through a window. Delicious grilled-cheese sandwiches and local wines and beers are also available—enjoy them at one of the sidewalk tables outside. **■TIP→ Ardent fans of this place might want to check out Rogue Creamery Dairy Farm, outside Grants Pass, and about 30 miles away from Central Point. Tours of the milking operations and the farm are available, and you can buy cheese and other gourmet goods there as well.** ✉ *311 N. Front St., Central Point* ☎ *541/665–1155* 🌐 *www.roguecreamery.com.*

Activities

GOLF

Eagle Point Golf Club

GOLF | One of the most challenging and best-designed in southern Oregon, this course is 10 miles northeast of Medford and was designed by legendary architect Robert Trent Jones Jr. and adjoins an upscale boutique resort. ✉ *100 Eagle Point Dr., Central Point* ☎ *541/826–8225* 🌐 *www.resortateaglepoint.com* 🎫 *$55* 🏌 *18 holes, 6576 yards, par 72.*

HIKING

Table Rock is one of the best venues for hiking in the Rogue Valley. You reach Lower Table Rock by way of a moderately challenging 5½-mile round-trip trail, and Upper Table Rock via a shorter (about 3 miles round-trip) and less-steep route. The trailheads to these formations are a couple of miles apart—just follow the road signs from Table Rock Road, north of TouVelle State Park (reached from Exit 33 of Interstate 5).

Jacksonville

5 miles west of Medford on Hwy. 238.

This perfectly preserved town founded in the frenzy of the 1851 gold rush has served as the backdrop for several western flicks. It's easy to see why. Jacksonville is one of only a small number of towns corralled into the National Register of Historic Places lock, stock, and barrel. These days, a bounty of lively shops, eateries, and inns set in downtown's historic buildings and the world-renowned Britt Festivals (held from late July to mid-August) of classical, jazz, and pop music are the draw, rather than gold. Trails winding up from the town's center lead to the festival amphitheater, mid-19th-century gardens, exotic madrona groves, and an intriguing pioneer cemetery. The surrounding countryside contains a number of noteworthy wineries, making Jacksonville one of the prime base camps in the Rogue Valley for winery touring.

GETTING HERE AND AROUND

Most visitors to Jacksonville come by way of Medford, 5 miles east, on Highway 238—it's a scenic drive over hilly farmland and past vineyards. Alternatively, you can reach the town coming the other way on Highway 238, driving southeast from Grants Pass. This similarly beautiful drive through the Applegate Valley takes about 45 minutes.

ESSENTIALS

VISITOR INFORMATION Jacksonville Visitor Information Center. ✉ *185 N. Oregon St.* ☎ *541/899–8118* 🌐 *www.jacksonville-oregon.com.*

Sights

★ Jacksonville Cemetery

CEMETERY | FAMILY | A trip up the winding road—or, better yet, a hike via the old cart track marked Catholic access—leads to the resting place of the clans (the Britts, the Beekmans, and the Orths) that built Jacksonville. You'll also get a fascinating, if sometimes unattractive, view of the social dynamics of the Old West: older graves (the cemetery is still in use) are strictly segregated, Irish Catholics from Jews from Protestants. A somber granite plinth marks the pauper's field, where those who found themselves on the losing end of gold-rush economics entered eternity anonymously. The cemetery closes at sundown, and guided daytime and sunset strolls are offered about once a month in summer. ✉ *Cemetery Rd. at N. Oregon St.* ☎ *541/826–9939* 🌐 *www.friendsjvillecemetery.org.*

Quady North Tasting Room

WINERY/DISTILLERY | You can try the complex, mostly Rhône-inspired wines—such as Viognier and Syrah, and Grenache—of this respected Rogue Valley producer that uses grapes from a few different area vineyards. The cute, cozy, brick tasting room is one of the only ones within walking distance of downtown Jacksonville inns and restaurants. ✉ *255 E. California St.* ☎ *541/702–2123* 🌐 *www.quadynorth.com* ⏲ *Closed Tues.*

Rellik Winery and Alpaca Farm

FARM/RANCH | FAMILY | Among the many vineyards throughout the Rogue Valley, Rellik stands out both for producing well-balanced wines (including a quite tasty oak-aged Cabernet Sauvignon) and for having a herd of curious, friendly alpacas, which makes this a fun stop for the entire family. You can admire and even pet the alpacas, and sip wine while snacking on cheese and charcuterie on the tasting room or on the shaded patio. The vineyard is just over a mile up the road from historic Jacksonville. ✉ *970 Old Stage Rd., Central Point* ☎ *541/499–0449* 🌐 *www.rellikwinery.com.*

Restaurants

Back Porch Bar & Grill

$$ | SOUTHERN | For an excellent, mid-priced alternative to Jacksonville's more upscale eateries, head to this roadhouse-style clapboard building six blocks northeast of the town's historic main drag. Authentic central Texas–style barbecue is served here: chargrilled red-hot sausage, slow-cooked pork ribs, and ½-pound burgers, plus a few steak and pasta dishes. **Known for:** tangy slow-cooked barbecue; down-home, Wild West decor; good selection of local wines. 💲 *Average main: $19* ✉ *605 N. 5th St.* ☎ *541/899–8821* 🌐 *www.backporchjacksonville.com.*

C Street Bistro

$$ | MODERN EUROPEAN | Casual and warmly decorated with shelves of cookbooks, pickled veggies, jams, and wine bottles, and with a few choice outdoor tables that you should definitely consider on a softly breezy summer day, this welcoming bistro is a perfect lunch or dinner stop after a tasting or two at a nearby winery. The kitchen specializes in creative takes on comfort fare, including house-made pastas, brioche-bun burgers with fingerling potatoes, and Alsatian-style pizzas with garlic bechamel sauce, smoked ham, and Swiss cheese. **Known for:** terrific wine list; the market-fresh red meat and fish of the day specials; organic-crust pizzas. 💲 *Average main: $20* ✉ *230 E. C St.* ☎ *541/261–7638* 🌐 *www.cstbistro.com* ⏲ *Closed Sun. and Mon. No dinner Wed.*

★ Gogi's

$$$ | MODERN AMERICAN | This low-key favorite among foodies and locals lies just down the hill from Britt Gardens and serves sophisticated contemporary cuisine and a discerning selection of local and international wines. The menu changes regularly, but might feature squash-and-ricotta ravioli with pancetta, shallot confit, and Marsala brown butter sauce; or white-wine-and-tomato-braised lamb shank with Parmesan polenta, grilled broccolini, and fresh horseradish gremolata. **Known for:** terrific wine list; artfully presented, innovative dishes; excellent cheese and charcuterie boards. *Average main: $28* *235 W. Main St.* *541/899–8699* *www.gogisrestaurant.com* *Closed Sun.–Tues. No lunch.*

Hotels

Jacksonville Inn

$$ | **B&B/INN** | The spotless pioneer period antiques and the wealth of well-chosen amenities (fireplaces, saunas, whirlpool tubs, double steam showers) at this eight-room 1861-vintage inn—with four additional luxury cottages—evoke the Wild West with an urbane, sophisticated aesthetic. **Pros:** in heart of downtown historic district; one of the town's most historically significant buildings; very good restaurant on-site. **Cons:** rather old-fashioned decor for some tastes; on busy street; often books up well ahead on summer weekends. *Rooms from: $165* *175 E. California St.* *541/899–1900, 800/321–9344* *www.jacksonvilleinn.com* *12 rooms* *Free breakfast.*

★ Magnolia Inn

$$ | **B&B/INN** | The nine warmly appointed, reasonably priced rooms in the Mediterranean-inspired 1920s inn steps from many of Jacksonville's best restaurants and boutiques have plush bedding, well-designed bathrooms, and tasteful but not overly frilly furnishings. **Pros:** walking distance from shops and dining; beautifully landscaped grounds; pet-friendly rooms. **Cons:** tends to book up far ahead on summer weekends; on a slightly busy street; excellent continental breakfast but no hot entrées. *Rooms from: $154* *245 N. 5th St.* *541/899–0255, 866/899–0255* *www.magnolia-inn.com* *9 rooms* *Free breakfast.*

Shopping

Jacksonville's historic downtown has several engaging galleries, boutiques, and gift shops. It's best just to stroll along California Street and its cross streets to get a sense of the retail scene.

The English Lavender Farm

SPECIALTY STORES | **FAMILY** | Part of the fun of browsing the lavender-infused essential oils, honeys, salted caramels, soaps, sachets, and other products here is visiting the pastoral Applegate Valley farm, which is about 20 miles southwest of Jacksonville. Although it's only open a few days a week in June and July, the farmstead has two big festivals each summer, and they sell their products throughout much of the rest of the year at farmers' markets in Jacksonville, Medford, and Grants Pass. *8040 Thompson Creek Rd., Applegate* *541/846–0375* *www.englishlavenderfarm.com.*

The Miners Bazaar

GIFTS/SOUVENIRS | **FAMILY** | An oddly endearing little gallery and gift shop that's set in a pretty, little, crooked, white house built during the town's mining heyday, the bazaar sells handmade jewelry, crafts, fiber arts, and other goods, and also offers its customers supplies and art kits to create their own DIY creations. It's great fun for kids and adults, and there's also a café serving locally sourced food as well as coffee and tea drinks, and local beer and wine. *235 E. California St.* *541/702–2380* *www.theminersbazaar.com.*

Ashland

20 miles southeast of Jacksonville and 14 miles southeast of Medford on I–5.

Known for its hilly streets dotted with restored Victorian and Craftsman houses, sophisticated restaurants and cafés, and surrounding natural scenery that's ideal for hiking, biking, rafting, and winery-hopping most of the year (and skiing in winter), Ashland's greatest claim to fame is the prestigious Oregon Shakespeare Festival, which attracts thousands of theater lovers every year, from late February to early November (prime season is June through September). The influx of visitors means that Ashland is more geared toward the arts, more eccentric, and more expensive than its size (about 21,000 people) might suggest. The mix of well-heeled theater tourists, bohemian students from Southern Oregon University, and dramatic show folk imbues the town with an urbane sensibility.

GETTING HERE AND AROUND

The southernmost community in the Rogue Valley, Ashland is also the first town you'll reach via Interstate 5 if driving north from California. You can also get here from Klamath Falls by driving west on winding, scenic Highway 66. Cascade Airport Shuttle offers door-to-door service from the airport to Ashland for about $30 to $35, and Uber and Lyft serve the area as well. A car isn't necessary to explore downtown and to get among many of the inns and restaurants, but it is helpful if you're planning to venture farther afield or visit more than one town, which most visitors do.

ESSENTIALS

VISITOR INFORMATION Ashland Chamber of Commerce and Visitors Information Center. ✉ *110 E. Main St.* ☎ *541/482–3486* 🌐 *www.ashlandchamber.com.*

Sights

Belle Fiore Winery

WINERY/DISTILLERY | As you pull up before this over-the-top, opulent, Mediterranean-inspired chateau nestled in the mountains a few miles east of downtown Ashland, it's easy to guess that it's a favorite destination for weddings. But the winery's elegant Pavilion Tasting Room is also a memorable spot to sip Belle Fiore's excellent Cabernet Franc, Riesling, and more than a dozen other finely crafted wines. There's an art gallery, too, and there's light dining on the upper level, with its gracious terrace. ✉ *100 Belle Fiore La.* ☎ *541/552–4900* 🌐 *www.bellefiorewine.com.*

★ Irvine & Roberts Winery

WINERY/DISTILLERY | This relatively young rising star among southern Oregon wineries specializes in two varietals the region generally isn't known for: Pinot Noir and Chardonnay. The vineyard's cooler, higher-elevation setting is perfect for these grapes usually associated with the Willamette Valley, and you can sample them, along with a refreshing, dry rosé of Pinot Noir—with one of their impressive cheese-and-charcuterie boards, perhaps—amid the cushy seating in the airy, modern tasting room and sweeping patio, with its grand mountain views. ✉ *1614 Emigrant Creek Rd.* ☎ *541/482–9383* 🌐 *www.irvinerobertsvineyards.com* 🕓 *Closed Mon. and Tues.*

★ Lithia Park

CITY PARK | FAMILY | The Allen Elizabethan Theatre overlooks this park, a wooded 93-acre jewel founded in 1916 that serves as Ashland's physical and psychological anchor. The park is named for the town's mineral springs, which supply water fountains by the band shell and on the town plaza—be warned that the slightly bubbly water has a strong and rather disagreeable taste. From morning through evening, picnickers, joggers, dog walkers, and visitors congregate amid this park's most popular areas, which include dozens of paved and unpaved trails, two duck ponds, a rose garden, a Japanese garden, and ice-skating rink, and a reservoir with a beach and swimming. A great way to get a sense of Lithia Park's vastness, and just how much wilderness there is in the northern section, is to make the 3-mile loop drive around its border. On weekends from mid-March through October, the park hosts a lively artisans' market, and free concerts take place Thursday evenings in summer. Each June the Oregon Shakespeare Festival opens its outdoor season by hosting the Feast of Will in the park, with music, dancing, bagpipes, and food. Tickets ($16) are available through the festival box office (☎ *541/482–4331* 🌐 *www.osfashland.org*). ✉ *N. Main St. at Winburn Way* 🌐 *www.ashland.or.us.*

★ Oregon Shakespeare Festival

FESTIVAL | From mid-February to early November, more than 100,000 Bard-loving fans descend on Ashland for some of the finest Shakespearean productions you're likely to see outside of London—plus works by both classic (Ibsen, O'Neill) and contemporary playwrights, including occasional world premieres. Eleven plays are staged in repertory in the 1,200-seat Allen Elizabethan Theatre, an atmospheric re-creation of the Fortune Theatre in London; the 600-seat Angus Bowmer Theatre, a state-of-the-art facility typically used for five different productions in a single season; and the 350-seat Thomas Theatre, which often hosts productions of new or experimental work. The festival, which dates to 1935, generally operates close to capacity, so it's important to book ahead. ✉ *15 S. Pioneer St.* ☎ *541/482–4331, 800/219–8161* 🌐 *www.osfashland.org.*

Schneider Museum of Art

MUSEUM | On the beautifully landscaped campus of Southern Oregon University, this museum includes a light-filled gallery devoted to special exhibits by Oregon, West Coast, and international artists. The permanent collection has grown considerably over the years, and includes pre-Columbian ceramics and works by such notables as Alexander Calder, George Inness, and David Alfaro Siqueiros. Hallways and galleries throughout the rest of the 66,000-square-foot complex display many works by students and faculty. **■ TIP→ Steps from the museum, the university's Hannon Library is a gorgeous building with a dramatic four-story atrium, plenty of comfy seating, and quite a few notable artworks as well.** ✉ *555 Indiana St.* ☎ *541/552–6245* 🌐 *www.sma.sou.edu* ⏲ *Closed Sun.*

ScienceWorks Hands-On Museum

MUSEUM | FAMILY | Geared toward kids but with some genuinely fascinating interactive exhibits that will please curious adults, too, this 26,000-square-foot science museum is close to the Southern Oregon University campus. In the main hall, you can explore touch-friendly exhibits on nanotechnology and sports science, and Discovery Island has curious games and puzzles geared to tots under age five. There's outdoor fun amid the plantings and pathways in the xeriscape Black Bear Garden, as well as a weather station, solar-power nursery, and kid-appropriate climbing wall. ✉ *1500 E. Main St.* ☎ *541/482–6767* 🌐 *www.scienceworksmuseum.org* 🎫 *$10* ⏲ *Closed Mon. and Tues.*

Weisinger Family Winery

WINERY/DISTILLERY | Just a short drive east of downtown, this long-established winemaker occupies a leafy hilltop with broad views of the surrounding mountains. Specialties include a fine Malbec, a well-respected Viognier, both conventional (crisp, minerally) and late-harvest (for dessert) Gewürztraminer, and a nicely balanced Tempranillo. The winery also rents out a stylish one-bedroom cottage with a kitchen and hot tub for overnight stays. ✉ *3150 Siskiyou Blvd.* ☎ *541/488–5989* 🌐 *www.weisingers.com.*

Ashland's 93-acre Lithia Park is named for the town's mineral springs, which supply water fountains by the band shell and on the town plaza.

Restaurants

Amuse

$$$$ | **PACIFIC NORTHWEST** | The Northwest-driven French cuisine here, which is infused with seasonal, organic meat and produce, changes regularly but might feature charcoal-grilled prawns, duck-leg confit, or braised pork shoulder. Try to save room for one of the local-fruit desserts, such as wild huckleberry tart with a pecan crust or Gravenstein apple crisp. **Known for:** intimate, romantic setting; reasonable $20 corkage fee to bring your own wine; delectable desserts and cheese-course options. *Average main: $31 15 N. 1st St. 541/488–9000 www.amuserestaurant.com Closed Mon. and Tues. No lunch.*

Hearsay

$$ | **MODERN AMERICAN** | The lush, tranquil garden patios of this sophisticated bar and bistro attached to the Oregon Cabaret Theatre and a short stroll from the Shakespeare Festival are so appealing it's easy to forget the charming interior, with its art deco–inspired paintings and live piano lounge. This restaurant inside a 1911 former church turns out eclectic, creative dishes like beer-cured salmon tartare and burgers topped with wild mushrooms, Rogue Oregonzola cheese, and truffle aioli, and the desserts are fabulous, too. **Known for:** romantic garden seating; creative craft cocktails; great happy hour deals (lounge only). *Average main: $22 40 S. 1st St. 541/625–0505 www.hearsayashland.com Closed Tues. No lunch.*

★ Hither Coffee & Goods

$$ | **MODERN AMERICAN** | Set in a minimalist downtown space with bare floors, a vaulted painted-white timber ceiling, and bounteous floral arrangements, Hither serves as an inviting coffeehouse and café by day, featuring heavenly pastries and artfully composed egg dishes and tartines. Later in the day, stop in for a light dinner of grilled duck breast with aioli and frites, or house-made pasta with 'nduja, bitter greens, and lemon bread crumbs, along with a glass or two from

the well-curated natural wine list. **Known for:** clean, uncluttered aesthetic; delicious sweets and baked goods; craft beverages, from Sightglass Coffee to local wines and beers. *Average main: $19* *376 E. Main St.* *541/625–4090* *www.hithermarket.com* *No dinner Sun.*

Larks

$$$ | **MODERN AMERICAN** | In a swanky yet soothing dining room off the lobby of the historic Ashland Springs Hotel, Larks pairs the freshest ingredients from local farms with great wines, artisanal chocolate desserts, and drinks, and features modern interpretations of classic comfort food, such as Southern fried chicken with bacon pan gravy. Dessert offerings include old-fashioned chocolate sundaes, s'mores, and a seasonal cheesecake selection. **Known for:** pretheater dining; outstanding Sunday brunch; fine cocktails in the adjoining 1920s bar. *Average main: $28* *Ashland Springs Hotel, 212 E. Main St.* *541/488–5558* *www.larksrestaurant.com.*

★ MÄS

$$$$ | **PACIFIC NORTHWEST** | Book ahead several days—or even weeks for Friday and Saturday—for the chance to dine at this intimate prix-fixe restaurant that features the modern, farm-to-table culinary masterpieces of young and extraordinary chef-owner Josh Dorcak. Feasts generally of 6 to 10 courses are available, with the seats at the cozy and lively chef's counter the most desirable—wine and sake pairings are available. **Known for:** exquisitely plated tasting menus; dining at the chef's counter; a hyper-local approach to Northwest cuisine. *Average main: $75* *141 Will Dodge Way* *Next to Yogurt Hut, off Lithia Way* *541/581–0090* *www.masashland.com* *Closed Mon.–Wed.*

Morning Glory

$ | **AMERICAN** | Expect a wait for a table, especially on weekend or summer mornings, when dining at this wildly popular, eclectically furnished, blue Craftsman-style bungalow across the street from Southern Oregon University. The extraordinarily good food emphasizes breakfast fare—omelets filled with crab, artichokes, Parmesan, and smoked-garlic cream and lemon-poppy waffles with seasonal berries—but the lamb burgers, pressed Cuban sandwiches, and other lunch items are tasty, too. **Known for:** large portions; long lines, especially for a table on the pretty patio; crab omelets and crab melts. *Average main: $14* *1149 Siskiyou Blvd.* *541/488–8636* *No dinner.*

★ New Sammy's Cowboy Bistro

$$$$ | **PACIFIC NORTHWEST** | Ardent foodies have been known to make reservations weeks in advance, especially for weekends, to dine in this stucco Southwest-style roadhouse a few miles northwest of Ashland. Surrounded by orchards and gardens, the menu finds its way into the exquisite—and mostly farm-to-table—Northwestern fare with typical dishes from the seasonal menu ranging from green-garlic flan with spiced Washington spot prawns, cherry tomatoes, avocado, and epazote to pan-roasted king salmon with garden gazpacho, three basils, and tapenade. **Known for:** artful desserts; funky yet romantic setting; nicely curated beer and wine list. *Average main: $32* *2210 S. Pacific Hwy.* *541/535–2779* *newsammys.com* *Closed Sun.–Tues.*

Peerless Restaurant & Bar

$$$ | **MODERN AMERICAN** | This hip neighborhood bistro and wine bar adjoins the stylish little Peerless Hotel and anchors the up-and-coming Railroad District, on the north side of downtown, just a few blocks from Main Street and the Shakespeare theaters. Regulars appreciate the well-crafted cocktails and thoughtful wine list as much as the consistently tasty locally sourced American food, such as fig-and-horseradish salad with apples and blue cheese and grilled lamb T-bone with apricot-glazed carrots and avocado-yogurt sauce. **Known for:** delicious

desserts with suggested drink pairings; first-rate cocktails; beautiful outdoor garden dining area. *Average main: $28* *265 4th St.* *541/488–6067* *www.peerlesshotel.com* *Closed Sun. and Mon. No lunch.*

Sammich

$ | **DELI** | In this unassuming deli tucked into a small shopping center across the street from Southern Oregon University, you'll find some of the biggest and tastiest sandwiches in the state—they've been featured on TV's *Diners, Drive-Ins and Dives,* and there's also a branch in Portland. Owner Melissa McMillan bases her menu on the Italian-style sandwiches of Chicago, where she's from, and unless you're absolutely starving, it's not a bad idea to order a half or share a whole with a friend. **Known for:** truly prodigious sandwiches; the Pastrami Zombie with Swiss, slaw, and Russian dressing on rye; grilled cheese with tomato soup. *Average main: $11* *424 Bridge St.* *541/708–6055* *www.sammichrestaurants.com* *No dinner.*

Coffee and Quick Bites

Noble Coffee Roasting

$ | **CAFÉ** | The fair-trade, organic beans used in the espresso drinks at Noble Coffee Roasting, in the hip Railroad District, are among the best in town. The spacious, high-ceilinged dining room is a comfy and attractive place to socialize or get work done while you sip and munch. **Known for:** cold-brew, ice-dripped, and other cool espresso drinks; tasty pastries; house-made Tonic sparkling beverage with coffee fruit, lemon, and agave. *Average main: $5* *281 4th St.* *541/488–3288* *www.noblecoffeeroasting.com.*

Hotels

The Oregon Shakespeare Festival has stimulated one of the most extensive networks of B&Bs in the Northwest—more than 30 in all. High season for Ashland-area bed-and-breakfasts is June–October.

Ashland B&B Network

The network provides referrals and has an online booking system for about a dozen of the town's top inns. *www.stayashland.com.*

★ Ashland Creek Inn

$$$$ | **B&B/INN** | Every plush suite in this converted late-19th-century mill has a geographic theme—the Normandy is outfitted with rustic country French prints and furniture, while Moroccan, Danish, and New Mexican motifs are among the designs in other units—and each sitting room–bedroom combo has its own entrance, a full kitchen or kitchenette, and a deck amid stunning gardens and just inches from burbling Ashland Creek. **Pros:** exceptionally good breakfasts; short walk to downtown shopping, Lithia Park, and theaters; enormous suites. **Cons:** among the priciest inns in town; limited common areas; two-night minimum stay most of the year. *Rooms from: $320* *70 Water St.* *541/482–3315* *www.ashlandcreekinn.com* *10 suites* *Free breakfast.*

★ Ashland Hills Hotel & Suites

$$ | **HOTEL** | Hoteliers Doug and Becky Neuman (who also run the excellent Ashland Springs Hotel and Lithia Springs Resort) transformed this long-shuttered '70s-era resort into a stylish yet affordable retro-cool compound, retaining the property's fabulous globe lights, soaring lobby windows, and beam ceilings while adding many period-style furnishings. **Pros:** great rates considering all the amenities; terrific restaurant on-site; attractive grounds, including patio and sundeck. **Cons:** just off the interstate a 10-minute drive from downtown; some rooms face parking lot; fitness rooms are small and dark. *Rooms from: $162* *2525 Ashland St.* *541/482–8310, 855/482–8310* *www.ashlandhillshotel.com* *173 rooms* *Free breakfast.*

Ashland Springs Hotel

$$ | **HOTEL** | Ashland's stately 1925 landmark hotel towers seven stories over the center of downtown, with 70 rooms done with a preponderance of gentle fall colors and unconventional decor—think French-inspired botanical-print quilts and lampshades with leaf designs. **Pros:** rich with history; upper floors have dazzling mountain views; the excellent Larks restaurant is on-site. **Cons:** central location translates to some street noise and bustle; many rooms are quite small; no gym (but discount at a local fitness center nearby). *Rooms from: $175* *212 E. Main St.* *541/488–1700, 888/795–4545* *www.ashlandspringshotel.com* *70 rooms* *Free breakfast.*

The Palm

$$ | **HOTEL** | This cheerfully restored, eco-friendly, midcentury modern complex has a hip, quirky vibe and offers the convenience of a downtown location with relatively moderate prices. **Pros:** retro-chic vibe; pretty gardens and a pool with cool deck chairs and cabanas; convenient location near Southern Oregon University and not far from theaters. **Cons:** on a busy street; the economical rooms are quite small; cabana rentals can be spendy on summer weekends. *Rooms from: $157* *1065 Siskiyou Blvd.* *541/482–2636, 800/691–2360* *www.palmcottages.com* *16 rooms* *No meals.*

The Winchester Inn

$$$$ | **B&B/INN** | **FAMILY** | Rooms and suites in this upscale Victorian have character and restful charm—some have fireplaces, refrigerators, and wet bars, and private exterior entrances, and most are well suited to having one or two children in the room. **Pros:** the adjacent Alchemy wine bar and restaurant serve outstanding international fare; one of the more child-friendly B&Bs in town; surrounded by lush gardens. **Cons:** among the more expensive lodgings in town; downtown location can feel a bit busy in summer; some rooms are reached via steep flights of stairs. *Rooms from: $295* *35 S. 2nd St.* *541/488–1113* *www.winchesterinn.com* *24 rooms* *Free breakfast.*

Nightlife

With its presence of college students, theater types, and increasing numbers of tourists (many of them fans of local wine), Ashland has developed quite a festive nightlife scene. Much of the activity takes place at bars inside some of downtown's more reputable restaurants in the center of town.

Caldera Brewery & Restaurant

BREWPUBS/BEER GARDENS | At this renowned brewery just off Interstate 5 you can sample the signature Hopportunity Knocks IPA, Old Growth Imperial Stout, and an extensive selection of tasty apps, burgers, and pub fare. *590 Clover La.* *541/482–4677* *www.calderabrewing.com.*

Ostras! Tapas + Bottle Shop

TAPAS BARS | There's definitely an impressive and extensive enough selection of beautifully plated Spanish tapas—half-shell oysters with cava mignonette, braised pork cheeks—to make this a sophisticated, high-ceilinged bar a dinner option (there's even paella). But, it's also one of the coolest little bars in southern Oregon, offering up a stellar list of Spanish and local wines as well as fine after-dinner drinks. *47 N. Main St.* *541/708–0528* *ostrasashland.com.*

Performing Arts

Oregon Cabaret Theatre

THEATER | Shakespeare isn't the only game in this town, although the presence of OSF no doubt contributes to the wealth of talented performers in Ashland. You can see some of the region's top talents in five or six musicals throughout the year at this handsome cabaret theater set inside a converted 1911 church, and the on-site restaurant serves tasty dinner and brunch fare to enjoy before each show. ✉ *241 Hargadine St.* ☎ *541/488–2902.*

Shopping

Bloomsbury Books

BOOKS/STATIONERY | If you're looking for a book copy of the work you're seeing at Oregon Shakespeare Festival, this cheerful, literary-minded indie bookshop in the center of town is sure to have it. Readings and book discussions are also offered regularly. ✉ *290 E. Main St.* ☎ *541/488–0029* 🌐 *www.bloomsburyashland.com.*

Gathering Glass Studio

CERAMICS/GLASSWARE | The striking, contemporary works of glassblower Keith Gabor are displayed in this spacious gallery and hot shop where you can also watch demonstrations and even take a class. ✉ *322 N. Pioneer St.* ☎ *541/488–4738* 🌐 *www.gatheringglass.com.*

Activities

MULTISPORT OUTFITTERS

Momentum River Expeditions

WHITE-WATER RAFTING | Known primarily for its multiday white-water rafting as well as fishing, hiking, trail running, and climbing trips, Momentum also offers excellent half- and full-day rafting adventures on the Rogue, Upper Klamath, and Scott rivers. ✉ *3195 E. Main St.* ☎ *541/488–2525* 🌐 *www.momentumriverexpeditions.com* ☞ *From $70.*

RAFTING

★ Noah's River Adventures

WHITE-WATER RAFTING | This long-running outfitter provides white-water rafting and wilderness fishing trips throughout the region—the company can lead single- or multiple-day adventures along the mighty Rogue River, the Upper Klamath, and—just across the border—in northern California, on the Salmon and Scott rivers. ✉ *53 N. Main St.* ☎ *541/488–2811, 800/858–2811* 🌐 *www.noahsrafting.com* ☞ *From $95.*

SKIING

Mt. Ashland Ski Area

SKIING/SNOWBOARDING | This winter-sports playground in the Siskiyou Mountains receives about 265 inches of snow annually and is halfway between San Francisco and Portland. The owners have invested heavily on upgrades in recent years, adding an impressive new chalet-style day lodge with rentals and a bar and restaurant. There are 23 trails, nearly all of them intermediate and advanced, in addition to chute skiing in a glacial cirque called the bowl. Two triple and two double chairlifts accommodate a vertical drop of 1,150 feet; the longest of the runs is 1 mile. A couple of days a week, usually Thursday and Friday, there's also lighted twilight skiing until 9 pm. Anytime of year the drive up the twisting road to the ski area is incredibly scenic, affording views of 14,162-foot Mt. Shasta, some 90 miles south in California. Free shuttle bus service from downtown Ashland is offered on weekends from mid-January through March. ✉ *Mt. Ashland Access Rd.* ✣ *Off Exit 6 from I–5, 18 miles south of downtown* ☎ *541/482–2897* 🌐 *www.mtashland.com* 🎫 *Lift ticket $52.*

Cave Junction

30 miles southwest of Grants Pass via U.S. 199, 60 miles west of Jacksonville via Hwy. 238 and U.S. 199.

One of southern Oregon's least populated and most pristine areas, Cave Junction and the surrounding Illinois Valley attract outdoors enthusiasts of all kinds for hiking, backpacking, camping, fishing, and hunting. Expect rugged terrain and the chance to view some of the tallest Douglas fir trees in the state. Other than those passing through en route from

Grants Pass to the northern California coast via U.S. 199, most visitors come here to visit Oregon Caves National Monument, one of the world's few marble caves (formed by erosion from acidic rainwater). Sleepy Cave Junction makes an engaging little base camp, its main drag lined with a handful of quirky shops, gas stations, and very casual restaurants.

GETTING HERE AND AROUND

Cave Junction lies along U.S. 199, the main road leading from Grants Pass. You can also get here by heading west from Jacksonville on Highway 238 to U.S. 199. From Cave Junction, head east on Highway 46 to reach Oregon Caves National Monument. Cave Junction is about a 75-minute drive southwest of Medford's regional airport. Alternatively, the small airport (served by Contour Airlines, with service from Oakland) in Crescent City, California, is the same distance.

ESSENTIALS

VISITOR INFORMATION Illinois Valley Chamber of Commerce. ✉ *201 Caves Hwy. (Hwy. 46)* ☎ *541/592–3326* 🌐 *www.ivchamberofcommerce.com.*

★ **Oregon Caves National Monument**

CAVE | Marble caves, large calcite formations, and huge underground rooms shape this rare adventure in geology. Guided cave tours take place late March through early November. The 90-minute half-mile tour is moderately strenuous, with low passageways, twisting turns, and more than 500 stairs; children must be at least 42 inches tall to participate. Cave tours aren't given in winter. Aboveground, the surrounding valley holds an old-growth forest with some of the state's largest trees, and offers some excellent and generally uncrowded hiking. Note that the park lodge, the Oregon Caves Chateau, is closed for a major renovation through 2020. ⚠ **GPS coordinates for the caves often direct drivers onto a mostly unpaved forest service road meant for four-wheel-drive vehicles. Instead, follow well-signed Highway 46 off U.S. 199 at Cave Junction, which is also narrow and twisting in parts; RVs or trailers more than 32 feet long are not advised.** ✉ *19000 Caves Hwy. (Hwy. 46)* ✣ *20 miles east of U.S. 199, 140 miles southwest of Crater Lake* ☎ *541/592–2100* 🌐 *www.nps.gov/orca* 🎫 *Park free, tours $10.*

Out 'n' About

$$ | **B&B/INN** | **FAMILY** | You sleep among the leaves in the tree houses of this extraordinary resort—the highest is 37 feet from the ground, one has an antique claw-foot bath, and another has separate kids' quarters connected to the main room by a swinging bridge. **Pros:** kids love the Swiss Family Robinson atmosphere; lots of fun activities are offered, from ziplining to horseback riding; amazingly quiet and peaceful. **Cons:** accommodations are extremely rustic; some units don't have private bathrooms; two-night minimum during week and three-night minimum weekends during spring to fall. [$] *Rooms from: $160* ✉ *300 Page Creek Rd.* ☎ *541/592–2208* 🌐 *www.treehouses.com* 🛏 *15 tree houses, 1 cabin* 🍽 *Free breakfast.*

Chapter 10

SEATTLE

Updated by AnnaMaria Stephens and Naomi Tomky

Sights ★★★★★

Restaurants ★★★★★

Hotels ★★★★☆

Shopping ★★★★☆

Nightlife ★★★☆☆

WELCOME TO SEATTLE

TOP REASONS TO GO

★ **Examine Seattle's architecture:** From the skyline-defining Space Needle to the architect-designed Seattle Center Library, the city offers aficionados plenty to admire.

★ **Appreciate art:** Visit the Seattle Art Museum and make time for a stroll in SAM's Olympic Sculpture Park on the Elliott Bay waterfront.

★ **Drink coffee:** Seattle may be the birthplace of Starbucks, but this is a city that takes coffee snobbery seriously, so be sure to explore.

★ **Cheer beer:** Tap into Seattle's craft beer scene, regularly ranked one of the best in the country.

★ **Indulge in fresh seafood:** First gawk at all the fabulous local produce and seafood at the Pike Place Market, and then visit some of Seattle's renowned restaurants to eat it.

1 **Downtown and Belltown.** Home to Pike Place Market and the Olympic Sculpture Park, respectively.

2 **South Lake Union and Queen Anne.** You'll find the Space Needle and the REI superstore here.

3 **Pioneer Square.** Seattle's oldest neighborhood.

4 **International District.** The Wing Luke Museum anchors this area.

5 **First Hill and the Central District.** Home to the Frye Art Museum.

6 **Capitol Hill.** The Hill is both young and hip and elegant and upscale.

7 **Fremont.** There is a mix of pricey boutiques and notable restaurants here.

8 **Ballard.** Visit Hiram M. Chittenden Locks.

9 **Wallingford.** At the ship canal is the wonderful waterfront Gas Works Park.

10 **The University District.** This area has all kinds of cuisine and a large student population.

11 **West Seattle.** California Avenue has lovely shops and restaurants.

12 **Puget Sound Islands.** Take a ferry to the islands of Bainbridge, Vashon, and Whidbey.

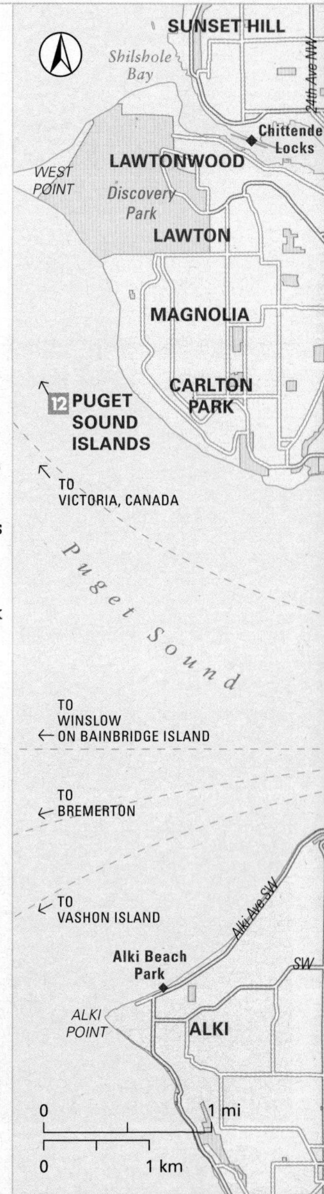

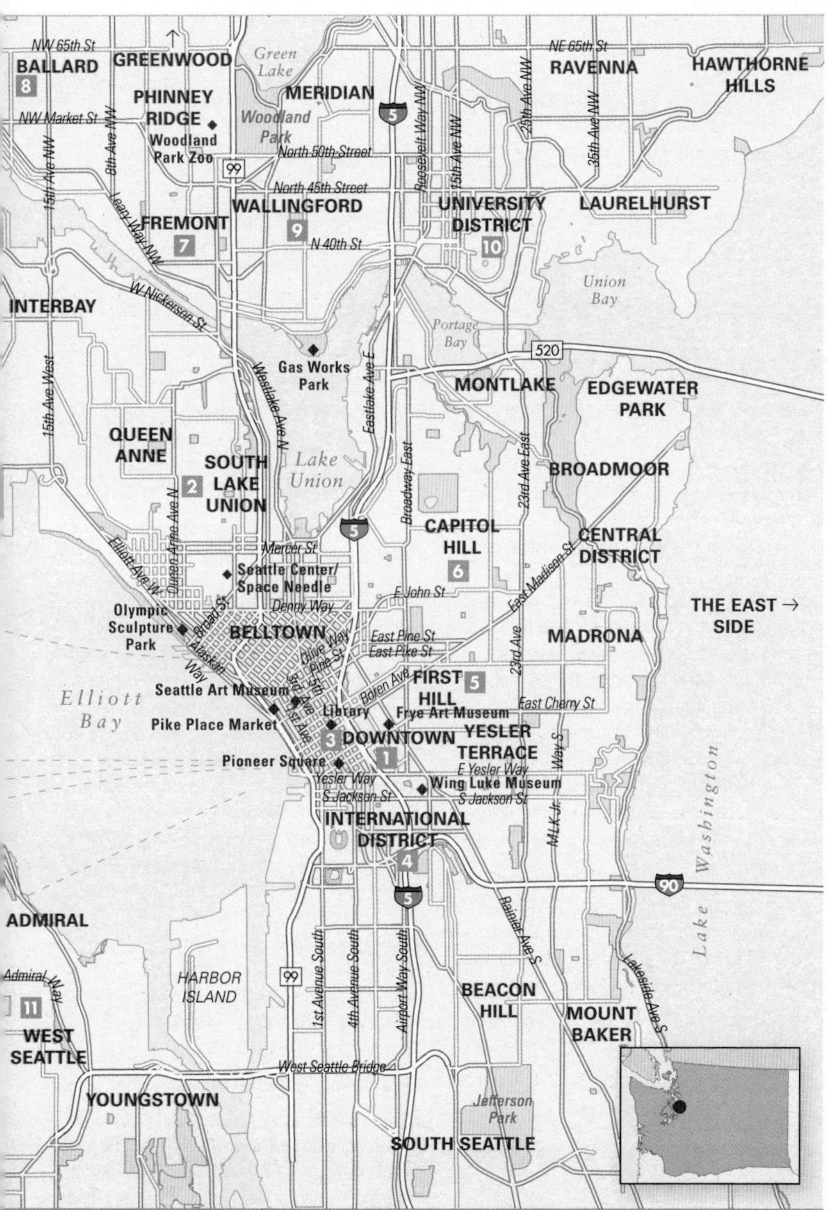
NW 65th St
BALLARD
8
GREENWOOD
Green Lake
PHINNEY RIDGE
MERIDIAN
NE 65th St
RAVENNA
HAWTHORNE HILLS
NW Market St
Woodland Park
Woodland Park Zoo
North 50th Street
99
North 45th Street
15th Ave NW
8th Ave NW
Leary Way NW
Roosevelt Way NW
15th Ave NW
25th Ave NW
35th Ave NW
WALLINGFORD
UNIVERSITY DISTRICT
LAURELHURST
FREMONT
7
9
N 40th St
10
Union Bay
W Nickerson St
INTERBAY
Portage Bay
520
Gas Works Park
Eastlake Ave E
MONTLAKE
EDGEWATER PARK
15th Ave West
Westlake Ave N
QUEEN ANNE
SOUTH LAKE UNION
2
Lake Union
Broadway East
23rd Ave East
BROADMOOR
5
CAPITOL HILL
6
CENTRAL DISTRICT
Elliott Ave W
Queen Anne Ave N
Mercer St
Seattle Center/ Space Needle
E John St
East Madison St
THE EAST SIDE
Olympic Sculpture Park
Broad St
Denny Way
BELLTOWN
Alaskan Way
Olive Way
Pine St
East Pine St
East Pike St
23rd Ave
MADRONA
Elliott Bay
Seattle Art Museum
3rd Ave
5th
1st Ave
Boren Ave
FIRST HILL
5
Library
Frye Art Museum
East Cherry St
Pike Place Market
3
DOWNTOWN
1
YESLER TERRACE
Pioneer Square
E Yesler Way
Yesler Way
S Jackson St
Wing Luke Museum
S Jackson St
M.L.K. Jr. Way S
INTERNATIONAL DISTRICT
4
Lake Washington
5
90
ADMIRAL
Rainier Ave S
Admiral Way
HARBOR ISLAND
99
1st Avenue South
4th Avenue South
Airport Way South
BEACON HILL
Lakeside Ave S
11
WEST SEATTLE
MOUNT BAKER
West Seattle Bridge
YOUNGSTOWN
Jefferson Park
SOUTH SEATTLE

Seattle is a city of many neighborhoods: eclectic, urban, outdoorsy, artsy, gritty, down-to-earth, or posh—it's all here, from the quirky character of the Seattle Waterfront and the eccentric "Republic of Fremont," to hipsters walking baby carriages past aging mansions on Capitol Hill. There's something for just about everyone within this vibrant Emerald City.

The city owes much of its appeal to its natural features—the myriad hills that did survive settlement offer views of mountain ranges and water, water, water. Outside Downtown and other smaller commercial cores, Seattle's neighborhoods fan out in tangles of tree-lined streets. Massive parks like Discovery, Magnuson, and Washington Park Arboretum make Seattle one of the greenest and most livable cities in the nation. From the peaks of the Olympics or Cascades to an artistically landscaped garden in front of a classic Northwest bungalow, nature is in full effect every time you turn your head.

Taking a stroll, browsing a bookstore, or enjoying a cup of coffee can feel different in every one of Seattle's neighborhoods. It's the adventure of exploring that will really introduce you to the character of Seattle.

Planning

When to Go

Unless you're planning an all-indoor museum trip, Seattle is most enjoyable May through October. June can be surprisingly rainy, but July through September is almost always dry, with warm days reaching into the mid-70s and 80s; nights are cooler, though it doesn't get dark until 9 or 10 pm. Although the weather can be dodgy, spring (particularly April) and fall are also excellent times to visit, as lodging and tour costs are usually much lower (and the crowds much smaller). In winter, the days are short, dark, and wet, but temperatures rarely dip below the low 40s and winter events—especially around the holidays—are plentiful.

FESTIVALS

The Seattle Convention and Visitors Bureau has a full calendar of events at 🌐 *www.visitseattle.org/cultural*. Foodies will want to hit up **Taste Washington** (spring 🌐 *www.tastewashington.org*) for the best of food and wine, as well as **Bite of Seattle** (July 🌐 *www.biteofseattle.com*), the Northwest Chocolate Festival (September 🌐 *www.nwchocolate.com*) and Seattle International Beer Fest (July 🌐 *www.seattlebeerfest.com*). The **Seattle International Film Festival** presents more than 200 features (May and June 🌐 *www.siff.net*).

Music lovers have three major events to keep them happy: **Bumbershoot** (September 🌐 *bumbershoot.org*) is Seattle's premier music festival, packed with major acts, as well as dance and theater, while Northwest Folklife Festival (May 🌐 *www.nwfolklife.org*) is a free, family-friendly event featuring folk music and dance from around the globe. Check out Capitol Hill Block Party (July 🌐 *www.capitolhill-blockparty.com*) for the best indie pop, rock, hip-hop, and alt-country.

The **Seattle Pride Festival** (June 🌐 *www.seattlepride.org*) has the Northwest's biggest gay, lesbian, and transgender pride parade. A local favorite, the quirky Fremont Fair Summer Solstice Parade (June 🌐 *www.fremontfair.org*) provides a glimpse into the true character of the city. **Seafair** (July and August 🌐 *www.seafair.com*) is the biggest summer festival; hydroplane races are just one major event.

Getting Here and Around

GETTING HERE

The major gateway is Seattle–Tacoma International Airport (SEA), known locally as Sea-Tac. The airport is south of the city and reasonably close to it—non-rush-hours trips to Downtown sometimes take less than a half hour. Sea-Tac is a midsize, modern airport that is usually pleasant to navigate. You can take Sound Transit's **Link light-rail** (🌐 *www.soundtransit.org*), which will take you right to Downtown or beyond in 35 minutes for just $3. As of 2019, a handful of flights also arrive and depart each day from Paine Field, about 35 minutes north of Downtown.

GETTING AROUND

Biking is a popular but somewhat tricky endeavor, thanks to a shortage of safe bike routes and some daunting hills. Walking is fun, though distances and rain can sometimes get in the way. Several neighborhoods—from Pioneer Square to Downtown, or from Belltown to Queen Anne, for example—are close enough to each other that even hills and moisture can't stop walkers.

The bus system will get you anywhere you need to go, although some routes require a time commitment and several transfers. Within the Downtown core, however, the bus is efficient and affordable. Another option for public transport is the bright red streetcars that connect Downtown to South Lake Union and Pioneer Square to Capitol Hill.

Access to a car is *almost* a necessity if you want to explore the residential neighborhoods beyond their commercial centers, but parking can cost upwards of $50 per night in the urban center. Alternatives like ShareNow, Lyft, or Uber are great options, and many high-end hotels offer complimentary town-car service around Downtown and the immediate areas.

Ferries are a major part of Seattle's transportation network, and they're the only way to reach Vashon Island and the San Juans. You'll get outstanding views of the skyline and the elusive Mt. Rainier from the ferry to Bainbridge.

Visitor Information

Contact the **Seattle Visitors Bureau and Convention Center** (🌐 *www.visitseattle.org* ☎ *206/461–5800*) for help with everything from sightseeing to booking spa services. You can also follow its Twitter feed (🌐 *twitter.com/seattlemaven*). The main visitor information center is

Downtown, at the Washington State Convention and Trade Center on 8th Avenue and Pike Street; it has a full-service concierge desk open daily 9 to 5 (in summer; weekdays only in winter). There's also an info booth at Pike Place Market.

Sights

Each of Seattle's neighborhoods has a distinctive personality, and taking a stroll, browsing a bookstore, or enjoying a cup of coffee can feel different in every one. It's the adventure of exploring that will really introduce you to the character of Seattle.

Dining

Thanks to inventive chefs, first-rate local produce, adventurous diners, and a bold entrepreneurial spirit, Seattle has become one of the culinary capitals of the nation. Fearless young chefs have stepped in and raised the bar. Nowadays, fresh and often foraged produce, local seafood, and imaginative techniques make the quality of local cuisine even higher.

Prices in the reviews are the average cost of a main course at dinner or, if dinner is not served, at lunch.

Hotels

Much like the eclectic city itself, Seattle's lodging offers something for everyone. There are grand, ornate vintage hotels; sleek and elegant modern properties; green hotels with yoga studios and enough bamboo for an army of pandas; and cozy bed-and-breakfasts with sweet bedspreads and home-cooked breakfasts. Travelers who appreciate the anonymity of high-rise chains can comfortably stay here, while guests who want to feel like family can find the perfect boutique inn to lay their heads.

Hotel reviews have been shortened. For full information, visit Fodors.com.

What It Costs in U.S. Dollars

	$	$$	$$$	$$$$
RESTAURANTS	under $16	$16–$24	$25–$32	over $32
HOTELS	under $180	$180–$265	$266–$350	over $350

Nightlife

Seattle's amazing musical legacy is well known, but there's more to the arts and nightlife scenes than live music. In fact, these days, there are far more swanky bars and inventive pubs than music venues in the city. To put it bluntly, Seattle's a dynamite place to drink. You can sip overly ambitious and ridiculously named specialty cocktails in trendy lounges, get a lesson from an enthusiastic sommelier in a wine bar or restaurant, or swill cheap beer on the patio of a dive bar. Though some places have very specific demographics, most Seattle bars are egalitarian, drawing loyal regulars of all ages.

In addition to its bars, Downtown and Belltown in particular have notable restaurants with separate bar areas. Most restaurants have impressive bar menus, and food is often served until 11 pm, midnight, or even 1 am in some spots.

Shopping

To find many of the stores that are truly special to Seattle—such as boutiques featuring handmade frocks from local designers, independent record stores run by encyclopedic-minded music geeks, cozy used-book shops that smell of paper and worn wood shelves—you'll have to branch out to Capitol Hill, Queen Anne, and northern neighborhoods like

Ballard. Shopping these areas will give you a better feel for the character of the city and its quirky inhabitants, all while you score that new dress or nab gifts for your friends.

Downtown and Belltown

Except for the busy areas around the Market and the piers, and the always-frenetic shopping district, a lot of Downtown can often seem deserted, especially at night. Still, while it may not be the soul of the city, it's definitely the heart, and there's plenty to do—nearly all of it easily reachable by foot.

Belltown is Downtown's younger sibling, just north of Virginia Street (up to Denny Way) and stretching from Elliott Bay to 6th Avenue. Today, Belltown is increasingly hip, with luxury condos, trendy restaurants, bustling bars, and a number of boutiques. (Most of the action happens between 1st and 4th avenues and between Bell and Virginia streets.)

Sights

★ Olympic Sculpture Park

PUBLIC ART | An outdoor branch of the Seattle Art Museum is a favorite destination for picnics, strolls, and quiet contemplation. Nestled at the edge of Belltown with views of Elliott Bay, the gently sloping green space features native plants and walking paths that wind past larger-than-life public artwork. On sunny days, the park frames an astounding panorama of the Olympic Mountains, but even the grayest afternoon casts a favorable light on the site's sculptures. The grounds are home to works by such artists as Richard Serra, Louise Bourgeois, and Alexander Calder, whose bright-red steel "Eagle" sculpture is a local favorite (and a nod to the bald eagles that sometimes soar above). "Echo," a 46-foot-tall elongated girl's face by Spanish artist Jaume Plensa, is a beautiful and bold presence on the waterfront. The park's PACCAR Pavilion has a gift shop, café, and information about the artworks. ✉ *2901 Western Ave., between Broad and Bay Sts., Belltown* ☎ *206/654–3100* 🌐 *www.seattleartmuseum.org* 🎫 *Free.*

★ Pike Place Market

MARKET | **FAMILY** | One of the nation's largest and oldest public markets dates from 1907, when the city issued permits allowing farmers to sell produce from parked wagons. At one time the market was a madhouse of vendors hawking their produce and haggling with customers over prices; now you might find fishmongers engaging in frenzied banter and hilarious antics, but chances are you won't get them to waver on prices. There are many restaurants, bakeries, coffee shops (including the flagship Starbucks), lunch counters, and ethnic eateries. Go to Pike Place hungry and you won't be disappointed. The flower market is also a must-see—gigantic fresh arrangements can be found for around $12. It's well worth wading through dense crowds to enjoy the market's many corridors, where you'll find specialty-food items, quirky gift shops, tea, honey, jams, comic books, beads, eclectic crafts, and cookware. In 2017, Pike Place Market debuted a significant expansion, fulfilling a decades-long vision for Seattle's Market Historic District. The market's new digs feature artisanal-food purveyors, an on-site brewery, four public art installations, seasonal pop-up vendors, and a 30,000-square-foot open public space with a plaza and a viewing deck overlooking Elliott Bay and the Seattle waterfront. ■ **TIP→ The famous "flying fish" fishmonger is located at the main entrance on Pike Street. Just be patient and eventually someone will toss a big fish through the air.** ✉ *Pike Pl. at Pike St., west of 1st Ave., Downtown* ☎ *206/682–7453* 🌐 *www.pikeplacemarket.org.*

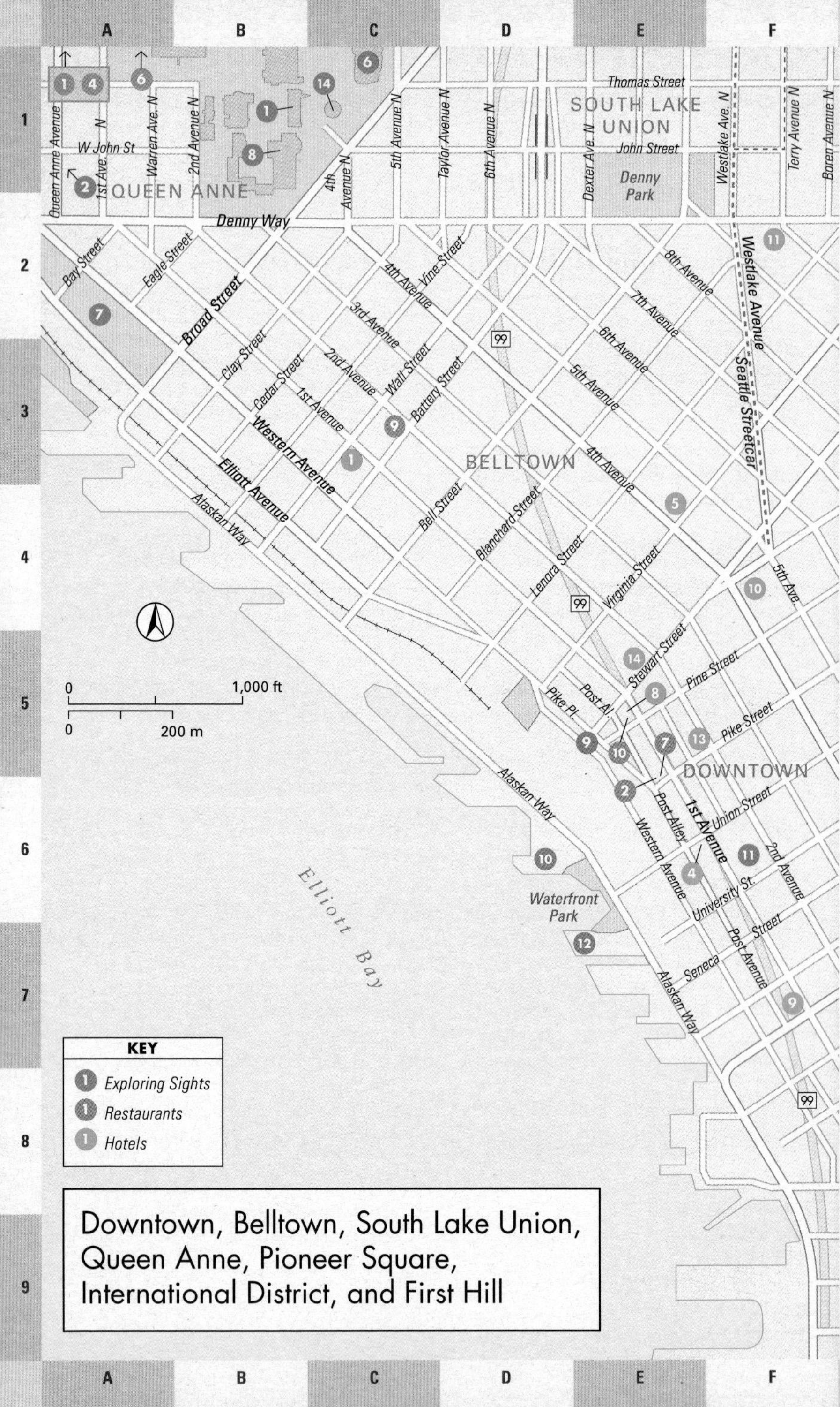

Downtown, Belltown, South Lake Union, Queen Anne, Pioneer Square, International District, and First Hill

Sights

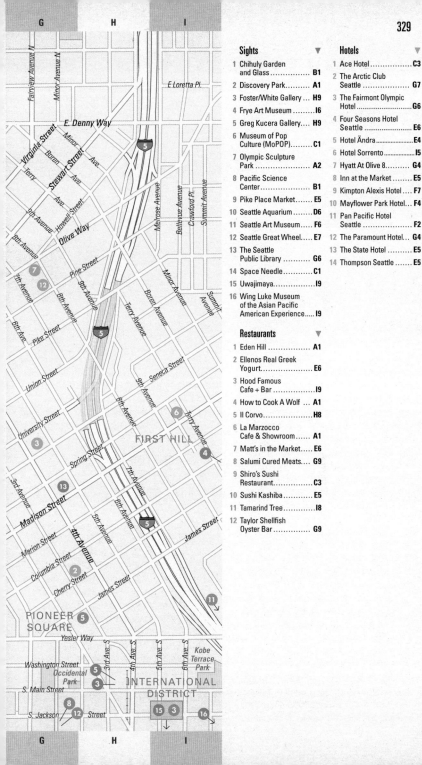

1 Chihuly Garden and Glass **B1**
2 Discovery Park.......... **A1**
3 Foster/White Gallery ... **H9**
4 Frye Art Museum **I6**
5 Greg Kucera Gallery.... **H9**
6 Museum of Pop Culture (MoPOP).........**C1**
7 Olympic Sculpture Park **A2**
8 Pacific Science Center.................... **B1**
9 Pike Place Market....... **E5**
10 Seattle Aquarium **D6**
11 Seattle Art Museum..... **F6**
12 Seattle Great Wheel..... **E7**
13 The Seattle Public Library **G6**
14 Space Needle...........**C1**
15 Uwajimaya.................**I9**
16 Wing Luke Museum of the Asian Pacific American Experience..... **I9**

Restaurants

1 Eden Hill **A1**
2 Ellenos Real Greek Yogurt..................... **E6**
3 Hood Famous Cafe + Bar **I9**
4 How to Cook A Wolf ... **A1**
5 Il Corvo.....................**H8**
6 La Marzocco Cafe & Showroom...... **A1**
7 Matt's in the Market..... **E6**
8 Salumi Cured Meats.... **G9**
9 Shiro's Sushi Restaurant................**C3**
10 Sushi Kashiba............ **E5**
11 Tamarind Tree.............**I8**
12 Taylor Shellfish Oyster Bar **G9**

Hotels

1 Ace Hotel..................**C3**
2 The Arctic Club Seattle **G7**
3 The Fairmont Olympic Hotel.............................**G6**
4 Four Seasons Hotel Seattle **E6**
5 Hotel Ändra........................**E4**
6 Hotel Sorrento....................**I5**
7 Hyatt At Olive 8.......... **G4**
8 Inn at the Market **E5**
9 Kimpton Alexis Hotel **F7**
10 Mayflower Park Hotel... **F4**
11 Pan Pacific Hotel Seattle **F2**
12 The Paramount Hotel... **G4**
13 The State Hotel **E5**
14 Thompson Seattle **E5**

A steel sculpture by Richard Serra at the Olympic Sculpture Park

★ Seattle Aquarium

ZOO | **FAMILY** | Located right at the water's edge, the Seattle Aquarium is one of the nation's premier aquariums. Among its most engaging residents are the sea otters—kids, especially, seem able to spend hours watching the delightful antics of these creatures and their river cousins. In the Puget Sound Great Hall, "Window on Washington Waters," a slice of Neah Bay life, is presented in a 20-foot-tall tank holding 120,000 gallons of water. The aquarium's darkened rooms and large, lighted tanks brilliantly display Pacific Northwest marine life, including clever octopuses and translucent jellyfish. The "Life on the Edge" tide pools re-create Washington's rocky coast and sandy beaches—kids can touch the starfish, sea urchins, and sponges. Huge glass windows provide underwater views of the harbor seal exhibit; go up top to watch them play in their pools. If you're visiting in fall or winter, dress warmly—the Marine Mammal area is outside on the waterfront and catches all of those chilly Puget Sound breezes. The café serves Ivar's chowder and kid-friendly food like burgers and chicken fingers; the balcony has views of Elliott Bay. ✉ *1483 Alaskan Way, Pier 59, Downtown* ☎ *206/386–4300* 🌐 *www.seattleaquarium.org* 🎫 *$34.95.*

★ Seattle Art Museum

MUSEUM | Sculptor Jonathan Borofsky's several-stories-high "Hammering Man" greets visitors to SAM, as locals call this pride of the city's art scene. SAM's permanent collection surveys American, Asian, Native American, African, Oceanic, and pre-Columbian art. Collections of African dance masks and Native American carvings are particularly strong. SAM's free floors have the best attractions for kids, including an installation of a massive tree-like sculpture hanging from the ceiling and the Chase OpenStudio. The museum's gift shop stocks serious eye candy for visitors of all ages. If you're interested in checking a special exhibition, consider buying tickets in advance as they can sell out. *The listed admission price to see the* *museum's general collections and installations is suggested pricing, though the museum charges fixed pricing for tickets that include special exhibitions. ✉ 1300 1st Ave., Downtown ☎ 206/654–3100 🌐 www.seattleartmuseum.org 🎫 $29.95; free 1st Thurs. of month ⏲ Closed Mon.-Tues.*

Seattle Great Wheel

AMUSEMENT PARK/WATER PARK | FAMILY | Want to hitch a ride to a soaring Seattle vantage point above the water? At the end of Pier 57, just steps from Pike Place Market and the Seattle Aquarium, the Seattle Great Wheel is a 175-foot (about 17 stories tall) Ferris wheel. As you round the top, enjoy views of the city skyline, Elliott Bay, the Olympic Mountains, and Mt. Rainier (on a clear day, of course). Rides are slow and smooth, lasting 15 to 20 minutes, with three revolutions total. Each climate-controlled gondola can hold six people (up to eight if some are children) and, generally speaking, parties will be able to sit together. The Seattle Great Wheel also lights up the waterfront after dark with dazzling colors. Advance tickets are recommended—you'll still have to wait in line, but the line is a lot shorter. **■ TIP→ If you're afraid of heights, you may want to skip this attraction.** *✉ 1301 Alaskan Way (Pier 56), Downtown ☎ 206/623–8600 🌐 www.seattlegreatwheel.com 🎫 $15.*

★ The Seattle Public Library

LIBRARY | The hub of Seattle's 26-branch library system is a stunning jewel of a building that stands out against the concrete jungle of Downtown. Designed by renowned Dutch architect Rem Koolhaas and Joshua Ramus, this 11-story structure houses more than 1 million books, a language center, terrific areas for kids and teens—plus hundreds of computers, an auditorium, a "mixing chamber" floor of information desks, and a café. The building's floor plan is anything but simple; stand outside the beveled glass-and-metal facade of the building and you can see the library's floors zigzagging upward. Tours are self-guided via a laminated sheet you can pick up at the information desk; there's also a number you can call on your cell phone for an audio tour. The reading room on the 10th floor has unbeatable views of the city and the water, and the building has Wi-Fi throughout (look for the network "spl-public"). Readings and free film screenings happen on a regular basis; check the website for more information. *✉ 1000 4th Ave., Downtown ☎ 206/386–4636 🌐 www.spl.org/locations/central-library.*

Restaurants

★ Ellenos Real Greek Yogurt

$ | FAST FOOD | When people walk by the Pike Place Market booth, they might think they're passing a gelato stand from the artful display, but in fact Ellenos is serving up the best (and best-looking) yogurt in the city—and possibly the country. Thicker and smoother than most commercial Greek yogurts, the Australian-Greek family behind the brand uses local milk and a slow culturing process to create their nearly ice cream-like treat. **Known for:** Greek yogurt with a cult following; fresh fruit toppings. *$ Average main: $4 ✉ 1500 Pike Pl., Downtown ☎ 206/535–7562 🌐 www.ellenos.com ⏲ No dinner.*

★ Matt's in the Market

$$$$ | PACIFIC NORTHWEST | One of the most beloved of Pike Place Market's restaurants, Matt's is all about intimate dining, fresh ingredients, and superb service. You can perch at the bar for pints and the signature deviled eggs or be seated at a table—complete with vases filled with flowers from the market—for a seasonal menu that synthesizes the best picks from the restaurant's produce vendors and an excellent wine list. **Known for:** wonderful Market and water views; a fresh catch of the day; daily late-night hours until 1 am. *$ Average main: $40 ✉ 94 Pike St., Downtown*

The stunning Seattle Central Library

☎ 206/467–7909 🌐 *www.mattsinthemarket.com.*

★ Shiro's Sushi Restaurant

$$$ | JAPANESE | Founder Shiro Kashiba is no longer here (he's now at Downtown's Sushi Kashiba), but this sushi spot is still the best in Belltown, with simple decor, ultra-fresh fish, and an omakase service that's a bit more affordable than at other spots. **Known for:** chef's choice omakase; simple ambience. *$ Average main: $28* ✉ *2401 2nd Ave., Belltown* ☎ *206/443–9844* 🌐 *www.shiros.com* ⏲ *No lunch.*

★ Sushi Kashiba

$$$$ | SUSHI | After decades spent earning a reputation as one of Seattle's top sushi chefs, Shiro Kashiba opened his own spot in a location as notable as his skill with seafood deserves. Diners in the spare-but-elegant Pike Place Market space can opt for the *omakase* (chef's choice) selection of the best fish from around the world and just up the street, or order from the menu of Japanese classics and sashimi. **Known for:** local celebrity chef; omakase is expensive but a memorable tasting experience; outstanding service. *$ Average main: $85* ✉ *86 Pine St., Suite 1, Downtown* ✣ *Inn at the Market* ☎ *206/441–8844* 🌐 *www.sushikashiba.com* ⏲ *No lunch.*

Hotels

★ Ace Hotel

$ | HOTEL | The Ace is a dream come true for anyone who appreciates unique minimalist decor, with touches like army-surplus blankets, industrial metal sinks, and street art breaking up any notion of austerity; the cheapest rooms share bathrooms, which have enormous showers. **Pros:** ultratrendy but with some of the most affordable rates in town; good place to meet other travelers; free Wi-Fi. **Cons:** half the rooms have shared bathrooms; not for people who want pampering; lots of stairs to get to lobby. *$ Rooms from: $149* ✉ *2423 1st Ave., Belltown* ☎ *206/448–4721* 🌐 *www.acehotel.com* *14 standard rooms, 14 deluxe rooms* *No meals.*

★ Kimpton Alexis Hotel
$$$ | **HOTEL** | The guestrooms received a top-to-bottom redo in 2019 at the boutique Alexis, which occupies a pair of historic buildings (on the National Register of Historic Places, in fact) near the waterfront; the new design features nautical- and Northwest-inspired hues, textures, and furnishings that complement the hotel's exposed brick and walls of windows. **Pros:** a short walk to the waterfront; chic modern rooms that appeal to design lovers; suites aren't prohibitively expensive. **Cons:** small lobby; not entirely soundproofed against old building and city noise; some rooms can be a bit dark. *Rooms from: $397 ✉ 1007 1st Ave., Downtown ☎ 206/624–4844, 888/850–1155 🌐 www.alexishotel.com ⇨ 88 rooms 🍽 No meals.*

★ The Arctic Club Seattle
$$$ | **HOTEL** | From the building's famous antique terra cotta walrus heads and Alaskan-marble-sheathed foyer to guest rooms with vintage bathroom tile and explorer-chic touches like steamer trunks for bedside tables, the Arctic Club pays homage to an era of gold-rush opulence (the early 1900s building was once a gentlemen's club). **Pros:** feels boutique but has Doubletree by Hilton level standards; a truly beautiful lobby, which includes the Polar Bar; light-rail and bus lines just outside the door. **Cons:** much closer to Pioneer Square than the heart of Downtown; rooms are a bit dark; style may be off-putting for travelers who like modern hotels. *Rooms from: $304 ✉ 700 3rd Ave., Downtown ☎ 206/340–0340, 800/445–8667 🌐 thearcticclubseattle.com ⇨ 120 rooms 🍽 No meals.*

★ The Fairmont Olympic Hotel
$$$$ | **HOTEL** | **FAMILY** | While the lobby of this glamorous luxury hotel sweeps guests away with Old World marble floors, soaring ceilings, massive chandeliers, and grand staircases, the guest rooms have a decidedly more modern feel, with mid century-inspired furnishings and all-marble bathrooms featuring rain showers and designer toiletries. **Pros:** impeccable service; a top-notch fitness center with an indoor pool; great on-site dining and amenities. **Cons:** not much in the way of views; valet parking is $60; some rooms on the small side. *Rooms from: $366 ✉ 411 University St., Downtown ☎ 206/621–1700, 888/363–5022 🌐 www.fairmont.com/seattle ⇨ 450 rooms 🍽 No meals.*

★ Four Seasons Hotel Seattle
$$$$ | **HOTEL** | **FAMILY** | Just south of the Pike Place Market and steps from the Seattle Art Museum, this Downtown gem overlooking Elliott Bay is polished and elegant, with spacious light-filled guest rooms that were renovated in 2019; the fresh new design features serene hues that nod to the hotel's surroundings, museum-quality art reproductions, and comfortable high-end modern furnishings. **Pros:** fantastic outdoor inifinity pool with views for miles; luxurious marble bathrooms with deep soaking tubs; lovely spa facility offering extensive treatments. **Cons:** Four Seasons regulars might not click with this modern take on the brand; street-side rooms not entirely soundproofed; some water-facing room views are partially obscured by industrial sites. *Rooms from: $720 ✉ 99 Union St., Downtown ☎ 206/749–7000, 800/332–3442 🌐 www.fourseasons.com/seattle ⇨ 134 rooms 🍽 No meals.*

★ Hotel Ändra
$$$ | **HOTEL** | Scandinavian sensibility and clean, modern lines define this sophisticated hotel on the edge of Belltown, where spacious, comfortable rooms have dark fabrics and light woods, with a few bright accents and geometric prints. **Pros:** hangout-worthy lobby lounge; on-trend Scandinavian vibe; very close to transit. **Cons:** some street noise; not family-friendly; small bathroom. *Rooms from: $295 ✉ 2000 4th Ave., Belltown ☎ 206/448–8600, 877/448–8600 🌐 www.*

hotelandra.com ⇨ *93 rooms, 4 studios, 22 suites* 🍴 *No meals.*

★ Hyatt at Olive 8

$$$$ | **HOTEL** | In a city known for environmental responsibility, being one of the greenest hotels in town is no small feat, and green is rarely this chic—rooms have floor-to-ceiling windows flooding the place with light along with enviro touches like dual-flush toilets, fresh-air vents, and low-flow showerheads. **Pros:** central location; serene indoor pool; one of Seattle's best day spas. **Cons:** standard rooms have showers only; guests complain of hallway and traffic noise; translucent glass bathroom doors offer little privacy. $ *Rooms from: $339* ✉ *1635 8th Ave., Downtown* ☎ *206/695–1234, 800/233–1234* 🌐 *www.olive8.hyatt.com* ⇨ *346 rooms* 🍴 *No meals.*

★ Inn at the Market

$$$$ | **HOTEL** | From its heart-stopping views to the fabulous location just steps from Pike Place Market, this is a place you'll want to visit again and again. **Pros:** outstanding views from most rooms; deals on rooms that don't have views, even in peak season; guests have access to the fabulous rooftop deck. **Cons:** not much indoor common space; some street and Market noise; not the easiest to get in and out by car. $ *Rooms from: $390* ✉ *86 Pine St., Downtown* ☎ *206/443–3600, 800/446–4484* 🌐 *www.innatthemarket.com* ⇨ *70 rooms* 🍴 *No meals.*

★ Mayflower Park Hotel

$$$ | **HOTEL** | Comfortable, old-world charm comes with sturdy antiques, Asian accents, brass fixtures, and florals, and though the hotel's main draw is its central location close to all the action, street noise isn't much of an issue thanks to the sturdy old construction of the historic 1927 building. **Pros:** close to light rail and Monorail; on-site Spanish restaurant Andaluca is well worth a visit; comfortable beds. **Cons:** some of the rooms are small; old-fashioned for some travelers; not all rooms have mini fridges. $ *Rooms from: $354* ✉ *405 Olive Way, Downtown* ☎ *206/623–8700, 800/426–5100* 🌐 *www.mayflowerpark.com* ⇨ *189 rooms* 🍴 *No meals.*

★ The Paramount Hotel

$$ | **HOTEL** | Good value meets great location at this comfortable boutique hotel with friendly service and tasteful contemporary furnishings, including a decent-size desk for business travelers. **Pros:** close to the Convention Center; clean, quiet rooms; ice chests instead of machines mean less noise. **Cons:** not much in the way of amenities; tiny fitness center; small lobby. $ *Rooms from: $240* ✉ *724 Pine St., Downtown* ☎ *206/292–9500* 🌐 *www.paramounthotelseattle.com* ⇨ *146 rooms* 🍴 *No meals.*

★ Hotel Sorrento

$$$$ | **HOTEL** | Built in 1906, the historic and serene Hotel Sorrento hits the perfect note between traditional and modern, with lovely Italianate architecture, carved wood moldings, white marble bathrooms, antique furnishings in sumptuous fabrics, and chic original contemporary artwork in the common spaces, including the Sorrento's stylish Dunbar Room restaurant. **Pros:** the elegant wood-paneled Fireside Room is perfect for cocktail hour; courteous guest service; comfortable beds. **Cons:** not central; rooms are a bit small (though corner suites are commodious); ho-hum views. $ *Rooms from: $424* ✉ *900 Madison St., First Hill* ☎ *206/622–6400, 800/426–1265* 🌐 *www.hotelsorrento.com* ⇨ *76 rooms* 🍴 *No meals.*

★ The State Hotel

$$ | **HOTEL** | From the huge exterior mural by artist Shepard Fairey to the gorgeous graphic wallpaper inspired by nearby Pike Place Market, every inch of this hip new boutique hotel is eye candy, including stylish rooms with sleek, tiled rain showers, an eclectic and welcoming lobby, and vibrant Ben Paris bar and restaurant,

Marijuana Legalization

In 2012, Washington voted to legalize recreational marijuana, one of the first two states in the United States to blaze the trail. Since 2014, when the first handful of legal locations opened in Washington, pot shops have cropped up in every Seattle neighborhood. Just two years after the initial roll out, state residents and visitors had consumed more than $1 billion in marijuana products, which generated roughly $250 million for the state through a 37% excise tax at the point of purchase. Steep taxes mean legal weed doesn't come as cheap as black-market goods, but as demand has grown, average prices have dropped significantly, from $25 per gram in 2014 to $10 per gram in 2016. That's good news for tourists who'd like to try it!

If you're inclined to explore the legal scene, it's a good idea to do a bit of research first. Shopping options range from hole-in-the-wall storefronts to upscale boutiques that stock impressive selections of marijuana along with various accessories. Check sites like *leafly.com* or *weedmaps.com* to locate stores and check on what strains they carry. You must be 21 or up with a valid ID to purchase marijuana in Washington. You can buy or possess an ounce of weed at a time, or up to 6 ounces of solid marijuana-infused edibles. When it comes to consumption, treat it like booze. Don't partake in public, and don't get high and drive. If you'd like a guided introduction to Emerald City's green offerings, check out Kush Tourism (*www.kushtourism.com*).

where neighborhood locals are as likely to hang out as tourists. **Pros:** minimal but well-appointed guest rooms, some with nice water views; really friendly service; great lobby coffee. **Cons:** some rooms are on the small side; not kid-friendly; rooftop patio only has a few tables. *Rooms from: $200* *1501 2nd Ave., Downtown* *800/827–3900* *www.statehotel.com* *91 rooms* *No meals.*

★ Thompson Seattle

$$$ | **HOTEL** | Designed by local starchitects Olson Kundig, the 12-story Thompson Seattle (a Hyatt hotel) makes an impression with a contemporary glass exterior and sophisticated guest rooms that feature floor-to-ceiling windows—some framing epic water views—hardwood floors, a crisp white-and-navy palette, and leather and smoked-glass accents. **Pros:** perfect for the style obsessed; very close to Pike Place Market; home to The Nest rooftop bar. **Cons:** blazing afternoon sun in some rooms; some small rooms; floor beneath rooftop bar can be noisy. *Rooms from: $279* *110 Stewart St., Downtown* *206/623–4600* *www.thompsonhotels.com/hotels/thompson-seattle* *158 rooms* *No meals.*

Nightlife

★ Zig Zag Café

BARS/PUBS | A mixed crowd of mostly locals hunts out this unique spot at Pike Place Market's Street Hill Climb (walk past the Gum Wall—yes, it really is as disgusting as it sounds—to find a nearly hidden stairwell leading down to the piers). In addition to pouring a perfect martini, Zig Zag features a revolving cast of memorable cocktails. A Mediterranean-inspired food menu offers plenty of tasty bites to accompany the excellent cocktails. A small patio is the place to be on a summery happy-hour evening. Zig Zag is friendly—retro without being obnoxiously ironic—and very Seattle, with the occasional live music show to boot. ✉ *1501 Western Ave., Downtown* ☎ *206/625–1146* 🌐 *zigzagseattle.com.*

LIVE MUSIC

★ The Crocodile

MUSIC CLUBS | The heart and soul of Seattle's music scene since 1991 has hosted the likes of the Beastie Boys, Pearl Jam, and Mudhoney, along with countless other bands. There's a reason *Rolling Stone* once called the 525-person Crocodile one of the best small clubs in America. Nightly shows are complemented by cheap beer on tap and pizza at the Back Bar. All hail the Croc! ✉ *2200 2nd Ave., Belltown* ☎ *206/441–7416* 🌐 *www.thecrocodile.com.*

Shopping

BOOKS AND PRINTED MATERIAL

★ Peter Miller Architectural & Design Books and Supplies

BOOKS/STATIONERY | Aesthetes and architects haunt this shop, which is stocked with all things design. Rare, international architecture, art, and design books (including titles for children) mingle with high-end products from Alessi and Iittala; sleek notebooks, bags, portfolios, and drawing tools round out the collection. This is a great shop for quirky, unforgettable gifts, like a pentagram typography calendar, an Arne Jacobsen wall clock, or an aerodynamic umbrella. ✉ *304 Alaskan Way South, Post Alley, Belltown* ✣ *entrance off alley* ☎ *206/441–4114* 🌐 *www.petermiller.com* 🕒 *Closed Sun.*

Phinney Books

BOOKS/STATIONERY | A gem of an independent bookstore, Phinney Books is owned by local eight-time "Jeopardy!" champ and reading enthusiast Tom Nissley, who's stocked his charming shop with an expertly curated selection of books, including many titles by local authors and a whimsical section for kids. ✉ *7405 Greenwood Ave. N, Seattle* ☎ *206/297–2665* 🌐 *www.phinneybooks.com.*

CHOCOLATE

★ Fran's Chocolates

FOOD/CANDY | A Seattle institution (helmed by Fran Bigelow) has been making quality chocolates for decades. Its world-famous salted caramels are transcendent—a much-noted favorite of the Obama family, in fact—as are delectable truffles, which are spiked with oolong tea, single-malt whiskey, or raspberry, among other flavors. This shop is housed in the elegant Four Seasons on 1st Avenue. ✉ *1325 1st Ave., Downtown* ☎ *206/682–0168* 🌐 *www.franschocolates.com.*

DEPARTMENT STORES

★ Nordstrom

DEPARTMENT STORES | Seattle's own retail giant sells quality clothing, accessories, cosmetics, jewelry, and lots of shoes—in keeping with its roots in footwear—including many hard-to-find sizes. Peruse the various floors for anything from trendy jeans to lingerie to goods for the home. A sky bridge on the store's fourth floor will take you to Pacific Place Shopping Center. Deservedly renowned for its impeccable customer service, the busy Downtown flagship has a concierge desk and valet parking. **■TIP→ The Nordstrom Rack store at 1st Avenue and Spring Street, close to Pike Place Market, has great deals on marked-down items.** ✉ *500 Pine St., Downtown* ☎ *206/628–2111* 🌐 *shop.nordstrom.com.*

WINE AND SPECIALTY FOODS

★ DeLaurenti Specialty Food and Wine

FOOD/CANDY | Attention foodies: clear out your hotel minibars and make room for delectable treats from DeLaurenti. And, if you're planning any picnics, swing by here first. Imported meats and cheeses crowd the deli cases, and packaged delicacies pack the aisles. Stock up on hard-to-find items like truffle-infused olive oil or excellent Italian vintages from the wine shop upstairs. Spring travelers will also want to stop by DeLaurenti's nosh nirvana, called Cheesefest, in May. ✉ *Pike Place Market, 1435 1st Ave., Downtown* ☎ *206/622–0141* 🌐 *www.delaurenti.com.*

South Lake Union and Queen Anne

Almost all visitors make their way to Seattle Center at some point, to visit the Space Needle or other key Seattle sites like MoPOP, the Pacific Science Center, or the stunning new Chihuly Garden and Glass. The neighborhoods that bookend Seattle Center couldn't be more different: Queen Anne is all residential elegance (especially on top of the hill), while South Lake Union, once completely industrial, is quickly becoming Seattle's next hot neighborhood.

Sights

★ Chihuly Garden and Glass

MUSEUM | Just steps from the base of the Space Needle, fans of Dale Chihuly's glass works will be delighted to trace the artist's early influences—neon art, Native American Northwest Coast trade baskets, and Pendleton blankets, to name a few—to the vibrant chandelier towers and architectural glass installations he is most known for today. There are eight galleries total, plus a 40-foot-tall "Glasshouse," and an outdoor garden that serves as a backdrop for colorful installations that integrate with a dynamic Northwest landscape, including native plants and a 500-year-old western cedar that washed up on the shores of Neah Bay. Chihuly, who was born and raised in Tacoma, was actively involved in the design of the exhibition as well as the whimsical Collections Cafe, where you'll find Chihuly's quirky personal collections on display—everything from tin toys to vintage cameras to antique shaving brushes. Indeed, so many of his personal touches are part of the exhibition space, you can almost feel his presence in every room (look for the guy with the unruly hair and the black eye patch). Chihuly is kid-friendly for all but the littlest ones. **■ TIP→ If you're also planning to visit the Space Needle, the combination ticket can save you some money.** ✉ *305 Harrison St., under Space Needle, Central District* ☎ *206/753–4940* 🌐 *www.chihulygardenandglass.com* 🎫 *$32* ⏲ *Discounts for evening tickets.*

★ Discovery Park

NATIONAL/STATE PARK | **FAMILY** | You won't find more spectacular views of Puget Sound, the Cascades, and the Olympics. Located on Magnolia Bluff, northwest of Downtown, Seattle's largest park covers 534 acres and has an amazing variety of terrain: shaded, secluded forest trails lead to meadows, saltwater beaches, sand dunes, a lighthouse, and 2 miles of protected beaches. The North Beach Trail, which takes you along the shore to the lighthouse, is a must-see. Head to the South Bluff Trail to get a view of Mt. Rainier. The park has several entrances—if you want to stop at the visitor center to pick up a trail map before exploring, use the main entrance at Government Way. The North Parking Lot is much closer to the North Beach Trail and to Ballard and Fremont, if you're coming from that direction. First-come, first-served beach parking passes for the disabled, elderly, and families with small children are available at the Learning Center. Note that the park is easily reached from Ballard and Fremont. It's easier to combine a park day with an exploration of those neighborhoods than with a busy Downtown itinerary. ✉ *3801 W. Government Way, Magnolia* ✣ *From Downtown, take Elliot Ave. W (which turns into 15th Ave. W), and get off at Emerson St. exit and turn left onto W Emerson. Make a right onto Gilman Ave. W (which eventually becomes W Government Way). As you enter park, road becomes Washington Ave.; turn left on Utah Ave.*

Continued on page 342

PIKE PLACE MARKET

Nine Acres of History & Quirky Charm

With more than a century of history tucked into every corner and plenty of local personality, the Market is one spot you can't miss. Office workers hustle past cruise-ship crowds to take a seat at lunch counters that serve anything from pizza to piroshkies to German sausage. Local chefs plan the evening's menu over stacks of fresh, colorful produce. At night, couples stroll in to canoodle by candlelight in tucked-away bars and restaurants. Sure, some residents may bemoan the hordes of visitors, and many Seattleites spend their dollars at a growing number of neighborhood farmers' markets. But the Market is still one of Seattle's best-loved attractions.

The Pike Place Market dates from 1907. In response to anger over rising food prices, the city issued permits for farmers to sell produce from wagons parked at Pike Place. The impromptu public market grew steadily, and in 1921 Frank Goodwin, a hotel owner who had been quietly buying up real estate around Pike Place for a decade, proposed to build a permanent space.

More than 250 businesses, including 70 eateries. Breathtaking views of Elliott Bay. A pedestrian-friendly central shopping arcade that buzzes to life each day beginning at 6:30 AM. Strumming street musicians. Cobblestones, flying fish, and the very first Starbucks. Pike Place Market—the oldest continuously operated public market in the United States and a beloved Seattle icon—covers all the bases.

The Market's vitality ebbed after World War II, with the exodus to the suburbs and the rise of large supermarkets. Both it and the surrounding neighborhoods began to deteriorate. But a group of dedicated residents, led by the late architect Victor Steinbrueck, rallied and voted the Market a Historical Asset in the early 1970s. Years of subsequent restoration turned the Market into what you see today.

Pike Place Market is many buildings built around a central arcade (which is distinguished by its huge red neon sign). Shops and restaurants fill buildings on Pike Place and Western Avenue. In the main arcade, dozens of booths sell fresh produce, cheese, spices, coffee, crafts, and seafood—which can be packed in dry ice for flights home. Farmers sell high-quality produce that helps to set Seattle's rigorous dining standards. The shopkeepers who rent store spaces sell art, curios, clothing, beads, and more. Most shops cater to tourists, but there are gems to be found.

EXPLORING THE MARKET

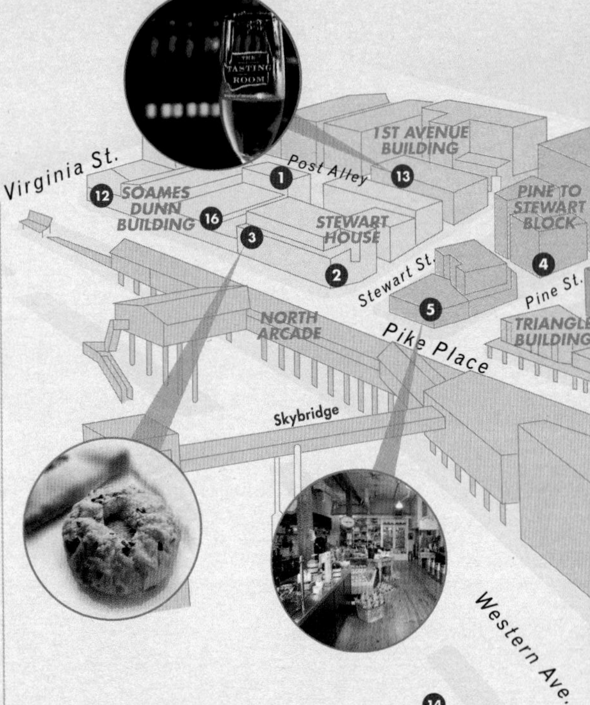

TOP EATS

❶ THE PINK DOOR. This adored (and adorable) Italian eatery is tucked into Post Alley. Whimsical decor, very good Italian food (such as the scrumptious *linguine alla vongole*), and weekend cabaret and burlesque make this gem a must-visit.

❷ LE PANIER. It's a self-proclaimed "Very French Bakery" and another Seattle favorite. The pastries are the main draw, but sandwiches on fresh baguettes and stuffed croissants offer more substantial snacks.

❸ PIROSHKY PIROSHKY. Authentic piroshky come in both standard varieties (beef and cheese) and Seattle-influenced ones (smoked salmon with cream cheese). There are plenty of sweet piroshky, too, if you need a sugar fix.

❹ CAMPAGNE. This French favorite and its charming attached café have you covered, whether you want a quick Croque Madame for lunch, a leisurely and delicious weekend brunch, or a white-tablecloth dinner.

❺ BEECHER'S. Artisanal cheeses—and mac-n-cheese to go—make this a spot Seattleites will brave the crowds for.

❻ THREE GIRLS BAKERY. This tiny bakery turns out piles of pastries and sandwiches on their fresh-baked bread (the baked salmon is a favorite).

❼ MATT'S IN THE MARKET. Matt's is the best restaurant in the Market, and one of the best in the city. Lunch is casual (try the catfish po'boy), and dinner is elegant, with fresh fish and local produce showcased on the small menu. Reservations are essential.

❽ DAILY DOZEN DONUTS. Mini-donuts are made fresh before your eyes and are a great snack to pick up before you venture into the labyrinth.

❾ MARKET GRILL. This no-frills counter serves up the market's best fish sandwiches and a great clam chowder.

❿ CHUKAR CHERRIES. Look for handmade confections featuring—but not restricted to—local cherries dipped in all sorts of sweet, rich coatings.

TOP SHOPS

⓫ MARKET SPICE TEA. For a tin of the Market's signature tea, Market Spice Blend, which is infused with cinnamon and clove oils, seek out Market Spice shop on the south side of the main arcade.

⓬ PIKE & WESTERN WINE SHOP. The Tasting Room in Post Alley may be a lovely place to sample Washington wines, but Pike and Western is the place where serious oenophiles flock.

⓭ THE TASTING ROOM. With one of the top wine selections in town, the Tasting Room offers Washington wines for the casual collector and the experienced connois-

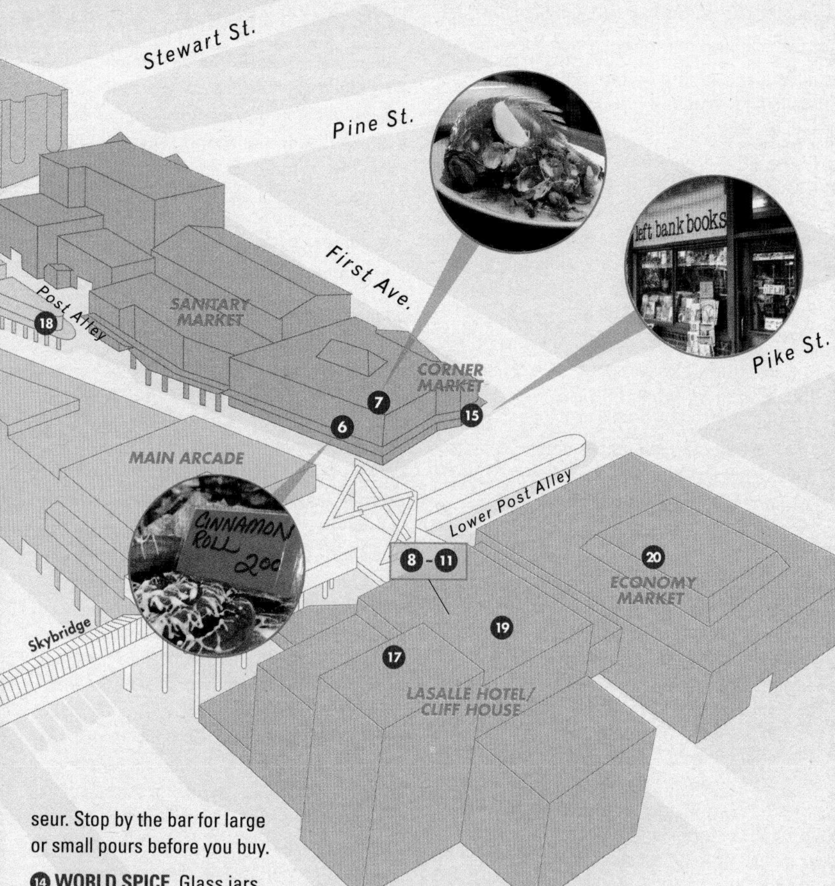

seur. Stop by the bar for large or small pours before you buy.

⓮ **WORLD SPICE.** Glass jars are filled with spices and teas from around the world here: Buy by the ounce or grab a pre-packaged gift set as a souvenir.

⓯ **LEFT BANK BOOKS.** A collective in operation since 1973, this tiny bookshop specializes in political and history titles and alternative literature.

⓰ **THE ORIGINAL STARBUCKS.** At 1912 Pike Place, you'll find the tiny store that opened in 1971 and started an empire. The shop is definitely more quaint and old-timey than its sleek younger siblings, and it features the original, uncensored (read: bare-breasted) version of the mermaid logo.

⓱ **RACHEL'S GINGER BEER.** The flagship store for Seattle's wildly popular ginger beer serves up delicious variations on its homemade brew, including boozy cocktails.

⓲ **PAPPARDELLE'S PASTA.** There's no type of pasta you could dream up that isn't already in a bin at Pappardelle's.

⓳ **DELAURENTI'S.** This amazing Italian grocery has everything from fancy olive oil to digestifs and wine to meats and fine cheeses.

☎ *206/386–4236* 🌐 *www.seattle.gov/parks/find/parks/discovery-park* 🎫 *Free.*

★ **Museum of Pop Culture (MoPOP)**

MUSEUM | **FAMILY** | Formerly EMP, Seattle's most controversial architectural statement is the 140,000-square-foot complex designed by architect Frank Gehry, who drew inspiration from electric guitars to achieve the building's curvy metallic design. It's a fitting backdrop for rock memorabilia from the likes of Bob Dylan and the grunge-scene heavies. A permanent exhibit provides a primer on the evolution of Seattle's music scene, focusing on Nirvana. In the Science Fiction and Fantasy Hall of Fame and related exhibits,you'll find iconic artifacts from sci-fi literature, film, television, and art, including an Imperial Dalek from *Doctor Who,* the command chair from the classic television series *Star Trek*, and Neo's coat from *The Matrix Reloaded.* ✉ *325 5th Ave. N , between Broad and Thomas Sts., Central District* ☎ *206/770–2700* 🌐 *www.mopop.org* 🎫 *$36 (less if purchased online).*

★ **Pacific Science Center**

MUSEUM | **FAMILY** | If you have kids, this nonprofit science center in the heart of Seattle is a must-visit, home to more than 200 indoor and outdoor hands-on exhibits, two IMAX theaters, a Laser Dome, a butterfly house, and a state-of-the-art planetarium. The dinosaur exhibit—complete with moving robotic reproductions—is a favorite, and tots can experiment with water at the ever-popular stream table. Machines analyze human physiology in the *Body Works* exhibit. When you need to warm up, the Tropical Butterfly House is 80°F and home to colorful butterflies from South and Central America, Africa, and Asia; other creatures live in the Insect Village and saltwater tide-pool areas. IMAX movies, planetarium shows, Live Science Shows, and Laser Dome rock shows run daily. Look for the giant white arches near the Space Needle and make a day of the surrounding sights. **■ TIP→ Pacific Science Center offers a number of lectures, forums, and "Science Cafes" for adults, plus a variety of educational programs for kids, including camp-ins, monthly parents' night outs, workshops, and more. See website for schedule information.** ✉ *200 2nd Ave. N, Queen Anne* ☎ *206/443–2001* 🌐 *www.pacsci.org* 🎫 *Center $29.95, IMAX $10.75–$16.95, laser shows $5–$14, combined museum/IMAX $34.95.*

Space Needle

BUILDING | **FAMILY** | Almost 60 years old, Seattle's most iconic building is as quirky and beloved as ever, and a recent remodel has restored and improved it. The distinctive, towering, 605-foot-high structure is visible throughout much of Seattle—but the view from the inside out is even better. A less-than-one-minute ride up to the observation deck yields 360-degree vistas of Downtown Seattle, the Olympic Mountains, Elliott Bay, Queen Anne Hill, Lake Union, and the Cascade Range through floor-to-ceiling windows, the open air observation area, and the rotating glass floor. Built for the 1962 World's Fair, the Needle has an app to guide you around and interactive experiences to leave your own mark, and a virtual reality bungee-jump. If the forecast says you may have a sunny day during your visit, schedule the Needle for that day! If you can't decide whether you want the daytime or nighttime view, for an extra 10 bucks you can buy a ticket that allows you to visit twice in one day. (Also look for package deals with Chihuly Garden and Glass.) ✉ *400 Broad St., Central District* ☎ *206/905–2100* 🌐 *www.spaceneedle.com* 🎫 *From $32.50.*

Restaurants

★ **Eden Hill**

$$$$ | **MODERN AMERICAN** | This tiny, 24-seat restaurant quietly turns out some of the most exciting and innovative food in the city in the form of visually stunning small plates. Tables are seated beside wide windows overlooking the serene side of Queen Anne. **Known for:** signature dessert "lick the bowl" made with foie gras; grand tasting menu requires reservations; daily changing menus. *Average main: $160 2209 Queen Anne Ave. N, Queen Anne 206/708–6836 www.edenhillrestaurant.com Closed Mon. No lunch.*

How to Cook a Wolf

$$ | ITALIAN | This sleek eatery features fresh, artisanal ingredients. Starters run the gamut from cured-meat platters to roasted almonds, pork terrine, chicken-liver mousse, and arugula salad, while tasty mains focus on simple handmade pastas—orecchiette with sausage, garlic, and ricotta. **Known for:** small plates; pasta. *Average main: $22 2208 Queen Anne Ave. N, Queen Anne 206/838–8090 www.ethanstowellrestaurants.com No lunch.*

★ La Marzocco Cafe & Showroom

$ | CAFÉ | Though better known for making espresso machines than espresso, La Marzocco brings a sprawling open café, gorgeous light, and incredible coffee and coffeemakers to Seattle Center. Sharing space with Seattle's cherished public radio station, KEXP, the café brings in a different roaster—their drinks, experts, and style—each month. **Known for:** elevated espresso drinks; monthly rotating roasters; inside KEXP space. *Average main: $3 KEXP Seattle Center Campus, 472 1st Ave. N, Lower Queen Anne 206/388–3500 www.lamarzoccousa.com/locations/ No dinner.*

Hotels

★ Pan Pacific Hotel Seattle

$$$$ | HOTEL | Located in one of Seattle's most vibrant and transforming neighborhoods, this hotel has undeniable draws, from the attractive and comfortable modern rooms to a happening lobby bar-restaurant serving Northwest cuisine and tapas, to the impressive views of the Space Needle and Lake Union. **Pros:** no touristy vibe like Downtown hotels; feels more luxurious than it costs; award-winning sustainability efforts. **Cons:** long walk to Downtown (though streetcar access and the hotel's free car service help with that); bathroom design isn't the most private. *Rooms from: $350 2125 Terry Ave., South Lake Union 206/264–8111 www.panpacific.com/seattle 131 rooms No meals.*

Pioneer Square

The Pioneer Square district, directly south of Downtown, is Seattle's oldest neighborhood. It attracts visitors with elegantly renovated (or in some cases replica) turn-of-the-20th-century redbrick buildings and art galleries. It's the center of Seattle's arts scene, and the galleries in this small neighborhood are a large part of the sights. In recent years, a growing number of new restaurants and businesses have opened, giving the neighborhood fresh appeal to locals and tourists alike.

Sights

Foster/White Gallery

MUSEUM | One of the Seattle art scene's heaviest hitters has digs as impressive as the works it shows: a century-old building with high ceilings and 7,000 square feet of exhibition space. Works by internationally acclaimed Northwest masters Kenneth Callahan, Mark Tobey, Alden Mason, and George Tsutakawa are on permanent display. *220 3rd Ave. S, Pioneer Square 206/622–2833 www.fosterwhite.com Free Closed Sun.–Mon.*

★ Greg Kucera Gallery

MUSEUM | One of the most important destinations on the First Thursday gallery walk, this gorgeous space is a top venue for national and regional artists. Be sure to check out the outdoor sculpture deck on the second level. If you have

Top Spots to Shop

Shopping becomes decidedly less fun when it involves driving around and circling for parking. You're better off limiting your all-day shopping tours to one of several key areas than planning to do a citywide search for a particular item. The following areas have the greatest concentration of shops and the greatest variety.

5th and 6th Avenues, Downtown. Depending on where you're staying, you may not need to drive to this area, but if you do, the parking garage at Pacific Place mall (at 600 Pine Street) always seems to have a space somewhere. Tackling either Pacific Place or the four blocks of 5th and 6th avenues between Olive Way and University Street will keep you very busy for a day.

1st Avenue, Belltown. From Wall Street to Pine Street, you'll find clothing boutiques, shoe stores, and some sleek home- and architectural-design stores. First Avenue and Pike Street brings you to the Pike Place Market. There are numerous pay parking lots on both 1st and 2nd avenues.

Pioneer Square. Walk or bus here if you can. Art galleries are the main draw, along with some home-decor and rug shops. If you do drive, many pay lots in the neighborhood participate in the "Parking Around the Square" program, which works with local businesses to offer shoppers validated parking; the website 🌐 *www.pioneersquare.org* lists the lots and stores that offer it.

International District. Parking in the I.D. can be hit or miss depending on the time of day. It's best if you can walk here from Downtown or take a quick bus ride over. If you do drive, go directly to the Uwajimaya parking lot. It validates for purchases, and it's a safe bet you'll be buying something here.

Pike–Pine Corridor, Capitol Hill. The best shopping in the Hill is on Pike and Pine Streets between Melrose Avenue and 10th Avenue East. Most of the stores are on Pike Street; Pine's best offerings are clustered on the western end of the avenue between Melrose and Summit. There are pay lots on Pike Street (near Broadway) and one on Summit by East Olive Way (next to the Starbucks).

Fremont and Ballard. Start in Fremont's small retail center, which is mostly along 36th Street. You may be able to snag street parking. After you've exhausted Fremont's shops, it's an easy drive over to Ballard. Ballard Avenue and N.W. Market Street are chockablock with great boutiques. Finding parking in Ballard can be tricky on weekends, but it's possible.

time for only one gallery visit, this is the place to go. You'll see big names that you might recognize—along with newer artists—and the thematic group shows are always thoughtful and well presented. ✉ *212 3rd Ave. S, Pioneer Square* ☎ *206/624–0770* 🌐 *www.gregkucera.com* 🎫 *Free* 🕒 *Closed Sun.–Mon.*

Restaurants

★ Salumi Cured Meats

$ | ITALIAN | The lines are long for hearty, unforgettable sandwiches filled with superior house-cured meats and more at this shop, originally founded by famed New York chef Mario Batali's father

Armandino. The oxtail sandwich special is unbeatable, but if it's unavailable or sold out (as specials often are by the lunchtime peak) order a salami, bresaola, porchetta, meatball, sausage, or lamb prosciutto sandwich with onions, peppers, cheese, and olive oil. **Known for:** cured meats; long lines; famous chef. *Average main: $10 ✉ 404 Occidental Ave. S, Pioneer Square ☎ 206/621–8772 🌐 www.salumicuredmeats.com ⏲ Closed Sat.–Sun.*

★ Taylor Shellfish Oyster Bar

$ | PACIFIC NORTHWEST | Oysters don't get any fresher than this: Taylor, a fifth-generation, family-owned company, opened its own restaurant in order to serve their products in the manner most befitting such pristine shellfish. The simple preparations—raw, cooked, and chilled—are all designed to best show off the seafood with light broths and sauces and a few accoutrements. **Known for:** popular with locals; expert shucking; unlikely pre-stadium tailgating stop. *Average main: $15 ✉ 410 Occidental Ave., Pioneer Square ☎ 206/501–4060 🌐 www.taylorshellfishfarms.com.*

Nightlife

BARS AND LOUNGES

Collins Pub

BARS/PUBS | The best beer bar in Pioneer Square features 22 rotating taps of Northwest (including Boundary Bay, Chuckanut, and Anacortes) and California beers and a long list of bottles from the region. Its upscale pub menu features local and seasonal ingredients. *✉ 526 2nd Ave., Pioneer Square ☎ 206/623–1016 🌐 www.collinspubseattle.com.*

Sake Nomi

BARS/PUBS | Whether you're a novice or expert, you'll appreciate the authentic offerings here. The shop and tasting bar is open until 10 pm Tuesday through Saturday and from noon to 6 on Sunday. Don't be shy—have a seat, try a few of the rotating samples, and ask a lot of questions. Sake can be served up in a variety of temperatures and styles. *✉ 76 S. Washington St., Pioneer Square ☎ 206/467–7253 🌐 www.sakenomi.us.*

Gallery Walks

It's fun to simply walk around Pioneer Square and pop into galleries. South Jackson Street to Yesler between Western and 4th Avenue South is a good area. The first Thursday of every month, galleries stay open late for First Thursday Art Walk, a neighborhood highlight. Visit 🌐 *www.firstthursdayseattle.com.*

International District

Bright welcome banners, 12-foot fiberglass dragons clinging to lampposts, and a traditional Chinese gate confirm you're in the International District. The I.D., as it's locally known, is synonymous with delectable dining—it has many inexpensive Chinese restaurants, but the best eateries reflect its Pan-Asian spirit: Vietnamese, Japanese, Malay, Filipino, Cambodian.

Sights

★ Uwajimaya

STORE/MALL | FAMILY | This huge, fascinating Japanese supermarket is a feast for the senses. A 30-foot-long red Chinese dragon stretches above colorful mounds of fresh produce and aisles of delicious packaged goods—colorful sweets and unique savory treats from countries throughout Asia. A busy food court serves sushi, Japanese bento-box meals, Chinese stir-fry combos, Korean barbecue, Hawaiian dishes, Vietnamese spring rolls, and an assortment of teas and tapioca drinks. You'll also find authentic housewares, cosmetics (Japanese-edition Shiseido), toys (Hello Kitty), and more. There's also a fantastic branch of the famous Kinokuniya bookstore chain, selling many Asian-language books. The large parking lot is free for one hour with a minimum $10 purchase or two hours with a minimum $20 purchase—don't forget to have your ticket validated by the cashiers. ✉ *600 5th Ave. S, International District* ☎ *206/624–6248* 🌐 *www.uwajimaya.com.*

★ Wing Luke Museum of the Asian Pacific American Experience

MUSEUM | FAMILY | One of the only museums in the United States devoted to the Asian Pacific American experience provides a sophisticated and often somber look at how immigrants and their descendants have transformed (and been transformed by) American culture. The evolution of the museum has been driven by community participation—the museum's library has an oral history lab, and many of the rotating exhibits are focused around stories from longtime residents and their descendants. Museum admission includes a guided walk-and-talk tour through the East Kong Yick building, where scores of immigrant workers from China, Japan, and the Philippines first found refuge in Seattle. ✉ *719 S King St., International District* ☎ *206/623–5124* 🌐 *www.wingluke.org* 🎫 *$17.*

Restaurants

★ Hood Famous Cafe + Bar

$ | PHILIPPINE | Starting out small and growing on word of mouth, as the name implies, Chera Amlag's bakery and bar sprouted from the popularity of the desserts she would make for her musician husband's Filipino pop-up dinners. Now in a cozy but elegant I.D. space, she serves the same dazzling purple ube cheesecake that got her here, alongside breakfast foods with Filipino touches, like longanisa (sausage) quiche, and butter mochi waffles with calamansi demerara syrup. **Known for:** ube cheesecake; innovative pastries. $ *Average main: $5* ✉ *504 5th Ave S, Suite 107A, International District* ☎ *206/485–7049* 🌐 *www.hoodfamousbakeshop.com.*

Tamarind Tree

$$ | VIETNAMESE | Wildly popular with savvy diners from all across the city, this Vietnamese haunt on the eastern side of the I.D. *really* doesn't look like much from the outside, especially because the entrance is through a cramped parking lot (which it shares with Sichuanese Cuisine restaurant), but once you're inside, the elegantly simple, large, and warm space is extremely welcoming. The food is the main draw—try the spring rolls, which are stuffed with fresh herbs, fried tofu, peanuts, coconut, jicama, and carrots; authentic bánh xèo; spicy pho; the signature "seven courses of beef"; and, to finish, grilled banana cake with warm coconut milk. **Known for:** great service; delicious cocktails; reservations recommended. $ *Average main: $21* ✉ *1036 S Jackson St., International District* ☎ *206/860–1404* 🌐 *www.tamarindtreerestaurant.com.*

First Hill

Smack between Downtown and Capitol Hill, First Hill is an odd mix of sterile-looking medical facilities (earning it the nickname "Pill Hill"), old brick buildings that look like they belong on a college campus, and newer residential towers.

Sights

Frye Art Museum

MUSEUM | In addition to its beloved permanent collection—predominately 19th- and 20th-century pastoral paintings—the Frye hosts eclectic and often avant-garde exhibits, putting this elegant museum on par with the Henry in the U-District. No matter what's going on in the stark,

Capitol Hill

Sights

1 Volunteer Park and the Seattle Asian Art Museum **B2**

2 Washington Park Arboretum .. **D1**

Restaurants

1 Altura **A3**

2 Cascina Spinasse.... **B5**

3 Dino's Tomato Pie.. **A4**

Hotels

1 11th Avenue Inn Seattle Bed & Breakfast... **B4**

2 Shafer Baillie Mansion Bed & Breakfast .. **B2**

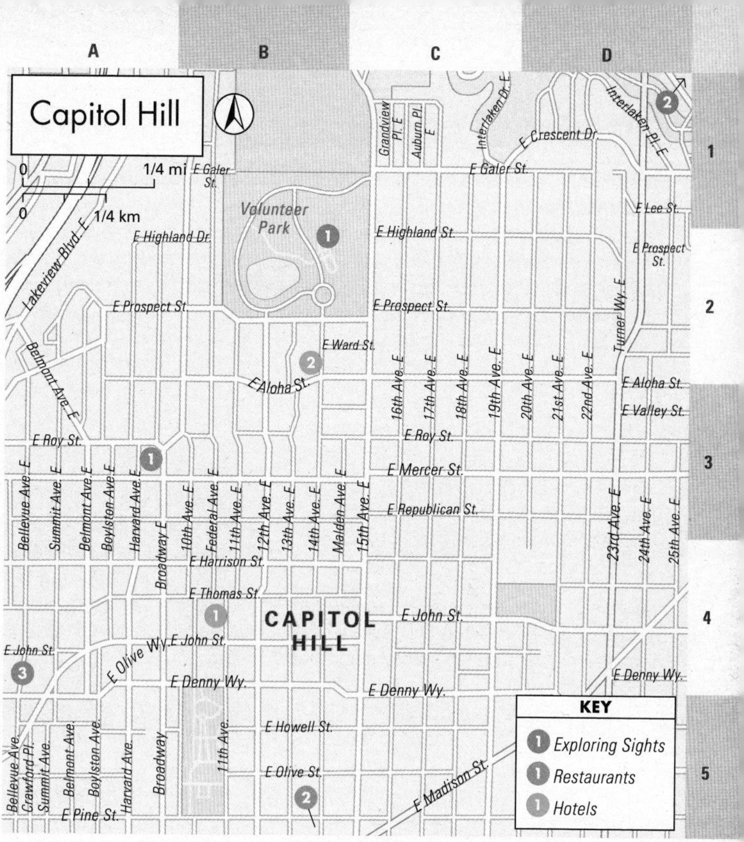

KEY

Exploring Sights

Restaurants

Hotels

brightly lighted back galleries, it always seems to blend well with the permanent collection, which is rotated regularly. Thanks to the legacy of Charles and Emma Frye, the museum is always free, and parking is free as well. ✉ *704 Terry Ave., First Hill* ☎ *206/622–9250* 🌐 *www.fryemuseum.org* 🎫 *Free.*

Capitol Hill

The Hill has two faces: on one side, it's young and edgy, full of artists, musicians, and students. Tattoo parlors and coffeehouses abound, as well as thumping music venues and bars. On the other side, it's elegant and upscale, with tree-lined streets, 19th-century mansions, and John Charles Olmsted's Volunteer Park. Converted warehouses, modern high-rises, colorfully painted two-story homes, and brick mansions all occupy the same neighborhood.

Sights

Volunteer Park and the Seattle Asian Art Museum

MUSEUM | Nestled among the grand homes of North Capitol Hill sits this 45-acre grassy expanse that's perfect for picnicking, sunbathing (or stomping in rain puddles), and strolling. You can tell this is one of the city's older parks by the size of the trees and the rhododendrons, many of which were planted more than a hundred years ago. The Olmsted Brothers, the premier landscape architects of the day, helped with the final design in 1904; the park has changed surprisingly little since then. In the center of the park is the recently remodeled **Seattle Asian Art Museum (SAAM, a branch of the Seattle**

Art Museum), housed in a 1933 art moderne–style edifice. It fits surprisingly well with the stark plaza stretching from the front door to the edge of a bluff, and with the lush plants of Volunteer Park. The museum's collections include thousands of paintings, sculptures, pottery, and textiles from China, Japan, India, Korea, and several Southeast Asian countries.

The Victorian-style Volunteer Park Conservatory greenhouse, across from the museum, has a magnificent collection of tropical pants. The five houses include the Bromeliad House, the Palm House, the Fern House, the Seasonal Display House, and the Cactus House. Admission is free.

A focal point of the park, at the western edge of the hill in front of the Asian Art Museum, is Isamu Noguchi's sculpture, *Black Sun,* a natural frame from which to view the Space Needle, the Puget Sound, and the Olympic Mountains. ✉ *Park entrance, 1400 E Prospect St., Capitol Hill* ☎ *206/654–3100 museum, 206/684–4743 conservatory* 🎫 *Park free; museum $5, free for all on the 1st Thursday of each month and for seniors on 1st Friday.*

★ Washington Park Arboretum

GARDEN | **FAMILY** | As far as Seattle's green spaces go, this 230-acre arboretum is arguably the most beautiful. On calm weekdays, the place feels really secluded. The seasons are always on full display: in warm winters, flowering cherries and plums bloom in its protected valleys as early as late February, while the flowering shrubs in Rhododendron Glen and Azalea Way bloom March through June. In autumn, trees and shrubs glow in hues of crimson, pumpkin, and lemon; in winter, plantings chosen specially for their stark and colorful branches dominate the landscape. In 2018, as part of a 20-year master plan, the arboretum completed a 1¼ mile trail that connects to an existing path to create a 2½-mile accessible loop, giving all guests access to areas that were previously hard to reach. March through October, visit the peaceful **Japanese Garden,** a compressed world of mountains, forests, rivers, lakes, and tablelands. The pond, lined with blooming water irises in spring, has turtles and brightly colored koi. An authentic Japanese tea house is reserved for tea ceremonies and instruction on the art of serving tea (visitors who would like to enjoy a bowl of tea and sweets can purchase a $10 "Chado" tea ticket at the Garden ticket booth). The Graham Visitors Center at the park's north end has descriptions of the arboretum's flora and fauna (which include 130 endangered plants), as well as brochures, a garden gift shop, and walking-tour maps. Free tours are offered most of the year; see website for schedule. There is a pleasant playground at the ball fields on the south end of the park. ✉ *2300 Arboretum Dr. E, Capitol Hill* ☎ *206/543–8800 arboretum, 206/684–4725 Japanese garden* 🌐 *botanicgardens.uw.edu/washington-park-arboretum/* 🎫 *Free, Japanese garden $8.*

Restaurants

★ Altura

$$$$ | **ITALIAN** | A hand-carved cedar angel statue watches over diners at this lively spot, where chef-owner Nathan Lockwood lends a Northwest focus to Italian cuisine. The set tasting menu weaves rare, intriguing, and fascinating local and global ingredients into classic Italian techniques. **Known for:** tasting menu; interesting ingredients. 💲 *Average main: $157* ✉ *617 Broadway E, Capitol Hill* ☎ *206/402–6749* 🌐 *www.alturarestaurant.com* 🕒 *Closed Sun.-Mon. No lunch.*

★ Cascina Spinasse

$$$ | **ITALIAN** | Wth cream-colored lace curtains and true Italian soul, Spinasse brings the cuisine of Piedmont to Seattle. Chef Stuart Lane makes the pasta fresh daily and with such sauces and fillings as short rib ragu, eggplant and anchovies, or simply, as in their signature dish, dressed in butter and sage. *Secondi* options can range from braised pork belly with cabbage to stewed venison served over polenta. **Known for:** handmade pasta; amaro. *Average main: $27 ✉ 1531 14th Ave., Capitol Hill ☎ 206/251–7673 ⊕ www.spinasse.com ⊙ No lunch.*

★ Dino's Tomato Pie

$ | PIZZA | Long hailed as the creator of Seattle's best pizza at his first shop, Delancey, Brandon Pettit perhaps even improves on his previous recipe as he re-creates the neighborhood joints of his New Jersey childhood. The thick, crisp corners of the square Sicilian pies caramelize in the hot oven into what is practically pizza candy, while lovers of traditional round pizza will enjoy the char on the classics. **Known for:** square pizza; creative cocktails; children are not allowed to dine. *Average main: $15 ✉ 1524 E Olive Way, Capitol Hill ☎ 206/403–1742 ⊕ www.dinostomatopie.com ⊙ No lunch.*

Hotels

★ 11th Avenue Inn Seattle Bed & Breakfast

$ | B&B/INN | The closest B&B to Downtown offers all the charm of a classic bed-and-breakfast (exquisitely styled with antique beds and Oriental rugs) with the convenience of being near the action. **Pros:** free on-site parking; oozes vintage charm; wonderful owner and staff. **Cons:** although most guests are courteous, sound does carry in old houses; no kids under 12; minimum three-night stay. *Rooms from: $169 ✉ 121 11th Ave. E, Capitol Hill ☎ 206/720–7161 ⊕ www.11thavenueinn.com 9 rooms Free Breakfast.*

★ Shafer Baillie Mansion Bed & Breakfast

$$ | B&B/INN | The opulent guest rooms and suites on the second floor are large, with private baths, antique furnishings, Oriental rugs, huge windows, and lush details like ornate four-poster beds; third-floor rooms, while lovely, have a more contemporary country feel, but still have private baths and large windows. **Pros:** wonderful staff; great interior and exterior common spaces; free Wi-Fi. **Cons:** no elevator and the walk to the third floor might be hard for some guests; while children are allowed, some guests say the mansion isn't kid-friendly; three-night minimum stay during summer weekends. *Rooms from: $199 ✉ 907 14th Ave. E, Capitol Hill ☎ 800/985–4654 ⊕ www.sbmansion.com 6 rooms, 2 suites Free Breakfast.*

Nightlife

★ Montana

BARS/PUBS | Lived-in booths and a welcoming atmosphere keep this place packed with everyone from couples on a first date to groups of old friends. As an anchor to the E Olive bar strip, it makes for excellent people-watching, either from the inside looking out or from the co-opted piece of sidewalk called a "parklet" that serves as the patio. *✉ 1506 E Olive Way, Capitol Hill ☎ 206/327–9362 ⊕ www.montanainseattle.com.*

Shopping

★ Elliott Bay Book Company

BOOKS/STATIONERY | A major reason to visit this landmark bookstore—formerly a longtime haunt in Pioneer Square, hence the name—is the great selection of Pacific Northwest history books and fiction titles by local authors, complete with handwritten recommendation cards from the knowledgeable staff. A big selection of bargain books, lovely skylights, and an appealing café all sweeten the deal—and the hundreds of author events held every year mean that nearly every day is an exciting one for dropping by. *✉ 1521 10th Ave., Capitol Hill ☎ 206/624–6600 ⊕ www.elliottbaybook.com.*

Fremont

For many years, Fremont enjoyed its reputation as Seattle's weirdest neighborhood, home to hippies, artists, bikers, and rat-race dropouts. But Fremont has lost most of its artist cachet as the stores along its main strip turned more upscale, and rising rents sent many longtime residents reluctantly packing (many to nearby Ballard).

Sights

Theo Chocolate Factory Tour

STORE/MALL | FAMILY | If it weren't for a small sign on the sidewalk pointing the way and the faint whiff of cocoa in the air, you'd never know that Fremont has its own artisanal chocolate factory with daily tours. Since it opened in 2005, Theo has become one of the Northwest's most familiar chocolate brands, sold in shops across the city. ✉ *3400 Phinney Ave. N, Fremont* ☎ *206/632–5100* 🌐 *www.theochocolate.com* 🎟 *Tour $12.*

Restaurants

★ Manolin

$$$ | SEAFOOD | Walking into the light-filled dining room of Manolin, with its horseshoe-shape bar framing the open kitchen, transports you straight to the sea. Blue tiles, the wood-fired oven in the center, the cool marble bar, and the seafood-laden menu all bring diners to the ambiguous maritime destination, where ceviches are inspired by coastal Mexico, plantain chips come from the Caribbean, smoked salmon has vaguely Scandinavian flavors, and the squid with black rice and ginger is as if from Asia, all mingling on the menu. **Known for:** a celebration of ceviche; creative cocktails; global flavors. *$ Average main: $30* ✉ *3621 Stone Way N, Fremont* ☎ *206/294–3331* 🌐 *www.manolinseattle.com* 🕒 *No lunch. Closed Mon.* 💳 *No credit cards.*

★ Vif

$ | BISTRO | Part coffee shop, part casual snack restaurant, and part wine retailer, Vif is all magic. The brainchild of a former pastry chef and wine director of one of Seattle's bygone restaurants, the menu brings the kind of nuance and skill that you'd expect from a pastry chef but the elegance of a wine expert. **Known for:** expertly prepared coffee; curated wine selection; light fare and "snackettes". *$ Average main: $9* ✉ *4401 Fremont Ave. N, Fremont* ☎ *206/557–7357* 🌐 *www.vifseattle.com* 🕒 *No dinner.*

Hotels

★ Chelsea Station Inn Bed & Breakfast

$$$ | B&B/INN | The four 900-square-foot suites in this 1920s brick colonial have distressed hardwood floors with colorful rugs, decorative fireplaces, sleeper sofas, contemporary furnishings, and a soft, modern color palette, and are a convenient and luxurious jumping-off point for all the north end has to offer. **Pros:** great, unobtrusive host; huge rooms and 1½ bathrooms per suite; fabulous breakfasts and complimentary snacks. **Cons:** far from Downtown; no TVs; no elevator. *$ Rooms from: $287* ✉ *4915 Linden Ave. N, Fremont* ☎ *206/547–6077* 🌐 *www.chelseastationinn.com* *4 suites* 🍽 *Free Breakfast.*

Ballard

Ballard is Seattle's sweetheart. This historically Scandinavian neighborhood doesn't have major sights outside of the Hiram M. Chittenden Locks, though it's also home to one of Seattle's most beloved and beautiful public beaches, Golden Gardens Park, which looks out at panoramic views of the Puget Sound and Olympic Mountains. The Ballard Avenue Historic District is a place to check out lovely old buildings, along with a happening nightlife, shopping, and restaurant scene. Every Sunday, rain or shine, Ballard hosts one of the best farmers' markets in town.

Sights

★ Hiram M. Chittenden Locks

LIGHTHOUSE | **FAMILY** | There's no doubt—there's something intriguing and eerie about seeing two bodies of water, right next to each other, at different levels. The Hiram M. Chittenden Locks (also known as "Ballard Locks") are an important passage in the 8-mile Lake Washington Ship Canal that connects Puget Sound to freshwater Lake Washington and Lake Union. In addition to boat traffic, the locks see an estimated half-million salmon and trout make the journey from saltwater to fresh each summer, with the help of a fish ladder. Families picnic beneath oak trees in the adjacent 7-acre Carl S. English Botanical Gardens; various musical performances (from jazz bands to chamber music) serenade visitors on summer weekends; and steel-tinted salmon awe spectators as they climb a 21-step fish ladder en route to their freshwater spawning grounds—a heroic journey from the Pacific to the base of the Cascade Mountains. Free guided tours of the locks depart from the visitor center and will give you far more information than the plaques by the locks. ✉ *3015 NW 54th St., Ballard* ✣ *From Fremont, head north on Leary Way NW, west on NW Market St., and south on 54th St.* ☎ *206/783–7059* 🌐 *www.ballardlocks.org* 🎟 *Free* 🕑 *No tours in Jan. or Feb.*

Restaurants

★ Delancey

$ | **PIZZA** | Brandon Pettit spent years developing his thin-but-chewy pizza crust, and the final product has made him a contender for the city's best pies. Pettit himself is occasionally manning the wood-fired oven at this sweetly sophisticated little spot north of downtown Ballard that he owns with partner Molly Wizenberg (author of the popular "Orangette" food blog). **Known for:** quality pizza toppings; desserts. $ *Average main: $16* ✉ *1415 NW 70th St., Ballard* ☎ *206/838–1960* 🌐 *www.delanceyseattle.com* 🕑 *Closed Mon. No lunch.*

Staple & Fancy

$$$$ | **MODERN ITALIAN** | The "Staple" side of this Ethan Stowell restaurant at the south end of Ballard Avenue might mean gnocchi served with corn and chanterelles or a whole grilled branzino. But visitors to the glam, remodeled, historic brick building are best served by going "fancy," meaning the chef's menu dinner where diners are asked about allergies and food preferences, then presented with several courses (technically four, but the appetizer usually consists of a few different plates) of whatever the cooks are playing with on the line that night—cured meats, salads made with exotic greens, handmade pastas, seasonal desserts. **Known for:** multicourse menu; pasta. $ *Average main: $33* ✉ *4739 Ballard Ave. NW, Ballard* ☎ *206/789–1200* 🌐 *www.ethanstowellrestaurants.com* 🕑 *No lunch.*

The Walrus and the Carpenter

$$$ | **SEAFOOD** | Chef-owner Renee Erickson was inspired by the casual oyster bars of Paris to open this bustling shoebox of a restaurant on the south end of Ballard Avenue (in the rear of a historic brick building, behind Staple & Fancy). Seats fill fast at the zinc bar and the scattered tall tables where seafood fans slurp on fresh-shucked Olympias and Blue Pools and other local oysters, but the menu also offers refined small plates like grilled sardines with shallots and walnuts or roasted greengage plums in cream. **Known for:** oysters; small plates; very popular (long wait times). $ *Average main: $27* ✉ *4743 Ballard Ave. NW, Ballard* ☎ *206/395–9227* 🌐 *www.thewalrusbar.com.*

Hotels

★ Hotel Ballard

$$ | HOTEL | A historic sandstone building features a modern gray-and-yellow palette that melds historical details with design accents that nod to the neighborhood's Scandinavian heritage, and many rooms include views of waterways and the Olympic Mountains; eight rooftop suites are especially inviting. **Pros:** in the heart of Ballard; $15 self park; free use of large gym with saltwater pool; fireplaces and soaking tubs in suites. **Cons:** not close to the majority of Seattle attractions. *$ Rooms from: $239 ✉ 5216 Ballard Ave. N.W., Ballard ☎ 206/789–5012 🌐 www.hotelballard.com 20 rooms, 8 suites No meals No credit cards.*

Wallingford and Greenlake

The laid-back neighborhood of Wallingford is directly east of Fremont—the boundaries actually blur quite a bit. There are several lovely parks and residential streets brimming with colorful Craftsman houses. The main drag, 45th Street NW, has an eclectic group of shops, from a gourmet beer store to an erotic bakery to a Hawaiian merchant, along with a few great coffeehouses, and several notable restaurants.

Sights

★ Gas Works Park

NATIONAL/STATE PARK | FAMILY | Far from being an eyesore, the hulking remains of an old 1907 gas plant actually lends quirky character to the otherwise open, hilly, 20-acre park. Get a great view of Downtown Seattle while seaplanes rise up from the south shore of Lake Union; the best vantage point is from the zodiac sculpture at the top of a very steep hill, so be sure to wear appropriate walking shoes. This is a great spot for couples and families alike; the enormous and recently remodeled playground has rope climbing structures, a variety of swings, and a padded floor. Crowds throng to picnic and enjoy outdoor summer concerts, movies, and the July 4th fireworks display over Lake Union. **■ TIP→ Gas Works can easily be reached on foot from Fremont Center, via the waterfront Burke-Gilman Trail.** *✉ 2101 N Northlake Way, at Meridian Ave. N (the north end of Lake Union), Wallingford.*

Hotels

★ Greenlake Guest House

$$ | B&B/INN | Outdoorsy types, visitors who want to stay in a low-key residential area, and anyone who wants to feel pampered and refreshed will enjoy this lovely B&B across the street from beautiful Green Lake. **Pros:** views; thoughtful amenities and wonderful hosts; can accommodate kids over four years old; short walk to restaurants. **Cons:** 5 miles from Downtown; on a busy street. *$ Rooms from: $229 ✉ 7630 E. Green Lake Dr. N, Green Lake ☎ 206/729–8700, 866/355–8700 🌐 www.greenlakeguesthouse.com 5 rooms Free Breakfast.*

University District

The U District, as everyone calls it, is the neighborhood surrounding the University of Washington (UW or "U Dub" to locals). The campus is extraordinarily beautiful (especially in springtime, when the cherry blossoms are flowering), and the Henry Art Gallery, on its western edge, is one of the city's best small museums. Beyond that, the appeal of the neighborhood lies in its variety of cheap, delicious ethnic eateries, its proximity to the waters of Portage and Union Bays and Lake Washington, and its youthful energy.

Sights

Burke Museum of Natural History and Culture

MUSEUM | FAMILY | Founded in 1885, the Burke is the state's oldest museum but just underwent a huge redesign and got a new building in 2019. It features exhibits that survey the natural history of the Pacific Northwest, but also a behind-the-scenes look at how museums work, with its open doors and windows. Highlights include artifacts from Washington's 35 Native American tribes, dinosaur skeletons, and dioramas depicting the traditions of Pacific Rim cultures. An adjacent ethnobotanical garden is planted with species that were important to the region's Native American communities, and the Native-owned cafe serves fry bread and indigenous foods. Check out the schedule for family events and adult classes. ✉ *University of Washington campus, 17th Ave. NE and NE 45th St., University District* ☎ *206/543–5590* 🌐 *www.burkemuseum.org* 🎫 *$22, free 1st Thurs. of month.*

★ Henry Art Gallery

MUSEUM | This large gallery is perhaps the best reason to take a side trip to the U-District and consistently presents sophisticated and thought-provoking contemporary work. Exhibits pull from many different genres and include mixed media, photography, and paintings. Richard C. Elliott used more than 21,500 bicycle and truck reflectors of different colors and sizes in his paintings that fit into the sculpture alcoves on the exterior walls of the museum; in another permanent installation, *Light Reign*, a "Skyspace" from artist James Turrell, an elliptical chamber allows visitors to view the sky. More than a few people have used this as a meditation spot; at night the chamber is illuminated by thousands of LED lights. ✉ *University of Washington campus, 15th Ave. NE and NE 41st St., University District* ☎ *206/543–2280* 🌐 *www.henryart.org* 🎫 *$10* ⏲ *Closed Mon. and Tues.*

West Seattle

Cross the bridge to West Seattle and it's another world altogether. Jutting out into Elliott Bay and Puget Sound, separated from the city by the Duwamish waterway, this out-of-the-way neighborhood covers most of the city's western peninsula—and, indeed, it has an identity of its own.

Sights

★ Alki Point and Beach

BEACH—SIGHT | FAMILY | In summer, this is as close to California as Seattle gets—and some hardy residents even swim in the cold, salty waters of Puget Sound here (water temperature ranges from 46°F to 56°F). This 2½-mile stretch of sand has views of the Seattle skyline and the Olympic Mountains, and the beachfront promenade is especially popular with skaters, joggers, strollers, and cyclists. Year-round, Seattleites come to build sand castles, beachcomb, and fly kites; in winter, storm-watchers come to see the crashing waves. Facilities include drinking water, grills, picnic tables, phones, and restrooms; restaurants line the street across from the beach. To get here from Downtown, take either Interstate 5 south or Highway 99 south to the West Seattle Bridge (keep an eye out, as this exit is easy to miss) and exit onto Harbor Avenue SW, turning right at the stoplight. Alki Point is the place where David Denny, John Low, and Lee Terry arrived in September 1851, ready to found a city. The Alki Point Lighthouse dates from 1913. One of 195 Lady Liberty replicas found around the country lives near the 2700 block of Alki Avenue SW. Miss Liberty (or Little Liberty) is a popular meeting point for beachfront picnics and dates. ✉ *1702 Alki Ave. SW, West Seattle.*

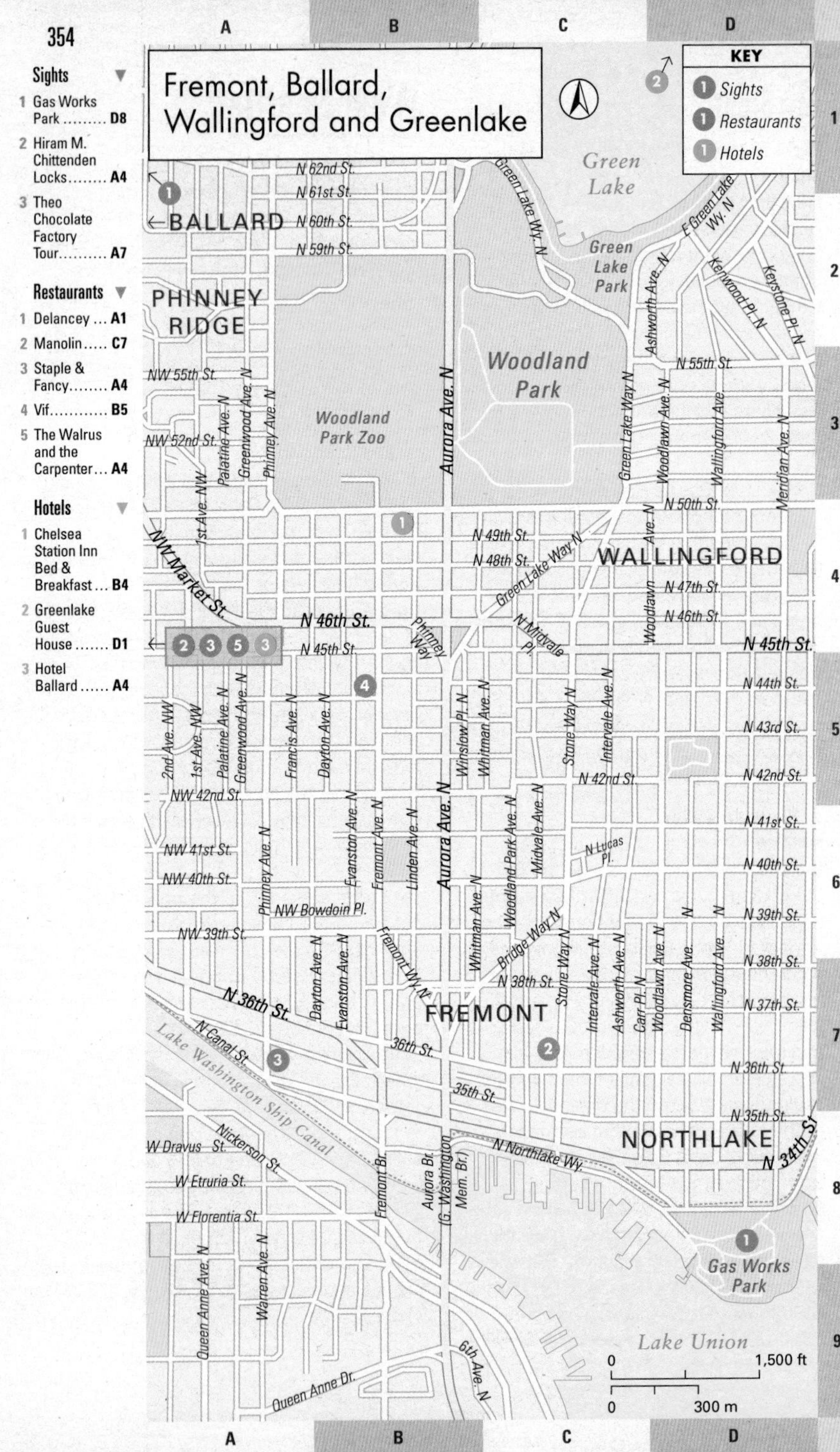
Sights
1 Gas Works Park D8
2 Hiram M. Chittenden Locks........ A4
3 Theo Chocolate Factory Tour.......... A7
Restaurants
1 Delancey ... A1
2 Manolin..... C7
3 Staple & Fancy........ A4
4 Vif............ B5
5 The Walrus and the Carpenter... A4
Hotels
1 Chelsea Station Inn Bed & Breakfast ... B4
2 Greenlake Guest House D1
3 Hotel Ballard A4
Fremont, Ballard, Wallingford and Greenlake
KEY
Sights
Restaurants
Hotels
A
B
C
D
1
2
3
4
5
6
7
8
9
BALLARD
PHINNEY RIDGE
WALLINGFORD
FREMONT
NORTHLAKE
Green Lake
Green Lake Park
Woodland Park
Woodland Park Zoo
Gas Works Park
Lake Union
Lake Washington Ship Canal
N 62nd St.
N 61st St.
N 60th St.
N 59th St.
NW 55th St.
N 55th St.
NW 52nd St.
N 50th St.
N 49th St.
N 48th St.
N 47th St.
N 46th St.
N 45th St.
N 44th St.
N 43rd St.
N 42nd St.
NW 42nd St.
N 41st St.
NW 41st St.
N 40th St.
NW 40th St.
NW Bowdoin Pl.
N 39th St.
NW 39th St.
N 38th St.
N 37th St.
N 36th St.
36th St.
35th St.
N 35th St.
N 34th St.
N Canal St.
N Northlake Wy.
NW Market St.
Green Lake Wy. N
E Green Lake Wy. N
Green Lake Way N
Ashworth Ave. N
Kenwood Pl. N
Keystone Pl. N
Woodlawn Ave. N
Wallingford Ave. N
Meridian Ave. N
Aurora Ave. N
Palatine Ave. N
Greenwood Ave. N
Phinney Ave. N
1st Ave. NW
2nd Ave. NW
Francis Ave. N
Dayton Ave. N
Phinney Way
N Midvale Pl.
Winslow Pl. N
Whitman Ave. N
Stone Way N
Intervale Ave. N
Evanston Ave. N
Fremont Ave. N
Linden Ave. N
Woodland Park Ave. N
Midvale Ave. N
N Lucas Pl.
Bridge Way N
Fremont Wy. N
Carr Pl. N
Densmore Ave.
Nickerson St.
W Dravus St.
W Etruria St.
W Florentia St.
Fremont Br.
Aurora Br. (G. Washington Mem. Br.)
Queen Anne Ave. N
Warren Ave. N
Queen Anne Dr.
6th Ave. N
0
1,500 ft
0
300 m

Woodinville Wineries

Walla Walla wine country is too far to go from Seattle if you've only got a few days; instead, check out Woodinville's excellent wineries. It's only about 22 miles from Seattle's city center. You'll need a car unless you sign up for a guided tour. Check out *www.woodinvillewinecountry.com* for a full list of wineries and touring maps.

Wineries

There are more than 50 wineries in Woodinville, though most of them don't have tasting rooms. This list provides a good survey, from the big guys to the smallest boutique producers:

Chateau Ste. Michelle (14111 N.E. 145th St. *www.ste-michelle.com*) is the grande dame of the Woodinville wine scene, and perhaps the most recognizable name nationwide. Guided tours of the winery and grounds (which do include a château) are available daily 10:30–4:30. The tasting room is open daily 10–5. Check the website for special events like dinners and concerts.

Columbia Winery (14030 N.E. 145th St. *www.columbiawinery.com*) is another major player with a grand house anchoring its winery. Columbia's tasting room is open Sunday–Tuesday 11–6 and Wednesday–Saturday 11–7. Regular tastings are $10 and private tastings are available for $25 per person.

Novelty Hill-Januik (*14710 Woodinville-Redmond Rd. NE* *www.noveltyhilljanuik.com*) is often described as the most Napa-esque experience in Woodinville. The tasting room (open daily 11–5) for these sister wineries is sleek and modern. Themed tastings are $7–$10 per person. Brick-oven pizza is available on weekends.

Ross Andrew (*14810 N.E. 145th St., No. A-2* *www.rossandrewwinery.com*) is a newcomer that is already at the top of many enthusiasts' lists for Cabs and Syrah from Columbia Valley grapes and Pinot Blanc and Pinot Gris from Oregon grapes. The tasting room is open Thursday–Monday noon–5 (Saturday until 6).

Restaurants

Ma'ono Fried Chicken & Whiskey
$$ | HAWAIIANKOREAN FUSION | A quietly hip vibe pervades this culinary beacon in West Seattle, where the vast bar surrounds an open kitchen. Diners of all stripes relish the Hawaiian spin on fresh and high-quality Pacific Northwest bounty. **Known for:** fried chicken; whiskey. *Average main: $18* *4437 California Ave. SW, West Seattle* *206/935–1075* *www.maonoseattle.com* *No lunch weekdays.*

Activities

The question in Seattle isn't "do you exercise?" Rather, it's "how do you exercise?" Athleticism is a regular part of most people's lives here, whether it's an afternoon jog, a sunrise rowing session, a lunch-hour bike ride, or an evening game of Frisbee.

PARKS INFORMATION

King County Parks and Recreation
PARK—SPORTS-OUTDOORS | This agency manages many of the parks outside city limits. *201 S. Jackson, Suite 700, Downtown* *206/477–4527 information*

🌐 *www.kingcounty.gov/services/parks-recreation/parks.*

Washington State Parks

PARK—SPORTS-OUTDOORS | The state manages several parks and campgrounds in greater Seattle. ✉ *1111 Israel Rd. SW, Olympia* ☎ *360/902–8844 for general information, 888/226–7688 for campsite reservations* 🌐 *www.parks.wa.gov.*

BIKING

Biking is probably Seattle's most popular sport. Thousands of Seattleites bike to work, and even more ride recreationally, especially on weekends. In the past, Seattle wasn't a particularly bike-friendly city. But the city government has adopted a sweeping Bicycle Master Plan that calls for 118 new miles of bike lanes, 19 miles of bike paths, and countless route signs and lane markings throughout the city by 2017. The plan can't erase the hills, though—only masochists should attempt Queen Anne Hill and Phinney Ridge. Fortunately, all city buses have easy-to-use bike racks (on the front of the buses, below the windshield) and drivers are used to waiting for cyclists to load and unload their bikes. If you're not comfortable biking in urban traffic—and there is a lot of urban traffic to contend with here—you can do a combination bus-and-bike tour of the city or stick to the car-free Burke-Gilman Trail.

Seattle drivers are fairly used to sharing the road with cyclists. With the exception of the occasional road-rager or clueless cell-phone talker, drivers usually leave a generous amount of room when passing; however, there are biking fatalities every year, so be alert and cautious, especially when approaching blind intersections, of which Seattle has many. You must wear a helmet at all times (it's the law) and be sure to lock up your bike—bikes do get stolen, even in quiet residential neighborhoods.

The Seattle Parks Department sponsors Bicycle Sundays on various weekends from May through September. On these Sundays, a 4-mile stretch of Lake Washington Boulevard—from Mt. Baker Beach to Seward Park—is closed to motor vehicles. Many riders continue around the 2-mile loop at Seward Park and back to Mt. Baker Beach to complete a 10-mile, car-free ride. Check with the **Seattle Parks and Recreation Department** (☎ *206/684–4075* 🌐 *www.seattle.gov/parks/bicyclesunday*) for a complete schedule.

The trail that circles **Green Lake** is popular with cyclists, though runners and walkers can impede fast travel. The city-maintained **Burke-Gilman Trail,** a slightly less congested path, follows an abandoned railroad line 14 miles roughly following Seattle's waterfront from Ballard to Kenmore, at the north end of Lake Washington. (From there, serious cyclists can continue on the Sammamish River Trail to Marymoor Park in Redmond; in all, the trail spans 42 miles between Seattle and Issaquah.) **Discovery Park** is a very tranquil place to tool around in. **Myrtle Edwards Park,** north of Pier 70, has a two-lane waterfront path for biking and running. The **islands of the Puget Sound** are also easily explored by bike (there are rental places by the ferry terminals), though keep in mind that Bainbridge, Whidbey, and the San Juans all have some tough hills.

King County has more than 100 miles of paved and nearly 70 miles of unpaved routes, including the Sammamish River, Interurban, Green River, Cedar River, Snoqualmie Valley, and Soos Creek trails. For more information, contact the **King County Parks and Recreation** office (☎ *206/296–8687*).

RENTALS

Montlake Bicycle Shop

BICYCLING | This shop a mile south of the University of Washington and within easy riding distance of the Burke-Gilman Trail rents mountain bikes, road bikes, basic cruisers, electric bikes, and tandems.

Prices range from $45 to $110 for the day, with discounts for longer rentals (credit card hold required). ✉ *2223 24th Ave. E, Montlake* ☎ *206/329–7333* 🌐 *www.montlakebike.com.*

BOATING AND KAYAKING

★ Agua Verde Cafe & Paddle Club

BOATING | Start out by renting a kayak and paddling along either the Lake Union shoreline, with its hodgepodge of funky-to-fabulous houseboats and dramatic Downtown vistas, or Union Bay on Lake Washington, with its marshes and cattails. Afterward, take in the lakefront as you wash down some Mexican food (halibut tacos, anyone?) with a margarita. Kayaks and stand-up paddleboards are available March through October and are rented by the hour—$20 for single kayaks, $26 for doubles, and $23 for SUPs. It pays to paddle midweek: if you go before early afternoon they offer weekday discounts. Email for winter paddling options or for a tour (tours@aguaverde.com). ✉ *1303 NE Boat St., University District* ☎ *206/545–8570* 🌐 *www.aguaverde.com.*

Alki Kayak Tours & Adventure Center

BOATING | For a variety of daylong guided kayak outings—from a Seattle sunset sea kayak tour to an Alki Point lighthouse tour—led by experienced, fun staff, try this great outfitter in West Seattle. In addition to kayaks, you can also rent stand-up paddleboards, skates, and longboards here. Custom sea-kayaking adventures can be set up, too. To rent a kayak without a guide, you must be an experienced kayaker; otherwise, sign up for one of the fascinating guided outings (the popular sunset tour is $69 per person). ✉ *1660 Harbor Ave. SW, West Seattle* ☎ *206/953–0237* 🌐 *kayakalki.com.*

The Center for Wooden Boats

BOATING | Located on the southern shore of Lake Union, Seattle's free maritime heritage museum is a bustling community hub. Thousands of Seattleites rent rowboats and small wooden sailboats here every year; the center also offers workshops, demonstrations, and classes. Rentals for nonmembers range from $30 to $65 per hour, and sailboats require a prescheduled sailing checkout test. Free half-hour guided sails and steamboat rides are offered on Sunday from 11 am to 3 pm (arrive an hour early to reserve a spot). ✉ *1010 Valley St., Lake Union* ☎ *206/382–2628* 🌐 *www.cwb.org.*

★ Green Lake Boathouse

BOATING | This shop is the source for canoes, paddleboats, sailboats, kayaks, stand-up paddleboards, and rowboats to take out on Green Lake's calm waters. On beautiful summer afternoons, however, be prepared to spend most of your time dealing with traffic, both in the parking lot and on the water. Fees are $24 an hour for paddleboats, single kayaks, rowboats, and stand-up paddleboards, $30 an hour for sailboats. Don't confuse this place with the Green Lake Small Craft Center, which offers sailing programs but no rentals. Golfing is available in the summer as well. **■ TIP→ Rent before noon to get the "Happy Hour" rate of $16.** ✉ *7351 E Green Lake Dr. N, Green Lake* ☎ *206/527–0171* 🌐 *www.greenlakeboatrentals.net.*

Northwest Outdoor Center

BOATING | This center on Lake Union's west side rents one- or two-person kayaks (it also has a few triples) by the hour or day, including equipment and wetsuits (much needed outside of summer). The hourly rate is $18 for a single and $25 for a double (costs are figured in 10-minute increments after the first hour). For the more vertically inclined, the center also rents out stand-up paddleboards for $20 an hour. NWOC also runs classes, sunset tours near Golden Gardens Park, and full moon moonlight paddles. Reservations recommended in summer. ✉ *2100 Westlake Ave. N, Lake Union* ☎ *206/281–9694* 🌐 *www.nwoc.com.*

GOLF

Gold Mountain Golf Complex

GOLF | Most people make the trek to Bremerton to play the Olympic Course, a beautiful and challenging par 72 that is widely considered the best public course in Washington. The older, less-sculpted Cascade Course is also popular; it's better suited to those new to the game. There are four putting greens, a driving range, and a striking clubhouse with views of the Belfair Valley. Rates vary but start as low as $20 for midweek, off-season tee times booked online. Carts are $16.50 prior to twilight and $10 after. You can drive all the way to Bremerton via Interstate 5, or you can take the car ferry to Bremerton from Pier 52. The trip will take roughly 1½ hours no matter which way you do it, but the ferry ride (60 minutes) might be a more pleasant way to spend a large part of the journey. Note, however, that the earliest departure time for the ferry is 6 am, so this option won't work for very early tee times. ✉ *7263 W Belfair Valley Rd., Bremerton* ☎ *360/415–5433* 🌐 *www.goldmt.com.*

Jefferson Park

GOLF | This golf complex has views of the city skyline *and* Mt. Rainier. The par-27, 9-hole course has a lighted driving range with heated stalls that's open from dusk until midnight. And the 18-hole, par-69 main course is one of the city's best. Greens fees are around $30 but are dynamic based on demand, so you could get a great deal on an off-time or weekday option. ✉ *4101 Beacon Ave. S., Beacon Hill* ☎ *206/762–4513* 🌐 *www.seattlegolf.com.*

HIKING

■ TIP→ Within Seattle city limits, the best nature trails can be found in Discovery Park, Lincoln Park, Seward Park, and at the Washington Park Arboretum. Some trailheads require parking permits, but they're marked and you can usually pay on-site.

Cougar Mountain Regional Wildland Park

HIKING/WALKING | This spectacular park in the "Issaquah Alps" has more than 38 miles of hiking trails and 12 miles of bridle trails within its 3,000-plus acres. The Indian Trail, believed to date back 8,000 years, was part of a trade route that Native Americans used to reach North Bend and the Cascades. Thick pine forests rise to spectacular mountaintop views; there are waterfalls, deep caves, and the remnants of a former mining town. Local residents include deer, black bears, bobcats, bald eagles, and pileated woodpeckers, among many other woodland creatures. ✉ *18201 SE Cougar Mountain Dr., Issaquah* ✣ *From Downtown Seattle take I–90 E; follow signs to park beyond Issaquah.*

Mt. Si

HIKING/WALKING | This thigh-buster is where mountaineers train to climb grueling Mt. Rainier. Mt. Si offers a challenging hike with views of a valley (slightly marred by the suburbs) and the Olympic Mountains in the distance. The main trail to Haystack Basin, 8 miles round-trip, climbs some 4,000 vertical feet, but there are several obvious places to rest or turn around if you'd like to keep the hike to 3 or 4 miles. Note that solitude is in short supply here—this is an extremely popular trail thanks to its proximity to Seattle. On the bright side, it's one of the best places to witness the local hikers and trail runners in all their weird and wonderful splendor. ✉ *North Bend* ✣ *Take I–90 E to Exit 31 (toward North Bend). Turn onto North Bend Way and then make left onto Mt. Si Rd. and follow that road to trailhead parking lot.*

★ Snow Lake

HIKING/WALKING | One of Washington State's most popular wilderness trails may be crowded at times, but the scenery and convenience of this hike make it a classic. Though very rocky in stretches—you'll want to wear sturdy shoes—the 8-mile round-trip sports a relatively modest 1,300-foot elevation gain; the views of the Alpine Lakes Wilderness are well worth the sweat. The glimmering waters of Snow Lake await hikers at the trail's end; summer visitors will find abundant wildflowers, huckleberries, and wild birds. ✉ *Snoqualmie Pass* ✢ *Take I–90 E to Exit 52 (toward Snoqualmie Pass West). Turn left (north), cross under freeway, and continue on to trailhead, located in parking lot at Alpental Ski Area* 🌐 *www.wta.org/go-hiking/hikes/snow-lake-1*.

Side Trips from Seattle: The Puget Sound Islands

The islands of Puget Sound—particularly Bainbridge, Vashon, and Whidbey—are easy and popular day trips for Seattle visitors, and riding the Washington State ferries is half the fun.

BAINBRIDGE ISLAND

35 minutes west of Seattle by ferry.

Of the three main islands in Puget Sound, Bainbridge has by far the largest population of Seattle commuters. Certain parts of the island are dense enough to have rush-hour traffic problems, while other areas retain a semirural, small-town vibe. Longtime residents work hard to keep parks and protected areas out of the hands of condominium builders, and despite the increasing number of stressed-out commuters, the island still has resident artists, craftspeople, and old-timers who can't be bothered to venture into the big city. Though not as dramatic as Whidbey or as idyllic as Vashon, Bainbridge always makes for a pleasant day trip.

The ferry, which departs from the Downtown terminal at Pier 52, drops you off in the charming village of Winslow. Along its compact main street, Winslow Way, it's easy to while away an afternoon among the antiques shops, art galleries, bookstores, and cafés. There are two bike-rental shops in Winslow, too, if you plan on touring the island on two wheels. Getting out of town on a bike can be a bit nerve-racking, as the traffic to and from the ferry terminal is thick, and there aren't a lot of dedicated bike lanes, but you'll soon be on quieter country roads. Be sure to ask for maps at the rental shop, and if you want to avoid the worst of the island's hills, ask the staff to go over your options with you before you set out.

Many of the island's most reliable dining options are in Winslow, or close to it. You'll also find the delightful Town & Country supermarket on the main stretch if you want to pick up some provisions for a picnic, though you can also easily do that in Seattle at the Pike Place Market before you get on the ferry.

GETTING HERE AND AROUND

Unless you're coming from Tacoma or points farther south, or from the Olympic Peninsula, the only way to get to Bainbridge is via the ferry from Pier 52 Downtown. Round-trip fares start at $7.70 per person; round-trip fare for a car and driver is $32.80. Crossing time is 35 minutes. If you confine your visit to the village of Winslow, as many visitors do, then you won't need anything other than a pair of walking shoes. Out on the island, besides driving or biking, the only way to get around is on buses provided by Kitsap Transit. Fares are only $2 one way, but note that since routed buses are for commuters, they may not drop you off quite at the doorstep of the park or attraction you're headed to. Be sure to study the route map carefully or call Kitsap at least a day in advance of your trip to inquire about its Dial-A-Ride services.

CONTACTS Kitsap Transit. ☎ *800/501–7433* 🌐 *www.kitsaptransit.com*.

ESSENTIALS

VISITOR INFORMATION Bainbridge Chamber of Commerce. ☎ *206/842–3700* 🌐 *www.bainbridgechamber.com.*

★ Bloedel Reserve

NATIONAL/STATE PARK | This 150-acre internationally recognized preserve is a stunning mix of natural woodlands and beautifully landscaped gardens—including a moss garden, Japanese garden, a reflection pool, and the impressive former Bloedel estate home. Dazzling rhododendrons and azaleas bloom in spring, and Japanese maples colorfully signal autumn's arrival. Picnicking is not permitted, and you'll want to leave the pooch behind—pets are not allowed on the property, even if they stay in the car. Check the website's events page for special events, lectures, and exhibits. ✉ *7571 NE Dolphin Dr., 6 miles west of Winslow, via Hwy. 305, Bainbridge Island* ☎ *206/842–7631* 🌐 *www.bloedelreserve.org* 🎫 *$17.*

Blackbird Bakery

$ | BAKERY | A great place to grab a cup of coffee and a snack before exploring the island serves up rich pastries and cakes along with quiche, soups, and a good selection of teas and espresso drinks. Though there is some nice window seating that allows you to watch the human parade on Winslow Way, the place gets very crowded, especially when the ferries come in, so you might want to take your order to go. **Known for:** draws big crowds; delicious pastries. 💲 *Average main: $5* ✉ *210 Winslow Way E, Winslow* ☎ *206/780–1322* 🌐 *www.blackbirdbakery.com* 💳 *No credit cards* 🕒 *No dinner.*

Harbour Public House

$ | SEAFOOD | An 1881 estate home overlooking Eagle Harbor was renovated to create this casual pub and restaurant at Winslow's Harbor Marina, where a complimentary boat tie-up is available for pub patrons. Local seafood—including steamed mussels, clams, and oyster sliders—plus burgers, fish-and-chips, and poutine are typical fare, and there are 12 beers on tap. **Known for:** destination for kayakers; harbor views; open mic Tuesday night. 💲 *Average main: $16* ✉ *231 Parfitt Way SW, Winslow* ☎ *206/842–0969* 🌐 *www.harbourpub.com.*

VASHON ISLAND

20 minutes by ferry from West Seattle.

Vashon is the most peaceful and rural of the islands easily reached from the city, home to fruit growers, commune-dwelling hippies, rat-race dropouts, and Seattle commuters.

Biking, beachcombing, picnicking, and kayaking are the main activities here. A tour of the 13-mile-long island will take you down country lanes and past orchards and lavender farms. There are several artists' studios and galleries on the island, as well as a small commercial district in the center of the island, where a farmers' market is a highlight every Saturday from May to October. The popular Strawberry Festival takes place every July.

GETTING HERE AND AROUND

Washington State Ferries leave from Fauntleroy in West Seattle (about 9 miles southwest of Downtown) for the 20-minute ride to Vashon Island. The ferry docks at the northern tip of the island. Round-trip fares are $5.20 per person or $22.05 for a car and driver. A water taxi also goes to Vashon from Pier 50 on the Seattle waterfront, but it's primarily for commuters, operating only on weekdays during commuter hours. One-way fares are $5. There's limited bus service on the island; the best way to get around is by car or by bicycle (bring your own or rent in Seattle. Note that there's a huge hill as you immediately disembark the ferry dock and head up to town). The site www.vashonchamber.com is also a good source of information.

ESSENTIALS

VISITOR INFORMATION Vashon-Maury Island Chamber of Commerce. *17141 Vashon Hwy. SW, Vashon* *206/463–6217* *www.vashonchamber.com.*

Sights

Jensen Point and Burton Acres Park

NATIONAL/STATE PARK | Vashon has many parks and protected areas. This park, on the lush Burton Peninsula overlooking Quartermaster Harbor, is home to 64 acres of secluded hiking and horseback-riding trails. The adjacent Jensen Point, a 4-acre shoreline park, has picnic tables, a swimming beach, and kayak and paddleboard rentals (May through September). *8900 SW Harbor Dr., Vashon* *From ferry terminal, take Vashon Hwy. SW to SW Burton Dr. and turn left. Turn left on 97 Ave. SW and follow it around as it becomes SW Harbor Dr.* *www.vashonparks.org.*

Point Robinson Park

NATIONAL/STATE PARK | You can stroll along the beach, which is very picturesque thanks to **Point Robinson Lighthouse.** The lighthouse is typically open to the public from noon to 4 on Sunday during the summer; call to arrange a tour or rent out one of the historic beachfront Keepers' Quarters (two multibedroom houses) by the week. If you're lucky, you might even see an orca swim surprisingly close to the shore. *3705 SW Pt. Robinson Rd., Vashon* *206/463–9602* *www.vashonparks.org.*

Restaurants

★ May Kitchen + Bar

$$ | **THAI** | This is where sophisticated foodies swoon over delectable and highly authentic Thai dishes. The ambience is scene-y (atypical for Vashon): dark with fully paneled walls in mahogany and teak—wood that owner May Chaleoy had shipped from Thailand, where it previously lived in the interior of a 150-year-old home. **Known for:** real-deal Thai food that goes way beyond pad Thai; vibrant atmosphere; unique cocktails. *Average main: $18* *17614 Vashon Hwy. SW, Vashon* *206/408–7196* *www.may-kitchen.com* *Closed Mon.–Tue.*

WHIDBEY ISLAND

20 minutes by ferry from Mukilteo (30 miles north of Seattle) to Clinton, at the southern end of Whidbey Island, or drive north 87 miles to Deception Pass at the north end of the island.

Whidbey is a blend of low pastoral hills, evergreen and oak forests, meadows of wildflowers (including some endemic species), sandy beaches, and dramatic bluffs with a few pockets of unfortunate suburban sprawl. It's a great place for a scenic drive, viewing sunsets over the water, taking ridge hikes that give you uninterrupted views of the Strait of Juan de Fuca, walking along miles of rugged seaweed-strewn beaches, and for boating or kayaking along the protected shorelines of Saratoga Passage, Holmes Harbor, Penn Cove, and Skagit Bay.

GETTING HERE AND AROUND

You can reach Whidbey Island by heading north from Seattle on Interstate 5, west on Route 20 onto Fidalgo Island, and south across Deception Pass Bridge. The Deception Pass Bridge links Whidbey to Fidalgo Island. From the bridge it's just a short drive to Anacortes, Fidalgo's main town and the terminus for ferries to the San Juan Islands. It's easier—and more pleasant—to take the 20-minute ferry trip from Mukilteo (30 miles northwest of Seattle) to Clinton, on Whidbey's south end, as long as you don't time your trip on a Friday evening, which could leave you waiting in the car line for hours. Fares are $4.80 per person for walk-ons (round-trip) and $10.30 per car and driver (one way). Be sure to look at a map before choosing your point of entry; the ferry ride may not make sense if your main destination is Deception Pass State Park. Buses on Whidbey Island, provided by Island Transit, are free. Routes are fairly comprehensive, but keep in mind that Whidbey is big—it takes at least 35 minutes just to drive from the southern ferry terminal to the midway point at Coupeville—and if your itinerary is far-reaching, a car is your best bet.

CONTACT Island Transit. *800/240–8747 www.islandtransit.org.*

ESSENTIALS

VISITOR INFORMATION Langley Chamber of Commerce. *208 Anthes Ave., Langley 360/221–6765 www.visitlangley.com.*

LANGLEY

The historic village of Langley, 7 miles north of Clinton on Whidbey Island, is above a 50-foot-high bluff overlooking Saratoga Passage, which separates Whidbey from Camano Island. A grassy terrace just above the beach is a great place for viewing birds on the water or in the air. On a clear day you can see Mt. Baker in the distance. Upscale boutiques selling art, glass, jewelry, books, and clothing line 1st and 2nd streets in the heart of town.

Restaurants

Prima Bistro

$$ | **BISTRO** | Langley's most popular gathering spot occupies a second-story space on 1st Street, right above the Star Store Grocery. Northwest-inspired French cuisine is the headliner here; classic bistro dishes like steak frites, salade nicoise, and confit of duck leg are favorites. **Known for:** Penn Cove mussels and oysters; patio views of Saratoga Passage and Camano Island; live music on Thursday nights. *Average main: $22 201½ 1st St., Langley 360/221–4060 www.primabistro.com.*

Hotels

★ Inn at Langley

$$$$ | **B&B/INN** | Perched on a bluff above the beach, this concrete-and-wood Frank Lloyd Wright–inspired structure is just steps from the center of town. **Pros:** no children under 12; stunning views of the Saratoga Passage; destination restaurant (with priority seating for inn guests). **Cons:** some rooms can be on the small side; expensive for the area; not family-friendly for young kids. *Rooms from: $375 400 1st St., Langley 360/221–3033 www.innatlangley.com 28 rooms Free Breakfast.*

COUPEVILLE

Restored Victorian houses grace many of the streets in quiet Coupeville, Washington's second-oldest city, on the south shore of Penn Cove, 12 miles north of Greenbank. It also has one of the largest national historic districts in the state, and has been used for filming movies depicting 19th-century New England villages. Stores above the waterfront have maintained their old-fashioned character. Captain Thomas Coupe founded the town in 1852. His house was built the following year, and other houses and commercial buildings were built in the late 1800s. Even though Coupeville is the Island County seat, the town has a laid-back, almost 19th-century air.

Sights

★ Ebey's Landing National Historic Reserve

BEACH—SIGHT | **FAMILY** | The reserve encompasses a sand-and-cobble beach, bluffs with dramatic views down the Strait of Juan de Fuca, two state parks (Ft. Casey and Ft. Ebey; see separate listings), and several privately held pioneer farms homesteaded in the early 1850s. The first and largest reserve of its kind holds nearly 400 nationally registered historic structures (including those located within the town of Coupeville), most of them from the 19th century. Miles of

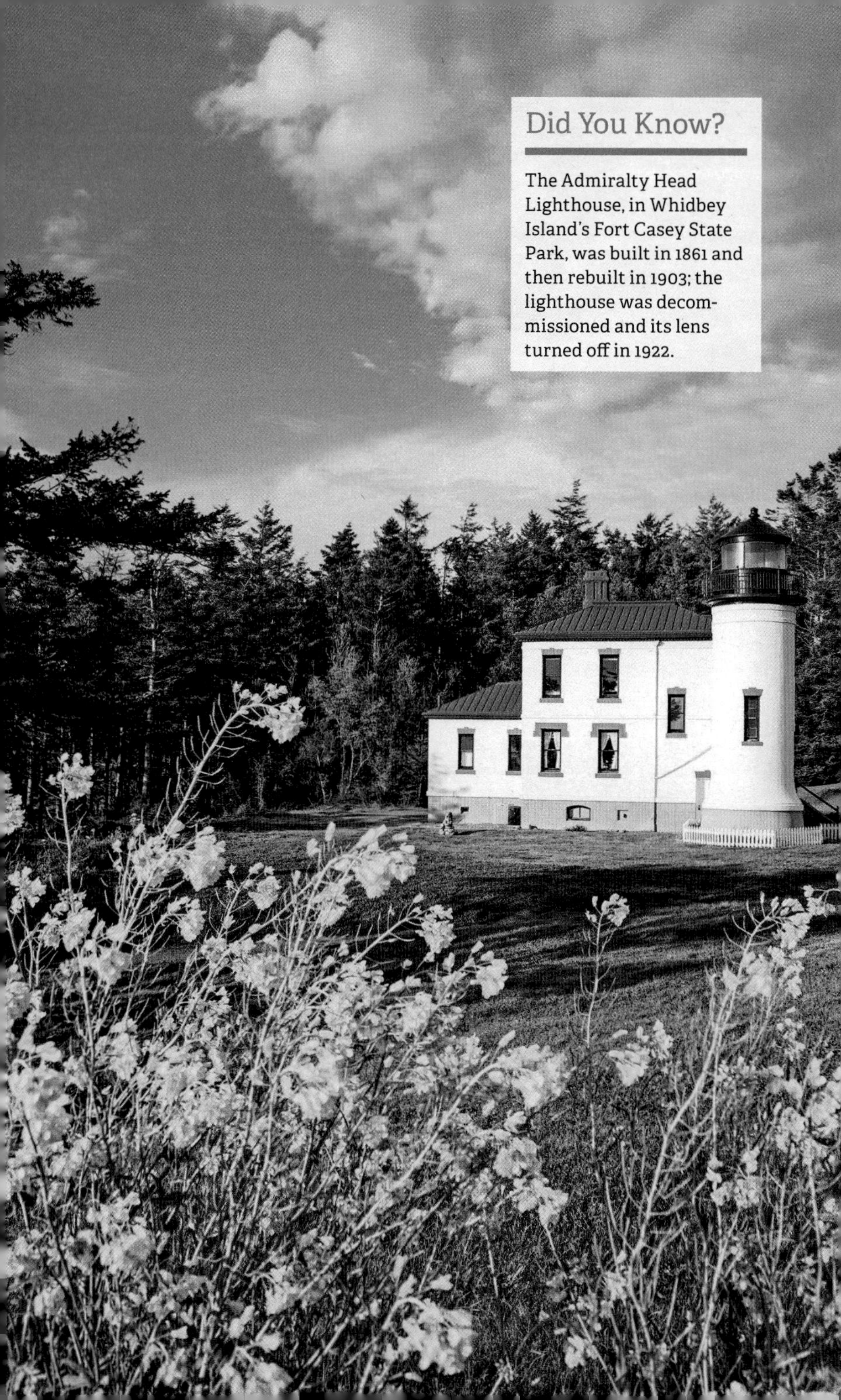

Did You Know?

The Admiralty Head Lighthouse, in Whidbey Island's Fort Casey State Park, was built in 1861 and then rebuilt in 1903; the lighthouse was decommissioned and its lens turned off in 1922.

trails lead along the beach and through the woods. Cedar Gulch, south of the main entrance to Ft. Ebey, has a lovely picnic area in a wooded ravine above the beach. ✉ *Coupeville* ✣ *From Hwy. 20, turn south on Main St. in Coupeville. This road turns into Engles Rd. as you head out of town. Turn right on Hill Rd. and follow it to reserve* 🌐 *www.nps.gov/ebla.*

Restaurants

★ The Oystercatcher

$$$$ | **SEAFOOD** | A dining destination for foodies from across the Northwest renowned for its local-inspired cuisine, the Oystercatcher features a simple menu that's heavily influenced by fresh in-season ingredients. The intimate, romantic dining space in the heart of town serves lunch Friday through Sunday, but it's the dinner scene that makes it a favorite spot for special occasions. **Known for:** pretty views of Penn Cove; farm-to-table; stellar wine list. $ *Average main: $38* ✉ *901 Grace St. NW, Coupeville* ☎ *360/678–0683* 🌐 *www.oystercatcher-whidbey.com* ⏲ *Closed Mon.–Tues. No lunch weekdays.*

Hotels

Captain Whidbey Inn

$$ | **B&B/INN** | Over a century old and steps from the shorefront of Penn Cove, this venerable historic lodge surrounded by old-growth firs was recently purchased by a young trio of investors from Portland, who refreshed the place with more of a hip boutique hotel vibe (think Ace Hotel) while maintaining the rustic charm that's made it a favorite for decades. **Pros:** a few lodging options, including private cabins with hot tubs; secluded "upscale summer camp" vibe; pedestal sinks in rooms. **Cons:** shared bathrooms; poor soundproofing in the main motel; spotty cell phone coverage. $ *Rooms from: $215* ✉ *2072 Captain Whidbey Inn Rd., off Madrona Way, Coupeville* ☎ *360/678–4097, 800/366–4097* 🌐 *www.captainwhidbey.com* *29 rooms, 2 suites, 4 cabins* 🍽 *Free Breakfast.*

Compass Rose Bed and Breakfast

$ | **B&B/INN** | Inside this stately 1890 Queen Anne Victorian on the National Register of Historic Places, a veritable museum of art, artifacts, and antiques awaits you. **Pros:** wonderful, interesting hosts; elegant breakfast with china, silver, linen, and lace; lots of eye candy for antiques lovers. **Cons:** only two rooms, so it gets booked up fast; too old-fashioned for some travelers; not kid-friendly (too many things to break). $ *Rooms from: $140* ✉ *508 S Main St., Coupeville* ☎ *360/678–5318, 800/237–3881* 🌐 *www.compassrosebandb.com* ▭ *No credit cards* *2 rooms* 🍽 *Free Breakfast.*

Chapter 11

WASHINGTON CASCADE MOUNTAINS AND VALLEYS

WITH TACOMA, OLYMPIA, AND MT. ST. HELENS

Updated by
Andrew Collins

Sights	Restaurants	Hotels	Shopping	Nightlife
★★★★★	★★★★★	★★★★☆	★★★☆☆	★★★☆☆

WELCOME TO WASHINGTON CASCADE MOUNTAINS AND VALLEYS

TOP REASONS TO GO

★ **Take flight:** See a Boeing jet in mid-construction or a World War II chopper up close at Everett's Paine Field.

★ **Tiptoe through the tulips:** Bike past undulating fields of tulips and other spring blooms in La Conner and Mount Vernon.

★ **Hang in glass houses:** Check out Dale Chihuly's biomorphic sculptures at Tacoma's Museum of Glass.

★ **View a volcano:** Visit Johnston Ridge Observatory, for an eerily close view of Mt. St. Helens.

★ **Paddle around Puget Sound:** Rent a kayak to explore the charming seaside communities of Poulsbo or Gig Harbor.

1 **Lynden.** This Dutch farming town on the Canadian border offers small-town charms and hosts one of the state's largest agricultural fairs.

2 **Mt. Baker.** The village of Glacier, the Nooksack River, and scenic Mt. Baker Highway are the gateways to Washington's third-highest mountain.

3 **Bellingham.** You'll find copious recreational opportunities and a hip dining and shopping scene in the largest city between Seattle and Vancouver.

4 **Bow-Edison.** These teensy twin villages on Samish Bay have become famous for artisan markets, oyster bars, and farm-to-table restaurants.

5 **Mount Vernon.** This historic river community is famous for its springtime tulip festival.

6 **La Conner.** One of the state's prettiest yet still somewhat underrated artists' communities, La Conner has three excellent small museums and a bustling riverfront.

7 **Camano Island.** Although it's one of the most accessible of the Puget Sound Islands, this peaceful expanse of forest and beaches is ideal for a relaxing getaway.

8 **Everett.** Visitors come from all over to tour the world-class aviation attractions of this small city north of Seattle.

9 **Edmonds.** Edmonds is a favorite weekend retreat on Puget Sound.

10 **Snoqualmie and North Bend.** The cult classic *Twin Peaks* was filmed in these rugged Cascade Mountains towns.

11 **Port Gamble.** This tiny, historic hamlet has beautifully preserved homes and water views galore.

12 **Poulsbo.** Dubbed "Little Norway," this cute village is a charming base for exploring the northern Kitsap Peninsula.

13 **Gig Harbor.** Home to both luxury pleasure boats and a prolific commercial fishing fleet, this town exudes nautical charm.

14 **Tacoma.** Those seeking an alternative to Seattle are transforming this hilly city.

15 **Olympia.** The state's political center has a lively downtown with waterfront parks and convivial restaurants and taverns.

16 **Ashford.** Rugged old-growth forests provide the picturesque scenery in this outdoor recreation hub just outside Mount Rainier National Park.

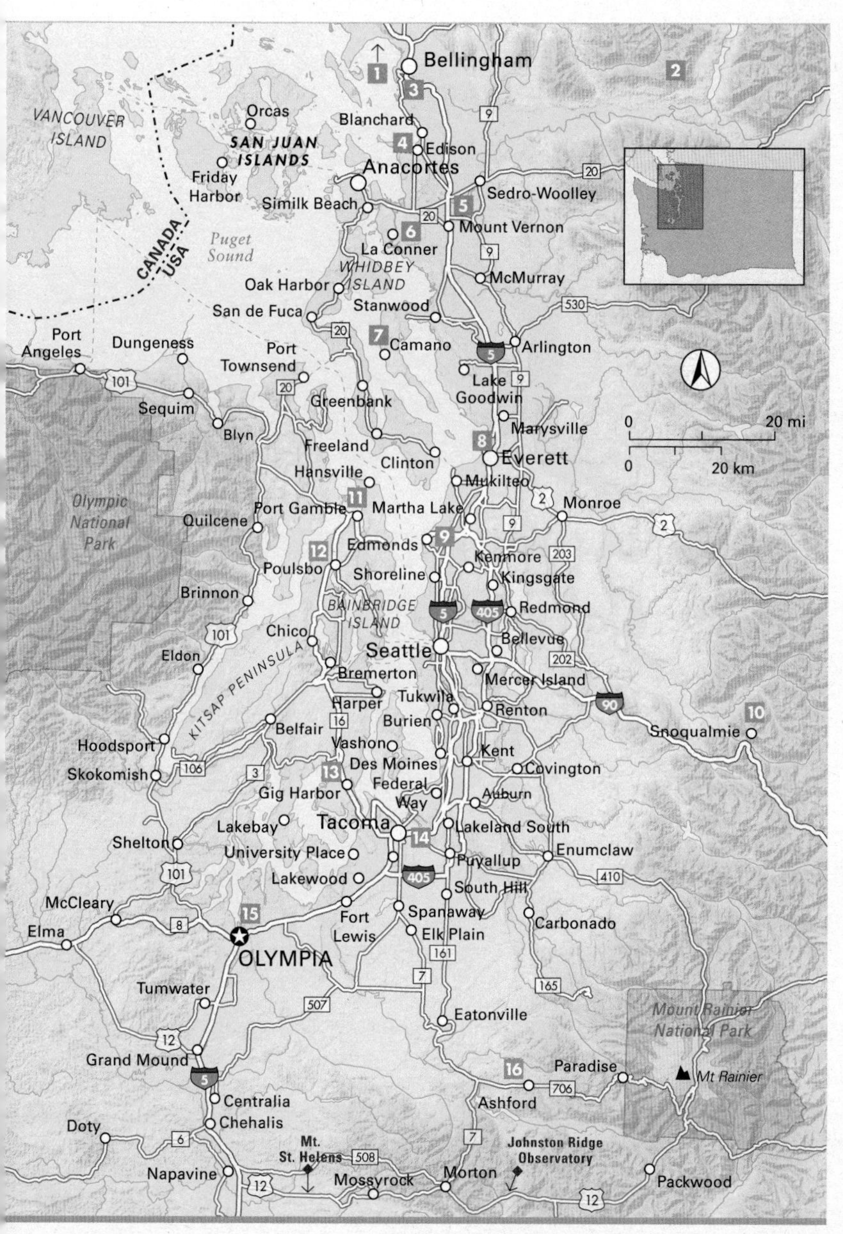

11

Washington Cascade Mountains and Valleys WELCOME TO WASHINGTON CASCADE MOUNTAINS AND VALLEYS

MT. ST. HELENS

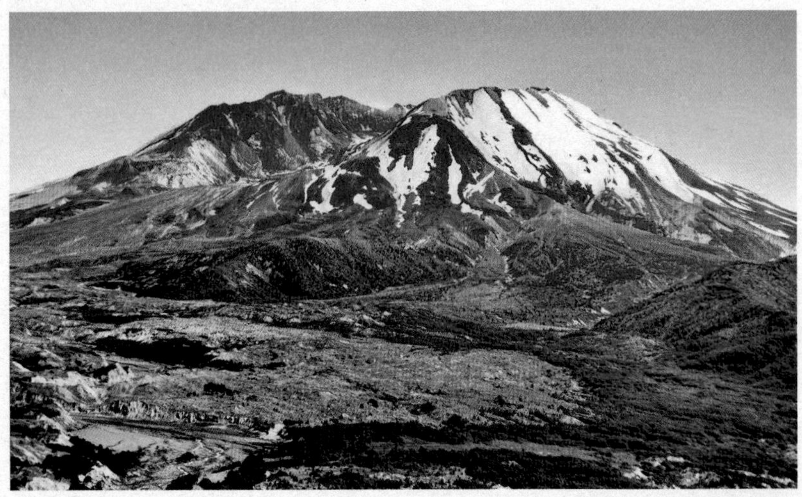

One of the most prominent peaks in the Northwest's rugged Cascade Range, Mount St. Helens National Volcanic Monument affords visitors an up-close look at the site of the most destructive volcanic blast in U.S. history.

Just 55 miles northeast of Portland and 155 miles southeast of Seattle, this once soaring, conical summit stood at 9,667 feet above sea level. Then, on May 18, 1980, a massive eruption launched a 36,000-foot plume of steam and ash into the air and sent nearly 4 million cubic yards of debris through the Toutle and Cowlitz river valleys. The devastating eruption leveled a 230-square-mile area, claiming 57 lives and more than 250 homes. The mountain now stands at 8,365 feet, and a horseshoe-shape crater—most visible from the north—now forms the scarred summit. A modern, scenic highway carries travelers to within about 5 miles of the summit, and the surrounding region offers thrilling opportunities for climbing, hiking, and learning about volcanology.

BEST TIME TO GO

It's best to visit from mid-May through late October, as the last section of Spirit Lake Highway, Johnston Ridge Observatory, and many of the park's forest roads are closed the rest of the year. The other visitor centers along the lower sections of the highway are open year-round, but overcast skies typically obscure the mountain's summit in winter.

PARK HIGHLIGHTS

APE CAVE

Measuring nearly 2½ miles in mapped length, Ape Cave is the longest continuous lava tube in the continental United States. Two routes traverse the tube. The lower route is an easy hour-long hike; the upper route is more challenging and takes about three hours. The park recommends bringing at least two light sources (you can rent lanterns from the headquarters for $5 in summer) and warm clothing. In high season ranger-led walks are sometimes available; inquire at the **Apes' Headquarters** (*360/449–7800*), off Forest Service Road 8303, 3 miles north of the junction of Forest Roads 83 and 90. Although Ape Cave is open year-round, the headquarters closes November through April. A Northwest Forest Pass ($5 daily) is required for parking (or a Sno-Park permit during winter). ✉ *Cougar* ☎ *360/449–7800* 🌐 *www.fs.usda.gov/giffordpinchot*.

JOHNSTON RIDGE OBSERVATORY

The visitor center closest to the summit is named for scientist David Johnston, who died in the mountain's immense lateral blast. Inside are fascinating exhibits on the mountain's geology, instruments measuring volcanic and seismic activity, and a theater that shows a riveting film that recounts the 1980 eruption. Several short trails afford spectacular views of the summit. ✉ *2400 Spirit Lake Hwy., Toutle* ☎ *360/274–2140* 🌐 *www.fs.usda.gov/giffordpinchot* 🎫 *$8 parking* ⏲ *Closed mid-May–early Nov.*

SPIRIT LAKE HIGHWAY

Officially known as Highway 504, this winding road rises 4,000 feet from the town of Castle Rock (just off I–5, Exit 49) to within about 5 miles of the Mt. St. Helens summit. Along this road are several visitor centers that explain the region's geology and geography, and several turnouts afford views of the destruction wrought upon the Toutle and Cowlitz river valleys.

STAY THE NIGHT

Your best nearby base is the Kelso-Longview area, which has several chain hotels and is about 10 to 15 miles south of the start of Spirit Lake Highway. You'll also find a wide selection of lodgings in Vancouver.

Fire Mountain Grill For good burgers, sandwiches, and beer and a memorable setting midway up Spirit Lake Highway, drop by this rustic roadhouse with a veranda overlooking the North Fork Toutle River. **Known for:** scenic river views; tasty desserts; comfort food. ✉ *9440 Spirit Lake Hwy., Toutle* ☎ *360/274–5217* ⏲ *Closed late Nov.–late Mar. No dinner.*

McMenamins Kalama Harbor Lodge In addition to 11 wood-panel rooms with king beds (some with riverfront balconies), you'll find four lively bars and a café. **Pros:** good base for Mt. St. Helens activities; pleasant views of the Columbia River; on-site food and drinks options. **Cons:** noise from passing trains; small bathrooms; food quality is uneven. ✉ *215 N. Hendrickson Dr.* ☎ *360/673–6970* 🌐 *www.mcmenamins.com/kalama-harbor-lodge* *11 rooms* *No meals.*

The San Juan Islands, the Olympic Peninsula, and the great swaths of midstate wilderness provide Washington's favorite photo ops, but there are plenty of adventures that don't require traveling on ferries or bumping along Forest Service roads.

Up and down Interstate 5 you'll find most of the state's major cities beyond Seattle: the ports of Tacoma, Olympia, and Bellingham each have enough cultural and outdoorsy attractions to warrant a long weekend.

Slightly farther afield you'll find smaller towns with some very specific draws: Poulsbo's proud Norwegian heritage, Port Gamble's painstakingly preserved mill-town vibe, Everett's enthusiasm for all things flight related, and North Bend and Snoqualmie's breathtaking alpine scenery and friendly feel. And south of Mt. Rainier, towns like Packwood and Ashford in the Cascades offer rugged scenery and jumping-off points for visiting both Rainier and Mt. St. Helens.

Exploring this part of the state, encompassing so many distinct geographical areas like the Kitsap Peninsula and the western fringe of the Skagit Valley, can bring you from industrial areas to tulip fields in one day. From naval warships to thundering falls, there's a lot to see within two hours of Seattle.

MAJOR REGIONS

Bellingham and Skagit Valley. The outdoorsy, artsy, and progressive college town of **Bellingham,** with its dramatic natural setting on Puget Sound and burgeoning craft-beer and food scenes, has become the coolest weekend getaway between Seattle and Vancouver. A bit farther north, you'll find ample opportunities for hiking, skiing, and rafting in Glacier and around **Mt. Baker,** as well as one-of-a-kind lodgings and eateries in the border towns of **Lynden** and Blaine. Between Everett and Canada are some lovely miles of coastline, impressive parks, and charming farm towns that appeal to foodies—all of which are easy to access from Interstate 5. Collectively, the somewhat underappreciated towns that anchor the northwestern corner of the state include **La Conner,** a pleasantly laid-back agrarian community; **Bow-Edison,** a pair of hamlets that have become renowned for their artisan food offerings; and **Mount Vernon,** a riverfront town with flower farms that draw big crowds in spring when the tulips bloom.

Snohomish County and the Cascade Foothills. North of Seattle are two notable port towns and a peaceful island community. **Edmonds** has more of a seaside vibe, with waterfront parks and trendy downtown restaurants and a ferry terminal serving the islands of Puget Sound. **Everett,** on the other hand, is devoted to flight, with its Boeing factory tours and museums devoted to the history of aviation, but the city center is also experiencing a gradual renaissance. From here, you're a short drive the pristine state parks of tranquil **Camano Island**. It's a short jaunt east from

Seattle via Interstate 90 to reach the spectacular hiking, biking, and skiing of Snoqualmie Pass, near which you can admire amazing waterfalls and spend a night or two in the cute neighboring towns of **Snoqualmie** and **North Bend.**

Kitsap Peninsula. On the quieter northern end of this scenic peninsula that juts into Puget Sound, the small port towns of **Poulsbo** and **Port Gamble** offer access to beach parks and glimpses of the region's Scandinavian and logging pasts—a nice snapshot of coastal Washington life that's more accessible than the Olympic Peninsula. The upscale boating community of **Gig Harbor** offers a bounty of distinctive shops, bars, and restaurants.

Tacoma and Olympia. Immortalized in song by Neko Case as the "dusty old jewel in the South Puget Sound," **Tacoma** is shining far more brightly these days, with a walkable waterfront that includes several impressive museums and a hip restaurant and bar scene. Farther south is the capital city **Olympia,** which is the perfect mix of quirky and stately.

Mt. Rainier Environs. Washington's rugged southern Cascades region is famous for two massive volcanic peaks, Mt. Rainier and Mt. St. Helens. Small, remote towns—notably **Ashford** is strung along winding, forested country highways that meander through this dramatic area within day-tripping distance of Olympia and Tacoma, or even Seattle.

Planning

When to Go

The climate throughout the Interstate 5 corridor, from the Skagit Valley down through Tacoma and Olympia, largely matches that of Seattle, with cool and damp winters (with low temperatures in the upper 30s) and largely dry and sunny summers, with temperatures in the 70s and low 80s. The more favorable weather of late spring through mid-October brings the largest crowds to the region. Rainy winter brings lower hotels rates—and on the Kitsap Peninsula or up in Bellingham and the Skagit Valley, can be charmingly stormy—ideal for cozying up by the fireplace in a toasty room. In the Mt. Baker and Snoqualmie areas, skiing and other winter sports are popular from December through April, when heavy snows come, although the towns in the foothills receive more rain than snow. In the communities around Mt. Rainier and Mt. St. Helens, winter snow often brings temporary road closures, and many restaurants, lodges, and attractions are closed or have limited hours from mid-fall through mid-spring; check forecasts and call ahead if venturing into the Cascades at this time.

FESTIVALS AND EVENTS

Northwest Washington Fair

FESTIVALS | **FAMILY** | This enormously popular six-day agricultural fair in Lynden dates to 1909 and features carnival amusements, a demolition derby, arts and crafts, live music, and plenty of great food. 🌐 *www.nwwafair.com.*

Skagit Valley Tulip Festival

FESTIVALS | **FAMILY** | April brings a month-long celebration of these iconic flowers that bloom by the millions throughout Mount Vernon and La Conner. 🌐 *www.tulipfestival.org.*

★ **Washington State Fair**

FESTIVALS | **FAMILY** | This fair in September brings thousands of visitors daily over three weeks to Puyallup, near Tacoma, and features concerts, a rodeo, art and cultural exhibits, agricultural shows, and amusement rides. There's also a shorter four-day version of the fair held in mid-April. 🌐 *www.thefair.com.*

Getting Here and Around

AIR

Seattle-Tacoma International Airport (Sea-Tac), 15 miles south of Seattle, is the hub for this region, although visitors to the southern part of the region might also consider flying into Oregon's user-friendly Portland International Airport. Additionally, Bellingham International Airport serves as a hub between northwestern Washington and greater Vancouver; it has direct flights to and from Seattle as well as Las Vegas, Los Angeles, Oakland, San Diego, Phoenix, and several other cities. And beside the Boeing factory in Everett, Paine Field opened a state-of-the-art commercial terminal in 2019; it offers nonstop service on Alaska and United to about 12 cities throughout the West.

CONTACTS Bellingham International. ✉ *4255 Mitchell Way, Bellingham* ☎ *360/676–2500* 🌐 *www.portofbellingham.com.* **Paine Field.** ✉ *3300 100th St. SW, Everett* ☎ *425/622–9040* 🌐 *www.flypainefield.com.*

AIRPORT TRANSFERS

Bremerton–Kitsap Airporter shuttles passengers from Sea-Tac to points in Tacoma, Bremerton, Port Orchard, Gig Harbor, and Poulsbo ($19–$30 one-way). The Airporter Shuttle/Bellair Charters makes numerous trips daily between Sea-Tac and Bellingham ($44 one-way), with a few stops in between; and between Sea-Tac and North Bend ($25 one way), continuing on to Yakima.

CONTACTS Airporter Shuttle/Bellair Charters. ☎ *866/235–5247* 🌐 *www.airporter.com.* **Bremerton–Kitsap Airporter.** ☎ *360/876–1737* 🌐 *www.kitsapairporter.com.*

BOAT AND FERRY

Washington State Ferries ply Puget Sound, with routes between Seattle and Bremerton and between Edmonds and Kingston on the Key Peninsula.

BUS

Greyhound Lines and Northwestern Trailways cover Washington and the Pacific Northwest. From Seattle, Greyhound connects to Tacoma, Olympia, Bellingham, and several other cities in the region. Pierce County Transit provides bus service around Tacoma. *For more on bus travel throughout the region, see Travel Smart.*

CONTACTS Pierce County Transit. ☎ *253/581–8000* 🌐 *www.piercetransit.org.*

CAR

Interstate 5 runs south from the Canadian border through Seattle, Tacoma, and Olympia to Oregon and California. Interstate 90 begins in Seattle and runs east through Snoqualmie and North Bend all the way to Idaho. U.S. 2 meanders east, parallel to Interstate 90, from Everett to Spokane. Highways 7 and 167 connect the Tacoma area with the towns around Mt. Rainier. U.S. 101 begins northwest of Olympia and traces the coast of the Olympic Peninsula.

TRAIN

Amtrak's Cascades line serves Centralia, Tacoma, Lacey (near Olympia), Seattle, Edmonds, Everett, Stanwood (near Camano Island), Mount Vernon, and Bellingham. From Seattle, Sound Transit's Sounder trains (commuter rail, weekdays only) run north to Edmonds, Mukilteo, and Everett, and south to Tacoma and few other suburbs.

TRAVELING FROM SEATTLE

Tacoma and Everett are good choices for day trips. Tacoma is only 30–40 minutes by car or train from Seattle; Everett is also easy to reach in under an hour, and seeing the exhibits on flight history doesn't require an overnight. Just don't get stuck driving the Interstate 5 corridor during weekday rush hours or on Sunday night in summer—the heavy traffic can be depressing.

Snoqualmie is also easily visited in a day, as it's close to Seattle, but because it's a popular base for outdoor recreation, many visitors overnight here.

Olympia is far enough from Seattle—it's only about 60 miles, but during the day you'll nearly always hit traffic, so expect a solid 1½ hours in the car—that it's often better for an overnight visit or as a stop on the way to Washington beach towns. Olympia is also a good leg-stretch between Seattle and Portland and can be part of an itinerary to Mount Rainier National Park or Mount St. Helens National Volcanic Monument—it's a good idea to spend the night near these parks if planning a visit, as they're a good drive from Seattle, and you'll want to get an early start if planning a hike or driving along these winding, narrow forest roads.

Restaurants

Olympia, Bellingham, and especially Tacoma have increasingly hip and sophisticated dining scenes, with everything from third-wave coffeehouses to seasonally driven restaurants with water views. After those cities, Gig Harbor, La Conner, Bow-Edison, and Edmonds have the best food scenes—they're not terribly big, but support fine little crops of notable restaurants, as do an increasing number of smaller towns in the region. You'll also find good brewpubs throughout the area, too.

Hotels

A few of the towns in this chapter are easy day trips from Seattle, so staying there is always an option, but you'll encounter much higher rates there as well. Tacoma, Olympia, and Bellingham have the widest variety of accommodations, with pricey hotels, midrange chains, and bed-and-breakfasts. There are a few other noteworthy hotels in these parts—the Chrysalis Inn and Hotel Leo in Bellingham, Channel Lodge in La Conner, and Salish Lodge in Snoqualmie. Many of the smaller towns in this region have a B&B or locally owned inn, but relatively prosaic chains dominate much of the lodging landscape. *Hotel reviews have been shortened. For full information, visit Fodors.com.*

What It Costs in U.S. Dollars

	$	$$	$$$	$$$$
RESTAURANTS	under $16	$16–$22	$23–$30	over $30
HOTELS	under $150	$150–$200	$201–$250	over $250

Lynden

45 miles southeast of Vancouver, BC, 100 miles north of Seattle.

Perhaps best known as home of the well-attended Northwest Washington Fair and Rodeo, which draws some 200,000 visitors to the area over six days in mid-August, this city of 14,500 in northern Whatcom County is a friendly, charming destination. Lynden is nearly at the Canadian border, a short drive from Vancouver, and with an urbane boutique hotel, one of the better small-town history museums in the state, and a cute downtown known for its Dutch architecture, it's a relaxing and picturesque spot for a quick getaway. It's also a good base for day trips to Mt. Baker or Bellingham.

GETTING HERE AND AROUND

Driving is the best way to explore this area. From the south, take Highway 539 north from Interstate 5, Exit 256; from the north, take Interstate 5 to Exit 270 and follow Birch Bay Lynden Road east into town.

ESSENTIALS

VISITOR INFORMATION Lynden Chamber of Commerce. ✉ *518 Front St.* ☎ *360/354–5995* 🌐 *www.lynden.org.*

Restaurants

★ Drayton Harbor Oyster Company

$ | **SEAFOOD** | With a dining room and deck that overlook the very bay that supplies this venerable seafood company's delicious, briny oysters, this funky spot serves bivalves in a variety of formats: raw on the half shell, in a creamy stew, fried in po' boys, or grilled with a garlic-butter-wine sauce and other tasty toppings. It's in downtown Blaine, less than a mile from the Canadian border, and 15 miles west of Lynden. **Known for:** frequently changing and reasonably priced daily specials; comfy dining room heated by a gas fireplace; fantastic selection of wine and beer. 💲 *Average main: $15* ✉ *685 Peace Portal Dr., Blaine* ☎ *360/656–5958* 🌐 *www.draytonharboroysters.com.*

The Mill

$ | **MODERN AMERICAN** | Beneath the 72-foot-tall Dutch windmill that brackets the west end of Lynden's tiny downtown, this cozy eatery with a fireplace, rich paneling, and dim lighting is a favorite gathering spot for both dinner and drinks (there's live music some evenings, too). Along with a variety of custom-produced house wines on tap as well as cocktails and craft beers, the Mill specializes in small plates, including artisan cheeses and fondue and pulled-pork paninis. **Known for:** reasonably priced Washington wines; flatbread pizzas with interesting toppings; rotating selection of local-berry desserts. 💲 *Average main: $14* ✉ *655 Front St., Blaine* ☎ *360/778–2760* 🌐 *www.themilllynden.com* ⏲ *Closed Sun.*

Hotels

★ Inn At Lynden

$$ | **HOTEL** | Several years after the historic Waples Mercantile Building in downtown Lynden was gutted by fire, a small group of friends transformed the building on the National Registry of Historic Places into a stunning boutique hotel with timber beams, wood floors, and rough-hewn walls. **Pros:** steps from downtown shopping and restaurants; home to outpost of Bellingham's Village Books; friendly, helpful staff. **Cons:** no gym on-site (but offers free day passes to two local gyms); breakfast not included; no pets allowed. 💲 *Rooms from: $179* ✉ *100 5th St.* ☎ *360/746–8597* 🌐 *www.innatlynden.com* 🛏 *35 rooms* 🍽 *No meals.*

Semiahmoo Resort

$$ | **RESORT** | **FAMILY** | This low-slung four-story resort with an acclaimed golf course, a full-service spa, several restaurants, and a slew of family and recreational activities enjoys one of the more dramatic settings of any hotel in the state, on the peninsula extending into Semiahmoo Bay and overlooking the Canadian shoreline near Vancouver. **Pros:** overlooks the boats of Drayton Harbor; first-rate golf course and spa on-site; good dining options. **Cons:** 15-minute drive from nearest town; pricey on summer weekends; rooms could use updating. 💲 *Rooms from: $195* ✉ *9565 Semiahmoo Pkwy., Blaine* ☎ *360/318–2000* 🌐 *www.semiahmoo.com* 🛏 *196 rooms* 🍽 *No meals.*

Sundara West B&B

$$ | **B&B/INN** | Although you'd swear it was built in the late 19th century, this stately Queen Anne–style inn about 8 miles southeast of Lynden was actually built in 1997, and the light-filled, tastefully appointed rooms feel both old-world and conveniently modern. **Pros:** cottage has its own kitchen and is ideal for longer stays; hot tub, fire pit, and seasonal heated pool; friendly, welcoming owners.

Cons: 15-minute drive from Lynden; can book up quickly in summer; few dining options nearby. *Rooms from: $155* *2265 Central Rd., Everson* *360/966–4959* *www.sundarawestbnb.com* *3 rooms* *Free breakfast.*

Shopping

★ Bellewood Acres

FOOD/CANDY | FAMILY | Both a farm market popular with kids and a craft distillery that's a hit with adults, this family-owned apple orchard on the main road between Lynden and Bellingham is a fun and tasty stop for stocking up on fresh produce and gourmet snacks and sampling house-made brandy, vodka, and gin. There's also a café on-site that's popular for breakfast and lunch, offers a good selection of hard ciders and beers on tap, and—naturally—serves delicious apple pie. *6140 Guide Meridian Rd. (Hwy. 539)* *360/318–7720* *www.bellewoodfarms.com.*

Glacier and Mt. Baker

30 miles east of Lynden, 35 miles east of Bellingham.

The canyon village of Glacier, an excellent base for visiting Mount Baker–Snoqualmie National Forest, has a few shops, cafés, and lodgings. Known as the Mt. Baker Highway, scenic Highway 542 twists and turns for about 60 miles east from Bellingham through Glacier into the forest through an increasingly steep-walled canyon. Beyond Glacier, the route is designated as a National Forest Scenic Byway—it passes 170-foot-high Nooksack Falls, about 5 miles east of Glacier, and travels up the north fork of the Nooksack River and the slopes of Mt. Baker. It ends at dramatic Artist Point, elevation 5,140 feet, where you'll find a picnic area and access to a number of notable trails.

GETTING HERE AND AROUND

Glacier is about an hour's drive from Bellingham on Highway 542, and it's another half-hour to Mt. Baker. Allow about 2½ hours to get to Glacier from Seattle, via Interstate 5, Highway 20, and Highway 9.

Sights

Mount Baker–Snoqualmie National Forest

NATIONAL/STATE PARK | A 2,694-square mile forest (it's a little bigger than Delaware), including much of the mountain and forest land around North Cascades National Park, this national forest has miles of trails, but because the snowline is quite low, the upper ridges and mountains are covered much of the year. This makes for a short hiking, climbing, and mountain-biking season, usually from mid-July to mid-September or early October—but winter brings skiing and snowmobiling. The wildflower season is also short, but it's spectacular; expect fall color by late August or early September. The 10,778-foot-high, snow-covered volcanic dome of **Mt. Baker** is visible from much of Whatcom County and from as far north as Vancouver and as far south as Seattle. The nearest year-round ranger office to this part of the forest is in Glacier, but there's also a summer office in Deming, known as the Heather Meadows Visitor Center, near Artist Point, at milepost 56 on the Mt. Baker Highway (Highway 542). At both centers, you can pick up trails maps and get advice on hiking and exploring the northern end of the forest. *Glacier Public Service Center, 10091 Mt. Baker Hwy. (Hwy. 542)* *360/783–6000 Everett office, 360/599–2714,* *www.fs.usda.gov/mbs* *$5 parking.*

Restaurants

North Fork Brewery

$ | PIZZA | Brewing memorabilia, including a big wall of vintage beer bottles known as the "beer shrine," greet patrons to this rambling roadhouse and brewery along the scenic Mt. Baker Highway, about 20 miles northeast of Bellingham. After a day of skiing or hiking, stop in for a pint of Bavarian-style hefeweizen or a heady barleywine, along with one of the filling pizzas. **Known for:** "the monster" pizza with nine toppings; well-crafted ales and lagers; beer flights. *Average main: $13 6186 Mt. Baker Hwy., Deming 360/599–2337 www.northforkbrewery.com.*

Yuki Yama

$ | **JAPANESE** | Dining options are limited along the arrestingly beautiful but sparsely populated Mt. Baker Highway, but this quirky little Japanese restaurant in the tiny hamlet of Maple Falls offers visitors filling, delicious sustenance at a reasonable price. The small menu focuses on gyozas, miso soup, and healthy rice bowls with a variety of proteins or veggies (ahi tuna teriyaki, red miso chicken). **Known for:** Wednesday night sushi rolls; fine sakes and craft beers; friendly atmosphere. *Average main: $14 7471 Mt. Baker Hwy. 360/389–5181 Closed Sun.–Tues. No lunch.*

Blue T Lodge

$ | **B&B/INN** | Skiers, hikers, rafters, and other outdoor adventurers appreciate this cheap and cheerful motel-style inn's location along Mt. Baker Highway, and that every room has a balcony or patio that overlooks a small lawn and garden shaded by soaring evergreens. **Pros:** excellent base for skiing or hiking at Mt. Baker; rustic wood furnishings; convenient location. **Cons:** in a quiet town with few dining options; rooms lack refrigerators and microwaves; compact rooms. *Rooms from: $119 10459 Mt. Bakery Hwy. 360/599–9944 www.bluetlodge.com 6 rooms No meals.*

Mt. Baker Ski Area

SKIING/SNOWBOARDING | At this day resort on one of the most famous mountains in the Pacific Northwest, you can snowboard and ski downhill on 31 trails from late November to the end of April. The mountain is served by eight lifts and a pair of rope tows, and there are three day lodges with rentals and casual dining options. The area receives the most snowfall of any ski resort in the world, about 660 inches per year; it set a world snowfall record in winter 1999 when some 1,140 inches of white stuff were dumped on these dramatic slopes *End of Hwy. 542 17 miles east of Glacier at end of Hwy. 542 360/734–6771, 360/671–0211 snow reports www.mtbaker.us Lift tickets $65.*

Bellingham

35 miles southwest of Glacier, 15 miles south of Lynden.

The fishing port and college city of Bellingham (population 90,000) has steadily transformed itself from a rough-and-tumble blue-collar town to the outdoor-recreation and pleasure-boating capital of Washington's northwest corner. The waterfront—dominated by lumber mills and shipyards in the early 1900s—is gradually morphing into a string of parks with connecting trails. Downtown and the historic Fairhaven community to the south both abound with hipster-favored cafés, craft breweries and cideries, specialty shops, and galleries. Colorful murals and street art appear on or in front of many of downtown's buildings. College students and professors from Western Washington University make up a sizable part of the town's population and contribute to its easygoing, progressive, and intellectual climate.

GETTING HERE AND AROUND

Although a car is the easiest way to reach town and explore the outlying region, it's possible to get here by Greyhound and Bolt Bus, Amtrak train, and even by commercial flights into the city's surprisingly large airport and then rely on public transit, bikes, and even walking to get around—both downtown and Fairhaven are quite pedestrian-friendly. Biking is popular in and around Bellingham, which has a series of designated bike paths and park trails. The Coast Millennium Trail will eventually connect Skagit and Whatcom counties to British Columbia. So far, about 15 miles of the 50-mile trail are open to bikes and walkers. Fairhaven Bike & Ski rents road bikes, full-suspension bikes, and standard mountain bikes starting at $50 per day.

CONTACTS Bellingham Whatcom County Tourism. ✉ *904 Potter St.* ☎ *360/671–3990* 🌐 *www.bellingham.org.* **City of Bellingham Bike Routes.** 🌐 *www.cob.org/transportation* . **Fairhaven Bicycles.** ✉ *1108 11th St.* ☎ *360/733–4433* 🌐 *www.fairhavenbicycles.com.*

Sights

Bloedel Donovan Park

CITY PARK | The only public access in Bellingham to rippling, 14-mile-long Lake Whatcom is at its north end, in this park about a 10-minute drive east of downtown. Locals swim in the sheltered waters of a cove, but you might find the water a bit cold. If so, spend some time trying to spot beavers, river otters, ducks, great blue herons, and yellow pond lilies at Scudder Pond, which is another 100 feet west (reached by trail from a parking area at Northshore and Alabama). ✉ *2114 Electric Ave.* ☎ *360/778–7000* 🌐 *www.cob.org.*

★ Boulevard Park

CITY PARK | **FAMILY** | With a long pier, a boardwalk over an old rail trestle, and a paved trail that skirts the waterfront overlooking the islands of Bellingham Bay, this leafy community park between downtown and Fairhaven is one of the loveliest spots in the area to stroll, jog, read a book, or watch the sailboats. At the center of the park is a branch of the popular local café Woods that offers sweeping water views. Other amenities include a playground, a small beach, barbecue grills, and picnic tables. ✉ *470 Bayview Dr.* 🌐 *www.cob.org.*

★ Chuckanut Drive

SCENIC DRIVE | Highway 11, also known as Chuckanut Drive, was once the only highway accessing Bellingham from the south. The drive begins in Fairhaven, reaches the flat farmlands of the Samish Valley near the village of Bow, and joins up with Interstate 5 at Burlington, in Skagit County. The full loop can be made in a couple of hours, but the many notable eateries along the route, especially around Bow—which even has a Bow-Edison Food Trail—may tempt you to linger. For a dozen miles this 23-mile road winds along the cliffs above beautiful Chuckanut and Samish bays. It twists its way past the sheer sandstone face of Chuckanut Mountain and crosses creeks with waterfalls. Turnouts are framed by gnarled madrona trees and pines and offer great views of the San Juan Islands. Bald eagles cruise along the cliffs or hang out on top of tall firs. Drive carefully: the cliffs are so steep in places that closures resulting from rock slides occasionally occur in winter. ✉ *Hwy. 11, starting in Fairhaven at 12th St. and Old Fairhaven Pkwy.*

★ Fairhaven

HISTORIC SITE | Just shy of 3 miles south of downtown Bellingham and at the beginning of Chuckanut Drive (Highway 11), this historic district was an independent city until 1903 and still retains its distinct identity as an intellectual and artistic center. The beautifully restored 1890s redbrick buildings of the Old Fairhaven District, especially on Harris Avenue between 10th and 12th streets, house restaurants, galleries, and stylish boutiques. The action is centered on Fairhaven Green, the site of festivals, concerts, outdoor movies, and other fun gatherings throughout the year. ✉ *Bellingham* 🌐 *www.fairhaven.com.*

★ Larrabee State Park

NATIONAL/STATE PARK | South of Fairhaven and accessed from Chuckanut Drive, this rugged 2,683-acre park offers both an 8,100-foot stretch of rocky shore with quiet, sandy coves and trails that climb high up along the slopes of Chuckanut Mountain. Even though the mountain has been logged repeatedly, there's still plenty of lush forest. Trails lead through ferny fir and maple forests to hidden lakes, caves, and cliff-top lookouts from which you can see all the way to the San Juan Islands—the 4½-mile round-trip Fragrance Lake loop is a particularly rewarding hike. At the shore there's a sheltered boat launch; you can go crabbing here or watch the birds—and the occasional harbor seal—that perch on the offshore rocks. The area west of Chuckanut Drive has picnic tables as well as tent and RV sites with hookups, which are open all year. ✉ *245 Chuckanut Dr.* ☎ *360/676–2093* 🌐 *www.parks.wa.gov* 🎫 *$10 parking.*

SPARK Museum of Electrical Invention

MUSEUM | FAMILY | At this quirky downtown museum, rooms filled with some of the world's earliest electrical appliances—light bulbs, phones, batteries, motors, radios, TVs—along with photos, news clippings, and interactive exhibits tell the story how electricity transformed our world. A particularly interesting exhibit sparked by the film *The Current War* traces the competitive battle for technological supremacy among Thomas Edison, George Westinghouse, and Nikola Tesla. A weekends at 2:30 pm, docents present a wildly entertaining electric light show, complete with 12-foot lightening bolts, in the museum theater. ✉ *1312 Bay St.* ☎ *360/738–3886* 🌐 *www.sparkmuseum.org* 🎫 *$8* 🕒 *Closed Mon. and Tues.*

★ Whatcom Museum

MUSEUM | FAMILY | Bellingham's art and history museum fills three buildings near one another downtown. At its centerpiece is the Lightcatcher, a LEED-certified (Leadership in Energy and Environmental Design) building with an 180-foot-long translucent wall. Rotating shows are presented here, as are permanent collections of contemporary Northwest artists. The second building, Bellingham's 1892 former city hall, is a redbrick structure that was converted into a museum in 1941 and contains historic exhibits. The third building, the Syre Education Center, contains a photographic archive. The museum's restaurant, Kismet Cafe & Wine Bar, is in the Lightcatcher and garners raves for its creative farm-to-table lunch and dinner fare. ✉ *250 Flora St.* ☎ *360/778–8930* 🌐 *www.whatcommuseum.org* 🎫 *$10* 🕒 *Closed Mon. and Tues.*

Restaurants

★ Bantam 46

$$ | SOUTHERN | At this convivial two-level downtown tavern with exposed brick walls and tall windows, boldly flavored Southern fare—prominently featuring rotisserie or fried (buttermilk or spicy-hot) chicken—rules the day. The chicken dishes come with a variety of sauces and sides, but if you aren't feelin' the bird, you can't go wrong with the sausage and grits or bacon cheeseburger. **Known for:** noteworthy roster of novel cocktails; pimento cheese hush puppies; biscuits and honey. 💲 *Average main: $21* ✉ *1327 Railroad Ave.* ☎ *360/788–4507* 🌐 *www.bantambellingham.com* 🕒 *Closed Sun. No lunch.*

Black Sheep

$ | MODERN MEXICAN | It's all about the fresh and flavorful tacos at this hip little tavern with exposed brick walls, a white tile and varnished wood bar, and a light-filled upstairs seating annex—oh, and the deftly poured cocktails, many of them featuring premium tequila and mezcal. The hand-pressed soft tacos are available in about 10 flavors, both meat and veggie, and are served with house-made salsas. **Known for:** creative fillings like rockfish, sweet potato, and gyro; well-crafted cocktails; delicious lamb pozole. *Average main: $11 ✉ 211 W. Holly St. ☎ 360/526–2109 🌐 www.blacksheepbellingham.com.*

Boundary Bay Brewery & Bistro
$ | **AMERICAN** | Long a top destination in downtown Bellingham, both for sampling distinctive, well-crafted microbrews and enjoying big portions of delicious pub fare, this convivial spot occupies a vintage former garage—the huge central door is rolled open in warm weather. Boundary Bay garners high marks among beer lovers for its ruby-red Scottish ale, smooth oatmeal stout, and rotating seasonal ales. **Known for:** delicious beef, lamb, and veggie burgers; satisfies every type of beer lover; a good-size side patio. *Average main: $15 ✉ 1107 Railroad Ave. ☎ 360/647–5593 🌐 www.bbaybrewery.com.*

★ Fork at Agate Bay
$$$ | **MODERN AMERICAN** | It's a scenic 20-minute drive east from downtown to reach this intimate but lively contemporary bistro near the north shore of Lake Whatcom, where the chefs emphasize local, seasonal ingredients. In the evening, you might start with Louisiana-style shrimp and grits or sautéed chicken livers with marsala cream, before moving on to rabbit pot pie or pork cheeks and belly with dill-mustard spaetzle. **Known for:** Cajun and European influenced brunch fare; strong commitment to sourcing locally; wood-fired flatbread pizzas. *Average main: $28 ✉ 2530 N. Shore Rd. ☎ 360/733–1126 🌐 www.theforkatagatebay.com ⏲ Closed Mon. and Tues. No lunch Wed.–Fri.*

★ Homeskillet
$ | **AMERICAN** | This decidedly offbeat breakfast and lunch spot in a quiet neighborhood just north of downtown stands out both for its prodigious portions of rib-sticking all-day breakfast fare and its funny (and often freaky) decorative elements, from dozens of clown paintings and figurines to its psychedelic color scheme. Prepare for a wait, especially on weekend mornings, and if you can possibly save room for dessert, the seasonal fruit (peach-blueberry, for example) bread puddings are to die for. **Known for:** wonderfully bizarre and kitschy decor; chicken-fried steak with chorizo gravy; homemade cinnamon-roll French toast. *Average main: $11 ✉ 521 Kentucky St. ☎ 360/676–6218 🌐 www.homeskilletinsunnyland.com ⏲ Closed Mon. No dinner.*

Old World Deli
$ | **DELI** | Epicureans flock to this bustling, high-ceilinged deli and specialty market in the heart of downtown for generously portioned sandwiches, salads, and charcuterie and cheese plates featuring the best goods from Portland's famed Olympia Provisions and Seattle's vaunted Salumi. The hot-pressed sub with mortadella, capicola, sopressata, fontina cheese, tomato, pepperoncini, and arugula on an Italian roll tastes right out of the best Little Italy neighborhoods of any East Coast metropolis. **Known for:** deli open for dinner Thursday through Saturday; excellent selection of Italian wines; muffaletta sandwiches. *Average main: $11 ✉ 1228 N. State St. ☎ 360/738–2090 🌐 www.oldworldbellingham.com ⏲ No dinner Sun.–Wed.*

Saltine
$$ | **MODERN AMERICAN** | Meals in this intimate, minimalist white-brick downtown bistro take full advantage of the area's local bounty of produce and artisan goods—the small but interesting printed menu is always supplemented by daily specials, maybe fried green tomatoes or

gnocchi with butternut squash, chanterelles,and a sage–brown butter sauce. Stars from the regular menu include addictive fried olives with yogurt and salsa verde, and the classic steak frites. **Known for:** fairly priced lineup of craft beer and wine; desserts are always worth saving room for; great seasonally driven daily specials. *Average main: $20 ✉ 114 Prospect St. ☎ 360/392–8051 🌐 www.saltinebellingham.com ⏲ Closed Sun. and Mon. No lunch.*

★ Willows Inn

$$$$ | PACIFIC NORTHWEST | You'll want to book well in advance for a chance to dine at this hallowed prix-fixe restaurant operated by Washington native Blaine Wetzel, who combines his years of knowledge working at Copenhagen's vaunted Noma with a passion for the farm-fresh produce and fresh seafood of the Puget Sound area. The dining room and outdoor deck afford sweeping views of the San Juan Islands to the west. **Known for:** exquisitely presented dishes; impressive (but steep) wine list; peaceful waterfront setting. *Average main: $225 ✉ 2579 W. Shore Dr. ☎ 360/758–2620 🌐 www.willows-inn.com ⏲ Closed Jan.–mid-Mar. and many weekdays.*

Coffee and Quick Bites

★ Camber

$ | CAFÉ | Equal parts artisan coffee roaster and casual-chic brunch room, this airy café on a busy downtown corner stands out both for the quality and creativity of its food and drink. Highlights on the food side include the rosemary lamb burger, and crisp rösti potatoes with fried eggs and bacon jam, while notable sippers range from a ginger-turmeric latte to local-blueberry mimosas. **Known for:** first-rate single-origin coffees and espresso drinks; impressive selection of wine, beer, and cocktails; inventive brunch fare. *Average main: $13 ✉ 221 W. Holly St. ☎ 360/656–5343 🌐 www.cambercoffee.com ⏲ No dinner.*

Mallard Ice Cream

$ | CAFÉ | Before you go ordering dessert from whichever restaurant you dine in Bellingham, keep in mind that this stellar artisan ice cream parlor is open until 10:30 or 11 every night, and the thick, creamy concoctions here are seriously superb. The team here has come up with literally hundreds of rotating flavors over the years, from yerba mate to burned sugar to vanilla black sesame. **Known for:** everything here is homemade; unusual roster of flavors; great ice-cream sundaes. *Average main: $5 ✉ 1323 Railroad Ave. ☎ 360/734–3884 🌐 www.mallardicecream.com.*

Hotels

Chrysalis Inn and Spa Bellingham

$$$ | HOTEL | In a gabled building rising above the waterfront between downtown and Fairhaven, these light-filled, contemporary rooms have fireplaces and offer the cushiest accommodations in town. **Pros:** rejuvenating facials, wraps, and massages in the tranquil spa; most rooms overlook Bellingham Bay; crackling fireplace in the lobby. **Cons:** some noise from train track behind the hotel; not within walking distance of downtown Bellingham; pricey in high season. *Rooms from: $219 ✉ 804 10th St. ☎ 360/756–1005 🌐 www.thechrysalisinn.com 45 rooms No meals.*

★ Fairhaven Village Inn

$$$ | HOTEL | On a slight bluff overlooking Fairhaven Village Green, this charming, historic inn overlooks Bellingham Bay; bay-view rooms have balconies and gas fireplaces, and a suite has french doors dividing a bedroom and sitting area. **Pros:** interesting part of town with good shops, galleries, and bookstores; convenient for exploring Chuckanut Scenic Drive; helpful and knowledgeable staff. **Cons:** two-night minimum stay at certain times; neighborhood can sometimes feel crowded; noise from occasional passing trains. *Rooms from: $224 ✉ 1200 10th St.*

☎ *360/733–1311, 877/733–1100* 🌐 *www.fairhavenvillageinn.com* 🛏 *22 rooms* 🍽 *Free Breakfast.*

★ Heliotrope Hotel

$ | **HOTEL** | Easily the best value in town, this small mid-century modern motel in a quiet neighborhood a mile west of downtown has been artfully updated with custom-built wood furniture, local art, and tiled bathrooms. **Pros:** lovely central lawn with picnic tables and a fire pit; perfect for those who like contemporary design; bargain rates. **Cons:** 15-minute walk from downtown; some rooms are a bit small; no breakfast. 💲 *Rooms from: $87* ✉ *2419 Elm St.* ☎ *360/201–2914* 🌐 *www.heliotropehotel.com* 🛏 *17 rooms* 🍽 *No meals.*

Hotel Bellwether

$$$$ | **HOTEL** | Bellingham's original waterfront hotel overlooks the entrance to bustling Squalicum Harbor, and its luxurious rooms have gas fireplaces, plush bathrooms with jetted tubs and separate glassed-in showers, and private balconies for lounging and dining. **Pros:** lighthouse suite is ensconced in its own tower; boutiques and restaurants within a short walk; wide variety of room configurations. **Cons:** can get crowded with groups and weddings; one of the more expensive options in town; a bit of a walk to downtown. 💲 *Rooms from: $269* ✉ *Squalicum Harbor Marina, 1 Bellwether Way* ☎ *360/392–3100, 877/411–1200* 🌐 *www.hotelbellwether.com* 🛏 *66 rooms* 🍽 *No meals.*

★ Hotel Leo

$$$ | **HOTEL** | Inside a striking tower dating from the 1880s, this smartly designed boutique hotel opened its doors in 2019. **Pros:** lots of great restaurants and shops within a short walk; rooms have high-tech touches like Bluetooth speakers; excellent fitness center and spacious common areas. **Cons:** economy rooms are quite small; not ideal for a quiet getaway; extra fee for parking. 💲 *Rooms from: $219* ✉ *1224 Cornwall Ave.* ☎ *360/739–0250* 🌐 *www.thehotelleo.com* 🛏 *40 rooms* 🍽 *No meals.*

MoonDance B&B

$ | **B&B/INN** | This handsomely restored 1930s lodge-style home with tastefully and quirkily furnished guest rooms is surrounded by colorful gardens and sits on the western shore of pristine Lake Whatcom—it's one of the most tranquil settings of any lodging in the area. **Pros:** expansive views of the landscape; kayaks for exploring the lake; family-friendly room. **Cons:** 5 miles east of downtown; two-night minimum during busy times; not many dining options nearby. 💲 *Rooms from: $145* ✉ *4737 Cable St.* ☎ *360/927–2599* 🌐 *www.bellinghambandb.com* 🛏 *5 rooms* 🍽 *Free Breakfast.*

Nightlife

★ Aslan Brewing

BREWPUBS/BEER GARDENS | One of the most esteemed of Bellingham's fast-growing number of highly regarded craft breweries occupies a sleek downtown building with soaring glass walls, an open floor plan, and plenty of sidewalk seating. The brewmasters here specialize in flavorful, small-batch beers, like faintly ginger-accented Irie Eyes Red Ale, and a rich, chocolaty dark lager called Cascadian. Part of the fun here is the bar food, including a rather decadent waffle-fry poutine, hefty bacon-bison burgers, and Chocolate Stout soft-serve ice cream topped with candied barley. ✉ *1330 N. Forest St.* ☎ *360/778–2088* 🌐 *www.aslanbrewing.com.*

★ Bellingham Cider Company

BREWPUBS/BEER GARDENS | With a dining room and spacious terrace overlooking the downtown's Waterfront District and Bellingham, this spacious craft cider taproom is an inviting place to sample the rotating selection of small-batch sippers, which come in flavors like blood orange and blackberry ginger. This is a legit dining option, too, with a kitchen that turns out well-crafted contemporary Northwest fare, from pastas to burgers, along with beer, wine, and cocktails. ✉ *205 Prospect St.* ☎ *360/510–8494* 🌐 *www.bellinghamcider.com.*

The Local

BREWPUBS/BEER GARDENS | This old-school downtown pub with a modern vibe and first-rate beer and food was opened by a trio of Western Washington University graduates who also happen to be talented beer makers (they own Menace Brewing). As you might guess, this laid-back spot with a conversation-friendly decibel level has a great list of rotating taps, featuring craft beers from throughout the Northwest. The locally driven food is tasty, too, from fried chicken and waffles during the popular weekend brunches to late-night pork-belly tacos and fish-and-chips. ✉ *1427 Railroad Ave.* ☎ *360/306–3731* 🌐 *www.menace-industries.com.*

Swim Club

BARS/PUBS | Historic Fairhaven's increasingly hip and modern cocktail scene is centered on this sleek lounge and its cushy armchairs, potted plants, and nifty curving marble bar. Tropical drinks—think mai tais and palomas—are a specialty. There's a great selection of contemporary bar snacks, too. ✉ *1147 11th St.* ☎ *360/393–3826* 🌐 *www.swimclubbar.com.*

Performing Arts

Mt. Baker Theatre

THEATER | The state's largest performing arts center north of Seattle occupies a restored vaudeville-era (1927) theater with a 110-foot-tall Moorish tower and a lobby fashioned after a Spanish galleon. It's home to the Whatcom Symphony Orchestra and is also a venue for movies, musicals, and headline performers. ✉ *104 N. Commercial St.* ☎ *360/734–6080* 🌐 *www.mountbakertheatre.com.*

★ Pickford Film Center

FILM | A host of local film festivals and a great place to see diverse indie, classic, and art-house movies, this handsome theater inside a restored historic downtown building offers a good selection of beer, wine, and snacks in the lobby. This nonprofit operation offers similar fare at the smaller Limelight Cinema, around the corner. ✉ *1318 Bay St.* ☎ *360/738–0735* 🌐 *www.pickfordfilmcenter.org.*

Shopping

Greenhouse

HOUSEHOLD ITEMS/FURNITURE | You'll discover a vast selection of both classic and contemporary housewares and furnishings in this two-story emporium in downtown Bellingham. Kitchen gadgets, bath and body products, and cool lighting and planters are among the top finds. ✉ *1235 Cornwall Ave.* ☎ *360/676–1161* 🌐 *www.greenhousehome.com.*

★ Village Books

BOOKS/STATIONERY | Since 1980, this enormous three-story bookstore has been an anchor of Fairhaven, bringing literary-minded folks to together to shop for recent releases, attend readings and discussions, and socialize amid the shop's several spaces for eating and mingling. These include the full-service restaurant, Colophon Cafe, and Evolve Chocolate + Cafe on the top floor, whose seating areas has grand views of Bellingham Bay. There's a newer branch in downtown Lynden. ✉ *1200 11th St.* ☎ *360/671–2626* 🌐 *www.villagebooks.com.*

Whatcom Art Market

ART GALLERIES | This well-established co-op gallery in Fairhaven showcases works in a wide variety of media by more than 45 of the region's top artists. ✉ *1103 11th St.* ☎ *360/738–8564* 🌐 *www.whatcomartmarket.org.*

Activities

WHALE-WATCHING

★ San Juan Cruises

WHALE-WATCHING | This popular whale-watching excursion company sails around Bellingham Bay and out to the San Juan Islands, where there's a stop for lunch and exploring in Friday Harbor on San Juan Island. Under the right conditions, the views of whales and sunsets cannot be beat. They also offer cruises with crab dinners, craft-beer, and Northwest wines. ✉ *Bellingham Cruise Terminal, 355 Harris Ave.* ☎ *360/738–8099, 800/443–4552* 🌐 *www.whales.com.*

Bow-Edison

20 miles south of Bellingham.

Long a hub of both fresh oysters and other shellfish sourced from the pristine Puget Sound waters of Samish and Padilla bays, these twin villages at the southern end of breathtaking Chuckanut Drive have in recent years become celebrated for their bounty of restaurants and purveyors of fine foods. Articles in *Food & Wine* and other respected publications have helped put this unassuming though beautiful swatch of the western Skagit Valley on the international foodie map. Most of the area's restaurants are in the slightly bigger of the two communities, Edison, whose tiny quadrant of narrow streets is jammed with fantastic places to eat, along with a few art galleries. Bow, on the other hand, has no real town center but is home to several remarkable farms open to the public. Beyond eating, Bow-Edison is also just a short drive from Bay View State Park and Padilla Bay National Estuarine Reserve.

GETTING HERE AND AROUND

You need a car to explore these neighboring villages and the surrounding farmlands. They're most easily reached from Bellingham or Mount Vernon via Interstate 5 to Exit 236, but the far more scenic and still relatively quick route from Bellingham is famous Chuckanut Drive (Highway 11), the southern end of which leads right into Bow.

Sights

Bay View State Park

NATIONAL/STATE PARK | Adjoining the small waterfront community of the same name, this scenic 25-acre park has a campground with cabins in the woods and picnic tables on the low grassy bluff above Padilla Bay, a national estaurine sanctuary. Canoers and kayakers take note: Padilla Bay runs almost dry at low tide, when water is restricted to a few creeklike tidal channels. ✉ *10905 Bay View–Edison Rd., Mount Vernon* ☎ *360/757–0227* 🌐 *www.parks.wa.gov* 🎫 *$10 parking.*

★ Bow-Edison Food Trail

TOUR—SIGHT | Just a 15-minute drive northwest of Mount Vernon, the twin villages of Bow-Edison have in just a relatively short time become one of Washington's premier foodie destinations. The region's bounty of farms, which produce everything from fresh berries to artisan cheese, and proximity to the fresh shellfish of Samish Bay inspired entrepreneurs to open restaurants, bakeries, and markets of a caliber you'd expect in a city 20 times the size (the combined population is about 200). Pick up a trail map or visit the website for the nearly 20 vendors in the area. ✉ *Bow* 🌐 *www.bowedisonfoodtrail.tumblr.com.*

★ Padilla Bay National Estuarine Reserve

NATURE PRESERVE | At this serene 8,000-acre wildlife preserve adjacent to Bayview State Park, the Breazeale Interpretive Center has great birding: there are black Brant (or Brent) geese, peregrine falcons, and bald eagles. Trails lead to an observation deck, into the woods, and to a rocky beach with more good bird-watching opportunities. This is also a popular place for kayaking. ✉ *10441 Bayview–Edison Rd., Mount Vernon* ☎ *360/428–1558* 🌐 *www.padillabay.gov* 🎟 *Free* ⏲ *Interpretive center closed Sun. and Mon.*

Restaurants

Chuckanut Manor

$$$$ | **AMERICAN** | This old-fashioned, glassed-in dining room and bar overlook the mouth of the Samish River, Samish Bay, and the mudflats, where great blue herons hang out and bald eagles are occasionally spotted gliding by. It's a popular spot for bird-watching, with finches, chickadees, and red-winged blackbirds at the feeders outside the picture windows. **Known for:** hosts a popular Champagne brunch on Sunday; sunset views of Samish Bay; tasty whiskey crab soup. $ *Average main: $32* ✉ *3056 Chuckanut Dr., Bow* ☎ *360/766–6191* 🌐 *www.chuckanutmanor.com* ⏲ *Closed Mon.*

★ Oyster Bar on Chuckanut Drive

$$$$ | **SEAFOOD** | Above the shore on a steep, wooded bluff in the northern reaches of Bow, this intimate restaurant is famous for having one of the best marine views of any Washington restaurant. People come here to dine on refined seafood, wild game, and steaks while watching the sun disappear behind the San Juan Islands to the west or the full moon reflect off the waters of Samish Bay. **Known for:** oyster fry with Parmesan–bread crumb crust; outstanding views of the water; well-chosen wine list. $ *Average main: $40* ✉ *2578 Chuckanut Dr., Bow* ☎ *360/766–6185* 🌐 *www.theoysterbar.net.*

Rhody Cafe

$$$ | **PACIFIC NORTHWEST** | Officially named the Rhododendron Cafe, this dapper, art-filled eatery has a lush garden terrace that makes it the perfect stop for a weekend brunch or leisurely dinner before or after a road trip along Chuckanut Drive. The menu changes to take advantage of what's in season, but you might start with butternut squash risotto topped with duck confit, before tucking into house-made fettuccine with Dungeness crab Alfredo sauce. **Known for:** waffles with huckleberry coulis for brunch; fresh farm-to-table cuisine; extensive, well-priced wine list. $ *Average main: $24* ✉ *5521 Chuckanut Dr., Bow* ☎ *360/766–6667* 🌐 *www.rhodycafe.com* ⏲ *Closed Mon. and Tues.*

Slough Food

$ | **CAFÉ** | With a name that's a play on the slow food movement and the Edison Slough, which runs through the tiny villages of Bow and Edison, this cozy café and deli is focused on two products that pair perfectly: wine and cheese. You'll discover an impressively curated selection of both, along with bountiful salads, soups, sandwiches, and other treats that showcase the area's seasonal ingredients. **Known for:** great selection of wine and craft beer by the glass; regularly scheduled paella parties; dining on the garden patio. $ *Average main: $12* ✉ *5766 Cains Ct., Bow* ☎ *360/766–4458* 🌐 *www.sloughfood.com* ⏲ *Closed Mon. and Tues. No dinner.*

★ Tweets

$$ | **CONTEMPORARY** | If you had time to dine in just one of the Bow-Edison's vaunted eateries, you'd be wise—and fortunate—to choose this quirky little café decorated with vintage mirrors and mismatched tables and chairs; just be sure to bring cash (credit cards aren't accepted) and take note of the limited hours. The menu changes daily and is presented on a chalkboard, but crowd-pleasing dishes that often appear include pork with salsa verde and a poached egg, shrimp and scallops with grits, and an artichoke-potato frittata with a garden salad. **Known for:** save room for a fresh-baked cookie or a slice of pie; farm-sourced breakfast and lunch fare; high-quality espresso drinks. $ *Average main: $16* ✉ *5800 Cains Ct., Bow*

360/820–9912 www.tweetscafe.com Closed Mon.–Thurs. No dinner No credit cards.

Shopping

Bow Hill Blueberries

FOOD/CANDY | Part of the fun in visiting this pastoral farmstead in Bow, apart from stocking up on fresh-picked (or pick-yourself) organic blueberries, is sampling the wide range of gourmet goodies. Bow Hill makes and sells juices, salad dressings, pickled preserves, and other treats made with local blueberries—there's blueberry ice cream, too. *15628 Bow Hill Rd., Bow 360/399–1006 www.bowhillblueberries.com.*

Breadfarm

FOOD/CANDY | A favorite stop on the Bow-Edison Food Trail, this cozy little purveyor of savory artisan breads and delectable pastries is a great place to stock up on picnic supplies before venturing up scenic Chuckanut Drive toward Bellingham. The offerings change regularly and features ingredients from local farms—you might find pumpkin brioche, herb focaccia, black olive baguettes, hand-and-cheese pastries, hazelnut espresso cookies, and chocolate babkas. The house-made granola is fantastic, too. *5766 Cains Ct., Bow 360/766–4065 www.breadfarm.com.*

★ Samish Bay Cheese

FOOD/CANDY | This 200-acre organic farm and dairy on the edge of Bow produces exceptional cow's-milk cheeses, plus kefir and yogurt. There's also a selection of pork and beef products, also raised on this beautiful farm. You can sample the goods in the tasting room or a bite to eat—cheese plates, mac and cheese, and labneh cheesecake are among the specialties. There's cider, beer, and coffee, too. *15115 Bow Hill Rd., Bow 360/766–6707 www.samishbay.com.*

★ Taylor Shellfish Farms

FOOD/CANDY | Run by the same family since 1890, this stunningly situated shellfish operation looks out over Samish Bay and is a memorable place to buy fresh oysters, Dungeness crab, clams, geoduck, and other fruits of the sea. You can take your purchases with you or enjoy them at one of the waterfront picnic tables, where you'll be encouraged to grill everything yourself on the barbecue. Beer and wine is available, too. *2182 Chuckanut Dr., Bow 360/766–6002 www.taylorshellfishfarms.com.*

Mount Vernon

12 miles southeast of Bow-Edison.

This attractive riverfront town, founded in 1871, is surrounded by dairy pastures, vegetable fields, and bulb farms—the town is famous for its annual Tulip Festival in April, when thousands of people visit to admire the floral exuberance. After a giant logjam on the lower Skagit was cleared, steamers began churning up the river, and Mount Vernon soon became the major commercial center of the Skagit Valley, a position it has never relinquished. Rising above downtown and the river, 972-foot-high Little Mountain is a city park with a view. It used to be an island until the mudflats were filled in by Skagit River silt. Glacial striations in rocks near the top of the mountain, dating from the last continental glaciation (10,000–20,000 years ago), were made when the mountain (and all of the Puget Sound region) was covered by some 3,500 feet of ice.

GETTING HERE AND AROUND

The best way to reach Mount Vernon is by car, taking Interstate 5 north to any of several exits right in town.

CONTACTS Mount Vernon Chamber of Commerce. *301 W. Kincaid St. 360/428–8547 www.mountvernonchamber.com.*

Sights

Little Mountain Park

CITY PARK | Atop the eponymous mountain at the southeastern edge of town, this 522-acre park, which rises to nearly 1,000 feet above sea level, has great views of the Skagit Valley (especially in March and April, when the daffodils and tulips are in full bloom), the San Juan Islands, Mount Baker, and the distant Olympic Mountains. It's a lovely spot for a picnic. ✉ *Little Mountain Rd., off E. Blackburn Rd., 4 miles southeast of downtown* ☎ *360/336–6213* 🌐 *www.mountvernonwa.gov* 🎟 *Free.*

RoozenGaarde

GARDEN | This 1,200-acre estate was established by the Roozen family and Washington Bulb Company in 1985—it's the world's largest family-owned tulip-, daffodil-, and iris-growing business. Sixteen acres of greenhouses are filled with multicolored blossoms, and more than 200,000 bulbs are planted in the show gardens each fall. The Skagit Valley Tulip Festival, held in April, is the main event, when the flowers pop up in neat, brilliant rows across the flat land, attracting thousands of sightseers. The garden and store are open year-round, and the staff is full of helpful advice for both novice and experienced gardeners. ✉ *15867 Beaver Marsh Rd.* ☎ *360/424–8531, 866/488–5477* 🌐 *www.tulips.com* 🎟 *Free.*

Restaurants

Il Granaio

$$$ | **ITALIAN** | Tucked deep into the town's historic Old Granery, amid displays of century-old farming equipment, is this cozy and rustic place where dark-wood floors, small tables, and lantern-like fixtures provide the authentic ambience of a local trattoria. The waitstaff is quick and knowledgeable, bringing out enormous pasta bowls, seafood salads, and panfried eggplant or salmon. **Known for:** extensive selection of Italian and Northwest wines; simple but richly satisfying desserts; popular cooking classes. $ *Average main: $25* ✉ *100 E. Montgomery St.* ☎ *360/419–0674* 🌐 *www.granaio.com* ⏲ *No lunch weekends.*

Taste of Thai by Wipa

$ | **THAI** | Some of the region's most flavorful Thai food is served in this cheerfully decorated restaurant in an unassuming Burlington strip mall. Helmed by a young, gracious chef owner who learned her trade at Bangkok's Thai Royal Grand Palace, the kitchen turns out authentic dishes, like a salad of poached chicken with coconut milk, banana blossoms, and fried shallots, and a fragrant massaman curry with fresh pineapple. **Known for:** flavorful Thai coffees and teas; gorgeous presentations; convivial dining room. $ *Average main: $15* ✉ *1038 S. Burlington Blvd., Burlington* ☎ *360/899–5823* 🌐 *www.tasteofthaibywipa.com* ⏲ *Closed Mon.*

★ The Upcountry

$$$ | **MODERN ASIAN** | This intimate downtown eatery—the handful of seats are set around an L-shape bar and overlook the kitchen—is one of the more memorable dining experiences in the region. It features a short, always-changing menu that showcases the region's freshest seasonal ingredients and the considerable talents of chef-owner Hiroki Inoue. **Known for:** Japanese-influenced farm-to-table fare; smart list of French and Italian wines; cozy, romantic ambience. $ *Average main: $28* ✉ *303 Pine St.* ☎ *360/588–4100* 🌐 *www.upcountryfood.com* ⏲ *Closed Mon.–Wed. No lunch.*

Valley Shine Distillery

$$ | **AMERICAN** | Although this craft distillery set in an early-20th-century downtown building is perhaps best known for the stellar spirits you can sample in the tasting room—including Benjamin's Bourbon, Bonfire Toffee Liqueur, and Red X Gin—it's also a terrific restaurant serving reasonably priced modern American fare. Barbecue brisket sandwiches, blackened-chicken chop salads, and baked meatballs with penne are among the standouts. **Known for:** creative cocktails using house-made spirits; hearty portions of pastas and steaks; handsome old-world dining room. *Average main: $18* *320 S. 1st St.* *360/588-4086* *www.valleyshinedistillery.com* *Closed Mon.*

La Conner

10 miles west of Mount Vernon, 14 miles southeast of Anacortes.

Morris Graves, Kenneth Callahan, Guy Anderson, Mark Tobey, and other painters set up shop in La Conner in the 1940s, and the village on the Swinomish Channel has been a haven for artists ever since. In recent years the community has become increasingly popular as a regional weekend escape—it's a fairly short drive from Seattle, but it feels refreshingly far from the bustle, and it's home to a number of distinctive inns and boutique hotels, making it the best lodging base in Skagit County. La Conner has several historic buildings near the waterfront or a short walk up the hill—you can walk up a flight of stairs leading up the bluff—as well as several inviting shops and restaurants. Parking can get a little challenging on summer weekends, when village fills with visitors. The flat land around La Conner makes for easy biking along levees and through the tulip and farm fields, several of which have stands selling produce during the growing season.

GETTING HERE AND AROUND

The center of La Conner is roughly 12 miles west of Interstate 5, Exit 221, via Highway 534. The town is very close to both Anacortes, where ferries depart for the San Juan Islands, and the northern tip of Whidbey Island. A car is by far the best way to reach and explore the area. Some hotels in the area lend bikes to their guests.

CONTACT La Conner Chamber of Commerce. *511 Morris St.* *360/466-4778* *www.lovelaconner.com.*

Sights

Museum of Northwest Art

MUSEUM | This striking, modern building displays some 2,500 works of regional creative minds past and present, including painters, sculptors, photographers, and other artists. Soaring spaces, circular exhibit rooms, a glass gallery, and a broad spiral staircase add to the free-form feeling of the displays. The small shop sells examples of what you see in the exhibits. *121 S. 1st St.* *360/466-4446* *www.museumofnwart.org* *Free* *Closed Mon. Jan.–early Mar.*

Pacific Northwest Quilt & Fiber Arts Museum

HOUSE | One of only a handful of fiber arts museums in the country is housed throughout three floors of the Queen Anne–style Gaches Mansion, which rises grandly over La Conner's downtown. Exhibits change throughout the year and feature both contemporary and historic quilts, wall hangings, and other textiles, most of them created in the Pacific Northwest. The lovingly restored mansion itself makes for an interesting tour, and there's an excellent museum shop on the ground floor. *703 S. 2nd St.* *360/466-4288* *$7* *Closed Mon. and Tues.*

Skagit County Historical Museum

MUSEUM | This hilltop museum surveys domestic life in early Skagit County and Northwest Coastal Native American history. There's an interesting gallery showcasing goods commonly found in the region's early general stores, and rotating exhibits interpret the different aspects of the community's rich heritage. *501 4th St.* *360/466-3365* *www.skagitcounty.net/museum* *$5* *Closed Mon.*

Restaurants

★ Anelia's Kitchen & Stage

$$ | POLISH | This airy and attractive downtown restaurant with a wall of windows and a timber ceiling serves hearty and healthy modern Polish fare, with dishes like elk-stuffed pierogis, beet-pickled deviled eggs, house-made sausage with beer-braised sauerkraut, and chicken-bacon *lazanki* (egg noodles) among the highlights. There's live music many evenings. **Known for:** classic cocktails and a good selection of wine and beer; artfully plated renditions of Polish classics; pierogies with several kinds of fillings. *Average main: $17* *513 1st St.* *360/399–1805* *www.aneliaskitchenandstage.com* *Closed Tues.*

Calico Cupboard

$ | CAFÉ | A local favorite, this storefront bakery, with branches nearby in Anacortes and Mount Vernon, turns out heavenly pastries, plus big portions of breakfast and lunch fare. Lunches focus on fresh and creative salads, soups, and burgers; huge and hearty breakfasts may leave you with little need for lunch—the roasted-butternut-squash hash and *migas* are a couple of favorites. **Known for:** deck seating overlooking Swinomish Channel; filling and delicious breakfasts served all day; rustic, savory breads. *Average main: $15* *720 S. 1st St.* *360/466–4451* *www.calicocupboardcafe.com* *No dinner.*

★ The Oyster and Thistle

$$$ | PACIFIC NORTHWEST | A couple of blocks from the river on a bluff with expansive views of the village, this homey restaurant with a rustic dark-wood interior serves some of the best seafood in the area, plus a few well-prepared French classics, such as cassoulet with duck confit and house-cured bacon, and fall-off-the-bone pork shank with wild-mushroom risotto. Simpler fare—caramelized-onion flatbread, shepherd's pie—is served in the adjoining pub. **Known for:** extensive selection of regional oysters; impressive list of Northwest and French wines; specialities like paella and bouillabaisse. *Average main: $29* *205 E. Washington St.* *360/766–6179* *www.theoysterandthistle.com* *No lunch Tues.–Thurs.*

Hotels

★ Channel Lodge

$$ | HOTEL | Most of the smartly furnished contemporary rooms at this chalet-style inn, trimmed with honey-colored wood and warmed with gas fireplaces, overlook the picturesque Swinomish Channel. **Pros:** rustic charm meets modern amenities; big stone fireplace in lobby; lovely waterfront setting. **Cons:** a handful of rooms don't overlook water; walls are a little thin; no gym or restaurant. *Rooms from: $172* *205 N. 1st St.* *360/466–1500, 888/466–4113* *www.laconnerchannellodge.com* *42 rooms* *Free Breakfast.*

Heron Inn

$ | B&B/INN | At this cheerfully decorated contemporary inn, wellness is the name of the game—there's a small but well-designed spa, reasonably priced packages include massage or other treatments, and a healthy breakfast buffet is served every morning. **Pros:** rooms have plush robes and bathrooms with radiant heat; a number of dining options within walking distance; high-tech touches like flat-screen TVs and Roku. **Cons:** no coffee in rooms (but it's always available in the lobby); several blocks from the waterfront; not a great option for kids. *Rooms from: $135* *117 Maple Ave.* *360/399–1074* *www.theheroninn.com* *12 rooms* *Free Breakfast.*

Hotel Planter

$ | B&B/INN | This warmly updated hotel dating from 1907, making it the oldest in La Conner, is located amid downtown's many atmospheric shops, galleries, and restaurants. **Pros:** most rooms overlook attractive courtyard; reasonably priced; historic charm. **Cons:** old-fashioned aesthetic isn't for everybody; no breakfast or on-site parking; some rooms get street noise. *Rooms from: $135* ✉ *715 1st St.* ☎ *360/466–4710* 🌐 *www.hotelplanter.com* *12 rooms* *No meals.*

La Conner Country Inn

$ | HOTEL | FAMILY | At this rambling motel-style property all the spacious rooms have private outdoor entrances, vaulted ceilings, gas fireplaces, refrigerators, and pleasant country-style furnishings; several have whirlpool baths. **Pros:** close to downtown shops and restaurants; spacious rooms make it popular with families; quiet but central location. **Cons:** rooms don't have a lot of character; no elevator to reach second floor; not on the waterfront. *Rooms from: $149* ✉ *107 S. 2nd St.* ☎ *360/466–1500, 888/466–4113* 🌐 *www.laconnercountryinn.com* *28 rooms* *Free Breakfast.*

★ Wild Iris

$ | B&B/INN | Lush gardens surround this Victorian-style inn, and the elegantly decorated interior begins with a river-rock fireplace and extends to spacious rooms done with luxe fabrics and polished wood accents. **Pros:** homemade cookies served upon arrival; great in-room amenities; excellent two-course breakfast. **Cons:** the least expensive rooms are quite small; several blocks from the waterfront; not appropriate for very young kids. *Rooms from: $144* ✉ *121 Maple Ave.* ☎ *360/466–1400, 800/477–1400* 🌐 *www.wildiris.com* *18 rooms* *Free Breakfast.*

Camano Island

20 miles south of La Conner.

Reached by bridge and much easier to reach from the mainland than Puget Sound's other islands, 40-square-mile Camano Island nevertheless remains lightly developed and largely unspoiled, a serene escape that's popular for outdoor recreation, getting away from it all, and experiencing the area as it might have felt long before Seattle's huge population boom. The island has a population of about 16,000 and is home to a number of farms as well as two beautiful state parks. The small town of Stanwood contains a greater selection of restaurants and shops, including a few notable eateries in its small but cute historic downtown.

GETTING HERE AND AROUND

You need a car to get around the island, which is reached from Interstate 5, Exit 212. Highway 532 leads directly from the mainland town of Standwood over the Camano Gateway Bridge.

ESSENTIALS

VISITOR INFORMATION Camano Island Chamber of Commerce. ✉ *370 NE Camano Dr.* ☎ *360/629–7136* 🌐 *www.camanoisland.org.*

★ Cama Beach Historical State Park

NATIONAL/STATE PARK | FAMILY | It feels as though you've stepped back in time nearly a century upon visiting this 486-acre waterfront park that occupies a former cabin resort that thrived from the 1930s to the 1950s. Situated on the hilly, densely wooded southwestern shoreline of Camano Island, the park maintains the resort's many buildings, including about 30 well-kept cedar cabins and bungalows set on or very near the sweeping beachfront with views to the west of Whidbey Island and the Olympic Mountains. Tasty breakfast and lunch fare is available to both day and overnight visitors in the cheerful Cama Beach Cafe, and you can rent kayaks, canoes, and rowboats from the park's Center for Wooden Boats. Hikers can explore more than 15 miles of woodland and beach trails, and rangers offer a range of guided walks, campfire talks, and other interpretive programs.

It's a wonderfully relaxing place to spend a few hours or a few days. ✉ *1880 W. Camano Dr.* ☎ *360/387–1550* 🌐 *www.parks.state.wa.us* 🎫 *$10 parking.*

Camano Island State Park

NATIONAL/STATE PARK | FAMILY | The smaller (at 244 acres) and generally less crowded of the island's two state parks, this peaceful tract of coniferous woodland includes nearly 7,000 feet of rugged, rocky shoreline that you can easily access via two meandering park roads. Picnic shelters, campsites (including a few rustic cabins), a boat launch, and scenic swimming, fishing, and crabbing spots look south across Saratoga Passage toward Whidbey Island. On clear days you can spy the snowy summit of Mt. Rainier. About 3 miles of fairly easy trails lace the park, and a well-maintained 1-mile trek connects with nearby Cama Beach Historical State Park. ✉ *2269 Lowell Point Rd.* ☎ *360/387–3031* 🌐 *www.parks.state.wa.us* 🎫 *$10 parking.*

Kristoferson Farm & Canopy Tours NW

FARM/RANCH | FAMILY | Owned by the same family since it was established in 1912, this idyllic farm with a giant red barn grows apples, lavender, pumpkins, and other goods that are available in the farm shop, along with rustic crafts. The farm also hosts five-course dinners with wine pairings once a month from spring through fall and hosts a number of popular seasonal events, from Midsommer in June to a fall festival in October. But the farm has become especially popular in recent years as the home of Canopy Tours NW (www.canopytoursnw.com). These tours include crossing a log bridge, walking on a couple of ferny forest trails, and zooming along six different zip-line trails. ✉ *332 NE Camano Dr.* ☎ *360/387–5807* 🌐 *www.kristofersonfarm.com.*

Matzke Fine Art and Design

MUSEUM | Tranquil fern-draped footpaths lead through groves cedar and Douglas fir to reveal a rich array of art installations at this delightful gallery and sculpture garden on the south side of Camano Island. More than 65 artists, many from the Pacific Northwest and Japan, show their work here, both in the sun-dappled garden and the indoor gallery. ✉ *2345 Blanche Way* ☎ *360/387–2759* 🌐 *www.matzkefineart.com* ⏲ *Closed Mon.–Thurs.*

Restaurants

Camano Commons Marketplace

$ | ECLECTIC | This bustling complex of eateries and shops, which you reach soon after driving onto the island, contains a counter-service bakery offering a great selection of espresso drinks, cookies and pastries, and ice cream, along with sit-down venues for breakfast, burgers, pizza, barbecue, and craft beer. It's a great option for a full meal or to pick up groceries and picnic supplies to take with you on your other adventures on the island. **Known for:** toothsome sweets and coffee drinks; dining options for every taste; gourmet picnic goods. 💲 *Average main: $12* ✉ *848 N. Sunrise Blvd.* ☎ *360/722–7459* 🌐 *www.camanocommons.com.*

Everett

30 miles southeast of Camano Island.

It's best known as the home of a massive Boeing Aircraft plant, so it's no surprise that Everett (population 110,000) has several world-class aviation museums that draw flight fans from around the world. It's also one of the largest Puget Sound ports, after Seattle and Tacoma, and the naval station here is home to a flotilla of destroyers and frigates. Much of this industrial city, including its steadily gentrifying downtown, sits high on a bluff above Port Gardner Bay and the Snohomish River. The waterfront was once lined by so many lumber, pulp, and shingle mills that Everett proudly called itself "the city of smokestacks." Downtown

Everett has many elegant old commercial buildings dating from the period when John D. Rockefeller heavily invested in the fledging town, hoping to profit from the nearby Monte Cristo mines—which turned out to be a flop. Another scheme failed when James J. Hill made Everett the western terminus of the Great Northern Railroad, hoping to turn it into Puget Sound's most important port.

The pleasant waterfront suburb of Mukilteo, about 5 miles southeast of Everett, is the main departure point for ferries to Clinton, on Whidbey Island, and the location of Paine Field, which opened to travelers in 2019. Marysville, 6 miles north of Everett, was set up as a trading post in 1877. Pioneers exchanged goods with the Snohomish people, who once occupied southeastern Whidbey Island and the lower Snohomish Valley. Today it's a thriving community and the home of the popular Tulalip (Too- *lay*-lip) Casino and the tribe's impressive Hibulb Cultural Center.

GETTING HERE AND AROUND

Everett is best explored by car; take Interstate 5 to Exit 192.

ESSENTIALS

VISITOR INFORMATION Seattle North Country. ☎ *425/348–5802, 888/338–0976* 🌐 *www.seattlenorthcountry.com.*

Sights

★ Boeing Future of Flight
FACTORY | This impressive facility showcases the Boeing Everett line (747, 767, 777, and 787 Dreamliner), and the 98-acre site holds the world's largest building—so big that it often creates its own weather system inside. You can see planes in various stages of production on a 90-minute tour of the Boeing factory and spend time in the gallery exhibits, with cutaways of airplane fuselages, up-close looks at the inner workings of navigation and hydraulic systems, and interactive exhibits on satellites, submarines, and space travel. You can even walk inside a space station module that was launched on an actual space shuttle mission. There's also a café, a kid-oriented family zone, and the Sky Deck atop the building, where you're treated to views of jets taking off and landing at adjacent Paine Field and impressive views of the surrounding mountains and Puget Sound. Note that no purses, backpacks, cameras, cell phones, or children under 48 inches tall are permitted on the factory tour (free lockers are provided); they are allowed on the Sky Deck and in the gallery exhibits. Reserving tour tickets a day in advance is recommended, but same-day tickets are always available. ✉ *8415 Paine Field Blvd., Mukilteo* ☎ *425/438–8100, 800/464–1476* 🌐 *www.boeingfutureofflight.com* 🎫 *$27.*

★ Flying Heritage & Combat Armor Museum
MUSEUM | Housed within two enormous airport hangars, this spectacular gathering of unique vintage aircraft, combat armor, and tanks belongs to local tycoon Paul Allen, who began collecting and restoring rare planes in 1998. The historic aircraft represent all of 20th-century military history, including the two world wars and other international battles. A favorite plane is the P-51D Mustang from World War II. Tours are self-guided; interactive exhibits like the thoughtful multimedia presentation "Why War: The Causes of Conflict" helps visitors understand the complexities of military engagements. In summer, try to time your visit for one of the Free Fly Days, when pilots are on-site to fly some of the craft as part of monthly maintenance. ✉ *Paine Field, 3407 109th St. SW* ☎ *206/342–4242* 🌐 *www.flyingheritage.com* 🎫 *$20* 🕒 *Closed Mon. in Sept.–May.*

Hibulb Cultural Center & Natural History Preserve

MUSEUM | **FAMILY** | This impressive contemporary museum and cultural center with a stunning cedar longhouse, intricate wood carvings, hand-crafted canoes, and engaging interactive exhibits reveals the rich history of the several tribes—including Snohomish, Skykomish, and Snoqualmie—that have thrived in the Puget Sound region for centuries. The center adjoins a 50-acre nature preserve with stands of cedar and hemlock trees, salmon-rich streams, preserved estuarial wetlands, and nature trails. Just off Interstate 5 near the town of Marysville, the waterfront Tulalip Reservation has more than 2,500 tribal members and is also home to the 370-room Tulalip Resort Casino and an outlet shopping center, which are just a few miles north of the cultural center. ✉ *6410 23rd Ave. NE, Marysville* ☎ *360/716–2600* 🌐 *www.hibulbculturalcenter.org* 🎫 *$10* 🕒 *Closed Mon.*

Imagine Children's Museum

MUSEUM | **FAMILY** | This engaging spot for kids is on a pioneer homestead built in the 1800s. Interactive exhibits and crafts are part of the fun; wee ones love the magic school bus as well. ✉ *1502 Wall St.* ☎ *425/258–1006* 🌐 *www.imaginecm.org* 🎫 *$13* 🕒 *Closed Mon.*

Jetty Island

NATURE PRESERVE | **FAMILY** | Open in summer only, this is a 2-mile-long, sand-fringed offshore haven full of wildlife and outdoor opportunities. Seasonal programs include guided walks, bonfires, and midsummer Jetty Island Days festivities. A ferry provides round-trip transportation. ✉ *West end of 10th St., off W. Marine View Dr.* ☎ *425/257–8304* 🌐 *www.everettwa.gov/jettyisland* 🎫 *$2 ferry, $3 parking* 🕒 *Closed early Sept.–early July.*

Museum of Flight Restoration Center

MUSEUM | At this branch of Seattle's Museum of Flight, vintage planes are restored by a volunteer staff that simply loves bringing vintage aircraft back to life. You can wander among the mix of delicate and behemoth planes on a leisurely, self-guided tour at Paine Field. ✉ *Paine Field, 2909 100th St. SW* ☎ *425/745–5150* 🌐 *www.museumofflight.org/restoration* 🎫 *$5* 🕒 *Closed Mon. and Tues.*

Schack Art Center

ARTS VENUE | **FAMILY** | This striking contemporary nonprofit art center has been a key part of downtown Everett's steady renaissance. It's spacious, high-ceilinged galleries mount diverse rotating exhibits throughout the year, and a gift shop carries works by nearly 200 regional artists. There's also a state-of-the-art hot shop where visitors can watch glass blowing. ✉ *2921 Hoyt Ave.* ☎ *425/259–5050* 🌐 *www.schack.org.*

 Restaurants

Anthony's Homeport

$$$ | **SEAFOOD** | Tucked into chic Marina Village, this handsome waterfront outpost of a popular Washington-based seafood chain has large windows opening to a panorama of Port Gardner Bay. The specials, which change daily, might include meaty Dungeness crab, wild chinook salmon, and other sea creatures caught just offshore. **Known for:** the clam chowder is justly renowned; weekday "sunset dinners" for $25; great views of the bay. 💲 *Average main: $24* ✉ *1726 W. Marine View Dr.* ☎ *425/252–3333* 🌐 *www.anthonys.com.*

Botan Ramen n' Bar

$ | **RAMEN** | A cherry tree in full bloom rises over the brick-walled dining room of this superb ramen and cocktail bar in Everett's steadily gentrifying downtown. Warm your soul with a steaming bowl of vegetarian shoyu, pork tonkatsu, spicy miso, or seafood ramen. **Known for:** authentic ramen and delicious appetizers; unique cocktails made with shochu;

generous portions. $ *Average main: $14* ✉ *2803 Colby Ave.* ☎ *425/595–4940.*

★ Narrative Coffee

$ | **CAFÉ** | Set in a dramatic 1920s downtown building with exposed rafters, big skylights, and plenty of seating, this well-respected third-wave coffeehouse is an inviting place to linger over a latte or cold brew. It's also one of Everett's best breakfast and lunch options, featuring ricotta toast, buttermilk biscuit breakfast sandwiches, and bacon-brussels sprouts salads. **Known for:** mochas made with artisan dark chocolate; hearty breakfast fare; cheerful living room-esque interior. $ *Average main: $10* ✉ *2927 Wetmore Ave.* ☎ *425/322–4648* 🌐 *www.narrative.coffee* ⏲ *No dinner.*

The Sisters

$ | **AMERICAN** | This funky breakfast and lunch café in Everett Public Market is as popular now as when it opened in 1983. Perhaps that's because the blueberry or pecan hotcakes, rich soups, and overflowing sandwiches are as good as ever. **Known for:** filling breakfast fare; fresh-berry pies; veggie, beef, and wild salmon burgers. $ *Average main: $10* ✉ *2804 Grand Ave.* ☎ *425/252–0480* 🌐 *www.thesistersrestaurant.com* ⏲ *Closed weekends. No dinner.*

Hotels

Best Western Plus Navigator Inn & Suites

$$ | **HOTEL** | Minutes from Boeing Future of Flight and Paine Field, this nicely maintained Best Western is a step up from many of the other chains in the area, especially considering the reasonable rates. **Pros:** close to the area's many aviation-related attractions; rates include very nice fitness club next door; lots of dining options nearby. **Cons:** suburban location isn't walkable; 15-minute drive south of downtown Everett; kitchens are small. $ *Rooms from: $169* ✉ *10210 Evergreen Way* ☎ *425/347–2555, 800/780–7234* 🌐 *www.navigatorsuites.com* *76 rooms* 🍽 *Free Breakfast.*

Hotel Indigo Seattle Everett Waterfront

$$ | **HOTEL** | This sleek, nautically themed hotel on northern Everett's bustling and attractive Port Gardner waterfront offers a number of pleasing features, including a pretty indoor pool, a state-of-the-art fitness center, and well-designed rooms with high-tech entertainment and work amenities. **Pros:** lively, attractive seafood restaurant; lovely spot overlooking Puget Sound; great for outdoors enthusiasts. **Cons:** a handful of rooms don't have water views; not within walking distance of downtown; compact rooms. $ *Rooms from: $155* ✉ *1028 13th St.* ☎ *425/217–2772* 🌐 *www.ihg.com* *142 rooms* 🍽 *No meals.*

Nightlife

★ Bluewater Distilling

BARS/PUBS | Known for producing acclaimed, organic Bluewater Vodka, Halcyon Gin, Wintersun Aquavit, and several flavored liqueurs, this industrial-chic operation on the Port Gardner waterfront also houses a trendy bar and bistro. Stop by for a tasting or a cocktail (try one of the house infusions), and check out the extensive selection of inventive tapas. ✉ *1205 Craftsman Way* ☎ *425/404–1408* 🌐 *www.bluewaterdistilling.com.*

Independent Beer Bar

BARS/PUBS | You'll find an impressive lineup of regional craft beers on tap at this welcoming, dog-friendly downtown bar that also serves Russian dumplings. ✉ *1801 Hewitt Ave.* ☎ *425/212–9517* 🌐 *www.theindependentbeerbar.com.*

Performing Arts

Historic Everett Theatre

THEATER | In this grand, painstakingly restored 1901 theater in downtown Everett, you can attend concerts, comedy shows, traveling theater productions, and occasional classic films. ✉ *2911 Colby Ave.* ☎ *425/258–6766* 🌐 *www.yourhistoriceveretttheatre.org.*

Edmonds

18 miles southwest of Everett, 15 miles north of Seattle.

On the east side of Puget Sound, Edmonds is a good gateway to the Kitsap Peninsula, as ferries from here connect to Kingston. This charming small city just north of Seattle has a waterfront lined by more than a mile of boutiques and restaurants, seaside parks and attractions, and a string of broad, windswept beaches. Just beyond is the small but lively downtown area, where you can wander into hip cafés and wine shops, peruse attractive antiques stores and chic galleries, and browse the colorful Summer Market, which runs Saturday 9 to 3 from mid-June through early October. The early-evening Third Thursday Art Walk—one of the state's largest such events—shows off the work of local artists, and numerous events and festivals take place year-round. On the east side of town, the many strip malls lining Highway 99 have attracted a slew of first-rate Asian and Latin American restaurants in recent years—it's one of the state's better concentrations of international dining.

GETTING HERE AND AROUND

From Seattle or Everett, take Interstate 5 to Highway 104 west, which leads downtown and to the ferry terminal.

ESSENTIALS

VISITOR INFORMATION Edmonds Chamber of Commerce. ✉ *121 5th Ave. N* ☎ *425/776–6711* 🌐 *www.edmondswa.com.*

Sights

Cascadia Art Museum

MUSEUM | One of the more imaginative adaptations you'll ever see of a mid-century modern grocery store, this sustainably designed regional art museum sits on the edge of downtown Edmonds, steps from the ferry terminal. The museum presents rotating exhibits that focus heavily on Pacific Northwest art from the mid-19th to mid-20th centuries, and the curators make it an important part of their mission to include female, minority, and LGBTQ representation. Classical music performances are held here monthly. ✉ *190 Sunset Ave.* ☎ *425/336–4809* 🌐 *www.cascadiaartmuseum.org* 🎫 *$10* 🕒 *Closed Mon. and Tues.*

Olympic Beach

BEACH—SIGHT | **FAMILY** | Get your dinner to go and watch the sun go down behind Whidbey Island and the Olympic Mountains at this lovely waterfront park. The Olympic Beach fishing pier attracts anglers all year and public art dots the landscape. In summer, a beach ranger station (open weekends noon–5) is a great place to pick up local info; kids like exploring the marine touch tank. ✉ *200 Admiral Way* ☎ *425/775–1344* 🌐 *www.edmondswa.gov.*

Restaurants

Bar Dojo

$$$ | **ASIAN FUSION** | A couple of miles east of downtown in a strip mall, this hot spot serves creative, often complex modern Asian fare, with an emphasis on local ingredients. Pork-belly ramen and fried soft-shell crab with tuna poke are stars among the noodle bowls, but also consider the grilled lemongrass chicken with a white wine–oyster sauce. **Known for:** great deals during late-night happy hour; Asian-inspired steaks and seafood grills; Asian-Latino taco nights on Tuesday.

$ Average main: $24 ✉ 8404 Bowdoin Way ☎ 425/967–7267 🌐 www.bardojo.com ⏲ No lunch.

★ Epulo Bistro

$$ | **MEDITERRANEAN** | Dimly lighted, smartly furnished, and urbane, this hip spot in the heart of downtown serves seasonally driven Mediterranean food with plenty of Northwestern influences. It's very easy to make a meal here of several tantalizing small plates, like sautéed brussels sprouts with bacon, chili, and garlic and Penn Cove mussels with saffron, orange, and leeks. **Known for:** wood-fired pizzas are a stellar options; cured meat boards and fresh burrata; Sunday half-price wine nights. *$ Average main: $22 ✉ 526 Main St. ☎ 425/678–8680 🌐 www.epulobistro.com ⏲ Closed Mon. No lunch.*

Fashion Dim Sum

$$ | **CHINESE** | Along Highway 99's "restaurant row" a few miles east of downtown Edmonds, this compact spot in an unassuming strip mall enjoys a sterling reputation for authentic dim sum. Bring a group of friends and select several plates per person, and don't miss the piggy buns (decorated with adorable piggy faces), salted egg yolk buns, shrimp-scallop shumai, crispy taro shrimp cakes, and sausage rice. **Known for:** impressive selection of buns and dumplings; a fun experience for family-style dining; no one leaves here hungry. *$ Average main: $16 ✉ 22923 Hwy. 99 ☎ 425/697–2886 🌐 www.fashiondimsum.com ⏲ Closed Wed.*

Maize & Barley

$ | **CARIBBEAN** | This friendly, upbeat downtown gastropub offers a menu of made-from-scratch Caribbean dishes, with an emphasis on healthy organic ingredients. There's always a good selection of local brews and ciders on tap, as well as Northwest wines, and dishes like Cuban-style borscht, smoked tofu with pineapple kraut, and spice-rubbed rockfish sandwiches burst with flavor. **Known for:** well-curated list of unusual Northwest beers; house-made cucumber, tamarind, and ginger sodas; mocha-stout bread pudding. *$ Average main: $9 ✉ 525 Main St. ☎ 425/835–0868 🌐 www.maizebarley.com ⏲ Closed Mon. and Tues.*

★ Milkie Milkie Dessert Cafe

$ | **KOREAN** | Edmonds is one the best Asian dining destinations outside Seattle, and this hip little café specializing in colorful—and highly Instagrammable—Korean *bingsoo* (shaved ice) desserts. These enormous, shareable concoctions are piled high with a variety of toppings—mangoes, rice cakes, bean paste, marshmallows, taro, coconut flakes, black sesame, and more—and are served with a side of sweet condensed milk. **Known for:** decadent shaved-ice bowls easily serve two to three people; a small assortment of savory Korean street foods; dessert toast toppings like green tea chocolate. *$ Average main: $10 ✉ 23830 Hwy. 99 ☎ 425/361–7696 🌐 www.milkiemilkie.com ⏲ Closed Tues. No lunch weekdays.*

Hotels

Best Western Plus Edmonds Harbor Inn

$$ | **HOTEL** | In downtown Edmonds, this well-maintained chain hotel has more luxury than you'd typically find at a Best Western, with comfortable country-style rooms updated in modern, easy-on-the-eyes beiges and earth tones; some have fireplaces, kitchens, or oversize jetted bathtubs. **Pros:** close to the ferry dock and train station; seasonal outdoor heated pool; full breakfast is included. **Cons:** no beach views; design is a bit cookie-cutter; some rooms get traffic noise. *$ Rooms from: $169 ✉ 130 W. Dayton St. ☎ 425/771–5021, 800/441–8033 🌐 www.bwedmondsharborinn.com 🛏 91 rooms 🍴 Free Breakfast.*

Snoqualmie and North Bend

30 miles east of Seattle.

Although it's just a 30-mile drive from downtown Seattle, much of the densely wooded town of Snoqualmie (sno- *qual*-mie) feels as though it could be hours away. Indeed, the rustic scenery and famed Snoqualmie Falls inspired David Lynch to film many of the exterior shots for *Twin Peaks* in and around the area—fans will recognize the luxurious Salish Lodge as the Great Northern Hotel, Twede's Cafe in North Bend as the Double R Diner, and the Roadhouse in nearby Fall City as the eponymous locale in the show. Although it's growing quickly (the population has skyrocketed from about 1,600 in 2000 to nearly 14,000 today) and becoming more suburban, it's still a popular getaway because of the falls, the luxurious Salish Lodge resort, and the impressive Northwest Railway Museum.

A few miles southeast, the small town of North Bend gets its name from a bend in the Snoqualmie River, which here turns toward Canada. The gorgeous scenery is dominated by 4,420-foot Mt. Washington, 4,788-foot Mt. Tenerife, and 4,167-foot Mt. Si. Named for early settler Josiah "Si" Merrit, Mt. Si can be climbed via a steep, four-hour trail that in summer provides views of the Cascade and Olympic peaks down to Puget Sound and Seattle. In winter, however, these mountains corner the rains: North Bend is one of the wettest places in western Washington, with an annual precipitation typically exceeding 65 inches (about double that of Seattle).

GETTING HERE AND AROUND

From Seattle, take Interstate 90 east to Exit 27. The Old Town area of Snoqualmie is very compact and walkable; the falls and Salish Lodge are a mile north. North Bend is 3 miles southeast.

Sights

Northwest Railway Museum

MUSEUM | FAMILY | Vintage cars line a paved path along Railroad Avenue, with signs explaining the origin of each engine, car, and caboose on display, with more history and memorabilia inside several different buildings, including the former waiting room of the stunning restored Snoqualmie depot. The Railway History Center, located in the train shed a mile south of the depot at 9312 Stone Quarry Road, displays photographs, documents, and exhibits related to the region's rail history. Several times a day on weekends, a train made of cars built in the mid-1910s for the Spokane, Portland, and Seattle Railroad travels between Snoqualmie Depot and North Bend. The 75-minute round-trip excursion passes through woods, past waterfalls, and around patchwork farmland. Crowds of families pack the winter Santa Train journeys and the midsummer Railroad Days rides, which features an annual parade. ✉ *Snoqualmie Depot, 38625 SE King St.* ☎ *425/888–3030* 🌐 *www.trainmuseum.org* 🎫 *Depot free; Railway History Center $10, train rides $20* ⏲ *No rides weekdays or Nov.–Apr. except during certain holidays periods. Railway History Center closed Tues. and Nov.–Mar.*

Sigillo Cellars

WINERY/DISTILLERY | Stop by this tasting room set inside a high-ceilinged former theater in Snoqualmie's Old Town to sample a selection of exceptional wines, most of them made with Bordeaux and Rhône grapes sourced from top vineyards around throughout the Columbia Valley. A variety of appetizers, including cheese and meat boards, are also available, and there's live music most Friday and Saturday evenings. Sigillo has a second tasting room in Chelan. ✉ *8086 Railroad Ave.* ☎ *425/292–0754* 🌐 *www.sigillocellars.com* ⏲ *Closed Mon.*

★ Snoqualmie Falls

BODY OF WATER | Spring and summer snowmelt turn the Snoqualmie River into a thundering torrent at Snoqualmie Falls. These sweeping cascades provided the backdrop for the *Twin Peaks* opening montage. The water pours over a 268-foot rock ledge (100 feet higher than Niagara Falls) to a 65-foot-deep pool. These cascades, considered sacred by the Native Americans, are Snoqualmie's biggest attraction. A privately owned 2-acre park with a gift shop and observation platform affords some of the best views of the falls and the surrounding area, as does the elegant Salish Lodge hotel. The 3-mile round-trip River Trail winds through trees and over open slopes to the base of the cascades. ✉ *6351 Railroad Ave. SE* ☎ *425/831–6525* 🌐 *www.snoqualmiefalls.com.*

Restaurants

Caadxi Oaxaca

$ | **MEXICAN** | Brightly painted *alebrijes* (carved wooden animal figurines) and folk art lend warmth and authenticity to this friendly Old Town restaurant and bar that specializes in the richly complex cuisine of Oaxaca as well as artisan mezcal. Start with a few *antojitos* (snacks), such as prawn ceviche, braised chicken tostadas, and *molotes* (potato and chorizo pastries), before moving on to a platter of pork in a fragrant red mole sauce or chile-cheese tamales. **Known for:** interesting mezcal and tequila cocktails; flavorful sauces made from scratch; hearty pozole and other soups. *$ Average main: $13* ✉ *8030 Railroad Ave.* ☎ *425/434–9587* *Closed Mon.*

Snoqualmie Taproom & Brewery

$ | **AMERICAN** | This bustling, spacious Old Town brewpub and casual restaurant is renowned for its craft beers, including a much-acclaimed Steam Train Porter, named for the town's historic rail line. Expect a range of hearty hot and cold sandwiches (the smoked turkey, provolone, jalapeño, and chipotle mayo on rosemary bread has plenty of kick), plus a variety of 12-inch pizzas and flatbreads. **Known for:** festive seasonal outdoor beer garden; house-brewed root beer; Washington apple flatbread. *$ Average main: $13* ✉ *8032 Falls Ave. SE* ☎ *425/831–2357* 🌐 *www.fallsbrew.com.*

Hotels

The Roadhouse

$ | **B&B/INN** | Fans of *Twin Peaks* will recognize the exterior of this rambling two-story tavern and inn (although interior scenes were shot elsewhere), but you needn't have watched the show to appreciate the clean, comfy, and affordable guest rooms. **Pros:** tasty comfort food served in the ground-floor pub; good base for hikes and waterfall exploring; reasonable rates. **Cons:** 10-minute drive from Old Town Snoqualmie restaurants; some rooms pick up noise from the bar or street traffic; breakfast not included. *$ Rooms from: $135* ✉ *4200 Preston-Fall City Rd. SE* ☎ *425/222–4800* 🌐 *www.fcroadhouse.com* *7 rooms* *No meals.*

Roaring River Bed & Breakfast

$ | **B&B/INN** | On 2½ acres above the Snoqualmie River, this secluded B&B a few miles east of North Bend has unbeatable mountain and wilderness views, and rooms, with wainscoting and fireplaces, have private entrances and decks. **Pros:** homemade goodies delivered to your room each morning; reasonably priced accommodations with lots of character; pretty, serene location. **Cons:** rustic country ambience isn't for everyone; not a lot of common areas; a slight drive to dining and shopping. *$ Rooms from: $139* ✉ *46715 SE 129th St., North Bend* ☎ *425/888–4834* 🌐 *www.theroaringriver.com* *5 rooms* *Free Breakfast.*

The Summit at Snoqualmie

★ Salish Lodge & Spa

$$$$ | **RESORT** | The stunning, chalet-style lodge—which you may recognize from the opening credits of *Twin Peaks*—sits dramatically over Snoqualmie Falls and offers a slew of creature comforts, including plush rooms with gas fireplaces, window seats or balconies, and a first-rate spa with sauna, steam room, and soaking tubs. **Pros:** spectacular waterfall setting; exceptional restaurants; great spa and soaking pools. **Cons:** additional resort fee (but it includes valet parking and other pluses); not within easy walking distance of town; books up way ahead on weekends. *Rooms from: $319* ✉ *6501 Railroad Ave. SE* ☎ *425/888–2556, 800/272–5474* 🌐 *www.salishlodge.com* *86 rooms* *No meals.*

Activities

HIKING

Twin Falls Trail

HIKING/WALKING | This relatively short though occasionally hilly 2½-mile round-trip trek through stands of old-growth conifers runs alongside a pristine stretch of the Snoqualmie River's south fork, a few miles southeast of North Bend. The reward is an expansive view of the waterfalls for which the trail is named. The trail also links with other good hikes in adjacent Iron Horse and Olallie state parks. Parking is $5. ✉ *SE 159th St., North Bend* ✣ *Off SE 468th Ave.*

SKIING

★ The Summit at Snoqualmie

SKIING/SNOWBOARDING | **FAMILY** | This winter sports destination, about 25 miles east of Snoqualmie, combines the Alpental, Summit West, Summit East, and Summit Central ski areas along Snoqualmie Pass. Spread over nearly 2,000 acres and with a vertical drop of nearly 2,300 feet, the facilities include 65 ski trails (86% of them intermediate and advanced), 25 chairlifts, and two terrain parks. Those seeking tamer pursuits can head to the Summit Nordic Center, with 30 miles of groomed trails and a tubing area. Shops, restaurants, lodges (none of which are slope-side), and ski schools are connected by shuttle vans; there's even child care. For a different take on the mountains, head up to the pass after dinner; this is one of the nation's largest night-skiing areas. Full-day lift tickets, good for any of the four mountains, start at $85. ✉ *1001 Hwy. 906, Snoqualmie Pass* ✥ *Exit 52 off I-90* ☎ *425/434–7669, 206/236–1600 snow conditions* 🌐 *www.summitatsnoqualmie.com.*

Port Gamble

14 miles west of Edmonds by ferry, 27 miles southeast of Port Townsend by road.

Residents from the opposite side of America founded Port Gamble around a sawmill in 1853, which is why its New England–style architecture mimicks founder Captain William Talbot's hometown of East Machias, Maine. Its setting amid the Kitsap Peninsula's tall stands of timber brought in great profits, but the mill was later destroyed by fire, and much of the forest has disappeared. A walk through town takes you past the 1870 St. Paul's Episcopal Church as well as the Thompson House, thought to be the state's oldest continuously lived-in home, and a handful of shops and restaurants. The town also stages the popular Kitsap Medieval Faire each summer.

GETTING HERE AND AROUND

Port Gamble is at the confluence of Highways 3 and 104 and easily reached from Poulsbo (10 miles south) as well as the Olympic Peninsula via Port Ludlow and the Hood Canal Floating Bridge.

Sights

★ Point No Point Lighthouse Park

LIGHTHOUSE | This small, scenic waterfront park in the village of Hansville sits at the very northeastern tip of the Kitsap Peninsula and is home to the oldest lighthouse on Puget Sound. The relatively small white building with a bright-red roof opened in 1879 and from April to September is open for tours from noon to 4 on weekends. Any day of the week, however, this is a pleasing spot for a picnic, a stroll along the beach, or simply the chance to sit and admire the views north and east of Whidbey Island and—in the distance—the Cascade Range. The adjacent lighthouse keeper's quarters can be rented overnight. ✉ *9009 NE Point No Point Rd.* ☎ *360/337–5350* 🌐 *www.kitsapgov.com.*

★ Port Gamble Historic Museum

MUSEUM | **FAMILY** | Beneath the town's quaint General Store, the Smithsonian-designed Port Gamble Historic Museum takes you through the region's timber heyday. Highlights include artifacts from the Pope and Talbot Timber Company, which built the town, and realistic ship's quarters. Above the General Store, the **Of Sea and Shore Museum** is open daily and houses more than 25,000 shells as well as displays on natural history. Kids love the weird bug exhibit. In between visits stop at the General Store for souvenirs or a huge ice-cream cone or hand-dipped milk shake, or stay for lunch or dinner in the excellent restaurant, Scratch Kitchen, in the back of the building. ✉ *32400 Rainier Ave. NE* ☎ *360/297–8078* 🌐 *www.portgamble.com/museum* 🎫 *Shell Museum free, Historic Museum $4* ⏲ *Closed Mon.–Thurs. in mid-Sept.–late May.*

Restaurants

★ Butcher & Baker Provisions

$$ | **MODERN AMERICAN** | You'll find everything from thoughtfully curated artisanal groceries and prepared foods to a selection of creative contemporary American and international fare in the cheerful dining room of this stylish market set inside a retrofitted auto repair shop. Try the chilaquiles or croque madame at breakfast, and later in the day sample the salmon gravlax bagels and whole fried rainbow trout with grilled asparagus. **Known for:** short walk from the Port Gamble Museum and General Store; hefty sandwiches with creative ingredients; great selection of gourmet picnic provisions. *Average main: $17* *4719 Hwy. 104* *360/297–9500* *www.butcherandbakerprovisions.com* *Closed Mon. and Tues.*

★ Peninsula Pies

$ | **ITALIAN** | One of only a handful of restaurants on the northern end of the Kitsap Peninsula, this dapper wood-fired-pizza parlor and wine bar is worth a trip for its blistered-crust pies topped with Sicilian olives, local Mt. Townsend cheese curds, Calabrese chilies, and other carefully—and often locally—sourced ingredients. The offerings also include farm-fresh salads and slow-cooked-pork porchetta panini. **Known for:** reasonably priced but interesting wine and beer; crispy-crust Neapolitan-style pizzas; luscious house-made tiramisu. *Average main: $12* *38955 Hansville Rd. NE* *360/860–1436* *www.peninsulapies.com* *Closed Sun.–Tues. No lunch.*

Poulsbo

10 miles south of Port Gamble, 12 miles northwest of Bainbridge Island.

Velkommen til Poulsbo (*pauls*-bo), a charming village on lovely Liberty Bay. Soon after it was settled by Norwegians in the 1880s, shops and bakeries sprang up along Front Street, as did a cod-drying facility to produce the Norwegian delicacy called lutefisk. Although it's no longer produced here commercially, lutefisk is still served at holiday feasts. Front Street is crammed with authentic Norwegian bakeries, eclectic Scandinavian crafts shops, small boutiques and bookstores, and art galleries. Norwegian flags flutter from the eaves of the town's chalet-style buildings. Grassy Liberty Bay Park is fronted by a network of slender docks where seals and otters pop in and out of the waves. One of the town's biggest events is the annual May Viking Festival (*www.vikingfest.org*), complete with Viking tents and weapons, costumed locals, and a lively parade.

GETTING HERE AND AROUND

To reach Poulsbo from Seattle, it's easiest to take the Washington State Ferries to Bainbridge Island and drive 12 miles from there via Highway 305 north across the Agate Pass Bridge. To get here from the mainland north of Seattle, you can also take the ferry from Edmonds to Kingston, where it's a 10-mile drive into Poulsbo.

ESSENTIALS

VISITOR INFORMATION Poulsbo Chamber of Commerce. *19735 10th Ave. NE, Suite S100* *360/779–4848, 877/768–5726* *www.poulsbochamber.com.*

Sights

SEA Discovery Center

MUSEUM | **FAMILY** | On the waterfront and at the edge of Liberty Bay Park, Western Washington University's small but well-designed marine center and aquarium is jam-packed with exhibits of local sea creatures. An intertidal touch tank lets kids feel sea anemones, sea urchins, and starfish, while other displays house crabs, jellyfish, and plants. Puppets, puzzles, murals, and videos help youngsters learn more about what they see. *18743*

Front St. NE ☎ 360/598–4460 🌐 wp.wwu.edu/seacenter 💳 Free ⏲ Closed Mon. and Tues.

Restaurants

Paella Bar

$$ | TAPAS | This warmly lighted, inviting downtown spot for Pacific Northwest–inspired Spanish tapas is adjacent to similarly excellent Burrata Bistro and is popular for its afternoon and late-night happy hours as well as for lunch and dinner. Paella is, of course, the big star here—it's studded with fresh local seafood, but you could also easily make a fine meal of delicious tapas, including achiote-marinated beef short ribs over golden polenta, cod fritters with chipotle aioli, and roasted brussels sprouts with pancetta and manchego cheese. **Known for:** good selection of sangria and Spanish wines; seafood and chicken paellas; potato tortillas with artichokes and aioli. *$ Average main: $19 ✉ 19006 Front St. ☎ 360/930–8446 🌐 www.burratabistro-paellabar.com.*

Hotels

Oxford Suites Silverdale

$$ | HOTEL | Overlooking Dyes Inlet, this contemporary five-story hotel in suburban Silverdale has spacious suites with nautical designs, some with balconies facing the water, and plenty of thoughtful extras, including a full breakfast. **Pros:** indoor pool, hot tub, sauna, and steam room; close to walking and biking trail; spacious gym. **Cons:** 15-minute drive to Poulsbo; surrounded by dull shopping centers; can get a little pricey in summer. *$ Rooms from: $179 ✉ 9550 Silverdale Way NW, Silverdale ☎ 360/698–9550 🌐 www.oxfordsuitessilverdale.com 104 rooms Free Breakfast.*

Suquamish Clearwater Casino Resort

$$ | RESORT | Whatever your feeling about casinos, this large contemporary resort just across the bridge to Bainbridge Island offers some of the most attractive and well-equipped rooms in the region, especially considering the reasonable rates and views from many rooms of Puget Sound's Agate Pass strait. **Pros:** plenty of on-site entertainment and dining options; most rooms have sweeping water views; 10-minute drive from downtown Poulsbo. **Cons:** not especially relaxing on busy weekends; casino can be a drawback for nongamers; breakfast not included. *$ Rooms from: $169 ✉ 15347 Suquamish Way NE ☎ 360/598–8700, 866/609–8700 🌐 www.clearwatercasino.com 186 rooms No meals.*

Shopping

★ Sluys Bakery

FOOD/CANDY | FAMILY | Rhyme it with "pies" and you'll sound like a local when you enter the town's most famous bakery, a fixture since the early 1900s. Gorgeous Norwegian pastries, braided bread, and *lefse* (traditional round flatbread) line the shelves. Kids often beg for one of the decorated cookies or frosted doughnuts displayed at eye level. There's only strong coffee and milk to drink, and there are no seats, but you can grab a bench along busy Front Street or take your goodies to the waterfront at Liberty Bay Park. *✉ 18924 Front St. ☎ 360/779–2798 🌐 www.sluyspoulsbobakery.com.*

Gig Harbor

22 miles south of Bremerton, 10 miles northwest of Tacoma.

One of the prettiest and most accessible waterfront communities on Puget Sound, Gig Harbor has a neat, circular bay dotted with sailboats and fronted by hills of evergreens and million-dollar homes. Expect spectacular views all along the town's winding, 2-mile, bay-side walkway, which is intermittently lined by boat docks, quirky shops, stylish eateries, and broad expanses of open water. The bay was a storm refuge for the 1841 survey team of Captain Charles Wilkes, who named the area after his small gig (boat). A decade later Croatian and Scandinavian immigrants put their fishing, lumber, and boatbuilding skills to profitable use, and the town still has strong seafaring traditions. By the 1880s, steamboats carried passengers and goods between the harbor and Tacoma, and auto ferries plied the narrows between the cities by 1917.

Surrounding Gig Harbor, pine forests and open woods alternate with rolling pastures; it's enjoyable scenery (even on rainy days) during the 10-minute drive to Fox Island. Crossing the Fox Island Bridge over Echo Bay, you'll see stunning views of the Olympic Mountains to the right and the Tanglewood Lighthouse against a backdrop of Mt. Rainier to the left. Tanglewood Island, the small drop of forest on which the Tanglewood Lighthouse sits, was once a Native American burial ground known as Grav Island. At low tide the boat ramp and boulder-strewn beach next to the bridge are scattered with stranded saltwater creatures.

GETTING HERE AND AROUND

From Seattle, the fastest way (if there's no traffic) to Gig Harbor is to take Interstate 5 south through Tacoma, and then take Highway 16 north via the Tacoma Narrows Bridge. A slightly longer approach—in minutes, not miles—is to take the ferry from the West Seattle terminal to the Southworth landing on the Kitsap Peninsula and take Highway 160 west to Highway 16 south. The ferry from Seattle to Bremerton also works—take Highway 3 south to Highway 16.

ESSENTIALS

VISITOR INFORMATION Gig Harbor Chamber of Commerce. ✉ *3125 Judson St.* ☎ *253/851–6865* 🌐 *www.gigharborchamber.net.*

Sights

Harbor History Museum

MUSEUM | An excellent collection of exhibits describes the city's maritime history, and there are photo archives, video programs, and a research library focusing on the area's pioneer and Native American ancestors. The facilities include a one-room, early-20th-century schoolhouse and a 65-foot, 1950s purse seiner, a type of fishing vessel from the community's famous seafaring fleets. News clippings and videos about "Galloping Gertie," the bridge over the Tacoma Narrows that famously collapsed in 1940, are particularly eerie. ✉ *4121 Harborview Dr.* ☎ *253/858–6722* 🌐 *www.harborhistorymuseum.org* ⏲ *Closed Sun. and Mon.*

Heritage Distilling Company

WINERY/DISTILLERY | Among the most acclaimed craft spirits producers in the country, Heritage Distilling is based in Gig Harbor, where it operates a pair of production facilities, both with tasting rooms, tours, and shops. Here at the downtown location, you can try a flight of samples—BSB Brown Sugar Bourbon, Elk Rider Gin, and Lavender Vodka are all popular—while taking in the views of Gig Harbor. The company's other location is a couple of miles south in a shopping center off Highway 16. ✉ *3118 Harborview Dr.* ☎ *253/514–8120* 🌐 *www.heritagedistilling.com.*

Kopachuck State Park

NATIONAL/STATE PARK | A 10-minute drive from Gig Harbor, this is a wonderful beachcombing area at low tide. Native American tribes once fished and clammed here, and you can still see people trolling the shallow waters or digging deep for razor clams in season. Children and dogs alike delight in discovering huge Dungeness crabs, sea stars, and sand dollars. Picnic tables and walking trails are interspersed throughout the 109 acres of steep, forested hills, and the campground is popular all summer.

⊠ 11101 56th St. NW ☎ 253/265–3606 ⊕ www.parks.wa.gov 🎫 $10 parking.

Skansie Brothers Park and Netshed

BUILDING | During the town's early years, Gig Harbor's waterfront was lined with wooden structures set on pilings over the water and used by fishermen to store gear and tackle. Today just 17 of these structures remain, with the town's still active commercial fishing fleet still using some of them. This 3-acre park preserves the historic home and netshed once owned by the Skansie Brothers, lifelong fishermen and boat builders. Festivals and a farmers market are held on the grassy lawn, which includes a pavilion, picnic tables, and a platform overlooking the harbor. ⊠ *3211 Harborview Dr.* ☎ *253/851–6170* ⊕ *www.skansiebrothersnetshed.com.*

Restaurants

Animarum

$$$$ | **PACIFIC NORTHWEST** | Exquisite farm-to-table Pacific Northwest fare stars at this dimly lighted bistro at the foot of the harbor, next to the Harbor History Museum. Dishes like roasted turkey leg with chopped pesto, walnut-crusted black cod with fennel and pea puree, and lamb rillettes with minted apple jelly reveal the deft touch and creative inspiration in the kitchen. **Known for:** summer dining on the charming side patio; romantic, intimate dining room; alluring selection of desserts. 💲 *Average main: $32* ⊠ *4107 Harborview Dr.* ☎ *253/720–6005* ⊕ *www.animarum253.com* ⏲ *Closed Sun.–Tues. No lunch.*

★ Brix 25°

$$$ | **MODERN AMERICAN** | Simple dishes and classic European fare are beautifully presented in this light-filled dining room with expansive outdoor terraces overlooking Gig Harbor. Dinners are elaborate affairs that feature seafood—perhaps Thai curry and coconut-steamed mussels—and rich classics such as grilled filet mignon with crab-compound butter. **Known for:** terrific daily happy hour in the bar; try booking one of the chef's dinners; sweeping harbor views. 💲 *Average main: $28* ⊠ *3315 Harborview Dr.* ☎ *253/858–6626* ⊕ *www.harborbrix.com* ⏲ *Closed Tues. No lunch.*

Gertie and The Giant Octopus

$$ | **MODERN EUROPEAN** | Try not to be put off by the setting of this quirky bistro and wine bar set in a modern shopping center off Highway 16. Named for the famed Tacoma Narrows Bridge, better known as Galloping Gertie, this festive spot has shimmering chandeliers, eclectic glass art, and an open loft that create an inviting environment for enjoying modern American and European fare, from lamb ragu with pappardelle pasta to olive oil–roasted Spanish octopus with chorizo. **Known for:** reasonably priced bistro fare; excellent wine list; afternoon happy hour. 💲 *Average main: $18* ⊠ *4747 Point Fosdick Dr.* ☎ *253/649–0921* ⊕ *facebook.com/Gertieandthegiantoctopus* ⏲ *Closed Sun. and Mon. No lunch.*

NetShed No. 9

$ | **MODERN AMERICAN** | In a converted historic netshed perched dramatically over the water in Gig Harbor, this is a lively and picturesque spot for breakfast or lunch—especially on warm days when you can soak up the soft breezes from a seat on the deck. Standout dishes include the fluffy biscuit stuffed with Portuguese sausage and Beecher's cheddar and topped with red gravy, and lemon curd and blueberry French toast. **Known for:** good variety of beers and brunch cocktails; creative sweet and savory breakfast fare; overstuffed sandwiches. 💲 *Average main: $13* ⊠ *3313 Harborview Dr.* ☎ *253/858–7175* ⊕ *www.netshed9.com* ⏲ *Closed Tues. and Wed. No dinner.*

Hotels

Inn at Gig Harbor

$$ | **HOTEL** | While it may look like a cookie-cutter chain hotel, many of the rooms at this midrange property set among tall trees have Mt. Rainier views, and suites have fireplaces or jetted tubs. **Pros:** short walk to Heritage Distilling and several restaurants; small spa offering a range of treatments; good fitness center. **Cons:** some rooms face a busy highway; not near the water; no pool. *Rooms from: $174* ✉ *3211 56th St. NW* ☎ *253/858–1111, 800/795–9980* 🌐 *www.innatgigharbor.com* *64 rooms* *Free Breakfast.*

Maritime Inn

$$ | **HOTEL** | On a hill across from Jersich Park, this lodging's individually decorated and themed rooms have unfussy, contemporary furnishings and gas fireplaces, and nearly every one overlooks the water; several have decks. **Pros:** short walk to several excellent restaurants; friendly staff and highly personal service; right on the waterfront. **Cons:** front rooms absorb traffic noise; some rooms are a little small; no restaurant. *Rooms from: $189* ✉ *3112 Harborview Dr.* ☎ *253/858–1818, 888/506–3580* 🌐 *www.maritimeinn.com* *15 rooms* *Free Breakfast.*

Waterfront Inn

$$ | **B&B/INN** | If you love being right on the water, this cozy inn set in a cute 1910s house has plenty going for it, including a spacious deck, a 150-foot dock, a couple kayaks you can use, and dramatic views from each of the five smartly appointed, contemporary rooms. **Pros:** gas fireplaces and jetted soaking tubs in every room; short walk to museums and restaurants; stunning harbor views. **Cons:** tight parking lot down a steep driveway; pricey on summer weekends; no breakfast. *Rooms from: $189* ✉ *9017 N. Harborview Dr.* ☎ *253/857–0770* 🌐 *www.waterfront-inn.com* *5 rooms* *No meals.*

Nightlife

7 Seas Brewing

BREWPUBS/BEER GARDENS | This esteemed craft brewery and taproom a few blocks from the waterfront specializes in complex, boldly flavored brews, like the crisp Axis Brut IPA and slightly tart, tangerine-infused Life Jacket Citrus IPA. There's a second location in downtown. ✉ *3006 Judson St.* ☎ *253/514–8129* 🌐 *www.7seasbrewing.com.*

Tides Tavern

BARS/PUBS | The legendary Tide's Tavern, right on the water in a weather-worn 1910 building that housed the town's original general store, has been a local hot spot for drinks, darts, and live music since the 1930s. ✉ *2925 Harborview Dr.* ☎ *253/858–3982* 🌐 *www.tidestavern.com.*

Tacoma

12 miles southeast of Gig Harbor, 34 miles southwest of Seattle.

After decades of decline, Tacoma (population 216,000) has been undergoing a renaissance in recent years, with development around the waterfront and in other parts of downtown showing dramatic progress—a number of urbane galleries, craft cocktail bars, and sophisticated restaurants have popped up around Union Station. North End neighborhoods like the Stadium District, with its grand Victorian homes (a handful of which are B&Bs), the Proctor District, and 6th Avenue abound with charming places to shop and eat.

Tacoma's got plenty of character, and there's easily enough to see and do to fill a weekend or even several days. The museums (which are vastly underrated), waterfront promenade, and lush and expansive Point Defiance Park make for an engaging adventure. The city's tourism office, Travel Tacoma–Mt. Rainier,

Gig Harbor

sells three- and seven-day attraction passes accessible via an app that save you about 50% admission to the city's top attractions. It's the most economical and convenient way to take everything in during one visit.

GETTING HERE AND AROUND

Tacoma is close enough to Seattle that many people commute in both directions. It's a straight 30-mile shot along Interstate 5 to Exit 133 toward the city center, but bear in mind that the miserable rush-hour traffic between the two cities can double your travel time. The city is also served by Greyhound and Amtrak, with connections north to Seattle and beyond, as well as south to Olympia. Tacoma is also served by Sound Transit's commuter rail, though trains are limited to rush hours.

If you're not planning to travel too far outside the downtown core—just seeing the museums and the waterfront—you don't absolutely need a car to get around, as Amtrak and Greyhound let you off within a few blocks of each other in the Dome district (by the Tacoma Dome, on Puyallup Avenue). From here, you can catch Sound Transit's free Link light-rail or use ride-share services like Uber and Lyft to get around the city.

ESSENTIALS

VISITOR INFORMATION Travel Tacoma–Mt. Rainier. ✉ *1516 Commerce St.* ☎ *253/284–3254, 800/272–2662* 🌐 *www.traveltacoma.com.*

Sights

Fort Nisqually

MILITARY SITE | This restored Hudson's Bay Trading Post—a British outpost on the Nisqually Delta in the 1830s—was moved to Point Defiance in 1935. The compound houses a trading post, granary, blacksmith's shop, bakery, and officers' quarters. Docents dress in 1850s attire and demonstrate pioneer skills like weaving and loading a rifle. Queen Victoria's birthday in May is a big event, and eerie candlelight tours are offered several days in October. ✉ *5400*

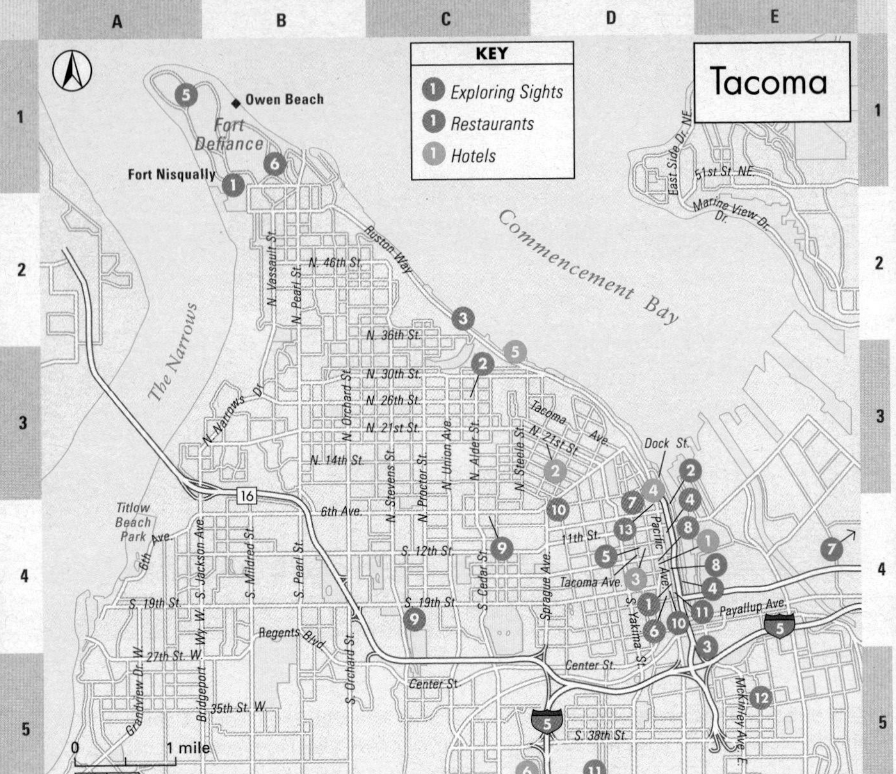

Sights

1 Fort Nisqually **B1**
2 Foss Waterway Seaport **D4**
3 LeMay—America's Car Museum **D4**
4 Museum of Glass **D4**
5 Point Defiance Park **A1**
6 Point Defiance Zoo & Aquarium............. **B1**
7 Rhododendron Species Botanical Garden........ **E4**
8 Tacoma Art Museum... **D4**
9 Tacoma Nature Center at Snake Lake **C4**
10 Union Station............ **D4**
11 Washington State History Museum **D4**

Restaurants

1 Anthem Coffee & Tea............ **D4**
2 Cooks Tavern............ **C3**
3 Duke's Chowder House.......... **C2**
4 En Rama **D4**
5 Honey Coffee + Kitchen................. **D4**
6 Indochine **D4**
7 Over The Moon Cafe ... **D4**
8 Pacific Grill.............. **D4**
9 Red Hot **C4**
10 Southern Kitchen **D4**
11 TibbittsFernHill **D5**
12 Top of Tacoma **E5**
13 Wooden City............ **D3**

Hotels

1 Courtyard Marriott Tacoma Downtown..... **D4**
2 Geiger Victorian Bed and Breakfast...... **D3**
3 Hotel Murano **D4**
4 McMenamins Elks Temple.............. **D4**
5 Silver Cloud Inn **C3**
6 Thornewood Castle **C5**

Chihuly Bridge of Glass, Tacoma

N. Pearl St. ☎ 253/404–3970 🌐 www.fortnisqually.org 🎫 $9 ⏲ Closed Mon. and Tues. in Oct.–Apr.

★ Foss Waterway Seaport

MUSEUM | With its beautiful setting right along the Thea Foss waterfront, this turn-of-the-20th-century structure—with a dramatic modern glass facade—is easily reached via a walk along the bay. Inside the enormous timber building, a museum devoted to the city's waterfront heritage contains displays about the history of Tacoma's brisk shipping business, the city's role as a major ship-to-rail center, and the indigenous Puyallup people's close relationship with local waterways. Extensive exhibits cover boat making, vintage scuba and diving gear, and fin and humpback whales. Photos and relics round out the exhibits, and children's activities are staged regularly. ✉ *705 Dock St. ☎ 253/272–2750 🌐 www.fosswaterwayseaport.org 🎫 $10 ⏲ Closed Mon. and Tues.*

★ LeMay—America's Car Museum

MUSEUM | **FAMILY** | About 350 meticulously restored automobiles, from some of the world's earliest models to brassy muscle cars from the late '60s, are displayed in this sleek, striking museum on the south side of downtown. It's one of the most impressive car museums in the country, with engaging exhibits on Route 66, alternative-fuel cars, NASCAR, and other aspects of automobile culture and history. The cars here were collected by the late Harold LeMay, whose entire inventory of some 4,000 autos is recognized by the *Guinness Book of World Records* as the largest privately owned collection in the world. Highlights include a 1906 Cadillac Model M, a 1926 Rolls-Royce Silver Ghost, a 1930 Lincoln L Brougham, a 1953 Citroen 2CV, a 1960 Corvette, and a 1963 Studebaker Avanti. The café serves diner classics, including very tasty banana splits. If you're an ardent car enthusiast, it's worth making the 15-minute drive south to the related LeMay Family Collection Foundation at the Marymount Event Center in the

Spanaway neighborhood of south Tacoma. ✉ *2702 E. D St.* ☎ *253/779–8490, 877/902–8490* 🌐 *www.lemaymuseum.org* 🎫 *$18.*

★ Museum of Glass

MUSEUM | The showpiece of this spectacular, 2-acre complex of delicate and creative art-glass installations is the 500-foot-long Chihuly Bridge of Glass, a tunnel of glorious color and light that stretches above Interstate 705. Cross it from downtown to reach the museum's grounds, which sit above the Foss Waterway and next to a shallow reflecting pool dotted with large modern-art sculptures. Inside, you can wander through the quiet, light-filled galleries that present a fascinating and compelling array of rotating exhibits, take a seat in the conical-roofed Hot Shop to watch glass-blowing artists, or try your own hand at arts and crafts in the studio. You'll also find an outstanding museum gift shop and café. ✉ *1801 E. Dock St.* ☎ *253/284–4750* 🌐 *www.museumofglass.org* 🎫 *$17* ⏲ *Closed Mon.*

★ Point Defiance Park

NATIONAL/STATE PARK | **FAMILY** | Jutting into Commencement Bay, this 760-acre park surrounds Five Mile Drive with hilly picnicking fields and patches of forest. Hiking trails, bike paths, and numerous gardens draw crowds year-round, particularly during summer festivals such as the Taste of Tacoma, in late June. The park begins at the north end of Pearl Street as you drive toward the Point Defiance Ferry Terminal, where vehicles depart for Vashon Island just across the Sound. A one-way road branches off the ferry lane, past a lake and picnic area, a rose garden, a spectacular 22-acre rhododendron garden, and a Japanese garden, finally winding down to the beach.

A half-mile past the gardens is **Owen Beach,** a driftwood-strewn stretch of pebbly sand near the ferry dock and a wonderful place for beachcombing and sailboat-watching. Kayak rentals and concessions are available in summer. Continue around the looping drive, which offers occasional views of the narrows. Cruise slowly to take in the scenes—and watch out for joggers and bikers. ✉ *5400 N. Pearl St.* 🌐 *www.metroparkstacoma.org/point-defiance-park.*

★ Point Defiance Zoo & Aquarium

ZOO | **FAMILY** | One of the Northwest's finest collections of regional and international animal species, this winding and hilly site includes tigers, elephants, tapirs, and gibbons in the Asian Forest Sanctuary, where paw-print trails lead between lookouts so even the smallest tots can spot animals. The impressive South Pacific and Pacific Seas aquariums are also fun to explore—they include a glass-walled, floor-to-ceiling shark tank (where eye-to-eye caged shark dives are offered). Other areas house such cold-weather creatures as beluga whales, Arctic foxes, polar bears, and penguins. Engaging zookeeper chats about different animals and up-close feedings are held throughout the day. The fantastic playground area has friendly farm animals running between the slides, and seasonal special events include a Halloween Zoo Boo trick-or-treat night and the famous nightly Zoolights holiday displays around Christmas. ✉ *Point Defiance Park, 5400 N. Pearl St.* ☎ *253/404–3800* 🌐 *www.pdza.org* 🎫 *$22* ⏲ *Closed Tues. and Wed. in Nov.–mid-Dec. and early Jan.–Feb.*

Rhododendron Species Botanical Garden

GARDEN | On Point Defiance Park's Five Mile Drive, this is a 22-acre expanse of more than 10,000 plants—some 700 species, including azaleas, blue poppies, and magnolias—that bloom in succession. It's one of the finest rhododendron collections in the world. ✉ *2525 S. 336th St., Federal Way* ☎ *253/838–4646* 🌐 *www.rhodygarden.org* 🎫 *$8* ⏲ *Closed Mon.*

★ Tacoma Art Museum

MUSEUM | Adorned in glass and steel, this Antoine Predock masterpiece wraps around a beautiful garden. Inside, you'll find paintings, ceramics, sculptures, and other creations dating from the 18th century to the present, with an emphasis on Western U.S. artists, including many indigenous talents. On view is the largest permanent collection of glass works by Dale Chihuly, and the stunning, light-filled Benaroya Wing—designed by Olson Kundig and opened in 2019—displays hundreds of new works, included pieces by artists trained at the prestigious Pilchuck Glass School. ✉ *1701 Pacific Ave.* ☎ *253/272–4258* 🌐 *www.tacomaart-museum.org* 🎫 *$18* 🕒 *Closed Mon.*

Tacoma Nature Center at Snake Lake
NATURE PRESERVE | **FAMILY** | Comprising 71 acres of marshland, evergreen forest, and a shallow lake that break up the urban sprawl of west Tacoma, the center shelters 20 species of mammals and more than 100 species of birds. The lake has nesting pairs of wood ducks, rare elsewhere in western Washington, and the interpretive center is a fun place for kids to look at small creatures, take walks and nature quizzes, and dress up in animal costumes. ✉ *1919 S. Tyler St.* ☎ *253/404–3930* 🌐 *www.metroparksta-coma.org/tacomanaturecenter* 🕒 *Center closed Sun.*

Union Station
TRANSPORTATION SITE (AIRPORT/BUS/FERRY/TRAIN) | This imposing structure dates from 1911, when Tacoma was the western terminus of the Northern Pacific Railroad. Built by Reed and Stem, architects of New York City's Grand Central Terminal, the copper-domed, beaux arts–style depot shows the influence of the Roman Pantheon and Italian baroque style. The station houses federal district courts, but its rotunda contains a gorgeous exhibit of glass sculptures by Dale Chihuly. Because it's a government facility, be prepared to walk through a metal detector and show photo ID. ✉ *1717 Pacific Ave.* ☎ *253/863–5173* 🌐 *www.unionstationro-tunda.org* 🎫 *Free* 🕒 *Closed weekends.*

★ **Washington State History Museum**
MUSEUM | Adjacent to Union Station, and with the same opulent architecture, Washington's official history museum presents interactive exhibits and multi-media installations about the exploration and settlement of the state. Exhibits are wide-ranging and artfully designed, and feature Native American, Inuit, and pioneer artifacts, and mining, logging, and railroad relics. The upstairs gallery hosts rotating exhibits, and summer programs are staged in the outdoor amphitheater. ✉ *1911 Pacific Ave.* ☎ *253/272–3500, 888/238–4373* 🌐 *www.washingtonhisto-ry.org* 🎫 *$14* 🕒 *Closed Mon.*

Restaurants

Anthem Coffee & Tea
$ | **CAFÉ** | The spacious, high-ceilinged downtown branch of this local chain is steps from the Museum of Glass and other attractions and is a great place to kick off the day with a well-crafted espresso drink and breakfast sandwich, or linger later in the day over a naan flatbread pizza. **Known for:** on warm days you can relax at an outdoor table; tall windows let in plenty of sunlight; craft beers and local wines. 💲 *Average main: $7* ✉ *1911 Pacific Ave.* ☎ *253/572–9705* 🌐 *myanthemcoffee.com* 🕒 *No dinner.*

Cooks Tavern
$$ | **INTERNATIONAL** | This warmly lighted tavern in the historic North End operates under a clever and ambitious premise: every four months the kitchen unveils a new menu dedicated to the cuisine of a different region of the Americas, from New Orleans to Montreal to Argentina. To keep fans with less adventurous tastes happy, the restaurant keeps a number of noteworthy dishes on every menu. **Known for:** owners run a craft-beer-focused establishment next door; burger topped with sharp cheddar, bacon, and fried egg; friendly staff. 💲 *Average main: $19* ✉ *3201 N. 26th St.* ☎ *253/327–1777* 🌐 *www.cookstavern.com.*

Duke's Chowder House

$$$ | **SEAFOOD** | One of several popular seafood restaurants along Ruston Way, Duke's is part of a regional chainlet that can be counted on for serving some of the freshest and most creative fare of the bunch—it's not just about the view here, although the tables on the patio do offer dazzling panoramas of Commencement Bay. Chowder fans having a tough time deciding what to try might want to order the "full fleet" sampler, with small servings of clam, lobster, crab bisque, chicken-corn, and Northwest seafood varieties. **Known for:** outdoor dining on Commencement Bay; food and drinks deals at happy hour; great for seafood lovers. *Average main: $25 3327 Ruston Way 253/752–5444 www.dukeschowderhouse.com.*

En Rama

$$ | **ITALIAN** | The rarefied setting—soaring ceilings, palladian windows, polished-wood tables—inside downtown's neoclassical 1910 post office building is one good reason to book a table here. But don't overlook the well-prepared classic Italian fare, which ranges from simple but hearty meatballs in red sauce and garganelli pasta with venison bolognese to the somewhat more delicately flavored roasted-chestnut soup and lasagna with parsnip cream. **Known for:** seats on the sidewalk terrace are in high demand; rich and robustly flavored pasta dishes; impressive selection of fine sherries. *Average main: $21 1102 A St. 253/223–7184 www.enramatacoma.com Closed Sun. and Mon.*

Honey Coffee + Kitchen

$ | **CAFÉ** | Step inside this chatter-filled café with comfy seating and views of pretty gardens to discover some of the best espresso drinks in town, including the signature honeybutt latte (with brown butter and honey). It's a great bet for breakfast, lunch, or even nighttime noshing, too, serving up boldly flavored shakshuka, sweet potato hash, and garlic-chicken melt sandwiches. **Known for:** pleasing teas, juices, and other coffee alternatives; inviting art-filled confines; leisurely breakfasts. *Average main: $11 1322 Fawcett Ave. 253/507–7289 www.almamatertacoma.com No dinner Sun. and Mon.*

Indochine

$$ | **ASIAN** | This sleekly modern, dimly lighted space with a gurgling stone and glass fountain in the center serves generous portions of pan-Asian fare. The well-prepared array of Thai, Chinese, Indian, and Japanese cuisines includes curries, stir-fries, soups, and seafood, from honey-glazed walnut prawns to Filipino pork adobo. **Known for:** convenient to downtown destinations; elegant, artfully designed dining room; flavorful Southeast Asian dishes. *Average main: $19 1924 Pacific Ave. 253/272–8200 www.indochinedowntown.com Closed Mon.*

Over The Moon Cafe

$$$ | **PACIFIC NORTHWEST** | Tucked down an alley near Wright Park, this quirky and cozy neighborhood bistro serves first-rate Northwest-influenced Italian fare, including bounteous salads and creative grills. It's worth seeking out this art-filled space with exposed-brick walls for such delectable fare as slow-cooked short-rib ragù over rigatoni and pan-seared, bourbon-glazed salmon fillet. **Known for:** desserts, including banana pie, are a major draw; decadent lobster mac and cheese; close to the theater district. *Average main: $28 709 Opera Alley 253/284–3722 www.overthemooncafe.net Closed Sun. and Mon.*

Pacific Grill

$$$$ | **MODERN AMERICAN** | With its clubby interior, huge wine list, and proximity to downtown attractions, it's easy to see how this flashy restaurant is a favorite for special occasions and high-end business meals. Here you can expect a menu of contemporary variations on seafood and steak, including Columbia

River steelhead with a maple-balsamic glaze and New York strip with red-flannel hash and a red-wine sauce; vegetarians shouldn't pass up the unusual roasted cauliflower "steak" served with olive gremolata, tomatoes, orange, and capers. **Known for:** terrific happy-hour deals on weekday afternoons; bottomless drinks during weekend brunch; raw bar appetizers. $ *Average main: $32* ✉ *1502 Pacific Ave.* ☎ *253/627–3535* 🌐 *www.pacificgrill-tacoma.com.*

★ Red Hot

$ | HOT DOG | The first thing you notice inside this bustling tavern and hot-dog joint are the dozens of beer taps hanging from the ceiling, each one representing a particular ale that's been poured here. Indeed, this quirky spot is a must for beer lovers, with plenty of interesting varieties on tap and available by the bottle, from Northwest craft brews to Belgian Trappist tripels. **Known for:** the place for German-style bratwurst; lots of great beers on tap; late-night dining. $ *Average main: $6* ✉ *2914 6th Ave.* ☎ *253/779–0229* 🌐 *www.redhottacoma.com.*

★ Southern Kitchen

$$ | SOUTHERN | Sure, it's awfully far north to be specializing in down-home Southern cooking, but this bustling, casual spot on Tacoma's north side, a little west of Wright Park, serves remarkably authentic and absolutely delicious soul food. In the morning, regulars swing by for heaping plates of chicken-fried steak with grits and eggs, or homemade biscuits and gravy. **Known for:** save room for the sweet-potato pie; hand-battered fried catfish; jalapeño hush puppies. $ *Average main: $16* ✉ *1716 6th Ave.* ☎ *253/627–4282* 🌐 *www.southernkitchen-tacoma.com.*

TibbittsFernHill

$$ | AMERICAN | On just about any morning it can be tough to score a table at this compact and quirky South Tacoma brunch destination featuring the wonderfully weird cuisine of chef-owner Shawn Tibbitts, hence the reservations-only policy on weekends (book well ahead). The payoff is the chance to stuff yourself with prodigious plates of candied-bacon-wrapped breakfast burritos and salted-caramel banana pancakes. **Known for:** heaping plates of wildly inventive breakfast fare; lively dining room filled with regulars; charismatic chef-owner. $ *Average main: $17* ✉ *8237 S. Park Ave.* ☎ *253/327–1334* 🌐 *www.tibbittsfernhill.com* ⏲ *Closed Mon. and Tues. No dinner.*

Top of Tacoma

$ | AMERICAN | This hillside neighborhood tavern just south of downtown makes a convivial option for lunch (or weekend brunch), dinner, or cocktails, as the drinks selection is extensive and the affordable food—from tacos to tofu—is a cut or two above your typical pub grub. Favorites include crispy pork-belly tacos with apple-cabbage slaw and tart cherries, Moroccan-style quinoa salad with harrisa-agave vinaigrette and seared tofu, and a commendable Reuben on rye bread. **Known for:** grab a seat on the sidewalk on warm days; jukebox with plenty of old-school tunes; some of the best sandwiches in town. $ *Average main: $12* ✉ *3529 McKinley Ave.* ☎ *253/272–1502.*

★ Wooden City

$$ | MODERN AMERICAN | Located on the edge of downtown's lively theater district, this swanky eatery with brick walls, high-top tables, and a bar lighted by dangling Edison bulbs is the perfect go-to spot for date night. The consistently outstanding food ranges from small, shareable plates of creamy burrata and garlic toast with pimento cheese to thin-crust pizzas topped with sausage and cremini mushrooms. **Known for:** festive and well-priced happy hour; imaginative cocktails; stylish yet casual vibe. $ *Average main: $21* ✉ *714 Pacific Ave.* ☎ *253/503–0762* 🌐 *www.woodencitytacoma.com* ⏲ *No lunch.*

Hotels

Courtyard Marriott Tacoma Downtown
$$$ | **HOTEL** | In the late-19th-century Waddell Building, this reliable chain hotel has spacious, modern rooms outfitted in bright Northwest colors with lots of 21st-century touches. **Pros:** near the Tacoma Convention & Trade Center; steps from many of the best museums; fitness center and indoor pool. **Cons:** rooms get some street noise; rates are little pricey; parking fee. *Rooms from: $224 1515 Commerce St. 253/591–9100 www.marriott.com 162 rooms No meals.*

Geiger Victorian Bed and Breakfast
$ | **B&B/INN** | With a quiet location in Tacoma's residential North Slope Historic District, this Stick Victorian mansion with four lavishly decorated rooms is an excellent choice if you want to be away from the urban bustle and close to some of the city's hippest shopping and dining districts. **Pros:** close to leafy Point Defiance Park; includes an excellent full breakfast; beautifully appointed rooms. **Cons:** not within walking distance of downtown; some rooms require climbing lots of stairs; not appropriate for very young children. *Rooms from: $139 912 N. I St. 253/383–3504 www.geigervictorian.com 4 rooms Free Breakfast.*

★ **Hotel Murano**
$$ | **HOTEL** | Named for the Venetian island where some of the world's best glass is created, this handsome high-rise hotel with an intimate ambience centers around exhibits by world-famous glass artists. **Pros:** range of treatments offered in the day spa; well-equipped fitness center; easy walk to many museums. **Cons:** sometimes fills up with conventions and meetings; parking fee; an uphill walk from downtown attractions. *Rooms from: $165 1320 Broadway Plaza 253/238–8000, 888/862–3255 www.hotelmuranotacoma.com 329 rooms No meals.*

McMenamins Elks Temple
$$ | **HOTEL** | The famously quirky McMenamins company opened this offbeat boutique hotel inside a dramatically refurbished 1916 Renaissance Revival landmark set high on hill on the north side of downtown and adjacent to Tacoma's famous Spanish Steps. **Pros:** beautiful renovation of a fascinating older building; some rooms have Puget Sound views; full of colorful common areas. **Cons:** noise from the music venue can be a problem; a bit of a walk from downtown attractions; no on-site parking. *Rooms from: $165 565 Broadway 425/219–4370 www.mcmenamins.com 44 rooms No meals.*

★ **Silver Cloud Inn**
$$$ | **HOTEL** | Tacoma's lone waterfront hotel juts out into the bay along picturesque Ruston Way and the historic Old Town. **Pros:** free wine-and-cheese receptions on Tuesday; Ruston Way walking paths and eateries nearby; tasty breakfast is included. **Cons:** area around hotel gets crowded on weekends; rates can get steep in the summer; not within walking distance of downtown. *Rooms from: $229 2317 N. Ruston Way 253/272–1300, 866/820–8448 www.silvercloud.com 90 rooms Free Breakfast.*

Thornewood Castle
$$$$ | **B&B/INN** | Spread over 3 lushly landscaped acres along beautiful American Lake, this 27,000-square-foot, Gothic-Tudor-style mansion built in 1908 has hosted two American presidents (William Howard Taft and Theodore Roosevelt) and surrounds current guests with medieval-style stained-glass windows, gleaming wood floors, large mirrors, antiques, fireplaces, and hot tubs. **Pros:** castlelike ambience; utterly romantic vibe; dramatic lakefront setting. **Cons:** one of the more expensive properties in the area; 15-minute drive from downtown Tacoma; weddings on most summer weekends. *Rooms from: $265 8601 N. Thorne*

La. SW, Lakewood ☎ *253/584–4393* 🌐 *www.thornewoodcastle.com* 🛏 *12 rooms* 🍽 *Free Breakfast.*

Nightlife

★ Bob's Java Jive

BARS/PUBS | Known for its setting inside a fabulous 1920s roadside building shaped like a coffee pot, Bob's is one of the city's most enduring landmarks—and it's a pretty fun dive bar for karaoke and cheap drinks. Fun facts: Indie singer Neko Case used to be a bartender here, and parts of the screwball comedy film *I Love You To Death* were filmed inside. ✉ *2102 S. Tacoma Way* ☎ *253/475–9843.*

★ Matriarch

BARS/PUBS | This sexy, contemporary cocktail bar in the Alma Mater arts venue is a snazzy spot for mingling and people-watching, whether at the buzzy bar or in a plush upholstered armchair. In addition to great mixology-minded drinks, there's a tempting array of food options, from sourdough toast with bone marrow to roasted maitake mushrooms with braised lentils and kale chips. ✉ *1322 Fawcett Ave.* ☎ *253/507–7289* 🌐 *www.almamatertacoma.com.*

The Mix

DANCE CLUBS | Tacoma has a sizable gay community, and this friendly, welcoming bar with a nice-size dance floor and fun karaoke parties is the top nightspot among LGBTQ folks. It's in the heart of the Theater District. ✉ *635 St. Helens Ave.* ☎ *253/383–4327* 🌐 *www.themixtacoma.com.*

Swiss Pub

BARS/PUBS | This lively downtown pub inside a historic building has a great selection of craft beers on tap, pool tables, and live music many evenings—there's also a Dale Chihuly glass installation above the bar. ✉ *1904 S. Jefferson Ave.* ☎ *253/572–2821* 🌐 *www.theswisspub.com.*

1022 South J

BARS/PUBS | You can't claim to have a sophisticated nightlife scene until someone in a vest is mixing artisanal cocktails, and 1022 South is one of Tacoma's top spots for fine drinks made with unusual infusions (nettles, yerba maté), house-made liqueurs, and premium liquors with hipster cachet (Crater Lake Pepper Vodka, for example). Daily happy hour is 4 to 7 pm (and all day Sunday), and the kitchen produces nosh-worthy nibbles, from cheese plates to burgers to smoked pork shoulder and cheddar grits. ✉ *1022 S. J St.* ☎ *253/627–8588.*

Performing Arts

★ Broadway Center for the Performing Arts

ARTS CENTERS | Cultural activity in Tacoma centers on the outstanding—and historic—Broadway Center for the Performing Arts, which comprises four distinct venues, including the gorgeous 1918 Pantages Theater, the beaux-arts Rialto, and the more contemporary Theatre on the Square. One of the largest performing arts center in the Pacific Northwest, the venue hosts pop concerts, touring Broadway shows, Symphony Tacoma performances, and more. ✉ *901 Broadway* ☎ *253/591–5894, 800/291–7593* 🌐 *www.broadwaycenter.org.*

Shopping

Tacoma's top shopping districts are Antique Row, along Broadway at St. Helen's Street, where upscale shops sell everything from collectibles to vintage paraphernalia, and the Proctor District, in the north end, where many specialty shops do business.

Ruston Mercantile

HOUSEHOLD ITEMS/FURNITURE | This hip and contemporary home-goods store on lively 6th Avenue carries a nicely curated mix of candles, vases, and shabby-chic furniture. ✉ *2503 6th Ave.* ☎ *253/534–8808.*

★ **Tacoma Night Market**

OUTDOOR/FLEA/GREEN MARKETS | Tacoma's increasingly vibrant maker culture is showcased at its highly popular night markets. Originally held monthly, the markets now take place more frequently and at several cool venues, including the Alma Mater arts and event space, the Museum of Glass, and—nearby in Gig Harbor—7 Seas Brewing. As many as 80 artists and makers sell their wares at these gatherings that run from 5 until 10 pm and feature music and a slew of food and drinks vendors. ✉ *Tacoma* ☎ *253/234–4198* 🌐 *www.tacomanight-market.com.*

Activities

★ **Chambers Bay Golf Course**

GOLF | This beautiful course modeled after the sweeping links-style courses of the United Kingdom revitalized a former sand and gravel quarry and has become one of the most celebrated public golf facilities in the country, hosting the U.S. Open in 2015. The par-72, 18-hole layout offers dramatic views of Puget Sound. Greens fees start as low as $90 on winter weekdays but can climb well above $200 during high-season weekends. ✉ *6320 Grandview Dr. W.* ✣ *8 miles west of Tacoma* ☎ *253/460–4653* 🌐 *www.chambersbaygolf.com.*

Olympia

30 miles southwest of Tacoma.

Olympia has been the capital of Washington since 1853, the beginning of city and state. It is small (population 54,000) for the capital city of a major state, but that makes it all the more pleasant to visit. The historic and charming downtown area is compact and easy on the feet, stretching between Capitol Lake and the gathering of austere government buildings to the south, the shipping and yacht docks around glistening Budd Inlet to the west, the colorful market area capping the north end of town, and Interstate 5 running along the eastern edge. There are small, unexpected surprises all through town, from pretty half-block parks and blossoming miniature gardens to clutches of hip bistros, third-wave coffeehouses, artisan cocktail bars, and indie boutiques. The imposing state capitol, finished in 1928, is set above the south end of town like a fortress, framed by a skirt of granite steps. The monumental 287-foot-high dome is the fourth-tallest masonry dome in the world (only St. Peter's in Rome, St. Paul's in London, and St. Isaac's Cathedral in St. Petersburg rise higher).

GETTING HERE AND AROUND

Downtown is off Interstate 5, Exit 105. This is an easy city to drive and park in, and a car is your best way around. Both Greyhound and Amtrak serve Olympia, but the Amtrak station is 8 miles away, so from Seattle, if you're not driving, taking the bus is actually more convenient, as the bus station is centrally located and the sights are clustered around downtown.

ESSENTIALS

VISITOR INFORMATION Olympia & Beyond. ✉ *2424 Heritage Ct. SW, Suite B* ☎ *360/704–7544, 877/704–7500* 🌐 *www.experienceolympia.com.*

Sights

Capitol Campus

GOVERNMENT BUILDING | These attractive grounds, sprawling around the buildings perched above the Capitol Lake bluffs, contain memorials, monuments, rose gardens, and Japanese cherry trees. Free 45-minute tours (weekdays 10–3, weekends 11–3) from the visitor center take you around the area. If you want to see state government in action, the legislature is in session for 30 or 60 days from the second Monday in January, depending on whether it's an even- or odd-numbered year. ✉ *Capitol Way, between 10th* *and 14th Aves.* ☎ *360/902–8880 tour information* 🌐 *www.des.wa.gov* 🎫 *Free.*

Hands On Children's Museum

MUSEUM | **FAMILY** | This fun spot in a handsome, modern building just off Marine Drive overlooking East Bay is where children can touch, build, and play with all sorts of crafts and exhibits. Dozens of interactive, cleverly designed stations include an art studio and a special gallery for kids four and under. During the city's First Friday art walks the museum is open late, offers free admission after 5 pm. ✉ *414 Jefferson St. NE* ☎ *360/956–0818* 🌐 *www.hocm.org* 🎫 *$15.*

★ Nisqually National Wildlife Refuge

NATURE PRESERVE | More than 200 different bird species along with a slew of reptiles, mammals, and amphibians thrive amid the marshes and grasslands of this 4,529-acre refuge—the largest estuary restoration in the Pacific Northwest—situated on the delta formed by the Nisqually River's confluence with Puget Sound. Just 8 miles east of downtown Olympia, the tranquil space feels a world away from civilization and is laced with 4 miles of trails, some of them along boardwalks. Naturalists lead guided walks and give lectures on weekends from April through September, and a visitor center contains exhibits and a nature store. ✉ *100 Brown Farm Rd.* ☎ *360/753–9467* 🌐 *www.fws.gov/refuge/Billy_Frank_Jr_Nisqually* 🎫 *$3* ⏲ *Visitor center closed Mon. and Tues.*

Olympia Farmers Market

MARKET | Neat, clean, and well run, this complex housing more than 100 covered fruit, vegetable, pastry, and craft stalls sits at the north edge of downtown. You'll find all sorts of oddities such as ostrich eggs, button magnets, and glass sculptures. With several tiny international eateries tucked in between the vendors, it's also a terrific place to grab a bite and then walk over to the waterfront. During high season (April to October), it's open Thursday–Sunday; the rest of the years, the market is open one or two days a week. ✉ *700 Capitol Way N* ☎ *360/352–9096* 🌐 *www.olympiafarmersmarket.com* 🎫 *Free.*

Percival Landing Waterfront Park

CITY PARK | Framing nearly 4 acres of landscaped desert gardens and bird-watching areas, this lovely waterfront spot stretches along a 1-mile boardwalk through a beachy section of the West Bay shoreline. The park overlooks yachts bobbing in the water at several marinas, and features include beach pavilions and a playground. You can see it all from three stories up by climbing the winding steps of the viewing tower at the north end of the complex, in Port Plaza, where open benches invite visitors to relax and enjoy the outlook. ✉ *217 Thurston Ave. NW* ☎ *360/753–8380* 🌐 *www.olympiawa.gov.*

Priest Point Park

NATURE PRESERVE | This leafy 314-acre tract is a beautiful section of protected shoreline and wetlands. Thick swaths of forest and glistening bay views are the main attractions, with picnic areas and playgrounds filling in the open spaces. The 3-mile **Ellis Cove Trail,** with interpretive stations, bridges, and nature settings, runs right through the Priest Point Park area and around the Olympia coast. ✉ *2600 East Bay Dr. NE* ☎ *360/753–8380* 🌐 *www.olympiawa.gov* 🎫 *Free.*

★ 222 Market

MARKET | One of Olympia's premier foodie destinations is this artisanal marketplace just a couple of blocks east of Percival Landing and a short walk south of the city's renowned Farmers Market. The warren of boutique restaurants and food purveyors includes the long-running Bread Peddler bakery along with about eight others outlets specializing in everything from sustainable shellfish and bone broths to small-batch whiskey and premium gelato. There's also a florist and gourmet market. ✉ *222 Capitol Way N* 🌐 *www.222market.com.*

Restaurants

★ Chelsea Farms Oyster Bar

$$$ | **SEAFOOD** | Arguably the best restaurant inside the bustling 222 Market food hall, and one of the top dining destinations in the city, this beautifully designed contemporary seafood restaurant with a marble-top bar and striking oyster-shell chandeliers is a winning choice for anything from a snack of oysters on the half shell to a grand feast. Consider sharing a couple of starters—maybe charred carrots with white-bean hummus and local mussels with mustard, cream, and cider, before diving into more substantial dishes, like whole Dungeness crab with brown butter, lemon, and capers. **Known for:** brunch on weekends is a popular affair; shellfish sourced locally and prepared in inventive ways; house-made focaccia with sea salt and sea bean powder. *Average main: $25* *222 Capitol Way N* *360/915–7784* *www.chelseafarms.net* *Closed Mon.*

Dillinger's Cocktails, Kitchen & Rum Room

$$ | **MODERN AMERICAN** | Although creative cocktails—of which many, many varieties are offered—are the biggest draw at this swanky downtown lounge set inside one of the Olympia's oldest buildings, Dillinger's offers up a commendable food menu, too. Friends might want to go in together on a few of the shareable platters, with crab cakes, foie gras, and artisan cheeses among the options, or consider one of the globally influenced dishes, such as ceviche or coconut-ginger soup. **Known for:** alluring speakeasy-inspired vibe; wallet-friendly afternoon and late-night deals; ambitious and impressive mixology program. *Average main: $19* *406 Washington St. SE* *360/515–0650* *www.dillingerscocktailsandkitchen.com* *No lunch.*

Dockside Bistro & Wine Bar

$$$ | **PACIFIC NORTHWEST** | The marina views are only part of the appeal of this bright, modern bistro overlooking West Bay. It's the innovative, beautifully presented dishes that delights patrons, not to mention the friendly and efficient service and stellar wine list. **Known for:** Pacific Northwest fare with Asian influences; well-chosen wine selection; views of West Bay. *Average main: $30* *501 Columbia St. NW* *360/956–1928* *www.docksidebistro.com* *Closed Mon. No lunch Sun.*

New Moon Cooperative Cafe

$ | **AMERICAN** | This cheery, simple downtown breakfast and lunch spot renowned for its house-made blackberry jam and funky vibe is a cooperative, owned entirely by its staff. The filling omelets, including the Northwestern (with smoked salmon, spinach, and cream cheese) and Benedicts are among the mainstays that keep regulars coming back, but the decadent blackberry French toast is the café's showstopper. **Known for:** New Moon burger topped with avocado, feta, and mushrooms; fills up on weekends, so expect a wait; burgers and salads at lunchtime. *Average main: $13* *113 4th Ave. W* *360/357–3452* *www.newmooncoop.com* *No dinner.*

Octapas Cafe

$$ | **TAPAS** | This playfully named restaurant with nautical artwork does indeed specialize in tapas, including—naturally—giant Pacific octopus, cured in olive oil and served with crusty house bread. Others treats from the seafood-centric menu include smoked oysters with lemon, mussels in a Thai lemongrass curry, and prawn tacos with pineapple salsa, but you'll find plenty of meat and veggie options, too. **Known for:** generous three-hour-long happy hour; live music and late hours on weekends; friendly vibe. *Average main: $21* *414 4th Ave. E* *360/878–9333* *www.octapascafe.com* *No lunch.*

Olympia Coffee Roasting

$ | **CAFÉ** | Stop by this sleek downtown coffee roastery with big windows and a retractable glass door that's opened on warm days for stellar espresso and java drinks, from rich mochas to nitro ice coffee. Light snacks and baked goods are also on offer. **Known for:** expertly roasted and brewed coffee; house-made syrups; mocha milk shakes. *Average main: $4 600 4th Ave. E 360/753–0066 www.olympiacoffee.com.*

Our Table

$ | **MODERN AMERICAN** | Locally sourced, sustainable ingredients take center stage in the artfully plated dishes at this otherwise simple-looking downtown diner popular for its affordable breakfast and lunch fare. Fluffy house-made biscuits with sausage gravy and the hangtown fry with local fried oysters, bacon, and house-made hot sauce are among noteworthy morning dishes. **Known for:** chocolate mousse is fluffy and delicious; locally sourced produce; duck-and-root-vegetable pâté. *Average main: $11 406 4th Ave. E 360/932–6030 Closed Tues. and Wed. No dinner.*

Hotels

Doubletree Olympia Hotel

$$$ | **HOTEL** | This reliable chain property has an ideal location steps from Percival Landing Park and the Budd Inlet waterfront and a couple of blocks from several excellent restaurants and the Farmers Market. **Pros:** nicest rooms of any chain property in town; 24-hour pool and fitness center; inexpensive parking. **Cons:** bland design inside and out; expensive during busy periods; valet parking not available. *Rooms from: $209 415 Capitol Way N 360/570–0555, 855/610–8733 www.hilton.com 102 rooms Free Breakfast.*

Hotel RL Olympia by Red Lion

$ | **HOTEL** | Views of Capitol Lake and the surrounding hills are highlights of this budget-minded property from which you can walk to many local sights. **Pros:** many rooms have water or park views; lobby and restaurant have crisp, clean design; many parts have been recently renovated. **Cons:** can get noisy during conventions; a bit of a walk to downtown restaurants; service is hit-or-miss. *Rooms from: $109 2300 Evergreen Park Dr. 360/943–4000 www.redlion.com 193 rooms Free Breakfast.*

★ **Inn At Mallard Cove**

$$ | **B&B/INN** | Although this beautifully decorated Tudor-style mansion has an Olympia address, it couldn't feel more removed from the bustle of the city. **Pros:** close to Billy Frank Jr. Nisqually National Wildlife Refuge; rates include lavish three-course breakfast; unbeatable views of Puget Sound. **Cons:** 15-minute drive from downtown; not suitable for younger kids; two-night minimum in high season. *Rooms from: $189 5025 Meridian Rd. NE 360/491–9795 www.theinnatmallardcove.com 3 rooms Free Breakfast.*

Swantown Inn & Spa

$$ | **B&B/INN** | Antiques and lace grace every room of this stylish, peak-roofed 1887 Queen Anne–Eastlake mansion that sits high above fragrant gardens and landscaped lawns. **Pros:** feels like you've stepped back in time; amenities for business travelers; delicious hot breakfasts. **Cons:** a 20-minute walk to downtown; ornate decor isn't to everyone's taste; sometimes fully booked for weddings. *Rooms from: $179 1431 11th Ave. SE 360/753–9123 www.swantown-inn.com 5 rooms Free Breakfast.*

Shopping

Ember Goods

HOUSEHOLD ITEMS/FURNITURE | This handsome boutique in the heart of downtown dispenses artisan coffee (and sells beans by the bag as well), along with a great selection Pacific Northwest–made men's and women's apparel, household goods, upcycled furnishings, and other intriguing goods. *422 Washington St. SE 360/338–0315 www.embergoods.com.*

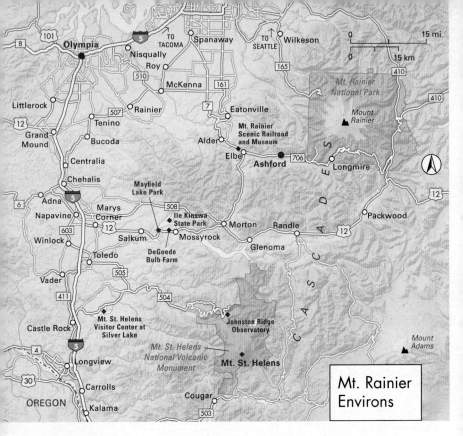

Mt. Rainier Environs

Ashford

60 miles east of Olympia, 85 miles south of Seattle, 130 miles north of Portland.

Adjacent to the Nisqually (Longmire) entrance to Mount Rainier National Park, Ashford draws around 2 million visitors every year. Long a transit route for local aboriginal tribes, its more recent history began when it became a logging terminal on the rail line and developed into a tourism hub with lodges, restaurants, groceries, and gift shops along Highway 706.

GETTING HERE AND AROUND

Ashford is easiest to reach from Seattle via Interstate 5 southbound to Highway 7, then driving southeast to Highway 706. An alternate route is via Interstate 5 southbound to Highway 167, then continuing south to Highway 161 through Eatonville to Highway 7, then east to Highway 706. From Portland, follow Interstate 5 northbound, then head east on Highway 12 to Morton and north via Highway 7 to Highway 706.

Sights

Mt. Rainier Scenic Railroad and Museum

TOUR—SIGHT | FAMILY | This trip takes you through lush forests and across scenic bridges, covering 14 miles of incomparable beauty. Trains depart from Elbe, 11 miles west of Ashford, then bring passengers to a lovely picnic area near Mineral Lake before returning. The trains run weekends from mid-May to June, then Friday–Sunday from July through Labor Day weekend, and Saturday through mid-October. Special pumpkin patch excursions operate for two weekends in late October, and Winter Polar

Mt. Rainier was named after British admiral Peter Rainier in the late 18th century.

Express trains run from mid-November to December on weekends (and daily during winter break, except Christmas Day). Prices start at $41 for basic excursions; special events—including wine and craft beer trains—cost more. At Mineral Lake, guests can tour the museum containing old train memorabilia and artifacts and exhibits on the area's old railroad camps. ✉ *54124 Mountain Hwy. E, Elbe* ☎ *360/492–6000* 🌐 *www.mtrainierrailroad.com* 🕒 *Closed Nov.–Apr. (except for holiday excursions).*

Restaurants

Copper Creek Restaurant

$$ | AMERICAN | FAMILY | This old-fashioned roadhouse, with rough-hewn fir floors and knotty-pine walls, is nestled beneath towering trees along the main road to Mt. Rainier from Eatonville. It's been a favorite lunch and dinner stop since it opened in the 1940s, and these days parkgoers still come by in droves to fill up on hearty, straightforward comfort fare, such as biscuits and gravy and chicken-fried steak and eggs in the morning, bacon-and-blue-cheese burgers at lunch, and wild Alaskan salmon with blackberry vinaigrette in the evening. **Known for:** save room for the blackberry pie à la mode; hearty, stick-to-your-ribs fare; rustic, family-friendly vibe. [$] *Average main: $18* ✉ *35707 Hwy. 706* ☎ *360/569–2799* 🌐 *www.coppercreekinn.com.*

Wildberry Restaurant

$ | ECLECTIC | If you're looking to fuel up before a big hike in the park, this festive restaurant with plenty of outdoor seating is a good bet. It's run by record-shattering Mt. Everest climber Lhakpa Gelu Sherpa and his wife, Fulamu, who helms the kitchen, serving up a mix of Nepalese and classic American dishes, including traditional thali chicken, mushroom, and garbanzo bean platters, pork momo dumplings, and sherpa stew. **Known for:** close to Nisqually Entrance of Mount Rainier National Park; mix of hearty American and Himalayan fare; homemade marionberry and blueberry pies.

$ Average main: $15 ✉ 37718 Hwy. 706 ☎ 360/569–2277 🌐 www.rainierwildberry.com ⊙ Closed Nov.–Mar.

Hotels

Alexander's Lodge
$ | **B&B/INN** | A mile from Mt. Rainier's Nisqually Entrance, this ideally located lodging's vintage furnishings lend romance to rooms in the main building, which dates back to 1912; there are also two adjacent guesthouses at the charming property. **Pros:** plenty of historical character; in-room spa services available; some rooms are pet-friendly. **Cons:** steep stairs to some units; decor is a bit old-fashioned; some rooms are quite small. *$ Rooms from: $139 ✉ 37515 Hwy. 706 ☎ 360/569–2300 🌐 www.alexanderslodge.com 21 rooms Free Breakfast.*

★ **Mountain Meadows Inn**
$$ | **B&B/INN** | This homey woodland hideaway, 6 miles southwest of Mount Rainier National Park's Nisqually Entrance, includes a lovingly restored Craftsman-style home with gorgeous Douglas fir floors, interesting antiques, and three guest rooms, as well as a separate modern chalet with three suites that have private entrances and kitchenettes. **Pros:** reasonable rates; thoughtful and friendly owners; lush grounds include a hot tub. **Cons:** no restaurants within walking distance; suites lack historic charm of main house; rooms in main house don't have TVs. *$ Rooms from: $160 ✉ 28912 Hwy. 706 ☎ 360/569–0507 🌐 www.mountain-meadows-inn.com 6 rooms Free Breakfast.*

Paradise Village Hotel
$ | **HOTEL** | A young Ukranian bought and completely revamped what had been a dated little lodging in the center of Ashford, giving it a fresh, distinctive look and a fun energy. **Pros:** restaurant and bakery serving hearty Eastern European and American dishes; great room amenities, from Bluetooth speakers to flat-screen TVs; has a young, hip vibe. **Cons:** some rooms are a little small; hourly charge for the hot tub; traffic noise, especially in summer. *$ Rooms from: $129 ✉ 31811 Hwy. 706 ☎ 360/255–0070 🌐 www.paradisevillagelodge.com 12 units No meals.*

Wellspring
$$ | **B&B/INN** | Deep in the woods outside Ashford, the accommodations at this tranquil alpine spa include tastefully designed log cabins, a tree house, a room adjoining a hot tub and sauna, and several other unique configurations. **Pros:** a wide range of spa treatments are offered; good for groups and families; relaxing soaking tubs. **Cons:** limited amenities; no cell service; no restaurant. *$ Rooms from: $155 ✉ 54922 Kernehan Rd. ☎ 360/569–2514 🌐 www.wellspringspa.com 17 units No meals.*

Chapter 12

THE SAN JUAN ISLANDS

12

Updated by
AnnaMaria Stephens

Sights ★★★★★
Restaurants ★★★☆☆
Hotels ★★★☆☆
Shopping ★★★☆☆
Nightlife ★☆☆☆☆

WELCOME TO THE SAN JUAN ISLANDS

TOP REASONS TO GO

★ **Whale watch:** Spot whales and other marine life from a tour boat or sea kayak.

★ **Taste local flavors:** Talented chefs have turned Orcas and San Juan Islands into hot spots for sophisticated, locavore-driven cuisine.

★ **Gallery hop:** Dozens of acclaimed artists live year-round or seasonally in the San Juans, and you can find their work in studio galleries and group cooperatives throughout the islands.

★ **Indulge in a spa day:** Work out the kayaking or hiking kinks with a massage at the lovely seaside Rosario Resort and Spa on Orcas Island or Afterglow Spa at Roche Harbor on San Juan Island.

★ **Bike beautiful terrain:** Rent a bike and cycle the scenic, sloping country roads—Lopez Island has the gentlest terrain for this activity.

Spending time on the San Juans is all about connecting with the sea, although there's plenty to see and do—especially on the two largest islands—away from the water, from mountain hiking to sophisticated gallery-hopping. A trip to the San Juans requires a bit of travel, planning, and expense, but visitors nevertheless flock here to spot whales, go kayaking, chill out in endearingly informal inns, and dine on creative, surprisingly urbane cuisine. The most popular boating activity is whale-watching, but each island has its share of parks, bluffs, and coastline to explore.

The San Juan Islands are part of the same archipelago as the Gulf Islands of British Columbia—they're actually far closer to Victoria, BC, than they are to Seattle. The closest mainland Washington city is Anacortes, about 90 minutes north of Seattle.

1 Lopez Island. The smallest, least populated, and most tranquil of the main islands is a largely rural and wonderfully restive place with a handful of charming cafés, a few inns, and traffic-free roads ideal for biking.

2 Orcas Island. The rugged and hilly terrain contains the highest point in the San Juans and is the largest in the archipelago, although the pace is easygoing and relaxed. The main village of Eastsound, however, contains a number of sophisticated restaurants and galleries, and you'll find several fine eateries, inns, and boutique resorts elsewhere on this verdant island.

3 San Juan Island. The political seat and commercial center of the archipelago, and the only one of the islands with direct ferry service to British Columbia, is home to the bustling town of Friday Harbor, which abounds with good shopping, cheery cafés, and a mix of midpriced and luxury inns and small hotels. Aside from cultural activities—including a national historic park, art museum, and sculpture garden—you'll enjoy fine beaches, great roads for biking, and marinas that rent kayaks and boats. Still, even in summer, you'll discover plenty of quiet, secluded areas on the island in which to commune with nature.

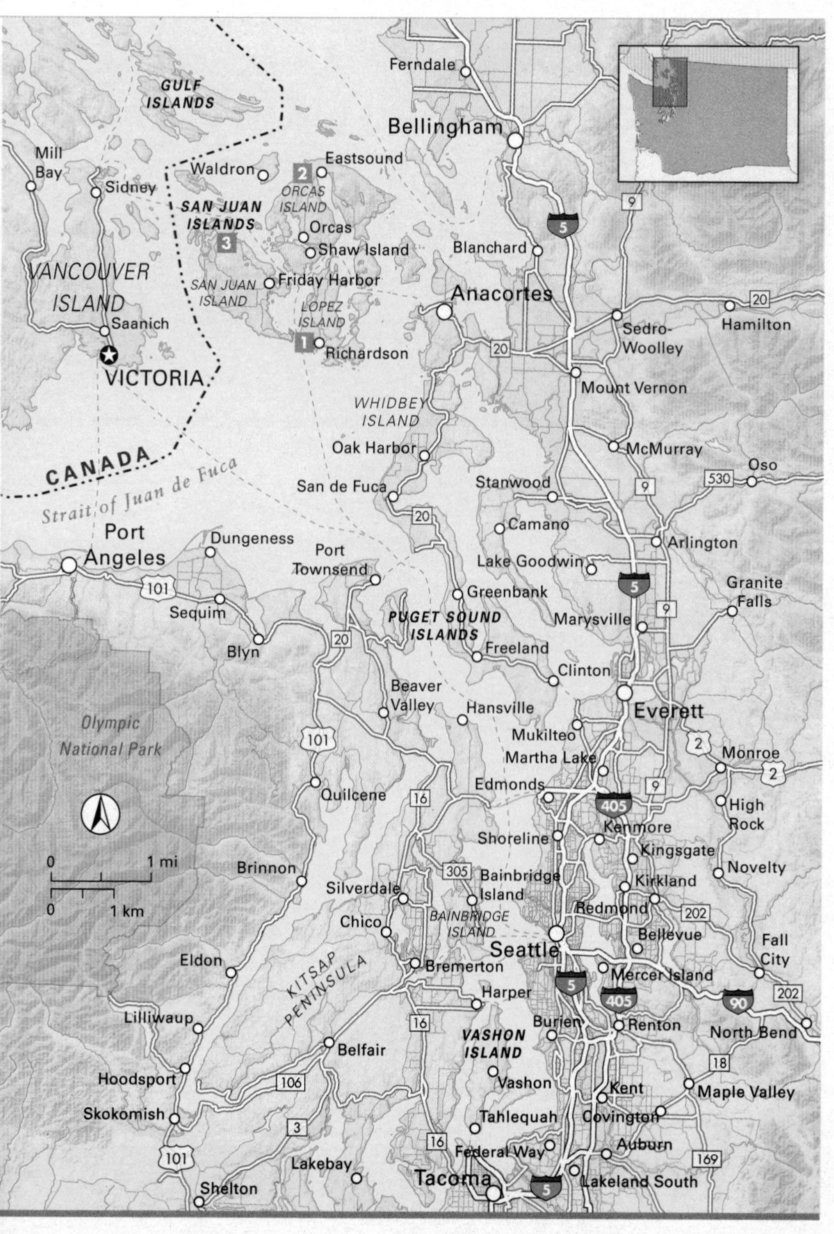
GULF ISLANDS
Ferndale
Bellingham
Mill Bay
Sidney
Waldron
2
Eastsound
ORCAS ISLAND
SAN JUAN ISLANDS
3
Orcas
Shaw Island
Blanchard
VANCOUVER ISLAND
SAN JUAN ISLAND
Friday Harbor
Anacortes
LOPEZ ISLAND
Saanich
1
Richardson
VICTORIA
20
Sedro-Woolley
Hamilton
Mount Vernon
WHIDBEY ISLAND
Oak Harbor
McMurray
CANADA
Strait of Juan de Fuca
San de Fuca
Stanwood
530
Oso
Camano
Arlington
Port Angeles
Dungeness
Port Townsend
Lake Goodwin
101
Sequim
Greenbank
Granite Falls
PUGET SOUND ISLANDS
Marysville
Blyn
Freeland
Clinton
Beaver Valley
Hansville
Everett
Olympic National Park
Mukilteo
Martha Lake
Monroe
2
Quilcene
Edmonds
16
405
High Rock
Kenmore
Shoreline
Kingsgate
0
1 mi
1 km
Brinnon
305
Bainbridge Island
Kirkland
Novelty
Silverdale
Redmond
202
Chico
BAINBRIDGE ISLAND
Bellevue
Seattle
Fall City
KITSAP PENINSULA
Eldon
Bremerton
Mercer Island
Harper
90
Lilliwaup
Burien
Renton
North Bend
VASHON ISLAND
Belfair
18
Hoodsport
106
Vashon
Kent
Maple Valley
Skokomish
Tahlequah
Covington
3
Federal Way
Auburn
169
Lakebay
Tacoma
Lakeland South
Shelton
5
9

About 100 miles northwest of Seattle, these romantic islands abound with breathtaking rolling pastures, rocky shorelines, and thickly forested ridges, and their quaint villages draw art lovers, foodies, and city folk seeking serenity. Inns are easygoing and well appointed, and many restaurants are helmed by highly talented chefs emphasizing local ingredients.

There are 172 named islands in the archipelago. Sixty are populated (though most have only a house or two), and 10 are state marine parks, some of which are accessible only to nonmotorized craft—kayakers, canoes, small sailboats—navigating the Cascadia Marine Trail.

Planning

When to Go

This part of Washington has a mild, maritime climate. Winter temperatures average in the low 40s, while summer temps hover in the mid 70s. July and August are by far the most popular months to visit the three main islands—they can get busy during this time, with resorts, boating tours, and ferries often at capacity. To beat the crowds and avoid the worst of the wet weather, visit in late spring or early fall—September and early October can be fair and stunningly gorgeous, as can May and early June. Hotel rates are generally lower everywhere during these shoulder seasons—and even lower once often drizzly winter starts.

Orcas, Lopez, and San Juan islands are extremely popular in high season; securing hotel reservations in advance is essential. If you're bringing a car to the islands, be sure to book a ferry reservation well in advance. Or if you're traveling light and plan to stay put in one place in the islands, consider walking or biking. Lot parking at Anacortes is $10 per day and $40 per week in summer and half that October–April.

■ TIP→ Though a few places close or have limited hours and the incredible views are frequently obscured by drizzle during the winter, the San Juan Islands are still worth a visit in the off-season, except in January, when many spots shutter for the entire month.

FESTIVALS

Orcas Island Chamber Music Festival

FESTIVALS | Around for more than two decades, this music festival comprises more than two weeks of "classical music with a view" in August. These concerts are immensely popular with chamber-music fans around the Pacific Northwest. ✉ *Orcas Island* ☎ *866/492–0003* 🌐 *www.oicmf.org.*

Savor the San Juans

FESTIVALS | Autumn has become increasingly popular thanks to the growth of this culinary festival, which runs about six weeks. It consists of an islands-wide series of events and gatherings celebrating local foods and beverages, including farm tours, film screenings, and harvest dinners. ☎ *360/378–3277* 🌐 *www.visitsanjuans.com/savor.*

Getting Here and Around

AIR

Port of Friday Harbor is the main San Juan Islands airport, but there are also small airports on Lopez, Shaw, and Orcas Islands. Seaplanes land on the waterfront at Friday Harbor and Roche Harbor on San Juan Island; Rosario Resort, Deer Harbor, and West Sound on Orcas Island; and Fisherman Bay on Lopez Island. Daily scheduled flights link the San Juan Islands with mainland airports at Anacortes, Bellingham, and Lake Washington, Renton, and Boeing Field near Seattle. Some airlines also offer charter services.

If traffic and ferry lines really aren't your thing, consider hopping aboard a seaplane for the quick flight from Seattle. **Kenmore Air** offers several daily departures from Lake Union, Lake Washington, and Boeing Field, and from May through September **Friday Harbor Seaplanes** has up to four daily departures from Renton to Friday Harbor. Flying isn't cheap—around $130–$170 each way—but the scenic, hour-long flight is an experience in itself. Flights on **San Juan Airlines** from Bellingham and Anacortes run about $96 each way.

AIR CONTACTS Friday Harbor Seaplanes. ☎ *425/277–1590,* 🌐 *www.fridayharborseaplanes.com.* **Kenmore Air.** ☎ *425/486–1257, 866/435–9524* 🌐 *www.kenmoreair.com.* **San Juan Airlines.** ☎ *800/874–4434* 🌐 *www.sanjuanairlines.com.*

CAR

Most visitors arrive by car, which is the best way to explore these mostly rural islands comprehensively, especially if you plan on visiting for more than a couple of days. You can also park your car at the Anacortes ferry terminal ($10 per day or $40 per week high season, and half that fall through spring), as fares are cheaper and lines much shorter for passengers without cars. B&B owners can often pick guests up at the ferry terminal by prior arrangement, and you can rely on bikes and occasional taxis or on-island car or moped rentals (on San Juan and Orcas) for getting around. Also, in summer, a shuttle bus makes its way daily around San Juan Island and on weekends on Orcas and Lopez islands. From Seattle, it's a 90-minute drive via Interstate 5 north and Highway 20 west to reach Anacortes.

Island roads are narrow and often windy, with one or two lanes. Slow down and hug the shoulder when passing another car on a one-lane road. Expect rough patches, some unpaved lanes, deer and rabbits, bicyclists, and other hazards—plus the distractions of sweeping water views. There are a few car-rental agencies on San Juan and Orcas, with daily rates running about $60 to $100 in summer, and as much as 25% less off-season. You'll likely save money renting a car on the mainland, even factoring in the cost of ferry transport (which in high season is about $45 to $65 for a standard vehicle including driver, plus around $14 per passenger, depending on which island you're headed to).

RENTAL CAR CONTACTS M and W Rental Cars. ✉ *725 Spring St., Friday Harbor* ☎ *360/376–5266 Orcas, 360/378–2794 San Juan* 🌐 *www.sanjuanauto.com.* **Orcas Island Rental Cars.** ☎ *360/376–7433* 🌐 *www.orcasislandshuttle.com.* **Susie's**

Mopeds. ✉ *125 Nichols St., Friday Harbor* ☎ *360/378–5244, 800/532–0087* 🌐 *www.susiesmopeds.com.*

FERRY

The Washington State Ferries system can become overloaded during peak travel times. Thankfully, a reservations system makes it far easier to plan trips and avoid lines. Reservations are highly recommended, especially in summer and on weekends, although a small number of spaces on every sailing are always reserved for standby. Always arrive at least 45 minutes ahead of your departure, and as much as two hours ahead at busy times if you don't have a reservation. You'll find information on the Washington State Ferries website on up-to-the-minute wait times as well as tips on which ferries tend to be the most crowded. It's rarely a problem to get a walk-on spot, although arriving a bit early to ensure you get a ticket is wise. **■ TIP→ Avoid returning to Anacortes on the daily ferries that originate in Sidney, BC; though they're more direct routes, domestic passengers have to wait in the Customs and Border Protection line to exit along with Canadian passengers, which can take a very long time.**

FERRY CONTACTS Washington State Ferries. ✉ *2100 Ferry Terminal Rd., Anacortes* ☎ *206/464–6400, 888/808–7977* 🌐 *www.wsdot.wa.gov/ferries.*

Restaurants

The San Juans have myriad small farms and restaurants serving local foods and fresh-harvested seafood, and culinary agritourism—visiting local farmers, growers, and chefs at their places of business—is on the rise.

Hotels

With the exception of Lopez Island, which has just a handful of inns, accommodations in the San Juans are quite varied and tend be plush, if also expensive during the high summer season. Rosario Resort & Spa on Orcas Island and Roche Harbor Resort on San Juan Island are favorite spots for special-occasion splurges, and both islands have seen an influx of either new or luxuriously updated inns in recent years. These places often have perks like lavish breakfasts and on-site outfitters and tour operators. *Hotel reviews have been shortened. For full information, visit Fodors.com.*

Visitor Information

Look to the San Juan Islands Visitors Bureau for general information on all the islands—the website is very useful.

CONTACTS San Juan Islands Visitors Bureau. ✉ *The Technology Center, 640 Mullis St., Suites 210–211, Friday Harbor* ☎ *360/378–3277, 888/468–3701* 🌐 *www.visitsanjuans.com.*

Lopez Island

45 mins by ferry from Anacortes.

Known affectionately as "Slow-pez," the closest significantly populated island to the mainland is a broad, bay-encircled bit of terrain set amid sparkling blue seas, a place where cabinlike homes are tucked into the woods, and boats are moored in lonely coves.

GETTING HERE AND AROUND

The Washington State Ferries crossing from Anacortes take about 45 minutes; round-trip peak-season fares are about $14 per person, $45 for a car and driver. One-hour flights from Seattle cost about $130 to $170 each way. You can get around the island by car (bring your own—there

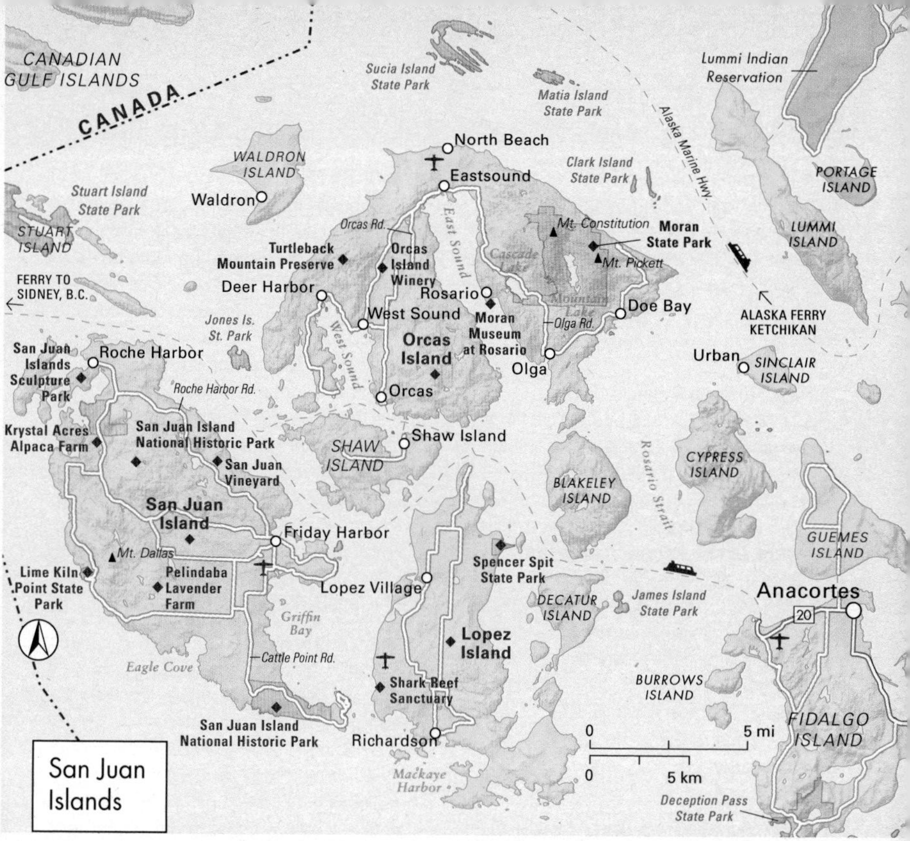

San Juan Islands

are no rentals) or bike; there are bike-rental facilities by the ferry terminal.

ESSENTIALS

VISITOR INFORMATION Lopez Island Chamber of Commerce. ✉ *Lopez Rd., at Tower Rd., Lopez* ☎ *360/468–4664* 🌐 *www.lopezisland.com.*

Sights

Lopez Island Historical Museum

MUSEUM | Artifacts from the region's Native American tribes and early settlers include some impressive ship and small-boat models and maps of local landmarks. You can also listen to fascinating digital recordings of early settlers discussing life on Lopez Island. ✉ *Weeks Rd. and Washburn Pl., Lopez* ☎ *360/468–2049* 🌐 *www.lopezmuseum.org* 🎟 *Free* ⏲ *Closed Mon.–Tues. and Oct.–Apr.*

★ Shark Reef Sanctuary

TRAIL | A quiet forest trail along beautiful Shark Reef leads to an isolated headland jutting out above the bay. The sounds of raucous barks and squeals mean you're nearly there, and eventually you may see throngs of seals and seagulls on the rocky islets across from the point. Bring binoculars to spot bald eagles in the trees as you walk and to view sea otters frolicking in the waves near the shore. The trail starts at the Shark Reef Road parking lot south of the airport, and it's a 15-minute walk to the headland. ✉ *Shark Reef Rd., Lopez* ✣ *2 miles south of Lopez Island Airport* 🎟 *Free.*

Spencer Spit State Park

NATIONAL/STATE PARK | Set on a spit along the Cascadia Marine Trail for kayakers, this popular spot for summer camping is on former Native American clamming, crabbing, and fishing grounds. A variety of campsites is available, from primitive tent sites to full hookups. This is one of the few Washington beaches where cars are permitted. *521 A Bakerview Rd., Lopez* *360/468–2251* *www.parks.wa.gov/parks* *$10.*

Restaurants

Haven Kitchen & Bar

$$ | **AMERICAN** | You'll find something for everyone at this Lopez eatery, which seems to have picked favorite dishes from various cuisines and created solid versions of them, sometimes with inventive twists (tater tots in a burrito, for example); they've got everything from Thai fresh rolls to gamberoni linguine with fresh, locally made pasta. **Known for:** eclectic menu; expansive flower-lined outdoor deck; well-crafted artisanal cocktails. *Average main: $22* *9 Old Post Rd., Lopez* *360/468–3272* *www.lopezhaven.com* *Closed Sun.–Tues.*

Ursa Minor

$$$$ | **PACIFIC NORTHWEST** | One of the latest upscale farm-to-table restaurants to put the San Juan Islands on the culinary map (reservations strongly recommended), Ursa Minor is helmed by Nick Coffey, formerly of the now-closed Sitka & Spruce in Seattle. He celebrates the Islands' incredible bounty with a creative seasonal menu featuring seafood, foraged mushrooms, and products from Lopez's longtime Jones Family Farm, which raises grass-fed livestock and cultivates a few types of shellfish, including a pink scallop that has Seattle chefs wait-listing for orders. **Known for:** airy, serene organic-modern space; island-sourced ingredients; unique Northwest fare. *Average main: $40* *210 Lopez Rd., Lopez* *360/622–2730* *www.ursaminorlopez.com* *Closed Mon.–Thu. and Jan.*

Coffee and Quick Bites

Holly B's Bakery

$ | **BAKERY** | Tucked into a small, cabinlike strip of businesses set back from the water, this cozy wood-paneled bakery has been a source of delicious fresh ham-and-Gruyère croissants, marionberry scones, slices of pizza, and other savory and sweet treats since 1977. Sunny summer mornings bring diners out onto the patio, where kids play and parents relax. **Known for:** ginormous, decadent cinnamon rolls; pizza by the slice; scones flavored with seasonal fruit. *Average main: $7* *Lopez Plaza, 211 Lopez Rd., Lopez* *360/468–2133* *www.hollybsbakery.com* *No credit cards* *Closed Dec.–Mar. No dinner.*

Isabel's Espresso

$ | **CAFÉ** | A favorite of Lopez locals, Isabel's sources its coffee from Fair Trade suppliers and its creamy dairy from the mainland's small Fresh Breeze Organic Dairy Farm. Housed in a charming rustic building in Lopez's tiny "downtown," the café also serves light fare like pastries and sandwiches. **Known for:** good coffee; outdoor seating with views. *Average main: $6* *308 Lopez Rd., Lopez* *360/468–4114* *www.isabelsespresso.com.*

Vita's Wildly Delicious

$ | **CAFÉ** | At this gourmet market and wine shop (open primarily during the daytime but until 8 pm on Friday), the proprietors create a daily-changing assortment of prepared foods and some made-to-order items, such as Reuben panini sandwiches. Other favorites include Dungeness crab cakes, hearty meat loaf, lobster mac-and-cheese, and an assortment of tempting desserts. **Known for:** Dungeness crab cakes; pretty garden-dining area; gourmet picnic supplies. *Average main: $11* *77 Village Rd., Lopez* *360/468–4268* *www.vitasonlopez.com* *Closed Sun., Mon., and late fall–late spring. No dinner.*

Hotels

Edenwild Inn

$$$ | **B&B/INN** | Thoughtful and friendly owners Anthony and Crystal Rovente operate this large Victorian-style farmhouse surrounded by gardens and framed by Fisherman Bay, where spacious rooms are each painted or papered in different pastel shades and furnished with simple antiques; some have claw-foot tubs and brick fireplaces. **Pros:** lovely outdoor spaces, including an outdoor veranda; nice breakfast buffet using local produce and homemade baked goods; handy location close to village restaurants. **Cons:** no TVs in rooms; decor is a bit plain; two-night minimum. *Rooms from: $229 ✉ 132 Lopez Rd., Lopez ☎ 360/468–3238 🌐 www.edenwildinn.com ⇔ 9 rooms 🍴 Free Breakfast.*

★ Mackaye Harbor Inn

$$ | **B&B/INN** | This former sea captain's house, built in 1904, rises two stories above the beach at the southern end of the island and accommodates guests in cheerfully furnished rooms with golden-oak and brass details and wicker furniture; three have views of MacKaye Harbor. **Pros:** fantastic water views; mountain bikes (free) and kayaks (reasonable daily fee) available; friendly and attentive hosts. **Cons:** on far end of the island; several miles from the ferry terminal and airport; some bathrooms are across the hall from rooms. *Rooms from: $195 ✉ 949 MacKaye Harbor Rd., Lopez ☎ 360/468–2253, 888/314–6140 🌐 www.mackayeharborinn.com ⇔ 5 rooms 🍴 Free Breakfast.*

Activities

BIKING

Bike rental rates start at around $7 an hour and $30 a day. Reservations are recommended, particularly in summer.

Lopez Bicycle Works

BICYCLING | At the marina 4 miles from the ferry, this full-service operation can bring bicycles right to you. In addition to cruisers and mountain bikes, the shop also rents tandem and recumbent bikes. *✉ 2847 Fisherman Bay Rd., Lopez ☎ 360/468–2847 🌐 www.lopezbicycleworks.com.*

Village Cycles

BICYCLING | This aptly named full-service rental and repair shop is in the heart of Lopez Village. *✉ 214 Lopez Rd., Lopez ☎ 360/468–4013 🌐 www.villagecycles.net.*

SEA KAYAKING

Cascadia Kayaks

KAYAKING | This company rents kayaks for half days or full days. The outfitter also organizes half-day, full-day, and two- to three-day guided tours. Hour-long private lessons are available, too, if you need a little coaching before going out on your own. *✉ 135 Lopez Rd., Lopez ☎ 360/468–3008 🌐 www.cascadiakayaks.com.*

Lopez Island Sea Kayak

KAYAKING | Open May to September at Fisherman Bay, this outfitter has a huge selection of kayaks, both plastic and fiberglass touring models. Rentals are by the hour or day, and the company can deliver kayaks to any point on the island for an additional fee. *✉ 2845 Fisherman Bay Rd., Lopez ☎ 360/468–2847 🌐 www.lopezkayaks.com.*

Shopping

Chimera Gallery

ART GALLERIES | This local artists' cooperative exhibits and sells crafts, jewelry, and fine art. *✉ Lopez Plaza, 211 Lopez Rd., Lopez ☎ 360/468–3265 🌐 www.chimeragallery.com.*

Lopez Bookshop

BOOKS/STATIONERY | This longtime bookseller is stocked with publications on San Juan Islands history and activities, as well as tomes about the Pacific Northwest. There's also a good selection of mysteries, literary novels, children's books, and craft kits, plus greeting cards, art prints, and maps. Many of the items sold here are the works of local writers, artists, and photographers. ✉ *Lopez Plaza, 211 Lopez Rd., Lopez* ☎ *360/468–2132* 🌐 *www.lopezbookshop.com.*

Orcas Island

75 mins by ferry from Anacortes.

Orcas Island, the largest of the San Juans, is blessed with wide, pastoral valleys and scenic ridges that rise high above the neighboring waters. (At 2,409 feet, Orcas's Mt. Constitution is the highest peak in the San Juans.) Spanish explorers set foot here in 1791, and the island is actually named for one of these early visitors, Juan Vicente de Güemes Padilla Horcasitas y Aguayo—not for the black-and-white whales that frolic in the surrounding waters. The island was also the home of Native American tribes, whose history is reflected in such places as Pole Pass, where the Lummi people used kelp and cedar-bark nets to catch ducks, and Massacre Bay, where in 1858 a tribe from southeast Alaska attacked a Lummi fishing village.

Today farmers, fishermen, artists, retirees, and summer-home owners make up the population of about 4,500. Houses are spaced far apart, and the island's few hamlets typically have just one major road running through them.

GETTING HERE AND AROUND

The Washington State Ferries crossing from Anacortes to Orcas Village, in the island's Westsound area, takes about 75 minutes; peak-season round-trip fares are about $14 per person, $55 for a car and driver. One-hour flights from Seattle cost about $130 to $170 each way. Planes land at Deer Harbor, Eastsound, Westsound, and at the Rosario Resort and Spa.

The best way to get around the island is by car—bikes will do in a pinch, but the hilly, curvy roads that generally lack shoulders make cycling a bit risky. Most resorts and inns offer transfers from the ferry terminal.

ESSENTIALS

VISITOR INFORMATION Orcas Island Chamber of Commerce & Visitor Center. ✉ *65 N Beach Rd.* ☎ *360/376–2273* 🌐 *www.orcasislandchamber.com.*

Sights

Moran Museum at Rosario

ARTS VENUE | This 1909 mansion that forms the centerpiece of Rosario Resort was constructed as the vacation home of Seattle shipping magnate and mayor Robert Moran. On the second floor is this fascinating museum that spans several former guest rooms and includes old photos, furniture, and memorabilia related to the Moran family, the resort's history, and the handsome ships built by Moran and his brothers. A highlight is the music room, which contains an incredible two-story 1913 aeolian pipe organ and an ornate, original Tiffany chandelier. Renowned musician Christopher Peacock discusses the resort's history and performs on the 1900 Steinway grand piano daily (except Sunday) at 4 pm in summer and on Saturday at 4 the rest of the year. The surrounding grounds make for a lovely stroll, which you might combine with lunch or a cocktail in one of the resort's water-view restaurants. ✉ *1400 Rosario Rd.* ☎ *360/376–2222* 🌐 *www.rosarioresort.com/museum* 🎫 *Free.*

★ Moran State Park

NATIONAL/STATE PARK | **FAMILY** | This pristine patch of wilderness comprises 5,252 acres of hilly, old-growth forests dotted

The view from Mount Constitution on Orcas Island, the highest point in the San Juans

with sparkling lakes, in the middle of which rises the island's highest point, 2,409-foot Mt. Constitution. A drive to the summit affords exhilarating views of the islands, the Cascades, the Olympics, and Vancouver Island, and avid hikers enjoy the strenuous but stunning 7-mile round-trip trek from rippling Mountain Lake to the summit (some 38 miles of trails traverse the entire park). The observation tower on the summit was built by the Civilian Conservation Corps in the 1930s. In summer, you can rent boats to paddle around beautiful Cascade Lake. ✉ *Mt. Constitution Rd.* ☎ *360/376–2326* 🌐 *www.parks.wa.gov/parks* 🎫 *Discover Pass (annual $30/day pass $10).*

Orcas Island Historical Museum

HISTORIC SITE | Surrounded by Eastsound's lively shops and cafés, this museum comprises several reassembled and relocated late-19th-century pioneer cabins. An impressive collection of more than 6,000 photographs, documents, and artifacts tells the story of the island's Native American and Anglo history, and in an oral-history exhibit longtime residents of the island talk about how the community has evolved over the decades. The museum also operates the 1888 Crow Valley Schoolhouse, which is open on summer Wednesdays and Saturdays; call the museum for hours and directions. ✉ *181 N Beach Rd.* ☎ *360/376–4849* 🌐 *www.orcasmuseum.org* 🎫 *$5* ⏲ *Closed Oct.–May, Sun.–Tues.*

Orcas Island Winery

WINERY/DISTILLERY | **FAMILY** | This boutique winery known on the island for its reds is under new ownership—a young married couple from Los Angeles was so awed by the area that they jumped at the chance to take over and have transformed the winery into a modern farmhouse-chic gathering space with picnic-table outdoor seating perfect for a sunny afternoon spent sipping wine and listening to concerts. ✉ *2371 Crow Valley Rd.* ☎ *360/797–5062* 🌐 *www.orcasislandwinery.com* ⏲ *Closed Mon.–Tue. and Jan.*

★ Turtleback Mountain Preserve

NATURE PRESERVE | A more peaceful, less crowded hiking and wildlife-watching alternative to Moran State Park, this 1,576-acre expanse of rugged ridges, wildflower-strewn meadows, temperate rain forest, and lush wetlands is one of the natural wonders of the archipelago. Because the San Juan County Land Bank purchased this land in 2006, it will be preserved forever for the public to enjoy. There are 8 miles of well-groomed trails, including a steep trek up to 1,519-foot-elevation Raven Ridge and a windy hike to Turtlehead Point, a soaring bluff with spectacular views west of San Juan Island and Vancouver Island beyond that—it's an amazing place to watch the sunset. You can access the preserve either from the North Trailhead, which is just 3 miles southwest of Eastsound on Crow Valley Road, or the South Trailhead, which is 3 miles northeast of Deer Harbor off Wild Rose Lane—check the website for a trail map and detailed directions. ✉ *North Trailhead parking, Crow Valley Rd., just south of Crow Valley Schoolhouse* ☎ *360/378–4402* 🌐 *www.sjclandbank.org/turtle_back.html* 🎫 *Free.*

Restaurants

★ Doe Bay Cafe

$$$ | PACIFIC NORTHWEST | Most of the tables in this warmly rustic dining room at Doe Bay Resort overlook the tranquil body of water for which the café is named. This is a popular stop for brunch or dinner before or after hiking or biking in nearby Moran State Park—starting your day off with smoked-salmon Benedict with Calabrian-chili hollandaise sauce will provide you with plenty of fuel for recreation. **Known for:** locally sourced and foraged ingredients; smoked-salmon Benedict; funky, rustic vibe. 💲 *Average main: $23* ✉ *107 Doe Bay Rd.* ☎ *360/376–8059* 🌐 *www.doebay.com* 🕓 *Closed Tues.–Wed. Limited hrs Oct.–May; call ahead.*

★ Hogstone's Wood Oven

$$ | PIZZA | An intimate, minimalist space with large windows and just a handful of tables, this hip locavore-minded pizza joint (a James Beard Award semifinalist in 2019) serves wood-fired pies with creative toppings—consider the one with new potatoes, crispy pork fat, chickweed, cultured cream, and uncured garlic. The bounteous, farmers'-market-sourced salads are another strength, and the wine list, with varietals from the Northwest and Europe, is exceptional. **Known for:** wildly inventive pizzas with unusual toppings; extensive wine list; long wait on the weekend (reservations not accepted). 💲 *Average main: $22* ✉ *460 Main St.* ☎ *360/376–4647* 🌐 *www.hogstone.com* 🕓 *Closed Tues.–Wed. (check for winter hours).*

Inn at Ship Bay

$$$ | PACIFIC NORTHWEST | This restaurant at this stylish, contemporary inn just a mile from Eastsound offers among the most memorable dining experiences on the island. Tucked into a renovated 1869 farmhouse, the dining room and bar serve food that emphasizes local, seasonal ingredients. **Known for:** outstanding wine list; house-made sourdough bread made from a century-old starter yeast; ingredients from on-site garden and orchard. 💲 *Average main: $26* ✉ *326 Olga Rd.* ☎ *360/376–5886* 🌐 *www.innatshipbay.com* 🕓 *Closed Sun. and Mon. and mid-Dec.–mid-Mar. No lunch.*

The Kitchen

$ | ASIAN | Seating at this casual, affordable Asian restaurant adjacent to the distinctive boutiques of Prune Alley is in a compact dining room or, when the weather is nice, at open-air picnic tables in a tree-shaded garden. The pan-Asian food here is filling and simple, using local seafood and produce, with plenty of vegetarian options. **Known for:** hearty ramen and Thai noodle soups; sustainable practices; nice selection of craft brews on tap. 💲 *Average main: $10* ✉ *249 Prune*

Alley ☎ 360/376–6958 🌐 www.thekitchenorcas.com ⏲ Closed Sun.

Mansion Restaurant

$$$$ | **PACIFIC NORTHWEST** | For a special-occasion dinner (or lunch on weekends), it's worth the drive to this grandly romantic dining room inside the historic main inn at Rosario Resort, which recently tapped a heavy-hitter restaurant-industry veteran from San Francisco to oversee the dining program at the historic hotel. Though some changes are in store, you'll still be treated to polished service, sweeping bay views, and exquisitely plated seasonal Northwest cuisine. **Known for:** lovely views of Cascade Bay; dinner service in the mahogany-clad fireside Moran Lounge; small portions for the price. *$ Average main: $40 ✉ 1400 Rosario Rd. ☎ 360/376–2222 🌐 www.rosarioresort.com ⏲ No lunch Mon.–Thurs.*

Mijitas

$$ | **MEXICAN** | **FAMILY** | A bustling family-friendly Mexican restaurant with a cozy dining room and a sprawling shaded garden patio is helmed by Raul Rios, who learned to cook during his years growing up outside Mexico City. The flavorful food here isn't entirely authentic—expect a mix of Mexican and Mexican-American dishes, many featuring local ingredients. **Known for:** sweet, tangy margaritas; expansive garden patio; braised short ribs with blackberry mole sauce. *$ Average main: $21 ✉ 310 A St. ☎ 360/376–6722 ⏲ No lunch.*

Roses Bakery & Cafe

$$ | **MODERN AMERICAN** | Set inside a cheerfully renovated former Eastsound fire station, this bustling café known for its house-baked breads and an impressive selection of artisanal gourmet groceries (from cheeses to fine wines) is also a fine spot for breakfast or lunch. The fare is French-Italian influenced but using local ingredients: try the croque monsieur or house-cured gravlax in the morning. **Known for:** rhubarb galette with fennel ice cream; outstanding assortment of cheese, sweets, and wines to go; budget-friendly premade sandwiches for picnic lunches. *$ Average main: $19 ✉ 382 Prune Alley ☎ 🌐 www.rosesbakerycafe.com ⏲ No dinner.*

Hotels

★ Outlook Inn

$ | **HOTEL** | This nice range of accommodations in the center of Eastsound includes small budget-oriented rooms with twin beds and shared bathrooms, rooms with queen or double beds, and rambling bay-view suites with gas fireplaces, kitchenettes, and two-person Jacuzzi tubs. **Pros:** steps from Eastsound dining and shops (and great restaurant on-site); friendly and helpful staff; broad mix of rates. **Cons:** in-town location can be a little noisy; only some rooms have water view; least expensive rooms have shared bath. *$ Rooms from: $124 ✉ 171 Main St. ☎ 360/376–2200, 888/688–5665 🌐 www.outlookinn.com 54 rooms 🍽 No meals.*

★ Rosario Resort and Spa

$$ | **RESORT** | **FAMILY** | Shipbuilding magnate Robert Moran built this Arts and Crafts–style waterfront mansion in 1909, and it is now the centerpiece of a gorgeous 40-acre resort that comprises several different buildings with sweeping views of Cascade Bay and Rosario Point—accommodations range from moderately priced standard guest rooms to deluxe one- and two-bedroom suites with fireplaces, decks, and full kitchens. **Pros:** water views from all buildings and many rooms; management continues to make improvements; first-rate spa and adults-only pool. **Cons:** often busy with weddings and special events; some rooms/common spaces need updating; 15-minute drive to Eastsound. *$ Rooms from: $185 ✉ 1400 Rosario Rd. ☎ 360/376–2222, 800/562–8820 🌐 www.rosarioresort.com 67 rooms 🍽 No meals.*

Nightlife

★ The Barnacle

BARS/PUBS | This quirky hole-in-the-wall bar with an insider-y, speakeasy vibe is across the lawn from the Kitchen restaurant, and has developed a cult following for its sophisticated, well-made craft cocktails—many infused with house-made bitters and local herbs and berries—and interesting wines. On this quiet, early-to-bed island, it's a nice late-night option. Light tapas are served, too. ✉ *249 Prune Alley* ☎ *206/679–5683.*

Activities

BIKING

Mountain bikes rent for about $30 per day or $100 per week. Tandem, recumbent, and electric bikes rent for about $50 per day.

Wildlife Cycles

BICYCLING | This trusty shop rents bikes and can recommend great routes all over the island. ✉ *350 N Beach Rd.* ☎ *360/376–4708* 🌐 *www.wildlifecycles.com.*

BOATING AND SAILING

Kruger Escapes

BOATING | Three-hour day adventures and sunset cruises around the islands are offered on two handsome sailboats that were both designed and formerly used for racing. The boats are also available for multiday charters. ✉ *Orcas Island* ☎ *360/201–0586* 🌐 *www.krugerescapes.com.*

Orcas Boat Rentals

BOATING | You can rent a variety of sailboats, outboards, and skiffs for full- and half-day trips, as well as book custom charter cruises, with this company. ✉ *5164 Deer Harbor Rd.* ☎ *360/376–7616* 🌐 *www.orcasboatrentals.com.*

West Beach Resort Marina

BOATING | This is a good option for renting motorized boats, kayaks and canoes, and fishing gear on the island's northwest shore. The resort is also a popular spot for divers, who can fill their tanks here. ✉ *190 Waterfront Way* ☎ *360/376–2240, 877/937–8224* 🌐 *www.westbeachresort.com.*

SEA KAYAKING

All equipment is usually included in a rental package or tour. Three-hour trips cost around $80; day tours, $110 to $135.

Orcas Outdoors Sea Kayak Tours

KAYAKING | This outfitter offers one-, two-, and three-hour journeys, as well as day trips, overnight tours, and rentals. ✉ *Orcas Ferry Landing* ☎ *360/376–4611* 🌐 *www.orcasoutdoors.com.*

Shearwater Kayak Tours

KAYAKING | This established company holds kayaking classes and runs three-hour, day, and overnight tours from Rosario, Deer Harbor, West Beach, and Doe Bay resorts. ✉ *138 N Beach Rd.* ☎ *360/376–4699* 🌐 *www.shearwaterkayaks.com.*

WHALE-WATCHING

Cruises, which run about four hours, are scheduled daily in summer and once or twice weekly at other times. The cost is around $100 to $120 per person, and boats hold 20 to 40 people. Wear warm clothing and bring a snack.

Deer Harbor Charters

BOATING | This eco-friendly tour company (the first in the San Juans to use biodiesel) offers whale-watching cruises around the island straits, with departures from both Deer Harbor Marina and Rosario Resort. Outboards and skiffs are also available, as is fishing gear. ✉ *Deer Harbor Rd.* ☎ *360/376–5989, 800/544–5758* 🌐 *www.deerharborcharters.com.*

Orcas Island Eclipse Charters
WHALE-WATCHING | In addition to tours that search around Orcas Island for whale pods and other sea life, this charter company offers lighthouse tours. ✉ *Orcas Island Ferry Landing* ☎ *360/376–6566* 🌐 *www.orcasislandwhales.com.*

Shopping

Darvill's Bookstore
BOOKS/STATIONERY | This island favorite, with a coffee bar and a couple of cozy seats with panoramic views of the water, specializes in literary fiction and nautical literature. ✉ *296 Main St.* ☎ *360/376–2135* 🌐 *www.darvillsbookstore.com.*

★ Doe Bay Wine Co.
WINE/SPIRITS | Owned by an Orcas Island–born sommelier who worked at restaurants in Vail and Vegas before returning home, this cheerful little bottle shop and tasting room in Eastsound has a great selection of wine, beer, and cider from around the world, including a wine series, the Orcas Project, that is produced in collaboration with Pacific Northwest winemakers and artists. Sample flights of Orcas Project wines daily. ✉ *109 N Beach Rd.* ☎ 🌐 *www.doebaywinecompany.com.*

Island Thyme and Crow Valley Shop and Gallery
ART GALLERIES | This colorful shop/gallery in Eastsound's village sells locally made soap and skin-care products and hosts occasional gallery shows. ✉ *296 Main St.* ☎ *360/376–4260* 🌐 *www.crowvalley.com.*

Kathryn Taylor Chocolates
FOOD/CANDY | This sweet sweetshop in Eastsound village sells the creative bonbons (pistachio-fig, black raspberry) of Kathryn Taylor. It's also a good stop for ice cream and Stumptown coffee drinks. ✉ *68 N Beach Rd.* ☎ *360/376–1030* 🌐 *www.kathryntaylorchocolates.com.*

★ Orcas Island Artworks Gallery
ART GALLERIES | Stop by this cooperative gallery to see the impressive displays pottery, sculpture, jewelry, art glass, paintings, and quilts by resident artists, including an upstairs gallery devoted to current original paintings by well-known Northwest landscape artist James Hardman. You'll find gifts in a wide price range at this wonderful space. ✉ *11 Point Lawrence Rd.* ☎ *360/376–4408* 🌐 *www.orcasartworks.com.*

★ Orcas Island Pottery
ART GALLERIES | A stroll through the historic house, outbuildings, and gardens of this enchanting arts complex on a bluff overlooking President Channel and Waldron Island is more than just a chance to browse beautiful pottery—it's a great spot simply to relax and soak up the views. More than a dozen regular and guest potters exhibit and sell their wares here, everything from functional dinnerware and mugs to fanciful vases and wall hangings. ✉ *338 Old Pottery Rd.* ☎ *360/376–2813* 🌐 *www.orcasislandpottery.com.*

San Juan Island

45 mins by ferry from Orcas Island, 75–90 mins by ferry from Anacortes or Sidney, BC (near Victoria).

San Juan is the cultural and commercial hub of the archipelago that shares its name. Friday Harbor, the county seat, is larger, more vibrant, and more crowded than any of the towns on Orcas or Lopez, yet San Juan still has miles of rural roads, uncrowded beaches, and rolling woodlands. It's easy to get here, too, making San Juan the preferred destination for travelers who have time to visit only one island.

GETTING HERE AND AROUND

With ferry connections from both Anacortes and Sidney, BC (on Vancouver Island, near Victoria), San Juan is the most convenient of the islands to reach, and the island is easily explored by car; public transportation and bicycles also work but require a bit more effort. However, if you're staying in Friday Harbor, you can get from the ferry terminal to your hotel as well as to area shops and restaurants easily on foot.

AIR

One-hour flights from Seattle to San Juan Airport, Friday Harbor, or Roche Harbor cost about $130 to $170 each way.

BUS

San Juan Transit & Tours operates shuttle buses daily from mid-May to mid-September. Hop on at Friday Harbor, the main town, to get to all the island's significant points and parks, including the San Juan Vineyards, Krystal Acres Alpaca Farm, Lime Kiln Point State Park, and Snug Harbor and Roche Harbor resorts. Different buses call on different stops, so be sure to check the schedule before you plan your day. Tickets are $5 one-way or $15 for a day pass. From mid-June through mid-September, the Friday Harbor Jolly Trolley offers trips around the island—also stopping at all of the key attractions—in an old-fashioned trolley-style bus; tickets cost $20 and are good for the entire day.

CONTACT Friday Harbor Jolly Trolley. ☎ *360/298–8873* 🌐 *www.fridayharborjollytrolley.com.* **San Juan Transit & Tours.** ✉ *Cannery Landing, Friday Harbor* ☎ *360/378–8887* 🌐 *sanjuantransit.com.*

BOAT AND FERRY

The Washington State Ferries crossings from Anacortes to Friday Harbor takes about 75 to 90 minutes; round-trip fares in high season are about $14 per person, $65 for a car and driver. It's about the same distance from Sidney, BC, on Vancouver Island—this service is available twice daily in summer and once daily spring and fall (there's no BC service in winter). Round-trip fares are about $25 per person, $85 for car and driver. Clipper Navigation operates the passenger-only *San Juan Clipper* jet catamaran service between Pier 69 in Seattle and Friday Harbor. Boats leave Seattle daily mid-June–early September, Thursday–Monday mid-May–mid-June, and weekends early September–early October at 8:15 am and return from Friday Harbor at 5 pm; reservations are strongly recommended. During peak season, fares start at $160 for a round-trip ticket, depending on the day and whether you purchase in advance (advance tickets are cheaper). Clipper also offers optional whale-watching excursions, which can be combined with ferry passage.

■ TIP→ Some points on the west end of San Juan Island are so close to BC, Canada (which is visible across the Haro Straight), that cell phones switch to roaming; it's a good idea to turn roaming off while touring the island to avoid unexpected charges.

CONTACTS Clipper Navigation. ☎ *206/448–5000, 800/888–2535* 🌐 *www.clippervacations.com.*

ESSENTIALS

The San Juan Island Chamber of Commerce has a visitor center (open daily 10 to 4) in Friday Harbor where you can grab brochures and ask for advice.

VISITOR INFORMATION San Juan Island Chamber of Commerce. ✉ *165 1st St., Friday Harbor* ☎ *360/378–5240* 🌐 *www.sanjuanisland.org.*

Sights

Krystal Acres Alpaca Farm

FARM/RANCH | FAMILY | Kids and adults love admiring the more than 70 alpacas from South America at this sprawling 80-acre ranch on the west side of the island. The shop in the big barn displays beautiful, high-quality clothing and crafts, all handmade from alpaca hair. ✉ *152 Blazing Tree Rd., Friday Harbor* ☎ *360/378–6125* 🌐 *www.krystalacres.com* 🎟 *Free.*

Historic Roche Harbor on San Juan provides a seaside escape.

★ Lime Kiln Point State Park

NATIONAL/STATE PARK | FAMILY | To watch whales cavorting in Haro Strait, head to these 36 acres on San Juan's western side just 9 miles from Friday Harbor. A rocky coastal trail leads to lookout points and a little 1919 lighthouse. The best time to spot whales is from the end of April through September, but resident pods of orcas regularly cruise past the point. This park is also a beautiful spot to soak in a summer sunset, with expansive views of Vancouver Island and beyond. ✉ *1567 Westside Rd.* ☎ *360/378–2044* 🌐 *www.parks.wa.gov/parks* 🎫 *$10* 🕑 *Interpretive center closed mid-Sept.–late May.*

Pelindaba Lavender Farm

FARM/RANCH | FAMILY | Wander a spectacular 20-acre valley smothered with endless rows of fragrant purple-and-gold lavender blossoms. The oils are distilled for use in therapeutic, botanical, and household products, all created on-site. The farm hosts the very popular San Juan Island Lavender Festival in mid- to late July. If you can't make it to the farm, stop at the outlet in the Friday Harbor Center at 150 1st Street, where you can buy their products and sample delicious lavender-infused baked goods, ice cream, and beverages. ✉ *33 Hawthorne La., Friday Harbor* ☎ *360/378–4248, 866/819–1911* 🌐 *www.pelindabalavender.com* 🎫 *Free* 🕑 *Closed Nov.–Apr.*

★ Roche Harbor

TOWN | FAMILY | It's hard to believe that fashionable Roche Harbor at the northern end of San Juan Island was once the most important producer of builder's lime on the West Coast. In 1882, John S. McMillin gained control of the lime company and expanded production. But even in its heyday as a limestone quarrying village, Roche Harbor was known for abundant flowers and welcoming accommodations. McMillin's former home is now a restaurant, and workers' cottages have been transformed into comfortable visitors' lodgings. With its rose gardens, cobblestone waterfront, and well-manicured lawns, Roche Harbor retains the flavor of its days as a hangout for McMillin's powerful friends—especially since the sheltered harbor is very popular with well-to-do pleasure boaters. *End of Roche Harbor Rd.* *www.rocheharbor.com.*

★ San Juan Island National Historic Park

NATIONAL/STATE PARK | **FAMILY** | Fortifications and other 19th-century military installments commemorate the Pig War, in which the United States and Great Britain nearly went into battle over their respective claims on the San Juan Islands. The park comprises two separate areas on opposite sides of the island. English Camp, in a sheltered cove of Garrison Bay on the northern end, includes a blockhouse, a commissary, and barracks. American Camp, on the southern end, has a visitor center and the remains of fortifications; it stretches along driftwood-strewn beaches. Great views greet you from the top of the Mt. Finlayson Trail—if you're lucky, you might be able to see Mt. Baker and Mt. Rainier along with the Olympics. From June to August you can take guided hikes and see reenactments of 1860s-era military life. *Park headquarters, 125 Spring St., American Camp, 6 miles southeast of Friday Harbor; English Camp, 9 miles northwest of Friday Harbor, Friday Harbor* *360/378–2240* *www.nps.gov/sajh* *Free* *American Camp visitor center closed mid-Dec.–Feb. English Camp visitor center closed early Sept.–late May.*

San Juan Islands Museum of Art

MUSEUM | Housed in a sleek, contemporary building, SJIMA presents rotating art shows and exhibits with an emphasis on island and Northwest artists, including the highly touted Artists' Registry Show in winter, which features works by nearly 100 San Juan Islands artists.

Housed in a sleek, contemporary building, SJIMA presents rotating art shows and exhibits with an emphasis on island and Northwest artists, including the highly touted Artists' Registry Show in winter, which features works by nearly 100 San Juan Islands artists. *540 Spring St., Friday Harbor* *360/370–5050* *www.sjima.org* *$10* *Closed Tue.–Wed. in summer, Tue.–Thu. off season.*

San Juan Islands Sculpture Park

PUBLIC ART | **FAMILY** | At this serene 20-acre park near Roche Harbor, you can stroll along five winding trails to view more than 150 colorful, in many cases large-scale sculptures spread amid freshwater and saltwater wetlands, open woods, blossoming fields, and rugged terrain. The park is also a haven for birds; more than 120 species nest and breed here. It's a great spot for picnicking, and dogs are welcome. *Roche Harbor Rd., just before entrance to Roche Harbor Resort, Roche Harbor* *www.sjisculpturepark.com* *$5 donation recommended.*

San Juan Historical Museum

MUSEUM | This museum in an old farmhouse presents island life at the turn of the 20th century through historic photography, documents, and buildings. *405 Price St., Friday Harbor* *360/378–3949* *www.sjmuseum.org* *$5* *Closed Nov.–Mar. except by appointment.*

San Juan Vineyard

WINERY/DISTILLERY | A remodeled 1895 schoolhouse serving estate-grown wines, this picturesque winery is worth a visit for the scenery and its award-winning Siegerrebe and Madeleine Angevine varietals (the winery belongs to the Puget Sound AVA, the coolest-climate growing region in Washington State). In 2018, the winery was purchased by new owners who also own other wineries and vineyards in Eastern Washington. The vineyard's wines show up on many local menus. *3136 Roche Harbor Rd.* *360/378–9463* *www.sanjuanvineyard.com.*

Whale Museum

MUSEUM | FAMILY | A dramatic exterior mural depicting several types of whales welcomes you into a world that is all about these behemoth beauties. Visitors will find models of whales and large whale skeletons, recordings of whale sounds, videos of whales, and information about the plight of the three local orca pods. Head around to the back of the first-floor gift shop to view maps of the latest orca trackings in the area. ✉ *62 1st St. N, Friday Harbor* ☎ *360/378–4710* 🌐 *www.whalemuseum.org* 🎟 *$9.*

Restaurants

★ Backdoor Kitchen

$$$ | ECLECTIC | This local favorite has become well-known beyond the San Juans, thanks to the stellar service and inventive, globally inspired cuisine and craft cocktails. As the name might indicate, it's a bit hard to find, tucked in an elegant courtyard a few blocks uphill from the water, but worth the search for dishes that include pan-seared scallops with ginger-sake beurre blanc, and pork chops topped with a poblano–goat cheese sauce and served with caramelized onions and smoked bacon. **Known for:** "noodle Bowl Monday" lunch specials; some of the best pan-Asian dishes on the island; relaxing and scenic outdoor dining in a landscaped courtyard. $ *Average main: $23* ✉ *400b A St., Friday Harbor* ☎ *360/378–9540* 🌐 *www.backdoorkitchen.com* 🕒 *Closed Mon., Tues., and additional days in winter; call off-season. No lunch Tues.–Sun.*

Downriggers

$$$ | PACIFIC NORTHWEST | This snazzy, contemporary, seafood-driven restaurant overlooking the harbor is helmed by one of the most celebrated chefs in the islands, Aaron Rock. The light-filled dining room is a terrific spot to watch boats and ferries come and go while sampling such tempting fare as Penn Cove mussels and pan-seared sockeye salmon with sweet-corn grits, and caramel-chicken and ginger-spiced waffles drizzled with warm honey. **Known for:** pub fare with creative twists; extensive list of craft cocktails; Asian-inspired chicken and waffles. $ *Average main: $23* ✉ *10 Front St., Friday Harbor* ☎ *360/378–2700* 🌐 *www.downriggerssanjuan.com.*

Ernie's Cafe

$ | ECLECTIC | Ask a local for the best lunch recommendation in town, and you may be surprised by the answer—plenty of folks will send you to this casual diner at the airport, where you can watch planes take off while you eat. You'll find a few Asian-fusion dishes on the menu, including Korean-style *bulgogi* (grilled marinated beef), and hearty noodle bowls, plus diner classics like hefty cheeseburgers, breakfast sandwiches, and flaky popovers. **Known for:** popovers at breakfast; several Korean-inspired dishes; watching airplanes. $ *Average main: $12* ✉ *744 Airport Circle Dr., Friday Harbor* ☎ *360/378–6605* 🕒 *Closed weekends. No dinner.*

★ Restaurant at Friday Harbor House

$$$ | PACIFIC NORTHWEST | Ingenuity and dedication to local ingredients are hallmarks of this stylish, contemporary restaurant, where locals and tourists alike come for dishes such as baked oysters, mushroom panzanella, San Juan Island–raised lamb shoulder cooked in fig leaves, and a popular house burger; during the summer, the hotel's outdoor Raw Bar serves up seafood and frozen cocktails. The brunch burger, topped with a fried egg and green-tomato-and-bacon jam, and breakfast poutine with duck confit and cheese curds make for decadent starts to your day. **Known for:** excellent cocktails with unique ingredients; a popular daily breakfast (until noon on the weekend); panoramic views of Friday Harbor. $ *Average main: $30* ✉ *Friday Harbor House, 130 West St., Friday Harbor* ☎ *360/378–8455* 🌐 *www.fridayharborhouse.com* 🕒 *No dinner Tues. and Wed.*

Coffee and Quick Bites

Bakery San Juan
$ | **BAKERY** | The fabulous aroma lets you know you're in for a treat at this popular island bakery, which makes fresh bread, cakes and pastries, sandwiches, and pizza. **Known for:** wild-yeasted baked goods; nice place for morning coffee. *Average main: $6* *775 Mullis St.* *360/378–5810.*

Hotels

★ Friday Harbor House
$$$$ | **HOTEL** | At this bluff-top getaway with floor-to-ceiling windows, sleek, modern wood furnishings, and fabrics in beige hues fill the rooms—all of which have gas fireplaces, deep jetted tubs, Chemex pour-over coffee carafes, and at least partial views of the marina, ferry landing, and San Juan Channel below (the ferries are especially enjoyable to watch dock after dark, when they're all lit up). **Pros:** some room views are breathtaking (request at booking); excellent restaurant and bar with views; free parking and just steps from downtown shopping and dining. **Cons:** two-night minimum at peak season; among the priciest hotels in the San Juan Islands; some early-morning noise from the ferry landing. *Rooms from: $429* *130 West St., Friday Harbor* *360/378–8455, 866/722–7356* *www.fridayharborhouse.com* *23 rooms* *Free Breakfast.*

★ Island Inn at 123 West
$$$ | **HOTEL** | There's a pretty striking contrast of accommodation styles at this cosmopolitan complex that tumbles down a hillside overlooking Friday Harbor, from intimate Euro-style rooms that lack exterior windows to expansive suites with water views to ginormous bilevel penthouses with two bedrooms, private decks, gorgeous full kitchens, and astounding views. **Pros:** penthouse suites are great for luxurious family getaways; Euro-style standard rooms are a good deal; handy in-town location. **Cons:** suites are quite spendy; standard rooms have no views; no on-site dining. *Rooms from: $279* *123 West St., Friday Harbor* *360/378–4400, 877/512–9262* *www.123west.com* *16 rooms* *No meals.*

Kirk House Bed & Breakfast
$$$ | **B&B/INN** | Rooms are all differently decorated in this 1907 Craftsman bungalow, the one-time summer home of steel magnate Peter Kirk: the Garden Room has a botanical motif, the sunny Trellis Room is done in soft shades of yellow and green, and the Arbor Room has French doors leading out to the garden. **Pros:** gorgeous house full of stained glass and other lovely details; within walking distance of town; nice breakfast in the parlor or in bed served on Limoges china. **Cons:** occasional noise from nearby airport; a couple of the rooms are on the small side; with only 4 rooms, inn itself may feel too cozy for some. *Rooms from: $245* *595 Park St., Friday Harbor* *360/378–3757, 800/639–2762* *www.kirkhouse.net* *4 rooms* *Free Breakfast.*

★ Lakedale Resort at Three Lakes
$$$ | **RESORT** | **FAMILY** | This 82-acre property may not have invented glamping, but it was one of the first to nail the travel trend, and the resort's hip 450-square-foot yurts—which share a private lakefront beach and fire pit—are as luxurious as they come, with fireplaces, kitchenettes, spacious bathrooms, and private decks with hot tubs; other options include real log cabins and the lodge, which sits on a scenic lake frequented by swans and geese. **Pros:** pretty grounds and fun amenities; close to Friday Harbor but feels secluded; serene hotel rooms at the lakefront lodge (16 and up only) were just renovated. **Cons:** some noise from nearby Roche Harbor Road; the grounds include a lot of camping spots, so the resort can feel crowded; books up way in advance. *Rooms from: $295* *4313 Roche Harbor Rd.*

☎ *360/378–2350* 🌐 *www.lakedale.com* 🛏 *10 rooms, 7 yurts, 6 cabins* 🍽 *Free Breakfast.*

★ Roche Harbor Resort
$$$ | RESORT | This sprawling resort, with several types of accommodations ranging from historic hotel rooms to luxurious contemporary waterfront suites, occupies the site of the lime works that made John S. McMillin his fortune in the late 19th century. **Pros:** lots of different options for families and groups; several on-site restaurants; gorgeous full-service spa. **Cons:** condos have less character and are away from the waterfront; a bit isolated from the rest of the island if you don't have a car; the least expensive rooms in Hotel de Haro have shared baths. $ *Rooms from: $277* ✉ *248 Reuben Memorial Dr., Roche Harbor* ☎ *360/378–2155, 800/451–8910* 🌐 *www.rocheharbor.com* 🛏 *16 rooms, 18 suites, 9 cottages, 20 condos* 🍽 *No meals.*

Activities

BEACHES

San Juan County Park
BEACH—SIGHT | You'll find a wide gravel beachfront at this park 10 miles west of Friday Harbor, overlooking waters where orcas often frolic in summer, plus grassy lawns with picnic tables and a small campground. **Amenities:** parking (free); toilets. **Best for:** walking. ✉ *380 Westside Rd., Friday Harbor* ☎ *360/378–8420* 🌐 *www.co.san-juan.wa.us.*

South Beach at American Camp
BEACH—SIGHT | This 2-mile public beach on the southern end of the island is part of San Juan Island National Historical Park. **Amenities:** parking (free); toilets. **Best for:** solitude; walking. ✉ *Off Cattle Point Rd.* 🌐 *www.nps.gov/sajh.*

BIKING

You can rent standard, mountain, and BMX bikes for $40 to $50 per day or about $200 to $240 per week. Tandem, recumbent, and electric-assist bikes rent for about $55 to $80 per day.

Discovery Adventure Tours
BICYCLING | The noted Friday Harbor outfitter (aka Discovery Sea Kayaks) also rents conventional road bikes and electric-assist bikes. ✉ *260 Spring St., Friday Harbor* ☎ *360/378–2559, 866/461–2559* 🌐 *www.discoveryadventuretours.com.*

Island Bicycles
BICYCLING | This full-service shop rents bikes. ✉ *380 Argyle Ave., Friday Harbor* ☎ *360/378–4941* 🌐 *www.islandbicycles.com.*

BOATING AND SAILING

At public docks, high-season moorage rates are $1.10 to $2.10 per foot (of vessel) per night.

Port of Friday Harbor
BOATING | The marina at the island's main port offers guest moorage, vessel assistance and repair, bareboat and skippered charters, overnight accommodations, and wildlife- and whale-watching cruises. ✉ *204 Front St., Friday Harbor* ☎ *360/378–2688* 🌐 *www.portfridayharbor.org.*

Roche Harbor Marina
BOATING | The marina at Roche Harbor Resort has a fuel dock, pool, grocery, and other guest services. ✉ *248 Reuben Memorial Dr., Roche Harbor* ☎ *360/378–2155* 🌐 *www.rocheharbor.com.*

Snug Harbor Resort Marina
BOATING | This well-located marina adjoins a popular, upscale small resort. It provides van service to and from Friday Harbor and rents small powerboats. ✉ *1997 Mitchell Bay Rd., Friday Harbor* ☎ *360/378–4762* 🌐 *www.snugresort.com.*

SEA KAYAKING

Crystal Seas Kayaking
KAYAKING | Sunset trips and multisport tours that might include biking, kayaking, yoga, and camping are among the options with this respected guide

company. ✉ *40 Spring St., Friday Harbor* ☎ *360/378–4223, 877/732–7877* 🌐 *www.crystalseas.com.*

Discovery Sea Kayaks
KAYAKING | This outfitter offers both sea-kayaking adventures, including sunset trips and multiday excursions and whale-watching paddles. ✉ *260 Spring St., Friday Harbor* ☎ *360/378–2559, 866/461–2559* 🌐 *www.discoveryseakayak.com.*

San Juan Kayak Expeditions
KAYAKING | This reputable company has been running kayaking and camping tours in two-person kayaks since 1980. ✉ *85 Front St., Friday Harbor* ☎ *360/378–4436* 🌐 *www.sanjuankayak.com.*

Sea Quest Expeditions
KAYAKING | Kayak eco-tours with guides who are trained naturalists, biologists, and environmental scientists are available through this popular outfitter. ✉ *Friday Harbor* ☎ *360/378–5767, 888/589–4253* 🌐 *www.sea-quest-kayak.com.*

WHALE-WATCHING

Whale-watching expeditions usually run three to four hours and cost around $100–$120 per person. Note that tours departing from San Juan Island typically get you to the best whale-watching waters faster than those departing from the mainland. ■ **TIP→ For the best experience, look for tour companies with small boats that carry under 30 people**. Bring warm clothing even if it's a warm day.

★ **Maya's Legacy Whale Watching**
WHALE-WATCHING | These informative tours on small, modern, and speedy boats ensure great views for every passengers; departures are from Friday Harbor and Snug Harbor Marina. ✉ *14 Cannery Landing, Friday Harbor* ☎ *360/378–7996* 🌐 *www.sanjuanislandwhalewatch.com.*

San Juan Excursions
WHALE-WATCHING | Whale-watching cruises are offered aboard a converted 1941 U.S. Navy research vessel. ✉ *40 Spring St., Friday Harbor* ☎ *360/378–6636, 800/809–4253* 🌐 *www.watchwhales.com.*

San Juan Island Whale & Wildlife Tours
WHALE-WATCHING | Tours from Friday Harbor leave daily at noon and are led by highly knowledgeable marine experts. ✉ *1 Front St., Friday Harbor* ☎ *360/298–0012* 🌐 *www.sanjuanislandwhales.com.*

Western Prince Whale & Wildlife Tours
WHALE-WATCHING | Narrated whale-watching tours last three to four hours. ✉ *1 Spring St., Friday Harbor* ☎ *360/378–5315, 800/757–6722* 🌐 *www.orcawhalewatch.com.*

Shopping

Friday Harbor is the main shopping area, with dozens of shops selling a variety of art, crafts, and clothing created by residents, as well as a bounty of island-grown produce.

Arctic Raven Gallery
ART GALLERIES | The specialty here is Northwest native art, including scrimshaw and wood carvings. ✉ *130 S. 1st St., Friday Harbor* ☎ *360/378–3433* 🌐 *www.arcticravengalleryfridayharbor.com.*

San Juan Island Farmers Market
OUTDOOR/FLEA/GREEN MARKETS | From April through October, this open-air market with more than 30 vendors selling local produce and crafts takes place at Friday Harbor Brickworks on Saturdays from 9:30 to 1. The market is also open once or twice a month on Saturdays in winter; check the website for the schedule. ✉ *150 Nichols St., Friday Harbor* 🌐 *www.sjifarmersmarket.com.*

Chapter 13

OLYMPIC NATIONAL PARK

Updated by
Shelly Arenas

Sights ★★★★★
Restaurants ★☆☆☆☆
Hotels ★★☆☆☆
Shopping ☆☆☆☆☆
Nightlife ☆☆☆☆☆

WELCOME TO OLYMPIC NATIONAL PARK

TOP REASONS TO GO

★ **Exotic rain forest:** A rain forest in the Pacific Northwest? Indeed, Olympic National Park is one of the few places in the world with this unique temperate landscape.

★ **Beachcombing:** Miles of rugged, spectacular coastline hemmed with sea stacks and tidal pools edge the driftwood-strewn shores of the Olympic Peninsula.

★ **Nature's hot tubs:** A dip in Sol Duc's natural geothermal mineral pools offers a secluded spa experience in the wooded heart of the park.

★ **Lofty vistas:** The hardy can hike up meadowed foothill trails or climb the frosty peaks throughout the Olympics—or just drive up to Hurricane Ridge for endless views.

★ **A sense of history:** Native American history is key to this region, where eight tribes have traditional ties to the park lands—there's 12,000 years of history to explore.

1 Coastal Olympic. Here the Pacific smashes endlessly into the rugged coastline, carving out some of the park's most memorable scenes in the massive, rocky sea stacks and islets just offshore. Back from the water are beaches and tide pools full of sea stars, crabs, and anemones.

2 The Rain Forest. Centered on the Hoh, Queets, and Quinault river valleys, this is the region's most unique landscape. Fog-shrouded Douglas firs and Sitka spruces, some more than 300 feet tall, huddle in this moist, pine-carpeted area, shading fern- and moss-draped cedars, maples, and alders.

3 The Mountains. Craggy gray peaks and snow-covered summits dominate the skyline. Low-level foliage and wildflower meadows make for excellent hiking in the plateaus. Even on the sunniest days, temperatures are brisk. Some roads are closed in winter months.

4 Alpine Meadows. In midsummer wildlife teems among the honeyed flowers. Trails are never prettier, and views are crisp and vast.

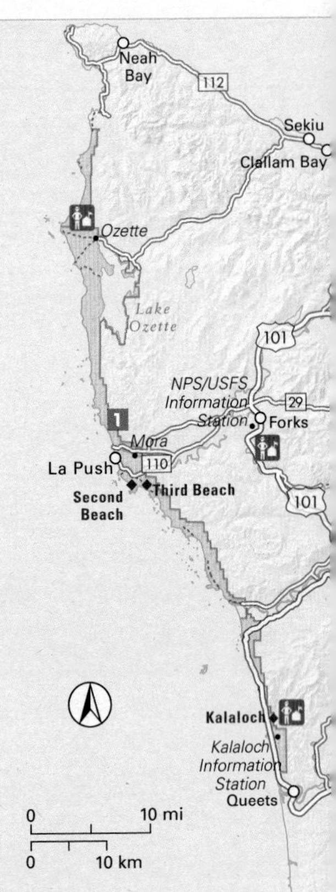

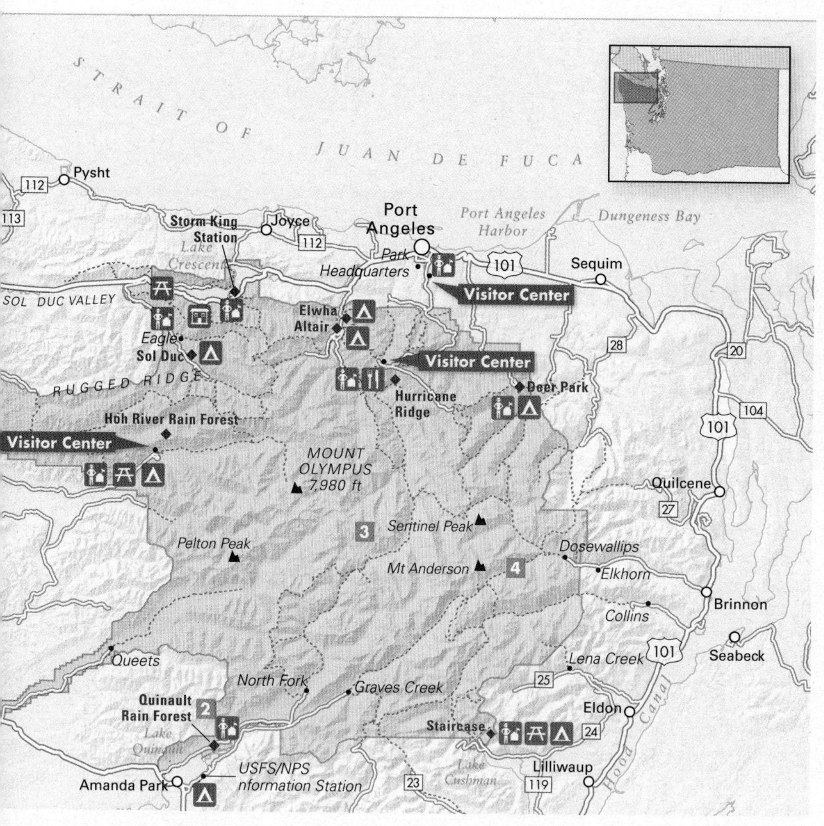
STRAIT OF JUAN DE FUCA
Pysht
Storm King Station
Joyce
Lake Crescent
Port Angeles
Park Headquarters
Visitor Center
Port Angeles Harbor
Dungeness Bay
Sequim
SOL DUC VALLEY
Elwha
Altair
Eagle
Sol Duc
Visitor Center
Hurricane Ridge
Deer Park
RUGGED RIDGE
Hoh River Rain Forest
Visitor Center
MOUNT OLYMPUS 7,980 ft
Quilcene
Sentinel Peak
Pelton Peak
Dosewallips
Mt Anderson
Elkhorn
Brinnon
Collins
Seabeck
Queets
Lena Creek
North Fork
Graves Creek
Quinault Rain Forest
Lake Quinault
Eldon
Staircase
Hood Canal
Lake Cushman
Lilliwaup
Amanda Park
USFS/NPS nformation Station

Edged on all sides by water, the forested landscape is remote and pristine, and works its way around the sharpened ridges of the snowcapped Olympic Mountains. Big lakes cut pockets of blue in the rugged blanket of pine forests.

Planning

When to Go

Summer, with its long stretches of sun-filled days, is prime touring time for Olympic National Park. June through September are the peak months; Hurricane Ridge, the Hoh Rain Forest, Lake Crescent, and Ruby Beach are bustling by 10 am.

Late spring and early autumn are also good bets for clear weather; anytime between April and October, you'll have a good chance of fair skies. Between Thanksgiving and Easter, it's a toss-up as to which days will turn out fair; prepare for heavy clouds, rain showers, and chilly temperatures, then hope for the best.

Winter is a great time to visit if you enjoy isolation. Locals are usually the only hardy souls here during this time, except for weekend skiers heading to the snowfields around Hurricane Ridge. Many visitor facilities have limited hours or are closed from October to April.

Planning Your Time

OLYMPIC IN ONE DAY

Start at the **Lake Quinault Lodge** in the park's southwest corner. From here, drive a half hour into the Quinault Valley via **South Shore Road.** Tackle the forested **Graves Creek Trail,** then head up **North Shore Road** to the Quinault Rain Forest Interpretive Trail. Next, head back to U.S. 101 and drive to **Ruby Beach,** where a shoreline walk presents a breathtaking scene of sea stacks and sparkling, pink-hue sands.

Forks and its **Timber Museum** are your next stop; have lunch here, then drive 20 minutes to the beach at **La Push.** Next, head to **Lake Crescent** around the corner to the northeast, where you can rent a boat, take a swim, or enjoy a picnic next to the sparkling teal waters. Drive through **Port Angeles** to **Hurricane Ridge**; count on an hour's drive from bottom to top if there aren't too many visitors. At the ridge, explore the visitor center or hike the 3-mile loop to **Hurricane Hill,** where you can see over the entire park north to Vancouver Island and south past Mt. Olympus.

Good Reads

■ Robert L. Wood's *Olympic Mountains Trail Guide* is a great resource for both day hikers and those planning longer excursions.

■ Craig Romano's *Day Hiking Olympic Peninsula: National Park/Coastal Beaches/Southwest Washington* is a detailed guide to day hikes in and around the national park.

■ Stephen Whitney's *A Field Guide to the Cascades and Olympics* is an excellent trailside reference, covering more than 500 plant and animal species found in the park.

■ The park's newspaper, the *Olympic Bugler*, is a seasonal guide for activities and opportunities in the park. You can pick it up at the visitor centers.

■ A handy online catalog of books, maps, and passes for northwest parks is available from Discover Your Northwest (🌐 *www.discovernw.org*).

Getting Here and Around

You can enter the park at a number of points, but because the park is 95% wilderness, access roads do not penetrate far. The best way to get around and to see many of the park's top sights is on foot.

AIR

Seattle–Tacoma International Airport is the nearest airport to Olympic National Park. It's roughly a two-hour drive from the park.

BOAT

Ferries provide another unique (though indirect) link to the Olympic area from Seattle; contact **Washington State Ferries** (☎ *800/843–3779, 206/464–6400* 🌐 *www.wsdot.wa.gov/ferries*) for information.

BUS

Grays Harbor Transit runs buses Monday through Saturday from Aberdeen and Hoquiam to Amanda Park, on the west end of Lake Quinault. Jefferson Transit operates a Forks–Amanda Park route Monday through Saturday.

BUS CONTACTS Grays Harbor Transit. ☎ *360/532–2770, 800/562–9730* 🌐 *www.ghtransit.com*. **Jefferson Transit.** ☎ *800/371–0497, 360/385–4777* 🌐 *www.jeffersontransit.com*.

CAR

U.S. 101 essentially encircles the main section of Olympic National Park, and a number of roads lead from the highway into the park's mountains and toward its beaches. You can reach U.S. 101 via Interstate 5 at Olympia, via Route 12 at Aberdeen, or via Route 104 from the Washington state ferry terminals at Bainbridge or Kingston.

Park Essentials

ACCESSIBILITY

There are wheelchair-accessible facilities—including trails, campgrounds, and visitor centers—throughout the park; contact visitor centers for information.

ADMISSION FEES AND PERMITS

Seven-day vehicle admission is $25; an annual pass is $50. Individuals arriving on foot, bike, or motorcycle pay $10. An overnight wilderness permit, available at visitor centers and ranger stations, is $7 per person per night. An annual wilderness camping permit costs $45. Fishing in freshwater streams and lakes within Olympic National Park does not require a Washington state fishing license; however, anglers must acquire a salmon-steelhead catch record card when fishing for those species. Ocean fishing and harvesting shellfish require licenses, which are available at sporting-goods and outdoor-supply stores.

ADMISSION HOURS

Six park entrances are open 24/7; gate kiosk hours (for buying passes) vary according to season and location, but most are staffed during daylight hours. Olympic National Park is in the Pacific time zone.

CELL PHONE RECEPTION

Note that cell reception is sketchy in wilderness areas. There are public telephones at the Olympic National Park Visitor Center, Hoh Rain Forest Visitor Center, and lodging properties within the park—Lake Crescent, Kalaloch, and Sol Duc Hot Springs. Fairholme General Store also has a phone.

Restaurants

The major resorts are your best bets for eating out in the park. Each has a main restaurant, café, and/or kiosk, as well as casually upscale dinner service, with regional seafood, meat, and produce complemented by a range of microbrews and good Washington and international wines. Reservations are either recommended or required.

Outside the park, small, easygoing cafés and bistros line the main thoroughfares in Sequim, Port Angeles, and Port Townsend, offering cuisine that ranges from hearty American-style fare to more eclectic local flavor.

Hotels

Major park resorts run from good to terrific, with generally comfortable rooms, excellent facilities, and easy access to trails, beaches, and activity centers. Midsize accommodations, like Sol Duc Hot Springs Resort, are often shockingly rustic—but remember, you're here for the park, not for the rooms.

The towns around the park have motels, hotels, and resorts for every budget. For a full beach-town vacation experience, base yourself in a home or cottage in the coastal community of Seabrook (near Pacific Beach). Sequim and Port Angeles have many attractive, friendly B&Bs, plus lots of inexpensive chain hotels and motels. Forks has mostly motels, with a few guesthouses on the fringes of town.

Hotel reviews have been shortened. For full information, visit Fodors.com.

Visitor Information

PARK CONTACT INFORMATION Olympic National Park. ✉ *Olympic National Park Visitor Center, 3002 Mount Angeles Rd., Port Angeles* ☎ *360/565–3130* 🌐 *www.nps.gov/olym.*

VISITOR CENTERS

Hoh Rain Forest Visitor Center

INFO CENTER | Pick up park maps and pamphlets, permits, and activities lists in this busy, woodsy chalet; there's also a shop and exhibits on natural history. Several short interpretive trails and longer wilderness treks start from here. ✉ *Hoh Valley Rd., Forks* ✣ *31 miles south of Forks* ☎ *360/374–6925* 🌐 *www.nps.gov/olym/planyourvisit/visitorcenters.htm* ⏲ *Closed Jan.–Feb., and Mon.–Thurs. off-season.*

Hurricane Ridge Visitor Center

INFO CENTER | The upper level of this visitor center has exhibits and nice views; the lower level has a gift shop and snack bar. Guided walks and programs start in late June. In winter, find details on the surrounding ski and sledding slopes and take guided snowshoe walks. ✉ *Hurricane Ridge Rd.* ☎ *360/565–3131 for road conditions* 🌐 *www.nps.gov/olym/planyourvisit/visitorcenters.htm* ⏲ *Operating hrs/days vary off-season.*

Olympic National Park Visitor Center

INFO CENTER | This modern, well-organized facility, staffed by park rangers, provides everything: maps, trail brochures, campground advice, weather forecasts, listings of wildlife sightings, educational programs and exhibits, information on road and trail closures, and a gift shop. ✉ *3002 Mount Angeles Rd., Port Angeles* ☎ *360/565–3130* 🌐 *www.nps.gov/olym/planyourvisit/visitorcenters.htm.*

South Shore Quinault Ranger Station

INFO CENTER | The National Forest Service's ranger station near the Lake Quinault Lodge has maps, campground information, and program listings. ✉ *353 S Shore Rd., Quinault* ☎ *360/288–2525* 🌐 *www.fs.usda.gov/main/olympic/home* ⏲ *Closed weekends after Labor Day until Memorial Day weekend.*

Wilderness Information Center (WIC)

INFO CENTER | Located behind Olympic National Park Visitor Center, this facility provides all the information you'll need for a trip in the park, including trail conditions, safety tips, and weather bulletins. The office also issues camping permits, takes campground reservations, and rents bear-proof food canisters. ✉ *3002 Mount Angeles Rd., Port Angeles* ☎ *360/565–3100* 🌐 *www.nps.gov/olym/planyourvisit/wic.htm* ⏲ *Hrs vary during off-season.*

Sights

Most of the park's attractions are found either off U.S. 101 or down trails that require hikes of 15 minutes or longer. The west-coast beaches are linked to the highway by downhill tracks; the number of cars parked alongside the road at the start of the paths indicates how crowded the beach will be.

SCENIC DRIVES

★ Port Angeles Visitor Center to Hurricane Ridge

VIEWPOINT | The premier scenic drive in Olympic National Park is a steep ribbon of curves that climbs from thickly forested foothills and subalpine meadows into the upper stretches of pine-swathed peaks. At the top, the visitor center at Hurricane Ridge has some spectacular views over the heart of the peninsula and across the Strait of Juan de Fuca. A mile past the visitor center, there are picnic tables in open meadows with photo-worthy views of the mountains to the east. Hurricane Ridge also has an uncommonly fine display of wildflowers in spring and summer. In winter, vehicles must carry chains, and the road is usually open Friday to Sunday only (call first to check conditions). ✉ *Olympic National Park* 🌐 *www.nps.gov/olym.*

HISTORIC SITES

La Push

BEACH—SIGHT | At the mouth of Quileute River, La Push is the tribal center of the Quileute Indians. In fact, the town's name is a variation on the French *la bouche,* which means "the mouth." Offshore rock spires known as sea stacks dot the coast here, and you may catch a glimpse of bald eagles nesting in the nearby cliffs. ✉ *Rte. 110, La Push* ✥ *14 miles west of Forks* 🌐 *www.nps.gov/olym/planyourvisit/upload/mora.pdf.*

Lake Ozette

BEACH—SIGHT | The third-largest glacial impoundment in Washington anchors the coastal strip of Olympic National Park at its north end. The small town of Ozette, home to a coastal tribe, is the trailhead for two of the park's better one-day hikes. Both 3-mile trails lead over boardwalks through swampy wetland and coastal old-growth forest to the ocean shore and uncrowded beaches. ✉ *Ozette* ✥ *At end of Hoko-Ozette Rd., 26 miles southwest*

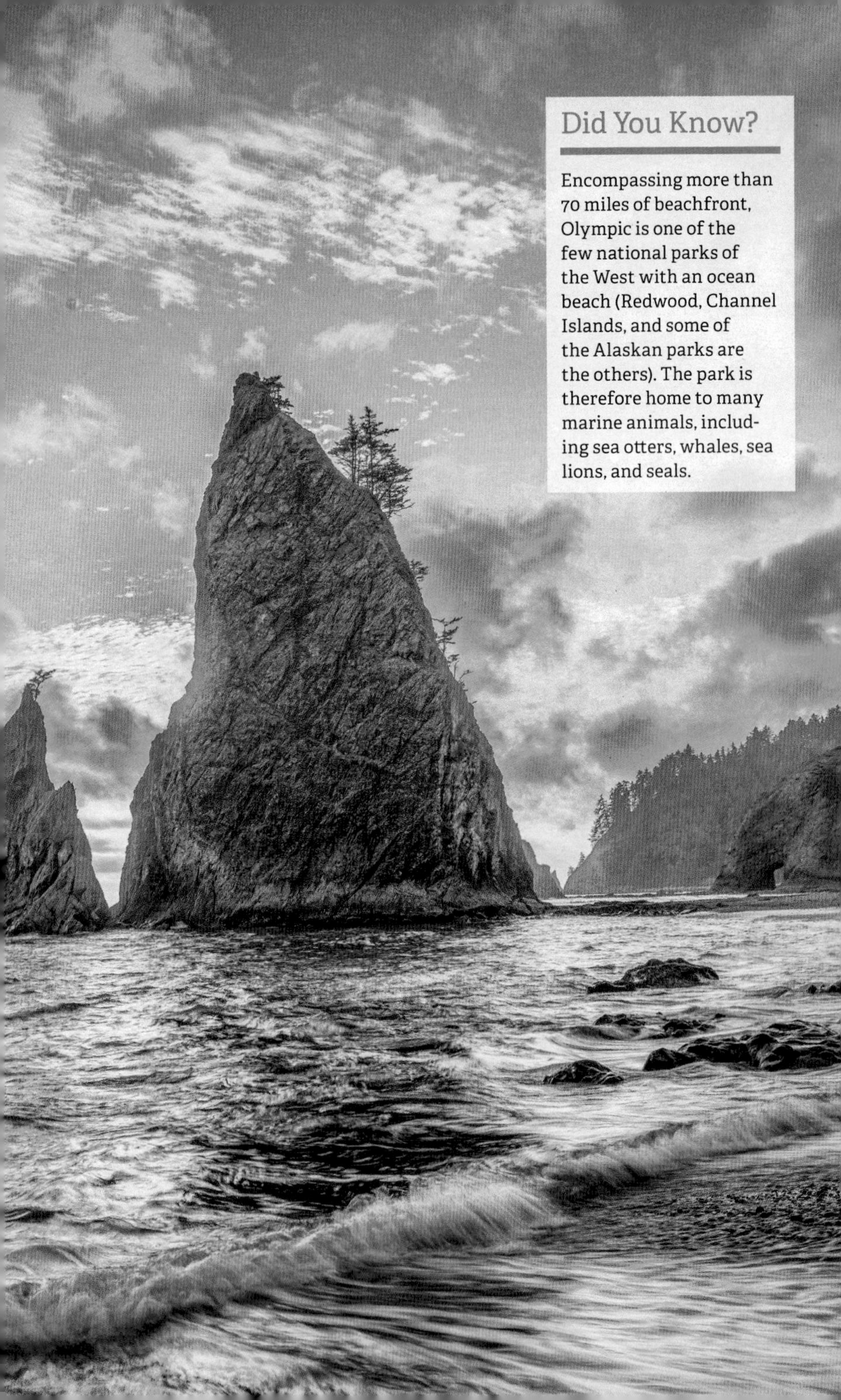

Did You Know?

Encompassing more than 70 miles of beachfront, Olympic is one of the few national parks of the West with an ocean beach (Redwood, Channel Islands, and some of the Alaskan parks are the others). The park is therefore home to many marine animals, including sea otters, whales, sea lions, and seals.

Plants and Wildlife in Olympic

Along the high mountain slopes hardy cedar, fir, and hemlock trees stand tough on the rugged land; the lower montane forests are filled with thickets of silver firs; and valleys stream with Douglas firs and western hemlock. The park's famous temperate rain forests are on the peninsula's western side, marked by broad western red cedars, towering red spruces, and ferns festooned with strands of mosses and patchwork lichens. This lower landscape is also home to some of the Northwest's largest trees: massive cedar and Sitka spruce near Lake Quinault can measure more than 700 inches around, and Douglas firs near the Queets and Hoh rivers are nearly as wide.

These landscapes are home to a variety of wildlife, including many large mammals and 15 creatures found nowhere else in the world. Hikers often come across Roosevelt's elk, black-tailed deer, mountain goats, beavers, raccoons, skunks, opossums, and foxes; Douglas squirrels and flying squirrels populate the heights of the forest. Less common are black bears (most prevalent from May through August); wolves, bobcats, and cougars are rarely seen. Birdlife includes bald eagles, red-tailed hawks, osprey, and great horned owls. Rivers and lakes are filled with freshwater fish, while beaches hold crabs, sea stars, anemones, and other shelled creatures. Get out in a boat on the Pacific to spot seals, sea lions, and sea otters—and perhaps a pod of porpoises, orcas, or gray whales.

Beware of jellyfish around the shores—beached jellyfish can still sting. In the woods, check for ticks after every hike and after each shower. Biting nasties include black flies, horseflies, sand fleas, and the ever-present mosquitoes. Yellow-jacket nests populate tree hollows along many trails; signs throughout the Hoh Rain Forest warn hikers to move quickly through these sections. If one or two chase you, remain calm and keep walking; these are just "guards" making sure you're keeping away from the hive. Poison oak is common, so familiarize yourself with its appearance. Bug repellent, sunscreen, and long pants and sleeves will go a long way toward making your experience more comfortable.

of Hwy. 112 near Sekiu ☎ 360/565–3130 Ozette Ranger Station 🌐 www.nps.gov/olym/planyourvisit/visiting-ozette.htm.

SCENIC STOPS

★ Hoh Rain Forest

FOREST | South of Forks, an 18-mile spur road links Highway 101 with this unique temperate rain forest, where spruce and hemlock trees soar to heights of more than 200 feet. Alders and big-leaf maples are so densely covered with mosses they look more like shaggy prehistoric animals than trees, and elk browse in shaded glens. Be prepared for precipitation: the region receives 140 inches or more each year. ✉ *Olympic National Park* ⊕ *From Hwy. 101, at about 20 miles north of Kalaloch, turn onto Upper Hoh Rd. 18 miles east to Hoh Rain Forest Visitor Center* ☎ *360/374–6925* 🌐 *www.nps.gov/olym/planyourvisit/visiting-the-hoh.htm.*

★ Hurricane Ridge

MOUNTAIN—SIGHT | The panoramic view from this 5,200-foot-high ridge encompasses the Olympic range, the Strait of Juan de Fuca, and Vancouver Island.

Hoh River Trail

Guided tours are given in summer along the many paved and unpaved trails, where wildflowers and wildlife such as deer and marmots flourish. ✉ *Hurricane Ridge Rd.* ✣ *17 miles south of Port Angeles* ☎ *360/565–3130 visitor center* 🌐 *www.nps.gov/olym/planyourvisit/visiting-hurricane-ridge.htm* ⊗ *Closed when road is closed.*

Kalaloch

BEACH—SIGHT | With a lodge and restaurant, a huge campground, miles of coastline, and easy access from the highway, this is a popular spot. Keen-eyed beachcombers may spot sea otters just offshore; they were reintroduced here in 1970. ✉ *Hwy. 101, Kalaloch* ✣ *32 miles northwest of Lake Quinault* ☎ *360/565–3130 visitor center, 360/962–2283 ranger station* 🌐 *www.nps.gov/olym/planyourvisit/visiting-kalaloch-and-ruby-beach.htm.*

Lake Crescent

BODY OF WATER | Visitors see Lake Crescent as Highway 101 winds along its southern shore, giving way to gorgeous views of teal waters rippling in a basin formed by Tuscan-like hills. In the evening, low bands of clouds caught between the surrounding mountains often linger over its reflective surface. ✉ *Hwy. 101* ✣ *16 miles west of Port Angeles and 28 miles northeast of Forks* ☎ *360/565–3130 visitor center* 🌐 *www.nps.gov/olym/planyourvisit/visiting-lake-crescent.htm.*

Lake Quinault

BODY OF WATER | This glimmering lake, 4½ miles long and 300 feet deep, is the first landmark you'll reach when driving the west-side loop of U.S. 101. The rain forest is thickest here, with moss-draped maples and alders, and towering spruce, fir, and hemlock. Enchanted Valley, high up near the Quinault River's source, is a deeply glaciated valley that's closer to the Hood Canal than to the Pacific Ocean. A scenic loop drive circles the lake and travels around a section of the Quinault River. ✉ *Hwy. 101* ✣ *38 miles north of Hoquiam* ☎ *360/288–2525 Quinault Rain Forest ranger station* 🌐 *www.nps.gov/olym/planyourvisit/visiting-quinault.htm.*

Second and Third Beaches

BEACH—SIGHT | During low tide these flat, driftwood-strewn expanses are perfect for long afternoon strolls. Second Beach, accessed via an easy forest trail through Quileute lands, opens to a vista of Pacific Ocean and sea stacks. Third Beach offers a 1¼-mile forest hike for a warm-up before reaching the sands. ✉ *Hwy. 101* ✣ *32 miles north of Lake Quinault* ☎ *360/565–3130 visitor center* 🌐 *www.nps.gov/olym.*

Sol Duc

BODY OF WATER | Sol Duc Valley is one of those magical places where all the Northwest's virtues seem at hand: lush lowland forests, sparkling river scenes, salmon runs, and serene hiking trails. Here, the popular Sol Duc Hot Springs area includes three attractive sulfuric pools ranging in temperature from 98°F to 104°F (admission to the pools costs $15). ✉ *Sol Duc Rd.* ✣ *South of U.S. 101, 12 miles past west end of Lake Crescent* ☎ *360/565–3130 visitor center* 🌐 *www.nps.gov/olym/planyourvisit/visiting-the-sol-duc-valley.htm.*

Staircase

INFO CENTER | Unlike the forests of the park's south and west sides, Douglas fir is the dominant tree on the east slope of the Olympic Mountains. Fire has played an important role in creating the majestic forest here, as the Staircase Ranger Station explains in interpretive exhibits. ✉ *Olympic National Park* ✣ *At end of Rte. 119, 15 miles from U.S. 101 at Hoodsport* ☎ *360/565–3130 visitor center* 🌐 *www.nps.gov/olym/planyourvisit/visiting-staircase.htm.*

Activities

BIKNG

The rough gravel car tracks to some of the park's remote sites were meant for four-wheel-drive vehicles but can double as mountain-bike routes. The Quinault Valley, Queets River, Hoh River, and Sol Duc River roads have bike paths through old-growth forest. Graves Creek Road, in the southwest, is a mountain-bike path; Lake Crescent's north side is also edged by the bike-friendly Spruce Railroad Trail. More bike tracks run through the adjacent Olympic National Forest. Note that U.S. 101 has heavy traffic and isn't recommended for cycling, although the western side has broad roads with beautiful scenery and can be biked off-season. Bikes are not permitted on foot trails.

Ben's Bikes

BICYCLING | This bike, gear, and repair shop is a great resource for advice on routes around the Olympic Peninsula, including the Olympic Discovery Trail. They can deliver bikes to local lodgings and to the ferry docks in Port Angeles and Port Townsend. They rent a variety of different styles, with rentals starting at $30 per day and $110 per week. ✉ *1251 W. Washington St., Sequim* ☎ *360/683–2666* 🌐 *www.bensbikessequim.com.*

Sound Bike & Kayak

BICYCLING | This sports outfitter rents and sells bikes, and sells kayaks, climbing gear, and related equipment. They offer several guided mountain climbs, day hikes, and custom trips, and a climbing wall to practice skills. Bike rentals start at $10 per hour and $45 per day. ✉ *120 E Front St., Port Angeles* ☎ *360/457–1240* 🌐 *www.soundbikeskayaks.com.*

CLIMBING

At 7,980 feet, Mt. Olympus is the highest peak in the park and the most popular climb in the region. To attempt the summit, climbers must register at the Glacier Meadows Ranger Station. Mt. Constance, the third-highest Olympic peak at 7,743 feet, has a well-traversed climbing route that requires technical experience; reservations are recommended for the Lake Constance stop, which is limited to 20 campers. Mt. Deception is another possibility, though tricky snows have caused fatalities and injuries in the last decade.

Climbing season runs from late June through September. Note that crevasse skills and self-rescue experience are highly recommended. Climbers must register with park officials and purchase wilderness permits before setting out. The best resource for climbing advice is the Wilderness Information Center in Port Angeles.

Mountain Madness

CLIMBING/MOUNTAINEERING | Adventure through the rain forest to the glaciated summit of Mt. Olympus on a five-day trip, offered several times per year by Mountain Madness. ☎ *800/328–5925, 206/937–8389* 🌐 *www.mountainmadness.com* 🎫 *From $1,390 for 5-day climb.*

FISHING

There are numerous fishing possibilities throughout the park. Lake Crescent is home to cutthroat and rainbow trout, as well as petite kokanee salmon; lakes Cushman, Quinault, and Ozette have trout, salmon, and steelhead. As for rivers, the Bogachiel and Queets have steelhead salmon in season. The glacier-fed Hoh River is home to chinook salmon April to November, and coho salmon from August through November; the Sol Duc River offers all five species of salmon. The Elwha River has been undergoing restoration since two dams were removed; strong salmon and steelhead runs are expected to return, although a fishing moratorium has been in place for several years. Other places to go after salmon and trout include the Dosewallips, Duckabush, Quillayute, Quinault, Salmon, and Skokomish rivers. A Washington state punch card is required during salmon-spawning months; fishing regulations vary throughout the park, and some areas are for catch and release only. Punch cards are available from sporting-goods and outdoor-supply stores.

Piscatorial Pursuits

FISHING | This company, based in Forks, offers salmon and steelhead fishing trips around the Olympic Peninsula from mid-October through May. ✉ *Forks* ☎ *866/347–4232* 🌐 *www.piscatorialpursuits.com* 🎫 *From $225 (rate per person for parties of two or more).*

HIKING

Know your tides, or you might be trapped by high water. Tide tables are available at all visitor centers and ranger stations. Remember that a wilderness permit is required for all overnight backcountry visits.

Cape Alava Trail

HIKING/WALKING | Beginning at Ozette, this 3-mile boardwalk trail leads from the forest to wave-tossed headlands. *Moderate.* ✉ *Ozette* ✣ *Trailhead: end of Hoko-Ozette Rd., 26 miles south of Hwy. 112, west of Sekiu* 🌐 *www.nps.gov/olym/planyourvisit/visiting-ozette.htm.*

Graves Creek Trail

HIKING/WALKING | This 6-mile-long moderately strenuous trail climbs from lowland rain forest to alpine territory at Sundown Pass. Due to spring floods, a fjord halfway up is often impassable in May and June. *Moderate.* ✉ *Olympic National Park* ✣ *Trailhead: end of S Shore Rd., 23 miles east of U.S. 101* 🌐 *www.nps.gov/olym.*

High Divide Trail

HIKING/WALKING | A 9-mile hike in the park's high country defines this trail, which includes some strenuous climbing on its last 4 miles before topping out at a small alpine lake. A return loop along High Divide wends its way an extra mile through alpine territory, with sensational views of Olympic peaks. This trail is only for dedicated, properly equipped hikers who are in good shape. *Difficult.* ✉ *Olympic National Park* ✣ *Trailhead: end of Sol Duc River Rd., 13 miles south of U.S. 101* 🌐 *www.nps.gov/olym/planyourvisit/high-divide-loop.htm.*

★ Hoh River Trail

HIKING/WALKING | **FAMILY** | From the Hoh Visitor Center, this rain-forest jaunt takes you into the Hoh Valley, wending its way for 17½ miles alongside the river, through moss-draped maple and alder trees and past open meadows where elk roam in winter. *Easy.* ✉ *Olympic National Park* ✣ *Trailhead: Hoh Visitor Center, 18 miles east of U.S. 101* 🌐 *www.nps.gov/olym/planyourvisit/hoh-river-trail.htm.*

Hurricane Ridge Meadow Trail

HIKING/WALKING | A ¼-mile alpine loop, most of it wheelchair accessible, leads through wildflower meadows overlooking numerous vistas of the interior Olympic peaks to the south and a panorama of the Strait of Juan de Fuca to the north. *Easy.* ✉ *Olympic National Park* ✣ *Trailhead: Hurricane Ridge Rd., 17 miles south of Port Angeles* 🌐 *www.nps.gov/olym/planyourvisit/visiting-hurricane-ridge.htm.*

★ Sol Duc River Trail

HIKING/WALKING | **FAMILY** | The 1½-mile gravel path off Sol Duc Road winds through thick Douglas fir forests toward the thundering, three-chute Sol Duc Falls. Just off the road, below a wooden platform over the Sol Duc River, you'll come across the 70-foot Salmon Cascades. In late summer and autumn, thousands of salmon negotiate 50 miles or more of treacherous waters to reach the cascades and the tamer pools near Sol Duc Hot Springs. The popular 6-mile **Lovers Lane Loop Trail** links the Sol Duc falls with the hot springs. You can continue up from the falls 5 miles to the **Appleton Pass Trail,** at 3,100 feet. From there you can hike on to the 8½-mile mark, where views at the High Divide are from 5,050 feet. *Moderate.* ✉ *Olympic National Park* ✣ *Trailhead: Sol Duc Rd., 12 miles south of U.S. 101* 🌐 *www.nps.gov/olym/planyourvisit/sol-duc-river-trail.htm.*

KAYAKING AND CANOEING

Lake Crescent, a serene expanse of teal-color waters surrounded by deep-green pine forests, is one of the park's best boating areas. Note that the west end is for swimming only; no speedboats are allowed here.

Lake Quinault has boating access from a gravel ramp on the north shore. From U.S. 101, take a right on North Shore Road, another right on Hemlock Way, and a left on Lakeview Drive. There are plank ramps at Falls Creek and Willoughby campgrounds on South Shore Drive, 0.1 mile and 0.2 mile past the Quinault Ranger Station, respectively.

Lake Ozette, with just one access road, is a good place for overnight trips. Only experienced canoe and kayak handlers should travel far from the put-in, since fierce storms occasionally strike—even in summer.

Fairholme General Store

CANOEING/ROWING/SKULLING | Kayaks and canoes on Lake Crescent are available to rent from $20 per hour to $60 for eight hours. The store is at the lake's west end, 27 miles west of Port Angeles. Closed after Labor Day until Memorial Day weekend. ✉ *221121 U.S. 101, Port Angeles* ☎ *360/928–3020* 🌐 *www.olympicnationalparks.com* ⏲ *Closed after Labor Day–Apr. and Mon.–Thurs. in May.*

Lake Crescent Lodge

CANOEING/ROWING/SKULLING | You can rent canoes, kayaks, and paddleboards here for $20 per hour and $60 for a full day. Two-hour guided kayak tours are offered and include instruction; they cost $55 in a single kayak and $75 in a double kayak. ✉ *416 Lake Crescent Rd.* ☎ *360/928–3211* 🌐 *www.olympicnationalparks.com* ⏲ *Closed Jan.–Apr.*

Log Cabin Resort

CANOEING/ROWING/SKULLING | This resort, 17 miles west of Port Angeles, has paddle boat, kayak, canoe, and paddleboard rentals for $20 per hour and $60 per day.

The dock provides easy access to Lake Crescent's northeast section. ✉ *3183 E Beach Rd., Port Angeles* ☎ *360/928–3325* 🌐 *www.olympicnationalparks.com* ⏲ *Closed Oct.–mid-May.*

Rainforest Paddlers

KAYAKING | This company takes kayakers down the Hoh River to explore the rain forest, and down the Quillayute through the estuary to La Push. Rafting trips are offered on both the Hoh and Sol Duc rivers. They also rent kayaks and mountain bikes. ✉ *4883 Upper Hoh Rd., Forks* ☎ *360/374–5254, 866/457–8398* 🌐 *www.rainforestpaddlers.com* 🎫 *Tours from $44; kayak rentals from $11/hr.*

RAFTING

Olympic has excellent rafting rivers, with Class II to Class V rapids. The Elwha River is a popular place to paddle, with some exciting turns. The Hoh is better for those who like a smooth, easy float.

Adventures Through Kayaking

WHITE-WATER RAFTING | This outfitter offers 3½-hour trips twice daily on the Sol Duc River in spring. Cost is $79/person and includes all gear. Beginners are welcome but kids must be 12 or older. Check-in is at the Sol Duc Hatchery. ✉ *Sol Duc Hatchery, 1423 Pavel Rd., Beaver* ☎ *360/417–3015* 🌐 *www.atkayaking.com.*

WINTER ACTIVITIES

Hurricane Ridge is the central spot for winter sports. Miles of downhill and Nordic ski tracks are open late December through March, and a ski lift, towropes, and ski school are open 10 to 4 weekends and holidays. A snow-play area for children ages eight and younger is near the Hurricane Ridge Visitors Center. Hurricane Ridge Road is open Friday through Sunday in the winter season; all vehicles are required to carry chains.

Hurricane Ridge Visitor Center

SNOW SPORTS | Rent snowshoes and ski equipment here December through March. ✉ *Hurricane Ridge Rd., Port Angeles* ☎ *360/565–3131 road condition information* 🌐 *www.nps.gov/olym/planyourvisit/hurricane-ridge-in-winter.htm* ⏲ *Closed Mon.–Thurs.*

Nearby Towns

Although most Olympic Peninsula towns have evolved from their exclusive reliance on timber, **Forks,** outside the national park's northwest tip, remains one of the region's logging capitals. Washington state's wettest town (100 inches or more of rain a year), it's a small, friendly place with just under 3,800 residents and a modicum of visitor facilities. **Port Angeles,** a city of around 20,000, focuses on its status as the main gateway to Olympic National Park and Victoria, British Columbia. Set below the Strait of Juan de Fuca and looking north to Vancouver Island, it's an enviably scenic settlement filled with attractive, Craftsman-style homes.

The Pacific Northwest has its very own "Banana Belt" in the waterfront community of **Sequim,** 15 miles east of Port Angeles along U.S. 101. The town of 6,900 is in the rain shadow of the Olympics and receives only 16 inches of rain per year (compared with the 140 to 170 inches that drench the Hoh Rain Forest just 40 miles away). The beach community of **Seabrook,** near Pacific Beach, is 25 miles from the southeast corner of the national park via the Moclips Highway. Created in 2004 as a pedestrian-friendly beach town, many of its several hundred Cape Cod–style cottage homes are available for short-term rentals; the community has parks, swimming pools, bike trails, beach access, special events, and a growing retail district.

VISITOR INFORMATION Forks Chamber of Commerce Visitor Center. ✉ *1411 S Forks Ave. (U.S. 101), Forks* ☎ *800/443–6757, 360/374–2531* 🌐 *www.forkswa.com.* **Port Angeles Chamber of Commerce Visitor Center.** ✉ *121 E Railroad Ave., Port Angeles* ☎ *360/452–2363* 🌐 *www.portangeles.*

org. **Sequim-Dungeness Valley Chamber of Commerce.** ✉ *1192 E Washington St., Sequim* ☎ *360/683–6197, 800/737–8462* 🌐 *www.sequimchamber.com.*

Sights

★ Dungeness Spit

NATURE PRESERVE | FAMILY | Curving nearly 6 miles into the Strait of Juan de Fuca, the longest natural sand spit in the United States is a wild, beautiful section of shoreline. More than 30,000 migratory waterfowl stop here each spring and fall, but you'll see plenty of birdlife any time of year. The entire spit is part of the **Dungeness National Wildlife Refuge** (🌐 *www.fws.gov/refuge/dungeness*). You can access it from the trail that begins in the 216-acre **Dungeness Recreation Area,** which serves as a portal to the shoreline. At the end of the spit is the towering white 1857 **New Dungeness Lighthouse** (🌐 *www.newdungenesslighthouse.com).* Tours, including a 74-step climb to the top, are available, though access is limited to those who can hike 5½ miles or paddle about 3½ miles out to the end of the spit—the closest launch is from Cline Spit County Park. You can also enroll to serve a one-week stint as a lighthouse keeper. If you'd prefer not to make the long trek all the way out to the lighthouse, an endeavor you should only attempt at low tide to avoid having to climb over massive driftwood logs, you can still take in plenty of beautiful scenery and spot myriad wildlife by hiking just a mile or so out along the spit and back. ✉ *554 Voice of America Rd. W, Sequim* ☎ *360/683–5847* 🌐 *www.clallam.net/parks* 💵 *$3 per group.*

Jamestown S'Klallam Tribe

NATIVE SITE | This village on the beach near the mouth of the Dungeness River has been occupied by the Jamestown S'Klallam tribe for thousands of years. The tribe, whose name means "strong people," was driven to the Skokomish Reservation on Hood Canal after the signing of the Treaty of Point No Point in 1855. However, in 1874, tribal leader James Balch and some 130 S'Klallam collectively purchased 210 acres where the community is today, and S'Klallam members have lived here ever since. An excellent gallery, Northwest Native Expressions, sells tribal artwork, including baskets, jewelry, textiles, and totems. Less than a mile away on U.S. 101, the tribe operates 7Cedars Casino along with a market and deli. As of this writing, the tribe was building a 100-room hotel adjacent to the casino and planned to open in late 2020. ✉ *Old Blyn Hwy. at U.S. 101, Sequim* 🌐 *www.jamestowntribe.org.*

Olympic Discovery Trail

TRAIL | Eventually, 140 miles of nonmotorized trail will lead from Port Townsend west to the Pacific Coast. As of this writing, 80 miles of the paved trail are complete and available for use by hikers, bikers, equestrians, and disabled users. The trail has been conceived as the northern portion of a route that will eventually encircle the entire Olympic Peninsula. 🌐 *www.olympicdiscoverytrail.org.*

Port Angeles Fine Arts Center

MUSEUM | With modern, funky, and intriguing exhibits by new and emerging artists, this small, beautifully designed modern museum is inside the former home of the late artist and publisher Esther Barrows Webster, one of Port Angeles's most energetic and cultured citizens. Outside, Webster's Woods Sculpture Park—open daily dawn to dusk—is dotted with oversize art installations set against a backdrop of the city and harbor. ✉ *1203 E. Lauridsen Blvd., Port Angeles* ☎ *360/457–3532* 🌐 *www.pafac.org* ⏲ *Closed Mon.–Wed. in Oct.–Mar.*

Sequim Bay State Park

BEACH—SIGHT | Protected by a sand spit 4 miles southeast of Sequim on Sequim Bay, this 92-acre woodsy inlet park has picnic tables, campsites, hiking trails, tennis courts, and a boat ramp. ✉ *269035 U.S. 101, Sequim* ☎ *360/683–4235* 🌐 *www.parks.state.wa.us* 💵 *Parking $10.*

Timber Museum

MUSEUM | The museum highlights Forks's logging history since the 1870s; a garden and fire tower are also on the grounds. *1421 S Forks Ave., Forks 360/374–9663 www.forkstimbermuseum.org $3.*

Restaurants

IN THE PARK

Creekside Restaurant

$$$ | AMERICAN | A tranquil country setting and ocean views at Kalaloch Lodge's restaurant create the perfect backdrop for savoring Pacific Northwest dinner specialties like grilled salmon, fresh shellfish, and elk burgers. Tempting seasonal desserts include local fruit tarts and cobblers in summer and organic winter squash bread pudding in winter; flourless chocolate torte is enjoyed year-round. **Known for:** locally sourced food; Washington wines. *Average main: $28 157151 Hwy. 101, Forks 866/662–9928, 360/962–2271 www.thekalalochlodge.com/dine-and-shop/creekside-restaurant.*

Lake Crescent Lodge

$$$ | AMERICAN | Part of the original 1916 lodge, the fir-paneled dining room overlooks the lake; you won't find a better spot for sunset views. Dinner entrées include wild salmon, brown butter–basted halibut, grilled steak, and roasted chicken breast; the lunch menu features elk cheeseburgers, inventive salads, and a variety of sandwiches. **Known for:** award-winning Pacific Northwest wine list; house-made lavender lemonade; certified green restaurant. *Average main: $29 416 Lake Crescent Rd., Port Angeles 360/928–3211 www.olympicnationalparks.com/lodging/dining/lake-crescent-lodge/ Closed Jan.–Apr.*

The Springs Restaurant

$$$ | AMERICAN | The main Sol Duc Hot Springs Resort restaurant is a rustic, fir-and-cedar-paneled dining room surrounded by trees. In summer big breakfasts are turned out daily—hikers can fill up on biscuits and sage-pork-sausage gravy, Grand Marnier French toast, and omelets before hitting the trails; for lighter fare, there's steel cut oatmeal and yogurt and granola parfaits. **Known for:** three breakfast mimosa choices; boxed lunches. *Average main: $24 12076 Sol Duc Rd. , at U.S. 101, Port Angeles 360/327–3583 www.olympicnationalparks.com/stay/dining/sol-duc-hot-springs-resort-.aspx Closed Nov.–late Mar.*

PICNIC AREAS

All Olympic National Park campgrounds have adjacent picnic areas with tables, some shelters, and restrooms, but no cooking facilities. The same is true for major visitor centers, such as Hoh Rain Forest. Drinking water is available at ranger stations, interpretive centers, and inside campgrounds.

East Beach Picnic Area

Set on a grassy meadow overlooking Lake Crescent, this popular swimming spot has six picnic tables and vault toilets. *E Beach Rd., Port Angeles At far east end of Lake Crescent, off Hwy. 101, 17 miles west of Port Angeles.*

La Poel Picnic Area

Tall firs lean over a tiny gravel beach at this small picnic area, which has several picnic tables and a splendid view of Pyramid Mountain across Lake Crescent. It's closed October to April. *Olympic National Park Off Hwy. 101, 22 miles west of Port Angeles Closed mid-Oct.–mid-May.*

Rialto Beach Picnic Area

Relatively secluded at the end of the road from Forks, this is one of the premier day-use areas in the park's Pacific coast segment. This site has 12 picnic tables, fire grills, and vault toilets. *Rte. 110, 14 miles west of Forks, Forks.*

Best Campgrounds in Olympic

Note that only a few places take reservations; if you can't book in advance, you'll have to arrive early to get a place. Each site usually has a picnic table and grill or fire pit, and most campgrounds have water, toilets, and garbage containers; for hookups, showers, and laundry facilities, you'll have to head into the towns or stay at a privately owned campground. Firewood is available from camp concessions, but if there's no store you can collect dead wood within 1 mile of your campsite. Dogs are allowed in campgrounds, but not on most trails or in the backcountry. Trailers should be 21 feet long or less (15 feet or less at Queets Campground), though a few campgrounds can accommodate up to 35 feet. There's a camping limit of two weeks. Nightly rates run $15–$22 per site.

If you have a backcountry pass, you can camp virtually anywhere throughout the park's forests and shores. Overnight wilderness permits are $8 per person per night and are available at visitor centers and ranger stations. Note that when you camp in the backcountry, you must choose a site at least ½ mile inside the park boundary.

Kalaloch Campground. Kalaloch is the biggest and most popular Olympic campground, and it's open all year. Its vantage of the Pacific is unmatched on the park's coastal stretch. ✉ *U.S. 101, ½ mile north of Kalaloch Information Station, Olympic National Park* ☎ 877/444–6777 or 🌐 *www.recreation.gov* for reservations.

Lake Quinault Rain Forest Resort Village Campground. Stretching along the south shore of Lake Quinault, this RV campground has many recreation facilities, including beaches, canoes, ball fields, and horseshoe pits. The 31 RV sites, which rent for $36 per night, are open year-round, but bathrooms are closed in winter. ✉ *3½ miles east of U.S. 101, South Shore Rd., Lake Quinault* ☎ *360/288–2535, 800/255–6936* 🌐 *www.rainforestresort.com.*

Mora Campground. Along the Quillayute estuary, this campground doubles as a popular staging point for hikes northward along the coast's wilderness stretch. ✉ *Rte. 110, 13 miles west of Forks* ☎ *No phone.*

Ozette Campground. Hikers heading to Cape Alava, a scenic promontory that is the westernmost point in the lower 48 states, use this lakeshore campground as a jumping-off point. ✉ *Hoko-Ozette Rd., 26 miles south of Hwy. 112* ☎ *No phone.*

Sol Duc Campground. Sol Duc resembles virtually all Olympic campgrounds save one distinguishing feature—the famed hot springs are a short walk away. ✉ *Sol Duc Rd., 11 miles south of U.S. 101* ☎ *877/444–6777* or 🌐 *www.recreation.gov* for reservations.

Staircase Campground. In deep woods away from the river, this campground is a popular jumping-off point for hikes into the Skokomish River Valley and the Olympic high country. ✉ *Rte. 119, 16 miles northwest of U.S. 101* ☎ *No phone.*

IN THE PARK

★ Kalaloch Lodge

$$$$ | **HOTEL** | **FAMILY** | Overlooking the Pacific, Kalaloch has cozy lodge rooms with sea views and separate cabins along the bluff. **Pros:** ranger tours; clam digging; supreme storm-watching in winter. **Cons:** no Internet and most units don't have TVs; some rooms are two blocks from main lodge; limited cell phone service. *Rooms from: $292 157151 U.S. 101, Forks 360/962–2271, 866/662–9928 www.thekalalochlodge.com 64 rooms No meals.*

Lake Crescent Lodge

$$$ | **HOTEL** | Deep in the forest at the foot of Mt. Storm King, this 1916 lodge has a variety of comfortable accommodations, from basic rooms with shared baths to spacious two-bedroom fireplace cottages. **Pros:** gorgeous setting; free wireless access in the lobby; lots of opportunities for off-the-grid fun outdoors. **Cons:** no laundry; Roosevelt Cottages often are booked a year in advance for summer stays; crowded with nonguest visitors. *Rooms from: $152 416 Lake Crescent Rd., Port Angeles 360/928–3211, 888/896–3818 www.olympicnationalparks.com Closed Jan.–Apr., except Roosevelt fireplace cabins open weekends 52 rooms No meals.*

Lake Quinault Lodge

$$$$ | **HOTEL** | On a lovely glacial lake in Olympic National Forest, this beautiful early-20th-century lodge complex is within walking distance of the lakeshore and hiking trails in the spectacular old-growth forest. **Pros:** boat tours of the lake are interesting; family-friendly ambience; year-round pool and sauna. **Cons:** no TV in some rooms; some units are noisy and not very private; service could be friendlier. *Rooms from: $341 345 South Shore Rd., Quinault 360/288–2900, 888/896–3818 www.olympicnationalparks.com 92 rooms No meals.*

Log Cabin Resort

$$ | **HOTEL** | **FAMILY** | This rustic resort has an idyllic setting at the northeast end of Lake Crescent with lodging choices that include A-frame chalet units, standard cabins, small camper cabins, motel units, and RV sites with full hookups. **Pros:** boat rentals available on-site; convenient general store; pets allowed in some cabins. **Cons:** cabins are extremely rustic; no plumbing in the camper cabins; no TVs. *Rooms from: $104 3183 E Beach Rd., Port Angeles 888/896–3818, 360/928–3325 www.olympicnationalparks.com Closed Oct.–late May 4 rooms, 20 cabins No meals.*

Sol Duc Hot Springs Resort

$$$$ | **HOTEL** | Deep in the brooding forest along the Sol Duc River and surrounded by 5,000-foot-tall mountains, the main draw of this remote 1910 resort is the pool area, with soothing mineral baths and a freshwater swimming pool. **Pros:** nearby trails; peaceful setting; some units are pet-friendly. **Cons:** units are dated; no air-conditioning, TV, or Internet access; pools get crowded. *Rooms from: $215 12076 Sol Duc Hot Springs Rd. 888/896–3818 www.olympicnationalparks.com Closed Nov.–late Mar. 32 cabins, 1 suite, 17 RV sites No meals.*

Chapter 14

OLYMPIC PENINSULA AND WASHINGTON COAST

Updated by
Andrew Collins

Sights	Restaurants	Hotels	Shopping	Nightlife
★★★★★	★★★★★	★★★★☆	★★☆☆☆	★★★☆☆

WELCOME TO OLYMPIC PENINSULA AND WASHINGTON COAST

TOP REASONS TO GO

★ **Soak up the scene in Port Townsend:** Washington's Victorian seaport offers historic lodgings, quirky eateries, and a variety of annual festivals celebrating everything from wooden boats to films to chamber music.

★ **Laze on the beach:** Coastal Washington's beach towns offer an abundance of memorable adventures.

★ **Follow the light:** Lighthouses and their histories beckon—from Point Wilson at Fort Worden, one of the state's best loved parks, to Grays Harbor.

★ **Meet the Makah:** Exhibits at Neah Bay's impressive Makah Cultural Center complex display authentic scenes of early life in the Northwest, and nearby tribal parks at Cape Flattery and Shi Shi Beach offer breathtaking scenery.

★ **Go locavore:** In addition to Port Townsend, the bustling downtowns of nearby Sequim and Port Angeles offer a growing number of farm-to-table restaurants and craft cideries, breweries, and coffeehouses.

1 **Hood Canal.** Scenic, low-keyed villages abundant with hiking and boating opportunities fringe this ancient fjord that forms the southeastern entry point to the peninsula.

2 **Port Townsend.** This Victorian seaport and artists community is an idyllic destination for a leisurely weekend of dining and shopping.

3 **Sequim.** Famous for its lavender farms and rugged swath of shoreline on the Strait of Juan de Fuca, Sequim has numerous first-rate eateries and inns.

4 **Port Angeles.** The largest town on the peninsula has an emerging restaurant scene and is a handy base for visiting Olympic National Park and ferrying to Victoria, BC.

5 **Neah Bay.** Secluded and ruggedly beautiful, this home base of the Makah Tribe rewards visitors with a top-notch museum and dramatic beach and forest hikes.

6 **Forks.** You'll find several small, charming lodgings in this lush village convenient for visiting the western reaches of Olympic National Park.

7 **Copalis Beach.** An abundance of vacation rentals and gorgeous windswept beaches are the draw of this quiet stretch of shoreline.

8 **Ocean Shores.** This bustling, family-friendly community is the closest ocean-beach town to Seattle.

9 **Westport.** An unpretentious fishing village with some lovely, budget-friendly lodgings, Westport is ideal for a quiet seaside getaway.

10 **Ilwaco.** Historic forts and lighthouses lie within a short drive of this colorful Columbia River port town on the way to the Long Beach Peninsula.

11 **Seaview.** This low-key village with a few terrific inns and eateries is close to some stunning beaches and Cape Disappointment State Park.

12 **Long Beach.** A retro shore community that teems with family-friendly amusements, this is a prime locale for beachcombing and surfing.

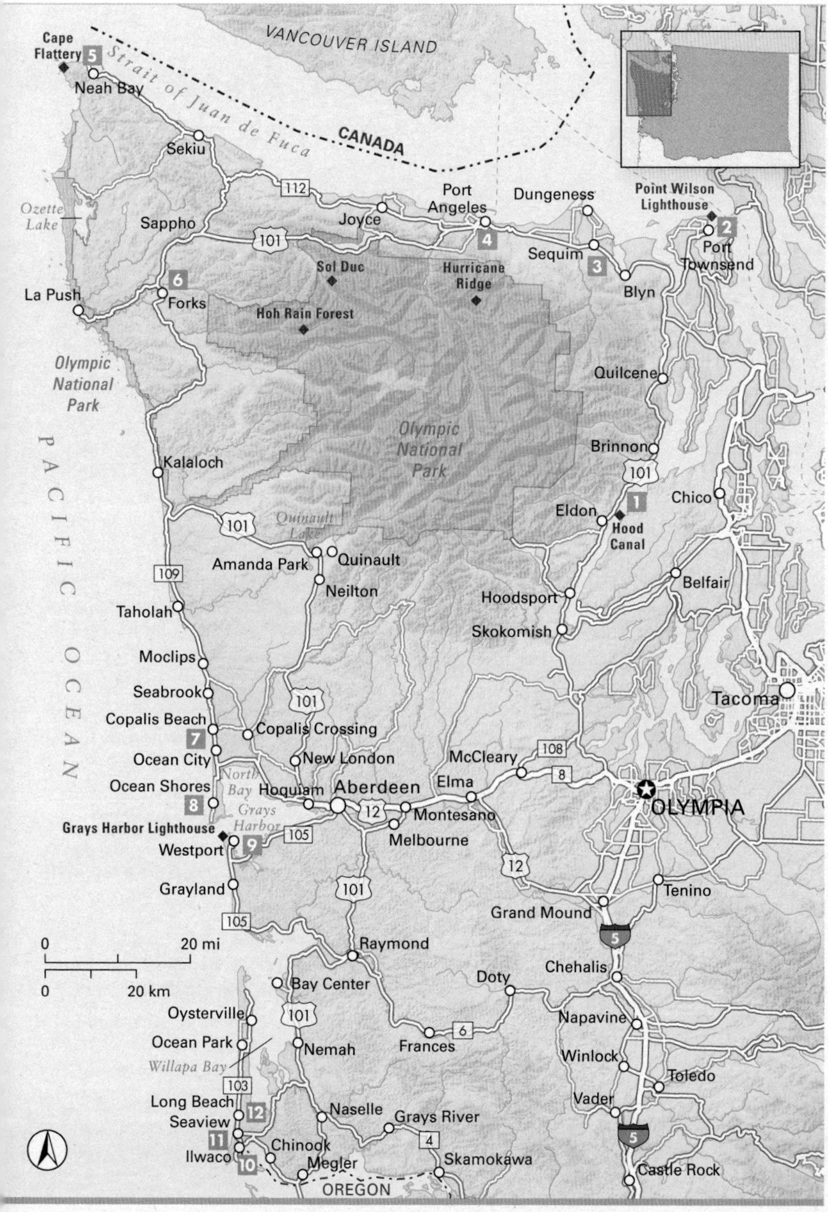

VANCOUVER ISLAND
CANADA
Strait of Juan de Fuca
Cape Flattery 5
Neah Bay
Sekiu
112
Port Angeles
Dungeness
Point Wilson Lighthouse
Ozette Lake
Sappho
Joyce
4
2
Port Townsend
101
Sequim
3
Blyn
Sol Duc
Hurricane Ridge
6
La Push
Forks
Hoh Rain Forest
Olympic National Park
Quilcene
Olympic National Park
Brinnon
PACIFIC OCEAN
Kalaloch
101
1
Chico
Eldon
Hood Canal
101
Quinault Lake
Amanda Park
Quinault
109
Neilton
Belfair
Hoodsport
Taholah
Skokomish
Moclips
Seabrook
101
Tacoma
Copalis Beach
Copalis Crossing
7
Ocean City
New London
McCleary
108
Ocean Shores
North Bay
Hoquiam
Aberdeen
Elma
8
OLYMPIA
8
Grays Harbor
12
Montesano
Grays Harbor Lighthouse
105
Melbourne
Westport
9
12
Grayland
101
Tenino
Grand Mound
105
5
0
20 mi
Raymond
Chehalis
0
20 km
Doty
Bay Center
Oysterville
101
Napavine
6
Frances
Ocean Park
Nemah
Winlock
Willapa Bay
103
Toledo
Long Beach
12
Vader
Naselle
Seaview
Grays River
5
11
4
Chinook
Ilwaco
10
Megler
Skamokawa
Castle Rock
OREGON

Wilderness envelops most of the Olympic Peninsula, an utterly enchanting land of craggy, snowcapped peaks, pristine evergreen forests, and driftwood-covered coastlines. This is a wonderland where the scent of saltwater and pine hang in the air and the entire world appears to be shades of blue and green. Historic lighthouses dot its shores and a majestic mountain range rises up from its heart.

The Olympic Mountains form the core of the peninsula, skirted by saltwater on three sides. The area's highest point, Mt. Olympus, stands nearly 8,000 feet above sea level. It's safeguarded in the 922,000-acre Olympic National Park *(see Chapter 13),* along with much of the extraordinary interior landscape. Several thousand acres more are protected in the Olympic National Forest. The peninsula also encompasses seven Native American reservations, five wilderness areas, five national wildlife refuges, the world's largest unmanaged herd of Roosevelt elk, and some of the wettest and driest areas in the coastal Pacific Northwest. The mountains catch penetrating Pacific storms, bringing an average annual rainfall of about 140 inches to the lush western river valleys and rain forests. The drier northeastern slopes of the peninsula's rain shadow see about 16 inches of precipitation per year, creating an ideal climate for the lavender that's grown commercially here.

Most residents live on the edges of the peninsula, anchored at its southwestern corner by Grays Harbor, named for Captain Robert Gray—in 1792, he became the first European American to enter the harbor. From there, the coast extends north to Cape Flattery and Neah Bay on the Makah Indian Reservation, then stretches east through the small city of Port Angeles through picturesque Sequim and onto the Victorian seaport of Port Townsend, on the tip of the Quimper Peninsula, a narrow, crooked elbow of land at the northeastern end of the larger land mass. Rugged terrain and few roads limit interior accessibility to backpackers and climbers. But the 330-mile outer loop of U.S. 101 offers breathtaking forest, ocean, and mountain vistas as well as rest stops at a variety of colorful outposts along the way.

MAJOR REGIONS

Northeastern Olympic Peninsula. The most populous and easily accessible part of the peninsula includes Port Townsend, a popular weekend retreat with folks from the Seattle-Tacoma region. Here, the protected waters of Hood Canal meet the Strait of Juan de Fuca, providing a backdrop for boating, bird-watching, and waterfront dining. Farther west, bucolic farmland abounds in the rain shadow surrounding Sequim. Port Angeles provides a launchpad for skiing, snowboarding, hiking, and biking at Hurricane Ridge, one of the most easily accessible parts of Olympic National Park.

Northwestern Olympic Peninsula. Driftwood-strewn secluded beaches and dense old-growth forests, featuring enormous ferns and moss-dripping evergreens, rule the rain-soaked west end. Marked by waterfalls, rivers, and mountain lakes, this part of the peninsula is home to Cape Flattery, the most northwesterly edge of the contiguous United States, and the old logging town of Forks, the setting for the *Twilight* novels.

Washington Coast. The communities along this stretch of Pacific coastline range from the Cape Cod–style homes in the development of Seabrook, where bikes and flip-flops provide the preferred means of transportation, to Ocean Shores and Westport, guarding the entry to Grays Harbor. Tucked inside is the historic lumber and fishing town of Aberdeen, home port of the state's official ship, the *Lady Washington*.

Long Beach Peninsula. Bookended by two state parks and bounded by the Pacific Ocean and the Columbia River, this narrow stretch of land offers a series of ocean-side retreats, oyster farms, cranberry bogs, and beach after beach to comb. Kite flying, kayaking, horseback riding, clam digging, and winter-storm watching are also popular pastimes. At the southern tip, Cape Disappointment is anything but, with two lighthouses, stunning views, miles of hiking trails, and the Lewis and Clark Interpretative Center.

Planning

When to Go

Visitors trek to the Olympic Peninsula year-round, but summer is prime touring time for this outdoors-lovers' paradise. June through September, when it's least likely to rain, is busiest. Beaches, campgrounds, and downtown areas bustle during the sun-filled summer months, and festivals attract additional crowds. This is also the time of peak lodging rates.

Spring and fall are likely to be less crowded, and typically the shoulder season also promises less expensive hotel rates. Anytime between April and October, there's a good chance of clear skies, even if temperatures dip. The rest of the year, prepare for heavy clouds, rain showers, and chilly temperatures.

Accommodations tend to fill up year-round on festival and holiday weekends. Some museums and other tourist attractions close or operate on a limited schedule in winter, when unrelenting storms pound Washington's Pacific coast. Mid-October through mid-March, pummeling waves crash into sea stacks and outcroppings, and wind speeds of up to 60 mph send rain spitting sideways. Winter-storm watchers, weekend skiers and snowboarders heading to Hurricane Ridge, and locals are often the only hardy souls around this time of the year. For some, that—coupled with off-season lodging rates—is a draw.

FESTIVALS AND EVENTS

The region has a number of festivals and events that are worth planning for.

Great Port Townsend Bay Kinetic Sculpture Race

FESTIVALS | FAMILY | Since 1983, contestants have been racing human-powered contraptions through sand, mud, and saltwater in the hope of winning the most coveted prize: the Mediocrity Award for finishing in the middle of the pack. The race takes place the first full weekend in October. Festivities include a parade, an art contest, and a fundraiser "kostume" ball on Saturday night. ✉ *Port Townsend* 🌐 *www.ptkineticrace.org.*

Irrigation Festival

FESTIVALS | FAMILY | Sequim has been celebrating the introduction of irrigation water to its once-parched prairie since 1896. The fest, held in May, features an antique-car show, art exhibit, street fair, parade, and Strongman Showdown, in which competitors put their muscles to the test in events like the arm-over-arm truck pull, log press, and car lift. ✉ *Sequim* 🌐 *www.irrigationfestival.com.*

Olympic Music Festival

MUSIC FESTIVALS | From mid-July through early September, concertgoers enjoy chamber music at the Wheeler Theater in Fort Worden State Park. ✉ *200 Battery Way, Port Townsend* ☎ *360/385–9699 festival office* 🌐 *www.olympicmusicfestival.org.*

Port Townsend Film Festival

FILM FESTIVALS | This mid-September fest features onstage discussions with Hollywood stars, a variety of documentary and narrative films, and the ever-popular outdoor screenings on Taylor Street in front of the 1907 Rose Theatre. More than 80 films are screened over three days at seven venues. ✉ *Port Townsend* ☎ *360/379–1333* 🌐 *www.ptfilmfest.com.*

Sequim Lavender Festival

FESTIVALS | FAMILY | A street fair and free self-guided farm tours celebrate Sequim's many fragrant lavender fields in mid-July. ✉ *Sequim* ☎ *360/681–3035* 🌐 *www.lavenderfestival.com.*

Wooden Boat Festival

FESTIVALS | Hundreds of wooden boats sail into Port Townsend Bay each September for a weekend of presentations, tours, and sea shanties. ✉ *Port Townsend* ☎ *360/385–3628* 🌐 *www.woodenboat.org.*

Getting Here and Around

BOAT AND FERRY

Washington State Ferries offer the most direct route from Seattle to the Olympic Peninsula. Options include crossing from Seattle to Bainbridge Island or Edmonds to Kingston and then driving across and up the Kitsap Peninsula. You can also take the ferry from Mukilteo to Clinton on Whidbey Island, drive to Coupeville, and then catch a second ferry to Port Townsend. Fares vary greatly depending on the route and season, but the trips described here will generally run from about $10 to $20 for a car and driver and $4 to $10 more for additional passengers or walk-ons.

From Port Angeles, travelers can travel to Victoria, British Columbia, on the M.V. *Coho,* which makes 1½-hour crossings four times daily from mid-May through mid-October and twice daily from mid-March to mid-May and mid-October to mid-January. Rates are $67 per car and driver, $19 per passenger, and $6.50 per bike; travelers can reserve ahead for an additional fee. *Coho,* operated by Black Ball Transport, departs from the ferry terminal at the foot of Laurel Street.

CONTACTS Black Ball Ferry Line. ☎ *360/457–4491, 888/993–3779* 🌐 *www.cohoferry.com.*

BUS

Traveling by bus isn't the speediest way to get to the Olympic Peninsula, but if you're spending most of your time in walkable Port Angeles and Port Townsend, it's an option. You'll find several major car rental agencies in Port Townsend, which will come in handy for exploring Olympic National Park and the countryside once you're here. Dungeness Line, a Greyhound affiliate, transports passengers twice daily from Sea-Tac

Airport ($49) and downtown Seattle ($39) to Port Angeles, Sequim, Discovery Bay, and Port Townsend.

CONTACTS Dungeness Line. ☎ *360/417-0700* 🌐 *www.dungeness-line.com.*

CAR

U.S. 101, the main thoroughfare around the Olympic Peninsula, is a well-paved two-lane highway. Rural back roads are blacktop or gravel, and tend to have potholes and get washed out during rains, and as you venture farther from the main population centers—Port Townsend to Port Angeles in the northeast, and the towns around Grays Harbor as well as the Long Beach Peninsula in the southwest—services are few and far between, and cell service is spotty to nonexistent. Always fill up your tank and plot your course before setting out—this is one part of the state where it's helpful to have print maps (or download them in advance on your phone). In winter, landslides and wet weather sometimes close roads.

Restaurants

Port Townsend reigns as the foodie capital of the Olympic Peninsula, where Pacific Northwest coastal cuisine prevails, but nearby Sequim has an arguably even more impressive clutch of restaurants, considering how much smaller it is. And don't overlook the formerly workaday city of Port Angeles, which has witnessed a culinary renaissance in recent years and also boasts a number of lively little nightspots. In all three communities, you'll find a good mix of approachable upscale dining options, worthy international—especially Asian—restaurants, and gastropubs and cafés pouring first-rate craft beer, Northwest wines, local ciders, and hosue-roasted espresso drinks. Elsewhere, from the remote northwestern reaches of the peninsula, where dining options are few, to the lively beach towns along the coast, you'll mostly encounter casual taverns and diners serving up traditional American grub, although the Long Beach Peninsula has a handful of truly destination worthy eateries. Naturally, seafood features prominently on menus throughout this entire peninsula, with local oysters, surf and razor clams, Dungeness crab, prawns, salmon, rockfish, halibut, albacore, and lingcod leading the way. *Restaurant reviews have been shortened. For full information, visit Fodors.com.*

Hotels

The Olympic Peninsula offers a wide range of lodging options, from Cape Cod–style cottages and rustic cabins to cushy timber-paneled lodges and clifftop inns. Many offer beach access or views of the water or mountains—or both. It can be challenging to find last-minute rooms in summer and during holidays—book ahead at these times, and prepare for two- or three-night minimum stays. Winter and shoulder seasons typically offer the most economical rates. Port Angeles has the largest selection of lodgings on the peninsula and is popular among skiers, snowboarders, and day hikers headed to Hurricane Ridge. Sequim and Port Townsend have the most distinctive and upscale lodgings. The Washington Coast and Long Beach Peninsula are the best destinations for winter-storm watchers and beachcombers—in these regions, vacation rentals, condo resorts, and retro motels abound. *Hotel reviews have been shortened. For full information, visit Fodors.com.*

What It Costs in U.S. Dollars

$	$$	$$$	$$$$
RESTAURANTS			
under $16	$16–$22	$23–$30	over $30
HOTELS			
under $150	$150–$200	$201–$250	Over $250

Visitor Information

CONTACTS Discover Your Northwest. ✉ *Olympic National Park Visitor Center, 3002 Mt. Angeles Rd., Port Angeles* ☎ *360/565–3195* 🌐 *www.discovernw.org.* **Olympic National Forest Office.** ✉ *1835 Black Lake Blvd. SW, Olympia* ☎ *360/956–2402* 🌐 *www.fs.usda.gov/olympic.* **Olympic Peninsula Tourism Commission.** ✉ *618 S. Peabody St., Port Angeles* ☎ *360/452–8552, 800/942–4042* 🌐 *www.olympicpeninsula.org.*

Hood Canal

40 miles northwest of Olympia.

The 50-mile-long Hood Canal is a narrow, naturally formed fjord that separates the Olympic Peninsula from the Kitsap Peninsula and is lined with small waterfront villages, such as Hoodsport and Lilliwaup. The canal is beautiful, averaging just 1½ miles across, and has long been famous for shellfish harvesting, especially oysters and clams. There are several reasons to take your time as you make your way through the Hood Canal region, and even a couple of notable places to spend the night in the scenic hamlet of Union, which flanks the canal just a few miles east of U.S. 101 where it hooks sharply to the northeast. Other draws include stunning hiking around Lake Cushman and Lake Lena, near the eastern border of Olympic National Park, and one of the Northwest's most famous little seafood markets and restaurants, Hama Hama Oyster Saloon.

GETTING HERE AND AROUND

If you're visiting this region from Tacoma, Olympia, or Portland, you'll likely get here by driving up U.S. 101. To get to Union, detour east along the canal via Highway 106.

ESSENTIALS

VISITOR INFORMATION Explore Hood Canal. ✉ *Hoodsport Visitor Center, 150 N. Lake Cushman Rd., Hoodsport* ☎ *360/877–2021* 🌐 *www.explorehoodcanal.com.*

 Sights

★ The Hardware Distillery

WINERY/DISTILLERY | Whether you're a serious fan of craft spirits or you're just looking for a fun diversion on your drive alongside Hood Canal, this distillery decorated with old tools and other memorabilia from the building's previous life as a hardware store offers informative tastings and, by appointment, entertaining tours. For a small operation, Hardware has developed a big following for its fruit-and-honey Bee's Knees liqueurs (the fig variety is a standout) as well as spicy Cardamom Aquavit, herbal-accented Dutch genever–style small-batch gin. ✉ *24210 U.S. 101, Hoodsport* ☎ *206/300–0877* 🌐 *www.thehardwaredistillery.com* ⏲ *Closed Mon.–Wed.*

★ Lake Cushman

BODY OF WATER | An 8-mile forest drive from Hoodsport along Highway 119 leads to this 4,000-acre glacial reservoir that hugs the less-visited southeastern border of Olympic National Park. It's a less-visited gem that's popular with hikers and campers but is also wonderful for canoeing and kayaking (there are a couple of rental outfitters along the shore) as well as fishing for salmon and trout. Relax on the beach or cool off with a dip at Skokomish Park on a summer day, or make your way to nearby Mt. Ellinor Trailhead, where there are both moderate and quite strenuous hikes into the mountains that rise above this glorious lake. ✉ *Skokomish Park, 7211 N. Lake Cushman Rd. (Hwy. 119), Hoodsport* ☎ *360/877–5656* 🌐 *www.skokomishtourism.com* *Parking $10.*

Potlatch State Park

NATIONAL/STATE PARK | As you drive up U.S. 101 along the eastern side of the peninsula, you'll pass right through this 84-acre park that offers some of the best access to and prettiest views of Hood Canal. It's a great place to launch a kayak, stop for a picnic beneath the moss-draped evergreens, or scamper along the beach. There's good fishing, clamming, and crabbing, too. ✉ *21020 U.S. 101, Shelton* ☎ *360/877–5361* 🌐 *www.parks.state.wa.us* *Parking $10.*

Restaurants

★ Hama Hama Oyster Saloon

$$ | **SEAFOOD** | You'll find Hama Hama oysters, which are harvested from this Hood Canal shellfish operation that's been going strong since 1922, on some of the top restaurants in the Pacific Northwest. Here at the farm store and saloon, you can enjoy these fresh-shucked bivalves (along with clams and mussels) raw, wood-roasted, or baked with pimento cheese, along with other tasty pub fare at lunch. **Known for:** local wines, ciders, and craft beers; spicy clams steamed in chili paste; expansive patio with water views. $ *Average main: $18* ✉ *35846 U.S. 101, Lilliwaup* ☎ *360/877–5811* 🌐 *www.hamahamaoysters.com* *No dinner.*

Hoodsport Coffee Company

$ | **CAFÉ** | Well-crafted espresso drinks made with house-roasted coffee are the main draw of this congenial roadside café with comfy seating and a gas fireplace. There's also a good selection of panini and bagel sandwiches, and—most famously—locally revered Olympic Mountain ice cream in unusual flavors like vanilla-habanero and huckleberry swirl. **Known for:** build-your-own breakfast sandwiches; white-chocolate mochas; sundaes and malted milk shakes. $ *Average main: $6* ✉ *24240 U.S. 101, Hoodsport* ☎ *360/877–6732* 🌐 *www.hoodsportcoffee.com* *No dinner.*

Union City Market

$$ | **SEAFOOD** | Operated by the nearby Alderbrook Resort, this restored market at the Hood Canal Marina is open most days for gourmet snacks and to-go items, local beer and wine, and nicely curated nautical souvenirs most days, and its Hook & Fork waterfront eatery serves afternoon appetizers on Friday and leisurely brunches on weekends. A juice bar doles out fresh-squeeze concoctions, and the rotating brunch menu features baked oysters, smoked-trout toast, and crab BLTs and Benedicts. **Known for:** locally caught clams, oysters, and crab; casual waterfront seating; monthly seafood cookouts. $ *Average main: $17* ✉ *5101 Hwy. 106, Union* ☎ *360/898–3500* 🌐 *www.unioncitymarket.com* *Closed Tues. and Wed.*

Hotels

★ Alderbrook Resort & Spa

$$$$ | **RESORT** | With a quiet setting on a scenic bend of Hood Canal, this elegant evergreen-shaded resort contains snazzy rooms overlooking the water, a courtyard, or a gurgling creek. **Pros:** gorgeous, tranquil setting right on the water; lots of recreation and spa options; memorable restaurant. **Cons:** somewhat remote location; sometimes crowded with weddings; waterfront rooms are spendy. $ *Rooms from: $289* ✉ *10 E. Alderbrook Dr., Union* ☎ *360/898–2200* 🌐 *www.alderbrookresort.com* *93 rooms* *No meals.*

Robin Hood Village Resort
$ | **B&B/INN** | This 1930s-era cabin compound on Hood Canal, built in a rustic fairytale style by the guy who designed the sets for Errol Flynn's *Robin Hood* movies, is ideal for a romantic yet reasonably priced woodland getaway, complete with an enchanting lodgelike restaurant and a pub offering live music. **Pros:** enchanting forest setting; within walking distance of Alderbrook Resort; free use of kayaks and paddle boats. **Cons:** some cabins don't have hot tubs; little space between some cabins; a bit too rustic for some tastes. *$ Rooms from: $140 ✉ 6790 Hwy. 106, Union ☎ 360/898–2163 🌐 www.robinhoodvillageresort.com 16 cabins No meals.*

Lena Lake Trail
HIKING/WALKING | Doable in a half-day, this well-maintained 6½-mile out-and-back trek through a pristine swatch of Olympic National Forest twists and rises—some 1,600 feet in elevation— through lush old-growth and second-growth conifer stands before it reaches a cool alpine lake. You can continue another 3 miles to Upper Lena Lake, but this part is fairly steep and enters Olympic National Park, so dogs aren't allowed and only fit, experienced hikers should attempt this extension. Parking is $5. *✉ N. Hamma Hamma Rd., Lilliwaup ✥ 7½ miles from U.S. 101 🌐 www.fs.usda.gov/recarea/olympic.*

Port Townsend

62 miles north from Hoodsport, 35 miles northwest of Kingston ferry terminal.

On its own rugged peninsula—the small, crooked arm of the Quimper on the northeastern tip of the larger, torch-shaped Olympic—Port Townsend is a center of maritime activity, artistic expression, entrepreneurial spirit, and natural beauty. Settled in 1851, Port Townsend was dubbed the "City of Dreams" because of the early promise that it would become the largest harbor on the West Coast with help from the impending railroad. Instead, the railroad opted to terminate in Seattle and Tacoma, and this former boomtown experienced a pronounced bust. But the town's maritime setting and its proliferation of handsome Victorian buildings imbue it with a sense of romance that makes it popular as both a place to visit and live—a different kind of city of dreams—to this day.

Ship captains from around the world once sailed into this port, known during its first 50 years for its parlors of ill repute, saloons, and other waterfront shenanigans. It developed into two separate urban centers: the rough-and-tumble downtown waterfront, which catered to hard-drinking sailors and other adventurers, and Uptown, on the cliff above the bay, where merchants and permanent residents lived and raised their families away from the riffraff. Today, both of these districts—which are connected by hilly streets and the picturesque Taylor Street Stairs—have become fashionable each in their own way, each teeming with galleries and trendy boutiques, coffeehouses, brew pubs, and upscale eateries.

GETTING HERE AND AROUND

From Seattle, it's fastest to get here via the Washington State Ferry, via Bainbridge Island or Kingston, and then driving northwest across the upper Kitsap Peninsula to the floating bridge near Port Ludlow. Both routes run roughly an hour and 45 minutes, not including waits for the ferries. From Olympia and points south, take U.S. 101 along Hood Canal to Highway 14. It's relatively easy to get here without a car, but driving is the best way to explore the greater area.

GUIDED TOURS

Port Townsend Walking Tours

WALKING TOURS | The Jefferson County Historical Society conducts hour-long walking tours of downtown Port Townsend on Saturdays from June through September for $15. Additional tours of other areas, including Uptown, are also offered occasionally. ✉ *540 Water St.* ☎ *360/385–1003* 🌐 *www.jchsmuseum.org.*

ESSENTIALS

VISITOR INFORMATION Port Townsend Visitor Information Center. ✉ *2409 Jefferson St.* ☎ *360/385–2722* 🌐 *www.enjoypt.com.*

Sights

Chetzemoka Park

BEACH—SIGHT | **FAMILY** | A lovely gazebo sits in the center of this gem of a city park, perched atop a bluff overlooking Admiralty Inlet. The 6 well-maintained acres are perfect for picnicking and encompass a pond, a footbridge, a playground, and a whimsical, trellis-covered pathway that teems with blooms in spring. The Port Townsend Summer Band performs concerts here (and at nearby Fort Worden). Access the sliver of beach below via a short footpath. ✉ *Jackson and Blaine Sts.* ☎ *360/379–5096* 🌐 *www.cityofpt.us/parksites.*

Fire Bell Tower

BUILDING | Set high along the bay-side bluffs, the tower is recognizable by its pyramid shape and red paint job. Built in 1890 to hold a 1,500-pound brass alarm bell, the 75-foot wooden structure was once the key alert center for local volunteer fire fighters. A century later it's considered one of the state's most valuable historic structures. Reach the tower by climbing the steep set of stairs behind Haller Fountain at the end of Taylor Street. The tenth-of-an-acre plot also holds a park bench and a few parking spots. ✉ *Tyler St. at Jefferson St.*

Fort Flagler Historical State Park

BEACH—SIGHT | This fort, along with Fort Worden in Port Townsend and Fort Casey on Whidbey Island, was constructed in 1897 as part of an "Iron Triangle" of defense for Puget Sound. Take in sweeping views of Whidbey Island's magnificent bluffs and Port Townsend's Victorian skyline from what is now a 784-acre park perched at the northern tip of Marrowstone Island. Surrounded by saltwater on three sides, Fort Flagler served as a military training center through the world wars, and still has old gun emplacements overlooking its rocky, log- and driftwood-strewn beaches. The park has RV and tent camping, 3½ miles of coastline, and 5 miles of hiking and biking trails. Island inlets are great for paddling around; you can rent canoes and kayaks—and stock up on picnic items—at Nordland General Store (*360/385–0777*), the island's only grocery store. ✉ *10341 Flagler Rd., Nordland* ☎ *360/385–1259* 🌐 *www.parks.wa.gov* 🎫 *Parking $10.*

★ Fort Worden State Park

MILITARY SITE | **FAMILY** | With restored Victorian officers' houses and pre–World War I–era bunkers, this fascinating 432-acre park served as the filming location for the 1982 film *An Officer and a Gentleman*. Built on Point Wilson in 1896 to guard the mouth of Puget Sound, the old fort provides myriad outdoor and cultural activities for kids and adults. A sandy beach leads to the graceful 1913 Point Wilson Lighthouse. Memory's Vault, a series of pillars hidden in the hill above the inlet, features inscriptions of works from local poet Sam Hamill. Touch tanks at Port Townsend Marine Science Center on the pier offer an up-close look at sea anemones and other underwater life. Kayak tours and rentals are also available. The fort also hosts music festivals in an old military balloon-hangar-turned-performing-arts-pavilion and exhibits in an artillery museum. Many of the old buildings can now be booked as overnight accommodations, and there are a couple of excellent dining options in the park: Reveille at the Commons serves breakfast, lunch, and coffee, and Taps at the Guardhouse is known for lunch, happy hour, and early dinners. ✉ *200 Battery Way* ☎ *360/344–4400* 🌐 *fortworden.org* 🎫 *$10 parking.*

Jefferson County Museum of Art & History
MUSEUM | The carved-sandstone 1892 City Hall building houses this history and art museum operated by the Jefferson County Historic Society. You can also see the old courtroom and the basement cells of the old city jail, where author Jack London spent a night on his way to the Klondike in the summer of 1879. There's a maritime display, clusters of Native American artifacts, vintage photos of the Olympic Peninsula, and exhibits chronicling Port Townsend's past. The society offers seasonal tours of two others sites in town, the period-decorated 1868 Rothschild House Museum, which sits on a bluff in Uptown, and the Commanding Officers Quarters building in Fort Worden State Park. ✉ *540 Water St.* ☎ *360/385–1003* 🌐 *www.jchsmuseum.org* 🎫 *From $6* ⏲ *Closed Tues.*

★ **Northwest Maritime Center**
COLLEGE | Port Townsend is one of only three Victorian-era seaports on the register of National Historic Sites, and you can learn all about it at this handsome building on the waterfront. It's the center of operations for the Wooden Boat Foundation, which stages the annual Wooden Boat Festival each September. The center has interactive exhibits, hands-on sailing instruction, boatbuilding workshops, a wood shop, and a pilot house where you can test navigational tools. You can launch a kayak or watch sloops and schooners gliding along the bay from the boardwalk, pier, and beach that fronts the buildings. There's also an excellent gift shop, The Chandlery, with a coffee bar. ✉ *431 Water St.* ☎ *360/385–3628* 🌐 *www.nwmaritime.org* 🎫 *Free.*

Port Townsend Marine Science Center
ZOO | Along the waterfront at Fort Worden State Park, the small but informative center is divided into two sections. The marine lab and aquarium building, in a former World War II military storage facility at the end of a pier, houses several aquarium displays, as well as touch tanks with sea stars, crabs, and anemones. The museum contains displays detailing the region's geography and marine ecology, including one of the only orca whale skeletons in the country. Beach walks, cruises, and camps and other programs are offered throughout the summer. ✉ *520 Battery Way* ☎ *360/385–5582* 🌐 *www.ptmsc.org* 🎫 *$7* ⏲ *Closed Mon.–Thurs. in early Sept.–late May.*

Restaurants

Ajax Cafe
$$ | **PACIFIC NORTHWEST** | For a relaxing waterfront feast of locally sourced seafood, game, and produce, drive 10 miles south to this quirky little bistro overlooking the southern end of Port Townsend Bay. On the seasonal menu, you might find fried Hood Canal oysters with cilanto-lime aioli; greens with local goat cheese, pistachios, and strawberries; and fall-of-the-bone braised lamb shank with chimichurri over a bed of sweet-corn polenta. **Known for:** colorful tchotchke-filled dining room; Washington-centric wine, beer, and cider list; weekend brunch with fresh-baked scones. 💲 *Average main: $20* ✉ *21 S. Water St., Port Hadlock* ☎ *360/385–1965* 🌐 *www.ajaxcafe.com* ⏲ *Closed Mon. and Tues. No lunch weekdays.*

★ **Blue Moose Cafe**
$ | **AMERICAN** | Convivial, cozy, and a bit off-the-wall, this is one Port Townsend's best sources of generous, unfussy breakfasts and lunches, like thick pancakes and amply stuffed omelets, plus hefty burgers and sandwiches. Long popular with sailors and shipwrights who work in the surrounding Port Townsend Boat

Haven, this cash-only hole in the wall fills up fast on weekends, but you can help yourself to a mug of drip coffee while you wait. **Known for:** kitschy artwork and dishy staff; peanut butter and banana pancakes; homemade chicken-fried steak. *Average main: $13 311 Haines Pl. 360/385–7339 No credit cards No dinner.*

★ Finistère

$$$ | **MODERN AMERICAN** | In an uncluttered, light-filled storefront space in Uptown, this hip neighborhood bistro opened by a husband-wife team with experience at some of New York City's and Seattle's top restaurants turns out some of the most flavorful locavore-driven cuisine on the peninsula. You might start with a bowl of sunchoke soup with chives and truffle oil, before graduating to rabbit lasagna with sofrito and mustard greens, or seared scallops with romesco, cauliflower, and Meyer lemon. **Known for:** romantic, candle-lit dining room; chicken liver pâté on toast with roasted-onion jam; house-made pastas with inventive sauces. *Average main: $27 1025 Lawrence St. 360/344–8127 www.restaurantfinistere.com Closed Mon. and Tues. No lunch weekdays.*

★ Fountain Café

$$ | **MEDITERRANEAN** | Local artwork lines the walls of this cozy, eclectic bistro tucked inside a historic clapboard building a block off the main drag, near the foot of the Taylor Street staircase. The delicious seafood- and pasta-intensive menu reveals Mediterranean and Pacific Northwest influences—think cioppino with local shellfish in a tomato-saffron broth, and roasted walnut and gorgonzola penne with wild boar. **Known for:** friendly, unpretentious service; fresh-baked baguette with herbed butter; warm gingerbread with vanilla custard. *Average main: $20 920 Washington St. 360/385–1364 www.fountaincafept.com.*

Hanazono Asian Noodle

$ | **JAPANESE** | This long, narrow Japanese sushi bar and noodle house offers a long menu of udon, ramen, and other hearty soups along with stir-fries, sushi rolls, and *donburi* rice bowls. Start with tofu fries, miso soup, seaweed salad, spring rolls, or *gyoza* (handmade pot stickers stuffed with cabbage, pork, and green onion). **Known for:** sushi rolls with local tempura ling cod and wasabi mayo; karaage-style fried chicken with ginger-garlic sauce; excellent sake menu. *Average main: $15 225 Taylor St. 360/385–7622 hanazonopt.com Closed Mon. and Tues.*

Lanza's Ristorante

$$ | **ITALIAN** | This intimate, romantic Uptown Italian eatery has been a local institution since the early 1980s, appealing to regulars with its welcoming and gracious staff, generous portions, and authentic old-country recipes. Share the ample antipasto platter while waiting for pastas ranging from classic spaghetti and meatballs to ravioli Florentine to penne with sausage, mushrooms, and spinach. **Known for:** white pizzas with kalamata olives and artichoke hearts; reasonably priced wine list; cozy brick-wall dining room. *Average main: $19 1020 Lawrence St. 360/379–1900 www.lanzaspt.com Closed Sun. and Mon. No lunch.*

123 Thai Food

$ | **THAI** | This cheap and cheerful eatery near the Port Townsend Boat Haven ranks among the best Thai restaurants in a region—stretching from Port Angeles to Port Townsend—that has dozens of great ones. Order at the counter and then take a seat at one of the little cafe tables while you enjoy classic fare like garlic-prawn rolls, Thai beef salad, tom kha soup, and green curry. **Known for:** low-frills, open-kitchen dining room; legit "bring tears to your eyes" spice, if requested; frequent locally caught salmon curry specials. *Average main: $12*

2219 E. Sims Way 360/344–3103
Closed Sun.

Owl Sprit Cafe

$$ | **ECLECTIC** | This cozy, eclectic little gem tucked away on a downtown side street uses locally sourced, organic ingredients in its healthful grilled sandwiches, burgers, burritos, and pasta dishes. A colorful owl mural on the back wall watches over a dining room full of plants, patterned tablecloths, and local works of art. **Known for:** fresh-squeezed juices and smoothies; pork carnitas burritos; coconut-pecan bread pudding. *Average main: $17* *218 Polk St.* *360/385–5275* *www.owlsprit.com* *Closed Sun. No dinner.*

Point Hudson Cafe

$ | **PACIFIC NORTHWEST** | Views of its namesake marina account for part of the popularity of this inviting spot with leather booths, local artwork, and a wall of windows overlooking the water. It's the creative cooking that keeps folks coming back, however, with a seasonally rotating menu including waffles with rhubarb syrup, smoked-salmon polenta hash, and regional oyster scrambles. **Known for:** crab cakes topped with poached eggs; excellent craft beer selection; well-prepared espresso drinks. *Average main: $13* *130 Hudson St.* *360/379–0592* *No dinner.*

Silverwater Cafe

$$$ | **PACIFIC NORTHWEST** | On the first two floors the 1889 Elks Lodge building, this elegant restaurant specializes in deftly prepared seafood, such as sashimi-grade seared lavender-pepper ahi tuna, lemon-dill-battered lingcod fish and chips, and local clams and mussels in garlic-shallot butter. You'll also find a selection of simpler fare, including Greek lamb burgers and Washington apple salads. **Known for:** traditional New England clam chowder; dinner before a movie next door at the Rose Theatre; creamy coconut flan. *Average main: $27* *237 Taylor St.* *360/385–6448* *www.silverwatercafe.com.*

Coffee and Quick Bites

Elevated Ice Cream Company

$ | **CAFÉ** | This venerable ice-cream parlor and candy shop has been a fixture downtown since 1977, doling out small-batch ice creams and Italian ices, and always featuring at least 30 flavors—many, such as pink gooseberry and strawberry-rhubarb, featuring ingredients sourced from local farms. If it's a warm day, bring your cone, shake, or sundae (or bag of chocolates) next door to Pope Marine Park and enjoy your dessert while watching ships in the bay. **Known for:** signature Swiss orange chocolate chip ice cream; old-timey atmosphere; classic banana splits. *Average main: $5* *627 Water St.* *360/385–1156* *www.elevatedicecream.com.*

Hotels

Bishop Victorian Hotel

$$ | **B&B/INN** | This downtown brick inn surrounded by gardens and a gazebo abounds with 19th-century charms, and most of the one- and two-bedroom suites, adorned with floral fabrics, well-chosen antiques, and authentic brass accents, have garden, mountain, or water views, as well as fireplaces. **Pros:** Victorian flair with contemporary conveniences; a stone's throw from waterfront restaurants and boutiques; some rooms have kitchenettes. **Cons:** very old-fashioned aesthetic; breakfast is nothing special; some steps to climb. *Rooms from: $158* *714 Washington St.* *360/385–6122, 833/254–2469* *www.bishopvictorian.com* *16 rooms* *Free Breakfast.*

Commander's Beach House

$ | **B&B/INN** | With a charmed waterfront location along the beach trail near Point Hudson Marina and a short walk from downtown, this 1930s colonial revival home has four cute rooms appointed with Victorian antiques. **Pros:** three room have water views; short walk to restaurants and marina; fantastic breakfast included. **Cons:** not ideal for young kids; may not suit modern tastes; some rooms share a bath. *Rooms from: $115 ✉ 400 Hudson St. ☎ 360/385–1778 🌐 www.commandersbeachhouse.com 4 rooms 🍴 Free Breakfast.*

★ Fort Worden

$$$ | **RENTAL** | You can choose from a variety of interesting accommodations among the restored buildings at this bluff-top waterfront fort, from a turreted castlelike cottage to six-bedroom former officers' quarters that are ideal for family and groups. **Pros:** distinctive accommodations with fascinating history; acres of trails and waterfront; excellent tavern and restaurant on-site. **Cons:** property is crowded in summer; not within walking distance of downtown; many of the accommodations are geared to groups. *Rooms from: $220 ✉ 200 Battery Way ☎ 360/344–4400 🌐 fortworden.org 42 units 🍴 No meals.*

★ Old Consulate Inn

$$ | **B&B/INN** | Perched on a bluff a couple of blocks from the bay, this elegant turreted Victorian mansion with a sweeping veranda and parklike gardens features well-appointed view rooms, some with brass beds and claw-foot tubs. **Pros:** lots of dining and shopping nearby; gorgeous grounds and views; an architectural treasure. **Cons:** not appropriate for kids; some steps to climb; near a busy road. *Rooms from: $160 ✉ 313 Walker St. ☎ 360/385–6753, 800/300–6753 🌐 www.oldconsulate.com 6 rooms 🍴 Free Breakfast.*

Palace Hotel

$ | **B&B/INN** | In a former bordello that retains its 19th-century grandeur, this budget-priced inn's light-filled rooms—many named for the women who used to work here—feature 14-foot ceilings, towering windows, and elegant period furnishings like hand-carved dressers, wrought-iron bed frames, and big claw-foot bathtubs. **Pros:** captures Port Townsend's rich history; steps from restaurants, boutiques, and bars; reasonable rates. **Cons:** Victorian style isn't to every taste; central location can get noisy; no elevator. *Rooms from: $80 ✉ 1004 Water St. ☎ 360/385–0773, 800/962–0741 🌐 www.palacehotelpt.com 19 rooms 🍴 No meals.*

★ Ravenscroft Inn

$$ | **B&B/INN** | This eight-room inn situated in a fairly peaceful residential neighborhood a short walk from both uptown and downtown eateries stands out for its sweeping double veranda, gracious gardens and lawns, and views of the bay and distant Cascade Mountains. **Pros:** hospitable innkeeper really knows the area; walking distance from many restaurants; some rooms have bay views. **Cons:** two- or three-night minimum during busy times; no phones or TVs in rooms; not a good choice for kids. *Rooms from: $155 ✉ 533 Quincy St. ☎ 360/205–2147 🌐 www.ravenscroftinn.com 8 rooms 🍴 Free Breakfast.*

Resort at Port Ludlow

$$ | **RESORT** | This boutique resort reached from Port Townsend via a pretty 18-mile country drive makes a good base for touring both the eastern Olympic and northern Kitsap peninsulas. **Pros:** sweeping waterfront views; great for outdoors lovers; peaceful setting. **Cons:** 30-minute drive from Port Townsend; some rooms could use updating; breakfast not included. *Rooms from: $189 ✉ 1 Heron Rd. ☎ 360/437–7412 🌐 www.portludlowresort.com 37 rooms 🍴 No meals.*

The Swan Hotel

$ | **B&B/INN** | On the northern edge of downtown overlooking Point Hudson Marina, this small four-story hotel features well-lighted, airy rooms with balconies and gorgeous sea views as well as roomy cottages, most with jetted tubs and fireplaces. **Pros:** central port-side location; majestic water views; private-entrance cottages. **Cons:** small, often crowded parking lot; neighborhood is busy in summer; plain decor. $ *Rooms from: $126* ✉ *216 Monroe St.* ☎ *360/385–1718, 800/776–1718* 🌐 *www.theswanhotel.com* *13 rooms* 🍽 *No meals.*

Washington Hotel

$ | **HOTEL** | With its sleek interiors and keyless entry, this apartment-style inn on the second floor of a historic building in the heart of downtown caters to independent travelers who prefer a more contemporary alternative to Port Townsend's Victorian sensibilities. **Pros:** stylish, urbane vibe; lots of dining options nearby; roomy suites. **Cons:** no common areas; little staff interaction; busy downtown location. $ *Rooms from: $130* ✉ *825 Washington St.* ☎ *360/774–0213* 🌐 *www.washingtonhotelporttownsend.com* *4 rooms* 🍽 *No meals.*

Nightlife

Cellar Door

BARS/PUBS | The entrance to this convivial subterranean lair can be difficult to spot—it's at the bottom of the Tyler Street Stairs. Inside you'll find a casually swank cocktail bar that melds vintage Victorian antiques and reclaimed wood with a rustic, industrial look. Most of the sodas, syrups, bitters, and infusions are made in-house. There's a good menu of creative bar bites, and most nights there's live jazz or acoustic music. ✉ *940 Water St.* ☎ *360/385–6959* 🌐 *www.cellardoorpt.com.*

★ Finnriver Farm and Cidery

BREWPUBS/BEER GARDENS | With an open-air deck overlooking an 80-acre orchard just south of Port Townsend, this hip, contemporary taproom has developed a national reputation for its handcrafted ciders, with bold flavor combinations like Forest Ginger and Cranberry-Rosehip. There's live music, poetry readings, and other performances many afternoons and early evenings, and the kitchen serves up creative gastropub fare. ✉ *124 Center Rd., Chimacum* ☎ *360/339–8478* 🌐 *www.finnriver.com.*

Port Townsend Brewing Company

BREWPUBS/BEER GARDENS | Boatyard workers and beer enthusiasts congregate at this casual but well-respected Boat Haven brewery to enjoy a pint and bowl of peanuts (don't worry about dropping the spent shells on the floor). There's an outdoor beer garden during warmer months, and live bands often perform. Regular brews include the English-style Bitter End IPA, lightly smoky Peeping Peater Scotch Ale, and crisply refreshing Yoda's Green Tea Gold. ✉ *330 10th St.* ☎ *360/385–9967* 🌐 *www.porttownsend-brewing.com.*

★ Pourhouse

BREWPUBS/BEER GARDENS | This gathering place for ardent beer enthusiasts features a dozen rotating taps, 200 bottles and cans of beer and hard cider, and wines by the glass. The waterfront beer garden offers sweeping views of Port Townsend Bay and the nearby harbor. Some snacks—like charcuterie or cheese plates—are served, or you can bring your own takeout. Most Friday and Saturday nights in summer, there's live music outside in the "Impound Lot." ✉ *2231 Washington St.* ☎ *360/379–5586* 🌐 *www.ptpourhouse.com.*

Performing Arts

★ Rose Theatre

FILM | This intimate cinema in the heart of downtown screens first-run films, with an emphasis on foreign and indie flicks, in a charming little theater with pressed-tin ceilings and a lobby concession serving craft beer, local wine, and elevated snacks. In the elegant Starlight Room, on the third floor, retro and other interesting film screenings take place, and food and drinks are served by the adjacent Silverwater Cafe. ✉ *235 Taylor St.* ☎ *360/385–1089* 🌐 *www.rosetheatre.com.*

Shopping

Conservatory Coastal Home

GIFTS/SOUVENIRS | With an array of upscale, seaside luxe-living essentials like soy candles (hand-poured on-site in small batches in scents like sailcloth, fog, moss, and water) this high-ceilinged, brick-walled home-design and gift boutique smells as good as it looks. Look for furniture fashioned from reclaimed wood, nautical-theme throw pillows, jewelry, seashells, and air plants in recycled-glass terrariums. ✉ *639 Water St.* ☎ *360/385–3857* 🌐 *www.conservatorycoastalhome.com.*

Getables

FOOD/CANDY | This bustling market is a fun stop for picnic supplies or treats to bring home with you—think chocolates, local coffee, finishing salts, cheeses, charcuterie, artisan cider and beer, handmade sugar scrubs and soaps, toys, and flasks. ✉ *810 Water St.* ☎ *360/385–5560* 🌐 *www.getablespt.com.*

★ Pane d'Amore

FOOD/CANDY | Pick up a baguette, loaf of fig-anise bread, chocolate-chip cookies, maple-pecan scones, or cinnamon buns at this top-notch bakery, tucked into a small storefront in the heart of the Uptown district. There's a selection of cheeses, jams, granola, kombucha, and other gourmet goods to go as well. ✉ *617 Tyler St.* ☎ *360/385–1199* 🌐 *www.panedamore.com.*

Port Townsend Antique Mall

ANTIQUES/COLLECTIBLES | The more than 40 dealers at the two-story Port Townsend Antique Mall sell merchandise ranging from pricey Victorian collectors' items to cheap flea-market kitsch. ✉ *802 Washington St.* ☎ *360/379–8069.*

Port Townsend Farmers' Market

OUTDOOR/FLEA/GREEN MARKETS | Port Townsend is proud of its long-standing farm-to-table ethic, and you can share in the region's bounty at this vibrant farmers market held Wednesdays downtown July–mid-September, Saturday Uptown late April–December, and Sunday at Chimacum Corner mid-June–late October. Approximately 70 vendors, including some 40 farmers, showcase their fare—fresh produce, flash-frozen salmon, artisan cheeses, ciders, prepared foods, and baked goods, along with crafts, flowers, and handmade soaps. ✉ *Port Townsend* ☎ *360/379–9098* 🌐 *www.jcfmarkets.org.*

★ Soak on the Sound

SPA/BEAUTY | At this boutique day spa overlooking Port Hudson, a variety hydrotherapy offerings will leave you rejuvenated and relaxed. Soak in one of the private candlelit saltwater tubs (reservations suggested) or in the first-come, first-serve community tub. Detox in the Finnish-style cedar sauna, or book a 75-minute essential-oil massage. ✉ *242 Monroe St.* ☎ *360/385–4100* 🌐 *www.soakonthesound.com.*

William James Bookseller

BOOKS/STATIONERY | Used and out-of-print books covering all fields—with an emphasis on nautical, regional history, and art titles—are arrayed from floor to ceiling of this jam-packed indie bookstore that also carries first editions and other rare finds. ✉ *829 Water St.* ☎ *360/385–7313* 🌐 *www.williamjamesbookseller.com.*

★ Wooden Boat Chandlery

SPECIALTY STORES | This vast retail space at the Northwest Maritime Center stocks a variety of nautical gifts and gear, from brass fittings and rigging supplies to galley wares, illustrated knot books, and boats in a bottle. There's also a great selection of fleeces, caps, packs, and other outerwear. In the well-lighted back corner overlooking the bay, Velocity Coffee Bar sells espresso and baked goods. ✉ *431 Water St.* ☎ *360/385–3628* 🌐 *www.woodenboatchandlery.org.*

Activities

BIKING

With its limited car traffic and alluring scenery Fort Worden State Park is an excellent close-in spot for cycling, but the entire Quimper Peninsula is bike-friendly and offers fantastic views all the way to Fort Flagler.

The Broken Spoke

BICYCLING | This bike retail, repair, and rental shop in the heart of downtown promotes cycling at all levels. ✉ *630 Water St.* ☎ *360/379–1295* 🌐 *www.thebrokenspokept.com.*

P. T. Cyclery

BICYCLING | Mountain, tandem, and road bikes are available for rent here, and the shop repairs flats and can advise you on where to start your journey. ✉ *252 Tyler St.* ☎ *360/385–6470* 🌐 *www.ptcyclery.com.*

BOAT CRUISES

Puget Sound Express

BIRD WATCHING | This family-run company runs whale-watching high-speed catamaran cruises between Port Townsend and Friday Harbor, San Juan Island, from May through September. Boats depart from Port Townsend at 9, arriving in Friday Harbor at noon; the return trip departs from Friday Harbor at 2:30 and arrives back in Port Townsend at 5. Four-hour whale-watching trips depart from Port Townsend from mid-March–April, and you're guaranteed to see migrating gray whales. Bird-watching and multiday wildlife-viewing cruises are also offered. ✉ *Port Hudson Marina, 227 Jackson St.* ☎ *360/385–5288* 🌐 *www.pugetsoundexpress.com* 🎫 *From $85.*

WATER SPORTS

Port Townsend Paddlesports

WATER SPORTS | This sea kayak and paddleboard rental company is located next to the beach in Fort Worden State Park. It's also a good place for bike rentals and beach umbrellas. ✉ *Fort Worden State Park, 532 Battery Way E* ☎ *360/379–3608* 🌐 *www.ptpaddlesports.com.*

Sequim

31 miles west of Port Townsend.

Sequim (pronounced *skwim*), incorporated in 1913, is an endearing old mill town and farming center between the northern foothills of the Olympic Mountains and the southeastern stretch of the Strait of Juan de Fuca. The youthful vibe of neighboring Port Townsend has crept this way, and a growing number of urbane eateries and hip boutiques have opened throughout Sequim's walkable downtown, which is marked by a historic grain elevator. A few miles to the north is the shallow and fertile Dungeness Valley, which enjoys some of the lowest rainfall in western Washington. Fragrant purple lavender flourishes in local fields. East of town, scenic Sequim Bay is home to the John Wayne Marina. The actor, who navigated local waters aboard his yacht, *Wild Goose,* donated land for the marina in 1975, four years before his death.

GETTING HERE AND AROUND

You'll want a car to explore this relatively rural community that easy to reach from both Port Townsend and Port Angeles.

ESSENTIALS

VISITOR INFORMATION Sequim-Dungeness Valley Chamber of Commerce. ✉ *1192 E. Washington St.* ☎ *360/683–6197, 800/737–8462* 🌐 *www.sequimchamber.com.*

Sights

★ Dungeness Spit

NATURE PRESERVE | **FAMILY** | Curving nearly 6 miles into the Strait of Juan de Fuca, the longest natural sand spit in the United States is a wild, beautiful section of shoreline. More than 30,000 migratory waterfowl stop here each spring and fall, but you'll see plenty of birdlife any time of year. The entire spit is part of the **Dungeness National Wildlife Refuge** (*www.fws.gov/refuge/dungeness*). You can access it from the trail that begins in the 216-acre **Dungeness Recreation Area,** which serves as a portal to the shoreline. At the end of the spit is the towering white 1857 **New Dungeness Lighthouse** (*www.newdungenesslighthouse.com*). Tours, including a 74-step climb to the top, are available, though access is limited to those who can hike 5½ miles or paddle about 3½ miles out to the end of the spit—the closest launch is from Cline Spit County Park. You can also enroll to serve a one-week stint as a lighthouse keeper. If you'd prefer not to make the long trek all the way out to the lighthouse, an endeavor you should only attempt at low tide to avoid having to climb over massive driftwood logs, you can still take in plenty of beautiful scenery and spot myriad wildlife by hiking just a mile or so out along the spit and back. *554 Voice of America Rd. W* *360/683–5847* *www.clallam.net/parks* *$3 per group.*

Jamestown S'Klallam Tribe

NATIVE SITE | This village on the beach near the mouth of the Dungeness River has been occupied by the Jamestown S'Klallam tribe for thousands of years. The tribe, whose name means "strong people," was driven to the Skokomish Reservation on Hood Canal after the signing of the Treaty of Point No Point in 1855. However, in 1874, tribal leader James Balch and some 130 S'Klallam collectively purchased 210 acres where the community is today, and S'Klallam members have lived here ever since. An excellent gallery, Northwest Native Expressions, sells tribal artwork, including baskets, jewelry, textiles, and totems. Less than a mile away on U.S. 101, the tribe operates 7Cedars Casino along with a market and deli. As of this writing, the tribe was building a 100-room hotel adjacent to the casino and planned to open in late 2020. *Old Blyn Hwy. at U.S. 101* *www.jamestowntribe.org.*

Olympic Game Farm

ZOO | FAMILY | For years, this 200-acre property—part zoo, part safari park—claimed Walt Disney Studios as its exclusive client, and many of the animals here are the offspring of former movie stars. On the hour-long, drive-through tour, which covers some 84 acres of the picturesque property, be prepared to see large animals like American bison surround your car and lick your windows. You'll also see zebras, llamas, lynx, lions, elk, Tibetan yak, emu, bobcat, Siberian and Bengal tigers, African lions, Kodiak and black bears, and many other kinds of animals. Facilities also include an aquarium, studio barn with movie sets, snack kiosk, and a gift shop. Guests are allowed to feed uncaged animals (with wheat bread only), except for the buffalo and elk at the entrance gates, but must stay in their vehicles. *1423 Ward Rd.* *360/683–4295, 800/778–4295* *www.olygamefarm.com* *$17.*

Purple Haze Organic Lavender Farm

FARM/RANCH | One of the best places to pick or even just stroll through Sequim's most famous agricultural product, this organic farm contains 12 acres of lavender fields as well as lawns for picnicking and a gift shop that carries bath and body products, honeys and jams, and other lavender-infused gifts. A little snack stand sells lavender ice cream and lemonade. The farm is open for visits late May through early September, but you can shop for Purple Haze products year-round at their downtown shop at 127 West Washington Street. *180 Bell Bottom Rd.* *360/582–1131* *www.purplehazelavender.com* *Closed early Sept.–late May.*

★ **Railroad Bridge Park**

CITY PARK | On 25 acres along the Dungeness River, this beautifully serene park is centered on a lacy ironwork bridge that was once part of the coastal rail line between Port Angeles and Port

Townsend. The River Walk hike-and-bike path leads from the Dungeness River Audubon Center—which has excellent natural history exhibits—into the woods, and a horseback track links Runnion Road with the waterway. In summer, you might picnic at the River Shed pavilion, and watch performances at the River Stage amphitheater. There are free guided bird walks Wednesday mornings from 8:30 to 10:30. ✉ *2151 Hendrickson Rd.* ☎ *360/681–4076* 🌐 *www.dungenessriver-center.org* 🎫 *Free.*

Sequim Bay State Park

BEACH—SIGHT | Protected by a sand spit 4 miles southeast of Sequim on Sequim Bay, this 92-acre woodsy inlet park has picnic tables, campsites, hiking trails, tennis courts, and a boat ramp. ✉ *269035 U.S. 101* ☎ *360/683–4235* 🌐 *www.parks.state.wa.us* 🎫 *Parking $10.*

Sequim Farmers Market

MARKET | You'll find honey, lavender, sea glass jewelry, pottery, and locally grown produce in abundance at this Saturday market, a tented affair with lots of color and live music, held 9 to 3 between mid-May and late October. ✉ *City Hall Plaza, 152 W. Cedar St.* ☎ *360/582–6218* 🌐 *www.sequimmarket.com.*

Restaurants

★ Alder Wood Bistro

$$$ | **PACIFIC NORTHWEST** | Look to this easygoing, art-filled restaurant for inventive, locally sourced and mostly organic dishes, including pizzas from the wood-fired with creative toppings like pesto, truffled goat cheese, and picked onions. The menu's sustainably harvested seafood selections highlight whatever is in season and also get the wood-fire treatment. **Known for:** alfresco dining in a garden courtyard; local craft beer and cider; crème brûlée with local lavender. [$] *Average main: $23* ✉ *139 W Alder St.* ☎ *360/683–4321* 🌐 *www.alderwoodbistro.com* 🕒 *Closed Sun.–Tues.*

Blondie's Plate

$$ | **MODERN AMERICAN** | An 1896 white clapboard former Episcopalian Church—with its Gothic windows, polished-wood floors, and soaring ceilings—has been converted into this buzzy neighborhood bistro that specializes in sophisticated cocktails and shareable plates of creative American fare. Notable offerings include a pickled-beet salad with goat cheese croutons, crispy-skin ginger-miso salmon, and house-made pasta with lamb ragout. **Known for:** liquid-smoke Manhattan cocktails; generous happy hours; flatbread with roasted-tomato pesto. [$] *Average main: $20* ✉ *134 S. 2nd Ave.* ☎ *360/683–2233* 🌐 *www.blondiesplate.com* 🕒 *Closed Sun. No lunch.*

Dockside Grill

$$$ | **SEAFOOD** | With memorable views of John Wayne Marina and Sequim Bay, this is a fun place to watch boats placidly sail by while nibbling on Dungeness crab fritters, steamed clams, bouillabaisse, cioppino, and seafood pastas. The kitchen also serves up an excellent cedar-plank rib-eye steak, coffee-rubbed and served with jalapeño-garlic butter. **Known for:** outdoor deck overlooking the water; oyster po'boys and crab melt sandwiches at lunch; espresso brownie à la mode. [$] *Average main: $27* ✉ *2577 W. Sequim Bay Rd.* ☎ *360/683–7510* 🌐 *www.docksidegrill-sequim.com* 🕒 *Closed Mon. and Tues.*

★ Nourish

$$$ | **PACIFIC NORTHWEST** | This greenhouse-enclosed restaurant with a sunny garden patio overlooks one of the region's oldest lavender and herb farms and features a seasonally inspired menu. The specialties change often but might include lamb burgers with turmeric-pickled onions and Dijon aioli, seared pork belly with tamari-ginger sauce, and chili-seared halibut with a rhubarb-tarragon salsa. **Known for:** rich selection of vegetarian, vegan, and gluten-free options; craft cocktails with herbal and fresh-fruit infusions; leisurely Sunday brunches. *Average main: $25* *101 Provence View La.* *360/797–1480* *www.nourishsequim.com* *Closed Mon. and Tues.*

Oak Table Cafe

$ | **AMERICAN** | Carefully crafted breakfasts and lunches are the focus of this well-run, family-friendly eatery, a Sequim institution since 1981. Breakfast is served throughout the day, and on Sunday morning the large, well-lit dining room is especially bustling. **Known for:** Eggs Nicole with veggies and hollandaise sauce on a croissant; huge soufflé-style apple-cinnamon pancakes; char-broiled burgers at lunch. *Average main: $13* *292 W. Bell St.* *360/683–2179* *www.oaktablecafe.com* *No dinner.*

★ Salty Girls Seafood

$$ | **SEAFOOD** | This hip, counter-service seafood bar with a mod-industrial vibe serves Puget Sound oysters and clams on the half shell—either raw or baked with seasonal compound butters—and several beers and ciders on tap to wash them down. Oyster shooters are another favorite, and there's a short menu of additional fish-centric dishes, from steamed Dungeness crab with clarified butter to chowder made with local clams. **Known for:** "grown-up" grilled cheese with bacon and shrimp; exceptional craft cocktails; sea-salt chocolate-chip cookies. *Average main: $18* *210 W. Washington St.* *360/775–3787* *www.saltygirlsseafood.com.*

Hotels

★ Dungeness Barn House B&B

$$ | **B&B/INN** | Smell the sea breeze and the scent of lavender from the grounds of this tranquil B&B fashioned out of a beautiful barn with wood floors, beadboard wainscoting, stained-glass windows, and an inviting great room with cathedral ceilings, a fireplace, a meditation loft. **Pros:** private deck with stairs leading down to beach; surrounded by seasonal gardens; farm-to-table breakfasts. **Cons:** need a car to get around; not ideal for young children; single-night stays cost more in high season. *Rooms from: $185* *42 Marine Dr.* *360/582–1663* *www.dungenessbarnhouse.com* *4 rooms* *Free Breakfast.*

Greenhouse Inn by the Sea

$$ | **B&B/INN** | All five rooms in this sweet, upscale B&B on a bluff overlooking the Strait of Juan de Fuca and Vancouver Island, just a short stroll from Cline Spit County Park, have private balconies with dramatic vistas, and some have fireplaces and soaking tubs. **Pros:** idyllic setting on Dungeness Bay; breakfast ingredients grown on property; rooms have sweeping views. **Cons:** not actually on the beach; 10-minute drive from downtown; least expensive room has bath on different floor. *Rooms from: $150* *15781 N.E. North Shore Rd.* *360/275–9313* *www.summertideresort.com* *5 rooms* *Free Breakfast.*

★ Lost Mountain Lodge

$$ | **B&B/INN** | In a beautiful foothills setting with Olympic Mountains views, this sumptuous 10-acre retreat offers tranquil grounds, spacious accommodations with luxe furnishings, and extras like in-room couples massage and other spa options. **Pros:** hearty breakfasts (for the suites without kitchens); quiet mountain-view setting; in-room spa services. **Cons:** 10-minute drive to downtown; books up well in advance in summer; not for families with small kids. *Rooms from: $190* *303 Sunny View Dr.* *360/683–2431* *www.lostmountainlodge.com* *6 rooms* *Free Breakfast.*

Red Caboose Getaway

$$$ | **B&B/INN** | Accommodations in this distinctive rail-theme B&B are inside six vintage cabooses with themes ranging from the Casey Jones (an original conductor's desk and other train memorabilia) to the Orient Express (a fireplace and

double whirlpool bath). Cupolas afford views of the Olympic Mountains. The Silver Eagle restaurant, in an elegant 1937 Zephyr dining car, turns out four-course breakfasts on fine china, crystal, and linens. vintage cabooses with themes ranging from the Casey Jones (an original conductor's desk and other train memorabilia) to the Orient Express (a fireplace and double whirlpool bath). **Pros:** one of the area's most memorable lodgings; a must for railroad enthusiasts; less than a mile from downtown. **Cons:** no kids under 12; less scenic part of town; rooms are a bit compact. *Rooms from: $222* *24 Old Coyote Way* *360/683–7350* *www.redcaboosegetaway.com* *6 suites* *Free Breakfast.*

Port Angeles

17 miles west of Sequim.

Sprawling along the hills above the deep-blue Strait of San Juan de Fuca, this logging and fishing town on the water's edge is drawing a steady stream of independently owned restaurants, shops, and bars, as well as a smattering of hotels (including a brand-new one built by the Lower Elwha Klallam tribe and slated to open in 2021). It's all set around a modern marina and the terminal for ferries bound for Victoria, British Columbia, 20 miles across the strait. With a population of about 20,000, the town is the largest on the Olympic Peninsula and the most prominent gateway to Olympic National Park. Summer foot traffic is shoulder-to-shoulder downtown, with travelers rushing to and from the ferry, strolling the waterfront, and relaxing at outdoor cafés and pubs.

The area was first settled by the Hoh, Makah, Quileute, Quinault, and S'Klallam tribes. Few others visited here until a Greek navigator named Apostolos Valerianus—aka Juan de Fuca—sailed into the strait in 1610. In 1791 Spanish explorer Juan Francisco de Eliza arrived and named the place Puerto de Nuestra Señora de Los Angeles, or Port of Our Lady of the Angels. George Vancouver shortened the name to Port Angeles in 1792, and the site was settled by pioneers in 1856. In the century that followed, Port Angeles became a timber-mill town, a military base, and a regional fishing port, and only since the mid-20th century has it become steadily popular with vacationers.

GETTING HERE AND AROUND

Port Angeles lies about an hour's drive west of Port Townsend and is most easily reached by car, although there are several car rental agencies in town, if you arrive here by ferry and bus and need a set of wheels to visit Olympic National Park or explore the shoreline.

ESSENTIALS

VISITOR INFORMATION Port Angeles Regional Chamber of Commerce. *121 E. Railroad Ave.* *360/452–2364* *www.portangeles.org.*

Sights

Feiro Marine Life Center

ZOO | **FAMILY** | Beside a small beach, this modest but nicely designed sea-life center has a perfect location right along the Port Angeles waterfront near the ferry terminal. Murals of historic Port Angeles scenes decorate the outside; inside are plenty of touch tanks where kids can say hello to sea creatures. *Port Angeles City Pier, 315 N. Lincoln St.* *360/417–6254* *www.feiromarinelifecenter.org* *$5.*

Port Angeles Fine Arts Center

MUSEUM | With modern, funky, and intriguing exhibits by new and emerging artists, this small, beautifully designed modern museum is inside the former home of the late artist and publisher Esther Barrows Webster, one of Port Angeles's most energetic and cultured citizens. Outside, Webster's Woods

Sculpture Park—open daily dawn to dusk—is dotted with oversize art installations set against a backdrop of the city and harbor. ✉ *1203 E. Lauridsen Blvd.* ☎ *360/457–3532* 🌐 *www.pafac.org* ⏲ *Closed Mon.–Wed. in Oct.–Mar.*

Restaurants

C'est Si Bon
$$$$ | **FRENCH** | With a fanciful dining room done up in bold red hues, with crisp white linens, huge oil paintings, and glittering chandeliers, this grand, solarium-style French restaurant is unabashedly old-school. The menu reads like a greatest hits of *Larousse Gastronomique,* with everything exquisitely prepared: French onion soup, salmon *en papillotte,* duck breast with berry sauce, steak au poivre. **Known for:** Parisian-inspired sophistication; deft, knowledgeable service; chocolate mousse and Irish coffee for dessert. 💲 *Average main: $38* ✉ *23 Cedar Park Rd.* ☎ *360/452–8888* 🌐 *www.cestsibon-frenchcuisine.com* ⏲ *Closed Mon. and Tues. No lunch.*

Dupuis Restaurant
$$ | **SEAFOOD** | This dimly lighted roadside log cabin, painted a cheery yellow, evokes the feeling of a bygone era with its wood paneling, exposed beams, and bric-a-brac-filled dining room. Local sustainable seafood, often with modern preparations, dominates the menu—consider Dungeness crab cakes with pineapple-cranberry compote, gnocchi with wild shrimp and shellfish, or cioppino with a side of creamy oyster stew. **Known for:** old-fashioned ambience; local-cod fish-and-chips; classic cocktails in the Forest Room lounge. 💲 *Average main: $22* ✉ *256861 U.S. 101* ☎ *360/457–8033* 🌐 *www.dupuis-restaurant.com* ⏲ *Closed Sun.–Tues. No lunch.*

Hotels

★ Colette's Bed & Breakfast
$$$$ | **B&B/INN** | This contemporary oceanfront mansion set on a 10-acre sanctuary of gorgeous gardens offers a level of service and luxury that's unmatched in the area, with water-view suites that have fireplaces, patios, and two-person spa tubs, and multicourse breakfasts featuring organic fresh local produce, decadent baked goods, and house specialties like Dungeness crab hash, smoked salmon frittata, and dill crepes. **Pros:** sweeping water views; highly professional staff; lush gardens and grounds. **Cons:** not suitable for kids; 15-minute drive from town; a bit spendy for the area. 💲 *Rooms from: $295* ✉ *339 Finn Hall Rd.* ☎ *360/457–9197, 888/457–9777* 🌐 *www.colettes.com* *5 suites* *Free Breakfast.*

Domaine Madeleine
$$$ | **B&B/INN** | Perched on a bluff above the Strait of Juan de Fuca, these opulent suites and cottages have updated contemporary decor, colorful murals, fireplaces, and water, mountain, and garden views. **Pros:** gorgeous gardens and water views; abundant wildlife viewing; large private decks or patios. **Cons:** no children under 10; breakfast costs extra; 15-minute drive from downtown. 💲 *Rooms from: $225* ✉ *146 Wildflower La.* ☎ *360/457–4174* 🌐 *www.domainemadeleine.com* *3 suites, 3 cottages* *No meals.*

Five SeaSuns Bed & Breakfast
$$ | **B&B/INN** | Less than a mile uphill from downtown, surrounded by meticulously cared for gardens, this cozy 1926 inn overlooks the mountains and the bay and contains elegant rooms with Victorian furnishings and wallpapers. **Pros:** lovely garden setting; excellent full breakfast; walking distance to restaurants and bars. **Cons:** on a busy street; rather frilly decor; not suitable for young kids. 💲 *Rooms from: $172* ✉ *1006 S. Lincoln St.* ☎ *360/452–8248* 🌐 *www.seasuns.com* *5 rooms* *Free Breakfast.*

★ **Sea Cliff Gardens Bed & Breakfast**

$$$$ | B&B/INN | A gingerbread-style porch fronts this Victorian on 2 landscaped acres of lush perennial gardens and a grand lawn dotted with Adirondack chairs that ends on a bluff overlooking Vancouver Island. **Pros:** sumptuous, romantic accommodations; gorgeous flower gardens; spectacular water views. **Cons:** a bit off the beaten path; among the most expensive lodgings in the area; not a good option for children. *Rooms from: $290* ✉ *397 Monterra Dr.* ☎ *360/452–2322* 🌐 *www.seacliffgardens.com* *5 suites* *Free Breakfast.*

Activities

BEACHES

Ediz Hook

PARK—SPORTS-OUTDOORS | FAMILY | At the western end of Port Angeles, this 3-mile-long natural sand spit protects the harbor from big waves and storms. The Hook is a fine place to take a walk along the water and watch shore- and seabirds, and to spot the occasional seal, orca, or gray whale. It's also a popular dive spot. ✉ *Ediz Hook Rd., off west end of Marine Dr.*

Neah Bay

70 miles northwest of Port Angeles.

One of the oldest villages in Washington, Neah (pronounced *nee*-ah) Bay has about 900 residents and is surrounded by the Makah Reservation at the northwestern tip of the Olympic Peninsula. It's a quiet seaside settlement of one-story homes, espresso stands, and bait shops stretched along about a mile of gravelly coastal road, which parallels the glistening, boat-filled bay. Although remote and relatively little visited, it's the gateway for some spectacular natural scenery, including Cape Flattery and Shi Shi Beach. In town, stroll along the docks to watch boot-clad fishermen and shaggy canines motoring out on warped and barnacled vessels, and peer into tidal pools for views of anemones and shellfish.

In 1778, explorer James Cook named Cape Flattery, the northwestern point in the Lower 48, when his ship missed the fog-smothered Strait of Juan de Fuca and landed here instead. In 1792 Spanish mariners established a short-lived fort, the first European settlement in what is now Washington State. The local Makah tribe is more closely related to the Nootka of Vancouver Island, just across the water, than to any Washington tribe.

GETTING HERE AND AROUND

Neah Bay is quite remote, accessed by Highway 112 west of Sekiu. It's about a 90-minute drive from Port Townsend.

Sights

★ **Cape Flattery**

LIGHTHOUSE | Part of the joy of visiting this windswept rocky outcropping that marks the northwesternmost point in the contiguous United States is making the picturesque 15-minute drive along winding Cape Loop Drive from Neah Bay. Once you've parked, follow the fairly easy ¾-mile trail, part of it along boardwalks and up and down wooden stairs, through a pristine evergreen forest to a wooden observation platform, from which you can see the 1854 Cape Flattery Lighthouse standing tall on a rocky island half a mile away. Keep an eye out for sea lions, eagles, migratory birds, and whales, which often appear in the rocky cove below. To park here on this land that's part of the Makah Reservation, you'll need to buy a $10 Makah Recreation Pass (also good for nearby Shi Shi Beach). ✉ *Cape Loop Rd.* 🌐 *www.makah.com* *$10 parking.*

★ **Makah Cultural and Research Center**

COLLEGE | FAMILY | Thousands of Makah artworks and artifacts, many eons old, fill a dramatically lighted space that's the perfect backdrop for the intriguing exhibits. The centerpiece is a full-size cedar longhouse, complete with handwoven baskets, fur skins, cattail wool, grass mats on the bed planks, with tribal music playing in the background. Another section showcases full-size whaling and seal-hunting canoes and weapons. Other areas show games, clothing, crafts, and relics from the ancient Ozette Village mudslide. The small but unusually good museum shop stocks a collection of locally made art crafts. ✉ *1880 Bayview Ave.* ☎ *360/645–2711* 🌐 *www.makahmuseum.com* 🎟 *$6.*

Makah National Fish Hatchery

FISH HATCHERY | At this facility with a picturesque setting on the Tsoo-Yess River, near Shi Shi Beach, visitors can view chinook salmon as they make their way over fish ladders to the hatchery's spawning area. Spawning months are October through December, and the salmon are released in late April. Smaller numbers of coho and chum salmon as well as steelhead trout also populate the hatchery. ✉ *897 Hatchery Rd.* ☎ *360/645–2521* 🌐 *www.fws.gov/makahnfh* ⏲ *Closed weekends.*

Beaches

★ Shi Shi Beach

BEACHES | Although it takes some effort to get to, and it can get quite crowded during the peak summer months, this spectacular crescent of beach strewn with massive boulders and otherworldly rock formations is well worth the trek, so allow yourself a full day to experience it. The trailhead and northern section of the beach are on the Makah Reservation, and hiking in is via a scenic 2-mile rainforest trail. Once you're at the beach, it's another 2½-mile trek along the sand to reach Shi Shi's most alluring featuring, the Point of Arches—a mile-long wonderland of dramatic sea stacks that look especially cool against the backdrop of the crashing surf and setting sun. The lower end of the beach and Point of Arches are within the border of Olympic National Park. A Makah Recreation Pass ($10) is required for parking, and a permit and, in summer, reservations must be obtained from the Wilderness Information Center in Port Angeles (see the Olympic National Park chapter). **Amenities:** parking. **Best for:** sunset, walking. ✉ *Tsoo-Yess Beach Rd.* ⊕ *6 miles south of Neah Bay; follow fish hatchery signs from Cape Flattery Rd.* 🌐 *www.makah.com* ☞ *Parking $10.*

Restaurants

Calvin's Crab House

$ | SEAFOOD | This friendly, no-frills seafood spot has a simple dining room as well as picnic tables and Adirondack chairs on the beach overlooking the Strait of San Juan de Fuca. On warm days it's an idyllic spot to enjoy fresh fish and chips (your choice of salmon, halibut, prawns, or oysters), plus hearty seafood chowder and Dungeness crab when it's in season. **Known for:** lightly battered fresh local seafood; thick, finger-size steak fries; iced and hot espresso drinks. 💲 *Average main: $15* ✉ *160 Bayview Ave.* ☎ *360/374–5630* ⏲ *Closed Sun. and Mon.*

Hotels

★ Chito Beach Resort

$$ | B&B/INN | Blissfully remote and breathtakingly scenic even by Olympic Peninsula standards, this collection of cabins between Clallam Bay and Neah Bay sits on a remote beach with panoramas across the Straight of San Juan de Fuca toward Vancouver Island. **Pros:** unobstructed Strait of Juan de Fuca views; cabins have fully stocked kitchens; peaceful setting. **Cons:** 15- to 20-minute drive from nearest town; not suitable for kids; two- to three-night minimum in summer. 💲 *Rooms from: $179* ✉ *7639 Hwy. 112, Sekiu* ☎ *360/963–2581* 🌐 *www.chitobeach.com* 🛏 *6 cabins* 🍽 *No meals.*

Makah Indian art

Inn at Neah Bay

$ | **B&B/INN** | This three-story, sky-gray chalet above the Strait of Juan de Fuca offers basic but comfortable rooms and suites with tile floors, microwaves and refrigerators, and shared porches with views of the Salish Sea. Some rooms can sleep four and have twin beds for kids. **Pros:** fire pit and barbecue grill; across the road from pristine beach; good choice for anglers. **Cons:** not well-suited for young kids; 5 miles from town; clean but fairly basic furnishings. *Rooms from: $112 ✉ 1562 Hwy. 112 ☎ 360/374–2225 🌐 www.theinnatneahbay.com 4 rooms Free Breakfast.*

Forks

49 miles south of Neah Bay.

The former logging town of Forks is named for two nearby river junctions: the Bogachiel and Calawah Rivers merge west of town, and a few miles farther they are joined by the Soleduck to form the Quillayute River, which empties into the Pacific at the Native American village of La Push. Forks is small and quiet with no major attractions per se, but is the gateway town for visiting Hoh River valley and the Pacific beaches of Olympic National Park. The surrounding countryside is exceptionally green, and the annual precipitation of more than 100 inches makes it one of the wettest places in the contiguous United States. As the setting for the popular *Twilight* movie series, the town has become a favorite destination for fans.

GETTING HERE AND AROUND

You definitely need a car to explore this rugged, rural area. Forks is a little more than an hour from Port Angeles and about two hours north of Aberdeen, by way of Lake Quinault.

ESSENTIALS

VISITOR INFORMATION Forks Chamber of Commerce. *✉ 1411 S. Forks Ave. ☎ 360/374–2531, 800/443–6757 🌐 www.forkswa.com.*

Beaches

★ Ruby Beach

BEACHES | The northernmost and arguably the most breathtaking of Olympic National Park's Kalaloch area beaches, this wild and windswept swath of shoreline is named for the rosy fragments of garnet that color its sands. From an evergreen-shaded bluff, a short trail winds down to the wave-beaten sands where Cedar Creek meets the ocean, and you may spy sea otters along with bald eagles, oystercatchers, cormorants, and other birdlife. Driftwood separates the woods from the sand—it's a good spot to set up a picnic blanket and watch the sun fall over the pounding surf. Up and down the coast, dramatic sea stacks and rock cairns frame beach, which is a favorite place for beachcombers, artists, and photographers. **Amenities:** toilets. **Best for:** sunset; walking. ✉ *U.S. 101, Kalaloch* ⊕ *28 miles south of Forks* 🌐 *www.nps.gov/olym.*

Restaurants

Blakeslee's Bar and Grill

$ | **AMERICAN** | In an area with precious few dining options, this casual tavern just a little south of downtown Forks is a sight for sore eyes and hungry stomachs, offering up big portions of reliably good pub food. After a day of hiking in the national park, tuck into the half-pound Mill Creek bacon and cheeseburger, a rib-eye steak, or a platter of batter-fried local seafood. **Known for:** nachos (both traditional and Irish-style); craft beer and creative cocktails; popular place for pool. $ *Average main: $14* ✉ *1222 S. Forks Ave.* ☎ *360/374–5003* ⏲ *Closed Mon.*

Hotels

Manitou Lodge

$$ | **B&B/INN** | Seclusion, quiet, and relaxation are assured at this cedar lodge in the rain forest, where five lodge rooms and two suites in the adjacent cottage have cedar paneling, handmade quilts, driftwood headboards, and oak furnishings; the large Sacagawea room even has a fireplace. **Pros:** warmly appointed rooms; tranquil Sol Duc River setting; short drive from Rialto Beach. **Cons:** no TV, phones, or cell service; modest breakfasts; remote location. $ *Rooms from: $178* ✉ *813 Kilmer Rd.* ☎ *360/374–6295* 🌐 *www.manitoulodge.com* *9 rooms* 🍴 *Free Breakfast.*

★ Miller Tree Inn Bed and Breakfast

$$ | **B&B/INN** | With country antiques, fluffy quilts, and big windows overlooking peaceful pastures, this 1916 farmhouse on the east side of downtown Forks is nicknamed the "Cullen House" for its resemblance to the description in Stephenie Meyer's *Twilight* books. **Pros:** some rooms have whirlpool tubs and gas fireplaces; nearby rivers offer prime salmon and steelhead fishing; children are welcome in some rooms. **Cons:** lots of Twilight-related tchotchkes; some rooms require climbing stairs; pricey in summer. $ *Rooms from: $190* ✉ *654 E. Division St.* ☎ *360/374–6806, 800/943–6563* 🌐 *www.millertreeinn.com* *8 rooms* 🍴 *Free Breakfast.*

Misty Valley Inn

$$ | **B&B/INN** | Tucked among towering trees a few miles north of Forks and close to the Sol Duc River, this peaceful little inn is a nature lover's dream, with fragrant roses and rhododendrons, hummingbirds darting about, and views east toward the Olympic Mountains. **Pros:** lush garden setting; delicious breakfasts; hot tub with woodland views. **Cons:** a few miles north of downtown; no kids under 12; near busy road. $ *Rooms from: $150* ✉ *194894 U.S. 101* ☎ *360/374–9389* 🌐 *www.mistyvalleyinn.com* *4 rooms* 🍴 *Free Breakfast.*

Pacific Inn Motel

$ | **HOTEL** | It may not look like much from the outside, but the only motel for 50 miles in either direction is a comfortable

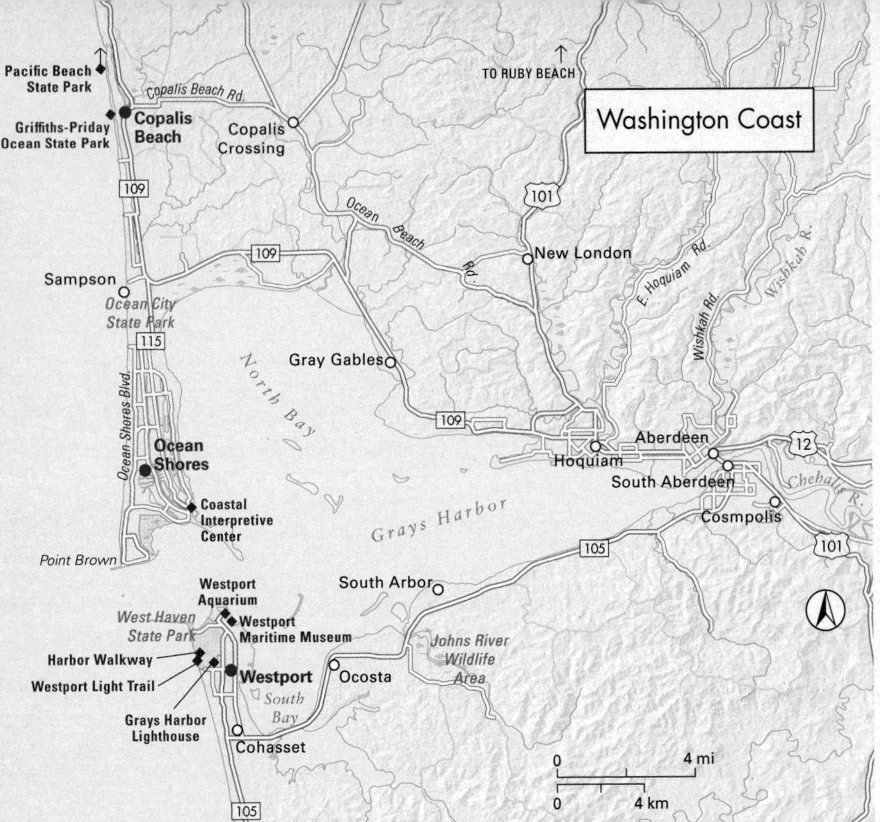

and clean budget choice and a handy base for exploring Olympic National Park, with spacious rooms with modern furnishings and framed landscape photos. **Pros:** cheap rates; central location; immaculately kept. **Cons:** no breakfast; low on frills; not in a scenic part of town. *Rooms from: $124* *352 Forks Ave.* *360/374–9400, 800/235–7344* *www.pacificinnmotel.com* *34 rooms* *No meals.*

Copalis Beach

74 miles west of Olympia, 100 miles south of Forks.

A Native American village for several thousand years, this small coastal town at the mouth of the Copalis (pronounced coh- *pah*-liss) River was settled by European Americans in the 1890s. The beach here is known locally for its innumerable razor clams, which can be gathered by the thousands each summer, and for its watchtowers, built between 1870 and 1903 to spot sea otters—the animals are now protected by Washington state law. Less developed and more low-key than Ocean Shores to the south, this scenery only becomes more beautiful as you venture north the shore to the upscale planned community of Seabrook and the laid-back village of Pacific Beach.

GETTING HERE AND AROUND

Copalis Beach is about 74 miles west of Olympia.

Sights

Griffiths-Priday Ocean State Park

NATIONAL/STATE PARK | You can hit the trails on foot or atop a horse in this 533-acre estuarial park stretching more than a mile along both the Pacific Ocean and the Copalis River. A boardwalk crosses low dunes to the broad, flat beach. The Copalis Spit section of the park is a designated wildlife refuge for thousands of snowy plovers and other birdlife. Favorite activities include picnicking, bird-watching, mountain biking, fishing, clamming, kite flying, and beachcombing. ✉ *3119 Hwy. 109* ☎ *360/902–8844* 🌐 *www.parks.state.wa.us* *Parking $10.*

Sandphifer Gallery

MUSEUM | In this cute clapboard cottage just north of Pacific Beach State Park, you can browse the mixed-media and colored-pencil wildlife drawings of Karin Phifer. The brilliantly colored sea creatures in her Fantasy Fish series offer a nice example of how she depicts animals' eyes, lips, and noses to accentuate their personalities. ✉ *102 1st St. N, Pacific Beach* ☎ *360/276–5029* 🌐 *www.sandphiferart.com* ⏲ *Closed weekdays early Sept.–late May.*

Beaches

Pacific Beach State Park

BEACH—SIGHT | Between Copalis Beach and the village of Moclips, this is a lovely spot for walking, surf-perch fishing, and razor-clam digging. There's also excellent fishing for sea-run cutthroat trout in the Moclips River—but be careful not to trespass onto the Quinault Reservation north of the river. The 17-acre park has developed tent and RV sites, as well as a few primitive beachfront campsites. **Amenities:** parking; toilets. **Best for :** solitude; sunset; walking. ✉ *49 2nd St., Pacific Beach* ☎ *360/276–4297* 🌐 *www.parks.state.wa.us* *Parking $10.*

Restaurants

★ **Frontager's Pizza**

$$ | **PIZZA** | One of the best restaurants in the beach community of Seabrook, this cosmopolitan bistro with white brick walls, a pressed-tin counter bar, and big windows produces tantalizing pies with blistered crusts and top-notch toppings. Consider the truffle bianca with locally foraged mushrooms and fresh oregano and sage, or the smoked-bacon pizza with basil pesto, fingerling potatoes, and two runny organic eggs. **Known for:** great selection of creative salads; thin-crust New York–style pizzas; small but thoughtful wine list. $ *Average main: $19* ✉ *21 Seabrook Ave., Pacific Beach* ☎ *360/276–0297* 🌐 *www.frontagerspizza.com.*

Green Lantern Pub

$ | **AMERICAN** | The Copalis River flows beside this cedar-shake-covered local favorite, in business since the 1930s and known for filling comfort food throughout the day, starting with bay shrimp breakfast scrambles and continuing later in the day with BLTs, burgers, grilled cheese, clam strips, and fish-and-chips served in baskets. The laid-back dining room has a 10-foot-long clam-digging shovel in the corner. **Known for:** picnic tables overlooking the river; prime-rib and barbecue rib specials; tasty fried seafood. $ *Average main: $13* ✉ *3119 Hwy. 109* ☎ *360/289–2297* *No credit cards.*

Hotels

★ **Iron Springs Resort**

$$$$ | **RESORT** | This 100-acre retreat dating back to the 1940s has gorgeously updated cabins, each decorated in earth tones with timber accents, beachy-elegant furnishings, and upscale kitchens. **Pros:** charming rustic-chic decor; gorgeous views and hiking trails; on a quiet stretch of beachfront. **Cons:** very secluded location; among the highest rates on the coast; some cabins are a bit small. $ *Rooms from: $269* ✉ *3707 Hwy. 109*

☎ *360/276–4230* ⊕ *www.ironspringsresort.com* ⇨ *28 cabins* 🍴 *No meals.*

Seabrook Cottage Rentals
$$ | **RENTAL** | **FAMILY** | Crushed seashells line pathways throughout the dapper planned beach resort town of Seabrook, where you'll find a collection of some 350 Cape Cod–style homes, more than half of which are available to rent. **Pros:** beach and forest within easy walking distance; attractive contemporary homes with lots of bells and whistles; some pet-friendly lodgings. **Cons:** homes are closely spaced on small lots; minimum two-night stay; outside the village center. $ *Rooms from: $155* ✉ *Hwy. 109 at Front St., Pacific Beach* ☎ *360/276–0265* ⊕ *www.seabrookwa.com* ⇨ *260 homes* 🍴 *No meals.*

Ocean Shores

10 miles south of Copalis Beach.

Ocean Shores, a long stretch of resorts, restaurants, shops, and beachfront, sits on the northern spit that encloses Grays Harbor. The whole area was planned by housing developers in the 1960s, and with its broad, flat, white beach, shallow surf, and sunset panoramas, it's been a favorite family getaway ever since, although its honky-tonk aesthetic and late-20th-century architecture hasn't aged especially well and is a deterrent to some. Come summer, dune buggies and go-carts buzz up and down the sand road, weaving around clusters of horses trotting tourists over the dunes. Colorful kites flap overhead, dogs romp in the waves, and tide pools are filled with huge orange Dungeness crabs, live sand dollars, and delicate snails, to the delight of small children. It's no tropical haven, however, as summer can bring chilly breezes, and the water never warms up much for swimming—jackets are needed sometimes even in July. A fog of sea mist often blows in during the late afternoon, and in winter dramatic storms billow onto land directly before the line of coastal hotels. An indoor pool and in-room fireplace are coveted amenities year-round in this cool climate.

GETTING HERE AND AROUND

Ocean Shores is the closest developed ocean-beach town to Seattle; it's about a 2½-hour drive by way of Olympia and Aberdeen. Weekend traffic can slow things considerably—especially in summer, try to avoid arriving on a Friday or departing on a Sunday.

ESSENTIALS

VISITOR INFORMATION Ocean Shores Visitor Information Center. ✉ *120 W. Chance a La Mer NW* ☎ *360/289–9586* ⊕ *www.tourismoceanshores.com.*

Coastal Interpretive Center
MUSEUM | **FAMILY** | A great stormy-day educational spot for families, this small natural history museum near the mouth of Grays Harbor highlights the seaside environment, local history, and Native American traditions. Displays include tsunami debris, artifacts from the founding of the city, and Native American basketry. Whale bones and a vast shell collection let you examine, and in many cases touch, the shoreline wildlife up close. ✉ *1033 Catala Ave. SE* ☎ *360/289–4617* ⊕ *www.interpretivecenter.org* 🎟 *Free* ⏲ *Closed Tues.–Thurs. in Feb. and Mar.*

Ocean Shores Beaches
BEACHES | **FAMILY** | Six miles of wide, sandy beaches line a peninsula trimmed by the Pacific Ocean on the west and Grays Harbor on the east. With five access roads, it's usually possible to find relatively secluded spots on the sand, despite this being the state's most visited public beach destination. Highest tides occur in July and December, the

latter when winter storm watching is at its peak. Motor vehicles are allowed on **City Beach,** a popular place for clam digging and kite flying. **Ocean City State Park,** a 257-acre oceanfront park 2 miles north, has year-round camping. Numerous hotels and resorts line the beach. **Amenities:** food and drink; parking; showers; toilets. **Best for:** sunrise; sunset; walking. *Sand Dune Ave. south from Hwy. 115* *www.oceanshores.org.*

Restaurants

Ocean Beach Roasters & Bistro
$$ | **PACIFIC NORTHWEST** | Espresso, beer, wine, and a variety of sweet baked goods—including memorable cinnamon rolls and lemon bars—are served in this inviting roastery and bistro with a gas fireplace, cathedral ceilings, and a cozy upstairs loft with armchairs and sofas. The kitchen doles out creative Pacific Northwestern fare, including duck hash with brussels sprouts and poached eggs, bouillabaisse with garlic-rubbed crostini, and zucchini lasagna. **Known for:** house-roasted coffee beans; live music some evenings; one of the best wine lists on the coast. *Average main: $20* *841 Point Brown Ave.* *360/289–3100* *oceanbeachroastersbistro.com* *No dinner Sun.–Tues.*

Oyhut Bay Grille
$$ | **PACIFIC NORTHWEST** | Located near the tip of the Point Brown Peninsula, this dapper contemporary bistro with ample seating in a festive courtyard draws discerning diners from up and down the coast. The eclectic cuisine draws relies heavily on local produce and seafood and includes flat-bread pizzas, blackened ahi with seasonal veggies, and hand-cut rib-eye steaks topped with grilled wild prawns. **Known for:** popular late-afternoon happy hour; inventive pizzas with great toppings; luscious cheesecake. *Average main: $22* *404 Salmonberry La. NW* *360/940–7138* *www.oyhutbay.com.*

Umi Sushi
$ | **SUSHI** | This casual Japanese restaurant set along the town's lively, if not especially charming, hotel strip serves superb sushi and sashimi along with ramen and udon noodle bowls, salmon teriyaki, and mixed tempura vegetables. Belly up to the bar for a traditional experience. **Known for:** mango-avocado Hawaiian ahi poke; two- and three-piece bento boxes; well-priced sushi combo platters. *Average main: $15* *698 Ocean Shores Blvd. NW* *360/289–2293.*

Hotels

Canterbury Inn
$$ | **HOTEL** | **FAMILY** | Families and groups of friends appreciate this dune-adjacent condo property with 45 owner-decorated studios and one- and two-bedroom suites, all of which share close proximity to the beach as well as Ocean Shores Golf Course. **Pros:** spacious suites with homelike comforts; private trails lead to the beach; nice indoor pool and fitness center. **Cons:** some units better decorated than others; a bit of a walk to most restaurants; crowded with families in summer. *Rooms from: $185* *643 Ocean Shores Blvd. NW* *360/289–3317* *www.canterburyinn.com* *45 rooms* *No meals.*

Nightlife

Elk Head Taproom
BREWPUBS/BEER GARDENS | Polished logs serve as bar stools in this tiny and rustic taproom, located in the back corner of a small, nondescript business plaza, its sign promising "cold beer and warm nuts to go." Elk Head produces a good range of flavorful beers, including hoppy West Coast–style IPAs. *739 Point Brown Ave. NW* *360/289–8277.*

Westport

43.5 miles south of Ocean Shores.

A picturesque, unpretentious bay-front fishing village on the southern spit that marks the entrance to Grays Harbor, Westport possesses stunning ocean beaches and a lively working marina from which numerous charter companies offer salmon, lingcod, rockfish, and albacore fishing trips, as well as whale-watching tours. If you're not taking a cruise, from the beaches you can often see gray whales migrating southward in November and December, toward their breeding grounds in Baja California, and northward in April and May, toward their feeding grounds in the Bering Sea. The serene beach is perfect for walking, surfing, or kite flying—although it's too dangerous for swimming and too cold for bathing. In winter it's one of the best spots on the coast to watch oncoming storms.

GETTING HERE AND AROUND

Westport is about an hour south of Ocean Shores via Highway 109 S and Highway 105 N.

ESSENTIALS

VISITOR INFORMATION Westport-Grayland Chamber of Commerce. ✉ *2985 S. Montesano St.* ☎ *360/268–9422, 800/345–6223* 🌐 *www.westportgrayland-chamber.org.*

Sights

★ Westport Maritime Museum

MUSEUM | Check out the 17-foot-tall Destruction Island Lens, a lighthouse beacon that was built in 1888 and weighs almost 6 tons, at this engaging maritime museum set inside a former Coast Guard station. It's filled with historic photos, equipment, clothing, and other relics from the life-saving service and artifacts related the area's local fishing, logging, and cranberry farming industries. The Westport South Beach Historical Society also operates the octagonal 1898 **Grays Harbor Lighthouse,** which at 107 feet is the tallest on the Washington coast. It's 2 miles south of the museum and adjacent to Westport Light State Park. Visiting the base is free; it costs extra to climb the 135 steps to the top. ✉ *2201 Westhaven Dr.* ☎ *360/268–0078* 🌐 *www.wsbhs.org* 🎫 *$5 each for museum and climbing lighthouse* ⏱ *Museum closed Tues. and Wed. Lighthouse Dec.and Jan. and Tues. and Wed. in Sept.–May.*

Westport Winery Garden Resort

GARDEN | About 10 miles east of Westport, stop by this winery anchored by a 40-foot-tall lighthouse first and foremost for a self-guided stroll through the 15 acres of gorgeously tended gardens and some 60 whimsical outdoor sculptures. Wine tastings are another popular activity, and about more than 30 varieties are offered, including a respectable Bordeaux blend, a Pinot Gris-Riesling blend, and an array of sweeter, sometimes fruit-based creations. There's also an attractive restaurant open daily for lunch and specializing in contemporary American fare, and a three-suite vacation rental. ✉ *1 S. Arbor Rd., Aberdeen* ☎ *360/648–2224* 🌐 *www.westportwinery.com.*

Beaches

Westport Light State Park

BEACH—SIGHT | The centerpiece of this 560-acre beach park is a paved promenade, sometimes called the Dunes Trail, that winds along the sandy beach north from the dunes near Grays Harbor Lighthouse, before exiting the park and curving along Half Moon Bay to the Westport Viewing Tower at the end of Westhaven Drive. The trail runs 2½ miles total, about half of it through the park, which is popular for beachcombing, bird-watching, and clamming, and has several picnic tables overlooking the sea. There's parking near downtown at the end of Jetty Haul Road and at the park's main entrance, at the end of West Ocean Avenue. **Amenities:**

parking; toilets. **Best for:** sunrise; sunset; walking ⊠ *End of W. Ocean Ave.* 🌐 *www.parks.state.wa.us* 🕒 *Parking $10.*

Restaurants

Aloha Alabama BBQ and Bakery

$ | **FUSION** | This funky eatery in Westport's marina district offers an unlikely trinity of traditional Southern barbecue, Hawaiian food, and the pub fare that's more typical of the area, and all of it is quite good. The island fare, includes kalua pork and Hawaiian barbecue chicken is particularly good, but regulars also swear by the fall-off-the-bone beef brisket and the panko-breaded Willapa Bay oysters and fries. **Known for:** refreshing cucumber margaritas; addictive smoked-pork egg rolls; garlic-smoked chicken platters. [$] *Average main: $14* ⊠ *2309 Westhaven Dr.* ☎ *360/268–7299* 🌐 *www.alohaalabama.com.*

Blue Buoy

$ | **AMERICAN** | Venture inside this endearingly dive-y diner with wood-paneled walls and nautical decor for formidable portions of stick-to-your-ribs breakfast and lunch fare. Consider the Dungeness crab omelet or fluffy biscuits and sausage gravy in the morning, while top lunch offerings include New England–style clam chowder and the shrimp Louie salad. **Known for:** fried oysters in everything from omelets to po'boys; marina view from tables in front; platters of assorted fish and shellfish. [$] *Average main: $15* ⊠ *2323 Westhaven Dr.* ☎ *360/268–7065* 🕒 *No dinner.*

Elixir Coffee Shop

$ | **CAFÉ** | A delightful stopover between the Long Beach Pensula and Westport, this stylish café with three walls of windows offering panoramic views of the Willapa River is decorated with colorfully painted chairs, hanging plants, and potted flowers. First-rate espresso drinks, chai teas, and light snacks—black currant scones, lavender-honey toast with goat cheese, bacon-tomato-avocado sandwiches—are offered. **Known for:** outdoor deck with river views; fresh-fruit smoothies; healthy and hearty salads. [$] *Average main: $7* ⊠ *1015 Robert Bush Dr. W, South Bend* ✥ *35 miles south of Westport* ☎ *360/875–8032* 🌐 *www.elixircoffeeshop.com* 🕒 *No dinner.*

Hotels

Glenacres Historic Inn

$ | **B&B/INN** | One of the better lodging deals in coastal Washington, this rambling, quirky old inn overlooking the South Bay of Grays Harbor offers eight guest rooms in the main building with country quilts and pretty antiques, as well as four cottages that offer more privacy and some kitchenettes. **Pros:** picturesque bayfront setting; reasonable rates; down-to-earth owner. **Cons:** not within walking distance of beaches; rooms aren't fancy; no breakfast in low season. [$] *Rooms from: $105* ⊠ *222 Montesano St.* ☎ *360/268–0958* 🌐 *www.glenacresinn.com* *12 rooms* *Free Breakfast.*

LOGE Westport

$ | **HOTEL** | Part of the outdoorsy-spirited boutique motel group, this handsomely updated mid-century motel lies a couple of miles south of downtown Westport on South Bay. Accommodations range from simple guest rooms to hostel-style bunks. **Pros:** hip, modern decor; verdant grounds; free bikes. **Cons:** youthful vibe isn't for everyone; on a busy road; not within walking distance of town. [$] *Rooms from: $133* ⊠ *1416 S. Montesano St.* ☎ *360/268–0091* 🌐 *www.logecamps.com* *31 rooms* *No meals.*

★ Westport Marina Cottages Motel

$$ | **HOTEL** | This cozy complex just across from downtown overlooks the marina on one side and Grays Harbor on the other. **Pros:** pretty waterfront setting; short walk to downtown dining; great for outdoors lovers. **Cons:** bayside cottages also

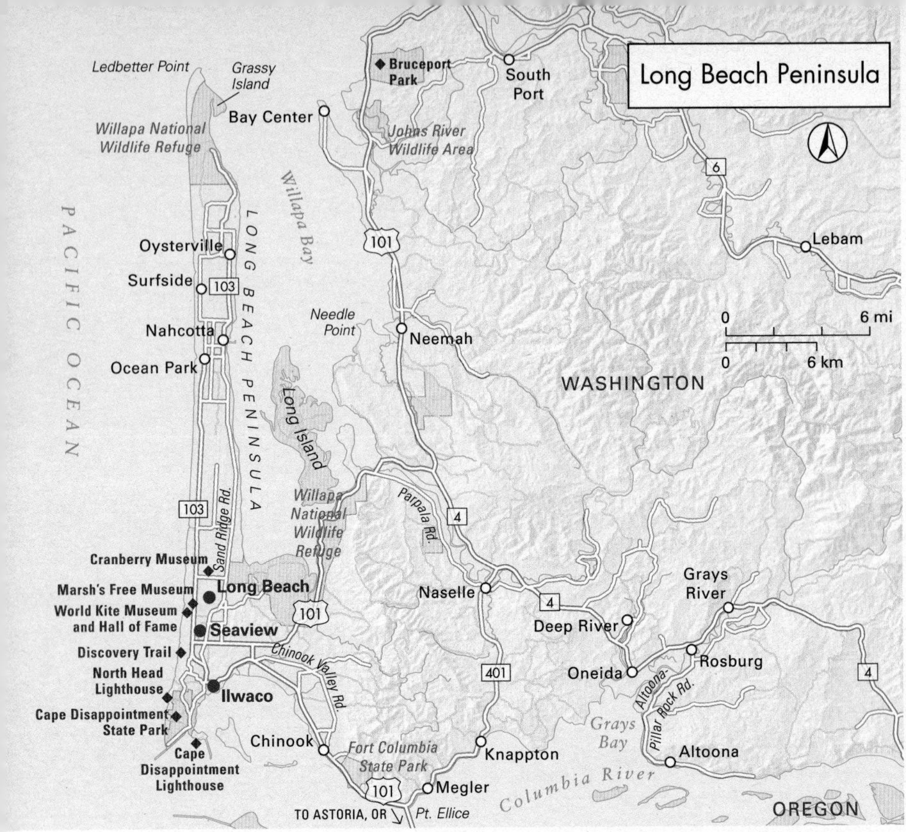

Long Beach Peninsula

overlook the road; books up well ahead in summer; no breakfast. $ *Rooms from: $169* ✉ *481 Neddie Rose Dr.* ☎ *360/268–7680* 🌐 *www.marinacottages.com* 🛏 *23 cottages* 🍴 *No meals.*

Ilwaco

80 miles south of Westport, 170 miles southwest of Seattle, 109 miles northwest of Portland, OR.

At the southern base of the Long Beach Peninsula, Ilwaco (ill- *wah*-co) has been a fishing port for thousands of years, first as a Native American village and later as an American settlement. From town, a 3-mile scenic loop winds through Cape Disappointment State Park to North Head Lighthouse, an ideal perch for viewing marine life, including gray whales during their winter (southerly) and spring (northerly) migrations. The colorful harbor is a great place for watching gulls and boats. Lewis and Clark camped here before moving their winter base to the Oregon coast at Fort Clatsop.

Sights

★ Cape Disappointment State Park

NATIONAL/STATE PARK | FAMILY | The cape and its treacherous neighboring sandbar—named in 1788 by Captain John Meares, an English fur trader who had been unable to find the Northwest Passage—has been the scourge of sailors since the 1800s, hence its reputation as the graveyard of the Pacific. More than 250 ships have sunk after running aground on its ever-shifting sands. Now a 2,023-acre state park contained within the Lewis and Clark National Historical

Park (which also has sections just across the Columbia River in Oregon), this dramatic cape with sheer sea cliffs and great stands of conifer forest was an active military installation until 1957. Emplacements for the guns that once guarded the Columbia's mouth remain, some of them hidden by dense vegetation. Some 8 miles of trails lead to stunning beaches, and opportunities to spy eagles, whales, sea lions, seat otters, and other wildlife abound. There are three lightkeepers' residences, dozens of campsites, several yurts, and three cabins available for rent. Exhibits at the park's free **Lewis & Clark Interpretive Center ,** which sits atop a 200-foot cliff with magnificent views, trace the cape's human and natural history. A more comprehensive permanent exhibit in the center, which costs $5 to enter, tells the tale of the duo's 8,000-mile round-trip expedition. Displays chronicle the Corps of Discovery, which arrived at Cape Disappointment in 1805. A ½-mile-long path from the center leads to the **Cape Disappointment Lighthouse.** Built in 1856, it's the oldest lighthouse on the West Coast that's still in use, and one of two lighthouses in the park, the other being North Head. ✉ *244 Robert Gray Dr.* ☎ *360/642–3078* 🌐 *www.parks.state.wa.us* 🎫 *$10 parking.*

Columbia Pacific Heritage Museum

MUSEUM | Dioramas of Long Beach towns illustrate the history of southwestern Washington, and other displays cover Native Americans; the influx of traders, missionaries, and pioneers; and the contemporary workers of the fishing, agriculture, and forest industries. The original Ilwaco Freight Depot and a Pullman car from the Clamshell Railroad highlight rail history. Also on display is a 26-foot surf boat used by the Klipsan Beach Lifesaving Service Station. ✉ *115 SE Lake St.* ☎ *360/642–3446* 🌐 *www.columbiapacificheritagemuseum.org* 🎫 *$5* ⏲ *Closed Sun. and Mon.*

Fort Columbia Historical State Park

NATIONAL/STATE PARK | This 618-acre park, part of the Lewis and Clark National Historical Park, blends so well into a rocky knob overlooking the river that it's all but invisible from land or water (U.S. 101 passes underneath, via a tunnel). The turn-of-the-20th-century military buildings offer great views of the river's mouth. In spring the slopes are fragrant with wildflowers, and there are 2 miles of hiking trails to explore the grounds. The interpretive center has displays on barracks life and Chinook Indian culture. Two historic buildings on the property are available for overnight rentals. ✉ *475 U.S. 101, Chinook* ☎ *360/777–8221* 🌐 *www.parks.state.wa.us* ⏲ *Parking $10.*

North Head Lighthouse

LIGHTHOUSE | Built in 1898, this red-roofed lighthouse helped skippers sailing from the north, whose view of Cape Disappointment Lighthouse was blocked by the cape itself. Rising high on a bluff amid the windswept trees, the lighthouse offers superb views of the Long Beach Peninsula. Tours of the lighthouse are given from May through September, but the grounds are open year-round. It's within Cape Disappointment State Park and reached from a well-marked parking area via a level half-mile trail that passes the Lighthouse Keepers' Residence, which is available for overnight rentals. ✉ *North Head Lighthouse Rd.* ☎ *360/642–3078* 🌐 *www.parks.state.wa.us* 🎫 *Parking $10, tours $3.*

Willipa National Wildlife Refuge

NATIONAL/STATE PARK | Headquartered about 11 miles north of downtown Ilwaco on U.S. 101, this 11,000-acre refuge comprises three main units: the largest is Long Island, an estuarine island with old-growth forest that's reached by kayak or canoe, most easily from the boat ramp across from the headquarters office. Accessed from Sandridge Road and 67th Place less than 2 miles east of the town of Long Beach, the South Bay unit comprises wetlands and marshes inhabited by bear, elk, bobcats, and all sorts of birds. Finally, the Leadbetter Point Unit, which adjoins Leadbetter State Park and is at the north end of the Long Beach Peninsula, 3 miles beyond Oysterville, is a great spot for bird-watching. Black brants, sandpipers, turnstones, yellowlegs, sanderlings, and knots are among the more than 100 species biologists have identified here. The dune area at the very end of the point is closed from March to September to protect the nesting snowy plover. From the parking lot, a ½-mile-long paved wheelchair-accessible path leads to the ocean, and a 2½-mile loop trail winds through the dunes along the ocean and Willapa Bay. Several trails along the loop lead to isolated patches of coastline. These trails flood in winter, often becoming impassable swamps, so pay attention to the warning signs. ✉ *Refuge Headquarters, 3888 U.S. 101* ☎ *360/484–3482* 🌐 *www.fws.gov/refuge/willapa* 🎫 *Parking $10.*

Hotels

Salt Hotel & Pub
$ | HOTEL | This family-friendly motel on Ilwaco Marina offers views of the Columbia River and easy access to nearby Cape Disappointment and Fort Columbia state parks and the lower reaches of Long Beach Peninsula. **Pros:** crowd-pleasing restaurant; scenic marina setting; great for outdoors lovers. **Cons:** 10-minute drive from nearest beach; nothing fancy about the furnishings; no water view from some rooms. 💲 *Rooms from: $130* ✉ *147 Howerton Ave.* ☎ *360/642–7258* 🌐 *www.salt-hotel.com* *21 rooms* 🍽 *No meals.*

Seaview

3 miles north of Ilwaco.

Seaview, an unincorporated town with perhaps 500 year-round residents and several homes that date from the 1800s, has a handful of good restaurants in its small village center, which is also where you'll find the region's well-stocked tourism information center, the Long Beach Peninsula Visitors Bureau, which is right on the main drag.

VISITOR INFORMATION Long Beach Peninsula Visitors Bureau. ✉ *3914 Pacific Way* ☎ *360/642–2400* 🌐 *www.visitlongbeachpeninsula.com.*

Restaurants

The Depot
$$$ | MODERN AMERICAN | Set inside a whimsically decorated 1905 railroad station with plenty of vintage train memorabilia and historic photos, this romantic yet unpretentious bistro serves up sophisticated Northwestern fare with international influences. Sustainably sourced seafood figures in a number of dishes, from wild-caught calamari tossed with a Thai-style cilantro peanut sauce to razor clams sauteed in garlic and white wine and served with bucatini pasta. **Known for:** rack of Oregon lamb with a verde sauce; exceptional clam chowder with a garlic-leek-cream base; velvety pot de crème. 💲 *Average main: $27* ✉ *1208 38th Pl.* ☎ *360/642–7880* 🌐 *www.depotrestaurantdining.com* 🕒 *No lunch.*

★ 42nd Street Cafe and Bistro
$$ | PACIFIC NORTHWEST | For nearly 30 years, this cheerful art-filled spot has been the go-to on the peninsula for celebrating special occasions and simply enjoying stellar comfort food with locally sourced ingredients. Consider kicking off your meal with Dungeness crab and shrimp beignets or a half pound of Willapa Bay clams steamed in white wine, before graduating to flash-fried razor clams with seasonal vegetables, or ravioli stuffed with butternut squash and topped with a cider-madeira glaze. **Known for:** New Orleans–style beignets at breakfast; exceptional Pacific Northwest wine list; house-made ice cream changes monthly.

Cape Disappointment State Park

Ⓢ *Average main: $22* ✉ *4201 Pacific Hwy.* ☎ *360/642–2323* 🌐 *www.42nd-streetcafe.com* ⏲ *Closed Mon. and Tues.*

Hotels

★ Shelburne Inn

$ | **B&B/INN** | A white picket fence and lovely gardens surround a Victorian hotel that's been continuously operating since it was built in 1896. **Pros:** inviting little pub serves lighter fare; historic charm in every room; steps from several good restaurants. **Cons:** breakfast not included in rates; some rooms are quite small; not on the beach. Ⓢ *Rooms from: $109* ✉ *4415 Pacific Way* ☎ *360/642–2442, 800/466–1896* 🌐 *www.theshelburneinn.com* *14 rooms* *No meals.*

Sou'wester Lodge and Cabins

$ | **RESORT** | For a bohemian and truly memorable Pacific Northwest experience, book one these eclectic accommodations—rustic cottages, a fleet of well-kept vintage travel trailers, and four second-floor suites carved out of a ballroom inside the 1892 summer retreat of former U.S. senator Henry Winslow Corbett. **Pros:** one-of-a-kind retro lodgings; cool shops and common spaces; fun, arty vibe. **Cons:** not for luxury seekers; some trailers don't have private baths; half-mile from the beach. Ⓢ *Rooms from: $108* ✉ *3728 J Pl.* ☎ *360/642–2542* 🌐 *www.souwester-lodge.com* *28 units* *No meals.*

Nightlife

★ North Jetty Brewing

BREWPUBS/BEER GARDENS | You can sample some of the finest craft beers in western Washington at this inviting taproom with a gas fireplace and comfy seating. Notable option include the refreshing Yellow Booth Kolsch and the roasty, Leadbetter Red Scottish Ale that'll warm your soul on a stormy winter evening. ✉ *4200 Pacific Way* ☎ *360/642–4234* 🌐 *www.northjettybrew.com.*

Long Beach

½ mile north of Seaview.

Similar to Seaside, a short way across the border in Oregon, Long Beach is a classic family beach town with a main thoroughfare lined with touristy amusements—you'll find everything from cotton candy and hot dogs to go-karts and bumper cars. This lively little community has the largest selection of restaurants and hotels, many of them with direct access along the town's gorgeous swath of dunes and beach. Development and vacation crowds thin the farther north you work you way up the peninsula from the town of Long Beach. You'll soon reach Ocean Park, the commercial center of the peninsula's quieter north end, then Nahcotta (*nuh*-caw-ta), on the bay side and known for its prolific oyster industry. Finally, there's sleepy Oysterville, a 19th-century waterfront village with pretty homes flanked by gardens.

Sights

Cranberry Museum

MUSEUM | Learn about the cranberry cultivation that's taken place since the early 1900s in coastal Washington by taking a self-guided walking tour through the bogs. Enjoy a dish of cranberry ice cream, and perhaps buying cranberry products to take home. ✉ *2907 Pioneer Rd.* ☎ *360/642–5553* 🌐 *www.cranberrymuseum.com* 🎫 *Free* ⏲ *Museum closed Sun.–Thurs. in mid-Dec.–Mar. Ground open year-round.*

Discovery Trail

TRAIL | FAMILY | Created to memorialize Lewis and Clark's explorations here in 1805–06, the 8½-mile Discovery Trail, which is paved or runs over boardwalk and is accessible to bikes and pedestrians, traces the explorers' moccasin steps from Ilwaco to north Long Beach. Along the way it passes plenty of sandy dunes and beaches. Access the trail from the beach parking lots on Sid Snyder Drive or Bolstad Street in Long Beach. Parking is also available at the Beard's Hollow lot in Cape Disappointment State Park. ✉ *Long Beach* 🌐 *www.visitlongbeachpeninsula.com.*

Leadbetter Point State Park

NATIONAL/STATE PARK | Located past Oysterville at the less-developed northern end of the peninsula, this 1,732-acre woodland and beach park adjoining part of Willapa National Wildlife Refuge offers 7 miles of trails through temperate dune forests and along Willapa Bay. It's one of the better migratory bird-watching habitats on Washington's coast, and as it receives far fewer visitors than the beaches farther south, it's also a great place to commune quietly with nature. ✉ *End of Stackpole Rd., Oysterville* ☎ *360/642–3078* 🌐 *www.parks.state.wa.us.*

Long Beach Boardwalk

BEACH—SIGHT | FAMILY | The ½-mile-long wooden boardwalk runs through the dunes parallel to the beach, and is a great place for strolling, bird-watching, or just sitting and listening to the wind and the roar of the surf. It runs between Bolstad Avenue and Sid Snyder Drive. ✉ *Long Beach* 🌐 *www.visitlongbeachpeninsula.com.*

Marsh's Free Museum

MUSEUM | FAMILY | If you're traveling with kids, or you simply an appreciation for seaside kitsch, drop by this quirky museum that's been around since 1921 and is best known for "Jake the Alligator Man," a mummified half-man, half-alligator. Marsh's is filled with plenty of other curiosities, like real shrunken heads, skeletons, and an eight-legged lamb. ✉ *400 S. Pacific Ave.* ☎ *360/642–2188* 🌐 *www.marshsfreemuseum.com* 🎫 *Free.*

World Kite Museum and Hall of Fame

MUSEUM | Each August, Long Beach hosts the Washington State International Kite Festival; the community is also home to the Northwest Stunt Kite Championships, a competition held each June. At the only U.S. museum focused solely on kites and kiting, you can view an array of kites and learn about kite making and history. *303 Sid Snyder Dr. SW* *360/642–4020* *www.kitefestival.com* *$5* *Hrs vary seasonally; call ahead.*

Beaches

Long Beach

BEACHES | The Long Beach Peninsula consists of 28 continuous miles of broad sandy beach, which fills with kite flyers, sand-castle builders, sunbathers, bicyclists, horseback riders, and drivers during summer months. Watch out for horses, cars, and other motor vehicles as you drive on the sand—some sections are open for driving year-round, while other parts don't allow it in summer. Bonfires are allowed. Bring a windbreaker—strong gusts are common near the water, which remains consistently frigid throughout the year. **Amenities:** parking, toilets. **Best for:** solitude; sunrise; sunset; walking. *End of Bolstad St. W* *www.visitlongbeachpeninsula.com.*

Restaurants

Beach Fire BBQ

$$ | **BARBECUE** | This cozy storefront café stands out among the more typical restaurants in touristy Long Beach for serving up legitimately mouthwatering Texas-style barbecue, along with boldly seasoned sides of potato salad, mac-and-cheese, and ranch beans. Standouts include brisket platters and smoked sausage sandwiches, but St. Louis–style ribs and pulled-pork sandwiches with Carolina-inspired mustard barbecue sauce are quite good, too. **Known for:** Oink and Moo (brisket, pulled pork, sausage) sandwich; massive family-style platters perfect for picnics on the beach; friendly, down-home service. *Average main: $17* *612 Pacific Ave. S* *360/777–3999* *www.beachfirebbq.com* *Closed Sun.–Tues.*

Pickled Fish

$$ | **MODERN AMERICAN** | Most of the seats in this third-floor restaurant at the Adrift Hotel offer panoramic views of the dunes and the ocean beyond, making this a popular—though sometimes a bit crowded—place for breakfast, lunch, and dinner in summer and on weekends. It's worth persevering for a table, though, as the creative renditions of classic beach fare are consistently excellent, from smoked salmon Benedicts and sticky salted-caramel buns in the morning to braised beef rib with red wine jus and charred-broccoli pizzas with chevre and Calabrian chiles later in the day. **Known for:** live jazz, blues, and folk most weekends; Dungeness crab melts with Brie and chevre; creative cocktails. *Average main: $21* *409 Sid Snyder Dr.* *360/642–2344* *www.pickledfishrestaurant.com.*

Hotels

Anchorage Cottages

$ | **RENTAL** | **FAMILY** | These sweet downtown cottages from the 1950s sleep from two to nine guests, overlook a grove of evergreens, and lead out to a private ¼-mile path that leads to the beach. **Pros:** pretty gardens and courtyard; affordable rates; near the beach. **Cons:** two-night minimum in high season; no beach view; not very private. *Rooms from: $109* *2209 Boulevard Ave. N* *800/646–2351, 360/642–2351* *www.theanchoragecottages.com* *10 cottages* *No meals.*

Boreas Bed and Breakfast

$$ | **B&B/INN** | Tasteful antiques and interesting books fill this vintage 1920s beach house, where rooms have balconies or decks with ocean views, a jetted spa tub sits in an enclosed glass-and-cedar gazebo that looks toward the ocean, and a private path leads through the dunes to the ocean and joining the Discovery Trail. **Pros:** many eateries and shops are just a few minutes' walk; extravagant three-course breakfasts; close to the ocean.

Cons: not directly on the beach; not good for families; in a busy part of town. *Rooms from: $199* *607 N. Ocean Beach Blvd.* *360/642–8069, 888/642–8069* *www.boreasinn.com* *5 rooms* *Free Breakfast.*

Campbell House

$$ | **B&B/INN** | One of the most peaceful getaways in the area, this contemporary B&B nestled amid the dunes on the quieter northern end of the Long Beach Peninsula has four simply but comfortably appointed rooms, each with big windows and beautiful sea views. **Pros:** views of the dunes from every room; set well away from the crowds; delicious breakfasts included. **Cons:** no dining within walking distance; two rooms share a bath; a little crowded when fully booked. *Rooms from: $175* *904 227th La., Ocean Park* *360/665–4030* *www.campbellhouse.us* *4 rooms* *Free Breakfast.*

★ Inn at Discovery Coast

$$$ | **HOTEL** | A favorite roost of young Seattle and Portland urbanites, this hip, eco-minded resort includes guest rooms with stylish mid-century modern decor and expansive sea views and sleek, contemporary studios in a poolhouse. **Pros:** shares amenities with adjoining Adrift Hotel; eye-catching contemporary design; scenic beach setting. **Cons:** no ocean view from poolhouse rooms; set along a busy section of beach; pricey in summer. *Rooms from: $209* *421 11th St. SW* *360/642–5265* *www.innatdiscoverycoast.com* *18 rooms* *Free Breakfast.*

Lighthouse Oceanfront Resort

$ | **RESORT** | **FAMILY** | A few miles north of downtown Long Beach, this sprawling, well-maintained compound set among the dunes includes modern suites, older cottages, and economical motel rooms. **Pros:** along a stunning stretch of beach; most units offer self-catering; indoor tennis center, pool, and gym. **Cons:** least expensive units are near the busy road; packed with families in summer; a long walk to restaurants. *Rooms from: $108* *12417 Pacific Way* *360/642–3622* *www.lighthouseresort.net* *42 units* *No meals.*

Chapter 15

NORTH CASCADES NATIONAL PARK

Updated by
Shelley Arenas

Sights	Restaurants	Hotels	Shopping	Nightlife
★★★★★	★★☆☆☆	★★☆☆☆	☆☆☆☆☆	☆☆☆☆☆

WELCOME TO NORTH CASCADES NATIONAL PARK

TOP REASONS TO GO

★ **Pure wilderness:** Spot bald eagles, deer, elk, and other wildlife on nearly 400 miles of mountain and meadow hiking trails.

★ **Majestic glaciers:** The North Cascades are home to several hundred moving ice masses, more than half of the glaciers in the United States.

★ **Splendid flora:** A bright palette of flowers blankets the hillsides in midsummer, while October's colors paint the landscape in vibrant autumn hues.

★ **Thrilling boat rides:** Lake Chelan, Ross Lake, and the Stehekin River are the starting points for kayaking, white-water rafting, and ferry trips.

★ **19th-century history:** Delve into the state's farming, lumber, and logging pasts in clapboard towns and homesteads around the park.

1 North Unit. The park's creek-cut northern wilderness, centered on snowy Mt. Challenger, stretches north from Highway 20 over the Picket Range toward the Canadian border. It's an endless landscape of pine-topped peaks and ridges.

2 South Unit. Hike lake-filled mountain foothills in summer to take in vistas of blue skies and flower-filled meadows. Waterfalls and wildlife are abundant here.

3 Ross Lake National Recreation Area. Drawing a thick line from British Columbia all the way down to the North Cascades Scenic Highway, placid Ross Lake is edged with pretty bays that draw swimmers and boaters.

4 Lake Chelan National Recreation Area. Ferries cruise between small waterfront villages along this pristine waterway, while kayakers and hikers follow quiet trails along its edges. This is one of the Northwest's most popular summer escapes, with nature-bound activities and rustic accommodations. See more information on Lake Chelan in the North Central Washington chapter.

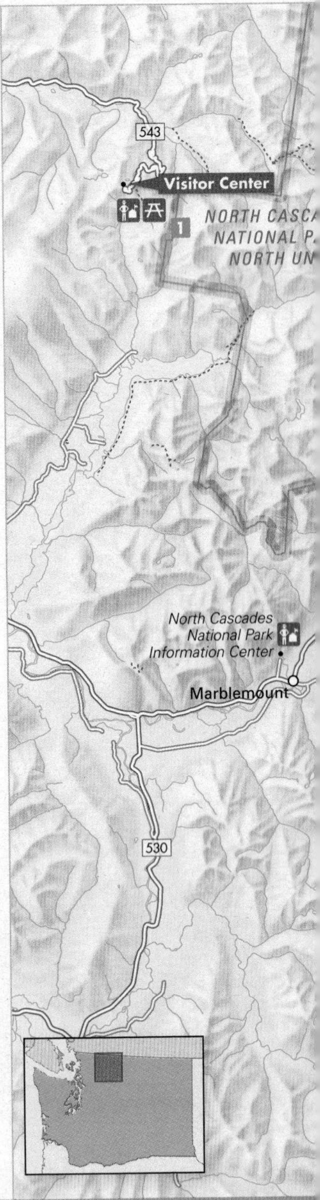

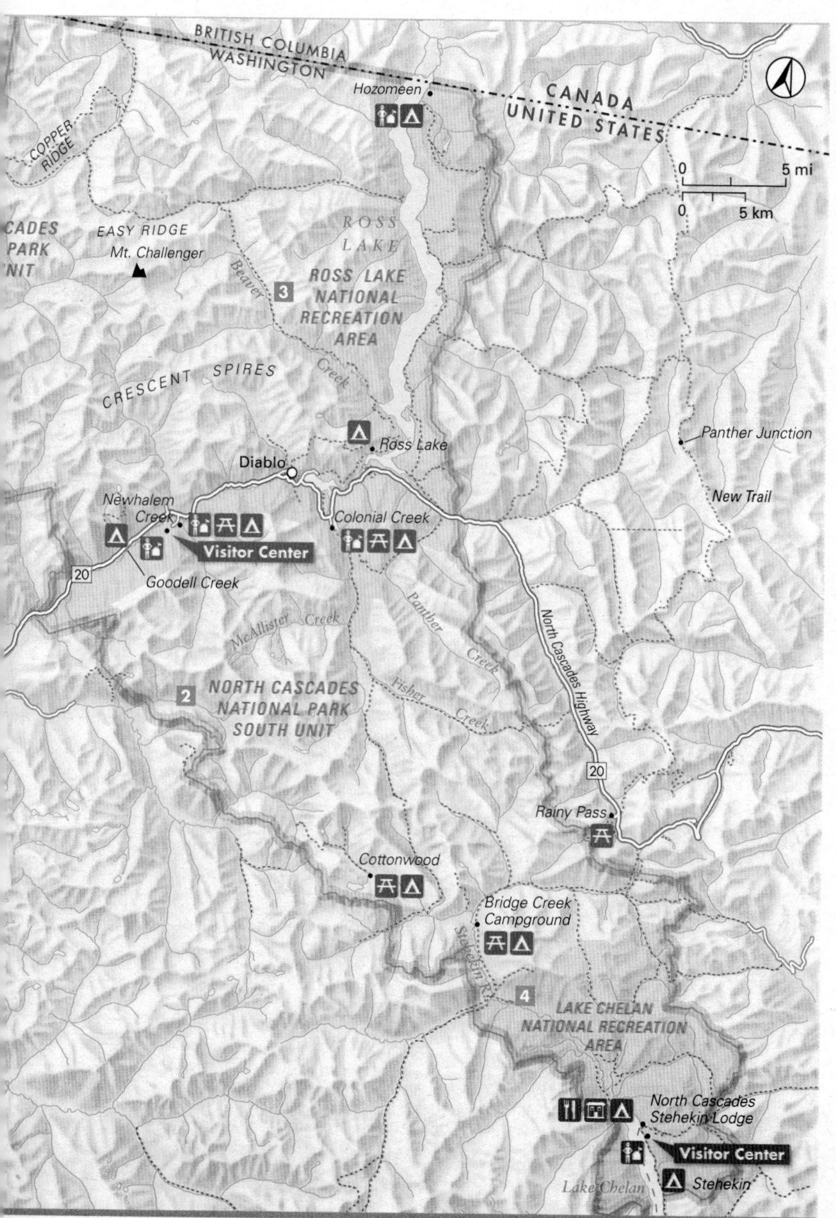
BRITISH COLUMBIA
WASHINGTON
CANADA
UNITED STATES
Hozomeen
COPPER RIDGE
EASY RIDGE
Mt. Challenger
ROSS LAKE
ROSS LAKE NATIONAL RECREATION AREA
Beaver Creek
CRESCENT SPIRES
Ross Lake
Diablo
Newhalem Creek
Visitor Center
Colonial Creek
Goodell Creek
20
McAllister Creek
Panther Creek
Fisher Creek
NORTH CASCADES NATIONAL PARK SOUTH UNIT
North Cascades Highway
Panther Junction
New Trail
0
5 mi
5 km
Rainy Pass
Cottonwood
Bridge Creek Campground
Stehekin R.
LAKE CHELAN NATIONAL RECREATION AREA
North Cascades Stehekin Lodge
Visitor Center
Lake Chelan
Stehekin

Countless snow-clad mountain spires dwarf narrow glacial valleys in this 505,000-acre expanse of the North Cascades, which encompasses three diverse natural areas. North Cascades National Park is the core of the region, flanked by Lake Chelan National Recreation Area to the south and Ross Lake National Recreation Area to the north.

Planning

When to Go

The spectacular, craggy peaks of the North Cascades—often likened to the Alps—are breathtaking anytime. Summer is peak season, especially along the alpine stretches of Highway 20; weekends and holidays can be crowded. Summer is short and glorious in the high country, extending from snowmelt (late May to July, depending on the elevation and the amount of snow) to early September.

The North Cascades Highway is a popular autumn drive in September and October, when the changing leaves put on a colorful show. The lowland forest areas, such as the complex around Newhalem, can be visited almost any time of year. These are wonderfully quiet in early spring or late autumn on mild rainy days. Snow closes the North Cascades Highway from mid-November through mid-April, and sometimes longer.

Planning Your Time

NORTH CASCADES IN ONE DAY

The **North Cascades Highway,** with its breathtaking mountain and meadow scenery, is one of the most memorable drives in the United States. Although many travelers first head northeast from Seattle into the park and make this their grand finale, if you start from Winthrop, at the south end of the route, traffic is lighter and there's less morning fog. Either way, the main highlight is **Washington Pass,** the road's highest point, where an overlook affords a sensational panorama of snow-covered peaks.

Rainy Pass, where the road heading north drops into the west slope valleys, is another good vantage point. Old-growth forest begins to appear, and after about an hour you reach **Gorge Creek Falls overlook** with its 242-foot cascade. Continue west to Newhalem and stop for lunch, then take a half-hour stroll along the **Trail**

AVERAGE HIGH/LOW TEMPERATURES					
JAN.	FEB.	MAR.	APR.	MAY	JUNE
39/30	43/32	49/34	56/38	64/43	70/49
JULY	AUG.	SEPT.	OCT.	NOV.	DEC.
76/52	76/53	69/49	57/42	45/36	39/31

of the Cedars. Later, stop at the **North Cascades Visitor Center** and take another short hike. It's an hour drive down the Skagit Valley to Sedro-Woolley, where bald eagles are often seen along the river in winter.

Getting Here and Around

AIR

The nearest commercial airports are in Bellingham to the northwest and in Wenatchee south of Chelan.

CAR

Highway 20, the North Cascades Highway, splits the park's north and south sections. The gravel Cascade River Road, which runs southeast from Marblemount, peels off Highway 20; Sibley Creek/Hidden Lake Road (USFS 1540) turns off Cascade River Road to the Cascade Pass trailhead. Thornton Creek Road is another rough four-wheel-drive track. For the Ross Lake area in the north, the unpaved Hozomeen Road (Silver–Skagit Road) provides access between Hope, British Columbia, and Silver Lake and Skagit Valley provincial parks. From Stehekin, the Stehekin Valley Road continues to High Bridge and Car Wash Falls—although seasonal floods may cause washouts. Note that roads are narrow and some are closed seasonally, many sights are off the beaten path, and the scenery is so spectacular that, once you're in it, you'll want to make more than a day trip.

Park Essentials

ACCESSIBILITY

Visitor centers along North Cascades Highway are accessible by wheelchair. Hikes include Sterling Munro, Skagit River Loop, and Rock Shelter, three short trails into lowland old-growth forest, all at mile 120 along Highway 20 near Newhalem, and the Happy Creek Forest Trail at mile 134.

PARK FEES AND PERMITS

There are no entrance fees to the national park and no parking fees at trailheads on park land. A Northwest Forest Pass, required for parking at Forest Service trailheads, is $5 per vehicle for a calendar day or $30 for a year. A free wilderness permit is required for all overnight stays in the backcountry; these are available in person only. Dock permits for boat-in campgrounds are $5 per day. Car camping is $10 per night at Gorge Lake Campground and $16 per night at Colonial Creek, Goodell Creek, and Newhalem Creek campgrounds during the summer (when water and other services are available) and free off-season; the primitive Hozomeen Campground is free all year. Passes and permits are sold at visitor centers and ranger stations around the park area.

PARK HOURS

The park never closes, but access is limited by snow in winter. Highway 20 (North Cascades Highway), the major access to the park, is partially closed from mid-November to mid-April, depending on snow levels.

CELL PHONE RECEPTION

Cell-phone reception in the park is unreliable. Public telephones are found at the North Cascades Visitor Center and Skagit Information Center in Newhalem and the Golden West Visitor Center and North Cascades Lodge in Stehekin.

Educational Offerings

Seattle City Light Information and Tour Center

TOUR—SIGHT | Based at a history museum that has exhibits about the introduction of electric power through the Cascade ranges, Seattle's public electric company offers tours and programs during summer. Several trails start at the building, and the group offers sightseeing excursions on Diablo Lake during the summer in partnership with the North Cascades Institute, Thursday through Monday lunch cruises by advance reservation, and afternoon cruises Friday through Sunday. The boat tour includes a visit to the Diablo Dam. Other tours include a visit to the powerhouse (with picnic lunch) on weekends, and an evening dinner and guided walk to Ladder Creek Falls on Thursday and Friday. Free 45-minute walking tours through the historic town of Newhalem are offered daily from July through Labor Day. ✉ *Milepost 120, North Cascades Hwy., Newhalem* ☎ *360/854–2589* 🌐 *www.skagittours.com* 🎫 *Walking tour free, other tours from $19* ⏲ *Closed Oct.–Apr.*

RANGER PROGRAMS

In summer, rangers conduct programs at the visitor centers, where you also can find exhibits and other park information. At the North Cascades Visitor Center in Newhalem you can learn about rain-forest ecology, while at the Golden West Visitor Center in Stehekin there's an arts-and-crafts gallery as well as audiovisual and children's programs. Check center bulletin boards for schedules.

Restaurants

There are no formal restaurants in North Cascades National Park, just a lakeside café at the North Cascades Environmental Learning Center. Stehekin has three options: the Stehekin Valley Ranch dining room, North Cascades Lodge, or the Stehekin Pastry Company; all serve simple, hearty, country-style meals and sweets. Towns within a few hours of the park on either side have a couple of small eateries, and a few lodgings have dining rooms with skilled chefs who craft high-end meals of locally grown products matched with extensive wine lists. Otherwise, don't expect fancy decor or gourmet frills—just friendly service and generally delicious homemade stews, roasts, grilled fare, soups, salads, and baked goods.

Hotels

Accommodations in North Cascades National Park are rustic, cozy, and comfortable. Options range from plush lodges and homey cabin rentals to spartan campgrounds. Expect to pay roughly $50 to $200 per night, depending on the rental size and the season. Book at least three months in advance, or even a year for popular accommodations in summer. Outside the park are numerous resorts, motels, bed-and-breakfasts, and even overnight boat rentals in Chelan, Concrete, Glacier, Marblemount, Sedro-Woolley, Twisp, and Winthrop. *Hotel reviews have been shortened. For full information, visit Fodors.com.*

What It Costs in U.S. Dollars

	$	$$	$$$	$$$$
RESTAURANTS				
	under $12	$12–$20	$21–$30	over $30
HOTELS				
	under $100	$100–$150	$151–$200	over $200

Tours

★ North Cascades Environmental Learning Center

TOUR—SIGHT | FAMILY | This is the spot for information on hiking, wildlife watching, horseback riding, climbing, boat rentals, and fishing in the park, as well as classroom education and hands-on nature experiences. Guided tours from the center include lake and dam visits, mountain climbs, pack-train excursions, and guided canoe trips on Diablo Lake. Other choices range from forest ecology and backpacking trips to writing and art retreats. Family getaway weekends in summer are a fun way to unplug from technology and introduce kids to nature. There's also a research library, a dock on Diablo Lake, an amphitheater, and overnight lodging. The center is operated by the North Cascades Institute in partnership with the National Park Service and Seattle City Light. ✉ *1940 Diablo Dam Rd., Diablo* ☎ *360/854–2599 headquarters, 206/526–2599 environmental learning center* 🌐 *www.ncascades.org* 🎫 *Day programs from $110; overnight lodging (including meals) from $226 per couple* ⏲ *Closed during winter months.*

Visitor Information

PARK CONTACT INFORMATION North Cascades National Park. ✉ *810 Rte. 20, Sedro-Woolley* ☎ *360/854–7200* 🌐 *www.nps.gov/noca.*

Wildlife in North Cascades

Bald eagles are present year-round along the Skagit River and the lakes—in December, hundreds flock to the Skagit to feed on a rare winter salmon run, and remain through January. Spring and early summer bring black bears to the roadsides in the high country. Deer and elk can often be spotted in early morning and late evening, grazing and browsing at the forest's edge. Other mountain residents include beaver, marmots, pika, otters, skunks, opossums, and other smaller mammals, as well as forest and field birds.

Sights

Buckner Homestead

FESTIVAL | Dating from 1889, this restored pioneer farm includes an apple orchard, farmhouse, barn, and many ranch buildings. You can pick up a self-guided tour booklet from the drop box. Feel free to enjoy apples from the trees in season. A harvest festival is held in October. ✉ *Stehekin Valley Rd., 3½ miles northwest of Stehekin Landing, Stehekin* 🌐 *www.bucknerhomestead.org.*

★ Mazama Store

GIFTS/SOUVENIRS | At this legendary family-run general store in tiny Mazama, the eastern gateway to North Cascades National Park, you'll find array of both practical and whimsical goods. Think organic soaps, outdoor gear (across the courtyard in the related Goat's Beard Mountain Supplies shop), and interesting gourmet snacks. You can also pick up espresso drinks, sweets, and sandwiches in the in-house bakery. ✉ *50 Lost River Rd., Mazama* ☎ *509/996–2855* 🌐 *www.themazamastore.com.*

North Cascades Highway

North Cascades Highway

SCENIC DRIVE | Also known as Highway 20, this classic scenic route first winds through the green pastures and woods of the upper Skagit Valley, the mountains looming in the distance. Beyond Concrete, a former cement-manufacturing town, the highway climbs into the mountains, passes the Ross and Diablo dams, and traverses Ross Lake National Recreation Area. Here several pull-outs offer great views of the lake and the surrounding snowcapped peaks. From June to September, the meadows are covered with wildflowers, and from late September through October, the mountain slopes glow with fall foliage. The pinnacle of this stretch is 5,477-foot-high Washington Pass: look east, to where the road descends quickly into a series of hairpin curves between Early Winters Creek and the Methow Valley. Remember, this section of the highway is closed from roughly November to April, depending on snowfall, and sometimes closes temporarily during the busy summer season due to mudslides from storms. From the Methow Valley, Highway 153 takes the scenic route along the Methow River's apple, nectarine, and peach orchards to Pateros, on the Columbia River; from here, you can continue east to Grand Coulee or south to Lake Chelan. 🌐 *www.cascadeloop.com*.

Skagit River Bald Eagle Interpretive Center

TOUR—SIGHT | Open on weekends in December and January to highlight the winter migration of bald eagles, the center offers guided hikes and educational presentations about the Skagit ecosystem. ✉ *52809 Rockport Park Rd., Rockport* ☎ *306/853–7626* 🌐 *www.skagiteagle.org*.

Restaurants

Developed picnic areas at both Rainy Pass (Highway 20, 38 miles east of the park visitor center) and Washington Pass (Highway 20, 42 miles east of the visitor center) have a half-dozen picnic tables, drinking water, and pit toilets. The vistas of surrounding peaks are sensational at

Best Campgrounds in North Cascades 

Tent campers can choose between forest sites, riverside spots, lake grounds, or meadow spreads encircled by mountains. Camping here is as easy or challenging as you want to make it; some campgrounds are a short walk from ranger stations, while others are miles from the highway. Note that many remote campsites, particularly those around Stehekin, lack road access, so you have to walk, boat, or ride a horse to reach them. Most don't accept reservations, and spots fill up quickly May through September. If there's no ranger on-site, you can often sign yourself in—and always check in at a ranger station before you set out overnight. Note that some areas are occasionally closed due to flooding, forest fires, or other factors.

Lake Chelan National Recreation Area. Many backcountry camping areas are accessible via park shuttles or boat. All require a free backcountry permit. Purple Point, the most popular campground due to its quick access to Stehekin Landing, has six tent sites, bear boxes, and nearby road access. ✉ *Stehekin Landing, Stehekin* ☎ *509/699–2080.*

these two overlooks. More picnic facilities are located near the visitor center in Newhalem and at Colonial Creek Campground, 10 miles east of the visitor center on Highway 20.

Restaurant at Stehekin Valley Ranch
$$ | **AMERICAN** | **FAMILY** | Meals in the rustic log ranch house, served at polished wood tables, include buffet dinners of steak, ribs, hamburgers, fish, salad, beans, and dessert. Note that breakfast is served 7 to 9, lunch is noon to 1, and dinner is 5:30 to 7; show up later than that and you'll find the kitchen is closed. **Known for:** hearty meals; fresh berries, fruit, and produce; communal dining. *$ Average main: $20 ✉ Stehekin Valley Rd., 9 miles north of Stehekin Landing, Stehekin ☎ 509/682–4677, 800/536–0745 🌐 www.stehekinvalleyranch.com ⏲ Closed Oct.–mid-June.*

Stehekin Pastry Company
$ | **BAKERY** | As you enter this lawn-framed timber chalet, you're immersed in the tantalizing aromas of a European bakery. Glassed-in display cases are filled with trays of homemade baked goods, and the pungent espresso is eye-opening. **Known for:** fruit pie; amazing pastries; hearty lunch food. *$ Average main: $9 ✉ Stehekin Valley Rd., Stehekin ✥ About 2 miles north of Stehekin Landing ☎ 509/682–7742 🌐 www.stehekinpastry.com ⏲ Closed mid-Oct.–mid-May.*

Hotels

North Cascades Lodge at Stehekin
$$$ | **HOTEL** | Crackling fires and Lake Chelan views are provided both in standard rooms in the Alpine House, with its shared lounge and lakeside deck, and in larger rooms in the Swiss Mont building, with private decks overlooking the water. **Pros:** on the water; recreation center with pool table; kayak and canoe rentals. **Cons:** no air-conditioning; TV is only available in the recreation building; limited Internet service and no cell phone service. *$ Rooms from: $151 ✉ 955 Stehekin Valley Rd., Stehekin ☎ 509/682–4494, 855/685–4167 reservations 🌐 www.lodgeatstehekin.com ⏲ General store and all but 7 rooms are closed mid-Oct.–mid-May 🛏 28 rooms, 1 house 🍽 No meals.*

Stehekin Valley Ranch
$$$$ | **ALL-INCLUSIVE** | **FAMILY** | Alongside pretty meadows at the edge of pine forest, this rustic ranch is a center for hikers and horseback riders, who stay in barnlike cabins with cedar paneling, tile floors, and a private bath, or canvas-roof tent cabins with bunk beds, kerosene lamps, and shared bathrooms. **Pros:** easy access to recreation; playground and outdoor game fields; hearty meals included. **Cons:** no bathrooms in tent cabins; many repeat guests so book early. *Rooms from: $280* ✉ *Stehekin Valley Rd., Stehekin* ✣ *9 miles north of Stehekin Landing* ☎ *509/682–4677, 800/536–0745* 🌐 *stehekinvalleyranch.com* ⏲ *Closed Oct.–mid-June* *15 cabins* *All meals.*

Chapter 16

NORTH CENTRAL WASHINGTON

Updated by
Andrew Collins

Sights ★★★★★ | Restaurants ★★★★☆ | Hotels ★★★★☆ | Shopping ★★☆☆☆ | Nightlife ★★☆☆☆

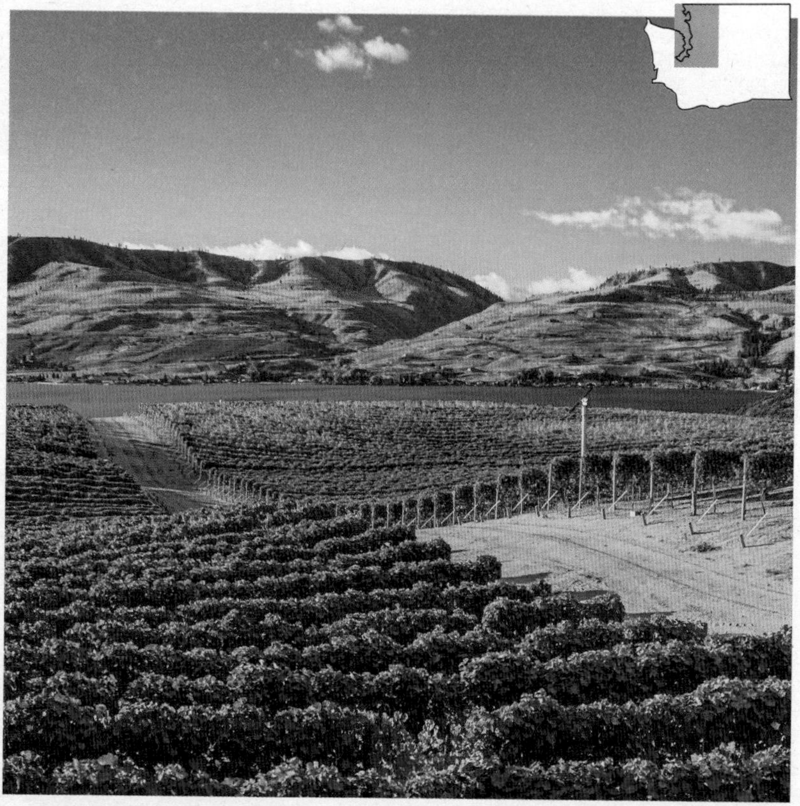

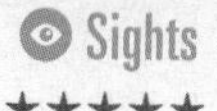

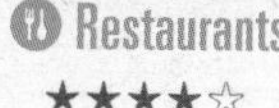

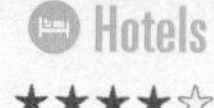

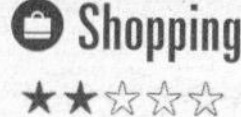

WELCOME TO NORTH CENTRAL WASHINGTON

TOP REASONS TO GO

★ **The great outdoors:** Stunning alpine and lakeside hikes draw recreation enthusiasts during the warmer months. In winter you'll find ample opportunities for skiing on the drier, sunnier side of the Cascades.

★ **Wine touring:** Fields around Chelan and Wenatchee have increasingly been planted with grapes, while Leavenworth has become a mini Woodinville in terms of tasting rooms.

★ **Cascade Loop:** This scenic byway circles through the mountains, offering some 400 miles of stunning vistas and delightful small-town diversions.

★ **The Old West:** With its wagon wheels, wooden sidewalks, false fronts, and hitching posts, riverside Winthrop celebrates Washington's vibrant frontier spirit.

★ **The Old World:** The Bavarian-inspired mountain town of Leavenworth buzzes with great food and drink all year and lights up for the holidays and many festivals.

1 **Winthrop.** This cowboy-theme village is the eastern gateway to North Cascades National Park and a lively hub of art, outdoor recreation, and wildlife viewing.

2 **Twisp.** The largest community in Methow Valley is Twisp, a funky, artsy little village.

3 **Chelan.** The most accessible town fringing the shores of fjordlike Lake Chelan abounds with wineries, restaurants, beaches, and family-friendly diversions.

4 **Wenatchee.** Famous for its prolific orchards, this laid-back city on the Columbia River is enjoying a resurgence fueled by outdoorsy newcomers and a growing craft-beer, wine, and food scene.

5 **Cashmere.** Small-town charms and grand river and mountain scenery reward visitors to this friendly community.

6 **Leavenworth.** This cute alpine town with a famously Bavarian look and style offers everything from old-world charm to proximity to skiing to a hip restaurant and bar scene.

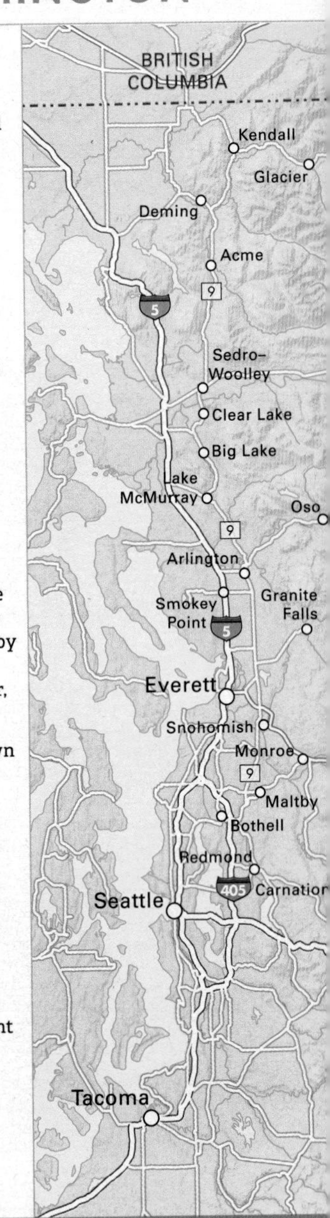

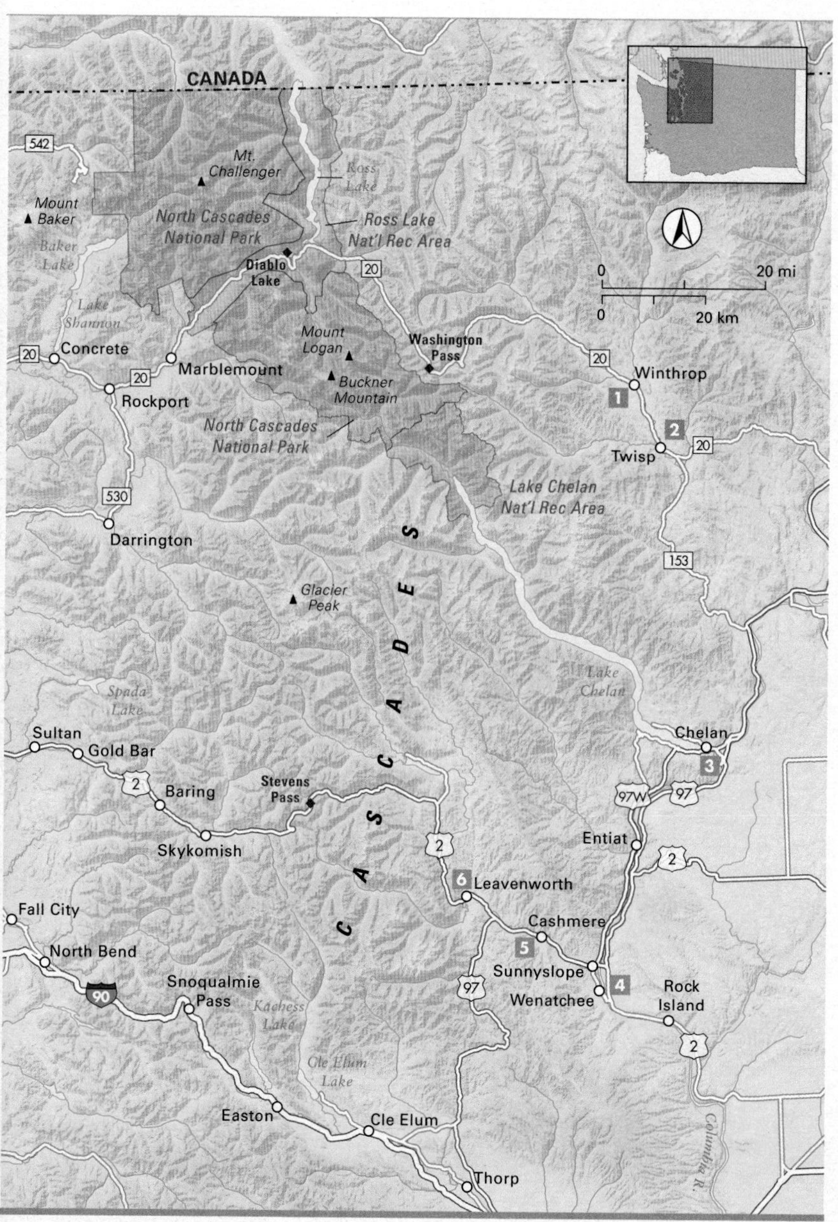
CANADA
542
Mt. Challenger
Ross Lake
Mount Baker
North Cascades National Park
Ross Lake Nat'l Rec Area
Baker Lake
Diablo Lake
20
0
20 mi
0
20 km
Lake Shannon
Mount Logan
Washington Pass
20
Concrete
Marblemount
20
Winthrop
Buckner Mountain
1
Rockport
North Cascades National Park
2
Twisp
20
Lake Chelan Nat'l Rec Area
530
Darrington
C A S C A D E S
153
Glacier Peak
Lake Chelan
Spada Lake
Sultan
Gold Bar
Chelan
3
2
Baring
Stevens Pass
97W
97
Skykomish
2
Entiat
2
6
Leavenworth
Fall City
Cashmere
North Bend
5
Sunnyslope
90
Snoqualmie Pass
97
4
Wenatchee
Rock Island
Kachess Lake
2
Cle Elum Lake
Easton
Cle Elum
Columbia R.
Thorp

Wilderness embraces much of North Central Washington, replete with cascading creeks, glacial peaks, low-hanging valleys dusted with wildflowers, and former timber and farming towns that now boast sophisticated inns, superb wineries, and buzzy art and food scenes. The region's natural beauty creates a feeling of journeying to an out-of-the-way, rural retreat. This is the quintessential Great Outdoors, and—despite a road closure that walls off the northern section from west of the Cascades in winter—it's surprisingly accessible.

Most of the region's permanent residents live along main two-lane highways that follow the Cascade Loop, on ranches and orchards and in mostly smaller towns, all gateways to the northern ridges of the Cascade Range. In winter, these peaks, which climb to more than 9,000 feet, have the greatest measured snowfall in North America—averaging more than 60 feet in some parts of the western slopes.

Getting to North Central Washington, especially if you're driving over one of the magnificent mountain passes in the Cascades, is a road-trippers dream. One of the most popular drives in the state, the Cascade Loop, encircles the region, albeit only part of the way in winter, when Highway 20 (the North Cascades Highway) is closed. In summer, however, you can drive from Interstate 5 in Burlington (between Mount Vernon and Bellingham) through North Cascades National Park and over Washington Pass and through the bustling riverside hamlets of Winthrop and Twisp. The Loop continues south, partly alongside the Columbia River, to the resort community of Chelan—it's at the southeastern tip of the eponymous 50-mile, glacier-fed lake and receives some 300 days of sunshine per year, a boon to the area's many wineries. The lake stretches 1½ miles at its widest and descends 1,486 feet at its deepest. The route continues south to the fruit-growing outdoor recreation hub of Wenatchee, where it joins U.S. 2 and cuts west through the dapper village of Cashmere and then to the considerable charms of Bavarian-style Leavenworth before climbing up through the Cascades and over Stevens Pass on a route that is maintained year-round, leading back to Interstate 5 in the northern Seattle suburbs. You can also reach the area year-round from Seattle via Interstate 90 and U.S. 97.

MAJOR REGIONS

East of Washington Pass and North Cascades National Park, Highway 20 descends into Okanogan County and the Methow (pronounced **met**-how) Valley, which includes rugged Mazama, Old West–style **Winthrop** and the quirky riverfront town of Twisp. Snowfall closes the pass from December through April, at which time you can access Methow Valley from the south, where you'll find not only the lakeside resort town of **Chelan,** but also sunny **Wenatchee**—the self-proclaimed "Apple Capital of Washington"—and the Bavarian-style village of **Leavenworth.** Bordered by the Columbia River to the east, the towns east of the Cascades offer a wealth of outdoor adventures as well as wine-tasting, apple-picking, and brewpub-hoppings.

Planning

When to Go

With its evergreen foothills and impressive peaks, the North Cascades—often likened to the Alps—is a popular destination year-round. Skiers, snowboarders, and snowshoers come here from December through March, relaxing après-ski in the area's lodges, small hotels, and bed-and-breakfasts. With Washington Pass closed in winter, however, visitors from the west can reach the area via U.S. 2 or Interstate 90. Year-round, you can reach virtually all of the area's foothills and valleys. Summer peak season extends from snowmelt (late May through July, depending on elevation) to early September. Many regular visitors to Lake Chelan book their lodgings for the following summer before leaving. Winter and summer weekends and holidays can get crowded throughout the region.

In the fall, when the North Cascades glow with crimson, saffron, and rust-color foliage against a backdrop of its evergreen trees, the Cascade Loop is a popular route. Leaf-peepers who don't mind the frequently rainy days of late autumn can enjoy otherwise mild temperatures and a quieter drive. Early spring also offers peace and quiet as well as the promise of alpine air. Many lodgings drop their rates during these shoulder seasons.

FESTIVALS AND EVENTS

If you want to match your visit up with a local event, there are highlights in each season.

Christkindlmarkt and Christmas Lighting Festival

CULTURAL FESTIVALS | FAMILY | Old-world holiday traditions blend with modern rituals to turn downtown Leavenworth into a glittering holiday wonderland, complete with carriage rides, carols, arts and crafts, tree lighting, children's activities, and performances by the Marlin Handbell Ringers, who help keep alive an 18th-century English tradition by jingling more than 100 bells. ⊠ *Leavenworth* 🌐 *www.christkindlmarktleavenworth.com.*

Lake Chelan Winterfest Fire and Ice

FESTIVALS | FAMILY | Held during two weekends in mid-January, this festival features a chili cook-off, music, wine and winter ale tastings, a fun run, ice slide, wine walk, polar bear dip, children's activities, ice sculpture, and fireworks. ⊠ *Chelan* 🌐 *www.lakechelanwinterfest.com.*

Maifest

CULTURAL FESTIVALS | FAMILY | Enjoy traditional German dancing, including an intricate old-world maypole dance, as well as a lederhosen contest and parade during this May weekend gathering in the flower-decked Bavarian-style village of Leavenworth. ✉ *Leavenworth* 🌐 *www.leavenworth.org.*

★ Oktoberfest

CULTURAL FESTIVALS | FAMILY | Show off your "chicken dance" and other oom-pah moves in Leavenworth at one of the most exuberant stateside celebrations of this German beer festival, complete with German food, German music, German dancing and, of course, beer. Lodgings fill up fast during this festive celebration held over the first three weekends of October. ✉ *Leavenworth* 🌐 *www.leavenworthoktoberfest.com.*

Winthrop Rhythm and Blues Festival

MUSIC FESTIVALS | The Blues Ranch, 1 mile west of Winthrop, hosts this nonprofit, volunteer-run July music festival—an outdoor Methow Valley tradition. ✉ *Winthrop* 🌐 *www.winthropbluesfestival.com.*

Getting Here and Around

AIR

It's a two- to five-hour drive to the region from Seattle's airports, or you can catch a commercial flight on Horizon Air from Sea-Tac to Wenatchee's Pangborn Memorial Airport, which has Budget and Enterprise car rental agencies. Additionally, Catlin Flying Service offers charter flights to Chelan, Winthrop, and Seattle's Boing Field.

CONTACTS Catlin Flying Service. ✉ *Winthrop* ☎ *509/429–2697* 🌐 *www.catlinflyingservice.com.* **Pangborn Memorial Airport.** ✉ *1 Pangborn Dr., East Wenatchee* ☎ *509/884–2494* 🌐 *www.flywenatchee.com.*

CAR

From roughly May through November, depending on snowfall, you can take Highway 20 (North Cascades Highway) from the Skagit Valley town of Burlington to Winthrop and Twisp. Year-round from Seattle and points west, you can take U.S. 2 to Leavenworth or Interstate 90 to U.S. 97, which leads north to Leavenworth and eventually, via Highway 153, Winthrop.

Restaurants

The region's dining options have expanded tremendously since the early 2000s, when it was mostly the domain of old-school diners, pubs, and pizzerias. Now even small towns like Twisp and Winthrop have a few chef-owned spots focused on seasonal and locally soured contemporary Pacific Northwest food, often with Asian, Mediterranean, and other international influences. Humbler establishments still abound, but the better ones feature inventive, carefully selected ingredients along with craft cocktails, local wines and beers, and craft coffees. In fact, the entire area has seen a huge boom in winemaking, especially around Lake Chelan, which is now a federally designated American Viticultural Area).

The area's largest city, Wenatchee, has the most diverse cuisine, with especially good Asian and Mexican eateries. When it comes to cosmopolitan dining and sipping, however, Bavarian-themed Leavenworth and wine-centric Chelan aren't far behind. And you'll find at least one notable craft brewer in even some of the little in-between villages in these parts. *Restaurant reviews have been shortened. For full information visit Fodors.com.*

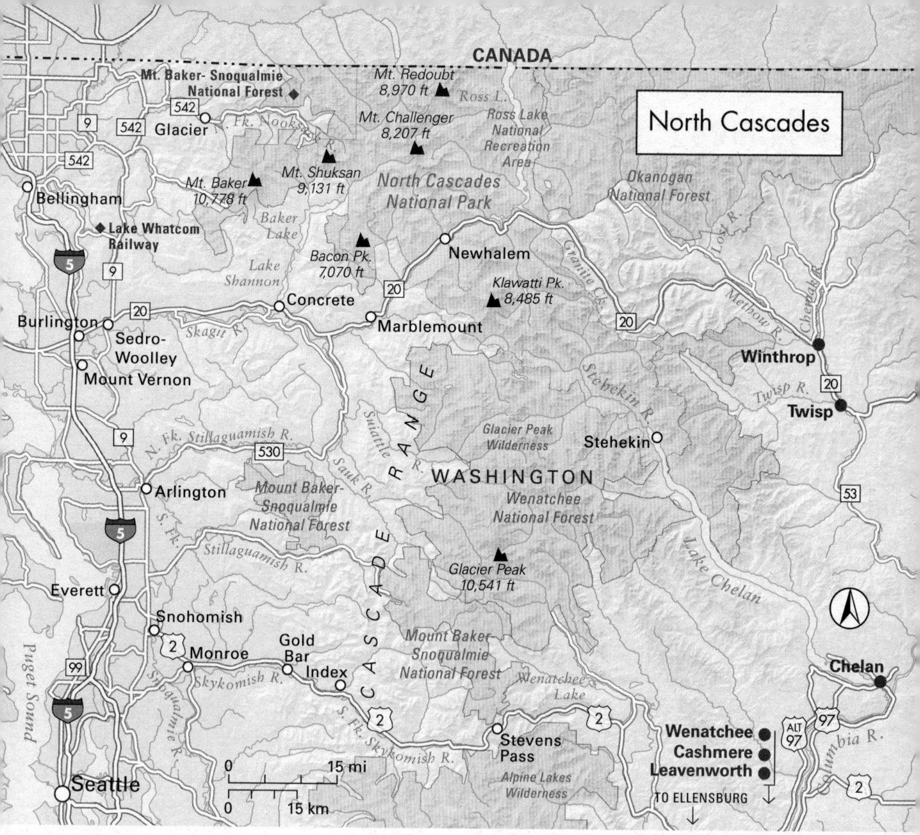

North Cascades

Hotels

Because a lot of visitors come from a long way and then stay for a while to take advantage of boating, skiing, hiking, and other recreational opportunities, many of the towns in the area offer a wealth of vacation rentals. Chelan and neighboring Manson, while hugely popular, have but a handful of official hotels. Winthrop has both rustic riverside cabins and one of the area's top resorts, Sun Mountain Lodge. Leavenworth has by far the largest inventory of accommodations in the region, offering everything from family-friendly motels with pools to sophisticated adult-only inns and even one superexclusive spa resort, the Posthotel. The more workaday city of Wenatchee is mostly the domain of chain hotels, but you'll find some appealing inns in the smaller towns to the west, such as Cashmere. Book well in advance for holiday and summer weekends, particularly during festivals and events, when many properties have two- or three-night minimums. And check hotel websites for package deals that include meals and outdoor activities. *Hotel reviews have been shortened. For full information, visit Fodors.com.*

What It Costs in U.S. Dollars

	$	$$	$$$	$$$$
RESTAURANTS				
	under $16	$16–$22	$23–$30	over $30
HOTELS				
	under $150	$150–$200	$201–$250	over $250

Winthrop

153 miles east of Bellingham, 240 miles northeast of Seattle.

As the eastern gateway to North Cascades National Park, Winthrop is an outdoor mecca with countless opportunities for amazing hiking, mountain biking, rock climbing, and fishing, and for cross-country skiing along the 120-mile Methow Trails network in winter. Methow Valley was historically a favorite gathering place for indigenous tribes, who dug the plentiful and nutritious bulbs and hunted deer while their horses fattened on the tall native grasses. Pioneering settlers began to arrive in the 1800s, when this burgeoning riverside settlement grew into a cattle-ranching town whose residents inspired some of Owen Wister's colorful characters in his novel *The Virginian.* In 1972, spurred by Leavenworth's Bavarian theme, Winthrop business owners enacted a plan to market the town's Old West feel, and many of the original, turn-of-the-20th-century buildings were restored or given vintage facades. Pedestrian bridges cross the Chewuch and Methow rivers on either side of this village's bustling commercial district, and from viewing platforms on both bridges, you can watch salmon spawn in May and June.

GETTING HERE AND AROUND

When the North Cascades Highway is open, Winthrop can be reached via that scenic route; it takes about three hours, 45 minutes from Seattle. The rest of the year, it will take about an extra hour via Stevens Pass (U.S. 2) or Snoqualmie Pass (Interstate 90 then Highway 970 to Highway 2) to Wenatchee then north via Highways 97, 153, and 20. From Spokane, Winthrop is about 3½ hours west via Highway 2, then Highways 174, 17, 97, 153, and 20.

ESSENTIALS

VISITOR INFORMATION Winthrop Chamber of Commerce. ✉ *202 Hwy. 20* ☎ *509/996–2125* 🌐 *www.winthropwashington.com.*

Sights

Shafer Historical Museum

HISTORIC SITE | Made up of several downtown buildings that trace to Winthrop's colorful mining and ranching past, including "the castle," a late-19th-century log house built by one of the town's founding fathers. Other structures include a country store, print shop, school house, women's dress shop, and an open-air display of vintage mining equipment. Although you can only go inside the buildings in summer, the grounds alone are worth a stroll and are open year-round. ✉ *285 Castle Ave.* ☎ *509/996–2712* 🌐 *www.shafermuseum.org* 🎟 *$5 donation suggested* ⏱ *Buildings closed early Sept.–late May.*

Restaurants

5B's Bakery and Eatery

$ | **BAKERY** | **FAMILY** | If you need a handy stop for breakfast or lunch, or take-out provisions for a picnic in the North Cascades, this gluten-free bakery featuring tasty, made-from-scratch baked goods and hearty meals is definitely worth a quick detour off the highway. The breakfast menu lists the usual quiches, hot cakes, and waffles, along with three-potato hash (with eggs, corned beef, veggies, or andouille sausage). **Known for:** gluten-free pastries, cookies, and breads; plenty of take-out options; locally sourced ingredients. 💲 *Average main: 13* ✉ *45597 Main St., Concrete* ☎ *360/853–8700* 🌐 *www.5bsbakery.com* ⏱ *Closed Tues.*

★ Arrowleaf Bistro

$$$$ | **PACIFIC NORTHWEST** | Locally sourced farm-to-table meals are the draw in this airy, casually elegant restaurant on the edge of downtown Winthrop. Notable examples of the deftly plated fare you might find here include parsnip bisque with curry oil, wild boar Bolognese, and smoked duck breast with Methow huckleberry sauce. **Known for:** great happy hour deals on craft cocktails; nightly sustainable-seafood special; sleek but unpretentious dining room. *Average main: $31 207 White Ave. 509/996–3919 www.arrowleafbistro.com Closed Mon. and Tues. No lunch.*

★ Dining Room at Sun Mountain Lodge
$$$$ | PACIFIC NORTHWEST | A sylvan hilltop overlooking the Methow Valley sets the scene for an extraordinary dining experience featuring upscale Pacific Northwest cuisine with local and often organic ingredients. Exquisite flavors match the artful presentation and elegant yet unpretentious lodgelike atmosphere. **Known for:** sophisticated Pacific Northwest fare; sweeping mountain views; extensive wine list. *Average main: $40 604 Patterson Lake Rd. 509/996–4707, 800/572–0493 www.sunmountainlodge.com/dining Limited hrs in winter and spring; closed 2 wks in Nov. No lunch.*

Methow Valley Ciderhouse
$ | AMERICAN | This chatter-filled, wood-paneled ciderhouse and taproom on the road to North Cascades National Park stands out for both its bright, crisp ciders and its elevated pub grub. Tuck into a plate of baby back ribs, Thai chicken sausage, or pulled-pork pizza, and consider a sampler of ciders—all of these sippers are produced with apples and other fruit grown in the immediate vicinity. **Known for:** mountain views from the patio; elevated comfort food; laid-back atmosphere. *Average main: $12 28 Hwy. 20 509/341–4354 www.methowvalleyciderhouse.com Closed Wed.*

Old Schoolhouse Brewery
$ | AMERICAN | Located in a long red building designed to resemble an old one-room schoolhouse, this craft brewpub sits between the town's main drag and the Chewuch River. While waiting for a burger or a bowl of chili, sip an Epiphany Pale, Hooligan Stout, or Ruud Awakening IPA. **Known for:** breezy rear deck in popular in summer; festive atmosphere; hearty pub grub. *Average main: $14 155 Riverside Ave. 509/996–3183 www.oldschoolhousebrewery.com No lunch Mon.–Thurs.*

Hotels

★ Freestone Inn
$$$$ | RESORT | FAMILY | At the heart of the 120-acre, historic Wilson Ranch, amid more than 2 million acres of forest, this upscale mountain retreat embraces the pioneer spirit in spacious rooms, suites, and cabins snuggled up to Early Winters Creek. **Pros:** two-story river-rock fireplace highlights the great room; groomed trails are used for year-round recreation; proximity to North Cascades National Park. **Cons:** limited cell phone and Wi-Fi service; amenities limited in shoulder season; cabins can be quite rustic. *Rooms from: $259 31 Early Winters Dr., Mazama About 14 miles northwest of Winthop 509/996–3906, 800/639–3809 www.freestoneinn.com 31 rooms Free Breakfast.*

Lakeside Lodge & Suites
$$$$ | HOTEL | FAMILY | Adjacent to Lakeside Park, a couple miles from downtown Chelan, this four-story property has all lake-facing rooms to enjoy sunset over the lake, and plenty of family-friendly amenities, including two pools and two hot tubs. **Pros:** lake views; adjacent to park with beach, playground, and sports courts; hot breakfast included. **Cons:** some room views are blocked by a giant tree; rooms open to outside (no halls); no on-site restaurant. *Rooms from: $260 2312 W. Woodin Ave., Chelan 800/468–2781, 509/682–4396 www.lakesidelodgeandsuites.com 93 rooms Free Breakfast.*

Mt. Gardner Inn
$ | **HOTEL** | With great views of the mountains to the west, this small hotel less than a mile from Winthrop's funky downtown sits just across Highway 20 from the scenic Methow River. **Pros:** close to several appealing restaurants; reasonable rates; friendly, thoughtful service. **Cons:** least expensive rooms are close to slightly busy road; two-night minimum stay on weekends; no breakfast. *Rooms from: $109* *611 Hwy. 20* *509/996–2000* *www.mtgardnerinn.com* *11 rooms* *No meals.*

★ River's Edge Resort
$ | **B&B/INN** | **FAMILY** | With an enviable location overlooking the Chewuch River and just a stone's throw from Winthrop's quirky shops and eateries, this small compound of one- to three-bedroom cabins with kitchens—and in most cases hot tubs and river views—is a terrific find and a great value. **Pros:** spacious accommodations with kitchens and living rooms; steps from village dining and shopping; great for families and groups. **Cons:** in the center of a sometimes busy village; two-night minimum stay on many weekends; no pets. *Rooms from: $140* *115 Riverside Ave.* *509/996–8000* *www.riversedgewinthrop.com* *6 cabins* *No meals.*

River Run Inn
$$$ | **B&B/INN** | **FAMILY** | The rooms and cabins are comfortable but not fancy here, but the inn's riverfront location and amenities—including picnic tables, hammocks, a playground, lawn games, and an indoor pool—make it a popular place to stay. **Pros:** free use of bikes; serene riverfront setting; free DVD library. **Cons:** hot tub is only big enough for a few people; bathrooms are small; just a few pet-friendly rooms. *Rooms from: $175* *27 Rader Rd.* *800/757–2709, 509/996–2173* *www.riverrun-inn.com* *16 rooms (plus 1 house)* *No meals.*

★ Sun Mountain Lodge
$$$$ | **RESORT** | The stunning North Cascades and all its attractions are the stars of this outdoor-oriented resort replete with luxurious accommodations, spectacular mountain views, and a range of activities that make it a year-round destination, whether the peaks are covered in snow or wildflowers. **Pros:** stunning setting; a wide array of outdoor activities year-round; panoramic views; award-winning dining; warm hospitality. **Cons:** limited cell service; roundabout route from Seattle in winter. *Rooms from: $265* *604 Patterson Lake Rd.* *509/996–2211, 800/572–0493* *www.sunmountainlodge.com* *Closed 2 wks in early Nov.* *112 rooms* *Free Breakfast.*

Copper Glance
BARS/PUBS | Amid Winthrop's old-fashioned Wild West storefronts, this swanky little cocktail bar with an ornate chandelier feels decidedly modern and urbane. It has creative bar nibbles and a stand-out selection of craft cocktails, many of them prepared with artisan spirits. There's also an extensive list of single-malt whiskeys. *134A Riverside Ave.* *509/433–7765* *www.copperglancewinthrop.com.*

Shopping

Sheri's Sweet Shoppe
FOOD/CANDY | Tucked into this Wild West–style clapboard building is a haven of treats: myriad candy bins, boxes of chocolate bars, and—behind the glass case—all kinds of house-made chocolates and fudge. Watch the staff make hand-dipped caramel apples. There's homemade ice cream, too. Shady tables on the patio provide respite for grown-ups, along with saddle-topped stools for the kids. Hot dogs, curly fries, and milk shakes are also available. *207 Riverside Ave.* *509/996–3834* *www.sherissweetshoppe.com.*

Activities

HIKING

Methow Valley Ranger District

HIKING/WALKING | Hundreds of miles of hiking trails, including the famed Pacific Crest Trail, crisscross the 1.3-million-acre Okanogan-Wenatchee National Forest and Pasayten wilderness, which surrounds Winthrop. You can pick up information and advice from this ranger station near downtown. ✉ *24 W. Chewuch Rd.* ☎ *509/996–4000* 🌐 *www.fs.usda.gov/okawen.*

North Cascades Mountain Guides

CLIMBING/MOUNTAINEERING | This outfitter provides guided backcountry-skiing and rock-climbing excursions for single and multiple days, as well as mountaineering courses. ✉ *Mazama* ☎ *509/996–3272* 🌐 *www.ncmountainguides.com.*

RAFTING

Methow River Raft + Kayak

WHITE-WATER RAFTING | This well-known outfitter offers a variety of half- and full-day white-water rafting trips in the area, from gentle floats to wilder rides along the Methow River. The company also offers tubing and river kayaking trips for all skill levels. ✉ *27 Radar Rd.* ☎ *509/866–6775* 🌐 *www.methowrafting.com.*

SKIING

★ Methow Valley Sport Trails Association

BICYCLING | The Methow Valley boasts one of the most extensive groomed cross-country ski trail systems in the country, some 120 miles in all. Fat bikes and snowshoes are also allowed. When there's no snow, the trails are among the best for dirt biking in the state. You can purchase day passes ($25 for skiing, $10 for fat bikes, $5 for snowshoeing) at the Methow Trails office as well as at many shops around the area. ✉ *309 Riverside Ave.* ☎ *509/996–3287* 🌐 *www.methowtrails.org.*

North Cascade Heli-Skiing

SKIING/SNOWBOARDING | If you can afford it, experienced skiers looking for fresh powder can get dropped off in virgin, backcountry snow by a helicopter for one day of runs ($1,300 per person). Three- or four-night yurt trips are also available ($1,350 to $1,500 per person). ✉ *Freestone Inn, 31 Early Winters Dr., Mazama* ☎ *509/996–3272* 🌐 *www.heli-ski.com.*

Twisp

8 miles south of Winthrop, 180 miles east of Seattle.

The largest community in Methow Valley is Twisp, a funky, artsy little village about 8 miles south of Winthrop. Its downtown buzzes with cool restaurants and galleries.

GETTING HERE AND AROUND

Winthrop and Twisp are sister communities, and many visitors shuttle from one to the other. Twisp is a 20-minute drive from Winthrop.

Confluence Gallery & Art Center

MUSEUM | Since it opened in the early 1990s, this nonprofit community art gallery has mirrored Twisp's growth into a renowned artists' colony. Set along the town's charming main commercial drag, the gallery hosts a half-dozen exhibits each year. In the outstanding gift shop you'll find an impressive selection of works, from paintings to postcards to pottery. ✉ *104 S. Glover St., Twisp* ☎ *509/997–2787* 🌐 *www.confluence-gallery.com* ⏲ *Closed Tues.*

Restaurants

Blue Star Coffee Roasters

$ | **CAFÉ** | Both serious coffee aficionados and casual sippers stop by this unassuming roaster and café a mile southeast of Twisp. Blue Star produces a number of fine roasts and blends, which you can sample in this casual spot along with decadent pastries and baked goods. **Known for:** superb house-roasted coffee; homemade mixed-berry pop tarts; pleasant patio seating. *Average main: $5* *3 Twisp Airport Rd., Twisp* *509/997–2583* *www.bluestarcoffeeroasters.com* *Closed Sun.*

★ Cinnamon Twisp Bakery

$ | **CAFÉ** | Tucked beside the popular Glover Street Market, this bakery is justly renowned for both savory and sweet treats, including—most famously—cinnamon "twisps" (the bakery's own decadent version of cinnamon rolls). There are also smoothies, milk shakes, and build-your-own sandwiches. **Known for:** impressive selection of rich sweets; refreshing house-made beverages; breakfast bagels. *Average main: $9* *116 N. Glover St., Twisp* *509/997–5030* *No dinner.*

★ Tappi

$$ | **ITALIAN** | The first thing you're likely to notice upon walking into this festive trattoria is the mammoth wood-fired brick oven, in which personable chef-owner John Bonica prepares such mouthwatering fare as roasted veggies over polenta, blistered-crust pizzas with creative toppings, and wine-braised roast beef. Several excellent pasta dishes are offered, too. **Known for:** sensational dishes from the wood-fired oven; seasonal fruit in the panna cotta; first-rate Italian wine list. *Average main: $17* *201 S. Glover St., Twisp* *509/997–3345* *www.tappitwisp.com* *Closed Tues. and Wed. and for 6 wks in late autumn. No lunch.*

Hotels

Twisp River Suites

$$$ | **HOTEL** | These chic, comfortable, and contemporary rooms and condominium-style suites filled with thoughtful extras hug the banks of the Twisp River, lined by ponderosa pine and frequented by bald eagles. **Pros:** riverfront views from many of the rooms; sleek and modern mountain feel; within walking distance of restaurants. **Cons:** not much to do in the little town of Twisp; 15-minute drive from Winthrop; two-night minimum stay in summer. *Rooms from: $209* *140 W. Twisp Ave., Twisp* *509/997–0100, 855/784–8328* *www.twispriversuites.com* *16 rooms* *Free Breakfast.*

★ Twisp Terrace Lodge

$$$$ | **B&B/INN** | Private, peaceful, pampering—this upscale boutique resort surrounded by a 300-acre high-desert has just 11 grand rooms, along with a sophisticated restaurant, a cozy old-fashioned pub, and an impressive 30,000-gallon seasonal pool. **Pros:** secluded, and beautiful, grounds; impressive three-course breakfast included; fire pit and golf driving range. **Cons:** steep rates for the area; guests under the age of 18 not permitted; 20-minute drive from Winthrop. *Rooms from: $259* *20556 Hwy. 20, Twisp* *888/550–5919* *www.twispterrace.com* *11 rooms* *Free Breakfast.*

Activities

SKIING

Loup Loup Ski Bowl

SKIING/SNOWBOARDING | Lift tickets at this small ski area east of Twisp, where you can downhill or telemark ski, cost $55 on weekends or holidays, and $48 on weekdays. *97 FS 4200100 Rd., Twisp* *Off Hwy. 20* *509/557–3401 office, 509/557–3405 conditions* *www.skitheloup.com.*

Stehekin River Valley

Chelan

60 miles south of Winthrop, 180 miles east of Seattle.

Lake Chelan, a sinewy, 50½-mile-long fjord—Washington's deepest lake—works its way from the town of Chelan (pronounced shuh- **lan**), at its south end, to Stehekin, on the northwest shore and located within North Cascades National Park. The surrounding mountains rise from a height of about 4,000 feet near Chelan to 8,000 and 9,000 feet closer to Stehekin—just south of the lake, 9,511-foot Bonanza Peak is Washington's tallest nonvolcanic peak. The scenery around the region is unparalleled, the lake's flat blue water encircled by plunging gorges, with a vista of snow-capped mountains beyond. The region serves as a favorite lake resort of western Washingtonians, with most visitors staying in vacation homes and condo rentals, although there are a few casual resorts and hotels.

A growing number of acclaimed wineries dot the warmer eastern shores, where temperatures often soar above 100° in summer. Chelan is one of the state's newest American Viticultural Areas, and has more than two-dozen tasting rooms, located both in the town of Chelan and in the village of Manson.

GETTING HERE AND AROUND

From Seattle, allow between 3½ and 4 hours to reach Chelan by either U.S. 2 or Interstate 90, then north via Highway 97.

ESSENTIALS

VISITOR INFORMATION Lake Chelan Chamber of Commerce. ✉ *216 E. Woodin Ave.* ☎ *509/682–3503* 🌐 *www.lake-chelan.com.*

Sights

Benson Vineyards

WINERY/DISTILLERY | The excellent wine is part of the reason to drop by this vineyard hugging a hillside on the north shore of the lake. You'll also want to soak up the sweeping Lake Chelan and mountain views, both from the tasting room—with its large south-facing windows—and the terrace. ✉ *754 Winesap Ave.* ☎ *509/687–0313* 🌐 *www.bensonvineyards.com.*

★ Hard Row to Hoe Vineyards

WINERY/DISTILLERY | One of Chelan's several acclaimed operations with female winemakers, this upper North Shore winery with a bordello-inspired tasting has a helpful staff and a pretty outdoor picnic area. The winery's playful approach extends to the interesting lineup, from spicy Gewürztraminer to a creamy yet lively methode champenoise Brut Rosé sparkler to a velvety red blend aptly called "The Coquette." There's also an aromatic Vermouth aperitif that's a perfect match with light tapas. ✉ *300 Ivan Morse Rd.* ☎ *509/687–3000* 🌐 *www.hardrow.com.*

★ Karma Vineyards

WINERY/DISTILLERY | With a gracious patio, koi pond, and fireplace overlooking the lake as well as a dark and inviting wine cave, this first-rate winery on the South Shore stands out for its superb Brut de Brut Champagne-style sparkler as well as for its Alsatian grapes, including Gewürztraminer and Riesling (and a pretty solid Pinot Noir). ✉ *1681 S. Lakeshore Rd.* ☎ *509/682–5538* 🌐 *www.goodkarmawines.com* ⏲ *Closed Mon.–Wed.*

★ Lake Chelan

BODY OF WATER | Tremendously popular in summer, this narrow, 50-mile-long fjord—Washington's largest natural lake—offers striking scenery year-round. The views include sparkling blue water with snow-capped peaks in the distance. The lake offers swimming, boating, fishing, and a chance to soak up the sun. By road, the only access to the shore is its southeastern end, but May through October you can explore the rest of the lake by boat. ✉ *U.S. 97A.*

Lake Chelan Boat Co.

TRANSPORTATION SITE (AIRPORT/BUS/FERRY/TRAIN) | The *Lady of the Lake II* makes journeys from May to October, departing Chelan at 8:30 and returning at 6 ($40.50 round-trip). The *Lady Express,* a speedy catamaran, runs between Stehekin, Holden Village, the national park, and Lake Chelan year-round; schedules vary with the seasons, with daily trips during summer and three to five trips weekly the rest of the year. Tickets are $61 round-trip May to October and $40.50 round-trip the rest of the year. The vessels also can drop off and pick up at lakeshore trailheads. ✉ *1418 Woodin Ave.* ☎ *509/682–4584, 888/682–4584* 🌐 *ladyofthelake.com.*

Lake Chelan State Park

NATIONAL/STATE PARK | On the lake's less crowded north shore, 9 miles west of Chelan, this 127-acre park with 6,000 feet of shoreline is a favorite hangout for soaking up sunshine and accessing the water. There are docks, a boat ramp, campsites, and plenty of picnic areas. ✉ *7544 S. Lakeshore Rd.* ☎ *509/687–3710* 🌐 *www.parks.wa.gov* 🎫 *$10 parking.*

Nefarious Cellars

WINERY/DISTILLERY | An intimate boutique winery on the South Shore with a devoted—and growing—following, especially for its compelling blends, like the bright and zesty off-dry Consequence (Sauvignon Blanc, Pinot Grigio, and Riesling) and the classic Rhône red, called RX. This estate with sweeping lake vistas also rents out a stunning two-bedroom guesthouse. ✉ *495 S. Lakeshore Rd.* ☎ *509/682–9505* 🌐 *www.nefariouscellars.com* ⏲ *Closed weekdays.*

Twenty-Five Mile Creek State Park

NATIONAL/STATE PARK | About 10 miles north of Lake Chelan State Park, this 232-acre park also abuts the lake's southern shore but attracts even fewer crowds. It's truly a place to get away from it all, and there are plenty of tent and RV sites as well as day-use amenities including picnic tables and a marina. ✉ *20530 S. Lakeshore Rd.* ☎ *509/687–3610* 🌐 *www.*

parks.wa.gov *$10 parking* *Closed Nov.–Mar.*

Wapato Point Cellars

WINERY/DISTILLERY | Home to the popular Winemaker's Grill restaurant, which serves dinner daily, this well-respected operation with a tasting room and wine bar is in the small North Shore town of Manson and makes a great stop whether you're thirsty, hungry, or both. In warm weather, have a seat on the patio and drink up the mountain views. *200 S. Quetilquasoon Rd.* *509/687–4000* *www.wapatopointcellars.com.*

Restaurants

Fox & Quail Cafe

$ | **ECLECTIC** | This casual, sunny eatery with big windows and bench seats occupies a charmingly converted house in downtown Chelan. Popular for lunch and dinner, Fox & Quail presents an international menu of creative small and large plates, including Swedish meat-balls with gravy, ahi tuna sushi towers, prawn po'boys, and Mexico City–inspired street tacos. **Known for:** globally inspired sandwiches and shareable appetizers; patio with brightly colored picnic tables; interesting cocktails and local wines. *Average main: $15* *303 E. Wapato Ave.* *509/682–4196* *Closed Sun. No dinner Mon.–Wed.*

★ **Riverwalk Inn & Cafe**

$ | **AMERICAN** | The cheerful café at this budget-minded downtown inn is open only seasonally, but it's one of the very best destinations in the area for lunch and, especially, breakfast. Plates heaping with raisin-walnut French toast, smoked salmon and poached eggs over sage bread, and several kinds of burrito wraps are the perfect sustenance for a day of hiking, boating, or wine-touring. **Known for:** hearty yet healthy breakfast fare; Blue Star coffee served here; good list of local wines. *Average main: $$13* *204 E. Wapato Ave.* *509/682–2627* *www.riverwalkinnchelan.com* *Closed Jan.–Mar. and Mon.–Wed. No dinner.*

Vin du Lac Winery

$$$ | **BISTRO** | Head to this north shore winery and bistro for wine tasting and dining on the terrace overlooking the Spaders Bay section of Lake Chelan. The lunch and dinner menus feature herbs and produce grown in Vin du Lac's own gardens, as well as meats, cheeses, and seafood sourced regionally as much as possible. **Known for:** tasting room with house-made wines; pretty patio with lake views; live music on Saturday. *Average main: $24* *105 Hwy. 150* *509/682–2882* *www.vindulac.com* *Closed Mon. and Tues.*

Hotels

Campbell's Resort

$$$$ | **RESORT** | **FAMILY** | A family favorite since 1901, this sprawling resort sits on beautifully landscaped grounds along-side a marina and pristine 1,200-foot beach on Lake Chelan, each room with balcony views of the lake or mountains, and some with kitchen or fireplace. **Pros:** short walk to dining and shopping; large private beach; lake and mountain views. **Cons:** pricey in summer; lots of families and groups; needs some updating. *Rooms from: $285* *104 W. Woodin Ave.* *509/682–2561, 800/553–8225* *www.campbellsresort.com* *170 rooms* *No meals.*

Howard's on the River

$$ | **HOTEL** | Located on a breathtaking bend in the Columbia River about 20 miles north of Chelan, this three-story motel-style property has handsome rooms, all of them with fireplaces and generously size balconies with water views. **Pros:** dazzling river views from rooms and patios; good base for exploring Methow Valley; short walk from a couple of good restaurants. **Cons:** room decor isn't especially memorable; not much to do in the tiny town of Pateros;

can get a little pricey on summer weekends. $ *Rooms from: $180* ✉ *233 Lakeshore Dr.* ☎ *509/923–9555* 🌐 *www.howardsontheriver.com* 🛏 *29 rooms* 🍽 *Free Breakfast.*

The Inn at Gamble Sands

$$$$ | HOTEL | Overlooking the fairways of the famed Gamble Sands course, the Columbia River, and the Cascade Range beyond, this collection of high-ceilinged, contemporary rooms and suites is a top destination among ardent golfers. **Pros:** adjoins world-class golf course; spacious, luxurious rooms; rates drop sharply in winter. **Cons:** remote location, 35 miles from Chelan; tends to book up fast in summer; not a lot to do if you're not a golfer. $ *Rooms from: $279* ✉ *200 Sands Trail Rd.* ☎ *509/436–8323* 🌐 *www.gamblesands.com* 🛏 *37 rooms* 🍽 *No meals.*

Lake's Edge Tuscan Lodge

$$ | B&B/INN | An intimate and elegant boutique resort set amid sloping vineyards near Lake Chelan's north shore, this upscale property with a pretty lawn and swimming pool has expansive views of Roses Lake and the mountains beyond. **Pros:** amenities like a swimming pool, hot tub, and exercise room; close to several of the region's iconic wineries; pretty hillside location by two small lakes. **Cons:** not a good fit for kids; short drive to Manson and Chelan restaurants; sometimes books up entirely for weddings or retreats. $ *Rooms from: $175* ✉ *3445 Wapato Lake Rd.* ☎ *509/630–5521* 🌐 *www.lakesedgechelan.com* 🛏 *8 rooms* 🍽 *Free Breakfast.*

Mountain View Lodge

$ | HOTEL | FAMILY | This reasonably priced family-run motor lodge in the laid-back town of Manson is just a 10-minute walk from the shore of Lake Chelan and several tasting rooms and restaurants. **Pros:** pretty outdoor pool and hot tub; friendly, helpful staff; nice views of the mountains. **Cons:** rooms could use an update; 15-minute drive from Chelan; not directly on the lake. $ *Rooms from: $149* ✉ *25 Wapato Point Pkwy.* ☎ *509/687–9505* 🌐 *www.mvlresort.com* 🛏 *33 rooms* 🍽 *No meals.*

Nightlife

Layla's

BARS/PUBS | A sleek taproom set along Chelan's main drag, Layla's is a hip, convivial destination for local wines, craft cocktails, and inventive bar food. ✉ *142–B E. Woodin Ave.* ☎ *509/888–0800* 🌐 *www.laylaschelan.com.*

Activities

★ **Gamble Sands Golf Course**

GOLF | Often ranked among the top 100 public golf courses in the country, this 115-acre links-style track sits alongside a beautiful stretch of the Columbia River about 35 miles northeast of Chelan. The undulating fairways afford dramatic views of the Cascade Range and offer plenty of challenging sand traps, pin placements, and dog legs. The property includes a 37-room inn and a restaurant. ✉ *200 Sands Trail Rd.* ☎ *509/436–8323* 🌐 *www.gamblesands.com* ☞ *From $99.*

Wenatchee

39 miles southwest of Chelan.

Gaining popularity with an outdoorsy crowd and sophisticated wine lovers, Wenatchee (we- *nat*-chee) is an attractive, fast-growing city of about 35,000 in a shallow valley at the confluence of the Wenatchee and Columbia Rivers. Surrounded by orchards, Wenatchee has traditionally been known as the "Apple Capital of Washington." Downtown has many old commercial buildings as well as apple-packing houses where visitors can buy locally grown apples by the case (at great prices, too). The paved Apple Valley Recreation Loop Trail runs for 26 miles on both sides of the Columbia River, crossing the water on bridges at the northern and southern ends of town and connecting several riverfront parks. Downtown has a growing arts scene, with a First Fridays Art Walk each month that offers a nice way to explore local galleries, and an Art on the Avenues loop trail that features more than 90 sculptures and public artworks.

GETTING HERE AND AROUND

Although a car is the best way to explore the region, you can also fly into Wenatchee's tiny Pangborn Memorial Airport via Horizon Air or take Amtrak's *Empire Builder* from Seattle or Spokane to downtown's Columbia Station. By car, it's a 2½- to 3-hour drive from Seattle via U.S. 2 or Interstate 90 and U.S. 97; from Spokane, it's 2½ to 3 hours via U.S. 2 or Interstate 90.

ESSENTIALS

VISITOR INFORMATION Wenatchee Chamber of Commerce and Visitor Center. ✉ *137 N. Wentachee Ave.* ☎ *509/662–2116, 800/572–7753* 🌐 *www.wenatchee.org.*

Sights

Martin Scott Winery

WINERY/DISTILLERY | With its terraces, lawns, and garden, this impressive winery overlooking the banks of the Columbia River lies about 7 miles southeast of Wenatchee. Martin Scott works with an astounding 17 varieties of grapes, from crisp Sauvignon Blancs to fruit-forward Malbecs. ✉ *3400 10th St. SE, East Wenatchee* ☎ *509/886–4596* 🌐 *www.martinscottwinery.com* ⏲ *Closed Sun.–Thurs.*

★ Ohme Gardens

GARDEN | At this lush green oasis, high atop bluffs near the confluence of the Columbia and Wenatchee Rivers, visitors can commune with a blend of native rocks, ferns, mosses, pools, waterfalls, rock gardens, and conifers. Herman Ohme purchased the land in 1929 as a private family retreat and developed the gardens—now owned and managed by Chelan County—for his wife, Ruth. ✉ *3327 Ohme Rd.* ☎ *509/662–5785* 🌐 *www.ohmegardens.org* 🎫 *$8* ⏲ *Closed mid-Oct.–mid-Apr.*

★ Pybus Public Market

MARKET | Set in a renovated warehouse along the Columbia River, this market hall modeled loosely on Seattle's Pike Place Market has been a cog in the revitalization of Wenatchee's riverfront since it opened in 2013. Inside you'll find several excellent restaurants as well as vendors selling fresh produce from nearby farms, artisanal cheeses and charcuterie, seafood, coffee, gelato, and baked goods. ✉ *3 N. Worthen St.* ☎ *509/888–3900* 🌐 *www.pybuspublicmarket.org.*

Rocky Reach Dam Park and Discovery Center

DAM | This 125-foot-tall hydroelectric dam on the Columbia River, about 8 miles north of Wenatchee, supplies power to about 7 million people. There's much for visitors to see and do here, including a 17-acre park with picnic shelters and great river views. The Discovery Center has interactive exhibits and fish-viewing windows, and the Museum of the Columbia contains the pilothouse of the late-19th-century sternwheeler *Columbia,* Native American tools and replica dwellings, and loggers' and railroad workers' tools. As of this writing, all of the dam's visitor facilities were undergoing a major expansion that's slated for completion in spring 2021. ✉ *6151 U.S. 97A* ☎ *509/663–7522* 🌐 *www.chelanpud.org* ⏲ *Visitor center closed Dec.–Mar.*

Stemilt Creek Winery

WINERY/DISTILLERY | Founded by fourth-generation farmers that have been growing fruit in the Wenatchee foothills since the 1890s, Stemilt Creek has developed a sterling reputation for its Cabernet Franc, Cabernet Sauvignon, and other Bordeaux wines. The tasting room in downtown Wenatchee adjoins the popular Wok About Grill restaurant. ✉ *110*

N. Wenatchee Ave. ☎ *509/665–3485* 🌐 *www.stemiltcreek.com.*

Wenatchee Valley Museum & Cultural Center

MUSEUM | Set inside two connected early 1900s former government buildings, the city's well-designed history museum contains Native American and pioneer artifacts, exhibits on Washington's famed apple industry and a display about the 1931 landing of the first-ever flight across the Pacific. Children enjoy the hands-on area and the model railway. There are also Northwest artist exhibits. ✉ *127 S. Mission St.* ☎ *509/888–6240* 🌐 *www.wenatcheevalleymuseum.org* 🎫 *$5* ⏲ *Closed Sun. and Mon.*

 Restaurants

Atlas Fare

$$$ | **CONTEMPORARY** | The name of this upbeat, contemporary downtown bistro reflects the kitchen's globally inspired approach in dishes from Thailand (tom kah soup), Mexico (poached shrimp ceviche), Italy (mushroom risotto), and the American South (shrimp and grits). Creative preparation, a full bar with an impressive wine and spirits selection, and knowledgeable service are further reasons this buzzy spot quickly found a loyal legion of fans following its 2020 opening. **Known for:** eclectic mix of Asian, European, and American fare; stylish art-filled dining room; well-prepared cocktails. 💲 *Average main: $25* ✉ *137 N. Wenatchee Ave.* ☎ *509/300–0303* 🌐 *www.atlasfare.com* ⏲ *Closed Mon.*

★ McGlinn's Public House

$ | **AMERICAN** | This beloved downtown gastropub, with its rustic brick walls and soaring wood-beam ceilings, serves elevated comfort fare, including cheddar-blue mac and cheese, lamb tzatziki burgers, and wood-fired pizzas with inventive toppings (the blueberry-prosciutto is a favorite). There's an extensive craft-beer list, and desserts are worth saving room for. **Known for:** salted caramel and berry campfire s'mores; selection of craft beers; lively, friendly crowd. 💲 *Average main: $15* ✉ *111 Orondo Ave.* ☎ *509/663–9073* 🌐 *www.mcglinns.com.*

Mela Coffee Roasting Company

$ | **CAFÉ** | Downtown Wenatchee's go-to for cappuccinos, lattes, and other finely crafted espresso drinks is a large, inviting space with brick walls and plenty of seating. The kitchen also serves tasty breakfast fare—sous vide steak burritos, mushroom omelets, brioche French toast—daily until 11 am (noon on Sunday). **Known for:** extensive drink menu, from coffee to kombucha; lots of good breakfast options; comfy dining room. 💲 *Average main: $7* ✉ *17 N. Wenatchee Ave.* ☎ *509/888–0374* 🌐 *www.melacoffee.com* ⏲ *No dinner.*

Om Cooking

$ | **THAI** | Opened by two women with extensive experience cooking Thai food, this casual spot in the heart of downtown Wenatchee turns out some of the best Southeast Asian cuisine in the region. Traditional khao soi egg noodles, pineapple curries, Thai basil–eggplant stir-fries, and seafood salads are among the most popular dishes from the extensive menu. **Known for:** savory noodle and rice dishes; authentic curries; mango sticky rice. 💲 *Average main: $14* ✉ *104 N. Wenatchee Ave.* ☎ *509/888–8188* ⏲ *Closed Sun.*

★ Pybus Bistro

$$$ | **BISTRO** | Part of the charm of dining in this French–meets–Pacific Northwest bistro is the buzzy, feel-good energy of its open-air setting inside Pybus Public Market. And then there's the food, courtesy of a young husband-and-wife team who source as much as they can locally to create flawless croque monsieur sandwiches and French toast with maple anglaise at brunch, and pan-roasted rockfish and duck confit in the evening. **Known for:** reasonably priced, well-selected wine list; brunch menu available daily;

bustling ambience. 💲 *Average main: $24* ✉ *Pybus Public Market, 7 N. Worthen St.* ☎ *509/888–7007* 🌐 *www.pybusbistro.com* ⏲ *No dinner Sun.*

Sage Hills Bakery

$ | **BAKERY** | Prodigious breakfast sandwiches with delicious fillings—such as the "monster biscuit" with ham, bacon, cheddar, egg, herbed cream cheese, and Mama Lil's peppers—are the specialty of this bright, contemporary bakery on the north side of downtown Wenatchee. You'll also find an array of classic lunchtime sandwiches on fresh-baked breads and generous salads, plus cookies, cinnamon rolls, and other sweet endings. **Known for:** a great stop for picnic fare; overstuffed sandwiches; sweet and savory scones. 💲 *Average main: $8* ✉ *826 N. Wenatchee Ave.* ☎ *509/888–3912* ⏲ *Closed Sun. No dinner.*

The Windmill

$$$$ | **AMERICAN** | This old-school roadhouse on the north side of downtown Wenetchee, topped by a windmill and built in 1931, is all about home-style food, particularly steaks, which include 18-ounce rib eyes and slow-roasted prime rib—lobster tail and jumbo prawns are available as add-ons. Other mainstays include wild-caught salmon with compound lobster butter and Alaskan Amber beer–battered cod fish and chips. **Known for:** hefty steaks and seafood platters; charming retro aesthetic; excellent regional wine list. 💲 *Average main: $33* ✉ *1501 N. Wenatchee Ave.* ☎ *509/665–9529* ⏲ *No lunch.*

Hotels

Coast Wenatchee Center Hotel

$ | **HOTEL** | A skywalk links these tidy, if blandly furnished, rooms to the downtown convention center, a bonus for travelers on business, but there are enough facilities and amenities, including indoor and outdoor pools, to appeal to vacationers, too. **Pros:** short walk to Riverfront Park and downtown restaurants; good views, especially from upper floors; indoor pool and 24-hour gym. **Cons:** hotel lacks personality; furnishings could use updating; breakfast not included in rate. 💲 *Rooms from: $139* ✉ *201 N. Wenatchee Ave.* ☎ *509/662–1234* 🌐 *www.wenatcheecenter.com* *147 rooms* *No meals.*

Hilton Garden Inn

$$$ | **HOTEL** | With a convenient and picturesque location steps from Pybus Public Market and the riverside trails that pass through Wenatchee Riverfront Park, this is downtown's most contemporary and well-outfitted accommodation, albeit with a predictable design that's typical of the brand. **Pros:** lots to eat, sip, and see within walking distance; river view from many rooms; pretty parkside setting. **Cons:** rates can get steep during busy periods; breakfast not included in rates; possible noise from passing trains. 💲 *Rooms from: $205* ✉ *25 N. Worthen St.* ☎ *509/662–0600* 🌐 *www.hilton.com* *176 rooms* *No meals.*

★ Warm Springs Inn & Winery

$$$ | **B&B/INN** | This 1917 mansion, set amid 10 acres of gardens, offers elegant, well-appointed rooms filled with art and antiques. **Pros:** peaceful, picturesque setting outside of town; wine tasting room overlooking the river; lavish breakfast included. **Cons:** sometimes booked up in advance for weddings; not suitable for young kids; a 10-minute drive from downtown. 💲 *Rooms from: $225* ✉ *1611 Love La.* ☎ *509/662–5863* 🌐 *www.warmspringsinn.com* *6 rooms* *Free Breakfast.*

Nightlife

Badger Mountain Brewing

BREWPUBS/BEER GARDENS | A large window lets guests sneak a peek at the brewing operation while they sample these well-crafted ales and lagers. The rich Crema Stout, with its chocolate and coffee tones, is a standout—it's also used in a Stout float on the dessert menu. The kitchen also turns out decent pizza, burgers, wings, sandwiches, and the like. ✉ *1 Orondo Ave.* ☎ *509/888–2234* 🌐 *www.badgermountainbrewing.com.*

★ Sidecar Lounge

BARS/PUBS | The success of this intimate, brick-wall bar with a top-notch mixology program is evidence of Wenatchee's continued ascendance with discerning bar goers. The staff uses house-made bitters, infusions, and syrups in both classic drinks and a seasonally changing roster of new creations. Meat and cheese boards are offered, too. ✉ *101 S. Wenatchee Ave.* ☎ *509/316–9112* 🌐 *www.thesidecarlounge.com.*

Stone Gastropub

BARS/PUBS | This rustic-chic downtown tavern stands out for its impressive selection of drinks for all tastes—interesting wines by the glass (both regional and international), flights of artisan whiskey, excellent craft beers, and well-poured cocktails. The food's good, too, ranging from light tapas to hearty steaks, but the beverage program is what really shines. ✉ *120 N. Wenatchee Ave.* ☎ *509/470–2296* 🌐 *www.stonesgastropub.com.*

Activities

HIKING

Saddle Rock Trail

HIKING/WALKING | For exceptional views of the Columbia River as it snakes through downtown Wenatchee, venture out along this 2-mile round-trip loop hike to Saddle Rock, which is really a ridge of jagged rocks that rise high above the valley. With an elevation gain of nearly 1,000 feet, it's a good workout, but this fairly short, well-marked trail is doable even for beginners. ✉ *1130 Circle St.* 🌐 *www.wta.org.*

SKIING

Mission Ridge Ski Area

SKIING/SNOWBOARDING | Four lifts, 36 downhill runs, powder snow, and some 30 miles of marked cross-country trails make Mission Ridge one of Washington's most popular ski and snowboard areas. There's a 2,250-foot vertical drop, and the snowmaker scatters whiteness from the top to bottom slopes during the season. Lift tickets cost $75. ✉ *7500 Mission Ridge Rd.* ☎ *509/663–6543, 509/663–3200 snow conditions* 🌐 *www.missionridge.com.*

Cashmere

11 miles northwest of Wenatchee.

Set amid rolling hills and acres of pear, apple, and orchards in the foothills just east of the Cascade Range, tiny Cashmere (population 3,150) sits along scenic bend of the Wenatchee River and is anchored by downtown's Cottage Avenue Historic District, a small quadrant of Craftsman bungalows and early-20th-century buildings, many of which now contains cute cafés, boutiques, and antiques shops. This friendly, old-fashioned waypoint between Leavenworth and Wenatchee has an excellent history museum, and there's great hiking and rafting in the vicinity.

GETTING HERE AND AROUND

A car is best for exploring this small town on U.S. 2 midway between Wenatchee and Leavenworth.

ESSENTIALS

VISITOR INFORMATION Cashmere Chamber of Commerce. ✉ *103 Cottage Ave.* ☎ *509/782–7404* 🌐 *www.cashmerechamber.org.*

Sights

Aplets and Cotlets Candy Kitchen

FACTORY | FAMILY | About 10 miles west of Wenatchee, Cashmere is the apple, apricot, and pear capital of the Wenatchee Valley. Part of Liberty Orchards, Aplets and Cotlets was founded by two Armenian brothers in the early 20th century. When area orchards hit a rough patch in the 1920s, the brothers began producing the dried-fruit confections of their homeland, naming them aplets (made from apples) and cotlets (made from apricots). Free samples are offered during the 15-minute tour of this little factory and candy store set amid the shops and cafes of charming downtown Cashmere. The shop also has displays about the company's history and sells many other specialty sweets, including Turkish Delight, fruit-and-nut Orchard Bars, and a great variety of chocolates. ✉ *117 Mission Ave.* ☎ *509/782–2191* 🌐 *www.libertyorchards.com* ⏲ *Closed weekends Jan.–Mar.*

Historic Cashmere Museum and Pioneer Village

MUSEUM | FAMILY | At this engaging living history museum on the edge of the historic hamlet of Cashmere—midway between Wenatchee and Leavenworth—you can explore an excellent collection of Native American artifacts, as well as 20 pre-1900 Chelan County buildings that have been reassembled and furnished with period furniture and other historic objects. Surrounded by snowcapped mountain peaks, Cashmere is one of Washington's oldest towns, founded by Oblate missionaries back in 1863, when the Wenatchi and their vast herds of horses still roamed free over the bunch grasslands of the region. ✉ *600 Cotlets Way* ☎ *509/782–3230* 🌐 *www.cashmeremuseum.org* 🎟 *$8* ⏲ *Closed Nov.–Mar.*

Peshastin Pinnacles State Park

NATIONAL/STATE PARK | Although just 34 acres, this high-desert park in Dryden, about midway between Wenatchee and Leavenworth, is a terrific spot to admire otherworldly, pinnacle-shape rock formations—it's also a favorite destination for rock climbing. A steep 1½-mile trail leads to a dramatic promontory with great views of Wenatchee Valley. ✉ *7201 N. Dryden Rd.* ☎ *509/884–8702* 🌐 *www.parks.state.wa.us* 🎟 *$10 parking.*

Restaurants

★ Anjou Bakery

$ | BAKERY | Located on the edge of a pear orchard in Cashmere, this family-owned bakeshop has an unusual and appealing industrial–vintage-farmhouse feel. It offers up some of the best breads and pastries in the region, from bread pudding to almond meringue cookies to lemon cheesecake. **Known for:** rustic apricot and pear danishes; superb hand-crafted savory breads; lovely outdoor patio. $ *Average main: $8* ✉ *3898 Old Monitor Rd.* ☎ *509/782–4360* 🌐 *www.anjoubakery.com* ⏲ *Closed Mon.–Wed. No dinner.*

Hotels

Cascade Valley Inn

$$ | B&B/INN | An appealing lodging option if you favor tranquil, rugged settings surrounded by the lush valleys and sweeping hills east of the Cascades, this angular, contemporary B&B is just outside the quirky little town of Cashmere, about midway between Leavenworth and Wenatchee. **Pros:** dramatic mountain views; contemporary, light, and airy design; delicious hot breakfast included. **Cons:** 20-minute drive from Wenatchee and Leavenworth; often books up well in advance on weekends; no guests under 21 permitted. $ *Rooms from: $160* ✉ *56 Mountainside Dr.* ☎ *509/782–0240* 🌐 *www.cascadevalleyinn.com* *4 rooms* 🍽 *Free Breakfast.*

Leavenworth

12 miles northwest of Cashmere, 118 miles east of Seattle.

A favorite weekend getaway, this charming (if a touch kitschy) Bavarian-style village thrives with both old-fashioned and perhaps surprisingly urbane and hip restaurants and inns, and it's a hub for some of the Northwest's best skiing, boating, hiking, and other outdoor fun. Popular, easily accessible hikes in the surrounding Okanogan-Wenatchee National Forest include Icicle Ridge, the Enchantments, Snow Lake, and Stuart Lake trails. The drive here over the Cascades and dramatic Stevens Pass, via U.S. 2, is one of the prettiest in the state. If you have time, make a day of it, stopping to admire Bridal Veil Falls (milepost 28) and Deception Falls (miles 56), and perhaps grabbing a bite to eat in Skyhomish at the historic Cascadia Inn.

A railroad and mining center for many years, Leavenworth fell on hard times around the 1960s, and civic leaders, looking for ways to capitalize on the town's alpine setting, convinced shopkeepers and other businesspeople to add a gingerbread-Bavarian architectural style to their buildings. The pedestrian-friendly village center bustles with tourists—in winter, the trees are strung with holiday lights, and kids love to go sledding in downtown's tiny Front Street Park.

GETTING HERE AND AROUND

From Seattle, it's 2½- to 3-hour drive via U.S. 2 over Stevens Pass or Interstate 90 over Snoqualmie Pass, then a short jog up U.S. 97 over Blewett Pass. Also, Amtrak's *Empire Builder* stops here daily en route between Spokane and Seattle.

ESSENTIALS

VISITOR INFORMATION Leavenworth Chamber of Commerce. ✉ *940 U.S. 2, Suite B* ☎ *509/548–5807* 🌐 *www.leavenworth.org.*

Sights

★ Leavenworth National Fish Hatchery
FISH HATCHERY | FAMILY | Self-guided tours reveal how chinook salmon are released into the Wenatchee River in the hope they will return someday to spawn and keep the species thriving. Even if nothing's spawning, the view of millions of eggs in the nursery or thousands of small, 4-inch "fries" wriggling in the aquarium is something to see. Be sure to set aside time to walk the pretty 1-mile Icicle Creek Nature Trail loop, an easy and enjoyable stroll with wildlife viewing platforms, interpretive signs, and great birdwatching. There's also a butterfly garden in front of the hatchery building. ✉ *12790 Fish Hatchery Rd.* ☎ *509/548–7641* 🌐 *www.fws.gov/leavenworthfisheriescomplex* 🎫 *Free.*

Nutcracker Museum and Shop
MUSEUM | FAMILY | Nearly 7,000 modern and antique nutcrackers—some of them centuries old—are displayed in this two-story museum. Upstairs you can view exhibits on the region's Native American heritage and pioneer families presented by the Upper Valley Historical Society. The museum gift shop stocks nutcrackers of all sizes and in the likeness of all kinds of characters. ✉ *735 Front St.* ☎ *509/548–4573* 🌐 *www.nutcrackermuseum.com* 🎫 *$5.*

Waterfront Park
NATIONAL/STATE PARK | FAMILY | A flat and easy 3-mile trail winds along this pretty city park on the banks of the Wenatchee River, just down the hill from downtown Leavenworth. The trail crosses Blackbird Island and has several patches of beach that are ideal for a dip on a hot summer day. It's a wonderful park and trail for wildlife watching. ✉ *1010 Main St.* 🌐 *www.leavenworth.org.*

★ Wine Cellar Leavenworth
MARKET | In the center of town—in full Bavarian-style, naturally—this two-story building contains hip eateries (Tumwater

Holiday season in Leavenworth

Bakery & Pizza, J5 Coffee, Post Office Saloon) at street level. Descend the staircase into the building's stylish subterranean cellar, however, and you'll discover six tasting rooms from some of the state's up-and-coming wineries, including Patterson, Forgeron, and Sigillo, plus the trendy cocktail bar, Pika Provisions. ✉ *217 9th St.*

WineGirl Wines

WINERY/DISTILLERY | You can sip the acclaimed creations of winemaker Angela Jacobs in this attractive downtown tasting room. Sourcing from vineyards in the Columbia Valley, Rattlesnake Hills, and Lake Chelan (where there's a second tasting room), WineGirl specializes in Bordeaux single varieties and blends. ✉ *217 8th St.* ☎ *509/393-4125* 🌐 *www.winegirlwines.com* 🕓 *Closed Tues. and Wed.*

Restaurants

Andreas Keller Restaurant

$$ | **GERMAN** | Merry "oompah" music bubbles out from marching accordion players at this festive, long-running restaurant, where the theme is "Germany without the Passport," and that adjoins two sister establishments, Mozart's Steakhouse and Gingerbread Factory bakery. Laughing crowds lap up strong, cold brews and feast on a selection of wursts—bratwurst, knackwurst, and weisswurst—Polish sausage, beef goulash, and schnitzel cordon bleu, all nestled into heaping sides of sauerkraut, tangy German potato salad, and thick, dark rye bread. **Known for:** convivial, old-world ambience; German sausages of all types; knockout apple strudel. 💲 *Average main: $20* ✉ *829 Front St.* ☎ *509/548–6000* 🌐 *www.andreaskellerrestaurant.com.*

★ **Blewett Brewing Company**

$ | **PIZZA** | With a festive sidewalk seating area and a rustic timber-clad dining room, this trendy spot offers some of the best craft beer in Leavenworth. There are several great IPAs on hand, as well as a rich Maple stout. **Known for:** complex, well-crafted beers; friendly, festive ambience; sunny outside patio. *Average main: $15 ✉ 911 Commercial St. ☎ 509/888–8809 🌐 www.blewettbrew.com.*

J5 Coffee

$ | **CAFÉ** | The flagship location of this outstanding local roaster is in the trendy Wine Cellar building and doubles as a cute mercantile stocked with artisan chocolates, local maple syrup, and other goodies. There's no seating, but it's a perfect spot to pick up an expertly crafted espresso drink for your stroll around town. **Known for:** sleek, contemporary decor; bourbon maple lattes; artisan chocolates. *Average main: $5 ✉ 215 9th St. ☎ 509/470–9495 🌐 www.j5coffee.com.*

★ **Mana**

$$$$ | **VEGETARIAN** | Set in buttery yellow cottage with just a touch of gingerbread, this unfussy eatery offers a refreshing break from Leavenworth's Bavaria-on-steroids exuberance. The kitchen presents artfully plated eight-course vegetarian meals of mostly organic, farm-sourced Northwestern fare. **Known for:** spectacular farm-to-table feasts; exquisite vegetarian fare; wine pairings. *Average main: $85 ✉ 1033 Commercial St. ☎ 509/548–1662 🌐 www.manamountain.com ⏲ Closed Mon.–Thurs. No lunch.*

Munchen Haus

$ | **GERMAN** | **FAMILY** | Bratwurst, beef franks, and brews abound at this outdoor Bavarian grill and beer garden, tucked into a cozy corner in downtown. It's perfect for hungry travelers seeking an affordable but filling meal. **Known for:** affordable German fare; outdoor picnic-table dining; plenty of great beers. *Average main: $8 ✉ 709 Front St. ☎ 509/548–1158 🌐 www.munchen-haus.com.*

South

$$ | **MODERN MEXICAN** | A fusion-y menu of modern Latin American (primarily Mexican) dishes provides a nice—and slightly spicy—alternative to Leavenworth's wealth of Bavarian food. Enjoy sweet-potato-and-roasted-poblano-chili enchiladas, pork belly tacos with pineapple salsa, and Michoacán-style carnitas platters, along with Argentine chimichurri steaks and Peruvian chicken. **Known for:** premium tequilas and mezcals; desserts like tres leche cake; generous helpings.

A fusion-y menu of modern Latin American (primarily Mexican) dishes provides a nice—and slightly spicy—alternative to Leavenworth's wealth of Bavarian food. Enjoy sweet-potato-and-roasted-poblano-chili enchiladas, pork belly tacos with pineapple salsa, and Michoacán-style carnitas platters, along with Argentine chimichurri steaks and Peruvian chicken. **Known for:** premium tequilas and mezcals; desserts like tres leche cake; generous helpings. *Average main: $18 ✉ 913 Front St. ☎ 509/888–4328 🌐 www.southrestaurants.com.*

★ **Watershed Cafe**

$$$$ | **PACIFIC NORTHWEST** | A significant player in Leavenworth's steady transformation into a hipper and more upscale destination, this warmly lighted farm-to-table bistro with hardwood floors and exposed-brick walls feels both appropriate for celebrating a special occasion and perfect for an unpretentious meal. The menu changes regularly, but typical creations include Oregon buffalo carpaccio and curry-rubbed wild cod with peach relish, wonton crunchies, and sweet-chile butter. **Known for:** first-rate cocktail and wine program; sophisticated farm-to-table cuisine; river and mountain views from deck. *Average main: $34 ✉ 221 8th St. ☎ 509/888–0214 🌐 www.watershedpnw.com ⏲ Closed Tues. and Wed. No lunch.*

Yodelin Broth Company

$ | **ECLECTIC** | In winter, its stone walls and varnished-wood tables impart a warm vibe, and in summer the sprawling beer garden with grand river and mountain views puts everyone in a happy mood. This hipster-approved, counter-service purveyor of fragrant, flavorful Asian-style bone broths and creative pub fare seems always to draw a big, chatty crowd. **Known for:** extensive selection of regional craft beers; great burgers and sandwiches; fun atmosphere. *Average main: $$15 633 Front St. 509/888–4555 www.yodelinrestaurantgroup.com.*

Hotels

★ Abendblume Pension

$$$$ | **B&B/INN** | Dazzling views of the mountains and valley are your at this Bavarian-style country chalet in a quiet setting a mile north of downtown. **Pros:** Bavarian breakfast is authentic and ample; utterly romantic atmosphere; exceptional hospitality. **Cons:** fills up quickly during festivals; 20-minute walk from downtown; on the pricey side. *Rooms from: $259 12570 Ranger Rd. 509/548–4059 www.abendblume.com 7 rooms Free Breakfast.*

Bavarian Lodge

$$$ | **HOTEL** | The handsome rooms at this warm and inviting downtown hotel come with atmospheric furnishings—some have gas fireplaces and jetted tubs—and include an ample complimentary breakfast of waffles, biscuits and gravy, ham and potatoes, and more. **Pros:** across the street from downtown shopping and restaurants; year-round outdoor swimming pool and two hot tubs; on-site dining and live music at Woodsman Pub. **Cons:** located on what can be a busy thoroughfare; some rooms face the parking lot; can be expensive on weekends. *Rooms from: $209 810 U.S. 2 888/717–7878, 509/548–7878 www.bavarianlodge.com 54 rooms Free Breakfast.*

Haus Rohrbach

$ | **B&B/INN** | **FAMILY** | Rooms at this alpine-style pension set on a bluff and beside an evergreen forest come with unobstructed views of either the valley or the woods. **Pros:** peaceful setting amid well-tended gardens; pleasant pool and hot tub; very welcoming to families. **Cons:** a half-hour walk from town; cheaper rooms have shared baths; homey ambience may not suit everyone. *Rooms from: $110 12882 Ranger Rd. 509/548–7024, 800/548–4477 www.hausrohrbach.com 10 rooms Free Breakfast.*

★ Hotel Pension Anna

$$$ | **B&B/INN** | This Bavarian-style lodging with flowers tumbling over the wooden balconies is decorated with sturdy alpine furniture, rich fabrics, and cozy comforters—some have hand-painted old-world bed frames and armoires. **Pros:** old-world European ambience; steps from restaurants and shops; hearty breakfasts. **Cons:** some steps to climb; no gym or recreational facilities; downtown location can get crowded. *Rooms from: $215 926 Commercial St. 509/548–6273 www.pensionanna.com 16 rooms Free Breakfast.*

Icicle Village Resort

$$$ | **RESORT** | **FAMILY** | This sprawling resort on the edge of downtown has an array of amenities, including two outdoor pools, a minigolf course, a full-service spa, and attractive rooms and suites decorated with modern, mountain-chic flair. **Pros:** spa offers a full range of pedicures, facials, and massages; condos in a separate building are great for groups; hot breakfast buffet included. **Cons:** some rooms overlook parking lot; long walk to downtown dining; no room service. *Rooms from: $209 505 U.S. 2 800/961–0162, 509/888–2776 www.iciclevillage.com 156 rooms Free Breakfast.*

Linderhof Inn
$$ | **HOTEL** | **FAMILY** | One of the best-value lodgings in Leavenworth is smack in the heart of downtown and offers modern and comfortable rooms with all of the usual amenities and a bit of chintz added for character. **Pros:** small seasonal swimming pool; steps from downtown eateries; free use of ski equipment. **Cons:** busy location can get crowded during festivals; two-night minimum stay during holidays; rooms don't have much character. *Rooms from: $165 690 U.S. 2 509/548–5283, 800/828–5680 www.linderhof.com 34 rooms Free Breakfast.*

LOGE Leavenworth
$$ | **HOTEL** | This fun, activity-focused cluster of smartly designed cabins and hostel bunks appeals to younger, outdoorsy guests with its inexpensive rates and myriad amenities, including bikes to borrow, outdoor music and movies on weekends, and plenty of attractive spaces to socialize, eat, and soak up views of the adjacent Wenatchee River. **Pros:** beautiful riverside setting beneath towering evergreens; friendly vibe that appeals to social butterflies; alternative to Leavenworth's kitsch. **Cons:** youthful vibe isn't for everyone; 10- to 15-minute walk into town; a bit of traffic noise. *Rooms from: $175 11798 U.S. 2 509/690–4106 www.logecamps.com 8 cabins No meals.*

★ Mountain Home Lodge
$$$$ | **B&B/INN** | This contemporary mountain inn, where peeled-pine and vine-maple furniture fills the rooms, is built of sturdy cedar and redwood and sits on a 20-acre alpine meadow with breathtaking Cascade Mountains views. **Pros:** opulent breakfast and afternoon appetizers and wine; stunning, pristine wilderness setting; luxurious accommodations. **Cons:** getting here can be challenging in winter weather; two-night minimum stay at busy times; 10-minute drive to downtown. *Rooms from: $390 8201 Mountain Home Rd. 509/548–7077 www.mthome.com 12 rooms Free Breakfast.*

★ Posthotel Leavenworth
$$$$ | **RESORT** | Washington's first true Alps-inspired luxury wellness spa sits on a quiet street overlooking the Wenatchee River in downtown Leavenworth, offering all the pampering you could ask for, including healthy breakfasts and lunches (included in the rates), a slew of soothing spa treatments, and access to gorgeously designed saltwater hydrotherapy pools, steam baths, saunas, and other water treatment options. **Pros:** the ultimate spot for rest and relaxation; many great dining options within five minutes; stellar amenities. **Cons:** downtown location can get crowded during busy times; no alcohol for sale (but you can bring your own); not suitable for kids. *Rooms from: $460 308 8th St. 509/548–7678 www.posthotelleavenworth.com 55 rooms Free Breakfast.*

★ Run of the River
$$$$ | **B&B/INN** | This intimate, relaxed mountain inn hugs the banks of the Wenatchee River near downtown Leavenworth. **Pros:** tranquil natural surroundings; generous, hearty breakfasts; free access to mountain bikes. **Cons:** not within walking distance of town; sometimes books up for weddings; kids not permitted. *Rooms from: $286 9308 E. Leavenworth Rd. 509/548–7171, 800/288–6491 www.runoftheriver.com 7 rooms Free Breakfast.*

Sleeping Lady Mountain Resort
$$$$ | **RESORT** | Fall asleep on a hand-hewn log bed under a down comforter along the banks of Icicle Creek at this quiet and scenic retreat in the heart of the Cascade Mountains, where lodgelike rooms are light and airy, with lots of wood accents, and activities include yoga, birding, hiking, horseback riding, white-water rafting, cross-country skiing, shoeshoeing, and more. **Pros:** a nice balance of activities and relaxation; spectacular

setting and scenery; spa, seasonal pool, and hot tub. **Cons:** 10-minute drive to downtown; no TVs (admittedly a plus for some); could use some updating. *Rooms from: $258* *7375 Icicle Rd.* *509/548–6344* *www.sleepinglady.com* *58 rooms* *Free Breakfast.*

Nightlife

Bushel & Bee Taproom

BARS/PUBS | Within a short drive of some of the world's most prolific apple orchards, this downtown taphouse specializes in local artisan ciders, with about 12 on tap, but you'll also find a great selection of beer as well as mead and even kombucha from Leavenworth's beloved Honey Jun. *900 Front St.* *509/818–3373* *www.bushelandbee.com.*

Icicle Brewing Company

BREWPUBS/BEER GARDENS | One of the foremost craft brewers in the state, Icicle Brewing boasts a large and cheery outdoor terrace as an attractive indoor taproom where you can view the company's massive brewing vats. Order a flight for a chance to sample the eclectic offerings, and be sure to include the signature Bootjack IPA in the mix. Warm pretzels and bowls of chili are great food choices. *935 Front St.* *509/548–2739* *www.iciclebrewing.com.*

★ Pika Provisions

BARS/PUBS | Painted canoe paddles line the walls of this speakeasy-inspired cocktail bar situated amid the tasting rooms in downtown's Wine Cellar building. Grab at seat at the bar or in one of the cozy booths and enjoy a well-prepared cocktail and maybe a snack or two from the small Spanish-inspired menu. *217 9th St., basement* *509/888–0746* *www.pikaprovisions.com.*

Shopping

The Cheesemonger's Shop

FOOD/CANDY | Pick up a snack or the makings of a picnic at this lively basement-level cheese shop, where applewood-smoked cheddar is the number one seller. *819 Front St.* *509/548–9011, 877/888–7389* *www.cheesemongersshop.com.*

Homefires Bakery

FOOD/CANDY | Tucked inside a back corner of Dan's Food Market, this homey little bakery turns out delicious breads, muffins, cookies, cakes, and pastries. Take a cinnamon roll or berry pie—and an espresso—to go. *1329 U.S. 2* *509/548–7362* *www.homefiresbakery.com.*

The Oil and Vinegar Cellar

FOOD/CANDY | In this basement-level specialty shop sample gourmet salts; aged balsamic vinegars in flavors like fig, honey ginger, pecan praline, and garlic cilantro; and infused olive oils such as basil, blood orange, garlic mushroom, and rosemary. *633 Front St.* *509/470–7684* *www.oilandvinegarcellar.com.*

Schocolat

FOOD/CANDY | Tucked in the back of the high-end home-decor and gourmet-kitchen store Ganz Klasse!, which offers handcrafted wooden cutting boards, table linens, and porcelain pieces, Schocolate sells fine handcrafted chocolates in flavors like brandied pear, burnt-caramel–salted almond, and Earl Grey. *834 Front St.* *509/548–7274* *www.schocolat.com.*

Activities

HORSEBACK RIDING

Eagle Creek Ranch

HORSEBACK RIDING | Take 2-, 3-, or 5-mile horse rides ($28 to $50) at this ranch in rugged Wenatchee National Forest, about a 15-minute drive northeast of town.

Seasonal sleigh rides are also available ($19–$38). ✉ *7951 Eagle Creek Rd.* ☎ *509/548–7798* 🌐 *www.eaglecreek.ws.*

Icicle Outfitters & Guides
HORSEBACK RIDING | You can enjoy 2- to 4-mile trail rides ($30–$60 per person), daylong rides with lunch ($185), and even two- to seven-day custom deluxe pack trips (starting at $225 per person per day). In winter, there are sleigh rides ($20). ✉ *7919 E. Leavenworth Rd.* ☎ *800/497–3912, 509/669–1518* 🌐 *www.icicleoutfitters.com.*

★ **Mountain Springs Lodge**
HORSEBACK RIDING | Horseback rides from 90 minutes to half-day ($67–$165) are offered at this pristine woodland property in the mountains near Lake Wenatchee, about 15 miles north of Leavenworth. Other fun includes sleigh rides ($26–$79) and snowmobile tours lasting one to five hours ($84–$284). In summer, there's ziplining ($89–$109). ✉ *19115 Chiwawa Loop Rd.* ☎ *509/763–2713, 800/858–2276* 🌐 *www.mtsprings.com.*

SKIING

Nearly 20 miles of cross-country ski trails lace the Leavenworth area, which is also a popular base for downhill skiers heading to Stevens Pass.

Leavenworth Ski Hill
SKIING/SNOWBOARDING | **FAMILY** | In winter enjoy a Nordic ski jump, snowboarding, tubing, fat-tire biking, and fun downhill and cross-country skiing at this small but beautiful family-friendly facility a mile north of Leavenworth. In summer, come for the wildflowers or to catch the Leavenworth Summer Theatre's production of *The Sound of Music.* ✉ *Ski Hill Dr.* ☎ *509/548–5477* 🌐 *www.skileavenworth.com.*

★ **Stevens Pass**
SKIING/SNOWBOARDING | There's snowboarding and cross-country skiing here at one of Washington's top ski areas, which offers 52 major downhill runs and slopes for skiers of every level. Skiing is on two different mountains, and the vertical drop is 1,800 feet. Lift tickets cost $84–$100, and there's night skiing, too. Summer weekends, the mountain is popular for mountain biking, hiking, and disc golf. ✉ *93001 N.E. Stevens Pass Hwy., Skykomish* ↔ *35 miles west of Leavenworth* ☎ *206/812–4510* 🌐 *www.stevenspass.com.*

WHITE-WATER RAFTING

Rafting is popular from March to July; the prime high-country runoff occurs in May and June. With its Class III rapids, the Wenatchee River runs through Leavenworth and is considered one of state's best white-water rivers.

Alpine Adventures
WHITE-WATER RAFTING | Challenging white-water and relaxing river floats through spectacular scenery are the options here. A Wenatchee River white-water trip with lunch costs $79; a scenic Skyhomish or Yakima River float trip runs $74. Methow River rafting costs $89. ✉ *Leavenworth* ☎ *800/723–8386, 509/470–7762* 🌐 *www.alpineadventures.com.*

★ **Leavenworth Outdoor Center**
BICYCLING | **FAMILY** | Rent tubes, rafts, kayaks, paddleboards, and bicycles at this shop, which provides a shuttle to the launch point along the Wenatchee River, and even outfits your pet pooch with a life jacket for a float downstream. ✉ *321 9th St.* ☎ *509/548–8823* 🌐 *www.leavenworthoutdoorcenter.com.*

Osprey Rafting Co.
WHITE-WATER RAFTING | **FAMILY** | This fun-focused outfitter offers a variety of trips on the Wenatchee River, priced $80–$120, including wet suits and booties, transportation, and options for barbecue lunches and live music. ✉ *9342 Icicle Rd.* ☎ *509/548–6800* 🌐 *www.ospreyrafting.com.*

Chapter 17

MOUNT RAINIER NATIONAL PARK

Updated by
Shelley Arenas

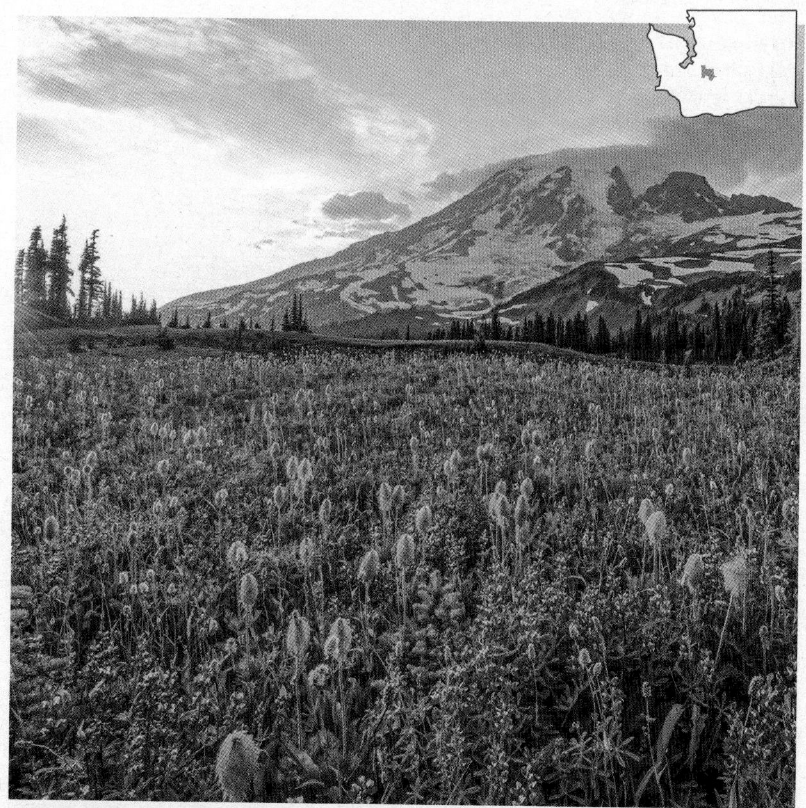

Sights ★★★★★ | Restaurants ★★★☆☆ | Hotels ☆☆☆☆☆ | Shopping ☆☆☆☆☆ | Nightlife ☆☆☆☆☆

WELCOME TO MOUNT RAINIER NATIONAL PARK

TOP REASONS TO GO

★ **The mountain:** Some say Mt. Rainier is the most magical mountain in America. At 14,411 feet, it is a popular peak for climbing, with more than 10,000 attempts per year—nearly half of which are successful.

★ **The glaciers:** About 35 square miles of glaciers and snowfields encircle Mt. Rainier, including Carbon Glacier and Emmons Glacier, the largest glaciers by volume and area, respectively, in the continental United States.

★ **The wildflowers:** More than 100 species of wildflowers bloom in the park's high meadows; the display dazzles from midsummer until the snow flies.

★ **Fabulous hiking:** More than 240 miles of maintained trails provide access to old-growth forest, river valleys, lakes, and rugged ridges.

★ **Unencumbered wilderness:** Under the provisions of the 1964 Wilderness Act and the National Wilderness Preservation System, 97% of the park is preserved as wilderness.

1 Longmire. Inside the Nisqually Gate explore Longmire historic district's museum and visitor center, ruins of the park's first hotel.

2 Paradise. The park's most popular destination is famous for wildflowers in summer and skiing in winter.

3 Ohanapecosh. Closest to the southeast entrance and the town of Packwood, the giant old-growth trees of the Grove of the Patriarchs are a must-see.

4 Sunrise and White River. Sunrise is the highest stretch of road in the park and a great place to take in the alpenglow—reddish light on the peak of the mountain near sunrise and sunset. Mt. Rainier's premier mountain-biking area, White River, is also the gateway to more than a dozen hiking trails.

5 Carbon River and Mowich Lake. Near the Carbon River Entrance Station is a swath of temperate forest, but to really get away from it all, follow the windy gravel roads to remote Mowich Lake.

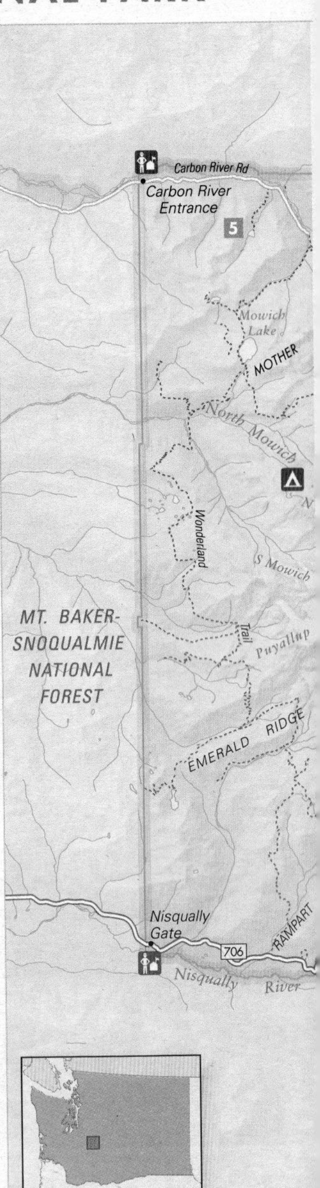

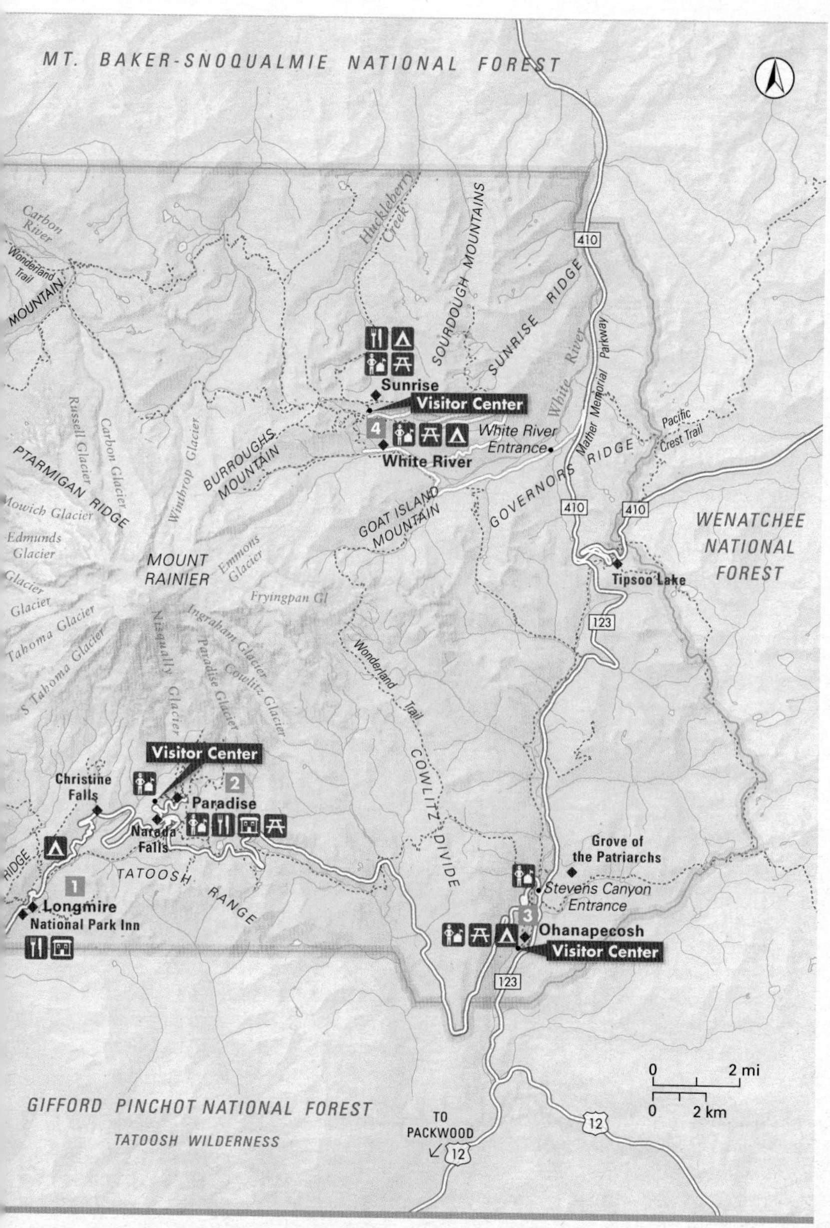
MT. BAKER-SNOQUALMIE NATIONAL FOREST
Carbon River
Wonderland Trail
MOUNTAIN
Huckleberry Creek
SOURDOUGH MOUNTAINS
SUNRISE RIDGE
410
White River
Mather Memorial Parkway
Sunrise
Visitor Center
4
White River Entrance
White River
Pacific Crest Trail
GOVERNORS RIDGE
Russell Glacier
Carbon Glacier
PTARMIGAN RIDGE
Mowich Glacier
Winthrop Glacier
BURROUGHS MOUNTAIN
GOAT ISLAND MOUNTAIN
WENATCHEE NATIONAL FOREST
Edmunds Glacier
MOUNT RAINIER
Emmons Glacier
Tipsoo Lake
Fryingpan Gl
123
Tahoma Glacier
S Tahoma Glacier
Nisqually Glacier
Ingraham Glacier
Paradise Glacier
Cowlitz Glacier
Wonderland Trail
COWLITZ DIVIDE
Visitor Center
Christine Falls
2
Paradise
Narada Falls
RIDGE
1
TATOOSH RANGE
Longmire
National Park Inn
Grove of the Patriarchs
Stevens Canyon Entrance
3
Ohanapecosh
Visitor Center
0 2 mi
0 2 km
GIFFORD PINCHOT NATIONAL FOREST
TATOOSH WILDERNESS
TO PACKWOOD
12

Mt. Rainier is the centerpiece of its namesake park. The impressive volcanic peak stands at an elevation of 14,411 feet, making it the fifth-highest peak in the lower 48 states. Nearly 2 million visitors a year enjoy spectacular views of the mountain and return home with a lifelong memory of its image.

On the lower slopes you find silent forests made up of cathedral-like groves of Douglas fir, western hemlock, and western red cedar, some more than 1,000 years old. Water and lush greenery are everywhere in the park, and dozens of thundering waterfalls, accessible from the road or by a short hike, fill the air with mist.

Planning

When to Go

Rainier is the Puget Sound's weather vane: if you can see it, skies will be clear. Visitors are most likely to see the summit July through September. Crowds are heaviest in summer, too, meaning the parking lots at Paradise and Sunrise often fill before noon, campsites are reserved months in advance, and other lodgings are reserved as much as a year ahead.

True to its name, Paradise is often sunny during periods when the lowlands are under a cloud layer. The rest of the year, Rainier's summit gathers flying-saucer-like lenticular clouds whenever a Pacific storm approaches; once the peak vanishes from view, it's time to haul out rain gear. The rare periods of clear winter weather bring residents up to Paradise for cross-country skiing.

Planning Your Time

MT. RAINIER IN ONE DAY

The best way to get a complete overview of Mt. Rainier in a day is to enter via Nisqually and begin your tour by browsing in **Longmire Museum.** When you're done, get to know the environment in and around Longmire Meadow and the overgrown ruins of Longmire Springs Hotel on the ½-mile **Trail of the Shadows** nature loop.

From Longmire, Highway 706 East climbs northeast into the mountains toward Paradise. Take a moment to explore two-tiered **Christine Falls,** just north of the road 1½ miles past Cougar Rock Campground, and the cascading **Narada Falls,** 3 miles farther on; both are spanned by graceful stone footbridges. Fantastic mountain views, alpine meadows crosshatched with nature trails, a welcoming lodge and restaurant, and the excellent **Jackson Memorial Visitor Center** combine to make lofty Paradise the primary goal of most park visitors. One outstanding (but challenging) way to explore the high country is to hike the 5-mile round-trip **Skyline Trail** to Panorama Point, which rewards you with stunning 360-degree views.

Continue eastward on Highway 706 East for 21 miles and leave your car to explore the incomparable, 1,000-year-old **Grove of the Patriarchs.** Afterward, turn your car north toward White River and **Sunrise Visitor Center,** where you can watch the alpenglow fade from Mt. Rainier's domed summit.

Getting Here and Around

AIR

Seattle–Tacoma International Airport, 15 miles south of downtown Seattle, is the nearest airport to the national park.

CAR

The Nisqually entrance is on Highway 706, 14 miles east of Route 7; the Ohanapecosh entrance is on Route 123, 5 miles north of U.S. 12; and the White River entrance is on Route 410, 3 miles north of the Chinook and Cayuse passes. These highways become mountain roads as they reach Rainier, winding up and down many steep slopes, so cautious driving is essential: use a lower gear, especially on downhill sections, and take care not to overheat brakes by constant use. These roads are subject to storms any time of year and are repaired in the summer from winter damage and washouts.

Side roads into the park's western slope are narrower, unpaved, and subject to flooding and washouts. All are closed by snow in winter except Highway 706 to Paradise and Carbon River Road, though the latter tends to flood near the park boundary. (Route 410 is open to the Crystal Mountain access road entrance.)

Park roads have a maximum speed of 35 mph in most places, and you have to watch for pedestrians, cyclists, and wildlife. Parking can be difficult during peak summer season, especially at Paradise, Sunrise, Grove of the Patriarchs, and at the trailheads between Longmire and Paradise; arrive early if you plan to visit these sites. All off-road-vehicle use—4X4 vehicles, ATVs, motorcycles, snowmobiles—is prohibited in Mount Rainier National Park.

Park Essentials

ACCESSIBILITY

The only trail in the park that is fully accessible to those with impaired mobility is Kautz Creek Trail, a ½-mile boardwalk that leads to a splendid view of the mountain. Parts of the Trail of the Shadows at Longmire and the Grove of the Patriarchs at Ohanapecosh are also accessible. Campgrounds at Cougar Rock and Ohanapecosh have several accessible sites. All main visitor centers, as well as National Park Inn at Longmire, are accessible. Wheelchairs are available at the Jackson Visitor Center for guests to use in the center.

PARK FEES AND PERMITS

The entrance fee of $30 per vehicle and $15 for those on foot, motorcycle, or bicycle is good for seven days. Annual passes are $55. Climbing permits are $51 per person per climb or glacier trek. Wilderness camping permits must be obtained for all backcountry trips, and advance reservations are highly recommended.

PARK HOURS

Mount Rainier National Park is open 24/7 year-round, but with limited access in winter. Gates at Nisqually (Longmire) are staffed year-round during the day; facilities at Paradise are open daily from late May to mid-October; and Sunrise is open daily July to early September. During off-hours you can buy passes at the gates from machines that accept credit and debit cards. Winter access to the park is limited to the Nisqually entrance, and the Jackson Memorial Visitor Center at Paradise is open on weekends and holidays in winter. The Paradise snow-play area is open when there is sufficient snow.

CELL PHONE RECEPTION

Cell phone reception is unreliable throughout much of the park, although access is clear at Paradise, Sunrise, and Crystal Mountain. Public telephones are at all park visitor centers, at the National Park Inn at Longmire, and at Paradise Inn at Paradise.

Educational Offerings

RANGER PROGRAMS

Junior Ranger Program

NATIONAL/STATE PARK | FAMILY | Youngsters ages 6 to 11 can pick up an activity booklet at a visitor center and fill it out as they explore the park. When they complete it, they can show it to a ranger and receive a Mount Rainier Junior Ranger badge. ✉ *Visitor centers, Mt. Rainier National Park* ☎ *360/569–2211* 🌐 *www.nps.gov/mora/learn/kidsyouth* 🎫 *Free with park admission.*

Ranger Programs

NATIONAL/STATE PARK | FAMILY | Park ranger-led activities include **guided snowshoe walks** in the winter (most suitable for those older than eight) as well as **evening programs** during the summer at Longmire/Cougar Rock, Ohanapecosh, and White River campgrounds, and at the Paradise Inn. Evening talks may cover subjects such as park history, its flora and fauna, or interesting facts on climbing Mt. Rainier. There are also daily guided programs that start at the Jackson Visitor Center, including meadow and vista walks, tours of the Paradise Inn, a morning ranger chat, and evening astronomy program. ✉ *Visitor centers, Mt. Rainier National Park* ☎ *360/569–2211* 🌐 *www.nps.gov/mora/planyourvisit/rangerprograms.htm* 🎫 *Free with park admission.*

Restaurants

A limited number of restaurants are inside the park, and a few worth checking out lie beyond its borders. Mt. Rainier's picnic areas are justly famous, especially in summer, when wildflowers fill the meadows. Resist the urge to feed the yellow pine chipmunks darting about.

Hotels

The Mt. Rainier area is remarkably bereft of quality lodging. Rainier's two national park lodges, at Longmire and Paradise, are attractive and well maintained. They exude considerable history and charm, especially Paradise Inn, but unless you've made summer reservations a year in advance, getting a room can be a challenge. Dozens of motels, cabin complexes, and private vacation-home rentals are near the park entrances; while they can be pricey, the latter are convenient for longer stays. *Hotel reviews have been shortened. For full information, visit Fodors.com.*

Visitor Information

PARK CONTACT INFORMATION Mount Rainier National Park. ✉ *55210 238th Ave. East, Ashford* ☎ *360/569–2211, 360/569–6575* 🌐 *www.nps.gov/mora.*

VISITOR CENTERS

Jackson Memorial Visitor Center

INFO CENTER | High on the mountain's southern flank, this center houses exhibits on geology, mountaineering, glaciology, and alpine ecology. Multimedia programs are staged in the theater; there's also a snack bar and gift shop. This is the park's most popular visitor destination, and it can be quite crowded in summer. ✉ *Hwy. 706 E, 19 miles east of Nisqually park entrance, Mt. Rainier National Park* ☎ *360/569–6571* 🌐 *www.*

nps.gov/mora/planyourvisit/paradise.htm ⏲ *Closed weekdays mid-Oct.–Apr.*

Longmire Museum and Visitor Center

INFO CENTER | Glass cases inside this museum preserve the park's plants and animals, including a stuffed cougar. Historical photographs and geographical displays provide a worthwhile overview of the park's history. The adjacent visitor center has some perfunctory exhibits on the surrounding forest and its inhabitants, as well as pamphlets and information about park activities. ✉ *Hwy. 706, 10 miles east of Ashford, Longmire* ☎ *360/569–6575* 🌐 *www.nps.gov/mora/planyourvisit/longmire.htm.*

Sunrise Visitor Center

INFO CENTER | Exhibits at this center explain the region's sparser alpine and subalpine ecology. A network of nearby loop trails leads you through alpine meadows and forest to overlooks that have broad views of the Cascades and Rainier. The visitor center has a snack bar and gift shop. ✉ *Sunrise Rd., 15 miles from White River park entrance, Mt. Rainier National Park* ☎ *360/663–2425* 🌐 *www.nps.gov/mora/planyourvisit/sunrise.htm* ⏲ *Closed mid-Sept.–June.*

Sights

Chinook Pass Road

SCENIC DRIVE | Route 410, the highway to Yakima, follows the eastern edge of the park to Chinook Pass, where it climbs the steep, 5,432-foot pass via a series of switchbacks. At its top, take in broad views of Rainier and the east slope of the Cascades. The pass usually closes for the winter in November and reopens by late May. ✉ *Mt. Rainier National Park* 🌐 *www.wsdot.wa.gov/traffic/passes/chinook-cayuse.*

Christine Falls

BODY OF WATER | These two-tiered falls were named in honor of Christine Louise Van Trump, who climbed to the 10,000-foot level on Mt. Rainier in 1889 at the age of nine, despite having a crippling nervous-system disorder. ✉ *Next to Hwy. 706, about 2½ miles east of Cougar Rock Campground, Mt. Rainier National Park* 🌐 *www.nps.gov/mora.*

★ **Grove of the Patriarchs**

TRAIL | Protected from the periodic fires that swept through the surrounding areas, this small island of 1,000-year-old trees is one of Mount Rainier National Park's most memorable features. A 1½-mile loop trail heads through the old-growth forest of Douglas fir, cedar, and hemlock. ✉ *Rte. 123, west of the Stevens Canyon entrance, Mt. Rainier National Park* 🌐 *www.nps.gov/mora/planyourvisit/ohanapecosh.htm.*

Mowich Lake Road

SCENIC DRIVE | In the northwest corner of the park, this 24-mile mountain road begins in Wilkeson and heads up the Rainier foothills to Mowich Lake, traversing beautiful mountain meadows along the way. Mowich Lake is a pleasant spot for a picnic. The road is open mid-July to mid-October. ✉ *Mt. Rainier National*

Plants and Wildlife

Wildflower season in the meadows at and above timberline is mid-July through August. Large mammals like deer, elk, black bears, and cougars tend to occupy the less accessible wilderness areas of the park and thus elude the average visitor. The best times to see wildlife are at dawn and dusk at the forest's edge, though you'll occasionally see bears ambling through meadows in the distance during the day. Fawns are born in May, and the bugling of bull elk on the high ridges can be heard in late September and October.

Only one hiker at a time should cross the 200-feet Tacoma Creek Suspension Bridge over the glacier-fed water.

Park ⊕ www.nps.gov/mora/planyourvisit/carbon-and-mowich.htm ⊙ Closed mid-Oct.–mid-July.

Narada Falls

BODY OF WATER | A steep but short trail leads to the viewing area for these spectacular 168-foot falls, which expand to a width of 75 feet during peak flow times. In winter the frozen falls are popular with ice climbers. ✉ *Along Hwy. 706, 1 mile west of turnoff for Paradise, 6 miles east of Cougar Rock Campground, Mt. Rainier National Park ⊕ www.nps.gov/mora/planyourvisit/longmire.htm.*

National Park Inn

BUILDING | Even if you don't plan to stay overnight, you can stop by year-round to view the architecture of this inn, built in 1917 and on the National Register of Historic Places. While you're here, relax in front of the fireplace in the lounge, stop at the gift shop, or dine at the restaurant. ✉ *Longmire Visitor Complex, Hwy. 706, 10 miles east of Nisqually entrance, Longmire ☎ 360/569–2411 ⊕ www.mtrainierguestservices.com/accommodations/national-park-inn.*

Paradise Road

SCENIC DRIVE | This 9-mile stretch of Highway 706 winds its way up the mountain's southwest flank from Longmire to Paradise, taking you from lowland forest to the ever-expanding vistas of the mountain above. Visit early on a weekday if possible, especially in peak summer months, when the road is packed with cars. The route is open year-round, though there may be some weekday closures in winter. From November through April, all vehicles must carry chains. ✉ *Mt. Rainier National Park ⊕ www.nps.gov/mora/planyourvisit/paradise.htm.*

Sunrise Road

SCENIC DRIVE | This popular (and often crowded) scenic road to the highest drivable point at Mt. Rainier carves its way 11 miles up Sunrise Ridge from the White River Valley on the northeast side of the park. As you top the ridge there are sweeping views of the surrounding lowlands. The road is usually open

July through September. ✉ *Mt. Rainier National Park* 🌐 *www.nps.gov/mora/planyourvisit/sunrise.htm* ⏲ *Usually closed Oct.–June.*

Tipsoo Lake

BODY OF WATER | FAMILY | The short, pleasant trail that circles the lake—ideal for families—provides breathtaking views. Enjoy the subalpine wildflower meadows during the summer months; in late summer to early fall there is an abundant supply of huckleberries. ✉ *Off Cayuse Pass east on Hwy. 410, Mt. Rainier National Park* 🌐 *www.nps.gov/mora/planyourvisit/sunrise.htm.*

Restaurants

National Park Inn Dining Room

$$$ | AMERICAN | Photos of Mt. Rainier taken by top photographers adorn the walls of this inn's large dining room, a bonus on the many days the mountain refuses to show itself. Meals are simple but tasty: rib-eye steak, lamb chops, cedar-plank trout, and blackberry cobbler à la mode. **Known for:** only restaurant open year-round in the park; hearty breakfast options. 💲 *Average main: $25* ✉ *Hwy. 706, Longmire* ☎ *360/569–2411* 🌐 *www.mtrainierguestservices.com.*

Paradise Camp Deli

$ | AMERICAN | FAMILY | Grilled meats, sandwiches, salads, and soft drinks are served daily from May through early October and on weekends and holidays the rest of the year. **Known for:** a quick bite to eat. 💲 *Average main: $10* ✉ *Jackson Visitor Center, Paradise Rd. E, Paradise* ☎ *360/569–6571* 🌐 *www.mtrainierguestservices.com* ⏲ *Closed weekdays early Oct.–Apr.*

Paradise Inn

$$$ | AMERICAN | Tall windows in this historic timber lodge provide terrific views of Rainier, and the warm glow of native wood permeates the large dining room, where hearty Pacific Northwest fare is served. Sunday brunch is legendary and served during the summer months; on other days and during the shoulder season there's a breakfast buffet. **Known for:** bourbon buffalo meat loaf; warm liquor drinks. 💲 *Average main: $27* ✉ *E. Paradise Rd., near Jackson Visitor Center, Paradise* ☎ *360/569–2275, 855/755–2275* 🌐 *www.mtrainierguestservices.com* ⏲ *Closed Oct.–mid-May.*

Sunrise Day Lodge Food Service

$ | AMERICAN | FAMILY | A cafeteria and grill serve tasty hamburgers, chili, hot dogs, and soft-serve ice cream from July through September. **Known for:** only food service in this part of the park; often busy. 💲 *Average main: $10* ✉ *Sunrise Rd., 15 miles from White River park entrance, Mt. Rainier National Park* ☎ *360/663–2425* 🌐 *www.mtrainierguestservices.com* ⏲ *Closed Oct.–June.*

PICNIC AREAS

Park picnic areas are usually open only from late May through September.

Paradise Picnic Area

NATIONAL/STATE PARK | This site has great views on clear days. After picnicking at Paradise, you can take an easy hike to one of the many waterfalls in the area—Sluiskin, Myrtle, or Narada, to name a few. ✉ *Hwy. 706, 11 miles east of Longmire, Mt. Rainier National Park* 🌐 *www.nps.gov/mora.*

Sunrise Picnic Area

NATIONAL/STATE PARK | Set in an alpine meadow that's filled with wildflowers in July and August, this picnic area provides expansive views of the mountain and surrounding ranges in good weather. ✉ *Sunrise Rd., 11 miles west of White River entrance, Mt. Rainier National Park* 🌐 *www.nps.gov/mora/planyourvisit/sunrise.htm* ⏲ *Road to Sunrise usually closed Oct.–June.*

Hotels

National Park Inn

$$ | **B&B/INN** | A large stone fireplace warms the common room of this country inn, the only one of the park's two inns that's open year-round, while rustic details such as wrought-iron lamps and antique bentwood headboards adorn the small rooms. **Pros:** classic national park lodge ambience; on-site restaurant with simple American fare; winter packages with perks like breakfast and free snowshoe use. **Cons:** jam-packed in summer; must book far in advance; some rooms have a shared bath. *Rooms from: $187* ✉ *Longmire Visitor Complex, Hwy. 706, 6 miles east of Nisqually entrance, Longmire* ☎ *360/569–2275, 855/755–2275* 🌐 *www.mtrainierguestservices.com* *43 rooms* *No meals.*

★ Paradise Inn

$$ | **HOTEL** | With its hand-carved Alaskan cedar logs, burnished parquet floors, stone fireplaces, Indian rugs, and glorious mountain views, this 1917 inn is a classic example of a national park lodge. **Pros:** central to trails; pristine vistas; nature-inspired details. **Cons:** rooms are small and basic; many rooms have shared bathrooms; no elevators, air-conditioning, cell service, TV, or Wi-Fi. *Rooms from: $138* ✉ *E Paradise Rd., near Jackson Visitor Center, Paradise* ☎ *360/569–2275, 855/755–2275* 🌐 *www.mtrainierguestservices.com* *Closed mid-Oct.–mid-May* *121 rooms* *No meals.*

Activities

MULTISPORT OUTFITTERS

RMI Expeditions

CLIMBING/MOUNTAINEERING | Reserve a private hiking guide through this highly regarded outfitter, or take part in its one-day mountaineering classes (mid-May through late September), where participants are evaluated on their fitness for the climb and must be able to withstand a 16-mile round-trip hike with a 9,000-foot gain in elevation. The company also arranges private cross-country skiing and snowshoeing guides. ✉ *30027 Hwy. 706 E, Ashford* ☎ *888/892–5462, 360/569–2227* 🌐 *www.rmiguides.com* *From $1,118 for 4-day package.*

Whittaker Mountaineering

TOUR—SPORTS | You can rent hiking and climbing gear, cross-country skis, snowshoes, and other outdoor equipment at this all-purpose Rainier Base Camp outfitter, which also arranges for private cross-country skiing and hiking guides. If you forget to bring tire chains (which all vehicles are required to carry in the national park in winter), they rent those too. ✉ *30027 SR 706 E, Ashford* ☎ *800/238–5756, 360/569–2982* 🌐 *www.whittakermountaineering.com.*

BIRD-WATCHING

Be alert for kestrels, red-tailed hawks, and, occasionally, golden eagles on snags in the lowland forests. Also present at Rainier, but rarely seen, are great horned owls, spotted owls, and screech owls. Iridescent rufous hummingbirds flit from blossom to blossom in the drowsy summer lowlands, and sprightly water ouzels flutter in the many forest creeks. Raucous Steller's jays and gray jays scold passersby from trees, often darting boldly down to steal morsels from unguarded picnic tables. At higher elevations, look for the pure white plumage of the white-tailed ptarmigan as it hunts for seeds and insects in winter. Waxwings, vireos, nuthatches, sapsuckers, warblers, flycatchers, larks, thrushes, siskins, tanagers, and finches are common throughout the park.

HIKING

Although the mountain can seem remarkably benign on calm summer days, hiking Rainier is not a city-park stroll. Dozens of hikers and trekkers annually lose their way and must be rescued—and lives are lost on the mountain each year. Weather that approaches cyclonic levels can appear quite suddenly, any month of the year. All visitors venturing far from vehicle access points, with the possible exception of the short loop hikes listed here, should carry day packs with warm clothing, food, and other emergency supplies.

Nisqually Vista Trail

HIKING/WALKING | Equally popular in summer and winter, this trail is a 1¼-mile round-trip through subalpine meadows to an overlook point for Nisqually Glacier. The gradually sloping path is a favorite venue for cross-country skiers in winter; in summer, listen for the shrill alarm calls of the area's marmots. *Easy.* ✉ *Mt. Rainier National Park* ✣ *Trailhead: at Jackson Memorial Visitor Center, Rte. 123, 1 mile north of Ohanapecosh, at high point of Hwy. 706* 🌐 *www.nps.gov/mora/planyourvisit/day-hiking-at-mount-rainier.htm.*

★ Skyline Trail

HIKING/WALKING | This 5-mile loop, one of the highest trails in the park, beckons day-trippers with a vista of alpine ridges and, in summer, meadows filled with brilliant flowers and birds. At 6,800 feet, Panorama Point, the spine of the Cascade Range, spreads away to the east, and Nisqually Glacier tumbles downslope. *Moderate.* ✉ *Mt. Rainier National Park* ✣ *Trailhead: Jackson Memorial Visitor Center, Rte. 123, 1 mile north of Ohanapecosh at high point of Hwy. 706* 🌐 *www.nps.gov/mora/planyourvisit/skyline-trail.htm.*

Sunrise Nature Trail

HIKING/WALKING | The 1½-mile-long loop of this self-guided trail takes you through the delicate subalpine meadows near the Sunrise Visitor Center. A gradual climb to the ridgetop yields magnificent views of Mt. Rainier and the more distant volcanic cones of Mt. Baker, Mt. Adams, and Glacier Peak. *Easy.* ✉ *Mt. Rainier National Park* ✣ *Trailhead: at Sunrise Visitor Center, Sunrise Rd., 15 miles from White River park entrance* 🌐 *www.nps.gov/mora/planyourvisit/sunrise.htm.*

Trail of the Shadows

HIKING/WALKING | This ¾-mile loop is notable for its glimpses of meadowland ecology, its colorful soda springs (don't drink the water), James Longmire's old homestead cabin, and the foundation of the old Longmire Springs Hotel, which was destroyed by fire around 1900. *Easy.* ✉ *Mt. Rainier National Park* ✣ *Trailhead: at Hwy. 706, 10 miles east of Nisqually entrance* 🌐 *www.nps.gov/mora/planyourvisit/day-hiking-at-mount-rainier.htm.*

Van Trump Park Trail

HIKING/WALKING | You gain an exhilarating 2,200 feet on this route while hiking through a vast expanse of meadow with views of the southern Puget Sound and Mt. Adams and Mt. St. Helens. On the way up is one of the highest water falls in the park, Comet Falls. The 5¾-mile track provides good footing, and the average hiker can make it up and back in five hours. *Moderate.* ✉ *Mt. Rainier National Park* ✣ *Trailhead: Hwy. 706 at Christine Falls, 4½ miles east of Longmire* 🌐 *www.nps.gov/mora/planyourvisit/van-trump-trail.htm.*

MOUNTAIN CLIMBING

Climbing Mt. Rainier is not for amateurs; each year adventurers die on the mountain, and many get lost and must be rescued. Near-catastrophic weather can appear quite suddenly any month of the year. If you're experienced in technical, high-elevation snow, rock, and ice-field adventuring, Mt. Rainier can be a memorable adventure. Climbers can fill out a climbing card at the Paradise, White River, or Carbon River ranger station and lead their own groups of two or more. Climbers must register with a ranger before leaving and check out on return. A $51 annual climbing fee applies to anyone heading above 10,000 feet or onto one of Rainier's glaciers. During peak season it is recommended that climbers make their camping reservations ($20 per site) in advance; reservations are taken by fax and mail beginning in mid-March on a first-come, first-served basis (find the reservation form at 🌐 *www.nps.gov/mora/planyourvisit/climbing.htm*).

SKIING AND SNOWSHOEING

Mt. Rainier is a major Nordic ski center for cross-country and telemark skiing. Although trails are not groomed, those around Paradise are extremely popular. If you want to ski with fewer people, try the trails in and around the Ohanapecosh–Stevens Canyon area, which are just as beautiful and, because of their more easterly exposure, slightly less subject to the rains that can douse the Longmire side, even in the dead of winter. Never ski on plowed main roads, especially around Paradise—the snowplow operator can't see you. Rentals aren't available on the eastern side of the park.

Deep snows make Mt. Rainier a snowshoeing pleasure. The Paradise area, with its network of trails, is the best choice. The park's east-side roads, Routes 123 and 410, are unplowed and provide other good snowshoeing venues, although you must share the main routes with snowmobilers.

General Store at the National Park Inn

SKIING/SNOWBOARDING | The store at the National Park Inn in Longmire rents cross-country ski equipment and snowshoes. It's open daily in winter, depending on snow conditions. ✉ *National Park Inn, Longmire* ☎ *360/569–2411* 🌐 *www.mtrainierguestservices.com/activities-and-events/winter-activities/cross-country-skiing*.

Paradise Snowplay Area and Nordic Ski Route

SKIING/SNOWBOARDING | Sledding on flexible sleds (no toboggans or runners), inner tubes, and plastic saucers is allowed only in the Paradise snow-play area adjacent to the Jackson Visitor Center. The area is open when there is sufficient snow, usually from late December through mid-March. The easy 3½-mile Paradise Valley Road Nordic ski route begins at the Paradise parking lot and follows Paradise Valley/Stevens Canyon Road to Reflection Lakes. Equipment rentals are available at Whittaker Mountaineering in Ashford or at the National Park Inn's General Store in Longmire. ✉ *Adjacent to Jackson Visitor Center at Paradise, Mt. Rainier National Park* ☎ *360/569–2211* 🌐 *www.nps.gov/mora/planyourvisit/winter-recreation.htm*.

Activities

Crystal Mountain Ski Area

HIKING/WALKING | Washington State's biggest and best-known ski area has nine lifts (plus a children's lift and a gondola) and 57 runs. In summer, it's open for hiking, rides on the Mt. Rainier Gondola, and meals at the Summit House, all providing sensational views of Rainier and the Cascades. **■ TIP→ Because of recent episodes of overcrowding at the ski resort, during which many people were turned away, Crystal no longer sells day-of tickets on weekends during peak winter season.** **Facilities:** 57 trails; 2,600 acres; 3,100-foot vertical drop; 11 lifts. ✉ *33914 Crystal Mountain Blvd. , off Rte. 410, Crystal Mountain* ☎ *360/663–2265* 🌐 *www.crystalmountainresort.com* 🎫 *From $24*.

Chapter 18

WASHINGTON WINE COUNTRY

YAKIMA RIVER VALLEY

Updated by
Andrew Collins

Sights	Restaurants	Hotels	Shopping	Nightlife
★★★★★	★★★☆☆	★★★☆☆	★☆☆☆☆	★★☆☆☆

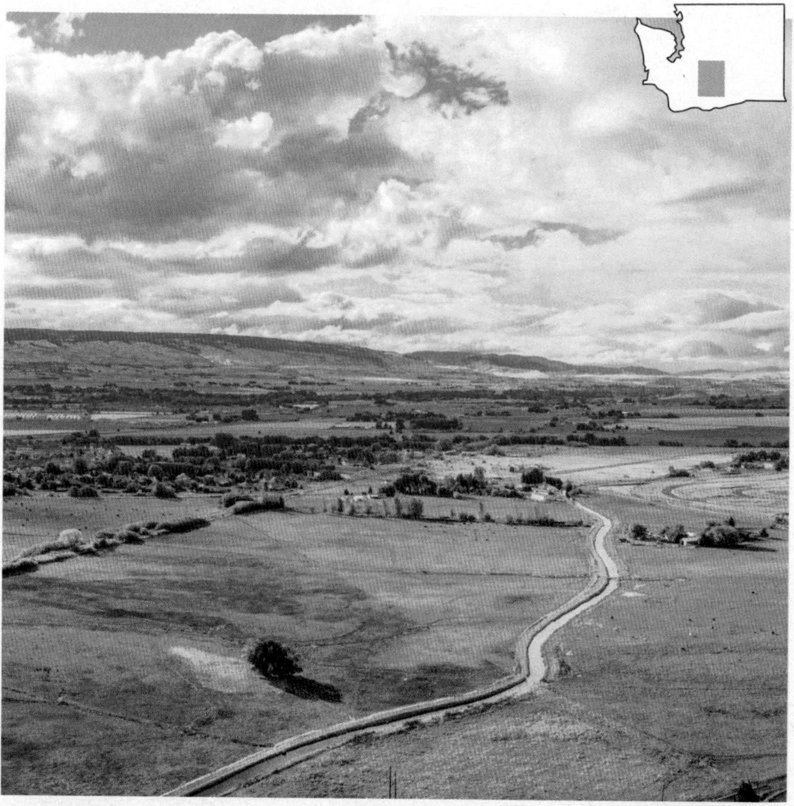

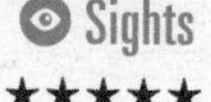

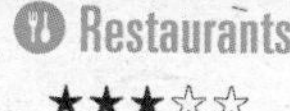

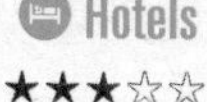

WELCOME TO WASHINGTON WINE COUNTRY

TOP REASONS TO GO

★ **Sip fine wine:** Yakima Valley is the state's oldest and one of its most respected wine regions, with more than 120 producers, most with public tasting rooms.

★ **College town charm:** The presence of Central Washington University has helped transform Ellensburg into a hip and lively regional hub of cool cafés, art centers, and convivial bars.

★ **Mine Washington history:** The former mining towns of Roslyn and Cle Elum honor their hardscrabble pasts with the Coal Mines Trail, which winds past several old mine sites, and exhibits at Northern Kittitas County Historical Society Museums.

★ **Enjoy the outdoors:** From world-class skiing and golfing to pleasant hikes and bike rides along the Yakima Greenway and Palouse to Cascades Trail, opportunities for recreation abound in this region.

★ **Hop to it:** Some of the Pacific Northwest's finest craft brewers thrive here in the region that produces about 75% of the country's hops.

1 Cle Elum and Roslyn. These quirky mining towns abound with colorful saloons and laid-back eateries, one reason why Roslyn was the location for TV's *Northern Exposure*.

2 Ellensburg. Both a progressive college town and a traditional ranching center, this lively small city offers a blend of artistic, historical, and culinary diversions.

3 Yakima. This workaday city—the region's largest—has a charming historic core with a growing crop of hip eateries and bars.

4 Zillah. One of the state's oldest winemaking centers, rural Zillah is home to several prominent vineyards and tasting rooms.

5 Sunnyside. Sunnyside has noteworthy wineries and one of the valley's top craft brewers.

6 Prosser. You'll find the Yakima Valley's largest concentration of tasting rooms in this charming little town that flanks the Horse Heaven Hills.

7 Benton City. Don't let that "City" in the name fool you—this tiny hamlet just west of the Tri-Cities is all about agriculture and wine-making and is home to the prestigious Red Mountain AVA.

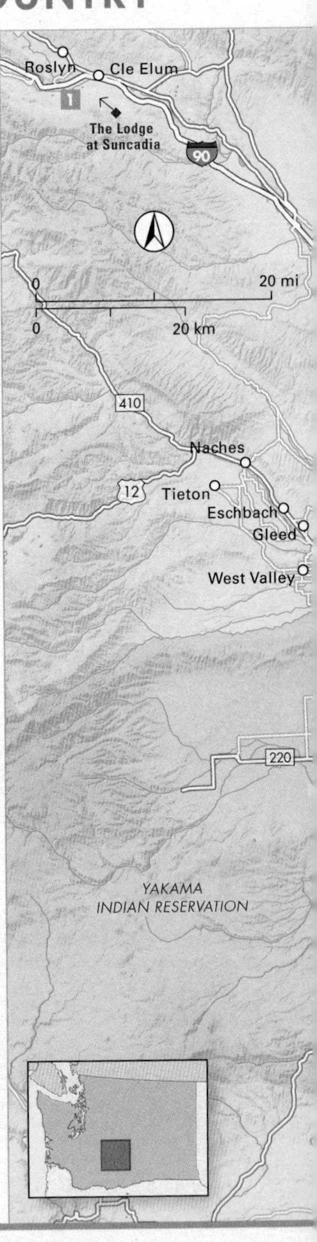

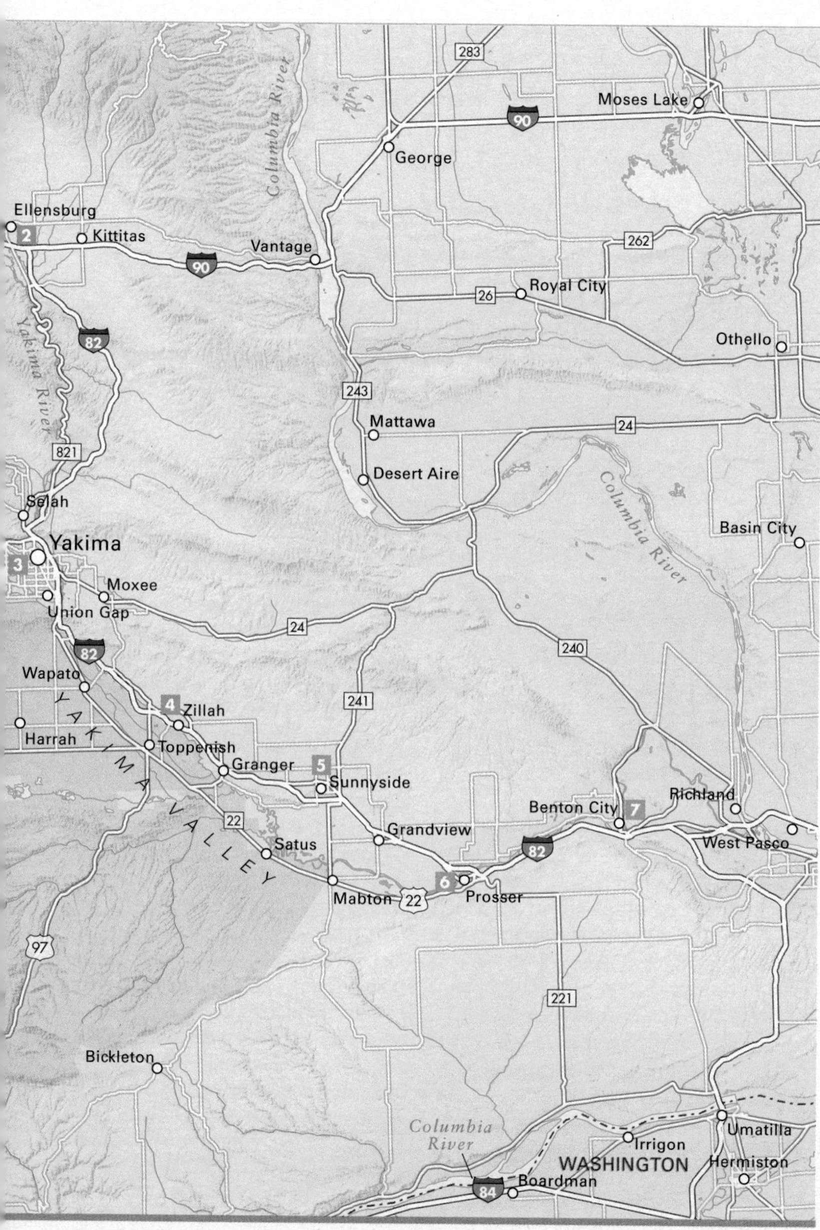
Moses Lake
George
Ellensburg
Kittitas
Vantage
Royal City
Othello
Mattawa
Desert Aire
Selah
Yakima
Moxee
Union Gap
Basin City
Wapato
Zillah
Harrah
Toppenish
Granger
Sunnyside
Benton City
Richland
West Pasco
Grandview
Satus
Mabton
Prosser
Bickleton
Umatilla
Irrigon
Hermiston
Boardman
WASHINGTON
YAKIMA VALLEY
Columbia River
Yakima River

The Yakima River binds a region of great contrasts. Snowcapped volcanic peaks and evergreen-covered hills overlook a natural shrub steppe turned green by irrigation. Famed throughout the world for its apples and cherries, its wine and hops, this fertile landscape is also the ancestral home of the Yakama people from whom it takes its name.

The river flows southeasterly from its source in the Cascade Mountains near Snoqualmie Pass. Between the college town of Ellensburg, at the heart of the Kittitas Valley, and Yakima, the region's largest city, the river cuts steep canyons through serried, sagebrush-covered ridges before merging with the Naches River. Then it breaks through Union Gap to enter its fecund namesake, the broad Yakima Valley. Some 200 miles from its source, the river makes one final bend around vineyard-rich Red Mountain before joining the mighty Columbia River at the Tri-Cities.

Broad-shouldered Mt. Adams is the sacred mountain of the Yakama people. The 12,276-foot-tall mountain marks the western boundary of their reservation, second largest in the Pacific Northwest. As they have for centuries, wild horses run free through the Yakama Nation and can sometimes be seen feeding along U.S. 97 south of Toppenish. Deer and elk roam the evergreen forests, eagles and ospreys soar overhead.

Orchards and vineyards dominate Yakima Valley's agricultural landscape. Cattle and sheep ranching initially drove the economy; apples and other produce came with the engineering of irrigation canals and outlets in the 1890s. The annual asparagus harvest begins in April, followed by cherries in June; apricots and peaches ripen in early to midsummer. Hops—more are grown here than anywhere else in the world—are ready by late August and used to brew beer; travelers may see the bushy vines spiraling up fields of twine. The apple harvest runs from late summer through October.

The valley's real fame, however, rests on its wine grapes. The area marks the birth of Washington's world-famous wine industry, and although exceptional wine regions now abound in many other parts of the state, Yakima Valley continues to claim some of the top vineyards and producers. Concord grapes were first planted here in the 1960s, and they still take up large tracts of land. But vinifera grapes, the noble grapes of Europe, now dominate the local wine industry. Merlot and Chardonnay first put the region on the map, followed by Cabernet Sauvignon and Franc, and then Syrah and its Rhône cousins, Grenache, Mourvèdre, and—on the white side—Viognier. The other grapes that Yakima wineries plant the most include Riesling, Gewürztraminer, Sémillon, Sauvignon Blanc, and Chenin Blanc among the whites, and Malbec, Sangiovese, Tempranillo, and Lemberger among the reds.

MAJOR REGIONS

Northern Yakima River Valley. Just 80 miles from Seattle over the Cascade Mountains, the historic mining towns of **Roslyn** and **Cle Elum** offer offbeat shops and one plush resort, the Hyatt Suncadia. Golf, fishing, hiking, biking, and cross-country skiing are popular pastimes in this area. As you follow the Yakima River down through attractive **Ellensburg** and then down into the region's largest city, **Yakima,** you can see how irrigation turns a virtual desert into one of the most agriculturally rich regions in the nation.

Southern Yakima River Valley. Traveling southeast from Yakima, the gateway to the region's wine country, visitors can sample wine at dozens of tasting rooms and snap up fresh fruits and vegetables at orchards and roadside farmstands in **Zillah, Sunnyside, Prosser,** and **Benton City.** History is rich here as well. The Yakama Indian Reservation occupies much of the land southwest of Interstate 82, and you can learn about the history of its people at a couple of museums around the region.

Planning

When to Go

Much of the area is considered semiarid shrub steppe, with annual rainfall of just 8 inches a year. But in winter, in the higher elevations, snowfall is quite common from November until March. This is a decidedly four-season region, with wet, cool, windy springs, beautiful warm summer days, and gorgeous falls with brilliant foliage. The most pleasant times to visit are April to June and September through October, when temperatures are moderate. Summer in the Lower Yakima Valley can be quite hot.

The main wine-tasting season begins in late April and runs to the end of the fall harvest in November. Wineries often reduce their hours in winter—it's best to check websites before visiting. Wine Yakima Valley (🌐 *www.wineyakimavalley.org*) publishes a map-brochure that lists wineries with tasting-room hours. As wine regions go, Yakima Valley is relatively unpretentious and very friendly, and you'll often have the chance to meet local winemakers when visiting tasting rooms.

Getting Here and Around

AIR

Although major airlines serve the region's two airports, most people fly into Seattle or Portland, Oregon—which offer far more airline and flight options—and drive here. Both Yakima and the Tri-Cities have service on Horizon (part of Alaska) to Seattle. The Tri-Cities are also served by Allegiant (to Las Vegas and Phoenix), Delta (to Minneapolis, Seattle, and Salt Lake City), and United (to Denver, Los Angeles, and San Francisco).

The Airporter Shuttle has five daily roundtrips from Sea-Tac airport to the Yakima airport ($52 one-way) or downtown Yakima ($47), with stops in downtown Seattle, Cle Elum ($37), and Ellensburg ($41).

AIRPORTS Tri-Cities Regional Airport. ✉ *3601 N. 20th Ave., Pasco* ☎ *509/547–6352* 🌐 *www.flytricities.com.* **Yakima Air Terminal.** ✉ *2300 W. Washington Ave., Yakima* ☎ *509/575–6149* 🌐 *www.yakimaairterminal.com.*

AIRPORT TRANSFERS Airporter Shuttle. ☎ *866/235–5247* 🌐 *www.airporter.com.*

CAR

You'll definitely want a car to explore this part of the state, as even cities like Yakima and smaller Ellensburg have a lot to see beyond the downtown cores. The Yakima Valley Highway, which turns into Wine Country Road just south of Sunnyside, is a reliable, less-traveled alternative to Interstate 82 for wine-country visits; but it can be slow, especially in downtowns, or if farm machinery is on the road.

Restaurants

Although more farm-to-table restaurants and hip coffeehouses and gastropubs have begun to open, especially in northern Yakima River Valley, this part of the state is still dominated by no-frills diners, traditional burger joints and steak houses, along with ubiquitous chains. The presence of so much freshly grown produce and terrific local wine is helping to improve the culinary scene, and Yakima Valley has seen a recent influx of exceptional craft breweries and cideries. South Central Washington also has a sizable Latino population, which has led to a great variety of excellent taco trucks and casual Mexican restaurants. *Restaurant reviews have been shortened. For full information, visit Fodors.com.*

Hotels

You'll find the highest concentration of lodging options along the Interstate 90 and Interstate 82 corridors, especially in Ellensburg and Yakima; however, cookie-cutter chain properties prevail. Fortunately, a smattering of notable boutique hotels and independent motels have opened in the area in recent years, and you'll also find a handful of distinctive inns and B&Bs as well as the famed Hyatt Suncadia Resort in Cle Elum, which offers among the poshest accommodations in the region. In towns with lots of wineries, book well ahead the third week in April for Spring Barrel Tasting, and on weekends from Memorial Day through Labor Day. *Hotel reviews have been shortened. For full information, visit Fodors.com.*

What It Costs in U.S. Dollars

	$	$$	$$$	$$$$
RESTAURANTS	under $16	$16–$22	$23–$30	over $30
HOTELS	under $150	$150–$200	$201–$250	over $250

Visitor Information

Wine Yakima Valley Association
🌐 *wineyakimavalley.org.*

Yakima Valley Visitor Information Center
✉ *101 N. Fair Ave., Yakima* ☎ *509/573–3388, 800/221–0751* 🌐 *www.visityakima.com.*

Cle Elum and Roslyn

86 miles southeast of Seattle.

A former railroad, coal, and logging town, Cle Elum (pronounced "klee *ell*-um") now caters to leisure travelers stopping for a breath of air before or after tackling Snoqualmie Pass. Outside the low-keyed downtown with its vintage storefronts and retro signs, vacationers in search of upscale R&R flock to the world-class Hyatt Suncadia Resort. It's actually closer to Roslyn, a former coal-mining town that gained notoriety as the stand-in for the fictional Alaskan village of Cicely on the 1990s TV show *Northern Exposure.* Today, Cicely's Gift Shop on the town's main drag sells memorabilia, and the show's radio-station set can be viewed a block away at the old Northwestern Improvement Co. building. Roslyn is also notable for its 26 ethnic cemeteries, established by communities of miners in the late 19th and early 20th centuries and clustered on a hillside west of town.

GETTING HERE AND AROUND

Cle Elum is just off Interstate 90, typically less than 90-minute drive from Seattle, and Roslyn is just a few miles north via Highway 903.

Sights

Northern Kittitas County Historical Society Museums

MUSEUM | The local historical society preserves two distinct aspects of the town's colorful history. At the three-story 1914 Carpenter House Museum, you can view rotating art exhibits and see furnishings, clothing, and historical documents that belonged to some of the community's founding families. A few blocks away on Cle Elum's main drag (221 East 1st Street, closed early September–late May), the Telephone Museum contains the manual switchboard that the town used until 1966 (the town was one of the last in the nation to switch to automated telephone exchanges), as well exhibits on the history of telephone technology and memorabilia related to the area's vibrant mining heritage. ✉ *Carpenter House Museum, 302 W. 3rd St.* ☎ *509/649–2880* 🌐 *www.nkcmuseums.org* 🎫 *Free* 🕑 *Closed Jan. and Mon.–Thurs.*

Palouse to Cascades State Park Trail

TRAIL | **FAMILY** | Although this rails-to-trails multiuse throughway stretches for 212 miles across Washington, following the former route of the Chicago, Milwaukee, St. Paul, and Pacific Railroad, this section over the Cascades and into Cle Elum is one of the more scenic and popular. Formerly known variously as the John Wayne Pioneer and Iron Horse Trail, it climbs over Snoqualmie Pass, passes through Snoqualmie Tunnel (it's closed in winter), and then runs alongside several alpine lakes on its way to the old rail station in South Cle Elum (an excellent place to pick up the trail). Here you can also continue east toward the Columbia River through Ellensburg, if you're up for a longer adventure. The headquarters of this linear park is at Lake Easton State Park, 15 miles west of Cle Elum and just off Interstate 90. The trail is open to hiking, jogging, biking, and horseback riding, as well as cross-country skiing and snowshoeing in winter. ✉ *South Cle Elum Depot, 801 Milwaukee Ave.* ☎ *509/656–2230* 🌐 *www.parks.state.wa.us* 🎫 *$10 parking.*

Restaurants

★ Basecamp Books and Bites

$$ | **MODERN AMERICAN** | Equal parts indie bookstore, bar, and coffee house, this hip hangout set in one of Roslyn's quirky Victorian storefronts turns out creatively prepared American classics morning to night, including elk sausage scrambles, candied-bacon and blue-cheese burgers, apple-maple salads, and turkey potpies. Espresso drinks are brewed using a beautiful teal La Marzocco machine, and craft cocktails are served in the cozy basement bar. **Known for:** terrific selection of outdoorsy books and gear; interesting cocktails and mocktails; fun, social vibe. $ *Average main: $16* ✉ *110 W. Pensylvania Ave., Roslyn* ☎ *509/649–3821* 🌐 *www.basecampbooks.com* 🕑 *No dinner Sun. and Mon.*

Red Bird Cafe

$ | **CAFÉ** | **FAMILY** | Have a seat at one of the red vintage tables and chairs in this charming breakfast and lunch café on the first floor of a sweet blue-and-red house built in 1906 near the town center. Standout dishes include the Gallic Rooster (a French toast sandwich filled with bacon, strawberry jam, goat cheese, and fried eggs) and meatballs and marinara hoagie. **Known for:** hefty sandwiches and salads with unusual ingredients; children's area with play kitchen; three cute guest rooms upstairs. $ *Average main: $12*

⊠ *102 E. Pennsylvania Ave., Roslyn* ☎ *509/649–3209* ⊙ *No dinner.*

Roslyn Cafe

$ | **AMERICAN** | Famed for its camel mural, which figured prominently in the intro of TV's *Northern Exposure*, this eclectic corner café is a reliable option for elevated America fare, but the main draw is the pop-culture cachet and the inviting space. There's a rustic dining room with stone and timber walls and a handful of sidewalk tables. **Known for:** prodigious breakfast portions; Vietnamese-inspired banh mi burger; bloody marys with all the garnishes. *$ Average main: $13* ⊠ *201 W. Pennsylvania Ave., Roslyn* ☎ *509/649–2763* 🌐 *www.theroslyncafe.com* ⊙ *Closed Tues.*

Stella's

$ | **CAFÉ** | This friendly daytime café is inside a quirky little cabin with a sunny deck beside Cle Elum's Flag Pole Park. Popular for a bite or a latte before or after hiking the nearby Coal Mines Trail or just strolling around downtown, Stella's specializes in overstuffed sandwiches—such as the Gobbler, with roast turkey, cranberry sauce, and Swiss—and well-prepared breakfasts featuring everything from French toast to steal-cut oatmeal to build-your-own egg scrambles. **Known for:** espresso drinks with house-made chocolate and caramel sauces; cute deck seating; friendly staff. *$ Average main: $8* ⊠ *316½ W. 1st St.* ☎ *509/674–6816* ⊙ *No dinner.*

Sunset Cafe and Loose Wolf Lounge

$ | **AMERICAN** | Since 1936 this family-run Western-theme restaurant has been serving breakfast delectables that include the signature "Texas-size cinnamon rolls," plus boneless pork chops and eggs, corned-beef-hash Benedicts, and astoundingly large pancakes filled with bananas, chocolate chips, and peanut butter. The rest of the day, count on traditional Italian and American fare like burgers and chicken Parmesan. **Known for:** colorful people-watching in the saloon; stick-to-your-ribs comfort fare; down-home diner-style vibe. *$ Average main: $14* ⊠ *318 E. 1st St.* ☎ *509/674–2241.*

★ **Swiftwater Cellars**

$$$$ | **MODERN AMERICAN** | Set in a grand stone-and-timber lodge that overlooks both the remains of the old Roslyn No. 9 mineshaft and the Hyatt Suncadia Resort's scenic Rope Rider Golf Course, this wine-centric dining room provides an elegant counterpoint to the area's quirky saloons. The menu mixes Pacific Northwestern and international recipes—think kung pao calamari, pear-pancetta flatbread, and Angus rib-eye steaks—and Swiftwater's own mostly Bordeaux-style wines are a delight. **Known for:** creatively prepared steak and seafood; on-site winery and tasting room; sunny terrace with sweeping views. *$ Average main: $36* ⊠ *301 Rope Rider Dr.* ☎ *509/674–6555* 🌐 *www.swiftwatercellars.com* ⊙ *Closed Mon. and Tues.*

Hotels

Hotel Roslyn

$$$ | **B&B/INN** | This sleek, smartly designed boutique inn opened in historic Rosyln in 2019, offering a mix of suites and two-bedroom town homes with a wealth of creature comforts, including private entrances, fully equipped kitchens, pretty patios, and separate sitting areas. **Pros:** wine happy hours Thursday to Saturday; close to Roslyn's dining and shopping; kitchenettes or kitchens in every unit. **Cons:** a little pricey for the area; lacks Roslyn's old-fashioned charm; no gym. *$ Rooms from: $230* ⊠ *103 W. Washington Ave., Roslyn* ☎ *509/649–3852* 🌐 *www.hotelroslyn.com* *10 rooms* *No meals.*

Huckleberry House

$ | **B&B/INN** | Set on a hill overlooking Roslyn's main street, this charming inn whose well-lighted rooms feature claw-foot tubs and wraparound porches is a short walk from Roslyn's atmospheric eateries and watering holes. **Pros:** picturesque perch; convenient, central location; very economical rates. **Cons:** downtown location can get a little noisy; old-fashioned feel isn't to everyone's taste; no breakfast. *Rooms from: $95 ✉ 301 Pennsylvania Ave., Roslyn ☎ 509/649–2900 🌐 www.huckleberry-house.com 3 rooms No meals.*

Hyatt Suncadia Resort
$$$$ | **RESORT** | Set on a ridge overlooking the Cle Elum River, with spectacular views of the pine-covered Cascade Mountains, this upscale resort offers elegant rooms in a stone-and-wood lodge, most with gas fireplaces. **Pros:** stunning mountain and forest views; activities abound for adults and children; feels like an alpine lodge. **Cons:** activity and meal costs can add up quickly; not within walking distance of Cle Elum or Roslyn; hefty daily resort fee. *Rooms from: $259 ✉ 3320 Suncadia Trail ☎ 509/649–6400, 866/904–6300 🌐 www.suncadia.com 272 rooms No meals.*

Iron Horse Inn Bed and Breakfast
$$ | **B&B/INN** | Near a former boardinghouse for rail workers, this offbeat collection of four restored cabooses filled with engaging railroad memorabilia is especially fun for fans of vintage trains, but individually decorated accommodations are quite comfy, too. **Pros:** one of the most memorable lodgings in the area; suites have jetted tubs and kitchenettes; good location for outdoors lovers. **Cons:** funky accommodations may not appeal to modernists; 15- to 20-minute walk from downtown Cle Elum; no breakfast. *Rooms from: $160 ✉ 526 Marie Ave. ☎ 509/674–5939, 800/228–9246 🌐 www.ironhorseinnbb.com 4 suites No meals.*

★ **Brick Tavern**
BARS/PUBS | Built in 1889 and rebuilt in 1898, this iconic corner saloon features hearty pub grub, a great selection of beer from the Pacific Northwest, a giant wood-burning stove, basement jail cells, and a 23-foot-long running-water spittoon, now used for annual miniboat races. There's live music on weekends, and the kitchen serves decent pub fare. *✉ 100 W. Pennsylvania Ave., Roslyn ☎ 509/649–2643 🌐 www.bricksaloon.com.*

Shopping

★ **Owens Meats**
FOOD/CANDY | The Owens family established this marvelous smokehouse in 1887 and has been running the self-proclaimed "candy store for the carnivore" ever since. You'll find no processed meats here—just the house-smoked and cured jerky, bacon, sausage, chicken breast, bone-in pork chops, and more, along with a big selection of sauces, condiments, and gourmet goodies. Meat vending machines located throughout the region, including outside this store, mean you can satisfy your cravings day or night. *✉ 502 E. 1st St. ☎ 509/674–2530 🌐 www.owensmeats.com.*

Ellensburg

25 miles southeast of Cle Elum.

Home to Central Washington University, this easygoing college towns has a handful of notable history and arts attractions as an increasingly noteworthy bar and restaurant scene centered around the stylish Hotel Windrow, which opened early in 2020. "Modern" Ellensburg had its origin in a July 4 fire that engulfed the original city in 1889. Almost overnight, Victorian brick buildings rose from the ashes, and many now house galleries, restaurants, and taverns.

One of central Washington's biggest events is the Ellensburg Rodeo, held Labor Day weekend. On the national circuit since the 1920s, the rodeo has a year-round headquarters on Main Street, where you can buy tickets and souvenirs.

You can also get a bird's-eye view of the rodeo grounds from Reed Park, in the 500 block of North Alder Street.

GETTING HERE AND AROUND

Ellensburg has two exits on Interstate 90. Follow Main Street north to reach the heart of downtown and Central Washington University.

ESSENTIALS

VISITOR INFORMATION Kittitas County Chamber of Commerce. ✉ *609 N. Main St.* ☎ *509/925–2002, 888/925–2204* 🌐 *www.kittitascountychamber.com.*

Sights

Central Washington University

BUILDING | Roughly 12,500 students learn and in many cases live on this pleasant, tree-shaded campus marked by formidable redbrick architecture and located on the north side of downtown. University Way contains several handsome buildings dating from the university's founding in 1891 as the State Normal School. Attractions near the center of campus include a serene Japanese garden and the Sarah Spurgeon Gallery, which features the work of regional and national artists. ✉ *400 E. University Way* ☎ *509/963–1111* 🌐 *www.cwu.edu.*

Clymer Museum & Gallery

LOCAL INTEREST | Half this museum set inside converted vintage downtown storefronts houses a collection of works by renowned painter John Clymer (1907–89), an Ellensburg native who was one of the most widely published illustrators of the American West, focusing many of his oils and watercolors on wildlife and indigenous culture. The other galleries mount rotating exhibitions featuring other established and emerging Western and wildlife artists. ✉ *416 N. Pearl St.* ☎ *509/962–6416* 🌐 *www.clymermuseum.org* 🎫 *Free* ⏲ *Closed Sun.*

Dick and Jane's Spot

HOUSE | FAMILY | The home of artists Jane Orleman and her late husband Dick Elliott is a continuously growing whimsical folk sculpture of outsider art: a collage of some 20,000 bottle caps, 1,500 bicycle reflectors, and other colorful, reused bits. Although you can't tour the house itself, you can view the fantastic exterior and art-strewn front and backyards from the sidewalk, and you're encouraged to sign the guest book mounted on the surrounding fence. ✉ *101 N. Pearl St.* ☎ *509/925–3224* 🌐 *www.reflectorart.com.*

★ Gallery One Visual Art Center

MUSEUM | You could lose yourself for at least an hour browsing the three floors of light-filled galleries within downtown's imposing 1889 Stewart Building. This community art center buzzes with creative energy, as artists often work on-site. Rotating exhibits showcase the area's considerable diversity of artistic talent, and there's a fantastic gift shop. Be sure to check out the top floor, which preserves many of the building's most striking Victorian architectural elements. ✉ *408 N. Pearl St.* ☎ *509/925–2670* 🌐 *www.gallery-one.org.*

Ginkgo Petrified Forest and Wanapum State Parks

NATIONAL/STATE PARK | About 30 miles east of Ellensburg via Interstate 90, these two adjoining state parks hug the western banks of the Columbia River. Ginkgo Petrified Forest preserves the remarkable petrified-wood logs that were once part of a thriving ginkgo forest. The 1½-mile-Trees of Stone Interpretative Trail loop leads from the interpretive center (closed some days mid-September–mid-May). Just south, Wanapum State Park has camping, swimming, and river access for boaters. ✉ *4511 Huntzinger Rd., Vantage* ☎ *509/856–2700* 🌐 *www.parks.wa.gov* 🎫 *Parking $10.*

Kittitas County Historical Museum

MUSEUM | The six galleries in this excellent regional history museum set inside the opulent Victorian Cadwell Building showcase one of the state's better pioneer artifact collections, ranging from Native American basketry to early-20th-century carriages. There's also an impressive collection of historic photos. ✉ *114 E. 3rd Ave.* ☎ *509/925–3778* 🌐 *www.kchm.org* ⏲ *Closed Sun.*

Wild Horse Renewable Energy Center

FACTORY | **FAMILY** | Wind power is one of the fastest-growing sustainable energy sources in the West, and this massive 273-megawatt desert wind farm 16 miles east of Ellensburg is a big one, powering 70,000 Washington homes with 149 turbines. On free guided tours, offered daily at 10 am and 2 pm from April through October, you'll step inside one of these 221-foot-tall turbines while also soaking up sweeping views of the Cascades. The contemporary visitor center also has exhibits and videos that further explain wind power and discuss other forms of energy used historically in the Pacific Northwest. ✉ *25905 Vantage Hwy.* ☎ *509/964–7815* 🌐 *www.pse.com* ⏲ *Closed Nov.–Mar.*

Restaurants

★ Basalt

$$$ | **PACIFIC NORTHWEST** | Opening its doors in early 2020, this attractive restaurant off the lobby of downtown's Hotel Windrow specializes in locally sourced and seasonally inspired steaks, seafood, and produce and has drawn both locals and out-of-towners for lively dinners, lunches, and breakfasts. In the morning, you might consider wild-mushroom hash or marinated flank steak and eggs, while evening favorites include over-roasted sockeye salmon and ricotta cavatelli with lamb sausage, goat cheese, and marinated peppers. **Known for:** well-prepared steaks with delicious sides; weekend brunch is always packed; well-chosen local wines and beers. $ *Average main: $28* ✉ *502 N. Main St.* ☎ *509/962–8002* 🌐 *www.basaltellensburg.com.*

Cornerstone Pie

$ | **PIZZA** | Set near the CWU campus and decorated with repurposed, reclaimed, and historical artifacts, this casual hangout with a great porch revolves around one central fixture, a wood-fire pizza oven. Out of that oven come pies and grinders with a focus on regional and seasonal ingredients—the salmon-caper and pulled-pork pizzas are among the favorites. **Known for:** Pacific Northwest craft beer on tap; bacon maple bars for dessert; nice selection of wines. $ *Average main: $14* ✉ *307 E. 5th Ave.* ☎ *509/933–3600* 🌐 *www.cornerstonepie.com.*

The Early Bird

$ | **MODERN AMERICAN** | From students recovering after a night of partying to hikers fueling up before hitting the trail, this cozy split-level café with counter service, big windows, and an expansive patio serves brunch daily—with cocktails, if you wish. Specialties include pork green chili with fried eggs, banana–and–macadamia nut waffles, and avocado toast on sourdough with eggs, cotija cheese, and cherry tomatoes. **Known for:** filling breakfast bowls; savory and sweet waffles; seasonally flavored mimosas. $ *Average main: $13* ✉ *108 S. Water St.* ☎ *509/968–5288* 🌐 *www.earlybirdeatery.com* ⏲ *Closed Tues.*

The Palace Cafe

$$ | **AMERICAN** | Hungry travelers and townsfolk have been fueling up in this rollicking Old West tavern with period wallpaper and pressed-tin ceilings since 1892, tucking into plates of old-school pub fare. The nachos, fish-and-chips, and steaks are just fine, while a handful of specialties—especially the prime rib with coconut prawns and open-faced chili burgers—keep regulars coming back again and again. **Known for:** ample, old-school breakfasts; delicious burgers;

colorful crowd. [$] *Average main: $17* ✉ *323 Main St.* ☎ *509/925–2327* 🌐 *www.thepalacecafe.net.*

★ The Pearl Bar & Grill

$$ | **AMERICAN** | In this warmly inviting storefront that morphs into a full-on bar and live music haunt after 9 pm, enjoy gastropub cooking that leans toward hearty—bourbon-glazed chicken, bacon-gorgonzola steaks, and pork belly Cubano sandwiches. Decked out with deep wooden booths, exposed brick walls, and vintage chandeliers, it's a classy joint, but with an "everybody knows your name" vibe. **Known for:** generous late-afternoon happy hour; robust burgers and chops; prohibition era–inspired cocktails. [$] *Average main: $20* ✉ *402 N. Pearl St.* ☎ *509/201–1042* 🌐 *www.thepearlbg.com* ⏲ *Closed Sun.*

Red Horse Diner

$ | **AMERICAN** | **FAMILY** | Step back in time to a 1930s-era service station that's been converted into a diner, serving up classic greasy-spoon fare, like steak and eggs, biscuits and gravy, charbroiled chicken sandwiches, banana splits, and the like. While you await your grub, check out the hundreds of vintage metal gas station signs and advertisements. **Known for:** old-fashioned burgers and fries; cool roadside memorabilia; luscious milk shakes. [$] *Average main: $13* ✉ *1518 W. University Way* ☎ *509/925–1956.*

★ Yellow Church Café

$$ | **MODERN AMERICAN** | Set inside a 1923 Lutheran church, this cheery yellow house of culinary worship now serves modern American fare with global accents inside the former nave and choir loft. Standouts at dinner include garam masala–crusted rack of lamb and oven-roasted cedar plank steelhead with lemon caper butter. **Known for:** charmingly quirky architecture and decor; praiseworthy list of Washington wines; memorable breakfasts on weekends. [$] *Average main: $21* ✉ *111 S. Pearl St.* ☎ *509/933–2233* 🌐 *www.theyellowchurchcafe.com.*

Hotels

Best Western Plus Ellensburg Hotel

$$ | **HOTEL** | One of the best budget-minded options in the area, this reliable chain property conveniently located on the south edge of downtown offers travelers plenty of elbow room in contemporary rooms with separate sitting areas and lots of amenities, including refrigerators and microwaves, and—in some suites—jetted tubs and kitchenettes. **Pros:** nice indoor pool and 24-hour gym; short drive from downtown; free breakfast. **Cons:** bland location near freeway; standard chain furnishings; some noise from nearby train tracks. [$] *Rooms from: $159* ✉ *211 W. Umptanum Rd.* ☎ *509/925–4244, 866/925–4288* 🌐 *www.bestwestern.com* *55 rooms* *Free Breakfast.*

Brew House Boarding

$ | **RENTAL** | An ideal option if you're seeking a home-away-from-home atmosphere, this dapper, distinctive hideaway above Thrall & Dodge wine-tasting room in the small town of Kittitas (8 miles east of Ellensburg) includes a pair of roomy suites with sitting areas, the larger one with a refrigerator and cool mid-century modern decor. **Pros:** TVs with Roku and Netflix; spacious apartment-style accommodations; wine bar and tasting room on ground floor. **Cons:** 10- to 15-minute drive from Ellensburg; host is not on the premises; not much going on in Kittitas. [$] *Rooms from: $119* ✉ *109 Main St., Kittitas* ☎ *509/968–3388* 🌐 *www.brewhouseboarding.com* *2 suites* *No meals.*

★ Hotel Windrow

$$ | **HOTEL** | Ellensburg's first downtown hotel in generations opened in early 2020 and comprises a masterfully designed four-story building incorporating parts of a historic Elks Club building, complete with

stylish high-ceilinged rooms, a sophisticated lobby restaurant, and a seasonal rooftop bar. **Pros:** steps from downtown dining and shopping; smart, contemporary rooms; excellent gym, restaurant, and rooftop bar. **Cons:** breakfast costs extra; central location can get a little busy; valet parking only (although it's not expensive). *Rooms from: $179 ⊠ 502 N. Main St. ☎ 509/962–8000 ⊕ www.hotelwindrow.com 59 rooms No meals.*

★ **Whipsaw Brewing**

BREWPUBS/BEER GARDENS | This unfussy brewpub on the northwest side of downtown has a pet-friendly patio and taproom with lumberjack-inspired decor (the owner is a former logger). It's one of the top craft brewers in the region, known especially for its refreshing blackberry wheat ale and potent Final Detonation Imperial Red. *⊠ 704 N. Wenas St. ☎ 509/968–5111 ⊕ www.whipsawbrewing.com.*

Umtanum Creek Falls

HIKING/WALKING | One of the region's best hikes, easily reached from Ellensburg and Yakima, leads to a 40-foot waterfall that yields breathtaking views year-round—it cascades down a mossy, fern-covered basalt ledge in summer, while in winter the pool into which it pours may be glistening with a sheet of ice. With an elevation gain of about 700 feet, the 3-mile round-trip trek through Douglas fir, ponderosa pine, and aspen groves offers a pretty good workout and great scenery, including the possibility of spying an elusive bighorn sheep. A Discover Pass ($10 per day) is required for parking. *⊠ 29360 N. Wenas Rd., Selah ⊕ www.wta.org.*

Yakima

38 miles south of Ellensburg.

The gateway to Washington's wine country is sunny Yakima (pronounced *yak*-imah), which has a metro population of about 130,000.

Yakima was settled in the late 1850s as a ranching center where Ahtanum Creek joins the Yakima River, on the site of earlier Yakama tribal villages at present-day Union Gap. When the Northern Pacific Railroad established its terminal 4 miles north in 1884, most of the town literally picked up and moved to what was then called "North Yakima."

The Central Washington State Fair draws more than 300,000 people to town in late September—it's an engaging showcase for the agricultural bounty of the area.

GETTING HERE AND AROUND

Yakima Air Terminal has commercial service on Horizon Air from Seattle daily, but most visitors get here by car via Interstate 82 from Ellensburg or the Tri-Cities. U.S. 12 and Highway 410, known respectively as White Pass and Chinook Pass, lead to either side of Mt. Rainier, and U.S. 97 leads south into central Oregon.

ESSENTIALS

VISITOR INFORMATION Yakima Valley Tourism. *⊠ 10 N. 8th St. ☎ 800/221–0751 ⊕ www.visityakima.com.*

Central Washington Agricultural Museum

MUSEUM | This underrated history museum is quite a sight to see, with rows and upon rows of antique farming equipment, including more than 150 tractors donated by families that have been farming the Yakima Valley for generations. This sprawling compound is devoted to preserving the state's agrarian heritage, with additional exhibits that include

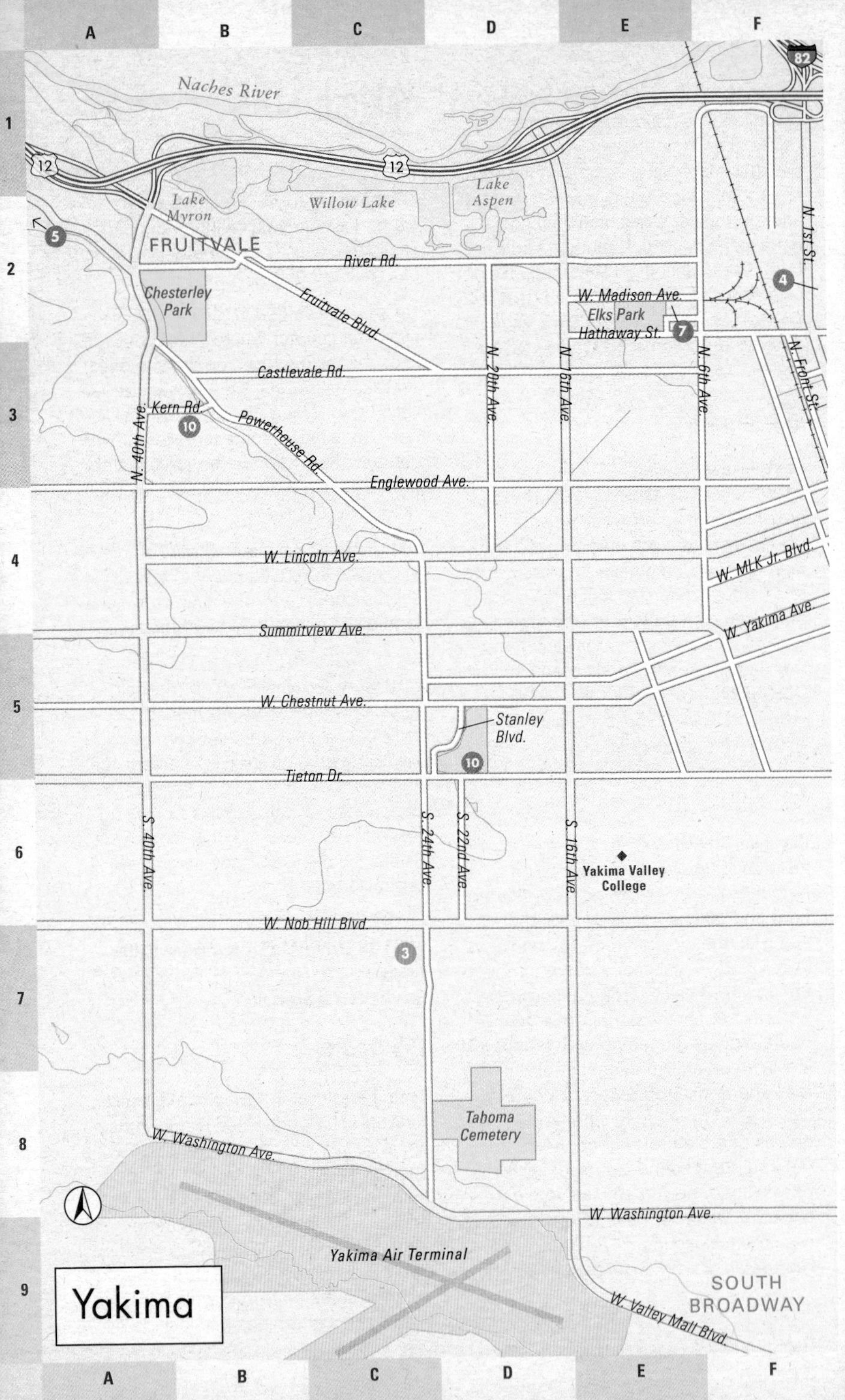

Yakima
A
B
C
D
E
F
1
2
3
4
5
6
7
8
9
Naches River
12
82
Lake Myron
Willow Lake
Lake Aspen
FRUITVALE
5
River Rd.
Chesterley Park
Fruitvale Blvd.
W. Madison Ave.
Elks Park
Hathaway St.
7
4
N. 1st St.
N. Front St.
N. 6th Ave.
N. 16th Ave.
N. 20th Ave.
Castlevale Rd.
Kern Rd.
10
Powerhouse Rd.
N. 40th Ave.
Englewood Ave.
W. Lincoln Ave.
W. MLK Jr. Blvd.
W. Yakima Ave.
Summitview Ave.
W. Chestnut Ave.
Stanley Blvd.
Tieton Dr.
S. 40th Ave.
S. 24th Ave.
S. 22nd Ave.
S. 16th Ave.
Yakima Valley College
W. Nob Hill Blvd.
3
Tahoma Cemetery
W. Washington Ave.
Yakima Air Terminal
SOUTH BROADWAY
W. Valley Mall Blvd.

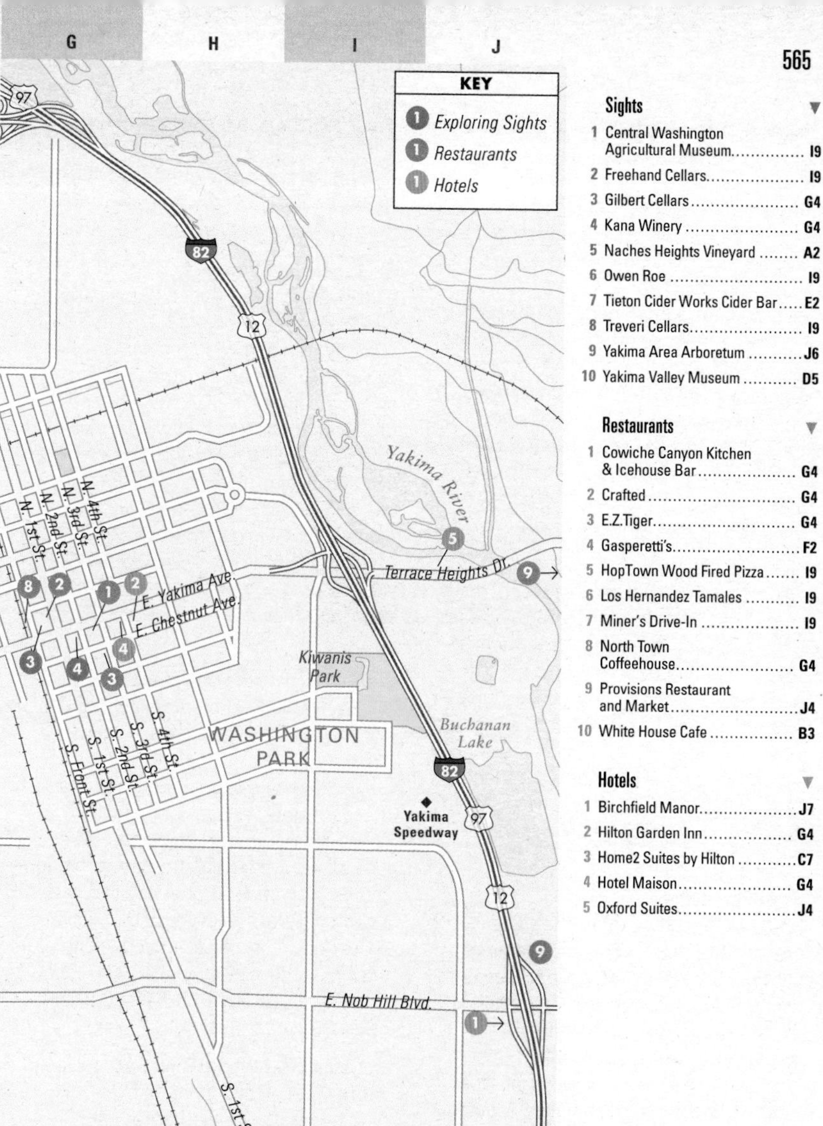

Sights

1 Central Washington Agricultural Museum.............. I9
2 Freehand Cellars.................... I9
3 Gilbert Cellars...................... G4
4 Kana Winery G4
5 Naches Heights Vineyard A2
6 Owen Roe I9
7 Tieton Cider Works Cider Bar..... E2
8 Treveri Cellars...................... I9
9 Yakima Area Arboretum J6
10 Yakima Valley Museum D5

Restaurants

1 Cowiche Canyon Kitchen & Icehouse Bar.................... G4
2 Crafted G4
3 E.Z.Tiger............................ G4
4 Gasperetti's..........................F2
5 HopTown Wood Fired Pizza I9
6 Los Hernandez Tamales I9
7 Miner's Drive-In I9
8 North Town Coffeehouse........................ G4
9 Provisions Restaurant and Market..........................J4
10 White House Cafe B3

Hotels

1 Birchfield Manor.....................J7
2 Hilton Garden Inn.................. G4
3 Home2 Suites by Hilton C7
4 Hotel Maison........................ G4
5 Oxford Suites.........................J4

pioneer-era homesteads and cabins, a vintage railroad boxcar, a vintage gas station, a blacksmith shop, a sawmill, an antique roy collection, and many more buildings. Located a couple of miles south of Yakima in one of the state's oldest towns, Union Gap, the museum occupies a good chunk of 15-acre Fullbright Park and offers access to trails along Ahtanum Creek and up into the high-desert hills. The museum grounds are generally open year-round, even when the buildings are closed. ✉ *4508 Main St., Union Gap* ☎ *509/457–8735* 🌐 *www.centralwaagmuseum.org* ⏲ *Museum buildings closed Mon. and Nov.–Mar.*

Freehand Cellars

WINERY/DISTILLERY | Established several miles south of Yakima in 2018 by a team of wine-loving architects, this stunning modern tasting room set on a hill with clear Mt. Adams views produces accessible Pinot Gris, Syrah, and several other balanced wines. The kitchen serves tasty flatbread pizzas and other wine-friendly fare. ✉ *420 Windy Point Dr., Wapato* ☎ *509/866–4664* 🌐 *www.freehandcellars.com.*

★ **Gilbert Cellars**

WINERY/DISTILLERY | In Yakima's Old North Historic District, this bustling tasting room pours selections from the beautiful family vineyards, specializing in blends of Rhône and Bordeaux varietals and both lightly oaked and unoaked Chardonnays. You can also order light tapas, such as bacon-wrapped dates, Marcona almonds, and cheese platters. There's live music some evenings. ✉ *5 N. Front St.* ☎ *509/249–9049* 🌐 *www.gilbertcellars.com.*

Kana Winery

WINERY/DISTILLERY | On the ground floor of downtown Yakima's handsome art deco A.E. Larson Building, this lively tasting room presents local rock and acoustic bands on Friday nights—the owner is a serious Grateful Dead fan, which shows in everything from the colorful retro-'70s decor to the Dead-inspired artwork and names (Dark Star red blend, Katie Mae Riesling) of the mostly Rhône-style wines. ✉ *10 S. 2nd St.* ☎ *509/453–6611* 🌐 *www.kanawinery.com.*

Naches Heights Vineyard

WINERY/DISTILLERY | About 10 miles northwest of Yakima in one of the state's more recently trending wine-growing areas, this organic and biodynamic vineyard sits at an elevation of 1,780 feet and produces friendly priced wines, including Spanish-style Albariño and Tempranillo, and some innovative red and white blends. The tasting room has ample seating inside and sometimes hosts live music. ✉ *1857 Weikel Rd.* ☎ *509/945–4062* 🌐 *www.nhvwines.com* ⏲ *Closed Mon. and Tues.*

★ **Owen Roe**

WINERY/DISTILLERY | This long-esteemed winemaker with operations in both Oregon's Willamette Valley and here in the Yakima Valley earns kudos from leading critics for estate-grown Riesling, Chardonnay, Cabernet Sauvignon, and several heady, aging-worthy red blends, plus less-expensive bottles from its approachable Sharecropper's label. Tastings are in a contemporary wine-making shed with big windows and a patio overlooking the vineyards in Wapato. ✉ *309 Gangl Rd., Wapato* ☎ *509/877–0454* 🌐 *www.owenroe.com.*

★ **Tieton Cider Works Cider Bar**

WINERY/DISTILLERY | Opened by a third-generation apple farmer, this 55-acre orchard and artisan cidery is one of the most celebrated in the country, turning out several year-round sippers, including a semi-sweet cherry and crisp dry-hopped apple variety, along with numerous seasonal varieties. Try a sampler at the tasting room, which also has a big outdoor patio, bocce ball court, and outdoor stage featuring live music. ✉ *619 W. J St.* ☎ *509/571–1430* 🌐 *www.tietonciderworks.com* ⏲ *Closed Tues.*

Yakima Valley vineyard

★ Treveri Cellars

WINERY/DISTILLERY | Enjoy Yakima Valley views from the tasting room and grounds of this esteemed winery that uses the long-standing Methodé Champenoise to produce Champagne-style sparkling wines that rank among the best in the country. Favorites from the reasonably priced portfolio include a creamy Chardonnay-based Blanc de Blanc, a minerally mid-priced Müller-Thurgau, and an elegant Syrah Brut. ✉ *71 Gangl Rd., Wapato* ☎ *509/877–0925* 🌐 *www.trevericellars.com.*

Yakima Area Arboretum

GARDEN | Just off Interstate 82 on the east side of the city, this 46-acre parklike property features hundreds of different plants, flowers, and trees. A Japanese garden and a wetland trail are highlights. The arboretum sits alongside the Yakima River and the 10-mile-long Yakima Greenway, a paved path that links a series of riverfront parks. ✉ *1401 Arboretum Dr.* ☎ *509/248–7337* 🌐 *www.ahtrees.org.*

Yakima Valley Museum

MUSEUM | **FAMILY** | Exhibits at this history museum on the west side of town focus on Yakama native, pioneer, and 20th-century history, ranging from horse-drawn vehicles to a "neon garden" of street signs. Highlights include seasonal beekeeping exhibit (on view spring through fall) and a model of Yakima native and Supreme Court Justice William O. Douglas's Washington, D.C., office. ✉ *2105 Tieton Dr.* ☎ *509/248–0747* 🌐 *www.yakimavalleymuseum.org* 🎫 *$7* 🕒 *Closed Sun. and Mon.*

Restaurants

★ Cowiche Canyon Kitchen & Icehouse Bar

$$$ | **CONTEMPORARY** | Named for the hiking trail that runs through an old railway route in a canyon west of Yakima, this hip downtown restaurant offers contemporary, elevated comfort fare like prawn spring rolls, prime rib dip sandwiches with horseradish sauce, and butcher's cut steaks with a chimichurri glaze. Notable for its sleek design, the restaurant uses antique ice hooks and smudge pots, which double as light fixtures, to pay homage to the region's past, and the high-ceilinged bar is lined with the wood used to mold the restaurant's board-formed concrete walls. **Known for:** extensive selection of regional and local beer; creative takes on modern American fare; cool, contemporary design. *Average main: $24 202 E. Yakima Ave. 509/457–2007 www.cowichecanyon.com.*

★ Crafted

$$$ | **MODERN AMERICAN** | The menu at this urbane farm-to-table downtown bistro changes according to whatever's fresh in the Yakima Valley, showcasing anything from braised short ribs with local cherries, horseradish, and pureed apples in summer to squash agnolotti with duck eggs and maitake mushrooms in autumn. Certain dishes you can always expect to find on the menu, like local oysters on the half-shell, and seasonal sorbets for dessert. **Known for:** beautiful minimalist aesthetic; late-night oyster happy hour; gorgeous presentation. *Average main: $24 22 N. 1st St. 509/426–2220 www.craftedyakima.com Closed Tues. and Wed. No lunch.*

E.Z Tiger

$$ | **MODERN ASIAN** | This hip pan-Asian joint with big windows and patio seating will satisfy your yearning for dumplings, steamed buns, and noodle bowls. Beyond the flavorful fare, which in many instances features regional ingredients, E.Z turns out fun cocktails like the Tiki Tiger, with whiskey, yuzu, grapefruit, pomegranate, honey, and lemon. **Known for:** great variety of dim sum starters; miso rib-eye steaks; mango sticky rice. *Average main: $20 222 E. Chestnut Ave. 509/571–1977 www.ez-tiger.com Closed Sun. and Mon.*

Gasperetti's

$$$ | **ITALIAN** | A beloved destination for hearty red-sauce Italian fare since 1966, elegant Gasperetti's sits like a diamond amid the uninspired strip malls north of downtown, doling out pasta, meat, and seafood entrées accented with locally grown produce—think filet mignon with gorgonzola-pecan sauce, and rigatoni with pesto Genovese. The cellar stocks an excellent selection of wines, with a decidedly Italian lean. **Known for:** extensive selection of mix-and-match pasta and sauce options; many dishes with Washington seafood; retro-cool ambience. *Average main: $24 1013 N. 1st St. 509/248–0628 www.gasperettis-restaurant.com Closed Sun. and Mon. No lunch Sat. or Tues.*

★ HopTown Wood Fired Pizza

$ | **PIZZA** | This down-home pizza parlor between Sunnyside and Yakima celebrates the produce of Yakima Valley with wood-fired pizzas topped with an array of interesting ingredients, such as roasted garlic, house-smoked mozzarella, blueberries, pine nuts, and—most notably—locally grown Cascade hops. Aptly, there's a great selection of hoppy Northwest ales, too. **Known for:** wood-fired elephant ear pastries with local honey; lots of great local beers; outdoor dining. *Average main: $14 2560 Donald Wapato Rd., Wapato 509/952–4414 www.hoptownpizza.com Closed Mon.*

★ Los Hernandez Tamales

$ | **MEXICAN** | From this humble mom-and-pop shop in Union Gap come heavenly tamales—shredded chicken and pork and, during spring, asparagus and pepper jack cheese. Order a pile of these delicacies that have been acclaimed by locals and critics alike—the restaurant even earned a vaunted James Beard Foundation award in the American Classics category. **Known for:** tender tamales bursting with flavor; simple, down-home dining room with just a few tables; friendly staff. *Average main: $6 3706 Main St., Union Gap 509/457–6003.*

Miner's Drive-In

$ | **AMERICAN** | **FAMILY** | This 1940s hamburger joint that's expanded from a drive-in to a family-friendly diner over the years is a Yakima Valley icon (actually located in Union Gap), doling out all sorts of comfort classics, from salads to fish-and-chips to enormous burgers. The real crowd pleaser is the gut-busting "Big Miner"—a hulking pile of meat that's best enjoyed with a basket of fries and a shake. **Known for:** old-fashioned ambience; mammoth burgers; 44-ounce milk shakes. *Average main: $10 2415 S. 1st St., Union Gap 509/457–8194.*

North Town Coffeehouse

$ | **CAFÉ** | Located in Yakima's atmospheric 1909 train depot, this first-rate coffeehouse offers plenty of seating surrounded by ornate pillars, molding, arched ceilings, and other architectural elements. Sit in a comfy armchair and savor a white chocolate mocha or potent cold brew. **Known for:** distinctive setting inside vintage station; great spot for chatting with friends; gelato and baked goods. *Average main: $5 32 N. Front St. 509/895–7600 www.northtowncoffee.com No dinner.*

Provisions Restaurant and Market

$$ | **MODERN AMERICAN** | A pantry full of carefully curated groceries, a bar with a notable beer and spirits list, and a chill neighborhood bistro with a postindustrial look and a large patio, Provisions successfully plays multiple roles as a destination for excellent food and drink. The locavore-minded menu changes seasonally, but might feature curried cauliflower with a dill-lemon sauce, grilled kale and Italian sausage pizza, and down-home fried chicken with mashed potatoes and gravy. **Known for:** creative Italian fare; delectable picnic supplies; desserts featuring local berries. *Average main: $19 2710 Terrace Heights Dr. 509/452–8100 www.provisionsyakima.com Closed Mon.*

White House Cafe

$ | **AMERICAN** | Set amid law offices on the north side of town, this dapper Craftsman-style home is an inviting spot for leisurely, if a touch decadent, brunches and lunches. Sit in the dining, living, or sun room—or, when the weather's nice, in the garden out back—and relish platters of egg, ham, and havarti croissant melts, prodigious sugar-dusted cinnamon rolls, and oven-roasted-chicken salad sandwiches, along with an array of daily-rotating desserts. **Known for:** quaintly decorated cottage setting; breakfast served all day Sunday; cupcakes in many flavors. *Average main: $13 3602 Kern Rd. 509/469–2644 www.whitehouseinyakima.com No dinner.*

Hotels

Birchfield Manor

$$ | **B&B/INN** | This dignified 1910 country inn—set on a plateau of vineyards and hops fields a few miles southeast of Yakima—consists of a manor house with an upscale restaurant, five traditionally furnished upstairs rooms, and a newer, more private cottage with six rooms that feature such cushy amenities as steam-sauna showers and gas fireplaces. **Pros:** peaceful, romantic getaway; elaborate breakfast included; very good restaurant on-site. **Cons:** a little off the beaten path; limited restaurant hours; sometimes booked up for weddings. *Rooms from: $170 2018 Birchfield Rd. 509/452–1960 www.birchfieldmanor.com 11 rooms Free Breakfast.*

Hilton Garden Inn

$$ | **HOTEL** | Modern, spacious, and comfortably furnished rooms in the heart of downtown are the draw of this surprisingly appealing property whose perks include a living room–style lobby with a two-sided glass fireplace, a casual restaurant, and a full-service spa. **Pros:** steps from downtown dining and shopping; lots of appealing common spaces; great

amenities. **Cons:** in the sometimes noisy downtown center; no distinctive style; no valet parking. *Rooms from: $155* ✉ *402 E. Yakima Ave.* ☎ *509/454–1111* 🌐 *www.hilton.com* *114 rooms* *No meals.*

Home2 Suites by Hilton

$$ | HOTEL | On the city's southwest side, this bright, attractive outpost of Hilton's popular extended-stay brand is great for families or those on longer trips, but its reasonable rates and handy features—patio with gas grills and a fire pit, big suites with well-designed kitchens—mean it appeals to all kinds of travelers. **Pros:** sleek, spacious rooms with kitchens; attractive indoor and outdoor common spaces; convenient to airport. **Cons:** anodyne suburban location; 10-minute drive from downtown; chain-hotel design. *Rooms from: $155* ✉ *2420 W. Nob Hill Blvd.* ☎ *509/453–1806* 🌐 *www.hilton.com* *107 rooms* *Free Breakfast.*

★ Hotel Maison

$$ | HOTEL | This strikingly handsome boutique hotel occupies a grand 1911 Masonic temple, and many of its architectural flourishes have been retained. **Pros:** within walking distance of shops and restaurants; complimentary glass of wine upon arrival; stylish modern furnishings. **Cons:** modern interior design doesn't capture building's historic architecture; no free parking; no bathtubs. *Rooms from: $189* ✉ *321 E. Yakima Ave.* ☎ *509/571–1900* 🌐 *www.thehotelmaison.com* *36 rooms* *Free Breakfast.*

Oxford Suites

$ | HOTEL | This low-slung property overlooking the Yakima Greenway and the Yakima River has good-size rooms, some of them full suites with separate sitting rooms, and many with river-view patios or balconies. **Pros:** Adjacent to Yakima River and Greenway; breakfast and evening reception included; indoor pool and fitness center. **Cons:** across from unattractive big-box store; not within walking distance of downtown; small parking. *Rooms from: $132* ✉ *1603 Terrace Heights Dr.* ☎ *509/457–9000, 800/404–7848* 🌐 *www.oxfordsuitesyakima.com* *108 rooms* *Free Breakfast.*

Nightlife

★ Bale Breaker Brewing Company

BREWPUBS/BEER GARDENS | It's appropriate that one of Yakima Valley's top breweries is surrounded by hop fields. First planted in 1932 by the great-grandparents of the three siblings who now own it, the fields supply fresh hops to the beloved Topcutter IPA, Bottomcutter Double IPA, and several other classic and seasonal brews. The "dealer's choice" sampler is a great, reasonably priced way to sample a range of beers, either in the glass-walled tap room or out on the covered patio and grassy lawn, complete with games and a taco truck doling short-order comfort fare. ✉ *1801 Birchfield Rd.* ☎ *509/424–4000* 🌐 *www.balebreaker.com.*

Mickey's Pub and Orion Cinema

BARS/PUBS | At this downtown three-screen cinema pub that shows first-run films and occasional classics, push a call button for seat-side service—including local beer, burgers, pizza, and the like—or just sit in the bar and mingle with locals or catch live music many weekends. ✉ *202 E. Chestnut Ave.* ☎ *509/248–0245* 🌐 *www.mickeyspubyakima.com.*

Single Hill Brewing

BREWPUBS/BEER GARDENS | A standout among downtown Yakima's growing crop of artisan beer makers, Single Hill occupies a stylish, contemporary space with high ceilings and exposed ducts. The brewery works with a variety of small farms throughout the valley to produce its hop-forward Eastside IPA and Hitched, a slightly sour fruit bomb brewed with local sourdough culture. ✉ *102 N. Naches Ave.* ☎ *509/367–6756* 🌐 *www.singlehillbrewing.com.*

Sports Center Yakima

BARS/PUBS | A Yakima standby on the town's main drag since 1904, this friendly dive is known for its signature neon sign, which depicts a sportsman pointing a rifle into the air. Inside, TV screens show pro and college games, and kitchen churns out pub favorites. ✉ *214 E. Yakima Ave.* ☎ *509/453–4647* 🌐 *www.sportscenteryakima.com.*

Shopping

★ Johnson Orchards
FOOD/CANDY | FAMILY | This company has been growing and selling fruit—including cherries, peaches, apples, and pears—on this site since 1904. There's also a bakeshop on-site. ✉ *4906 Summitview Ave.* ☎ *509/966–7479* 🌐 *www.johnsonorchardsfruit.com.*

GOLF

★ Apple Tree Golf Course
GOLF | This exacting, meticulously maintained layout, cut through the apple orchards of west Yakima, consistently ranks among the state's most acclaimed public courses. The signature 17th hole is shaped like a giant apple and is surrounded by a lake. ✉ *8804 Occidental Rd.* ☎ *509/966–5877* 🌐 *www.appletreeresort.com* 🎫 *From $52* ⛳ *18 holes, 6900 yards, par 72.*

SKIING

White Pass Ski Area
SKIING/SNOWBOARDING | This family-friendly 1,400-acre ski resort 50 miles west of Yakima toward Mt. Rainier is the home mountain of 1980s Olympic medalists Phil and Steve Mahre. Eight lifts serve 45 trails on a vertical drop of 2,000 feet from the 6,500-foot summit. Here you'll find condominiums, a gas station, grocery store, and snack bar. Open woods are popular with cross-country skiers and summer hikers. Lift tickets are $73. ✉ *48935 U.S. 12, Naches* ☎ *509/672–3101* 🌐 *www.skiwhitepass.com.*

Zillah

15 miles southeast of Yakima.

The south-facing slopes above Zillah, a tiny town named after the daughter of a railroad manager, are covered with orchards and vineyards. Several wineries are in or near the community.

GETTING HERE AND AROUND

Zillah sits right on Interstate 82, southeast of Yakima. Downtown Zillah is just up the hill a half mile or so, and most of the wineries are to the north and east.

American Hop Museum
MUSEUM | The Yakima Valley grows about 75% of the nation's hops, and the industry's story is well told at this museum housed in a 1917 creamery in Toppenish whose facade is covered with murals of hop farming. Exhibits describe the history, growing process, and unique biology of the plant, a primary ingredient that gives beer its strikingly bitter taste. ✉ *22 S. B St., Toppenish* ☎ *509/865–4677* 🌐 *www.americanhopmuseum.org* 🎫 *$5* ⏲ *Closed Mon., Tues., and Oct.–Apr.*

Bonair Winery
WINERY/DISTILLERY | This family-run winery's tasting room, reminiscent of a European chalet, sits among vineyards near a duck pond that's lovely for picnics. A valley stalwart since 1985, Bonair has garnered dozens of awards for its Cabernet Franc, Cabernet Sauvignon, Riesling, and Chardonnay. ✉ *500 S. Bonair Rd.* ☎ *509/829–6027* 🌐 *www.bonairwine.com.*

Fort Simcoe Historical State Park
MILITARY SITE | FAMILY | This 1856 fort and its several outbuildings are situated on 196 acres on the Yakama Indian Reservation in the town of White Swan. Particularly impressive is the commanding officers' quarters, which looks like a Victorian summer retreat and now

contains a museum (open Saturday, April–October) with exhibits that focus on relations between the Yakama people and American settlers. The Military Days celebration in May features reenactments. Popular activities include bird-watching and picnicking. ✉ *5150 Ft. Simcoe Rd., Toppenish* ☎ *509/874–2372* 🌐 *www.parks.wa.gov* 🎫 *$10 parking.*

Hyatt Vineyards

WINERY/DISTILLERY | Sourcing from 180 acres of vineyards in Zillah, Hyatt has long been respected for Merlot and Syrah, as well as a dessert-friendly late-harvest Riesling. The well-appointed tasting room and well-manicured gardens and lawns are nice for picnicking and offer grand views to the west of the Cascades. ✉ *2020 Gilbert Rd.* ☎ *509/829–6333* 🌐 *www.hyattvineyards.net.*

★ J Bell Cellars

WINERY/DISTILLERY | At this 30-acre lavender farm and wine-making operation set in a stylishly modernized farmhouse a little northwest of Zillah, you can sample first-rate, mostly Bordeaux- and Rhône-style vino, along with a brick-oven-baked pizza made with a dough recipe passed down by one of the owner's Ukrainian families. You can also attend concerts, chef dinners, and other special events. ✉ *73 Knight Hill Rd.* ☎ *509/865–1935* 🌐 *www.jbellcellars.com* ⏲ *Closed Mon.–Thurs.*

Portteus Vineyards

WINERY/DISTILLERY | One of the early Yakima Valley wineries, established in 1981, Portteus is beloved by red-wine drinkers and offers one of the better tasting deals in the region: eight of the winery's many varieties for $5. Options includes Malbec, Syrah, Zinfandel, and several Italian grapes, with Barbera leading the pack. The modest tasting room sits among acres of vineyards with nice Mt. Adams views. ✉ *5201 Highland Dr.* ☎ *509/829–6970* 🌐 *www.portteus.com.*

Silver Lake

WINERY/DISTILLERY | Often on summer weekends, bands serenade picnickers on what the winery calls their "viniferanda," above their historic estate on the 1,200-foot southern slopes of the Rattlesnake Hills. With both a large deck and well-manicured lawn with a soothing fountain, the winery offers views of vineyards planted chiefly with Cabernet Sauvignon, Riesling, Merlot, and Chardonnay. ✉ *1500 Vintage Rd.* ☎ *509/829–6235* 🌐 *www.silverlakewinery.com* ⏲ *Closed Mon. and Tues.*

Toppenish

PUBLIC ART | This small, friendly town a few miles from Zillah is worth a stop for its more than 75 colorful murals adorning the facades and exterior walls. Commissioned since 1989 by the Toppenish Mural Association and done in a variety of styles by regional artists, they commemorate the town's history and Western spirit. The town lies within the nearly 2,200-square-mile Yakama Reservation and is home to a number of affordable, family-run Mexican restaurants—more than 85% of its 8,800 residents identify as Hispanic or Latino. ✉ *Toppenish Chamber of Commerce, 504 S. Elm St., Toppenish* ☎ *509/865–3262* 🌐 *www.visittoppenish.com.*

★ Two Mountain Winery

WINERY/DISTILLERY | This winery and tasting room occupies an attractive Western-style building with outdoor tables made from wine barrels. It's named for the two mountains that you can see on the western horizon, Mt. Adams and Mt. Rainier. The wines are entirely estate grown and include Chardonnay with just a hint of toasty vanilla notes, a terrific off-dry Riesling, a peppery Lemberger, and a dry but berry-intensive Rosé that often sells out ahead of the rest (try to visit in late spring or summer when there's a decent supply). ✉ *2151 Cheyne Rd.* ☎ *509/829–3900* 🌐 *www.twomountainwinery.com.*

Yakama Nation Cultural Center

NATIVE SITE | **FAMILY** | This six-building complex just outside Toppenish has a fascinating museum of history and culture related to the Yakama Nation, which occupies a 2,200-square-mile reservation. (It's a little bigger than the state of Delaware.) Holdings include costumes, basketry, beadwork, and reconstructions of traditional lodges. Tribal dances and other cultural events are often staged in the Heritage Theater. The complex also includes a gift shop and library. ✉ *Buster Dr. at U.S. 97, Toppenish* ☎ *509/865–2800* 🌐 *www.yakamamuseum.com* 🎟 *$6.*

Restaurants

El Porton

$ | **MEXICAN** | Sample some of the tastiest Mexican-American fare in the valley at this friendly, no-frills establishment. The savory seafood dishes, such as sautéed prawns with mushrooms and garlic, are among the standouts, and traditional offerings like pork chile verde burritos and shredded-beef chimichangas round out the menu. **Known for:** delicious flavored margaritas; reasonably priced meals; fried ice cream with strawberry sauce. $ *Average main: $12* ✉ *905 Vintage Valley Pkwy.* ☎ *509/829–9100.*

Hotels

Best Western Plus Vintage Valley Inn

$ | **HOTEL** | Large, comfortable rooms, a business center, gym, and an indoor pool and spa make this stop just a few steps from Claar Cellars ideal for wine lovers and families alike. **Pros:** short walk from El Porton restaurant; indoor heated pool, spa, and gym; breakfast included. **Cons:** some noise from nearby highway; not much curb appeal; prosaic decor. $ *Rooms from: $124* ✉ *911 Vintage Valley Pkwy.* ☎ *509/829–3399* 🌐 *www.vintagevalleyinn.com* *40 rooms* 🍽 *Free Breakfast.*

Zillah Lakes Inn

$ | **B&B/INN** | In a small residential community a short drive from many of Zillah's top wineries, this modern apartment-style inn and its stone patio, fire pit, and dock overlook the lake for which it's named. **Pros:** guests can use rowboats and canoes on the lake; good base for local wine tours; steps from 6-hole golf course. **Cons:** some rooms don't have lake views; not many dining options nearby; sometimes fully booked for weddings. $ *Rooms from: $145* ✉ *701 Fountain Blvd.* ☎ *509/581–0522* 🌐 *www.zillahlakesinn.com* *7 rooms* 🍽 *No meals.*

Sunnyside

14 miles southeast of Zillah.

The largest community in the lower Yakima Valley, Sunnyside runs along the sunny southern slopes of the Rattlesnake Hills. Not the most charming town in the valley, it nevertheless has a few notable wineries and dining and lodging options, making it a convenient stopover.

GETTING HERE AND AROUND

Interstate 82 runs right past Sunnyside on its way through the lower Yakima Valley.

Sights

★ Co Dinn Cellars

WINERY/DISTILLERY | Co Dinn, the owner of this downtown Sunnyside operation, spent nearly 20 years as the winemaker at renowned Hogue Cellars before establishing his own boutique winery. Top wine publications have taken notice and lavished praise on the complex unfiltered Chardonnay and juicy southern Rhône GSM (Grenache-Syrah-Mourvèdre). The tasting room is in a neatly transformed deco-style former water utility building. ✉ *501 Grant Ave.* ☎ *509/840–2314* 🌐 *www.codinncellars.com* ⏲ *Closed Mon. and Tues.*

Côte Bonneville

WINERY/DISTILLERY | Set in Sunnyside's white-clapboard rail depot, Côte Bonneville winery has earned cult status among discerning sippers for its expressive wines produced from low-yield grape vines on the steep, rocky, south-facing slopes of nearby DuBrul Vineyard. Drop by this art-filled tasting room to sample the superb Cabernet Franc Rosé or one of the richly textured Bordeaux blends. ✉ *1413 E. Edison Ave., Zillah* ☎ *509/840–4596* 🌐 *www.cotebonneville.com* ⏲ *Closed Mon. and Tues.*

Restaurants

Bon Vino's

$ | **AMERICAN** | Look to this casual bakery in downtown Sunnyside for fresh and filling breakfast and lunch fare, from smoked-salmon crepes and mascarpone-stuffed French toast in the morning to caprese paninis and beef or salmon burgers for lunch. There's also a bakery case filled with decadent treats. **Known for:** sweet-savory breakfast combo plates; good stock of local wines; four-layer carrot cake. $ *Average main: $13* ✉ *122 N. 16th St.* ☎ *509/837–3936* 🌐 *www.bonvinosbistro.com* ⏲ *No dinner.*

Hotels

★ **Cozy Rose Inn**

$$$ | **B&B/INN** | Plan a relaxing, pastoral idyll in one of the six extravagantly decorated accommodations at this sunny, refined country inn. **Pros:** full breakfast delivered to your room; wonderfully tranquil setting; convenient to local wineries. **Cons:** somewhat remote location; two-night minimum most weekends; among the highest rates in the area. $ *Rooms from: $229* ✉ *1220 Forsell Rd., Grandview* ☎ *509/882–4669* 🌐 *www.cozyroseinn.com* *6 rooms* *Free Breakfast.*

Sunnyside Inn Bed & Breakfast

$ | **B&B/INN** | Consisting of two neighboring buildings that were constructed in 1919 as a doctor's residence and office, this economical 13-room inn sits in the center of Sunnyside and offers everything from simple, snug rooms to rangy suites with kitchenettes and separate sunrooms. **Pros:** within walking distance of tasting rooms and restaurants; a short drive to several different wineries; reasonable rates. **Cons:** in a busy downtown area; old-fashioned decor; some rooms are dark. $ *Rooms from: $105* ✉ *800–804 E. Edison Ave.* ☎ *509/839–5557, 800/221–4195* 🌐 *www.sunnysideinn.com* *13 rooms* *Free Breakfast.*

Nightlife

★ **Varietal Beer Company**

BREWPUBS/BEER GARDENS | Arguably the most accomplished artisan beer maker in the Lower Valley, Varietal produces an extensive roster of both traditional and experimental brews—including a coffee-infused British style dark ale—as well as first-rate ciders (the one infused with hibiscus is fantastic). Enjoy your sipping at the counter, or head to the back to play some old-school arcade games. ✉ *416 E. Edison Ave.* ☎ *509/515–2222* 🌐 *www.varietalbeer.com.*

Prosser

13 miles southeast of Sunnyside.

On the south bank of the Yakima River, this slice of small-town America has become one of Washington's most illustrious wine-making regions, thanks in part to the proximity of the Horse Heaven Hills AVA (American Viticultural Area). There are now two big clusters of tasting rooms in Prosser, including a number of acclaimed up-and-comers, plus several more wine-making operations on the town's outskirts.

GETTING HERE AND AROUND

On the lower end of the Yakima Valley, Prosser is just off Interstate 82.

ESSENTIALS

VISITOR INFORMATION Prosser Chamber of Commerce. ✉ *1230 Bennett Ave.* ☎ *509/786–3177, 866/343–5101* 🌐 *www.prosserchamber.org.*

Sights

Airfield Estates Winery

WINERY/DISTILLERY | In a cool industrial building designed to resemble a small airplane hangar (there's even a little turret that looks like an air traffic control tower), Airfield is one of the best known and most respected of the several outfits in Vintner's Village, offering a nice range of wine varieties that thrive in these parts—think bold, full-bodied reds. On warm days, bring your dog with you to the landscaped patio. ✉ *560 Merlot Dr.* ☎ *509/203–7646* 🌐 *www.airfieldwines.com.*

★ Alexandria Nicole Cellars

WINERY/DISTILLERY | With an attractive tasting room in the up-and-coming Port of Benton Food and Wine Park on the east side of town, Alexandria Nicole opened its eco-minded winery near the Columbia River—about 35 miles south—in 2004 and has steadily developed into one of the region's stars. The refreshing Viognier and lightly floral Shepherds Market Roussanne-based blend regularly score high marks from *Wine Spectactor,* while the cherry- and plum-inflected Tempranillo is a stellar choice among the reds. Ask about the four tiny houses for rent at the vineyard. ✉ *2880 Lee Rd.* ☎ *509/786–3497* 🌐 *www.alexandrianicolecellars.com.*

★ Desert Wind Winery

WINERY/DISTILLERY | This expansive, airy tasting room housed in an elegant Santa Fe–style building featuring a vast patio overlooking the Yakima River is one of the highlights of any wine tour in the valley. Notable bottles include the Sémillon, Barbera, Petit Verdot, and a crowd-pleasing everyday red blend, the Ruah. For the ultimate experience, book a full tour of the winery, which includes barrel tastings and pairings with light snacks. Just off Interstate 82, this family-owned winery also includes a luxurious four-room inn as well as a gift shop with Yakima Valley edibles. ✉ *2258 Wine Country Rd.* ☎ *509/786–7277* 🌐 *www.desertwindwinery.com.*

14 Hands Winery

WINERY/DISTILLERY | One of the largest and most widely distributed wine producers in Washington, equestrian-theme 14 Hands is perhaps best known for its Hot to Trot, Stampede, and other wallet-friendly blends, but a visit to the winery provides you with the chance to sample some harder-to-find bottles. Consider the Reserve Petit Verdot, dry sparkling Brut, and peach- and melon-accented Reserve Chenin Blanc. The tasting room occupies a sleek, angular building made from reclaimed barn wood that's flanked by a large patio. ✉ *660 Frontier Rd.* ☎ *509/786–5514* 🌐 *www.14hands.com.*

Kestrel Vintners

WINERY/DISTILLERY | Don't be put off by the industrial look of the Port of Benton's Wine and Food Park—it's home to several superb wineries, including Kestrel, which has long been acclaimed for its full-bodied reds (Cabernet Sauvignon, Merlot, and Syrah) and eclectic mix of whites (Chardonnay, Viognier, and Sauvignon Blanc). They're made from grapes—some of them estate grown—that are deliberately stressed to increase the intensity of their flavors. The tasting room sells cheeses and deli items, too. ✉ *2890 Lee Rd.* ☎ *509/786–2675* 🌐 *www.kestrelwines.com* ⊙ *Closed Mon.–Thurs.*

★ Martinez & Martinez Winery

WINERY/DISTILLERY | Opened by the son of an immigrant farm worker who first began planting grapes in Horse Heaven Hills back in 1981, this small winery with an in-the-know following focuses mostly on reds, including a renowned Carménère. A favorite draw on hot days in their tasting room inside the Tuscan-style Winemakers Loft building is the Rosérita wine slushie. ✉ *357 Port Ave* ☎ *509/786–2392* 🌐 *www.martinezwine.com.*

Thurston Wolfe

WINERY/DISTILLERY | Established in 1987, one of Prosser's top mid-price wineries features Wade Wolfe's unusual blends, including a tropical fruit–forward white Pinot Gris–Viognier and a seductive Zinfandel, Petite Sirah, Lemberger blend known as Dr. Wolfe's Family Red. ✉ *588 Cabernet Ct.* ☎ *509/786–3313* 🌐 *www.thurstonwolfe.com* ⏲ *Closed Mon.–Wed. and additional days in winter (call first).*

★ **Walter Clore Wine & Culinary Center**

MARKET | Although not a winery per se, this handsome tasting room, market, and education center exists to help educate the public about wine-making. Interactive displays inside this nonprofit center trace the history of the state's viticulture, including a tribute to wine pioneer Walter Clore. Big wall maps show the state's key grape growing regions, and you can sample a rotating selection of wines at the tasting bar. Wine-friendly appetizers are also available Thursday through Saturday. ✉ *2140A Wine Country Dr.* ☎ *509/786–1000* 🌐 *www.theclorecenter.org.*

Wautoma Springs

WINERY/DISTILLERY | One of Yakima Valley's most buzzed-about up-and-coming wine operations, Wautoma Springs was founded by Jessica Munnell and Tom Merkle, two highly respected names in the state's viticultural community. They've quickly developed a following for a crisp Sauvignon Blanc with melon and grapefruit notes, and an inky reserve Malbec (it's literally named Inky) that you'll want to serve at your next steak dinner. The tasting room is in a newer section of Vintner's Village, in an airy, high-ceilinged building with comfy seating. ✉ *236 Port Ave.* 🌐 *www.wautomasprings.com* ⏲ *Closed Mon.–Thurs.*

★ **Wit Cellars**

WINERY/DISTILLERY | Another of Prosser's crop of young wineries that have quickly developed a big reputation, Wit Cellars offers tastings in a dapper little space in the Port of Benton Food and Wine Park. In addition to producing an eclectic array of superb wines, from a old-world-style Cabernet Franc to a late-harvest Riesling and a port-style Petit Verdot dessert wines, the winery stands out for its exceptionally welcoming staff. ✉ *2880 Lee Rd.* ☎ *509/786–1311* 🌐 *www.witcellars.com* ⏲ *Closed Mon.–Wed.*

Restaurants

Brewminatti

$ | CAFÉ | Whether for a morning macchiato, a bagel breakfast sandwich, a lunchtime panini, or a late-afternoon slice of cake, this roomy coffeehouse with hardwood floors, comfy armchairs, and café tables works nicely for a quick pick-me-up or a more leisurely meal. Although generally open only during the day, this downtown hangout opens many weekend evenings to host live rock, jazz, and country musicians. **Known for:** well-crafted espresso drinks; excellent breakfast and lunch sandwiches; friendly vibe. $ *Average main: $6* ✉ *713 6th St.* ☎ *509/786–2269* 🌐 *www.brewminatti.com* ⏲ *Closed Sun. No dinner.*

Horse Heaven Saloon

$$ | AMERICAN | Named for the nearby rolling hills that have become synonymous with some of Yakima Valley's top vineyards, this convivial Wild West–inspired saloon-meets-gastropub does pour a variety of local wines, but it also serves hop-forward craft brews from adjoining Heaven Hills Brewery. In a fun space decorated with murals of galloping steeds and old-time street scenes, feast on smoked tri-tip, country-style meat loaf, beer-baked mac and cheese, and eight types of burgers. **Known for:** tender steaks and prodigious burgers; excellent craft beer and local wine list; engaging old-time-saloon vibe. 💲 *Average main: $18* ✉ *615 6th St.* ☎ *509/781–6228* 🌐 *www.horseheavensaloonprosser.com* 🕒 *Closed Mon.*

Whitstran Steaks & Spirits
$$ | **STEAKHOUSE** | In a modern, stylish building on the north edge of downtown, close to Prosser's winery districts, this unpretentious steak and seafood restaurant with black-leather booths and banquette seating offers plenty of great dishes to pair with Yakima Valley wines (of which it stocks a considerable selection). Filet mignon, steak frites, and classic Caesar salads star on a menu that also includes a variety of sandwiches, burgers, and taco plates. **Known for:** hearty, meat-centric American fare; pleasant seasonal patio; New York–style cheesecake. 💲 *Average main: $22* ✉ *1427 Wine Country Rd.* ☎ *509/781–6266* 🕒 *Closed Sun.*

★ **Wine o'Clock**
$$ | **MODERN AMERICAN** | Smack in the center of Vintner's Village, steps from more than a dozen tasting rooms, this smartly casual bistro is a delightful spot for a relaxing lunch, with its open kitchen, fresh flowers on the tables, and handful of outside seats set among the restaurant's herb and vegetable gardens. Share a few small plates with friends—maybe goat cheese fondue with fresh fruit or crisp-crust pizza with seasonal ingredients from the wood-fired oven—or consider a more substantial meal, such as bouillabaisse or pork tenderloin with apple compote. **Known for:** antipasto plates and light tapas; one of the best local wine selections; dark-chocolate truffled brownies. 💲 *Average main: $22* ✉ *548 Cabernet Ct.* ☎ *509/786–2197* 🌐 *www.bunnellfamilycellar.com* 🕒 *Closed Tues. and Wed.*

★ **Inn at Desert Wind**
$$$$ | **B&B/INN** | The four cushiest guest suites in the Yakima Valley occupy the upper floors of the beautiful Desert Wind Winery, and each of these Santa Fe–style hideaways abounds with warm, inviting features—kiva-style gas fireplaces, leather armchairs, hardwood floors, Oriental rugs, and balconies overlooking a sunny courtyard, the Yakima River, and Mt. Adams. **Pros:** gorgeous bathrooms with top-of-the-line beauty products; large suites with endless views; Walter Clore Wine Center is next door. **Cons:** no indoor common spaces except for tasting room; often books up well in advance on weekends; no restaurants within walking distance. 💲 *Rooms from: $255* ✉ *2258 Wine Country Rd.* ☎ *509/786–7277* 🌐 *www.desertwindwinery.com* *4 rooms* *Free Breakfast.*

Shopping

Chukar Cherries
FOOD/CANDY | Since 1988, this shop featuring chocolates, sauces, relishes, and dozens of other gourmet goods made with Bing, Rainier, Black Forest, and other cherries grown on the family orchard has been a favorite stop for foodies. Help yourself to the many free samples. ✉ *320 Wine Country Rd.* ☎ *800/624–9544* 🌐 *www.chukar.com.*

Benton City

16 miles east of Prosser.

Benton City, with a mere 3,300 residents, sits on a bluff west of the river facing vineyard-cloaked Red Mountain. High-carbonate soil, a location in a unique high-pressure pocket, and geographical anomalies have led to this district's being given its own appellation. You can access most of the wineries from Highway 224.

GETTING HERE AND AROUND

You'll find Benton City just off Interstate 82 and the very end of the lower Yakima Valley—it bumps right up against West Richland and the Tri-Cities region.

Sights

★ Fidelitas Wines

WINERY/DISTILLERY | This vaunted boutique winery with sweeping views specializes is a darling of critics who appreciate its exceptional Bordeaux wines, including one of the state's most accomplished Malbecs. The tasting room is modern, bright, and airy, and outdoor seating areas provide a spectacular backdrop for indulging in these rich wines. ⊠ *51810 N. Sunset Rd.* ☎ *509/588–3469* 🌐 *www.fidelitaswines.com.*

Frichette Winery

WINERY/DISTILLERY | This husband-and-wife-owned estate is one of Benton City's younger properties, but it has quickly developed a strong fan base for its polished, mostly Bordeaux-style wines, including a velvety Merlot and a refreshing Semillon that's a perfect match with Northwest seafood. The airy, industrial-chic tasting room has comfy armchairs and a patio overlooking the vineyards. ⊠ *39412 N. Sunset Rd.* ☎ *509/426–3227* 🌐 *www.frichettewinery.com.*

Hedges Family Estate

WINERY/DISTILLERY | The most recognized of Red Mountain's many acclaimed wineries occupies a spectacular hillside château that looks like it could have been plucked straight out of the Bordeaux countryside. Indeed, the estate specializes in the classic French wines that excel in Benton City, with Cabernet Sauvignon and Syrah leading the charge. On cool days, sip your wine by the fire in the grand tasting room; in summer, have a seat on the patio overlooking the neatly groomed gardens. ⊠ *53511 N. Sunset Rd.* ☎ *509/588–3155* 🌐 *www.hedgesfamilyestate.com* ⏲ *Closed Sun. and Mon. in Dec.–Mar. and Mon. and Tues. in Apr.–Nov.*

★ Kiona Vineyards Winery

WINERY/DISTILLERY | John Williams planted the first grapes on Red Mountain in 1975, made his first Kiona Vineyards wines in 1980, and produced the first commercial Lemberger, a light German red, in the United States. Today the winery boasts a beautiful 10,000-square-foot tasting room with 180-degree views of Red Mountain and the Rattlesnake Hills, an idyllic setting for sampling top-notch Mourvèdre Rosé, late harvest Riesling, Chenin Blanc ice wine, Gewürztraminer, Sangiovese, and many others. You can order charcuterie and cheese plates to enjoy inside or on the patio. ⊠ *44612 N. Sunset Rd.* ☎ *509/588–6716* 🌐 *www.kionawine.com.*

Terra Blanca

WINERY/DISTILLERY | It's named for the calcium carbonate in the earth beneath it—Terra Blanca is Latin for "white earth"—and from this favorable soil grow wine grapes that produce the winery's specialties: Syrah, Merlot, Cabernet Sauvignon, and Chardonnay. This picturesque estate winery offers sweeping views of the Red Mountain region, and also has one of the only restaurants in Benton City, serving refined Pacific Northwest fare. ⊠ *34715 N. Demoss Rd.* ☎ *509/588–6082* 🌐 *www.terrablanca.com.*

Upchurch Vineyard

WINERY/DISTILLERY | This timber-frame winery and tasting room was opened on a sunny slope at the south end of Benton City by Chris Upchurch, founding winemaker of acclaimed DeLille Cellars and one of Washington's pioneers in aging wines in concrete tanks, a practice with Roman roots. Focused on sustainable vineyard management, his winery produces a short but critically acclaimed list of mostly Bordeaux-style wines. ⊠ *32901 Vineyard View PR NE* ☎ *425/298–4923* 🌐 *www.upchurchvineyard.com* ⏲ *Closed Mon.–Wed.*

Chapter 19

SPOKANE AND EASTERN WASHINGTON

Updated by
Shelley Arenas

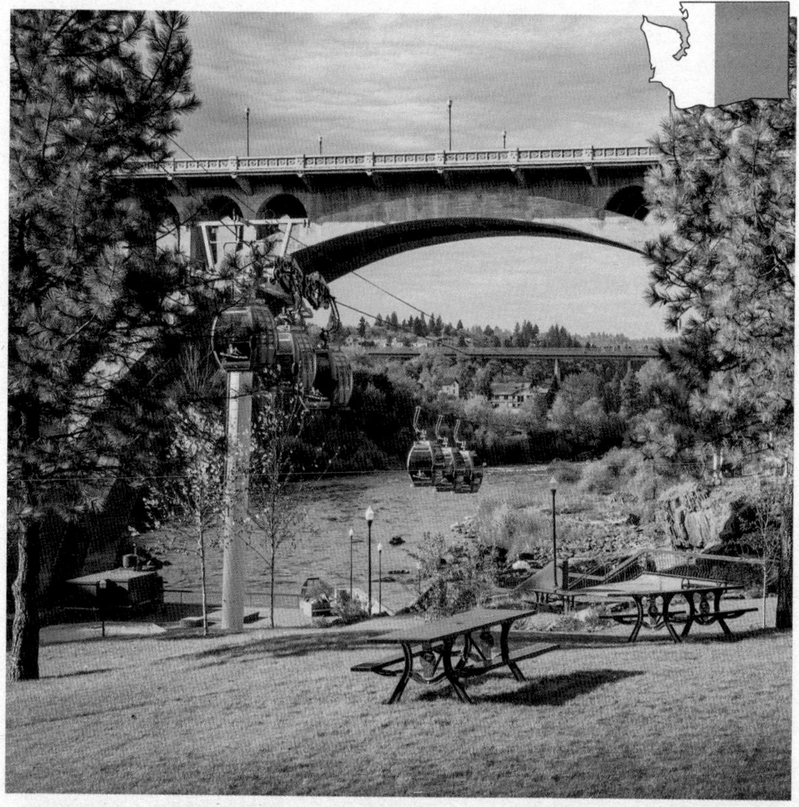

Sights ★★★★★ | Restaurants ★★★★☆ | Hotels ★★★☆☆ | Shopping ★☆☆☆☆ | Nightlife ☆☆☆☆☆

WELCOME TO SPOKANE AND EASTERN WASHINGTON

TOP REASONS TO GO

★ **Historic lodgings:** Take a step back in time. Visit the historic hotels and inns in Spokane and Walla Walla, which have been updated with modern amenities and high-tech touches, yet retain the flavor of yesteryear.

★ **Natural wonders:** Get off the beaten path to experience the unique waters of Soap Lake, see the cliffs and canyons along the Columbia River, and hike in national forests.

★ **Wineries:** Explore the many wineries in Walla Walla, Tri-Cities, and Spokane.

★ **Family attractions:** Slip in a little education on your family vacation by visiting pioneer museums, then play at water parks and Spokane's sprawling Riverfront Park.

★ **Big sporting events:** Join more than 50,000 runners in one of the largest timed running races in the nation—Spokane's annual 12K Bloomsday Run. And take to the streets for the biggest 3-on-3 basketball tournament in the world, Spokane's annual Hoopfest.

1 **Richland.** Richland has more than 100 wineries.

2 **Pasco.** The Lewis and Clark Expedition passed through here.

3 **Kennewick.** Kennewick has the largest population of the Tri-Cities.

4 **Walla Walla.** Walla Walla is a mecca for wine lovers.

5 **Dayton.** Dayton is known for its buildings on the National Register of Historic Places.

6 **Pullman.** Home to Washington State University, Pullman has a freewheeling style.

7 **Spokane.** Spokane has impressive waterfalls and eateries.

8 **Moses Lake.** Moses Lake is in the desert part of the state.

9 **Quincy.** Home to the award-winning concert venue, the Gorge.

10 **Ephrata.** This pleasant farm town is the closest community to Soap Lake.

11 **Coulee Dam National Recreation Area.** This mile-long concrete dam is an impressive sight.

12 **Omak.** Omak is in the heart of Okanogan Valley.

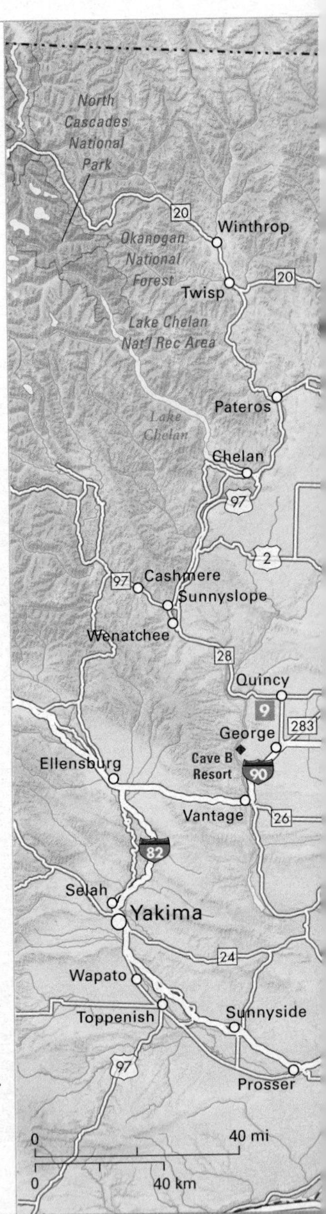

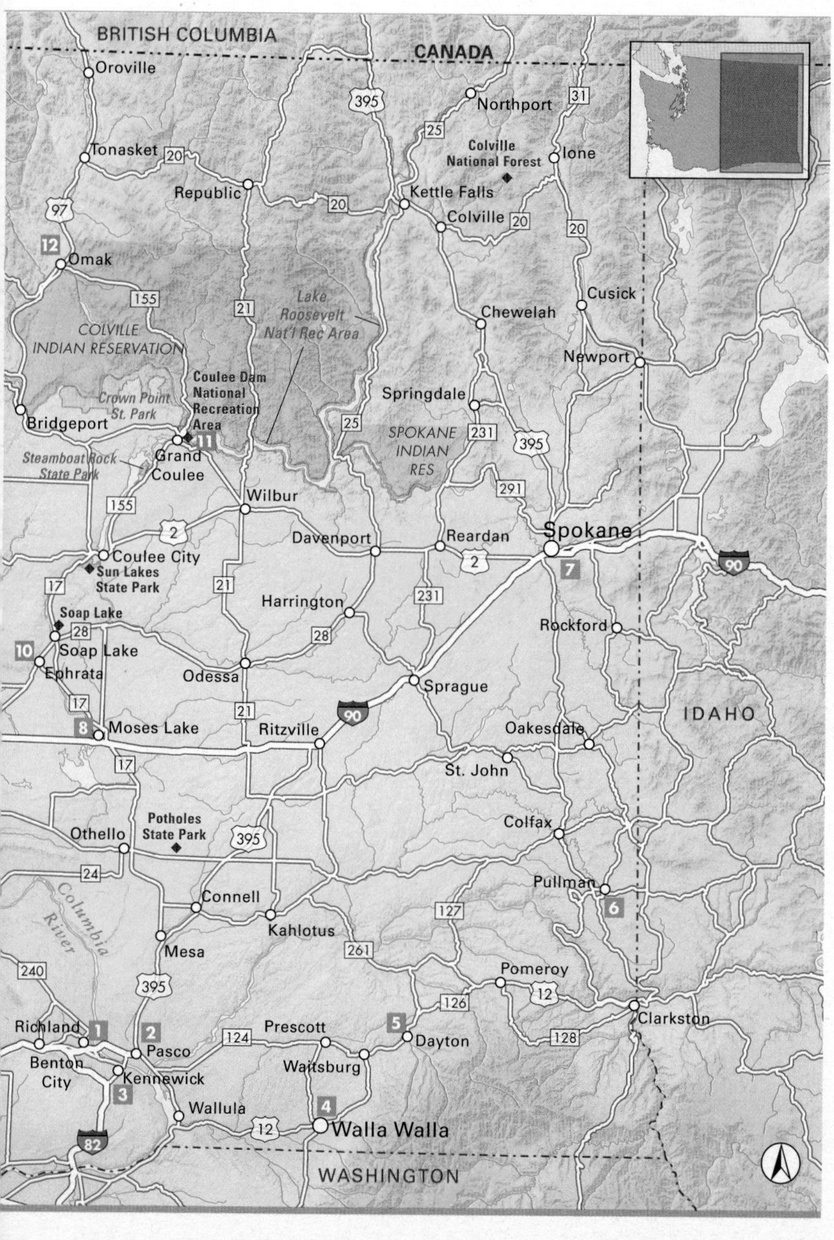
BRITISH COLUMBIA
CANADA
Oroville
Northport
Tonasket
Colville National Forest
Ione
Republic
Kettle Falls
Colville
Omak
Cusick
Lake Roosevelt Nat'l Rec Area
Chewelah
COLVILLE INDIAN RESERVATION
Newport
Coulee Dam National Recreation Area
Crown Point St. Park
Springdale
Bridgeport
SPOKANE INDIAN RES
Steamboat Rock State Park
Grand Coulee
Wilbur
Davenport
Reardan
Spokane
Coulee City
Sun Lakes State Park
Harrington
Soap Lake
Rockford
Soap Lake
Ephrata
Odessa
Sprague
Moses Lake
Ritzville
Oakesdale
IDAHO
St. John
Potholes State Park
Othello
Colfax
Columbia River
Connell
Pullman
Kahlotus
Mesa
Pomeroy
Clarkston
Richland
Prescott
Dayton
Pasco
Benton City
Waitsburg
Kennewick
Wallula
Walla Walla
WASHINGTON
395
31
25
20
97
155
21
231
291
2
90
17
28
24
240
127
261
126
12
124
128
82
1
2
3
4
5
6
7
8
10
11
12

The Columbia Plateau was created by a series of lava flows that were later deeply cut by glacial floods. Because its soil is mostly made up of alluvial deposits and windblown silt (known to geologists as loess), it's very fertile. But little annual rainfall means that its vast central section—more than 30,000 square miles from the foothills of the Cascades and the northeastern mountains east to Idaho and south to Oregon—has no forests. In fact, except for a few scattered pine trees in the north, oaks in the southwest, and willows and cottonwoods along creeks and rivers, it has no trees.

This treeless expanse is part of an even larger steppe and desert region that runs north into Canada and south to California and the Sea of Cortez. There is water, however, carried from the mountains by the great Columbia and Snake Rivers and their tributaries. Irrigation provides the region's cities with shrubs, trees, and flowers, and its fields bear a great variety of crops: asparagus, potatoes, apples, peaches, alfalfa, sweet corn, wheat, lentils, and much more. This bounty of agriculture makes the region prosperous, and provides funds for symphony halls and opera houses, theaters, art museums, and universities.

Southeast of the Columbia Plateau lies a region of rolling hills and fields. Farmers of the Palouse region and of the foothills of the Blue Mountains don't need to irrigate their fields, as rain here produces record crops of wheat, lentils, and peas. It's a blessed landscape, flowing green and golden under the sun in waves of loam. In the Walla Walla Valley the traditional crops of wheat and sweet onions remain, but more than 2,800 acres of grapes now supply nearly 150 wineries that have opened in the past few decades. The region is not only fertile, it is historically significant as well. The Lewis and Clark expedition passed through the Palouse in 1805, and Walla Walla was one of the earliest settlements in the Inland Northwest. You can learn about its past by visiting the local museum and national historic site, then indulge in the food, wine, and luxurious lodgings of present-day Walla Walla.

The northeastern mountains, from the Okanogan to the Pend Oreille Valley, consist of granite peaks, glaciated cliffs, grassy uplands, and sunlit forests. Few Washingtonians seem to know about this region's attractions, however. Even at the height of the summer its roads and trails are rarely crowded and today's explorers of these wild areas are rewarded with up-close views of wildlife and natural beauty. The Grand Coulee Dam, which took nearly a decade to build in the 1930s, created the 150-mile-long Lake Roosevelt, where recreational activities abound.

While eastern Washington's stunning natural features, varied topography, agricultural bounty, and abundant outdoor recreation contribute to a sense of spaciousness that is remote and rural, the area is also home to Washington's second-largest city, Spokane. Known as the "Capital of the Inland Empire," Spokane is the cultural and financial center of the Inland Northwest, with a rich history. Its dry, hot summers and excellent urban parks, golf courses, and nearby lakes and the Spokane River, make it easy to plan golf, fishing, and hiking excursions. Snowy winters mean plenty of time to enjoy skiing, snowboarding, and sledding, too.

MAJOR REGIONS

Southeastern Washington. In the wide-open areas of the Walla Walla and Columbia Valleys, hillsides are covered with rows of grapevines and wind turbines. Lodging, restaurants, museums, and wine-tasting opportunities can be found in Walla Walla and the Tri-Cities. Farther east are historic Dayton and the college town of Pullman.

Spokane. The second-largest city in Washington is home to one of the state's best hotels, the restored Davenport, and several other historic lodgings. There are numerous restaurants, from fine dining to family-friendly; a fun kids' museum and science museum, and an interesting history museum; and two especially notable parks (Manito, with its duck pond and Japanese Garden, and Riverfront, with lots of activities for the whole family).

East Central Washington. The highway through central Washington's desert lands can seem endless, but the farmers of Grant County's irrigated lands perk things up a bit with crop signs in the fences and lighted holiday displays. Venture off the main route to discover the stunning Cave B Resort by the Columbia River, see pioneer-history displays in Ephrata, and experience the healing waters of Soap Lake, before heading back on Interstate 90 through Moses Lake.

Northeastern Washington. Travelers to this region will find the "Eighth Technological Wonder of the World"—the Grand Coulee Dam—which features a daily laser-light show in summer. Further exploration brings you to the Colville and Okanogan national forests, and the small towns of Grand Coulee, Coulee City, and Omak.

Planning

When to Go

Eastern Washington has four distinct seasons, with generally very hot summers and sometimes very snowy winters. Recreational activities are geared to the specific season, with several downhill ski resorts open for skiing and snowboarding, and Nordic skiing available in the national forests, too. In summer, water activities on the lakes and rivers are popular, and there are many places to pursue hiking, backpacking, cycling, and fishing. Eastern Washington rarely feels crowded, though popular campgrounds may fill in summer. Lodging rates tend to be higher between Memorial Day and Labor Day, so visiting off-season can reduce costs. Spring and fall are both beautiful seasons to explore the region. In smaller towns certain attractions are open only from May through September, so call ahead to plan visits to sights.

FESTIVALS AND EVENTS

The region's rich bounty of viniculture and agriculture is celebrated with festivals throughout the year.

Bloomsday

FESTIVAL | On the first Sunday of May, more than 50,000 runners course 12 km (7½ miles) through downtown Spokane and the northwest part of the city. ✉ *Spokane* ☎ *509/838–1579* 🌐 *www.bloomsdayrun.org.*

Farmer Consumer Awareness Day

FESTIVAL | Farms and processing plants in Quincy throw an open house on a Saturday every September so consumers can get a closer look at where their food comes from. There are exhibits, food booths, and a farmers' market. ✉ *Quincy* ☎ *509/787–2140* 🌐 *www.quincyfarmer-consumer.com.*

Green Bluff Growers Festivals

FESTIVAL | The association of small farms and food stands in Green Bluff (about 20 miles northeast of downtown Spokane) presents several festivals as orchard fruits come into season. Strawberries are celebrated in late June and early July, cherries in July, peaches mid-August through Labor Day, and apples late September through late October. There's also a Holiday Festival in November and December. ✉ *Hwy. 2 and Green Bluff Rd., Colbert* 🌐 *www.greenbluffgrowers.com.*

Hoopfest

FESTIVAL | The last weekend in June, basketball mania descends on downtown Spokane as Hoopfest comes to town, a mega tournament with more than 6,000 teams and 24,000 players playing 3-on-3 basketball on more than 400 courts on 45 city blocks. It's the world's largest event of its type, with 250,000 fans in attendance. ✉ *Spokane* ☎ *509/624–2414* 🌐 *www.spokanehoopfest.net.*

Pig Out in the Park

FESTIVAL | Locals and tourists flock to Riverfront Park over Labor Day for a six-day food fest featuring local fare and nonstop live music. ✉ *Riverfront Park, 507 N. Howard St., Spokane* ☎ *509/921–5579* 🌐 *www.spokanepigout.com.*

Spokane Lilac Festival

FESTIVAL | Parades and other events honor the flower that gives Spokane the moniker "Lilac City." ✉ *Spokane* ☎ *509/535–4554* 🌐 *www.spokanelilacfestival.org.*

Walla Walla Wine Festivals

FESTIVAL | The Walla Walla Valley Wine Alliance coordinates Walla Walla Valley Wine Month in April; Spring Release Weekend in May; Fall Release Weekend in November; and Holiday Barrel Tasting in December. ✉ *Walla Walla* ☎ *509/526–3117* 🌐 *www.wallawallawine.com.*

Getting Here and Around

AIR

Spokane International Airport is the main hub for air travel in eastern Washington. Smaller airports include Pullman, Tri-Cities, Walla Walla, and Lewiston, Idaho (across the border from Clarkston). Spokane International Airport is served by Alaska, American, Delta, Southwest, and United; the Tri-Cities Airport is served by Alaska, Allegiant, Delta, and United. Horizon Air has service to Walla Walla, and Alaska serves Pullman.

CONTACTS Lewiston-Nez Perce County Airport. ✉ *406 Burrell Ave., Lewiston* ☎ *208/746–4471* 🌐 *www.golws.com.* **Pullman-Moscow Regional Airport.** ✉ *3200 Airport Complex N, Pullman* ☎ *509/338–3223* 🌐 *www.flypuw.com.* **Spokane International Airport.** ✉ *9000 W. Airport*

Dr., Spokane ☏ *509/455–6455* 🌐 *www.spokaneairports.net.* **Tri-Cities Airport.** ✉ *3601 N. 20th Ave., Pasco* ☏ *509/547–6352* 🌐 *www.flytricities.com.* **Walla Walla Regional Airport.** ✉ *45 Terminal Loop Rd., Walla Walla* ☏ *509/525–3100* 🌐 *www.wallawallaairport.com.*

CAR

Interstate 90 is the most direct route from Seattle to Spokane over the Cascade Mountains (Snoqualmie Pass). U.S. 2 (Stevens Pass), an alternate route, begins north of Seattle near Everett, and passes through Wenatchee and Coulee City. South of Interstate 90, U.S. 395 leads to the Tri-Cities from the east; the Tri-Cities can also be accessed via Interstate 82 from the west. Past the Tri-Cities, continue on Interstate 82 then U.S. 12 to reach Walla Walla. U.S. 195 traverses southeastern Washington to Pullman. Leave U.S. 195 at Colfax, heading southwest on Highway 26 and then 127, and finally U.S. 12 to Dayton and Walla Walla. Gas stations along the main highways cater to truckers, and some are open 24 hours.

Restaurants

Local diners and cafés are great spots for getting a hearty breakfast of traditional favorites like farm-fresh eggs or biscuits and gravy. Spokane has a good diversity of cuisines and some highly acclaimed restaurants, but up-and-coming Walla Walla is also becoming a hot spot for foodies and wine lovers.

Hotels

Family-owned motels and budget chains are prevalent in small towns like Grand Coulee, Moses Lake, Omak, Pullman, and Soap Lake. Several pleasant bed-and-breakfasts with friendly innkeepers are found in Spokane, Walla Walla, and Uniontown (near Pullman), but with no more than seven suites at each it's necessary to call ahead for a reservation. There are several historic hotels built in the early 1900s and restored in recent years that are definitely worth visiting in Spokane, Walla Walla, and Dayton. The Inn at Abeja, just outside Walla Walla on a historic farm site, offers unique, high-end lodging. A stay at the Cave B Resort by the Columbia River—in one of its cliff houses, cavern rooms, or luxury yurts—is a recommended destination experience, too. *Hotel reviews have been shortened. For full information, visit Fodors.com.*

What It Costs in U.S. Dollars

	$	$$	$$$	$$$$
RESTAURANTS	under $16	$16–$22	$23–$30	over $30
HOTELS	under $150	$150–$200	$201–$250	over $250

Richland

202 miles southeast of Seattle, 145 miles southwest of Spokane.

Richland is the northernmost of the three municipalities along the bank of the Columbia River known as the Tri-Cities (the others are Pasco and Kennewick). Founded in the 1880s, Richland was a pleasant farming village until 1942, when the federal government built a nuclear reactor on the nearby Hanford Nuclear Reservation. The Hanford site was instrumental in the building of the Tri-Cities, and still plays a major role in the area's economy. In recent years this has also become a major wine-producing area. You can find more than 100 wineries within a 50-mile radius, many with tasting rooms.

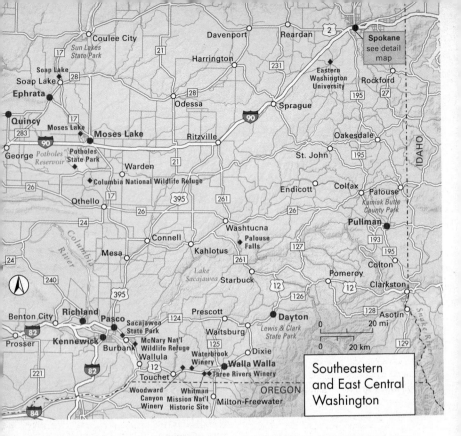

Southeastern and East Central Washington

GETTING HERE AND AROUND

The Tri-Cities Airport in Pasco is served by Alaska, Allegiant, Delta, and United. Taxis and rental cars are available there. Some hotels also offer an airport shuttle. Greyhound Bus Lines and Amtrak's Empire Builder both stop in Pasco. Ben Franklin Transit serves all three cities. By car, Interstate 82 is the main east–west highway; from Ritzville or Spokane, take Highway 395 to reach the Tri-Cities; from Ellensburg and Yakima, take Highway 82 south and east.

CONTACT Ben Franklin Transit. ☎ *509/735–5100* 🌐 *www.bft.org.*

ESSENTIALS

VISITOR INFORMATION Richland Visitor's Center. ✉ *Richland City Hall, 625 Swift Blvd.* ☎ *800/254–5824* 🌐 *www.visittri-cities.com.* **Tri-Cities Visitor and Convention Bureau.** ✉ *7130 W. Grandridge Blvd., Suite B, Kennewick* ☎ *800/254–5824, 509/735–8486* 🌐 *www.visittri-cities.com.*

Sights

Barnard Griffin Winery and Tasting Room

WINERY/DISTILLERY | Owners Rob Griffin and Deborah Barnard offer a variety of fine wines, including excellent Merlot and Cabernet. The Kitchen at Barnard Griffin features farm-to-table cuisine to enjoy with wine pairings; there's live music some nights, too. The art gallery adds class to the wine-tasting experience. ✉ *878 Tulip La.* ☎ *509/627–0266* 🌐 *www.barnardgriffin.com* ⏲ *Restaurant closed Mon. and Tues. No dinner Sun.*

Bookwalter Winery

WINERY/DISTILLERY | Next door to Barnard Griffin Winery, Bookwalter produces red wines aged in French oak barrels and whites that are 100% stainless-steel fermented. The classic Merlot is celebrated. Blends are prevalent in both reds and whites. The on-site restaurant, Fiction, has made the top 10 on several "best winery restaurant" lists. ✉ *894 Tulip La.* ☎ *509/627–5000* 🌐 *www.bookwalterwines.com.*

The REACH (*The Hanford Reach Interpretive Center*)
MUSEUM | Here's the place to learn about the Hanford Reach National Monument, an area that encompasses the Hanford Reach of the Columbia River and greater Columbia Basin and surrounds the former site of the Hanford Nuclear Reservation. The interpretive center highlights the region's history, culture, science and technology, natural resources and agriculture, and arts. The exhibit area has permanent exhibits on the Columbia Basin Project's irrigated agriculture, the history of the atomic age and Hanford's contribution to ending World War II, and the Columbia River's role in producing electrical power. Special events include tours, classes, and culinary events highlighting the area's wineries and agriculture. The 18-acre setting on the Columbia River includes outdoor exhibits, a nature trail, and a stage where concerts are held in the summer. ✉ *1943 Columbia Park Trail* ☎ *509/943–4100* 🌐 *www.visitthereach.org* 🎫 *$10* ⏲ *Closed Mon., closed Sun. early Sept.–mid-May.*

Restaurants

Anthony's at Columbia Point
$$$$ | **SEAFOOD** | The Anthony's chain is renowned for fine waterfront dining in western Washington, and this outpost on the Columbia River waterfront continues the tradition. Seafood is the specialty—from fish-focused appetizers, including panfried Willapa Bay oysters and fresh Northwest littleneck clams, to entrées with Dungeness crab (whole, in fettuccine, or in crab cakes), Idaho rainbow trout, Alaskan weathervane scallops, char-grilled Alaskan halibut, and salmon. **Known for:** weekday sunset three- and four-course dinners; fresh seafood from the Northwest and Alaska regions; moorage for guests arriving by boat. 💲 *Average main: $32* ✉ *550 Columbia Point Dr.* ☎ *509/946–3474* 🌐 *www.anthonys.com.*

Atomic Ale Brewpub and Eatery
$$ | **AMERICAN** | The staff is friendly at this small, casual brewpub, which serves several house-brewed beers to go with the delicious wood-fired pizzas, sandwiches (the hot grinder is a specialty), salads, and soups. Local memorabilia is displayed throughout the restaurant, and the history of the Hanford Nuclear Site is depicted in photos on the walls. **Known for:** red-potato soup made with in-house brew; spicy "nuclear butter" adds heat to dishes; delicious desserts. 💲 *Average main: $18* ✉ *1015 Lee Blvd.* ☎ *509/946–5465* 🌐 *www.atomicalebrewpub.com.*

Monterosso's Italian Restaurant
$$ | **ITALIAN** | In a refurbished railroad dining car, this small and charming Italian restaurant is fun for the whole family, but it's also a nice choice for a romantic meal. The traditional fare includes bruschetta, chicken and veal Parmesan, and several steak and seafood options. **Known for:** homemade tiramisu and cheesecake; more than a dozen wine choices; authentic Italian dishes. 💲 *Average main: $20* ✉ *1026 Lee Blvd.* ☎ *509/946–4525* 🌐 *www.monterossos.com* ⏲ *Closed Sun. No lunch Mon. and Sat.*

Hotels

Lodge at Columbia Point
$$$$ | **HOTEL** | This hotel has a luxurious feel inside and out, thanks to its handsome facade overlooking the river or facing the mountains. **Pros:** the only four-star hotel in the area; 1-mile River Walk right outside; easy access to marina. **Cons:** customer service has been inconsistent; some rooms prone to noise from outside; minimum stay on weekends.

Rooms from: $250 ✉ 530 Columbia Pt. Dr. ☎ 509/713–7423, 844/200–8641 🌐 lodgeatcolumbiapoint.com 82 rooms Free Breakfast.

Riverfront Hotel

$ | **HOTEL** | **FAMILY** | Given a head-to-toe renovation in 2020, this lodging on the Columbia River has a fresh look and up-to-date amenities (coffeemakers, microwaves, refrigerators, and fold-down ironing units) that make it convenient for both business and leisure guests. **Pros:** easy access to trails and parks; pleasant riverfront location; family-friendly vibe. **Cons:** rooms near the outdoor pool can be noisy; ask for a pet-free room if you have allergies; no elevators. *Rooms from: $129 ✉ 50 Comstock St. ☎ 509/946–4661 🌐 www.richlandriverfronthotel.com 136 rooms Free Breakfast.*

Pasco

10 miles east of Richland.

Tree-shaded Pasco, a college town and the Franklin County seat, is an oasis of green on the Columbia River near a site where the Lewis and Clark expedition made camp in 1805. The city began as a railroad switchyard and now has a busy container port. The neoclassical Franklin County Courthouse (1907) is worth a visit for its fine marble interior.

The Pasco Basin has first-rate vineyards and wineries and some of the state's most fertile land. You can purchase the regional bounty at the farmers' market, held downtown every Wednesday and Saturday morning during the growing season.

GETTING HERE AND AROUND

The Tri-Cities Airport is in Pasco; Alaska, Allegiant, Delta, and United operate there. Taxis and rental cars are both available, and some hotels offer an airport shuttle. Ben Franklin Transit serves all three cities. By car, Interstate 82 is the main east–west highway; from Ritzville or Spokane, take Highway 395 to reach the Tri-Cities; from Ellensburg and Yakima, take Interstate 82 south and east.

ESSENTIALS

VISITOR INFORMATION City of Pasco. *☎ 509/544–3080 🌐 www.pasco-wa.gov.*

Sights

Franklin County Historical Museum

MUSEUM | Here you'll find numerous items illustrating local history, including Native American artifacts. Revolving exhibits have featured the Lewis and Clark expedition, the railroad, World War II, agriculture, and aviation. *✉ 305 N. 4th Ave. ☎ 509/547–3714 🌐 www.franklincountyhistoricalsociety.org $5 Closed Sun. and Mon.; Jan. and Feb.*

Sacajawea State Park

NATIONAL/STATE PARK | At the confluence of the Snake and Columbia Rivers, this park occupies the site of Ainsworth, a railroad town that flourished from 1879 to 1884. It's named for the Shoshoni woman who guided the Lewis and Clark expedition over the Rocky Mountains and down the Snake River. The 284-acre day-use park has an interpretive center and a large display of Native American tools. A beach, boat launch, picnic area, and children's playground round out the facilities; sand dunes, marshes, and ponds are great for watching wildlife. *✉ 2503 Sacajawea Park Rd. Off U.S. 12, 5 miles southeast of Pasco ☎ 509/545–2361 🌐 parks.state.wa.us/575/Sacajawea Day pass $10 per vehicle; annual Discovery Pass $30 (valid at all state parks) Facilities closed Dec.–Mar.*

Hotels

Best Western Premier Pasco Inn & Suites

$$ | **HOTEL** | A favorite of travelers for years, this reliable chain hotel has a warm and welcoming vibe (there's even fresh hot cookies in the evening).

Pros: on-site market is open around the clock; a filling hot breakfast; close to the airport with free shuttle. **Cons:** not many dining options nearby; location is a bit secluded; restaurant doesn't offer lunch. *Rooms from: $189 2811 N. 20th Ave. 509/543–7722, 800/780–7234 reservations www.bestwestern.com 110 rooms Free Breakfast.*

Kennewick

3 miles southwest of Pasco, directly across the Columbia River.

In its 100-year history, Kennewick (*ken-uh-wick*) evolved from a railroad town to a farm-supply center and then to a bedroom community for Hanford workers and a food-processing capital for the Columbia Basin. The name Kennewick translates as "grassy place," and Native Americans had winter villages here long before Lewis and Clark passed through. Arrowheads and other artifacts aside, the 9,000-year-old skeleton of Kennewick Man was studied by scientists at the University of Washington to determine whether its features are Native American or, as some claim, Caucasian. Nearly two decades after its discovery, it was finally confirmed to be Native American and turned over to tribes for burial.

GETTING HERE AND AROUND

The Tri-Cities Airport is in nearby Pasco, served by Alaska, Allegiant, Delta, and United. Taxis and rental cars are available and some hotels offer an airport shuttle. Ben Franklin Transit serves all three cities. By car, Interstate 82 is the main east–west highway; from Ritzville or Spokane, take Highway 395 to reach the Tri-Cities; from Ellensburg and Yakima, take Interstate 82 south and east.

ESSENTIALS

VISITOR INFORMATION City of Kennewick. *509/585–4200 www.go2kennewick.com.*

Sights

Badger Mountain Vineyard

WINERY/DISTILLERY | A beautiful view of the valley and wine made without pesticides or preservatives is what you'll find here. Badger Mountain was the first wine-grape vineyard in Washington State to be certified organic. *1106 N. Jurupa St. 800/643–9463 www.badgermtnvineyard.com.*

Columbia Park

CITY PARK | FAMILY | Adjacent to the Columbia River, this is one of Washington's great parks. Its 4½-mile-long riverfront has boat ramps, a golf course, picnic areas, playgrounds (including an aquatic one), train ride, skate park, and family fishing pond. In summer, hydroplane races are held here. *Columbia Trail Dr., between U.S. 240 and Columbia River 509/585–4293 www.go2kennewick.com.*

East Benton County Historical Museum

MUSEUM | The entire entryway to the museum is made of petrified wood. Photographs, agricultural displays, petroglyphs, and a large collection of arrowheads interpret area history. Kennewick's oldest park, Keewaydin, is across the street. *205 W. Keewaydin Dr. 509/582–7704 www.ebchs.org $5 Closed Sun. and Mon.*

Ice Harbor Lock and Dam

DAM | At 103 feet, the single-lift locks here are among the world's highest. Inside the visitor center, there's a fish ladder viewing room where you can see salmon and steelhead on their annual migration. Exhibits and films provide information about the Salmon River and the area's history. As this is a federal facility, government identification is required for entry. *2763 Monument Dr., Burbank About 12 miles southeast of Kennewick 509/547–7781 www.nww.usace.army.mil/Locations/District-Locks-and-Dams/Ice-Harbor-Lock-and-Dam/ Closed Nov.–Mar.*

McNary National Wildlife Refuge

NATURE PRESERVE | FAMILY | More than 200 species of birds have been identified here, and many waterfowl make it their winter home. But the 15,000 acres of water and marsh, croplands, grasslands, trees, and shrubs are most enjoyable in spring and summer. The Environmental Education Center features hands-on exhibits. A self-guided 2-mile trail winds through the marshes, and a cabinlike blind hidden in the reeds allows you to watch wildlife up close. Other recreation includes boating, fishing, hiking, and horseback riding. ✉ *64 Maple Rd., Burbank* ✣ *¼ mile east of U.S. 12, south of Snake River Bridge* ☎ *509/546–8300* 🌐 *www.fws.gov/refuge/McNary.*

Restaurants

Ice Harbor at the Marina

$ | AMERICAN | There are 11 ales on tap at Ice Harbor Brewery's restaurant, along with a good selection of cocktails and local wines. You can order your favorite bar snacks like nachos, wings, and pretzels with beer cheese, along with more substantial fare including chicken pesto flatbread, panfried salmon, beer-battered halibut, and grilled New York steak. **Known for:** six types of tasty burgers; cool location at the marina; beer sampler trays. 💲 *Average main: $15* ✉ *350 Clover Island Dr.* ☎ *509/586–3181* 🌐 *www.iceharbor.com/ice-harbor-brewing-company-at-the-marina.*

Hotels

Springhill Suites

$ | HOTEL | FAMILY | An indoor swimming pool and hot tub are two of the draws at this modern chain hotel with spacious suites with separate living areas. **Pros:** walking distance of a shopping mall; rooms can sleep up to five people; on-site restaurant is open for dinner. **Cons:** some bathrooms don't have tubs; some awkward room layouts; a/c can be noisy. 💲 *Rooms from: $149* ✉ *7048 W. Grandridge Blvd.* ☎ *509/820–3026, 844/833–6503* 🌐 *www.marriott.com/hotels/travel/kwcsh-springhill-suites-kennewick-tri-cities/* *116 suites* 🍴 *Free Breakfast.*

Walla Walla

52 miles southeast of Kennewick.

A successful downtown restoration has earned Walla Walla high praise. The heart of downtown, at 2nd and Main Streets, looks as pretty as it did 60 years ago, with beautifully maintained old buildings and newer structures that add to the overall vibe. Walla Walla's Main Street is the winner of the "Great American Main Street Award" from the National Trust for Historic Preservation. Residents and visitors come here to visit shops, wineries, cafés, and restaurants.

Walla Walla, founded in the 1850s on the site of a Nez Perce village, was Washington's first metropolis. As late as the 1880s its population was larger than that of Seattle. Walla Walla occupies a lush green valley below the rugged Blue Mountains. Its beautiful downtown boasts old residences, green parks, and the campus of Whitman College, Washington's oldest institution of higher learning.

West of town, the green Walla Walla Valley—famous for asparagus, sweet onions, cherries, and wheat—has emerged as Washington's premier viticultural region. Tall grain elevators mark Lowden, a few miles west of Walla Walla, a wheat hamlet that now has several wineries.

GETTING HERE AND AROUND

Coming from points west, Walla Walla is reached via Interstate 82 east of the Tri-Cities, then Highway 12, which is still a two-lane highway in places but has recently been expanded west of Walla

Walla and into the town. From Spokane and the northeast, travel is all by two-lane highway, going south on Highway 195 to Colfax, then southwest via Highways 26 and 127 to Highway 12, then continuing south through Dayton and Waitsburg. Horizon Air runs two daily flights (one on Saturday) each way between Walla Walla and Seattle.

ESSENTIALS

VISITOR INFORMATION Walla Walla Valley Chamber of Commerce. ✉ *29 E. Sumach St.* ☎ *509/525–0850* 🌐 *www.wwvchamber.com.*

Sights

Canoe Ridge Vineyards

WINERY/DISTILLERY | Owned by Precept Wine, this vineyard produces Merlot, Cabernet Sauvignon, Chardonnay, Rosé, and a red blend. The tasting room is in Walla Walla's historic Engine House. ✉ *45 E. Main St.* ☎ *509/525–1843* 🌐 *www.canoeridgevineyard.com.*

Fort Walla Walla Museum

MUSEUM | FAMILY | On 15 acres at Fort Walla Walla Park, a 17-building pioneer village depicts the region's life in the 1800s, and five halls house military, agricultural, textile, and transportation exhibits. ✉ *755 Myra Rd.* ☎ *509/525–7703* 🌐 *www.fwwm.org* 🎫 *$9.*

L'Ecole No. 41

WINERY/DISTILLERY | Housed in the lower floors of a circa-1915 schoolhouse, this winery is one of the oldest in the Walla Walla Valley. It produces outstanding Bordeaux blends from single vineyards, among other wines. The tasting room is in one of the old classrooms, and details like chalkboards and books add to the ambience. ✉ *41 Lowden School Rd., Lowden* ☎ *509/525–0940* 🌐 *www.lecole.com.*

Long Shadows Vintners

WINERY/DISTILLERY | Long Shadows partners with international winemakers to create their Cabernet Sauvignon, Merlot, and red blends. Their Riesling, called Poet's Leap, is a collaboration with German winemaker Armin Diel. You can sample them all in the stunning tasting room that features glass art by noted artist Dale Chihuly. ✉ *1604 Frenchtown Rd.* ☎ *509/526–0905* 🌐 *longshadows.com.*

Pioneer Park

CITY PARK | FAMILY | Planted with native and exotic flowers and trees, this turn-of-the-20th-century park has a fine aviary. It was originally landscaped by sons of Frederick Law Olmsted, who designed New York City's Central Park. ✉ *E. Alder St. and Division St.* 🌐 *www.wallawallawa.gov.*

Seven Hills Winery

WINERY/DISTILLERY | Owner Casey McClellan makes well-balanced Cabernet Sauvignon, Malbec, Merlot, and other reds, as well as Sauvignon Blanc and a dry Rosé. The winery is in Walla Walla's historic Whitehouse-Crawford building. ✉ *212 N. 3rd Ave.* ☎ *509/529–7198, 877/777–7870* 🌐 *www.sevenhillswinery.com.*

Three Rivers Winery

WINERY/DISTILLERY | Surrounded by vineyards, this winery produces premium Cabernet Sauvignon, Merlot, Chardonnay, Riesling, and others. It has a nice tasting room, a gift shop, summer concerts, and a 3-acre lawn where you can play games like cornhole. ✉ *5641 Old Hwy. 12* ☎ *509/526–9463* 🌐 *www.threeriverswinery.com.*

Waterbrook Winery

WINERY/DISTILLERY | Set on 75 acres, this tasting room has a spacious patio with an outdoor fireplace, hillside views, and beautiful landscaping and ponds. Waterbrook is best known for Merlot, Chardonnay, and Cabernet that is often served at restaurants in the area. An on-site cafe is open Thursday to Monday. ✉ *10518 W. U.S. Hwy. 12* ☎ *509/522–1262* 🌐 *www.waterbrook.com.*

Whitman College

COLLEGE | Large, tree-lined lawns surround the many beautiful 19th-century stone and brick structures of the Whitman College campus. The school began as a seminary in 1859 and became a college in 1883. ✉ *345 Boyer Ave.* ☎ *509/527–5111* 🌐 *www.whitman.edu.*

Whitman Mission National Historic Site

HISTORIC SITE | **FAMILY** | This is a reconstruction of Waiilatpu Mission, a Presbyterian outpost established on Cayuse lands in 1836. The park preserves the foundations of the mission buildings, a short segment of the Oregon Trail, and, on a nearby hill, the graveyard where the Native American victims of an 1847 measles epidemic and subsequent uprising are buried. ✉ *328 Whitman Mission Rd.* ✢ *7 miles west of downtown* ☎ *509/522–6360 park headquarters, 509/522–6357 visitor info* 🌐 *www.nps.gov/whmi* ⏲ *Visitor center closed Dec. and Jan., and Mon. and Tues. in Oct., Nov., and Feb.–mid-May.*

Woodward Canyon Winery

WINERY/DISTILLERY | Lovers of fine wines make pilgrimages to this winery, 12 miles west of Walla Walla, for the superb Cabernet Sauvignon and Merlot. Its 2017 Chardonnay was named "Best Splurge" by *Seattle Magazine*. The winery has a second label, Nelms Road, that focuses on more affordable red wines. ✉ *11920 W. U.S. 12, Lowden* ☎ *509/525–4129* 🌐 *www.woodwardcanyon.com.*

Restaurants

Hattaway's on Alder

$$$ | **SOUTHERN** | Downtown Walla Walla is home to some excellent eateries, and Hattaway's on Alder has continued to raise the bar even higher with innovative and delicious dishes like fish and grits or panfried trout and a green-tomato relish made with local tomatoes. The grilled pork collar comes with smoked smashed potatoes, and the red beans and rice gets an updated treatment with Cajun smoked tofu. **Known for:** inventive menu with both Southern and Northwest influences; creative cocktails and many wine choices; save room for the delicious bread pudding. $ *Average main: $25* ✉ *125 W. Alder St.* ☎ *509/525–4433* 🌐 *hattawaysonalder.com* ⏲ *No lunch. No dinner weekends.*

TMACS

$$$ | **ITALIAN** | This local favorite expanded into a larger space just up the street, so now even more people can enjoy the contemporary Italian food, along with the neighborly feel of the two-level dining room, the cozy bar, and the hip upstairs lounge. The menu focuses on bold flavors and fresh, local, and organic ingredients for dishes like prosciutto carbonara, grilled king salmon, and braised lamb chop. **Known for:** white truffle mac and cheese is rich and delicious; all the decadent desserts are made in-house; half-price appetizers during happy hour. $ *Average main: $30* ✉ *80 N. Colville St.* ☎ *509/522–4776* 🌐 *www.tmacsww.com.*

★ Whitehouse-Crawford Restaurant

$$$$ | **AMERICAN** | In a former wood mill, this fine-dining destination has gained a reputation for quality and excellence, thanks to chef-owner Jamie Guerin. Local is the watchword here, where hamburgers are made with grass-fed beef from Blue Valley Meats, and other nearby purveyors supply produce, cheese, meat, eggs, and even popcorn for the bar. **Known for:** extensive wine list features many Walla Walla Valley winemakers; house-made ice cream and sorbet; more casual dining at bar. $ *Average main: $35* ✉ *55 W. Cherry St.* ☎ *509/525–2222* 🌐 *www.whitehousecrawford.com* ⏲ *Closed Mon. and Tues. No lunch.*

Hotels

The Barn B&B Walla Walla

$$$$ | **B&B/INN** | One of the area's newest lodgings, the Barn B&B Walla Walla is also one of the most unique, with one suite called the Granary that has rounded walls because it's inside an actual silo. **Pros:** beautiful art and furniture the owners collected while living abroad; complimentary Thursday night dinners with the hosts; special golfing, wine, and cooking packages. **Cons:** pool may detract from sense of solitude and privacy; about 9 miles from downtown Walla Walla; two-night minimum stay. *Rooms from: 400* *1624 Stovall Rd.* *509/398–8422* *www.bnbwallawalla.com* *7 suites* *Free Breakfast.*

The Finch

$$$ | **HOTEL** | A former motel has been reborn as this hip hotel with a mission to be your base for exploring all that's wonderful about Walla Walla, with helpful maps to help guide your discoveries. **Pros:** off-season and midweek rates are good value; common areas encourage guests to socialize; helpful, friendly staff. **Cons:** most of the rooms have outdoor entrances; might be too minimalist for some; no phones in rooms. *Rooms from: $229* *325 East Main St.* *509/956–4994* *finchwallawalla.com* *80 rooms* *No meals.*

Green Gables Inn

$$ | **B&B/INN** | One block from the Whitman College campus, this 1909 Arts and Crafts–style mansion sits among flowering plants and shrubs on a quaint, tree-lined street and offers charming guest rooms. **Pros:** three-bedroom Violet Vale Guest House is great for families; rooms individually decorated with Victorian antiques; delicious gourmet breakfasts. **Cons:** two-night minimum stay on weekends; only two rooms allow children; limited availability for pets. *Rooms from: $179* *922 Bonsella St.* *509/876–4373* *www.greengablesinn.com* *7 rooms* *Free Breakfast.*

★ Inn at Abeja

$$$$ | **B&B/INN** | Set on 35 acres of gardens, lawns, and vineyards, the incredibly stylish, beautifully furnished guest cottages and suites have a serene, relaxing, and secluded feel. **Pros:** multicourse breakfast can be delivered to your room or the patio; a short drive to both downtown Walla Walla and valley wineries; rooms have binoculars for enjoying the views. **Cons:** two-night minimum stay on weekends; fills up fast with repeat guests; no children under 13. *Rooms from: $359* *2014 Mill Creek Rd.* *509/522–1234* *www.abeja.net* *8 rooms* *Free Breakfast.*

Inn at Blackberry Creek

$$$ | **B&B/INN** | Centrally located, yet with a secluded feel, this 1906 Kentucky farmhouse-style home with cozy, traditionally furnished accommodations sits on a 2-acre lot in a residential area, with Blackberry Creek running through the backyard. **Pros:** wonderful breakfast consisting of several choices; rooms are well stocked with lots of extras; hosts are warm and friendly. **Cons:** books up fast on wine-event weekends; not walking distance to town; no children under 12. *Rooms from: $209* *1126 Pleasant St.* *509/522–5233* *www.innatblackberrycreek.com* *4 rooms* *Free Breakfast.*

★ Marcus Whitman Hotel

$$ | **HOTEL** | This 1928 hotel is *the* landmark in downtown Walla Walla, and guest quarters include spacious two-room parlor suites and spa suites in the historic tower building—adorned with Italian furnishings and lots of amenities, these rooms are well worth the splurge. **Pros:** four boutique winery tasting rooms are adjacent to the lobby; full breakfast buffet fuels you up for a day of exploring; parking and other extras are included. **Cons:** West Wing rooms are standard hotel style; no bathtubs in historic rooms; some bathrooms are small. *Rooms from: $189* *6 W. Rose St.* *509/525–2200, 866/937–7713* *www.marcuswhitmanhotel.com* *133 rooms* *Free Breakfast.*

Dayton

31 miles northeast of Walla Walla.

The tree-shaded county seat of Columbia County is the kind of Currier & Ives place many people conjure up when they imagine the best qualities of rural America. This tidy town has 117 buildings listed on the National Register of Historic Places, including the state's oldest railroad depot and courthouse.

GETTING HERE AND AROUND

Dayton is northeast of Walla Walla via Highway 12. From the Spokane area, take Highway 195 to Colfax, then veer southwest via Highways 26 and 127 before reaching Highway 12 and continuing into the town.

Sights

Dayton Historical Depot Society

MUSEUM | At Washington's oldest standing depot, the society houses exhibits illustrating the history of Dayton and surrounding communities. *222 E. Commercial Ave. 509/382–2026 www.daytonhistoricdepot.org Closed Sun.–Tues.*

Palouse Falls State Park

NATIONAL/STATE PARK | Just north of its confluence with the Snake River, the Palouse River gushes over a basalt cliff higher than Niagara Falls and drops 198 feet into a steep-walled basin. Those who are sure-footed can hike to an overlook above the falls, which are at their fastest during spring runoff in March. Just downstream from the falls at the Marmes Rock Shelter, remains of the earliest-known inhabitants of North America, dating back 10,000 years, were discovered by archaeologists. The park has 11 primitive campsites, open year-round, but with no water November through March. *Palouse Falls Rd. and Ste. Rte. 261 38 miles north of Dayton 509/646–9218 parks.state.wa.us/559/Palouse-Falls Day pass $10 per vehicle; annual Discovery Pass $30 (valid at all state parks); campsites $12.*

Restaurants

Weinhard Café and Bakery

$$ | **AMERICAN** | The past seems to echo through this restaurant, which is across the street from the Weinhard Hotel in what was once the town's pharmacy. The menu changes frequently to highlight seasonal specialties and local purveyors; some signature items include the chef's salad, rib-eye steak, and dark chocolate cake. **Known for:** great variety of baked desserts and breads; Thursday night spaghetti specials; satisfying wine list. *Average main: $22 258 E. Main St. 509/382–1681 www.weinhardcafe.com Closed Sun.-Tues.*

Pullman

75 miles south of Spokane.

This funky, liberal town—home of Washington State University—is in the heart of the rather conservative Palouse agricultural district. The town's freewheeling style can perhaps be explained by the fact that most of the students come from elsewhere in Washington.

The Palouse River, the upper course of which flows though the town, is an exception among Washington rivers: because of the high erosion rate of the light Palouse loess soil it usually runs muddy and almost gruel-like during floods (most Washington rivers run clear, even after major storms). The 198-foot-high Palouse Falls farther downstream, near Washtucna, dramatically drop as a thin sheet of water into a steep box canyon.

GETTING HERE AND AROUND

Alaska flies into the local airport, where taxis and rental cars are available to get you to your destination. Most of the hotels have free airport shuttles, too.

Pullman is reached via Highway 195, about 75 miles from Spokane.

ESSENTIALS

VISITOR INFORMATION Pullman Chamber of Commerce. ✉ *415 N. Grand Ave.* ☎ *509/334–3565, 800/365–6948* 🌐 *www.pullmanchamber.com.*

Charles R. Conner Museum of Zoology

MUSEUM | On the campus of Washington State University, this museum has the finest collection of stuffed birds and mammals and preserved invertebrates in the Pacific Northwest; more than 700 are on display. ✉ *Abelson Hall, Library Rd. and College Ave.* ☎ *509/592–8922* 🌐 *sbs.wsu.edu/connermuseum* ⏲ *Closed school holidays.*

Jordan Schnitzer Museum of Art

MUSEUM | FAMILY | Washington State University's outstanding Museum of Art has more than 3,500 pieces in its permanent collection, including works by regional, national, and international artists. Its six galleries showcase art from the university's collections and hosts visiting exhibits. The architecturally stunning building nicknamed the "Crimson Cube" opened in 2018 ✉ *WSU Fine Arts Center, 1535 NE Wilson Rd.* ☎ *509/335–1910* 🌐 *museum.wsu.edu* ⏲ *Closed Sun., Mon. and school holidays. Closed Sat. in summer.*

Kamiak Butte County Park

CITY PARK | The 3,640-foot-tall butte is part of a mountain chain that was here long before the lava flows of the Columbia basin erupted millions of years ago. The park has great views of the Palouse hills and Idaho's snowcapped peaks to the east, as well as eight primitive campsites, a picnic area, and a 1-mile trail to the top of the butte. ✉ *902 Kamiak Butte Park Rd., Palouse* ✥ *12 miles north of Pullman* ☎ *509/397–6238* 🌐 *www.whitmancounty.org* 🎟 *Free; campsite $15.*

Steptoe Butte State Park

NATIONAL/STATE PARK | The park dotted with picnic tables is named after an army officer who lost a battle in 1858 against Native Americans at nearby Rosalia. The lieutenant colonel and other survivors sneaked away at night—a retreat historians think was permitted by their adversaries. The hike to the summit of the 3,600-foot-high butte rewards hikers with panoramic views 200 miles in the distance. ✉ *Garfield* ✥ *32 miles north of Pullman via U.S. 195 and Hume Rd.* ☎ *509/337–6457* 🌐 *parks.state.wa.us/592/Steptoe-Butte* 🎟 *Day pass $10 per vehicle; annual Discovery Pass $30 (valid at all state parks).*

Washington State University

COLLEGE | Opened in 1892 as the state's agriculture school, Washington State University today sprawls almost all the way to the Idaho state line. Besides checking out the interesting architecture of 19th century buildings like Bryan Hall with its clocktower that lights up and night and Thompson Hall with its castle-like turrets, a visit to the new Jordan Schnitzer Museum of Art is a must. To park on campus, pick up a parking pass in the Security Building on Wilson Road. ✉ *1 S.E. Stadium Way* ☎ *509/335–3564* 🌐 *www.wsu.edu.*

Sella's Calzone and Pastas

$ | PIZZA | Made daily from scratch, the calzones are always fresh at this cozy storefront and include the most popular, Coug (pepperoni, mushrooms, and black olives), followed by the Gourmet (artichoke hearts, sun-dried tomatoes, and pesto sauce). Pizzas, sandwiches, pastas, and salads are also served. **Known for:** affordable daily lunch specials; bright and airy dining room; friendly service. $ *Average main: $11* ✉ *1115 E. Main St.* ☎ *509/334–1895* 🌐 *www.sellascalzone.com.*

Hotels

Churchyard Inn

$ | **B&B/INN** | Registered as a national and state historic site, this 1905 Flemish-style inn, 15 miles southeast of Pullman in Uniontown, was once a parish house for the adjacent church; some of the homey, traditionally furnished rooms have views of the countryside, and one suite has its own kitchen. **Pros:** welcoming and helpful innkeepers; cookies and wine when you arrive; quiet and scenic location. **Cons:** two-night minimum on game weekends (but no increase in rates); about 20 minutes from Pullman; no TVs in most rooms. *Rooms from: $125* *206 St. Boniface St., Uniontown* *509/229–3200* *www.churchyardinn.com* *Closed Jan. and Feb.* *7 rooms* *Free Breakfast.*

Holiday Inn Express & Suites

$ | **HOTEL** | **FAMILY** | You can count on this member of the national chain for cleanliness, comfortable beds, and friendly service, and all rooms include a refrigerator, microwave, and flat-screen TV. **Pros:** near a walking and biking trail; free shuttle to campus; lovely indoor pool. **Cons:** no restaurant on-site; high rates during events; books up far in advance. *Rooms from: $145* *1190 SE Bishop Blvd.* *509/334–4437, 888/465–4329* *www.holidayinnexpress.com* *130 rooms* *Free Breakfast.*

Shopping

Ferdinand's

STORE/MALL | On weekdays or any Saturday when there's a football home game, you can pop into Ferdinand's, an ice-cream and cheese shop in Washington State University's food-science building, to buy Aged Cougar Gold, a cheddar-type cheese in a can. Ice cream is made daily from milk from the university's dairy cows. *2035 NE Ferdinand's La.* *800/457–5442* *creamery.wsu.edu* *Closed weekends and school breaks.*

Spokane

75 miles north of Pullman, 282 miles east of Seattle.

Washington's second-largest city, Spokane (spo- *can,* not spo- *cane*) takes its name from the Spokan tribe of Salish Native Americans. It translates as "Children of the Sun," a fitting name for this sunny city. It's also a city of flowers and trees, public gardens, parks, and museums. Spokane's magnificent waterfalls form the heart of downtown's Riverfront Park, and the city rises from the falls in a series of broad terraces to the valley's rim.

Spokane began as a Native American village at a roaring waterfall where each autumn salmon ascended in great numbers. American settlers built a sawmill at the falls in 1873. Several railroads arrived after 1881, and Spokane soon became the transportation hub of eastern Washington. In 1885 Spokane built the first hydroelectric plant west of the Mississippi. Downtown boomed after the fire of 1889, as the city grew rich from mining ventures in Washington, Idaho, and Montana, and from shipping the wheat grown on the Palouse hills.

GETTING HERE AND AROUND

Spokane can be reached by Interstate 90 from the east or west. U.S. 395 runs north from Spokane to Colville and the Canadian border. Downtown Spokane is laid out along a true grid: streets run north–south, avenues east–west; many are one way. Spokane's heaviest traffic is on Interstate 90 between Spokane and Spokane Valley on weekday evenings. Metered parking is available on city streets; there are also several downtown lots.

AIRPORT TRANSFERS

Many hotels offer a free airport shuttle service. Spokane Transit runs between the airport and downtown, every half hour 6:40 am–6:40 pm (then hourly until 11 pm) weekdays, and hourly on weekends: 6:05 am–9:05 pm Saturday and 8:04–6:04 Sunday; the 20-minute bus ride costs $2. Wheatland Express has shuttle service between the Spokane Airport and Pullman and Moscow, Idaho. Reservations are recommended; the cost is $38 one-way. City Cab serves the Spokane area. Metered fares run about $2.60 a mile. A taxi ride from the Spokane airport to downtown costs about $25. Lyft and Uber both serve the airport; rates depend on time of day and level of service but generally range from $17 to $20 to downtown.

CONTACTS City Cab. ☎ *509/455–3333* 🌐 *www.spokanecitycab.com.* **Spokane Transit Authority.** ☎ *509/328–7433* 🌐 *www.spokanetransit.com.* **Wheatland Express.** ☎ *509/334–2200* 🌐 *www.wheatlandexpress.com.*

BUS

Spokane has an extensive local bus system. The fare is $1.75; exact change or a token is required. Pick up schedules, maps, and tokens at the bus depot or the Plaza, the major downtown transfer point.

CONTACTS The Plaza. ✉ *Bus Shop at the Plaza, 701 W. Riverside Ave.* ☎ *509/456–7277* 🌐 *www.spokanetransit.com.*

TRAIN

Amtrak's Empire Builder runs daily between Spokane and Seattle and between Spokane and Portland, stopping at points in between (including Ephrata and Pasco). Reservations are recommended. Round-trip fares to Seattle or Portland, vary depending on season, but are usually around $120.

ESSENTIALS

VISITOR INFORMATION Spokane Area Visitors Information. ✉ *620 W. Spokane Falls Blvd.* ☎ *509/624–1341, 888/776–5263* 🌐 *www.visitspokane.com.*

Sights

Arbor Crest Wine Cellars

WINERY/DISTILLERY | On the grounds of the eclectic 1924 mansion of Royal Riblet, the inventor of a square-wheel tractor and the poles that hold up ski lifts, you can sample Arbor Crest wines, enjoy the striking view of the Spokane River, or meander through the impeccably kept grounds (the house isn't open to tours). Arbor Crest's wines include Cabernet Sauvignon and Chardonnays from the Columbia Valley. Enjoy Sunday-evening concerts (5:30–sunset) outside from early May through September; in winter there's live music by the fireside in the Wine Bar on Friday and Saturday nights (5:30–7:30). ✉ *4705 N. Fruithill Rd.* ☎ *509/927–9463* 🌐 *www.arborcrest.com.*

Bing Crosby House Museum

MUSEUM | Crooner Bing Crosby grew up in Spokane in a Craftsman-style house built in 1911 by his father and uncles. The house museum has hundreds of items (out of the thousands in Gonzaga University's Crosby Collection) on display, including his Oscar for the film *Going My Way*, his gold records, and other memorabilia. ✉ *508 E. Sharp Ave.* ☎ *509/313–3873* 🌐 *researchguides.gonzaga.edu/bingcrosbyhouse* ⏲ *Closed Sun.*

Cat Tales Zoological Park

ZOO | **FAMILY** | Among the large cats living at this wildlife refuge and rescue sanctuary are lions, tigers, bobcats, pumas, and lynxes. You'll also see bears and foxes. Guided tours give background information on the animals. While it's not a zoo in the traditional sense, the mission of the nonprofit that runs it is a worthy one. ✉ *17020 N. Newport Hwy., Mead* ✣ *12 miles north of I–90* ☎ *509/238–4126* 🌐 *www.cattales.org* 🎫 ***$12*** ⏲ *Closed Mon.*

Cathedral of St. John the Evangelist

RELIGIOUS SITE | This architectural masterpiece, considered one of America's most important and beautiful Gothic

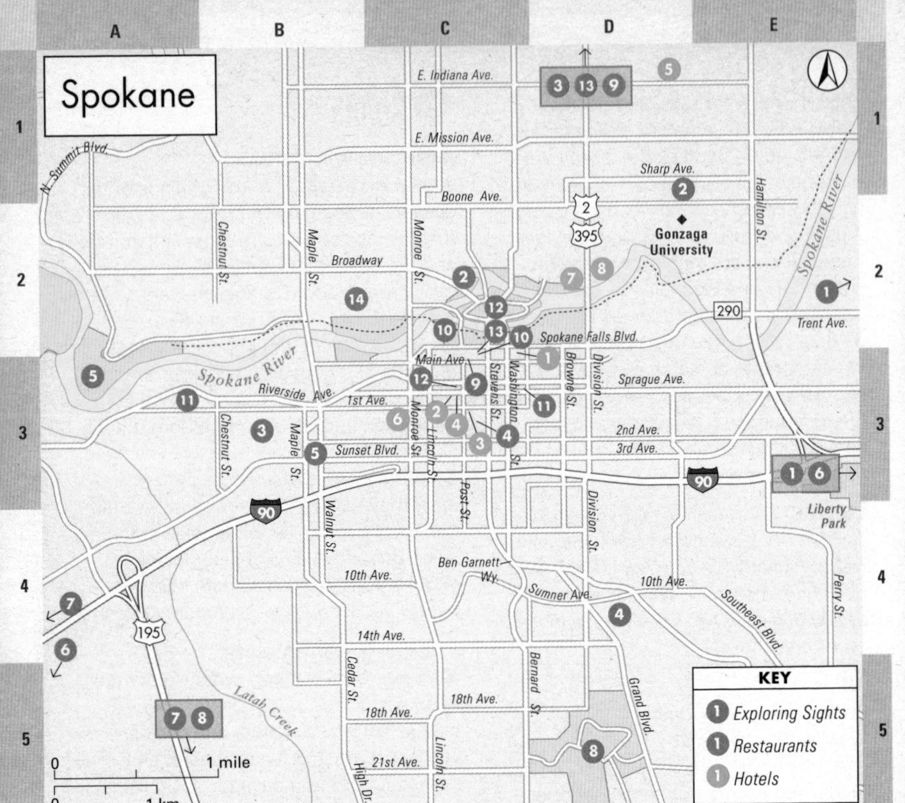

Sights

1 Arbor Crest Wine Cellars.............. E2
2 Bing Crosby House Museum......... D1
3 Cat Tales Zoological Park......... D1
4 Cathedral of St. John the Evangelist........... D4
5 Centennial Trail......... A3
6 Eastern Washington University................ A4
7 Finch Arboretum........ A4
8 Manito Park and Gardens............. D5
9 Mobius Children's Museum...... C3
10 Mobius Science Center.......... C2
11 Northwest Museum of Arts and Culture..... A3
12 Riverfront Park........... C2
13 Townshend Cellar...... D1

Restaurants

1 Casper Fry................ E3
2 Clinkerdagger............ C2
3 Elk Public House........ B3
4 Europa Restaurant and Bakery............... C3
5 Frank's Diner............ B3
6 Fresh Soul................. E3
7 Latah Bistro............. A5
8 Luna...................... A5
9 Mary Lou's Milk Bottle.............. D1
10 Mizuna.................... C2
11 Onion..................... C3
12 Post Street Ale House................ C3
13 Steelhead Bar & Grille.............. C2
14 The Wandering Table.................... B2

Hotels

1 The Davenport Grand... C2
2 The Davenport Lusso...................... C3
3 The Davenport Tower...................... C3
4 The Historic Davenport Hotel....................... C3
5 Marianna Stoltz House.................... D1
6 Montvale Hotel.......... C3
7 Oxford Suites............ D2
8 Ruby River Hotel....... D2

Spokane's scenic Monroe Street Bridge at night.

cathedrals, was constructed in the 1920s with sandstone from Tacoma and Boise and limestone from Indiana. The cathedral's renowned 49-bell carillon has attracted international guest musicians. ✉ *127 E. 12th Ave.* ☎ *509/838–4277* 🌐 *www.stjohns-cathedral.org.*

★ Centennial Trail

TRAIL | **FAMILY** | This trail—which starts near Nine Mile Falls, northwest of Spokane, then runs through downtown, along Riverfront Park, and then stretches east to the Idaho border—is perfect for a hike, bike, or run. Roughly 40 miles long, the path follows the Spokane River. ✉ *Along Spokane River* 🌐 *spokanecentennialtrail.org.*

Eastern Washington University

COLLEGE | The entrance to the tree-shaded Cheney campus is marked by the Pillars of Hercules; built in 1915, they include granite from the original Cheney Normal School that was destroyed by fire a few years earlier. Six campus buildings are on the National Register of Historic Places. Walk through the EWU Historic District to learn about the university's founding as the state's first institution for training teachers and to see the early-1900 buildings where students lived and studied. ✉ *526 5th St., Cheney* ✣ *About 20 miles west of Spokane* ☎ *509/359–6200* 🌐 *www.ewu.edu.*

Finch Arboretum

GARDEN | This mile-long green patch along Garden Springs Creek has an extensive botanical garden with more than 2,000 labeled trees, shrubs, and flowers. Follow the walking tour on well-manicured paths along the creek, or follow your whim—depending on the season—through flowering rhododendrons, hibiscus, magnolias, dogwoods, hydrangeas, and more. ✉ *3404 W. Woodland Blvd.* ☎ *509/363–5466* 🌐 *my.spokanecity.org/urbanforestry/programs/finch-arboretum.*

★ Manito Park and Gardens

GARDEN | **FAMILY** | A pleasant place to stroll in summer, this 90-acre park has a formal Renaissance-style garden, Japanese garden, duck pond, and rose and perennial gardens. There's also a conservatory that's especially fun to visit during the last half of December when it's illuminated with 30,000 lights for the free Holiday Lights display. A café is open daily from Memorial Day through Labor Day and features live music on Friday nights. Snowy winters find the park's hills full of sledders and its frozen pond packed with skaters. ✉ *1702 S. Grand Blvd.* ☎ *509/625–6200* 🌐 *my.spokanecity.org/parks/major/manito/* ⏲ *Japanese Garden closed Nov.–Mar.*

Mobius Children's Museum

MUSEUM | FAMILY | Spokane's museum for children is in the lower level of River Park Square and has interactive galleries for hands-on learning. Activity areas include a miniature city that teaches little ones about safety, an art studio, a forest-themed play area for infants and toddlers, and a stage with theater equipment and costumes. A partner facility, Mobius Science Center, is a five-minute walk north. ✉ *808 W. Main Ave.* ☎ *509/321–7121* 🌐 *www.mobiusspokane.org* 🎟 *From $10* ⏲ *Closed Mon.*

Mobius Science Center

MUSEUM | FAMILY | In the historic Washington Water Power building, this hands-on museum features interactive science and technology exhibits that change every several years as technology advances. ✉ *331 N. Post St.* ☎ *509/321–7133* 🌐 *www.mobiusspokane.org* 🎟 *From $10* ⏲ *Closed Mon.*

Northwest Museum of Arts and Culture

MUSEUM | FAMILY | Affectionately known as the MAC, the museum is in an impressive six-level glass-and-wood structure filled with audiovisual displays and artifacts that trace Spokane's history. There's also a fine Native American collection that includes baskets and beadwork of the Plateau nation. Wander to the adjacent Victorian home, the Campbell House, to admire the interior or view mining-era exhibits; guided tours are offered four times a day except Saturday (register when you arrive). ✉ *2316 W. 1st Ave.* ☎ *509/456–3931* 🌐 *www.northwestmuseum.org* 🎟 *$20* ⏲ *Closed Mon.*

★ Riverfront Park

CITY PARK | FAMILY | The 100-acre park is what remains of Spokane's Expo '74. Sprawling across several islands in the Spokane River, the park was developed from old railroad yards, where the stone clock tower of the former Great Northern Railroad Station still stands. The modernist Washington State pavilion, built as an opera house, is now the INB Performing Arts Center. A 1909 carousel, hand-carved by master builder Charles I.D. Looff, is a local landmark. Another family favorite is the giant red slide shaped like a Radio Flyer wagon. Thanks to a multiyear redevelopment effort, the iconic U.S. Pavilion reopened in 2019 as the Pavilion at Riverfront, an event space that hosts concerts, festivals, and an eye-catching light display on weekends. For a great view of the river and falls, walk across Post Street Bridge or take the sky ride over Spokane Falls. ✉ *507 N. Howard St.* ☎ *509/625–6600* 🌐 *www.spokanefrontpark.com* 🎟 *Free.*

Townshend Cellar

WINERY/DISTILLERY | A drive to the Green Bluff countryside leads wine lovers to this small winery and its tasting room. It's won awards for its Cabernet Sauvignon, and also produces Merlot, Chardonnay, Syrah, Riesling, and several blends, offering more than 20 wines. Huckleberries from nearby Idaho are used in dessert wine. ✉ *8022 E. Greenbluff Rd., Colbert* ✥ *13 miles northeast of Spokane* ☎ *509/238–1400* 🌐 *www.townshendcellar.com* ⏲ *Closed Mon.–Thurs.*

Restaurants

Casper Fry

$$ | SOUTHERN | In Spokane's South Perry District, this restaurant has food and ambience that would fit right into a hip Seattle or Portland foodie neighborhood, the menu includes such comfort foods as cast-iron-skillet mac and cheese, buttermilk fried chicken, blackened catfish, po' boys, and shrimp and grits. Biscuits (with sausage gravy or fried chicken), beef brisket, and cinnamon French toast are some of the fare served up at weekend brunch. **Known for:** barrel-aged cocktails and an impressive list of whiskeys; dishes hot from a charcoal-burning oven; great brunch spot. *$ Average main: $19 ✉ 928 S. Perry ☎ 509/535–0536 🌐 www.casperfry.com ⏲ Closed Mon.*

★ Clinkerdagger

$$$$ | SEAFOOD | FAMILY | In a former flour mill with great views of the Spokane River, Clink's has been a Spokane institution since 1974. The seafood, steaks, and prime rib are excellent; the Maytag blue cheese salad and beer-battered fish-and-chips are both popular at lunch. **Known for:** excellent happy hour; favorite for special occasions; delicious desserts. *$ Average main: $33 ✉ 621 W. Mallon Ave. ☎ 509/328–5965 🌐 www.clinkerdagger.com ⏲ No lunch Sun.*

Elk Public House

$ | AMERICAN | This casual eatery in the relaxed Browne's Addition neighborhood serves tasty pub food like grilled lamb sandwiches, panko fried chicken, and a spicy gumbo, and you can wash it all down with one of the 16 beers on tap. A copper bar stands along one wall, backed by a mirror and lots of memorabilia, giving the interior a saloonlike appearance. **Known for:** good selection of microbrews, most from the Northwest; hipster vibe, but families are just as welcome; nice patio for outdoor dining. *$ Average main: $15 ✉ 1931 W. Pacific Ave. ☎ 509/363–1973 🌐 www.wedonthaveone.com.*

Europa Restaurant and Bakery

$$ | ITALIAN | FAMILY | Artisanal pizza is featured here (including gluten-free), along with lots of pastas, calzones, salads, seafood, steak, and chicken dishes. Candles on the tables, murals, exposed brick, and wood beams give a European flavor to the dining room and adjacent pub. **Known for:** a popular spot for happy hour; really good desserts; easygoing atmosphere. *$ Average main: $20 ✉ 125 S. Wall St. ☎ 509/455–4051.*

★ Frank's Diner

$ | DINER | FAMILY | Right off the Maple Street Bridge, this is the state's oldest railroad-car restaurant; built as an observation car in 1906, it has original light fixtures, stained-glass windows, and mahogany details. Generously sized breakfasts are the specialty here, including unique items like Creole Benedict with lobster and crab. **Known for:** very popular, so be prepared for a wait; everything is made from scratch; many items can be gluten-free. *$ Average main: $15 ✉ 1516 W. 2nd Ave. ☎ 509/747–8798 🌐 www.franksdiners.com.*

Fresh Soul

$$ | SOUTHERN | Operated by a neighborhood nonprofit that helps young people learn job skills, Fresh Soul blends a worthy purpose with really good Southern food. At lunchtime, a pulled pork or catfish sandwich will hit the spot, and for dinner, the big combo meals (think fried chicken legs with cornbread) are tasty and filling. **Known for:** tasty ribs are fall-off-the-bone tender; favorite beverages include sweet tea; family combos are a good value. *$ Average main: $16 ✉ 3029 E. 5th Ave. ☎ 509/242–3377 🌐 www.freshsoulrestaurant.com ⏲ Closed Sun.-Mon.*

Latah Bistro

$$ | ECLECTIC | Tucked into a strip mall in south Spokane near the Creek at Qualchan Golf Course, this neighborhood restaurant serves a wide-ranging menu that changes frequently. Some standards include glazed pork tenderloin, seared scallops, spinach salad with hot bacon, and rich desserts. **Known for:** pizzas baked in a wood-burning oven; diverse wine list; fun menu of martinis. *$ Average main: $22 ✉ 4241 S. Cheney–Spokane Rd.*

Riverfront Park

509/838–8338 www.latahbistro.com Brunch on Sun. only.

Luna

$$$ | **ECLECTIC** | You'll find inventive approaches to classics here, from grass-fed beef burgers to citrus-cured salmon. Weekend brunch has sweet treats like beignets with chocolate sauce as well as many savory offerings, including butternut-squash hash, smoked-salmon scramble, and brisket hash and peppers. **Known for:** rose terrace and courtyard dining in summer; tasty wood-fired pizzas; extensive wine list. *Average main: $30 5620 S. Perry St. 509/448–2383 www.lunaspokane.com.*

Mary Lou's Milk Bottle

$ | **AMERICAN** | **FAMILY** | Built in 1933, this restaurant is shaped like a gigantic milk bottle; since 1978 the eatery has been selling homemade ice cream. Fries are made from hand-cut potatoes, buns are made in-house, and burgers, sandwiches, salads, and soup (in winter only) round out the menu. **Known for:** huckleberry shakes; reasonable prices; memorable building. *Average main: $11 802 W. Garland Ave. 509/325–1772 www.facebook.com/milkbtl/ No credit cards No dinner Sun.*

Mizuna

$$$ | **ECLECTIC** | Fresh flowers and redbrick walls lend color and charm to this downtown eatery, where a patio is open for outdoor dining when the weather gets warms. Depending on the season, the daily seafood might be swordfish, salmon, or halibut, usually served with grilled vegetables. **Known for:** an entire menu of vegetarian and vegan dishes; cheese plate gets rave reviews; Northwest regional wines. *Average main: $32 214 N. Howard St. 509/747–2004 www.mizuna.com No lunch Sun.*

Onion

$$ | **AMERICAN** | Pressed-tin ceilings, vintage photographs, and a century-old bar with ornate columns evoke the past at this former saloon and pharmacy, enthusiastically serving American fare for decades. There are dozens of sandwiches and burgers on the menu, along with

heartier dishes like pot roast dinner, two kinds of fish-and-chips, wild Alaskan salmon, and huckleberry barbecue ribs. **Known for:** great happy hour menu on weekdays; late night menu for night owls; salads are a meal on their own. *Average main: $17* *302 W. Riverside Ave.* *509/747–3852* *theonion.biz.*

Post Street Ale House

$ | **AMERICAN** | Adjacent to The Davenport Lusso, this casual eatery offers standard pub fare like fish-and-chips, barbecue pork sliders, and several kinds of burgers. Starters include the signature fried pickles, hand-cut onion rings, and wings with your choice of sauce. **Known for:** more than 25 beers are on tap; late-night bar menu; speedy service. *Average main: $14* *1 N. Post St.* *509/789–6900* *www.davenporthotelcollection.com/our-hotels/the-davenport-lusso/dining/.*

Steelhead Bar & Grille

$$ | **AMERICAN** | This pub-style eatery, housed in one of Spokane's many historic brick buildings, has an urban contemporary vibe thanks to lots of burnished-metal artwork by local artists. Sandwiches and burgers make this a handy place for lunch; fish-and-chips with huckleberry coleslaw, pan-roasted halibut with citrus creamed corn, and (of course) a steelhead fillet with lemon-dill butter are heartier fare at dinner. **Known for:** dig into the half-pound bison burger; chocolate huckleberry truffles; everything is locally sourced. *Average main: $17* *218 N. Howard St.* *509/747–1303* *www.steelheadbarandgrille.com.*

The Wandering Table

$ | **AMERICAN** | If you're adventurous, the chef will create your meal based on what is in season, and is likely to include some of the house standards, such as deviled eggs with maple-bacon filling, fried brussels sprouts, and albacore tuna ceviche. The many small plates make this a popular spot for both a light lunch and tapas-style dinner. **Known for:** three different tasting menus are available each night; happy hour food menu is a great bargain; most food locally sourced. *Average main: $16* *1242 W. Summit Pkwy.* *509/443–4410* *www.thewanderingtable.com* *No lunch Sun. and Mon.*

Hotels

The Davenport Grand

$$ | **HOTEL** | Across from the INB Performing Arts Center and Riverfront Park, Spokane's largest lodging features business-friendly amenities (there is a skybridge directly to the convention center) that make it popular with traveling executives. **Pros:** convenient downtown location; nice views from upper floors; discounted rates often available. **Cons:** hotel can be noisy during conventions; no bathtubs; no swimming pool. *Rooms from: $169* *333 W. Spokane Falls Blvd.* *800/918–9344, 509/458–3330* *www.davenporthotelcollection.com* *716 rooms* *No meals.*

The Davenport Lusso

$$ | **HOTEL** | With a name that's Italian for "luxury," you won't be surprised that this European-style hotel combines elegant furnishings and many modern amenities like flat-screen TVs. **Pros:** suites are tasteful and elegantly appointed; access to amenities at sister property; attentive service. **Cons:** standard rooms aren't as special; some rooms face an alley; daily amenity fee. *Rooms from: $169* *808 W. Sprague Ave.* *509/747–9750, 800/918–9343* *www.davenporthotelcollection.com* *48 rooms* *No meals.*

The Davenport Tower

$$ | **HOTEL** | **FAMILY** | The lively Safari Room Grill has delightful scenes from the African savanna, and that motif continues in a subtle way through the rest of this 21-story tower. **Pros:** downtown location in the heart of the action; very affordable rates off-season; great happy-hour deals. **Cons:** noise from nearby trains and other rooms; parking is expensive; inconsistent service. *Rooms from: $189* *111 S.*

Post St. ☎ *509/789–6965, 800/899–1482* 🌐 *www.davenporthotelcollection.com* ⇆ *328 rooms* 🍽 *No meals.*

★ The Historic Davenport Hotel

$$ | HOTEL | FAMILY | More than a century old, this longtime landmark known for its stunning ballrooms and public spaces reopened in the early 2000s with beautiful accommodations featuring hand-carved mahogany furniture and fine Irish linens, marble bathrooms with big soaking tubs and separate showers. **Pros:** historic restoration makes it one of the city's jewels; abundant amenities make it feel like a resort; art gallery in lobby. **Cons:** some guests have noted service issues; can hear trains at night from some rooms; extra charges can add up. $ *Rooms from: $181* ✉ *10 S. Post St.* ☎ *509/455–8888, 800/899–1482* 🌐 *www.davenporthotel.com* ⇆ *284 rooms* 🍽 *No meals.*

Marianna Stolz House

$ | B&B/INN | On a tree-lined street across from Gonzaga University, this American foursquare home built in 1908 is listed on Spokane's historic register and is decorated with leaded-glass china cabinets, Renaissance Revival armchairs, and original dark-fir woodwork. **Pros:** convenient location for college events; innkeeper makes everyone feel welcome; lovely wrap-around porch and parlor. **Cons:** shared bathrooms in some rooms; minimum stay for some dates; online booking not available. $ *Rooms from: $115* ✉ *427 E. Indiana Ave.* ☎ *509/483–4316, 800/978–6587* 🌐 *www.mariannastoltzhouse.com* ⇆ *4 rooms* 🍽 *Free Breakfast.*

★ Montvale Hotel

$ | HOTEL | In a recently restored historic building, this intimate boutique hotel has spacious, stylish rooms with comfortable beds, flat-screen TVs, microwaves, and refrigerators. **Pros:** convenient location in theater district; great value for well-equipped rooms; abundant options for dining and drinking. **Cons:** noise from trucks, trains, and nearby nightlife can be distracting; very small hotel, so few activities; no on-site parking. $ *Rooms from: $116* ✉ *105 1st Ave.* ☎ *509/624–1518,* 🌐 *montvalespokane.com* ⇆ *36 rooms* 🍽 *No meals.*

Oxford Suites

$ | HOTEL | FAMILY | Located on the north side of the Spokane River, this three-story hotel of well-equipped studio suites is convenient to downtown and Riverfront Park, as well as the Spokane Arena and Gonzaga University. **Pros:** free drinks and appetizers in the evenings; indoor pool, hot tub, sauna, and steam room; airport shuttle available. **Cons:** two-night minimum stay most weekends; book ahead for popular events; some baths on the smaller side. $ *Rooms from: $129* ✉ *115 W. North River Dr.* ☎ *509/353–9000, 800/774–1877* 🌐 *www.oxfordsuitesspokane.com* ⇆ *125 rooms* 🍽 *Free Breakfast.*

Ruby River Hotel

$ | HOTEL | This sprawling riverfront hotel on 8 acres was reinvented as an urban resort in 2020, with two outdoor swimming pools, a lively restaurant, and free live music on the patio in the summer. **Pros:** parking is free and a shuttle runs to downtown and the airport; riverside rooms are worth the slight extra charge; convenient to downtown destinations. **Cons:** can get noisy with sports teams staying here; parking lot view from some rooms; no elevators. $ *Rooms from: $139* ✉ *700 N. Division St.* ☎ *509/326–5577* 🌐 *rubyriverspokane.com* ⇆ *245 rooms* 🍽 *No meals.*

Nightlife

The Ridler Piano Bar

PIANO BARS/LOUNGES | Every Thursday through Saturday pianists duke it out on the ivories, playing both popular and offbeat tunes—and, of course, they take requests. Country night is every Tuesday and includes swing dancing lessons.

✉ *718 W. Riverside Ave.* ☎ *509/822–7938* 🌐 *ridlerpiano.bar/welcome.*

Performing Arts

The Bing Crosby Theater

THEATER | The Bing, built in 1915, is one of America's few remaining palace-style theaters. It was renamed for hometown hero Bing Crosby; he performed skits here in between the showing of silent films. In addition to a varied roster from comedy to music, it also hosts the Bing Crosby Holiday Film Festival every December, which highlights some of Crosby's best films from his storied career. ✉ *901 W. Sprague Ave.* ☎ *509/227–7638* 🌐 *www.bingcrosbytheater.com.*

The Garland Theater

FILM | FAMILY | Spokane's only independent movie theater, the Garland has "bottomless bags" of popcorn, booze, and grub (pulled pork shoulder, pizzas, and more) that you can take into the cinema. Bring the kids to the free morning showings during the summer. ✉ *924 W. Garland Ave.* ☎ *509/327–2509* 🌐 *garlandtheater.com* 🎟 *$5.*

The Knitting Factory Concert House

CONCERTS | National acts, ranging from rapper Tech N9ne to country legend Tanya Tucker, are hosted in this 1,500-seat venue. ✉ *919 W. Sprague Ave.* ☎ *509/244-3279* 🌐 *sp.knittingfactory.com.*

Spokane Symphony

CONCERTS | Classical and pops concerts are presented from September through May in the historic Martin Woldson Theater at The Fox, plus special events such as the *Nutcracker* at the INB Performing Arts Center and free outdoor concerts at city parks in summer. ✉ *Fox Theater, 1001 W. Sprague* ☎ *509/624–1200* 🌐 *www.spokanesymphony.org/.*

Shopping

Boo Radley's

GIFTS/SOUVENIRS | Part curiosity shop, part vintage toy store, this eclectic spot is great for unusual gifts or to spend some time browsing. Original and creative toys, cards, games, T-shirts, masks and statuettes are just some of the treasures you'll find here. ✉ *232 N. Howard St.* ☎ *509/456–7479.*

Activities

GOLF

The Creek at Qualchan

GOLF | In a city with several stand-out municipal courses, Creek at Qualchan is a favorite to many golfers. It has some fabulous views and plenty of opportunities to spot wildlife. Greens fees are $45 and carts are $36. ✉ *301 E. Meadowlane Rd.* ☎ *509/448–9317* 🌐 *my.spokanecity.org/golf/qualchan* ⛳ *18 holes, 6559 yards, par 72.*

Indian Canyon

GOLF | On the slope of a basalt canyon, this 18-hole course has great views of Mt. Spokane. It's been frequently named as one of the top 25 public courses in the United States. The greens fees are $45; golf carts are $36. ✉ *1000 S. Assembly* ☎ *509/747–5353* 🌐 *my.spokanecity.org/golf/courses/indian-canyon* ⛳ *18 holes, 6255 yards, par 72.*

MeadowWood

GOLF | This is a Scottish-style course that has been ranked in Washington's top 10 municipal courses. Greens fees are $39 weekdays, $42 weekends. Golf carts are $36 for the day.

This is a Scottish-style course that has been ranked in Washington's top 10 municipal courses. Greens fees are $39 weekdays, $42 weekends. Golf carts are $36 for the day. ✉ *24501 E. Valleyway Ave., Liberty Lake* ☎ *509/255–9539* 🌐 *www.spokanecounty.org/1234/MeadowWood* ⛳ *18 holes, 6874 yards, par 70.*

HIKING

The hills around Spokane are laced with trails, almost all of which connect with 37-mile-long **Centennial Trail,** which winds along the Spokane River. Beginning in Nine Mile Falls, northwest of Spokane, the well-marked trail ends in Idaho. Maps are available at the visitor center at Riverfront Park. Northwest of downtown at **Riverside State Park,** a paved trail leads through a 17-million-year-old fossil forest in Deep Creek Canyon. From there it's easy to get to the western end of the Centennial Trail by crossing the suspension bridge at the day-use parking lot; trails heading both left and right will lead to the Centennial.

Riverside State Park

HIKING/WALKING | The park has 55 miles of trails for walking, hiking, and biking. Snowshoeing and cross-country skiing are popular activities in the winter. There's also a campground and water recreation on the Spokane and Little Spokane rivers. A $10 daily parking permit is required (or $30 annual Discover Pass that can be used at all Washington state parks). ✉ *9711 W. Charles Road* ☎ *509/465–5064* 🌐 *parks.state.wa.us/573/Riverside.*

SKIING

49° North

SKIING/SNOWBOARDING | An hour north of Spokane in the Colville National Forest, this is a 2,325-acre family-oriented resort. Lift tickets cost $57 to $65; snowboards and ski package rentals are $38. ✉ *U.S. 395, 3311 Flowery Trail Rd., Chewelah* ☎ *509/935–6649* 🌐 *www.ski49n.com.*

Mt. Spokane

SKIING/SNOWBOARDING | This modest downhill resort, 28 miles northeast of downtown Spokane, has a 2,000-foot drop and 10 miles of groomed cross-country ski trails. Snowshoeing and tubing are also options. There's night skiing Wednesday–Saturday. Lift tickets cost $46 to $62. A Discover Pass is required for all vehicles ($10 for one day or $30 annually) when visiting in summer. A Sno-Park permit is also required for parking at Nordic skiing trailheads. ✉ *29500 N. Mt. Spokane Park Dr., Mead* ☎ *509/238–2220* 🌐 *www.mtspokane.com.*

Moses Lake

105 miles west of Spokane.

The natural lake from which this sprawling town takes its name seems to be an anomaly in the dry landscape of East Central Washington. But ever since the Columbia Basin Project took shape, there's been water everywhere. Approaching Moses Lake from the west on Interstate 90, you'll pass lushly green irrigated fields; to the east lie vast stretches of wheat. The lakes of this region have more shorebirds than Washington's ocean beaches. Potholes Reservoir is an artificial lake that supports as much wildlife as does the Columbia Wildlife Refuge. The Winchester Wasteway, west of Moses Lake, is a great place to paddle a kayak or canoe and watch birds as you glide along the reedy banks.

GETTING HERE AND AROUND

Moses Lake straddles Interstate 90; it's about 100 miles from Spokane and 175 miles from Seattle. To the north, Highway 17 connects Moses Lake to Ephrata and points north, including Soap Lake and Coulee City.

ESSENTIALS

VISITOR INFORMATION Moses Lake Area Chamber of Commerce. ✉ *324 S. Pioneer Way* ☎ *509/765–7888, 800/992–6234* 🌐 *www.moseslake.com.*

Sights

Columbia National Wildlife Refuge

NATURE PRESERVE | A great number of birds are attracted to this reserve: hawks, falcons, golden eagles, ducks, sandhill cranes, herons, American avocets, black-necked stilts, and yellow-headed and red-winged blackbirds. The refuge is also home to beavers, muskrats, badgers, and coyotes. ✉ *51 S Morgan Lake Rd., Othello* ✣ *7 miles northwest of Othello* ☎ *509/488–3140* 🌐 *www.fws.gov/refuge/columbia* 🎟 *Free.*

Moses Lake

BODY OF WATER | Claw-shape, 38-foot-deep, 18-mile-long Moses Lake is filled by Crab Creek—which originates in the hills west of Spokane—with three side branches known as Parker Horn, Lewis Horn, and Pelican Horn. The city of Moses Lake sprawls over the peninsulas formed by these "horns," and can therefore be a bit difficult to get around. This is the state's second-largest lake. ✉ *Hwy. 17* ✣ *Off I–90.*

Moses Lake Museum and Art Center

MUSEUM | Exhibits include a collection of Native American artifacts and some on local history. Regional artists are featured in the gallery, and the giant Columbian Mammoth metal sculpture is a fun photo opp. ✉ *Moses Lake Civic Center, 401 S. Balsam St.* ☎ *509/764–3830* 🌐 *www.cityofml.com* ⏲ *Closed Sun.*

Potholes State Park

NATIONAL/STATE PARK | This park is 25 miles southwest of Moses Lake on the west side of O'Sullivan Dam next to the Potholes Reservoir, an artificial lake in a natural depression carved by the huge Spokane Floods. Open year-round, it's a great fishing lake, with trout in the fall, winter, and early spring, and ice fishing in the winter. Camping, boating, and wildlife viewing are other popular diversions. Five cabins are available to rent. ✉ *6762 Hwy. 262 E, Othello* ☎ *509/346–2759, 888/226–7688 campsite reservations* 🌐 *parks.state.wa.us/568/Potholes* 🎟 *Day pass $10 per vehicle.*

Surf 'n Slide Water Park

AMUSEMENT PARK/WATER PARK | **FAMILY** | This is a great place to cool off from the hot central Washington sunshine, with an Olympic-size pool, two 200-foot waterslides, a tube slide, a "baby octopus" slide, and diving boards. ✉ *McCosh Park, 401 W. 4th Ave.* ☎ *509/764–3805* 🌐 *www.cityofml.com* 🎟 *$15* ⏲ *Closed Labor Day–Memorial Day.*

Restaurants

Michael's on the Lake

$$$ | **AMERICAN** | As the late-afternoon rays of sunlight wash over the dining room and deck at this lakeside restaurant, you can indulge in main courses like Parmesan-crusted halibut over linguine and prime rib or share several of the smaller plates like ginger-chicken lettuce wraps, mahimahi tacos, and lobster mac and cheese. Chocolate lovers will appreciate the mile-high mud pie, half-baked chocolate-chip cookies, and chocolate-banana bread pudding. **Known for:** half-price appetizers during happy hour; decadent dessert menu; more than a dozen salads. $ *Average main: $24* ✉ *910 W. Broadway Ave.* ☎ *509/765–1611* 🌐 *www.michaelsonthelake.com.*

Porter House Steakhouse

$$ | **STEAKHOUSE** | **FAMILY** | The owners of one of Moses Lake's oldest restaurants set out to make it a favorite family gathering place where, as the name implies, steaks are the main event, ranging from an 8-ounce sirloin to a 24-ounce porterhouse. There's even a 4-ounce steak on the children's menu. **Known for:** a variety of chicken, seafood, and pasta dishes; extensive cocktail menu; friendly service. $ *Average main: $22* ✉ *217 N. Elder St.* ☎ *509/766–0308* 🌐 *www.porterhousesteakhouse.net* ⏲ *No lunch Sun.*

Comfort Suites

$$ | **HOTEL** | **FAMILY** | Spacious and comfortable rooms—considered suites because there's a separate sitting area—shine with modern style and conveniences. **Pros:** modern accommodations; nice swimming pool; friendly service. **Cons:**

no restaurant; prices steep during some events; a/c units can get noisy. *Rooms from: $152* *1700 E. Kittleson Rd.* *509/765–3731, 877/424–6423* *www.comfortsuitesmoseslake.com* *60 suites* *Free Breakfast.*

Shopping

Moses Lake Farmers Market
OUTDOOR/FLEA/GREEN MARKETS | Vendors come here each Saturday from May to October to sell fresh produce and handmade arts and crafts. *McCosh Park, 401 W. 4th Ave.* *509/750–7831* *www.moseslakefarmersmarket.com.*

Quincy

34 miles northwest of Moses Lake.

On the fences along Interstate 90 to Gorge and north on Highway 281 to Quincy, crop-identification signs highlight what the Quincy Valley is known for: agriculture. From Thanksgiving to New Year's Eve, these same fields are filled with Christmas motion-light displays, powered by electricity from farmers' irrigation lines—a delightful sight for highway travelers in the dark winter nights.

GETTING HERE AND AROUND

Quincy is 11 miles north of Interstate 90's Exit 149, via Highway 281. It's about two hours, 45 minutes from Seattle and two hours, 30 minutes from Spokane.

Sights

Gorge Amphitheatre
ARTS VENUE | This 27,500-seat amphitheater has won accolades as best outdoor concert venue due to its fine acoustics and stunning vistas of the Columbia River—a setting compared to the Grand Canyon's. Set in one of the sunniest parts of the state, the concert season runs from May to September. Concertgoers often overnight at the adjacent campground or at motels and hotels in Quincy, Soap Lake, Moses Lake, and Ellensburg. *754 Silica Rd. NW, George* *509/785–6262.*

Hotels

★ Cave B Inn and Spa Resort
$$ | RESORT | Built on (and into) ancient basalt cliffs 900 feet above the Columbia River; this resort's 15 cliff houses, 12 cavern rooms, and inn are all designed to blend into the natural environment and offer casually elegant, comfortable accommodations with fireplaces, soaking tubs, and other luxuries. **Pros:** hikes down to the river and past waterfalls; seasonal yurts have views of nearby vineyards; dogs welcome in some units. **Cons:** no local meal options besides on-site restaurant; summer weekend reservations fill up quickly; expensive during concerts. *Rooms from: $159* *344 Silica Rd. NW* *509/787–8000,* *www.cavebinn.com* *Closed mid-Dec.–early Feb.; yurts closed Nov.–Mar.* *58 rooms* *No meals.*

Ephrata

18 miles northeast of Quincy.

Ephrata (e- *fray*-tuh), a pleasant, small farm town and the Grant County seat, is in the exact center of Washington. It was settled quite early because its abundant natural springs made it an oasis in the dry steppe country of the Columbia Basin. Native Americans visited the springs, as did cattle drovers after American ranchers stocked the open range. Ephrata began to grow after the Great Northern Railroad established a terminal here in 1892. Cattlemen took advantage of the railroad to round up and ship out thousands of wild horses that roamed the range. The last great roundup was held in 1906, when the remaining 2,400 horses of a herd that once numbered some 25,000 were corralled and shipped off. Just north of Ephrata, the little town of Soap Lake is an interesting place to stretch your legs and watch summer vacationers cover themselves with mud.

GETTING HERE AND AROUND

Ephrata is about 20 miles north of Moses Lake via Highway 17. Continuing north on the highway leads to the town of Soap Lake, then past state parks, up to Coulee City.

Sights

Grant County Historical Museum and Village

MUSEUM | FAMILY | More than 30 pioneer-era buildings have been brought here from other parts of Grant County. They include a blacksmith forge, saloon, barbershop, and printing office. ✉ *742 Basin St. N* ☎ *509/754–3334* *$4* *Closed Oct.–Apr.*

Soap Lake

BODY OF WATER | The water is high in dissolved carbonates, sulfates, and chlorides, and the lake has long been famous for its mineral waters and therapeutic mud baths; in fact it was called the "World's Greatest Medical Marvel" more than a century ago. Yet the eponymous small town has never quite succeeded as a modern-day resort—perhaps because the miraculous waters have been heavily diluted by irrigation waters. Still, a loyal contingent of believers return to the lakeshore each year to cover themselves in the mud that they find healing. ✉ *Soap Lake* *6 miles north of Ephrata* *www.visitsoaplake.com.*

Hotels

Inn at Soap Lake

$$ | B&B/INN | FAMILY | Because this inn opened in 1915 during Soap Lake's heyday as a destination for health treatments, most rooms have a soaking tub with the natural mineral-rich water on tap. **Pros:** beautifully landscaped gardens; private beach has lounge chairs; pets allowed in some cottages. **Cons:** cottages often booked up with return guests; registration desk is not staffed; strict cancellation policy. *Rooms from: $150* ✉ *226 Main Ave. E, Soap Lake* ☎ *509/246–0462, 800/524–0558* *soaplakeresort.com/inn-soap-lake* *28 rooms* *No meals.*

Notaras Lodge

$$$ | HOTEL | FAMILY | The spacious rooms at this rustic lodge on the shore of Soap Lake are individually decorated, but they all have quirky touches like split-stump stools and beds with log frames, as well as photos and other artifacts from the original owner. **Pros:** one of the region's most unique lodgings; rooms are like historical museums; interesting grounds. **Cons:** not all rooms have lake views; two-night minimum on weekends; some units are in basement. *Rooms from: $210* ✉ *236 Main Ave. E, Soap Lake* ☎ *509/246–0462, 800/524–0558* *soaplakeresort.com/notaras-lodge* *15 rooms* *No meals.*

Coulee Dam National Recreation Area

60 miles northeast of Ephrata, 239 miles northeast of Seattle, 87 miles northwest of Spokane.

Grand Coulee Dam is the one of the world's largest concrete structures. At almost a mile long, it justly deserves the moniker "Eighth Technological Wonder of the World." Beginning in 1932, 9,000 men excavated 45 million cubic yards of rock and soil and dammed the Grand Coulee, a gorge created by the Columbia River, with 12 million cubic yards of concrete—enough to build a sidewalk the length of the equator. By the time the dam was completed in 1941, 77 men had perished and 11 towns were submerged under the newly formed Roosevelt Lake. The waters backed up behind the dam turned eastern Washington's arid soil

Northeastern Washington

into fertile farming land, but not without consequence: salmon-fishing stations that were a source of food and spiritual identity for Native Americans were destroyed.

In 1946 most of Roosevelt Lake and the grassy and pine woodland hills surrounding it were designated the Coulee Dam National Recreation Area. Crown Point Vista, about 5 miles west of Grand Coulee on Highway 174, may have the best vantage for photographs of the dam, Roosevelt Lake, Rufus Woods Lake (below the dam), and the town of Coulee Dam.

GETTING HERE AND AROUND

From Ephrata, take Highway 17 north to reach Grand Coulee. From the Spokane area, U.S. 2 to Highway 174 is the most direct route.

ESSENTIALS

VISITOR INFORMATION Grand Coulee Dam Area Chamber of Commerce. ✉ *17 Midway Ave., Grand Coulee* ☎ *509/633–3074* 🌐 *www.grandcouleedam.org.*

Sights

Colville Indian Reservation

NATIVE SITE | Highway 155 passes through the Colville Indian Reservation, one of the largest reservations in Washington, with about 7,700 enrolled members of the Colville Confederated Tribes. This was the final home for Chief Joseph and the Nez Perce, who fought a series of fierce battles with the U.S. Army in the 1870s after the U.S. government enforced a treaty that many present-day historians agree was fraudulent. Chief Joseph lived on the Colville reservation until his death in 1904. There's a memorial to him off Highway

155 east of the town of Nespelem, 17 miles north of the dam; four blocks away (two east and two north) is his grave. You can drive through the reservation's undeveloped landscape, and except for a few highway signs you'll feel like you've time-traveled to pioneer days. The **Colville Tribal Museum** (*512 Mead Way, Coulee Dam, 509/633–0751, open Tuesday–Saturday 8:30–5*) is worth a visit. ✉ *Coulee Dam* 🌐 *www.colvilletribes.com.*

Grand Coulee Dam Visitor Center

DAM | FAMILY | Colorful displays about the dam, a 13-minute film on the site's geology and the dam's construction, and information about the 30-minute laser-light show (held nightly from Memorial Day weekend through September) are here. The U.S. Bureau of Reclamation, which oversees operation and maintenance of the dam, conducts tours daily April through October, weather and maintenance schedules permitting. You can also pick up a self-guided historical walking tour that will take you from the visitor center through the old part of town, across the bridge, and into the old engineers' town. ✉ *Hwy. 155, Coulee Dam* ☎ *509/633–9265* 🌐 *www.usbr.gov/pn/grandcoulee.*

Lake Roosevelt National Recreation Area

NATIONAL/STATE PARK | The 150-mile-long lake was created by the Columbia River when it was backed up by Grand Coulee Dam. Several Native American villages, historic sites, and towns lie beneath the waters. Visitors find abundant opportunities for outdoor recreation on the lake, including fishing, swimming, and boating. The Fort Spokane Visitor Center and Museum operates from the former guardhouse and provides detailed and interesting information about the area's history, including its use as a military fort and later a boarding school for Native Americans and a tuberculosis hospital. ✉ *Headquarters, 1008 Crest Dr., Coulee Dam* ☎ *509/754–7800* 🌐 *www.nps.gov/laro* 🎫 *Free; camping $18 May–Sept., $9 Oct.–Apr.*

Steamboat Rock State Park

NATIONAL/STATE PARK | Here, a 2,200-foot-high flat-topped lava butte rises 1,000 feet above Banks Lake, the 31-mile-long irrigation reservoir filled with water from Lake Roosevelt by giant pumps and siphons. Water is distributed from the south end of the lake throughout the Columbia Basin. The state park has campsites, three cabins, a swimming area, and boat ramps. In summer it's popular with boaters and anglers, and in winter there's Nordic skiing, snowshoeing, and ice fishing. ✉ *51052 Hwy. 155, Electric City* ✥ *16 miles north of Coulee City* ☎ *509/633–1304, 888/226–7688* 🌐 *parks.state.wa.us/590/Steamboat-Rock* 🎫 *Day pass $10 per vehicle.*

★ **Sun Lakes-Dry Falls State Park**

NATURE SITE | A high point in the coulee, this park has picnic areas, campgrounds, boat rentals, and a state-run golf course that attracts visitors year-round; in summer the lakes bristle with boaters. From the bluffs on U.S. 2, west of the dam, you can get a great view over this enormous canyon. ✉ *34875 Park Lake Rd. NE, Coulee City* ☎ *509/632–5583, 888/226–7688 campsite reservations* 🌐 *parks.state.wa.us/298/Sun-Lakes-Dry-Falls* 🎫 *Day pass $10 per vehicle.*

Restaurants

Fusion Cafe

$ | AMERICAN | This spot is a bit of a hidden gem; it doesn't look too exciting inside or out, but all the food is made from scratch and expertly prepared. There are rotating specials along with the standard favorites, including burgers, soups, and salads. **Known for:** people rave about the cheesecake; excellent selection of burgers; a favorite with families. 💲 *Average main: 10* ✉ *302 Coulee Blvd. E, Electric City* ☎ *509/631–3011* ⏲ *Closed weekends and mid-Dec.–Jan 1.*

Hotels

Columbia River Inn

$ | **HOTEL** | The well-appointed rooms all have private decks at this roadside lodging across from Grand Coulee Dam, with easy access to hiking trails and fishing. **Pros:** rooms have microwaves and refrigerators; the views are definitely a plus; ideal locations. **Cons:** basic rooms on the small side; some visitors complain about noise; no food service on-site. *Rooms from: $120* ✉ *10 Lincoln St., Coulee Dam* ☎ *509/633-2100, 800/633-6421* 🌐 *www.columbiariverinn.com* *37 rooms* *No meals.*

Omak

52 miles northwest of Grand Coulee Dam.

Omak is a small mill and orchard town in the beautifully rustic Okanogan Valley of north-central Washington. Lake Omak to the southeast, on the Colville Reservation, is part of an ancient channel of the Columbia River, which ran north prior to the last ice age before turning south at Omak in what is now the lower Okanogan Valley.

For years Omak has been criticized by animal lovers for its mid-August Omak Stampede and Suicide Race. During the annual event, which started as a rodeo in 1933, wild horses race down a steep bluff and across the Okanogan River. Some horses have been killed and riders seriously injured. Many of the riders are from the Colville Reservation, and elders defend the race as part of Native American culture.

GETTING HERE AND AROUND

Omak can be reached from the west via Highway 20 from the Methow Valley area. From Ephrata, head north via Highway 17, then Highway 97. From Grand Coulee Dam, take WA 155N.

Sights

Okanogan County Historical Museum

MUSEUM | **FAMILY** | Okanogan pioneer life is portrayed in the displays here, and there's a replica of an Old West town. Outside are Okanogan's oldest building, a 19th-century log cabin, and antique farm equipment. ✉ *1410 2nd Ave. N, Okanogan* ☎ *509/422-4272* 🌐 *okanoganhistory.org* *$2* *Closed after Labor Day; reopens Memorial Day weekend.*

Okanogan National Forest

FOREST | This is a region of open woods, meadows, and pastoral river valleys in the Okanogan highlands. There's lots of wildlife: deer, black bears, coyotes, badgers, bobcats, cougars, grouse, hawks, and golden eagles. Campgrounds are scattered throughout the region. There are 11 Sno-Parks with groomed trails for snowmobilers, and open areas for cross-country skiing. Ski areas are at Loup Loup Pass (Nordic and alpine) and Sitzmark (alpine only). ✉ *Forest Headquarters, 215 Melody La., Wenatchee* ☎ *509/664-9200* 🌐 *www.fs.usda.gov/okawen* *Free; permits required at Sno-Parks.*

Restaurants

★ **Breadline Cafe**

$$ | **ECLECTIC** | Since the early 1980s, Breadline has been a top dining destination in the Okanogan Valley for hearty servings of eclectic fare. The menu features local organic produce, a variety of freshly baked breads, and locally raised natural Angus beef. **Known for:** the brandied bread pudding is a local favorite; soda fountain treats like root beer floats; Saturday buffet brunch. *Average main: $22* ✉ *102 S. Ash St.* ☎ *509/826-5836* 🌐 *www.breadlinecafe.com* *Closed Sun. and Mon. No breakfast Tues.–Fri.*

Chapter 20

VANCOUVER AND VICTORIA

Updated by Jennifer Foden, Sue Kernaghan, Chris McBeath, Lesley Mirza, Vanessa Pinniger

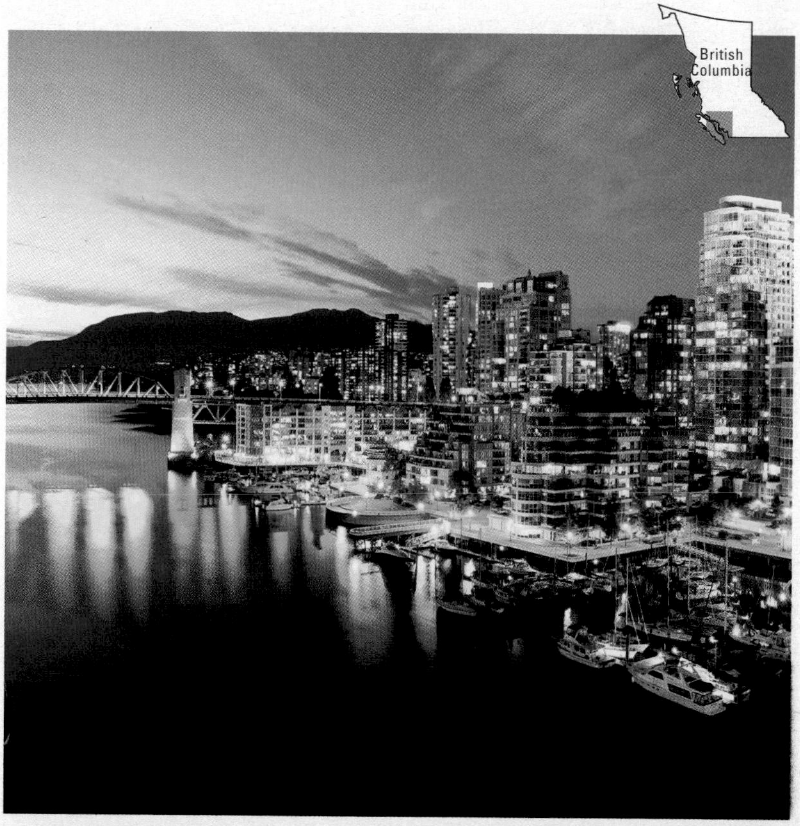

Sights ★★★★★ | Restaurants ★★★★★ | Hotels ★★★★★ | Shopping ★★★★★ | Nightlife ★★★★★

WELCOME TO VANCOUVER AND VICTORIA

TOP REASONS TO GO

★ **Stanley Park:** The views, the activities, and the natural wilderness beauty here are quintessential Vancouver.

★ **Granville Island:** Ride the miniferry across False Creek to the Granville Island Public Market, where you can shop for delicious lunch fixings; eat outside when the weather's fine.

★ **Museum of Anthropology at the University of British Columbia:** The phenomenal collection of First Nations art and cultural artifacts, and the incredible backdrop, make this a must-see.

★ **The Journey here:** Yes, getting here is one of the best things about Victoria: whether by ferry meandering past the Gulf or San Juan Islands, by floatplane (try to travel at least one leg this way), or on a whale-watching boat, getting to Victoria from the mainland is memorable.

★ **Butchart Gardens:** Nearly a million and a half visitors can't be wrong—these lavish gardens north of town live up to the hype.

Most of Vancouver is on a peninsula, which makes it compact and easy to explore on foot. To get your bearings, use the mountains as your "true north" and you can't go too far wrong.

Victoria, at the southern tip of Vancouver Island, is farther south than most of Canada, giving it the mildest climate in the country, with virtually no snow and less than half the rain of Vancouver.

The names can get confusing so here's what to remember: the city of Victoria is on Vancouver Island (not Victoria Island). The city of Vancouver is on the British Columbia mainland, not on Vancouver Island, or on Victoria Island (which isn't in British Columbia but rather way up north, spanning parts of Nunavut and the Northwest Territories).

1 Downtown and the West End.

2 Stanley Park.

3 Gastown and Chinatown.

4 Yaletown.

5 The West Side.

6 North Shore.

7 Downtown Victoria.

8 Brentwood Bay.

9 Rockland.

10 Salt Spring Island.

11 Galiano Island.

12 Tofino.

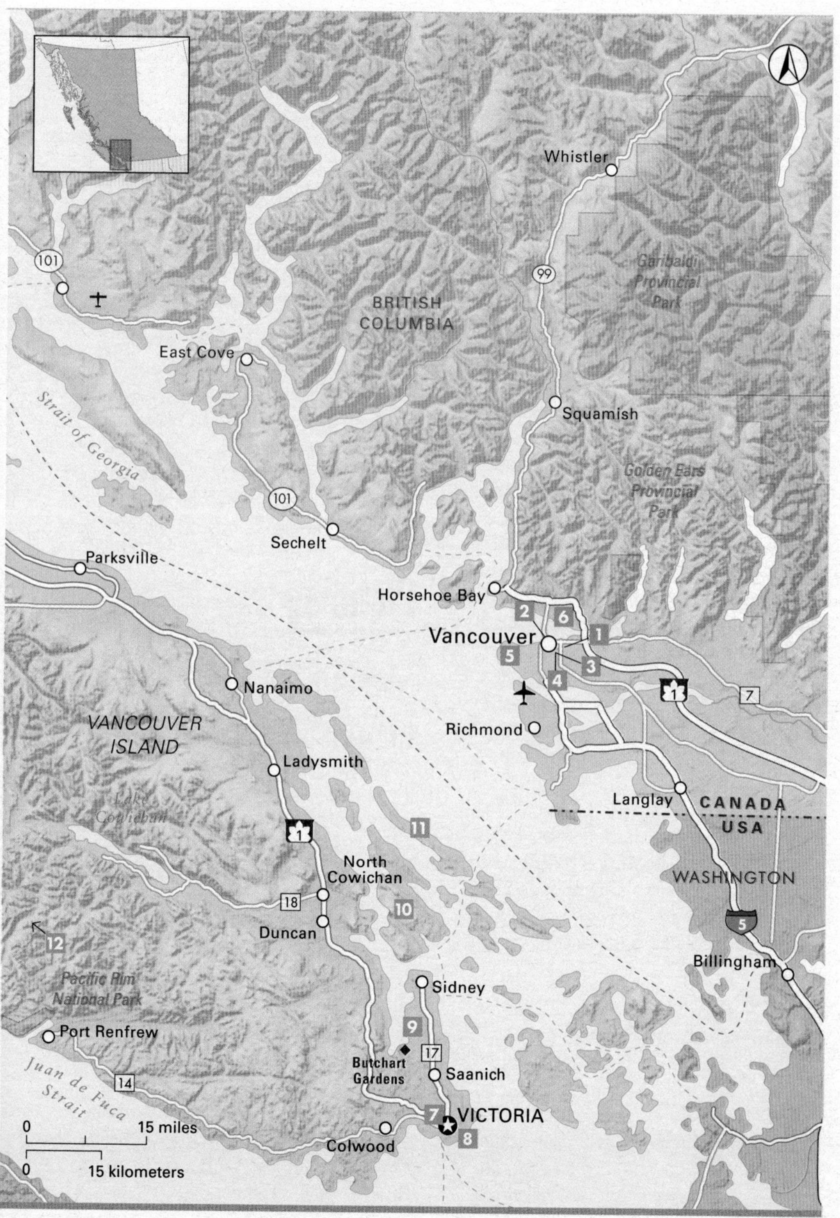

Whistler
101
99
Garibaldi Provincial Park
BRITISH COLUMBIA
East Cove
Strait of Georgia
Squamish
Golden Ears Provincial Park
101
Sechelt
Parksville
Horsehoe Bay
2
6
Vancouver
1
5
3
4
Nanaimo
1
7
VANCOUVER ISLAND
Richmond
Ladysmith
Langlay
CANADA
USA
Lake Cowichan
1
11
North Cowichan
WASHINGTON
18
10
Duncan
5
12
Pacific Rim National Park
Billingham
Sidney
Port Renfrew
9
17
Butchart Gardens
Saanich
Juan de Fuca Strait
14
7
VICTORIA
0
15 miles
8
Colwood
0
15 kilometers

Set on Canada's West Coast, Vancouver and Victoria blend urban sophistication and multicultural vitality with spectacular settings near mountains, ocean, and rain forest.

Both cities are famously livable: Vancouver gleams with towering skyscrapers; the smaller Victoria charms with its historic waterfront. To see the appeal, stroll and bike in Vancouver's Stanley Park, eat fresh seafood, sip cocktails, browse boutiques, and visit renowned museums and gardens. Sure, it rains out here, but take a cue from the laid-back locals in their chic, all-weather clothes. Vancouver is a delicious juxtaposition of urban sophistication and on-your-doorstep wilderness adventure. The mountains and seascape make the city an outdoor playground for hiking, skiing, kayaking, cycling, and sailing—and so much more—while the cuisine and arts scenes are equally diverse, reflecting the makeup of Vancouver's ethnic (predominantly Asian) mosaic. Victoria, British Columbia's photogenic capital, is a walkable, livable seaside city of fragrant gardens, waterfront paths, engaging museums, and beautifully restored 19th-century architecture. In summer, the Inner Harbour—Victoria's social and cultural center—buzzes with visiting yachts, horse-and-carriage rides, street entertainers, and excursion boats heading out to visit pods of friendly local whales.

MAJOR REGIONS

Vancouver. Many people say that Vancouver is the most gorgeous city in North America, and situated as it is, between mountains and water, it's hard to disagree. The Vancouver area actually covers a lot of ground, but the central core—Downtown, Gastown, Yaletown, Chinatown, Stanley Park, and Granville Island—is fairly compact. An excellent public transportation system makes getting around a snap. When in doubt, remember that the mountains are north.

Victoria. British Columbia's capital city, Victoria, is a lovely, walkable city with waterfront paths, lovely gardens, fascinating museums, and splendid 19th-century architecture. In some senses remote, it's roughly midway between Vancouver and Seattle and about three hours by car and ferry from either city.

Planning

Making the Most of Your Time

If you don't have much time in Vancouver, you'll probably still want to spend at least a half day in Stanley Park. A couple of hours at the Granville Island Public Market are also a must—plan to have breakfast or lunch, and, if you have time, check out the crafts stores. Walking the Downtown core is a great way to get to know the city. Start at Canada Place and head east to Gastown and Chinatown; that's a good half day. Then head north to Yaletown, perhaps for a glass of wine and dinner. If you're traveling with children, make sure to check out Science World, Grouse Mountain, and the Capilano Suspension Bridge or Lynn Canyon. For museums, adults and older children love the displays of Northwest Coast First Nations art at the Museum of Anthropology. The Bill Reid Gallery also has an impressive collection of aboriginal art.

You can see most of the sights in Downtown Victoria's compact core in a day, although there's enough to see at the main museums to easily fill two days. You can save time by prebooking tea at the Empress Hotel and buying tickets online for the Royal British Columbia Museum. You should also save at least half a day or a full evening to visit Butchart Gardens.

An extra day allows for some time on the water, either on a whale-watching trip—it's fairly easy to spot orcas in the area during summer—or on a Harbour Ferries tour, with stops for tea at Point Ellice House or fish-and-chips at Fisherman's Wharf. You can also explore the shoreline on foot, following all, or part, of the 7-mile waterfront walkway.

When to Go

July and August, with the best weather, are peak season on Vancouver Island. September, with its quieter pace, harvest festivals, and lingering sunshine, may be the perfect time to visit. Increasingly, storm-watchers are flocking to Tofino and Ucluelet in winter to watch dramatic tempests pound the coast. April is also a prime month for the west coast: that's when 20,000 gray whales swim by on their way to Alaska and when the Pacific Rim Whale Festival welcomes visitors. Victoria has the warmest, mildest climate in Canada: snow is rare and flowers bloom in February. Summers are mild, too, rarely topping 75°F. Between May and October is when the streets come to life with crafts stalls, street entertainers, blooming gardens, and the inevitable tour buses.

Getting Here and Around

Central Vancouver is extremely walkable, and the public transit system—a mix of bus, ferry, and SkyTrain (a fully automated rail system)—is efficient and easy to use. The hop-on, hop-off Vancouver Trolley buses circle the city in a continuous loop and are a great way to see the sites—especially on a rainy day; the same company runs the seasonal Stanley Park Shuttle.

It's easy to visit Victoria without a car. Most sights, restaurants, and hotels are in the compact walkable core, with bikes, ferries, horse-drawn carriages, double-decker buses, step-on tour buses, taxis, and pedicabs on hand to fill the gaps. For sights outside the core—Butchart Gardens, Hatley Castle, Scenic Marine Drive—tour buses are your best bet if you don't have your own vehicle. Bike paths lace Downtown and run along much of Victoria's waterfront, and long-haul car-free paths run to the ferry terminals and as far west as Sooke. Most buses and ferries carry bikes.

CONTACTS Vancouver Trolley Company. ☎ *604/801–5515* 🌐 *www.westcoastsightseeing.com.*

AIR

Air Canada, Pacific Coastal Airlines, and WestJet fly to Victoria from Vancouver International Airport. Alaska Airlines (under its Horizon Air division) flies between Seattle and Victoria. Victoria International Airport is 25 km (15 miles) north of Downtown Victoria. The flight from Vancouver to Victoria takes about 25 minutes. There is floatplane service to Victoria's Inner Harbour in Downtown Victoria with Harbour Air Seaplanes. Harbour Air also flies from Whistler to Downtown Victoria, May–September. Kenmore Air has daily floatplane service from Seattle to Victoria's Inner Harbour. Helijet has helicopter service from Downtown

Vancouver and Vancouver International Airport to Downtown Victoria.

BUS AND RAPID-TRANSIT

TransLink, Metro Vancouver's public transport system, includes bus service, a rapid transit system called SkyTrain, and a 400-passenger commuter ferry (SeaBus) that connects Downtown to the North Shore.

TransLink offers an electronic Compass Card system for single-fare tickets or stored-value cards, to be purchased at station vending machines before boarding. You "tap in" your ticket or card to the electronic reader when you board the SkyTrain or SeaBus; you "tap out" when you exit, which subtracts the fare from your card (you only have to "tap in" on buses). Cash fares (exact change required) can only be used for bus travel (single-fare tickets and stored-value cards are good for bus travel as well); SkyTrain and SeaBus fares must be purchased from machines (correct change isn't necessary). All fares are valid for 90 minutes and allow travel in any direction on the buses, SkyTrain, or SeaBus. Your Compass Card or single fare ticket must be carried with you as proof of payment. SkyTrain and SeaBus fares are based on zones (bus travel is considered one zone) and whether you have a stored-value Compass Card or single fare ticket: one zone (C$2.75 single fare, C$2.10 stored-value), two zones (C$4 single fare, C$3.15 stored-value), or three zones (C$5.50 single fare, C$4.20 stored-value). Fares go down in zones two and three in off-peak hours. Travel within the Vancouver city limits is a one-zone trip; traveling between Vancouver and the North Shore or from Vancouver to Richmond is two zones. You can also buy a day pass (on a Compass Card or single fare ticket) if you're planning to use the system frequently in one day (C$11 single/cash fare, C$9.75 stored-value, good all day across all zones).

A stored-value Compass Card does have its price: a C$6 refundable deposit. However, at a savings of 65 cents per ride in zone one (versus the single fare ticket), it'll pay off in just 10 rides. You can also get your deposit back if you return your card to the Customer Service Centre at Stadium-Chinatown Station. Also, note: all SkyTrain rides leaving YVR airport add a C$5 fee to your fare. If you're traveling to the airport, the same fee does not apply.

■ **TIP→ SkyTrain is convenient for transit between Downtown, BC Place Stadium, Pacific Central Station, Science World, and Vancouver International Airport. SeaBus is the fastest way to travel between Downtown and the North Shore (there are bus connections to Capilano Suspension Bridge and Grouse Mountain). There is also a free shuttle from Canada Place to Capilano Suspension Bridge and Grouse Mountain in the summer.**

CONTACTS TransLink. ☎ *604/953–3333* 🌐 *www.translink.ca.*

FERRY

Twelve- and 20-passenger Aquabus Ferries and False Creek Ferries bypass busy bridges and are a key reason why you don't need a car in Vancouver. Both of these are private commercial enterprises—not part of the TransLink system—that provide passenger services between key locales on either side of False Creek. Single-ride tickets range from C$3.25 to C$5.50 depending on the route; day passes are C$15. Aquabus Ferries connections include The Village (Science World and the Olympic Village), Plaza of Nations, Yaletown, Spyglass Place, Stamp's Landing, David Lam Park, Granville Island, and the Hornby Street dock. False Creek Ferries provides service between all of these stops (with the exception of the Hornby Street dock), and instead stops at the Aquatic Centre on Beach Avenue and the Maritime Museum in Kitsilano. The large SeaBus ferries (via TransLink, *see above*) travel between Waterfront Station and Lonsdale Quay in North Vancouver.

FROM THE BC MAINLAND

BC Ferries has daily service between Tsawwassen, about an hour south of Vancouver, and Swartz Bay, at the end of Highway 17 (the Patricia Bay Highway), about 30 minutes north of Victoria. Sailing time is about 1½ hours. An excellent option combines four hours of whale-watching with travel between Vancouver and Victoria, offered by the Prince of Whales. The 74-passenger boat leaves the Westin Bayshore Hotel in Downtown Vancouver daily at 9 am (June–mid-September), arriving in Victoria at 1 pm; there are also departures from Victoria's Inner Harbour at 1:45 pm (one-way C$200). Quadras and Cortes Islands (the most popular of the Discovery Islands wedged between BC Mainland and Vancouver Island) can also be reached by ferry (🌐 *www.discoveryislands.ca)*.

WITHIN VICTORIA

The Victoria Harbour Ferry serves the Inner Harbour; stops include the Fairmont Empress, Chinatown, Point Ellice House, the Delta Victoria Ocean Pointe Resort, and Fisherman's Wharf. Fares start at C$5. Boats make the rounds every 15 to 20 minutes. They run 10 to 9 from mid-May through mid-September and 11 to 5 from March through mid-May and mid-September to late October. The ferries don't run from November through February. The 45-minute harbor tours cost C$22, and gorge cruises cost C$26. At 10:45 am on summer Sundays, the little ferries perform a water ballet set to classical music in the Inner Harbour.

CONTACTS Victoria Harbour Ferry.
☎ *250/708–0201* 🌐 *www.victoriaharbourferry.com.*

Sights

Vancouver's Downtown core includes the main business district between Robson Street and the Burrard Inlet harbor front; the West End that edges up against English Bay; Stanley Park; trendy Yaletown; and Gastown and Chinatown, which are the oldest parts of the city. Main Street, which runs north–south, is roughly the dividing line between the east and west sides. The entire Downtown district sits on a peninsula bordered by English Bay and the Pacific Ocean to the west; by False Creek to the south; and by Burrard Inlet, the city's working port, to the north, where the North Shore Mountains loom. Home to the vast majority of Victoria's sights, hotels, and eateries, Downtownis Victoria for most visitors. At its heart is the Inner Harbour.

Restaurants

From inventive neighborhood bistros to glamorous Downtown dining rooms to ethnic restaurants that rival those in the world capitals, Vancouver has a diverse array of gastronomic options. Many cutting-edge establishments are perfecting what we call Modern Canadian fare, which—at the western end of the country—incorporates regional seafood (notably salmon, halibut, and spot prawns) and locally grown produce. Vancouver is all about "localism," with many restaurants emphasizing the provenance of their ingredients and embracing products that hail from within a 100-mile-or-so radius of the city, or at least from within BC.

With at least 40% of the region's population of Asian heritage, it's no surprise that Asian eateries abound in Vancouver. From mom-and-pop noodle shops, curry houses, and corner sushi bars to elegant and upscale dining rooms, cuisine from China, Taiwan, Hong Kong, Japan, and India (and to a lesser extent, from Korea,

Thailand, Vietnam, and Malaysia) can be found all over town.

Victoria has a tremendous number and variety of restaurants for such a small city; this fact, and the glorious pantry that is Vancouver Island—think local fish, seafood, cheese, and organic fruits and veggies—keeps prices down (at least compared to Vancouver) and standards up. Restaurants in the region are generally casual. Smoking is banned in all public places, including restaurant patios, in Greater Victoria and on the Southern Gulf Islands. Victorians tend to dine early—restaurants get busy at 6 and many kitchens close by 9. Pubs, lounges, and the few open-late places mentioned here are your best options for an after-hours nosh.

Afternoon tea is a Victoria tradition, as is good coffee—despite the Starbucks invasion, there are plenty of fun and funky local caffeine purveyors around town.

Hotels

Vancouver is a pretty compact city, but each neighborhood has a distinct character and its own style of accommodations options. From hip boutique hotels to historic bed-and-breakfasts to sharp-angled glass-and-mirror towers, there are lodging choices for every style and budget. You can choose to be in the center of the shopping action on Robson Street, among the gracious tree-lined boulevards near Stanley Park, or in close proximity to the pulsing heart of the city's core.

Most hotels let children under 18 stay free in their parents' room, though you may be charged extra for more than two adults. Parking runs about C$25 to C$40 per day at Downtown hotels, and can be free outside the Downtown core. Watch out for phone and Internet charges, which can add up. You'll also be charged a 1.5% accommodations tax, a 10% Provincial Sales Tax (PST), and a 5% Goods and Services Tax (GST) for a total levy of 16.5%.

Victoria has a vast range of accommodations, with what seems like whole neighborhoods dedicated to hotels. Options range from city resorts and full-service business hotels to midpriced tour-group haunts and family-friendly motels, but the city is especially known for its lavish B&Bs in beautifully restored Victorian and Edwardian mansions. Outlying areas, such as Sooke and Saanich, pride themselves on destination spa resorts and luxurious country inns, though affordable lodgings can be found there, too.

Hotel reviews have been shortened. For full information, visit Fodors.com.

What It Costs in Canadian Dollars

	$	$$	$$$	$$$$
RESTAURANTS				
	under C$13	C$13–C$20	C$21–C$30	over C$30
HOTELS				
	under C$125	C$125–C$195	C$196–C$300	over C$300

Nightlife

Vancouver might be best known for its outdoors activities but this hip city delivers plenty of entertainment once the sun goes down. Look for modern craft breweries, wine bars showcasing wines from the nearby Okanagan Valley, and some excellent music venues.

Shopping

Art galleries, ethnic markets, gourmet-food shops, and high-fashion boutiques abound in Vancouver. Shopping here is more unique than in many other North American cities because of the prevalence of Asian and First Nations influences in crafts, home furnishings, and foods. In the art scene, look for First Nations and other aboriginal art, from souvenir trinkets to stellar contemporary art; many galleries showcasing First Nations artists are in Gastown. Area artisans also create a variety of fine crafts, exhibiting and selling their wares at Granville Island galleries.

In Victoria, as in the rest of British Columbia, the most popular souvenirs are First Nations arts and crafts, which you can pick up at shops, galleries, street markets, and—in some cases—directly from artists' studios. Look for silver jewelry and cedar boxes carved with traditional images and, especially around Duncan (in the Cowichan Valley), the thick hand-knit sweaters made by the Cowichan people. BC wines, from shops in Victoria or directly from the wineries, make good souvenirs, as most are unavailable outside the province. Shopping in Victoria is easy: virtually everything is in the Downtown area on or near Government Street stretching north from the Fairmont Empress hotel.

Vancouver

Downtown and the West End

Vancouver's compact Downtown juxtaposes historic architecture with gleaming brand-new buildings. There are museums and galleries to visit, as well as top-notch shopping, most notably along Robson Street, which runs into the city's West End. The harbor front, with the green-roofed convention center, has a fabulous water's edge path all the way to Stanley Park—walk along here to get a feel for what Vancouver is all about.

Sights

★ Bill Reid Gallery

MUSEUM | Named after one of British Columbia's preeminent artists, Bill Reid (1920–98), this small aboriginal gallery is as much a legacy of Reid's works as it is a showcase of current First Nations artists. Displays include wood carvings, jewelry, print, and sculpture, and programs often feature artist talks and themed exhibitions such as basket weaving. Reid is best known for his bronze statue *The Spirit of Haida Gwaii, The Jade Canoe*—measuring 12 feet by 20 feet; it is displayed at the Vancouver International Airport, and its image was on the back of Canadian $20 bills issued between 2004 and 2012. More Bill Reid pieces are at the Museum of Anthropology. ✉ *639 Hornby St., Downtown* ☎ *604/682–3455* 🌐 *www.billreidgallery.ca* 🎫 *C$13* ⏲ *Closed Mon. and Tues., Oct.–May.*

Olympic Cauldron

PUBLIC ART | A four-pronged sculpture towering more than 30 feet, the Olympic Cauldron is next to the Vancouver Convention Centre's West Building. In 2010, when Vancouver hosted the Winter Olympic and Paralympic Games, it burned with the Olympic flame and it's relit occasionally, for Canada Day and other special events. The Cauldron overlooks the Burrard Inlet on Jack Poole Plaza, which is named for the Canadian businessman who led the bid to bring the Olympics to Vancouver. Sadly, Poole died of cancer just one day after the flame for the Olympic torch relay was lit in Olympia, Greece, at the start of its journey to Vancouver. ✉ *Foot of Thurlow St., at Canada Pl., Downtown.*

Robson Street

NEIGHBORHOOD | Running from the Terry Fox Plaza outside BC Place Stadium down to the West End, Robson is Vancouver's busiest shopping street, where fashionistas hang out at see-and-be-seen sidewalk cafés, high-end boutiques, and chain stores. Most of the designer action takes place between Jervis and Burrard streets, and that's also where you can find buskers and other entertainers in the evenings. ✉ *Downtown* 🌐 *www.robsonstreet.ca.*

Vancouver Public Library

LIBRARY | The Victoria Public Library, centered on Library Square, is enclosed in a free-standing elliptical. Bridges and wells filled with natural sunlight take you to different sections of the nine-story building. Movies and shows including *Battlestar Gallactica* have been filmed in the iconic structure. ✉ *350 W. Georgia St., Downtown* ☎ *604/331–3603* 🌐 *www.vpl.ca.*

Restaurants

Chambar

$$$$ | **BELGIAN** | In this hip, brick-walled eatery, classic Belgian dishes are reinvented with flavors from North Africa and beyond. The *moules* (mussels) are justifiably popular, either steamed in white wine or sauced with exotic smoked chilis, cilantro, and coconut cream. **Known for:** moules frites; Belgian beer; specialty meats. $ *Average main: C$32* ✉ *568 Beatty St., Downtown* ☎ *604/879–7119* 🌐 *www.chambar.com.*

Kingyo Izakaya

$$ | **JAPANESE** | Behind its ornate wooden door, this *izakaya* occupies the stylish end of the spectrum, with a carved wood bar, lots of greenery, and sexy mood lighting. The intriguing Japanese small plates, from salmon carpaccio to grilled miso-marinated pork cheeks to the spicy *tako-wasabi* (octopus), are delicious, and the vibe is bustling and fun. **Known for:** Japanese small plates; shochu and sake; stylish room. $ *Average main: C$16* ✉ *871 Denman St., West End* ☎ *604/608–1677* 🌐 *www.kingyo-izakaya.ca* 💳 *No credit cards.*

Hotels

★ **Rosewood Hotel Georgia**

$$$$ | **HOTEL** | The classy Rosewood is one of the city's most historic properties: the 1927 Georgian Revival building once welcomed prestigious guests such as Elvis Presley and Katharine Hepburn. **Pros:** at the center of the city's action; top-rated spa; destination restaurant. **Cons:** expensive valet parking; restaurant can get very busy; on Vancouver's busiest thoroughfare. $ *Rooms from: C$566* ✉ *801 W. Georgia St., Downtown* ☎ *604/682–5566, 888/767–3966* 🌐 *www.rosewoodhotels.com/en/hotel-georgia-vancouver/* *156 rooms* 🍽 *No meals.*

★ **Times Square Suites Hotel**

$$$ | **HOTEL** | **FAMILY** | You can't get much closer to Stanley Park than this chic but understated all-suites hotel near plenty of restaurants. **Pros:** next to Stanley Park; good location for restaurants; roof deck for guest use. **Cons:** on a very busy intersection; back rooms overlook noisy-at-night alley; lack of storage for large suitcases. $ *Rooms from: C$266* ✉ *1821 Robson St., West End* ☎ *604/684–2223* 🌐 *www.timessquaresuites.com* *42 rooms* 🍽 *No meals.*

★ **Wedgewood Hotel & Spa**

$$$$ | **HOTEL** | A member of the exclusive Relais & Châteaux group, the luxurious, family-owned Wedgewood is all about pampering. **Pros:** personalized service; great location close to shops; Bacchus Lounge is a destination in its own right. **Cons:** hotel fills up quickly, book well ahead; Bacchus Lounge can get very busy; no pool. $ *Rooms from: C$435* ✉ *845 Hornby St., Downtown* ☎ *604/689–7777, 800/663–0666* 🌐 *www.wedgewoodhotel.com* *83 rooms* 🍽 *No meals.*

Nightlife

BARS

★ Tap & Barrel

BARS/PUBS | The 360-degree views from this convention center patio take in Stanley Park, the seaplane terminal, and the North Shore Mountains. You can sit inside, amid the wooden casks of wine, but waiting for a seat on the deck is worth it if the weather even hints at sunshine. There's another location—and similarly large patio—on False Creek (*75 Athlete's Way*), and yet another at North Vancouver's Shipyards district with equally stunning harbor views on a giant patio. ✉ *1055 Canada Pl., Downtown* ☎ *604/235–9827* 🌐 *www.tapandbarrel.com.*

Shopping

SPECIALTY STORES

★ Silk Road Tea Store

FOOD/CANDY | Tea aspires to new heights in this chic emporium at the edge of Chinatown. Shelves are stacked with more than 300 intriguing varieties; some you can enjoy in flights at an impressive tasting bar, and others have been restyled into aromatherapy remedies and spa treatments, including a green tea facial, which you can try out in the tiny spa downstairs. Or check out Silk Road's afternoon teas at Hotel Grand Pacific (reservations: 250/380-4458). ✉ *1624 Government St., Downtown* ☎ *250/382-0006* 🌐 *www.silkroadtea.com.*

MacLeod's Books

BOOKS/STATIONERY | One of the city's best antiquarian and used-book stores, this jam-packed shop is a treasure trove of titles from mainstream to wildly eclectic. ✉ *455 W. Pender St., Downtown* ☎ *604/681–7654.*

Munro's Books

BOOKS/STATIONERY | Move over, Chapters-Indigo: this beautifully restored 1909 former bank now houses one of Canada's best-stocked independent bookstores. Deals abound in the remainders bin. ✉ *1108 Government St., Downtown* ☎ *250/382–2464* 🌐 *www.munrobooks.com.*

★ lululemon athletica

CLOTHING | Power-yoga devotees, soccer moms, and anyone who likes casual, comfy clothes covets the fashionable, well-constructed workout wear with the stylized "A" insignia from this Vancouver-based company. In addition to the flagship location at 2123 West 4th Avenue in Kitsilano, there are several branches around town, including a lululemon lab at 50 Powell Street in Gastown that showcases the latest athleisure lines. ✉ *970 Robson St., Downtown* ☎ *604/681–3118* 🌐 *www.lululemon.com.*

★ Roots

CLOTHING | For outdoorsy clothes that double as souvenirs (many sport maple-leaf logos), check out these Canadian-made sweatshirts, leather jackets, and other comfy casuals for men, women and kids. In addition to this Downtown flagship store, there's a smaller branch down the street at 1153 Robson Street, branches on South Granville Street and on West 4th Avenue in Kitsilano, and a number of outlet stores, called Roots 73, in the suburbs. ✉ *1001 Robson St., West End* ☎ *604/683–4305* 🌐 *www.roots.com.*

Stanley Park

A 1,000-acre wilderness park, only blocks from the Downtown section of a major city, is a rare treasure and Vancouverites make use of it to bike, walk, jog, in-line skate, and go to the beach.

Sights

★ Stanley Park Seawall

TRAIL | Vancouver's seawall path includes a 9-km (5½-mile) paved shoreline section within Stanley Park. It's one of several car-free zones in the park and it's popular with walkers and cyclists. If you have the time (about a half day) and the energy, strolling the entire seawall is an exhilarating experience. ✉ *Stanley Park.*

★ Vancouver Aquarium

ZOO | FAMILY | Massive floor-to-ceiling windows let you get face-to-face with sea otters, sea lions, dolphins, and harbor seals at this award-winning research and educational facility. In the Amazon Gallery you walk through a rain-forest jungle populated with piranhas, caimans, and tropical birds; in summer, hundreds of free-flying butterflies add to the mix. The Tropic Zone is home to exotic freshwater and saltwater life, including clown fish, moray eels, and black-tip reef sharks. Other displays, many with hands-on features for kids, show the underwater life of coastal British Columbia and the Canadian Arctic. Sea lion and dolphin shows, as well as dive shows (where divers swim with aquatic life, including sharks) are held daily. Be sure to check out the stingray touch pool, as well as the "4-D" film experience (it's a multisensory show that puts mist, smell, and wind into the 3-D equation). For an extra fee, you can help the trainers feed and train otters, belugas, and sea lions. There's also a café and a gift shop. Be prepared for lines on weekends and school holidays. In summer, the quietest time to visit is before 11 am or after 4 pm; in other seasons, the crowds are smaller before noon or after 2 pm. ✉ *845 Avison Way, Stanley Park* ☎ *604/659–3474 information line* 🌐 *www.vanaqua.org* 🎫 *C$40.*

Restaurants

The Teahouse in Stanley Park

$$$$ | CANADIAN | The former officers' mess at Ferguson Point in Stanley Park is a prime location for water views by day, and for watching sunsets at dusk. The Pacific Northwest menu is not especially innovative, but its broad appeal will please those looking for local fish, rack of lamb, steaks, and a host of other options, including gluten-free pasta. **Known for:** tasting boards; lovely patio; Pacific Northwest cuisine. $ *Average main: C$33* ✉ *7501 Stanley Park Dr., Stanley Park* ✣ *At Ferguson Point* ☎ *604/669–3281* 🌐 *www.vancouverdine.com/teahouse.*

Gastown and Chinatown

Historic Gastown and adjacent Chinatown are full of character. They're favorite destinations for visitors and residents alike, and easily explored together. Both neighborhoods are experiencing gentrification as historic buildings get a new lease on life.

Sights

★ Dr. Sun Yat-Sen Classical Chinese Garden

GARDEN | The first authentic Ming Dynasty–style garden outside China, this small garden was built in 1986 by 52 Chinese artisans from Suzhou. No power tools, screws, or nails were used in the construction. It incorporates design elements and traditional materials from several of Suzhou's centuries-old private gardens. Guided tours (45 minutes long), included in the ticket price, are conducted on the hour between mid-June and the end of August (call ahead or check the website for off-season tour times); these are valuable for understanding the philosophy and symbolism that are central to the garden's design. Covered walkways make this a good rainy-day choice. A concert series, including classical, Asian, world, jazz, and sacred music, plays on Thursday evenings in July and August. The free public park next door is a pleasant place to sit, but lacks the context that you get with a tour of the Sun Yat-Sen garden. ✉ *578 Carrall St., Chinatown* ☎ *604/662–3207* 🌐 *www.vancouverchinesegarden.com* 🎫 *C$13.33* 🕒 *Closed Mon., Oct.–Apr.* Ⓜ *Stadium-Chinatown.*

Restaurants

★ Ask For Luigi

$$$ | ITALIAN | Neighborhood residents queue before opening to secure one of the 30 seats in this cozy Italian bistro serving up house-made pasta and Prosecco on tap. Antipasti like smoked mackerel, crispy polenta, and—of course—meatballs, are served family-style, so bring some friends for the best experience. **Known for:** family-style dining; Italian antipasti; house-bottled Spritz. *Average main: C$25* ✉ *305 Alexander St., Gastown* ☎ *604/428–2544* 🌐 *www.askforluigi.com* ⏲ *Closed Mon.*

★ Pidgin

$$$ | ASIAN FUSION | The menu in this glossy white space draws inspiration from Asia for inventive sharing plates that are some of Vancouver's most exciting eating options. From the ever-changing menu, you might choose chicken *karaage* with spicy yuzu kosho mayo and tosazu pickle daikon, a foie-gras rice bowl with chestnuts, daikon, and a unagi glaze, or the Korean rice cake with gochujang bolognese and spiced hazelnut. **Known for:** inventive sharing plates; creative cocktails; bold flavors. *Average main: C$26* ✉ *350 Carrall St., Gastown* ☎ *604/620–9400* 🌐 *www.pidginvancouver.com* ⏲ *No lunch.*

Nightlife

BARS

★ The Keefer Bar

BARS/PUBS | The Keefer Bar has fully capitalized on its Chinatown connection, using ingredients sourced from local herbalists (magnolia bark anyone?)—ginseng, tea-based tinctures, or astragalus root, for example. Small plates of Asian dishes make good nibbling. The decor is dark and red, with hanging cylindrical neon lights that layer a sultry, hidden vibe over nights of live music and DJs. ✉ *135 Keefer St., Chinatown* ☎ *604/688–1961* 🌐 *www.thekeeferbar.com.*

Shopping

ART AND ANTIQUES

★ Hill's Native Art

ART GALLERIES | This highly respected store has Vancouver's largest selection of First Nations art. The place is crammed with souvenirs, keepsakes, and high-quality pieces, including carvings, masks, and drums. If you think that's impressive, head for one-of-a-kind collector pieces and limited editions. Its recent move from Gastown to East Broadway makes it a 10-minute cab ride from Downtown, but the larger and brighter space makes for easy browsing. ✉ *120 E. Broadway, Mt. Pleasant* ☎ *604/685–4249, 866/685–5422* 🌐 *www.hills.ca.*

SHOES AND ACCESSORIES

★ John Fluevog

SHOES/LUGGAGE/LEATHER GOODS | You might have seen John Fluevog shops in New York and Los Angeles, but did you know that these funky shoes were created by a Vancouverite? The Gastown location is worth a look for the store itself, with its striking glass facade and soaring ceilings. There's another branch Downtown at 837 Granville Street. ✉ *65 Water St., Gastown* ☎ *604/688–6228* 🌐 *www.fluevog.com.*

Yaletown

Yaletown is one of Vancouver's most fashionable areas and one of the most impressive urban-redevelopment projects in North America. The brick warehouses were turned into apartment buildings and offices, and the old loading docks are now terraces for cappuccino bars and trendy restaurants. There are brewpubs, day spas, retail and wholesale fashion outlets, and shops selling upscale home decor.

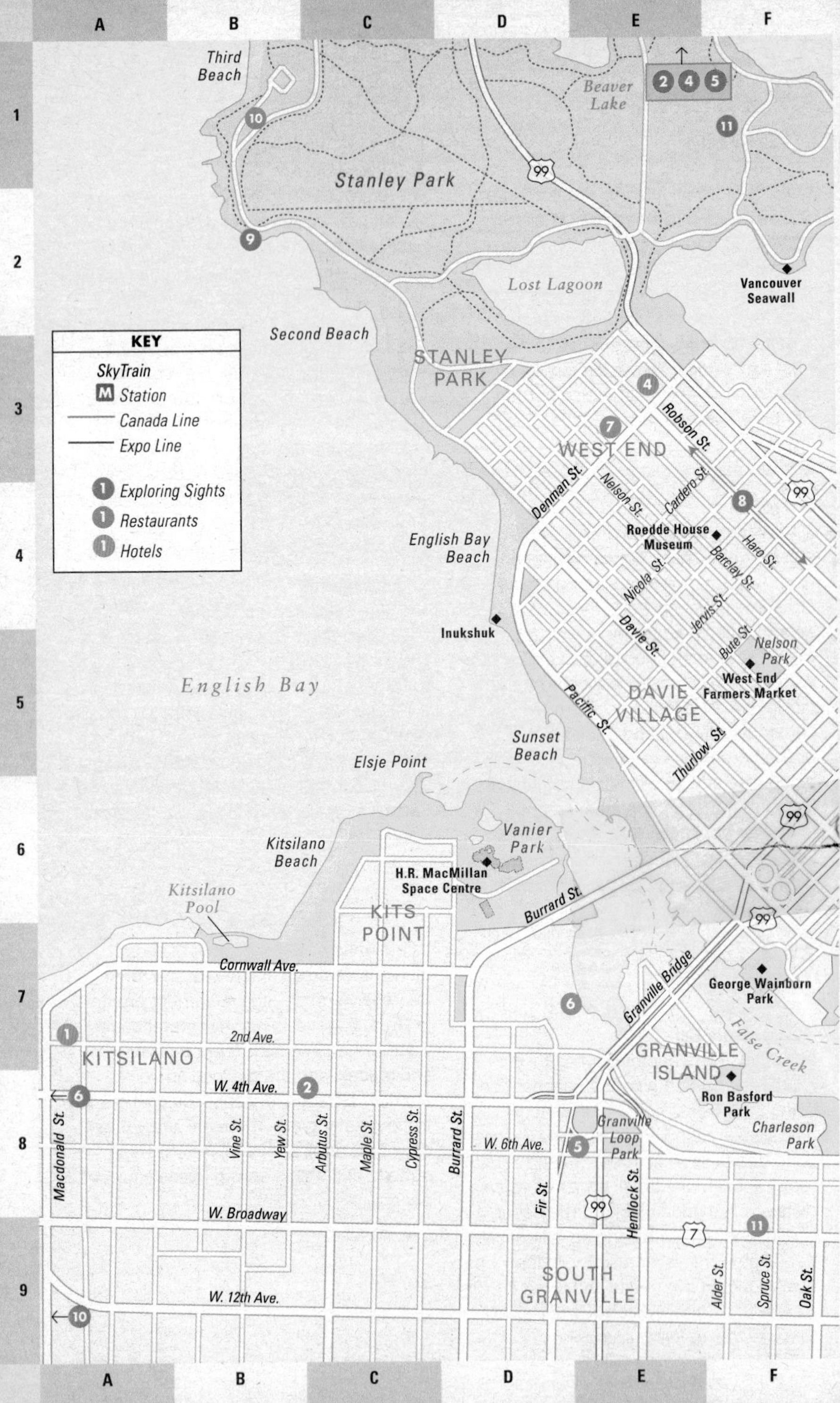

A
B
C
D
E
F
1
2
3
4
5
6
7
8
9
Third Beach
Beaver Lake
Stanley Park
Lost Lagoon
Vancouver Seawall
KEY
SkyTrain
Station
Canada Line
Expo Line
Exploring Sights
Restaurants
Hotels
Second Beach
STANLEY PARK
WEST END
Robson St.
Denman St.
Nelson St.
Cardero St.
Roedde House Museum
Haro St.
Barclay St.
English Bay Beach
Nicola St.
Jervis St.
Davie St.
Bute St.
Nelson Park
Inukshuk
West End Farmers Market
English Bay
Pacific St.
DAVIE VILLAGE
Sunset Beach
Thurlow St.
Elsje Point
Vanier Park
Kitsilano Beach
H.R. MacMillan Space Centre
Kitsilano Pool
KITS POINT
Burrard St.
Cornwall Ave.
Granville Bridge
George Wainborn Park
False Creek
2nd Ave.
KITSILANO
GRANVILLE ISLAND
W. 4th Ave.
Ron Basford Park
Granville Loop Park
Charleson Park
Macdonald St.
Vine St.
Yew St.
Arbutus St.
Maple St.
Cypress St.
Burrard St.
W. 6th Ave.
Fir St.
Hemlock St.
W. Broadway
SOUTH GRANVILLE
W. 12th Ave.
Alder St.
Spruce St.
Oak St.

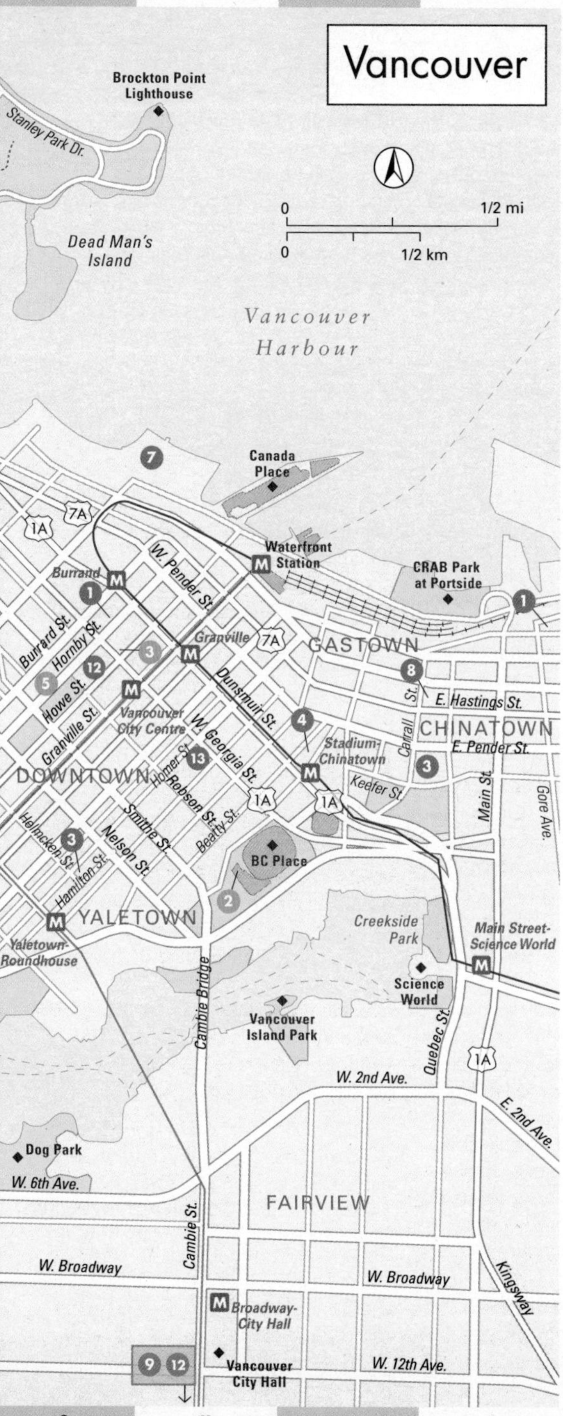

Sights

1 Bill Reid Gallery G4
2 Capilano Suspension Bridge E1
3 Dr. Sun Yat-Sen Classical Chinese Garden..................... J5
4 Grouse Mountain E1
5 Lynn Canyon Park and Suspension Bridge E1
6 Museum of Anthropology......... A8
7 Olympic Cauldron................. H3
8 Robson Street....................... F4
9 Stanley Park Seawall B2
10 University of British Columbia Botanical Garden A9
11 Vancouver Aquarium............... F1
12 Vancouver Art Gallery............. G5
13 Vancouver Public Library......... H5

Restaurants

1 Ask for Luigi J4
2 Bishop's.............................. B8
3 Blue Water Cafe G6
4 Chambar I6
5 Farmer's Apprentice................ E8
6 Go Fish D7
7 Kingyo Izakaya...................... E3
8 Pidgin J5
9 Seasons in the Park H9
10 The Teahouse in Stanley Park.... B1
11 Tojo's F9
12 Vij's H9

Hotels

1 Corkscrew Inn A7
2 Douglas Hotel H6
3 Rosewood Hotel Georgia G5
4 Times Square Suites Hotel E3
5 Wedgewood Hotel & Spa......... G5

Restaurants

★ Blue Water Cafe

$$$$ | **SEAFOOD** | Executive chef Frank Pabst focuses his menu on both popular and lesser-known local seafood (including frequently overlooked varieties like mackerel or herring) at his widely heralded, fashionable fish restaurant. You can dine in the warmly lighted interior or outside on the former loading dock that's now a lovely terrace. **Known for:** seafood-centric menu; top-notch sushi; great local wine list. *Average main: C$38 ✉ 1095 Hamilton St., Yaletown ☎ 604/688–8078 🌐 www.bluewatercafe.net ⏲ No lunch.*

Hotels

★ Douglas Hotel

$$$$ | **RESORT** | The Douglas, an Autograph Collection Hotel, is a stunning one-of-a-kind property created by Marriott and situated within the city's newest entertainment destination, Parq Vancouver. **Pros:** steps from False Creek and the seawall; multiple dining options; dog-friendly. **Cons:** strong signature fragrance in lobby; several minutes' walk to the heart of Downtown; hotel parking is expensive. *Rooms from: C$320 ✉ Parq Vancouver, 39 Smithe St., Yaletown ☎ 604/676-0889 🌐 thedouglasvancouver.com 288 rooms No meals.*

The West Side

The West Side, the set of diverse neighborhoods just south of Downtown, has some of Vancouver's best gardens and natural sights as well as some chic shopping. "Kits," as the locals refer to Kitsilano, though, is really where all the action is: the once-hippie neighborhood has evolved into an upscale district of shops, restaurants, museums, and one of the city's best people-watching beaches.

Sights

★ Museum of Anthropology

MUSEUM | Part of the University of British Columbia, the MOA has one of the world's leading collections of Northwest Coast First Nations art. The Great Hall has dramatic cedar poles, bentwood boxes, and canoes adorned with traditional Northwest Coast–painted designs. On clear days, the gallery's 50-foot-tall windows reveal a striking backdrop of mountains and sea. *✉ University of British Columbia, 6393 N.W. Marine Dr., Point Grey ☎ 604/822–5087 🌐 www.moa.ubc.ca C$18; Thurs. 5–9 pm C$10 ⏲ Closed Mon. mid-Oct.–mid-May.*

University of British Columbia Botanical Garden

GARDEN | **FAMILY** | Ten thousand trees, shrubs, and rare plants from around the world thrive on this 70-acre research site on the university campus, which edges on Pacific Spirit Park. The complex feels as far away from the city as you can get, with forested walkways through an Asian garden, a garden of medicinal plants, and an alpine garden with some of the world's rarest plants. A Walk in the Woods is a 20-minute loop that takes you through more than 1,000 species of coastal plant life. The garden gift store is one of the best of its kind. One-hour guided tours, free with garden admission, are offered on certain days; call or check the website for schedule. A UBC Museums and Gardens Pass will save you money if you're planning to visit several attractions at UBC.

✉ 6804 S.W. Marine Dr., Point Grey ☎ 604/822–4208 🌐 www.botanicalgarden.ubc.ca C$10; C$26 includes Nitobe Memorial Garden and Greenheart TreeWalk.

Restaurants

★ Bishop's

$$$$ | **MODERN CANADIAN** | Before "local" and "seasonal" were all the rage, this highly regarded restaurant was serving West Coast cuisine with an emphasis on organic regional produce. Menu highlights include starters like tuna tartare with pickled garlic scapes and arugula seed pods, while Haida Gwaii halibut with broccoli puree, roasted cauliflower, and crispy potato, and heritage pork with clams are among the tasty main dishes. **Known for:** impeccable service; extensive local wine list; West Coast cuisine. *$ Average main: C$42 ✉ 2183 W. 4th Ave., Kitsilano ☎ 604/738–2025 ⊕ www.bishopsonline.com ⏲ Closed Sun. and Mon. No lunch.*

★ Go Fish

$$ | **SEAFOOD** | If the weather's fine, head for this seafood stand on the seawall overlooking the docks beside Granville Island. The menu is short—highlights include fish-and-chips, grilled salmon or tuna sandwiches, and fish tacos—but the quality is first-rate. **Known for:** seaside location; fish-and-chips; long queues. *$ Average main: C$12 ✉ Fisherman's Wharf, 1505 W. 1st Ave., Kitsilano ☎ 604/730–5040 ⏲ Closed Mon. No dinner.*

★ Farmer's Apprentice

$$$ | **MODERN CANADIAN** | Book ahead to nab one of the 30 or so seats in this cozy bistro, voted one of Canada's 100 Best restaurants, where chef Bardia Ilbeiggi and his team in the open kitchen craft wildly creative "vegetable forward" set menus. It's not a vegetarian restaurant, but fresh local produce plays starring roles both the "omnivore" and "herbivore" (C$65) menus, each featuring six courses that change daily to feature seasonal ingredients like garlic ramps, heirloom tomatoes, and black garlic. **Known for:** six-course menus; seasonal ingredients; great vegetarian dining. *$ Average main: C$30 ✉ 1535 W. 6th Ave., South Granville ☎ 604/620–2070 ⊕ www.farmersapprentice.ca ⏲ Closed Mon.*

★ Seasons in the Park

$$$$ | **PACIFIC NORTHWEST** | A perennial favorite with locals for special occasions, this restaurant boasts spectacular views overlooking the city and mountains from its perch at the highest point in Queen Elizabeth Park. Service is excellent in the white-tableclothed dining room and the menu showcases regional West Coast cuisine. **Known for:** panoramic views; special occasions; fine dining. *$ Average main: C$32 ✉ Queen Elizabeth Park, West 33rd Ave. at Cambie, Cambie ☎ 604/874-8008 ⊕ www.vancouverdine.com.*

★ Tojo's

$$$$ | **JAPANESE** | Hidekazu Tojo is a sushi-making legend in Vancouver, with thousands of special preparations stored in his creative mind. The first to introduce omakase to Vancouver, he is also the creator of the '"Inside out"' Tojo Roll, now universally known as the "California Roll." In this bright modern, high-ceilinged space, complete with a separate sake lounge, the prime perch is at the sushi bar, a convivial ringside seat for watching the creation of edible art. **Known for:** omakase; top-notch sushi; sake lounge. *$ Average main: C$36 ✉ 1133 W. Broadway, Cambie ☎ 604/872–8050 ⊕ www.tojos.com ⏲ Closed Sun. No lunch.*

★ Vij's

$$$ | **INDIAN** | Long lauded as Vancouver's most innovative Indian restaurant, and always on the Top Ten lists of restaurants in the country, this dining destination, run by genial proprietor Vikram Vij and his ex-wife Meeru Dhalwala, uses local ingredients to create exciting takes on South Asian cuisine. Mark Bittman said in the *New York Times* it is "easily among the finest Indian restaurants in the world." Dishes such as lamb "popsicles" in a creamy curry or BC rainbow trout

in coconut masala served with a wheat berry pilaf are far from traditional but are beautifully executed. **Known for:** one of the best Indian restaurants in North America; rooftop patio; warm, welcoming service. *$ Average main: C$30 ✉ 3106 Cambie St., Cambie ☎ 604/736–6664 🌐 www.vijs.ca ⏲ No lunch.*

Hotels

★ Corkscrew Inn

$$$ | B&B/INN | This restored 1912 Craftsman-style house near the beach in Kitsilano combines the comforts of a B&B with a quirky tribute to the humble corkscrew: guests are encouraged to explore the small wine paraphernalia museum. **Pros:** great local neighborhood; delicious breakfast; free parking. **Cons:** not Downtown; a 15-minute bus ride to the Canada Line airport connection; no pets. *$ Rooms from: C$295 ✉ 2735 W. 2nd Ave., Kitsilano ☎ 604/733–7276, 877/737–7276 🌐 www.corkscrewinn.com 5 rooms Free breakfast.*

Shopping

FOOD

★ Les Amis du Fromage

FOOD/CANDY | If you love cheese, don't miss the mind-boggling array of selections from BC, the rest of Canada, and elsewhere at this family-run shop of delicacies. Owner Allison Spurrell and her extremely knowledgeable staff encourage you to taste before you buy. Yum. The fromagerie is located between Granville Island and Kitsilano Beach—useful to keep in mind if you're assembling a seaside picnic. There's a second location at 843 East Hastings Street on Vancouver's East Side. *✉ 1752 W. 2nd Ave., Kitsilano ☎ 604/732–4218 🌐 www.buycheese.com.*

North Shore

The North Shore and its star attractions—the Capilano Suspension Bridge, Grouse Mountain, Lonsdale Quay, and, farther east, the lovely hamlet of Deep Cove—are just a short trip from Downtown Vancouver. The North Shore is where people come to kayak up fjords, and hike, ski, and explore the forest and mountainous terrain. The two main communities on the North Shore are North Vancouver and West Vancouver.

Sights

★ Capilano Suspension Bridge

BRIDGE/TUNNEL | FAMILY | At Vancouver's oldest tourist attraction (the original bridge was built in 1889), you can get a taste of rain forest scenery and test your mettle on the swaying, 450-foot cedar-plank suspension bridge that hangs 230 feet above the rushing Capilano River. Across the bridge is the Treetops Adventure, where you can walk along 650 feet of cable bridges suspended among the trees. If you're even braver, you can follow the **Cliffwalk**, a series of narrow cantilevered bridges and walkways hanging out over the edge of the canyon. Without crossing the bridge, you can enjoy the site's viewing decks, nature trails, and totem park, as well as history and forestry exhibits. There's also a massive gift shop in the original 1911 teahouse, and a restaurant. May through October, guides in 19th-century costumes conduct free tours on themes related to history, nature, or ecology, while fiddle bands, and other entertainers keep things lively. In December, more than 1.5 million lights illuminate the canyon during the Canyon Lights winter celebration. Catch the attraction's free shuttle service from Canada Place; it also stops at hotels along Burrard and Robson streets. *✉ 3735 Capilano Rd., North Vancouver ☎ 877/985-7474 🌐 www.capbridge.com C$53.95; Parking: $7.50.*

Grouse Mountain

VIEWPOINT | FAMILY | Enjoy city views from a mountain gondola and a wealth of alpine activites on Grouse Mountain. ✉ *6400 Nancy Greene Way, North Vancouver* ☎ *604/980–9311* 🌐 *www.grousemountain.com* 🎫 *Skyride and many activities C$59* ⏲ *Closed late October to early November.*

↗ Lynn Canyon Park and Suspension Bridge
With a steep canyon landscape, a temperate rain forest complete with waterfalls, and a suspension bridge (circa 1912) 166½ feet above raging Lynn Creek, this 617-acre park provides thrills to go with its scenic views. The park has many hiking trails, including a short walk to a popular swimming hole, and another trail leading to a double waterfall. Longer walks in the park link to trail networks in nearby Lynn Headwaters Regional Park and the Lower Seymour Conservation Reserve. The park's on-site Ecology Centre distributes trail maps, as well as information about the local flora and fauna. There's also a gift shop and a café here. To get to the park, take the Lions Gate Bridge and Capilano Road, go east on Highway 1, take Exit 19, the Lynn Valley Road exit, and turn right on Peters Road. From Downtown Vancouver, you can take the SeaBus to Lonsdale Quay, then Bus 228 or 229 from the quay; both stop about a 15-minute walk from the park. **■ TIP→ The suspension bridge here is shorter than the Capilano Suspension Bridge (157 feet versus 450 feet at Capilano) so the experience is less thrilling, but also less touristy—and it's free.** ✉ *3663 Park Rd. at end of Peters Rd., North Vancouver* ☎ *604/990–3755 Ecology Centre, 604/739-3663 café* 🌐 *lynncanyonecologycentre.ca* 🎫 *Ecology Centre by donation, suspension bridge free.*

Victoria

Downtown Victoria

Home to the vast majority of Victoria's sights, hotels, and eateries, Downtown *is* Victoria for most visitors. At its heart is the Inner Harbour. Busy with yachts, passenger ferries, whale-watching boats, and floatplanes, and framed by such iconic buildings as the Fairmont Empress hotel, this pedestrian-friendly area is busy with horse-and-carriage rides, street entertainers, tour buses, and, yes, tourists—all summer long. The south shore of the harbor, extending to the Dallas Road waterfront and Beacon Hill Park, is known as James Bay. Two key sites, the Parliament Buildings and the Robert Bateman Centre, are here, but if you stroll just a block south, you'll find a peaceful residential district of modest historic homes, and such interesting historic sites as Emily Carr House. North of the Inner Harbour, a straight shot up Government Street leads to some great shopping and to more historic areas: Bastion Square, Market Square, and Chinatown. Founded in 1858, Victoria's Chinatown, along Fisgard Street between Government and Store streets, is the oldest such district in Canada. At just two square blocks, it's much smaller than Vancouver's but still pleasant to stroll through, particularly as hip boutiques and eateries have moved into the district. If you enter from Government Street, you'll pass under the elaborate Gate of Harmonious Interest, made of Taiwanese ceramic tiles and decorative panels.

Sights

Emily Carr House

LOCAL INTEREST | One of Canada's most celebrated artists and a respected writer, Emily Carr (1871–1945) lived in this extremely proper, wooden Victorian house before she abandoned her

More than 3,300 lights outline Victoria's Parliament Buildings; like the Fairmont Empress hotel, the buildings have a prominent position in the Inner Harbor, and were designed by the same architect: Francis Rattenbury.

middle-class life to live in the wilds of British Columbia. Carr's own descriptions, from her autobiography *Book of Small,* were used to restore the house. Art on display includes reproductions of Carr's work—visit the Art Gallery of Greater Victoria or the Vancouver Art Gallery to see the originals. ✉ *207 Government St., James Bay, Downtown* ☎ *250/383–5843* 🌐 *www.emilycarr.com* 🎟 *C$8* ⏲ *Closed Sun.–Mon. May–Sept.; closed Oct.–Apr.*

★ The Bateman Foundation Gallery of Nature

MUSEUM | This small but impressive gallery displays more than 100 works—from etchings to paintings—spanning seven decades in the career of Canada's best-known wildlife artist. One gallery, where paintings are matched to birdsongs, is especially innovative. The historic waterfront building, Victoria's original steamship terminal, is also home to a waterfront restaurant and a shop selling high-end local art. Proceeds from gallery admissions go to support the Bateman Foundation's conservation work. ✉ *470 Belleville St., James Bay* ☎ *250/940–3630* 🌐 *batemancentre.org* 🎟 *C$10.*

Fairmont Empress

BUILDING | Opened in 1908 by the Canadian Pacific Railway, the Empress is one of the grand château-style railroad hotels that grace many Canadian cities. Designed by Francis Rattenbury, who also designed the Parliament Buildings across the way, the solid Edwardian grandeur of the Empress has made it a symbol of the city. The elements that made the hotel an attraction for travelers in the past—old-world architecture, ornate decor, and a commanding view of the Inner Harbour—are still here although they exude a fresh, contemporary air. Nonguests can reserve ahead for afternoon tea (the dress code is smart casual) in the chandelier-draped Tea Lobby, meet for Pimm's cocktails or enjoy superb Pacific Northwest cuisine at the Q Lounge and Restaurant, or enjoy a treatment at the hotel's Willow Stream spa. In summer, lunch, snacks, and cocktails are served on the veranda overlooking the Inner Harbour. ✉ *721 Government St., Downtown* ☎ *250/384–8111, 250/389–2727 tea reservations* 🌐 *www.fairmont.com/empress* 🎫 *Free; afternoon tea C$82.*

Fisherman's Wharf

MARINA | **FAMILY** | This favorite nautical spot is only a 20-minute walk from Downtown, along a waterfront path just west of the Inner Harbour. Or you can get here by hopping aboard one of the many Victoria Harbour Ferries. You can watch fishers unload their catches and admire the various vessels, or picnic in the shoreside park. If you stroll the docks and walk among the colorful houseboats, you'll come across several floating shacks where you can buy ice cream, fish tacos, and live crabs, take kayak tours, or buy tickets for whale-watching cruises. Other booths sell fish to feed the harbor seals who often visit the quay (you can even watch them on the underwater "seal cam"). The busiest vendor is Barb's, an esteemed fish-and-chips spot that is open only in the summer, from May through October. ✉ *Corner of Dallas Rd. and Erie St., James Bay, Downtown* 🌐 *fishermanswharfvictoria.com.*

Parliament Buildings

BUILDING | Officially the British Columbia Provincial Legislative Assembly Buildings, these massive stone structures are more popularly referred to as the Parliament Buildings. Designed by Francis Rattenbury (who also designed the Fairmont Empress hotel) when he was just 25 years old, and completed in 1897, they dominate the Inner Harbour. Atop the central dome is a gilded statue of Captain George Vancouver (1757–98), the first European to sail around Vancouver Island. A statue of Queen Victoria (1819–1901) reigns over the front of the complex. More than 3,300 lights outline the buildings at night. The interior is lavishly done with stained-glass windows, gilt moldings, and historic photographs, and in summer actors play historic figures from British Columbia's past. When the legislature is in session, you can sit in the public gallery and watch British Columbia's democracy at work (custom has the opposing parties sitting 2½ sword lengths apart). Free, informative, 30- to 45-minute tours run every 20 to 30 minutes in summer and several times a day in the off-season (less frequently if school groups or private tours are coming through). Tours are obligatory on summer weekends (mid-May until Labor Day) and optional the rest of the time. Self-guided booklets are available online. ✉ *501 Belleville St., James Bay, Downtown* ☎ *250/387–3046* 🌐 *www.leg.bc.ca* 🎫 *Free.*

★ **Royal British Columbia Museum**

MUSEUM | **FAMILY** | This excellent museum, one of Victoria's leading attractions, traces several thousand years of British Columbian history. Especially strong is its First Peoples Gallery, home to a genuine Kwakwaka'wakw big house, an intriguing exhibit on First Nations languages, and a dramatically displayed collection of masks and other artifacts. Special exhibits, usually held between mid-May and mid-November, attract crowds despite the higher admission prices. You can skip (sometimes very long) ticket lines by booking online. In front of the museum, at Government and Belleville streets, is the **Netherlands Centennial Carillon.** With 62 bells, it's the largest bell tower in Canada; the Westminster chimes ring out every hour, and free recitals are occasionally held on Sunday afternoon. The Native Plant Garden at the museum's entrance showcases 400 indigenous plant species. Behind the main building, bordering Douglas Street, are the grassy lawns of **Thunderbird Park,** home to 10 totem poles (carved replicas of originals that are preserved in the museum). One of the oldest houses in BC, **Helmcken House** (*open late May–early Sept., daily noon–4*) was built in 1852 for pioneer doctor and statesman John Sebastian Helmcken. Inside are displays of the

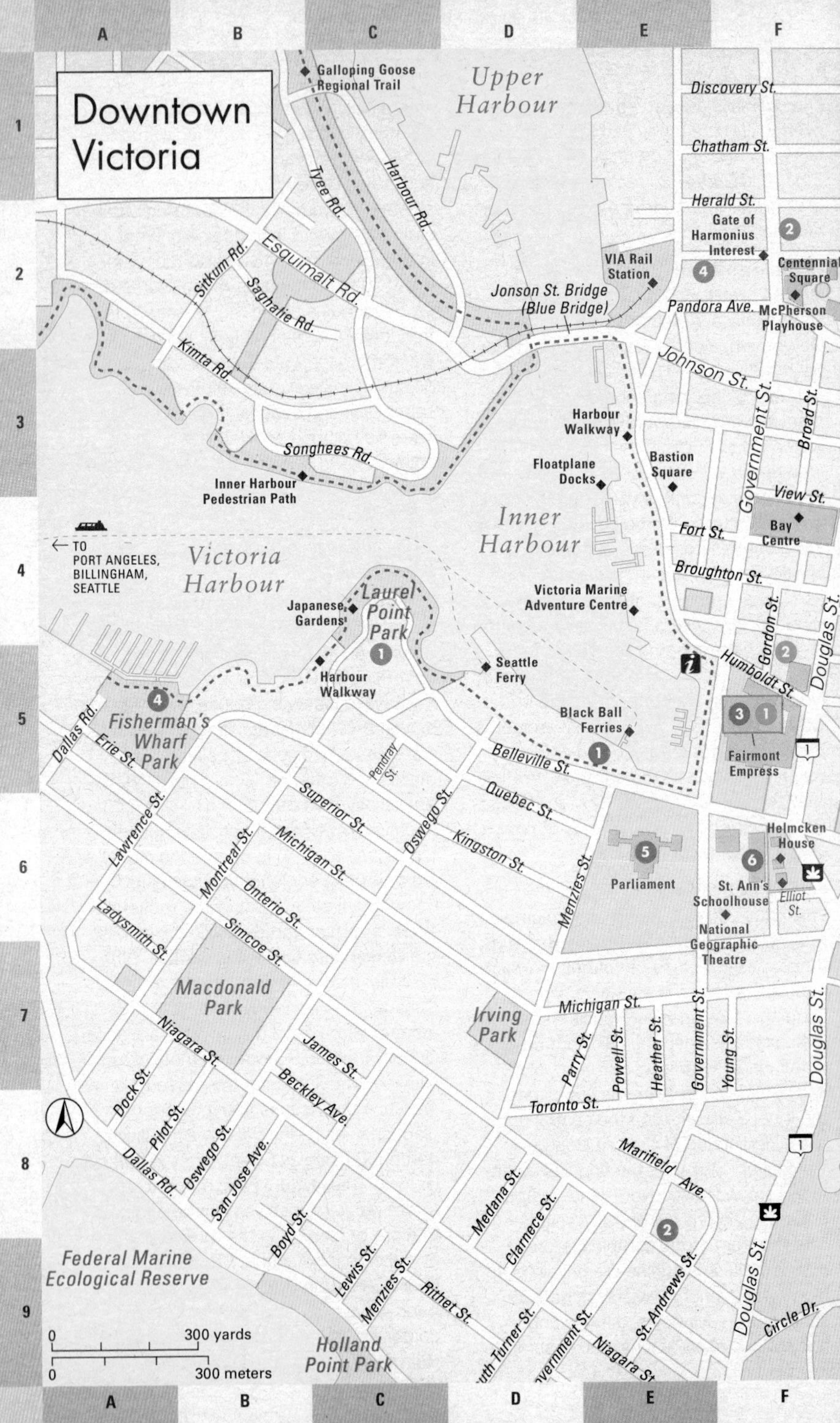

Downtown Victoria
Upper Harbour
Galloping Goose Regional Trail
Tyee Rd.
Harbour Rd.
Esquimalt Rd.
Sitkum Rd.
Saghalie Rd.
Kimta Rd.
Songhees Rd.
Inner Harbour Pedestrian Path
VIA Rail Station
Jonson St. Bridge (Blue Bridge)
Discovery St.
Chatham St.
Herald St.
Gate of Harmonius Interest
Centennial Square
Pandora Ave.
McPherson Playhouse
Johnson St.
Government St.
Broad St.
Harbour Walkway
Bastion Square
Floatplane Docks
View St.
Bay Centre
Fort St.
Inner Harbour
Victoria Harbour
TO PORT ANGELES, BILLINGHAM, SEATTLE
Broughton St.
Victoria Marine Adventure Centre
Gordon St.
Douglas St.
Laurel Point Park
Japanese Gardens
Harbour Walkway
Seattle Ferry
Humboldt St.
Black Ball Ferries
Fairmont Empress
Fisherman's Wharf Park
Dallas Rd.
Erie St.
Pendray St.
Belleville St.
Quebec St.
Superior St.
Oswego St.
Kingston St.
Lawrence St.
Montreal St.
Michigan St.
Menzies St.
Parliament
Helmcken House
St. Ann's Schoolhouse
Elliot St.
National Geographic Theatre
Onterio St.
Ladysmith St.
Simcoe St.
Macdonald Park
Irving Park
Michigan St.
Niagara St.
James St.
Parry St.
Powell St.
Heather St.
Government St.
Young St.
Beckley Ave.
Dock St.
Toronto St.
Pilot St.
Oswego St.
San Jose Ave.
Marifield Ave.
Dallas Rd.
Medana St.
Clarnece St.
Boyd St.
Federal Marine Ecological Reserve
Lewis St.
Menzies St.
Rithet St.
St. Andrews St.
Douglas St.
Circle Dr.
Holland Point Park
Niagara St.
0 300 yards
0 300 meters
A B C D E F
1 2 3 4 5 6 7 8 9

Sights

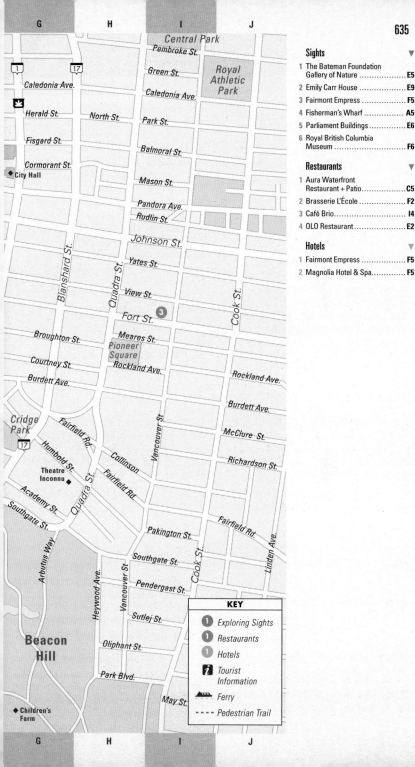

1 The Bateman Foundation Gallery of Nature E5
2 Emily Carr House E9
3 Fairmont Empress F5
4 Fisherman's Wharf A5
5 Parliament Buildings E6
6 Royal British Columbia Museum F6

Restaurants

1 Aura Waterfront Restaurant + Patio C5
2 Brasserie L'École F2
3 Café Brio I4
4 OLO Restaurant E2

Hotels

1 Fairmont Empress F5
2 Magnolia Hotel & Spa F5

family's belongings, including the doctor's medical tools. Behind it is **St. Ann's School House,** built in 1858. One of British Columbia's oldest schools, it is thought to be Victoria's oldest building still standing. Both buildings are part of the Royal British Columbia Museum. ✉ *675 Belleville St., Downtown* ☎ *250/356–7226, 888/447–7977 museum, 877/480–4887 IMAX theater* 🌐 *www.royalbcmuseum.bc.ca* 🎫 *C$26.95, IMAX theater C$11.95; combination ticket C$36.90.*

Restaurants

★ Aura Waterfront Restaurant + Patio
$ | **PACIFIC NORTHWEST** | After a 12-month renovation program, the critically acclaimed Aura re-opened November 2019, with inspired west coast-Asian fusion cuisine to rival its drop-dead gorgeous backdrop of the Inner Harbour. Think BBQ sambal skate on banana leaf with XO sauce and jicama slaw and house-made fried spam with crispy rice, aged cheddar, soft-poached egg, and cilantro oil. **Known for:** waterfront patio; imaginative fusion cuisine; stylish dining room. $ *Average main: C$12* ✉ *Inn at Laurel Point, 680 Montreal St., James Bay, Downtown* ☎ *250/414–6739* 🌐 *www.aurarestaurant.ca.*

★ Brasserie L'École
$$$ | **FRENCH** | French-country cooking shines at this informal Chinatown bistro, and the historic room—once a schoolhouse for the Chinese community—evokes a timeless brasserie, from the patina-rich fir floors to the chalkboards above the slate bar listing the day's oyster, mussel, and steak options. Owner Sean Brennan, one of the city's better-known chefs, works with local farmers and fishermen to source the best seasonal, local, and organic ingredients. **Known for:** seasonal menus; French-country fare; French wine and Belgian beers. $ *Average main: C$30* ✉ *1715 Government St., Downtown* ☎ *250/475–6260* 🌐 *www.lecole.ca* ⏲ *Closed Sun. and Mon. No lunch.*

★ Café Brio
$$$$ | **MODERN CANADIAN** | This intimate yet bustling Italian villa–style room has long been a Victoria favorite, mainly because of its Mediterranean-influenced atmosphere and cuisine, which is prepared primarily with locally raised ingredients. The menu changes almost daily, but you might find local rockfish paired with peperonata (sweet roasted red onion and heirloom tomato syrup), maple-glazed quail, or even an apricot dessert soup. **Known for:** house-made charcuterie; 400-label wine list; seasonal dishes. $ *Average main: C$32* ✉ *944 Fort St., Downtown* ☎ *250/383–0009, 866/270–5461* 🌐 *www.cafe-brio.com* ⏲ *No lunch. Closed Sun.–Mon. and two weeks in Jan.*

★ OLO Restaurant
$$$ | **MODERN CANADIAN** | Victoria's foodies rave about this small Chinatown bistro that serves up some of the city's most innovative fare, simply yet superbly. Many items like the smoked salmon and pasta are crafted in-house, and the locally sourced menu changes often, often with a French flair. **Known for:** grass-fed beef; unusual pavlovas; tasting menus. $ *Average main: C$30* ✉ *509 Fisgard St., Downtown* ☎ *250/590–8795* 🌐 *www.olorestaurant.com* ⏲ *No lunch.*

Hotels

★ Fairmont Empress
$$$$ | **HOTEL** | Opened in 1908, this harborside château and city landmark has aged gracefully. **Pros:** central location; professional service; great spa and restaurant. **Cons:** small- to average-size rooms and bathrooms; pricey all round; restaurant and spa get booked up quickly with non-guests. $ *Rooms from: C$563* ✉ *721 Government St., Downtown* ☎ *250/384–8111, 866/540–4429 central reservations* 🌐 *www.fairmont.com/empress* *477 rooms* *No meals.*

Butchart Gardens

★ **Magnolia Hotel & Spa**

$$$$ | **HOTEL** | From the on-site spa to the soaker tubs, sauna, and herb tea, this locally owned boutique hotel, without actually saying so, caters beautifully to the female traveler—though the attention to detail, hop-to-it staff, and central location won't be lost on men either. **Pros:** great location; friendly and helpful service; welcoming lobby with fireplace, tea, and coffee. **Cons:** no on-site pool or hot tub; some rooms have limited views; valet parking C$30. *Rooms from: C$379* ✉ *623 Courtney St., Downtown* ☎ *250/381–0999, 877/624–6654* 🌐 *www.magnoliahotel.com* *64 rooms* *Free breakfast.*

Brentwood Bay

Sights

★ **The Butchart Gardens**

GARDEN | This stunning 55-acre garden and national historic site has been drawing visitors since it was started in a limestone quarry in 1904. Highlights include the dramatic 70-foot Ross Fountain, the formal Japanese garden, and the intricate Italian garden complete with a gelato stand. Kids will love the old-fashioned carousel and will likely enjoy the 45-minute miniboat tours around Tod Inlet. From mid-June to mid-September the gardens are illuminated at night with hundreds of hidden lights. In July and August, jazz, blues, and classical musicians play at an outdoor stage each evening, and fireworks draw crowds every Saturday night. The wheelchair- and stroller-accessible site is also home to a seed-and-gift shop, a plant-identification center, two restaurants (one offering traditional afternoon tea), and a coffee shop; you can even call ahead for a picnic basket on fireworks nights. ✉ *800 Benvenuto Ave., Brentwood Bay* ☎ *250/652–5256, 866/652–4422* 🌐 *www.butchartgardens.com* *C$35* ☞ *Rates are lower between Oct. and mid-June.*

Hotels

★ Brentwood Bay Resort & Spa
$$$$ | **RESORT** | Every room has a private ocean-view patio or balcony at this adult-oriented boutique resort in a tiny seaside village. **Pros:** magnificent setting; close to The Butchart Gardens; free Wi-Fi. **Cons:** pricey rates; 30-minute drive from Downtown; spa service inconsistent. *Rooms from: C$364* *849 Verdier Ave., Brentwood Bay* *250/544–2079, 888/544–2079* *www.brentwoodbay-resort.com* *33 rooms, 2 villas* *No meals.*

Rockland

Hotels

★ Abbeymoore Manor Bed & Breakfast Inn
$$$ | **B&B/INN** | This 1912 mansion has the wide verandas, dark wainscoting, and high ceilings of its era, but the attitude is informal and welcoming, from the superhelpful hosts to the free snacks to the coffee on tap all day. **Pros:** good value; friendly hosts; excellent service. **Cons:** a mile from the Inner Harbour; often booked in advance; very quiet neighborhood. *Rooms from: C$279* *1470 Rockland Ave., Rockland* *250/370–1470, 888/801–1811* *www.abbeymoore.com* *7 rooms* *Free breakfast.*

Salt Spring Island

52.7 km from Downtown Victoria.

With its wealth of studios, galleries, restaurants, and B&Bs, Salt Spring is the most developed, and most visited, of the Southern Gulf Islands. It's home to the only town in the archipelago (Ganges) and, although it can get busy on summer weekends, has not yet lost its relaxed rural feel. Outside Ganges, the rolling landscape is home to small organic farms, wineries, forested hills, quiet white-shell beaches, and several swimming lakes.

Hotels

★ Hastings House Country House Hotel
$$$$ | **HOTEL** | The centerpiece of this 22-acre Relais & Châteaux seaside estate—with its gardens, meadows, and harbor views—is a 1939 country house, built in the style of an 11th-century Sussex manor. **Pros:** wonderful food; top-notch service; historic character. **Cons:** no pool; some rooms overlook a nearby pub; pricey. *Rooms from: C$485* *160 Upper Ganges Rd., Ganges, Salt Spring Island* *250/537–2362, 800/661–9255* *www.hastingshouse.com* *Closed Nov.–Feb.* *18 suites and cottages* *Free breakfast.*

Shopping

To visit local artists in their studios, follow the Salt Spring Studio Tour map, listing more than 30 locations. You can either download the map from *www.saltspringstudiotour.com* or pick it up at any of the local artist studios, Salt Spring Island Cheese, or at any of the island's hotels.

★ Salt Spring Island Saturday Market
OUTDOOR/FLEA/GREEN MARKETS | Locals and visitors alike flock to Ganges for the famous Saturday Market, held in Centennial Park from Easter through October. It's one of the island's most popular attractions. Everything sold at this colorful outdoor bazaar is made or grown on the island; the array and quality of crafts, food, and produce is dazzling. Centennial Park also hosts a farmers' market on summer Tuesdays. *Centennial Park, Fulford-Ganges Rd., Ganges, Salt Spring Island* *250/537–4448* *www.saltspringmarket.com.*

Galiano Island

68.8 km from Victoria.

With its 26km-long (16-mile-long) eastern shore and cove-dotted western coast, Galiano is arguably the prettiest of the Southern Gulf islands. It's certainly the best for hiking and mountain biking, with miles of trails through the Douglas fir and Garry Oak forest. Mt. Galiano and Bodega Ridge are classic walks, with far-reaching views to the mainland. Most shops and services—including cash machines, gas pumps, galleries, and a bookstore—are clustered near the Sturdies Bay ferry terminal. A visitor information booth is to your right as you leave the ferry.

Restaurants

★ **pilgrimme**

$$$$ | **CANADIAN** | This small restaurant in the woods has garnered all sorts of accolades since it first opened in 2014. Here chef Jesse McCleery, who spent a winter in the kitchen at Noma in Copenhagen, focuses on locally sourced food and unusual ingredients presented in the most imaginative ways. **Known for:** one of Canada's best restaurants; homey setting; charming staff. *Average main: C$75* *2806 Montague Rd., Galiano Island* *250/539–5392* *www.pilgrimme.ca* *Closed Mon. to Wed. No lunch* *7-course fixed-price menu.*

Hotels

★ **Galiano Oceanfront Inn & Spa**

$$$ | **RESORT** | Just a block from the ferry and local shops, this inviting waterfront retreat on Sturdies Bay, which has both a nice restaurant and great spa, is an ideal spot for a car-free vacation. **Pros:** staff pick you up at the ferry; lovely spa; quiet environment. **Cons:** no pool; no hot tub; no fitness center. *Rooms from: C$299* *134 Madrona Dr., Galiano Island* *250/539–3388, 877/530–3939* *www.galianoinn.com* *10 rooms, 10 suites* *No meals.*

Tofino

42 km (26 miles) northwest of Ucluelet, 337 km (209 miles) northwest of Victoria.

Tofino may be the birthplace of North American storm-watching, but the area's tempestuous winter weather and roiling waves are only two of the many stellar attractions you'll find along British Columbia's wildest coastline. Exquisite tide pooling, expansive wilderness beaches, excellent surfing, and the potential to see some of the continent's largest sea mammals lure thousands of visitors each year.

Sights

★ **Pacific Rim National Park Reserve**

NATIONAL/STATE PARK | This national park has some of Canada's most stunning coastal and rain-forest scenery, abundant wildlife, and a unique marine environment. It comprises three separate units—Long Beach, the Broken Group Islands, and the West Coast Trail—for a combined area of 123,431 acres, and stretches 130 km (81 miles) along Vancouver Island's west coast.

More than 100 islands of the Broken Group Islands archipelago in Barkley Sound can be reached only by boat. The islands and their clear waters are alive with sea lions, seals, and whales, and because the inner waters are much calmer than the surrounding ocean, they provide an excellent environment for kayaking. Guided kayak and charter-boat tours are available from outfitters in Ucluelet, Bamfield, and Port Alberni.

The most popular part of the park, and the only section that can be reached by car, is the Long Beach section. Besides the beach, the Long Beach section of the park is home to rich stands of old-growth forest, a wealth of marine and terrestrial wildlife (including black bears, cougars, and sea lions), and a network of coastal and rain-forest hiking paths. A first stop for any first-timer is the visitor center, which doubles as the Ucluelet Visitor Information Office. You can pick up maps and information, and pay park entrance fees here. ✉ *2791 Pacific Rim Hwy., Ucluelet* ☎ *250/726–4600* 🌐 *www.pc.gc.ca* 🎟 *Park admission is C$7.80 per person per day.*

Restaurants

★ The Pointe

$$$$ | **CANADIAN** | With 180-degree views of the crashing surf, the Pointe is *the* top-notch Tofino dining experience. It's renowned for its refined west coast cuisine, which is superbly presented and excellently paired with options from the award-winning wine list—an impressive 11,000-bottle wine cellar is the latest jewel in this grande dame's crown. **Known for:** impeccable service; incredible views; an unforgettable dining experience. $ *Average main: C$46* ✉ *The Wickaninnish Inn, 500 Osprey La.* ☎ *250/725–3106* 🌐 *thepointerestaurant.ca.*

★ Schooner Restaurant

$$$$ | **SEAFOOD** | An institution in downtown Tofino (it's been operating since 1949), the Schooner's main-floor dining room is comfortable and casually upscale. The seafood dishes change frequently, but ask for the signature halibut filet stuffed with Brie, crab, and shrimp in an apple-peppercorn brandy sauce. **Known for:** serving epic seafood and steaks since 1949; great views; stuffed halibut. $ *Average main: C$38* ✉ *331 Campbell St.* ☎ *250/725–3444* 🌐 *www.schoonerrestaurant.ca* ⏲ *Closed Mon. No lunch.*

★ Sobo

$$$$ | **ECLECTIC** | **FAMILY** | The name, short for "sophisticated bohemian," sums up the style here: a classically trained chef serving casual fare influenced by international street food. The offbeat concept started in a purple truck before finding a permanent home in this light-filled café and bistro. **Known for:** fresh seafood; fish tacos; international street food influence. $ *Average main: C$31* ✉ *311 Neill St.* ☎ *250/725–2341* 🌐 *www.sobo.ca.*

★ The Wolf in the Fog

$$$$ | **CANADIAN** | Chef Nick Nutting and his crew present a unique west-coast dining experience here that puts an inspired twist on freshly caught seafood and foraged local ingredients; think seaweed combed from the shore and wild forest mushrooms. The big platters of charred octopus and steamed mussels beg to be shared. **Known for:** award winning; innovative hyper-local cuisine; foraged ingredients. $ *Average main: C$32* ✉ *150 4th St.* ☎ *250/725–9653* 🌐 *www.wolfinthefog.com.*

Hotels

★ Chesterman Beach Bed & Breakfast

$$$$ | **B&B/INN** | This charming beachside inn, opened as Tofino's first B&B in 1984, is the kind of intimate seaside getaway that brought people to Vancouver Island's west coast in the first place. **Pros:** gracious owners knowledgeable about area; private; scenic. **Cons:** 10-minute drive to restaurants; breakfast not actually included in rates; breakfast not available at the cottage. $ *Rooms from: C$420* ✉ *1345 Chesterman Beach Rd.* ☎ *250/725–3726* 🌐 *www.tofinoaccommodation.com* 🛏 *2 suites; 1 1-bedroom cottage* 🍽 *No meals.*

★ Clayoquot Wilderness Resort

$$$$ | **RESORT** | **FAMILY** | People from around the globe arrive via floatplane or a 30-minute boat ride from Tofino to

experience this Relais & Châteaux property, one of the region's top wilderness resorts. **Pros:** escapism at its best, with no phone or other distractions; excellent food; a ton of outdoorsy activities. **Cons:** it's extremely pricey; fairly isolated; requires a long trip to reach the property. *Rooms from: C$6,201 1 Clayoquot 250/266–0397, 888/333–5405 www.wildretreat.com Closed Oct.–mid-May 25 tents, 20 with private bath All-inclusive Actual price is per-person for three nights.*

★ The Wickaninnish Inn

$$$$ | **RESORT** | On a rocky promontory with open ocean on three sides and old-growth forest as a backdrop, this cedar-sided inn is exceptional in every sense. **Pros:** at the end of a superb crescent beach; the silence of storms through triple-glazed windows is surreal; excellent staff. **Cons:** no swimming pool; pricey; no hot tub. *Rooms from: C$680 500 Osprey La., at Chesterman Beach 250/725–3100, 800/333–4604 www.wickinn.com Pointe Building: 45 rooms. Beach Building: 18 rooms, 12 suites No meals.*

Vancouver and Victoria Activities

Blessed with a mild climate, fabulous natural setting, and excellent public-use facilities, Vancouverites, unsurprisingly, are an outdoorsy lot. The Downtown peninsula of Vancouver is entirely encircled by a seawall along which you can walk, in-line skate (which is still quite popular in Vancouver), cycle, or otherwise propel yourself for more than 22 km (13½ miles), with plenty of picturesque jumping on and off points.

You'll find rental equipment and tour operators in Vancouver for every imaginable outdoor activity, from tandem bikes for Stanley Park trails to stand-up paddleboards on Granville Island. Yoga studios seem to be around every corner and hiking trails materialize just at the end of the road. Hotel concierges can recommend the best wilderness trails just as easily as they can top sushi spots. To buy or rent gear, head to the Mountain Equipment Co-op, a local institution (⇨ *see Shopping*).

★ Richmond Olympic Oval

ICE SKATING | **FAMILY** | This speed-skating oval was built alongside the Fraser River for the 2010 Olympics. The state-of-the-art facility, with a gorgeous glass-and-steel design, contains world-class ice rinks and a huge fitness center with a climbing wall. It also houses Canada's only official Olympic museum, the Olympic Experience at the Richmond Olympic Oval. Here you can channel your inner athlete on sports simulators, experiencing what it's like to compete in events such as bobsledding and ski jumping. It's a 15-minute walk from the Canada Line Lansdowne Station. The C94 Community Shuttle runs to the front door of the Oval from the Canada Line Brighouse Station. *6111 River Rd., Richmond 778/296–1400 www.richmondoval.ca C$20 Olympic Experience closed Mon. to Wed.*

Sea to Sky Highway

Drive the Sea to Sky Highway along Howe Sound for a memorable experience. Stop in Squamish for a visit to the Stawamus Chief, one of the largest granite monoliths in the world.

Beaches

Greater Vancouver is well endowed with beaches but the waters are decidedly cool, with summer water temperatures ranging from 12 to 18°C (54 to 64°F). Aside from kids and the intrepid, most stick to quick dips, sunbathing, or wearing a wet suit for water activities.

English Bay Beach

BEACH—SIGHT | The city's best-known beach, English Bay, lies just to the east of Stanley Park's southern entrance. A long stretch of golden sand, a waterslide, volleyball courts, kayak rentals, and food trucks keep things interesting all summer. Known locally for being gay-friendly, it draws a diverse crowd. Special events include summer Celebration of Light fireworks and a New Year's Day swim. The oversized *A-maze-ing Laughter* sculptures will make you smile. **Amenities:** food and drink; lifeguards; parking (fee); toilets; water sports. **Best for:** atmosphere; partiers; sunset; swimming; walking. ✉ *1700 Beach Ave., between Gilford and Bidwell Sts., West End* ☎ *604/665–3424* 🌐 *www.vancouver.ca/parks-recreation-culture/english-bay-beach.aspx.*

★ Kitsilano Beach

BEACH—SIGHT | West of the southern end of the Burrard Bridge, Kits Beach is the city's busiest beach—Frisbee tossers, beach volleyball players, and sleek young people are ever present. Facilities include a playground, restaurant, concession stand, and tennis courts. **Kitsilano Pool** is here: at 137.5 meters (451 feet), it's the longest pool in Canada and one of the few heated saltwater pools in the world (open May to September). Just steps from the sand, the Boathouse on Kits Beach serves lunch, dinner, and weekend brunch inside and on its big ocean-view deck. There's also a take-out concession at the same site. Inland from the pool, the Kitsilano Showboat, an outdoor amphitheater hosts music and dance performances during the summer. **Amenities:** food and drink; lifeguards; parking (fee); toilets; water sports. **Best for:** atmosphere; sunrise; sunset; swimming; walking. ✉ *Kits Beach, Kitsilano* ☎ *604/731–0011* 🌐 *www.vancouver.ca/parks-recreation-culture/kitsilano-beach.aspx.*

★ Stanley Park Beaches

BEACH—SIGHT | There are two fine beaches accessed from Stanley Park, with other unnamed sandy spots dotted along the seawall. The most popular with families is **Second Beach,** which has a playground and large heated pool with slides. **Third Beach** is a little more removed than the other central beaches. It has a larger stretch of sand, fairly warm water, and unbeatable sunset views. It's a popular evening picnic spot. **Amenities:** food and drink; lifeguards; parking (fee); toilets. **Best for:** sunset; swimming; walking. ✉ *7495 Stanley Park Dr., Stanley Park* 🌐 *www.vancouver.ca/parks-recreation-culture/third-beach.aspx.*

Biking

Vancouver's most popular bike path is the 9-km (5½-mile) **Stanley Park Seawall**, which follows the park's perimeter, hugging the harbor along the way. The views of Lions Gate Bridge and the mountains to the north are breathtaking. The path connects at both ends with the city's longer seawall path, if you feel like making a day of it. Rent your bike near the entrance to Stanley Park, in the West End, as there are no rentals once you're inside the park.

For biking on city streets, Downtown Vancouver's "separated bike lanes" have made biking even easier—most bike lanes have a barrier between them and the traffic. Especially useful ones are along Hornby and Dunsmuir streets. These lanes are in addition to the city's many bikeways, identified by green bicycle signs. There are detailed maps and other information on the website operated by the City of Vancouver (🌐 *www.vancouver.ca/streets-transportation/biking-and-cyclists.aspx*). Cycling maps are also available from most bike shops and bike-rental outlets. Helmets are required by law, and a sturdy lock is essential.

Victoria is a bike-friendly town with more bicycle commuters than any other city in Canada. Bike racks on city buses, bike lanes on Downtown streets, and tolerant drivers all help, as do the city's three long-distance cycling routes, which mix car-free paths and low-traffic scenic routes.

BIKE ROUTES

Galloping Goose Regional Trail

BICYCLING | Following an old rail bed, this 55-km (35-mile) route officially starts at the Vic West end of Johnson Street Bridge, which connects Downtown Victoria to Vic West. The multiuse trail runs across old rail trestles and through forests west to the town of Sooke, finishing just past Sooke Potholes Provincial Park. Just north of Downtown it links with the Lochside Regional Trail to the BC Ferries terminal at Swartz Bay, creating a nearly continuous 55-mile car-free route. It has earned many accolades, deservedly so. ✉ *Johnson St. Bridge, Vic West* ☎ *250/478–3344* 🌐 *www.crd.bc.ca/parks* 🎫 *Free.*

Lochside Regional Trail

BICYCLING | This fairly level, mostly car-free route follows an old rail bed for 29 km (18 miles) past farmland, wineries, and beaches from the ferry terminals at Swartz Bay and Sidney to Downtown Victoria. It joins the Seaside Touring Route at Cordova Bay and meets the Galloping Goose Trail just north of Downtown Victoria. ✉ *Sidney* ☎ *250/360-3000* 🌐 *www.crd.bc.ca/parks.*

★ Seawall

BICYCLING | The paved bike paths of Vancouver's 28-km (17-mile) seawall start Downtown at Canada Place, go around Stanley Park (for 9km/5.5-miles), and follow False Creek to Kitsilano and the University of British Columbia. It is one of the longest seashore paths of its kind in the world. ✉ *Downtown* 🌐 *www.vancouver.ca/parks-recreation-culture/seawall.aspx.*

Victoria Seaside Touring Route

BICYCLING | This vista-inspired, self-guided cycling tour starts at the corner of Government and Belleville streets on the Inner Harbour. It's a 39-km (24-mile) route along city streets and coastal roads, marked with bright yellow signs, that leads past Fisherman's Wharf and along the Dallas Road waterfront to Beacon Hill Park. It then follows the seashore to Cordova Bay, where it connects with Victoria's other two long-distance routes: the Lochside and Galloping Goose regional trails. ✉ *Government St. at Belleville St., Inner Harbour, Downtown.*

BIKE RENTALS AND TOURS

Cycle BC Rentals

BICYCLING | This centrally located shop rents bikes for adults and children, as well as bike trailers, motorcycles, and scooters. ✉ *685 Humboldt St., Downtown* ☎ *250/380–2453, 866/380–2453* 🌐 *www.victoria.cyclebc.ca.*

Seawall Adventure Centre

BICYCLING | Besides renting bikes, this company runs bike tours of Victoria, multiday trips to the Gulf Islands, and vineyard tours of the Saanich Peninsula and the Cowichan Valley. Their self-guided trips include bikes, maps, and a ride to Butchart Gardens or the end of the Galloping Goose or Lochside trail so that you can pedal back. ✉ *950 Wharf St., Downtown* ☎ *250/414-4284* 🌐 *www.seawalladventurecentre.com.*

Spokes Bicycle Rentals

BICYCLING | Near Stanley Park, Spokes has a wide selection of mountain bikes, tandem bikes, e-bikes, and children's bikes. Everything from hourly to weekly rentals are available. Helmets, locks, and route maps are complimentary. ✉ *1798 W. Georgia St., West End* ☎ *604/688–5141* 🌐 *www.spokesbicyclerentals.com.*

Ecotours and Wildlife Viewing

Given a temperate climate and forest, mountain, and marine environments teeming with life, it's no surprise that wildlife-watching is an important pastime and growing business in and around Vancouver.

★ Sewell's Marina

WILDLIFE-WATCHING | This marina in the village of Horseshoe Bay, runs two-hour ecotours of the marine and coastal mountain habitat of Howe Sound.

Sightings range from swimming seals to soaring eagles. High-speed rigid hull inflatable boats are used. They also offer guided salmon-fishing charters. *6409 Bay St., West Vancouver* *604/921–3474* *www.sewellsmarina.com* *No tours Nov. 1 to March 31.*

Hiking

With its expansive landscape of mountains, inlets, alpine lakes, and approachable glaciers, as well as low-lying rivers, hills, dikes, and meadows, southwestern British Columbia is a hiker's paradise. For easy walking and hiking, you can't beat Stanley Park in Downtown Vancouver but for more strenuous hiking, there are fabulous parks not far away. With their photo-worthy profile, the North Shore Mountains may appear benign, but this is a vast and rugged territory filled with natural pitfalls and occasionally hostile wildlife.

HIKING TRAILS

★ Garibaldi Provincial Park

PARK—SPORTS-OUTDOORS | A vast wilderness on Whistler's doorstep, Garibaldi Provincial Park is a serious hiker's dream. You can't miss it: the 2,678-meter (8,786-foot) peak of Mount Garibaldi kisses the heavens just north of Squamish. Alpine meadows and wildlife-viewing await you on trails leading to Black Tusk, Diamond Head, Cheakamus Lake, Elfin Lakes, and Singing Pass. Mountain goats, black bears, and bald eagles are found throughout the park. This is truly one of Canada's most spectacular wildernesses, and being easily accessible from Vancouver makes it even more appealing. A compass is mandatory, as are food and water, rain gear, a flashlight, and a first-aid kit. There are also two medium to advanced mountain bike trails. Take seriously the glacier hazards and avalanche warnings. Snow tires are necessary in winter. Garibaldi Provincial Park is serviced by Parkbus, a seasonal shuttle bus, from Downtown Vancouver (*www.parkbus.ca* or *800/928–7101*). *Hwy. 99, between Squamish and Pemberton, Whistler* *800/689–9025 Discover Camping campsite reservations, 800/928–7101 Parkbus* *www.env.gov.bc.ca/bcparks/explore/parkpgs/garibaldi.*

↗ PEAK 2 PEAK Gondola

Located about two hours from Vancouver in Whistler, the longest and tallest gondola in the world when it opened, the PEAK 2 PEAK delivers jaw-dropping views as it travels 4.3 km (2.7 miles) from Whistler's Roundhouse to Blackcomb's Rendezvous Lodge, which sits at an elevation of 7,000 feet. Two gondolas have a glass-floor viewing area that are worth the extra few minutes' wait; there's a separate lineup for these. A day pass may seem costly until you realize that you can ride PEAK 2 PEAK as many times as you wish, plus travel up and down both Whistler and Blackcomb on a fully enclosed gondola system, a 13.5 km (8.3 miles) loop forming the longest continuous lift system in the world. In summer, the ski runs and the rest of the mountainsides open up to 50 km (31 miles) of incredible hiking. Discounts are offered for multiple days. *Roundhouse Lodge, Whistler Mountain, Whistler* *800/766–0449* *www.whistlerblackcomb.com* *C$65* *Closed weekdays mid-Sept.–mid-Oct.; closed mid-Oct.–mid-Nov. and mid-Apr.–mid-May.*

Grouse Grind

PARK—SPORTS-OUTDOORS | Vancouver's most famous, or infamous, hiking route, the Grind, is about a 3-km (about 2-mile) climb straight up 853 meters (2,799 feet) to the top of Grouse Mountain. Thousands do it annually, but climbers are advised to be experienced and in excellent physical condition. The route is open daily during daylight hours, from spring through autumn (conditions permitting). Hikers can ride the Grouse Mountain Skyride back down for $15 (a round-trip is C$59; hiking down is not permitted). Hiking trails in the adjacent Lynn Headwaters Regional Park are accessible from the gondola, including the **4-hour Goat Mountain Trail**. ✉ *Grouse Mountain, 6400 Nancy Greene Way, North Vancouver* ☎ *604/980–9311* 🌐 *www.grousemountain.com.*

Mount Douglas Regional Park
HIKING/WALKING | Trails through the forest to the 260-meter (853-foot) summit of Mt. Douglas reward hikers with a 360-degree view of Victoria, the Saanich Peninsula, and the mountains of Washington State. ✉ *Off Cedar Hill Rd., Saanich* ☎ *250/475–5522* 🌐 *www.saanich.ca.*

GUIDED HIKING TOURS

Novice hikers and serious walkers can join guided trips or do self-guided walks of varying approach and difficulty. **Grouse Mountain** hosts several daily "eco-walks" along easy, meandering paths, including a discussion of flora and fauna and a visit to the Refuge for Endangered Wildlife. They're free with admission to Grouse Mountain Skyride.

Stanley Park Ecology Centre
WILDLIFE-WATCHING | FAMILY | A calendar of guided nature walks and discovery sessions is filled with fun, kid-friendly options. Despite its urban access, Stanley Park offers incredible wildlife diversity—from the namesake rodents in Beaver Lake to a rookery of great blue herons near the tennis courts. The organization also operates the Stanley Park Nature House on the shores of Lost Lagoon. A park ranger station also operates daily beside the concession stand at Second Beach. ✉ *Alberni St. at Chilco St., Stanley Park* ✣ *Southeast corner of Lost Lagoon* ☎ *604/257–8544, 604/718–6522* 🌐 *www.stanleyparkecology.ca* 🎫 *Free.*

Whale-Watching

Between April and October pods of orca whales migrate through the Strait of Georgia, near Vancouver. The area is also home to year-round pods of harbor seals, elephant seals, minke whales, porpoises, and a wealth of birdlife, inlcuding bald eagles. Other migrating whales include humpbacks and grays.

The following companies provide whale-watching excursions from Vancouver and Victoria.

Orca Spirit Adventures
WILDLIFE-WATCHING | FAMILY | This company offers year-round tours with both Zodiacs and covered vessels. Boats are equipped with hydrophones and all guides are marine biologists. In summer a three-hour tour starts at C$129. The outfitter offers free hotel pickup/drop-off service. A second location is at the Marina Level outside the Victoria Coast Hotel, 146 Kingston St. ✉ *950 Wharf St., Victoria* ☎ *250/383–8411, 888/672–6722* 🌐 *www.orcaspirit.com.*

Prince of Whales
WILDLIFE-WATCHING | FAMILY | Victoria's biggest whale-watching company offers a whole range of marine excursions, from three-hour boat or Zodiac tours from Victoria, to five-hour trips that include a stop at Butchart Gardens, to one-way or round-trip crossings between Vancouver and Victoria; all sailings have naturalists on board. Zodiac trips cost C$130 and leave year-round; covered boat sailings on the *Ocean Magic II* are C$130 and run from April to October; and Victoria to Butchart Gardens trips run from late May to late September (the C$160 fare includes admission to the gardens). The company's Vancouver to Victoria crossings, running from late May to late September on the 94-passenger *Salish Sea Dream*, are a great time-saver, combining a sailing to or from Victoria with a whale-watching trip. A stop at The Butchart Gardens or return flights by floatplane or helicopter are options, too. The most popular trip, billed as The Ultimate Day Trip, includes a whale-watching trip from Vancouver to Victoria, a stop in Downtown Victoria, a bus transfer to Butchart Gardens, and a sunset sailing back to Vancouver. This C$340 trip runs daily from late May to late September. The

company's Victoria office is on the Inner Harbour Causeway, below the Visitor Info Centre. ✉ *812 Wharf St., Lower Causeway Level, Downtown* ☎ *250/383–4884, 888/383–4884* 🌐 *www.princeofwhales.com.*

Wild Whales Vancouver

WHALE-WATCHING | Boats leave Granville Island in search of orca pods in the Strait of Georgia, often traveling as far as Victoria. Rates are C$145 for a three- to six-hour trip in either an open or glass-domed boat (trip lengths depend on where the whales are hanging out on a particular day). Each boat leaves once daily, April through October, conditions permitting. ✉ *1806 Mast Tower Rd., Granville Island* ☎ *604/699–2011* 🌐 *www.whalesvancouver.com.*

Winter Sports

SKIING, SNOWBOARDING, SNOWSHOEING, AND SNOW-TUBING

★ Cypress Mountain Ski Resort

SKIING/SNOWBOARDING | Just 30 minutes from Downtown, the ski facilities at Cypress Mountain include six quad or double chairs, 53 downhill runs, and a vertical drop of 610 meters (2,001 feet). The resort has a snow-tubing area and snowshoe tours. This is also a major cross-country skiing area. Summer activities at Cypress Mountain include hiking, geocaching, wildlife-viewing, and mountain biking. To get there without a car, ride the SeaBus to Lonsdale Quay and catch the privately run Cypress Mountain Express Bus (🌐 *www.cypresscoachlines.com*). ✉ *Cypress Provincial Park, 6000 Cypress Bowl Rd., West Vancouver* ☎ *604/926–5612* 🌐 *www.cypressmountain.com.*

Grouse Mountain Ski Resort

SKIING/SNOWBOARDING | **FAMILY** | A 25-minute drive from Downtown Vancouver, the Skyride gondola takes skiers up to the ski resort on a slope overlooking the city. The views are fine on a clear day, but at night they're spectacular, and the area is known for its night skiing. Facilities include four quad chairs, 33 skiing and snowboarding runs, and several all-level freestyle-terrain parks. There's a choice of upscale and casual dining in a handsome stone-and-timber lodge. ✉ *6400 Nancy Greene Way, North Vancouver* ☎ *604/980–9311, 604/986–6262 snow report* 🌐 *www.grousemountain.com.*

SKATING RINKS

Robson Square Ice Rink

ICE SKATING | **FAMILY** | Rent skates and lace them up tight to enjoy this free ice-skating rink in the city center. It's the best of indoor and outdoor skating combined—with a glass dome covering the open-air rink. The season runs December through February. ✉ *800 Robson St., Downtown* ☎ *604/646–3554* 🌐 *www.robsonsquare.com* 🎫 *Free.*

Index

A

A. R. Bowman Memorial Museum, *276*
Abacela Vineyards and Winery, *299*
Abbeymoore Manor , *638*
Abendblume Pension , *535*
Abigail Hall (bar), *78*
Ace Hotel (Seattle) , *332*
Adelsheim Vineyard, *182, 193*
Afuri Ramen ✕, *110*
Agua Verde Cafe & Paddle Club, *357*
Air travel, *46*
Airfield Estates Winery, *575*
Albany, OR, *174*
Alberta Arts District, *101*
Alder Wood Bistro ✕, *480*
Alderbrook Resort & Spa , *469*
Alderhouse Glassblowing (shop), *148*
Alexander Nicole Cellars, *575*
Alfred A. Loeb State Park, *171*
Alki Point and Beach, *35, 353*
Alton Baker Park, *210*
Altura ✕, *348*
American Hop Museum, *571*
Analemma Winery, *238–239*
Anderson Homestead, *239*
Anelia's Kitchen & Stage ✕, *388*
Aniche Cellars, *236*
Anjou Bakery ✕, *531*
Anna's by the Sea ✕, *170*
Ape Cave (lava tube), *369*
Aplets and Cotlets Candy Kitchen, *531*
Apple Tree Golf Course, *571*
Aramenta Cellars, *182, 193*
Arbor Crest Wine Cellars, *597*
Arch Rock, *121*
Archery Summit Winery, *194, 196*
Arctic Club Seattle, The , *333*
Argyle Winery, *194, 196*
Arlene Schnitzer Concert Hall, *78*
Arrowhead Bistro ✕, *518–519*
Ashford, WA, *366, 371, 418–420*
Ashland, OR, *292, 295, 313–3197*
Ashland Creek Inn , *317*
Ashland Hills Hotel & Suites , *317*
Asian Art Museum, *347–348*
Asian Brewing (bar), *381*
Ask For Luigi ✕, *625*
Astoria, OR, *118, 123, 126–133*
Astoria Column, *127*
Astoria Riverfront Trolley, *127*
Ataula ✕, *89*
Atticus Hotel , *202*
Aura Waterfront Restaurant ✕, *636*
Ava Gene's ✕, *110–111*

B

Backdoor Kitchen ✕, *439*
Bagdad Theater, *116*
Bainbridge Island, WA, *26, 359–360*
Bale Breaker Brewing Company, *570*
Ballard (Seattle), *322, 350–352*
Ballard Locks, *351*
Ballooning, *185*
Bandon, OR, *118, 123, 163, 165–167*
Bandon Dunes Golf Resort , *166, 167*
Bandon Historical Society Museum, *165*
Bantam *46* ✕, *378*
Barnacle, The (bar), *434*
Basalt ✕, *561*
Basecamp Books and Bites ✕, *557*
Bateman Foundation Gallery of Nature, The, *632*
Bay Area (Oregon Coast), *160–163*
Bay Point Landing , *162*
Bay View State Park, *383*
Beach Street Kitchen ✕, *156*
Beaches, *35*
Olympic National Park, 444, 449, 451, 452, 453, 457
Olympic Peninsula and Washington Coast, 471, 480, 484, 485, 487, 489, 490–491, 492–493, 498, 499
Oregon Coast, 118, 120–121, 135–136, 141–142, 143, 165–166, 169, 171
San Juan Islands, 441
Seattle, 353, 362, 364
Vancouver and Victoria, 641–642
Washington Cascade Mountains and Valleys, 394, 408
Beacon Rock State Park, *34, 227*
Beam & Anchor (shop), *100–101*
Bed-and-breakfasts, *51*
Belle Fiore Winery, *313*
Bellingham, WA, *366, 370, 376–383*
Bellingham Cider Company, *381–382*
Belltown (Seattle), *322, 327, 330–337*
Bellewood Acres, *375*
Bend, OR, *252, 257–268*
Bend Film Festival, *256*
Benson Vineyards, *523–524*
Benton City, WA, *552, 577–578*
Bergstrom Winery, *183, 193*
Bernard Griffin Winery, *586*
Bethel Heights Vineyard, *203*
Betsy & Iya (shop), *92*
Beverly Beach State Park, *151*
Bible Club (bar), *115*
Bicycling, *36*
Central Oregon, 257, 266
Columbia River Gorge and Mt. Hood, 230
North Central Washington, 521
Olympic National Park, 453
Olympic Peninsula and Washington Coast, 478
Portland, 68, 79–80, 92
San Juan Islands, 422, 429, 434, 441
Seattle, 356–357
Vancouver and Victoria, 642–643
Willamette Valley and Wine Country, 214
Bill Reid Gallery, *621*
Bing Crosby House Museum, *597*
Bird-watching, *149, 478, 548*
Bishop's ✕, *629*
Bistro Bar, *194, 196*
Black Squid Beer House, *148*
Blackfish Café ✕, *145*
Blewett Brewing Company ✕, *534*
Bloedel Donovan Park, *377*
Bloedel Reserve, *360*
Blue Moose Cafe ✕, *472–473*
Blue Water Cafe ✕, *628*
Bluewater Distilling, *303*
Boat and ferry travel, *46–47, 62, 372, 426, 436, 447, 466, 618–619*
Boating
Central Oregon, 266–267
Crater Lake National Park, 284
Olympic Peninsula and Washington Coast, 478
Oregon Coast, 151, 170–171
San Juan Islands, 429, 434, 441–442
Seattle, 356
Bob's Java Jive (bar), *413*
Boeing Future of Flight, *391*
Bonair Winery, *571*
Bonneville Dam, *225*
Bonneville Fish Hatchery, *225*
Books and movies, *42, 447*
Bookwalter Winery, *586–587*
Border crossing, *48*
Bos Taurus ✕, *261*
Botanist Bar PDX, *87*
Bow-Edison, WA, *366, 370, 383–385*
Box Factory (shop), *265*
Brasada Ranch , *278*
Brasserie L'École ✕, *636*
Bravura Cellars, *183, 192*
Breadline Cafe ✕, *612*
Brentwood Bay (Victoria), *638*
Brick Tavern, *559*
Bridge of the Gods, *227–228*
British Columbia. ⇨ **See Vancouver; Victoria**
Brix 25 ✕, *403*
Broadway Center for the Performing Arts, *413*
Broder ✕, *111*
Brookings, OR, *118, 123, 171–172*
Buckner Homestead, *507*
Bull Run Distilling, *88*
Bullard ✕, *73*
Bullards Beach State Park, *165*
Buoy Beer Co. ✕, *130*
Burke Museum of Natural History and Culture, *14, 353*
Bush's Pasture Park, *203*
Butchart Gardens, *614, 637*
Butcher & Baker Provisions ✕, *400*

C

Café Brio ✕, *636*
Cama Beach Historical State Park, *389–390*
Camano Island, WA, *366, 371, 389–390*
Camano Island State Park, *390*
Camber ✕, *380*
Camp 1805 (bar), *234–235*
Camp Sherman, *268*
Camping, *51, 289, 459, 509*
Cannabis, *18, 44*
Cannery Pier Hotel , *131*
Cannon Beach, OR, *35, 118, 121, 123, 135–138*
Cannon Beach and Ecola State Park, *136*
Cannon Beach Hardware and Public House, *138*
Canoe (shop), *79*
Canoe Ridge Vineyards, *591*
Canoeing, *455*
Canopy by Hilton Portland , *87*
Cape Arago Lighthouse, *161*
Cape Arago State Park, *161*
Cape Blanco State Park, *168*
Cape Disappointment Lighthouse, *495*
Cape Disappointment State Park, *34, 494–495*
Cape Flattery, *484*
Cape Foulweather, *150*
Cape Kiwanda State Natural Area, *35, 143*
Cape Perpetua Scenic Area, *35, 155*
Cape Sebastian State Scenic Corridor, *169*
Capilano Suspension Bridge, *14, 630*
Capitol Campus, *414–415*
Capitol Hill (Seattle), *322, 347–349*
Car travel and rentals, *47–50*
Carlton Winemakers Studio, *195, 199*
Cascade Brewing, *115*
Cascade Head Preserve, *145*
Cascade Lakes Scenic Byway, *259*
Cascade Locks, OR, *216, 219, 225–227*
Cascades Raptor Center, *210*
Cascadia Art Museum, *394*
Cascina Spinasse ✕, *348–349*
Cashmere, WA, *512, 530–531*
Castle Crest Wildflower Trail, *288*
Cat Tales Zoological Park, *597*
Cathedral of St. John the Evangelist, *597, 599*
Cathedral Park, *94*
Catherine Creek Recreation Area, *236*
Cave B Inn and Spa Resort , *608*
Cave Junction, OR, *292, 295, 319–320*
Celilo Inn , *240–241*
Central Coast (Oregon Coast), *123*
Central Eastside (Portland), *106*
Central Oregon, *20, 252–278*
Central Washington Agricultural Museum, *563, 565*
Central Washington University, *560*
Centennial Trail, *599*
Chambers Bay Golf Course, *414*

D

E

F

G

H

I

J

K

L

Photo Credits

Front Cover: Inge Johnsson / Alamy [Description: Larch trees at Asgaard Pass in the Enchantment Lakes wilderness of Washington state]. **Back cover, from left to right:** zack schnepf/iStockphoto, Mike Fitzpatrick/iStockphoto, cdrin/Shutterstock. Spine: Panachai Cherdchucheep/Shutterstock. **Interior, from left to right:** EB Adventure Photography/Shutterstock (1). Ahorica/iStockphoto (2). Mark B. Bauschke/Shutterstock (5). **Chapter 1: Experience Pacific Northwest:** AndrewSoundarajan/iStockphoto (8-9). zschnepf/Shutterstock (10). All rights Heath Moffatt Photography (11). Stephen Moehle/Shutterstock (11). Tourism Vancouver / Harbour Air (12). Joshua Rainey Photography/Shutterstock (12). Nicole Lohse, Tourism Tofino (12). Laura Ragsdale Photo/Shutterstock (13). Taylor Higgins (13). Courtesy of Capilano Suspension Bridge Park (14). Heath Moffatt (14). Burke Museum/Visit Seattle (14). Josemaria Toscano/Shutterstock (15). Carolyn Wells-Kramer (16). Torsten Kjellstrand/Travel Portland (16). Juntinglin/Dreamstime (16). Spotmatik/Dreamstime (16). Courtesy of Bard on the Beach Shakespeare Festival (17). Jeanne Provost/Shutterstock (17). cdrin/Shutterstock (17). Ronnie Chua/Shutterstock (17). SERRA (18). LeonWang/Shutterstock (18). T. Charles Erickson/Oregon Shakespeare Festival (18). Cory Dawson, courtesy of the Museum of Anthropology at UBC (18). Felipecbit/Shutterstock (19). Jeffclimer/Dreamstime (24). BobNoah/Shutterstock (25). John Cameron (26). Russ Heinl/Shutterstock (26). Jessica Kirkwood (26). Sean Lahusen/Parks Canada (27). J A Uppendahl/Shutterstock (27). Darius Kuzmickas (28). Denise Lett / Alamy Stock Photo (28). Mario Gallucci (28). Courtesy of Elliott Bay Book Company (28). Courtesy_Vancouver Public Library (29). Courtesy of Wayne Templeton (29). Courtesy_The Seattle Public Library (29). Courtesy of Phinney Books (29). Marek Rybar/Dreamstime (30). AllTrails (30). Aaron Hinckley/Dreamstime (30). Mark Mackay/Tourism Whistler (30). Jim Vaillancourt/AllTrails (31). Stuart Westmorland / age fotostock (37). Dorling Kindersley (38) (All). Thomas Kitchin Vict / age fotostock (39). San Juan Safaris (40). Sylvain Grandadam / age fotostock (41). **Chapter 3: Portland:** Torsten Kjellstrand (63). Strekoza2/Dreamstime (84). Jamie Francis (86). Joshuarainey photography/Dreamstime (98). Appalachianviews/Dreamstime (111). **Chapter 4: Oregon Coast:** Glebtarro/Dreamstime (117). Tom Wald/iStockphoto (120). Scott Catron/ wikipedia.org (121). John Norris/Flickr, [CC BY-ND 2.0] (121). Oregon Coast Aquarium (154). Greg Vaughn (163). **Chapter 5: Willamette Valley and Wine Country:** Dennis Frates / Alamy (173). GREG VAUGHN (182). Jason Tomczak (186). GREG VAUGHN (186-187). REX HILL, Newberg, OR (188). REX HILL, Newberg, OR (190). Jason Tomczak (190). Doreen L. Wynja (191). Polara Studio All Rights Reseved (192). Kent Derek (193). REX HILL, Newberg, OR (193). Norman Eder/iStockphoto (193). Polara Studio All Rights Reseved (195). Andrea Johnson Photography (195). Dundee Bistro (195). Jpldesigns/Dreamstime (206). **Chapter 6: Columbia River Gorge and Mt. Hood:** William Blacke/iStockphoto (215). zschnepf/Shutterstock (224). Melissa & Bryan Ripka/Flickr, [CC BY-ND 2.0] (244). **Chapter 7: Central Oregon:** Livingstonatlarge/Dreamstime (251). Svetlana55/Dreamstime (262). Sunriver Resort (267). davemantel/iStockphoto (274). **Chapter 8: Crater Lake National Park:** William A. McConnell (279). Photographer and videographer from Ukraine/iStockphoto (287). **Chapter 9: Southern Oregon:** Greg Vaughn (291). nwrafting/Flickr, [CC BY-ND 2.0] (301). Viviansviews/Dreamstime (315). **Chapter 10: Seattle:** Jose Fuste Raga / age fotostock (321). Mariusz S. Jurgielewicz/Shutterstock (330). jeffwilcox/Flickr, [CC BY-ND 2.0] (332). Charles Amundson/Shutterstock (338). Mark B. Bauschke/Shutterstock (338-339). The Tasting Room (340). piroshky bakery (340). Courtesy of Beecherís Handmade Cheese (340). eng1ne/Flickr, [CC BY-ND 2.0] (341). Photo courtesy of Nick Jurich of flashpd.com (341). Phillie Casablanca (341). Richard Cummins / age fotostock(363). **Chapter 11: Washington Cascade Mountains and Valleys:** Carlos Arguelles/Shutterstock (365). Tusharkoley/ Dreamstime.com (368). Bjulien03/Dreamstime.com (369). Bpperry/Dreamstime.com (369). John Carlson (398). Richard Cummins / age fotostock (405). amanderson2/Flickr, [CC BY-ND 2.0] (407). tusharkoley/Shutterstock (419). **Chapter 12: The San Juan Islands:** Edmund Lowe Photography/Shutterstock (421). Jdanne/Dreamstime.com (431). Cascade Creatives/Shutterstock (437). **Chapter 13: Olympic National Park:** Galyna Andrushko/Shutterstock (443). Sean Pavone/Shutterstock (450). TomKli/Shutterstock (452). **Chapter 14: Olympic Peninsula and Washington Coast:** Roman Khomlyak/Shutterstock (461). Konrad Wothe / age fotostock (486). Alan Majchrowicz / age fotostock (497). **Chapter 15: North Cascades National Park:** Serge Skiba/Dreamstime (501). Edmund Lowe/Dreamstime (508). **Chapter 16: North Central Washington:** ARSimonds/Shutterstock (511). brewbooks/Flickr, [CC BY-ND 2.0] (523). Natalia Bratslavsky/Shutterstock (533). **Chapter 17: Mount Rainier National Park:** Dene Miles/Shutterstock (539). Jon Marc Lyttle/Shutterstock (546). **Chapter 18: Washington Wine Country, Yakima River Valley:** Cascade Creatives/Shutterstock (551). waterfordyork/iStockphoto (567). Chapter 19: Spokane and Eastern Washington: Inge Johnsson / Alamy Stock Photo (579). Alex Grichenko/Dreamstime (599). Alexander Cimbal/ Dreamstime (602). **Chapter 20: Vancouver and Victoria:** Dan Breckwoldt/shutterstock (613). North Light Images / age fotostock (632). Jim Lawrence/Dreamstime (637). **About Our Writers:** All photos are courtesy of the writers. *Every effort has been made to trace the copyright holders, and we apologize in advance for any accidental errors. We would be happy to apply the corrections in the following edition of this publication.

Fodor's PACIFIC NORTHWEST

Publisher: Stephen Horowitz, *General Manager*

Editorial: Douglas Stallings, *Editorial Director*, Jill Fergus, Jacinta O'Halloran, Amanda Sadlowski, *Senior Editors*; Kayla Becker, Alexis Kelly, Rachael Roth, *Editors*

Design: Tina Malaney, *Director of Design and Production*; Jessica Gonzalez, *Graphic Designer;* Mariana Tabares, *Design and Production Intern*

Production: Jennifer DePrima, *Editorial Production Manager*, Elyse Rozelle, *Senior Production Editor;* Monica White, *Production Editor*

Maps: Rebecca Baer, *Senior Map Editor*, Mark Stroud (Moon Street Cartography), David Lindroth, *Cartographers*

Photography: Viviane Teles, *Senior Photo Editor;* Namrata Aggarwal, Ashok Kumar, Carl Yu, *Photo Editors;* Rebecca Rimmer, *Photo Intern*

Business and Operations: Chuck Hoover, *Chief Marketing Officer*, Robert Ames, *Group General Manager*, Devin Duckworth, *Director of Print Publishing*; Victor Bernal, *Business Analyst*

Public Relations and Marketing: Joe Ewaskiw, *Senior Director Communications & Public Relations*

Fodors.com: Jeremy Tarr, *Editorial Director;* Rachael Levitt, *Managing Editor*

Technology: Jon Atkinson, *Director of Technology;* Rudresh Teotia, *Lead Developer*, Jacob Ashpis, *Content Operations Manager*

Writers: Shelley Arenas, Margot Bigg, Andrew Collins, Jennifer Foden, Sue Kernaghan, Chris McBeath, Lesley Mirza, Vanessa Pinniger, Jon Shadel, AnnaMaria Stephens, Naomi Tomky

Editor: Rachael Roth

Production Editor: Jennifer DePrima

22nd Edition

ISBN 978-1-64097-304-6

ISSN 1098-6774

SPECIAL SALES

This book is available at special discounts for bulk purchases for sales promotions or premiums. For more information, e-mail SpecialMarkets@fodors.com.

PRINTED IN THE UNITED STATES OF AMERICA

10 9 8 7 6 5 4 3 2 1

About Our Writers

Shelley Arenas has written for Fodor's for more than a decade, contributing to several editions of Pacific Northwest. She co-authored a book about Seattle for families and has written for regional magazines. She loves to explore national parks and has contributed to the last four editions of the Complete Guide to the National Parks of the West. She updated the Bryce Canyon National Park, Capitol Reef National Park, Zion National Park, and Travel Smart chapters of this book.

Margot Bigg is a freelance travel writer and editor based in Portland, Oregon. She's lived and worked all over the world, most recently in India, where she worked at *Time Out Magazine* and contributed to the last three editions of *Fodor's Essential India*. Though now back in the States, she continues to contribute to a variety of Indian publications, including local editions of *Rolling Stone* and *National Geographic Traveler*, as well as U.S. publications ranging from *Sunset Magazine* to *VICE*. Margot updated the Willamette Valley chapter for this edition.

Andrew Collins, a former Fodor's editor, updated Experience Pacific Northwest, Portland, Oregon Coast, Columbia River Gorge and Mt. Hood, Crater Lake National Park, Southern Oregon, Washinton Cascade Mountains and Valleys, and The San Juan Islands chapters this edition. A resident of both Portland and Mexico City who travels frequently throughout the Northwest, he has authored more than a dozen guidebooks, and is editor in chief of three magazines, including *The Pearl* (about Portland's hip Pearl District). He also writes about restaurants, art, and design for *Four Seasons Magazine* and travel for *New Mexico Magazine*; teaches food writing and travel writing for Gotham Writers' Workshop; and has contributed to *Travel + Leisure, Sunset*, and dozens of other periodicals.

Jennifer Foden is an award-winning freelance writer and editor who relocated from Toronto to Vancouver—for the mountains. She writes about travel, sustainability, social justice, architecture, and food and drink for a variety of publications. When she's not working with words, she's traveling, watching sports, or Face Timing her niece and nephew.

Freelance writer **Sue Kernaghan** has written about British Columbia for dozens of publications and websites around the world, including several editions of *Fodor's Vancouver and British Columbia*. A fourth-generation British Columbian, she now lives and writes on Salt Spring Island.

Award-winning freelance travel writer **Chris McBeath's** more than 25 years in the tourism industry have given her an insider's eye about what makes a great vacation. British Columbia is her home, so whether routing through backcountry or discovering a hidden-away inn, Chris has combined history, insight, and anecdotes into her contribution to this book. Many of Chris's articles can be found at 🌐 *www.greatestgetaways.com*; her destination videos are available on YouTube.

Born in Canada and raised in the UK, **Lesley Mirza** was introduced to the pleasure of travel at an early age by her globetrotting parents. Now back in Canada, and living in Vancouver, BC, with her husband and two senior

About Our Writers

pugs, Lesley works as a freelance writer, penning travel and lifestyle stories for a variety of publications.

Vanessa Pinniger is a freelance journalist from Vancouver, who has been exploring the West Coast her whole life. As Pacific Newspaper Group's Specialty Publications editor, she was responsible for the Travel sections of Vancouver's two daily newspapers and was editor-in-chief of the award-winning Westcoast Homes and Design magazine. She traded in her desk job for life on the road in 2015 and has been travelling ever since. Her stories and photos have appeared in The Vancouver Sun, The Province, Montreal Gazette, Ottawa Citizen and on canada.com.

Jon Shadel is a Portland-based writer, editor, and multimedia journalist, whose work appears in *The Washington Post*, *VICE*, Condé Nast's *them.*, *The Atlantic CityLab*, and many other outlets. Prior to embarking on a career as a roving freelancer, they worked as the top editor at MEDIAmerica, a publisher of Pacific Northwest magazines and travel guides. Learn more about their work covering culture, travel, and technology at 🌐 *www.jdshadel.com.*

AnnaMaria Stephens is a Seattle-based freelance writer who covers travel, design, food, and more. She's a fan of everything her city has to offer, from the coffee and culture to the countless views of mountains and water. She also firmly believes that Seattle's spectacular summers are worth a few months of drizzle.

Naomi Tomky lives and writes in Seattle, where she's the city's biggest cheerleader and most enthusiastic eater. She writes about Seattle's food scene for local and national publications and received the Association of Food Journalist's Best Food and Travel Award for 2016.